Y0-CMM-007

1996 PGA TOUR

Official Media Guide of the PGA TOUR

TABLE OF CONTENTS

TABLE OF CONTENTS

1996 PGA TOUR TOURNAMENT SCHEDULE

( )—1995 Purses

Date	Tournament Dir./Media Contact	Location (Par/Yardage)	Prize Money	Pro-Am	TV	1995 Winner
Jan 4-7	**Mercedes Championships** Mike Crosthwaite/Sarah Suggs 619-438-9111 x4612	La Costa Resort & Spa (72/7022) 2100 Costa del Mar Road Carlsbad, CA 92009	$1,000,000	$10,000	ESPN/ABC	Steve Elkington
Jan 11-14	**Nortel Open** Judy McDermott/Ted Doe 520-571-0400	Tucson National Golf Resort (72/7148) Starr Pass Golf Club (71/6,942) 2727 West Club Drive Tucson, AZ 85741	$1,250,000	$15,000	ESPN	Phil Mickelson
Jan 17-21	**Bob Hope Chrysler Classic** Edward Heorodt/Connie Whelchel 619-346-8184	Indian Ridge Country Club (72/7037) Bermuda Dunes Country Club (72/6927) Indian Wells Country Club (72/6478) Tamarisk Country Club (72/6881) Palm Desert, CA 92211	$1,300,000	$21,000	NBC	Kenny Perry
Jan 24-27	**Phoenix Open presented by the Dial Corp.** Ed Grant/Drew Wathey 602-870-0163	TPC of Scottsdale (71/6992) 17020 North Hayden Road Scottsdale, AZ 85255	$1,300,000	$ 7,500	ESPN	Vijay Singh
Feb 1-4	**AT&T Pebble Beach National Pro-Am** Lou Russo/Cathy Scherzer 408-649-1533	Pebble Beach Golf Links (72/6799) Spyglass Hill Golf Course (72/6810) Poppy Hills (72/6850) Pebble Beach, CA 93953	$1,500,000	$70,000	USA/CBS	Peter Jacobsen
Feb 8-11	**Buick Invitational** Tom Wilson/Rick Schloss 619-281-4653	Torrey Pines Golf Course South Course (72/7000) North Course (72/6592) 11480 Torrey Pines Road La Jolla, CA 92037	$1,200,000	$10,000	ESPN/NBC	Peter Jacobsen
Feb 15-18	**United Airlines Hawaiian Open** Chester Kahapea/Bill Bachran 808-526-1232	Waialae Country Club (72/6975) 4997 Kahala Avenue Honolulu, HI 96816	$1,200,000	$10,000	ABC	John Morse
Feb 22-25	**Nissan Open** Tom Pulchinski/Toby Zwikel 213-482-1311	Riviera Country Club (71/6946) 1250 Capri Drive Pacific Palisades, CA 90272	$1,200,000	$ 7,500	USA/CBS	Corey Pavin

1996 PGA TOUR TOURNAMENT SCHEDULE *continued*

( )—1995 Purses

Date	Tournament Dir./Media Contact	Location (Par/Yardage)	Prize Money	Pro-Am	TV	1995 Winner
Feb 29-3	**Doral-Ryder Open** Scott Montgomery/Judy Janofsky 305-477-4653	Doral Resort & Country Club Blue Course (72/6939) 4400 NW 87th Avenue Miami, FL 33178	$1,800,000	$ 7,500	USA/CBS	Nick Faldo
Mar 7-10	**The Honda Classic** Cliff Danley/Gary Ferman 954-346-4000	TPC at Eagle Trace (72/7040) 1111 Eagle Trace Boulevard Coral Springs, FL 33071	$1,300,000	$ 7,500	USA/NBC	Mark O'Meara
Mar 14-17	**Bay Hill Invitational Presented by Office Depot** Jim Bell/Jennifer Eberlein 407-876-2888	Bay Hill Club & Lodge (72/7207) 9000 Bay Hill Boulevard Orlando, FL 32819	$1,200,000	$10,000	USA/NBC	Loren Roberts
Mar 21-24	**Freeport•McDermott Classic** Thomas Wulff/Mark Romig 504-831-4653	English Turn Golf & Country Club (72/7116) One Clubhouse Drive New Orleans, LA 70131	$1,200,000	$ 7,500	ESPN/NBC	Davis Love III
Mar 28-31	**THE PLAYERS Championship** Henry Hughes 904-285-7888	TPC at Sawgrass—Stadium (72/6896) 110 TPC Boulevard Ponte Vedra Beach, FL 32082	($3,000,000)		ESPN/NBC	Lee Janzen
Apr 4-7	**BellSouth Classic** Dave Kaplan/John Marshall 770-951-8777	Atlanta Country Club (72/7018) 500 Atlanta Country Club Drive Marietta, GA 30067	$1,300,000	$ 7,500	CBS	Mark Calcavecchia
Apr 11-14	**•Masters Tournament** Walton Johnson 706-667-6000	Augusta National Golf Club (72/6925) 2604 Washington Road Augusta, GA 30904	($2,200,000)		USA/CBS	Ben Crenshaw
Apr 18-21	**MCI Classic** Michael Stevens/Arnie Burdick 803-671-2448	Harbour Town Golf Links (71/6912) Hilton Head Island, SC 29928	$1,400,000	$ 7,500	CBS	Bob Tway
Apr 22-23	**+U.S. Championship/Andersen Consulting WCOG** Dick McClean 808-669-4844	Reynolds Plantation Great Waters Course (72/7048) Lake Oconee, GA (Mailing address: 100 Linger Longer Road; Greensboro, GA 60342)	$3,650,000 (full tournament)		ESPN	To be determined. December 31

1996 PGA TOUR TOURNAMENT SCHEDULE *continued*

( )—1995 Purses

Date	Tournament Dir./Media Contact	Location (Par/Yardage)	Prize Money	Pro-Am	TV	1995 Winner
Apr 25-28	**Kmart Greater Greensboro Open** Sabrah Hardin/Patricia Cook 910-379-1570	Forest Oaks Country Club (72/7062) 4600 Forest Oaks Drive Greensboro, NC 27406	$1,500,000	$ 7,500	USA/CBS	Jim Gallagher, Jr.
May 2-5	**Shell Houston Open** Eric Fredricksen/Burt Darden 713-367-7999	TPC at The Woodlands (72/7045) 1730 South Millbend Drive The Woodlands, TX 77380	$1,500,000	$ 7,500	ABC	Payne Stewart
May 9-12	**GTE Byron Nelson Classic** Janie Henderson/Charlie Seay 214-717-1200	TPC at Four Seasons Resort/ Las Colinas (70/6899) Cottonwood Valley Golf Course (70/6846) 4200 North MacArthur Boulevard Irving, TX 75038	$1,500,000	$15,000	ABC	Ernie Els
May 16-19	**MasterCard Colonial** Floyd Wade/Jerre Todd 817-927-4277	Colonial Country Club (70/7010) 3735 Country Club Circle Ft. Worth, TX 76109	$1,500,000	$ 7,500	USA/CBS	Tom Lehman
May 23-26	**Kemper Open** Ben Brundred/Charlie Brotman 301-469-3737	TPC at Avenel (71/7005) 10000 Oaklyn Drive Potomac, MD 20854	$1,500,000	$ 7,500	CBS	Lee Janzen
May 30-2	**Memorial Tournament** Jim Wisler/Kip Eriksen 614-889-6700	Muirfield Village Golf Club (72/7104) P.O. Box 565 5750 Memorial Drive Dublin, OH 43017	$1,800,000		ESPN/ABC	Greg Norman
June 6-9	**Buick Classic** Dede Patterson/Barbara Richardson 914-967-5356	Westchester Country Club (71/6779) West Course 99 Biltmore Avenue Rye, NY 10580	$1,200,000	$ 7,500	USA/CBS	Vijay Singh
June 13-16	**•US Open** Mike Davis 908-234-2300	Oakland Hills Country Club (70/6990) P.O. Box 111 3451 West Maple Road Bloomfield Hills, MI 48301	($2,000,000)		ESPN/NBC	Corey Pavin
June 20-23	**FedEx St. Jude Classic** Dwight Drinkard/Phil Cannon 901-748-0534	TPC at Southwind (71/7006) 3325 Club at Southwind Memphis, TN 38125	$1,350,000	$ 7,500	CBS	Jim Gallagher, Jr.

1996 PGA TOUR TOURNAMENT SCHEDULE *continued*

( )—1995 Purses

Date	Tournament Dir./Media Contact	Location (Par/Yardage)	Prize Money	Pro-Am	TV	1995 Winner
June 27-30	**Canon Greater Hartford Open** Eric Cormier/Mary Engvall 203-522-4171	TPC at River Highlands (70/6820) Golf Club Road Cromwell, CT 06416	$1,500,000	$ 7,500	ESPN/CBS	Greg Norman
July 4-7	**Motorola Western Open** Greg McLaughlin/Gary Holaway 708-724-4600	Cog Hill Golf & Country Club (72/7073) 12294 Archer Avenue Lemont, IL 60439	$2,000,000	$ 7,500	USA/CBS	Billy Mayfair
July 11-14	**Michelob Championship at Kingsmill** Johnnie Bender 804-253-3985	Kingsmill Golf Club (71/6797) River Course 100 Golf Club Road Williamsburg, VA 23185	$1,250,000	$20,000	ESPN	Ted Tryba
July 18-21	**Deposit Guaranty Golf Classic** Robert Morgan 601-544-0262	Annandale Golf Club (72/7157) 837 Mannsdale Road Madison, MS 39110	$1,000,000	$ 7,500	TGC	Ed Dougherty
July 18-21	**•British Open** 011-44-1334-472112	Royal Lytham & St. Annes Golf Club (71/6857) Links Gate Lytham St. Annes Lancashire FY8 3LQ ENGLAND	($2,000,000)		ESPN/ABC	John Daly
July 25-28	**CVS Charity Classic** Stephen Mingolla/Jennifer Toland 508-865-1491	Pleasant Valley Country Club (71/7110) Armsby Road Sutton, MA 01590	$1,200,000	$ 7,500	TGC	Fred Funk
Aug 1-4	**Buick Open** J. Schaffer/Dave Roman 810-293-9435	Warwick Hills Golf & Country Club (72/7105) G-9057 South Saginaw Street Grand Blanc, MI 48439	$1,200,000	$ 7,500	CBS	Woody Austin
Aug 8-11	**•PGA Championship** Tara Hipp 502-254-1996	Valhalla Golf Club (72/7115) P.O. Box 43819 Louisville, KY 40253-0819	($2,000,000)		TBS/CBS	Steve Elkington
Aug 15-18	**The Sprint International** Larry Thiel/Buddy Martin 303-660-8000	Castle Pines Golf Club (72/7559) 1000 Humingbird Drive Castle Rock, CO 80104	$1,600,000	$10,000	ESPN/CBS	Lee Janzen
Aug 22-25	**NEC World Series of Golf** Jim Cook 216-644-2299	Firestone Country Club (70/7149) South Course 452 East Warner Road Akron, OH 44319	$2,000,000	$ 7,500	USA/CBS	Greg Norman

1996 PGA TOUR TOURNAMENT SCHEDULE *continued*

( )—1995 Purses

Date	Tournament Dir./Media Contact	Location (Par/Yardage)	Prize Money	Pro-Am	TV	1995 Winner
Aug 22-25	**Greater Vancouver Open** Marty Zlotnik/Brad Ewart 604-899-4641	Northview Golf & Country Club The Ridge Course (71/6900) 6857 168th Street Cloverdale, British Columbia CANADA V3S 8E7	$1,000,000	$ 7,500	TSN	First-year event
Aug 29-1	**Greater Milwaukee Open presented by Lite Beer** Tom Strong/Dan Blackman 414-365-4466	Brown Deer Park Golf Course (71/6739) 835 North Green Bay Avenue Milwaukee, WI 53209	$1,200,000	$ 7,500	ABC	Scott Hoch
Sept 5-8	**Bell Canadian Open** Bill Paul/David Jones 905-849-9700	Glen Abbey Golf Club (72/7102) 1333 Dorval Drive, R.R. 2 Oakville, Ontario CANADA L6J 4Z3	$1,500,000	$ 7,500	ESPN	Mark O'Meara
Sept 12-15	**Quad City Classic** TBD/Curt Burnett 309-762-4653	Oakwood Country Club (70/6796) Route 6 Coal Valley, IL 61240	$1,000,000	$ 7,500	TGC	D.A. Weibring
Sept 12-15	**The Presidents Cup** Henry Hughes 904-285-7888	Robert Trent Jones Golf Club (72/7238) One Turtle Point Drive Lake Manassas, VA 22065	(No purse/proceeds to charity)		ESPN/CBS	
Sept 19-22	**B.C. Open** Mike Norman/Pat Vavra 607-785-3722	En-Joie Golf Club (71/6966) 722 West Main Street Endicott, NY 13760	$1,000,000	$ 7,500	TGC	Hal Sutton
Sept 26-29	**Buick Challenge** Bob Berry/Jim Visser 706-324-0411	Callaway Gardens (72/7057) Mountain View Course Highway 27 Pine Mountain, GA 31822	$1,000,000	$ 7,500	ESPN	Fred Funk
Oct 2-6	**Las Vegas Invitational** Charlie Baron/Rob Dondbru 702-382-6616	TPC at Summerlin (72/7243) 1700 Village Center Circle Las Vegas, NV 89134	$1,600,000	$18,000	ESPN	Jim Furyk
Oct 10-13	**LaCantera Texas Open** Tony Piazzi/Jerry Grotz 210-341-0823	LaCantera Golf Club (72/6899) 16401 LaCantera Parkway San Antonio, TX 78256	$1,200,000	$ 7,500	TGC	Duffy Waldorf

1996 PGA TOUR TOURNAMENT SCHEDULE *continued*

( )—1995 Purses

Date	Tournament Dir./Media Contact	Location (Par/Yardage)	Prize Money	Pro-Am	TV	1995 Winner
Oct 17-20	**Walt Disney World/Oldsmobile Golf Classic** Michael McPhillips 407-824-2250	Magnolia Course (72/7190) Palm Course (72/6957) Lake Buena Vista Golf Course (72/6819) Lake Buena Vista, FL 32830	$1,200,000	$25,000	TGC	Brad Bryant
Oct 24-27	**THE TOUR Championship** Marlene Livaudais 918-497-4653	Southern Hills Country Club (70/6834) 2636 East 61st Street Tulsa, OK 74136	$3,000,000	$10,000	ESPN/ABC	Billy Mayfair
Nov 7-10	**+Lincoln-Mercury Kapalua Int'l** Margaret A. Santos/Linn Nishikawa 808-669-0244	Plantation Course at Kapalua (73/7263) Bay Course at Kapalua Resort (71/6531) 2000 Plantation Club Drive Lahaina, Maui, HI 96761	$1,100,000		ESPN/ABC	Jim Furyk
Nov 14-17	**+Franklin Templeton Shark Shootout** Eric Jonke/Steve Brener 216-436-3440	Sherwood Country Club (72/7025) 2215 West Stafford Road Thousand Oaks, CA 91361	$1,100,000		CBS	Mark Calcavecchia/ Steve Elkington
Nov 21-24	**+The World Cup of Golf** Jack Warfield/Tom Place 513-624-2100	Erinvale Golf Club P.O. Box 16 Somerset West (Cape Town) South Africa 7129	($1,500,000)		NBC	United States (Fred Couples/ Davis Love III)
Nov 28-1	**+Skins Game** Chuck Gerber/Steve Brener 310-358-5300	Rancho La Quinta Country Club 48500 Washington Street La Quinta, CA 32253	($540,000)		ABC	Fred Couples
Dec 5-8	**+JCPenney Classic** Gerald Goodman/Dick Dailey 813-942-5566	Innisbrook Hilton Resort Copperhead Course (71/7054) 36750 U.S. Highway 19 North Palm Harbor, FL 34684	$1,300,000	$10,000	ESPN/ABC	Davis Love III/ Beth Daniel
Dec 12-15	**+Diners Club Matches** Bill Jones 619-777-0150	PGA West (Nicklaus Course) 55-955 PGA Boulevard La Quinta, CA 92253-4604	$ 890,000		ESPN/ABC	Tom Lehman/ Duffy Waldorf
Jan 4-5 1997	**+Andersen Consulting WCOG** Dick McClean 808-669-4844	Grayhawk Golf Club 7001 North Scottsdale Road, #1034 Scottsdale, AZ 85253	$3,650,000 (full tournament)		ESPN/ABC	To be determined December 31

• Non-PGA TOUR cosponsored event

+ Unofficial event

A BRIEF HISTORY OF THE PGA TOUR

It is not always easy to discover the exact beginning of something. So it is with the PGA TOUR. Certainly there were professionals who competed against each other from the earliest days of the game.

In 1895, 10 professional golfers and one amateur played in the first U.S. Open in Newport, RI. Shortly thereafter, tournaments began to pop up across the country. There was the Western Open in 1899. But this was not "tour" golf. The events lacked continuity.

Interest in the game, however, continued to grow. American professionals were rapidly improving. And when John McDermott became the first American-born player to win the U.S. Open, enthusiasm for the game blossomed.

Adding to this growth was a commercially backed exhibition by Englishmen Harry Vardon and Ted Ray. The duo travelled across the country and attracted good crowds wherever they stopped during the warmer months of 1913. A 20-year-old, Francis Ouimet, defeated the pair in a playoff for the United States Open Championship at Brookline, MA. Suddenly golf became front page news and a game for everyone.

In the early '20s, the PGA TOUR saw its first development. Tournaments were held on the West Coast, Texas and Florida. These events were held in the winter, and the golfers played their way east and up to Pinehurst in the spring. By the middle of the decade, the TOUR was doing relatively well--offering $77,000 in total prize money.

The TOUR became more structured following World War II and exploded in the late 1950s and early '60s. Flip through the **Facts and Figures** section of this book and look at such areas as leading money-winners and rising tournament purses to witness the continuing growth.

When television became a player in the game, the eyes of the world were on golf. This exposure inspired millions to try the game and, at the same time, TV rights fees sent purses soaring. The bulk of these rights fees, which are distributed by the PGA TOUR to all co-sponsors, have gone back into the purses, accounting for the tripling of prize money in the last decade.

The touring professionals began to gain control of the TOUR in late 1968. Joseph C. Dey was the first Commissioner of what was then called the Tournament Players Division. He served from early 1969 through February 28, 1974, and was succeeded by Deane R. Beman, who took office March 1, 1974.

During Beman's administration, the value of tournament purses escalated at an unprecedented rate: PGA TOUR assets grew from $730,000 in 1974 to over $200 million, and total revenues increased from $3.9 million to $229 million in 1993.

Timothy W. Finchem, previously the TOUR's Deputy Commissioner and Chief Operating Officer, became third Commissioner on June 1, 1994. In 1995, Finchem undertook a restructuring program designed to strengthen the PGA TOUR's core business, which is its competitions; expand the TOUR's international scope and prepare it to enter the 21st Century.

Since 1938, PGA TOUR events have made donations approaching $300 million to charity. Of that total, more than $134 million has been raised in the 1990s. The 1994 season produced a one-year record $24,701,631 for charity; in 1995, the total was yet another record: $25.2 million.

The competitive scope of the PGA TOUR also is much broader today. The Senior PGA TOUR is considered by many the sports success story of the 1980s. In 1996, the NIKE TOUR will enjoy its seventh season as a proving ground for professionals, taking golf to 30 additional markets and paving the way for the future John Dalys, Jeff Maggerts, Tom Lehmans and David Duvals of the PGA TOUR.

Also continuing to grow is the Tournament Players Club Network. When the PGA TOUR opened the Tournament Players Club at Sawgrass in 1980, it introduced the era of Stadium Golf and record-breaking attendance. Owned and operated by the TOUR, the concept means these courses are the only major league sports arenas owned by the players themselves.

The TPC Network now includes facilities in Japan, Thailand and China as well as the United States. In November 1995, the TPC at Mission Hills, near Shenzhen, served as the venue for the 41st World Cup of Golf, the first major international golf competition held in the People's Republic of China.

CHRONOLOGY OF PGA TOUR

1895 -- First U.S. Open (won by Horace Rawlins) played at Newport (RI) Golf Club

1899 -- Inaugural Western Open (won by Willie Smith) played at Glenview (IL) Golf Club

1900 -- Harry Vardon tour of United States generates widespread interest in game

1913 -- Francis Ouimet captures U.S. Open playoff with Vardon and Ted Ray

1914 -- Walter Hagen wins first of 11 major titles in U.S. Open at Midlothian Country Club outside Chicago

1916 -- PGA of America formed; Jim Barnes wins first PGA Championship over Jock Hutchison at Siwanoy CC in Bronxville, NY

1922 -- Gene Sarazen (age 20) wins U.S. Open (Skokie Country Club in Glencoe, IL); also wins PGA Championship (Oakmont CC), becoming first to hold both titles at once

1926 -- Los Angeles Open offers $10,000 purse

1927 -- First Ryder Cup matches played, won by United States [Worcester (MA) Country Club]

A BRIEF HISTORY OF THE PGA TOUR (cont'd.)

1930 -- Bob Harlow named manager of PGA Tournament Bureau and broaches idea of year-round tournament circuit;raises annual purse money on the Tour from $77,000 to $130,000 in first year on job; instrumental in creating volunteer system by which TOUR functions to this day; Code of Conduct drawn up

1931 -- Golf Ball and Golf Club Manufacturers Association puts up $5,000 to support sponsors during 1931-32 winter swing

1932 -- "Playing Pros" organization formed, pre-dating by 36 years formation of current PGA TOUR organization

1933 -- Hershey Chocolate Company, at least unofficially, first corporate sponsor on PGA TOUR with Hershey Open

1934 -- Group of players meets to discuss possibilities of year-round tournament circuit; Horton Smith wins first Masters at Augusta National Golf Club; leading money winner for year Paul Runyan earns $6,767

1937 -- First Bing Crosby Pro-Am/"Clambake" played at San Diego's Rancho Santa Fe CC; Sam Snead becomes nationally recognized figure in golf by winning Oakland Open

1938 -- Palm Beach Invitational makes first TOUR contribution to charity, $10,000

1945 -- Byron Nelson captures 11 consecutive tournament starts, seven other official events and one unofficial, a total of 19 wins in one year; voted 1945 Associated Press Male Athlete of Year; Tam O'Shanter All-American offers $60,000 purse

1947 -- U.S. Open televised live in St. Louis area

1949 -- Ben Hogan critically injured in head-on collision of his automobile with Greyhound bus

1950 -- Ben Hogan returns to competitive golf in Los Angeles Open, starting with two-under-par 34 on his front nine and eventual 280 total tied by Sam Snead; loses playoff eight days later

1953 -- Ben Hogan wins three major championships: the Masters, U.S. Open and the only British Open he ever played
Lew Worsham wins first PGA TOUR event to appear live on national television, Tam O'Shanter World Championship
Golf's "color barrier" broken with PGA constitutional amendment allowing for "Approved Entries," nonmembers who could play in tournaments if invited by sponsors

1954 -- USGA begins to televise U.S. Open for national audience

1955 -- World Championship of Golf offers first $100,000 purse in PGA TOUR history

1956 -- Masters Tournament televised for the first time

1957 -- "All-Star Golf," first series of matches between pros filmed for television, has its debut

1961 -- Caucasians-only clause stricken from PGA constitution; PGA TOUR officially integrated

1962 -- "Shell's Wonderful World of Golf" begins nine-year run

1965 -- Inaugural Qualifying School held at PGA National Golf Club in Palm Beach Gardens, FL; John Schlee first medalist

1968 -- Association of Professional Golfers (APG), an autonomous tournament players' organization, forms in breakaway from PGA. As compromise, Tournament Players Division of PGA formed under aegis of 10-man policy board late in year

1969 -- Joe Dey becomes first Commissioner of Tournament Players Division

1974 -- Deane Beman succeeds Dey as Commissioner on March 1
Jack Nicklaus captures inaugural Tournament Players Championship (now THE PLAYERS Championship) at Atlanta CC

1977 -- Al Geiberger records first sub-60 round in PGA TOUR history on June 10, a 59 in Danny Thomas Memphis Classic at Colonial CC

1978 -- First "Legends of Golf" played at Onion Creek CC in Austin, TX, precursor of Senior PGA TOUR

1979 -- PGA TOUR Headquarters relocated from Washington, D.C. to Ponte Vedra Beach, FL

1980 -- Senior PGA TOUR organized with four tournaments
First Tournament Players Club opens, the TPC at Sawgrass in Ponte Vedra, FL

1983 -- All-Exempt TOUR put in place, virtually eliminating Monday qualifying; top 125 players exempt; Tournament Players Series (TPS) begins three-year run; PGA TOUR Pension Program begins

1985 -- PGA TOUR Productions created

1986 -- Panasonic Las Vegas Invitational offers first $1 million purse in PGA TOUR history

1987 -- PGA TOUR surpasses $100 million in charitable contributions

1988 -- 30 players compete at Pebble Beach for $2 million in Nabisco Championships, predecessor of THE TOUR Championship

1990 -- Ben Hogan Tour comes into existence as developmental circuit, succeeded by NIKE TOUR beginning in 1993

1991 -- Chip Beck matches Geiberger's 1977 feat on October 11, carding a 59 at Sunrise Golf Club during Las Vegas Invitational

1992 -- PGA TOUR surpasses $200 million in charitable contributions

1993 -- The PGA TOUR boasts a record five $1 million winners

1994 -- Tim Finchem succeeds Beman as Commissioner on June 1
Inaugural Presidents Cup Match played; U.S. defeats Internationals 20-12

1995 -- PGA TOUR initiates staff reorganization to strengthen core business: competitions; first major international golf competition held in People's Republic of China, World Cup of Golf, played at TPC at Mission Hills

PGA TOUR POLICY BOARD

The PGA TOUR Policy Board establishes goals and policies for the operation of the PGA TOUR. The nine-member Board is composed of the following:

Four Player Directors elected by the PGA TOUR membership. A Player Director also serves as Vice President of the PGA of America.

Four Independent Directors, representing the public interest. One serves as Chairman of the Board.

One PGA of America Director, who is a national officer of the PGA of America.

A Players Advisory Council consults with the Policy Board.

The Policy Board appoints the Commissioner as chief executive and administrative officer of the PGA TOUR. The tournament staff, serving under the Commissioner, conducts tournament play.

Richard J. Ferris
Northbrook, IL
Chairman

Victor F. Ganzi
New York, NY
Independent Director

James F. Nordstrom
Seattle, WA
Independent Director

Harold "Red" Poling
Dearborn, MI
Independent Director

Jay Haas
Greenville, SC
Player Director

Tom Lehman
Scottsdale, AZ
Player Director

Davis Love III
Sea Island, GA
Player Director

Mark O'Meara
Windermere, FL
Player Director

Tom Addis III
El Cajon, CA
PGA Director

PGA TOUR GOLF COURSE PROPERTIES BOARD

H. James Griggs
Chairman

An advisory board of the PGA TOUR Policy Board, the Golf Course Properties Board makes reports and recommendations relating to the development and operational functions of the Tournament Players Club (TPC) Network, domestically and internationally.

Directors of the Golf Course Properties Board are experts in the fields of development, finance, construction, law, international business and other specialties related to property development.

See pages 506-507 for information on the Tournament Players Club Network.

Edward W. Brown III

James Clark

Wayne S. Doran

W.J. "Jim" Smith

John L. Steffens

Carl Ware

ABOUT THE COMMISSIONER

Timothy W. Finchem

Commissioner

Timothy W. Finchem became the third Commissioner in the 25-year history of the PGA TOUR on June 1, 1994.

Finchem, 48, succeeded Deane R. Beman, who had served as Commissioner for 20 years. The late Joseph C. Dey was the first Commissioner of the PGA TOUR, serving from 1969 until 1974.

A 4-handicapper, Finchem combines a love of the game and a respect for its traditions with a vision that will carry the PGA TOUR successfully into the future. In 1995, he oversaw a restructuring designed to prepare the TOUR to move forward into the 21st century and expand golf's international horizons.

A graduate of the University of Virginia School of Law, Finchem began his career as an associate of the Norfolk, VA law firm of Babalas & Ermlich in 1973 and became a partner in the firm of Croshaw, Finchem and Williams in Virginia Beach, VA in 1976.

Finchem served in the White House as the Deputy Advisor to the President for Economic Affairs in 1978 and 1979, then became National Staff Director of the Carter-Mondale Presidential Campaign in 1980.

In 1981, Finchem became President of Beckel, Finchem, Torricelli and Associates before becoming co-founder of National Strategies and Marketing Group, a Washington, DC consulting and marketing firm, in 1984. He was a consultant to the PGA TOUR while with NSMG.

Finchem joined the TOUR staff as Vice President of Business Affairs in 1987 and became Deputy Commissioner and Chief Operating Officer in 1989.

Born in Ottawa, IL on April 19, 1947, Finchem was graduated from Princess Anne High School in Virginia Beach. He attended the University of Richmond on a debate scholarship and received his Bachelor of Arts degree from the school in 1969. He received his degree from the University of Virginia Law School in 1973.

A physical fitness devotee, Finchem is a member of the President's Council on Physical Fitness.

Married to the former Holly Bachand, Finchem is the father of four. The Finchems live in Ponte Vedra Beach, FL.

Billy Mayfair experienced the greatest one-season earnings gain in TOUR history, a jump of $1,385,033 over 1994, with $540,000 of that coming from his 1995 TOUR Championship victory. He also won the Motorola Western Open.

ALL-EXEMPT TOUR PRIORITY RANKINGS

Each PGA TOUR player has earned a position on the priority ranking system that will be used to select tournament fields. The complete ranking system, in order of priority, is as follows:

I. SPECIAL EXEMPTIONS

1. Winners of PGA Championship or U.S. Open prior to 1970 or in the last 10 calendar years.

Paul Azinger, Jack Burke, Billy Casper, John Daly, Ernie Els, Steve Elkington, Dow Finsterwald, Jack Fleck, Ray Floyd, Doug Ford, Ed Furgol, Al Geiberger, Wayne Grady, Jay Hebert, Lionel Hebert, Hale Irwin, Don January, Lee Janzen, Tom Kite, Gene Littler, Dave Marr, Orville Moody, Larry Nelson, Bobby Nichols, Jack Nicklaus, Arnold Palmer, Corey Pavin, Gary Player, Nick Price, Bob Rosburg, Scott Simpson, Jeff Sluman, Sam Snead, Payne Stewart, Curtis Strange, Lee Trevino, Bob Tway, Ken Venturi

2. Winners of the THE PLAYERS Championship in the last 10 calendar years.

Davis Love III, Sandy Lyle, John Mahaffey, Mark McCumber, Jodie Mudd, Greg Norman

3. Winners of the NEC World Series of Golf in the last 10 calendar years.

Fulton Allem, David Frost, Dan Pohl, Tom Purtzer, Mike Reid, Craig Stadler

4. Winners of the Masters Tournament in the last 10 calendar years.

Fred Couples, Ben Crenshaw, Nick Faldo, Larry Mize

5. Winners of the British Open in the last 10 calendar years (1990-present).

Ian Baker-Finch

6. The leader in PGA TOUR official earnings in each of the last five calendar years.

7. Winners of PGA TOUR cosponsored or approved events (except team events) within the last two calendar years, or during the current year; winners receive an additional year of exemption for each additional win, up to five years.

Woody Austin, Mark Brooks, Brad Bryant, Mark Calcavecchia, Ed Dougherty, Bob Estes, Rick Fehr, Fred Funk, Jim Furyk, Jim Gallagher, Jr., Bill Glasson, Mike Heinen, Brian Henninger, Scott Hoch, John Huston, Peter Jacobsen, Neal Lancaster, Tom Lehman, Bruce Lietzke, Steve Lowery, Andrew Magee, Billy Mayfair, Phil Mickelson, Johnny Miller, John Morse, Mark O'Meara, Brett Ogle, Kenny Perry, Dicky Pride, Loren Roberts, Vijay Singh, Mike Springer, Mike Sullivan, Hal Sutton, Ted Tryba, Duffy Waldorf, D.A. Weibring

8. Members of the last-named U.S. Ryder Cup team.

Brad Faxon, Jay Haas, Jeff Maggert

9. Leaders in official PGA TOUR career earnings, as follows:

   a. Players among the Top 50 in career earnings as of the end of the preceding calendar year may elect to use a one-time, one-year exemption for the next year.

   Wayne Levi, Steve Pate

   b. Players among the Top 25 in career earnings as of the end of the preceding calendar year may elect to use this special exemption for a second year, provided that the player remains among the Top 25 on the career money list.

10. Sponsor exemptions (a maximum of eight, which may include amateurs with handicaps of two or less), on the following basis:

    a. Not less than two sponsor invitees shall be PGA TOUR Regular, Life or Past Champion members not otherwise exempt.

    b. Not less than two of the top 50 finishers from the last Qualifying Tournament, if not all of them can otherwise be accommodated (Note: PGA TOUR members may receive unlimited number of sponsor invitations. Non-TOUR members may receive maximum of five per year.)

11. Two foreign players designated by the Commissioner.

12. The current PGA Club Professional Champion for a maximum of three open events, in addition to any sponsor selections.

    Steve Schneiter

13. PGA Section Champion of the Section in which the tournament is played.

14. Two members of the PGA Section in which the tournament is played, who qualify through sectional qualifying competitions.

15. Four low scorers at Open Qualifying, which shall normally be held on Monday of tournament week.

16. Past champions of the particular event being contested that week, if co-sponsored by the PGA TOUR and the same tournament sponsor (except for Team events), as follows:
    Winners prior to July 28, 1970--unlimited exemptions for such events.
    Winners after July 28, 1970—ten years of exemptions for such events.
17. Life Members (who have been active members of the PGA TOUR for 15 years and have won at least 20 cosponsored events).
    Tom Watson
    Lanny Wadkins

II. TOP 125, PREVIOUS YEAR'S OFFICIAL MONEY LIST—If not exempt under "Special Exemptions, the top 125 PGA TOUR members on the previous year's Official Money List, in order of their positions on the list.

David Duval
Justin Leonard
Kirk Triplett
Steve Stricker
Jim McGovern
Lennie Clements
Jay Don Blake
Scott Verplank
Bob Lohr
Gene Sauers
Mike Hulbert
Guy Boros
Craig Parry
Joe Ozaki
Robin Freeman
Billy Andrade
Marco Dawson
Gil Morgan
John Adams
Brian Claar
Grant Waite
Blaine McCallister
Nolan Henke
Steve Jones
Jay Delsing
Doug Martin
Don Pooley
David Edwards
Jesper Parnevik
Michael Bradley
Brandel Chamblee
Dillard Pruitt
Robert Gamez
Joey Sindelar
Glen Day
Mike Brisky
Dan Forsman
Jonathan Kaye
Lee Rinker
John Cook
Scott Gump
Jim Carter
Charlie Rymer
Mike Standly
Curt Byrum
Ken Green
Kelly Gibson
Fuzzy Zoeller
Chip Beck
Mark Wiebe
Bobby Wadkins
Tommy Tolles
Brian Kamm
Partick Burke
Phil Blackmar
David Ogrin
Dave Stockton, Jr.
John Wilson
Joe Acosta, Jr.
Scott McCarron
Paul Goydos
Keith Fergus

III. SPECIAL MEDICAL EXTENSION—If granted by the Commissioner, if not otherwise eligible, and if needed to fill the field, Special Medical Extension.

Rocco Mediate
John Inman
Ed Fiori
Jim Thorpe
Denis Watson

IV. TOP FIVE MONEY WINNERS ON 1995 NIKE TOUR

Allen Doyle
Sean Murphy
Jerry Kelly
Stuart Appleby
Franklin Langham

V. TOP 10 FINISHERS—The top 10 professionals and those tied for 10th in an open tournament whose victory has official status are exempt into the next open tournament whose victory has official status.

VI. QUALIFYING TOURNAMENT—The low 40 scorers and ties from the previous year's PGA TOUR Qualifying Tournament , in order of their finish in the tournament, and players 6-10 on the 1995 NIKE TOUR money list.

Carl Paulson
Omar Uresti
Steve Hart
Shane Bertsch
Joey Gullion
Tom Byrum
Tom Scherrer
Olin Browne
Chris Smith
Kevin Sutherland
Sean Murphy
Tim Herron
Hugh Royer III
Russ Cochran
Brad Fabel
Steve Jurgensen
Clarence Rose
Scott Medlin
David Peoples
Robert Wrenn
Paul Stankowski
Hisayuki Sasaki
Lucas Parsons
Brian Tennyson
Billy Ray Brown
Frank Lickliter, Jr.
Len Mattiace
Jeff Gallagher
Steve Rintoul
Ronnie Black
Scott Dunlap
Joe Daley
Bart Bryant
Taylor Smith
Jarmo Sandelin
John Maginnes
Jeff Julian
Greg Kraft
Jay Williamson
Mike Swartz
Joel Edwards
Ron Whittaker
Gary Rusnak
Jeff Hart
John Elliott
Andy Bean
Bryan Gorman

VII. NEXT 25 MEMBERS AFTER TOP 125 MEMBERS FROM PREVIOUS YEAR'S OFFICIAL MONEY LIST—If needed to fill the field, the next 25 PGA TOUR members after the top 125 PGA TOUR members from the previous year's Official Money List, in order of their positions on the list.

Russ Cochran
Tom Byrum
Paul Stankowski
Pete Jordan
Donnie Hammond
Howard Twitty
Bob Gilder
Greg Kraft
Emlyn Aubrey
Tommy Armour III
Tray Tyner
Ronnie Black
Jay Williamson
Bart Bryant
Dave Barr
Dudley Hart
Joel Edwards
Chris Perry
Tony Sills
Steve Rintoul
J.P. Hayes
Bruce Fleisher
Omar Uresti

VIII. SPECIAL MEDICAL EXTENSION BEYOND THE 126-150 FINISHERS

Mark Lye

IX. PAST CHAMPION MEMBERS—If not otherwise eligible and if needed to fill the field, Past Champion Members, in order of the total number of cosponsored or approved events won, excluding Team events. If two or more players are tied, the player who is higher on the PGA TOUR Career Money List shall be eligible.

X. SPECIAL TEMPORARY—If during the course of a PGA TOUR season, a nonmember of the PGA TOUR wins an amount of official money (e.g., by playing in PGA TOUR events through sponsor exemptions, Open Qualifying, etc.) equal to the amount won in the preceding year by the 154th finisher on the official money winning list will be eligible for the remainder of the year.

XI. TEAM CHAMPIONSHIP WINNERS—If not otherwise eligible and if needed to fill the field, winners of cosponsored team championships, in order of the total number of team championship tournaments won. If two or more players are tied based on the number of such tournaments won, the player who is higher on the official PGA TOUR career money list shall be eligible.

XII. VETERAN MEMBERS—If not otherwise eligible and if needed to fill the field, Veteran Members (players who have made a minimum of 150 cuts during their career), in order of their standing on the PGA TOUR career money list.

JOE ACOSTA, JR. *(uh-COST-uh)*

EXEMPT STATUS: 127th on 1995 money list
FULL NAME: Joe Angel Acosta, Jr.
HEIGHT: 6'3" **WEIGHT:** 170
BIRTH DATE: October 25, 1973 **BIRTHPLACE:** San Diego, CA
RESIDENCE: Visalia, CA
FAMILY: Single **COLLEGE:** Fresno State University
SPECIAL INTERESTS: Basketball
TURNED PROFESSIONAL: 1994
Q SCHOOL: 1994

BEST CAREER FINISH: T3 -- 1995 Greater Milwaukee Open

BEST 1995 FINISHES: T3 -- Greater Milwaukee Open; T4 -- Walt Disney World Oldsmobile Classic

1995 SEASON: As the youngest member of the PGA TOUR in 1995, Acosta got off to a slow start, but two top-four finishes in September and October helped him retain his playing privileges for 1996...earned just $8,714 in his first 14 starts, missing the cut in 12 of them...that long dry spell ended with his first top-20 finish, a T18 at the Anheuser-Busch Golf Classic...he made his next three cuts before his breakthrough week at the Greater Milwaukee Open...was in fourth place after the second and third rounds, just two strokes off the lead...went on to tie for third, five strokes behind Scott Hoch, worth $52,000...only player in field with all four rounds in 60s (68-69-69-68)...after the GMO, made four of his next five cuts, the final one at the Walt Disney World/Oldsmobile Classic...he was tied for 22nd with 18 holes to go in the rain-shortened event, but a final-round 66 at the Palm Course lifted him into a tie for fourth, three strokes behind winner Brad Bryant...the $49,600 paycheck guaranteed Acosta's return to the TOUR in 1996.

CAREER HIGHLIGHTS: Earned a spot on TOUR in 1995 by finishing 27th at the 1994 Qualifying Tournament...a second-team All-American at Fresno State in 1993 and 1994...was the 1994 Western Athletic Conference individual champion and led Fresno State to the team title...was named 1994 WAC Player of the Year...a two-time California Junior champion.

PERSONAL: Left Fresno State early to turn professional...knew by age 14 he wanted to be a professional golfer...at the time, was seeing the same teaching pro in Visalia, CA, as Mike Springer.

PGA TOUR CAREER SUMMARY — **PLAYOFF RECORD: 0-0**

Year	Events Played	Cuts Made	1st	2nd	3rd	Top 10	Top 25	Earnings	Rank
1995	26	11			1	2	4	$147,745	127
Total	26	11			1	2	4	$147,745	369

NIKE TOUR SUMMARY

Year	Events Played	Cuts Made	1st	2nd	3rd	Top 10	Top 25	Earnings	Rank
1994	1								
1995	3	2				1	1	$5,320	153
Total	4	2				1	1	$5,320	
COMBINED TOTAL MONEY								$153,065	

1996 PGA TOUR CHARITY TEAM : Mercedes Championships

1995 PGA TOUR STATISTICS

Statistic	Value	Rank
Scoring	71.85	(153T)
Driving	270.7	(36T)
Driving Accuracy	64.0	(165)
Greens in Regulation	66.9	(66T)
Putting	1.784	(79T)
All Around	781	(110T)
Sand Saves	47.8	(144T)
Total Driving	201	(117T)
Eagles	10	(15T)
Birdies	253	(123T)

MISCELLANEOUS STATISTICS

Statistic	Value	Rank
Scoring Avg Before Cut	71.80	(150)
Scoring Avg 3rd Rnd	70.15	(28)
Scoring Avg Final Rnd	71.18	(89T)
Birdies Conversion %	28.6	(95T)
Par Breakers	19.9	(62T)

1995 Low Round: 66: 3 times, most recent 1995 Walt Disney World/ Oldsmobile Classic/3
Career Low Round: 66: 2 times, most recent 1995 Walt Disney World/ Oldsmobile Classic/3
Career Largest Paycheck: $52,000: 1995 Greater Milwaukee Open/T3

John Adams

EXEMPT STATUS: 74th on 1995 money list
FULL NAME: John Gregg Adams
HEIGHT: 6'3" **WEIGHT:** 220
BIRTH DATE: May 5, 1954 **BIRTHPLACE:** Scottsdale, AZ
RESIDENCE: Scottsdale, AZ
FAMILY: Wife, Jane; Benjamin Craig (6/20/83), Kimberly Jill (10/23/85)
COLLEGE: Arizona State University **SPECIAL INTERESTS:** Hunting, fishing
TURNED PROFESSIONAL: 1976
Q SCHOOL: Spring 1978; Fall 1979; Fall 1985

BEST CAREER FINISH: 2 -- 1982 Hall of Fame Classic

BEST 1995 FINISHES: 4 -- Kmart Greater Greensboro Open; T7 -- Phoenix Open; T9 -- AT&T Pebble Beach National Pro-Am

1995 SEASON: After finishing 151st on the 1994 money list and regaining his playing privileges as last qualifier at the Qualifying Tournament, had his most successful year on TOUR...took advantage of a sponsor's exemption at the Phoenix Open by finishing T7, then finished T9 at AT&T Pebble Beach the following week...was one stroke behind leader Ben Crenshaw after the third round at Phoenix...his third top-10 of the year, fourth place at Kmart Greater Greensboro Open, guaranteed a finish in top 125...was tied for fourth after 54 holes at Greensboro, five strokes off the lead and two ahead of eventual winner Jim Gallagher, Jr....the $72,000 check he earned at KGGO is largest of his career...was not in top 10 after KGGO, but did post top-25 finishes at Kemper (T16), Deposit Guaranty (T11) and Buick Challenge (T20)...shot an opening-round 65 at the PGA Championship, but finished with 76-71-70 to place T49...finished the year in the top 10 in four statistical categories -- fourth in eagles (13), sixth in driving distance (278.9), eighth in all-around (381) and 10th in par breakers (.215).

CAREER HIGHLIGHTS: Best chance to win came at the 1982 Hall of Fame Classic played at Pinehurst No. 2...made a bogey on the second playoff hole and lost to Jay Haas...best finish since was a tie for third at the 1992 Las Vegas Invitational, four strokes behind winner John Cook...had his best season prior to 1995 in 1993, when he earned $221,753 on the strength of two top-10 finishes...finished T11 at the 1993 U.S. Open to earn his first Masters appearance in 1994...led the PGA TOUR in Greens in Regulation in 1988 (73.9%) and was third in Driving Distance in 1992 (275.8)...won the 1975 Arizona State Amateur.

PERSONAL: Started playing golf as soon as he could hold a club...held the club and putter cross-handed, "but gave that up when I was about three years old"...while at Arizona State, was coached by Bill Mann, who now is a scorekeeper on the PGA TOUR...father was a golf professional.

CAREER SUMMARY **PLAYOFF RECORD: 0-1**

Year	Events Played	Cuts Made	1st	2nd	3rd	Top 10	Top 25	Earnings	Rank
1973	1	1						$511	267
1978	10	2					1	$2,025	196
1979	11	3						$1,785	224
1980	22	9				1	3	$19,895	125
1981	25	10				1	3	$17,898	140
1982	27	16		1		2	5	$54,014	86
1983	34	17			1	3	4	$59,287	87
1984	27	19			1	2	8	$73,567	80
1985	24	9						$9,613	181
1986	30	19				2	6	$64,906	124
1987	33	20					4	$51,976	149
1988	19	15				1	4	$64,341	140
1989	30	14				2	6	$106,824	120
1990	32	13				2	4	$127,733	122
1991	30	16				2	3	$117,549	125
1992	31	17			1	1	7	$173,069	89
1993	29	18				2	7	$221,753	78
1994	32	11				1	3	$106,689	151
1995	25	16				3	7	$243,366	74
Total	472	245		1	3	25	75	$1,516,801	136

1996 PGA TOUR CHARITY TEAM : Honda Classic

TOP TOURNAMENT SUMMARY

YEAR	80	81	82	83	84	85	86	87	89	90	91	92	93	94	95
Masters Tournament														CUT	
U.S. Open	CUT	CUT		W/D			CUT		CUT		62	CUT	T11	CUT	
PGA Championship				T55	CUT								74		T49
THE PLAYERS Championship		CUT	CUT	T35	CUT	CUT	CUT	CUT		W/D	T52	CUT	CUT	T78	

John Adams...continued

1995 PGA TOUR STATISTICS		
Scoring	70.96	(66)
Driving	278.9	(6T)
Driving Accuracy	64.7	(160)
Greens in Regulation	69.2	(22T)
Putting	1.771	(44T)
All Around	381	(8)
Sand Saves	59.0	(18)
Total Driving	166	(64T)
Eagles	13	(4)
Birdies	300	(61)

MISCELLANEOUS STATISTICS		
Scoring Avg Before Cut	70.55	(29T)
Scoring Avg 3rd Rnd	70.41	(43T)
Scoring Avg Final Rnd	70.94	(70)
Birdies Conversion %	29.7	(60T)
Par Breakers	21.5	(10T)

1995 Low Round: **65:** 1995 PGA Championship/1
Career Low Round: **63:** 1993 Sprint Western Open/3
Career Largest Paycheck: $72,000: 1995 Kmart Greater Greensboro Open/4

Fulton Allem *(AL-ehm)*

EXEMPT STATUS: Winner, 1993 NEC World Series of Golf
FULL NAME: Fulton Peter Allem
HEIGHT: 5'11" **WEIGHT:** 215
BIRTH DATE: September 15, 1957 **BIRTHPLACE:** Kroonstad, South Africa
RESIDENCE: Heathrow, FL
FAMILY: Wife, Colleen; Nadia (7/7/86), Nicholas (1/1/91)
SPECIAL INTERESTS: Riding horses, breeding horses, fishing & hunting
TURNED PROFESSIONAL: 1976
JOINED TOUR: Fall 1987

TOUR VICTORIES (3): 1991 Independent Insurance Agent Open. **1993** Southwestern Bell Colonial, NEC World Series of Golf

INTERNATIONAL VICTORIES (14): 1985 Palaborwa Classic, Million Dollar Challenge. **1986** Minolta Match Play Championship, Palaborwa Classic, South African PGA. **1987** South African PGA, Palaborwa Classic. **1988** Palaborwa Classic, Million Dollar Challenge. **1989** Minolta Match Play Championship. **1990** Lexington PGA Championship, Twee Jongezellen Masters, Goodyear Classic. **1991** ICL International. (All South Africa).

BEST 1995 FINISH: T12 -- Doral-Ryder Open

1995 SEASON: Had his second consecutive sub-par season after his breakthrough year in 1993...made just eight of 21 cuts, with his best finish coming at Doral-Ryder Open where he finished tied for 12th...his opening-round 66 left him one stroke off the lead at that point...only other top-25 finish came in June -- T21 at the Kemper Open, where his third-round 65 was his best of the year...only once was he able to string together two made-cuts -- at the Canon Greater Hartford Open and FedEx St. Jude Classic, where he placed T59 and 69, respectively...his 1995 earnings of $54,239 were the least of his nine-year PGA TOUR career.

CAREER HIGHLIGHTS: His two victories in 1993 came on two of the most storied courses on TOUR, Colonial and Firestone...outdueled Greg Norman for his second career TOUR title at the Southwestern Bell Colonial...second-round 63 put him in contention, and closing 67 gave a one-stroke victory over Norman...that win got him into NEC World Series of Golf, where a final-round 62 brought him the $360,000 first-place check and 10-year TOUR exemption...earned his first TOUR victory in the final week of the 1991 season at the rescheduled Independent Insurance Agent Open (the tournament had been rained out in April)...played last two rounds in 11-under-par to edge Billy Ray Brown, Mike Hulbert and Tom Kite by single stroke...had been No. 143 on money list going into IIAO, but with victory came two-year exemption...second-place finish in 1987 World Series brought him TOUR card without having to go to Qualifying Tournament...Captain's Choice for International Team in inaugural Presidents Cup Match...was 1-3 in foursome and four-ball matches, teaming with Mark McNulty to defeat Jim Gallagher, Jr.-John Huston in four-ball...halved Sunday singles match with Phil Mickelson.

FULTON ALLEM...*continued*

PERSONAL: Started playing golf at age seven with encouragement from father...countryman Gary Player had large influence on him...had 18 second-place finishes before breaking through with first win on South African Tour.

CAREER SUMMARY						PLAYOFF RECORD: 0-0			
Year	**Events Played**	**Cuts Made**	**1st**	**2nd**	**3rd**	**Top 10**	**Top 25**	**Earnings**	**Rank**
1986	2								
1987	6	3		1		1	1	$88,734	105
1988	22	12			1	3	5	$163,911	73
1989	26	18					10	$134,706	104
1990	23	14				1	5	$132,493	116
1991	23	13	1			2	5	$229,702	71
1992	29	21				2	7	$209,982	74
1993	28	19	2			4	8	$851,345	9
1994	28	17				1	3	$166,144	109
1995	21	8					2	$54,239	199
Total	208	125	3	1	1	14	46	$2,031,256	96

1996 PGA TOUR CHARITY TEAM : Buick Open

TOP TOURNAMENT SUMMARY										
YEAR	**86**	**87**	**88**	**89**	**90**	**91**	**92**	**93**	**94**	**95**
Masters Tournament							T52		T38	
U.S. Open						CUT		T52	T33	CUT
British Open Championship	CUT	T44				T44		CUT	CUT	
PGA Championship			CUT	CUT			T40	T31	T47	
THE PLAYERS Championship			T3	T14	T11	CUT	CUT	T20	T55	CUT
THE TOUR Championship								T12		

NATIONAL TEAMS: Presidents Cup, 1994.

1995 PGA TOUR STATISTICS		
Scoring	72.18	(174T)
Driving	254.9	(159T)
Driving Accuracy	77.7	(11)
Greens in Regulation	60.6	(183)
Putting	1.817	(172T)
All Around	1,129	(177T)
Sand Saves	51.1	(106T)
Total Driving	170	(70T)
Eagles	3	(137T)
Birdies	148	(187)

MISCELLANEOUS STATISTICS		
Scoring Avg Before Cut	72.58	(184T)
Scoring Avg 3rd Rnd	72.44	(168)
Scoring Avg Final Rnd	71.50	(113T)
Birdies Conversion %	24.8	(178T)
Par Breakers	15.3	(187)

1995 Low Round: 65: 1995 Kemper Open/3
Career Low Round: 62: 1993 NEC World Series of Golf/4
Career Largest Paycheck: $360,000: 1993 NEC World Series of Golf/1

Did You Know?

For the second year in a row, Joe Acosta, Jr., is the youngest member of the PGA TOUR. Joe was born October 25, 1973. Also for the second year in a row, Justin Leonard, born June 15, 1972, is the PGA TOUR's second youngest member.

BILLY ANDRADE *(ANN-drade)*

EXEMPT STATUS: 69th on 1995 money list
FULL NAME: William Thomas Andrade
HEIGHT: 5' 8" **WEIGHT:** 155
BIRTH DATE: January 25, 1964 **BIRTHPLACE:** Fall River, MA
RESIDENCE: Bristol, RI and Atlanta, GA
FAMILY: Wife, Jody; Cameron James (4/5/94)
COLLEGE: Wake Forest University (1987, Sociology)
SPECIAL INTERESTS: All sports
TURNED PROFESSIONAL: 1987 **Q SCHOOL:** Fall 1987, 1988

TOUR VICTORIES (2): 1991 Kemper Open, Buick Classic

BEST 1995 FINISHES: T7 -- BellSouth Classic; T8 -- THE PLAYERS Championship, Canon Greater Hartford Open.

1995 SEASON: An off-year for the Wake Forest graduate, whose earnings fell for the second consecutive season...best finish came at the BellSouth Classic, where a final-round 67 lifted him to a tie for seventh place...his biggest check of the year came at THE PLAYERS Championship, where his T8 was worth $87,000...also T8 at Canon GHO, thanks largely to a third-round 62, a course record at the TPC at River Highlands...it was the low round of his PGA TOUR career, bettering the opening-round 63 he fired at the 1993 Northern Telecom Open...was one stroke off the lead after an opening-round 65 at Colonial, eventually finishing T15...after a T18 at the Ideon Classic at Pleasant Valley, made just two more cuts in his final eight events of the season.

CAREER HIGHLIGHTS: Enjoyed memorable two-week June stretch in 1991, when he became the first player since John Fought in 1979 to win his first two PGA TOUR events in consecutive weeks...defeated Jeff Sluman on the first playoff hole to capture the Kemper Open after both had carded tournament-record 21-under-par 263s...edged Brad Bryant by one stroke at Westchester Country Club to win the Buick Classic...carded final-round 67 at 1993 Buick Southern Open to get into five-man playoff won by John Inman...three-time All-American at Wake Forest and a member of the Demon Deacons' 1986 NCAA Championship team...winner 1986 Sunnehanna and North and South Amateurs...recipient of Arnold Palmer Scholarship to Wake Forest...teamed with Kris Tschetter to win the 1992 JCPenney Classic.

PERSONAL: Started playing golf at age five, won first tournament at 11...No. 1 ranked junior player in nation in 1981...named to Rhode Island all-state high school basketball team (he would remind you it is a small state).

CAREER SUMMARY **PLAYOFF RECORD: 1-1**

Year	Events Played	Cuts Made	1st	2nd	3rd	Top 10	Top 25	Earnings	Rank
1983(Am.)	1								
1986(Am.)	2	2					2		
1987(Am.)	1								
1987	4	3						$4,001	235
1988	34	17				1	7	$74,950	134
1989	31	17		1		3	6	$202,242	69
1990	28	25				1	12	$231,362	64
1991	29	19	2			4	10	$615,765	14
1992	28	16			1	2	8	$202,509	76
1993	29	18		1	1	7	10	$365,759	40
1994	26	18		1	1	3	5	$342,208	48
1995	29	16				3	8	$276,494	69
Total	242	151	2	3	3	24	68	$2,315,291	79

1996 PGA TOUR CHARITY TEAM: Bay Hill Invitational presented by Office Depot

TOP TOURNAMENT SUMMARY

YEAR	87	88	89	90	91	92	93	94	95
Masters Tournament	CUT					T54	61		
U.S. Open		CUT			CUT	T6	T33		T21
British Open Championship	T54					T25	CUT		CUT
PGA Championship			CUT	T14	T32	T12	CUT	T47	CUT
THE PLAYERS Championship				CUT	T27	CUT	T20	CUT	T8
THE TOUR Championship					T13				

NATIONAL TEAMS: Junior World Cup, 1981 (won team title with Sam Randolph at Portmarnock, Ireland); World Amateur Team Championship, 1986; Walker Cup, 1987.

BILLY ANDRADE...continued

1995 PGA TOUR STATISTICS		
Scoring	71.12	(79T)
Driving	254.9	(159T)
Driving Accuracy	63.5	(169)
Greens in Regulation	65.8	(111T)
Putting	1.786	(86T)
All Around	812	(121)
Sand Saves	56.2	(44)
Total Driving	328	(186)
Eagles	6	(69T)
Birdies	277	(95T)

MISCELLANEOUS STATISTICS		
Scoring Avg Before Cut	71.34	(103T)
Scoring Avg 3rd Rnd	71.39	(113)
Scoring Avg Final Rnd	72.00	(153T)
Birdies Conversion %	26.6	(147T)
Par Breakers	17.5	(150T)

1995 Low Round: **62:** 1995 Canon Greater Hartford Open/3
Career Low Round: **62:** 1995 Canon Greater Hartford Open/3
Career Largest Paycheck: $180,000: 2 times, most recent 1991 Buick Classic/1

STUART APPLEBY *(APPLE-bee)*

EXEMPT STATUS: 5th on 1995 NIKE TOUR money list
FULL NAME: Stuart Appleby
HEIGHT: 6'1" **WEIGHT:** 185
BIRTH DATE: May 1, 1971 **BIRTHPLACE:** Cohuna, Australia
RESIDENCE: Sydney, Australia
FAMILY: Single
SPECIAL INTERESTS: Action sports, motor racing
TURNED PROFESSIONAL: 1992
JOINED TOUR: 1996

BEST CAREER FINISH: First year on PGA TOUR

NIKE TOUR VICTORIES (2): 1995 NIKE Monterrey Open, NIKE Sonoma County Open

BEST 1995 FINISHES: 1—NIKE Monterrey Open, NIKE Sonoma County Open; T2—NIKE Ozarks Open; T6—NIKE Miami Valley Open; T7—NIKE TOUR Championship; T8—NIKE Boise Open; T9—NIKE Texarkana Open.

BEST 1995 FINISH: Did not play PGA TOUR in 1995

1995 SEASON: Became only the eighth player in history to win his first-ever NIKE TOUR event...defeated Rafael Alarcon in a seven-hole playoff to win the NIKE Monterrey Open...the seven-hole affair was the second longest in NIKE TOUR history, behind only the eight-hole playoff won by Tom Lehman at the 1991 Mississippi Gulf Coast Classic...added his second title of the year at the NIKE Sonoma County Open, winning by four strokes...nearly earned another title in August, losing in a playoff to Mike Schuchart at the NIKE Ozarks Open...a great finisher, 29 of his 32 third and fourth rounds last season were par or better...ranked fourth on the NIKE TOUR with a 70.04 scoring average.

CAREER HIGHLIGHTS: Won four tournaments on the Australasian PGA Tour's Foundation Tour in 1994: the Victorian PGA Championship, South Australia PGA Championship, Nedlands Masters and the Tassie Classic...won the 1991 Queensland Open Championship as an amateur...won the 1991 Victorian Amateur Championship and Australian Junior Championship.

PERSONAL: His fiancee, Renay White, serves as his caddy...during the two-week break in the NIKE TOUR schedule following his Sonoma County win, stayed at Orlando home of PGA TOUR member and fellow Australian Ian Baker-Finch.

NIKE TOUR CAREER SUMMARY

Year	Events Played	Cuts Made	1st	2nd	3rd	Top 10	Top 25	Earnings	Rank
1995	22	17	2	1		7	15	$144,419	5
Total	22	17	2	1		7	15	$144,419	

1995 NIKE TOUR STATISTICS		
Scoring	70.04	(4)
Eagles	9	(21T)
Birdies	294	(29T)

1995 NIKE TOUR STATISTICS

1995 Low Round: **65:** 1995 NIKE Sonoma County Open/3
Career Low Round: **65:** 1995 NIKE Sonoma County Open/3
Career Largest Paycheck: $40,500: 1995 NIKE Monterrey Open/1

Woody Austin

EXEMPT STATUS: 1995 tournament winner
FULL NAME: Albert Woody Austin
HEIGHT: 6' **WEIGHT:** 170
BIRTH DATE: January 27, 1964 **BIRTHPLACE:** Tampa, FL
RESIDENCE: Tampa, FL
FAMILY: Wife, Shannon
COLLEGE: University of Miami
SPECIAL INTERESTS: Sports
TURNED PROFESSIONAL: 1987 **Q SCHOOL:** 1994

TOUR VICTORIES (1): 1995 Buick Open

BEST 1995 FINISHES: 1 -- Buick Open; 4 -- Colonial National Invitation; T4 -- MCI Classic, THE TOUR Championship; T6 -- Northern Telecom Open; T7 -- Doral-Ryder Open; T10 -- Motorola Western Open.

1995 SEASON: Smashing debut for the medalist from 1994 PGA TOUR Qualifying Tournament...his performance resulted in PGA TOUR Rookie of the Year honors...one of three rookies in 1995 to qualify for THE TOUR Championship...year's highlight was his playoff victory over Mike Brisky at the Buick Open...after an opening 63 gave him a two-stroke lead, he lost the lead to Payne Stewart after the second round...through 54 holes, he was tied for sixth, three strokes behind Jeff Sluman...a final-round 68 earned him spot in the playoff, which he won with a par on the first extra hole...the win was worth $216,000...showed his talents early in the year as 13 of his first 14 rounds were par or better...during that stretch, earned his first career top-10 finish with a T6 at the Northern Telecom Open...guaranteed himself a place on TOUR in 1996 after the TOUR moved to Florida...tied for seventh at the Doral-Ryder Open after an opening-round 66 placed him just one stroke off the lead...after top-20 finishes at the Honda and Freeport-McMoRan Classics, he notched a T4 at the MCI Classic...entering the final round tied for 43rd, he fired a 64 and finished just one stroke out of three-man playoff eventually won by Bob Tway...fourth at Colonial and T10 at the Motorola Western Open followed...had made 10 of 12 cuts leading up to THE TOUR Championship...after 36 holes at Southern Hills, he stood alone in third, two strokes behind Billy Mayfair...went on to tie for fourth with Scott Simpson...only Ted Tryba, Paul Goydos and Greg Kraft played in more events than Austin's 34.

CAREER HIGHLIGHTS: Finished 23rd on 1994 NIKE TOUR money list...had six top-10 finishes in 26 starts, including second at NIKE Sonoma County Open and T3 at Boise Open...prior to 1995, had only one PGA TOUR start, a missed cut at 1992 Buick Southern Open...played in Japan (1989-90) and on mini-tours (1992-93).

PERSONAL: Tore tendons and cartilage in left knee during 1987 Q-Tournament...injury sidelined him for two years...worked for years as credit union bank clerk during off season.

PGA TOUR CAREER SUMMARY — **PLAYOFF RECORD: 1-0**

Year	Events Played	Cuts Made	1st	2nd	3rd	Top 10	Top 25	Earnings	Rank
1992	1								
1995	34	22	1			7	12	$736,497	24
Total	35	22	1			7	12	$736,497	214

NIKE TOUR SUMMARY

Year	Events Played	Cuts Made	1st	2nd	3rd	Top 10	Top 25	Earnings	Rank
1990	1								
1993	1	1						$383	274
1994	26	18		1	1	6	10	$72,206	23
1995	1								
Total	29	19		1	1	6	10	$72,588	
COMBINED TOTAL MONEY								$809,085	

1996 PGA TOUR CHARITY TEAM : Buick Open

TOP TOURNAMENT SUMMARY

YEAR	95
PGA Championship	T23
THE TOUR Championship	T4

1995 PGA TOUR STATISTICS

Scoring	70.99	(67)
Driving	277.5	(9)
Driving Accuracy	65.3	(151T)
Greens in Regulation	66.6	(80T)
Putting	1.805	(139T)
All Around	521	(38)
Sand Saves	54.3	(68)
Total Driving	160	(58)
Eagles	12	(5T)
Birdies	404	(2T)

MISCELLANEOUS STATISTICS

Scoring Avg Before Cut	70.93	(60T)
Scoring Avg 3rd Rnd	70.50	(52T)
Scoring Avg Final Rnd	70.70	(41T)
Birdies Conversion %	29.6	(64T)
Par Breakers	20.3	(40T)

1995 Low Round: **63:** 1995 Buick Open/1
Career Low Round: **63:** 1995 Buick Open/1
Career Largest Paycheck: **$216,000:** 1995 Buick Open/1

Paul Azinger *(Ā-zing-r)*

EXEMPT STATUS: Winner, 1993 PGA Championship
FULL NAME: Paul William Azinger
HEIGHT: 6' 2" **WEIGHT:** 175
BIRTH DATE: January 6, 1960 **BIRTHPLACE:** Holyoke, MA
RESIDENCE: Bradenton, FL
FAMILY: Wife,Toni; Sarah Jean (12/28/85), Josie Lynn (4/21/89)
COLLEGE: Brevard JC and Florida State University
SPECIAL INTERESTS: Fishing
TURNED PROFESSIONAL: 1981 **Q SCHOOL:** Fall 1981, 1983, 1984

TOUR VICTORIES (11): 1987 Phoenix Open, Panasonic-Las Vegas Invitational, Canon-Sammy Davis Jr.-Greater Hartford Open. **1988** Hertz Bay Hill Classic. **1989** Canon Greater Hartford Open. **1990** MONY Tournament of Champions.**1991** AT&T Pebble Beach National Pro-Am. **1992** TOUR Championship.**1993** Memorial Tournament, New England Classic, PGA Championship.

INTERNATIONAL VICTORIES (2): 1990 BMW International Open (Eur). **1992** BMW International Open (Eur).

BEST 1995 FINISH: T4 -- United Airlines Hawaiian Open

1995 SEASON: Completed his first full season after chemotherapy and radiation treatments for lymphoma diagnosed in Dec. 1993...a closing 66 gave him a tie for fourth in his first event of 1995, the United Airlines Hawaiian Open...he earned his biggest check of the year there -- $49,600 -- but it would be his only top-10 finish of the year...played consistently, though not spectacularly, after Hawaii, making seven of the next 10 cuts...tied for 17th at the Masters...only other top-20 finish came at the Canon Greater Hartford Open, where rounds of 67-70-66-70--273 were good for a T15...U.S. region semifinalist in Andersen Consulting World Championship of Golf.

CAREER HIGHLIGHTS: Best year of career, 1993, ended in diagnosis of lymphoma in right shoulder blade...suffered from pain in shoulder for years, had one operation in 1991...captured first major by defeating Greg Norman on second hole of a sudden-death playoff for 1993 PGA Championship at Inverness...earlier won Memorial Tournament in dramatic fashion, holing out from greenside bunker on 72nd hole...third-round 64 put him in position for New England Classic win...10 top-three finishes that year were the most since Tom Watson in 1980...finished second on money list to Nick Price...had at least one win per year from 1987 through 1993...a three-time winner in 1987, when again second on money list and won PGA Player of Year honors...runner-up 1987 British Open...1984 Qualifying Tournament medalist...winner of the Fred Meyer Challenge in 1988 with Bob Tway and in 1991 with Ben Crenshaw.

PERSONAL: Has dedicated himself to being an inspiration to others ("I have a chance to reach out to thousands of people")...wrote book, Zinger, about fight against cancer...is host of Zinger Stinger Pro-Am each November to raise money for lymphoma research...event has raised more than $500,000 in two years...recipient of GWAA Ben Hogan Trophy in 1995, given to the individual who has continued to be active in golf despite physical handicap...credits much of success to teacher John Redman...started playing golf at age 5, but success didn't come immediately...couldn't break 40 for nine holes as high school senior...made broadcasting debut as on-course reporter for NBC at 1995 Ryder Cup.

CAREER SUMMARY **PLAYOFF RECORD: 1-2**

Year	Events Played	Cuts Made	1st	2nd	3rd	Top 10	Top 25	Earnings	Rank
1982	21	10				1	1	$10,655	174
1983	2								
1984	21	14					3	$27,821	144
1985	33	18				3	6	$81,179	93
1986	30	25		2	2	7	13	$254,019	29
1987	27	22	3		1	9	15	$822,481	2
1988	27	21	1	1	1	10	16	$594,850	11
1989	25	21	1	2	4	13	16	$951,649	3
1990	26	22	1	3		12	18	$944,731	4
1991	21	18	1	2	2	6	13	$685,603	9
1992	23	20	1	1	3	10	14	$929,863	7
1993	24	17	3	1	6	12	13	$1,458,456	2
1994	4	2					1	$13,422	242
1995	23	15				1	5	$182,595	100
Total	307	225	11	12	19	84	134	$6,957,324	8

1996 PGA TOUR CHARITY TEAM : Canon Greater Hartford Open

PAUL AZINGER...*continued*

TOP TOURNAMENT SUMMARY

YEAR	83	85	86	87	88	89	90	91	92	93	94	95
Masters Tournament				T17	CUT	T14	CUT	52	T31	CUT		T17
U.S. Open	CUT	CUT	34	CUT	T6	T9	T24	CUT	T33	T3		CUT
British Open Championship				T2	T48	T8	T48		T59	T59		CUT
PGA Championship		CUT	CUT	CUT	2	CUT	T31		T33	1	CUT	T31
THE PLAYERS Championship		CUT	T64	6	T30	T14	CUT	T3	T29	T6		CUT
THE TOUR Championship				4	T17	T3	11	T24	1	21		

NATIONAL TEAMS: Ryder Cup (3), 1989, 1991, 1993; World Cup, 1989; Co-captain Presidents Cup, 1994

1995 PGA TOUR STATISTICS

Scoring	**71.13**	**(82T)**
Driving	**265.0**	**(80T)**
Driving Accuracy	**65.7**	**(147)**
Greens in Regulation	**65.9**	**(108T)**
Putting	**1.751**	**(7T)**
All Around	**619**	**(63)**
Sand Saves	**53.7**	**(77)**
Total Driving	**227**	**(150T)**
Eagles	**15**	**(2)**
Birdies	**259**	**(116T)**

MISCELLANEOUS STATISTICS

Scoring Avg Before Cut	**71.58**	**(132T)**
Scoring Avg 3rd Rnd	**70.67**	**(60)**
Scoring Avg Final Rnd	**70.20**	**(17)**
Birdies Conversion %	**29.5**	**(68T)**
Par Breakers	**20.0**	**(56T)**

1995 Low Round: 66: 2 times, most recent 1995 Canon Greater Hartford Open/3
Career Low Round: 62: 2 times, most recent 1989 Texas Open/2
Career Largest Paycheck: $360,000: 1992 TOUR Championship/1

IAN BAKER-FINCH

EXEMPT STATUS: Winner, 1991 British Open
FULL NAME: Ian Baker-Finch
HEIGHT: 6'4" **WEIGHT:** 190
BIRTH DATE: October 24, 1960 **BIRTHPLACE:** Nambour, Australia
RESIDENCE: Sanctuary Cove, Queensland, Australia; plays out of Sanctuary Cove
FAMILY: Wife, Jennie; Hayley (2/7/89), Laura (10/7/91)
SPECIAL INTERESTS: Water sports, wine, tennis, sports
TURNED PROFESSIONAL: 1979 **JOINED TOUR:** Fall 1988

TOUR VICTORIES (1): 1989 Southwestern Bell Colonial

INTERNATIONAL VICTORIES (15): 1983 New Zealand Open (Aus). **1984** Western Australian Open (Aus), New South Wales Open (Aus), PGA Championship of Queensland (Aus). **1985** Victorian Open (Aus), Scandinavian Enterprise Open (Eur). **1987** Australian Match Play Championship (Aus), Polaroid Cup Golf Digest (Jpn). **1988** Australian Masters (Aus), Pocari Sweat Open (Jpn), Bridgestone ASO Open (Aus). **1990** Coolum Classic (Aus), Queensland Open (Aus). **1991** British Open (Eur). **1993** Australian PGA Championship (Aus).

1995 SEASON: After making only six of 20 cuts in 1994, Ian failed to make a cut in 18 starts...his string of missed cuts stretches back to the 1994 NEC World Series of Golf -- a total of 20 events...hampered by shoulder and back problems...took six weeks off April to mid-May...didn't touch a club during that stretch.

CAREER HIGHLIGHTS: Captured 120th British Open at Royal Birkdale in 1991...closed with rounds of 64-66 to defeat countryman Mike Harwood by two strokes...birdied five of first seven holes Sunday to set stage for victory...lone PGA TOUR victory to date came in 1989 Southwestern Bell Colonial by four strokes over David Edwards...amassed 15 top-10s during 1990-91 TOUR seasons, earning more than $600,000 each year...qualified for the PGA TOUR by finishing third at the 1988 World Series of Golf, worth $75,840...led 1984 British Open at St. Andrews through three rounds before a final-round 79 left him tied for ninth...first check in the United States came in 1984 with T16 in Charley Pride Fiesta, a Tournament Players Series event...winner of events in Australia, Japan and Europe, most notable of which 1988 Australian Masters and most recent 1993 Ford Australian PGA Championship...1994 injury problems involved shoulder and knee, as well as recovery from eye surgery.

PERSONAL: Comes from same "neighborhood" as Greg Norman and Wayne Grady in Queensland, Australia...has worked with sports psychologist Jim Loehr, who has helped tennis players Pete Sampras and Jim Courier.

Ian Baker-Finch...*continued*

Year	Events Played	Cuts Made	1st	2nd	3rd	Top 10	Top 25	Earnings	Rank
CAREER SUMMARY					**PLAYOFF RECORD: 0-1**				
1984	1								
1985	8	5					1	$4,825	202
1988	4	4			1	2	3	$75,840	133
1989	18	14	1			1	5	$253,309	53
1990	24	19		3	2	6	10	$611,492	16
1991	21	19		3	1	9	14	$649,513	13
1992	19	13		1		3	6	$261,817	58
1993	20	12			1	1	4	$140,621	114
1994	20	6				1	1	$81,326	167
1995	18								
Total	153	92	1	7	5	23	44	$2,078,743	98

1996 PGA TOUR CHARITY TEAM: Greater Milwaukee Open

TOP TOURNAMENT SUMMARY

YEAR	84	85	86	87	88	89	90	91	92	93	94	95
Masters Tournament		CUT					CUT	T7	T6	T54	T10	CUT
U.S. Open								T44	T13	T19	CUT	CUT
British Open Championship	T9	T20	CUT	CUT	CUT	T30	T6	1	T19	T70	CUT	CUT
PGA Championship						T34	T57	CUT	T69	66	CUT	CUT
THE PLAYERS Championship						CUT	T46	T41	T2	T39	T69	W/D
THE TOUR Championship							T3	T10				

NATIONAL TEAMS: Dunhill Cup (2), 1989, 1992; Four Tours World Championship of Golf (3), 1989, 1990, 1991; Australian World Cup, 1985; Nissan Cup (2), 1985, 1986; Kirin Cup (4), 1987, 1988.

1995 PGA TOUR STATISTICS

Scoring	**76.64**	**(N/A)**
Driving	**245.7**	**(N/A)**
Driving Accuracy	**45.0**	**(N/A)**
Greens in Regulation	**49.6**	**(N/A)**
Putting	**1.874**	**(N/A)**
Sand Saves	**52.5**	**(N/A)**
Total Driving	**1,998**	**(N/A)**
Eagles	**1**	**(N/A)**
Birdies	**54**	**(N/A)**

MISCELLANEOUS STATISTICS

Scoring Avg Before Cut	**76.57**	**(N/A)**
Scoring Avg 3rd Rnd	**77.00**	**(N/A)**
Birdies Conversion %	**20.6**	**(N/A)**
Par Breakers	**9.8**	**(N/A)**

1995 Low Round: 71: 4 times, most recent 1995 Las Vegas Invitational/1
Career Low Round: 62: 1991 Anheuser-Busch GC/1
Career Largest Paycheck: $180,000: 1989 S/West Bell Colonial/1

Chip Beck

EXEMPT STATUS: 111th on 1995 money list
FULL NAME: Charles Henry Beck
HEIGHT: 5' 10" **WEIGHT:** 170
BIRTH DATE: September 12, 1956 **BIRTHPLACE:** Fayetteville, NC
RESIDENCE: Lake Forest, IL; plays out of Royal Melbourne, Long Grove, IL
FAMILY: Wife, Karen; Charles (11/12/83), Elizabeth (3/16/87), Mary Catherine (7/7/90), Anne Marie (5/28/92), John (5/17/93), Carl Henry (10/30/95)
COLLEGE: University of Georgia (1978, Journalism)
SPECIAL INTERESTS: Tennis, landscaping, water skiing
TURNED PROFESSIONAL: 1978 **Q SCHOOL: Fall** 1978

TOUR VICTORIES (4) : 1988 Los Angeles Open, USF&G Classic. **1990** Buick Open. **1992** Freeport-McMoRan Classic.

BEST 1995 FINISH: 9 -- United Airlines Hawaiian Open.

1995 SEASON: A second consecutive disappointing year for Beck, whose earnings fell to their lowest point in a decade...dropped out of the top 100 on the money list for the first time since 1981, his third year on TOUR...had his best finish of 1995 in his first start

Chip Beck...continued

-- T9 at the United Airlines Hawaiian Open...the $34,800 he earned at Waialae was his largest check of the year...after a T16 at the Buick Invitational of California in February, was in the top 25 only three more times -- T18 at Buick Classic in May, T25 at Motorola Western Open in July and T15 at Walt Disney World/Oldsmobile Classic...an opening 66 at the PGA Championship placed him tied for fifth, three strokes off Michael Bradley's lead...he closed with rounds of 74-73-68 to finish T44...that round, along with a second-round 66 at Disney, was his lowest of the year.

CAREER HIGHLIGHTS: Recorded 59 on October 11, 1991, during third round of Las Vegas Invitational at Sunrise GC...made 13 birdies during bogey-free round, sinking three-foot putt on 18th hole to join Al Geiberger as only sub-60 shooters in TOUR history...received $500,000 from Hilton Hotels for historic feat, with another $500,000 designated for charity...set up Chip Beck Scholarship Fund for distribution of monies...best year on TOUR was1988, when he won L.A. Open and USF&G Classic...repeated as New Orleans winner in 1992...had two runner-up finishes in 1993, at Masters Tournament and in Anheuser-Busch Golf Classic...A-B finish enabled him to make third Ryder Cup team...singles victory over Barry Lane at The Belfry gave United States second consecutive victory...winner 1988 Vardon Trophy...won the 1989 and 1992 Merrill Lynch Shoot-Out Championships.

PERSONAL: Without question, possesses the sunniest disposition on the PGA TOUR...started playing golf during summer of 10th year, won Pee Wee division by end of that summer...three time All-American at Georgia, where majored in journalism...named UGA Athlete of Year as senior.

CAREER SUMMARY — **PLAYOFF RECORD: 0-2**

Year	Events Played	Cuts Made	1st	2nd	3rd	Top 10	Top 25	Earnings	Rank
1979	15	5						$4,166	197
1980	25	13				1	2	$17,109	134
1981	27	13				1	5	$30,034	112
1982	29	15			1	2	6	$57,608	77
1983	32	25		2		5	12	$149,909	33
1984	31	20			4	7	10	$177,289	34
1985	30	18				1	7	$76,038	97
1986	31	21		2		6	13	$215,140	39
1987	28	19		2	3	7	14	$523,003	9
1988	25	23	2	3		11	17	$916,818	2
1989	23	18		3	1	10	16	$694,087	9
1990	25	20	1			7	11	$571,816	17
1991	26	22		1	2	7	15	$578,535	16
1992	26	21	1	2	2	7	10	$689,704	17
1993	27	19		2		5	13	$603,376	25
1994	27	19			1	1	8	$281,131	68
1995	29	19				1	5	$170,081	111
Total	456	310	4	17	14	79	164	$5,755,844	16

1996 PGA TOUR CHARITY TEAM: Motorola Western Open

TOP TOURNAMENT SUMMARY

YEAR	80	81	82	83	84	85	86	87	88	89	90	91	92	93	94	95
Masters Tournament				T32	CUT			T12	T21	T8	T39	CUT	CUT	2	T15	T35
U.S. Open	56	CUT	T12	T10	T21		T2	CUT	T21	T2	T29	CUT	CUT	T25	T25	CUT
British Open Championship			CUT						T28	T26	CUT	T17	T12	CUT	CUT	
PGA Championship			CUT	T23	T25	CUT	T16	T56	T31	T34	T5	T23	CUT	CUT	T36	T44
THE PLAYERS Championship		CUT	CUT	CUT	T29	CUT	CUT	T44	T11	2	T66	T52	T49	CUT	T27	T61
THE TOUR Championship								2	T24	T9	6	T5	T20	T12		

NATIONAL TEAMS: Ryder Cup (3), 1989,1991, 1993; Dunhill Cup, 1988; Kirin Cup, 1988; Asahi Glass Four Tours World Championship of Golf, 1989.

1995 PGA TOUR STATISTICS

Scoring	**71.35**	**(103T)**
Driving	**260.2**	**(117)**
Driving Accuracy	**68.2**	**(113T)**
Greens in Regulation	**64.9**	**(124T)**
Putting	**1.782**	**(74T)**
All Around	**774**	**(108)**
Sand Saves	**54.9**	**(62)**
Total Driving	**230**	**(154)**
Eagles	**3**	**(137T)**
Birdies	**312**	**(44T)**

MISCELLANEOUS STATISTICS

Scoring Avg Before Cut	**71.21**	**(92T)**
Scoring Avg 3rd Rnd	**72.00**	**(149T)**
Scoring Avg Final Rnd	**71.94**	**(149T)**
Birdies Conversion %	**28.7**	**(92T)**
Par Breakers	**18.8**	**(106T)**

1995 Low Round: **66:** 4 times, most recent 1995 Walt Disney World/Oldsmobile Classic/2
Career Low Round: **59:** 1991 Las Vegas Invitation/3
Career Largest Paycheck: **$216,000:** 1987 Nabisco Championship/2

PHIL BLACKMAR

EXEMPT STATUS: 121st on 1995 money list
FULL NAME: Philip Arnold Blackmar
HEIGHT: 6' 7" **WEIGHT:** 245
BIRTH DATE: September 22, 1957 **BIRTHPLACE:** San Diego, CA
RESIDENCE: Corpus Christi, TX; plays out of Kings Crossing CC
FAMILY: Wife, Carol; Kristin Ashley(3/21/84), Kelli Michelle (9/20/85), Philip James (5/9/88), Mark Fredrik (4/28/92)
COLLEGE: Universty of Texas (1979, Finance)
SPECIAL INTERESTS: Fishing
TURNED PROFESSIONAL: 1980 **Q SCHOOL:** Fall 1984, 1994

TOUR VICTORIES (2) : 1985 Canon Sammy Davis, Jr. Greater Hartford Open. **1988** Provident Classic.

BEST 1995 FINISH: T4 -- Las Vegas Invitational

1995 SEASON: After surviving his first trip to the Qualifying Tournament in 10 years, retained his playing privileges for 1996 with a strong finish at the Las Vegas Invitational...tied for 42nd after the third round of the 90-hole event, shot 64-65 in the final two rounds to finish T4...the $62,000 paycheck, his largest since 1993, moved him into the top 125...LVI finish his first top-10 since 1993 Canadian Open (T8)...the 64 at the TPC at Summerlin was his low round of 1995...after missing the cut in his first five events of 1995, earned a check in 15 of 19 the rest of the way...had consecutive top-20 finishes at the Shell Houston Open (T19) and BellSouth Classic (T18)...made seven consecutive cuts from the Anheuser-Busch Golf Classic through the Quad City Classic, including a T14 at the Bell Canadian Open.

CAREER HIGHLIGHTS: Has two career victories, both in playoffs...defeated Dan Pohl and Jodie Mudd with a birdie at the first extra hole at the 1985 Canon Sammy Davis, Jr.-Greater Hartford Open...that year finished 28th on the money list and was named Rookie of the Year...second win came in 1988, when he sank a long birdie putt on the first extra hole to defeat Payne Stewart at the Provident Classic...led 1991 PLAYERS Championship until ball found water on 71st hole at famed island green...also was in contention through 70 holes of 1992 PLAYERS until again met watery fate...best chance at victory since then may have come at the 1993 International...trailed Mark O'Meara by one point through 36 holes before finishing third...finished runner-up to Paul Azinger at the 1984 Qualifying Tournament...was second at the 1985 National Long Drive Championship...1983 Missouri State Amateur champion...three times an all-Southwest Conference selection at Texas.

PERSONAL: Father won the National Left-Handers title in 1965 and introduced him to the game at an early age...graduated from the University of Texas with a degree in finance and worked at a bank for several months before he began entering mini-tour events in 1980.

CAREER SUMMARY					PLAYOFF RECORD: 1-1				
Year	Events Played	Cuts Made	1st	2nd	3rd	Top 10	Top 25	Earnings	Rank
1984	1	1						$3,374	210
1985	27	16	1			4	7	$198,537	28
1986	29	17			2	4	9	$191,228	43
1987	32	19		1		1	8	$99,581	97
1988	29	9	1			1	3	$108,403	105
1989	27	15				2	6	$140,949	100
1990	30	15			1	2	9	$200,796	78
1991	27	13			1	3	5	$218,838	77
1992	24	17		1		2	5	$242,783	63
1993	30	17			1	2	6	$207,310	83
1994	30	5					1	$28,159	213
1995	24	15				1	5	$154,801	121
Total	310	159	2	2	5	22	64	$1,794,760	111

1996 PGA TOUR CHARITY TEAM: Bell Canadian Open

TOP TOURNAMENT SUMMARY

YEAR	84	85	86	87	88	89	90	91	92	93	94
Masters Tournament			T45								
U.S. Open	T43	CUT	T35				CUT	CUT	CUT		
PGA Championship		T65	T53	T40		T53		T73	CUT		
THE PLAYERS Championship		T64	CUT	CUT	CUT	CUT	CUT	T3	T2	CUT	CUT

PHIL BLACKMAR...continued

1995 PGA TOUR STATISTICS		
Scoring	71.56	(121T)
Driving	268.8	(49)
Driving Accuracy	61.1	(177)
Greens in Regulation	63.5	(154T)
Putting	1.777	(58T)
All Around	733	(97)
Sand Saves	57.4	(34T)
Total Driving	226	(147T)
Eagles	9	(20T)
Birdies	255	(120)

MISCELLANEOUS STATISTICS		
Scoring Avg Before Cut	71.60	(135)
Scoring Avg 3rd Rnd	71.69	(135T)
Scoring Avg Final Rnd	71.67	(125T)
Birdies Conversion %	29.3	(77T)
Par Breakers	19.3	(89T)

1995 Low Round: **64:** 1995 Las Vegas Invitational/4
Career Low Round: **63:** 1992 GTE Byron Nelson Cl./1
Career Largest Paycheck: $118,800: 1992 PLAYERS Championship/T2

JAY DON BLAKE

EXEMPT STATUS: 54th on 1995 money list
FULL NAME: Jay Don Blake
HEIGHT: 6' 2" **WEIGHT:**180
BIRTH DATE: October 28, 1958 **BIRTHPLACE:** St. George, UT
RESIDENCE: St. George, UT
FAMILY: Jamie Dawn (10/1/79), Bridgette (4/11/83)
COLLEGE: Utah State University
SPECIAL INTERESTS: Fishing, hunting, all sports
TURNED PROFESSIONAL: 1981 **Q SCHOOL:** Fall 1986

TOUR VICTORIES (1): 1991 Shearson Lehman Brothers Open

INTERNATIONAL VICTORIES (1): 1991 Argentina Open.

BEST 1995 FINISHES: T2 -- Nissan Open; T5 -- GTE Byron Nelson Classic; T6 -- LaCantera Texas Open.

1995 SEASON: Another solid year for the Utah native, who pushed his career earnings over the $2 million mark...his three top-10 finishes included a T2 at the Nissan Open...a third-round 66 moved him to within two strokes of Kenny Perry's lead...after a closing 69, finished tied with Perry, three strokes behind Corey Pavin...his $105,600 check was the third-largest of his career, surpassed by his $180,000 winner's check at 1991 Shearson Lehman Brothers Open and $108,000 check for his second at the 1992 BellSouth Classic...at GTE Byron Nelson, an opening 64 was one stroke off Glen Day's lead...he closed 69-69-66 to finish tied for fifth...two weeks later, a final-round 64 lifted him to T15 at Colonial...his best chance to win likely came at the final full-field event of the season, the LaCantera Texas Open...two rounds of 67 placed him alone in second, two strokes behind Duffy Waldorf after 36 holes...a third-round 70 in blustery conditions cut Waldorf's lead in half...a disastrous 9 on the 16th hole in the final round, combined with Waldorf's closing 65, left Blake tied for sixth, 13 strokes behind the leader...the $38,225 check pushed him over $300,000 for the second year in a row and the third time in his career.

CAREER HIGHLIGHTS: Best year of career came in 1991, when captured only tournament title, Shearson Lehman Brothers Open...closed with consecutive 67s at Torrey Pines to edge Bill Sander by two strokes...had five other top-10 finishes during that campaign, which produced earnings of $563,854 and only Top-30 money list placing to date -- 21st...went over $200,000 in earnings for first time in 1989, with best finish T3 in BellSouth Atlanta Classic...tied for second with Steve Stricker, Vijay Singh and Loren Roberts at 1994 Northern Telecom Open, two strokes behind Andrew Magee...had pair of T4s in 1993, in Buick Invitational of California and at Buick Open, his top finishes that year...posted solo second in 1991 BellSouth Classic, three strokes behind Tom Kite...led TOUR in putting in 1991, averaging 1.733 putts per green in regulation...finished in top 10 in putting the next year, as well...winner 1988 Utah State Open.

PERSONAL: Winner of 1980 NCAA Championship during junior year at Utah State, runner-up in 1981...named College Player of Year in 1981...knew by age 12 wanted to be professional golfer...attended, with three TOUR fellows, National Hot Rod Association driving school in Gainesville, FL in December 1995.

JAY DON BLAKE...continued

CAREER SUMMARY — **PLAYOFF RECORD: 0-0**

Year	Events Played	Cuts Made	1st	2nd	3rd	Top 10	Top 25	Earnings	Rank
1987	31	19				1	9	$87,634	106
1988	31	24				2	8	$131,937	90
1989	27	16			1	3	9	$200,499	71
1990	30	16					8	$148,384	106
1991	27	23	1			6	14	$563,854	21
1992	24	15		1		4	8	$299,298	51
1993	26	15				3	6	$202,482	86
1994	25	20		1		2	9	$309,351	55
1995	26	17		1		3	9	$333,551	54
Total	247	165	1	3	1	24	80	$2,276,989	83

1996 PGA TOUR CHARITY TEAM: MCI Classic

TOP TOURNAMENT SUMMARY

YEAR	87	88	89	90	91	92	93	94	95
Masters Tournament					T27	CUT	T45		
U.S. Open	T24		T18	CUT		T6	T62	CUT	
British Open Championship					T64				
PGA Championship		T25	CUT	W/D	T13	T76		T66	CUT
THE PLAYERS Championship	CUT	T34	CUT	CUT	T27	T40	W/D	T35	CUT
THE TOUR Championship					T13				

1995 PGA TOUR STATISTICS

Scoring	70.84	(59T)
Driving	263.5	(89T)
Driving Accuracy	70.3	(86T)
Greens in Regulation	68.9	(28T)
Putting	1.793	(105T)
All Around	614	(61)
Sand Saves	48.9	(134)
Total Driving	175	(79)
Eagles	7	(51T)
Birdies	299	(62)

MISCELLANEOUS STATISTICS

Scoring Avg Before Cut	70.91	(57T)
Scoring Avg 3rd Rnd	70.00	(19T)
Scoring Avg Final Rnd	70.65	(34T)
Birdies Conversion %	28.0	(120T)
Par Breakers	19.8	(71T)

1995 Low Round: 64: 2 times, most recent 1995 Colonial National Invitation/4
Career Low Round: 63: 1994 Bell Canadian Open/2
Career Largest Paycheck: $180,000: 1991 Shearson Lehman Bros/1

GUY BOROS *(BORE-ohs)*

EXEMPT STATUS: 62nd on 1995 money list
FULL NAME: Guy Donald Boros
HEIGHT: 6'1" **WEIGHT:** 240
BIRTH DATE: September 4, 1964 **BIRTHPLACE:** Ft. Lauderdale, FL
RESIDENCE: Ft. Lauderdale, FL
FAMILY: Wife, Kim
COLLEGE: University of Iowa
SPECIAL INTERESTS: Hunting, fishing
TURNED PROFESSIONAL: 1986 **Q SCHOOL:** 1993

BEST TOUR CAREER FINISH: T3 -- 1994 Deposit Guaranty Golf Classic

INTERNATIONAL VICTORIES (2): 1989 Atlantic Classic (Can). **1991** B.C. Open (Can).

BEST 1995 FINISHES: T4 -- BellSouth Classic, Buick Challenge; T6 -- AT&T Pebble Beach National Pro-Am; T7 -- Kmart Greater Greensboro Open.

GUY BOROS...*continued*

1995 SEASON: Despite missing more cuts than he made, easily retained his playing privileges thanks to four top-10 finishes, two in the top five...after three missed cuts to open year, T6 at AT&T Pebble Beach was worth $46,900...broke a later string of five missed cuts with a T7 at Kmart GGO...two weeks later, posted one of two T4s on the year at BellSouth Classic...the $53,733 check was largest of his career...made five consecutive cuts, his longest string of the year, from the U.S. Open through the Ideon Classic at Pleasant Valley...in that stretch, recorded a T11 at Canon Greater Hartford Open and, at one point, had 15 of 16 rounds of par or better...second T4 also came in Georgia, thanks to a closing 65 at the Buick Challenge...low round of the year was a third-round 64 at Canon GHO, where he finished T11.

CAREER HIGHLIGHTS: After four years on the Canadian Tour and two on the Australian Tour, qualified for PGA TOUR by finishing T18 in 1993 Qualifying Tournament...had four top-10 finishes in 1994 to finish 76th on the money list, sixth among rookies...shot 69-67 in the rain-shortened, 36-hole 1994 Deposit Guaranty Classic to tie for third, his best TOUR finish...led 1991 Canadian Tour Order of Merit...finished 13th on 1993 NIKE TOUR money list with $75,104, with a second at the NIKE South Texas Open and a T3 at the NIKE Miami Valley Open to his credit.

PERSONAL: Son of two-time U.S. Open champion Julius Boros...was competing in the 1994 Southwestern Bell Colonial when his father died...all-Big Ten golfer 1984-85-86 at University of Iowa.

PGA TOUR CAREER SUMMARY — **PLAYOFF RECORD: 0-0**

Year	Events Played	Cuts Made	1st	2nd	3rd	Top 10	Top 25	Earnings	Rank
1990	1								
1991	1								
1994	30	19			1	4	8	$240,775	76
1995	34	14				4	9	$303,654	62
Total	66	33			1	8	17	$544,429	244

NIKE TOUR SUMMARY

Year	Events Played	Cuts Made	1st	2nd	3rd	Top 10	Top 25	Earnings	Rank
1991	1								
1993	28	22		1	1	8	14	$75,104	13
1994	1								
Total	30	22		1	1	8	14	$75,104	
COMBINED TOTAL MONEY								$619,533	

1996 PGA TOUR CHARITY TEAM: Buick Classic

TOP TOURNAMENT SUMMARY

YEAR	95
U.S. Open	T36
PGA Championship	CUT
THE PLAYERS Championship	CUT

1995 PGA TOUR STATISTICS

Scoring	71.04	(72T)
Driving	271.0	(33)
Driving Accuracy	64.3	(162)
Greens in Regulation	66.5	(82T)
Putting	1.780	(66T)
All Around	586	(53)
Sand Saves	50.9	(112T)
Total Driving	195	(107T)
Eagles	8	(36T)
Birdies	343	(23)

MISCELLANEOUS STATISTICS

Scoring Avg Before Cut	71.51	(124T)
Scoring Avg 3rd Rnd	70.56	(55)
Scoring Avg Final Rnd	70.07	(13)
Birdies Conversion %	29.5	(68T)
Par Breakers	20.1	(53T)

1995 Low Round: **64:** 1995 Canon Greater Hartford Open/3
Career Low Round: **63:** 2 times, most recent 1994 Las Vegas Invitational/2
Career Largest Paycheck: **$53,733:** 1995 BellSouth Classic/T4

MICHAEL BRADLEY

EXEMPT STATUS: 85th on 1995 money list
FULL NAME: Michael John Bradley
HEIGHT: 6' **WEIGHT:** 180
BIRTH DATE: July 17, 1966 **BIRTHPLACE:** Largo, FL
RESIDENCE: Valrico, FL; plays out of Bloomingdale Golfers' Club, Brandon, FL
FAMILY: Wife, Jennifer
COLLEGE: Oklahoma State University
SPECIAL INTERESTS: Sports
TURNED PROFESSIONAL: 1988 **Q SCHOOL:** 1992

BEST TOUR CAREER FINISH: T3 -- 1993 Kemper Open

INTERNATIONAL VICTORIES (2): 1989 Ontario Open (Can). **1990** Quebec Open (Can).

BEST 1995 FINISHES: T8 -- Honda Classic, Canon Greater Hartford Open.

1995 SEASON: Improved upon prior year's earnings once again in 1995, topping $200,000 for the first time...had two top-10s during the year, both T8s...shot 73-69-73-68--283 for T8 at the Honda Classic in March...shot four rounds in the 60s at the Canon GHO in June to finish T8 and earn his largest check of the year, $34,800...shot a 63, his best round of 1995, in the first round of the PGA Championship...only previous PGA Championship first-round 63 posted by Ray Floyd in 1982...led by one stroke at the time, but finished T54 after closing with 73-73-74...made 18 of 27 cuts on the year, including six in a row beginning at the Doral-Ryder Open...that stretch included three top-15 finishes...a later string of five consecutive made cuts, from the Motorola Western Open through the Sprint International, included a T11 at the Anheuser-Busch Golf Classic...closed with a 65 to finish T22 at the Ideon Classic at Pleasant Valley.

CAREER HIGHLIGHTS: Top finish of first three years on TOUR was T3 in 1993 Kemper Open...closed with rounds of 69-68 at TPC at Avenel, tying Scott Hoch for third, two strokes behind winner Grant Waite...check for $74,500 is the largest of career...had three top-10s in 1994, including a T4 at Anheuser-Busch, where he posted four rounds in the 60s...missed a month of the 1994 season after hurting his elbow in a pick-up basketball game following the Buick Open...winner of two Canadian Tour events...finished 52nd on Australasian Tour Order of Merit in 1992...shot 59 in Willows Classic pro-am in Saskatoon, Saskatchewan.

PERSONAL: 1987-88 All-American at Oklahoma State.

CAREER SUMMARY **PLAYOFF RECORD: 0-0**

Year	Events Played	Cuts Made	1st	2nd	3rd	Top 10	Top 25	Earnings	Rank
1988	2	1						$1,664	281
1990	1								
1992	1								
1993	25	14			1	1	3	$126,160	121
1994	29	15				3	4	$175,137	104
1995	27	18				2	6	$214,469	85
Total	85	48			1	6	13	$517,429	256

1996 PGA TOUR CHARITY TEAM: MasterCard Colonial

TOP TOURNAMENT SUMMARY

YEAR	90	92	94	95
U.S. Open	CUT	CUT	CUT	
PGA Championship				T54
THE PLAYERS Championship			CUT	T29

1995 PGA TOUR STATISTICS

Scoring	71.00	(68)
Driving	274.0	(19)
Driving Accuracy	60.4	(180)
Greens in Regulation	64.1	(144T)
Putting	1.772	(49T)
All Around	585	(52)
Sand Saves	54.6	(66T)
Total Driving	199	(113T)
Eagles	12	(5T)
Birdies	303	(54T)

MISCELLANEOUS STATISTICS

Scoring Avg Before Cut	70.73	(39T)
Scoring Avg 3rd Rnd	71.11	(88)
Scoring Avg Final Rnd	71.18	(89T)
Birdies Conversion %	29.9	(52T)
Par Breakers	19.9	(62T)

1995 Low Round: 63: 1995 PGA Championship/1
Career Low Round: 62: 1994 Hardee's Classic/3
Career Largest Paycheck: $75,400: 1993 Kemper Open/T3

Mike Brisky

EXEMPT STATUS: 92nd on 1995 money list
FULL NAME: Michael Charles Brisky
HEIGHT: 6' 1" **WEIGHT:** 185
BIRTH DATE: May 28, 1965 **BIRTHPLACE:** Brownsville, TX
RESIDENCE: Orlando, FL
FAMILY: Wife, Judy; Jacob (6/15/94)
COLLEGE: Pan American University
SPECIAL INTERESTS: Fishing, movies, Bible study
TURNED PROFESSIONAL: 1987 **Q SCHOOL:** 1993, 1994

BEST CAREER FINISH: 2 -- 1995 Buick Open

NIKE TOUR VICTORIES (1): 1994 NIKE Texarkana Open.

BEST 1995 FINISH: 2 -- Buick Open

1995 SEASON: Showed how one week can make a season...with rounds of 67-68-67-68--270, he earned a spot in a playoff with Woody Austin at the Buick Open...a bunkered approach on the first extra hole led to a bogey, and Austin won the tournament with a par...before collecting the $129,600 runner-up check, Brisky had recorded career earnings of just $79,392...began the year by making the cut in just three of his first 12 events, then finished T18 at the Buick Classic, worth $14,100...made five consecutive cuts from the U.S. Open through the Deposit Guaranty Golf Classic, but finished no better than T28 (at DGGC) during the stretch...after a missed cut at the Ideon Classic came his career week in Flint...closed the year with his third top-25 finish, T15 at the LaCantera Texas Open, where he shot a second-round 65, tying his third-round performance at the Canon GHO for best round of the year.

CAREER HIGHLIGHTS: First earned his PGA TOUR playing privileges at the 1993 Qualifying Tournament, where he tied for 37th place...in 1994, played in 14 events and made the cut six times...his best finishes came at the Deposit Guaranty Golf Classic and Buick Southern Open, T11 each time...also played in eight NIKE TOUR events in 1994 and won the NIKE Texarkana Open by seven strokes...returned to the Qualifying Tournament after finishing 200th on the money list and regained his card with a 10th-place finish.

PERSONAL: A two-time winner on the T.C. Jordan Tour.

PGA TOUR CAREER SUMMARY — **PLAYOFF RECORD: 0-1**

Year	Events Played	Cuts Made	1st	2nd	3rd	Top 10	Top 25	Earnings	Rank
1989	1								
1994	14	6					2	$38,713	200
1995	30	14		1		1	3	$194,874	92
Total	45	20		1		1	5	$233,587	333

NIKE TOUR SUMMARY

Year	Events Played	Cuts Made	1st	2nd	3rd	Top 10	Top 25	Earnings	Rank
1992	3	2					1	$1,627	206
1994	8	5	1			2	2	$46,938	37
1995	1								
Total	12	7	1			2	3	$48,565	
COMBINED TOTAL MONEY								$282,152	

1996 PGA TOUR CHARITY TEAM: LaCantera Texas Open

TOP TOURNAMENT SUMMARY

YEAR	89	95
U.S. Open	CUT	T67

1995 PGA TOUR STATISTICS

Scoring	71.84	(152)
Driving	253.9	(167)
Driving Accuracy	71.5	(70)
Greens in Regulation	61.9	(177)
Putting	1.772	(49T)
All Around	795	(115T)
Sand Saves	55.8	(45T)
Total Driving	237	(158T)
Eagles	8	(36T)
Birdies	272	(99T)

MISCELLANEOUS STATISTICS

Scoring Avg Before Cut	72.05	(161)
Scoring Avg 3rd Rnd	72.63	(176)
Scoring Avg Final Rnd	72.00	(153T)
Birdies Conversion %	28.0	(120T)
Par Breakers	17.9	(136T)

1995 Low Round: 65: 2 times, most recent 1995 LaCantera Texas Open/2
Career Low Round: 65: 2 times, most recent 1995 LaCantera Texas Open/2
Career Largest Paycheck: $129,600: 1995 Buick Open/2

Mark Brooks

EXEMPT STATUS: 1994 tournament winner
FULL NAME: Mark David Brooks
HEIGHT: 5' 9" **WEIGHT:** 150
BIRTH DATE: March 25, 1961 **BIRTHPLACE:** Fort Worth, TX
RESIDENCE: Fort Worth, TX
FAMILY: Wife, Cynthia; Lyndsay (1/24/86), Hollie (9/21/89)
COLLEGE: University of Texas
SPECIAL INTERESTS: All sports, cooking
TURNED PROFESSIONAL: 1983 **Q SCHOOL:** Fall 1983, 1984, 1985, 1987

TOUR VICTORIES (4): 1988 Canon Sammy Davis, Jr-Greater Hartford Open. **1991** Kmart Greater Greensboro Open, Greater Milwaukee Open. **1994** Kemper Open

BEST 1995 FINISHES: T3 -- British Open; T7 -- United Airlines Hawaiian Open, Bob Hope Chrysler Classic.

1995 SEASON: A tie for third at the British Open highlighted Brooks's 12th PGA TOUR season...after rounds of 70-69, trailed John Daly, Brad Faxon and Katsuyoshi Tomori by one stroke after 36 holes...fell back to T8 after a third-round 73, then closed with 71 to tie with Steven Bottomley and Michael Campbell, one stroke out of the John Daly-Costantino Rocca playoff...his two other top-10 finishes came in his first five events...T7 at United Airlines Hawaiian and at Bob Hope Chrysler...a fourth-round 65 at La Quinta Country Club pulled Brooks to within four strokes of leader Kenny Perry...a final-round 70 left him tied for seventh...also T11 at GTE Byron Nelson and FedEx St. Jude...final top-15 finish came at the Bell Canadian Open, where he tied for 14th despite a final-round 77.

CAREER HIGHLIGHTS: Best season to date--1991--featured pair of victories, in Kmart Greater Greensboro Open and Greater Milwaukee Open...fired 8-under-par 64 on final day to catch Gene Sauers, then defeated him with par on third extra hole for GGO title...later edged Robert Gamez by one stroke after opening with 9-under-par 63 in GMO...first TOUR victory, in 1988 Canon Sammy Davis, Jr.-Greater Hartford Open, came in playoff with Joey Sindelar and Dave Barr...sank 10-foot birdie putt on second extra hole for the win...fourth TOUR win came at 1994 Kemper Open, a three-stroke victory over D.A. Weibring and Bobby Wadkins...posted 11 top-10 finishes in 1992, going over $600,000 mark for second time in career...was part of five-man playoff won by John Inman at 1993 Buick Southern Open...finished second in eagles (15) and third in birdies (372) in 1994.

PERSONAL: Two-time All-American at University of Texas...was introduced to golf by his grandfather at age of eight...is host to an annual golf tournament, Hal Brooks Memorial, in memory of father...event benefits Brooks House, also founded in father's memory, which provides counseling for teens.

CAREER SUMMARY — **PLAYOFF RECORD: 2-2**

Year	Events Played	Cuts Made	1st	2nd	3rd	Top 10	Top 25	Earnings	Rank
1983(Am.)	1								
1983	6	2					1	$6,924	194
1984	35	17				1	4	$40,438	122
1985	32	11					3	$32,094	141
1986	32	19				1	5	$47,264	140
1987	32	17					2	$42,100	165
1988	30	22	1	1		2	11	$280,636	36
1989	30	15				1	3	$112,838	115
1990	33	23			2	5	10	$307,948	45
1991	30	24	2			5	11	$667,263	11
1992	29	24			3	11	16	$629,754	21
1993	31	19		1		3	10	$249,696	66
1994	33	23	1			4	8	$523,285	31
1995	29	17			1	3	10	$366,860	48
Total	383	233	4	2	6	36	94	$3,307,100	51

1996 PGA TOUR CHARITY TEAM: Diners Club Matches

TOP TOURNAMENT SUMMARY

YEAR	84	85	86	87	88	89	90	91	92	93	94	95
Masters Tournament						CUT		T35	CUT	CUT		CUT
U.S. Open	CUT		CUT	CUT	CUT		T5	T19	T44	T46	CUT	
British Open Championship								T80	T55		T20	T3
PGA Championship					CUT	CUT	T26	CUT	T15	CUT	CUT	T31
THE PLAYERS Championship	CUT	CUT		T63		CUT	T36	CUT	T9	CUT	CUT	CUT
THE TOUR Championship								T24	T27		T29	

Mark Brooks...continued

1995 PGA TOUR STATISTICS		
Scoring	70.87	(62)
Driving	262.0	(100T)
Driving Accuracy	72.6	(53T)
Greens in Regulation	69.1	(25)
Putting	1.770	(42T)
All Around	423	(16T)
Sand Saves	51.7	(101)
Total Driving	153	(48T)
Eagles	11	(12T)
Birdies	338	(28T)

MISCELLANEOUS STATISTICS		
Scoring Avg Before Cut	70.79	(43T)
Scoring Avg 3rd Rnd	70.82	(69)
Scoring Avg Final Rnd	70.76	(52T)
Birdies Conversion %	30.5	(40)
Par Breakers	20.8	(28T)

1995 Low Round: 65: 3 times, most recent 1995 FedEx St. Jude Classic/2
Career Low Round: 61: 1990 Shearson Lehman Hutton Open/2
Career Largest Paycheck: $234,000: 1994 Kemper Open/1

Brad Bryant

EXEMPT STATUS: 1995 tournament winner
FULL NAME: Bradley Dub Bryant
HEIGHT: 5' 10" **WEIGHT:** 170
BIRTH DATE: December 11, 1954 **BIRTHPLACE:** Amarillo, TX
RESIDENCE: Windermere, FL
FAMILY: Wife, Sue; William Jamieson (1/27/91); Jonathan David (4/26/93)
COLLEGE: University of New Mexico
SPECIAL INTERESTS: Bass fishing, hunting
TURNED PROFESSIONAL: 1976 **Q SCHOOL:** Fall 1978, 1987, 1988

TOUR VICTORIES (1): 1995 Walt Disney World/Oldsmobile Classic

BEST 1995 FINISHES: 1 -- Walt Disney World/Oldsmobile Classic; T4 -- Las Vegas Invitational; T6 -- THE PLAYERS Championship; T7 -- THE TOUR Championship; T8 -- Freeport-McMoRan Classic.

1995 SEASON: In his 18th year on the PGA TOUR, competing in his 475th official event, Brad Bryant recorded his first victory...his one-stroke victory at the rain-shortened Walt Disney World/Oldsmobile Classic ended his reign as the leading money-winner in TOUR history among non-winners...Bryant grabbed a share of the lead with Carl Paulson, thanks to a second-round 63 at Lake Buena Vista...round featured tounament record-tying 29 for nine holes...a final-round 68 at the Magnolia Course earned him the victory...the win was his third top-10 of the season; the first two came in consecutive weeks in the spring -- T6 at THE PLAYERS, T8 at Freeport-McMoRan...was the only player in field at THE PLAYERS to shoot par-or-better every round...72-72-72-71--286 trailed winner Lee Janzen by three strokes...at English Turn, was one stroke off the lead after an opening 65 but followed with 74-69-70 to finish four strokes behind Davis Love III-Mike Heinen playoff...two more top-10s came after his win...T4 at the Las Vegas Invitational and T8 at THE TOUR Championship...was tied for the lead with Billy Mayfair after 17 holes of the third round at Southern Hills, but a double-bogey and a Mayfair birdie left him three strokes behind with 18 holes to play...went to the hospital Sunday morning with a severe case of the flu but was able to play the final round, shooting 76.

CAREER HIGHLIGHTS: Had four top-three finishes in 1994 (T2 at Doral-Ryder and Kmart GGO and 3 at Buick Southern and TOUR Championship) and was part of a five-man playoff at the Buick Southern Open in 1993...TOUR Championship finish earned him largest paycheck of his career before this year --$207,000...before this year, his best shot at winning came at 1993 Bell Canadian Open...held one-stroke lead entering final round but closed with 74 to finish third behind David Frost...other runnerup finishes came in 1991 Buick Classic, 1983 Byron Nelson, 1982 Tournament Players Championship and 1982 Quad Cities...led TOUR in birdies in 1994 with 397.

PERSONAL: Played hurt from 1984 until undergoing shoulder surgery in 1985...took until 1988 for full recovery, since which has been solid performer...an avid fisherman...nickname "Dr. Dirt" bestowed by Gary McCord...return to form due in part to work with David Leadbetter, who at least allowed him to continue playing righthanded.

BRAD BRYANT...*continued*

CAREER SUMMARY — **PLAYOFF RECORD: 0-1**

Year	Events Played	Cuts Made	1st	2nd	3rd	Top 10	Top 25	Earnings	Rank
1978	11	7					1	$4,350	174
1979	29	21				5	8	$63,013	66
1980	32	24				3	10	$56,115	69
1981	29	19				3	9	$52,070	82
1982	29	18		2		4	5	$99,576	38
1983	30	20		1		2	8	$93,021	61
1984	31	16					3	$36,805	127
1985	16	2						$1,683	232
1986	20	8					2	$11,290	202
1987	7	4					2	$17,090	191
1988	26	15				2	3	$62,614	141
1989	32	22				1	8	$174,393	84
1990	31	15			1	5	7	$189,795	86
1991	29	9		1		1	3	$152,202	99
1992	33	26				3	8	$227,529	69
1993	30	21		1	1	3	4	$230,139	74
1994	32	25		2	2	6	11	$687,803	18
1995	31	20	1			5	14	$723,834	25
Total	478	292	1	7	4	43	106	$2,866,233	61

1996 PGA TOUR CHARITY TEAM: JCPenney Classic

TOP TOURNAMENT SUMMARY

YEAR	80	81	82	83	84	89	90	91	92	93	94	95
Masters Tournament												CUT
U.S. Open				CUT			CUT		T23		CUT	T13
British Open Championship												CUT
PGA Championship	71	CUT	T61	CUT	CUT	T58	CUT		T48		CUT	CUT
THE PLAYERS Championship	T14	CUT	T2	CUT	CUT	T59	CUT	CUT	CUT	T52	T74	T6
THE TOUR Championship											3	T7

1995 PGA TOUR STATISTICS

Scoring	70.48	(39)
Driving	268.3	(52)
Driving Accuracy	70.4	(85)
Greens in Regulation	67.9	(47T)
Putting	1.770	(42T)
All Around	397	(10T)
Sand Saves	51.9	(99T)
Total Driving	137	(30T)
Eagles	10	(15T)
Birdies	353	(18T)

MISCELLANEOUS STATISTICS

Scoring Avg Before Cut	70.90	(54T)
Scoring Avg 3rd Rnd	70.33	(38T)
Scoring Avg Final Rnd	70.89	(65)
Birdies Conversion %	31.0	(27T)
Par Breakers	21.2	(15T)

1995 Low Round: **63:** 1995 Walt Disney World/Oldsmobile Classic/2
Career Low Round: **63:** 1995 Walt Disney World/Oldsmobile Classic/2
Career Largest Paycheck: $216,000: 1995 Walt Disney World/Oldsmobile Classic/1

Did You Know?

With the victories by Brad Bryant and Duffy Waldorf in the final weeks of the 1995 season, Bobby Wadkins finds himself with a sizeable lead on the career money list among non-winners. Wadkins begins 1996 with $2,448,213; his closest pursuer is Kirk Triplett with $1,752,830.

PATRICK BURKE

EXEMPT STATUS: 119th on 1995 money list
FULL NAME: Patrick Thomas Burke
HEIGHT: 5' 5" **WEIGHT:** 165
BIRTH DATE: March 17, 1962 **BIRTHPLACE:** Hollywood, FL
RESIDENCE: Azusa, CA
FAMILY: Wife, Jody; Jaime (10/12/93)
COLLEGE: Citrus College
SPECIAL INTERESTS: Ice Hockey
TURNED PROFESSIONAL: 1986 **Q SCHOOL:** 1989, 1991, 1994

BEST TOUR CAREER FINISH: T6 -- 1992 BellSouth Classic

INTERNATIONAL VICTORIES (2): 1994 Optus Players Championship (Aus), Victorian Open (Aus).

BEST 1995 FINISH: T7 -- Walt Disney World/Oldsmobile Classic

1995 SEASON: With nearly $55,000 in earnings in October, Patrick earned a place in the top 125...it marked the first time since joining the TOUR in 1990 that he avoided a return trip to the Qualifying Tournament...at the Walt Disney World/Oldsmobile Classic, he was one stroke behind Carl Paulson and Brad Bryant after 36 holes of the rain-shortened, 54-hole tournament...a final-round 71 dropped him into a tie for seventh, but still earned $31,275...two weeks later he strung together five rounds in the 60s and tied for 15th at the Las Vegas Invitational, worth another $23,250...made seven of nine cuts to start the year, including three top-20 finishes -- T13 at the Honda Classic, T14 at the Nestle Invitational and T18 at the United Airlines Hawaiian Open...although he made cut regularly throughout the year (16 in 24 starts), his next top-20 finish did not come until Disney.

CAREER HIGHLIGHTS: A two-time winner on the Australasian Tour in 1994...captured the Australian TPC (earning a trip to the NEC World Series of Golf) and the Victoria Open...runner-up at the 1994 Alfred Dunhill Masters...medalist at the 1987 Australian Tour Qualifying School...has advanced to the PGA TOUR three times through the Qualifying Tournament...tied for seventh to earn his card in 1994.

PERSONAL: Finished third 1994 Australian Order of Merit, from which earned berth in 1995 British Open.

CAREER SUMMARY **PLAYOFF RECORD: 0-0**

Year	Events Played	Cuts Made	1st	2nd	3rd	Top 10	Top 25	Earnings	Rank
1990	23	3						$5,228	247
1992	28	19				1	2	$101,513	129
1993	17	11				1	5	$100,717	144
1994	10	2						$5,034	276
1995	24	16				1	5	$162,892	119
Total	102	51				3	12	$375,384	290

NIKE TOUR SUMMARY

Year	Events Played	Cuts Made	1st	2nd	3rd	Top 10	Top 25	Earnings	Rank
1991	17	6				1	2	$10,373	92
1993	1								
1994	6	2				1	1	$3,988	147
Total	24	8				2	3	$14,360	
COMBINED TOTAL MONEY								$389,744	

1996 PGA TOUR CHARITY TEAM: Walt Disney World/Oldsmobile Classic

TOP TOURNAMENT SUMMARY

YEAR	92	95
U.S. Open	CUT	
British Open Championship		T79

1995 PGA TOUR STATISTICS

Scoring	71.38	(107)
Driving	264.1	(87T)
Driving Accuracy	69.3	(100)
Greens in Regulation	69.3	(21)
Putting	1.781	(68T)
All Around	736	(98)
Sand Saves	43.9	(176)
Total Driving	187	(96T)
Eagles	6	(69T)
Birdies	266	(108)

MISCELLANEOUS STATISTICS

Scoring Avg Before Cut	71.47	(114T)
Scoring Avg 3rd Rnd	70.93	(76T)
Scoring Avg Final Rnd	69.36	(2)
Birdies Conversion %	30.2	(45T)
Par Breakers	20.3	(40T)

1995 Low Round: 65: 1995 Walt Disney World/Oldsmobile Classic/2
Career Low Round: 65: 2 times, most recent 1995 Walt Disney World/Oldsmobile Classic/2
Career Largest Paycheck: $34,750: 1992 BellSouth Classic/T6

Curt Byrum

EXEMPT STATUS: 107th on 1995 money list
FULL NAME: Curt Allen Byrum
HEIGHT: 6' 2" **WEIGHT:** 190
BIRTH DATE: December 28,1958 **BIRTHPLACE:** Onida, SD
RESIDENCE: Scottsdale, AZ; plays out of Desert Mountain GC
FAMILY: Wife, Cyndi; Christina Suzanne (10/13/90), Jake (6/11/92)
COLLEGE: University of New Mexico
SPECIAL INTERESTS: All sports
TURNED PROFESSIONAL: 1982 **Q SCHOOL:** 1982

TOUR VICTORIES (1): 1989 Hardee's Golf Classic

BEST 1995 FINISH: T8 -- Quad City Classic

1995 SEASON: After finishing in the top 125 in 1994 by the slimmest of margins, had a bit more cushion in 1995...T8 at Quad City Classic, his sole top-10 finish of the year, put him over the top...opening-round 66 left him two strokes behind leaders...closed with 68-69 in rain-shortened event to earn $30,000...biggest payday of 1995 came at THE PLAYERS Championship, where T18 was worth $39,120...made the cut in the last seven tournaments he entered...shot 65 in the third round of the Walt Disney World/Oldsmobile Classic and the second round of the Las Vegas Invitational, his lowest rounds of the year...after opening with 66-65, was tied for second, one stroke behind Bob Tway at Las Vegas...after closing with 70-72-70, finished T30.

CAREER HIGHLIGHTS: Earned final position in top 125 in 1994 despite being disqualified in final event of the year...had Jose Maria Olazabal decided to join TOUR, would have been odd man out...was at top of game in 1989, when went over $200,000 for third consecutive year and captured Hardee's Golf Classic...that victory, coupled with brother Tom's Kemper Open win seven weeks earlier, made Byrums first brothers to win in same year since Dave and Mike Hill in 1972...fell first to 129th, then to 148th, during two seasons under victory exemption...plunge continued in 1992, with elbow trouble finally leading to December surgery...played on NIKE TOUR in 1993 and regained PGA TOUR playing privileges by finishing 10th on money list...went over $200,000 for first time in 1987...teamed with Bobby Nichols to win 1986 Showdown Classic at Jeremy Ranch, a PGA TOUR/Senior PGA TOUR event...winner 1979 Pacific Coast Amateur...four-time winner South Dakota State Juniors, five-time winner South Dakota State Amateur...1980 All-American at New Mexico.

PERSONAL: Exceptional high school athlete, all-state in both football and basketball...named South Dakota Athlete of Year in 1977...learned to play on nine-hole course he and brother Tom used to mow in South Dakota.

PGA TOUR CAREER SUMMARY — **PLAYOFF RECORD: 0-0**

Year	Events Played	Cuts Made	1st	2nd	3rd	Top 10	Top 25	Earnings	Rank
1982	4	2						$1,247	268
1983	31	17				1	2	$30,772	130
1984	26	14				1	2	$27,836	143
1985	13	6						$6,943	193
1986	10	6		1	1	2	2	$79,454	108
1987	33	24		1		5	9	$212,450	46
1988	31	19			1	3	8	$208,853	55
1989	33	15	1			1	5	$221,702	64
1990	31	17					5	$117,134	129
1991	31	18				1	1	$78,725	148
1992	14	7					1	$31,450	194
1994	28	13				2	5	$137,587	128
1995	33	21				1	4	$173,838	107
Total	318	179	1	2	2	17	44	$1,327,991	151

NIKE TOUR SUMMARY

Year	Events Played	Cuts Made	1st	2nd	3rd	Top 10	Top 25	Earnings	Rank
1991	1	1				1	1	$5,750	127
1992	16	9		2	1	3	7	$40,742	35
1993	19	14	1	1	1	7	10	$88,757	10
1994	1								
Total	37	24	1	3	2	11	18	$135,249	
COMBINED TOTAL MONEY								$1,463,240	

1996 PGA TOUR CHARITY TEAM: Las Vegas Invitational

CURT BYRUM...continued

TOP TOURNAMENT SUMMARY

YEAR	85	87	88	89	90	95
Masters Tournament					CUT	
U.S. Open	T64					T36
PGA Championship		T14	CUT	70		T71
THE PLAYERS Championship		T32	T3	CUT	CUT	T18

1995 PGA TOUR STATISTICS

Scoring	71.22	(93T)
Driving	271.7	(28)
Driving Accuracy	64.4	(161)
Greens in Regulation	67.6	(53T)
Putting	1.799	(124T)
All Around	663	(76)
Sand Saves	47.6	(147T)
Total Driving	189	(100T)
Eagles	7	(51T)
Birdies	380	(6T)

MISCELLANEOUS STATISTICS

Scoring Avg Before Cut	70.99	(69)
Scoring Avg 3rd Rnd	71.67	(130T)
Scoring Avg Final Rnd	71.57	(119T)
Birdies Conversion %	29.5	(68T)
Par Breakers	20.3	(40T)

1995 Low Round: 65: 2 times, most recent 1995 Las Vegas Invitational/2
Career Low Round: 63: 1983 Miller High LIfe QCO/1
Career Largest Paycheck: $126,000: 1989 Hardees Golf Classic/1

MARK CALCAVECCHIA *(CAL-kuh-VECK-ee-uh)*

EXEMPT STATUS: 1995 tournament wnner
FULL NAME: Mark John Calcavecchia
HEIGHT: 6' **WEIGHT:** 200
BIRTH DATE: June 12, 1960 **BIRTHPLACE:** Laurel, NE
RESIDENCE: West Palm Beach, FL
FAMILY: Wife, Sheryl; Brittney Jo (8/8/89), Eric Jordan (1/1/94)
COLLEGE: University of Florida
SPECIAL INTERESTS: Bowling, music
TURNED PROFESSIONAL: 1981 **Q SCHOOL:** Spring 1981; Fall 1982, 1983

TOUR VICTORIES (7): 1986 Southwest Golf Classic. **1987** Honda Classic. **1988** Bank of Boston Classic. **1989** Phoenix Open, Nissan Los Angeles Open. **1992** Phoenix Open. **1995** BellSouth Classic.

INTERNATIONAL VICTORIES (3): 1988 Australian Open. **1989** British Open. **1993** Argentine Open.

BEST 1995 FINISHES: 1 -- BellSouth Classic; T2 -- Buick Invitational of California, Memorial Tournament; 5 -- Kmart Greater Greensboro Open; T7-- Phoenix Open

1995 SEASON: Mark's seventh TOUR win highlighted the best earnings year of his 15-year career...trailed Jim Gallagher, Jr., and club pro Stephen Keppler by two strokes entering the BellSouth Classic's final round...a closing 66 gave him a two-stroke victory worth $234,000, his best-ever payday...began 1995 by making 17 consecutive cuts...recorded all six of his top-10 finishes in that stretch, including two T2s -- Buick Invitational of California and Memorial Tournament...low round of the year came at the GTE Byron Nelson Classic...first-round 64 at Cottonwood Valley Course left him just behind leader Glen Day...eventually tied for 16th...second half of the year less lucrative, but he still made eight of his last 12 cuts and easily qualified for THE TOUR Championship for the seventh time...by tying for 27th there, he pushed his earnings to $843,552, slightly more than his previous best earnings year of 1990...won Franklin Templeton Shark Shootout with Steve Elkington.

CAREER HIGHLIGHTS: Captured 1989 British Open at Troon...defeated Wayne Grady and Greg Norman in the first playoff using the Royal and Ancient's multi-hole playoff system...his 5-iron shot to seven feet from 190 yards on fourth and final playoff hole sealed the victory...earlier that year won twice during TOUR's West Coast swing -- Phoenix Open (by seven strokes) and Nissan Los Angeles Open...won at the TPC of Scottsdale again in 1992, this time by five strokes...had a string of four years with a victory from 1986 to 1989, beginning with his first TOUR win, the 1986 Southwest Golf Classic, played in Abilene...playoff loser to Billy Mayfair in 1993 Greater Milwaukee Open when Mayfair chipped in from 20 feet on fourth extra hole...a December 1993 skiing accident hampered him early in 1994...after surgery to repair cartilage damage and a torn ACL, he finished T9 at the Buick Invitational of California...the 1988 Australian Open champion.

Mark Calcavecchia...*continued*

PERSONAL: Winner 1976 Florida State Junior Championship and Orange Bowl Championship...first-team All-SEC in 1979...thrilled when family moved from Nebraska to Florida when he was 13, because he could play golf every day...attributed BellSouth win to "Billy," putter he used to win Honda Classic, Australian Open and 1989 Phoenix and L.A. Opens.

CAREER SUMMARY — **PLAYOFF RECORD: 0-3**

Year	Events Played	Cuts Made	1st	2nd	3rd	Top 10	Top 25	Earnings	Rank
1981	7	1						$404	313
1982	25	14				1	5	$25,064	135
1983	20	9				1	2	$16,313	161
1984	25	14				1	1	$29,660	140
1985	15	7					2	$15,957	162
1986	17	9	1			5	8	$155,012	58
1987	26	20	1	2	3	9	12	$522,398	10
1988	33	28	1	4	1	12	18	$751,912	6
1989	25	18	2	1	2	10	13	$807,741	5
1990	27	22		5	1	9	14	$834,281	7
1991	24	17			1	6	8	$323,621	50
1992	27	22	1			4	6	$377,234	39
1993	30	20		3		6	13	$630,366	21
1994	27	18		1	2	6	13	$533,201	30
1995	29	25	1	2		6	13	$843,552	13
Total	357	244	7	18	10	76	128	$5,866,716	14

1996 PGA TOUR CHARITY TEAM: Phoenix Open

TOP TOURNAMENT SUMMARY

YEAR	86	87	88	89	90	91	92	93	94	95
Masters Tournament		T17	2	T31	T20	T12	T31	T17	CUT	T41
U.S. Open	14	T17	T62	T61	CUT	T37	T33	T25	CUT	CUT
British Open Championship		T11	CUT	1	CUT	CUT	T28	T14	T11	T24
PGA Championship		CUT	T17		CUT	T32	T48	T31	CUT	CUT
THE PLAYERS Championship		T50	T64	CUT	2	CUT	73	CUT	T23	T18
THE TOUR Championship		T5	T3	T9	T14			T7	T24	T27

NATIONAL TEAMS: Ryder Cup (3), 1987, 1989, 1991; Kirin Cup 1987; Asahi Glass Four Tours World Championship of Golf (2), 1989, 1990; Dunhill Cup (2), 1989, 1990.

1995 PGA TOUR STATISTICS

Statistic	Value	Rank
Scoring	70.28	(22T)
Driving	272.5	(25)
Driving Accuracy	68.2	(113T)
Greens in Regulation	66.9	(66T)
Putting	1.777	(58T)
All Around	350	(5)
Sand Saves	55.2	(53T)
Total Driving	138	(32T)
Eagles	12	(5T)
Birdies	372	(8)

MISCELLANEOUS STATISTICS

Statistic	Value	Rank
Scoring Avg Before Cut	70.80	(45T)
Scoring Avg 3rd Rnd	70.58	(56)
Scoring Avg Final Rnd	70.58	(30T)
Birdies Conversion %	30.6	(38T)
Par Breakers	20.3	(40T)

1995 Low Round: **64:** 1995 GTE Byron Nelson Classic/1
Career Low Round: **63:** 2 times, most recent 1992 NEC World Series/3
Career Largest Paycheck: **$234,000:** 1995 BellSouth Classic/1

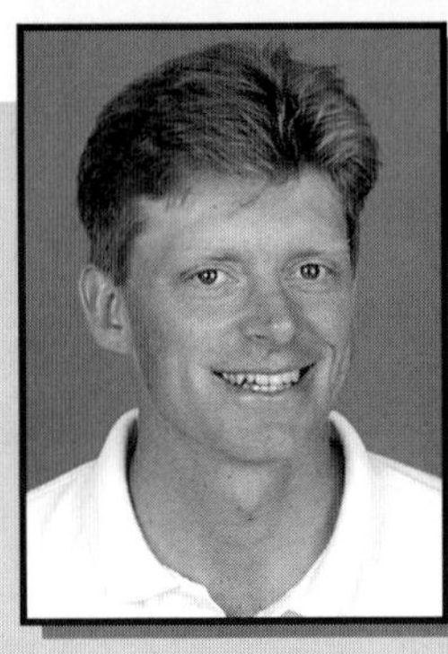

Jim Carter

EXEMPT STATUS: 102nd on 1995 money list
FULL NAME: Jim Laver Carter
HEIGHT: 6'0" **WEIGHT:** 175
BIRTH DATE: June 24, 1961 **BIRTHPLACE:** Spring Lake, NC
RESIDENCE: Scottsdale, AZ
FAMILY: Wife, Cyndi; Shane (10/5/91); Brant (3/7/95)
COLLEGE: Arizona State University (1984, Business)
SPECIAL INTERESTS: Music, sports, family
TURNED PROFESSIONAL: 1985 **Q SCHOOL:** Fall 1985, 1986

BEST TOUR CAREER FINISH: T3 -- 1989 AT&T Pebble Beach National Pro-Am, 1995 Anheuser-Busch Golf Classic.

NIKE TOUR VICTORIES (1): 1994 NIKE New Mexico Charity Classic

BEST 1995 FINISH: T3 -- Anheuser-Busch Golf Classic

1995 SEASON: After a missed cut in Hawaii to open 1995, Jim made his next eight to get his year off to solid start...trailed Ben Crenshaw and Hale Irwin by two strokes after a second-round 64 at the Phoenix Open...shot 73-67 in the final two rounds to finish T12...the 64 was his low round of the year, later matched in the second round at FedEx St. Jude...the $24,700 he earned at the TPC of Scottsdale was his largest check of the year until Anheuser-Busch...one stroke out of the lead after the first and second rounds at Kingsmill, he held the lead alone after a third-round 68, one stroke ahead of Jim Gallagher, Jr., Blaine McCallister and Ted Tryba...finished T3 after an even-par 71 on the final day, two strokes behind Tryba...the finish equalled the best of his career and the $57,200 paycheck was his best ever.

CAREER HIGHLIGHTS: Finished 33rd on PGA TOUR money list in 1989, a year that saw him record six top-10 finishes...his 11-under-par 61 during second round of 1989 Centel Classic (Tallahassee, FL) was tournament record in last year of the event...lost his card the following year when he fell to 172nd on the money list...a win at the 1994 NIKE New Mexico Charity Classic and three second-place finishes helped him finish fourth on the 1994 NIKE TOUR money list and earned a return trip to the PGA TOUR...enjoyed brilliant collegiate career at Arizona State, capped by winning NCAA Championship in 1983...named university's Athlete-of-the-Year in 1984...two-time winner of Arizona State Amateur and the Southwest Amateur championships.

PERSONAL: Began golfing at age 13 and soon was traveling around state with his father, competing in junior tournaments...inducted into Arizona State Sports Hall of Fame in 1995...you may see him sporting a goatee, but never for long.

PGA TOUR CAREER SUMMARY — **PLAYOFF RECORD: 0-0**

Year	Events Played	Cuts Made	1st	2nd	3rd	Top 10	Top 25	Earnings	Rank
1985(Am.)	1								
1987	32	20				1	5	$60,102	134
1988	30	19				5	10	$191,489	60
1989	32	22			1	6	13	$319,719	33
1990	32	12					2	$54,392	172
1991	7	1						$2,450	278
1993	1	1						$2,753	289
1994	1								
1995	30	19			1	1	3	$180,664	102
Total	166	94			2	13	33	$811,568	200

NIKE TOUR SUMMARY

Year	Events Played	Cuts Made	1st	2nd	3rd	Top 10	Top 25	Earnings	Rank
1991	16	9					5	$10,265	94
1992	4	2						$1,755	200
1993	23	18		1		6	11	$49,922	32
1994	20	18	1	3		8	12	$142,750	4
Total	63	47	1	4		14	28	$204,691	
COMBINED TOTAL MONEY								$1,016,260	

1996 PGA TOUR CHARITY TEAM: Phoenix Open

TOP TOURNAMENT SUMMARY

YEAR	87	88	89	90
U.S. Open	T71	T55	CUT	
PGA Championship		T66	CUT	
THE PLAYERS Championship		T58	T45	CUT

JIM CARTER...continued

1995 PGA TOUR STATISTICS		
Scoring	71.12	(79T)
Driving	260.3	(115T)
Driving Accuracy	72.2	(59)
Greens in Regulation	68.3	(38T)
Putting	1.808	(148T)
All Around	549	(42T)
Sand Saves	58.9	(19T)
Total Driving	174	(77T)
Eagles	7	(51T)
Birdies	318	(40)

MISCELLANEOUS STATISTICS		
Scoring Avg Before Cut	70.65	(37)
Scoring Avg 3rd Rnd	71.37	(111T)
Scoring Avg Final Rnd	71.68	(128)
Birdies Conversion %	26.9	(142)
Par Breakers	18.8	(106T)

1995 Low Round: 64: 2 times, most recent 1995 FedEx St. Jude Classic/2
Career Low Round: 61: 1989 Centel Classic/2
Career Largest Paycheck: $57,200: 1995 Anheuser-Busch Golf Classic/T3

BRANDEL CHAMBLEE *(BRAN-dl SHAM-blee)*

EXEMPT STATUS: 86th on 1995 money list
FULL NAME: Brandel Eugene Chamblee
HEIGHT: 5' 10" **WEIGHT:** 155
BIRTH DATE: July 2, 1962 **BIRTHPLACE:** St. Louis, MO
RESIDENCE: Phoenix, AZ
FAMILY: Wife, Karen
COLLEGE: University of Texas
SPECIAL INTERESTS: Tennis, horses
TURNED PROFESSIONAL: 1985 **Q SCHOOL:** 1987,1990, 1991,1992

BEST TOUR CAREER FINISH: 3 -- 1994 Honda Classic

NIKE TOUR VICTORIES (1): 1990 New England Classic

BEST 1995 FINISHES: T5 -- FedEx St. Jude Classic; T7 -- BellSouth Classic; T8 -- Buick Invitational of California

1995 SEASON: Brandel's earnings exceeded $200,000 for the first time in 1995...in each of his six years on TOUR, his earnings have increased over the previous season...opened his season with seven consecutive made cuts, including the year's first top-10 finish -- T8 at Buick Invitational of California...held the lead after 36 holes at Torrey Pines thanks to consecutive 66s...fell to T7 after a third-round 74, then closed with a 70 to finish seven strokes behind Peter Jacobsen...four sub-par rounds at Atlanta Country Club led to his second top-10 finish, a T7 at BellSouth...closed with 65-66 at TPC at Southwind to gain a T5 at the FedEx St. Jude Classic...65 was his low round of 1995...year slowed after that as he made the cut in only two of last eight events he entered.

CAREER HIGHLIGHTS: Best chance to win may have come at the 1994 Honda Classic...held a two-stroke lead over Davis Love III after 54 holes...closing 71 left him two strokes behind Nick Price...member of Ben Hogan Tour (now the NIKE TOUR)) in its inaugural season of 1990...posted one victory, winning New England Classic at Woodlands CC in Falmouth, ME...at conclusion of 54-hole event was only golfer under par, at 1-under 215...finished seventh on money list with $73,251...winner 1986 TPA Sun City Classic...enjoyed excellent collegiate career at Texas...winner 1982 Bluebonnet Tournament and 1983 Rice Planters Championship...winner 1983 Southwest Conference Championship and 1984 Morris Williams Tournament...selected first-team All-American in 1983, second-team 1982 and 1984.

PERSONAL: Now known as "8 1/2 D" after magazine article he wrote in February 1995 elicited strong response from readers seeking to accept his offer of slightly used golf shoes.

PGA TOUR CAREER SUMMARY **PLAYOFF RECORD: 0-0**

Year	Events Played	Cuts Made	1st	2nd	3rd	Top 10	Top 25	Earnings	Rank
1983(Am.)	1	1							
1984(Am.)	2								
1985	1	1						$1,190	239
1987	4								
1988	29	10				1	1	$33,618	166
1989	4								
1991	30	12				1	3	$64,141	161

continued on page 44

BRANDEL CHAMBLEE...*continued*

PGA TOUR CAREER SUMMARY...*continued*

Year	Events Played	Cuts Made	1st	2nd	3rd	Top 10	Top 25	Earnings	Rank
1992	28	15					6	$97,921	133
1993	29	13				2	4	$126,940	119
1994	27	20			1	1	3	$161,018	111
1995	25	13				3	8	$213,796	86
Total	180	85			1	8	25	$698,624	221

NIKE TOUR SUMMARY

Year	Events Played	Cuts Made	1st	2nd	3rd	Top 10	Top 25	Earnings	Rank
1990	28	22	1	1		10	16	$73,251	7
1991	1	1				1	1	$4,050	141
Total	29	23	1	1		11	17	$77,301	
COMBINED TOTAL MONEY								$775,925	

1996 PGA TOUR CHARITY TEAM: Nortel Open

TOP TOURNAMENT SUMMARY

YEAR	87	92	94	95
U.S. Open	CUT	CUT		
British Open Championship	T66			CUT
PGA Championship				CUT
THE PLAYERS Championship			T69	CUT

1995 PGA TOUR STATISTICS

Scoring	71.26	(97)
Driving	260.9	(109T)
Driving Accuracy	72.7	(50T)
Greens in Regulation	66.4	(90T)
Putting	1.769	(39T)
All Around	649	(71)
Sand Saves	53.9	(70T)
Total Driving	159	(57)
Eagles	5	(88T)
Birdies	267	(106T)

MISCELLANEOUS STATISTICS

Scoring Avg Before Cut	71.65	(139T)
Scoring Avg 3rd Rnd	70.29	(34T)
Scoring Avg Final Rnd	70.85	(60)
Birdies Conversion %	30.8	(32T)
Par Breakers	20.3	(40T)

1995 Low Round: 65: 1995 FedEx St. Jude Classic/3
Career Low Round: 64: 2 times, most recent 1993 Hardee's Classic/2
Career Largest Paycheck: $74,800: 1994 Honda Classic/3

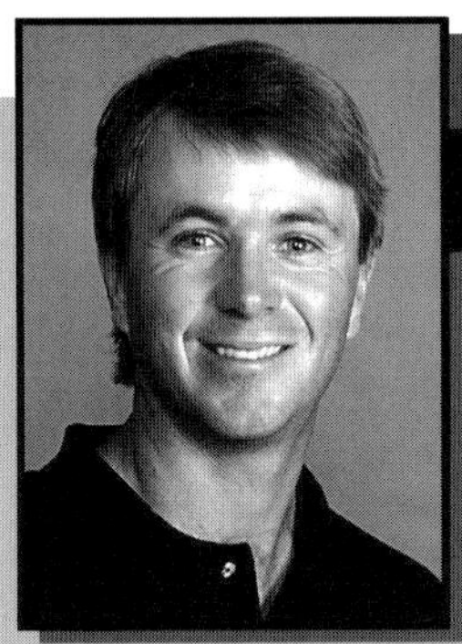

BRIAN CLAAR *(CLARE)*

EXEMPT STATUS: 75th on 1995 money list
FULL NAME: Brian James Claar
HEIGHT: 5' 8" **WEIGHT:** 150
BIRTH DATE: July 29, 1959 **BIRTHPLACE:** Santa Monica, CA
RESIDENCE: Palm Harbor, FL; plays out of East Lake Woodlands CC
FAMILY: Wife, Tracy; Zackary (7/15/90), Cassidy (9/8/93)
COLLEGE: University of Tampa (1981)
SPECIAL INTERESTS: Fishing, Tampa Bay Bucs
TURNED PROFESSIONAL: 1981 **Q SCHOOL:** Fall 1985, 1989.

BEST TOUR CAREER FINISH: T2 -- 1991 AT&T Pebble Beach National Pro-Am

INTERNATIONAL VICTORIES (2): 1989 Johnnie Walker Hong Kong Open (Asia), Thailand Open (Asia).

BEST 1995 FINISHES: T6 -- Shell Houston Open; T8 -- Honda Classic; T10 -- Freeport-McMoRan Classic.

1995 SEASON: Another solid year from the University of Tampa graduate...his earnings of $241,107 were the second-most of his 10-year career...had his most successful stretch of the year during the TOUR's Florida swing...T8 at the Honda Classic, T11 at THE

BRIAN CLAAR...continued

PLAYERS Championship and T10 at Freeport-McMoRan Classic came in consecutive starts...$69,000 earned at THE PLAYERS was largest check of 1995...final top-10 came at Shell Houston Open...after an opening 73, came back with rounds of 68-67-71...had a later string of four consecutive cuts made, including the British Open and PGA Championship...open qualified for his first British Open...made just one cut in seven starts after the PGA.

CAREER HIGHLIGHTS: Arrived on TOUR with a flourish in 1986, finishing 75th on the money list and being named Rookie of the Year...was unable to match early success during the next three years, but showed some of his old form by finishing fifth at the 1989 U.S. Open at Oak Hill...closed with rounds of 68-69 (the only player to better par in each of the final two rounds) to finish within two strokes of Curtis Strange...regained his playing privileges on TOUR at the 1989 Qualifying Tournament...tied Corey Pavin for second at 1991 AT&T, four strokes behind Paul Azinger...tied for third at 1994 B.C. Open...led Asian Tour Order of Merit in 1989, when won Hong Kong and Thailand Opens.

PERSONAL: Knew he wanted to play TOUR by junior year of college...introduced to game by neighbor, who watched him hitting golf balls with baseball bat.

CAREER SUMMARY — **PLAYOFF RECORD: 0-0**

Year	Events Played	Cuts Made	1st	2nd	3rd	Top 10	Top 25	Earnings	Rank
1986	27	20				4	12	$117,355	75
1987	37	18					2	$43,111	162
1988	11	7					5	$30,276	172
1989	13	9				1	4	$88,010	133
1990	25	19				2	5	$161,356	98
1991	31	21		1	1	3	5	$251,309	67
1992	29	20				3	5	$192,255	78
1993	32	24				1	5	$202,624	85
1994	31	19			1	2	3	$165,370	110
1995	30	17				3	5	$241,107	75
Total	266	174		1	2	19	51	$1,492,773	140

1996 PGA TOUR CHARITY TEAM: United Airlines Hawaiian Open

TOP TOURNAMENT SUMMARY

YEAR	87	89	90	91	92	93	94	95
Masters Tournament			CUT					
U.S. Open		5	T29		CUT	T46		
British Open Championship								T49
PGA Championship				CUT	T9	CUT		T49
THE PLAYERS Championship	CUT			T41	T49	T28	T55	T11

1995 PGA TOUR STATISTICS

Scoring	71.34	(102)
Driving	257.6	(138T)
Driving Accuracy	74.1	(29T)
Greens in Regulation	64.6	(131)
Putting	1.805	(139T)
All Around	714	(88T)
Sand Saves	57.8	(30T)
Total Driving	167	(66)
Eagles	6	(69T)
Birdies	287	(76)

MISCELLANEOUS STATISTICS

Scoring Avg Before Cut	71.34	(103T)
Scoring Avg 3rd Rnd	70.86	(70T)
Scoring Avg Final Rnd	72.22	(165)
Birdies Conversion %	26.8	(143T)
Par Breakers	17.0	(167T)

1995 Low Round: 65: 1995 Canon Greater Hartford Open/3
Career Low Round: 62: 1991 Anheuser-Busch GC/3
Career Largest Paycheck: $96,800: 1991 AT&T Pebble Beach/T2

LENNIE CLEMENTS *(CLEM-ents)*

EXEMPT STATUS: 51st on 1995 money list
FULL NAME: Leonard Clyde Clements
HEIGHT: 5' 8" **WEIGHT:** 160
BIRTH DATE: January 20, 1957 **BIRTHPLACE:** Cherry Point, NC
RESIDENCE: San Diego, CA
FAMILY: Wife, Jan; Elizabeth (11/19/83), Christopher (7/16/86)
COLLEGE: San Diego State University
SPECIAL INTERESTS: Family activities, all sports
TURNED PROFESSIONAL: 1980
JOINED TOUR: 1981 **Q SCHOOL:** 1992

BEST TOUR CAREER FINISH: T2 -- 1994 Bob Hope Chrysler Classic.

INTERNATIONAL VICTORIES (1): 1982 Timex Open (France).

NIKE TOUR VICTORIES (1): 1992 Greater Ozarks Open.

BEST 1995 FINISHES: T3 -- Anheuser-Busch Golf Classic; T4 -- Ideon Classic at Pleasant Valley; T7 -- BellSouth Classic; T10 - Freeport-McMoRan Classic.

1995 SEASON: Another solid year for one of the TOUR's steadiest performers...made the cut in 21 of 24 events in 1995...over the past two years, he has cashed in 42 of 46 starts...had a stretch of 11 consecutive made cuts from Nissan Open in February through FedEx St. Jude Classic in July...string began with four consecutive top-25 finishes, including the first top-10 of the year at Freeport-McMoRan...four weeks later, posted a T7 at the BellSouth Classic...low round of the year was an opening 64 at Colonial...shared the lead with Clark Dennis after 18 holes but went on to finish T23...was three strokes off the lead with 18 holes to play at Anheuser-Busch...a final 68 left him tied for third, two strokes behind Ted Tryba...in his next start, an opening 67 left him just two strokes behind Ronnie Black at the Ideon Classic at Pleasant Valley...rounds of 68-69-67 followed for a 13-under-par 271 total, good for a T4, three strokes behind winner Fred Funk...those two top-four finishes began a string of eight made cuts through the end of the year, which also included T17 at the Greater Milwaukee Open and T15 at Las Vegas Invitational...TOUR leader in greens hit in regulation.

CAREER HIGHLIGHTS: The best season of his career was certainly 1994, when he finished 39th on the money list and posted six top-10 finishes...five of those top-10s came in his first seven starts...shot a third-round 61 during the 90-hole Bob Hope Chrysler Classic that year...eventually tied for second behind winner Scott Hoch...his $82,133 Bob Hope check is his career best...before the 1994 Hope, his best finish was way back in 1983 -- a T3 at the Miller High Life Quad Cities Open...vaulted into contention with a third-round 65...finished one stroke behind playoff participants Danny Edwards and Morris Hatalsky...winner 1982 Timex Open (France) and 1983 Sierra Nevada Open...winner 1988 Spalding Invitational on Monterey Peninsula...had a successful amateur career, winning 1975 California State High School Championship...medalist 1979 California State Amateur...winner 1979 Southwestern Amateur...two-time All-American at San Diego State.

PGA TOUR CAREER SUMMARY **PLAYOFF RECORD: 0-0**

Year	Events Played	Cuts Made	1st	2nd	3rd	Top 10	Top 25	Earnings	Rank
1980	1	1						$1,695	240
1981	24	12				1	3	$19,819	134
1982	23	12				2	6	$44,796	98
1983	29	14			1	1	6	$44,455	110
1984	31	13					2	$25,712	146
1985	24	16				1	6	$49,383	120
1986	28	19				4	11	$112,642	79
1987	25	15				3	7	$124,989	83
1988	33	21				3	3	$86,332	120
1989	29	13				1	4	$69,399	147
1990	29	12				1	4	$80,096	146
1991	15	10					3	$62,827	163
1992	10	8						$30,121	198
1993	25	16				2	6	$141,526	113
1994	22	21		1		6	11	$416,880	39
1995	24	21			1	4	12	$355,130	51
Total	372	224		1	2	29	84	$1,665,804	121

NIKE TOUR SUMMARY									
Year	Events Played	Cuts Made	1st	2nd	3rd	Top 10	Top 25	Earnings	Rank
1991	6	5					3	$6,913	118
1992	13	12	1		1	6	10	$73,253	11
Total	19	17	1		1	6	13	$80,166	
COMBINED TOTAL MONEY								$1,745,969	

1996 PGA TOUR CHARITY TEAM: United Airlines Hawaiian Open

TOP TOURNAMENT SUMMARY										
YEAR	82	83	84	85	86	87	88	89	94	95
Masters Tournament			CUT	T36			CUT			
U.S. Open		T13	T16		T24	T9	CUT		T28	
British Open Championship									T67	
PGA Championship	74				67	CUT			T30	T39
THE PLAYERS Championship	CUT	T19	70		CUT	T44	T42	CUT	T27	T18

1995 PGA TOUR STATISTICS		
Scoring	70.30	(26)
Driving	254.7	(163T)
Driving Accuracy	78.3	(7)
Greens in Regulation	72.3	(1)
Putting	1.771	(44T)
All Around	516	(36)
Sand Saves	48.6	(138T)
Total Driving	170	(70T)
Eagles	4	(116T)
Birdies	346	(21T)

MISCELLANEOUS STATISTICS		
Scoring Avg Before Cut	70.04	(6)
Scoring Avg 3rd Rnd	70.43	(45)
Scoring Avg Final Rnd	70.86	(61)
Birdies Conversion %	28.6	(95T)
Par Breakers	20.9	(23T)

1995 Low Round: **64:** 1995 Colonial National Invitation/1
Career Low Round: **61:** 1994 Bob Hope Chrysler Classic/3
Career Largest Paycheck: **$82,133:** 1994 Bob Hope Chrysler Classic/T2

JOHN COOK

EXEMPT STATUS: 97th on 1995 money list
FULL NAME: John Neuman Cook
HEIGHT: 6' **WEIGHT:** 175
BIRTH DATE: October 2, 1957 **BIRTHPLACE:** Toledo, OH
RESIDENCE: Rancho Mirage, CA
FAMILY: Wife, Jan; Kristin (7/20/81), Courtney (4/11/84), Jason (1/10/86)
COLLEGE: Ohio State University
SPECIAL INTERESTS: Auto racing, skiing, all sports
TURNED PROFESSIONAL: 1979 **Q SCHOOL:** Fall 1979

TOUR VICTORIES (6): **1981** Bing Crosby National Pro-Am. **1983** Canadian Open. **1987** The International. **1992** Bob Hope Chrysler Classic, United Airlines Hawaiian Open, Las Vegas Invitational

INTERNATIONAL VICTORIES (2): **1982** Sao Paulo-Brazilian Open. **1995** Mexican Open.

BEST 1995 FINISHES: T5 -- FedEx St. Jude Classic

1995 SEASON: The 16-year PGA TOUR veteran saw his earnings and money-list rank fall to their lowest levels since 1989, a season cut short by hand surgery...after T17 in season's second week at Northern Telecom Open, next top-25 finish didn't come until April at Shell Houston Open...was one stroke behind leader Steve Rintoul after opening 67 and was tied for second through 54 holes, five strokes behind Scott Hoch...closing 75 dropped him to 11th, still five strokes back...at FedEx St. Jude Classic, shot 65-70-67-68 -- 270 for T5, three strokes behind Jim Gallagher, Jr....had two top-15 finishes in October...66-68-69 -- 203 good for T15 at rain-curtailed Walt Disney World/Oldsmobile Classic...the following week, second-round 64, low round of year, helped him to 14th at Las Vegas Invitational...won first Ernst Championship, Fred Couples' charity tournament, in August...in post-season, won Mexican Open.

JOHN COOK...*continued*

CAREER HIGHLIGHTS: Had string of solid finishes in majors from 1992-94 -- 1994 U.S. Open (5), 1994 PGA Championship (T4), 1993 PGA Championship (T6), 1992 British Open (2), 1992 PGA Championship (T2)...surpassed $1 million in earnings in 1992, when won three times...captured five-man playoff at Bob Hope Chrysler Classic, outlasting Gene Sauers with three birdies and an eagle over four holes...posted two-stroke victories in United Airlines Hawaiian Open and Las Vegas Invitational...first victory came in 1981 Bing Crosby, winning another five-man playoff...defeated Johnny Miller at 1983 Canadian Open on the sixth playoff hole...other title was in 1987 International...winner of numerous amateur titles, principal among which 1978 U.S. Amateur...winner 1982 Sao Paulo-Brazilian Open...teamed with Rex Caldwell to win 1983 World Cup...a three-time All-American (1977-79)...member 1979 Ohio State NCAA Championship Team.

PERSONAL: Although born in Ohio, grew up in Southern California...was persuaded by Jack Nicklaus and Tom Weiskopf to attend Ohio State.

CAREER SUMMARY — **PLAYOFF RECORD: 3-3**

Year	Events Played	Cuts Made	1st	2nd	3rd	Top 10	Top 25	Earnings	Rank
1978(Am.)	1	1					1		
1979(Am.)	3	3							
1980	30	19				2	6	$43,316	80
1981	30	23	1			3	12	$127,608	25
1982	28	21				3	6	$57,483	78
1983	28	27	1		2	7	12	$216,868	16
1984	28	20				1	5	$65,710	89
1985	29	17				1	5	$63,573	106
1986	30	20		2	1	6	13	$255,126	27
1987	32	19	1			6	10	$333,184	29
1988	29	21				2	9	$139,916	84
1989	12	6				1	2	$39,445	172
1990	27	20		2		4	10	$448,112	28
1991	25	21		1	2	8	12	$546,984	26
1992	21	18	3	2	1	8	13	$1,165,606	3
1993	23	19				5	13	$342,321	45
1994	24	16			1	6	11	$429,725	37
1995	27	17				1	5	$186,977	97
Total	427	308	6	7	7	64	145	$4,461,954	33

1996 PGA TOUR CHARITY TEAM: Quad City Classic

TOP TOURNAMENT SUMMARY

YEAR	79	80	81	82	83	84	85	86	87	88	89	90	91	92	93
Masters Tournament	39		T21	CUT		CUT			T24	CUT			CUT	T54	T39
U.S. Open	T53	T51	T4	CUT		CUT	CUT	T35	T36	T50			T19	T13	T25
British Open Championship		CUT												2	CUT
PGA Championship			T19	T34	T20	CUT		T53	T28	T48			CUT	T2	T6
THE PLAYERS Championship			CUT	T41	T3	T44	CUT	T7	CUT	CUT	CUT		T3	CUT	CUT
THE TOUR Championship												T22	28	T13	

TOP TOURNAMENT SUMMARY (cont.)

YEAR	94	95
The Masters Tournament	T46	CUT
U.S. Open	5	T62
British Open Championship	T55	T40
PGA Championship	T4	CUT
THE PLAYERS Championship	T23	W/D

NATIONAL TEAMS: World Cup, 1983; World Amateur Team Championship, 1979; Ryder Cup, 1993.

1995 PGA TOUR STATISTICS

Scoring	**71.29**	**(101)**
Driving	**256.4**	**(147T)**
Driving Accuracy	**71.3**	**(74)**
Greens in Regulation	**69.0**	**(26T)**
Putting	**1.809**	**(150T)**
All Around	**920**	**(140T)**
Sand Saves	**38.5**	**(187)**
Total Driving	**221**	**(142T)**
Eagles	**4**	**(116T)**
Birdies	**257**	**(119)**

MISCELLANEOUS STATISTICS

Scoring Avg Before Cut	**71.20**	**(91)**
Scoring Avg 3rd Rnd	**71.63**	**(128)**
Scoring Avg Final Rnd	**71.40**	**(108T)**
Birdies Conversion %	**26.0**	**(161T)**
Par Breakers	**17.4**	**(152T)**

1995 Low Round: **64:** 1995 Las Vegas Invitational/2
Career Low Round: **62:** 1992 Las Vegas Invitational/3
Career Largest Paycheck: **$234,000:** 1992 Las Vegas Invitational/1

Fred Couples

EXEMPT STATUS: Winner, 1992 Masters Tournament
FULL NAME: Frederick Stephen Couples
HEIGHT: 5' 11" **WEIGHT:** 185
BIRTH DATE: October 3, 1959 **BIRTHPLACE:** Seattle, WA
RESIDENCE: Dallas, TX
FAMILY: Single
COLLEGE: University of Houston
SPECIAL INTERESTS: All sports, tennis, antiques, bicycling, vintage cars
TURNED PROFESSIONAL: 1980 **Q SCHOOL:** Fall 1980

TOUR VICTORIES (11): 1983 Kemper Open. **1984** Tournament Players Championship. **1987** Byron Nelson Golf Classic. **1990** Nissan Los Angeles Open. **1991** Federal Express St. Jude Classic, B.C. Open. **1992** Nissan Los Angeles Open, Nestle Invitational, Masters. **1993** Honda Classic. **1994** Buick Open

INTERNATIONAL VICTORIES (5): 1991 Johnnie Walker World Championship. **1994** World Cup (Indiv.). **1995** Dubai Desert Classic (Eur), Johnnie Walker Classic (Eur).

BEST 1995 FINISHES T5 -- Mercedes Championships; 6 -- Buick Open; T6 -- NEC World Series of Golf; T10 -- Masters Tournament.

1995 SEASON: A second season interrupted by back problems for the 15-year PGA TOUR veteran...without a victory for the first time since 1989, ending what had been the longest existing streak on TOUR...opened year with T5 at Mercedes Championships and made five consecutive cuts after that, culminating with T10 at the Masters...trailed leaders Ben Crenshaw and Brian Henninger by one stroke heading into the final round, but fell back with closing 75...after missing first cut of year the following week at MCI Classic, Fred left the TOUR for nearly two months due to resumption of back trouble...problem diagnosed as a closing of the space between the disc and spinal cord...after rest and treatment, returned in June for Kemper Open...missed cut there and following week at U.S. Open, the first string of three consecutive missed cuts since 1990...two starts later, picked up third top-10 finish by shooting 16-under-par 272 for solo sixth at the Buick Open...recovered from second-round 76 with 68-68 on weekend to finish T6 at NEC World Series of Golf...once again, November was a banner month as he teamed with Davis Love III for fourth consecutive World Cup of Golf triumph at Shenzhen, China and won his first Skins Game title...continued off-season success with playoff win over Loren Roberts and Vijay Singh in Johnnie Walker World Championship...began 1995 with back-to-back victories on PGA European Tour; first American since Charles Coody (1973) to perform that feat...also first time in career had consecutive wins...had 2-1 record as captain's choice in Ryder Cup...concluded year by winning second Johnnie Walker World Championship in playoff with Loren Roberts and Vijay Singh.

CAREER HIGHLIGHTS: Fred's career year came in 1992, when won three events including the Masters Tournament and over $1.3 million...named PGA TOUR Player of Year 1991 and 1992...won 1994 Buick Open by two strokes over Corey Pavin...second-extra-hole winner over Robert Gamez at 1993 Honda Classic...holed out from bunker on No. 17 to force eventual playoff...first TOUR win came in five-man playoff at 1983 Kemper Open...captured Tournament Players Championship in 1984, carding TPC at Sawgrass course-record 64 in process...lowered mark to 63 in 1992 PLAYERS Championship...claimed first of two Nissan Los Angeles Open titles in 1990...multiple winner for first time in 1991...won 1991 Johnnie Walker World Championship of Golf in Jamaica...teamed with Raymond Floyd to win 1990 RMCC Invitational hosted by Greg Norman and with Brad Faxon to win 1994 Shark Shootout...winner (with Mike Donald) of 1990 Sazale Classic...winner of Vardon Trophy 1991-92, Arnold Palmer Award 1992, PGA Player of Year 1992.

PERSONAL: Teammate of Blaine McCallister and CBS-TV broadcaster Jim Nantz at University of Houston...three have teamed for annual Three Amigos Celebrity Tournament...his charity Millie Medin Violet Sobich Couples Fund, in memory of mother...also hosts another charity event, the Ernst Championship, in hometown of Seattle...introduced to golf by father, who worked in Seattle Parks and Recreation Department...announced engagement to girlfriend Tawnya Dodd during 1995 Ryder Cup.

CAREER SUMMARY **PLAYOFF RECORD: 4-4**

Year	Events Played	Cuts Made	1st	2nd	3rd	Top 10	Top 25	Earnings	Rank
1979(Am.)	1	1							
1981	25	19		1	1	4	9	$78,939	53
1982	28	18			1	2	9	$77,606	54
1983	30	23	1		1	7	15	$209,733	19
1984	26	24	1		2	9	19	$334,573	7
1985	26	23				7	10	$171,272	38
1986	26	16		1		1	6	$116,065	76
1987	27	21	1			9	15	$441,025	19
1988	27	25		1	1	10	19	$489,822	21
1989	24	21		1	2	9	17	$653,944	11

continued on page 50

FRED COUPLES...*continued*

PGA TOUR CAREER SUMMARY *...continued*

Year	Events Played	Cuts Made	1st	2nd	3rd	Top 10	Top 25	Earnings	Rank
1990	22	17	1	1	3	9	12	$757,999	9
1991	21	20	2		4	9	12	$791,749	3
1992	22	20	3	2	3	12	19	$1,344,188	1
1993	19	17	1	2		9	15	$796,579	10
1994	15	15	1	2		4	7	$625,654	23
1995	15	12				4	7	$299,259	63
Total	354	292	11	11	18	105	191	$7,188,408	5

1996 PGA TOUR CHARITY TEAM: Greater Milwaukee Open

TOP TOURNAMENT SUMMARY

YEAR	79	82	83	84	85	86	87	88	89	90	91	92	93	94	95
Masters Tournament			T32	10	T10	T31		T5	T11	5	T35	1	T21		T10
U.S. Open	T48	CUT	CUT	T9	T39		T46	T10	T21	CUT	T3	T17	T16	T16	CUT
British Open Championship				T4		T46	T40	T4	T6	T25	T3	CUT	T9		
PGA Championship		T3	T23	T20	T6	T36	CUT	CUT	CUT	2	T27	T21	T31	T39	T31
THE PLAYERS Championship		CUT	CUT	1	T49	CUT	CUT	T23	T4	CUT	T23	T13	T39		T29
THE TOUR Championship							T12	7	T7	T22	T16	T5	T10	T29	

NATIONAL TEAMS: U.S.A. vs. Japan, 1984; Ryder Cup (4), 1989, 1991, 1993, 1995; Asahi Glass Four Tours World Championship of Golf (2), 1990, 1991; Dunhill Cup (4), 1991, 1992,1993,1994; World Cup (4), 1992,1993,1994, 1995 (won individual title 1994); Presidents Cup, 1994.

1995 PGA TOUR STATISTICS

Scoring Leaders	70.22	(15T)
Driving Leaders	276.3	(10)
Driving Accuracy	65.8	(145T)
Greens in Regulation	68.9	(28T)
Putting Leaders	1.763	(27T)
All Around	572	(48)
Sand Saves	47.6	(147T)
Total Driving	155	(50T)
Eagle Leaders	8	(36T)
Birdie Leaders	206	(164T)

MISCELLANEOUS STATISTICS

Scoring Avg Before Cut	70.79	(43T)
Scoring Avg 3rd Rnd	69.83	(13)
Scoring Avg Final Rnd	71.75	(133T)
Birdie Conversion %	30.7	(36T)
Par Breakers	22.0	(5T)

1995 Low Round: **66:** 1995 PGA Championship/4
Career Low Round: **62:** 1990 Nissan LA Open/3
Career Largest Paycheck: **$270,000:** 1992 Masters Tournament/1

Fred Couples accepts the green jacket from Ian Woosnam after winning the 1992 Masters. Couples finished 1992 as the leading money winner on the PGA TOUR with $1,344,188.

Ben Crenshaw

EXEMPT STATUS: Winner, 1995 Masters Tournament
FULL NAME: Ben Daniel Crenshaw
HEIGHT: 5' 9" **WEIGHT:** 165
BIRTH DATE: January 11, 1952 **BIRTHPLACE:** Austin, TX
RESIDENCE: Austin, TX; plays out of Barton Creek Club in Austin
FAMILY: Wife, Julie; Katherine Vail (10/6/87), Claire Susan (4/23/92)
COLLEGE: University of Texas
SPECIAL INTERESTS: Fishing, bird watching, golf artifacts, golf course architecture, country music
TURNED PROFESSIONAL: 1973 **JOINED TOUR:** Fall 1973

TOUR VICTORIES (19): 1973 San Antonio-Texas Open. **1976** Bing Crosby National Pro-Am, Hawaiian Open, Ohio Kings Island Open. **1977** Colonial National Invitation. **1979** Phoenix Open, Walt Disney World Team Championship (with George Burns). **1980** Anheuser-Busch Classic. **1983** Byron Nelson Classic. **1984** Masters Tournament. **1986** Buick Open, Vantage Championship. **1987** USF&G Classic. **1988** Doral Ryder Open. **1990** Southwestern Bell Colonial. **1992** Centel Western Open. **1993** Nestle Invitational.**1994** Freeport-McMoRan Classic. **1995** Masters Tournament.

INTERNATIONAL VICTORIES (2): 1976 Irish Open (Eur). **1988** World Cup (Indiv.).

BEST 1995 FINISHES: 1 -- Masters Tournament; 3 -- Phoenix Open; T5 -- Mercedes Championships, Memorial Tournament

1995 SEASON: In the year's most poignant moment, Ben won his second Masters Tournament title after serving as a pall bearer at the funeral of his long-time teacher Harvey Penick earlier in the week...shot rounds of 70-67-69-68 -- 274 to defeat Davis Love III by one stroke...posted top-10 finishes in first two events of 1995...after T5 at Mercedes Championships, shot second-round 64 at Phoenix Open to claim share of lead...third-round 70 enough to take one stroke lead over five golfers through 54 holes...closed with 69 for solo third, two strokes out of playoff won by Vijay Singh...T13 at AT&T Pebble Beach the following week...after Masters, posted one more top-10 finish, T5 at Memorial Tournament...opening 67 at British Open good for share of first round lead...shot 72-76-72 thereafter for T15...finished T25 at TOUR Championship after undergoing treatment for kidney stone just before the event...in November, won PGA Grand Slam of Golf by holing a 60-yard wedge shot for eagle on final hole.

CAREER HIGHLIGHTS: Has produced win-a-year since turning 40...prior to Masters victory, forty-something titles include 1992 Western Open, 1993 Nestle Invitational and 1994 Freeport-McMoRan Classic...from July 1992 through April 1994 his only three top-10 finishes were victories...one of his biggest victories came at 1984 Masters Tournament, where final-round 68 for 277 gave him two-stroke decision over Tom Watson...first triumph came in first start as official member of PGA TOUR, 1973 San Antonio-Texas Open...winner of two events at Colonial CC 13 years apart, 1977 Colonial National Invitation and 1990 Southwestern Bell Colonial...most recent of three multiple victory seasons 1986, when he claimed Buick Open and Vantage Championship, precursor of TOUR Championship...winner of 1983 Byron Nelson Classic...won 1973 Qualifying Tournament by then-record 12 strokes...winner 1971-72-73 NCAA Championships, co-winner with Tom Kite 1972...winner of Fred Haskins Award as nation's outstanding collegiate golfer each of those years...won William Richardson Award in 1989, Bob Jones Award in 1991.

PERSONAL: Noted golf historian...enjoys golf course architecture...fought winning battle against Graves disease in mid-1980s...bothered by calcium deposits and bone spur on toe in 1995.

CAREER SUMMARY **PLAYOFF RECORD: 0-8**

Year	Events Played	Cuts Made	1st	2nd	3rd	Top 10	Top 25	Earnings	Rank
1970(Am.)	1	1							
1971(Am.)	3	3				1	2		
1972(Am.)	4	4			1	1	4		
1973(Am.)	3	3				1	3		
1973	5	5	1	1		3	4	$76,749	34
1974	27	22		2		6	11	$71,065	31
1975	28	20			3	6	8	$63,528	32
1976	28	27	3	3		14	17	$257,759	2
1977	24	19	1	1	2	6	11	$123,841	16
1978	27	24		1	2	5	12	$108,305	21
1979	25	20	2	4		9	17	$236,769	5
1980	26	24	1	2	1	10	13	$237,727	5
1981	25	20		2	1	9	14	$151,038	20
1982	22	15				2	8	$54,277	84
1983	21	18	1	2	2	9	14	$275,474	7
1984	24	20	1		1	9	13	$270,989	16
1985	22	8					2	$25,814	149

continued on page 52

CAREER SUMMARY ...*continued*

Year	Events Played	Cuts Made	1st	2nd	3rd	Top 10	Top 25	Earnings	Rank
1986	26	22	2			5	12	$388,169	8
1987	24	19	1	1	1	14	15	$638,194	3
1988	26	25	1	1	1	8	21	$696,895	8
1989	23	18		1	1	5	12	$443,095	21
1990	21	15	1			2	8	$351,193	33
1991	21	10			2	4	7	$224,563	75
1992	24	19	1	1		4	7	$439,071	31
1993	22	15	1			1	7	$318,605	51
1994	24	20	1			6	13	$659,252	21
1995	23	17	1		1	4	7	$737,475	23
Total	549	433	19	22	19	144	262	$6,845,235	9

1996 PGA TOUR CHARITY TEAM: Kmart Greater Greensboro Open

TOP TOURNAMENT SUMMARY

YEAR	70	71	72	73	74	75	76	77	78	79	80	81	82	83	84
Masters Tournament			T19	T24	T22	T30	2	T8	T37		T6	T8	T24	T2	1
U.S. Open	T36	T27				T3	T8	T49		T11	T31	T11	T19	CUT	CUT
British Open Championship					T28			T5	T2	T2	3	T8	T15	CUT	T22
PGA Championship					T63	T10	T8		T16	2	T41	CUT	CUT	T9	CUT
THE PLAYERS Championship					T39	T55	T70		T4		2	T63	CUT	T10	T26

TOP TOURNAMENT SUMMARY (cont.)

YEAR	85	86	87	88	89	90	91	92	93	94	95
The Masters Tournament	T57	T16	T4	4	T3	T14	T3	46	CUT	T18	1
U.S. Open	CUT	T6	T4	T12	CUT	CUT				T33	T71
British Open Championship	T35	T21	T4	T16	T52	T31	T80		CUT	T77	T15
PGA Championship	T59	T11	T7	T17	T17	T31	W/D	T73	T61	T9	T44
THE PLAYERS Championship	T33	T54	T9	T11	T11	CUT	CUT	T29	CUT	T19	CUT
THE TOUR Championship			T5	T21	T14					T13	T25

NATIONAL TEAMS: Ryder Cup (4), 1981, 1983, 1987, 1995; World Cup (2), 1987, 1988 (won individual title in 1988); U.S. vs. Japan, 1983; Kirin Cup, 1988; Dunhill Cup, 1995.

1995 PGA TOUR STATISTICS

Scoring	**70.86**	**(61)**
Driving	**253.1**	**(172)**
Driving Accuracy	**70.6**	**(79T)**
Greens in Regulation	**63.2**	**(159T)**
Putting	**1.772**	**(49T)**
All Around	**784**	**(112)**
Sand Saves	**61.4**	**(6)**
Total Driving	**251**	**(165T)**
Eagles	**3**	**(137T)**
Birdies	**254**	**(121T)**

MISCELLANEOUS STATISTICS

Scoring Avg Before Cut	**71.16**	**(85T)**
Scoring Avg 3rd Rnd	**72.00**	**(149T)**
Scoring Avg Final Rnd	**71.06**	**(75)**
Birdies Conversion %	**29.4**	**(76)**
Par Breakers	**17.8**	**(140T)**

1995 Low Round: 64: 2 times, most recent 1995 Buick Invitational of California/2
Career Low Round: 61: 1979 Phoenix Open/2
Career Largest Paycheck: $396,000: 1995 Masters Tournament/1

JOHN DALY

EXEMPT STATUS: Winner, 1995 British Open
FULL NAME: John Patrick Daly
HEIGHT: 5' 11" **WEIGHT:** 175
BIRTH DATE: April 28,1966 **BIRTHPLACE:** Carmichael, CA
RESIDENCE: Germantown, TN
COLLEGE: University of Arkansas
FAMILY: Wife, Paulette; Shynah Hale (6/10/92), Sierra Lynn (6/1/95)
SPECIAL INTERESTS: Most sports
TURNED PROFESSIONAL: 1987 **Q SCHOOL:** Fall 1990

TOUR VICTORIES (4): 1991 PGA Championship. **1992** B.C. Open. **1994** BellSouth Classic. **1995** British Open.

INTERNATIONAL VICTORIES (2): 1990 AECI Charity Classic (Afr), Hollard Royal Swazi Sun Classic (Afr).

NIKE TOUR VICTORIES (1): 1990 Utah Classic.

BEST 1995 FINISH: 1 -- British Open.

1995 SEASON: A year with only one top-10 finish normally would not go down as one of John's best, except that the win came in the British Open at St. Andrews...held a share of the first- and second-round lead at the Old Course before a third-round 73 dropped him into a tie for fourth, four strokes behind Michael Campbell...a closing 71 would have been enough to win by one stroke if not for the miraculous 70-foot putt from off the green by Costantino Rocca, which forced a four-hole playoff...won the playoff handily with a birdie and three pars to Rocca's bogey-par-triple bogey 7- birdie...became the youngest active player on TOUR with two major victories to his credit... since World War II Nicklaus, Watson, Miller and Daly only Americans to win two majors before turning 30...made the cut in 15 of 23 tournaments...aside from the British Open win, best finish came in defending his BellSouth Classic title...led after two rounds of 67 at Atlanta CC...fell two strokes back after a third-round 71...a closing 72 left him T12...gave fans a thrill Sunday by driving 335-yard par-4 14th hole, narrowly missing hole-in-one...was tied for second after two rounds at MCI Classic, four strokes behind Tom Lehman...finished T13...second-round 65 at GTE Byron Nelson Golf Classic was his low round of 1995, when he finished T41...led the driving distance category on the PGA TOUR for the fourth time in last five years...his 289.0 average was the longest since record-keeping began in 1980.

CAREER HIGHLIGHTS: A crowd-pleaser each time he takes driver out of bag, delighted golf world with surprising victory at 1991 PGA Championship at Crooked Stick...as ninth and last alternate in field, saw Crooked Stick for first time during Round 1...opening 69 left him two strokes out of lead...added rounds of 67-69-71 for three-stroke win over Bruce Lietzke...completed rookie season with third-place finish in TOUR Championship at Pinehurst No. 2...named PGA TOUR Rookie of Year... won 1992 B.C. Open by six strokes...after serving a PGA TOUR suspension early in 1994, earned his third TOUR victory at 1994 BellSouth Classic...grabbed the lead with a second-round 64, then fought off challenges of Nolan Henke and Brian Henninger...played Ben Hogan Tour in 1990 after winning only Hogan Tour Qualifying Tournament...won 1990 Ben Hogan Utah Classic...finished ninth on money list with over $64,000...won several events on South African Tour...winner 1987 Missouri Open.

PERSONAL: Served as non-paid assistant coach for University of Arkansas golf team during hiatus between 1994-95 TOUR seasons...started playing as youngster after father gave him full-sized set of clubs...experienced mid-year headaches in 1995 related to his on-going alcohol rehabilitation.

PGA TOUR CAREER SUMMARY — **PLAYOFF RECORD: 1-0**

Year	Events Played	Cuts Made	1st	2nd	3rd	Top 10	Top 25	Earnings	Rank
1986	1								
1989	6	3					1	$14,689	200
1990	3	2					1	$10,000	230
1991	33	21	1		2	4	11	$574,783	17
1992	25	15	1	1		5	8	$387,455	37
1993	24	15			1	1	5	$225,591	76
1994	17	9	1			3	4	$340,034	49
1995	23	15	1			1	4	$321,748	57
Total	132	80	4	1	3	14	34	$1,874,299	106

NIKE TOUR SUMMARY

Year	Events Played	Cuts Made	1st	2nd	3rd	Top 10	Top 25	Earnings	Rank
1990	18	14	1	3		6	11	$64,692	9
1991	1	1						$673	276
Total	19	15	1	3		6	11	$65,365	
COMBINED TOTAL MONEY								$1,939,664	

1996 PGA TOUR CHARITY TEAM: Buick Challenge

JOHN DALY...continued

NATIONAL TEAMS: Dunhill Cup, 1993.

TOP TOURNAMENT SUMMARY

YEAR	86	89	91	92	93	94	95
Masters Tournament				T19	T3	T48	T45
U.S. Open	CUT	T69		CUT	T33	CUT	T45
British Open Championship				75	T14	81	1
PGA Championship			1	82	T51	CUT	CUT
THE PLAYERS Championship			CUT	72	CUT	CUT	
THE TOUR Championship			3				

1995 PGA TOUR STATISTICS

Scoring	71.60	(127)
Driving	289.0	(1)
Driving Accuracy	56.8	(184)
Greens in Regulation	59.3	(185)
Putting	1.781	(68T)
All Around	823	(124)
Sand Saves	55.1	(58T)
Total Driving	185	(92T)
Eagles	6	(69T)
Birdies	246	(131T)

MISCELLANEOUS STATISTICS

Scoring Avg Before Cut	71.19	(89T)
Scoring Avg 3rd Rnd	73.00	(183)
Scoring Avg Final Rnd	73.20	(185)
Birdies Conversion %	32.5	(13T)
Par Breakers	18.7	(108T)

1995 Low Round: **65:** 1995 GTE Byron Nelson Classic/2
Career Low Round: **63:** 2 times, most recent 1991 Las Vegas Invitation/2
Career Largest Paycheck: **$230,000:** 1991 PGA Championship/1

MARCO DAWSON

EXEMPT STATUS: 71st on 1995 money list
FULL NAME: Marco Thomas Dawson
HEIGHT: 6' **WEIGHT:** 195
BIRTH DATE: November 17, 1963 **BIRTHPLACE:** Freising, Germany
RESIDENCE: Lakeland, FL
COLLEGE: Florida Southern University
FAMILY: Single
SPECIAL INTERESTS: Boxing, sport fishing, all sports
TURNED PROFESSIONAL: 1986 **Q SCHOOL:** 1990, 1991, 1994

BEST CAREER FINISH: 2 -- 1995 Greater Milwaukee Open

BEST 1995 FINISHES: 2 -- Greater Milwaukee Open; T6 -- Anheuser-Busch Golf Classic

1995 SEASON: After four years on TOUR, during which he hung on the edge of finishing within the top 125 at the end of the year, Marco put together the best year of his career with $261,214, good for 71st on the money list...nearly earned his first PGA TOUR victory at Greater Milwaukee Open...a second-round 65 earned him a share of the lead with Richard Zokol...when Scott Hoch closed with two 65s of his own, Marco claimed second, three strokes back at 272...$108,000 runner-up share was largest payday of his career...first top-10 finish came at Anheuser-Busch Golf Classic...a closing 63, his low round of the year, moved him from T48 into a share of sixth place, three strokes behind Ted Tryba...the next two weeks, recorded back-to-back T11s at Deposit Guaranty Golf Classic and Ideon Classic at Pleasant Valley...T7 at Lincoln-Mercury Kapalua International.

CAREER HIGHLIGHTS: Finished 20th at the Qualifying Tournament last fall after finishing 139th on the money list in 1994...1994 earnings of $121,025 actually were slightly higher than his 1993 total, when he retained his card...best 1994 finish came at Greater Milwaukee Open, T7...prior to 1995, best career finishes were two Texas T5s...a second-round 63 at the rain-shortened Byron Nelson Classic helped earn his first T5...in 1993, four rounds in the 60s, including a third-round 65, led to his H-E-B Texas Open T5...finished 31st on the 1990 Ben Hogan Tour money list.

PERSONAL: Attended Florida Southern and was a college teammate of Lee Janzen and Rocco Mediate.

MARCO DAWSON...continued

PGA TOUR CAREER SUMMARY — **PLAYOFF RECORD: 0-0**

Year	Events Played	Cuts Made	1st	2nd	3rd	Top 10	Top 25	Earnings	Rank
1986	1	1					1	$2,080	249
1990	2	1						$2,154	272
1991	29	12				2	3	$96,756	137
1992	28	14				2	4	$113,464	123
1993	32	21				1	4	$120,462	124
1994	30	13				1	4	$121,025	139
1995	25	14		1		2	7	$261,214	71
Total	147	76		1		8	23	$717,154	220

NIKE TOUR SUMMARY

Year	Events Played	Cuts Made	1st	2nd	3rd	Top 10	Top 25	Earnings	Rank
1990	24	15			1	3	12	$29,972	31
1991	4	3				3	3	$9,071	102
Total	28	18			1	6	15	$39,044	
COMBINED TOTAL MONEY								$756,198	

1996 PGA TOUR CHARITY TEAM: Nissan Open

TOP TOURNAMENT SUMMARY

YEAR	93	94
THE PLAYERS Championship	T46	CUT

1995 PGA TOUR STATISTICS

Scoring	71.14	(84T)
Driving	267.9	(56)
Driving Accuracy	62.6	(172)
Greens in Regulation	66.9	(66T)
Putting	1.783	(77T)
All Around	758	(104)
Sand Saves	50.4	(122T)
Total Driving	228	(152T)
Eagles	4	(116T)
Birdies	296	(65T)

MISCELLANEOUS STATISTICS

Scoring Avg Before Cut	71.15	(83T)
Scoring Avg 3rd Rnd	72.31	(166)
Scoring Avg Final Rnd	69.27	(1)
Birdies Conversion %	30.0	(50T)
Par Breakers	20.3	(40T)

1995 Low Round: **63:** 1995 Anheuser-Busch Golf Classic/4
Career Low Round: **61:** 1991 Chattanooga Classic/1
Career Largest Paycheck: $108,000: 1995 Greater Milwaukee Open/2

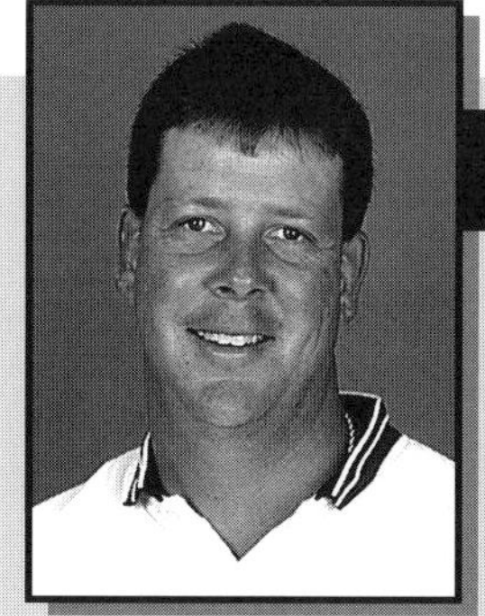

GLEN DAY

EXEMPT STATUS: 91st on 1995 money list
FULL NAME: Glen Edward Day
HEIGHT: 5' 10" **WEIGHT:** 170
BIRTH DATE: November 16, 1965 **BIRTHPLACE:** Mobile, AL
RESIDENCE: Little Rock, AR; plays out of Waverly GC, West Point, MS
FAMILY: Wife, Jennifer Ralston-Day; Whitney Elizabeth (7/26/94)
COLLEGE: University of Oklahoma
SPECIAL INTERESTS: Hunting
TURNED PROFESSIONAL: 1988 **Q SCHOOL:** 1993

BEST TOUR CAREER FINISH: 2 -- 1994 Anheuser-Busch Golf Classic

INTERNATIONAL VICTORIES (1): **1990** Benson & Hedges Malaysian Open (Asia).

BEST 1995 FINISH: T7 -- Las Vegas Invitational

1995 SEASON: While he didn't match his 1994 numbers, Glen retained his playing privileges for 1996 with a 91st place money-list finish...broke slowly in 1995, missing six of his first seven cuts and finishing T71 in the one cut he made -- Nissan Open...after

GLEN DAY...continued

a T24 at Honda Classic, two impressive first rounds led to high finishes in the spring...finished T11 at GTE Byron Nelson Golf Classic after an opening 63...after a career-best 62 at FedEx St. Jude Classic, he shared the lead with Mike Standly...fell from contention after a second-round 74 and went on to finish T21...recorded top-20 finishes at Anheuser-Busch (T11), Deposit Guaranty (T18), Sprint International (T17) and Buick Challenge (T12) before breaking into the top 10 at Las Vegas...closing 66 at TPC at Summerlin good for a T7, five strokes behind Jim Furyk...$46,750 paycheck was largest of the year.

CAREER HIGHLIGHTS: Rookie of Year candidate in 1994 after finishing third on money list among first-year players...trailed just Ernie Els and Mike Heinen with $357,236...went over $100,000 for season in early April by cashing in seven consecutive events, following missed cut in first start, United Airlines Hawaiian Open...T9 at Canon Greater Hartford Open featured two holes-in-one in the second round...after opening with season-low 64, stood three strokes off lead from start to finish in Anheuser-Busch Golf Classic...second-place finish behind Mark McCumber was worth $118,800...earned TOUR playing privileges with T11 in 1993 Qualifying Tournament...winner 1989 Malaysian Open... also played three years in Europe... 1987-88 All-American at University of Oklahoma.

PERSONAL: Making his first foray into the golf course design business in conjuction with Nicklaus Design...the course, Salem Glen, near Winston-Salem, NC slated to open in late 1996...plays with a picture of his daughter clipped to his hat...father-in-law, Bob Ralston, made 1995 FedEx St. Jude Classic field...the two first competed against one another at 1988 Arkansas Open won by Glen...credits grandfather with encouraging his pursuit of a professional career...grandfather co-signed $20,000 loan so he could play in Asia and Europe...Glen is an avid duck hunter.

CAREER SUMMARY — **PLAYOFF RECORD: 0-0**

Year	Events Played	Cuts Made	1st	2nd	3rd	Top 10	Top 25	Earnings	Rank
1994	30	18		1		4	10	$357,236	45
1995	32	15				1	8	$201,809	91
Total	62	33		1		5	18	$559,046	241

NIKE TOUR SUMMARY

Year	Events Played	Cuts Made	1st	2nd	3rd	Top 10	Top 25	Earnings	Rank
1990	1								
1992	1	1					1	$1,116	220
1993	3	2					1	$2,816	168
Total	5	3					2	$3,932	
COMBINED TOTAL MONEY								$562,978	

1996 PGA TOUR CHARITY TEAM: Deposit Guaranty Golf Classic

TOP TOURNAMENT SUMMARY

YEAR	93	94	95
U.S. Open		CUT	CUT
British Open Championship	CUT		
PGA Championship		T15	CUT
THE PLAYERS Championship			CUT

1995 PGA TOUR STATISTICS

Scoring	71.41	(110)
Driving	261.9	(102T)
Driving Accuracy	69.8	(91T)
Greens in Regulation	64.8	(126T)
Putting	1.781	(68T)
All Around	744	(102)
Sand Saves	47.1	(152T)
Total Driving	193	(105T)
Eagles	7	(51T)
Birdies	312	(44T)

MISCELLANEOUS STATISTICS

Scoring Avg Before Cut	71.79	(149)
Scoring Avg 3rd Rnd	69.87	(15T)
Scoring Avg Final Rnd	70.71	(44T)
Birdies Conversion %	29.5	(68T)
Par Breakers	19.5	(80T)

1995 Low Round: 62: 1995 FedEx St. Jude Classic/1
Career Low Round: 62: 1995 FedEx St. Jude Classic/1
Career Largest Paycheck: $118,800: 1994 Anheuser-Busch Golf Classic/2

JAY DELSING

EXEMPT STATUS: 80th on 1995 money list
FULL NAME: James Patrick Delsing
HEIGHT: 6' 5" **WEIGHT:** 200
BIRTH DATE: October 17, 1960 **BIRTHPLACE:** St. Louis, MO
RESIDENCE: St. Louis, MO; plays out of CC of St. Albans, MO
FAMILY: Wife, Kathy; Mackenzie (5/31/89), Gemma (12/9/91), Brennan (9/21/93)
COLLEGE: UCLA (1983, Economics)
SPECIAL INTERESTS: Fishing, all sports
TURNED PROFESSIONAL: 1984 **Q SCHOOL:** Fall 1984, 1988, 1989

BEST CAREER FINISH: T2 -- 1993 New England Classic, 1995 FedEx St. Jude Classic

BEST 1995 FINISHES: T2 -- FedEx St. Jude Classic; 3 -- Quad City Classic

1995 SEASON: Recorded only three top-25 finishes, but two of those were a tie for second at FedEx St. Jude Classic and a third at Quad City Classic...moved into contention at FedEx after a second-round 63, his low round of the year, left him tied for fourth...was sixth after a third-round 69, but a closing 67 moved him into a tie for second with Ken Green, one stroke behind Jim Gallagher, Jr...shared the lead with Jonathan Kaye after a second-round 64 at the rain-shortened Quad City Classic...a final-round 67 left him alone in third behind Kaye and winner D.A. Weibring...leading up to his FedEx finish, Jay was suffering through a horrible slump, having made just 2 of 15 cuts worth $8,437...the T2 at TPC at Southwind was the first of four consecutive cuts made...closed the year by making five of six cuts, including Quad City...first in that stretch was his other top 25 -- T24 at Bell Canadian Open.

CAREER HIGHLIGHTS: As slowly as Jay started in 1995, that's how quickly he started the year before...made 10 of his first 11 cuts in 1994, including a T7 at AT&T Pebble Beach and T8 at Nissan...went over $200,000 three of four years 1990-1993 (exception 1991)...first T2 placing of 10-year career came at 1993 New England Classic, four strokes behind Paul Azinger...climbed hill steadily, but was unable to overcome 10-stroke deficit he faced after Round 1...closing 67 brought him $88,000 payday...very next week carded course-record, 10-under-par 61 in final round at TPC at Southwind, vaulting into T8...earned $121,000 for those two weeks...posted four top-10 finishes, including T4s Phoenix and Canadian Opens, solo fourth Hardee's Golf Classic, during 1992 campaign, his best to date.

PERSONAL: Father, Jim Delsing, who played for New York Yankees, Chicago White Sox, St. Louis Browns and Kansas City A's, was the pinchrunner for Eddie Gaedel, the midget Bill Veeck used as a pinchhitter in 1951...teammates at UCLA included Corey Pavin, Steve Pate and Duffy Waldorf...was two-time All-American at UCLA.

CAREER SUMMARY **PLAYOFF RECORD: 0-0**

Year	Events Played	Cuts Made	1st	2nd	3rd	Top 10	Top 25	Earnings	Rank
1985	27	14				2	3	$46,480	125
1986	33	17				2	5	$65,850	123
1987	35	13				1	4	$58,657	136
1988	30	10				1	3	$45,504	152
1989	23	10					1	$26,565	187
1990	29	20			1	4	7	$207,740	74
1991	31	15					7	$149,775	100
1992	29	20				4	9	$296,740	52
1993	29	20		1		3	6	$233,484	71
1994	27	16				2	3	$143,738	124
1995	27	11		1	1	2	3	$230,769	80
Total	320	166		2	2	21	51	$1,505,302	137

1996 PGA TOUR CHARITY TEAM: CVS Charity Classic

TOP TOURNAMENT SUMMARY

YEAR	85	86	87	90	91	92	93	94	95
U.S. Open					CUT	T33			
British Open Championship									T88
PGA Championship				T63	CUT		CUT		
THE PLAYERS Championship	CUT	CUT	CUT	CUT	T13	CUT	CUT	T27	CUT

1995 PGA TOUR STATISTICS

Scoring	71.70	(136T)
Driving	264.8	(82T)
Driving Accuracy	66.7	(136T)
Greens in Regulation	62.5	(171)
Putting	1.812	(161T)
All Around	963	(153)
Sand Saves	55.6	(49)
Total Driving	218	(139T)
Eagles	5	(88T)
Birdies	237	(140)

MISCELLANEOUS STATISTICS

Scoring Avg Before Cut	71.76	(146T)
Scoring Avg 3rd Rnd	71.71	(138T)
Scoring Avg Final Rnd	72.17	(162)
Birdies Conversion %	29.1	(80)
Par Breakers	17.6	(147T)

1995 Low Round: **63:** 1995 FedEx St. Jude Classic/2
Career Low Round: **61:** 1993 Federal Express St. Jude Classic/4
Career Largest Paycheck: **$110,000:** 1995 FedEx St. Jude Classic/T2

Ed Dougherty *(DOCK-er-tee)*

EXEMPT STATUS: 1995 tournament winner
FULL NAME: Edward Matthew Dougherty
HEIGHT: 6' 1" **WEIGHT:** 225
BIRTH DATE: November 4, 1947 **BIRTHPLACE:** Chester, PA
RESIDENCE: Linwood, PA
FAMILY: Wife, Carolyn
SPECIAL INTERESTS: Lionel toy trains, Old Gottlieb pinball machines
TURNED PROFESSIONAL: 1969
Q SCHOOL: Fall 1975, 1986, 1989

TOUR VICTORIES (1): 1995 Deposit Guaranty Golf Classic

BEST 1995 FINISH: 1 -- Deposit Guaranty Golf Classic

1995 SEASON: After finishing 157th on the 1994 money list, Ed lost his exempt status and was reclassified as a Veteran Member (with 150 or more career made cuts)...idled early in year by shoulder injured while lifting one of his vintage pinball machines...as a result, the Deposit Guaranty Classic in July was only his third start of 1995...after rounds of 68-68-70, he began the final round tied for seventh, three strokes behind Dicky Thompson...his final-round 66, which included a 32 on the second nine, earned a two-stroke victory over Gil Morgan...it was the first PGA TOUR win in his career, which began in 1975...was the oldest first-time winner since John Barnum captured the 1962 Cajun Classic at 51...the two-year exemption will take him past his 50th birthday...after the win, Dougherty resumed the schedule pace he had maintained in 1990-93 when he was among the busiest players on TOUR...wasn't able to regain the form he displayed in Mississippi and, in his final 12 starts, his best finish was a T33 at NEC World Series of Golf.

CAREER HIGHLIGHTS: Had three second-place finishes to his credit prior to his win last year...lost in a playoff to Jim Gallagher, Jr., at 1990 Greater Milwaukee Open...also was second at Anheuser-Busch Golf Classic and Chattanooga Classic in 1992...that year he had his career-best earnings ($237,525) and money-list finish (66th)...was the 1985 PGA of America Club Professional of the Year, the year he won the Club Pro Championship...first joined the TOUR in 1975, but left in 1982 to become the golf professional at Edgewood CC in Pennsylvania...regained his TOUR card at the 1989 Qualifying Tournament.

PERSONAL: A serious model train enthusiast who visits train stores in most cities on TOUR...more recently has begun restoring old pinball machines...during his enforced absence from the TOUR in early 1995, admitted he did "absolutely nothing"...nickname, based on pronunciation of last name, is "Doc"...one of few remaining Vietnam vets active on PGA TOUR.

CAREER SUMMARY				PLAYOFF RECORD: 0-1					
Year	Events Played	Cuts Made	1st	2nd	3rd	Top 10	Top 25	Earnings	Rank
1975	17	9					4	$9,374	129
1976	26	14			1	1	1	$17,333	113
1977	26	17				2	5	$17,606	113
1978	20	7				1	3	$9,936	141
1979	26	12				2	3	$24,802	115
1980	25	7					1	$9,113	168
1981	22	13				1	3	$22,096	128
1982	26	15				1	3	$27,948	129
1983	18	8					1	$9,422	180
1984	1								
1985	1								
1986	8	3					1	$11,743	200
1987	27	17				1	6	$76,705	115
1988	36	10						$22,455	195
1989	3	1						$1,800	267
1990	27	12		1		1	3	$124,505	123
1991	36	20			1	2	5	$201,958	82
1992	36	19		2		2	4	$237,525	66
1993	34	22				3	5	$167,651	99
1994	33	18					4	$96,987	157
1995	15	7	1			1	1	$154,007	122
Total	463	231	1	3	2	18	53	$1,241,542	158

Ed Dougherty...continued

NIKE TOUR SUMMARY

Year	Events Played	Cuts Made	1st	2nd	3rd	Top 10	Top 25	Earnings	Rank
1995	1	1						$440	269
Total	1	1						$440	
COMBINED TOTAL MONEY								$1,241,982	

1996 PGA TOUR CHARITY TEAM: JCPenney Classic

TOP TOURNAMENT SUMMARY

YEAR	75	77	80	82	85	86	87	88	90	91	92	93	94	95
U.S. Open						CUT	T51	CUT	CUT	CUT				
PGA Championship	T22				CUT	CUT				T43	CUT			T58
THE PLAYERS Championship	T67	T34	CUT	T65				CUT		T27	T54	T61	CUT	

1995 PGA TOUR STATISTICS

Scoring	72.28	(N/A)
Driving	261.7	(N/A)
Driving Accuracy	68.2	(N/A)
Greens in Regulation	61.8	(N/A)
Putting	1.831	(N/A)
Sand Saves	50.0	(N/A)
Total Driving	1,998	(N/A)
Eagles	1	(N/A)
Birdies	123	(N/A)

MISCELLANEOUS STATISTICS

Scoring Avg Before Cut	72.48	(N/A)
Scoring Avg 3rd Rnd	74.11	(N/A)
Scoring Avg Final Rnd	70.38	(N/A)
Birdies Conversion %	25.7	(N/A)
Par Breakers	16.0	(N/A)

1995 Low Round: **66:** 1995 Deposit Guaranty Golf Classic/4
Career Low Round: **62:** 1992 Chattanooga Classic/3
Career Largest Paycheck: $126,000: 1995 Deposit Guaranty Golf Classic/1

Allen Doyle

EXEMPT STATUS: 2nd on 1995 NIKE TOUR money list
FULL NAME: Allen Michael Doyle
HEIGHT: 6'3" **WEIGHT:** 210
BIRTH DATE: June 26, 1948 **BIRTHPLACE:** Woonsocket, RI
RESIDENCE: La Grange, GA
FAMILY: Wife, Kate; Erin (8/22/79); Michelle (10/26/80)
COLLEGE: Norwich University
SPECIAL INTERESTS: Family
TURNED PROFESSIONAL: 1995 **JOINED TOUR:** 1996

BEST TOUR CAREER FINISH: T64—1991 Memorial Tournament, 1994 Memorial Tournament

NIKE TOUR VICTORIES (3): 1995 NIKE Mississippi Gulf Coast Classic, NIKE Texarkana Open, NIKE TOUR Championship

BEST 1995 FINISH: 74—Memorial Tournament

BEST NIKE TOUR 1995 FINISHES: 1—NIKE Mississippi Gulf Coast Classic, NIKE Texarkana Open, NIKE TOUR Championship; 2—NIKE Philadelphia Classic; T5—NIKE Tallahassee Open, NIKE Central Georgia Open; T9—NIKE Cleveland Open; T10—NIKE Miami Valley Open.

1995 SEASON: At 47 is the oldest rookie in PGA TOUR history...following an outstanding amateur career, joined the NIKE TOUR in March and won his second event...defeated his former Walker Cup teammate Franklin Langham in a playoff at the NIKE Mississippi Gulf Coast Classic...had gained entrance into the field by finishing tied for 21st in his debut the previous week at the NIKE Pensacola Classic...earned his second victory of the season in August at the NIKE Texarkana Open, where he defeated Gary Rusnak by one stroke...became the season's only three-time winner when he defeated John Maginnes in a playoff at the NIKE TOUR Championship...at 47 years, two months and 26 days when he won the NIKE TOUR Championship, he bettered his own record as the oldest winner in NIKE TOUR history...earned $176,652 in only 20 events...led the NIKE TOUR in scoring with 69.79 average...played in two PGA TOUR events in 1995, missing the cut in the BellSouth Classic and finishing 74th in the Memorial Tournament.

ALLEN DOYLE...continued

CAREER HIGHLIGHTS: Celebrated amateur who was a member of the 1989, 1991 and 1993 Walker Cup teams...also represented the United States on the 1990, 1992 and 1994 World Amateur Cup teams...six-time winner of the Georgia State Open, in 1978-79, 1982, 1987-88 and 1990...in 1994, his final year of amateur competition, won five significant amateur titles: the Porter Cup, Sunnehanna Amateur, Cardinal Amateur, Dogwood Amateur and the Rice Planters Invitational...semi-finalist in 1992 U.S. Amateur...has played in the Memorial Tournament every year since 1991, making the cut three times.

PERSONAL: Was inducted into the Norwich University Sports Hall of Fame as a hockey player...says his unorthodox swing developed from practicing in a low-ceiling room as a youngster in Massachusetts.

PGA TOUR CAREER SUMMARY — **PLAYOFF RECORD: 0-0**

Year	Events Played	Cuts Made	1st	2nd	3rd	Top 10	Top 25	Earnings	Rank
1991(Am.)	2	1							
1992(Am.)	1								
1993(Am.)	1								
1994(Am.)	1	1							
1995	2	1						$3,264	314
Total	7	3						$3,264	

NIKE TOUR CAREER SUMMARY

Year	Events Played	Cuts Made	1st	2nd	3rd	Top 10	Top 25	Earnings	Rank
1995	20	16	3	1		8	12	$176,652	2
Total	20	16	3	1		8	12	$176,652	34
COMBINED TOTAL MONEY								$179,916	

1996 PGA TOUR CHARITY TEAM: Motorola Western Open.

TOP TOURNAMENT SUMMARY

YEAR	91
U.S. Open	CUT

NATIONAL TEAMS: Walker Cup (3), 1989, 1991, 1993; World Amateur Cup (3), 1990, 1992, 1994.

1995 PGA TOUR STATISTICS

Scoring	75.03	(N/A)
Driving	239.1	(N/A)
Driving Accuracy	95.2	(N/A)
Greens in Regulation	62.0	(N/A)
Putting	1.925	(N/A)
Sand Saves	50.0	(N/A)
Total Driving		(N/A)
Eagles		(N/A)
Birdies	11	(N/A)

MISCELLANEOUS STATISTICS

Scoring Avg Before Cut	74.50	(N/A)
Scoring Avg 3rd Rnd	76.00	(N/A)
Scoring Avg Final Rnd	74.00	(N/A)
Birdies Conversion %	16.4	(N/A)
Par Breakers	10.2	(N/A)

1995 Low Round: 72: 1995 Memorial Tournament/2
Career Low Round: 71: 1991 Memorial Tournament/2
Career Largest Paycheck: $3,264: 1995 Memorial Tournament/74

Scoring	69.79	(1)
Eagles	4	(66T)
Birdies	282	(37)

1995 Low Round: 64: 1995 NIKE Philadelphia Classic/4
Career Low Round: 64: 1995 NIKE Philadelphia Classic/4
Career Largest Paycheck: $45,000: 1995 NIKE TOUR Championship/1

DAVID DUVAL *(due-VAHL)*

EXEMPT STATUS: 11th on 1995 money list
FULL NAME: David Robert Duval
HEIGHT: 6' **WEIGHT:** 195
BIRTH DATE: November 9, 1971 **BIRTHPLACE:** Jacksonville, FL
RESIDENCE: Ponte Vedra Beach, FL
FAMILY: Single
COLLEGE: Georgia Tech
SPECIAL INTERESTS: Mountain bikes, reading
TURNED PROFESSIONAL: 1993

BEST TOUR CAREER FINISHES: 2 -- 1995 AT&T Pebble Beach National Pro-Am, 1995 Bob Hope Chrysler Classic; T2 -- 1995 Memorial Tournament

NIKE TOUR VICTORIES (2) : 1993 NIKE Wichita Open, NIKE TOUR Championship

BEST 1995 FINISHES: 2 -- AT&T Pebble Beach National Pro-Am, Bob Hope Chrysler Classic; T2 -- Memorial Tournament; 3 -- Freeport-McMoRan Classic; 5 -- Sprint International; T6 -- Northern Telecom Open; T8 -- Buick Classic; T9 -- THE TOUR Championship.

1995 SEASON: Although he did not win a tournament in 1995, David still laid claim to one of the most successful rookie seasons in TOUR history...after T14 in his first start at United Airlines Hawaiian Open, recorded two runner-up finishes and a tie for sixth in his next four tournaments...only three strokes off lead after 54 holes at Northern Telecom Open before a closing 70 left him T6, five strokes behind Phil Mickelson...two weeks later, at Bob Hope Chrysler Classic, again near the lead after 54 holes and tied for second, three behind Kenny Perry...final 67 was enough to overtake Perry, but left him alone in second, two behind Peter Jacobsen, who closed with 65...the $151,200 was his largest payday on TOUR...moved into contention at Bob Hope Chrysler Classic after third-round 65 left alone in third...shared second place, again behind Kenny Perry through 72 holes of the five-round event...finished one stroke behind Perry after a closing 69...shared the lead after two rounds at Freeport-McMoran Classic ...71-69 on weekend left him in third place, one stroke out of Davis Love III-Mike Heinen playoff...despite a second-round 75, came back with rounds of 67-70 to earn T8 at Buick Classic...third runner-up finish came at Memorial...moved into contention with third-round 64, but closing 68 could not overtake Greg Norman, who won by four...after missing cut at Buick Open and PGA (only consecutive cuts all year), finished solo fifth at Sprint International...completed his year with T9 at THE TOUR Championship, giving him $881,436 on the year, a rookie earnings record...passed Ernie Els with Memorial T2, which lifted him to $691,633...Els' 1994 rookie standard was $684,440...began year No. 437 in Sony Ranking but made fastest climb in history into top 50.

CAREER HIGHLIGHTS: Won 1993 NIKE Wichita Open and 1993 NIKE TOUR Championship...finished 11th on money list in 1993 despite playing just nine events...finished eighth on 1994 NIKE TOUR money list...during Georgia Tech career, joined Phil Mickelson and Gary Hallberg as only four-time Division I first-team All-Americans...1993 collegiate Player of the Year...had five wins and 11 seconds in college career.

PERSONAL: Father and uncle are both golf professionals...donated $5,000 check for winning BellSouth Merrill Lynch Shoot-Out to Atlanta Junior Golf Association...was American Junior Golf Association Player of Year in 1989.

PGA TOUR CAREER SUMMARY — **PLAYOFF RECORD: 0-0**

Year	Events Played	Cuts Made	1st	2nd	3rd	Top 10	Top 25	Earnings	Rank
1990(Am.)	1	1							
1992(Am.)	5	2					2		
1993	5	4					1	$27,181	201
1994	6	4				1	1	$44,006	195
1995	26	20		3	1	8	14	$881,436	11
Total	43	31		3	1	9	18	$952,623	189

NIKE TOUR SUMMARY

Year	Events Played	Cuts Made	1st	2nd	3rd	Top 10	Top 25	Earnings	Rank
1993	9	8	2		1	5	6	$85,882	11
1994	22	17		1	3	10	15	$126,430	8
Total	31	25	2	1	4	15	21	$212,312	
COMBINED TOTAL MONEY								$1,164,935	

1996 PGA TOUR CHARITY TEAM: Sprint International

DAVID DUVAL...continued

TOP TOURNAMENT SUMMARY

YEAR	90	92	95
U.S. Open	T56	CUT	T28
British Open Championship			T20
PGA Championship			CUT
THE PLAYERS Championship			CUT
THE TOUR Championship			T9

1995 PGA TOUR STATISTICS

Scoring	70.35	(29T)
Driving	274.3	(16T)
Driving Accuracy	70.3	(86T)
Greens in Regulation	67.4	(59T)
Putting	1.784	(79T)
All Around	348	(4)
Sand Saves	57.4	(34T)
Total Driving	102	(9)
Eagles	9	(20T)
Birdies	341	(25T)

MISCELLANEOUS STATISTICS

Scoring Avg Before Cut	70.91	(57T)
Scoring Avg 3rd Rnd	70.11	(25)
Scoring Avg Final Rnd	70.53	(29)
Birdies Conversion %	33.1	(6T)
Par Breakers	21.8	(7T)

1995 Low Round: 64: 3 times, most recent 1995 Memorial Tournament/3
Career Low Round: 64: 2 times, most recent 1995 Memorial Tournament/3
Career Largest Paycheck: $151,200: 1995 AT&T Pebble Beach National Pro-Am/2

DAVID EDWARDS

EXEMPT STATUS: 83rd on 1995 money list
FULL NAME: David Wayne Edwards
HEIGHT: 5' 8" **WEIGHT:** 165
BIRTH DATE: April 18, 1956 **BIRTHPLACE:** Neosho, MO
RESIDENCE: Stillwater, OK; plays out of Karsten Creek GC
FAMILY: Wife, Jonnie; Rachel Leigh (12/21/85), Abby Grace (11/22/93)
COLLEGE: Oklahoma State University
SPECIAL INTERESTS: Cars, motorcycles, radio controlled miniature cars, flying
TURNED PROFESSIONAL: 1978 **Q SCHOOL:** Fall 1978

TOUR VICTORIES (4): 1980 Walt Disney World National Team Championship (with Danny Edwards).**1984** Los Angeles Open.**1992** Memorial Tournament.**1993** MCI Heritage Classic.

BEST 1995 FINISHES: T7 -- MCI Classic, Las Vegas Invitational

1995 SEASON: Although his 17th TOUR campaign was his least successful since 1990, still earned $225,857 to finish 83rd on the money list...made four of first five cuts, but best finish during the stretch was a T27 at United Airlines Hawaiian Open...after a T24 at Masters (earning an invitation in 1996), posted first top-10 finish of year at MCI Classic...rounds of 70-69-66 gave him a piece of the 54-hole lead with David Frost, Mark McCumber and Gene Sauers...closing 72 dropped him to T7, just two strokes out of playoff won by Bob Tway...T11 at Canon Greater Hartford Open was top finish of summer...finished year in fine style with four made cuts, including T12 at B.C. Open, T20 at Quad City Classic and T7 at Las Vegas Invitational...shared 54-hole LVI lead with Jim Furyk at 18-under-par 197 and was only two strokes out after 72 holes...closed with 70 to finish five strokes off Furyk's pace...finished fourth on TOUR in driving accuracy, category he led in 1994.

CAREER HIGHLIGHTS: Four consecutive top-10 finishes highlighted 1994 campaign -- MCI Heritage (T4), Kmart GGO (T8), GTE Byron Nelson (T2 as part of six-man playoff) and Memorial (5)... after having not won on TOUR for eight years, collected pair of victories in 11 months: 1992 Memorial and 1993 MCI Heritage Classic...shared 36- and 54-hole leads in Heritage, where closing 69 on 37th birthday provided two-stroke win over David Frost...broke victory drought by winning Memorial in darkness, defeating Rick Fehr on second playoff hole...second-round 65 at Muirfield Village vaulted into contention, closing 67 left tied with Fehr...final-round 65 at Texas Open, good for T3 and $46,800 in final full-field event of season, bumped Ben Crenshaw for 30th and final spot in 1992 TOUR Championship...teamed with brother Danny to win 1980 Walt Disney World National Team Championship...four years later won Los Angeles Open by three strokes over Jack Renner...winner 1978 NCAA Championship...All-American selection 1977-78...winner 1973 Oklahoma State Junior title.

DAVID EDWARDS...*continued*

PERSONAL: Member of PGA TOUR "Air Force," flies own plane to most tournament stops. . . started tagging along with older brother Danny to golf course when about 12 years old. . . joined Mike Hulbert briefly in 1995 one-handed putting club, shooting 72 in first round of Memorial.

CAREER SUMMARY — **PLAYOFF RECORD: 1-1**

Year	Events Played	Cuts Made	1st	2nd	3rd	Top 10	Top 25	Earnings	Rank
1978(Am.)	1	1							
1979	27	18				4	5	$44,456	88
1980	28	12	1			4	6	$35,810	95
1981	27	17			1	4	5	$68,211	65
1982	21	13				4	5	$49,896	91
1983	25	18		1		5	9	$114,037	48
1984	19	15	1	1	1	5	9	$236,061	23
1985	26	12						$21,506	157
1986	24	16				4	7	$122,079	71
1987	21	14		1		3	8	$148,217	73
1988	23	16		1		1	4	$151,513	76
1989	27	17		1		2	8	$238,908	57
1990	22	13				4	7	$166,028	95
1991	27	20		2		5	11	$396,695	38
1992	26	21	1		1	4	9	$515,070	27
1993	21	17	1		1	6	11	$653,086	20
1994	23	20		1		6	12	$458,845	34
1995	22	15				2	7	$225,857	83
Total	410	275	4	8	4	63	123	$3,645,275	41

1996 PGA TOUR CHARITY TEAM: Nissan Open

TOP TOURNAMENT SUMMARY

YEAR	79	80	81	82	83	84	85	86	87	88	89	90	91	92	93
Masters Tournament						T3	T41								T54
U.S. Open	T53	T27					CUT			54	CUT				T11
British Open Championship			CUT												CUT
PGA Championship		T30	T16		CUT	T37		68	T14	T25	T41		T32	T40	CUT
THE PLAYERS Championship		79	CUT	CUT	T35	T15	CUT	T19	T32	T48	T21	T36	T41	T35	T46
THE TOUR Championship														T22	T12

TOP TOURNAMENT SUMMARY (cont.)

YEAR	94	95
Masters Tournament	T18	T24
U.S. Open	T13	T62
British Open Championship	T47	
PGA Championship	T44	
THE PLAYERS Championship	T51	CUT

1995 PGA TOUR STATISTICS

Scoring	**70.54**	**(41)**
Driving	**253.5**	**(169T)**
Driving Accuracy	**79.1**	**(4)**
Greens in Regulation	**67.9**	**(47T)**
Putting	**1.790**	**(95T)**
All Around	**626**	**(65)**
Sand Saves	**57.2**	**(41)**
Total Driving	**173**	**(75T)**
Eagles	**5**	**(88T)**
Birdies	**236**	**(141)**

MISCELLANEOUS STATISTICS

Scoring Avg Before Cut	**71.07**	**(74T)**
Scoring Avg 3rd Rnd	**69.13**	**(2)**
Scoring Avg Final Rnd	**70.93**	**(67T)**
Birdies Conversion %	**26.1**	**(157T)**
Par Breakers	**18.1**	**(127T)**

1995 Low Round: **64:** 1995 Las Vegas Invitational/3
Career Low Round: **61:** 1987 Bob Hope Chrysler/1
Career Largest Paycheck: **$234,000:** 1992 Memorial Tournament/1

Steve Elkington

EXEMPT STATUS: Winner, 1995 PGA Championship
FULL NAME: Stephen John Elkington
HEIGHT: 6' 2" **WEIGHT:** 190
BIRTH DATE: December 8, 1962 **BIRTHPLACE:** Inverell, Australia
RESIDENCE: Sydney, Australia and Houston, TX; plays out of Champions GC
FAMILY: Wife, Lisa; Annie Elizabeth (3/24/95)
COLLEGE: University of Houston (1985, Recreation)
SPECIAL INTERESTS: Character drawing, fishing, hunting, gardening
TURNED PROFESSIONAL: 1985 **Q SCHOOL:** Fall 1986

TOUR VICTORIES (6): 1990 Kmart Greater Greensboro Open. **1991** THE PLAYERS Championship. **1992** Infiniti Tournament of Champions. **1994** Buick Southern Open. **1995** Mercedes Championships, PGA Championship.

INTERNATIONAL VICTORIES (1): 1992 Australian Open (Aus).

BEST 1995 FINISHES: 1 -- Mercedes Championships, PGA Championship; T2 -- Memorial Tournament, THE TOUR Championship; T4 -- Doral-Ryder Open; T5 -- Masters Tournament; T6 -- British Open.

1995 SEASON: With two wins and more than $1 million in earnings, Steve enjoyed most successful season of his nine-season PGA TOUR career...passed Nick Price at TOUR Championship to win Vardon Trophy with 69.62 scoring average...opened year with his second Mercedes Championships title...he and Bruce Lietzke each shot closing 67s to tie at 278...a birdie on the second extra hole sealed the win...T21 after 36 holes at Doral-Ryder Open, shot 67-69 on weekend to finish T4...after withdrawing from THE PLAYERS Championship after 18 holes when his daughter was born, tied for fifth at the Masters...was one stroke behind Ben Crenshaw and Brian Henninger after three rounds, but could not mount a charge on Sunday, finishing five back...final-round 67 enough to share second at Memorial, four strokes behind Greg Norman...second top-10 major finish came at the British Open...trailed Michael Campbell by two strokes through 54 holes, but a 74 on Sunday left him T6...next TOUR start was at the PGA...trailing Ernie Els by six strokes after third round, shot 31 on the front nine on Sunday on his way to 64, forcing a playoff with Colin Montgomerie...sank a 25-foot birdie putt on the same line Montgomerie had in regulation to make birdie moments before to win first major title...267 totals he and Montgomerie produced in regulation bettered Nick Price's 1994 record by two strokes...total also equaled Greg Norman for lowest ever in major (1993 British Open)...with a third-round 67 (low round of the week), was T2 through 54 holes at THE TOUR Championship...closing 73 good enough to hold position, T2 three behind Billy Mayfair...second on TOUR in sand saves (68.2%)...won Franklin Templeton Shark Shootout with Mark Calcavecchia.

CAREER HIGHLIGHTS: First TOUR victory came in 1990 Kmart Greater Greensboro Open, where final-day 66 brought him from seven strokes back for win...scored biggest triumph by outdueling Fuzzy Zoeller to win THE PLAYERS Championship in 1991...collected $288,000 paycheck and 10-year TOUR exemption...won 1992 Infiniti Tournament of Champions in playoff with Brad Faxon...late in year lost H-E-B Texas Open playoff to Nick Price...made all 23 cuts in 1993, when best performance was playoff loss to Rocco Mediate in Kmart GGO...runnerup finish witnessed by parents, visiting from Australia...also finished T3 in '93 Masters...missed part of 1994 season after sinus surgery...came back with T7 at PGA Championship and a five-stroke win at Buick Southern Open...winner 1993 Fred Meyer Challenge (with Tom Purtzer)...winner 1992 Australian Open...runner-up 1986 Qualifying Tournament...winner 1980 Australia-New Zealand Amateur...winner 1981 Australian Amateur and Doug Sanders Junior World Championship...two-time All-American at Houston, where teammates included Billy Ray Brown...two-time Southwest Conference Champion...member 1984-85 NCAA Championship teams.

PERSONAL: Idol growing up was fellow Aussie Bruce Devlin...while in college, worked as usher at The Summit sports arena...one of four PGA Champion members at Champions GC in Houston (Jack Burke, Jr., Jay Hebert, Dave Marr).

CAREER SUMMARY **PLAYOFF RECORD: 1-2**

Year	Events Played	Cuts Made	1st	2nd	3rd	Top 10	Top 25	Earnings	Rank
1984(Am.)	1	1							
1985(Am.)	2	2							
1985	5	5					1	$9,897	180
1986	5	3					1	$12,705	194
1987	35	19				2	7	$75,738	118
1988	29	19				2	9	$149,972	79
1989	29	21		1	1	3	9	$231,062	61
1990	26	24	1			4	14	$548,564	18
1991	28	17	1			4	10	$549,120	25
1992	24	21	1	2	3	9	14	$746,352	12
1993	23	23		1	1	8	14	$675,383	17
1994	20	15	1			2	5	$294,943	62
1995	21	16	2	2		7	11	$1,254,352	5
Total	248	186	6	6	5	41	95	$4,548,089	31

1996 PGA TOUR CHARITY TEAM: THE TOUR Championship

STEVE ELKINGTON...*continued*

NATIONAL TEAMS: Presidents Cup, 1994; World Cup, 1994; Dunhill Cup (2), 1994, 1995.

YEAR	87	88	89	90	91	92	93	94	95
Masters Tournament					T22	T37	T3	CUT	T5
U.S. Open			T21	T21	T55	CUT	T33		T36
British Open Championship				CUT	T44	T34	T48	T67	T6
PGA Championship		T31	T41	CUT	T32	T18	T14	T7	1
THE PLAYERS Championship	CUT	T54	CUT	T16	1	CUT	T16	T51	W/D
THE TOUR Championship				10	9	T22	T23		T2

1995 PGA TOUR STATISTICS

Scoring	69.59	(2)
Driving	270.6	(38T)
Driving Accuracy	70.6	(79T)
Greens in Regulation	68.9	(28T)
Putting	1.790	(95T)
All Around	450	(23)
Sand Saves	68.2	(2)
Total Driving	117	(16)
Eagles	5	(88T)
Birdies	258	(118)

MISCELLANEOUS STATISTICS

Scoring Avg Before Cut	70.83	(48)
Scoring Avg 3rd Rnd	69.27	(5)
Scoring Avg Final Rnd	69.53	(4)
Birdies Conversion %	30.8	(32T)
Par Breakers	20.5	(35T)

1995 Low Round: 64: 1995 PGA Championship/4
Career Low Round: 62: 2 times, most recent 1991 Southwestern Bell/3
Career Largest Paycheck: $360,000: 1995 PGA Championship/1

ERNIE ELS *(Else)*

EXEMPT STATUS: Winner, 1994 U.S. Open
FULL NAME: Theodore Ernest Els
HEIGHT: 6' 3" **WEIGHT:** 210
BIRTH DATE: October 17, 1969 **BIRTHPLACE:** Johannesburg, South Africa
RESIDENCE: Orlando, FL
FAMILY: Single
SPECIAL INTERESTS: Movies, reading, sports
TURNED PROFESSIONAL: 1989
JOINED TOUR: 1994

TOUR VICTORIES (2): 1994 U.S. Open. **1995** GTE Byron Nelson Classic

INTERNATIONAL VICTORIES (13): 1992 Protea Assurance South Africa Open (Afr), Lexington PGA Championship (Afr), South African Masters (Afr), Hollard Royal Swazi Sun Classic (Afr), First National Bank Players' Championship (Afr), Goodyear Classic (Afr). **1993** Dunlop Phoenix Tournament (Jap). **1994** Dubai Desert Classic (Eur), Toyota World Match Play Championship (Eur), Johnnie Walker World Championship (Eur), Gene Sarazen World Open. **1995** Lexington South African PGA Championship (Eur), Toyota World Match Play Championship (Eur).

BEST 1995 FINISHES: 1 -- GTE Byron Nelson Classic; 2 -- Sprint International; T3 -- Buick Open, PGA Championship; T4 -- Buick Classic; T7 -- MCI Classic

1995 SEASON: Improved on his rookie season with four top-three finishes, including a win at GTE Byron Nelson Classic...victory at Las Colinas highlighted by a second-round course-record 61 over the Cottonwood Valley Course, which tied him with Robin Freeman after 36 holes...a third-round 65 gave him a three-stroke lead which, after a closing 68, was the margin of victory...final 263 broke Sam Snead's 1957 tournament record by one stroke...at Buick Classic the following week, was one stroke off the lead after 36 holes, but dropped to T24 after a third-round 75...a Sunday 68 (low round of day) moved him to T4...after T13 at The Memorial and T11 at British Open, had three consecutive top-three finishes...six strokes off lead after an opening 69, finished with 68-66-68 to climb to T3 at Buick Open...shared second-round lead and held three-stroke edge alone at PGA Championship...131 equaled 36-hole record, 197 bettered 54-hole standard by three strokes...closing 72 succumbed to charges of Steve Elkington and Colin Montgomerie...finished two strokes out of their playoff...took lead during final round of Sprint International with birdies on 12, 13 and 14, but Lee Janzen drew even with a birdie at 17...Janzen won with a par on 18 to Els's bogey...tied for third on TOUR in scoring (69.81) and tied for seventh in sand saves (61.3)...won second consecutive Toyota World Match Play Championship by defeating Steve Elkington, 2 & 1...second to win event in first two appearances.

ERNIE ELS...continued

CAREER HIGHLIGHTS: Although well known in Europe and his native South Africa, win at 1994 U.S. Open, in a playoff over Loren Roberts and Colin Mongomerie, was his introduction to American golf fans...finished second to Lee Janzen at Buick Classic the previous week...tied for seventh at 1993 U.S. Open...played in six TOUR events in 1993, three in 1992...top '92 finish T31 at International...also competed in 1991 International, 1990 Buick Southern Open...participated in eight Ben Hogan Tour events in 1991, with top finish T9 in Tulsa Open...placed T6 in 1993 British Open (first to record four rounds in 60s), T5 in 1992...winner six 1992 tournaments in Africa, including South African Open, South African PGA Championship, South African Masters...Gary Player only other to win those three events in same year...defeated Phil Mickelson for Junior World Golf title in San Diego.

PERSONAL: Started playing golf at age 9...also was an accomplished junior tennis player, but turned sole focus to golf at 14...did 22 months mandatory service in South African Army in 1988-89.

CAREER SUMMARY **PLAYOFF RECORD: 1-0**

Year	Events Played	Cuts Made	1st	2nd	3rd	Top 10	Top 25	Earnings	Rank
1990	1								
1991	1	1						$2,647	274
1992	3	2						$18,420	213
1993	6	2				1	1	$38,185	190
1994	11	10	1	1		4	6	$684,440	19
1995	18	14	1	1	2	6	10	$842,590	14
Total	40	29	2	2	2	11	17	$1,586,282	135

NIKE TOUR SUMMARY

Year	Events Played	Cuts Made	1st	2nd	3rd	Top 10	Top 25	Earnings	Rank
1991	8	5				1	2	$6,143	123
Total	8	5				1	2	$6,143	
COMBINED TOTAL MONEY								$1,592,425	

1996 PGA TOUR CHARITY TEAM: Honda Classic

TOP TOURNAMENT SUMMARY

YEAR	89	92	93	94	95
Masters Tournament				T8	CUT
U.S. Open			T7	1	CUT
British Open Championship	CUT	T5	T6	T24	T11
PGA Championship		CUT	CUT	T25	T3
THE PLAYERS Championship			CUT	T45	T68
THE TOUR Championship				T17	T16

NATIONAL TEAMS: Dunhill Cup (4) 1992, 1993, 1994, 1995; World Cup (2) 1992, 1993

1995 PGA TOUR STATISTICS

Scoring	69.81	(3T)
Driving	274.3	(16T)
Driving Accuracy	68.4	(110T)
Greens in Regulation	64.5	(132T)
Putting	1.771	(44T)
All Around	580	(51)
Sand Saves	61.3	(7T)
Total Driving	126	(23)
Eagles	4	(116T)
Birdies	216	(152T)

MISCELLANEOUS STATISTICS

Scoring Avg Before Cut	70.22	(14)
Scoring Avg 3rd Rnd	70.92	(74T)
Scoring Avg Final Rnd	71.00	(72T)
Birdies Conversion %	33.2	(5)
Par Breakers	20.4	(38T)

1995 Low Round: **61:** 1995 GTE Byron Nelson Classic/2
Career Low Round: **61:** 1995 GTE Byron Nelson Classic/2
Career Largest Paycheck: **$320,000:** 1994 U.S. Open/1

Bob Estes *(ES-tis)*

EXEMPT STATUS: 1994 tournament winner
FULL NAME: Bob Alan Estes
HEIGHT: 6' 1" **WEIGHT:** 175
BIRTH DATE: February 2, 1966 **BIRTHPLACE:** Graham, TX
RESIDENCE: Austin, TX; plays out of The Hills of Lakeway, near Austin
FAMILY: Single
COLLEGE: University of Texas
SPECIAL INTERESTS: Music, hunting
TURNED PROFESSIONAL: 1988 **Q SCHOOL:** Fall 1988

TOUR VICTORIES (1): 1994 Texas Open.

BEST 1995 FINISHES: T6 -- Motorola Western Open, PGA Championship; T8 -- Canon Greater Hartford Open; British Open; T10 -- Greater Milwaukee Open

1995 SEASON: Played steady early in 1995, but caught fire in second half of year with five top-10 finishes in seven starts...made his first nine cuts, including three top-20 finishes -- Mercedes Championships (T12), Buick Invitational of California (T16), Nissan Open (T14)...T8 at Canon Greater Hartford Open after sharing first-round lead with Kirk Triplett at 64...after T14 at FedEx St. Jude Classic, finished T6 at Motorola Western Open ...rounds of 72-70-71-72 good for T8 at British Open...four rounds in the 60s also led to top-10 finish at PGA Championship, T8...closing 64 earned a T10 at Greater Milwaukee Open...took six weeks off after GMO to work with strength coaches at University of Texas...in defense of his 1994 Texas Open title, finished T22...switched to baseball grip for BellSouth Classic after reading article about it...hit 16 greens in regulation and shot 67 in first effort.

CAREER HIGHLIGHTS: Much anticipated first TOUR win came at 1994 Texas Open...opened with course-record-tying 62 at Oak Hills CC, then cruised to wire-to-wire win...had early close call with winning in Rookie-of-Year season of 1989...lost B.C. Open playoff to Mike Hulbert on first extra hole...participant in five-man playoff at 1993 Buick Southern Open won by John Inman...two weeks later, third-round 64 helped to solo fourth in Texas Open...with T3 at Las Vegas Invitational, missed final berth in 1993 TOUR Championship by just $1,135...one stroke out of lead after 54 holes of '93 PGA Championship, held lead during final round, only to finish with 73 and T6...won first professional event, Bogey Hills Invitational in St. Charles, MO in 1988...won numerous amateur events, including 1983 Texas High School Championship, 1985 Trans-Mississippi Amateur, 1988 Texas State Amateur...named Fred Haskins and Jack Nicklaus Award winners as 1988 College Player of Year.

PERSONAL: First played golf at four, set sights on TOUR career at 12...high school teammate of Mike Standly (Standly senior during his sophomore year)...Cathy Gerring, the LPGA Player whose hands were burned in a hospitality tent accident, was his caddie for Round 2 of Memorial.

CAREER SUMMARY **PLAYOFF RECORD: 0-2**

Year	Events Played	Cuts Made	1st	2nd	3rd	Top 10	Top 25	Earnings	Rank
1988	5	4						$5,968	237
1989	27	14		1		2	5	$135,628	102
1990	28	18				4	9	$212,090	69
1991	32	19				1	7	$147,364	105
1992	28	18			1	2	4	$190,778	80
1993	28	23		1	1	5	12	$447,187	32
1994	27	23	1	1	1	8	17	$765,360	14
1995	24	21				5	12	$433,992	41
Total	199	140	1	3	3	27	66	$2,338,367	78

1996 PGA TOUR CHARITY TEAM: Buick Open

TOP TOURNAMENT SUMMARY

YEAR	90	91	92	93	94	95
Masters Tournament					CUT	T29
U.S. Open		CUT	T44	T52		CUT
British Open Championship	CUT				T24	T8
PGA Championship	CUT		T76	T6	T47	T6
THE PLAYERS Championship	T70	CUT	T70	T20	T35	T34
THE TOUR Championship					T15	

BOB ESTES...*continued*

1995 PGA TOUR STATISTICS		
Scoring	70.34	(27T)
Driving	261.1	(108)
Driving Accuracy	67.3	(127T)
Greens in Regulation	64.8	(126T)
Putting	1.751	(7T)
All Around	507	(34)
Sand Saves	60.7	(11)
Total Driving	235	(157)
Eagles	6	(69T)
Birdies	333	(32T)

MISCELLANEOUS STATISTICS		
Scoring Avg Before Cut	70.50	(25T)
Scoring Avg 3rd Rnd	70.24	(33)
Scoring Avg Final Rnd	70.33	(24)
Birdies Conversion %	32.8	(12)
Par Breakers	20.7	(30T)

1995 Low Round: 64: 2 times, most recent 1995 Greater Milwaukee Open/4
Career Low Round: 61: 1991 Chattanooga Classic/2
Career Largest Paycheck: $180,000: 1994 Texas Open/1

NICK FALDO

EXEMPT STATUS: Winner, 1992 British Open
FULL NAME: Nicholas Alexander Faldo
HEIGHT: 6' 3" **WEIGHT:** 195
BIRTH DATE: July 18, 1957 **BIRTHPLACE:** Welwyn Garden City, England
RESIDENCE: Orlando, FL and Windlesham, England
FAMILY: Wife, Gill; Natalie (9/18/86), Matthew (3/17/89),Georgia (3/20/93)
SPECIAL INTERESTS: Fly fishing, flying helicopters
TURNED PROFESSIONAL: 1976
JOINED TOUR: 1981, 1995

TOUR VICTORIES (4): 1984 Sea Pines Heritage Classic. **1989** Masters Tournament. **1990** MastersTournament. **1995** Doral-Ryder Open.

INTERNATIONAL VICTORIES (33): 1977 Skol Lager (Eur). **1978** Colgate PGA Championship (Eur). **1979** ICL International (Afr). **1980** Sun Alliance PGA Championship (Eur). **1981** Sun Alliance PGA Championship (Eur). **1982** Haig Whisky TPC (Eur). **1983** Paco Rabanne French Open (Eur), Martini International (Eur), Car Care Plan International (Eur), Lawrence Batley International (Eur), Ebel Swiss Open-European Masters (Eur). **1984** Car Care Plan International (Eur). **1987** Peugeot Spanish Open (Eur), British Open (Eur). **1988** Peugeot French Open (Eur), Volvo Masters (Eur). **1989** Volvo PGA Championship (Eur), Dunhill British Masters (Eur), Peugeot French Open (Eur), Suntory World Match Play Championship (Eur). **1990** British Open (Eur), Johnnie Walker Classic (Hong Kong). **1991** Carroll's Irish Open (Eur). **1992** Carroll's Irish Open (Eur), British Open (Eur), Scandinavian Masters (Eur), GA European Open (Eur), Toyota World Match Play Championship (Eur), Johnnie Walker World Championship of Golf. **1993** Johnnie Walker Classic (Eur), Carroll's Irish Open (Eur). **1994** Alfred Dunhill Open (Eur), Nedbank Million Dollar Challenge (Afr).

BEST 1995 FINISHES: 1 -- Doral-Ryder Open; 2 -- Honda Classic; T4 -- MCI Classic, Buick Classic; T5 -- Nestle Invitational; T9 -- AT&T Pebble Beach National Pro-Am.

1995 SEASON: Wisdom of decision to play PGA TOUR full-time evident early in year...four top-10 finishes in first seven events, including victory at Doral, first on American soil since 1990...in third start of 1995, was one stroke out of lead after first-round 66 at AT&T Pebble Beach National Pro-Am, before finishing T9...two starts later at Doral, Nick trailed Peter Jacobsen and Greg Norman by three strokes after 54 holes...he took the lead with a birdie at the 14th hole, but a bogey at 18 dropped him into a tie with Norman...when Norman's approach found the water and he made bogey, Faldo won by one...victory came 4 years, 10 months, 24 days after previous PGA TOUR win at 1990 Masters...nearly won the following week as well, but a Honda Classic closing 69 was not enough to catch Mark O'Meara, who led by three entering the round...closing with 66-68 earned T5 at Nestle Invitational...followed an opening 74 with rounds of 64-70-68 for T4 at MCI Classic, one stroke out of playoff won by Bob Tway...final top-10 of year came in May at Buick Classic...two back after 54 holes, a closing 72 left him T4, still two strokes off the pace...though without another top-10 after May, recorded T13 at Memorial, T12 at NEC World Series of Golf and T13 at THE TOUR Championship...as a member of victorious European Ryder Cup Team, had a 2-3 record, including a 1-up win over Curtis Strange on Sunday...T4 in scoring for 1995 (69.85) and T9 in driving accuracy (77.8%).

CAREER HIGHLIGHTS: One of game's finest technicians, has earned five major titles: 1987-90-92 British Opens, 1989-90 Masters Tournaments...finished second to Greg Norman in 1993 British Open, third to Paul Azinger in 1993 PGA Championship...held second-round lead at Royal St. George's, then shared 54-hole lead with Corey Pavin before finishing two strokes behind Norman...first foreigner to win PGA Player of Year Award in 1990...playoff loser to Curtis Strange in 1988 U.S. Open...rejoined TOUR in September 1994 as fulltime member for 1995...played in nine TOUR events in 1994, posting top-10 finishes in two: PLAYERS Championship and PGA Championship...first win in U.S. came at 1984 Sea Pines Heritage Classic, by one over Tom Kite...led Sony World Ranking for record 81 weeks in 1993-94...led European Tour Order of Merit (money list) in 1983 and 1992...1977 European Tour Rookie of Year...1977 Ryder Cup victory over Tom Watson at Royal Lytham highlight of start of career...winner British PGA Championship 1978-80-81...had 11 top-10 finishes in 16 European Tour starts in 1983, compiling 69.03 stroke average.

PERSONAL: Decided to give golf a try at age 14, after watching Jack Nicklaus on television...rebuilt swing completely under watchful eye of David Leadbetter...won 1975 British Youths Amateur and English Amateur Championships...awarded MBE (Member of British Empire) in 1987.

CAREER SUMMARY — **PLAYOFF RECORD: 2-1**

Year	Events Played	Cuts Made	1st	2nd	3rd	Top 10	Top 25	Earnings	Rank
1979	2	2						$2,613	214
1981	12	10			1	2	4	$35,349	102
1982	15	14				2	9	$56,667	80
1983	13	8		1		2	5	$67,851	79
1984	19	14	1			4	9	$166,845	38
1985	17	13				2	5	$54,060	117
1986	16	9			1	1	5	$52,965	135
1987	6	5		1		1	2	$36,281	169
1988	9	7		1	1	3	3	$179,120	64
1989	16	14	1			2	9	$327,981	31
1990	7	7	1		1	2	6	$345,262	37
1991	7	7				2	5	$127,156	117
1992	7	6		2		4	6	$345,168	42
1993	6	6			1	2	3	$188,886	91
1994	9	6				2	3	$221,146	83
1995	19	17	1	1		6	12	$790,961	19
Total	180	145	4	6	5	37	86	$2,998,312	99

1996 PGA TOUR CHARITY TEAM: Doral-Ryder Open

TOP TOURNAMENT SUMMARY

YEAR	76	77	78	79	80	81	82	83	84	85	86	87	88	89	90
Masters Tournament				40				T20	T15	T25			T30	1	1
U.S. Open									T55				2	T18	T3
British Open Championship	T28	T62	T7	T19	T12	T11	T4	T8	T6	T53	5	1	3	T11	1
PGA Championship							T14	CUT	T20	T54	CUT	T28	T4	T9	T19
THE PLAYERS Championship							T35	T35	T20	CUT	CUT		CUT		

TOP TOURNAMENT SUMMARY (cont.)

YEAR	91	92	93	94	95
Masters Tournament	T12	T13	T39	32	T24
U.S. Open	T16	T4	T72	CUT	T45
British Open Championship	T17	1	2	T8	T40
PGA Championship	T16	T2	3	T4	T31
THE PLAYERS Championship	T57	T2		5	CUT
THE TOUR Championship					T13

NATIONAL TEAMS: Ryder Cup (10) 1977, 1979, 1981, 1983, 1985, 1987, 1989, 1991, 1993, 1995. Dunhill Cup (6) 1985, 1986, 1987, 1988, 1991, 1993. World Cup (2) 1977, 1991. Nissan Cup, 1986. Kirin Cup, 1987. Asahi Glass Four Tours, 1990. Hennessy Cognac Cup (4) 1978, 1980, 1982, 1984. Double Diamond, 1977.

1995 PGA TOUR STATISTICS

Statistic	Value	Rank
Scoring	**69.85**	**(5T)**
Driving	**258.1**	**(133T)**
Driving Accuracy	**77.8**	**(9T)**
Greens in Regulation	**68.5**	**(35T)**
Putting	**1.784**	**(79T)**
All Around	**600**	**(57)**
Sand Saves	**54.6**	**(66T)**
Total Driving	**142**	**(36)**
Eagles	**3**	**(137T)**
Birdies	**243**	**(136)**

MISCELLANEOUS STATISTICS

Statistic	Value	Rank
Scoring Avg Before Cut	**70.49**	**(24)**
Scoring Avg 3rd Rnd	**70.94**	**(78T)**
Scoring Avg Final Rnd	**69.82**	**(7T)**
Birdies Conversion %	**29.0**	**(81T)**
Par Breakers	**19.0**	**(96T)**

1995 Low Round: **64:** 1995 MCI Classic/2
Career Low Round: **62:** 1981 Hawaiian Open/2
Career Largest Paycheck: **$270,000:** 1995 Doral-Ryder Open/1

Brad Faxon

EXEMPT STATUS: Member, 1995 Ryder Cup Team
FULL NAME: Bradford John Faxon, Jr.
HEIGHT: 6' 1" **WEIGHT:** 170
BIRTH DATE: August 1, 1961 **BIRTHPLACE:** Oceanport, NJ
RESIDENCE: Barrington, RI
FAMILY: Wife, Bonnie, Melanie (1/3/89), Emily (5/13/91), Sophie Lee (9/10/95)
COLLEGE: Furman University (1983, Economics)
SPECIAL INTERESTS: All sports, except hunting and fishing; family
TURNED PROFESSIONAL: 1983 **Q SCHOOL:** Fall 1983

TOUR VICTORIES (4): 1986 Provident Classic.**1991** Buick Open. **1992** New England Classic, The International.

INTERNATIONAL VICTORIES (1): 1993 Heineken Australian Open (Aus).

BEST 1995 FINISHES: 2 -- Nestle Invitational; 5 -- PGA Championship; T5 -- Colonial National Invitation; T6 -- AT&T Pebble Beach National Pro-Am; T7 -- Kmart Greater Greensboro Open

1995 SEASON: Brad's 12th PGA TOUR season featured five top-10 finishes and his first selection to the Ryder Cup Team...most memorable performance certainly his closing 63 to finish fifth at PGA Championship...front-nine 28 was a PGA Championship record and only the second in major championship history (Denis Durnian, 1983 British Open the other)...1-2 in his Ryder Cup Matches...year's first top-10 came in second event at AT&T Pebble Beach National Pro-Am...held lead after a second-round 64, but closing 72-72 dropped him to T6...another 64 placed him second after three rounds at Nestle Invitational...final-round 71 left him in second, two behind Loren Roberts...opened with 65 to share lead at Kmart Greater Greensboro Open before shooting 71-71-72 to finish T7...moved from T33 to T5 with a closing 64 at Colonial National Invitation...shared lead with John Daly and Katsuyoshi Tomori through 36 holes at British Open, but fell to T15...left course during second round of Greater Milwaukee Open to be with wife in labor... $471,887 earned was third-best total of career...teamed with Greg Norman to win Fred Meyer Challenge...ranked fifth in putting (1.749 putts per GIR).

CAREER HIGHLIGHTS: Career year came in 1992, when he captured pair of titles...won on home turf in New England Classic and at International...won by two strokes at Pleasant Valley, had 14-point performance on Sunday to capture International...also lost 1992 playoffs at Tournament of Champions and Buick Open...first TOUR win came at 1986 Provident Classic, powered by final-round 63...scored playoff win over Chip Beck at 1991 Buick Open...slowed by a rib cage injury in 1993...won 1993 Heineken Australian Open...winner 1983 Fred Haskins, *Golf Magazine* and NCAA Coaches Awards as nation's outstanding collegiate player...member 1983 Walker Cup team...1982-83 All-American selection...winner 1980-81 New England Amateur...winner 1979-80 Rhode Island Amateur.

PERSONAL: As youngster, played golf with father on course grandmother owned on Cape Cod.

CAREER SUMMARY **PLAYOFF RECORD: 1-2**

Year	Events Played	Cuts Made	1st	2nd	3rd	Top 10	Top 25	Earnings	Rank
1981(Am.)	1	1							
1983(Am.)	1	1							
1983	8	5				1	2	$16,526	160
1984	32	19			1	2	6	$71,688	82
1985	31	15				1	6	$46,813	124
1986	34	16	1			1	2	$92,716	90
1987	28	19				2	10	$113,534	90
1988	29	15			1	3	8	$162,656	74
1989	28	20		2		2	5	$222,076	63
1990	28	16			1	3	8	$197,118	81
1991	28	23	1		1	4	11	$422,088	34
1992	26	20	2	2		7	12	$812,093	8
1993	25	20				4	11	$312,023	55
1994	25	23			2	6	10	$612,847	24
1995	25	19		1		5	8	$471,887	37
Total	349	232	4	5	6	41	99	$3,554,065	44

1996 PGA TOUR CHARITY TEAM: Franklin Templeton Shark Shootout

BRAD FAXON...*continued*

NATIONAL TEAMS: Walker Cup, 1983. Ryder Cup, 1995.

TOP TOURNAMENT SUMMARY

YEAR	83	84	85	86	87	88	89	90	91	92	93	94	95
Masters Tournament										T31	T9	T15	T17
U.S. Open	T50		57			CUT	T33	66	CUT	CUT	T68	T33	T56
British Open Championship			CUT			T11	T73				CUT	7	T15
PGA Championship			CUT	CUT	CUT	CUT	CUT	CUT	T48	T15	T14	T30	5
THE PLAYERS Championship		T33	CUT	CUT	CUT	CUT	T17	T70	CUT	T67	DQ	T6	T49
THE TOUR Championship										T7		T26	

1995 PGA TOUR STATISTICS		
Scoring	70.40	(36)
Driving	261.2	(107)
Driving Accuracy	69.1	(102T)
Greens in Regulation	63.6	(153)
Putting	1.749	(5)
All Around	492	(32)
Sand Saves	59.7	(15T)
Total Driving	209	(124T)
Eagles	9	(20T)
Birdies	303	(54T)

MISCELLANEOUS STATISTICS		
Scoring Avg Before Cut	70.47	(22T)
Scoring Avg 3rd Rnd	71.16	(92T)
Scoring Avg Final Rnd	70.84	(59)
Birdies Conversion %	32.1	(19)
Par Breakers	20.0	(56T)

1995 Low Round: 63: 1995 PGA Championship/4
Career Low Round: 62: 1986 Provident Classic/2
Career Largest Paycheck: $216,000: 1992 The International/1

RICK FEHR *(FAIR)*

EXEMPT STATUS: 1994 tournament winner
FULL NAME: Richard Elliott Fehr
HEIGHT: 5' 11" **WEIGHT:** 170
BIRTH DATE: August 28, 1962 **BIRTHPLACE:** Seattle, WA
RESIDENCE: Redmond, WA; plays out of Desert Canyon Golf Resort, Orondo, WA
FAMILY: Wife, Terri; J.D. (1/26/91), Mitchell (10/26/93)
COLLEGE: Brigham Young University (1984, Finance)
SPECIAL INTERESTS: Family, gardening, Christianity
TURNED PROFESSIONAL: 1984 **Q SCHOOL:** Fall 1985.

TOUR VICTORIES (2): 1986 B.C. Open. **1994** Walt Disney World/Oldsmobile Classic

BEST 1995 FINISHES: T5 -- Mercedes Championships; T10 -- Las Vegas Invitational

1995 SEASON: An off-year for Fehr, whose earnings and money-list rank fell to their lowest points since 1989...first year since then that earnings had not increased over previous year...opened year on a high note with a closing 66 at Mercedes Championships for T5...also had T18 at Phoenix Open as part of four consecutive made cuts to start 1995...went his next 17 events with nine missed cuts and no finish in the top 30...broke that string with a T28 at B.C. Open...second top-10 finish came at Las Vegas...trailed Joe Ozaki by one after a first-round 64...went on to finish T10...$36,000 paycheck was largest of 1995.

CAREER HIGHLIGHTS: Had planned to have hernia surgery week of 1994 Walt Disney World/Oldsmobile Classic, but decided to delay operation and went on to win by two strokes over Craig Stadler and Fuzzy Zoeller...win qualified him for THE TOUR Championship for second consecutive year...first victory came at 1986 B.C. Open, where began play simply hoping to retain card and finished with two-stroke win over Larry Mize...with '94 second at Sprint International, has seven runnerup finishes since 1991...1991: Federal Express St. Jude Classic, Canon Greater Hartford Open (playoff loss to Billy Ray Brown); 1992: Bob Hope Chrysler Classic (five-man playoff won by John Cook), Memorial Tournament (playoff loss to David Edwards); 1993: Bob Hope (with fourth-round 62 at Indian Wells) and Federal Express St. Jude Classic...low amateur 1984 Masters and 1984 U.S. Open...winner 1979 Washington State Junior and PGA National Junior Championships...winner 1982 Western Amateur...two-time All-American at Brigham Young.

PERSONAL: Member PGA TOUR Policy Board from 1992-1995.

RICK FEHR...continued

CAREER SUMMARY — **PLAYOFF RECORD: 0-4**

Year	Events Played	Cuts Made	1st	2nd	3rd	Top 10	Top 25	Earnings	Rank
1983(Am.)	2	1							
1984(Am.)	2	2					1		
1985	15	11				1	4	$40,101	133
1986	28	20	1			4	7	$151,162	61
1987	24	8		1		3	4	$106,808	94
1988	28	11				1	2	$79,080	130
1989	21	16				1	4	$93,142	131
1990	28	17			1	2	4	$149,867	105
1991	26	14		2		3	5	$288,983	55
1992	26	18		2		4	12	$433,003	33
1993	26	23		2		6	13	$556,322	28
1994	25	16	1	1		4	9	$573,963	27
1995	24	14				2	3	$147,766	126
Total	275	171	2	8	1	31	68	$2,620,197	72

1996 PGA TOUR CHARITY TEAM: Shell Houston Open

TOP TOURNAMENT SUMMARY

YEAR	83	84	85	86	87	88	90	91	92	93	94	95
Masters Tournament	CUT	T25		T36	CUT						CUT	47
U.S. Open		T43	T9	T62				T26	CUT	T46	CUT	CUT
PGA Championship					CUT		CUT	T27	T18	T56	CUT	
THE PLAYERS Championship					CUT	CUT	CUT	CUT	T21	T52	T45	CUT
THE TOUR Championship										6	T15	

NATIONAL TEAMS: Walker Cup, 1983

1995 PGA TOUR STATISTICS

Scoring	71.27	(98)
Driving	263.1	(92)
Driving Accuracy	69.7	(95)
Greens in Regulation	64.5	(132T)
Putting	1.764	(30T)
All Around	800	(118)
Sand Saves	44.8	(170T)
Total Driving	187	(96T)
Eagles	6	(69T)
Birdies	262	(114T)

MISCELLANEOUS STATISTICS

Scoring Avg Before Cut	71.58	(132T)
Scoring Avg 3rd Rnd	69.87	(15T)
Scoring Avg Final Rnd	70.93	(67T)
Birdies Conversion %	29.7	(60T)
Par Breakers	19.6	(77T)

1995 Low Round: **64:** 1995 Las Vegas Invitational/1
Career Low Round: **62:** 1993 Bob Hope Chrysler Classic/4
Career Largest Paycheck: $198,000: 1994 Walt Disney World/Oldsmobile Classic/1

KEITH FERGUS *(FUR-gus)*

EXEMPT STATUS: 130th on 1995 money list
FULL NAME: Keith Carlton Fergus
HEIGHT: 6' 2" **WEIGHT:** 200
BIRTH DATE: March 3, 1954 **BIRTHPLACE:** Temple, TX
RESIDENCE: Sugarland, TX
FAMILY: Wife, Cindy; Steven (9/4/79), Laura (3/5/84)
COLLEGE: University of Houston
SPECIAL INTERESTS: Fishing
TURNED PROFESSIONAL: 1976 **Q SCHOOL:** Fall 1976, 1994

TOUR VICTORIES (3): **1981** Memorial. **1982** Georgia-Pacific Atlanta Classic. **1983** Bob Hope Desert Classic.

NIKE TOUR VICTORIES (2): **1994** NIKE Panama City Beach Classic, NIKE Boise Open.

BEST 1995 FINISH: T8 -- Honda Classic

1995 SEASON: With five non-members among the top 125, the magic number to retain TOUR playing privileges became 130...with a T28 at LaCantera Texas Open, Keith claimed that spot by $696 over Russ Cochran...first year back on TOUR full-time since serving as University of Houston golf coach from 1988-94...finished 33rd at 1994 Qualifying Tournament to regain card...shot first-round 67 to share lead in his first tournament, United Airlines Hawaiian Open, where he finished T14...shot 68-72-71-71 -- 283 for T8 at Honda Classic, lone top-10 finish of year...T11 at GTE Byron Nelson Classic with 67-66-71-66...opening 64 over Palm Course at WDW/Oldsmobile Classic, where he finished T28, was low round of year...at LaCantera, opened with 68-72, then hung on through worsening weather to shoot 74-74 on weekend for 288 and the $7,480 needed to return in 1996.

CAREER HIGHLIGHTS: Made debut on TOUR in 1977...winner of three PGA TOUR events...defeated Jack Renner by one stroke at 1981 Memorial...birdied first playoff hole to defeat Raymond Floyd at 1992 Georgia-Pacific Atlanta Classic...won 1983 Bob Hope Desert Classic over Rex Caldwell with par on first extra hole, part of best earnings year on TOUR -- $155,922...lost card in 1986, finishing 142 on money list...returned to alma mater as golf coach two years later...began comeback in 1994 on NIKE TOUR and won NIKE Panama City Classic and NIKE Boise Open...13th on 1994 NIKE TOUR money list...three-time All-American at Houston (1974-75-76)...runner-up to Jay Haas at 1975 U.S. Amateur.

PERSONAL: Started playing golf at age eight...played football and basketball in high school, but enjoyed practicing golf more than the other sports.

PGA TOUR CAREER SUMMARY | **PLAYOFF RECORD: 2-0**

Year	Events Played	Cuts Made	1st	2nd	3rd	Top 10	Top 25	Earnings	Rank
1976	1	1						$645	245
1977	27	20				2	9	$29,558	84
1978	33	27				4	10	$55,773	59
1979	29	24			1	7	13	$97,045	37
1980	23	23			3	5	15	$119,614	33
1981	25	22	1	1		5	9	$150,792	21
1982	28	18	1		1	3	9	$122,265	30
1983	25	20	1			3	10	$155,922	31
1984	26	15			1	3	7	$78,758	78
1985	26	21				3	11	$136,352	60
1986	29	15					4	$45,548	142
1987	6	3						$4,033	234
1988	3	1						$2,002	274
1989	2								
1991	1	1						$2,532	276
1992	1								
1993	1								
1994	5	3					1	$16,749	231
1995	26	17				1	4	$146,359	130
Total	317	231	3	1	6	36	102	$1,162,301	

NIKE TOUR SUMMARY

Year	Events Played	Cuts Made	1st	2nd	3rd	Top 10	Top 25	Earnings	Rank
1991	1								
1993	2	2				1	1	$6,725	125
1994	18	14	2		1	6	9	$107,053	13
1995	1	1		1		1	1	$22,700	83
Total	22	17	2	1	1	8	11	$136,478	
COMBINED TOTAL MONEY								$1,298,779	

1996 PGA TOUR CHARITY TEAM: Buick Invitational

TOP TOURNAMENT SUMMARY

YEAR	78	79	80	81	82	83	84	85	86
Masters Tournament		T26	T37	T33	T16	CUT			
U.S. Open	T9	T3	T43	CUT	T39				
PGA Championship	T38	T60	T50	T4	CUT	T14	T20	CUT	
THE PLAYERS Championship	T28		T14	T56	T75	T13	T20	T40	T21

KEITH FERGUS...continued

1995 PGA TOUR STATISTICS		
Scoring	71.22	(93T)
Driving	268.0	(55)
Driving Accuracy	69.8	(91T)
Greens in Regulation	67.5	(55T)
Putting	1.788	(89T)
All Around	603	(58)
Sand Saves	53.2	(83)
Total Driving	146	(42T)
Eagles	7	(51T)
Birdies	283	(86)

MISCELLANEOUS STATISTICS		
Scoring Avg Before Cut	70.74	(41)
Scoring Avg 3rd Rnd	72.06	(155T)
Scoring Avg Final Rnd	71.88	(143T)
Birdies Conversion %	28.4	(103T)
Par Breakers	19.6	(77T)

1995 Low Round: 64: 2 times, most recent 1995 Las Vegas Invitational/1
Career Low Round: 64: 2 times, most recent 1995 Las Vegas Invitational/1
Career Largest Paycheck: $67,500: 1983 Hope Desert Classic/1

ED FIORI *(fee-OR-ee)*

EXEMPT STATUS: Special Medical Extension
FULL NAME: Edward Ray Fiori
HEIGHT: 5' 7" **WEIGHT:** 190
BIRTH DATE: April 21, 1953 **BIRTHPLACE:** Lynwood, CA
RESIDENCE: Sugarland, TX
FAMILY: Wife, Debbie; Kelly Ann (1/29/82), Michael Ray (10/22/84)
COLLEGE: University of Houston
SPECIAL INTERESTS: Fishing, bird hunting
TURNED PROFESSIONAL: 1977 **Q SCHOOL:** Fall 1977

TOUR VICTORIES (3): 1979 Southern Open. **1981** Western Open. **1982** Bob Hope Desert Classic.

BEST 1995 FINISH: T12 -- Shell Houston Open

1995 SEASON: Playing in 1996 under a special medical extension...will have 10 tournaments to earn $62,507 and be fully exempt for rest of year...missed first 15 weeks of season with a rotator cuff injury and, as a result, had earnings of less than $100,000 for first time since 1986...made debut at Kmart Greater Greensboro Open, finishing T61...in next start the following week at Shell Houston Open, shot 71-70-71-70 -- 282 for T12, his best finish of year...in September, had back-to-back T17s at Greater Milwaukee Open and B.C. Open...low round of year came in first round of Walt Disney World/Oldsmobile Classic, a 66 over the Magnolia Course...finished T37.

CAREER HIGHLIGHTS: All three of Ed's wins came in a four-year span...scored first victory in second season on TOUR in a playoff over Tom Weiskopf at 1979 Southern Open...finished 67-69-67 for a four-stroke victory at 1981 Western Open...the following year, defeated Tom Kite in a playoff at Bob Hope Desert Classic...held 36-hole lead at 1994 New England Classic and shared lead with David Feherty through 54...closing 70 left him alone in third, four strokes behind winner Kenny Perry...top earnings year was 1988 when T2 at Honda Classic and T4 at Los Angeles Open helped him earn $193,765, 58th on money list...attended Wharton Junior College for a semester, then moved on to the University of Houston, where he was a member of the 1977 NCAA Championship team...1977 All-American.

PERSONAL: Nicknamed "The Grip" because of -- surprise -- his overly strong grip...while growing up, used to sneak onto nine-hole course near home.

Ed Fiori...*continued*

CAREER SUMMARY — **PLAYOFF RECORD: 2-0**

Year	Events Played	Cuts Made	1st	2nd	3rd	Top 10	Top 25	Earnings	Rank
1978	25	11				1	4	$19,846	109
1979	27	17	1			1	5	$64,428	65
1980	30	22				4	11	$79,488	52
1981	33	17	1			4	8	$105,510	48
1982	31	23	1			2	6	$91,599	45
1983	29	23		1	1	5	10	$175,619	26
1984	32	16					5	$41,582	119
1985	29	19			1	5	8	$116,002	71
1986	32	16				2	6	$70,828	119
1987	28	18				2	5	$104,570	95
1988	29	25		1		2	9	$193,765	58
1989	29	22			1	2	7	$188,637	77
1990	33	22				1	4	$108,816	133
1991	29	21					7	$120,722	123
1992	31	18				2	5	$124,537	115
1993	31	16				2	4	$117,617	127
1994	15	8			1	1	1	$108,259	150
1995	15	10					3	$83,852	170
Total	508	324	3	2	4	36	108	$1,912,684	101

NIKE TOUR SUMMARY

Year	Events Played	Cuts Made	1st	2nd	3rd	Top 10	Top 25	Earnings	Rank
1991	1	1					1	$1,150	215
1995	1	1						$740	242
Total	2	2					1	$1,890	
COMBINED TOTAL MONEY								$1,914,574	

TOP TOURNAMENT SUMMARY

YEAR	78	79	80	81	82	83	84	85	86	87	88	89	90	92	93
Masters Tournament			T6	CUT	CUT		CUT								
U.S. Open	T35						CUT	T46				CUT			
PGA Championship			CUT	T33	T54	T55	CUT	T51			T52	T9	T69		
THE PLAYERS Championship		T14	W/D	T51	T51	T8	CUT	T27	CUT	CUT	T23	T59	T66	CUT	W/D

TOP TOURNAMENT SUMMARY (cont.)

YEAR	94
THE PLAYERS Championship	T27

1995 PGA TOUR STATISTICS

Scoring	**71.21**	**(N/A)**
Driving	**245.7**	**(N/A)**
Driving Accuracy	**79.3**	**(N/A)**
Greens in Regulation	**65.6**	**(N/A)**
Putting	**1.815**	**(N/A)**
Sand Saves	**54.3**	**(N/A)**
Total Driving	**1,998**	**(N/A)**
Eagles	**1**	**(N/A)**
Birdies	**138**	**(N/A)**

MISCELLANEOUS STATISTICS

Scoring Avg Before Cut	**70.83**	**(N/A)**
Scoring Avg 3rd Rnd	**71.50**	**(N/A)**
Scoring Avg Final Rnd	**71.40**	**(N/A)**
Birdies Conversion %	**24.1**	**(N/A)**
Par Breakers	**15.9**	**(N/A)**

1995 Low Round: **66:** 1995 Walt Disney World/Oldsmobile Classic/1
Career Low Round: **35:** 1992 Greater Milwaukee/2
Career Largest Paycheck: $68,000: 2 times, most recent 1989 Kmart GGO/3

RAYMOND FLOYD

EXEMPT STATUS: Winner, 1986 U.S. Open
FULL NAME: Raymond Loran Floyd
HEIGHT: 6' 1" **WEIGHT:** 200
BIRTH DATE: Sept. 4, 1942 **BIRTHPLACE:** Fort Bragg, NC
RESIDENCE: Miami, FL; plays out of The Bahama Club, Great Exuma, Bahamas
FAMILY: Wife, Maria; Raymond Jr. (9/20/74), Robert Loran (1/23/76), Christina Loran (8/29/79)
COLLEGE: University of North Carolina
SPECIAL INTERESTS: Sports, golf course design
TURNED PROFESSIONAL: 1961 **JOINED TOUR:** 1963

TOUR VICTORIES (22): **1963** St. Petersburg Open. **1965** St. Paul Open. **1969** Jacksonville Open, American Golf Classic, PGA Championship. **1975** Kemper Open. **1976** Masters, World Open. **1977** Byron Nelson Classic, Pleasant Valley Classic. **1979** Greensboro Open. **1980** Doral-Eastern Open. **1981** Doral-Eastern Open, Tournament Players Championship, Manufacturers Hanover-Westchester Classic. **1982** Memorial Tournament, Danny Thomas-Memphis Classic, PGA Championship. **1985** Houston Open. **1986** U.S. Open, Walt Disney/Oldsmobile Classic. **1992** Doral Ryder Open.

SENIOR PGA TOUR VICTORIES (12): **1992** GTE North Classic, Ralphs Senior Classic, Senior TOUR Championship. **1993** Gulfstream Aerospace Invitational, Northville Long Island Classic. **1994** The Tradition, Las Vegas Senior Classic, Cadillac NFL Golf Classic, Golf Magazine, Senior TOUR Championship. **1995** PGA Seniors' Championship, Burnet Senior Classic, Emerald Coast Classic.

BEST 1995 PGA TOUR FINISH: T17 -- Doral-Ryder Open, Masters

BEST SENIOR PGA TOUR 1995 FINISHES: 1—PGA Seniors' Championship, Burnet Senior Classic, Emerald Coast Classic; 2—Royal Caribbean Classic, The Intellinet Challenge, Energizer SENIOR TOUR Championship; T2—SBC presents the Dominion Seniors, Las Vegas Senior Classic, PaineWebber Invitational, Cadillac NFL Golf Classic; 3—Vantage Championship; T5—Ameritech Senior Open; T6—Senior Tournament of Champions, The Tradition; T7—Brickyard Crossing Championship; T8—GTE Suncoast Classic, U.S. Senior Open; T9—Bruno's Memorial Classic; T10—FORD SENIOR PLAYERS Championship.

1995 SEASON: For second consecutive year, made only four appearances on PGA TOUR...as in 1994, was in money in all four...played 21 Senior TOUR tournaments...T17 in first two PGA TOUR starts...shot 72-71-68-69 -- 280 at Doral and 71-70-70-74 -- 285 at Masters...low round of year on PGA TOUR was closing 67 at U.S. Open where finished T36...final TOUR appearance was T58 at British Open.

CAREER HIGHLIGHTS: Last PGA TOUR victory 1992 Doral-Ryder Open, which he won at 49...later that year, after turning 50 and becoming eligible for Senior TOUR events, captured GTE North Classic...two victories made him first to win on PGA TOUR and Senior PGA TOUR in same year...joined Sam Snead as only players to win TOUR events in four different decades...1986 U.S. Open victory made him oldest to win Open, distinction taken away in 1990 by Hale Irwin...first major title came at 1976 Masters Tournament...captured PGA Championships in 1969 and 1982...also won 1981 Tournament Players Championship...winner 1983 Vardon Trophy...1989 Ryder Cup captain...winner 1985 Chrysler Team Championship (with Hal Sutton)...winner 1988 Skins Game...winner 1990 RMCC Invitational (with Fred Couples), winner 1993 Franklin Funds Shark Shootout (with Steve Elkington).

PERSONAL: Son of career Army man, grew up in Fort Bragg, NC... devoted Chicago Cubs fan, chose golf over possible career in professional baseball...1992 Doral-Ryder Open victory saga made even more stirring by fact win came two weeks after Miami home burned...son Robert plays golf at University of Florida, Raymond, Jr. at Wake Forest.

CAREER SUMMARY **PLAYOFF RECORD: 4-11**

Year	Events Played	Cuts Made	1st	2nd	3rd	Top 10	Top 25	Earnings	Rank
1963	17	17	1	1		3	5	$10,529	58
1964	23	23			2	4	11	$21,407	30
1965	20	20	1			3	9	$36,692	25
1966	21	21		1	1	6	12	$29,712	32
1967	25	25			1	3	9	$25,254	47
1968	22	22		1	2	7	16	$63,002	26
1969	28	22	3			6	10	$109,957	8
1970	24	17			1	3	11	$47,632	24
1971	31	21		2		5	12	$70,607	32
1972	24	15				4	7	$35,624	70
1973	23	17		1		2	7	$39,646	77
1974	26	22		3	1	8	14	$119,385	18
1975	26	21	1	1		5	12	$103,627	13

(NOTE: 1963-1968 entries do not include missed cuts)

Year	Events Played	Cuts Made	1st	2nd	3rd	Top 10	Top 25	Earnings	Rank
1976	23	21	2	1	1	9	16	$178,318	7
1977	24	23	2			8	15	$163,261	7
1978	26	20		1		4	14	$77,595	30
1979	26	19	1			6	10	$122,872	26
1980	27	24	1	1		9	15	$192,993	10
1981	23	23	3	2		14	18	$359,360	2
1982	23	18	3	3		9	16	$386,809	2
1983	22	22		1		8	18	$208,353	20
1984	23	18				2	8	$102,813	68
1985	22	20	1	2	1	9	15	$378,989	5
1986	23	19	2	1		5	15	$380,508	9
1987	20	12				2	9	$122,880	86
1988	19	16				3	8	$169,549	69
1989	17	13				1	2	$74,699	145
1990	17	11		1	1	3	6	$264,078	55
1991	17	15			1	5	10	$284,897	56
1992	15	15	1	2	1	5	11	$741,918	13
1993	6	5				2	4	$126,516	120
1994	4	4				1	3	$95,017	158
1995	4	4					2	$65,031	180
Total	691	585	22	25	13	164	350	$5,194,044	23

SENIOR PGA TOUR CAREER SUMMARY **PLAYOFF RECORD: 2-0**

Year	Events Played	Cuts Made	1st	2nd	3rd	Top 10	Top 25	Earnings	Rank
1992	7		3	1		6	6	$436,991	14
1993	14		2	4	2	12	14	$713,168	9
1994	20		4	5	2	17	20	$1,382,762	2
1995	21		3	7	1	19	21	$1,419,545	2
Total	62		12	17	5	54	61	$3,952,465	
COMBINED TOTAL MONEY								$9,146,778	

TOP TOURNAMENT SUMMARY

YEAR	63	64	65	66	67	68	69	70	71	72	73	74	75	76	77
Masters Tournament				T8		T7	T35		T13		54	T22	T30	1	T8
U.S. Open		T14	T6		T38		T13	T22	8		16	T15	T12	13	T47
British Open Championship							T34	CUT					T23	4	8
PGA Championship	T57		T17	T18	T20	T41	1	T8		T4	T35	T11	T10	T2	T40
THE PLAYERS Championship												T24	T21	T12	T13

TOP TOURNAMENT SUMMARY (cont.)

YEAR	78	79	80	81	82	83	84	85	86	87	88	89	90	91	92
Masters Tournament	T16	T17	T17	T8	T7	T4	T15	T2	CUT	CUT	T11	T38	2	T17	2
U.S. Open	T12		T45	T37	T49	T13	T52	T23	1	T43	T17	T26	CUT	T8	T44
British Open Championship	T2	T36		T3	T15	T14	CUT		T16	T17	CUT	T42	T39	CUT	T12
PGA Championship	T50	T62	T17	T19	1	T20	13	CUT	CUT	T14	T9	T46	T49	T7	T48
THE PLAYERS Championship		T14	CUT	1	T22	T23	T12	T33	T21	CUT	DQ	CUT	CUT		
THE TOUR Championship															T5

TOP TOURNAMENT SUMMARY (cont.)

YEAR	93	94	95
Masters Tournament	T11	T10	T17
U.S. Open	T7		T36
British Open Championship	T34		T58
PGA Championship	CUT	T61	

NATIONAL TEAMS: Ryder Cup (8), 1969, 1975, 1977, 1981, 1983, 1985,1991, 1993. Captain of 1989 Ryder Cup team. U.S. vs. Japan, 1982. Nissan Cup, 1985.

RAYMOND FLOYD...*continued*

SENIOR PGA TOUR TOP TOURNAMENT SUMMARY

YEAR	92	93	94	95
The Tradition		T3	1	T6
U.S. Senior Open		T7	12	T8
PGA Seniors' Championship		T13	T3	1
FORD SENIOR PLAYERS Championship		2	T3	T10
Energizer SENIOR TOUR Championship	1	T2	1	2

1995 PGA TOUR STATISTICS

Scoring	70.47	(N/A)
Driving	268.1	(N/A)
Driving Accuracy	76.8	(N/A)
Greens in Regulation	57.4	(N/A)
Putting	1.758	(N/A)
Sand Saves	60.0	(N/A)
Total Driving	1,998	(N/A)
Eagles	1	(N/A)
Birdies	57	(N/A)

MISCELLANEOUS STATISTICS

Scoring Avg Before Cut	72.00	(N/A)
Scoring Avg 3rd Rnd	71.50	(N/A)
Scoring Avg Final Rnd	71.50	(N/A)
Birdies Conversion %	46.0	(N/A)
Par Breakers	20.1	(N/A)

1995 Low Round: **67:** 1995 U.S. Open/4
Career Low Round: **63:** 2 times, most recent 1992 MCI Heritage GC/2
Career Largest Paycheck: **$252,000:** 1992 Doral Ryder Open/1

1995 SENIOR PGA TOUR STATISTICS

Scoring	69.47	(1)
Driving	268.1	(6)
Driving Accuracy	74.6	(10)
Greens in Regulation	75.3	(1)
Putting	1.753	(4T)
All Around	89	(1)
Sand Saves	50.5	(17T)
Total Driving	16	(1)
Eagles	7	(13T)
Birdies	277	(37T)

MISCELLANEOUS SENIOR STATISTICS

1995 Low Round: **65:** 3 times, most recent 1995 Brickyard Crossing Championship/1
Career Low Round: **62:** 1992 Ralphs Sr. Classic/3
Career Largest Paycheck: **$240,000:** 1994 Golf Magazine SENIOR TOUR Championship/1

DAN FORSMAN *(FORS-mun)*

EXEMPT STATUS: 93rd on 1995 money list
FULL NAME: Daniel Bruce Forsman
HEIGHT: 6' 4" **WEIGHT:** 195
BIRTH DATE: July 15, 1958 **BIRTHPLACE:** Rhinelander, WI
RESIDENCE: Provo, UT; plays out of Riverside CC
FAMILY: Wife, Trudy; Ricky (1/18/85), Thomas (12/15/89)
COLLEGE: Arizona State University
SPECIAL INTERESTS: Snow skiing, reading, fly fishing, all sports
TURNED PROFESSIONAL: 1982 **Q SCHOOL:** Fall 1982

TOUR VICTORIES (4): 1985 Lite Quad Cities Open. **1986** Hertz Bay Hill Classic. **1990** Shearson Lehman Hutton Open. **1992** Buick Open.

BEST 1995 FINISH: T8 -- Ideon Classic at Pleasant Valley, Sprint International

1995 SEASON: Earned $194,539 in 1995, with most coming in second half of year when he made nine of final 10 cuts...after missing cut in first start, made his next six, including T22 at Phoenix Open and T20 at Nestle Invitational, each worth $13,000...year's first top-10 (his first in 40 tournaments) came at Ideon Classic...after second-round 65, his low round of 1995, was T3 and was alone in third after a third-round 67...closed with 71 for T8, four strokes behind Fred Funk...after a T24 the following week at Buick Open, finished T8 again at Sprint International worth $43,500, largest check of year...T11 at Bell Canadian Open despite closing 75.

DAN FORSMAN...continued

CAREER HIGHLIGHTS: Best season and No. 10 spot on money list came in1992, when captured Buick Open and finished second in three other events...fired final-round 67 at Warwick Hills to enter three-man playoff with Steve Elkington and Brad Faxon...par on second playoff hole gave him fourth TOUR title...runner-up finishes came in Federal Express St. Jude Classic, Chattanooga Classic and Canon Greater Hartford Open...missed but one cut in 29 starts...first TOUR victory came in 1985 Lite Quad Cities Open...the next year captured rain-shortened Hertz Bay Hill Classic...became three-time winner at 1990 Shearson Lehman Hutton Open...had another Canon GHO runner-up in 1993, when carded final-round 65 to finish one stroke behind Nick Price...earlier that year finished T7 in Masters Tournament after being tied for second (with Chip Beck) after three rounds...winner 1987 MCI Long Distance Driving Competition...1987-88 birdies leader...two-time All-American at Arizona State.

PERSONAL: Grew up in San Francisco Bay Area...learned game at Los Altos G&CC...took six weeks off during 1995 season to coach son's Little League team.

CAREER SUMMARY — **PLAYOFF RECORD: 1-0**

Year	Events Played	Cuts Made	1st	2nd	3rd	Top 10	Top 25	Earnings	Rank
1982	1								
1983	30	14				1	5	$37,859	118
1984	32	16				2	6	$52,152	105
1985	26	16	1			4	8	$150,334	53
1986	27	16	1			2	6	$169,445	54
1987	33	29		1		1	7	$157,728	63
1988	35	26		1	2	4	10	$269,440	40
1989	30	15				4	5	$141,174	99
1990	26	19	1			4	7	$319,160	43
1991	26	19			1	2	7	$214,175	78
1992	29	28	1	3		8	14	$763,190	10
1993	25	19		1		6	11	$410,150	36
1994	23	13					6	$160,805	112
1995	23	18				2	6	$194,539	93
Total	366	248	4	6	3	40	98	$3,040,150	56

1996 PGA TOUR CHARITY TEAM: AT&T Pebble Beach National Pro-Am

TOP TOURNAMENT SUMMARY

YEAR	82	84	85	86	87	88	89	90	91	92	93	94	95
Masters Tournament				CUT				CUT			T7	14	T35
U.S. Open	CUT	T60					T33	CUT		T60	T19		
British Open Championship											T73		
PGA Championship			CUT	CUT	CUT		CUT	CUT	T32	T7	T44		
THE PLAYERS Championship		CUT	T13	CUT	T61	CUT	CUT	T36	75	63	T11	83	CUT
THE TOUR Championship										T7			

1995 PGA TOUR STATISTICS

Scoring	**71.16**	**(87)**
Driving	**265.6**	**(71)**
Driving Accuracy	**69.0**	**(106)**
Greens in Regulation	**68.3**	**(38T)**
Putting	**1.788**	**(89T)**
All Around	**671**	**(77)**
Sand Saves	**46.7**	**(156)**
Total Driving	**177**	**(81)**
Eagles	**10**	**(15T)**
Birdies	**265**	**(109T)**

MISCELLANEOUS STATISTICS

Scoring Avg Before Cut	**71.09**	**(76T)**
Scoring Avg 3rd Rnd	**70.65**	**(58T)**
Scoring Avg Final Rnd	**71.88**	**(143T)**
Birdies Conversion %	**28.0**	**(120T)**
Par Breakers	**19.8**	**(71T)**

1995 Low Round: **65:** 1995 Ideon Classic at Pleasant Valley/2
Career Low Round: **62:** 1988 Bob Hope Chrysler Cl/2
Career Largest Paycheck: **$180,000:** 1992 Buick Open/1

Robin Freeman

EXEMPT STATUS: 68th on 1995 money list
FULL NAME: Robin Lee Freeman
HEIGHT: 6' **WEIGHT:** 185
BIRTH DATE: May 7, 1959 **BIRTHPLACE:** St. Charles, MO
RESIDENCE: Rancho Mirage, CA; plays out of PGA West, La Quinta, CA
FAMILY: Wife, K.C.; Chase Kiner (6/20/93), Kyle Scott (8/8/95)
COLLEGE: University of Central Oklahoma
SPECIAL INTERESTS: All sports
TURNED PROFESSIONAL: 1982 **Q SCHOOL:** 1988, 1991, 1992, 1993

BEST CAREER FINISH: T2 -- 1995 GTE Byron Nelson Classic

BEST 1995 FINISHES: T2 -- GTE Byron Nelson Classic; 3 -- Kemper Open

1995 SEASON: Easily retained his card for second consecutive year on the strength of two top-three finishes...made eight of his first 13 cuts, but could finish no better than T31 at AT&T Pebble Beach National Pro-Am and Honda Classic...shot low round of year in that stretch -- 64 at Bob Hope Chrysler Classic...breakthrough came at GTE Byron Nelson Classic...opened with back-to-back 65s to share 36-hole lead with Ernie Els...trailed Els by three after third-round 68...after another 68, finished T2 with D.A. Weibring and Mike Heinen, still three behind Els...$97,067 share is largest career payday...four weeks later at Kemper Open, was T4, three strokes out of lead through 54 holes before closing 68 placed him third, one stroke out of Lee Janzen-Corey Pavin playoff...missed next two cuts, but made nine of 11 thereafter...T12 at Quad City Classic with rounds of 68-68-69 -- 205.

CAREER HIGHLIGHTS: Only two-time medalist in PGA TOUR Qualifying Tournament history (1988, 1993)...prior to 1995, best TOUR finish came in 1993 Northern Telecom Open, where final-round 66 lifted him to T3 with Jim Gallagher, Jr., and Michael Allen, three strokes behind winner Larry Mize...had first top-10 in '92, T4 at Buick Open after closing 69-66-68, his first year to surpass $100,000 in earnings...top 1989 finish T24 in GTE Byron Nelson Classic...first-team NAIA All-American in 1981-82.

PERSONAL: Got into golf at 14 after fracturing a leg (had been involved in all sports)...worked as club pro for five years at Oak Tree and PGA West...father-in-law is Baseball Hall of Famer Ralph Kiner.

PGA TOUR CAREER SUMMARY **PLAYOFF RECORD: 0-0**

Year	Events Played	Cuts Made	1st	2nd	3rd	Top 10	Top 25	Earnings	Rank
1983	1								
1988	1	1						$1,508	288
1989	30	9					1	$26,517	188
1990	2								
1992	31	10				1	3	$101,642	128
1993	30	14			1	1	1	$92,096	148
1994	29	20				3	7	$177,044	103
1995	30	19		1	1	2	4	$283,756	68
Total	154	73		1	2	7	16	$682,564	223

NIKE TOUR SUMMARY

Year	Events Played	Cuts Made	1st	2nd	3rd	Top 10	Top 25	Earnings	Rank
1992	1	1						$733	266
1994	1								
Total	2	1						$733	
COMBINED TOTAL MONEY								$683,297	

1996 PGA TOUR CHARITY TEAM: Bob Hope Chrysler Classic

TOP TOURNAMENT SUMMARY

YEAR	95
PGA Championship	T49
THE PLAYERS Championship	CUT

ROBIN FREEMAN...*continued*

1995 PGA TOUR STATISTICS		
Scoring	71.14	(84T)
Driving	270.8	(34T)
Driving Accuracy	66.2	(142T)
Greens in Regulation	66.0	(106T)
Putting	1.793	(105T)
All Around	630	(67)
Sand Saves	53.9	(70T)
Total Driving	176	(80)
Eagles	6	(69T)
Birdies	348	(20)

MISCELLANEOUS STATISTICS		
Scoring Avg Before Cut	70.90	(54T)
Scoring Avg 3rd Rnd	71.85	(144)
Scoring Avg Final Rnd	71.26	(95)
Birdies Conversion %	30.2	(45T)
Par Breakers	20.3	(40T)

1995 Low Round: **64:** 1995 Bob Hope Chrysler Classic/1
Career Low Round: **63:** 2 times, most recent 1994 United Airlines Hawaiian Open/1
Career Largest Paycheck: **$97,066:** 1995 GTE Byron Nelson Classic/T2

DAVID FROST

EXEMPT STATUS: Winner, 1989 NEC World Series of Golf
FULL NAME: David Laurence Frost
HEIGHT: 5' 11" **WEIGHT:** 172
BIRTH DATE: Sept. 11, 1959
BIRTHPLACE: Cape Town, South Africa
RESIDENCE: Dallas, TX; plays out of Preston Trail GC
FAMILY: Sean (2/24/88), Noelle (1/15/90)
SPECIAL INTERESTS: All sports, rugby
TURNED PROFESSIONAL: 1981 **Q SCHOOL:** Fall 1984

TOUR VICTORIES (9): 1988 Southern Open, Northern Telecom Tucson Open. **1989** NEC World Series of Golf. **1990** USF&G Classic. **1992** Buick Classic, Hardee's Golf Classic. **1993** Canadian Open, Hardee's Golf Classic. **1994** Canon Greater Hartford Open.

INTERNATIONAL VICTORIES (8): 1984 Air France Cannes Open (Eur). **1989** Million Dollar Challenge (Afr). **1990** Million Dollar Challenge (Afr). **1992** Million Dollar Challenge (Afr), Dunlop Phoenix (Jpn). **1993** Kent Hong Kong Open (Asia). **1994** Lexington PGA Championship (Afr), Hong Kong Open (Asia).

BEST 1995 FINISHES: T2 -- MCI Classic; T5 -- Masters Tournament, Memorial Tournament

1995 SEASON: Fell from ranks of top 30 for first time since 1991, finishing 50th on money list with $357,658...failed to win for first time since 1991, but came closest at MCI Classic...after third-round 66, was tied for lead with David Edwards, Mark McCumber and Gene Sauers...closing 70 left him tied with Bob Tway and Nolan Henke at 9-under-par 275...he bogeyed the first extra hole and was eliminated; Tway won with a par on the next hole...his first top-10 of the year came the week before at the Masters...shared lead with Phil Mickelson and Jose Maria Olazabal after first-round 66...after three 71s, finished tied with Steve Elkington for fifth, five strokes behind Ben Crenshaw...T15 at Colonial National Invitation, then had second T5 at Memorial the following week...moved to within two strokes of lead after third-round 65, low round of year, then closed with 70...T14 at Bell Canadian Open his best finish for rest of year...with wins over Eduardo Romero, Steve Elkington and Robert Allenby, represented "Rest of the World" in finals of Andersen Consulting World Championship of Golf.

CAREER HIGHLIGHTS: Most recent win came at 1994 Canon Greater Hartford Open...shared lead after first and third rounds, then held on for one-stroke victory over Greg Norman...enjoyed finest season of career in 1993, when collected two wins, two seconds and one third and surpassed $1 million in earnings for first time...recorded back-to-back victories at Canadian Open and in Hardee's Golf Classic...by so doing, became first since Johnny Miller (1975) to successfully defend one title the week after winning another tournament...259 Hardee's total two strokes off TOUR record for 72 holes...two-time winner for second time in 1992, when claimed Buick Classic and Hardee's Classic...holed out from bunker on 72nd hole of 1990 USF&G Classic to defeat Greg Norman...scored biggest win of career at 1989 NEC World Series of Golf...second-hole playoff victory over Ben Crenshaw provided 10-year TOUR exemption...won twice in 1988, Southern Open (beat Bob Tway in playoff) and Northern Telecom Open...carded career-low 60 in Round 2 of 1990 Northern Telecom...winner 1987 Merrill Lynch Shoot-Out Final.

PERSONAL: Was bearded winner of 1992 Hardee's Golf Classic...shaved trademark mustache in Feb. 1993...first played in U.S. in 1981, returning in 1985.

DAVID FROST...continued

CAREER SUMMARY						PLAYOFF RECORD: 2-3			
Year	Events Played	Cuts Made	1st	2nd	3rd	Top 10	Top 25	Earnings	Rank
1983	1	1							
1985	28	18		1		3	8	$118,537	70
1986	28	20		1	1	6	14	$187,944	46
1987	27	24		3		12	19	$518,072	11
1988	25	18	2	3	3	11	13	$691,500	9
1989	26	23	1	1	1	8	12	$620,430	12
1990	26	15	1			4	8	$372,485	32
1991	28	18				2	8	$171,262	93
1992	25	16	2	1		6	11	$717,883	15
1993	22	15	2	2	1	9	15	$1,030,717	5
1994	23	20	1		1	6	10	$671,683	20
1995	21	15		1		3	5	$357,658	50
Total	280	203	9	13	7	70	123	$5,458,172	20

1996 PGA TOUR CHARITY TEAM: Buick Invitational

TOP TOURNAMENT SUMMARY

YEAR	83	84	85	86	87	88	89	90	91	92	93	94	95
Masters Tournament					T45	8	T18	CUT	T32		CUT	T35	T5
U.S. Open			T23	T15	T17	CUT	T18	T33	CUT		CUT	CUT	CUT
British Open Championship	CUT	T47	T28	CUT	6	T7	CUT	CUT	CUT		T24	T51	T31
PGA Championship			CUT	T21	T10	CUT	T27	T31	T48	T73	CUT	T25	T67
THE PLAYERS Championship				T48	T15	T3	T8	CUT	T41	CUT	CUT	CUT	T37
THE TOUR Championship					T17	T17	T11			T7	T2	T4	

NATIONAL TEAMS: Presidents Cup, 1994

1995 PGA TOUR STATISTICS		
Scoring	70.72	(53T)
Driving	254.0	(166)
Driving Accuracy	71.4	(71T)
Greens in Regulation	61.2	(181)
Putting	1.758	(19T)
All Around	801	(119)
Sand Saves	66.9	(3)
Total Driving	237	(158T)
Eagles	2	(161T)
Birdies	224	(147)

MISCELLANEOUS STATISTICS		
Scoring Avg Before Cut	71.32	(99T)
Scoring Avg 3rd Rnd	71.25	(101)
Scoring Avg Final Rnd	71.47	(111T)
Birdies Conversion %	29.9	(52T)
Par Breakers	17.4	(152T)

1995 Low Round: **65:** 1995 Memorial Tournament/3
Career Low Round: **60:** 1990 Tucson Open/2
Career Largest Paycheck: **$216,000:** 1994 Canon Greater Hartford Open/1

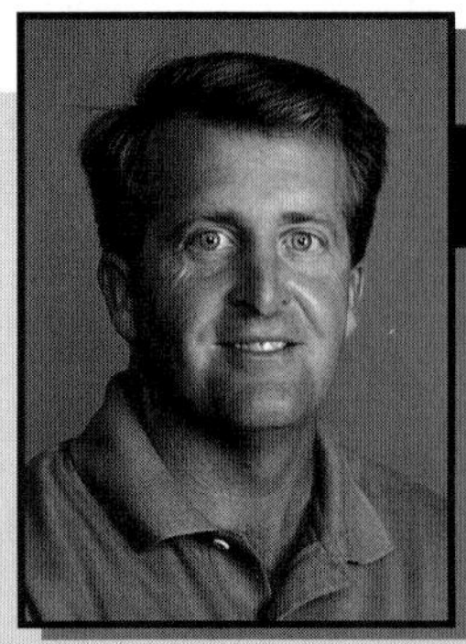

FRED FUNK

EXEMPT STATUS: 1995 tournament winner
FULL NAME: Frederick Funk
HEIGHT: 5'8" **WEIGHT:** 165
BIRTH DATE: June 14, 1956 **BIRTHPLACE:** Takoma Park, MD
RESIDENCE: Ponte Vedra Beach, FL
FAMILY: Wife, Sharon; Eric (8/2/91), Taylor Christian (10/30/95)
COLLEGE: University of Maryland (1980, Law Enforcement)
SPECIAL INTERESTS: Water, snow skiing
TURNED PROFESSIONAL: 1981 **Q SCHOOL:** Fall 1988, 1989.

TOUR VICTORIES (3): **1992** Shell Houston Open. **1995** Ideon Classic at Pleasant Valley, Buick Challenge.

INTERNATIONAL VICTORIES: **1993** Mexican Open.

BEST 1995 FINISHES: 1 -- Ideon Classic at Pleasant Valley, Buick Challenge; T4 -- Buick Classic; T8 -- Anheuser-Busch Golf Classic.

Fred Funk...*continued*

1995 SEASON: Enjoyed most successful year on TOUR with two wins, four top-10s and 11 top-25s...qualified for THE TOUR Championship for the first time...made 15 of his first 17 cuts, including T16 at Nestle Invitational, T12 at Shell Houston Open and his first top-10 of year, T4 at Buick Classic...was T12, just four strokes off Vijay Singh's lead after 54 holes of Buick Classic...closing 70 moved him to T4, two strokes out of Singh-Doug Martin playoff...after missing three consecutive cuts (Kemper, U.S. Open, Western), began hottest stretch of year with T8 at Anheuser-Busch...followed that with T11 at Deposit Guaranty, then earned first win since 1992 at Ideon Classic...was one of 10 one stroke off lead after first-round 66, then broke from pack with second-round 63 to lead by three...extended lead to four with third-round 66, then hung on with closing 73 to win by one over Jim McGovern...another T11 at Buick Open followed...third career victory came at Buick Challenge...gained share of lead with Steve Stricker after third-round 69, then closed with 67 to earn one-stroke victory over John Morse and Loren Roberts...each win worth $180,000...T6 in birdies category (380).

CAREER HIGHLIGHTS: Course-record 62 in Round 3, followed by closing 70, gave him victory in 1992 Shell Houston Open...held off Kirk Triplett by two strokes at TPC at The Woodlands...always one of busiest players on TOUR with 34 starts in 1993, 30 in 1994 and 32 last year...won 1984 Foot-Joy National Assistant Pro Championship...shot 59 on Desert Course at TPC of Scottsdale during separate pro-am at 1992 Phoenix Open...winner 1993 Mexican Open.

PERSONAL: Golf coach at University of Maryland from 1982-88 before joining TOUR...majored in Law Enforcement at Maryland...the "Other Fred" on TOUR, "Poof Poof" to Fred Couples' "Boom Boom"...tore left rotator cuff August 1986...reinjured shoulder and underwent surgery after 1991 "boogie board" accident.

CAREER SUMMARY — **PLAYOFF RECORD: 0-0**

Year	Events Played	Cuts Made	1st	2nd	3rd	Top 10	Top 25	Earnings	Rank
1982	3	2						$1,779	251
1985	1	1					1	$6,345	196
1986	3								
1987	2	1						$2,400	255
1988	2	1						$1,552	285
1989	29	17			1	2	3	$59,695	157
1990	29	13			1	3	7	$179,346	91
1991	31	17				5	9	$226,915	73
1992	32	24	1		1	3	9	$416,930	34
1993	34	24				5	11	$309,435	56
1994	30	23				4	8	$281,905	67
1995	32	26	2			4	11	$717,232	26
Total	228	149	3		3	26	59	$2,203,534	89

1996 PGA TOUR CHARITY TEAM: Mercedes Championships

TOP TOURNAMENT SUMMARY

YEAR	85	86	87	89	91	92	93	94	95
Masters Tournament							CUT	T38	
U.S. Open	T23	CUT	CUT	CUT	CUT	T33	T7	T44	CUT
British Open Championship						73			
PGA Championship			T47		T57	CUT	T44	T55	T39
THE PLAYERS Championship					CUT	T60	T39	T78	T61
THE TOUR Championship									T27

1995 PGA TOUR STATISTICS

Statistic	Value	Rank
Scoring	70.71	(51T)
Driving	256.8	(145)
Driving Accuracy	81.3	(1)
Greens in Regulation	67.7	(51T)
Putting	1.784	(79T)
All Around	482	(31)
Sand Saves	60.6	(12T)
Total Driving	146	(42T)
Eagles	3	(137T)
Birdies	380	(6T)

MISCELLANEOUS STATISTICS

Statistic	Value	Rank
Scoring Avg Before Cut	70.86	(51T)
Scoring Avg 3rd Rnd	70.44	(46T)
Scoring Avg Final Rnd	71.08	(77T)
Birdies Conversion %	27.9	(123T)
Par Breakers	19.0	(96T)

1995 Low Round: 63: 1995 Ideon Classic at Pleasant Valley/2
Career Low Round: 62: 2 times, most recent 1992 Shell Houston Open/3
Career Largest Paycheck: $216,000: 1992 Shell Houston Open/1

JIM FURYK *(FYUR-ik)*

EXEMPT STATUS: 1995 tournament winner
FULL NAME: James Michael Furyk
HEIGHT: 6' 2" **WEIGHT:** 200
BIRTH DATE: May 12, 1970 **BIRTHPLACE:** West Chester, PA
RESIDENCE: Ponte Vedra Beach, FL
FAMILY: Single
COLLEGE: University of Arizona
SPECIAL INTERESTS: All sports
TURNED PROFESSIONAL: 1992 **Q SCHOOL:** 1993

TOUR VICTORIES (1): 1995 Las Vegas Invitational

NIKE TOUR VICTORIES (1): 1993 NIKE Mississippi Gulf Coast Classic

BEST 1995 FINISHES: 1 -- Las Vegas Invitational; 5 -- Northern Telecom Open; T9 -- Nissan Open

1995 SEASON: Utilizing the TOUR's most unorthodox swing, gained first victory at Las Vegas Invitational, by one stroke over Billy Mayfair...grabbed share of lead with David Edwards after third-round 65 at TPC at Summerlin...after fourth-round 67, shared lead with Mayfair...took a two-stroke lead after Sunday's front nine, then shot two-under 34 on the back to seal victory...win moved him to 32nd on money list, but prior commitment in Japan kept him from making final run at top 30...as in 1994, first top-10 came at Northern Telecom Open...T21 after 36 holes, finished 67-67 for solo fifth, three strokes behind Phil Mickelson...T9 at Nissan Open featured third-round 65...second-round 62 at Buick Open was Warwick Hills CC course record, finished T11...T13 at PGA Championship the following week...won 1995 Lincoln-Mercury Kapalua International (unofficial)...led TOUR in putting (1.708 putts per GIR), T2 in birdies (404).

CAREER HIGHLIGHTS: Recorded three top-10s in his rookie season of 1994...shared third-round lead at Northern Telecom, then closed with 71 for T7...best chance to win came at Las Vegas Invitational when, after holding 72-hole lead, shot 70 to finish T5...qualified for PGA TOUR with T37 in 1993 Qualifying Tournament...finished No. 26 on 1993 NIKE TOUR money list with $58,240...won NIKE Mississippi Gulf Coast Classic, defeating Robert Friend on first playoff hole...lost NIKE Bakersfield Classic in playoff with Clark Dennis...twice named to First-Team All-PAC-10...two-time All-American selection.

PERSONAL: Parents have home adjoining Tucson National Resort...played course often while at University of Arizona...learned cross-handed putting stroke from father at age seven...works on swing only with his father.

CAREER SUMMARY — **PLAYOFF RECORD: 0-0**

Year	Events Played	Cuts Made	1st	2nd	3rd	Top 10	Top 25	Earnings	Rank
1988(Am.)	1								
1990(Am.)	1								
1991(Am.)	1								
1993	1								
1994	31	17				3	7	$236,603	78
1995	31	22	1			3	10	$535,380	33
Total	66	39	1			6	17	$771,983	209

NIKE TOUR CAREER SUMMARY

Year	Events Played	Cuts Made	1st	2nd	3rd	Top 10	Top 25	Earnings	Rank
1993	25	13	1	1		3	6	$58,240	26
1994	1	1				1	1	$3,815	153
Total	26	14	1	1		4	7	$62,055	
COMBINED TOTAL								$834,038	

1996 PGA TOUR CHARITY TEAM: Greater Vancouver Open

TOP TOURNAMENT SUMMARY

YEAR	94	95
U.S. Open	T28	
PGA Championship	T13	
THE PLAYERS Championship		CUT

JIM FURYK...continued

1995 PGA TOUR STATISTICS		
Scoring	71.04	(72T)
Driving	256.2	(149)
Driving Accuracy	69.2	(101)
Greens in Regulation	63.1	(161T)
Putting	1.708	(1)
All Around	574	(49T)
Sand Saves	55.4	(52)
Total Driving	250	(164)
Eagles	8	(36T)
Birdies	404	(2T)

MISCELLANEOUS STATISTICS		
Scoring Avg Before Cut	70.94	(63T)
Scoring Avg 3rd Rnd	70.14	(26T)
Scoring Avg Final Rnd	71.10	(81)
Birdies Conversion %	34.9	(2)
Par Breakers	22.4	(3)

1995 Low Round: **62:** 1995 Buick Open/2
Career Low Round: **62:** 1995 Buick Open/2
Career Largest Paycheck: **$270,000:** 1995 Las Vegas Invitational/1

JIM GALLAGHER, JR.

EXEMPT STATUS: 1995 tournament winner
FULL NAME: James Thomas Gallagher, Jr.
HEIGHT: 6' **WEIGHT:** 195
BIRTH DATE: March 24, 1961 **BIRTHPLACE:** Johnstown, PA
RESIDENCE: Greenwood, MS; plays out of Brickyard Crossing, Indianapolis, IN
FAMILY: Wife, Cissye; Mary Langdon (1/13/92), James Thomas III (12/1/93)
COLLEGE: University of Tennessee (1983, Marketing)
SPECIAL INTERESTS: Music, duck hunting, following family golf careers
TURNED PROFESSIONAL: 1983 **Q SCHOOL:** Fall 1983, 1984

TOUR VICTORIES (5): **1990** Greater Milwaukee Open. **1993** Anheuser-Busch Golf Classic, THE TOUR Championship. **1995** Kmart Greater Greensboro Open, FedEx St. Jude Classic.

BEST 1995 FINISHES: 1 -- Kmart Greater Greensboro Open, FedEx St. Jude Classic; 2 -- BellSouth Classic; T2 -- Northern Telecom Open; T3 -- Greater Milwaukee Open; T6 -- NEC World Series of Golf

1995 SEASON: For the second time in three years, won two tournaments and surpassed $1 million in earnings...second-round 64 moved him into second place behind Phil Mickelson at Northern Telecom Open...shared 54-hole lead with Mickelson and Brett Ogle after a third-round 69...closing 69 lost out to Mickelson's 68...trailed Kenny Perry by one after opening 64 at Bob Hope Chrysler Classic before finishing T14...fourth TOUR victory came at Kmart GGO...T10 and trailing leader Jeff Sluman by seven strokes entering final round, shot 66 on frigid Sunday to notch one-stroke victory over Sluman and Peter Jacobsen...one of two seven-stroke, final-day comebacks on TOUR in 1995 (Payne Stewart, Shell Houston Open, the other)...nearly won his next start at BellSouth...shared first-round lead with Bill Porter at 65 and third-round lead with club pro Stephen Keppler at 203...succumbed to Mark Calcavecchia's closing 66, finishing two back...after a second-round 62 at FedEx St. Jude, his low round of year, held two-stroke edge...Gene Sauers' third-round 63 cut lead to one, but closing 72 was enough to defeat Ken Green and Jay Delsing by a stroke...led by one after 18 and 36 holes at NEC World Series of Golf, then closed with 70-73 for T6, two strokes out of playoff won by Greg Norman...final top-10 came at site of first TOUR win -- Greater Milwakuee Open...274 was good for T3, five strokes behind Scott Hoch.

CAREER HIGHLIGHTS: 1993 season one to be remembered...captured Anheuser-Busch Golf Classic (second TOUR title) and then TOUR Championship...final-day 65 at A-B Classic provided two-stroke win over Chip Beck and enough points for first Ryder Cup berth...finished off U.S. victory with 3-and-2 defeat of Seve Ballesteros in singles...opened TOUR Championship with Olympic Club course-record 63...edged Greg Norman and David Frost by one stroke...no wins in 1994, but represented U.S. at inaugural Presidents Cup, where his record was 3-1, including singles win over Tsukasa Watanabe...first victory came in 1990 Greater Milwaukee Open, where he was given sponsor's exemption in 1988 and finished second...two years later defeated Ed Dougherty and Billy Mayfair on first playoff hole at Tuckaway CC...leading money winner on Tournament Players Series in 1985.

PERSONAL: Member of golfing family...father Jim, PGA Professional in Marion, IN, started him in game at age two... wife Cissye, former LSU golfer, also was member of LPGA...sister Jackie Gallagher-Smith is LPGA member...brother Jeff NIKE TOUR member since 1990 who qualified for 1996 PGA TOUR.

JIM GALLAGHER, JR....*continued*

CAREER SUMMARY					PLAYOFF RECORD: 1-1				
Year	**Events Played**	**Cuts Made**	**1st**	**2nd**	**3rd**	**Top 10**	**Top 25**	**Earnings**	**Rank**
1984	25	13				1	2	$22,249	148
1985	16	8					2	$19,061	159
1986	36	21			1	3	6	$79,967	107
1987	36	17				1	2	$39,402	166
1988	19	14		1		1	2	$83,766	124
1989	34	24				3	13	$265,809	50
1990	34	25	1		1	5	10	$476,706	25
1991	32	25		1	3	6	11	$570,627	18
1992	28	25		3	1	7	15	$638,314	19
1993	27	18	2	1	1	6	8	$1,078,870	4
1994	27	16		1		4	8	$325,976	51
1995	27	22	2	2	1	6	12	$1,057,241	8
Total	341	228	5	9	8	43	91	$4,657,989	29

1996 PGA TOUR CHARITY TEAM: Memorial Tournament

TOP TOURNAMENT SUMMARY										
YEAR	**86**	**87**	**88**	**89**	**90**	**91**	**92**	**93**	**94**	**95**
Masters Tournament						T17	T25	CUT	CUT	
U.S. Open			CUT	CUT	T33	T11	T57	CUT	T47	T62
British Open Championship							CUT	CUT	T47	T55
PGA Championship				T12	CUT	3	T2	CUT	CUT	T44
THE PLAYERS Championship	CUT	CUT		T34	T29	CUT	T60	T39	T27	T23
THE TOUR Championship					27	T5	T25	1		T25

NATIONAL TEAMS: Four Tours World Championship of Golf, 1991; Ryder Cup, 1993; Presidents Cup, 1994

1995 PGA TOUR STATISTICS		
Scoring	70.37	(33)
Driving	275.4	(12)
Driving Accuracy	64.9	(158T)
Greens in Regulation	66.9	(66T)
Putting	1.753	(13T)
All Around	353	(6)
Sand Saves	55.2	(53T)
Total Driving	170	(70T)
Eagles	12	(5T)
Birdies	360	(13T)

MISCELLANEOUS STATISTICS		
Scoring Avg Before Cut	70.45	(20T)
Scoring Avg 3rd Rnd	71.48	(118T)
Scoring Avg Final Rnd	71.27	(96T)
Birdies Conversion %	31.5	(22T)
Par Breakers	20.9	(23T)

1995 Low Round: **62:** 1995 FedEx St. Jude Classic/2
Career Low Round: **61:** 1991 Las Vegas Invitation/4
Career Largest Paycheck: **$540,000:** 1993 TOUR Championship/1

ROBERT GAMEZ *(GAM-ez)*

EXEMPT STATUS: 89th on 1995 money list
FULL NAME: Robert Anthony Gamez
HEIGHT: 5'9" **WEIGHT:** 170
BIRTH DATE: July 21, 1968 **BIRTHPLACE:** Las Vegas, NV
RESIDENCE: Las Vegas, NV; plays out of Ko Olina GC, Ewa Beach, Oahu, HI
FAMILY: Wife, Machala
COLLEGE: University of Arizona
SPECIAL INTERESTS: Music, movies
TURNED PROFESSIONAL: 1989 **Q SCHOOL:** Fall 1989

TOUR VICTORIES (2): **1990** Northern Telecom Tucson Open, Nestle Invitational.

INTERNATIONAL VICTORIES (1): **1994** Casio World Open (Jpn).

BEST 1995 FINISHES: T5 -- Memorial Tournament; 6 -- Bob Hope Chrysler Classic; T10 -- Greater Milwaukee Open

ROBERT GAMEZ...continued

1995 SEASON: Least productive year since joining TOUR in 1990...first year without at least a runner-up finish to his credit...after a T12 at United Airlines Hawaiian Open and two missed cuts in Arizona, finished sixth at Bob Hope Chrysler Classic...final three rounds of 66-68-66 moved him from T45 to final position, three strokes behind Kenny Perry...68-67 gave him share of lead at Memorial...fell one stroke behind after third-round 69 and finished T5, six back...opened with 65, low round of 1995, to share first-round Kemper Open lead with Vijay Singh but, largely due to third-round 77, finished T42...missed next six cuts after Kemper...final top-10 was T10 at Greater Milwaukee...finished T2 at Dunlop Phoenix (Japan), one stroke behind Jumbo Ozaki...finished second with Helen Alfredsson at JCPenney Classic for second consecutive year.

CAREER HIGHLIGHTS: Won first official start on PGA TOUR, capturing Northern Telecom Open by four strokes over Mark Calcavecchia in 1990...two months later electrified golf world by holing 7-iron from 176 yards for eagle-2 at 72nd hole of Nestle Invitational for one-stroke victory over Greg Norman...two victories and first-year earnings of $461,407 led to PGA TOUR Rookie of the Year honors...runner-up at 1994 Las Vegas Invitational worth $162,000 -- along with two winner's shares in 1990, his biggest paydays...playoff loser to Fred Couples in wind-shortened 1993 Honda Classic...blistered Tuckaway CC with opening-round 61 en route to runner-up finish in 1991 Greater Milwaukee Open...also had solo second in 1991 Buick Southern Open and T2 in 1992 Federal Express St. Jude Classic...1989 Fred Haskins and Jack Nicklaus Award winner as collegiate player of year...winner 1989 Porter Cup...member 1989 Walker Cup team.

PERSONAL: Host to annual charity tournament each February in Las Vegas...event benefits Robert Gamez Foundation, managed by brother Randy, who carried bag in both wins.

CAREER SUMMARY — **PLAYOFF RECORD: 0-1**

Year	Events Played	Cuts Made	1st	2nd	3rd	Top 10	Top 25	Earnings	Rank
1988(Am.)	1	1							
1989	3	1					1	$4,827	237
1990	25	16	2			2	6	$461,407	27
1991	27	13		2		3	7	$280,349	59
1992	25	13		1		3	3	$215,648	72
1993	25	15		1		3	4	$236,458	70
1994	23	15		1		5	7	$380,353	44
1995	27	13				3	5	$206,588	89
Total	156	87	2	5		19	33	$1,785,629	113

1996 PGA TOUR CHARITY TEAM: Shell Houston Open

TOP TOURNAMENT SUMMARY

YEAR	90	91	92	93	94	95
Masters Tournament	CUT	CUT				
U.S. Open	T61	CUT		88	CUT	CUT
British Open Championship	T12	T44				
PGA Championship	T49		T79	CUT		CUT
THE PLAYERS Championship	T46	CUT	CUT	CUT	84	T49
THE TOUR Championship	30					

NATIONAL TEAMS: Walker Cup, 1989

1995 PGA TOUR STATISTICS

Scoring	71.58	(124T)
Driving	275.8	(11)
Driving Accuracy	67.7	(122T)
Greens in Regulation	63.8	(148T)
Putting	1.790	(95T)
All Around	739	(100)
Sand Saves	52.0	(98)
Total Driving	133	(25)
Eagles	5	(88T)
Birdies	304	(53)

MISCELLANEOUS STATISTICS

Scoring Avg Before Cut	71.35	(105T)
Scoring Avg 3rd Rnd	71.67	(130T)
Scoring Avg Final Rnd	72.57	(172)
Birdies Conversion %	32.3	(16T)
Par Breakers	20.9	(23T)

1995 Low Round: **65:** 1995 Kemper Open/1
Career Low Round: **61:** 1991 Milwaukee Open/1
Career Largest Paycheck: $162,000: 3 times, most recent 1990 Tucson Open/1

KELLY GIBSON

EXEMPT STATUS: 109th on 1995 money list
FULL NAME: Kelly Michael Gibson
HEIGHT: 5'10" **WEIGHT:** 175
BIRTH DATE: May 2, 1964 **BIRTHPLACE:** New Orleans, LA
RESIDENCE: New Orleans, LA
FAMILY: Single
COLLEGE: Lamar University
SPECIAL INTERESTS: New Orleans Saints Football
TURNED PROFESSIONAL: 1986 **Q SCHOOL:** 1991, 1994

BEST TOUR CAREER FINISH: T4 -- 1992 Buick Southern Open

NIKE TOUR VICTORIES (1): 1991 Tri-Cities Open

BEST 1995 FINISH: T7 -- Bob Hope Chrysler Classic

1995 SEASON: After suffering through a stretch when he made just three of 13 cuts, came back to cash in eight of final nine and earn playing privileges for 1996...early season highlighted by lone top-10 finish of year -- T7 at Bob Hope Chrysler Classic...was only two back after first-round 65, but fell back with 71 the next day...closing 67-67-69 worth $34,920...recovered from opening 74 to finish T13 in MCI Classic...from final week of April through mid-July, managed only T61 at Kemper in nine starts...rebounded with T11 at Anheuser- Busch and T20 at Deposit Guaranty...began end-of-the-year comeback with 23rd at Sprint International and sealed return trip to TOUR with T15 at Las Vegas Invitational...was only one stroke behind leader Bob Tway through 36 holes, but third-round 74 dropped him to T31...65-69 finish earned $23,250 to push him safely into top 125...led TOUR in eagles with 16, one more than Paul Azinger, and fifth in driving distance at 280.2 yards.

CAREER HIGHLIGHTS: Best TOUR finish came in his rookie season at 1992 Buick Southern Open...part of five-way tie for lead after opening 67...closed with 72-71 in rain-shortened event to finish T4, four strokes behind Gary Hallberg...though without a top-10 in 1993, earned $148,003 to finish 110th on money list and retain his card...best finish came at Bob Hope Chrysler Classic, where he was within two strokes of lead after 54 holes before finishing T12...lost card after 1994 season despite largest career payday at Motorola Western Open...closing 67 moved him from T36 to T6, three strokes behind Nick Price...earned $41,700...finished 14th on 1991 Ben Hogan Tour money list with $50,097, including win at Ben Hogan Tri-Cities Open...four-year member of Canadian Tour...was third on its Order of Merit in 1991...led Canadian Tour in scoring average in 1991 (69.75).

PERSONAL: In addition to being an avid fan of the New Orleans Saints, supports all Louisiana State University teams.

PGA TOUR CAREER SUMMARY — **PLAYOFF RECORD: 0-0**

Year	Events Played	Cuts Made	1st	2nd	3rd	Top 10	Top 25	Earnings	Rank
1989	1	1						$502	298
1990	2								
1991	2	1						$2,140	288
1992	33	14				3	5	$137,984	105
1993	33	20					6	$148,003	110
1994	33	14				2	4	$134,841	129
1995	33	19				1	6	$173,425	109
Total	137	69				6	21	$596,896	234

NIKE TOUR SUMMARY

Year	Events Played	Cuts Made	1st	2nd	3rd	Top 10	Top 25	Earnings	Rank
1990	28	18		1		5	12	$33,550	26
1991	17	13	1	1		4	7	$50,098	14
1992	2								
Total	47	31	1	2		9	19	$83,648	
COMBINED TOTAL MONEY								$680,544	

1996 PGA TOUR CHARITY TEAM: Franklin Templeton Shark Shootout

TOP TOURNAMENT SUMMARY

YEAR	90	93	94
U.S. Open	CUT	CUT	
THE PLAYERS Championship		CUT	CUT

KELLY GIBSON...continued

1995 PGA TOUR STATISTICS		
Scoring	71.48	(116)
Driving	280.2	(5)
Driving Accuracy	61.8	(174T)
Greens in Regulation	65.8	(111T)
Putting	1.791	(99T)
All Around	606	(59)
Sand Saves	52.8	(89T)
Total Driving	179	(84)
Eagles	16	(1)
Birdies	361	(11T)

MISCELLANEOUS STATISTICS		
Scoring Avg Before Cut	71.41	(108T)
Scoring Avg 3rd Rnd	71.32	(106T)
Scoring Avg Final Rnd	71.61	(123)
Birdies Conversion %	30.2	(45T)
Par Breakers	20.7	(30T)

1995 Low Round: 65: 4 times, most recent 1995 Las Vegas Invitational/4
Career Low Round: 63: 1992 Chattanooga Classic/4
Career Largest Paycheck: $41,700: 1994 Motorola Western Open/T6

BILL GLASSON *(GLASS-n)*

EXEMPT STATUS: 1994 tournament winner
FULL NAME: William Lee Glasson, Jr.
HEIGHT: 5' 11" **WEIGHT:** 165
BIRTH DATE: April 29, 1960 **BIRTHPLACE:** Fresno, CA
RESIDENCE: Stillwater, OK
FAMILY: Wife, Courtney; Maxwell Alexander (9/30/88); Dakota Jade (2/26/92)
COLLEGE: Oral Roberts University (1982, Business)
SPECIAL INTERESTS: Flying own plane
TURNED PROFESSIONAL: 1983 **Q SCHOOL:** Fall 1983, 1984

TOUR VICTORIES (6): 1985 Kemper Open. **1988** B.C. Open, Centel Classic. **1989** Doral-Ryder Open. **1992** Kemper Open. **1994** Phoenix Open

BEST 1995 FINISHES: 3 -- Mercedes Championships; T4 -- United Airlines Hawaiian Open, U.S. Open; T5 -- Bell Canadian Open; T10 -- Las Vegas Invitational

1995 SEASON: Though without a victory in 1995, still had the third-best earnings year of his 12-year career...got off to quick start with a third and T4 in his first two events...a closing 67 at Mercedes Championships moved him from eighth to third, one stroke out of the Steve Elkington-Bruce Lietzke playoff...the following week, again finished well, with 68-66 on weekend at United Airlines Hawaiian Open to tie Paul Azinger for fourth...had two top-20 finishes in Florida --T17 at Doral and T20 at Nestle -- before missing next four cuts...ended that streak with T13 at Memorial and T16 at Kemper...was T5 after 36 holes at U.S. Open, before third-round 76 dropped him to T15...closing 69 moved him to T4, four strokes behind Corey Pavin...despite opening 77, recorded T13 at Motorola Western Open...another strong weekend performance at Bell Canadian Open...T21 through 36 holes, moved to T7 after third-round 68 and T5 with closing 70...same scenario at Las Vegas Invitational, where he was T58 after 54 holes, then closed 65-65 for T10 and his final top-10 finish of 1995...ranked sixth on TOUR in total driving (51st in driving distance and 31st in driving accuracy for 82).

CAREER HIGHLIGHTS: Sat out most of 1991 season due to lower back problems...almost filed for permanent disability, but trouble corrected via injections...sixth TOUR title came at 1994 Phoenix Open, where he made up two-stroke deficit after 54 holes with closing 64...held second- and third-round lead at 1994 TOUR Championship before finishing T4...started 1992 under special medical extension, later that season ended 38-month winless skein by capturing second Kemper Open title...first TOUR victory came at 1985 Kemper, when he sank a 40-foot birdie putt on final hole to defeat Larry Mize and Corey Pavin by one stroke...two-time winner in 1988, collecting titles at B.C. Open and Centel Classic...one-stroke victory over Fred Couples in 1989 Doral-Ryder Open produced biggest paycheck, $234,000...led TOUR in Driving Distance (276.5 yards per drive) in rookie season...two-time All-American selection at Oral Roberts.

PERSONAL: Possesses one of the lengthiest medical histories on TOUR, including elbow surgery, four sinus operations, four knee surgeries and lip surgery...flies own plane to many TOUR stops...teacher Ken Cayce was head pro at Congressional, site of first Kemper win.

BILL GLASSON...*continued*

CAREER SUMMARY — **PLAYOFF RECORD: 0-0**

Year	Events Played	Cuts Made	1st	2nd	3rd	Top 10	Top 25	Earnings	Rank
1984	19	6					3	$17,845	162
1985	28	20	1		1	4	6	$195,449	29
1986	28	24				3	8	$121,516	72
1987	29	19		2	1	4	6	$151,701	69
1988	28	19	2	1		6	11	$380,651	30
1989	23	19	1		1	5	9	$474,511	19
1990	23	11				4	6	$156,791	100
1991	11	5					1	$46,995	178
1992	19	11	1			2	4	$283,765	54
1993	22	16			1	6	10	$299,799	57
1994	21	16	1		1	7	14	$689,110	17
1995	22	15			1	5	11	$412,094	43
Total	273	181	6	3	6	46	89	$3,230,227	54

1996 PGA TOUR CHARITY TEAM: B.C. Open

TOP TOURNAMENT SUMMARY

YEAR	84	85	86	87	88	89	90	91	93	94	95
Masters Tournament			T25			CUT	T33		CUT	T18	CUT
U.S. Open	T25	T39	T53	CUT		T21	T51		CUT		T4
British Open Championship							CUT				T24
PGA Championship		T54	CUT		W/D		W/D			T19	CUT
THE PLAYERS Championship		CUT	CUT	T7	CUT	W/D	T24	T41	CUT	CUT	CUT
THE TOUR Championship						29				T4	

1995 PGA TOUR STATISTICS

Scoring	70.45	(38)
Driving	268.4	(51)
Driving Accuracy	73.9	(31T)
Greens in Regulation	67.1	(64T)
Putting	1.760	(23T)
All Around	423	(16T)
Sand Saves	52.3	(94)
Total Driving	82	(6)
Eagles	9	(20T)
Birdies	271	(102T)

MISCELLANEOUS STATISTICS

Scoring Avg Before Cut	71.05	(72)
Scoring Avg 3rd Rnd	70.73	(64T)
Scoring Avg Final Rnd	69.64	(6)
Birdies Conversion %	32.5	(13T)
Par Breakers	21.3	(14)

1995 Low Round: 65: 2 times, most recent 1995 Las Vegas Invitational/5
Career Low Round: 62: 1985 Panasonic Las Vegas/1
Career Largest Paycheck: $234,000: 1989 Doral Ryder Open/1

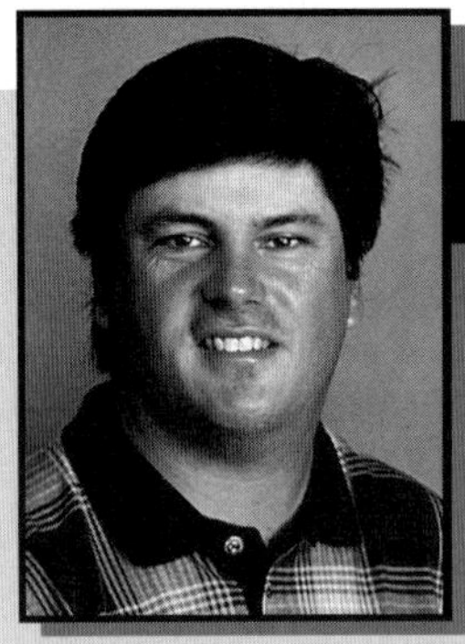

PAUL GOYDOS *(GOY-dose)*

EXEMPT STATUS: 129th on 1995 money list
FULL NAME: Paul David Goydos
HEIGHT: 5' 9" **WEIGHT:** 190
BIRTH DATE: June 20, 1964 **BIRTHPLACE:** Long Beach, CA
RESIDENCE: Long Beach, CA; plays out of Virginia CC, Long Beach, CA
FAMILY: Wife, Wendy; Chelsea (8/21/90), Courtney (9/8/92)
COLLEGE: Long Beach State University
SPECIAL INTERESTS: Sports
TURNED PROFESSIONAL: 1989 **Q SCHOOL:** 1992, 1993

BEST TOUR CAREER FINISH: T7 -- 1994 B.C. Open

NIKE TOUR VICTORIES (1): 1992 Ben Hogan Yuma Open

BEST 1995 FINISH: T15 -- Las Vegas Invitational

PAUL GOYDOS...continued

1995 SEASON: By earning $33,462 in last two tournaments, Paul retained his card for 1996 despite not recording a top-10 finish...made first three cuts of 1995 -- with best finish a T32 at Northern Telecom Open -- then missed five of next six...broke string with a T26 at Nestle Invitational...after T24 at MCI Classic, forced to withdraw from Kmart GGO with chicken pox ...after an opening 76, shot 66-68-69 for T21 at Kemper...first top-20 was T18 at Anheuser-Busch, which included third-round 65...tied for second after opening 65 at Buick Open, but fell to T40...after opening with 72 at Las Vegas, finished 65-68-66-68 for T15 and biggest check of year, $23,250...in final event, LaCantera Texas Open, closing 71 moved him from T33 to T22, worth $10,212...his 35 tournaments played was most on TOUR along with Ted Tryba and Greg Kraft.

CAREER HIGHLIGHTS: Finished 75th on 1994 PGA TOUR money list, making 22 of 31 cuts with three top-10 finishes...best finish was T7 at B.C. Open...T13 in 1993 Qualifying Tournament...best finish of rookie season also T13, in 1993 Buick Open...No. 17 on 1992 Ben Hogan Tour money list with $61,104...winner 1992 Ben Hogan Yuma Open...finished 39th on 1991 Hogan list with $30,237...winner 1990 Long Beach Open...Pacific Coast Athletic Association All-Conference 1985-86.

PERSONAL: Frequent visitor to TOUR press rooms, which led to prominent role in best-selling book about the TOUR......former school teacher in Long Beach, CA, and a big Long Beach State fan...nickname is "Sunshine," a tongue-in-cheek label bestowed because of his ability to find something negative in the most positive performance.

PGA TOUR CAREER SUMMARY — **PLAYOFF RECORD: 0-0**

Year	Events Played	Cuts Made	1st	2nd	3rd	Top 10	Top 25	Earnings	Rank
1993	30	18					4	$87,804	152
1994	31	22				3	9	$241,107	75
1995	35	21					6	$146,423	129
Total	96	61				3	19	$475,334	262

NIKE TOUR CAREER SUMMARY

Year	Events Played	Cuts Made	1st	2nd	3rd	Top 10	Top 25	Earnings	Rank
1991	25	13		1		4	7	$30,237	39
1992	29	17	1		2	3	8	$61,104	17
1993	2	2						$615	246
Total	56	32	1	1	2	7	15	$91,955	42
COMBINED TOTAL MONEY								$567,289	

1996 PGA TOUR CHARITY TEAM: LaCantera Texas Open

TOP TOURNAMENT SUMMARY

YEAR	94	95
U.S. Open	T44	T62
THE PLAYERS Championship	T62	T49

1995 PGA TOUR STATISTICS

Scoring	71.19	(89T)
Driving	265.1	(79)
Driving Accuracy	71.7	(66T)
Greens in Regulation	66.5	(82T)
Putting	1.816	(169T)
All Around	795	(115T)
Sand Saves	42.6	(184)
Total Driving	145	(39T)
Eagles	4	(116T)
Birdies	366	(10)

MISCELLANEOUS STATISTICS

Scoring Avg Before Cut	71.15	(83T)
Scoring Avg 3rd Rnd	71.32	(106T)
Scoring Avg Final Rnd	71.75	(133T)
Birdies Conversion %	28.1	(119)
Par Breakers	18.9	(102T)

1995 Low Round: 65: 4 times, most recent 1995 Las Vegas Invitational/2
Career Low Round: 65: 2 times, most recent 1995 Las Vegas Invitational/2
Career Largest Paycheck: $31,200: 1994 United Airlines Hawaiian Open/T8

Wayne Grady

EXEMPT STATUS: Winner, 1990 PGA Championship
FULL NAME: Wayne Desmond Grady
HEIGHT: 5' 9" **WEIGHT:** 160
BIRTH DATE: July 26, 1957 **BIRTHPLACE:** Brisbane, Australia
RESIDENCE: Queensland, Australia; plays out of Royal Pines Resort
FAMILY: Wife, Lyn; Samantha (11/23/86)
SPECIAL INTERESTS: Cricket, fishing, all sports
TURNED PROFESSIONAL: 1978 **Q SCHOOL:** Fall 1984

TOUR VICTORIES (2): 1989 Manufacturers Hanover Westchester Classic. **1990** PGA Championship.

INTERNATIONAL VICTORIES (4): 1978 Westlakes Classic (Aus). **1984** German Open (Eur). **1988** Australian PGA Championship (Aus). **1991** Australian PGA Championship (Aus).

BEST 1995 FINISH: T21 -- Kemper Open

1995 SEASON: Earned $45,218 in 16 starts in 1995, his lowest total since joining the PGA TOUR in 1985...opened with 69 at the Masters, then shot 73-74-74 for T35...best finish of year came at Kemper Open...was only one stroke out of lead after an opening 66, his low round of 1995... with a second-round 69, was just four back...third-round 75 dropped him from contention...only other top-25 finish came at Buick Open, where he shot 67-73-67-71-- 278 for T24.

CAREER HIGHLIGHTS: Biggest victory of career came in 1990 PGA Championship at Shoal Creek...was never headed after second-round 67...closed 72-71 for 282 total and three-stroke win over Fred Couples...first TOUR victory came in 1989 Manufacturers Hanover-Westchester Classic...finished at 7-under-par 277, then defeated Ronnie Black with birdie on first hole of their playoff...playoff loser (along with Greg Norman) to Mark Calcavecchia in 1989 British Open... first played Asian Tour with limited success, then started playing in Europe in 1983...won 1984 German Open...qualified for PGA TOUR by finishing sixth in 1984 Qualifying Tournament...winner 1988 and 1991 Australian PGA Championships...member of 1978-83-89 Australian World Cup teams...played for Australia in 1989-90 Dunhill Cups and Four Tours World Championship of Golf.

PERSONAL: As youngster, dreamed about someday becoming pilot in Australian Air Force...turned professional at 16, then regained amateur status...turned pro again at 21...worked for several years under Charley Earp at Royal Queensland (Earp also worked with Greg Norman).

CAREER SUMMARY — **PLAYOFF RECORD: 1-0**

Year	Events Played	Cuts Made	1st	2nd	3rd	Top 10	Top 25	Earnings	Rank
1984	9	3						$2,457	217
1985	30	26		1		4	11	$167,497	41
1986	32	14				1	5	$49,417	137
1987	16	11		1		2	3	$73,552	122
1988	22	12				3	6	$111,536	102
1989	26	16	1			4	10	$402,364	27
1990	22	19	1			5	10	$527,185	21
1991	19	13				3	4	$126,650	118
1992	21	14				1	9	$183,361	83
1993	20	8					1	$45,959	187
1994	19	10				1	4	$120,901	140
1995	16	8					2	$45,218	210
Total	252	154	2	2		24	65	$1,856,096	105

1996 PGA TOUR CHARITY TEAM: Las Vegas Invitational

TOP TOURNAMENT SUMMARY

YEAR	79	83	84	85	86	87	88	89	90	91	92	93	94	95
Masters Tournament									T27	CUT	T13	CUT	T41	T35
U.S. Open			CUT			T43	CUT	CUT	CUT	T63	T17	T81	CUT	CUT
British Open Championship	CUT	CUT	CUT			T17	T38	T2	CUT	T26	T39	T9	T60	CUT
PGA Championship					T21		CUT	T46	1	T43	CUT	CUT	T30	CUT
THE PLAYERS Championship				CUT	CUT		CUT	CUT	T29	CUT	T29	CUT	T45	CUT
THE TOUR Championship								T22	9					

WAYNE GRADY...continued

NATIONAL TEAMS: Australian World Cup (3) 1978, 1983, 1989; Australian Nissan Cup, 1985; Australian Four Tours World Championship of Golf (2), 1989, 1990. Dunhill Cup (2), 1989,1990.

1995 PGA TOUR STATISTICS		
Scoring	72.08	(N/A)
Driving	251.7	(N/A)
Driving Accuracy	71.7	(N/A)
Greens in Regulation	62.5	(N/A)
Putting	1.806	(N/A)
Sand Saves	73.0	(N/A)
Total Driving	1,998	(N/A)
Eagles	1	(N/A)
Birdies	135	(N/A)

MISCELLANEOUS STATISTICS		
Scoring Avg Before Cut	71.81	(N/A)
Scoring Avg 3rd Rnd	72.50	(N/A)
Scoring Avg Final Rnd	72.43	(N/A)
Birdies Conversion %	26.4	(N/A)
Par Breakers	15.9	(N/A)

1995 Low Round: **65:** 1995 Northern Telecom Open/2
Career Low Round: **63:** 1991 Hardee's Golf Cl/2
Career Largest Paycheck: $225,000: 1990 PGA Championship/1

KEN GREEN

EXEMPT STATUS: 108th on 1995 money list
FULL NAME: Kenneth J. Green
HEIGHT: 5' 10" **WEIGHT:** 175
BIRTH DATE: July 23, 1958 **BIRTHPLACE:** Danbury, CT
RESIDENCE: West Palm Beach, FL; plays out of Breakers West
FAMILY: Kenny (12/19/81), Hunter (9/30/88)
COLLEGE: Palm Beach JC
SPECIAL INTERESTS: Bowling, platform tennis
TURNED PROFESSIONAL: 1979 **Q SCHOOL:** Fall 1981, 1982, 1984

TOUR VICTORIES (5): 1985 Buick Open. **1986** The International. **1988** Canadian Open, Greater Milwaukee Open. **1989** Kmart Greater Greensboro Open.

INTERNATIONAL VICTORIES (2): 1988 Dunlop Phoenix (Jpn). **1990** Martell Hong Kong Open (Asia).

BEST 1995 FINISH: T2 -- FedEx St. Jude Classic

1995 SEASON: Wielding son Hunter's 26-inch putter, Ken nearly broke his six-year winless stretch at FedEx St. Jude Classic...moved into contention in the third round by shooting 65, his year's best...despite being seven strokes behind with 11 to play on Sunday, came back to tie Jay Delsing, just one stroke behind winner Jim Gallagher, Jr....made first cut of 1995 in his sixth start, THE PLAYERS Championship, finishing T61...was one of 10 players one stroke off the lead through 18 holes at Ideon Classic, but a shoulder injury in the final round caused him to withdraw...only other top-25 finish of year came in his final event...T22 at LaCantera Texas Open.

CAREER HIGHLIGHTS: Has captured five titles since joining TOUR in 1982...first victory came in 1985 Buick Open, where posted 20-under-par 268 to win by four strokes...repeated at inaugural International in 1986...turned discouraging 1988 campaign around by winning Canadian Open and Greater Milwaukee Open back-to-back...second-day 65 helped set up Glen Abbey win, while used third-round Tuckaway CC course-record 61 as springboard to easy GMO victory...earlier in '88 campaign three-putted final hole to drop into playoff with Sandy Lyle in Kmart Greater Greensboro Open, which he lost...made up for that loss by winning 1989 Kmart GGO...lost (along with Greg Norman and David Frost) playoff to Seve Ballesteros in '89 Manufacturers Hanover-Westchester Classic...three-putted final hole in 1989 Pensacola Classic to finish second...winner 1985 and 1992 Connecticut Opens...winner 1988 Dunlop Phoenix (Japan) and 1990 Hong Kong Open...member 1989 Ryder Cup team.

PERSONAL: Started playing golf at age 12 in Honduras, where father was principal of the American School–and only sports choices were golf or soccer...once described by Johnny Miller as best fairway wood player in the game.

CAREER SUMMARY **PLAYOFF RECORD: 0-2**

Year	Events Played	Cuts Made	1st	2nd	3rd	Top 10	Top 25	Earnings	Rank
1982	22	7					1	$11,899	170
1983	33	19				1	4	$40,263	114
1984	34	12				1	2	$20,160	156

continued on page 94

KEN GREEN...continued

Year	Events Played	Cuts Made	1st	2nd	3rd	Top 10	Top 25	Earnings	Rank
1985	30	24	1			2	6	$151,355	52
1986	30	19	1		1	3	7	$317,835	16
1987	26	23		1		4	9	$273,271	36
1988	29	21	2	3	1	10	15	$779,181	4
1989	27	16	1			1	6	$304,754	37
1990	25	20				5	7	$267,172	54
1991	29	19			1	5	8	$263,034	65
1992	26	18		2		5	9	$360,397	41
1993	22	10			1	3	6	$229,750	75
1994	28	18				2	5	$155,156	116
1995	23	13		1		1	2	$173,577	108
Total	384	239	5	7	4	43	87	$3,347,802	49

1996 PGA TOUR CHARITY TEAM: BellSouth Classic

TOP TOURNAMENT SUMMARY

YEAR	82	83	84	85	86	87	88	89	90	91	92	93	94	95
Masters Tournament					44	CUT		T11	CUT	T35				
U.S. Open	CUT	T26	CUT	T61	W/D	T31	T32	T46		W/D	CUT		CUT	
British Open Championship						T29		T61	CUT					T49
PGA Championship					T26	CUT	CUT	W/D		T16	W/D	W/D		
THE PLAYERS Championship			CUT		T33	T24	CUT	T21	T5	T27	DQ	T6	CUT	T61
THE TOUR Championship							T3							

NATIONAL TEAMS: Ryder Cup, 1989; Four Tours World Championship of Golf, 1989

1995 PGA TOUR STATISTICS		
Scoring	71.66	(132T)
Driving	258.0	(136)
Driving Accuracy	68.2	(113T)
Greens in Regulation	64.4	(136T)
Putting	1.807	(145T)
All Around	925	(142)
Sand Saves	58.2	(26)
Total Driving	249	(163)
Eagles	6	(69T)
Birdies	201	(168T)

MISCELLANEOUS STATISTICS		
Scoring Avg Before Cut	71.48	(116T)
Scoring Avg 3rd Rnd	71.00	(80T)
Scoring Avg Final Rnd	71.67	(125T)
Birdies Conversion %	27.6	(127T)
Par Breakers	17.2	(161T)

1995 Low Round: **65:** 1995 FedEx St. Jude Classic/3
Career Low Round: **61:** 1988 Milwaukee Open/3
Career Largest Paycheck: $180,000: 2 times, most recent 1986 The International/1

SCOTT GUMP

EXEMPT STATUS: 99th on 1995 money list
FULL NAME: Scott Edward Gump
HEIGHT: 6'2" **WEIGHT:** 165
BIRTH DATE: December 17, 1965 **BIRTHPLACE:** Rockledge, FL
RESIDENCE: Orlando, FL
FAMILY: Wife, Chris
COLLEGE: University of Miami
SPECIAL INTERESTS: Whitewater rafting, music, movies
TURNED PROFESSIONAL: 1988 **Q SCHOOL:** 1990

BEST TOUR CAREER FINISH: T2 -- 1991 International

NIKE TOUR VICTORIES (2): **1994** NIKE Monterrey Open, NIKE Greater Greenville Classic

BEST 1995 FINISH: T10 -- Motorola Western Open

SCOTT GUMP...*continued*

1995 SEASON: Just one top-10 finish in 1995, but still finished 99th on money list with $184,828, his second-best year on TOUR...first of five top-25 finishes came at Honda Classic...even-par 284 at windswept Weston Hills enough for T13...T10 at Western Open first of four consecutive cuts made, longest streak of year...T37 after 54 holes, final-round 66 moved him to T10 worth $50,000, his biggest payday of year...two starts later, T22 at Ideon Classic...back-to-back top-15s in October completed year...67-68 on weekend key to T12 at Buick Challenge...second-round 64 at WDW/Oldsmobile Classic was low round of 1995 and moved him to within three of lead...finished T15 after closing 70.

CAREER HIGHLIGHTS: Enjoyed best PGA TOUR finish at 1991 International...posted five birdies and three bogeys on final day, earned seven points and tie for second behind Jose Maria Olazabal...that finish produced biggest paycheck of PGA TOUR career, $82,133...top finish on PGA TOUR money list was 80th in 1991, when he earned $207,809...first-year member of NIKE TOUR in 1990, earning $20,863 to finish 50th on that money list...that finish earned exemption into second stage of Q-School, where he earned first PGA TOUR card for 1991...after losing card in 1993, returned to NIKE TOUR and finished second on 1994 money list with $161,035...in 24 NIKE TOUR starts had nine top-10 finishes, including wins at Monterrey, Mexico and Greenville SC...also had one T2 and one T3.

PERSONAL: Received as much attention for his name as for his game the last two years after earning the nickname "Forrest"...dreading release of the movie sequel.

CAREER SUMMARY — **PLAYOFF RECORD: 0-0**

Year	Events Played	Cuts Made	1st	2nd	3rd	Top 10	Top 25	Earnings	Rank
1988(Am.)	1	1							
1988	1								
1989	1								
1991	29	18		1		2	7	$207,809	80
1992	33	24				1	5	$148,696	102
1993	31	17					4	$96,822	147
1994	3	2						$4,181	286
1995	29	19				1	5	$184,828	99
Total	128	81		1		4	21	$642,336	228

NIKE TOUR SUMMARY

Year	Events Played	Cuts Made	1st	2nd	3rd	Top 10	Top 25	Earnings	Rank
1990	29	22				3	8	$20,864	50
1991	3	2				1	1	$4,071	139
1994	24	21	2	1	1	9	16	$161,035	2
Total	56	45	2	1	1	13	25	$185,970	14
COMBINED TOTAL MONEY								$828,306	

1996 PGA TOUR CHARITY TEAM: Deposit Guaranty Golf Classic

TOP TOURNAMENT SUMMARY

YEAR	88	91	92	93
Masters Tournament	CUT			
U.S. Open		CUT	T51	
PGA Championship			T79	
THE PLAYERS Championship			66	CUT

1995 PGA TOUR STATISTICS

Scoring	71.06	(75)
Driving	259.7	(122T)
Driving Accuracy	76.9	(15)
Greens in Regulation	70.7	(6)
Putting	1.809	(150T)
All Around	540	(41)
Sand Saves	58.1	(27T)
Total Driving	137	(30T)
Eagles	5	(88T)
Birdies	302	(57T)

MISCELLANEOUS STATISTICS

Scoring Avg Before Cut	71.17	(88)
Scoring Avg 3rd Rnd	70.30	(36T)
Scoring Avg Final Rnd	71.78	(138)
Birdies Conversion %	25.5	(170T)
Par Breakers	18.3	(115T)

1995 Low Round: **64:** 1995 Walt Disney World/Oldsmobile Classic/2
Career Low Round: **64:** 2 times, most recent 1995 Walt Disney World/Oldsmobile Classic/2
Career Largest Paycheck: $82,133: 1991 The International/T2

JAY HAAS *(HAWES)*

EXEMPT STATUS: Member, 1995 Ryder Cup Team
FULL NAME: Jay Dean Haas
HEIGHT: 5' 10" **WEIGHT:** 180
BIRTH DATE: December 2, 1953 **BIRTHPLACE:** St. Louis, MO
RESIDENCE: Greenville, SC; plays out of Thornblade GC
FAMILY: Wife, Janice; Jay, Jr. (3/8/81), William Harlan (5/24/82), Winona Haley (1/18/84); Emily Frances (9/25/87), Georgia Ann (3/12/92)
COLLEGE: Wake Forest University **SPECIAL INTERESTS:** All sports
TURNED PROFESSIONAL: 1976 **Q SCHOOL:** Fall 1976

TOUR VICTORIES (9): 1978 Andy Williams-San Diego Open. **1981** Greater Milwaukee Open, B.C. Open. **1982** Hall of Fame Classic, Texas Open. **1987** Big "I" Houston Open. **1988** Bob Hope Chrysler Classic. **1992** Federal Express St. Jude Classic. **1993** H-E-B Texas Open.

INTERNATIONAL VICTORIES (1): 1991 Mexican Open.

BEST 1995 FINISHES: T2 -- Motorola Western Open; T3 -- Masters Tournament, Sprint International; T4 -- U.S. Open; T5 -- Nestle Invitational, Memorial Tournament, B.C. Open; T7 -- Nissan Open; 8 -- LaCantera Texas Open; T8 -- PGA Championship; T10 -- Greater Milwaukee Open

1995 SEASON: An exceptional year for the 19-year veteran, even without a victory...led the TOUR in top-10 finishes with 11 and had his best earnings year with $822,259...up-and-down start to the year with three top-10s and nine missed cuts in first 13 starts...after four missed cuts, a closing 67 led to T7 at Nissan Open...moved from T18 to T5 with final-round 68 at Nestle Invitational...third top-10 came at Masters Tournament, where second-round 64 gave him one-stroke lead...one stroke behind through 54 holes, closed with 70 to finish three strokes off lead...four missed cuts followed, then shot 66-65 on weekend at Memorial for T5...closing 69 good for T4 at U.S. Open...led after 36 holes at Motorola Western Open, finishing 73-70 for T2, one stroke behind Billy Mayfair...third top-10 in a major came at PGA, where third-round 64 moved him into top 10...closed with 70 for T8...PGA first of five consecutive top-10s...T3 at Sprint International, T10 at Greater Milwaukee Open, T5 at B.C. Open (with closing 64) and 8th at La Cantera Texas Open followed...played on second Ryder Cup Team, winning one of four matches.

CAREER HIGHLIGHTS: Defeated Bob Lohr with birdie on second extra hole to win playoff and capture 1993 H-E-B Texas Open, his ninth TOUR title...closed with consecutive 64s on the weekend to win 1992 FedEx St. Jude Classic...opened with 63 en route to victory in 1988 Bob Hope Chrysler Classic...won 1987 Big "I" Houston Open by making 70-foot putt on 72nd hole, then defeating Buddy Gardner in playoff...first-time winner at 1978 Andy Williams-San Diego Open...won twice in 1981 and 1982, capturing first Texas Open in 1982...captain's choice on 1994 U.S. Presidents Cup team, where his record was 3-2...winner 1976 Southwestern and Missouri Opens...winner 1991 Mexican Open...member 1983 and 1995 Ryder Cup teams...won 1975 NCAA Championship at Wake Forest...winner 1975 Fred Haskins Award as outstanding collegiate player...1975-76 All-American selection.

PERSONAL: Uncle, former Masters champion Bob Goalby, got him started in golf...won first trophy at National Pee Wee Championship in Orlando, FL at age seven...brother Jerry a past member of PGA TOUR...brother-in-law is TOUR member Dillard Pruitt.

CAREER SUMMARY **PLAYOFF RECORD: 3-0**

Year	Events Played	Cuts Made	1st	2nd	3rd	Top 10	Top 25	Earnings	Rank
1973(Am.)	1	1							
1974(Am.)	1	1							
1975(Am.)	1	1					1		
1976	3	3						$1,882	205
1977	30	18				2	5	$32,326	77
1978	29	20	1			4	9	$77,176	31
1979	28	20		1		7	12	$102,515	34
1980	30	26			1	7	14	$114,102	35
1981	30	25	2			6	13	$181,894	15
1982	29	27	2		1	10	15	$229,746	13
1983	28	25		2	1	8	15	$191,735	23
1984	27	20		1	1	3	12	$146,514	45
1985	29	20				3	7	$121,488	69
1986	29	17				7	12	$189,204	45
1987	29	24	1			5	10	$270,347	37
1988	29	22	1	1		6	12	$490,409	20
1989	30	17		2		5	8	$248,831	54
1990	28	17		1		1	5	$180,023	89
1991	29	18			1	3	8	$200,637	84
1992	28	24	1	1	1	6	16	$632,628	20
1993	29	27	1			6	15	$601,603	26
1994	30	25			1	5	14	$593,386	25
1995	27	18		1	2	11	14	$822,259	16
Total	554	416	9	10	9	105	217	$5,428,703	22

1996 PGA TOUR CHARITY TEAM: CVS Charity Classic

JAY HAAS...continued

TOP TOURNAMENT SUMMARY

YEAR	74	75	77	78	79	80	81	82	83	84	85	86	87	88	89
Masters Tournament				T47		T17	T31	44	T27	T21	5	T6	T7	CUT	T46
U.S. Open	T54	T18	T5			T25	CUT	T6	T43	T11	T15	CUT		T25	CUT
British Open Championship								T27	T19	T36			T35	T38	
PGA Championship				T58	T7	T50	T19	T5	T9	T39	T38	T53	T28	T38	CUT
THE PLAYERS Championship				T57	T9	T8	T29	T27	W/D	T29	T55	T7	T50	DQ	CUT
THE TOUR Championship														T14	

TOP TOURNAMENT SUMMARY (cont.)

YEAR	90	91	92	93	94	95
Masters Tournament				38	T5	T3
U.S. Open	CUT		T23	T77	CUT	T4
British Open Championship						T79
PGA Championship	CUT		T62	T20	14	T8
THE PLAYERS Championship	CUT	CUT	CUT	T20	T55	CUT
THE TOUR Championship			T7	T10	6	T20

NATIONAL TEAMS: Ryder Cup (2), 1983, 1995. Walker Cup, 1975. Presidents Cup, 1994.

1995 PGA TOUR STATISTICS

Scoring	70.18	(13)
Driving	262.5	(95T)
Driving Accuracy	72.1	(60T)
Greens in Regulation	66.8	(73T)
Putting	1.751	(7T)
All Around	398	(12)
Sand Saves	52.7	(91)
Total Driving	155	(50T)
Eagles	12	(5T)
Birdies	303	(54T)

MISCELLANEOUS STATISTICS

Scoring Avg Before Cut	71.06	(73)
Scoring Avg 3rd Rnd	69.28	(6)
Scoring Avg Final Rnd	69.82	(7T)
Birdies Conversion %	30.0	(50T)
Par Breakers	19.9	(62T)

1995 Low Round: **64:** 3 times, most recent 1995 B.C. Open/4
Career Low Round: **63:** 2 times, most recent 1990 Nissan LA Open/3
Career Largest Paycheck: **$198,000:** 1992 Fed Exp St. Jude/1

MIKE HEINEN *(HIGH-nen)*

EXEMPT STATUS: 1994 tournament winner
FULL NAME: William Michael Heinen, Jr.
HEIGHT: 6' 1" **WEIGHT:** 195
BIRTH DATE: January 17, 1967 **BIRTHPLACE:** Rayne, LA
RESIDENCE: Lake Charles, LA
FAMILY: Wife, Kathy
COLLEGE: University of Southwestern Louisiana
SPECIAL INTERESTS: Hunting, fishing
TURNED PROFESSIONAL: 1989 **Q SCHOOL:** 1993

TOUR VICTORIES (1): **1994** Shell Houston Open

BEST 1995 FINISHES: 2 -- Freeport-McMoRan Classic; T2 -- GTE Byron Nelson Classic; T7 -- Walt Disney World/Oldsmobile Classic

1995 SEASON: No sign of a sophomore jinx as Mike put together another solid season and nearly returned to the winner's circle...after managing no better than a T24 at Mercedes Championships in his first nine starts, returned to his home state for Freeport-McMoRan Classic...two back after opening 66, two 71s dropped him to T11 after 54 holes...closing 66, despite double-bogey 6 on 18th, forced playoff with Davis Love III, which Love won with birdie on second extra hole...four starts later, recorded second runner-

MIKE HEINEN...*continued*

up finish, this time at GTE Byron Nelson Classic...shot 67-66-67-66 to tie D.A. Weibring and Robin Freeman, three strokes behind Ernie Els...summer-long slump followed as he missed nine of 10 cuts from mid-May through mid-September...righted ship by making final five paydays, including T12 at Buick Challenge, with a course-record final-round 63, and T7 at WDW/Oldsmobile Classic, where he opened with 65.

CAREER HIGHLIGHTS: Won in just his 10th TOUR start, a three-stroke victory over Tom Kite, Jeff Maggert and Hal Sutton at 1994 Shell Houston Open...shared lead with Maggert and Kite through 54, but closing 68 earned title...second to only Ernie Els in rookie earnings with $390,963...finished T26 in 1993 Qualifying Tournament...placed 16th on 1993 NIKE TOUR money list with $71,706...finished second to Dave Stockton, Jr. in 1993 NIKE Hawkeye Open...played Canadian Tour before the NIKE TOUR...two-time NCAA Division I All-American at Southwestern Louisiana.

PERSONAL: Hal Sutton was his golf idol while growing up in Louisiana.

CAREER SUMMARY — **PLAYOFF RECORD: 0-1**

Year	Events Played	Cuts Made	1st	2nd	3rd	Top 10	Top 25	Earnings	Rank
1991	1								
1994	27	12	1			3	5	$390,963	40
1995	29	16		2		3	6	$350,920	52
Total	57	28	1	2		6	11	$741,883	212

NIKE TOUR SUMMARY

Year	Events Played	Cuts Made	1st	2nd	3rd	Top 10	Top 25	Earnings	Rank
1990	1								
1992	3	1						$888	242
1993	29	17		1		7	11	$71,706	16
1994	1								
Total	34	18		1		7	11	$72,593	
COMBINED TOTAL MONEY								$814,477	

1996 PGA TOUR CHARITY TEAM: Kmart Greater Greensboro Open

TOP TOURNAMENT SUMMARY

YEAR	94	95
Masters Tournament		CUT
U.S. Open		CUT
PGA Championship	CUT	CUT
THE PLAYERS Championship		T37

1995 PGA TOUR STATISTICS

Scoring	71.13	(82T)
Driving	272.4	(26)
Driving Accuracy	65.8	(145T)
Greens in Regulation	67.4	(59T)
Putting	1.784	(79T)
All Around	628	(66)
Sand Saves	45.7	(166T)
Total Driving	171	(73T)
Eagles	9	(20T)
Birdies	305	(51T)

MISCELLANEOUS STATISTICS

Scoring Avg Before Cut	71.36	(107)
Scoring Avg 3rd Rnd	71.06	(85)
Scoring Avg Final Rnd	70.69	(39T)
Birdies Conversion %	28.9	(84T)
Par Breakers	20.1	(53T)

1995 Low Round: **63:** 1995 Buick Challenge/4
Career Low Round: **63:** 1995 Buick Challenge/4
Career Largest Paycheck: **$234,000:** 1994 Shell Houston Open/1

NOLAN HENKE *(HEN-key)*

EXEMPT STATUS: 78th on 1995 money list
FULL NAME: Nolan Jay Henke
HEIGHT: 6' **WEIGHT:** 165
BIRTH DATE: November 25, 1964 **BIRTHPLACE:** Battle Creek, MI
RESIDENCE: Fort Myers, FL; plays out of Vines CC
FAMILY: Single
COLLEGE: Florida State University
SPECIAL INTERESTS: Jet ski, tennis
TURNED PROFESSIONAL: 1987 **Q SCHOOL:** Fall 1988, 1989.

TOUR VICTORIES (3): 1990 B.C. Open. **1991** Phoenix Open. **1993** BellSouth Classic.

BEST 1995 FINISHES: T2 -- MCI Classic; T8 -- Buick Invitational of California

1995 SEASON: Uneven year for Nolan, who nearly reached winner's circle at MCI Classic, yet recorded second-lowest earnings of seven-year career...shared lead at Harbour Town after opening 66 but, after second-round 72, was six back...was T16 but just three off lead through 54 holes...final-round 67 forced playoff with Bob Tway and David Frost...after he and Tway parred the first extra hole, eliminating Frost, Tway won with par at the second...was only two strokes off lead through 36 at Buick Invitational of California before third-round 73 dropped him to T10...finished T8 after closing 69...after MCI, made 12 of next 15 cuts, with best finishes coming at Greater Milwaukee Open (T17) and PGA Championship (T23)...missed final four cuts.

CAREER HIGHLIGHTS: Final-round 67 brought victory in 1993 BellSouth Classic, a two-stroke win over Nick Price, Tom Sieckmann and Mark Calcavecchia...entered final round four strokes behind Price, left it with biggest check ($216,000) of career...had best finish of 1994 in defense of BellSouth title...eagled 72nd hole to tie Brian Henninger, one stroke behind John Daly...had pair of solid performances in '93 majors, T7 in U.S. Open and T6 at PGA Championship...was 7-under-par for the weekend in PGA at Inverness...first TOUR win came in 1990 B.C. Open, where he defeated Mark Wiebe by three strokes...second-round 64 keyed En-Joie GC win...enjoyed winning experience so much, staged repeat at 1991 Phoenix Open...although led by four strokes at start of Sunday's round, had to make 18-foot birdie putt on 72nd hole to clinch victory over formidable trio of Tom Watson, Curtis Strange and Gil Morgan at TPC of Scottsdale...outstanding collegiate golfer who won seven tournaments while at Florida State...first-team All-American in 1987...runnerup 1987 NCAA Championship...winner 1986 Porter Cup, 1987 American Amateur, 1987 Monroe Invitational..

CAREER SUMMARY **PLAYOFF RECORD: 0-1**

Year	Events Played	Cuts Made	1st	2nd	3rd	Top 10	Top 25	Earnings	Rank
1986(AM.)	1	1							
1987	2	2					1	$9,072	208
1989	26	13				1	3	$57,465	159
1990	29	16	1			5	8	$294,592	48
1991	27	20	1		1	6	13	$518,811	28
1992	27	16		1	1	4	11	$326,387	45
1993	26	20	1			4	9	$502,375	31
1994	26	12		1		3	5	$278,419	70
1995	25	14		1		2	5	$237,141	78
Total	189	114	3	3	2	25	55	$2,224,261	87

1996 PGA TOUR CHARITY TEAM: Phoenix Open

TOP TOURNAMENT SUMMARY

YEAR	89	91	92	93	94	95
Masters Tournament		T53	T6	T27	CUT	
U.S. Open	T21	7	CUT	T7	CUT	
British Open Championship		T38				
PGA Championship		T57	CUT	T6	CUT	T23
THE PLAYERS Championship		CUT	CUT	T65	T9	T61
THE TOUR Championship		T5		T23		

NOLAN HENKE...continued

1995 PGA TOUR STATISTICS		
Scoring	71.82	(149T)
Driving	256.6	(146)
Driving Accuracy	71.2	(75)
Greens in Regulation	64.3	(138T)
Putting	1.788	(89T)
All Around	897	(134T)
Sand Saves	59.6	(17)
Total Driving	221	(142T)
Eagles	1	(174T)
Birdies	265	(109T)

MISCELLANEOUS STATISTICS		
Scoring Avg Before Cut	71.98	(158T)
Scoring Avg 3rd Rnd	70.44	(46T)
Scoring Avg Final Rnd	71.13	(82T)
Birdies Conversion %	28.3	(108T)
Par Breakers	18.2	(122T)

1995 Low Round: 66: 3 times, most recent 1995 Greater Milwaukee Open/2
Career Low Round: 63: 1992 Las Vegas Invitation/4
Career Largest Paycheck: $216,000: 1993 BellSouth Classic/1

BRIAN HENNINGER *(HEN-in-grr)*

EXEMPT STATUS: 1994 tournament winner
FULL NAME: Brian Hatfield Henninger
HEIGHT: 5' 8" **WEIGHT:** 155
BIRTH DATE: October 19, 1962 **BIRTHPLACE:** Sacramento, CA
RESIDENCE: Canby, OR; plays out of The Oregon GC
FAMILY: Wife, Catherine; Carlin (6/10/93), Hunter (11/18/95)
COLLEGE: University of Southern California (1987, Psychology)
SPECIAL INTERESTS: Hunting, fishing, and horses
TURNED PROFESSIONAL: 1987 **JOINED TOUR:** 1993

TOUR VICTORIES (1): 1994 Deposit Guaranty Golf Classic

NIKE TOUR VICTORIES (3): 1992 South Texas Open, Macon Open, Knoxville Open

BEST 1995 FINISHES: T5 -- Canon Greater Hartford Open; T10 -- Masters Tournament

1995 SEASON: An inconsistent year for the Oregon native, who made just 11 cuts in 28 starts...will be remembered for challenging for Masters title through 54 holes...rounds of 70-68-68 tied him for lead at Augusta with Ben Crenshaw, one stroke ahead of five others...chances of winning Masters Tournament in first appearance disappeared when he turned in 39 on final day and trailed Crenshaw by five...closing 76 left him T10, eight strokes behind...was just two strokes off lead through two rounds at Canon Greater Hartford Open...third-round 72 dropped him to T20, but closed with 65 to finish T5...low round of 1995 was second-round 64 at FedEx St. Jude Classic, but rounds of 74-64-74-66 left him T45...thereafter, made just one of eight cuts -- T64 at Las Vegas Invitational.

CAREER HIGHLIGHTS: Earned first TOUR victory at weather-plagued 1994 Deposit Guaranty Golf Classic...over first three days, shot 67-68 to share lead with Mike Sullivan...when Sunday's final round was cancelled, he and Sullivan played off for title...won with birdie on first extra hole...$128,000 check is career best...daring approach on 72nd hole of 1994 BellSouth Classic set up an eagle-3 and T2 finish... top finish of rookie season T4 in 1993 Sprint Western Open...two weeks later posted only other top-25 of first-year campaign, T19 at New England Classic...missed Top 125 by just two positions, since 125 actually went to 128 because of non-members and other factors...finished second to John Flannery on 1992 Ben Hogan Tour money list to earn PGA TOUR playing privileges for 1993...won $128,301 and three '92 Hogan Tour events: Texas Open, Macon Open, Knoxville Open...one of seven players to win three times in season on NIKE/Hogan Tour...89th on 1991 Hogan Tour money list with $10,877...posted record 25-under-par 263 in second stage of 1991 Qualifying Tournament...won 1989 Queen Mary Open...first on 1989 Golden State Order of Merit...won Pacific Coast Amateur.

PERSONAL: Outstanding prep tennis player who switched to golf as high school junior... reached state tennis semifinals as sophomore and junior...won Oregon high school AAAA golf title...made college golf team as walk-on...teammates included Sam Randolph and John Flannery.

PGA TOUR CAREER SUMMARY — **PLAYOFF RECORD: 1-0**

Year	Events Played	Cuts Made	1st	2nd	3rd	Top 10	Top 25	Earnings	Rank
1993	30	16				1	3	$112,811	130
1994	21	16	1	1		2	2	$294,075	63
1995	28	11				2	3	$166,730	114
Total	79	43	1	1		5	8	$573,616	237

BRIAN HENNINGER...continued

NIKE TOUR SUMMARY

Year	Events Played	Cuts Made	1st	2nd	3rd	Top 10	Top 25	Earnings	Rank
1990	2	2					1	$2,325	158
1991	27	10					5	$10,878	89
1992	28	15	3		1	7	11	$128,301	2
1994	4	2		1		1	1	$23,905	59
Total	61	29	3	1	1	8	18	$165,409	
COMBINED TOTAL MONEY								$739,025	

1996 PGA TOUR CHARITY TEAM: AT&T Pebble Beach National Pro-Am

TOP TOURNAMENT SUMMARY

YEAR	94	95
Masters Tournament		T10
PGA Championship	T75	CUT
THE PLAYERS Championship		CUT

1995 PGA TOUR STATISTICS

Scoring	72.06	(165)
Driving	265.5	(72T)
Driving Accuracy	69.9	(90)
Greens in Regulation	64.1	(144T)
Putting	1.804	(136T)
All Around	946	(148)
Sand Saves	47.0	(154)
Total Driving	162	(61)
Eagles	7	(51T)
Birdies	244	(134T)

MISCELLANEOUS STATISTICS

Scoring Avg Before Cut	72.24	(174)
Scoring Avg 3rd Rnd	71.00	(80T)
Scoring Avg Final Rnd	71.45	(110)
Birdies Conversion %	26.8	(143T)
Par Breakers	17.7	(144T)

1995 Low Round: 64: 1995 FedEx St. Jude Classic/2
Career Low Round: 64: 2 times, most recent 1995 FedEx St. Jude Classic/2
Career Largest Paycheck: $126,000: 1994 Deposit Guaranty Golf Classic/1

SCOTT HOCH *(HOKE)*

EXEMPT STATUS: 1995 tournament winner
FULL NAME: Scott Mabon Hoch
HEIGHT: 5' 11" **WEIGHT:** 170
BIRTH DATE: November 24, 1955 **BIRTHPLACE:** Raleigh, NC
RESIDENCE: Orlando, FL
FAMILY: Wife, Sally; Cameron (5/1/84), Katie (5/16/86)
COLLEGE: Wake Forest University (1978, BA in Communications)
SPECIAL INTERESTS: All sports
TURNED PROFESSIONAL: 1979 **Q SCHOOL:** Fall 1979

TOUR VICTORIES (6): 1980 Quad Cities Open. **1982** USF&G Classic. **1984** Lite Quad Cities Open. **1989** Las Vegas Invitational. **1994** Bob Hope Chrysler Classic. **1995** Greater Milwaukee Open

INTERNATIONAL VICTORIES (6): 1982 Pacific Masters (Jpn), Casio World Open (Jpn). **1986** Casio World Open (Jpn). **1990** Korean Open (Asia). **1991** Korean Open (Asia). **1995** Heineken Dutch Open (Eur).

BEST 1995 FINISHES: 1 -- Greater Milwaukee Open; 2 -- Shell Houston Open; T3 -- Anheuser-Busch Golf Classic; T5 -- Quad City Classic; T7 -- Masters Tournament, BellSouth Classic; T8 -- Buick Challenge; T10 -- Motorola Western Open

1995 SEASON: Although he wasn't quite able to match his earnings of 1994, another outstanding year for the 16-year TOUR veteran...his $792,643 total was second-highest of his career...collected eight top-10 finishes, including a win at Greater Milwaukee Open...hit his stride at Masters Tournament...one stroke off lead through 36 and 54 holes, finished T7, six back...after T20 at MCI Classic, held five-stroke lead after three rounds of Shell Houston Open, but shot 75 on Sunday and lost on the first playoff hole to Payne Stewart...shot a closing 65 the following week to finish T7 at BellSouth Classic...had consecutive top-10s again in July -- T10 at Motorola Western Open and T3 at Anheuser-Busch Golf Classic...after missing cut at PGA, had three consecutive top-10s...T12 after

Scott Hoch...*continued*

36 holes at Greater Milwaukee Open, finished 65-65 for sixth career victory by three strokes...finished 65-66 at rain-shortened Quad City Classic for T5...closing 67 at Buick Challenge moved him from T17 to T8...second to Jim Furyk in putting (1.737 putts per GIR)...ninth in birdies (371)...won Heineken Dutch Open, first American to do so since Payne Stewart in 1991.

CAREER HIGHLIGHTS: Win at 1994 Bob Hope Chrysler Classic highlighted best year on TOUR...also runner-up at NEC World Series of Golf on way to $804,559, 11th on money list...had arthroscopic surgery in Feb. 1992 to correct shoulder impingement...start of season delayed until May,...enjoyed top money-list finish in 1989, when won Las Vegas Invitational and placed No. 10...Las Vegas triumph came in playoff with Robert Wrenn, just three weeks after Masters Tournament playoff loss to Nick Faldo...first win came in first year on TOUR, 1980 Quad Cities Open, which he won again in 1984, two years after capturing 1982 USF&G Classic...won 1986 Vardon Trophy...winner 1986 Chrysler Team Championship (with Gary Hallberg)...runner-up 1978 U.S. Amateur...1977-78 All-America selection...member 1975 NCAA Championship team...winner 1977-78 ACC Tournament...winner 1977 Northeast Amateur, 1976-79 North Carolina Amateurs

PERSONAL: Donated $100,000 of Las Vegas Invitational winner's share to Arnold Palmer Children's Hospital in Orlando...son Cameron successfully treated elsewhere for rare bone infection in right leg, but he and wife Sally continue to be strong supporters of A-P Hospital...brother Buddy a professional golfer, father won All-American honors in baseball at Wake Forest...in first round of Bob Hope Chrysler Classic title defense in 1995, played with tournament host, President Clinton and former Presidents Bush and Ford.

CAREER SUMMARY — **PLAYOFF RECORD: 1-2**

Year	Events Played	Cuts Made	1st	2nd	3rd	Top 10	Top 25	Earnings	Rank
1979(Am.)	1	1							
1980	18	6	1			1	4	$45,600	77
1981	31	19				2	7	$49,606	87
1982	28	23	1	1		8	17	$193,862	16
1983	25	20			1	7	11	$144,605	37
1984	26	22	1	1	3	7	13	$224,345	27
1985	30	24		1	1	6	13	$186,020	35
1986	28	23		1	3	6	13	$222,077	36
1987	27	23			4	8	12	$391,747	20
1988	31	26				10	18	$397,599	26
1989	27	21	1	1	1	6	12	$670,680	10
1990	26	19			1	7	13	$333,978	40
1991	31	26		1	1	9	14	$520,038	27
1992	16	13					3	$84,798	146
1993	28	18			1	6	15	$403,742	37
1994	28	21	1	1	2	7	14	$804,559	11
1995	28	23	1	1	1	8	14	$792,643	18
Total	429	328	6	8	19	98	193	$5,465,898	19

1996 PGA TOUR CHARITY TEAM: Lincoln-Mercury Kapalua International

TOP TOURNAMENT SUMMARY

YEAR	79	80	81	82	83	84	85	86	87	88	89	90	91	92	93
Masters Tournament	T34		T37		T27		T53			CUT	2	T14	T35		
U.S. Open			CUT	W/D	T48		T34		T36	T21	T13	T8	6	CUT	T5
British Open Championship												CUT			
PGA Championship		CUT	CUT		T61	T48	T12	T41	T3	T25	T7	T49	T43	CUT	T6
THE PLAYERS Championship			T37	T13	CUT	T44	CUT	T14	T39	CUT	CUT	W/D	CUT		CUT
THE TOUR Championship									T12	28	T7		T21		

TOP TOURNAMENT SUMMARY (cont.)

YEAR	94	95
Masters Tournament	CUT	T7
U.S. Open	T13	T56
British Open Championship		T68
PGA Championship	CUT	CUT
THE PLAYERS Championship	CUT	W/D
THE TOUR Championship	T20	T27

NATIONAL TEAMS: World Amateur Team Championship, 1978. Walker Cup, 1979. Presidents Cup, 1994.

1995 PGA TOUR STATISTICS

Scoring	70.39	(35)
Driving	265.5	(72T)
Driving Accuracy	67.3	(127T)
Greens in Regulation	66.3	(93T)
Putting	1.737	(2)
All Around	452	(24)
Sand Saves	54.8	(63T)
Total Driving	199	(113T)
Eagles	7	(51T)
Birdies	371	(9)

MISCELLANEOUS STATISTICS

Scoring Avg Before Cut	70.39	(18)
Scoring Avg 3rd Rnd	70.22	(31T)
Scoring Avg Final Rnd	70.91	(66)
Birdies Conversion %	32.4	(15)
Par Breakers	21.0	(19T)

1995 Low Round: 64: 3 times, most recent 1995 Walt Disney World/Oldsmobile Classic/2
Career Low Round: 62: 1994 Bob Hope Chrysler Classic/2
Career Largest Paycheck: $225,000: 1989 Las Vegas Invit./1

MIKE HULBERT *(HULL-bert)*

EXEMPT STATUS: 61st on 1995 money list
FULL NAME: Michael Patrick Hulbert
HEIGHT: 6' **WEIGHT:** 175
BIRTH DATE: April 14, 1958 **BIRTHPLACE:** Elmira, NY
RESIDENCE: Orlando, FL; plays out of Bay Hill and Lake Nona
FAMILY: Wife, Teresa; Justin Michael (7/25/93)
COLLEGE: East Tennessee State University (1980, Business Management)
SPECIAL INTERESTS: Fishing, exercising
TURNED PROFESSIONAL: 1981 **Q SCHOOL:** Fall 1984; 1985

TOUR VICTORIES (3): 1986 Federal Express-St. Jude Classic. **1989** B.C. Open. **1991** Anheuser-Busch Golf Classic.

BEST 1995 FINISHES: T2 -- Buick Invitational of California; T7 -- Walt Disney World/Oldsmobile Classic; T9 -- Nissan Open

1995 SEASON: It is safe to say that, in his 11 years on TOUR, nothing Mike has done caused as much of a stir as when he began putting one-handed at the AT&T Pebble Beach National Pro-Am, a practice he continued through most of year, concluding at the Sprint International...had the third-best earnings year of his career and his best since 1991...began seeing positive results from change in putting almost immediately...moved into contention at Buick Invitational with second-round 65...closed with 70-68 for T2, four strokes behind Peter Jacobsen...in next start, at Nissan Open, finished T9...also T13 at Honda Classic as he made first eight cuts of 1995...after missing next four cuts, made seven in a row, including T18 at Buick Classic and T15 at Colonial National Invitation...streaky year continued with four more missed cuts...closed year making six of seven, beginning with consecutive T17s at Sprint International and Greater Milwaukee Open...final top 10 came at WDW/Oldsmobile Classic...shot 68-66-68 in rain-shortened event for T7.

CAREER HIGHLIGHTS: Last of three TOUR victories came in 1991 Anheuser-Busch Golf Classic...two-putted for par from 40 feet on first playoff hole to defeat Kenny Knox in near darkness...first win came in very first season, one-stroke victory over childhood friend Joey Sindelar in 1986 Federal Express St. Jude Classic...triumph in 1989 B.C. Open was special, since he grew up in Horseheads, NY, less than an hour from En-Joie GC...playoff victory over Bob Estes one of seven top-10 finishes in 1989, year which also included Canadian Open runner-up and earnings of $477,621...winner 1987 Chrysler Team Championship (with Bob Tway)...also won 1991 Ping Kapalua International in playoff with Davis Love III...1979-80 All-America selection at East Tennessee State.

PERSONAL: Avid fisherman who, when son Justin was born weighing 8 lb., 1/2 oz. in 1993, said he was "just perfect for mounting"...has been best friends with Joey Sindelar since age 9 in hometown of Horseheads, NY.

CAREER SUMMARY — **PLAYOFF RECORD: 2-0**

Year	Events Played	Cuts Made	1st	2nd	3rd	Top 10	Top 25	Earnings	Rank
1983	1								
1985	26	12					1	$18,368	161
1986	37	26	1	1	1	5	13	$276,687	21
1987	36	23		1	1	6	10	$204,375	49
1988	35	21				1	8	$127,752	94
1989	34	26	1	1		7	13	$477,621	18
1990	31	26				3	6	$216,002	67
1991	31	24	1	1		5	13	$551,750	24
1992	32	24				3	11	$279,577	55
1993	31	21					6	$193,833	89
1994	31	21			1	2	5	$221,007	84
1995	31	22		1		3	8	$311,055	61
Total	356	246	3	5	3	35	94	$2,878,027	60

1996 PGA TOUR CHARITY TEAM: Greater Milwaukee Open

TOP TOURNAMENT SUMMARY

YEAR	86	87	88	89	90	91	92	93	94	95
Masters Tournament		48			T45		T19	CUT		
U.S. Open	CUT	CUT	CUT		T29		T6	T62	CUT	T28
British Open Championship					T39					
PGA Championship	T7	CUT	CUT	T27	T49	T23	T28	T31		CUT
THE PLAYERS Championship	T58	T24	T16	T59	T61	CUT	CUT	T11	T35	CUT
THE TOUR Championship				T14		30				

MIKE HULBERT...*continued*

1995 PGA TOUR STATISTICS		
Scoring	70.68	(49T)
Driving	259.3	(125T)
Driving Accuracy	68.1	(118T)
Greens in Regulation	68.6	(33T)
Putting	1.797	(121T)
All Around	705	(86)
Sand Saves	51.1	(106T)
Total Driving	243	(161)
Eagles	3	(137T)
Birdies	355	(16)

MISCELLANEOUS STATISTICS		
Scoring Avg Before Cut	70.98	(68)
Scoring Avg 3rd Rnd	70.29	(34T)
Scoring Avg Final Rnd	70.76	(52T)
Birdies Conversion %	28.2	(113T)
Par Breakers	19.5	(80T)

1995 Low Round: 65: 1995 Buick Invitational of California/2
Career Low Round: 63: 2 times, most recent 1993 Southwestern Bell Colonial/4
Career Largest Paycheck: $180,000: 1991 Anheuser-Busch GC/1

JOHN HUSTON *(HOUSTON)*

EXEMPT STATUS: 1994 tournament winner
FULL NAME: Johnny Ray Huston
HEIGHT: 5' 10" **WEIGHT:** 155
BIRTH DATE: June 1, 1961 **BIRTHPLACE:** Mt. Vernon, IL
RESIDENCE: Palm Harbor, FL; plays out of Innisbrook Hilton Golf Resort
FAMILY: Wife, Suzanne; Jessica (11/9/87), Travis (3/29/93)
COLLEGE: Auburn University
SPECIAL INTERESTS: All sports
TURNED PROFESSIONAL: 1983 **Q SCHOOL:** Fall 1987

TOUR VICTORIES (3): 1990 Honda Classic.**1992** Walt Disney World/Oldsmobile Classic. **1994** Doral-Ryder Open

BEST 1995 FINISHES: T6 -- Motorola Western Open; T7 -- United Airlines Hawaiian Open; T8 -- Buick Invitational of California, Buick Challenge; T9 -- Mercedes Championships

1995 SEASON: An off-year for the eight-year veteran, who saw his earnings drop to their lowest level since 1989...year opened with promise as he posted three top-10s in first four starts...led after first, second and third rounds of Mercedes Championships before closing 77 dropped him to T9, four strokes back...T7 at United Airlines Hawaiian Open the following week, thanks to final-round 66...after missed cut at Phoenix, T8 at Buick Invitational of California...was one stroke off lead through 36 holes of Masters, opening 70-66...was two behind through 54 holes after a 72, closing 77 dropped him to T17...T11 at FedEx St. Jude Classic, then earned T6 at Motorola Western Open, only two strokes behind winner Billy Mayfair...final top-10 came at Buick Challenge, where he was two strokes off lead after an opening 67...finished T8 at 276, four strokes off Fred Funk's winning score.

CAREER HIGHLIGHTS: Certainly no surprise all victories have been in Florida...as young player, enjoyed great success on Florida mini-tours, winning 10 events...first TOUR win came in wind-swept 1990 Honda Classic, where held off strong Mark Calcavecchia challenge to win by two strokes...fired closing 62 to pass Mark O'Meara to win 1992 Walt Disney World/Oldsmobile Classic...Disney-winning 26-under-par 262 one stroke off all-time TOUR record for most strokes under par...third win and biggest TOUR payday came at 1994 Doral-Ryder Open...closing 66 turned four-stroke deficit into three-stroke victory worth $252,000...lost playoff to Jim McGovern at 1993 Shell Houston Open...finished '93 campaign with TOUR Championship T2, knotting Greg Norman, Scott Simpson and David Frost, one stroke behind Jim Gallagher, Jr...won 1988 JCPenney Classic (with Amy Benz)...medalist in 1987 Qualifying Tournament...won 1985 Florida Open.

PERSONAL: Says would be mini-tour professional if not a member of PGA TOUR...father first put golf club in his hands at age seven.

CAREER SUMMARY **PLAYOFF RECORD: 0-1**

Year	Events Played	Cuts Made	1st	2nd	3rd	Top 10	Top 25	Earnings	Rank
1987	1	1						$1,055	287
1988	31	17			1	2	6	$150,301	78
1989	29	14		1		2	5	$203,207	68
1990	25	16	1		1	3	7	$435,690	30
1991	27	23			1	5	13	$395,853	40

continued on page 105

JOHN HUSTON...continued

Year	Events Played	Cuts Made	1st	2nd	3rd	Top 10	Top 25	Earnings	Rank
1992	32	23	1		1	4	15	$515,453	26
1993	30	26		2		6	15	$681,441	15
1994	25	19	1		1	8	11	$731,499	16
1995	27	15				5	7	$294,574	64
Total	227	154	3	3	5	35	79	$3,409,073	46

1996 PGA TOUR CHARITY TEAM: Walt Disney World/Oldsmobile Classic

TOP TOURNAMENT SUMMARY

YEAR	88	89	90	91	92	93	94	95
Masters Tournament			T3	T29	T25	59	T10	T17
U.S. Open		CUT	T14	CUT		CUT	CUT	CUT
British Open Championship			CUT			T48	CUT	T31
PGA Championship		CUT	T57	T7	T18	T44	CUT	DQ
THE PLAYERS Championship	68	CUT		T15	T40	CUT	T35	CUT
THE TOUR Championship			T28		T13	T2	T10	

NATIONAL TEAM: Presidents Cup, 1994

1995 PGA TOUR STATISTICS

Scoring	71.20	(91T)
Driving	273.9	(20)
Driving Accuracy	66.7	(136T)
Greens in Regulation	64.0	(146)
Putting	1.758	(19T)
All Around	574	(49T)
Sand Saves	53.4	(79T)
Total Driving	156	(52T)
Eagles	9	(20T)
Birdies	298	(63T)

MISCELLANEOUS STATISTICS

Scoring Avg Before Cut	71.19	(89T)
Scoring Avg 3rd Rnd	71.00	(80T)
Scoring Avg Final Rnd	72.21	(163T)
Birdies Conversion %	33.6	(4)
Par Breakers	21.1	(18)

1995 Low Round: 65: 3 times, most recent 1995 Las Vegas Invitational/2
Career Low Round: 62: 1992 WDW/Oldsmobile Classic./4
Career Largest Paycheck: $252,000: 1994 Doral-Ryder Open/1

JOHN INMAN

EXEMPT STATUS: Special Medical Extension
FULL NAME: John Samuel Inman
HEIGHT: 5' 10"
WEIGHT: 155
BIRTH DATE: November 26, 1962
BIRTHPLACE: Greensboro, NC
RESIDENCE: Roswell, GA
FAMILY: Wife, Patti
COLLEGE: University of North Carolina
SPECIAL INTERESTS: Fishing, music
TURNED PROFESSIONAL: 1985
Q SCHOOL: Fall 1986, 1990

TOUR VICTORIES (2): 1987 Provident Classic.**1993** Buick Southern Open.

1995 SEASON: His 1995 ended almost before it began... a back injury diagnosed as two herniated disks sidelined John in January after only three starts...was granted a special medical extention for 22 events in 1996, in which he must earn $146,359...missed cut at United Airlines Hawaiian Open and Northern Telecom Open to start year, then withdrew from Phoenix Open.

CAREER HIGHLIGHTS: First TOUR victory came at 1987 Provident Classic... he shot 65-67-67-66--265 to defeat Rocco Mediate and Bill Glasson by one stroke...second victory at 1993 Buick Southern Open contributed to best year on TOUR, when he made $242,140...victory at Callaway Gardens came on second hole of a five-man sudden-death playoff which also included Bob Estes, Billy Andrade, Mark Brooks and Brad Bryant...shot 64 in third round to move into contention...closing 70 earned spot in playoff...also posted T10 at 1993 Kemper Open...had pair of top-10s in 1992 -- T6 at Freeport-McMoRan Classic and T7 at Chattanooga Classic...has four holes-in-one in 1990s, all with five-irons...winner 1984 NCAA Championship...winner of 1984 Fred Haskins Award as nation's outstanding collegiate golfer.

PERSONAL: Wife Patti is active in TOUR Wives Association...older brother Joe won 1976 Kemper Open and still plays on TOUR occasionally.

CAREER SUMMARY — **PLAYOFF RECORD: 1-0**

Year	Events Played	Cuts Made	1st	2nd	3rd	Top 10	Top 25	Earnings	Rank
1984(Am.)	1								
1985(Am.)	1	1							
1985	6	1						$844	260
1986	2								
1987	32	17	1			3	5	$148,386	72
1988	35	15					2	$66,305	137
1989	30	17				1	4	$99,378	126
1990	32	18					4	$85,289	143
1991	32	17					2	$84,501	145
1992	31	20				2	6	$173,828	87
1993	32	18	1			2	4	$242,140	69
1994	34	15					5	$117,356	144
1995	3								
Total	271	139	2			8	32	$1,018,027	180

NIKE TOUR SUMMARY

Year	Events Played	Cuts Made	1st	2nd	3rd	Top 10	Top 25	Earnings	Rank
1991	1								
Total	1								
COMBINED TOTAL MONEY:								$1,018,027	

TOP TOURNAMENT SUMMARY

YEAR	85	87	88	90	91	93	94
Masters Tournament	59				CUT		CUT
U.S. Open	CUT			T14	T53		
PGA Championship			T58				T66
THE PLAYERS Championship		T44	CUT	CUT		CUT	CUT

1995 PGA TOUR STATISTICS

Scoring	73.24	(N/A)
Driving	243.6	(N/A)
Driving Accuracy	58.6	(N/A)
Greens in Regulation	55.6	(N/A)
Putting	1.820	(N/A)
Sand Saves	66.7	(N/A)
Total Driving	1,998	(N/A)
Eagles		(N/A)
Birdies	14	(N/A)

MISCELLANEOUS STATISTICS

Scoring Avg Before Cut	73.80	(N/A)
Birdies Conversion %	28.0	(N/A)
Par Breakers	15.6	(N/A)

1995 Low Round: **68:** 1995 Northern Telecom Open/2
Career Low Round: **64:** 2 times, most recent 1994 MCI Heritage Golf Classic/2
Career Largest Paycheck: **$126,000:** 1993 Buick Southern Open/1

Did You Know?

John Inman entered 1995 with a string of four consecutive years (1991-1994) with a hole-in-one in a PGA TOUR event, the longest such string on TOUR. Inman missed most of 1995 with a back injury and was unable to extend his streak. The longest current string of years with a hole-in-one is three by Willie Wood.

HALE IRWIN

EXEMPT STATUS: Winner, 1990 U.S. Open
FULL NAME: Hale S. Irwin
HEIGHT: 6' **WEIGHT:** 180
BIRTH DATE: June 3, 1945 **BIRTHPLACE:** Joplin, MO
RESIDENCE: Frontenac, MO
FAMILY: Wife, Sally Stahlhuth; Becky (12/15/71), Steven (8/6/74)
COLLEGE: University of Colorado (1968, Marketing)
SPECIAL INTERESTS: Fishing, hunting, golf course design
TURNED PROFESSIONAL: 1968 **Q SCHOOL:** Spring 1968

TOUR VICTORIES (20): 1971 Heritage Classic. **1973** Heritage Classic. **1974** U. S. Open. **1975** Western Open, Atlanta Classic. **1976** Glen Campbell Los Angeles Open, Florida Citrus Open. **1977** Atlanta Classic, Hall of Fame Classic, San Antonio-Texas Open. **1979** U. S. Open. **1981** Hawaiian Open, Buick Open. **1982** Honda-Inverrary Classic. **1983** Memorial Tournament. **1984** Bing Crosby Pro-Am. **1985** Memorial Tournament. **1990** U.S. Open, Buick Classic. **1994** MCI Heritage Classic.

SENIOR PGA TOUR VICTORIES (2): 1995 Ameritech Senior Open, Vantage Championship

INTERNATIONAL VICTORIES (8): 1974 Piccadilly World Match Play Championship (Eur). **1975** Piccadilly World Match Play Championship (Eur). **1978** Australian PGA Championship (Aus). **1979** South African PGA Championship (Afr), World Cup (Ind.). **1981** Bridgestone Classic (Aus). **1982** Brazilian Open. **1986** Bahamas Classic.

BEST 1995 PGA TOUR FINISHES: T7 -- Phoenix Open, Doral-Ryder Open

1995 SEASON: Played 12 PGA TOUR events before turning 50 on June 3 and focusing his attention on the Senior TOUR...made his first nine cuts of the year, including two T7s...opened with 66-66 at Phoenix Open to share 36-hole lead with Ben Crenshaw...fell two strokes off pace after third-round 72, then closed with 69 for T7...also T7 at Doral-Ryder Open, three strokes behind Nick Faldo...shot par or better all four rounds at Masters to finish T14...only two PGA TOUR starts after birthday -- missed cut at U.S. Open, T54 at PGA...on Senior TOUR, collected two victories (Ameritech Senior Open and Vantage Championship) and 11 top-10s in 12 starts...finished 10th on Senior TOUR money-list with $799,175.

CAREER HIGHLIGHTS: One of only 32 players in PGA TOUR history with 20 or more career victories...owns three U.S. Open titles, last of which came in grueling 19-hole playoff with Mike Donald at Medinah in 1990...sank 45-foot putt on final hole to force playoff...by ending playoff with 10-foot birdie putt became, at age 45, oldest to win Open...followed that victory with another the very next week at Buick Classic...two wins combined to help produce career-best $838,249...other two Open victories came at Winged Foot in 1974 and Inverness in 1979...first of 20 career wins (and first of three at Harbour Town) came in 1971 Heritage Classic...repeated there two years later...also two-time winner of Atlanta Classic (1975-77) and Memorial Tournament (1983-85)...from early 1975 through 1978, played 86 tournaments without missing cut, third best streak in TOUR history...first United States Presidents Cup Captain in 1994...also played on the team, compiling a 2-1 match record, including a singles victory over Robert Allenby as U.S. defeated International Team 20-12.

PERSONAL: Unusual two-sport participant at University of Colorado: 1967 NCAA Champion in golf, also two-time All-Big Eight selection as football defensive back...holds annual golf event to benefit St. Louis Children's Hospital...on the tournament's 20th anniversary in 1995, hospital dedicated Hale Irwin Pediatric Cancer Center.

PGA TOUR CAREER SUMMARY **PLAYOFF RECORD: 4-5**

Year	Events Played	Cuts Made	1st	2nd	3rd	Top 10	Top 25	Earnings	Rank
1966(Am.)	1	1							
1967(Am.)	1	1							
1968	10	10					2	$9,093	117
1969	32	20				1	6	$18,571	88
1970	36	26		1		4	15	$46,870	49
1971	34	27	1	2	1	7	13	$99,473	13
1972	33	26		3	3	10	16	$111,539	13
1973	32	25	1	1	1	12	18	$130,388	7
1974	23	21	1	2		8	15	$152,529	7
1975	22	21	2	1	1	14	17	$205,380	4
1976	21	21	2	3	2	12	17	$252,719	3
1977	23	23	3	1	1	8	13	$221,456	4
1978	22	22		2	4	13	17	$191,666	7
1979	23	17	1		3	6	12	$154,169	19

continued on page 108

HALE IRWIN...continued

Year	Events Played	Cuts Made	1st	2nd	3rd	Top 10	Top 25	Earnings	Rank
1980	25	18			1	9	14	$109,810	38
1981	23	21	2	4	1	8	12	$276,499	7
1982	23	20	1	1		4	11	$173,719	19
1983	20	20	1			9	15	$232,567	13
1984	20	16	1			6	11	$183,384	31
1985	20	14	1			2	8	$195,007	31
1986	25	15				1	3	$59,983	128
1987	22	14				2	7	$100,825	96
1988	23	14		1		2	7	$164,996	72
1989	19	14			1	2	6	$150,977	93
1990	17	15	2	1	2	6	11	$838,249	6
1991	17	15		1	2	6	7	$422,652	33
1992	20	13				1	2	$98,208	131
1993	21	15				2	9	$252,686	65
1994	22	19	1	1	1	6	11	$814,436	10
1995	14	11				2	5	$190,961	95
Total	644	515	20	25	24	163	300	$5,845,024	15

SENIOR PGA TOUR CAREER SUMMARY

Year	Events Played	Cuts Made	1st	2nd	3rd	Top 10	Top 25	Earnings	Rank
1995	12		2	3		11	12	$799,175	10
Total	12		2	3		11	12	$799,175	70
COMBINED TOTAL MONEY								$6,644,199	

1996 PGA TOUR CHARITY TEAM: MCI Classic

TOP TOURNAMENT SUMMARY

YEAR	66	70	71	72	73	74	75	76	77	78	79	80	81	82	83
Masters Tournament			T13			T4	T4	T5	5	8	T23	CUT	T25	CUT	T6
U.S. Open	T61		T19	T36	T20	1	T3	T26	T41	T4	1	T8	T58	T39	T39
British Open Championship						T24	9	T32	T46	T24	6				T2
PGA Championship		T31	T22	T11	T9		T5	T34	T44	T12		T30	T16	T42	T14
THE PLAYERS Championship						T34	7	T17	T3	T42		T14	T51	T19	T49

TOP TOURNAMENT SUMMARY (cont.)

YEAR	84	85	86	87	88	89	90	91	92	93	94	95
Masters Tournament	T21	T36	CUT					T10	47	T27	T18	T14
U.S. Open	6	14	CUT	CUT	T17	T54	1	T11	T51	T62	T18	CUT
British Open Championship	T14						T53	T57	T19			
PGA Championship	T25	T32	T26		T38		T12	T73	T66	T6	T39	T54
THE PLAYERS Championship	T15	T5	CUT	T24	CUT	CUT	T5	T27	CUT	CUT	4	T55
THE TOUR Championship							T19				T22	

SENIOR PGA TOUR TOP TOURNAMENT SUMMARY

YEAR	95
US Senior Open	T5
FORD SENIORPLAYERS Championship	T10
Energizer SENIOR TOUR Championship	T8

NATIONAL TEAMS: World Cup (2), 1974, 1979 (won individual title in 1979). Ryder Cup (5), 1975, 1977, 1979, 1981, 1991. U.S. vs. Japan, 1983. Presidents Cup (playing captain), 1994.

1995 PGA TOUR STATISTICS

Scoring	**70.73**	**(N/A)**
Driving	**244.7**	**(N/A)**
Driving Accuracy	**80.0**	**(N/A)**
Greens in Regulation	**68.9**	**(N/A)**
Putting	**1.798**	**(N/A)**
Sand Saves	**46.3**	**(N/A)**
Total Driving		**(N/A)**
Eagles		**(N/A)**
Birdies	**163**	**(N/A)**

MISCELLANEOUS STATISTICS

Scoring Avg Before Cut	**70.66**	**(N/A)**
Scoring Avg 3rd Rnd	**71.45**	**(N/A)**
Scoring Avg Final Rnd	**71.10**	**(N/A)**
Birdies Conversion %	**26.8**	**(N/A)**
Par Breakers	**18.5**	**(N/A)**

1995 Low Round: **66:** 3 times, most recent 1995 GTE Byron Nelson Classic/1
Career Low Round: **61:** 1982 Southern Open/4
Career Largest Paycheck: **$225,000:** 1994 MCI Heritage Golf Classic/1

HALE IRWIN...*continued*

1995 SENIOR PGA TOUR STATISTICS

Scoring	68.85	(N/A)
Driving	253.8	(N/A)
Driving Accuracy	82.2	(N/A)
Greens in Regulation	78.1	(N/A)
Putting	1.730	(N/A)
Sand Saves	51.7	(N/A)
Total Driving		(N/A)
Eagles	2	(N/A)
Birdies	173	(N/A)

MISCELLANEOUS SENIOR STATISTICS

1995 Low Round: ---------- 63: 1995 Ameritech Senior Open/2
Career Low Round: --------- 63: 1995 Ameritech Senior Open/2
Career Largest Paycheck: - $225,000: 1995 Vantage Championship/1

PETER JACOBSEN

EXEMPT STATUS: 1995 tournament winner
FULL NAME: Peter Erling Jacobsen
HEIGHT: 6' 3" **WEIGHT:** 200
BIRTH DATE: March 4, 1954 **BIRTHPLACE:** Portland, OR
RESIDENCE: Portland, OR; plays out of Waikoloa Resort, HI
FAMILY: Wife, Jan; Amy (7/19/80), Kristen (2/23/82), Mickey (10/12/84)
COLLEGE: University of Oregon
SPECIAL INTERESTS: Music, antique car collection
TURNED PROFESSIONAL: 1976 **Q-SCHOOL:** Fall 1976

TOUR VICTORIES (6): 1980 Buick-Goodwrench Open. **1984** Colonial National Invitation, Sammy Davis, Jr.-Greater Hartford Open. **1990** Bob Hope Chrysler Classic. **1995** AT&T Pebble Beach National Pro-Am, Buick Invitational of California.

INTERNATIONAL VICTORIES (3): 1979 Western Australian Open (Aus). **1981** Johnnie Walker Cup (Spain). **1982** Johnnie Walker Cup (Spain).

BEST 1995 FINISHES: 1 -- AT&T Pebble Beach National Pro-Am, Buick Invitational of California; T2 -- Doral-Ryder Open, Kmart Greater Greensboro Open; 3 -- Nestle Invitational

1995 SEASON: With two victories and more than $1 million in earnings, easily the best season of his 19-year career...first player to win back-to-back tournaments on PGA TOUR since David Frost in 1993...win came 5 years, 15 days after previous victory (1990 Bob Hope)...T20 after two rounds at AT&T, moved into a tie for second after third-round 66...closing 65 gave him two-stroke victory ...one stroke off lead through 36 holes at Buick Invitational of California, took lead for good with third-round 68...finished with another 68 for four-stroke victory...passed on chance to win three in a row at Bob Hope Chrysler Classic to give wife Jan a 40th birthday party...after T35 at Nissan Open, shared lead with Greg Norman through 54 holes at Doral-Ryder Open, but closed with 73 to finish T2...fourth top-3 finish in five starts came at Nestle Invitational...shot 70-68-68-69 to finish third, three strokes behind Loren Roberts...final top-10 finish, another T2, came at Kmart Greater Greensboro Open...was in second after second and third rounds...even-par 72 on frigid Sunday left him T2 with Jeff Sluman behind Jim Gallagher, Jr....though without a top-10 the rest of the year, continued solid play... seven top-25 finishes in final 13 events...made 22 of 25 cuts on year...third in total driving (26th in distance, 50th in accuracy for total of 76) and 10th in scoring (70.03).

CAREER HIGHLIGHTS: Before 1995, last TOUR victory was one-stroke win over Scott Simpson in 1990 Bob Hope Chrysler Classic...earned pair of titles in 1984, when finished top 10 on money list for second time...defeated Payne Stewart in playoff for Colonial title, which he dedicated to his father, who had just undergone very serious surgery...later captured Sammy Davis, Jr.-Greater Hartford Open...came from six strokes back on final day to claim first win, 1980 Buick-Goodwrench Open...won Oregon Open and Northern California Open after turning professional in 1976...winner 1986 Fred Meyer Challenge (with Curtis Strange)...three-time All-American 1974-76...winner 1974 Pac-8 Conference title.

PETER JACOBSEN...*continued*

PERSONAL: Has own event management company, Peter Jacobsen Productions...founded "Jake Trout and the Flounders," musical group featuring Payne Stewart, Mark Lye and Larry Rinker which used to perform at TOUR events...Player Director TOUR Policy Board 1983-85, again 1990-92...devoted final chapter of his book, Buried Lies, to brother Paul, an AIDS victim.

CAREER SUMMARY — **PLAYOFF RECORD: 1-3**

Year	Events Played	Cuts Made	1st	2nd	3rd	Top 10	Top 25	Earnings	Rank
1977	22	9					3	$12,608	129
1978	27	14			1	2	4	$34,188	82
1979	33	22				2	6	$48,848	44
1980	28	23	1	1		5	12	$138,562	8
1981	23	17		1		3	7	$85,624	44
1982	24	23		2		7	10	$145,832	25
1983	26	22			1	5	12	$158,765	29
1984	23	20	2		1	6	12	$295,025	10
1985	21	16		2		7	13	$214,959	23
1986	23	17			1	1	5	$112,964	78
1987	25	19				1	5	$79,924	111
1988	25	19		3		6	11	$526,765	16
1989	24	20		1		3	9	$267,241	48
1990	22	20	1		2	5	12	$547,279	19
1991	23	13		2		2	5	$263,180	64
1992	27	18					4	$106,100	127
1993	23	17				3	9	$222,291	77
1994	19	15				3	7	$211,762	88
1995	25	22	2	2	1	5	13	$1,075,057	7
Total	463	346	6	14	7	66	159	$4,547,564	30

1996 PGA TOUR CHARITY TEAM: United Airlines Hawaiian Open

TOP TOURNAMENT SUMMARY

YEAR	78	79	80	81	82	83	84	85	86	87	88	89	90	91	92
Masters Tournament				T11	T20	T20	T25	CUT	T25			T34	T30	T17	T61
U.S. Open			T22	T37		T34	T7	T31	T59	T24	T21	8	CUT	T31	63
British Open Championship						T12	T22	T11	CUT	WD		T30	T16	T73	
PGA Championship		T23	T10	T27	T34	3	T18	T10	3	20	47	T27	T26		T28
THE PLAYERS Championship	T52	T14	T5	CUT	T27	T16	T51	CUT	T33	CUT	T16	T70	T29	CUT	CUT
THE TOUR Championship											6		T19		

TOP TOURNAMENT SUMMARY (cont.)

YEAR	93	94	95
Masters Tournament			T31
U.S. Open	CUT		T51
British Open Championship		T32	T31
PGA Championship	T28		T23
THE PLAYERS Championship		CUT	T29
THE TOUR Championship			T16

NATIONAL TEAMS: Ryder Cup (2), 1985,1995. Dunhill Cup, 1995. U.S. vs. Japan, 1984.

1995 PGA TOUR STATISTICS

Scoring	70.03	(10)
Driving	272.9	(24)
Driving Accuracy	73.8	(36T)
Greens in Regulation	70.2	(12)
Putting	1.801	(130T)
All Around	425	(18)
Sand Saves	48.5	(141)
Total Driving	60	(3)
Eagles	8	(36T)
Birdies	325	(36)

MISCELLANEOUS STATISTICS

Scoring Avg Before Cut	69.92	(5)
Scoring Avg 3rd Rnd	70.30	(36T)
Scoring Avg Final Rnd	71.77	(137)
Birdies Conversion %	28.9	(84T)
Par Breakers	19.9	(62T)

1995 Low Round: 64: 1995 Doral-Ryder Open/3
Career Low Round: 62: 1982 Westchester Classic/2
Career Largest Paycheck: $252,000: 1995 AT&T Pebble Beach National Pro-Am/1

Lee Janzen

EXEMPT STATUS: Winner, 1995 PLAYERS Championship
FULL NAME: Lee MacLeod Janzen
HEIGHT: 6' **WEIGHT:** 175
BIRTH DATE: August 28, 1964 **BIRTHPLACE:** Austin, MN
RESIDENCE: Orlando, FL and Las Sendas GC in Mesa, AZ
FAMILY: Wife, Beverly; Connor MacLeod (10/20/93)
SPECIAL INTERESTS: Music, movies, snow skiing, all sports
COLLEGE: Florida Southern University (1986, Marketing)
TURNED PROFESSIONAL: 1986 **JOINED TOUR:** Fall 1989.

TOUR VICTORIES (7): 1992 Northern Telecom Open. **1993** Phoenix Open, U.S. Open. **1994** Buick Classic. **1995** THE PLAYERS Championship, Kemper Open, Sprint International.

BEST 1995 FINISHES: 1 -- THE PLAYERS Championship, Kemper Open, Sprint International; T9 -- Mercedes Championships

1995 SEASON: Won three tournaments on his way to the seventh-highest earnings total in PGA TOUR history...his three wins in 1995 matched only by Greg Norman...T9 at year's first tournament, Mercedes Championships, where he shot a second-round 63, his low round of year...first victory came at THE PLAYERS Championship...moved into third place, one stroke behind co-leaders Corey Pavin and Bernhard Langer, with third-round 69...had sole possession of lead by third hole of final round and held on for one-stroke win over Langer, worth $540,000...T12 at Masters in next start...T18 at Buick Classic and T19 at Memorial before picking up second win at Kemper Open... didn't lead until he birdied the 18th hole on Sunday to catch Corey Pavin...then birdied the 18th in the playoff (his fifth birdie of the week at the hole) to defeat Pavin...T13 the following week at U.S. Open...third win came at Sprint International by one point over Ernie Els...birdies at 14, 15, 16 and 17 on Sunday keys to victory.

CAREER HIGHLIGHTS: Owns seven wins but just two runner-up finishes, both in 1992: to Brad Faxon at the International and to Paul Azinger (tied with Corey Pavin) at TOUR Championship...earned biggest victory of career in head-to-head battle with Payne Stewart at 1993 U.S. Open...posted four rounds in 60s, good for two-stroke win over Stewart at Baltusrol...272 total tied Jack Nicklaus for lowest cumulative score in Open history...triumph provided $290,000 payday...fourth start that season produced second TOUR win, two-stroke Phoenix Open victory over Andrew Magee...won 1994 Buick Classic by three strokes over Ernie Els who, the following week, won U.S. Open...earned first title at 1992 Northern Telecom Open, where he was 17-under-par over last three rounds, which included final-round 65...leading money winner on U.S. Golf Tour in 1989...winner 1986 Division II National Championship... First-Team All-American in 1985-86.

PERSONAL: Started to take golf seriously at age 14 after family moved to Florida from Maryland, where he played Little League baseball...won first tournament at 15 as member of Greater Tampa Junior Golf Association...still an avid baseball fan...enrolled, at suggestion of wife Bev, in Dave Pelz Short Game School after winning PLAYERS Championship.

PGA TOUR CAREER SUMMARY — **PLAYOFF RECORD: 1-0**

Year	Events Played	Cuts Made	1st	2nd	3rd	Top 10	Top 25	Earnings	Rank
1985	1								
1988	2	1					1	$3,686	256
1989	2	1						$5,100	233
1990	30	20				2	6	$132,986	115
1991	33	23				2	11	$228,242	72
1992	32	21	1	2	1	6	15	$795,279	9
1993	26	23	2		1	7	15	$932,335	7
1994	26	19	1			2	8	$442,588	35
1995	28	22	3			4	14	$1,378,966	3
Total	180	130	7	2	2	23	70	$3,919,183	35

NIKE TOUR SUMMARY

Year	Events Played	Cuts Made	1st	2nd	3rd	Top 10	Top 25	Earnings	Rank
1990	2	1					1	$1,125	204
Total	2	1					1	$1,125	
COMBINED TOTAL MONEY								$3,920,308	

1996 PGA TOUR CHARITY TEAM: FedEx St. Jude Classic

LEE JANZEN...continued

TOP TOURNAMENT SUMMARY

YEAR	85	91	92	93	94	95
Masters Tournament			T54	T39	T30	T12
U.S. Open	CUT	CUT	CUT	1	CUT	T13
British Open Championship			T39	T48	T35	T24
PGA Championship			T21	T22	T66	T23
THE PLAYERS Championship		CUT	CUT	T34	T35	1
THE TOUR Championship			T2	22		T20

NATIONAL TEAMS: Ryder Cup, 1993. Dunhill Cup, 1995.

1995 PGA TOUR STATISTICS

Statistic	Value	Rank
Scoring	70.58	(42T)
Driving	267.8	(57)
Driving Accuracy	70.6	(79T)
Greens in Regulation	66.1	(100T)
Putting	1.771	(44T)
All Around	558	(45)
Sand Saves	52.2	(95T)
Total Driving	136	(28T)
Eagles	4	(116T)
Birdies	341	(25T)

MISCELLANEOUS STATISTICS

Statistic	Value	Rank
Scoring Avg Before Cut	71.09	(76T)
Scoring Avg 3rd Rnd	70.73	(64T)
Scoring Avg Final Rnd	71.57	(119T)
Birdies Conversion %	31.2	(24T)
Par Breakers	20.0	(56T)

1995 Low Round: 63: 1995 Mercedes Championships/2
Career Low Round: 61: 1993 Southwestern Bell Colonial/4
Career Largest Paycheck: $540,000: 1995 THE PLAYERS Championship/1

STEVE JONES

EXEMPT STATUS: 79th on 1995 money list
FULL NAME: Steven Glen Jones
HEIGHT: 6' 4" **WEIGHT:** 200
BIRTH DATE: December 27, 1958 **BIRTHPLACE:** Artesia, NM
RESIDENCE: Phoenix, AZ; plays out of Desert Mountain GC
FAMILY: Wife, Bonnie Buckingham; Cy Edmond (2/27/91), Stacey Jane (2/21/93)
COLLEGE: University of Colorado
SPECIAL INTERESTS: Basketball, fly fishing
TURNED PROFESSIONAL: 1981 **Q SCHOOL:** Fall 1981, 1984, 1986

TOUR VICTORIES (4): 1988 AT&T Pebble Beach National Pro-Am; **1989** MONY Tournament of Champions, Bob Hope Chrysler Classic, Canadian Open.

BEST 1995 FINISHES: T4 -- Phoenix Open; T5 -- FedEx St. Jude Classic

1995 SEASON: Played his first full season on PGA TOUR since Nov. 25, 1991 dirt-bike accident sidelined him for nearly three years...ligament and joint damage to left ring finger left him unable to grip club properly...developed reverse overlapping grip to compensate...an inconsistent start to year...missed five of first seven cuts, but finished T22 at United Airlines Hawaiian Open and T4 at Phoenix Open in two cuts made...shot 68-69-68-67 -- 272 at Phoenix to finish three strokes out of lead...only one stroke behind leader Davis Love III through 54 holes at Freeport-McMoRan Classic, but fell to T15 with final-round 76...shot 65-68 on weekend to finish T5, three strokes behind Jim Gallagher, Jr., at FedEx St. Jude Classic...finished year with top-20 finishes in three of last four tournaments ...T20 at Quad City Classic, T18 at Buick Challenge and T11 at LaCantera Texas Open.

CAREER HIGHLIGHTS: Made first PGA TOUR appearance since dirt-bike accident at 1994 B.C. Open...shot 67-70-70-74-- 281 for T40...T31 at other 1994 start at Hardee's Golf Classic...had finest season of first eight on TOUR in 1989, with three victories and earnings of $745,578...opened year with back-to-back wins in MONY Tournament of Champions and Bob Hope Chrysler Classic...tied Paul Azinger and Sandy Lyle at end of Hope regulation, then birdied first playoff hole for win...captured Canadian Open for third title of year...has been in two other playoffs, defeating Bob Tway for 1988 AT&T Pebble Beach National Pro-Am title and losing

STEVE JONES...continued

to Payne Stewart at 1990 MCI Heritage Classic...also finished T3 in 1990 PLAYERS Championship...had four top-10 finishes in 1991, including third in Greater Milwaukee Open...GMO finish one of seven consecutive top-25s to end final season until 1994...winner 1987 JCPenney Classic (with Jane Crafter)...medalist 1986 Qualifying Tournament...second-team All-American at University of Colorado...semifinalist 1976 USGA Junior Championship.

PERSONAL: Played golf and ran track in high school, where he also earned all-state honors in basketball before concentrating on golf alone at Colorado.

PGA TOUR CAREER SUMMARY — **PLAYOFF RECORD: 2-1**

Year	Events Played	Cuts Made	1st	2nd	3rd	Top 10	Top 25	Earnings	Rank
1984	1	1						$788	264
1985	21	12				1	7	$43,379	129
1986	23	14				2	5	$51,473	136
1987	30	20		1		2	6	$154,918	66
1988	25	19	1			3	6	$241,877	45
1989	26	22	3			6	11	$745,578	8
1990	24	16		1	1	5	12	$350,982	34
1991	27	19			1	4	11	$294,961	54
1994	2	2						$8,740	254
1995	24	16				2	9	$234,749	79
Total	203	141	4	2	2	25	67	$2,127,442	91

NIKE TOUR SUMMARY

Year	Events Played	Cuts Made	1st	2nd	3rd	Top 10	Top 25	Earnings	Rank
1994	2	2				1	1	$5,195	140
Total	2	2				1	1	$5,195	
COMBINED TOTAL MONEY								$2,132,637	

1996 PGA TOUR CHARITY TEAM: Buick Challenge

TOP TOURNAMENT SUMMARY

YEAR	87	88	89	90	91
Masters Tournament		T30	T31	T20	CUT
U.S. Open			T46	T8	CUT
British Open Championship			CUT	T16	T64
PGA Championship	T61	T9	T51	CUT	
THE PLAYERS Championship	T15	T48	T41	T3	T41
THE TOUR Championship			T14		

1995 PGA TOUR STATISTICS

Scoring	70.53	(40)
Driving	270.6	(38T)
Driving Accuracy	68.1	(118T)
Greens in Regulation	69.6	(17T)
Putting	1.782	(74T)
All Around	553	(44)
Sand Saves	46.5	(157T)
Total Driving	156	(52T)
Eagles	8	(36T)
Birdies	291	(73)

MISCELLANEOUS STATISTICS

Scoring Avg Before Cut	70.18	(13)
Scoring Avg 3rd Rnd	69.76	(11)
Scoring Avg Final Rnd	72.13	(161)
Birdies Conversion %	29.0	(81T)
Par Breakers	20.8	(28T)

1995 Low Round: **64:** 1995 GTE Byron Nelson Classic/2
Career Low Round: **63:** 2 times, most recent 1991 Las Vegas Invitation/3
Career Largest Paycheck: **$180,000:** 1989 Bob Hope Chrysler Cl/1

Brian Kamm

EXEMPT STATUS: 118th on 1995 money list
FULL NAME: Brian Thomas Kamm
HEIGHT: 5'6" **WEIGHT:** 160
BIRTH DATE: September 3, 1961 **BIRTHPLACE:** Rochester, NY
RESIDENCE: Tampa, FL
FAMILY: Wife, Yvette; Brandy (11/7/84), Michael (5/3/87)
COLLEGE: Florida State University
SPECIAL INTEREST: All sports
TURNED PROFESSIONAL: 1985 **Q-SCHOOL:** Fall 1989, 1990

BEST TOUR CAREER FINISH: T6 -- 1994 Bell Canadian Open

NIKE TOUR VICTORIES (1): 1992 Panama City Beach Classic

BEST 1995 FINISHES: T9 -- Nissan Open, Bell Canadian Open

1995 SEASON: Earnings dropped slightly in 1995, but still retained playing privileges for 1996...after T12 at Buick Invitational of California, posted first top-10 finish at Nissan Open...recovered from second-round 74 to finish 67-68 for T9...recorded back-to-back top-25 finishes at MCI Classic (T24) and Kmart Greater Greensboro Open (T19)...largest check of 1995 came at Bell Canadian Open...shot 74-71-70-69 -- 284 for T9, worth $36,400...shot 68-66-70 for T21 at Walt Disney World/Oldsmobile Classic.

CAREER HIGHLIGHTS: Best finish of six-year PGA TOUR career came at 1994 Bell Canadian Open...shot 71-71-69-68 -- 279 for T6, four strokes behind winner Nick Price...$43,550 payday is largest of his career...finished T7 at 1993 Canon Greater Hartford Open...closed with 6-under-par 64 at TPC at River Highlands to finish six strokes behind winner Price...had two other top-10s in '93, when fashioned solid season and retained playing privileges with No. 94 money-list finish...three consecutive 69s, followed by 67, provided T8 at Greater Milwaukee Open...closing 68 gave him T10 and $35,000 payday at Las Vegas Invitational...had moment in sun at 1991 U.S. Open, where first-round 69 had him just two strokes off early lead (ultimately finished T31)...finished seventh on 1992 Ben Hogan Tour money list with $88,608 to advance to finals of Qualifying Tournament, where he earned his TOUR card for 1993...had nine top-10 finishes, including win in fifth Hogan start...final-round 69 good for one-stroke victory over Jeff Gallagher in Ben Hogan Panama City Beach Classic...winner 1987 North Dakota Open...won two collegiate tournaments while at Florida State.

PGA TOUR CAREER SUMMARY — **PLAYOFF RECORD: 0-0**

Year	Events Played	Cuts Made	1st	2nd	3rd	Top 10	Top 25	Earnings	Rank
1986	1	1						$538	292
1988	1	1						$1,163	302
1990	21	5						$8,775	237
1991	27	11				1	4	$81,932	146
1992	4	1					1	$20,020	211
1993	27	17				3	7	$183,185	94
1994	32	16				3	5	$181,884	98
1995	29	17				2	6	$165,235	118
Total	142	69				9	23	$642,733	229

NIKE TOUR SUMMARY

Year	Events Played	Cuts Made	1st	2nd	3rd	Top 10	Top 25	Earnings	Rank
1990	2	1						$690	251
1991	4	2				1	2	$3,619	147
1992	23	16	1	1	1	9	14	$88,608	7
Total	29	19	1	1	1	10	16	$92,917	
COMBINED TOTAL MONEY								$735,650	

1996 PGA TOUR CHARITY TEAM: THE PLAYERS Championship

TOP TOURNAMENT SUMMARY

YEAR	91	94	95
U.S. Open	T31	CUT	
PGA Championship			70
THE PLAYERS Championship		CUT	CUT

BRIAN KAMM...continued

1995 PGA TOUR STATISTICS		
Scoring	71.81	(148)
Driving	266.6	(63T)
Driving Accuracy	67.6	(124T)
Greens in Regulation	63.0	(163T)
Putting	1.764	(30T)
All Around	722	(91)
Sand Saves	48.2	(142T)
Total Driving	187	(96T)
Eagles	10	(15T)
Birdies	319	(37T)

MISCELLANEOUS STATISTICS		
Scoring Avg Before Cut	71.66	(141)
Scoring Avg 3rd Rnd	71.18	(94T)
Scoring Avg Final Rnd	72.76	(177)
Birdies Conversion %	31.2	(24T)
Par Breakers	20.3	(40T)

1995 Low Round: 66: 4 times, most recent 1995 Walt Disney World/ Oldsmobile Classic/2
Career Low Round: 64: 2 times, most recent 1994 Las Vegas Invitational/1
Career Largest Paycheck: $43,550: 1994 Bell Canadian Open/T6

JONATHAN KAYE

EXEMPT STATUS: 94th on 1995 money list
FULL NAME: Jonathan Andrew Kaye
HEIGHT: 5'11" **WEIGHT:** 160
BIRTH DATE: August 2, 1970 **BIRTHPLACE:** Denver, CO
RESIDENCE: Phoenix, AZ
FAMILY: Single
COLLEGE: University of Colorado
SPECIAL INTERESTS: Fine dining, floating in the pool, dominos
TURNED PROFESSIONAL: 1993 **Q-SCHOOL:** Fall 1994

BEST EVER FINISH: 2 -- 1995 Quad City Classic

BEST 1995 FINISHES: 2 -- Quad City Classic; T9 -- Buick Open

BEST NIKE TOUR 1995 FINISHES: T9—NIKE Inland Empire Open

1995 SEASON: After being slowed by a shoulder injury during the first half of 1995, rebounded in the second half to finish 94th on the money list in his rookie season...top performance came at Quad City Classic, where he came to the tee at the final hole with a one- stroke lead over D.A. Weibring...a bogey, combined with Weibring's birdie, dropped him to second...67-66-65 -- 198 in rain-shortened event earned $108,000 and assured his return in 1996...T27 at United Airlines Hawaiian Open in first start on TOUR, then failed to cash in next 12 tournaments...streak ended at Anheuser-Busch (T27) ... the following week finished T11 at Deposit Guaranty Golf Classic...carded third-round 63 at Annandale GC, a course record...was T5, three strokes behind, after opening 67-66-67 at Las Vegas Invitational...T6 after fourth-round 69, but fell to T30 after closing 74.

CAREER HIGHLIGHTS: Joined PGA TOUR in 1994 after tying for 32nd at 1994 Qualifying Tournament...while playing for Colorado, won 1992 Ping Intercollegiate tournament, defeating Phil Mickelson in a playoff.

PERSONAL: Coincidentally or not, change of fortunes in 1995 occurred at approximately same time that girlfriend Jennifer Sweeney began caddying for him.

PGA TOUR CAREER SUMMARY — **PLAYOFF RECORD: 0-0**

Year	Events Played	Cuts Made	1st	2nd	3rd	Top 10	Top 25	Earnings	Rank
1995	25	8		1		2	4	$191,883	94
Total	25	8		1		2	4	$191,883	346

JONATHAN KAYE...continued

NIKE TOUR SUMMARY

Year	Events Played	Cuts Made	1st	2nd	3rd	Top 10	Top 25	Earnings	Rank
1995	3	2				1	2	$6,747	142
Total	3	2				1	2	$6,747	
COMBINED TOTAL MONEY								$198,631	

1996 PGA TOUR CHARITY TEAM: JCPenney Classic

1995 PGA TOUR STATISTICS

Scoring	71.55	(118T)
Driving	270.3	(42)
Driving Accuracy	69.1	(102T)
Greens in Regulation	64.3	(138T)
Putting	1.794	(110T)
All Around	764	(106)
Sand Saves	55.2	(53T)
Total Driving	144	(37T)
Eagles	7	(51T)
Birdies	219	(150)

MISCELLANEOUS STATISTICS

Scoring Avg Before Cut	71.94	(156T)
Scoring Avg 3rd Rnd	68.56	(1)
Scoring Avg Final Rnd	69.63	(5)
Birdies Conversion %	29.3	(77T)
Par Breakers	19.5	(80T)

1995 Low Round: 63: 1995 Deposit Guaranty Golf Classic/3
Career Low Round: 63: 1995 Deposit Guaranty Golf Classic/3
Career Largest Paycheck: $108,000: 1995 Quad City Classic/2

JERRY KELLY

EXEMPT STATUS: 1st on 1995 NIKE TOUR money list
FULL NAME: Jerry Patrick Kelly
HEIGHT: 5'11" **WEIGHT:** 165
BIRTH DATE: November 23, 1966 **BIRTHPLACE:** Madison, WI
RESIDENCE: Madison, WI
FAMILY: Wife, Carol
COLLEGE: University of Hartford (Finance and Insurance, 1989)
SPECIAL INTERESTS: Hockey, surfing
TURNED PROFESSIONAL: 1989 **JOINED TOUR:** 1996

BEST TOUR CAREER FINISH: T34—1995 Greater Milwaukee Open

NIKE TOUR VICTORIES (2): 1995 NIKE Alabama Classic, NIKE Buffalo Open

BEST 1995 PGA TOUR FINISH: T34—Greater Milwaukee Open

BEST NIKE TOUR 1995 FINISHES: 1—NIKE Alabama Classic, NIKE Buffalo Open; T2—NIKE Sonoma County Open; 4—NIKE Monterrey Open, NIKE Louisiana Open; T4—NIKE Greater Greenville Classic; T5—NIKE Central Georgia Open, NIKE Tri-Cities Open; T6—NIKE Philadelphia Classic; T7—NIKE Mississippi Gulf Coast Classic; T8—NIKE Shreveport Open; T9—NIKE Permian Basin Open; T10—NIKE Dominion Open, NIKE Gateway Classic, NIKE Utah Classic.

1995 SEASON: Set the NIKE TOUR record for single-season earnings with $188,878, eclipsing Chris Perry's 1994 mark of $167,148...earned victories in the NIKE Alabama Classic and the NIKE Buffalo Open...finished strong in each of his victories ...in Alabama he closed eagle-birdie-birdie to force a playoff with Buddy Gardner...in Buffalo he finished with three consecutive birdies to defeat Tim Simpson by one stroke...had 15 top-10 finishes in 28 events...led the NIKE TOUR in birdies (392) and eagles (15) and tied for the lead in par breakers (24.1%)...finished third on the NIKE TOUR with a 69.93 scoring average...played in two PGA TOUR events in 1995, missing the cut in the Motorola Western Open and tying for 34th in the Greater Milwaukee Open.

CAREER HIGHLIGHTS: Member of the NIKE TOUR 1993-95...1995 win in Alabama ended a stretch of 12 top-10 finishes without a victory...finished 26th on the 1994 NIKE TOUR money list with $60,928...in 1993 finished 25th on the money list with $61,074...career-best finish prior to 1995 was second in the 1993 NIKE Cleveland Open...winner of the 1992 and 1994 Wisconsin State Opens.

JERRY KELLY...continued

PERSONAL: Was an all-city hockey player in high school, and has said that his hockey background may have hurt his golf game in the past by bringing too much aggressiveness to his game...wife Carol has served as his caddy...Carol's brother Jim Schuman was a member of the NIKE TOUR from 1990-93.

PGA TOUR CAREER SUMMARY — **PLAYOFF RECORD: 0-0**

Year	Events Played	Cuts Made	1st	2nd	3rd	Top 10	Top 25	Earnings	Rank
1991	1								
1992	1								
1993	2								
1995	2	1						$4,733	306
Total	6	1						$4,733	

NIKE TOUR SUMMARY

1993	28	15		1		3	10	$61,074	25
1994	26	19				8	11	$60,928	26
1995	28	22	2	1		15	19	$188,878	1
Total	82	56	2	2		26	40	$310,881	
COMBINED TOTAL MONEY								$315,614	

1996 PGA TOUR CHARITY TEAM: Greater Milwaukee Open

1995 PGA TOUR STATISTICS

Scoring	71.01	(N/A)
Driving	285.6	(N/A)
Driving Accuracy	58.8	(N/A)
Greens in Regulation	69.4	(N/A)
Putting	1.880	(N/A)
Sand Saves	56.3	(N/A)
Total Driving		(N/A)
Eagles	1	(N/A)
Birdies	19	(N/A)

MISCELLANEOUS STATISTICS

Scoring Avg Before Cut	72.50	(N/A)
Scoring Avg 3rd Rnd	71.00	(N/A)
Scoring Avg Final Rnd	69.00	(N/A)
Birdies Conversion %	25.3	(N/A)
Par Breakers	18.5	(N/A)

1995 Low Round: **68:** 1995 Greater Milwaukee Open/2
Career Low Round: **68:** 1995 Greater Milwaukee Open/2
Career Largest Paycheck: $4,733: 1995 Greater Milwaukee Open/T34

1995 NIKE TOUR STATISTICS

Scoring	69.93	(3)
Eagles	15	(1)
Birdies	392	(1)

1995 Low Round: **64:** 2 times, most recent 1995 NIKE Louisiana Open/1
Career Low Round: **64:** 2 times, most recent 1995 NIKE Louisiana Open/1
Career Largest Paycheck: $36,000: 2 times, most recent 1995 NIKE Alabama Classic/1

Did You Know?

Scott Hoch's lead after the third round of the Shell Houston Open was five strokes, the largest 54-hole lead on TOUR in 1995, yet he lost in a playoff to Payne Stewart. It was the first time since 1989 that the holder of the year's largest 54-hole lead did not win the tournament. That year, John Daly led the Chattanooga Classic by four strokes, but Stan Utley won the tounament.

Tom Kite

EXEMPT STATUS: Winner, 1992 U.S. Open
FULL NAME: Thomas Oliver Kite, Jr.
HEIGHT: 5' 8" **WEIGHT:** 155
BIRTH DATE: December 9, 1949 **BIRTHPLACE:** Austin, TX
RESIDENCE: Austin, TX
FAMILY: Wife, Christy; Stephanie Lee (10/7/81), David Thomas and Paul Christopher (9/1/84)
COLLEGE: University of Texas **SPECIAL INTERESTS:** Landscaping
TURNED PROFESSIONAL: 1972 **Q SCHOOL:** Fall 1972

TOUR VICTORIES (19): 1976 IVB-Bicentennial Golf Classic. **1978** B.C. Open. **1981** American Motors-Inverrary Classic. **1982** Bay Hill Classic. **1983** Bing Crosby National Pro-Am. **1984** Doral-Eastern Open, Georgia-Pacific Atlanta Classic. **1985** MONY Tournament of Champions. **1986** Western Open. **1987** Kemper Open. **1989** Nestle Invitational, THE PLAYERS Championship, Nabisco Championships. **1990** Federal Express St. Jude Classic. **1991** Infiniti Tournament of Champions. **1992** BellSouth Classic, U.S. Open. **1993** Bob Hope Chrysler Classic, Nissan Los Angeles Open

INTERNATIONAL VICTORIES (1): 1980 European Open (Eur).

BEST 1995 FINISH: T6 -- Northern Telecom Open.

1995 SEASON: A decidedly down season for the 24-year veteran ended on a high note when he was named to captain the 1997 U.S. Ryder Cup team...season presented his lowest earnings ($178,580) since 1980 and his lowest finish on the money list since joining the TOUR full-time in 1973...without a win since 1993 Nissan Los Angeles Open, the first time he has gone two full seasons without a win since 1979-80...sole top-10 of 1995 came at Northern Telecom Open in January...T7, only three strokes off lead through 54 holes, closed with 70 to finish T6, five strokes behind Phil Mickelson...made 21 of 25 cuts in 1995, but only other top-20 finish was T11 at Sprint International...relinquished top position on career money-list to Greg Norman after NEC World Series of Golf.

CAREER HIGHLIGHTS: Greatest victory came in 1992 U.S. Open at Pebble Beach, where even-par 72 in tough Sunday conditions gave him two-stroke win over Jeff Sluman...win earlier that year in BellSouth Classic ended 16-month victory drought...got off to blazing start in 1993, posting two wins, a second and eighth in five starts before March back injury slowed him ...was untouchable in '93 Bob Hope Chrysler Classic, closing with rounds of 64-65-62 to set TOUR record for most strokes under par in 90-hole event...finished at 35-under 325, which also was good for six-stroke win over Rick Fehr...in next start, Nissan Los Angeles Open, even weather couldn't stop him...4-under-par 67 on final day of rain-shortened event produced 19th career victory...owns two Arnold Palmer Awards as TOUR's leading money-winner -- in 1981, when he earned $375,699, and in 1989, when he earned more than $1 million more ($1,395,278)...THE PLAYERS Championship one of three victory highlights of million-dollar campaign, which culminated in win at season-ending Nabisco Championships...1981 GWAA Player of Year...1989 PGA Player of Year...winner 1979 Bob Jones Award...Rookie of Year for 1973...winner 1981-82 Vardon Trophies...co-winner with Ben Crenshaw of 1972 NCAA Championship.

PERSONAL: Three of last four victories came on holidays: BellSouth Classic/Mother's Day, U.S. Open/Father's Day, Bob Hope Chrysler Classic/Valentine's Day...serves as spokesman for Chrysler Junior Golf Scholarship program...started playing golf at six, won first tournament at 11.

PGA TOUR CAREER SUMMARY **PLAYOFF RECORD: 6-3**

Year	Events Played	Cuts Made	1st	2nd	3rd	Top 10	Top 25	Earnings	Rank
1971(Am.)	1	1							
1972(Am.)	4	4					2		
1972	3	3						$2,582	233
1973	34	31				2	15	$54,270	56
1974	28	27			1	8	18	$82,055	26
1975	26	21		1	1	9	14	$87,045	18
1976	27	25	1			8	15	$116,180	21
1977	29	27		1	3	7	16	$125,204	14
1978	28	25	1	1	3	8	15	$161,370	11
1979	28	24			3	11	15	$166,878	17
1980	26	22		1		10	18	$152,490	20
1981	26	26	1	3	3	21	24	$375,699	1
1982	25	24	1	4	1	15	17	$341,081	3

TOM KITE...continued

Year	Events Played	Cuts Made	1st	2nd	3rd	Top 10	Top 25	Earnings	Rank
1983	25	21	1	2		8	16	$257,066	9
1984	25	21	2	1		10	14	$348,640	5
1985	24	21	1	1	1	6	11	$258,793	14
1986	26	24	1	1	1	9	13	$394,164	7
1987	24	21	1	2		11	18	$525,516	8
1988	25	21		3	1	10	16	$760,405	5
1989	23	23	3	1		10	14	$1,395,278	1
1990	22	21	1		1	9	15	$658,202	15
1991	25	19	1	1	1	4	9	$396,580	39
1992	23	22	2	1	1	9	17	$957,445	6
1993	20	14	2	2		8	10	$887,811	8
1994	23	18		1	1	8	12	$658,689	22
1995	25	21				1	4	$178,580	104
Total	595	527	19	27	22	202	338	$9,335,434	2

1996 PGA TOUR CHARITY TEAM: Canon Greater Hartford Open

TOP TOURNAMENT SUMMARY

YEAR	71	72	74	75	76	77	78	79	80	81	82	83	84	85	86
Masters Tournament	T42	T27		T10	T5	T3	T18	5	T6	T5	T5	T2	T6	CUT	T2
U.S. Open		T19	T8			T27	T20		CUT	T20	29	T20	CUT	13	T35
British Open Championship					T5		T2	T30	T27		CUT	T29	T22	T8	CUT
PGA Championship			T39	T33	T13	T13		T35	T20	T4	T9	T67	T34	T12	T26
THE PLAYERS Championship			T19	T40	T17		T28	T9	T31	DNS	T27	T27	T51	T64	T4

TOP TOURNAMENT SUMMARY (cont.)

YEAR	87	88	89	90	91	92	93	94	95
Masters Tournament	T24	44	T18	T14	56		CUT	4	CUT
U.S. Open	T46	T36	T9	T56	T37	1	CUT	T33	T67
British Open Championship	T72	T20	T19	CUT	T44	T19	T14	T8	T58
PGA Championship	T10	T4	T34	T40	T52	T21	T56	T9	T54
THE PLAYERS Championship	T9	T11	1	T5	CUT	T35	CUT	T9	T43
THE TOUR Championship	T17	2	1	18		T13	T7	T22	

NATIONAL TEAMS: Ryder Cup (7), 1979, 1981, 1983, 1985, 1987, 1989, 1993. World Cup (2), 1984, 1985. Dunhill Cup (4), 1989, 1990, 1992, 1994. Kirin Cup, 1987. U.S. vs. Japan (3), 1982, 1983, 1984. Asahi Glass Four Tours, 1989. Walker Cup, 1971.

1995 PGA TOUR STATISTICS

Scoring	**71.08**	**(77)**
Driving	**260.7**	**(112)**
Driving Accuracy	**74.1**	**(29T)**
Greens in Regulation	**69.6**	**(17T)**
Putting	**1.791**	**(99T)**
All Around	**656**	**(73)**
Sand Saves	**50.0**	**(126T)**
Total Driving	**141**	**(35)**
Eagles	**3**	**(137T)**
Birdies	**301**	**(59T)**

MISCELLANEOUS STATISTICS

Scoring Avg Before Cut	**70.56**	**(31T)**
Scoring Avg 3rd Rnd	**71.45**	**(117)**
Scoring Avg Final Rnd	**72.25**	**(166)**
Birdies Conversion %	**28.9**	**(84T)**
Par Breakers	**19.4**	**(85T)**

1995 Low Round: 64: 1995 Bob Hope Chrysler Classic/3
Career Low Round: 62: 4 times, most recent 1993 Bob Hope Chrysler Classic/5
Career Largest Paycheck: $450,000: 1989 Nabisco/1

NEAL LANCASTER

EXEMPT STATUS: 1994 tournament winner
FULL NAME: Grady Neal Lancaster
HEIGHT: 6' **WEIGHT:** 170
BIRTH DATE: September 13,1962 **BIRTHPLACE:** Smithfield, NC
RESIDENCE: Smithfield, NC; plays out of Johnston County CC
FAMILY: Wife, Lou Ann
SPECIAL INTERESTS: Fishing, movies
TURNED PROFESSIONAL: 1985 **Q SCHOOL:** 1989, 1990

TOUR VICTORIES (1) : 1994 GTE Byron Nelson Classic.

BEST 1995 FINISH: T4 -- U.S. Open

1995 SEASON: Enjoyed second-best earnings total of his six-year career, bettered only by 1994...highlight came at U.S. Open, where he became the first player in the championship's history to shoot 29 for nine holes...T46 through 54 holes, shot 36-29--65 in final round to finish T4, four strokes behind Corey Pavin...made consecutive birdies on 11-14 at Shinnecock Hills, including a 65-foot birdie putt on No. 13...also birdied 16 and 17...carded 65 in third round of Kemper Open the previous week and stood T4 through 54 holes, three strokes off lead...closing 73 left him T16...final top-20 finish came at B.C. Open...shot 70-70-67-68 -- 275 for T15.

CAREER HIGHLIGHTS: Winner of the 1994 "Half-Nelson," the GTE Byron Nelson Classic shortened to 36 holes by rain...birdied his final two holes in regulation to earn place in TOUR record six-man playoff...birdied first playoff hole to defeat David Ogrin, David Edwards, Tom Byrum, Mark Carnevale and Yoshinori Mizukami...$216,000 payday more than he had earned in any other year on TOUR...best previous finish was T5 in 1991 Greater Milwaukee Open...opened with rounds of 67 and 66 at Tuckaway CC...GMO payday $38,000...registered pair of top-10s in 1993...closed with 1-under-par 71 over windswept English Turn, good for T6 in Freeport-McMoRan Classic...final 67 gave him T9 in Buick Open...only 1992 top-10 also Freeport-McMoRan T6...had two other top-10s in 1991, T9 at Northern Telecom Open and T8 in Canadian Open...latter secured playing privileges for first time in career ...winner of PineTree Open in Birmingham, AL and Utah State Open in 1989...also mini-tour leading money winner that year.

PERSONAL: Took first golf lesson in 1992, having self-taught through golf magazine pictures until then...that first lesson came from L.B. Floyd, Raymond's father and fellow North Carolina resident...a former club pro who, in his own unique way, once noted: "I gave some lessons, but I kind of didn't know what I was doing."

PGA TOUR CAREER SUMMARY — **PLAYOFF RECORD: 1-0**

Year	Events Played	Cuts Made	1st	2nd	3rd	Top 10	Top 25	Earnings	Rank
1990	26	11				2	7	$85,769	142
1991	33	22				3	5	$180,037	90
1992	35	23				1	4	$146,867	103
1993	32	19				2	5	$149,381	107
1994	29	19	1			1	2	$305,038	58
1995	29	18				1	4	$182,219	101
Total	184	112	1			10	27	$1,049,311	175

NIKE TOUR SUMMARY

Year	Events Played	Cuts Made	1st	2nd	3rd	Top 10	Top 25	Earnings	Rank
1990	4	4				2	2	$4,516	118
Total	4	4				2	2	$4,516	
COMBINED TOTAL MONEY								$1,053,827	

1996 PGA TOUR CHARITY TEAM: Buick Challenge

TOP TOURNAMENT SUMMARY

YEAR	91	92	93	94	95
Masters Tournament					CUT
U.S. Open					T4
PGA Championship		T84		T44	
THE PLAYERS Championship	T20	T40	CUT	T35	CUT

NEAL LANCASTER...*continued*

1995 PGA TOUR STATISTICS		
Scoring	71.64	(130)
Driving	270.6	(38T)
Driving Accuracy	60.6	(179)
Greens in Regulation	62.4	(172T)
Putting	1.767	(36T)
All Around	797	(117)
Sand Saves	50.0	(126T)
Total Driving	217	(137T)
Eagles	6	(69T)

MISCELLANEOUS STATISTICS		
Scoring Avg Before Cut	71.88	(154)
Scoring Avg 3rd Rnd	71.44	(115T)
Scoring Avg Final Rnd	72.35	(168)
Birdies Conversion %	30.7	(36T)
Par Breakers	19.5	(80T)

1995 Low Round: **65:** 2 times, most recent 1995 U.S. Open/4
Career Low Round: **64:** 2 times, most recent 1992 Southwestern Bell Colonial/4
Career Largest Paycheck: **$216,000:** 1994 GTE Byron Nelson Classic/1

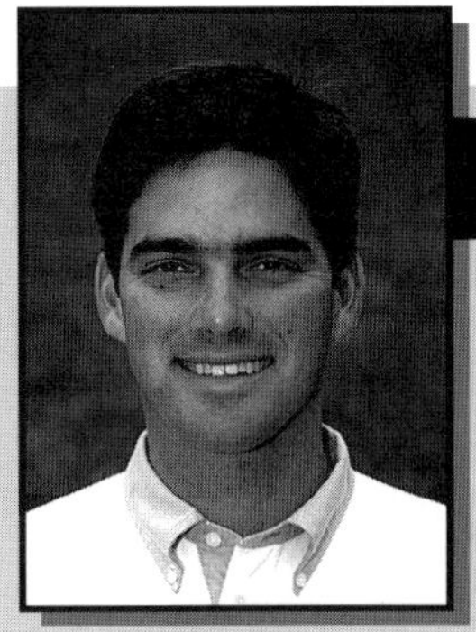

FRANKLIN LANGHAM

EXEMPT STATUS: 4th on 1995 NIKE TOUR money list
FULL NAME: James Franklin Langham
HEIGHT: 6'1" **WEIGHT:** 165
BIRTH DATE: May 8, 1968 **BIRTHPLACE:** Augusta, GA
RESIDENCE: Peachtree City, GA
FAMILY: Wife, Ashley
COLLEGE: University of Georgia (Risk Management & Insurance, 1991)
SPECIAL INTERESTS: Hunting, fishing
TURNED PROFESSIONAL: 1991 **JOINED TOUR:** 1996

BEST TOUR CAREER FINISH: First year on PGA TOUR.

NIKE TOUR VICTORIES (1): 1993 NIKE Permian Basin Open.

BEST 1995 FINISH: Did not play PGA TOUR in 1995.

BEST 1995 NIKE TOUR FINISHES: 2--NIKE Mississippi Gulf Coast Classic, NIKE Tri-Cities Open; T2--NIKE Permian Basin Open, NIKE Utah Classic; 3--NIKE Greater Greenville Classic; T3-- NIKE Central Georgia Open; T4--NIKE San Jose Open; T5--NIKE Tallahassee Open; T8--NIKE Boise Open, NIKE Sonoma County Open; T9--NIKE TOUR Championship; T10--NIKE Alabama Classic.

1995 SEASON: Established the NIKE TOUR record for single-season earnings without a victory with $158,990, eclipsing the $126,430 earned by David Duval in 1994...among his 12 top-10 finishes were four runner-up placings...lost in a playoff to former Walker Cup teammate Allen Doyle at the NIKE Mississippi Gulf Coast Classic...finished a stroke behind Hugh Royer III at the NIKE Permian Basin Open...lost playoffs in consecutive weeks at the NIKE Utah Classic and NIKE Tri-Cities Open...lost to Frank Lickliter, Jr. in Utah and to Jeff Gove in Tri-Cities...ranked second on the NIKE TOUR in birdies with 367 and fourth in par breakers at 23.6%...tied for fifth with a 70.17 scoring average.

CAREER HIGHLIGHTS: Member of the NIKE TOUR from 1993-95...won the 1993 NIKE Permian Basin in a playoff over Doug Martin...finished 18th on the money list that year with $71,235...fell to 55th the following year with $27,957 before rebounding with his very successful 1995 season...1991 All-America selection and a member of the Walker Cup team.

PERSONAL: Wife Ashley often serves as his caddy...on the NIKE TOUR, Ashley worked for the Darrell Survey and was president of the NIKE TOUR Wives Association...the couple was profiled in a "Week on the NIKE TOUR" feature in the August 1995 issue of ON TOUR Magazine.

PGA TOUR CAREER SUMMARY **PLAYOFF RECORD: 0-0**

Year	Events Played	Cuts Made	1st	2nd	3rd	Top 10	Top 25	Earnings	Rank
1992	1								
1994	1								
Total	2								

FRANKLIN LANGHAM...*continued*

NIKE TOUR CAREER SUMMARY

Year	Events Played	Cuts Made	1st	2nd	3rd	Top 10	Top 25	Earnings	Rank
1992	1								
1993	27	17	1			5	8	$71,235	18
1994	25	11				3	4	$27,957	55
1995	28	18		4	2	12	15	$158,990	4
Total	81	46	1	4	2	20	27	$258,182	
COMBINED TOTAL MONEY								$258,182	

1996 PGA TOUR CHARITY TEAM: THE TOUR Championship

1995 NIKE TOUR STATISTICS

Scoring ---------------------- **70.17 (5)**
Eagles ----------------------- **7 (32)**
Birdies ---------------------- **367 (2)**

MISCELLANEOUS NIKE TOUR STATISTICS

1995 Low Round: 64: 1995 NIKE Greater Greenville Classic/4
Career Low Round: 64: 2 times, most recent 1995 NIKE Greater Greenville Classic/4
Career Largest Paycheck: $27,000: 1995 NIKE Permian Basin Open/1

NATIONAL TEAM: Walker Cup, 1991

TOM LEHMAN *(LAY-mun)*

EXEMPT STATUS: 1995 tournament winner
FULL NAME: Thomas Edward Lehman
HEIGHT: 6' 2" **WEIGHT:** 190
BIRTH DATE: March 7, 1959 **BIRTHPLACE:** Austin, MN
RESIDENCE: Scottsdale, AZ; plays out of Desert Mountain GC
FAMILY: Wife, Melissa; Rachael (5/30/90), Holly (8/13/92), Thomas Andrew (7/24/95)
COLLEGE: University of Minnesota
SPECIAL INTERESTS: Hunting, church activities
TURNED PROFESSIONAL: 1982

TOUR VICTORIES (2): 1994 Memorial Tournament. **1995** Colonial National Invitation.

INTERNATIONAL VICTORIES (1): 1993 Casio World Open (Japan).

NIKE TOUR VICTORIES (4): 1990 Reflection Ridge. **1991** Gulf Coast Classic, South Carolina Classic, Santa Rosa Open.

BEST 1995 FINISHES: 1 -- Colonial National Invitation; T2 -- United Airlines Hawaiian Open; 3 -- U.S. Open; T5 -- Mercedes Championships; T9 -- Buick Open

1995 SEASON: Another outstanding year for the University of Minnesota product...despite playing in only 18 tournaments, earned $830,231 to finish 15th on money list...earned his second career victory at Colonial National Invitation...was two strokes behind leader Craig Parry after opening 67-68-68...caught Parry with a birdie at the 12th hole Sunday and, after Parry birdied 14, earned the win with birdies at 17 and 18...opened year with two top-10s...closed with 66 for T5 at Mercedes Championships...67-67 on weekend at United Airlines Hawaiian Open moved him into T2, three strokes behind John Morse...T14 at THE PLAYERS Championship...missed month after MCI Classic recovering from colon surgery...came back in fine style with T14 at Buick Classic and Colonial win...tied for lead with Greg Norman through 54 holes of U.S. Open...closing 74 at Shinnecock Hills left him in third, three strokes behind Corey Pavin... at next TOUR appearance, Buick Open, finished T9...closed year with three top-15 finishes -- Sprint International (T14), NEC World Series of Golf (T12), THE TOUR Championship (12)...T5 in scoring (69.85), T9 in greens in regulation (70.4%)...posted 2-1 record in first Ryder Cup...teamed with Duffy Waldorf to win Diners Club Matches.

TOM LEHMAN...*continued*

CAREER HIGHLIGHTS: Finest year on TOUR came in 1994, when he captured his first TOUR victory at Memorial Tournament and earned more than $1 million...four consecutive 67s and Memorial record 268 led to five-stroke victory over Greg Norman...six weeks earlier, finished runner-up to Jose Maria Olazabal at Masters Tournament...nine top-10 finishes in 1994...member of inaugural Presidents Cup team...following three years of limited success (1983-85), left to play in Asia, South Africa and elsewhere...used Ben Hogan Tour as road back to PGA TOUR...he won 1990 Hogan Reflection Ridge Open, then captured three events among 11 top-10 finishes in 1991...named Ben Hogan Tour Player of Year for 1991...returned to PGA TOUR with nine top-10 finishes in 1992, including T2 at Hardee's Golf Classic...finished tied with fellow first-time 1994 winner Loren Roberts, three strokes behind David Frost...two-time runner-up for Big 10 golf championship.

PERSONAL: Credits marriage with giving him focus to do well on TOUR...mini-tours experience included PGT, Dakotas, Golden State, South Florida and Carolinas...is host to annual tournament in Minneapolis to raise money for the Children's Cancer Research Fund...introduced to golf by his father at age 5...represented by his brother, Jim, Jr.

PGA TOUR CAREER SUMMARY — **PLAYOFF RECORD: 0-0**

Year	Events Played	Cuts Made	1st	2nd	3rd	Top 10	Top 25	Earnings	Rank
1983	22	9					1	$9,413	182
1984	26	9						$9,382	184
1985	26	10					2	$20,232	158
1986	2								
1987	1								
1990	1								
1992	29	25		1	1	9	15	$579,093	24
1993	27	20			1	6	12	$422,761	33
1994	23	21	1	1	1	9	15	$1,031,144	4
1995	18	16	1	1	1	5	12	$830,231	15
Total	175	110	2	3	4	29	57	$2,902,257	59

NIKE TOUR SUMMARY

Year	Events Played	Cuts Made	1st	2nd	3rd	Top 10	Top 25	Earnings	Rank
1990	18	12	1			5	8	$41,338	17
1991	28	27	3	3		11	24	$141,934	1
Total	46	39	4	3		16	32	$183,272	
COMBINED TOTAL MONEY								$3,085,529	

1996 PGA TOUR CHARITY TEAM: Las Vegas Invitational

TOP TOURNAMENT SUMMARY

YEAR	86	87	90	92	93	94	95
Masters Tournament					T3	2	40
U.S. Open	CUT	CUT	CUT	T6	T19	T33	3
British Open Championship					T59	T24	
PGA Championship					CUT	T39	CUT
THE PLAYERS Championship				T13	T11	CUT	T14
THE TOUR Championship				T13		28	12

NATIONAL TEAMS: Presidents Cup, 1994. Ryder Cup, 1995.

1995 PGA TOUR STATISTICS

Scoring	**69.85**	**(5T)**
Driving	**264.8**	**(82T)**
Driving Accuracy	**72.6**	**(53T)**
Greens in Regulation	**70.4**	**(9T)**
Putting	**1.820**	**(180)**
All Around	**732**	**(95T)**
Sand Saves	**50.0**	**(126T)**
Total Driving	**135**	**(27)**
Eagles	**4**	**(116T)**
Birdies	**210**	**(161T)**

MISCELLANEOUS STATISTICS

Scoring Avg Before Cut	**70.55**	**(29T)**
Scoring Avg 3rd Rnd	**70.75**	**(67)**
Scoring Avg Final Rnd	**70.73**	**(48)**
Birdies Conversion %	**25.5**	**(170T)**
Par Breakers	**18.3**	**(115T)**

1995 Low Round: **65:** 1995 MCI Classic/2
Career Low Round: **63:** 1993 H.E.B. Texas Open/2
Career Largest Paycheck: **$270,000:** 1994 The Memorial Tournament/1

Justin Leonard

EXEMPT STATUS: 22nd on 1995 money list
FULL NAME: Justin Charles Garret Leonard
HEIGHT: 5' 9" **WEIGHT:** 160
BIRTH DATE: June 15, 1972 **BIRTHPLACE:** Dallas, TX
RESIDENCE: Dallas, TX; plays out of Kiawah Island, SC
FAMILY: Single
COLLEGE: University of Texas (Business, 1994)
SPECIAL INTEREST: Fishing
TURNED PROFESSIONAL: 1994 **JOINED TOUR:** 1994

BEST EVER FINISH: 2 -- 1995 LaCantera Texas Open; T2 -- Motorola Western Open.

BEST 1995 FINISHES: 2 -- LaCantera Texas Open; T2 -- Motorola Western Open; T4 -- Doral-Ryder Open, Kemper Open; T5 -- Colonial National Invitation; T7 -- THE TOUR Championship; T8 -- PGA Championship.

1995 SEASON: One of three rookies to qualify for THE TOUR Championship, Justin finished 22nd on the money list with $748,793...made TOUR Championship with second-place finish at LaCantera Texas Open, last full-field event of year...missed first three cuts of year, but only three thereafter...first top-10 came at Doral-Ryder Open...T3 after 36 holes, fell to T13 with third-round 71, but closed with 68 to finish T4 two strokes behind Nick Faldo...shot 68-68 on weekend at Colonial National Invitation to finish T5...two weeks later, closing 67 led to T4 at Kemper Open...T11 through 54 holes at Motorola Western Open, shot final-round 67 to finish T2, one stroke behind Billy Mayfair...$132,000 payday was largest of year and brief career...at PGA, was alone in third through two rounds, three strokes behind Ernie Els and Mark O'Meara...closed with 70-70 for T8...at LaCantera, shot 67-70-69-68 -- 274 to finish alone in second, six strokes behind Duffy Waldorf and six strokes ahead of John Mahaffey, John Morse and Loren Roberts, who were T3...made final 11 cuts leading up to THE TOUR Championship...at Southern Hills, was at even-par 140, only three strokes off lead through 36 holes, then finished 72-74 for T7.

CAREER HIGHLIGHTS: Played eight TOUR events as amateur, making cut in five...earned TOUR privileges without trip to qualifying school by finishing 126th on 1994 money list with $140,143...finished third at Anheuser-Busch Classic in third pro start, worth $74,800...won 1994 NCAA Championship at 17-under-par 271, equalling NCAA record set by Phil Mickelson in 1992...only golfer in Southwest Conference history to win four consecutive conference championships...winner 1992 U.S. Amateur...First-Team All-American 1993-94...winner Texas 5A State Championship 1989-90.

PERSONAL: TOUR mentors include all-time University of Texas greats Ben Crenshaw and Tom Kite.

CAREER SUMMARY **PLAYOFF RECORD: 0-0**

Year	Events Played	Cuts Made	1st	2nd	3rd	Top 10	Top 25	Earnings	Rank
1993(Am.)	7	5					1		
1994	13	5			1	2	4	$140,413	126
1995	31	25		2		7	13	$748,793	22
Total	51	35		2	1	9	18	$889,206	193

1996 PGA TOUR CHARITY TEAM: Bell Canadian Open.

TOP TOURNAMENT SUMMARY

YEAR	93	95
Masters Tournament	CUT	
U.S. Open	T68	
British Open Championship	CUT	T58
PGA Championship		T8
THE PLAYERS Championship		T34
THE TOUR Championship		T7

NATIONAL TEAMS: Walker Cup,1993. U.S. World Amateur, 1992.

1995 PGA TOUR STATISTICS

Scoring	70.23	(17T)
Driving	259.3	(125T)
Driving Accuracy	77.1	(13)
Greens in Regulation	66.8	(73T)
Putting	1.757	(16T)
All Around	323	(1)
Sand Saves	57.3	(38T)
Total Driving	138	(32T)
Eagles	8	(36T)
Birdies	386	(5)

MISCELLANEOUS STATISTICS

Scoring Avg Before Cut	70.14	(12)
Scoring Avg 3rd Rnd	71.33	(108T)
Scoring Avg Final Rnd	70.21	(18T)
Birdies Conversion %	30.3	(42T)
Par Breakers	19.9	(62T)

1995 Low Round: **65:** 1995 Greater Milwaukee Open/4
Career Low Round: **65:** 1995 Greater Milwaukee Open/4
Career Largest Paycheck: **$132,000:** 1995 Motorola Western Open/T2

WAYNE LEVI *(LEV-ee)*

EXEMPT STATUS: Top 50 on PGA TOUR career money list
FULL NAME: Wayne John Levi
HEIGHT: 5' 9" **WEIGHT:** 165
BIRTH DATE: February 22, 1952 **BIRTHPLACE:** Little Falls, NY
RESIDENCE: New Hartford, NY
FAMILY: Wife, Judy; Michelle (7/29/79), Lauren (1/20/83), Christine (12/30/84); Brian (5/1/88)
COLLEGE: Oswego (NY) State
SPECIAL INTERESTS: Financial and stock markets, reading
TURNED PROFESSIONAL: 1973 **Q SCHOOL:** Spring 1977

TOUR VICTORIES (12): 1978 Walt Disney World National Team Play (with Bob Mann) **1979** Houston Open. **1980** Pleasant Valley-Jimmy Fund Classic. **1982** Hawaiian Open, LaJet Classic. **1983** Buick Open. **1984** B.C. Open. **1985** Georgia-Pacific Atlanta Classic. **1990** BellSouth Atlanta Classic, Centel Western Open, Canon Greater Hartford Open, Canadian Open.

BEST 1995 FINISHES: T20 -- MCI Classic, B.C. Open

1995 SEASON: After falling from top 125 for first time since his rookie year in 1977, Wayne is exempt in 1996 for being in top 50 on PGA TOUR career money list, an exemption he can use only once...made only six of 20 cuts in 1995, earning $46,095...best finishes of year were two T20s...at MCI Classic, shot 71-71-66-71 -- 279...at B.C. Open, shot 68-70-69-70 -- 277...low round of year came in second round of Las Vegas Invitational, a 65 at Las Vegas CC...shot third-round 79 to miss cut.

CAREER HIGHLIGHTS: Had career year in 1990, for which he was selected by his peers as the first PGA TOUR Player of the Year...collected four victories from May to September, making him first since Curtis Strange in 1988 to win four times...became fifth player to earn more than $1 million in one season as he finished second to Greg Norman on the money list...won BellSouth Classic, which he also won in 1985, in near darkness by one stroke over Keith Clearwater, Larry Mize and Nick Price...two weeks later, captured Centel Western Open by four over Payne Stewart...shot 67-66-67-67 -- 267 for a two-stroke victory at Canon Greater Hartford Open...fourth victory came at Canadian Open, by one stroke over Ian Baker-Finch and Jim Woodward...first TOUR victory came with Bob Mann in 1978 Walt Disney World National Team...upstate New York native captured 1984 B.C. Open at Endicott, NY...won 1982 Hawaiian Open with an orange ball, the first player to win with a ball that wasn't white...won 1988 Chrysler Team Championship with George Burns.

PERSONAL: Family man who prefers to spend much of his time at home...avid follower of financial markets.

CAREER SUMMARY — **PLAYOFF RECORD: 2-1**

Year	Events Played	Cuts Made	1st	2nd	3rd	Top 10	Top 25	Earnings	Rank
1976	1	1						$1,412	217
1977	13	7					3	$8,136	159
1978	23	16	1		1	1	5	$25,039	99
1979	29	24	1	1		6	14	$141,612	20
1980	32	19	1			5	10	$120,145	32
1981	30	24				2	11	$62,177	69
1982	27	22	2	1	1	9	18	$280,681	8
1983	22	20	1		1	6	13	$193,252	22
1984	28	22	1	1		7	16	$252,921	20
1985	23	21	1			5	14	$221,425	22
1986	28	20				5	9	$154,777	59
1987	27	16		2		5	7	$203,322	53
1988	23	19		1		4	8	$190,073	61
1989	26	17		1	1	7	11	$499,292	16
1990	23	14	4		1	5	6	$1,024,647	2
1991	25	12			1	3	6	$195,861	87
1992	25	17				3	7	$237,935	65
1993	22	15				2	6	$179,521	95
1994	24	17				4	7	$200,476	91
1995	20	6					2	$46,095	208
Total	471	329	12	7	6	79	173	$4,238,799	34

TOP TOURNAMENT SUMMARY

YEAR	76	78	79	80	81	82	83	84	85	86	87	88	89	90	91
Masters Tournament				CUT	T25	T24	T12	T11	T18	35				CUT	T32
U.S. Open	T28	T46	T25	T43			T43	W/D	T46	T55				CUT	T49
PGA Championship				CUT	T49	CUT		CUT	T18	T30	CUT				T16
THE PLAYERS Championship		T63	T5	W/D	T26	W/D	T13	T20	CUT	T48	CUT	T8	T50	CUT	CUT
THE TOUR Championship													T3	T3	

WAYNE LEVI...*continued*

TOP TOURNAMENT SUMMARY (cont.)

YEAR	92	93	94	95
U.S. Open		T25	T47	
PGA Championship	CUT	T31		
THE PLAYERS Championship	T17	CUT	T27	T43

NATIONAL TEAMS: Four Tours World Championship, 1990; Ryder Cup, 1991; World Cup, 1991

1995 PGA TOUR STATISTICS

Scoring	72.12	(172T)
Driving	253.5	(169T)
Driving Accuracy	73.0	(45T)
Greens in Regulation	64.3	(138T)
Putting	1.801	(130T)
All Around	1,035	(162T)
Sand Saves	58.1	(27T)
Total Driving	214	(133)
Eagles	1	(174T)
Birdies	174	(180)

MISCELLANEOUS STATISTICS

Scoring Avg Before Cut	72.39	(179T)
Scoring Avg 3rd Rnd	70.88	(72)
Scoring Avg Final Rnd	71.71	(130)
Birdies Conversion %	29.3	(77T)
Par Breakers	18.9	(102T)

1995 Low Round: **65:** 1995 Las Vegas Invitational/2
Career Low Round: **62:** 1989 GTE Byron Nelson/1
Career Largest Paycheck: $180,000: 4 times, most recent 1990 BellSouth Atlanta/1

BRUCE LIETZKE *(LITZ-kee)*

EXEMPT STATUS: 1994 tournament winner
FULL NAME: Bruce Alan Lietzke
HEIGHT: 6' 2" **WEIGHT:** 185
BIRTH DATE: July 18, 1951 **BIRTHPLACE:** Kansas City, KS
RESIDENCE: Dallas, TX
FAMILY: Wife, Rosemarie; Stephen Taylor (10/5/83), Christine (10/11/85)
COLLEGE: University of Houston
SPECIAL INTERESTS: Serious fishing, racing cars
TURNED PROFESSIONAL: 1974 **Q SCHOOL:** Spring 1975

TOUR VICTORIES (13): 1977 Joe Garagiola-Tucson Open, Hawaiian Open. **1978** Canadian Open. **1979** Joe Garagiola-Tucson Open. **1980** Colonial National Invitation. **1981** Bob Hope Desert Classic, Wickes-Andy Williams San Diego Open, Byron Nelson Classic. **1982** Canadian Open. **1984** Honda Classic. **1988** GTE Byron Nelson Classic. **1992** Southwestern Bell Colonial. **1994** Las Vegas Invitational.

BEST 1995 FINISHES: 2 -- Mercedes Championsips; T4 -- Phoenix Open

1995 SEASON: Another light schedule for the 21-year veteran...made 12 cuts in 16 starts, including two top-10s in January...erased six-stroke deficit with final-round 67 at Mercedes Championships to force playoff with Steve Elkington...lost playoff to Elkington's 25-foot birdie putt on second extra hole...typically, had not touched club in six weeks prior to Mercedes event...in third start, shot 72-65-69-66 at Phoenix Open for T4, three strokes behind Vijay Singh-Billy Mayfair playoff...shot 68-67 and was only one stroke off pace after 36 holes at Memorial Tournament, then finished with 70-72 for T13...took customary two-month hiatus after Memorial, reappearing at PGA Championship, where he finished T23...fifth in driving accuracy on TOUR (78.8%).

CAREER HIGHLIGHTS: Won 13th career title, 1994 Las Vegas Invitational worth $270,000, to earn unexpected spot in TOUR Championship...closing 65 enough to defeat Robert Gamez by one stroke...finest season on TOUR produced earnings of $703,805 in 1992, when he won Southwestern Bell Colonial for second time...recorded weekend rounds of 64-66 to finish tied with Corey Pavin at 13-under-par 267...birdie on first playoff hole brought first victory since 1988, when he captured GTE Byron Nelson Classic...also claimed Nelson Classic in 1981...all told, has won four events twice: Colonial and Nelson, Joe Garagiola-Tucson Open (1977-79), Canadian Open (1978-82)...first victory came in 1977 Tucson Open, where he defeated Gene Littler on fourth playoff hole...playoff loser to Greg Norman in 1992 Canadian Open...closed with 67 to miss by one stroke three-man 1993 Greater Milwaukee Open playoff won by Billy Mayfair.

BRUCE LIETZKE...*continued*

PERSONAL: Plays limited schedule in order to spend as much time as possible with family. . .enjoys coaching teams on which his children play. . .holds distinction of being only player in both fields when Al Geiberger (1977) and Chip Beck (1991) shot their 59s . . .an avid Dallas Cowboys fan. . .attended National Hot Road Association driving school in Gainesville, FL in December 1995.

CAREER SUMMARY — **PLAYOFF RECORD: 6-3**

Year	Events Played	Cuts Made	1st	2nd	3rd	Top 10	Top 25	Earnings	Rank
1975	14	8				5	6	$30,780	74
1976	31	25			2	6	13	$69,229	40
1977	27	25	2	2		7	18	$202,156	5
1978	27	19	1	1		7	11	$113,905	18
1979	27	23	1	2		10	17	$198,439	8
1980	24	19	1	1		6	15	$163,884	16
1981	24	22	3	2	1	13	18	$343,446	4
1982	24	21	1	1		6	14	$217,447	14
1983	20	18			2	6	11	$153,255	32
1984	21	18	1	3	1	7	12	$342,853	6
1985	18	13				5	9	$136,992	59
1986	22	20				5	10	$183,761	47
1987	21	15				2	9	$154,383	68
1988	25	20	1	2	1	10	12	$500,815	19
1989	20	18			2	3	9	$307,987	36
1990	18	16			3	4	11	$329,294	41
1991	19	16		1	1	7	13	$566,272	19
1992	18	17	1	2		7	12	$703,805	16
1993	16	10				2	4	$163,241	101
1994	18	13	1			4	10	$564,926	28
1995	16	12		1		2	5	$269,394	70
Total	450	368	13	18	13	124	239	$5,713,762	17

1996 PGA TOUR CHARITY TEAM: GTE Byron Nelson Classic

TOP TOURNAMENT SUMMARY

YEAR	76	77	78	79	80	81	82	83	84	85	86	87	88	89	90
Masters Tournament		T28		6	CUT	T11	T20	T42	T33	T6	T31	49		T34	
U.S. Open	T47	T19	T20	T41	T37	T17	CUT	CUT		T31					
British Open Championship					T19	T6	CUT								
PGA Championship	T38	T15	62	T16	T30	T4	T16	T6	T65	T18	T5	T28	T62	T46	CUT
THE PLAYERS Championship		T40			T24	T4	4	T3	T12	T7	T40	CUT	CUT	3	T11
THE TOUR Championship													T8		

TOP TOURNAMENT SUMMARY (cont.)

YEAR	91	92	93	94	95
Masters Tournament		T13	T31		T31
PGA Championship	2	T73	CUT		T23
THE PLAYERS Championship	T6	T46	T28	CUT	T43
THE TOUR Championship	4	T20		T10	

NATIONAL TEAMS: Ryder Cup, 1981. U.S. vs. Japan, 1984.

1995 PGA TOUR STATISTICS

Scoring	71.03	(70T)
Driving	265.2	(78)
Driving Accuracy	78.8	(5)
Greens in Regulation	67.9	(47T)
Putting	1.815	(168)
All Around	855	(128)
Sand Saves	45.1	(169)
Total Driving	83	(7)
Eagles	3	(137T)
Birdies	172	(181)

MISCELLANEOUS STATISTICS

Scoring Avg Before Cut	71.00	(70)
Scoring Avg 3rd Rnd	72.55	(173)
Scoring Avg Final Rnd	71.09	(79T)
Birdies Conversion %	26.5	(150T)
Par Breakers	18.3	(115T)

1995 Low Round: 65: 1995 Phoenix Open/2
Career Low Round: 62: 1993 GTE Byron Nelson Classic/2
Career Largest Paycheck: $270,000: 1994 Las Vegas Invitational/1

BOB LOHR *(LORE)*

EXEMPT STATUS: 59th on 1995 money list
FULL NAME: Robert Harold Lohr
HEIGHT: 6' 1" **WEIGHT:** 185
BIRTH DATE: November 2, 1960 **BIRTHPLACE:** Cincinnati, OH
RESIDENCE: Orlando, FL
FAMILY: Wife, Marie; Matthew Robert (7/15/91)
COLLEGE: Miami University, OH (1983, Marketing)
SPECIAL INTERESTS: Hunting, fishing, snow skiing
TURNED PROFESSIONAL: 1983 **Q SCHOOL:** Fall, 1984

TOUR VICTORIES (1): 1988 Walt Disney World/Oldsmobile Classic.

INTERNATIIONAL VICTORIES (1): 1990 Mexican Open.

BEST 1995 FINISHES: 2 -- Bell Canadian Open; T5 -- Nestle Invitational

1995 SEASON: Nearly captured second career victory at Bell Canadian Open...took one-stroke lead after 36 holes, shooting 68-67...extended lead to three over Mark O'Meara with third-round 69...through 14 holes of the final round, Lohr trailed by three, but by birdieing three of the last four holes, he forced a playoff which O'Meara won with a par at the first extra hole...made 16 of first 17 cuts...low round of year was 64 in third round of Bob Hope Chrysler Classic at La Quinta CC...T3 after 54 holes at Nestle Invitational, finished T5 with closing 72, six strokes behind Loren Roberts...T12 at Buick Challenge despite opening 74 at Callaway Gardens...closed with 68-65-70...the following week, four strokes off lead through two rounds at 54-hole Walt Disney World/ Oldsmobile Classic, then shot 70 in final round for T21.

CAREER HIGHLIGHTS: Only TOUR victory came via playoff at 1988 Walt Disney World/Oldsmobile Classic...birdied final hole to close regulation play at 25-under-par 263, in deadlock with Chip Beck...birdied fifth extra hole while Beck bogeyed in near darkness...had opened Disney play with 62 on Palm Course...shot 10-under-par 61 in first round of 1994 Anheuser-Busch Golf Classic...went on to finish T7...T5 at Kmart Greater Greensboro Open was best 1994 finish... lost playoff to Jay Haas at 1993 H-E-B Texas Open...posted second- and fourth-round 64s to finish at 21-under-par 263...Haas won with birdie on second extra hole at Oak Hills CC...also in 1993 had solo third in Sprint Western Open, where he closed with 63, and T4 at Bob Hope Chrysler Classic...seven top-10 finishes, including pair of second-place ties (Southwestern Bell Colonial and International), keyed career year with $386,759 in 1991...winner 1990 Mexican Open...named All Mid-America Conference three years while at Miami (Ohio) University...Honorable Mention All-American in 1983.

PERSONAL: Golf had stiff competition from baseball when he was youngster...outstanding pitcher through high school, but golf won out at Miami of Ohio–where both sports played in spring...inducted into Miami Hall of Fame 1993.

CAREER SUMMARY **PLAYOFF RECORD: 1-2**

Year	Events Played	Cuts Made	1st	2nd	3rd	Top 10	Top 25	Earnings	Rank
1985	30	18		1		2	7	$93,651	81
1986	35	18				3	6	$85,949	99
1987	33	18		1	1	3	7	$137,108	80
1988	33	23	1		1	5	10	$315,536	32
1989	31	19			1	3	7	$144,242	98
1990	30	20				2	3	$141,260	109
1991	26	15		2	1	7	9	$386,759	41
1992	30	16				2	5	$128,307	112
1993	26	17		1	1	3	6	$314,982	54
1994	28	16				2	7	$225,048	80
1995	28	22		1		2	6	$314,947	59
Total	330	202	1	6	5	34	73	$2,287,789	82

1996 PGA TOUR CHARITY TEAM: Doral-Ryder Open

TOP TOURNAMENT SUMMARY

YEAR	85	86	87	88	89	90	91	92	93	94	95
Masters Tournament					T46						
U.S. Open		CUT	T58	CUT		T33					
British Open Championship											T79
PGA Championship	CUT	CUT	CUT	CUT	T41	CUT	CUT	CUT	CUT	CUT	
THE PLAYERS Championship	CUT	CUT	71	T51	T59	T68	T9	T21	T28	CUT	T55

Bob Lohr...continued

1995 PGA TOUR STATISTICS		
Scoring	70.95	(64T)
Driving	251.2	(179T)
Driving Accuracy	73.9	(31T)
Greens in Regulation	64.8	(126T)
Putting	1.761	(25)
All Around	634	(68)
Sand Saves	55.5	(50T)
Total Driving	210	(126T)
Eagles	4	(116T)
Birdies	314	(43)

MISCELLANEOUS STATISTICS		
Scoring Avg Before Cut	70.93	(60T)
Scoring Avg 3rd Rnd	71.48	(118T)
Scoring Avg Final Rnd	71.29	(99T)
Birdies Conversion %	29.6	(64T)
Par Breakers	18.6	(111T)

1995 Low Round: **64:** 1995 Bob Hope Chrysler Classic/3
Career Low Round: **61:** 1994 Anheuser-Busch Golf Classic/1
Career Largest Paycheck: **$140,400:** 1995 Bell Canadian Open/2

Davis Love III

EXEMPT STATUS: Winner, 1992 PLAYERS Championship
FULL NAME: Davis Milton Love III
HEIGHT: 6' 3" **WEIGHT:** 175
BIRTH DATE: April 13, 1964 **BIRTHPLACE:** Charlotte, NC
RESIDENCE: Sea Island, GA; plays out of Sea Island
FAMILY: Wife, Robin; Alexia (6/5/88), Davis IV (12/4/93)
COLLEGE: University of North Carolina
SPECIAL INTERESTS: Fishing, reading novels, hunting
TURNED PROFESSIONAL: 1985 **Q SCHOOL:** Fall, 1985

TOUR VICTORIES (9): 1987 MCI Heritage Classic. **1990** The International. **1991** MCI Heritage Classic. **1992** THE PLAYERS Championship, MCI Heritage Classic, Kmart Greater Greensboro Open. **1993** Infiniti Tournament of Champions, Las Vegas Invitational. **1995** Freeport-McMoRan Classic.

INTERNATIONAL VICTORIES (1): 1995 World Cup (individual title).

BEST 1995 FINISHES: 1 -- Freeport-McMoRan Classic; 2 -- Masters Tournament; T3 -- AT&T Pebble Beach National Pro-Am; T4 -- Doral-Ryder Open, Kemper Open, U.S. Open; T6 -- THE PLAYERS Championship; T7 -- Las Vegas Invitational; T8 -- Sprint International

1995 SEASON: Rebounded from sub-par 1994 with second $1 million season of his 10-year PGA TOUR career...first three months occupied with chase for Masters invitation...earned trip to Augusta with playoff victory over Mike Heinen at Freeport-McMoRan Classic the week before...birdied second extra hole for ninth career win...prior to New Orleans, had several close calls -- T3 at AT&T Pebble Beach National Pro-Am after opening 65; 36-hole leader at Doral-Ryder Open, finished T4; two strokes off lead through 36 at Nestle Invitational, fell to T16; trailed by one through two rounds at THE PLAYERS Championship, finished T6...at Augusta National, was T11, three strokes behind leaders through 54 holes...closed with 66 to finish one stroke behind winner Ben Crenshaw...had two-stroke lead following second-round 63 at Kemper Open...led by one after 54 holes, then closed with 73 to finish T4, three strokes behind Corey Pavin-Lee Janzen playoff...the following week, shot 72-68-73-71 -- 284 for T4 at U.S. Open...final top-10s were T8 at Sprint International and T7 at Las Vegas Invitational...teamed with Fred Couples for record fourth consecutive World Cup title...captured first individual World Cup crown at TPC at Mission Hills in Shenzhen, China...member of second Ryder Cup Team, where his record was 3-2...second in driving distance (284.4 yards), a title he won in 1986 and 1994...third in eagles (14).

CAREER HIGHLIGHTS: Enjoyed finest season in 1992, when he won three times...began with four-stroke victory at PLAYERS Championship...three weeks later, successfully defended at MCI Heritage Classic (event also won for first title in 1987), then very next week captured Kmart Greater Greensboro Open...final 62 at Greensboro brought him from three strokes off Rocco Mediate lead for win...started and ended 1993 in winning fashion, beginning with Infiniti Tournament of Champions (one stroke over Tom Kite) and closing with Las Vegas Invitational...captured 1990 International by three points...winner 1984 North and South Amateur and ACC Championship.

PERSONAL: Father, who died in 1988 plane crash, a highly regarded teacher...Davis III was born shortly after Davis Jr. contended in 1964 Masters...enjoys hunting and fishing, North Carolina basketball, Atlanta Braves baseball, stock car racing...attended National Hot Road Association driving school in Gainesville, FL in Dec. 1995...conducts annual charity event for Safe Harbor each fall...brother Mark is his caddy.

CAREER SUMMARY — **PLAYOFF RECORD: 1-3**

Year	Events Played	Cuts Made	1st	2nd	3rd	Top 10	Top 25	Earnings	Rank
1985(Am.)	1								
1986	31	22			1	2	7	$113,245	77
1987	26	18	1	1		4	9	$297,378	33
1988	29	17				3	9	$156,068	75
1989	24	17		1	1	4	10	$278,760	44
1990	27	20	1		1	4	12	$537,172	20
1991	28	23	1	1	1	8	14	$686,361	8
1992	25	22	3	1	1	9	15	$1,191,630	2
1993	26	23	2	1		5	12	$777,059	12
1994	28	21		1		4	9	$474,219	33
1995	24	22	1	1	1	9	15	$1,111,999	6
Total	269	205	9	7	6	52	112	$5,623,890	18

1996 PGA TOUR CHARITY TEAM: Deposit Guaranty Golf Classic

TOP TOURNAMENT SUMMARY

YEAR	86	87	88	89	90	91	92	93	94	95
The Masters Tournament			CUT			T42	T25	T54	CUT	2
U.S. Open			CUT	T33		T11	T60	T33	T28	T4
British Open Championship		CUT	CUT	T23	CUT	T44	CUT	CUT	T38	T98
PGA Championship	T47	CUT		T17	T40	T32	T33	T31	CUT	CUT
THE PLAYERS Championship	T14	CUT	DQ	CUT	T24	CUT	1	T67	T6	T6
THE TOUR Championship					T12	T19	T25	27		T16

NATIONAL TEAMS: Walker Cup, 1985. Dunhill Cup, 1992. World Cup (4), 1992,1993,1994,1995. Ryder Cup (2), 1993, 1995. Presidents Cup, 1994.

1995 PGA TOUR STATISTICS

Scoring	**70.09**	**(12)**
Driving	**284.6**	**(2)**
Driving Accuracy	**69.1**	**(102T)**
Greens in Regulation	**66.5**	**(82T)**
Putting	**1.753**	**(13T)**
All Around	**399**	**(13)**
Sand Saves	**47.3**	**(151)**
Total Driving	**104**	**(11)**
Eagles	**14**	**(3)**
Birdies	**329**	**(34)**

MISCELLANEOUS STATISTICS

Scoring Avg Before Cut	**69.80**	**(2)**
Scoring Avg 3rd Rnd	**72.05**	**(154)**
Scoring Avg Final Rnd	**70.71**	**(44T)**
Birdies Conversion %	**32.3**	**(16T)**
Par Breakers	**21.4**	**(12T)**

1995 Low Round: **63:** 1995 Kemper Open/2
Career Low Round: **60:** 1994 United Airlines Hawaiian Open/2
Career Largest Paycheck: $324,000: 1992 PLAYERS Championship/1

Did You Know?

Only twice in the 1980s were three eagles recorded in one round -- Bruce Lietzke at the 1981 Hawaiian Open and Howard Twitty in the 1991 Pensacola Open. Already in the 1990s, it has happened seven times, including twice last year -- Tommy Tolles at the Bell Canadian Open and John Adams at the Buick Challenge.

STEVE LOWERY *(LAU-ree)*

EXEMPT STATUS: 1994 tournament winner
FULL NAME: Stephen Brent Lowery
HEIGHT: 6'2" **WEIGHT:** 225
BIRTH DATE: October 12, 1960 **BIRTHPLACE:** Birmingham, AL
RESIDENCE: Orlando, FL
FAMILY: Wife, Kathryn; Kristen Branch (12/27/91), Lauren Elizabeth (5/30/95)
COLLEGE: University of Alabama
SPECIAL INTEREST: Sports
TURNED PROFESSIONAL: 1983 **Q SCHOOL:** Fall 1987

TOUR VICTORIES (1): 1994 Sprint International

NIKE TOUR VICTORIES (1): 1992 Ben Hogan Tulsa Open

BEST 1995 FINISHES: T6 -- Motorola Western Open, Greater Milwaukee Open; T7 -- Phoenix Open, MCI Classic; T8 -- PGA Championship; T10 -- Doral Ryder Open

1995 SEASON: Another consistent year for the Alabama native who made 25 of 30 cuts, recorded 15 top-25 finishes and put together his second-best year on TOUR...first of five top-10s came at Phoenix Open, where third-round 65 left him one stroke behind Ben Crenshaw...closing 70 left him T7, four strokes behind Vijay Singh-Billy Mayfair playoff...T21 at AT&T Pebble Beach the following week, including third-round 64 at Spyglass Hill...opened with 65 at Doral-Ryder Open for share of 18-hole lead before finishing T10...trailed by only two after 54 holes at MCI Classic...final-round 70 left him T7, still two strokes off lead...made up 46 places with closing 62 at GTE Byron Nelson Classic, finishing T11...shared 54-hole lead with Brett Ogle at Motorola Western Open, before Sunday 72 placed him T6, two strokes behind winner Mayfair...T8 at PGA Championship with rounds of 69-68-68-69 -- 274...closing 65 at Greater Milwaukee Open enough for T6...led TOUR in birdies with 410.

CAREER HIGHLIGHTS: First TOUR victory came at 1994 Sprint International...tied with Rick Fehr with 35 points after 72 holes, won with par at first extra hole after Fehr's ball found water...victory worth $252,000, more than he had earned in any prior year on TOUR...earned $188,287 in 1993, including more than $60,000 by time TOUR left West Coast...made money in 25 of 32 events, with best finish being T10 in New England Classic...played Tournament Players Series 1983-84...first appeared on TOUR after finishing 12th in 1987 Qualifying Tournament...secured special temporary membership in 1990 and 1991 by earning as much as 150th-place finisher on previous year's money list...T3 at 1991 Chattanooga Classic, four strokes behind winner Dillard Pruitt...finished third on 1992 Hogan Tour money list, good for PGA TOUR membership in 1993...won Ben Hogan Tulsa Open over Jeff Coston on second playoff hole...1982 Southern Amateur champion...1982-83 All-American...1982-83 SEC Player of Year.

PERSONAL: Alabama Crimson Tide football fan...received 1995 Sington Award as Outstanding Professional Athlete in Alabama.

PGA TOUR CAREER SUMMARY **PLAYOFF RECORD: 1-0**

Year	Events Played	Cuts Made	1st	2nd	3rd	Top 10	Top 25	Earnings	Rank
1983	2								
1984	1								
1986	1	1						$666	287
1987	4	2						$4,190	233
1988	34	17					2	$44,327	157
1989	11	7				3	3	$38,699	174
1990	8	6				2	2	$68,524	159
1991	10	7			1	2	3	$87,597	143
1992	7	4					2	$22,608	207
1993	32	25				1	8	$188,287	92
1994	30	20	1	1	1	5	9	$794,048	12
1995	30	25				6	15	$463,858	38
Total	170	114	1	1	2	19	44	$1,712,804	120

NIKE TOUR SUMMARY

Year	Events Played	Cuts Made	1st	2nd	3rd	Top 10	Top 25	Earnings	Rank
1990	3	2					1	$1,420	179
1991	5	2		1		1	1	$10,363	93
1992	21	19	1	2	1	7	14	$114,553	3
Total	29	23	1	3	1	8	16	$126,336	
COMBINED TOTAL MONEY								$1,839,140	

1996 PGA TOUR CHARITY TEAM: Bay Hill Invitational presented by Office Depot.

STEVE LOWERY...continued

TOP TOURNAMENT SUMMARY

YEAR	88	93	94	95
The Masters Tournament				CUT
U.S. Open	CUT	T33	T16	T56
British Open Championship				T79
PGA Championship			CUT	T8
THE PLAYERS Championship			T6	DQ
THE TOUR Championship			T8	

1995 PGA TOUR STATISTICS

Scoring	70.38	(34)
Driving	269.2	(47)
Driving Accuracy	66.8	(135)
Greens in Regulation	67.2	(61T)
Putting	1.751	(7T)
All Around	395	(9)
Sand Saves	52.2	(95T)
Total Driving	182	(89)
Eagles	10	(15T)
Birdies	410	(1)

MISCELLANEOUS STATISTICS

Scoring Avg Before Cut	70.54	(28)
Scoring Avg 3rd Rnd	70.08	(22T)
Scoring Avg Final Rnd	70.68	(38)
Birdies Conversion %	32.9	(10T)
Par Breakers	21.8	(7T)

1995 Low Round: **62:** 1995 GTE Byron Nelson Classic/4
Career Low Round: **62:** 2 times, most recent 1995 GTE Byron Nelson Classic/4
Career Largest Paycheck: $252,000: 1994 The Sprint International/1

SANDY LYLE

EXEMPT STATUS: Winner,1988 Masters Tournament
FULL NAME: Alexander Walter Barr Lyle
HEIGHT: 6' **WEIGHT:** 187
BIRTH DATE: February 9, 1958 **BIRTHPLACE:** Shrewsbury, England
RESIDENCE: West Linton, Scotland
FAMILY: Wife, Jolande; Stuart (1983), James (1986), Alexandra (1993)
SPECIAL INTEREST: Motorcycles, cars, airplanes
TURNED PROFESSIONAL: 1977

TOUR VICTORIES (5): 1986 Greater Greensboro Open. **1987** Tournament Players Championship. **1988** Phoenix Open, Kmart Greater Greensboro Open, Masters Tournament.

INTERNATIONAL VICTORIES (20): 1979 Jersey Open, Scandinavian Enterprise Open, European Open, Scottish Pro Championship. **1980** Coral Classic, World Cup (Indiv.). **1981** Paco Rabanne French Open, Lawrence Batley International. **1982** Lawrence Batley International. **1983** Cepsa Madrid Open. **1984** Italian Open, Lancome Trophy. **1985** British Open, Benson and Hedges International Open. **1987** German Masters. **1988** Dunhill British Masters, Suntory World Match Play Championship. **1991** BMW International Open. **1992** Lancia-Martini Italian Open, Volvo Masters. (with exception of 1980 World Cup, all Europe)

BEST 1995 FINISH: T32 -- Freeport-McMoRan Classic.

1995 SEASON: As he prepared for a full-time return to the PGA TOUR in 1996, Sandy made four of seven cuts in 1995, including final three...shot 69-72-71-71 -- 283 to finish T32 at Freeport-McMoRan Classic, his best finish of year...at British Open, which he won in 1985, was four strokes off lead after opening 71-71, then shot 79-75 on weekend to finish T79...opened with 67 at PGA Championship, finishing T39...in final PGA TOUR start, finished T74 at Bell Canadian Open...will be fully exempt in 1996 based on the 10-year exemption he received for winning 1988 Masters Tournament.

CAREER HIGHLIGHTS: Best year in U.S. came in 1988...won three times on American soil and finished seventh on money list with $726,934...seven strokes behind Davis Love III entering the final round of 1985 Phoenix Open, shot 65 to reach playoff with Fred Couples, which he won with a bogey at third playoff hole, the last time bogey won a playoff on TOUR...moved into contention at Kmart Greater Greensboro Open with second-round 63...held three-stroke lead through 54 holes, then shot closing 72 and met Ken Green in playoff...birdied first extra hole for victory...the following week, took two-stroke lead after second round of Masters, then held on for one-stroke victory over Mark Calcavecchia. . .defeated Jeff Sluman in playoff to win 1987 Tournament Players Championship. . .first U.S. victory was two-stroke triumph over Andy Bean at 1986 Greater Greensboro Open. . .came from three strokes back on the final day to win 1985 British Open at Royal St. George's by one stroke over Payne Stewart. . .individual champion at 1980 World Cup. . .played for Great Britain and Ireland in 1977 Walker Cup Match.

PERSONAL: After becoming first British golfer to win Masters, put haggis on the menu at the Champions' Dinner the following year. . . awarded Member of British Empire.

CAREER SUMMARY — **PLAYOFF RECORD: 3-1**

Year	Events Played	Cuts Made	1st	2nd	3rd	Top 10	Top 25	Earnings	Rank
1980	5	3					2	$8,950	175
1981	3	1						$2,350	225
1982	3	1						$804	284
1983	1								
1984	6	4					3	$15,532	169
1985	13	11					5	$40,452	132
1986	13	9	1			1	4	$143,415	64
1987	15	11	1			4	7	$286,176	34
1988	17	14	3	1		5	13	$726,934	7
1989	17	9		2	1	4	4	$292,293	43
1990	15	7				1	2	$51,280	175
1991	8	5					3	$59,794	166
1992	9	5				1	2	$73,459	154
1993	7	5				1	2	$86,121	153
1994	7	5				1	1	$47,538	191
1995	7	4						$22,908	235
Total	146	94	5	3	1	18	48	$1,858,004	

1996 PGA TOUR CHARITY TEAM: BellSouth Classic

TOP TOURNAMENT SUMMARY

YEAR	80	81	83	85	86	87	88	89	90	91	92	93	94	95
Masters Tournament	48	T28	CUT	T25	T11	T17	1	CUT	CUT	CUT	T37	T21	T38	CUT
U.S. Open	CUT	CUT			T45	T36	T25	CUT	CUT	T16	T51	T52		
British Open Championship														T79
PGA Championship		CUT								T16	CUT	T56	T73	T39
THE PLAYERS Championship				CUT	CUT	1	CUT	CUT	CUT	CUT	CUT		T74	CUT
THE TOUR Championship							T17							

NATIONAL TEAMS: European Ryder Cup (5), 1979, 1981, 1983, 1985, 1987. Nissan Cup (2), 1985, 1986 (medalist in 1985). Kirin Cup, 1987, 1988. World Cup (3), 1979, 1980, 1987 (medalist in 1980). Dunhill Cup (6), 1985, 1986, 1987, 1988, 1989, 1990. Hennesy Cognac Cup (3), 1980, 1982, 1984. British Walker Cup, 1977.

1995 PGA TOUR STATISTICS

Statistic	Value	Rank
Scoring	72.08	(N/A)
Driving	275.0	(N/A)
Driving Accuracy	57.5	(N/A)
Greens in Regulation	59.3	(N/A)
Putting	1.797	(N/A)
Sand Saves	44.4	(N/A)
Total Driving		(N/A)
Eagles	1	(N/A)
Birdies	69	(N/A)

MISCELLANEOUS STATISTICS

Statistic	Value	Rank
Scoring Avg Before Cut	72.57	(N/A)
Scoring Avg 3rd Rnd	74.00	(N/A)
Scoring Avg Final Rnd	73.75	(N/A)
Birdies Conversion %	35.9	(N/A)
Par Breakers	17.7	(N/A)

1995 Low Round: 67: 1995 PGA Championship/1
Career Low Round: 63: 1988 K-Mart GGO/2
Career Largest Paycheck: $183,800: 1988 Masters/1

Andrew Magee

EXEMPT STATUS: 1994 tournament winner
FULL NAME: Andrew Donald Magee
HEIGHT: 6' **WEIGHT:** 180
BIRTH DATE: May 22, 1962 **BIRTHPLACE:** Paris, France
RESIDENCE: Paradise Valley, AZ
FAMILY: Wife, Susan; Lindsey Ellenberg (6/23/81), Campbell Joseph (11/27/88), Oliver Andrew (9/5/91)
COLLEGE: University of Oklahoma (1984)
SPECIAL INTERESTS: Travel, swimming, fishing, whistling
TURNED PROFESSIONAL: 1984 **Q SCHOOL:** Fall 1984

TOUR VICTORIES (4): 1988 Pensacola Open. **1991** Nestle Invitational, Las Vegas Invitational. **1994** Northern Telecom Open.

BEST 1995 FINISHES: 4 -- Honda Classic; T5 -- Bell Canadian Open; T10 Greater Milwaukee Open

1995 SEASON: Posted three top-10 finishes on way to $256,918 on year, lowest total since 1990...made first six cuts in 1995, sixth coming at Honda Classic...T2 after 36 holes at Weston Hills with rounds of 69-67...third-round 76 dropped him to T9, but rebounded with closing 67 for fourth, four strokes behind Mark O'Meara...$57,600 payday was largest of 1995...next top-10 didn't come until September, when closing 66 good for T10 at Greater Milwaukee Open...the following week, two 68s put him in second, one stroke off lead at Bell Canadian Open...T3 after third-round 73, but five strokes back...finished T5 at Glen Abbey after closing 71...shot second-round 65, low round of year, at Quad City Classic on way to T27.

CAREER HIGHLIGHTS: First TOUR win came in 1988 Pensacola Open, where he rallied from four strokes back to claim title...climaxed strong early-season run in 1991 with second career victory in Nestle Invitational...severe weather ended Bay Hill event after 54 holes...made eagle-3 with 30-foot putt on 16th hole to gain two-stroke win...later in year posted 31-under-par 329 to force playoff with D.A. Weibring at Las Vegas Invitational, a PGA TOUR 90-hole record at the time...posted career-low 62 in fourth round at Las Vegas CC... defeated Weibring with par on second extra hole...two 1991 wins helped produce best season to date...won 1994 Northern Telecom Open with closing 67 to defeat Loren Roberts, Vijay Singh, Jay Don Blake and Steve Stricker by two strokes...led through 36 and 54 holes the following week at Phoenix Open, but final-round 73 dropped him to T13...three-time All-America at University of Oklahoma...won 1979 Doug Sanders Junior Invitational.

PERSONAL: Born in Paris, where his father was working in the oil business.

CAREER SUMMARY **PLAYOFF RECORD: 1-0**

Year	Events Played	Cuts Made	1st	2nd	3rd	Top 10	Top 25	Earnings	Rank
1984	3	1						$1,701	238
1985	30	18				4	5	$75,593	99
1986	33	17				1	5	$69,478	120
1987	33	18				2	7	$94,598	99
1988	30	17	1		1	4	8	$261,954	43
1989	33	19				3	5	$126,770	109
1990	30	22				3	8	$210,507	71
1991	28	19	2			7	12	$750,082	5
1992	28	21				3	12	$285,946	53
1993	25	14		1		2	7	$269,986	62
1994	25	20	1			3	9	$431,041	36
1995	27	18				3	5	$256,918	72
Total	325	204	4	1	1	35	83	$2,834,575	63

1996 PGA TOUR CHARITY TEAM: CVS Charity Classic

TOP TOURNAMENT SUMMARY

YEAR	85	86	87	88	89	90	91	92	93	94	95
Masters Tournament					CUT		T7	T19	T31	T41	
U.S. Open		CUT		CUT		CUT	CUT	T17			CUT
British Open Championship				CUT			T57	T5	T39	CUT	
PGA Championship		CUT		69	CUT	T45	T13	T56	T51	T47	
THE PLAYERS Championship	CUT	CUT	CUT	CUT	CUT	T36	CUT	T17	T20	T45	T37
THE TOUR Championship							T19				

ANDREW MAGEE...continued

1995 PGA TOUR STATISTICS		
Scoring	70.78	(55T)
Driving	271.4	(29T)
Driving Accuracy	67.1	(132T)
Greens in Regulation	68.2	(42T)
Putting	1.781	(68T)
All Around	442	(22)
Sand Saves	55.8	(45T)
Total Driving	161	(59T)
Eagles	9	(20T)
Birdies	305	(51T)

MISCELLANEOUS STATISTICS		
Scoring Avg Before Cut	70.64	(36)
Scoring Avg 3rd Rnd	71.18	(94T)
Scoring Avg Final Rnd	71.47	(111T)
Birdies Conversion %	28.9	(84T)
Par Breakers	20.3	(40T)

1995 Low Round: **65:** 1995 Quad City Classic/2
Career Low Round: **62:** 1991 Las Vegas Invitation/4
Career Largest Paycheck: **$270,000:** 1991 Las Vegas Invitation/1

JEFF MAGGERT *(MAG-ert)*

EXEMPT STATUS: Member, 1995 Ryder Cup Team
FULL NAME: Jeffrey Allan Maggert
HEIGHT: 5' 9" **WEIGHT:** 165
BIRTH DATE: Feb. 20, 1964 **BIRTHPLACE:** Columbia, MO
RESIDENCE: The Woodlands, TX
FAMILY: Wife, Kelli; Matt (12/10/88), Macy (10/26/90)
COLLEGE: Texas A&M
SPECIAL INTERESTS: Fishing, hunting, camping, sporting events
TURNED PROFESSIONAL: 1986 **JOINED TOUR:** 1991

TOUR VICTORIES (1): **1993** Walt Disney World/Oldsmobile Classic.

INTERNATIONAL VICTORIES (2): **1989** Malaysian Open (Asia). **1990** Vines Classic (Aus).

NIKE TOUR VICTORIES (2): **1990** Knoxville Open, Buffalo Open.

BEST 1995 FINISHES: T2 -- Motorola Western Open; T3 -- PGA Championship; T4 -- U.S. Open; T5 -- Freeport-McMoRan Classic; T8 -- Colonial National Invitation

1995 SEASON: Earnings decreased for first time in career, but still finished 34th on money-list with $527,952...first of five top-10 finishes came at Freeport-McMoRan Classic...shot 72-66-70-69 -- 277 to finish T5, three strokes back...at Colonial National Invitation, was two strokes off lead after shooting 66-68, before 74-69 on weekend dropped him to T8...third top-10 came at U.S. Open, when a closing 66 at Shinnecock Hills offset a third-round 77 and lifted him from T35 to T4...opened 74-73 at Motorola Western Open before a 69-64 finish left him only one stroke behind Billy Mayfair...T2 with Mark O'Meara through 54 holes of PGA Championsip after third-round 65...finished T3 after 69 on Sunday, two strokes out of Steve Elkington-Colin Montgomerie playoff...in first Ryder Cup appearance, compiled 2-2 record.

CAREER HIGHLIGHTS: Leading point-getter among qualifiers for first Presidents Cup Team in 1994...had 2-2 record, including 2-1 victory over Bradley Hughes in singles...broke through in Oct. 1993 for first win, a three-stroke victory over Greg Kraft at Walt Disney World/Oldsmobile Classic...victory came under floodlights at conclusion of day in which he was forced to play 36 holes because of earlier weather delays...prior to Disney win, achieved best career finishes in 1993 at Northern Telecom (2) and FedEx St. Jude Classic (T2)...briefly held final-round lead in 1992 PGA Championship...course-record 65 in Round 3 of PGA at Bellerive CC moved him into second-place tie before eventual final-round 74 produced sixth-place finish...led 1991 Independent Insurance Agent Open through three rounds on home course at The Woodlands before faltering...as PGA TOUR rookie in '91, ranked behind only John Daly in earnings with $240,940...T5 in first TOUR start in Northern Telecom Open...1990 Ben Hogan Tour Player of Year with top earnings of $108,644 and victories in Hogan Knoxville and Buffalo Opens...gained international experience in 1989-90...won 1989 Malaysian Open on Asian Tour, 1990 Vines Classic on Australasian Tour...All-America at Texas A&M in 1986 ...winner 1980 Texas State Junior, 1988 and 1990 Texas State Opens, 1989 Louisiana Open...won inaugural Diners Club Matches with Jim McGovern in 1994.

PERSONAL: At 16, caddied for Scott Simpson in Houston Open.

PGA TOUR CAREER SUMMARY								PLAYOFF RECORD: 0-0	
Year	Events Played	Cuts Made	1st	2nd	3rd	Top 10	Top 25	Earnings	Rank
1986	4	1				1	1	$13,400	192
1987	4	1						$936	293
1990	2	1						$2,060	277
1991	29	17				2	9	$240,940	68
1992	26	19			2	4	9	$377,408	38
1993	28	17	1	2	1	6	13	$793,023	11
1994	26	22		2	2	11	14	$814,475	9
1995	23	17		1	1	5	10	$527,952	34
Total	142	95	1	5	6	29	56	$2,770,193	66

NIKE TOUR SUMMARY

Year	Events Played	Cuts Made	1st	2nd	3rd	Top 10	Top 25	Earnings	Rank
1990	22	20	2	3	1	13	17	$108,644	1
Total	22	20	2	3	1	13	17	$108,644	

COMBINED TOTAL MONEY: $2,878,838

1996 PGA TOUR CHARITY TEAM: Shell Houston Open

TOP TOURNAMENT SUMMARY

YEAR	86	87	91	92	93	94	95
Masters Tournament					T21	T50	CUT
U.S. Open	CUT	CUT			T52	T9	T4
British Open Championship				CUT	CUT	T24	T68
PGA Championship				6	T51	CUT	T3
THE PLAYERS Championship			CUT	T54	CUT	3	T18
THE TOUR Championship					15	7	

NATIONAL TEAMS: Presidents Cup, 1994

1995 PGA TOUR STATISTICS

Scoring	70.61	(45)
Driving	266.2	(65)
Driving Accuracy	72.3	(58)
Greens in Regulation	66.1	(100T)
Putting	1.763	(27T)
All Around	624	(64)
Sand Saves	48.8	(135T)
Total Driving	123	(20)
Eagles	3	(137T)
Birdies	302	(57T)

MISCELLANEOUS STATISTICS

Scoring Avg Before Cut	70.85	(50)
Scoring Avg 3rd Rnd	71.33	(108T)
Scoring Avg Final Rnd	70.65	(34T)
Birdies Conversion %	33.0	(9)
Par Breakers	20.9	(23T)

1995 Low Round: **64:** 1995 Motorola Western Open/4
Career Low Round: **64:** 2 times, most recent 1995 Motorola Western Open/4
Career Largest Paycheck: **$198,000:** 1993 Walt Disney World/Oldsmobile Classic/1

Did You Know?

Hal Sutton's closing 61 to win the B.C. Open was the lowest final-round score posted by a winner on TOUR since Johnny Miller shot a final-round 61 in winning the 1975 Dean Martin Tucson Open. One big difference, however -- Miller won by nine strokes, Sutton won by one.

JOHN MAHAFFEY *(muh-HAFF-ee)*

EXEMPT STATUS: Winner, 1986 Tournament Players Championship
FULL NAME: John Drayton Mahaffey
HEIGHT: 5' 9" **WEIGHT:** 160
BIRTH DATE: May 9, 1948 **BIRTHPLACE:** Kerrville, TX
RESIDENCE: Houston, TX; plays out of The Woodlands Resort
FAMILY: Wife, Denise; John D. Mahaffey III (8/8/88), Meagan (6/12/92)
COLLEGE: University of Houston (1970, Psychology)
SPECIAL INTERESTS: Fishing
TURNED PROFESSIONAL: 1971 **Q SCHOOL:** 1971

TOUR VICTORIES (10): 1973 Sahara Invitational. **1978** PGA Championship, American Optical Classic. **1979** Bob Hope Desert Classic. **1980** Kemper Open. **1981** Anheuser-Busch Classic. **1984** Bob Hope Classic. **1985** Texas Open. **1986** Tournament Players Championship. **1989** Federal Express St. Jude Classic.

INTERNATIONAL VICTORIES (1): 1978 World Cup (Indiv.).

BEST 1995 FINISHES: T3 -- LaCantera Texas Open; T9 -- Kemper Open.

1995 SEASON: On the strength of a T3 in year's last full-field event, the LaCantera Texas Open, John had his best year since 1990, earning $156,608 and finishing in the top 125 on the money list...with rounds of 67-71-71-71, he was one of only four players to better par all four days at LaCantera...tied with John Morse and Loren Roberts for third...year's first top-10 finish -- his first since 1992 Chattanooga Classic -- came at Kemper Open...third-round 65 at TPC at Avenel, his low round of year, lifted him to within four strokes of leader Davis Love III...final-round 70 good for T9...made 15 of 25 cuts in 1995.

CAREER HIGHLIGHTS: High point came in 1978 PGA Championship at Oakmont...won in playoff with Tom Watson and Jerry Pate...followed next week with triumph in American Optical Classic at Sutton, MA...earned 10-year exemption with one-stroke victory over Larry Mize in 1986 Tournament Players Championship...fired third-round 7-under-par 65 on Stadium Course at TPC at Sawgrass to move into position to win...last victory came in '89 Federal Express St. Jude Classic, where he closed with rounds of 66-65 on new TPC at Southwind course to win by three strokes...member 1979 Ryder Cup team, 1978-79 World Cup squads (medalist in '78)...captured 1990 Merrill Lynch Shoot-Out final and $90,000 at Troon North in Scottsdale, AZ...led TOUR in Greens in Regulation 1985-86.

PERSONAL: Had spendid amateur career, including 1970 NCAA Championship for University of Houston...professional career has been injury-plagued, starting with hyperextended tendon in left elbow suffered in 1976 PGA Championship...made it virtually impossible for him to play in 1977...past player director on PGA TOUR Policy Board.

CAREER SUMMARY **PLAYOFF RECORD: 3-2**

Year	Events Played	Cuts Made	1st	2nd	3rd	Top 10	Top 25	Earnings	Rank
1970(AM.)	1	1							
1971	1	1					1	$2,010	230
1972	31	24		1	1	4	6	$57,779	39
1973	36	30	1		1	12	21	$112,536	12
1974	25	24		3	1	7	17	$115,073	18
1975	25	21		4		10	16	$141,471	8
1976	26	24		1		6	12	$77,843	33
1977	14	5					4	$9,847	150
1978	28	23	2		1	5	12	$153,520	12
1979	20	16	1		1	2	5	$90,193	42
1980	24	20	1		2	5	12	$165,827	15
1981	25	15	1			5	10	$128,795	24
1982	26	20		1		2	9	$77,047	57
1983	28	20		1	1	4	9	$126,915	44
1984	30	21	1	1	1	8	15	$252,548	21
1985	29	26	1	4		9	18	$341,595	9
1986	27	23	1	1		6	13	$378,172	11
1987	29	23				6	13	$193,938	57
1988	30	21			1	3	15	$266,416	41
1989	31	24	1			2	8	$400,467	29
1990	28	20		2		3	8	$325,115	42
1991	21	13					2	$64,403	159
1992	28	8				2	4	$101,512	130
1993	27	11						$36,913	192
1994	26	10					2	$65,380	177
1995	25	15			1	2	2	$156,608	120
Total	641	459	10	19	11	103	234	$3,829,253	37

1996 PGA TOUR CHARITY TEAM: NEC World Series of Golf

JOHN MAHAFFEY...continued

TOP TOURNAMENT SUMMARY

YEAR	70	73	74	75	76	78	79	80	81	82	83	84	85	86	87
Masters Tournament					T39			T44	T8	CUT	T40	CUT	T14	T42	T35
U.S. Open	T36	T29	T12	2	T4		T36	T27	CUT	T22	T34	T30	T39	CUT	T24
British Open Championship			T44	T10				T32						T30	
PGA Championship		T30	T9	T28	W/D	1	T51	T15	CUT	T42	CUT	T20	T23	CUT	T65
THE PLAYERS Championship			T19	T11	T34	T12		T5	T19	T35	T3	T10	CUT	1	T32

TOP TOURNAMENT SUMMARY (cont.)

YEAR	88	89	90	91	92	93	94	95
Masters Tournament			T42					
U.S. Open		T46	CUT			CUT	CUT	CUT
PGA Championship	T15	CUT	T40	CUT	CUT	CUT	CUT	CUT
THE PLAYERS Championship	T27	T45	CUT	CUT	T9	CUT	T27	T55
THE TOUR Championship		27						

NATIONAL TEAMS: Ryder Cup, 1979; World Cup (2) 1978, 1979 (medalist in 1978).

1995 PGA TOUR STATISTICS

Statistic	Value	Rank
Scoring	71.35	(103T)
Driving	259.9	(119T)
Driving Accuracy	74.7	(26)
Greens in Regulation	69.7	(15T)
Putting	1.819	(179)
All Around	728	(93)
Sand Saves	53.9	(70T)
Total Driving	145	(39T)
Eagles	5	(88T)
Birdies	249	(128T)

MISCELLANEOUS STATISTICS

Statistic	Value	Rank
Scoring Avg Before Cut	71.55	(127T)
Scoring Avg 3rd Rnd	70.63	(57)
Scoring Avg Final Rnd	71.07	(76)
Birdies Conversion %	24.5	(182)
Par Breakers	17.4	(152T)

1995 Low Round: **65:** 1995 Kemper Open/3
Career Low Round: **63:** 2 times, most recent 1985 USF&G Classic/1
Career Largest Paycheck: **$180,000:** 1989 Fed Ex / St Jude/1

DOUG MARTIN

EXEMPT STATUS: 81st on 1995 money list
FULL NAME: Douglas Allan Martin
HEIGHT: 6' **WEIGHT:** 190
BIRTH DATE: December 8, 1966 **BIRTHPLACE:** Bluffton, OH
RESIDENCE: Florence, KY
FAMILY: Wife, Gaylyn; Cody Allan (12/24/90)
COLLEGE: University of Oklahoma
SPECIAL INTERESTS: Family, sports, Notre Dame football
TURNED PROFESSIONAL: 1989 **Q SCHOOL:** 1991

BEST PGA TOUR CAREER FINISH: T2 -- 1995 Buick Classic

NIKE TOUR VICTORIES (1): **1993** NIKE South Texas Open

BEST 1995 FINISH: T2 -- Buick Classic

1995 SEASON: After finishing 11th at the 1994 Qualifying Tournament, guaranteed his first finish among the top 125 on the PGA TOUR at Buick Classic...after an opening 67, led five golfers by one stroke...one stroke off pace after second-round 70...fell to T5, three strokes back after 72 in third round...by birdieing 15, 17 and 18, he finished at six-under-par 278 and tied with Vijay Singh, who won the playoff with a birdie at the fifth extra hole...trailed Ernie Els and Robin Freeman by one stroke after two rounds of GTE Byron Nelson Classic the previous week...followed opening 65-66 with 72-74 to finish T55...Walt Disney World/Oldsmobile Classic was only other top-25 finish...rounds of 69-68-66 at rain-shortened tournament good for T15.

Doug Martin...continued

CAREER HIGHLIGHTS: First joined PGA TOUR in 1992 after finishing T18 at 1991 Qualifying Tournament...earned $77,204 in 32 starts in 1992...best finish that year was seventh at Nissan Los Angeles Open...concentrated on NIKE TOUR in 1993, entering 20 tournaments and finishing second on money list...win at NIKE South Texas Open one of 13 top-10 finishes...T4 at Deposit Guaranty Classic that year one of five PGA TOUR starts...168th-place finish on 1994 PGA TOUR money list sent him back to qualifying tournament...three-time all-American at Oklahoma, where he was member of 1989 national championship team...member of 1989 Walker Cup team after reaching semifinals of U.S. Amateur.

PERSONAL: Huge Notre Dame football fan who spends several Saturdays each fall on sidelines as guest of Coach Lou Holtz...father gave him first club before he could walk...entered his first tournament at age 7...an all-state selection in basketball.

PGA TOUR CAREER SUMMARY — **PLAYOFF RECORD: 0-1**

Year	Events Played	Cuts Made	1st	2nd	3rd	Top 10	Top 25	Earnings	Rank
1989	1	1						$1,234	287
1990	2	1						$1,819	284
1992	32	12				1	2	$77,204	150
1993	5	4				1	1	$21,381	212
1994	33	8				1	4	$81,201	168
1995	29	18		1		1	2	$227,463	81
Total	102	44		1		4	9	$410,301	275

NIKE TOUR SUMMARY

Year	Events Played	Cuts Made	1st	2nd	3rd	Top 10	Top 25	Earnings	Rank
1991	30	19		2		9	16	$51,782	12
1992	1	1					1	$1,116	220
1993	20	19	1	3	1	13	17	$147,003	2
1995	1								
Total	52	39	1	5	1	22	34	$199,901	
COMBINED TOTAL MONEY								$610,202	

1996 PGA TOUR CHARITY TEAM: Memorial Tournament

TOP TOURNAMENT SUMMARY

YEAR	94	95
U.S. Open	T60	CUT
PGA Championship		CUT

NATIONAL TEAM: Walker Cup, 1989

1995 PGA TOUR STATISTICS

Scoring	71.22	(93T)
Driving	250.9	(181)
Driving Accuracy	72.9	(47T)
Greens in Regulation	66.4	(90T)
Putting	1.805	(139T)
All Around	781	(110T)
Sand Saves	51.5	(103)
Total Driving	228	(152T)
Eagles	7	(51T)
Birdies	286	(77T)

MISCELLANEOUS STATISTICS

Scoring Avg Before Cut	71.10	(79T)
Scoring Avg 3rd Rnd	71.16	(92T)
Scoring Avg Final Rnd	70.88	(62T)
Birdies Conversion %	26.0	(161T)
Par Breakers	17.7	(144T)

1995 Low Round: 65: 2 times, most recent 1995 Las Vegas Invitational/1
Career Low Round: 65: 2 times, most recent 1995 Las Vegas Invitational/1
Career Largest Paycheck: $129,600: 1995 Buick Classic/2

Billy Mayfair

EXEMPT STATUS: 1995 tournament winner
FULL NAME: William Fred Mayfair
HEIGHT: 5' 8" **WEIGHT:** 175
BIRTH DATE: August 6, 1966 **BIRTHPLACE:** Phoenix, AZ
RESIDENCE: Scottsdale, AZ; Plays out of Troon North GC
FAMILY: Wife, Tammy
COLLEGE: Arizona State
SPECIAL INTERESTS: All sports
TURNED PROFESSIONAL: 1988 **Q SCHOOL:** Fall 1988

TOUR VICTORIES (3): 1993 Greater Milwaukee Open. **1995** Motorola Western Open, THE TOUR Championship

BEST 1995 FINISHES: 1 -- Motorola Western Open, THE TOUR Championship; 2 -- Phoenix Open, Las Vegas Invitational; T2 - -- NEC World Series of Golf; T8 -- Colonial National Invitation

1995 SEASON: With two wins and three seconds (including two playoff losses), Billy finished second on the money list wth second-highest earnings in PGA TOUR history, $1,543,192...in so doing, he improved on his 1994 earnings by $1,385,033, a record...first playoff appearance came at Phoenix Open...trailed Ben Crenshaw by one stroke after 54 holes, then shot final-round 66 to tie Vijay Singh at 15-under-par 269...Singh won with par at first extra hole...second career victory came at Motorola Western Open...began final round at Cog Hill T6, three strokes off lead...closed with 67 to win by one stroke and earn $360,000...three strokes off lead beginning final round at NEC World Series of Golf, he shot a front-nine 32 Sunday to lead by three strokes, but bogeyed three of last four to join Nick Price and Greg Norman in playoff...Norman chipped in on first extra hole for victory...third runner-up finish came at Las Vegas Invitational, where he was one stroke off lead through 36 and 54 holes and tied with Jim Furyk after 72...Furyk took two-stroke lead on front nine of fifth round and held on for one-stroke victory...at THE TOUR Championship, held three-stroke lead after three rounds and won by that margin after a closing 73, earning $540,000...even-par victory at Southern Hills first on TOUR since Corey Pavin at 1995 U.S. Open...led TOUR in sand saves (68.6%).

CAREER HIGHLIGHTS: First tasted victory in 1993 Greater Milwaukee Open, defeating Mark Calcavecchia on fourth playoff hole by sinking 20-foot chip...earned $693,658 in 1990, a year in which he lost in playoffs twice -- to Jim Gallagher, Jr., at GMO and to Jodie Mudd in season-ending Nabisco Championships...had five other top-10 finishes that year...celebrated amateur player who won 1987 U.S. Amateur and 1986 U.S. Public Links...member 1987 Walker Cup team...1987 Fred Haskins Award recipient as outstanding college player of year...1985-87 Arizona Stroke Play champion...four-time winner Arizona State Juniors...member 1991 Four Tours World Championship of Golf team.

PERSONAL: Married the former Tammy McIntire on the 18th green at TPC at Las Colina on Tuesday of 1994 GTE Byron Nelson Classic, explaining: "We're going to be spending the rest off our lives on a golf course. We thought we might as well be married on one."...close friend of Phoenix Suns' Charles Barkley.

CAREER SUMMARY **PLAYOFF RECORD: 1-4**

Year	Events Played	Cuts Made	1st	2nd	3rd	Top 10	Top 25	Earnings	Rank
1987(Am.)	3	1							
1988(Am.)	3	2					1		
1988	5	3					1	$8,433	220
1989	33	18					6	$111,998	116
1990	32	23		2		7	15	$693,658	12
1991	33	20				1	7	$185,668	89
1992	33	23				1	9	$191,878	79
1993	32	22	1	1		5	8	$513,072	30
1994	32	18				1	7	$158,159	113
1995	28	21	2	3		6	9	$1,543,192	2
Total	234	151	3	6		21	63	$3,406,058	47

1996 PGA TOUR CHARITY TEAM: MasterCard Colonial

TOP TOURNAMENT SUMMARY

YEAR	88	89	90	91	92	93	94	95
Masters Tournament	CUT			T12	T42		CUT	
U.S. Open	T25	T33	CUT	T37	T23		CUT	
PGA Championship			T5	CUT	CUT	T28	T39	T23
THE PLAYERS Championship		CUT	CUT	T73	T67	T52	CUT	T18
THE TOUR Championship			2			30		1

NATIONAL TEAMS: Walker Cup, 1987; Four Tours World Championship of Golf, 1991.

BILLY MAYFAIR...continued

1995 PGA TOUR STATISTICS		
Scoring	70.29	(24T)
Driving	264.4	(85)
Driving Accuracy	73.9	(31T)
Greens in Regulation	66.3	(93T)
Putting	1.788	(89T)
All Around	420	(15)
Sand Saves	68.6	(1)
Total Driving	116	(14T)
Eagles	6	(69T)
Birdies	338	(28T)

MISCELLANEOUS STATISTICS		
Scoring Avg Before Cut	70.73	(39T)
Scoring Avg 3rd Rnd	70.00	(19T)
Scoring Avg Final Rnd	70.52	(28)
Birdies Conversion %	28.6	(95T)
Par Breakers	19.3	(89T)

1995 Low Round: 65: 1995 Las Vegas Invitational/2
Career Low Round: 61: 1993 GTE Byron Nelson Classic/2
Career Largest Paycheck: $540,000: 1995 THE TOUR Championship/1

BLAINE MCCALLISTER

EXEMPT STATUS: 77th on 1995 money list
FULL NAME: Blaine McCallister
HEIGHT: 5' 10" **WEIGHT:** 190
BIRTH DATE: October 17, 1958 **BIRTHPLACE:** Ft. Stockton, TX
RESIDENCE: Ponte Vedra Beach, FL; plays out of Ft. Stockton GC
FAMILY: Wife, Claudia
COLLEGE: University of Houston
SPECIAL INTERESTS: Hunting, fishing, tennis, baseball
TURNED PROFESSIONAL: 1981 **Q SCHOOL:** Fall 1981; 1982; 1985

TOUR VICTORIES (5): 1988 Hardee's Golf Classic. **1989** Honda Classic, Bank of Boston Classic. **1991** H-E-B. Texas Open. **1993** B.C. Open.

INTERNATIONAL VICTORIES: 1991 Vines Classic (Aus).

BEST 1995 FINISHES: 5 -- Honda Classic; T8 -- Buick Classic

1995 SEASON: Recorded fifth $200,000 season in a row and his seventh in 12 PGA TOUR seasons...recorded three top-25 finishes in five West Coast starts...opened Florida swing with fifth-place finish at Honda Classic...tied for second after 36 holes at Weston Hills, closed with 73-71 to finish five strokes behind Mark O'Meara...closing 65 at MCI Classic, low round of year, lifted him to T13...second top-10 came at Buick Classic...tied for fifth after 54 holes, three strokes off lead, shot final-round 72 for T8...trailed by one after three rounds at Anhesuer-Busch Classic, but closing 75 dropped him to T18.

CAREER HIGHLIGHTS: Fashioned pair of victories in best season to date, 1989...with 65-64 finish, captured Honda Classic by four strokes over Payne Stewart...later in 1989, fired closing-round 66 to win Bank of Boston Classic by one shot over Brad Faxon; lost 1986 Boston event in playoff with Gene Sauers...became part of TOUR history in winning 1988 Hardee's Golf Classic...middle rounds of 62-63--125 matched Gay Brewer's standard established in 1967 Pensacola Open...battled mononucleosis in early 1990, rebounded with fourth victory in 1991 Texas Open...plagued by illness in 1993 (missed April due to tonsilectomy), came back next month to score one-stroke win over Denis Watson in B.C. Open.

PERSONAL: Wife Claudia suffers from rare eye disease pseudoxanthoma elasticum (PXE)...actively involved with eyesight organizations because of Claudia's affliction...roomed with Fred Couples for one year and CBS-TV sportscaster Jim Nantz for three while at University of Houston...has joined with Couples and Nantz in Three Amigos Celebrity Tournament, first held Oct. 1994...natural lefthander who plays game righthanded but putts southpaw...suited up with Seattle Mariners during 1995 spring training, but struck out against junior college pitcher.

BLAINE McCALLISTER...*continued*

CAREER SUMMARY					PLAYOFF RECORD: 1-1				
Year	**Events Played**	**Cuts Made**	**1st**	**2nd**	**3rd**	**Top 10**	**Top 25**	**Earnings**	**Rank**
1982	22	7					1	$7,894	186
1983	24	6						$5,218	201
1984	1								
1986	35	17		1		1	3	$88,732	94
1987	35	19				2	6	$120,005	87
1988	34	23	1			3	11	$225,660	49
1989	31	20	2			5	11	$523,891	15
1990	30	18				2	5	$152,048	103
1991	26	22	1		1	4	11	$412,974	36
1992	28	19			2	4	7	$261,187	59
1993	27	16	1		1	2	5	$290,434	61
1994	27	20			1	7	11	$351,554	47
1995	26	18				2	8	$238,847	77
Total	346	205	5	1	5	32	79	$2,678,444	68

1996 PGA TOUR CHARITY TEAM: LaCantera Texas Open

TOP TOURNAMENT SUMMARY

YEAR	84	87	88	89	90	91	92	93	94	95
Masters Tournament				CUT	CUT		T48		CUT	
U.S. Open	CUT		CUT		T56	T46		T19		CUT
British Open Championship					T57					
PGA Championship		CUT	T25	T17	T19	T57	T62		T36	CUT
THE PLAYERS Championship		69	CUT	CUT		T23	T54	CUT	CUT	CUT
THE TOUR Championship				T22						

1995 PGA TOUR STATISTICS		
Scoring	70.78	(55T)
Driving	261.7	(105)
Driving Accuracy	76.1	(20)
Greens in Regulation	66.5	(82T)
Putting	1.792	(103T)
All Around	618	(62)
Sand Saves	50.6	(115T)
Total Driving	125	(21T)
Eagles	5	(88T)
Birdies	306	(50)

MISCELLANEOUS STATISTICS		
Scoring Avg Before Cut	70.82	(47)
Scoring Avg 3rd Rnd	71.21	(98T)
Scoring Avg Final Rnd	71.89	(146T)
Birdies Conversion %	28.4	(103T)
Par Breakers	19.2	(93T)

1995 Low Round: **65:** 1995 MCI Classic/4
Career Low Round: **62:** 1988 Hardee's Classic/2
Career Largest Paycheck: **$162,000:** 1991 H.E.B. Texas Open/1

A natural lefthander, Blaine McCallister learned to play golf righthanded (those were the only clubs available) but turned his game around by reverting to his more natural southpaw side for putting.

SCOTT MCCARRON *(muh-CARE-uhn)*

EXEMPT STATUS: 128th on 1995 money list
FULL NAME: Scott Michael McCarron
HEIGHT: 5' 10" **WEIGHT:** 170
BIRTH DATE: July 10, 1965 **BIRTHPLACE:** Sacramento, CA
RESIDENCE: Rancho Murieta, CA
FAMILY: Wife, Jennifer; Courtney (10/31/95)
COLLEGE: UCLA (1988, History)
SPECIAL INTERESTS: Flying, skiing, mountain biking, sky diving
TURNED PROFESSIONAL: 1992 **Q SCHOOL:** Fall 1994

BEST EVER FINISH: 3 -- 1995 Las Vegas Invitational

BEST 1995 FINISH: 3 -- Las Vegas Invitational

BEST NIKE TOUR CAREER FINISH: T20— 1995 NIKE Shreveport Open

1995 SEASON: Return trip to Qualifying Tournament took a pleasant detour in Las Vegas...prior to Las Vegas Invitational, had earned $40,751 and ranked 212th on money list...solo third and $108,000 check at Las Vegas moved him to 128th, a position he maintained the following week at LaCantera Texas Open...T31 after 54 holes of the 90-hole LVI, moved into the top 10 with a fourth-round 64...shot 33-32 -- 65 in final round to post 334, 25-under-par...when Mark O'Meara bogeyed the 18th, McCarron had third place by himself...earned his final $4,620 of year by finishing T38 at LaCantera Texas Open to keep his card by $2,708...made only two of first 11 cuts...best finish of year before Las Vegas came at Buick Challenge, T24.

CAREER HIGHLIGHTS: Joined TOUR in 1994 after finishing 31st at Qualifying Tournament...was a member of the Canadian Tour in 1993 and the Hooters Tour in 1994...won the 1994 Long Beach Open...was a member of UCLA's national championship team in 1988.

PERSONAL: Introduced to the sport at age 3 by his father.

PGA TOUR CAREER SUMMARY — **PLAYOFF RECORD: 0-0**

Year	Events Played	Cuts Made	1st	2nd	3rd	Top 10	Top 25	Earnings	Rank
1995	25	12			1	1	2	$147,371	128
Total	25	12			1	1	2	$147,371	370

NIKE TOUR SUMMARY

Year	Events Played	Cuts Made	1st	2nd	3rd	Top 10	Top 25	Earnings	Rank
1992	1	1						$720	268
1995	3	1					1	$1,950	204
Total	4	2					1	$2,670	
COMBINED TOTAL MONEY								$150,041	

1996 PGA TOUR CHARITY TEAM: Bob Hope Chrysler Classic

1995 PGA TOUR STATISTICS

Scoring	71.59	(126)
Driving	271.1	(32)
Driving Accuracy	64.9	(158T)
Greens in Regulation	65.1	(116T)
Putting	1.810	(153T)
All Around	741	(101)
Sand Saves	57.7	(32)
Total Driving	190	(103T)
Eagles	11	(12T)
Birdies	264	(112)

MISCELLANEOUS STATISTICS

Scoring Avg Before Cut	71.48	(116T)
Scoring Avg 3rd Rnd	71.93	(147T)
Scoring Avg Final Rnd	71.15	(86)
Birdies Conversion %	29.5	(68T)
Par Breakers	20.0	(56T)

1995 Low Round: **64:** 1995 Las Vegas Invitational/4
Career Low Round: **64:** 1995 Las Vegas Invitational/4
Career Largest Paycheck: **$102,000:** 1995 Las Vegas Invitational/3

Mark McCumber

EXEMPT STATUS: Winner, 1988 THE PLAYERS Championship
FULL NAME: Mark Randall McCumber
HEIGHT: 5' 8" **WEIGHT:** 170
BIRTH DATE: September 7, 1951 **BIRTHPLACE:** Jacksonville, FL
RESIDENCE: Jacksonville, FL
FAMILY: Wife, Paddy; Addison (1/28/76), Megan (6/14/80), Mark Tyler (4/4/91)
SPECIAL INTERESTS: Family activities, golf course architecture
TURNED PROFESSIONAL: 1974 **Q SCHOOL:** Spring 1978

TOUR VICTORIES (10): 1979 Doral-Eastern Open. **1983** Western Open, Pensacola Open **1985** Doral-Eastern Open. **1987** Anheuser-Busch Classic. **1988** THE PLAYERS Championship. **1989** Beatrice Western Open. **1994** Anheuser-Busch Classic, Hardee's Golf Classic, The TOUR Championship.

BEST 1995 FINISH: T4 -- MCI Classic; T5 -- Nestle Invitational, Colonial National Invitation

1995 SEASON: Unable to match the lofty standard he set in 1994, still a solid season for the 18-year veteran...after T16 at Mercedes Championships, resumed his year on the East Coast with two top-10s in next six starts...T12 at Doral-Ryder Open and T13 at Honda Classic before shooting 69-70-69-70 -- 278 at Nestle Invitational for T5...third-round 64 at MCI Classic, low round of year, lifted him into share of lead...final-round 71 left him at 8-under-par 276, one stroke out of three-man playoff won by Bob Tway...T5 two starts later at Colonial...T36 after opening 67-73, shot 68-68 on weekend to finish five strokes behind Tom Lehman...final-round 68 at U.S. Open good for T13...after first-round 74 in defense of Anheuser-Busch title, shot 68-69-67 to finish T11...with wins over Lehman, Corey Pavin and Loren Roberts, represented United States in final four of Andersen Consulting World Championship of Golf.

CAREER HIGHLIGHTS: With three wins, including season-ending TOUR Championship, enjoyed his best year on TOUR in 1994...first win came at Anheuser-Busch Classic, by three strokes over Glen Day...one-stroke victory over Kenny Perry at Hardee's Golf Classic gave him first multiple win season since 1983...defeated Fuzzy Zoeller on first extra hole of TOUR Championship at The Olympic Club by sinking a 40-foot birdie putt...achieved popular hometown victory in 1988 by winning THE PLAYERS Championship...captured first win, 1979 Doral-Eastern Open, in second year on TOUR, but in only his 12th tournament...hit stride in 1983 with victories in Western and Pensacola Opens...repeat victor in Doral-Eastern Open (1985) and Beatrice Western Open (1989), latter in playoff with Peter Jacobsen...1994 victory in A-B Classic gave him pair of titles in three different events, since also won at Williamsburg in 1987...with increased involvement in golf course design projects affecting his game, made decision in 1993 to put full focus on golf when playing tournaments...that call produced immediate results, including best money-list finish since 1989...member 1989 Ryder Cup team and 1988 and 1989 World Cup squads...he and Ben Crensaw won World Cup title in 1988.

PERSONAL: Making impact in golf course design with Mark McCumber and Associates, design arm of McCumber Golf, company he helps operate with his brothers...one of their designs, TPC at Heron Bay in Coral Springs, FL, will be site of 1997 Honda Classic...nephew Josh McCumber up-and-coming golfer at the University of Florida...member American Society of Golf Course Architects.

CAREER SUMMARY **PLAYOFF RECORD: 2-0**

Year	Events Played	Cuts Made	1st	2nd	3rd	Top 10	Top 25	Earnings	Rank
1978	8	6				1	1	$6,948	160
1979	31	15	1			1	4	$67,886	60
1980	30	15				2	6	$36,985	88
1981	25	15				2	4	$33,363	103
1982	26	18				1	5	$31,684	119
1983	29	20	2	2		8	13	$268,294	8
1984	26	19				5	10	$133,445	50
1985	24	14	1	1		3	8	$192,752	32
1986	28	21				1	10	$110,442	80
1987	29	24	1		1	5	14	$390,885	22
1988	22	21	1	1		5	12	$559,111	13
1989	20	15	1	1		7	13	$546,587	14
1990	24	20				3	6	$163,413	97
1991	23	17				1	5	$173,852	92
1992	24	17				1	4	$136,653	106
1993	21	18		1	1	3	11	$363,269	41
1994	20	18	3			6	13	$1,208,209	3
1995	19	14				3	12	$375,923	47
Total	429	307	10	6	2	58	151	$4,799,702	26

1996 PGA TOUR CHARITY TEAM: THE PLAYERS Championship

MARK McCUMBER...continued

TOP TOURNAMENT SUMMARY

YEAR	79	80	81	82	83	84	85	86	87	88	89	90	91	92	93
Masters Tournament						T35	T18	T11	T12	24	T43	T36	T17	T37	CUT
U.S. Open			CUT	CUT		T16		T8	T51	T32	T2	T47	CUT	T13	T46
British Open Championship						8	CUT			T48	T46	T31			
PGA Championship	T28		T56	CUT	CUT	T48	W/D	T53	T5	CUT	65	T49	T52	CUT	T31
THE PLAYERS Championship	T35	CUT	T45	CUT	T49	DQ	CUT	CUT	T12	1	T6	T9	T13	T40	T20
THE TOUR Championship									26	T14	T19				

TOP TOURNAMENT SUMMARY (cont.)

YEAR	94	95
Masters Tournament		T35
U.S. Open		T13
British Open Championship		CUT
PGA Championship	T19	CUT
THE PLAYERS Championship	T62	T23
THE TOUR Championship	1	

NATIONAL TEAMS: World Cup (2), 1988, 1989; Ryder Cup 1989.

1995 PGA TOUR STATISTICS

Scoring	70.27	(21)
Driving	264.1	(87T)
Driving Accuracy	72.9	(47T)
Greens in Regulation	64.9	(124T)
Putting	1.805	(139T)
All Around	827	(125)
Sand Saves	50.9	(112T)
Total Driving	134	(26)
Eagles	3	(137T)
Birdies	212	(160)

MISCELLANEOUS STATISTICS

Scoring Avg Before Cut	71.50	(122T)
Scoring Avg 3rd Rnd	69.87	(15T)
Scoring Avg Final Rnd	70.93	(67T)
Birdies Conversion %	28.3	(108T)
Par Breakers	18.1	(127T)

1995 Low Round: **64:** 1995 MCI Classic/3
Career Low Round: **63:** 1980 San Antonio-Texas/2
Career Largest Paycheck: **$540,000:** 1994 TOUR Championship/1

JIM McGOVERN

EXEMPT STATUS: 44th on 1995 money list
FULL NAME: James David McGovern
HEIGHT: 6'2" **WEIGHT:** 195
BIRTH DATE: February 5, 1965 **BIRTHPLACE:** Teaneck, NJ
RESIDENCE: Oradell, NJ; plays out of Hackensack GC
FAMILY: Wife, Lauren; Melanie Sue (2/5/95)
COLLEGE: Old Dominion University
SPECIAL INTERESTS: All sports
TURNED PROFESSIONAL: 1988 **Q SCHOOL:** 1991

TOUR VICTORIES (1): **1993** Shell Houston Open.

NIKE TOUR VICTORIES (3): **1990** Lake City Classic, New Haven Open, Texarkana Open

BEST 1995 FINISHES: 2 -- Ideon Classic at Pleasant Valley, B.C. Open; 4 -- Quad City Classic.

1994 SEASON: With two second-place finishes and a fourth, recorded his second-best year on TOUR...opening 65 at Honda Classic gave him one-stroke lead, then shot 74-75-70 -- 284 to finish T13...third-round 65 at Buick Classic moved him into T5, three strokes behind Vijay Singh...dropped to T14 after Sunday 74...second place at Ideon Classic after opening 66-66...still second through 54 holes, four strokes behind Fred Funk...finished one stroke behind Funk after closing 70 to earn $108,000...at B.C. Open, was T13 after 54 holes, four strokes behind leader Skip Kendall...closing 63, low round of year, moved him into second, but Hal Sutton earned win with final-round 61...opened following week with 64 at Quad City Classic to share 18-hole lead...finished 71-66 in rain-shortened tournament for solo fourth, four strokes behind D.A. Weibring.

JIM McGOVERN...continued

CAREER HIGHLIGHTS: "Jersey Kid" captured first PGA TOUR victory with birdie on second playoff hole of weather-shortened 1993 Shell Houston Open to defeat John Huston...after back-to-back bogeys in final round, hit fairway driver to within three feet for eagle on No. 15, then sank eight-footer for par on final hole to tie Huston...win at The Woodlands earned him an invitation to the 1994 Masters, where he shot 72-70-71-72 -- 285 for T5...prior to Houston victory, top TOUR finish had been solo fourth in 1992 Federal Express St. Jude Classic...Memphis appearance featured TPC at Southwind record-tying 62 in second round...qualified for first year on TOUR in 1991 by finishing second on 1990 Ben Hogan Tour money list...played 29 of 30 Hogan Tour events in 1990, also winning Texarkana and New Haven Opens...led Hogan Tour in birdies with 292 in 1990...won inaugural Diners Club with Jeff Maggert in 1994.

PERSONAL: Withdrew from 1995 AT&T Pebble Beach National Pro-Am after third round to be at birth of first child...Megan born five minutes into her father's 30th birthday...first exposed to game when parents bought house adjacent to Hackensack (NJ) Golf Club...because of minimum age restriction, couldn't gain admittance to club until tree knocked down connecting fence during storm, then with brothers hit balls on course until late at night...brother Rob played linebacker in NFL...wife Lauren an attorney.

PGA TOUR CAREER SUMMARY — **PLAYOFF RECORD: 1-0**

Year	Events Played	Cuts Made	1st	2nd	3rd	Top 10	Top 25	Earnings	Rank
1989	2								
1991	34	14				1	4	$88,869	141
1992	33	19				1	8	$169,888	92
1993	34	27	1			3	14	$587,495	27
1994	30	18				1	6	$227,764	79
1995	31	19		2		3	8	$402,587	44
Total	164	97	1	2		9	40	$1,476,603	139

NIKE TOUR SUMMARY

Year	Events Played	Cuts Made	1st	2nd	3rd	Top 10	Top 25	Earnings	Rank
1990	29	23	3	2		7	14	$99,841	2
Total	29	23	3	2		7	14	$99,841	
COMBINED TOTAL MONEY								$1,576,444	

1996 PGA TOUR CHARITY TEAM: Diners Club Matches

TOP TOURNAMENT SUMMARY

YEAR	89	91	92	93	94	95
Masters Tournament					T5	CUT
U.S. Open	CUT	CUT	CUT		T13	T45
British Open Championship				CUT	CUT	
PGA Championship				T22	CUT	CUT
THE PLAYERS Championship				CUT	T55	CUT
THE TOUR Championship				T16		

1995 PGA TOUR STATISTICS

Scoring	70.58	(42T)
Driving	262.2	(99)
Driving Accuracy	70.6	(79T)
Greens in Regulation	66.9	(66T)
Putting	1.786	(86T)
All Around	539	(40)
Sand Saves	51.0	(110T)
Total Driving	178	(82T)
Eagles	8	(36T)
Birdies	346	(21T)

MISCELLANEOUS STATISTICS

Scoring Avg Before Cut	71.10	(79T)
Scoring Avg 3rd Rnd	70.21	(30)
Scoring Avg Final Rnd	70.83	(58)
Birdies Conversion %	29.6	(64T)
Par Breakers	20.3	(40T)

1995 Low Round: **63:** 1995 B.C. Open/4
Career Low Round: **62:** 1992 Federal Express St. Jude Classic/2
Career Largest Paycheck: $234,000: 1993 Shell Houston Open/1

Rocco Mediate *(MEE-dee-ATE)*

EXEMPT STATUS: Special medical extension
FULL NAME: Rocco Anthony Mediate
HEIGHT: 6' 1" **WEIGHT:** 200
BIRTH DATE: December 17, 1962 **BIRTHPLACE:** Greensburg, PA
RESIDENCE: Ponte Vedra Beach, FL
FAMILY: Wife, Linda; Rocco Vincent (9/19/90), Nicco Anthony (1/29/93)
COLLEGE: Florida Southern University
SPECIAL INTERESTS: Photography, music, collecting trading cards
TURNED PROFESSIONAL: 1985 **Q SCHOOL:** Fall 1985, 1986

TOUR VICTORIES (2): 1991 Doral-Ryder Open. **1993** Kmart Greater Greensboro Open.

INTERNATIONAL VICTORIES (1): 1992 Perrier French Open.

BEST 1995 FINISHES: T5 -- FedEx St. Jude Classic; T8 -- Colonial National Invitation

1995 SEASON: Limited to 18 events in 1995, during which he earned $105,618...received medical extension at end of season, giving him seven more tournaments in 1996 to earn the $40,741 he would have needed to finish within top 125...still recovering from July 1994 surgery to remove fragmented disc...still managed two top-10 finishes in 1995...shot 69-68-70-70 at Colonial National Invitation to finish T8...opened with 65 at FedEx St. Jude Classic, low round of year...went on to finish T5, three strokes behind Jim Gallagher, Jr....final start came at Buick Open in July...in wake of back problems, developed bursitis in hip and ankle...decided to shut down season and pursue aggressive therapy program to prepare for 1996.

CAREER HIGHLIGHTS: Captured second TOUR title in April 1993, birdieing fourth playoff hole to defeat Steve Elkington and win Kmart Greater Greensboro Open...GGO triumph climaxed five-tournament string that featured four top-10 finishes...had finished ninth at Forest Oaks CC in 1992...earned first TOUR title in sixth season...Doral-Ryder Open victory on Blue Monster course came in playoff with Curtis Strange...caught Strange with birdies on 17th and 18th holes...sank 10-footers on each green...captured playoff and $252,000 winner's check by making five-foot birdie putt on first extra hole after Curtis missed 15-foot attempt...got out of blocks in spectacular fashion in 1991, posting six top-10 finishes in first seven starts...winner 1992 Perrier French Open.

PERSONAL: Was using long putter before back problems began...in fact, was first to win PGA TOUR event using elongated putter...in that respect, has said he's well ahead of game in terms of getting ready for Senior TOUR...grew up in Greensburg, PA, not far from Latrobe home of Arnold Palmer...played golf with Palmer for first time at age 19...attended California (PA) State College before transferring to Florida Southern.

CAREER SUMMARY **PLAYOFF RECORD: 2-0**

Year	Events Played	Cuts Made	1st	2nd	3rd	Top 10	Top 25	Earnings	Rank
1984(Am.)	1								
1985	2								
1986	27	10				1	4	$20,670	174
1987	32	19		1		1	7	$112,099	91
1988	32	25				1	9	$129,829	92
1989	30	23					8	$132,501	108
1990	27	17		1	1	3	5	$240,625	62
1991	25	19	1			7	14	$597,438	15
1992	25	17			2	6	8	$301,896	49
1993	24	22	1	1		6	10	$680,623	16
1994	6	4				1	2	$45,940	193
1995	18	8				2	2	$105,618	155
Total	249	164	2	3	3	28	69	$2,367,238	77

1996 PGA TOUR CHARITY TEAM: Kemper Open

TOP TOURNAMENT SUMMARY

YEAR	84	87	88	89	90	91	92	93	94	95
Masters Tournament						T22	T37			
U.S. Open	CUT					CUT	T44	T25	W/D	
British Open Championship						CUT	T45	T39		
PGA Championship			T31		T69	T16	T40	T68		
THE PLAYERS Championship		T50	CUT	T11	T11	T15	CUT	T6		T55
THE TOUR Championship						T26		T23		

Rocco Mediate...*continued*

1995 PGA TOUR STATISTICS		
Scoring	71.62	(128T)
Driving	260.3	(115T)
Driving Accuracy	69.6	(96)
Greens in Regulation	65.1	(116T)
Putting	1.806	(144)
All Around	960	(151T)
Sand Saves	57.3	(38T)
Total Driving	211	(128T)
Eagles	3	(137T)
Birdies	151	(186)

MISCELLANEOUS STATISTICS		
Scoring Avg Before Cut	71.82	(152)
Scoring Avg 3rd Rnd	72.75	(177)
Scoring Avg Final Rnd	70.75	(50T)
Birdies Conversion %	26.0	(161T)
Par Breakers	17.2	(161T)

1995 Low Round: 65: 1995 FedEx St. Jude Classic/1
Career Low Round: 63: 2 times, most recent 1991 Bob Hope Chrysler/2
Career Largest Paycheck: $270,000: 1993 Kmart Greater Greensboro Open/1

Phil Mickelson

EXEMPT STATUS: 1995 tournament winner
FULL NAME: Phil A. Mickelson
HEIGHT: 6' 2" **WEIGHT:** 190
BIRTH DATE: June 16, 1970 **BIRTHPLACE:** San Diego, CA
RESIDENCE: Scottsdale, AZ; plays out of Grayhawk GC
FAMILY: Single
COLLEGE: Arizona State University
SPECIAL INTERESTS: Snow and water skiing **JOINED TOUR:** June 1992

TOUR VICTORIES (5): 1991 Northern Telecom Open. **1993** Buick Invitational of California, The International. **1994** Mercedes Championships. **1995** Northern Telecom Open.

BEST 1995 FINISHES: 1 -- Northern Telecom Open; T4 -- U.S. Open, NEC World Series of Golf; T7 -- Masters Tournament.

1995 SEASON: With victory at Northern Telecom Open, become first in PGA TOUR history to win same tournament as an amateur and a professional...shared first-round lead with Tom Purtzer after 65 and followed with second-round 66 for one-stroke advantage...fell into tie with Jim Gallagher, Jr., and Brett Ogle after a Saturday 70...after Gallagher three-putted 18 on Sunday, Mickelson made par for the win...three weeks later, shared first-round lead with four others at Buick Invitational of California...finished T16...recovered from opening 78 to finish T14 at THE PLAYERS Championship...tied for lead at Masters Tournament after opening 66 and was only one stroke behind leaders after 54 holes...closing 73 left him T7...next top-10 came at next major, the U.S. Open...again trailed leaders by one stroke with 18 to play...74 on Sunday led to T4, four strokes behind Corey Pavin...fired closing 66 at NEC World Series of Golf to finish T4...3-0 in first Ryder Cup.

CAREER HIGHLIGHTS: Earned second and third titles in just second year as TOUR member in 1993...those wins also his initial two as professional, since first came as amateur in 1991...playing before home crowd, captured Buick Invitational of California after opening with 75 (highest first round for winner in '93)...closed with 65, good for four-shot win over Dave Rummells...followed T6 in PGA Championship with second victory of campaign, an eight-point win over Mark Calcavecchia at The International worth $234,000 (largest check of career)...turned professional at 1992 U.S. Open...finished second in third professional start at New England Classic, worth $108,000...while still playing for Arizona State, captured 1991 Northern Telecom Open by one stroke over Bob Tway and Tom Purtzer...winner 1989-90-92 NCAA Championships for ASU...won 1990 U.S. Amateur, only lefthander to do so...became only player other than Jack Nicklaus to win NCAA and U.S. Amateur titles in same year...one of four collegians (Ben Crenshaw, Curtis Strange, Billy Ray Brown) to win NCAA title in freshman year...four-time first-team All-America 1989-92 (only Gary Hallberg and David Duval have achieved same status)...winner 1990-92 collegiate player of year...1991 Golf World Amateur Player of Year...1989-91 Walker Cupper...low amateur 1990-91 U.S. Opens, 1991 Masters Tournament.

PERSONAL: Started hitting balls at 1 1/2...righthanded in everything but golf (his father demonstrated right-handed; Phil followed along left-handed).

PHIL MICKELSON...continued

CAREER SUMMARY									PLAYOFF RECORD: 1-0
Year	**Events Played**	**Cuts Made**	**1st**	**2nd**	**3rd**	**Top 10**	**Top 25**	**Earnings**	**Rank**
1988(Am.)	2								
1989(Am.)	1								
1990(Am.)	2	2					1		
1991(Am.)	7	6	1			1	1		
1992(Am.)	7	1							
1992	10	7		1		2	4	$171,714	90
1993	24	14	2			4	7	$628,735	22
1994	18	17	1		3	9	10	$748,316	15
1995	24	15	1			4	9	$655,777	28
Total	95	62	5	1	3	20	32	$2,204,542	88

1996 PGA TOUR CHARITY TEAM: Nortel Open

TOP TOURNAMENT SUMMARY						
YEAR	**90**	**91**	**92**	**93**	**94**	**95**
Masters Tournament		T46		T34		T7
U.S. Open	T29	T55	CUT		T47	T4
British Open Championship		T73			CUT	T40
PGA Championship				T6	3	CUT
THE PLAYERS Championship			CUT	CUT		T14
THE TOUR Championship				28	T17	24

NATIONAL TEAMS: Walker Cup, 1989,1991; Presidents Cup, 1994.

1995 PGA TOUR STATISTICS		
Scoring	70.59	(44)
Driving	270.7	(36T)
Driving Accuracy	71.1	(76T)
Greens in Regulation	66.1	(100T)
Putting	1.774	(54T)
All Around	528	(39)
Sand Saves	50.7	(114)
Total Driving	112	(13)
Eagles	9	(20T)
Birdies	284	(84T)

MISCELLANEOUS STATISTICS		
Scoring Avg Before Cut	71.07	(74T)
Scoring Avg 3rd Rnd	71.56	(124T)
Scoring Avg Final Rnd	71.13	(82T)
Birdies Conversion %	32.3	(16T)
Par Breakers	20.9	(23T)

1995 Low Round: **65:** 3 times, most recent 1995 Las Vegas Invitational/2
Career Low Round: **63:** 2 times, most recent 1994 Las Vegas Invitational/5
Career Largest Paycheck: **$234,000:** 1993 The International/1

JOHNNY MILLER

EXEMPT STATUS: 1994 tournament winner
FULL NAME: John Laurence Miller
HEIGHT: 6'2" **WEIGHT:** 180
BIRTH DATE: April 29, 1947 **BIRTHPLACE:** San Francisco, CA
RESIDENCE: Napa, CA
FAMILY: Wife, Linda Strouse; John S. (6/2/70), Kelly (12/26/72), Casi (7/30/74), Scott (5/12/76), Brent (2/3/78), Todd (1/22/80); 2 grandchildren
COLLEGE: Brigham Young University (Physical Education, 1969)
SPECIAL INTERESTS: Fishing, church activities, course architecture, golf club design
TURNED PROFESSIONAL: 1969 **JOINED TOUR:** Spring 1969

TOUR VICTORIES (24): 1971 Southern Open. **1972** Heritage Classic. **1973** U.S. Open. **1974** Bing Crosby Pro-Am, Phoenix Open, Dean Martin-Tucson Open, Heritage Classic, Tournament of Champions, Westchester Classic, World Open, Kaiser International. **1975** Phoenix Open, Dean Martin Tucson Open, Bob Hope Desert Classic, Kaiser International. **1976** NBC Tucson Open, Bob Hope Desert Classic. **1980** Jackie Gleason Inverrary Classic. **1981** Joe Garagiola Tucson Open, Glen Campbell Los Angeles Open. **1982** Wickes Andy Williams San Diego Open. **1983** Honda Inverrary Classic. **1987** AT&T Pebble Beach National Pro-Am. **1994** AT&T Pebble Beach National Pro-Am.

INTERNATIONAL VICTORIES (5): 1973 World Cup (Indiv.). **1974** Dunlop Phoenix. **1975** World Cup (Indiv.). **1976** British Open (Eur). **1979** Trophee Lancome (Eur).

1995 SEASON: While concentrating on his work as a golf analyst for NBC (and continuing to be plagued by bad knees), entered only two events...withdrew after three rounds from Mercedes Championships...missed cut in defense of AT&T Pebble Beach National Pro-Am title.

CAREER HIGHLIGHTS: In one of the true Cinderella stories of recent years, Johnny won his 24th PGA TOUR title at 1994 AT&T Pebble Beach National Pro-Am...moved into contention with third-round 67, one stroke behind Dudley Hart...shot closing 74, but it was good enough to hold off runners-up Tom Watson, Corey Pavin, Jeff Maggert and Kirk Triplett...owns two major titles...claimed 1973 U.S. Open at Oakmont, winning by five strokes over John Schlee, after a final-round 63...that 63 first of what still stands as lowest 18-hole score in majors history...defeated Jack Nicklaus and Seve Ballesteros by six strokes at Royal Birkdale...enjoyed lion's share of success on West Coast, winning 13 events in California and Arizona, including four times (1974-76 and 1981) in Tucson...most recent Pebble Beach win came 20 years after his first there; in between was 1987 Pebble victory, his last career triumph prior to 1994...first TOUR victory was in 1971 Southern Open...ranks fifth on all-time list with eight victories in single season (1974)...PGA TOUR's leading money winner in 1974, the only golfer other than Nicklaus or Watson to win the money title between 1971 and 1980...winner 1983 Chrysler Team Championship (with Nicklaus)...member 1975 and 1981 Ryder Cup teams, where compiled a 2-2-2 record (won both foursomes matches, lost both singles matches and halved both four-ball matches)...1973-75-80 World Cup teams (won individual and team title in 1973 and 1975)...1974 PGA Player of Year...winner 1964 U.S. Junior Amateur Championship.

PERSONAL: Unexpected 1994 AT&T Pebble Beach National Pro-Am win made him most recent grandfather to win a TOUR event (first since Art Wall, Jr. at 1975 Greater Milwaukee Open).

CAREER SUMMARY **PLAYOFF RECORD: 1-5**

Year	Events Played	Cuts Made	1st	2nd	3rd	Top 10	Top 25	Earnings	Rank
1966(Am.)	1	1				1	1		
1967(Am.)	1	1							
1969(Am.)	1	1							
1969	17	12					3	$8,364	135
1970	33	26				7	16	$52,391	40
1971	33	27	1	1	1	9	15	$91,081	18
1972	29	24	1	1	1	6	14	$99,348	17
1973	21	21	1	2	1	10	17	$127,833	9
1974	20	19	8		1	12	14	$353,021	1
1975	21	19	4	2		11	15	$226,118	2
1976	17	16	2	1		7	12	$135,888	14
1977	24	16		2	1	4	7	$61,025	48
1978	16	9				1	2	$17,440	111
1979	20	11		1		2	4	$49,266	78
1980	16	15	1	1		6	11	$127,117	30
1981	17	15	2	1		5	11	$193,167	12
1982	17	14	1	1	2	6	8	$169,065	20
1983	19	16	1	2	1	5	11	$230,186	14
1984	15	11			1	5	8	$139,422	47
1985	19	17				5	10	$126,616	64
1986	15	12			1	1	4	$71,444	118
1987	17	8	1			1	1	$139,398	78
1988	13	9					2	$31,989	169
1989	11	7				1	2	$66,171	150
1990	1	1					1	$8,900	235
1991	1	1						$2,864	269
1992	2	2						$4,312	269
1993	1								
1994	4	1	1			1	1	$225,000	81
1995	2	1							
Total	424	333	24	15	10	106	190	$2,746,424	67

TOP TOURNAMENT SUMMARY

YEAR	66	67	69	70	71	72	73	74	75	76	77	78	79	80	81
The Masters Tournament		T53			T2		T6	T15	T2	T23	T35	T32		T38	T2
U.S. Open	T8		T42	T18	T5	7	1	T35	T38	10	T27	T6		CUT	T23
British Open Championship					T47	T15	T2	10	T3	1	T9	CUT	T57	CUT	T39
PGA Championship				T12	T20	T20	T18	T39			T11	T38		T68	CUT
THE PLAYERS Championship										T39	W/D			T31	T37

JOHNNY MILLER...continued

TOP TOURNAMENT SUMMARY (cont.)

YEAR	82	83	84	85	86	87	88	89	91	94
Masters Tournament	CUT	T12	CUT	T25	T28	T42				CUT
U.S. Open	T45	CUT	T4	8	T45	CUT				CUT
British Open Championship	T22		T31		CUT		T53	T49	CUT	
PGA Championship	T32	T30	W/D	CUT	W/D	W/D				
THE PLAYERS Championship	CUT	T16	T29	CUT	CUT	CUT	CUT	CUT		

NATIONAL TEAMS: Ryder Cup (2), 1975, 1981; World Cup (3), 1973, 1975, 1980 (individual winner in 1973 and 1975).

1995 PGA TOUR STATISTICS

Scoring	73.10	(N/A)
Driving	230.3	(N/A)
Driving Accuracy	79.5	(N/A)
Greens in Regulation	69.4	(N/A)
Putting	1.840	(N/A)
Sand Saves	61.5	(N/A)
Total Driving		(N/A)
Eagles		(N/A)
Birdies	17	(N/A)

MISCELLANEOUS STATISTICS

Scoring Avg Before Cut	72.20	(N/A)
Scoring Avg 3rd Rnd	76.00	(N/A)
Birdies Conversion %	22.7	(N/A)
Par Breakers	15.7	(N/A)

1995 Low Round: 71: 3 times, most recent 1995 AT&T Pebble Beach National Pro-Am/2

Career Low Round: 61: 3 times, most recent 1975 Dean Martin Tucson Open/4

Career Largest Paycheck: $225,000: 1994 AT&T Pebble Beach National Pro-Am/1

LARRY MIZE

EXEMPT STATUS: Winner, 1987 Masters Tournament
FULL NAME: Larry Hogan Mize
HEIGHT: 6' **WEIGHT:** 165
BIRTH DATE: Sept. 23, 1958 **BIRTHPLACE:** Augusta, GA
RESIDENCE: Columbus, GA
FAMILY: Wife, Bonnie; David (4/17/86), Patrick (2/12/89), Robert (4/2/93)
COLLEGE: Georgia Tech
SPECIAL INTERESTS: Fishing, all sports, piano
TURNED PROFESSIONAL: 1980 **Q SCHOOL:** Fall 1981

TOUR VICTORIES (4): 1983 Danny Thomas-Memphis Classic. **1987** Masters Tournament. **1993** Northern Telecom Open, Buick Open.

INTERNATIONAL VICTORIES (4): 1988 Casio World Open (Jpn). **1989** Dunlop Phoenix (Jpn). **1990** Dunlop Phoenix (Jpn). **1993** Johnnie Walker World Championship.

BEST 1995 FINISHES: T5 -- FedEx St. Jude Classic; T8 -- THE PLAYERS Championship; T9 -- Kemper Open

1995 SEASON: Earned $289,576 in 14th PGA TOUR season, good for 67th on the money list, his lowest standing since his first year on TOUR...first of three top-10 finishes of year came at THE PLAYERS Championship...was T3 after opening 69 but fell well off pace with second-round 77...closed with 72-69 for T8, four strokes behind Lee Janzen...$87,000 payday was largest of year...shot 67-70-70-69 -- 276 for T9 at Kemper Open...at FedEx St. Jude Classic, rounds of 65-64-70-71 -- 270 left him T5, three strokes behind Jim Gallagher, Jr....opening 66 at Buick Challenge good for T2, one stroke behind leader Bill Porter...finished T40...third on TOUR in driving accuracy (79.6%).

CAREER HIGHLIGHTS: Captured two titles in season for first time in 1993, winning Northern Telecom and Buick Opens...those victories his first since 1987 Masters...gained final-round lead at Tucson National when 54-hole co-leaders Dudley Hart and Phil Mickelson faltered, then held off Jeff Maggert for third career win...came from four strokes off Fuzzy Zoeller's third-round lead to claim Buick Open...played just three tournaments in two months preceding Buick event, missing cut in each and taking July away from TOUR entirely...probably best known for "impossible" shot which captured Masters...finished regulation tied with Greg Norman and Seve Ballesteros after birdieing final hole...after Ballesteros went out on first playoff hole, used sand wedge to sink 140-foot pitch from right of green on second extra hole...first victory was in 1983 Danny Thomas-Memphis Classic, where sank 25-foot birdie putt to edge

LARRY MIZE...*continued*

Zoeller, Sammy Rachels and Chip Beck...lost playoff to Norman in 1986 Kemper Open, Payne Stewart in 1990 MCI Heritage Classic...underwent arthroscopic knee surgery in March 1994...T5 at Nestle Invitational one week later...winner 1993 Johnnie Walker World Championship (and $550,000) as last alternate in field of Jamaica event...winner 1988 Casio World Open, 1989-90 Dunlop Phoenix (Japan) ...member 1987 Ryder Cup team.

PERSONAL: Plays somewhat limited schedule each year, preferring to keep large measure of focus on young family...Player Director, PGA TOUR Policy Board 1987-90...winner Atlanta Amateur Championship ...played No. 1 three years at Georgia Tech, captain for two.

CAREER SUMMARY **PLAYOFF RECORD: 1-2**

Year	Events Played	Cuts Made	1st	2nd	3rd	Top 10	Top 25	Earnings	Rank
1980	2	1						$1,189	251
1981	2								
1982	28	13				1	4	$28,787	125
1983	35	25	1		1	3	7	$146,325	35
1984	31	26			1	6	13	$172,513	36
1985	28	25		1	1	8	17	$231,041	17
1986	25	22		3		6	11	$314,051	17
1987	23	16	1	2		9	15	$561,407	6
1988	24	17				3	10	$187,823	62
1989	25	22				7	11	$278,388	45
1990	23	21		3	2	7	16	$668,198	14
1991	25	22				4	12	$279,061	60
1992	24	18			1	5	10	$316,428	47
1993	22	17	2		1	7	11	$724,660	13
1994	22	18			1	4	9	$386,029	42
1995	22	15				3	7	$289,576	67
Total	361	278	4	9	8	73	153	$4,585,476	28

1996 PGA TOUR CHARITY TEAM: Lincoln-Mercury Kapalua International

TOP TOURNAMENT SUMMARY

YEAR	81	82	83	84	85	86	87	88	89	90	91	92	93	94	95
Masters Tournament				T11	T47	T16	1	T45	T26	T14	T17	T6	T21	3	CUT
U.S. Open	CUT	CUT			T39	T24	T4	T12	T33	T14	T55	CUT	CUT	CUT	CUT
British Open Championship				CUT		T46	T26	CUT	T19	T31	CUT	CUT	T27	T11	CUT
PGA Championship			T47	T6	T23	T53	CUT	CUT	T17	T12	CUT	T40	CUT	T15	CUT
THE PLAYERS Championship			T13	T15	CUT	2	T12	CUT	T70	CUT	CUT	T54	CUT	CUT	T8
THE TOUR Championship							T12			T28			T18		

NATIONAL TEAMS: Ryder Cup, 1987.

1995 PGA TOUR STATISTICS

Scoring	70.81	(57)
Driving	255.8	(150T)
Driving Accuracy	79.6	(3)
Greens in Regulation	69.2	(22T)
Putting	1.772	(49T)
All Around	609	(60)
Sand Saves	55.0	(60T)
Total Driving	153	(48T)
Eagles	3	(137T)
Birdies	246	(131T)

MISCELLANEOUS STATISTICS

Scoring Avg Before Cut	71.24	(94T)
Scoring Avg 3rd Rnd	69.86	(14)
Scoring Avg Final Rnd	70.79	(54T)
Birdies Conversion %	29.0	(81T)
Par Breakers	19.8	(71T)

1995 Low Round: **66:** 3 times, most recent 1995 Walt Disney World/Oldsmobile Classic/2
Career Low Round: **62:** 1985 Los Angeles Open/2
Career Largest Paycheck: **$198,000:** 1993 Northern Telecom Open/1

GIL MORGAN

EXEMPT STATUS: 73rd on 1995 money list
FULL NAME: Gilmer Bryan Morgan
HEIGHT: 5' 9" **WEIGHT:** 175
BIRTH DATE: Sept. 25, 1946 **BIRTHPLACE:** Wewoka, OK
RESIDENCE: Oak Tree Golf Club, Edmond, OK
FAMILY: Wife, Jeanine; Molly (5/18/81), Maggie (8/10/82), Melanie (9/24/84)
COLLEGE: East Central State College (1968, B.S.), Southern College of Optometry (1972, Doctor of Optometry)
SPECIAL INTERESTS: Cars
TURNED PROFESSIONAL: 1972 **Q SCHOOL:** Fall 1973

TOUR VICTORIES (7): 1977 B.C. Open. **1978** Glen Campbell-Los Angeles Open, World Series of Golf. **1979** Danny Thomas-Memphis Classic. **1983** Joe Garagiola-Tucson Open, Glen Campbell-Los Angeles Open. **1990** Kemper Open.

BEST 1995 FINISHES: 2 -- Deposit Guaranty Golf Classic; T5 -- GTE Byron Nelson Classic; T7 -- MCI Classic

1995 SEASON: In his last full season before his 50th birthday, did not play after first week of September due to neck injury, but earned $255,565, 73rd on money list...made first four cuts of 1995, with best finish a T29 at Phoenix Open, then missed next three...first top-10 came two starts later at MCI Classic...third-round 62, low round of his 23-year PGA TOUR career, moved him within one stroke of leaders...closing 71 left him T7, two strokes out of playoff won by Bob Tway...shot 68-66-68-66 -- 268 for T5 at GTE Byron Nelson Classic...nearly claimed eighth career victory at Deposit Guranty Golf Classic...after opening 69-69, moved into serious contention with third-round 67, which left him T4, two strokes behind Dicky Thompson...closed with 69 for 274 but was overtaken by Ed Dougherty, whose final-round 66 earned him the two-stroke victory...T11 at next start at Buick Open.

CAREER HIGHLIGHTS: Had leg up on one of great U.S. Opens of all time in 1992...became first to reach 10-under-par in Open early in Round 3, then climbed to 12-under through 43 holes before falling to eventual T13...handled tournament adversity and post-Open followup head-on and with dignity...biggest victory came in 1978 World Series of Golf...defeated Hubert Green in playoff to emerge year's No. 2 money winner behind Tom Watson...had left shoulder rotator cuff surgery in September 1986...after nine-month layoff, returned to TOUR in early May 1987 and was near top of game by midsummer...enjoyed most successful year in 1990...captured Kemper Open in early June, first victory since 1983 and seventh career...finished in top eight in seven straight tournaments...won first two events of '83, Joe Garagiola-Tucson Open in playoff with Lanny Wadkins and Glen Campbell-Los Angeles Open...recorded nine top-10 finishes in 1993...in 1994, finished runner-up to Bob Estes at Texas Open...member of 1979 and 1983 Ryder Cup teams when his record was 1-2-3.

PERSONAL: Holds Doctor of Optometry Degree (1972) from Southern College of Optometry, but has never practiced...during junior year at East Central State (OK) decided to pursue career in golf, but waited until earned doctor's degree before turning professional...named to NAIA Hall of Fame 1982.

CAREER SUMMARY **PLAYOFF RECORD: 3-4**

Year	Events Played	Cuts Made	1st	2nd	3rd	Top 10	Top 25	Earnings	Rank
1973	3	1					1	$3,800	204
1974	30	16				3	6	$23,880	94
1975	27	17		1	1	2	7	$42,772	60
1976	32	24		1		6	10	$61,372	42
1977	33	25	1		1	5	10	$104,817	24
1978	28	24	2	2		11	18	$267,459	2
1979	25	19	1			2	11	$115,857	29
1980	25	19		1	2	7	10	$135,308	28
1981	24	19		3	2	6	12	$171,184	18
1982	25	20		1	2	8	14	$139,652	26
1983	25	23	2	2	1	10	16	$306,133	5
1984	23	19		1	5	8	16	$281,948	13
1985	25	18		1	1	3	10	$133,941	62
1986	15	9			1	3	5	$98,770	84
1987	16	10		1		3	7	$133,980	81
1988	23	14		1	1	7	7	$288,002	34
1989	25	19			1	6	9	$300,395	39
1990	24	18	1	2	1	5	12	$702,629	11
1991	24	16		1		2	8	$232,913	70
1992	23	20				3	11	$272,959	56
1993	23	20			2	9	14	$610,312	24
1994	18	14		1		3	9	$309,690	54
1995	21	14		1		3	5	$255,565	73
Total	537	398	7	20	21	115	228	$4,989,013	24

1996 PGA TOUR CHARITY TEAM: THE TOUR Championship

Gil Morgan...continued

TOP TOURNAMENT SUMMARY

YEAR	74	75	76	77	78	79	80	81	82	83	84	85	86	87	88
Masters Tournament					T18	T31	T19	T21	CUT	T8	T3	CUT			
U.S. Open				T41			T16	CUT	T22	3	T21	T23		T51	CUT
British Open Championship						CUT	T10		CUT		T22				
PGA Championship		T17	T8	T15	T4	T28	T3	T19	T22	T55	CUT	T28	CUT	T21	CUT
THE PLAYERS Championship	T58		T65	T40	T20	T12	T31	T12	T47	T23	T44	CUT	T58		T6

TOP TOURNAMENT SUMMARY (cont.)

YEAR	89	90	91	92	93	94	95
Masters Tournament			CUT		T50	CUT	
U.S. Open	W/D	T56	CUT	T13	CUT	CUT	
British Open Championship			T64		T14	CUT	
PGA Championship	CUT	3	T16	T21	CUT	T39	T31
THE PLAYERS Championship	T6	CUT	CUT	CUT	T3		T68
THE TOUR Championship		T14			T18		

NATIONAL TEAMS: Ryder Cup (2), 1979, 1983.

1995 PGA TOUR STATISTICS

Scoring	70.71	(51T)
Driving	264.2	(86)
Driving Accuracy	72.0	(62T)
Greens in Regulation	69.5	(19)
Putting	1.779	(64T)
All Around	588	(54)
Sand Saves	49.6	(131)
Total Driving	148	(44)
Eagles	8	(36T)
Birdies	238	(139)

MISCELLANEOUS STATISTICS

Scoring Avg Before Cut	71.09	(76T)
Scoring Avg 3rd Rnd	69.14	(3)
Scoring Avg Final Rnd	70.64	(32T)
Birdies Conversion %	26.8	(143T)
Par Breakers	19.2	(93T)

1995 Low Round: **62:** 1995 MCI Classic/3
Career Low Round: **62:** 2 times, most recent 1995 MCI Classic/3
Career Largest Paycheck: $180,000: 1990 Kemper/1

John Morse

EXEMPT STATUS: 1995 tournament winner
FULL NAME: John Paul Morse
HEIGHT: 5' 10" **WEIGHT:** 180
BIRTH DATE: February 16, 1958 **BIRTHPLACE:** Marshall, MI
RESIDENCE: Casselberry, FL; plays out of Marshall (MI) CC
FAMILY: Wife, Kelly; Christina (7/31/92)
COLLEGE: University of Michigan
SPECIAL INTERESTS: Fishing
TURNED PROFESSIONAL: 1981 **JOINED TOUR:** 1994

TOUR VICTORIES (1): 1995 United Airlines Hawaiian Open

INTERNATIONAL VICTORIES (4): 1989 Quebec Open (Can). **1990** Australian Open (Aus), Nedlands Masters (Aus). **1991** Air New Zealand/Shell Open (Aus).

NIKE TOUR VICTORIES (1): 1993 NIKE New England Classic

BEST 1995 FINISHES: 1 -- United Airlines Hawaiian Open; T2 -- Buick Challenge; T3 -- LaCantera Texas Open

JOHN MORSE...*continued*

1995 SEASON: Ended any talk of sophomore jinx in season's first week, when he won the United Airlines Hawaiian Open...after an opening 71, shot back-to-back 65s to take a two-stroke lead after 54 holes...closed with 68 for a three-stroke victory at $216,000...took advantage of par-5s at Waialae CC, playing them in 18 under par, including eagle on final hole... T18 at Phoenix Open two weeks later...in next 15 starts, posted no better than T56 and failed to cash in 10 tournaments...recovered by making final six cuts of year and nearly returning to winner's circle at Buick Challenge...with rounds of 71-68-67 was T3, one stroke behind Fred Funk and Steve Stricker...final-round 67 not enough to catch Funk as he finished T2, one stroke behind...in final official start, shot 70-69-71-70 for T3 at LaCantera Texas Open, one of only four golfers to better par each day.

CAREER HIGHLIGHTS: Qualified for TOUR in 1994 by finishing fifth on 1993 NIKE TOUR money list...in rookie season, retained card for 1995 with quick start which included T14 at United Airlines Hawaiian Open, T12 at Freeport-McMoRan Classic and T6 at Kmart Greater Greensboro Open...winner of '93 NIKE New England Classic...year also featured pair of consecutive T2 finishes (New Mexico and Wichita), followed by T3 at Texarkana last three weeks of August...also had T3 at Hawkeye Open...played Australasian Tour from 1989-92...returned to Australia following conclusion of '93 NIKE TOUR for select events...winner of 1990 Australian Open in playoff with Craig Parry...that victory provided spot in 1991 NEC World Series of Golf, where T27 brought check for $9,116 (only PGA TOUR payday prior to 1994)...former Big 10 champion.

PERSONAL: Very much enjoyed Australian experience...decision to play 1993 NIKE TOUR rather than in Australia based on birth of daughter Christina...failed six times to earn playing card at Qualifying Tournament...all-conference high school basketball selection.

PGA TOUR CAREER SUMMARY — **PLAYOFF RECORD: 0-0**

Year	Events Played	Cuts Made	1st	2nd	3rd	Top 10	Top 25	Earnings	Rank
1984	2								
1987	1								
1988	1								
1991	3	1						$9,117	230
1994	26	12				1	4	$146,137	122
1995	24	12	1	1	1	3	4	$416,803	42
Total	57	25	1	1	1	4	8	$572,056	240

NIKE TOUR SUMMARY

Year	Events Played	Cuts Made	1st	2nd	3rd	Top 10	Top 25	Earnings	Rank
1993	26	19	1	2	2	9	12	$122,627	5
1994	2								
Total	28	19	1	2	2	9	12	$122,627	
COMBINED TOTAL MONEY								$694,684	

1996 PGA TOUR CHARITY TEAM: Honda Classic

TOP TOURNAMENT SUMMARY

YEAR	84	87	94	95
Masters Tournament				CUT
U.S. Open	CUT	CUT	CUT	
British Open Championship				CUT
PGA Championship				CUT
THE PLAYERS Championship				CUT

1995 PGA TOUR STATISTICS

Scoring	71.46	(113T)
Driving	255.7	(153T)
Driving Accuracy	75.8	(21T)
Greens in Regulation	66.9	(66T)
Putting	1.810	(153T)
All Around	876	(130)
Sand Saves	47.8	(144T)
Total Driving	174	(77T)
Eagles	6	(69T)
Birdies	214	(157T)

MISCELLANEOUS STATISTICS

Scoring Avg Before Cut	71.76	(146T)
Scoring Avg 3rd Rnd	70.92	(74T)
Scoring Avg Final Rnd	71.50	(113T)
Birdies Conversion %	25.8	(166)
Par Breakers	17.2	(161T)

1995 Low Round: **65:** 2 times, most recent 1995 United Airlines Hawaiian Open/3

Career Low Round: **65:** 2 times, most recent 1995 United Airlines Hawaiian Open/3

Career Largest Paycheck: $216,000: 1995 United Airlines Hawaiian Open/1

Jodie Mudd

EXEMPT STATUS: Winner, 1990 THE PLAYERS Championship
FULL NAME: Joseph Martin Mudd
HEIGHT: 5' 11" **WEIGHT:** 150
BIRTH DATE: April 23, 1960 **BIRTHPLACE:** Louisville, KY
RESIDENCE: Finchville, KY
FAMILY: Single
COLLEGE: Georgia Southern University
SPECIAL INTERESTS: Thoroughbred racing, outdoors
TURNED PROFESSIONAL: 1982 **JOINED TOUR:** April 1982

TOUR VICTORIES (4): 1988 Federal Express St. Jude Classic. **1989** GTE Byron Nelson Golf Classic. **1990** THE PLAYERS Championship, Nabisco Championships.

BEST 1995 FINISH: 6 -- Nissan Open

1995 SEASON: Continued to be part-time player...made only nine starts in 1995, none after July...made just one cut, but made it count at Nissan Open...shared lead with Billy Mayfair after an opening 66...second-round 71 dropped him to T8, five strokes off pace...six back after a third-round 69, then closed with 67 to finish alone in sixth at 273, five strokes behind Corey Pavin...it was his first top-10 finish in 35 starts dating back to the 1993 Nissan Los Angeles Open, when he finished T6.

CAREER HIGHLIGHTS: Enjoyed finest season in 1990, when won twice and finished fifth on money list with earnings over $900,000...'90 victories came in THE PLAYERS and Nabisco Championships, TOUR's two richest events...earned 10-year exemption in THE PLAYERS, battling Mark Calcavecchia to wire and making clutch birdie on treacherous 17th at TPC at Sawgrass...in Nabisco Championships birdied last two holes, then birdied first playoff hole to defeat Billy Mayfair and earn $450,000 first-place check...tailed off in '91, collecting three top-10 finishes, including T7 at Masters and T8 in next start at BellSouth Atlanta Classic...joined TOUR week after finishing low amateur in '82 Masters...two weeks later tied for fifth at USF&G Classic, earning over $10,000...U.S. Public Links champion 1980-81...winner 1981 Sunnehanna Amateur.

PERSONAL: Raises thoroughbreds in Kentucky...three-time All-America at Georgia Southern...Valhalla GC, site of 1996 PGA Championship, about 15 minutes from his home...goal is to earn enough money breeding horses to buy land for public golf course.

CAREER SUMMARY **PLAYOFF RECORD: 2-2**

Year	Events Played	Cuts Made	1st	2nd	3rd	Top 10	Top 25	Earnings	Rank
1982(Am.)	2	2					2		
1982	21	11				1	4	$34,216	115
1983	33	16					1	$21,515	145
1984	25	16					4	$42,244	114
1985	31	21		3		6	10	$186,648	34
1986	20	16		2	1	4	7	$182,812	48
1987	30	19		1		4	10	$203,923	51
1988	31	23	1			4	15	$422,022	23
1989	27	19	1			3	8	$404,860	26
1990	23	18	2		1	4	7	$911,746	5
1991	18	11				3	4	$148,453	102
1992	20	13				1	3	$88,081	141
1993	20	9				1	4	$89,366	150
1994	15	7						$27,868	214
1995	9	1				1	1	$43,200	212
Total	325	202	4	6	2	32	80	$2,806,955	65

TOP TOURNAMENT SUMMARY

YEAR	82	83	85	86	87	88	89	90	91	92	93	94	95
Masters Tournament	T20	T42			T4	CUT	7	T30	T7	CUT			
U.S. Open		CUT		T15	T17		T51	CUT	T26				
British Open Championship							5	T4	T5	T28			
PGA Championship				T41	CUT	T52	67		T32				
THE PLAYERS Championship		CUT	T40	CUT	W/D	T36	CUT	1	CUT	CUT	CUT	CUT	CUT
THE TOUR Championship						T8	T14	1					

NATIONAL TEAMS: World Cup, 1990; Four Tours World Championship of Golf, 1990; Walker Cup, 1981.

JODIE MUDD...continued

1995 PGA TOUR STATISTICS		
Scoring	72.56	(N/A)
Driving	265.3	(N/A)
Driving Accuracy	60.3	(N/A)
Greens in Regulation	62.7	(N/A)
Putting	1.803	(N/A)
Sand Saves	40.0	(N/A)
Total Driving		(N/A)
Eagles		(N/A)
Birdies	53	(N/A)

MISCELLANEOUS STATISTICS		
Scoring Avg Before Cut	73.63	(N/A)
Scoring Avg 3rd Rnd	69.00	(N/A)
Scoring Avg Final Rnd	67.00	(N/A)
Birdies Conversion %	26.1	(N/A)
Par Breakers	16.4	(N/A)

1995 Low Round: 66: 1995 Nissan Open/1
Career Low Round: 63: 1986 Bob Hope Classic/3
Career Largest Paycheck: $450,000: 1990 Nabisco Championship/1

LARRY NELSON

EXEMPT STATUS: Winner, 1987 PGA Championship
FULL NAME: Larry Gene Nelson
HEIGHT: 5' 9" **WEIGHT:** 150
BIRTH DATE: Sept. 10, 1947 **BIRTHPLACE:** Ft. Payne, AL
RESIDENCE: Marietta, GA; plays out of Centennial
FAMILY: Wife, Gayle; Drew (10/7/76), Josh (9/28/78)
COLLEGE: Kennesaw Junior College (1970)
SPECIAL INTERESTS: Golf course architecture, snow skiing
TURNED PROFESSIONAL: 1971 **Q SCHOOL:** Fall 1973

TOUR VICTORIES (10): 1979 Jackie Gleason-Inverrary Classic, Western Open. **1980** Atlanta Classic. **1981** Greater Greensboro Open, PGA Championship. **1983** U.S. Open. **1984** Walt Disney World Golf Classic. **1987** PGA Championship, Walt Disney World/Oldsmobile Classic. **1988** Georgia-Pacific Atlanta Classic.

INTERNATIONAL VICTORIES (4): 1980 Tokai Classic (Jpn). **1983** Dunlop International Open (Jpn). **1989** Suntory Open (Jpn). **1991** Dunlop Phoenix (Jpn).

BEST 1995 FINISH: T8—Buick Challenge

1995 SEASON: While year was a disappointment overall, T8 in Buick Challenge renewed hope for return to winning form...fired second-round 65, then started final day one stroke behind Steve Stricker and eventual winner Fred Funk...final-round 70 produced finish four strokes back and the comment: "I don't wonder anymore. I know for sure I want to win again and I think it is only a matter of time."...Callaway Gardens finish his best since T7 in 1992 Doral-Ryder Open...increased schedule to 21 events after playing only 17 in 1994 and 15 in 1993...made just six cuts in those 21 starts, failing to earn money in consecutive starts and missing three cuts in a row twice.

CAREER HIGHLIGHTS: With exception of 1979 Western Open and 1983 U.S. Open, all career victories have been achieved in Southeastern U.S.: four in Florida (including 1987 PGA Championship at PGA National), three in Georgia (including 1981 PGA at Atlanta Athletic Club) and one in North Carolina...last TOUR victory, 1988 Georgia-Pacific Atlanta Classic, came 300 yards from his house at Atlanta Country Club...finest year on TOUR 1987, when he won PGA Championship in playoff with Lanny Wadkins at Palm Beach Gardens...later in year captured second Walt Disney World/Oldsmobile Classic en route to earnings of over $500,000 for only time in career...made just 16 starts in 1991, with three top-10 finishes...fired final-round 68 at Hazeltine National to finish T3, three strokes out of Payne Stewart-Scott Simpson U.S. Open playoff...posted 9-3-1 Ryder Cup record in three appearances (1979-81-87).

PERSONAL: Former Player Director, PGA TOUR Tournament Policy Board...didn't start playing golf until after return from military service in Vietnam...broke 100 first time he ever played.

LARRY NELSON...*continued*

CAREER SUMMARY						PLAYOFF RECORD: 3-2			
Year	**Events Played**	**Cuts Made**	**1st**	**2nd**	**3rd**	**Top 10**	**Top 25**	**Earnings**	**Rank**
1973	3	1						$356	287
1974	25	14				2	6	$24,022	93
1975	30	19				5	8	$39,810	66
1976	34	27		1		4	11	$66,482	41
1977	33	24		3	1	6	10	$99,876	26
1978	31	22			1	4	12	$65,686	45
1979	26	22	2	2	2	9	14	$281,022	2
1980	29	22	1		1	9	16	$182,715	11
1981	28	21	2			4	14	$193,342	10
1982	25	18		1		8	13	$159,134	21
1983	23	13	1			3	7	$138,368	40
1984	20	11	1			4	8	$154,689	42
1985	21	19				5	13	$143,993	54
1986	23	10			1	3	3	$124,338	69
1987	22	14	2	1		7	9	$501,292	14
1988	18	17	1	1	1	6	10	$411,284	25
1989	17	12		1		2	5	$186,869	79
1990	15	10				2	5	$124,260	124
1991	16	8			2	3	4	$160,543	96
1992	15	9				1	3	$94,930	135
1993	18	9					2	$54,870	177
1994	17	8				1	1	$66,831	175
1995	21	6				1	1	$40,689	214
Total	510	336	10	10	9	89	175	$3,318,317	50

TOP TOURNAMENT SUMMARY

YEAR	**75**	**76**	**77**	**78**	**79**	**80**	**81**	**82**	**83**	**84**	**85**	**86**	**87**	**88**	**89**
Masters Tournament					T31	T6	CUT	T7	CUT	5	T36	T36	CUT	T33	CUT
U.S. Open		T21	T54		T4	T58	T20	T19	1	CUT	T39	T35	CUT	T62	T13
British Open Championship						T12		T32	T53	CUT	T55	CUT	T48	T13	CUT
PGA Championship		T34	T54	T12	T28	CUT	1	CUT	T36	CUT	T23	CUT	1	T38	T46
THE PLAYERS Championship	T72	T39	T8	T4	T20	DQ	CUT	T10	CUT	T62	CUT	CUT	CUT	CUT	T59
THE TOUR Championship													T21	T26	

TOP TOURNAMENT SUMMARY (cont.)

YEAR	**90**	**91**	**92**	**93**	**94**	**95**
Masters Tournament	48	55	DQ			
U.S. Open	T14	T3	CUT	T46	CUT	
PGA Championship	CUT	CUT	T28	T56	CUT	CUT
THE PLAYERS Championship	T16	T23	CUT	CUT	T55	CUT

NATIONAL TEAMS: Ryder Cup (3) 1979, 1981, 1987.

1995 PGA TOUR STATISTICS		
Scoring	**72.38**	**(182)**
Driving	**258.9**	**(130)**
Driving Accuracy	**72.5**	**(55T)**
Greens in Regulation	**63.4**	**(156T)**
Putting	**1.817**	**(172T)**
All Around	**1,114**	**(176)**
Sand Saves	**50.5**	**(118T)**
Total Driving	**185**	**(92T)**
Eagles	**4**	**(116T)**
Birdies	**157**	**(185)**

MISCELLANEOUS STATISTICS		
Scoring Avg Before Cut	**72.42**	**(182)**
Scoring Avg 3rd Rnd	**72.25**	**(162T)**
Scoring Avg Final Rnd	**71.86**	**(142)**
Birdies Conversion %	**24.6**	**(181)**
Par Breakers	**16.0**	**(183T)**

1995 Low Round: **64:** 1995 FedEx St. Jude Classic/2
Career Low Round: **63:** 2 times, most recent 1989 GTE Byron Nelson/1
Career Largest Paycheck: **$150,000:** 1987 PGA Championship/1

JACK NICKLAUS *(NICK-lus)*

EXEMPT STATUS: Winner, 1962 United States Open
FULL NAME: Jack William Nicklaus
HEIGHT: 5' 11" **WEIGHT:** 190
BIRTH DATE: Jan. 21, 1940 **BIRTHPLACE:** Columbus, OH
RESIDENCE: North Palm Beach, FL, Muirfield Village, OH; plays out of Muirfield Village
FAMILY: Wife, Barbara Bash; Jack II(9/23/61), Steven(4/11/63), Nancy Jean(5/5/65), Gary(1/15/69), Michael(7/24/73)
COLLEGE: Ohio State University
SPECIAL INTERESTS: Fishing, hunting, tennis and skiing
TURNED PROFESSIONAL: 1961 **JOINED TOUR:** 1962

PGA TOUR VICTORIES (70): 1962 U.S. Open, Seattle World's Fair, Portland. **1963** Palm Springs, Masters Tournament, Tournament of Champions, PGA Championship, Sahara. **1964** Portland, Tournament of Champions, Phoenix, Whitemarsh. **1965** Portland, Masters Tournament, Memphis, Thunderbird Classic, Philadelphia. **1966** Masters Tournament, Sahara. **1967** U.S. Open, Sahara, Bing Crosby, Western, Westchester. **1968** Western, American Golf Classic. **1969** Sahara, Kaiser, San Diego. **1970** Byron Nelson, Four-Ball (with Arnold Palmer). **1971** PGA Championship, Tournament of Champions, Byron Nelson, National Team (with Arnold Palmer), Disney World. **1972** Bing Crosby, Doral-Eastern, Masters Tournament, U.S. Open, Westchester, Match Play, Disney. **1973** Bing Crosby, New Orleans, Tournament of Champions, Atlanta, PGA Championship, Ohio Kings Island, Walt Disney. **1974** Hawaii, Tournament Players Championship. **1975** Doral-Eastern Open, Heritage Classic, Masters Tournament, PGA Championship, World Open. **1976** Tournament Players Championship, World Series of Golf. **1977** Gleason Inverrary, Tournament of Champions, Memorial. **1978** Gleason Inverrary, Tournament Players Championship, IVB-Philadelphia Classic. **1980** U.S. Open, PGA Championship. **1982** Colonial National Invitation. **1984** Memorial. **1986** Masters Tournament.

INTERNATIONAL VICTORIES (14): 1963 World Cup (Indiv.). **1964** Australian Open (Aus), World Cup (Indiv.). **1966** British Open (Eur). **1968** Australian Open (Aus). **1970** British Open (Eur), Piccadilly World Match Play Championship (Eur). **1971** Australian Open (Aus), Dunlop International (Aus), World Cup (Indiv.). **1975** Australian Open (Aus). **1976** Australian Open (Aus). **1978** British Open (Eur), Australian Open (Aus).

BEST 1995 PGA TOUR FINISH: T6—AT&T Pebble Beach National Pro-Am.

SENIOR PGA TOUR VICTORIES (8): 1990 Tradition at Desert Mountain, Mazda Senior TPC. **1991** The Tradition, PGA Seniors' Championship, U.S. Senior Open. **1993** U.S. Senior Open. **1994** Mercedes Championships. **1995** The Tradition.

BEST SENIOR PGA TOUR 1995 FINISHES: 1—The Tradition; 2—U.S. Senior Open; 2—FORD SENIOR PLAYERS Championship; 3—Bell Atlantic Classic; T5—GTE Suncoast Classic; 8—PGA Seniors' Championship; 9—Senior Tournament of Champions.

1995 SEASON: Started year with T6 at AT&T Pebble Beach National Pro-Am...first top-10 PGA TOUR finish since T10 in 1993 Doral-Ryder Open...best placing since 1991 T5 at Doral...third-round 67 equaled his lowest TOUR round of the year...10-under his lowest score ever on Monterey Peninsula...made cut in three of four major championships (T35 Masters, T79 British Open, T67 PGA Championship)...had missed cut in eight of 12 majors prior to 1995.

CAREER HIGHLIGHTS: Considered by many to be greatest player in history of golf...named "Golfer of the Century" in 1988, Sports Illustrated Athlete of the Decade for the 1970s, 1978 Sports Illustrated Sportsman of the Year, PGA Player of the Year five times (1967-72-73-75-76)...inducted into World Golf Hall of Fame in 1974...finished first in scoring eight times and was runner-up six...first TOUR player to reach $2 million (12/1/73), $3 million (5/2/77), $4 million (2/6/83) and $5 million (8/20/88) in career earnings...co-holds with Arnold Palmer TOUR record for most years winning at least one TOUR event, 17 (1962-78)...105 consecutive cuts made (11/70-9/76) is second to Byron Nelson's 113...dominated golf in 1960s and '70s...1962-69 finished in top 10 in 122 of 186 events played (66%); 1970-79 finished among top 10 in 121 of 171 events played (71%)...in remarkable three-year period from 1971-73, finished in top 10 45 of 55 events (82%)...among 45 top 10s, posted 19 victories and seven seconds...performance in majors is unmatched...winner of 18 professional major championships: six Masters, five PGA Championships, four United States Opens and three British Opens...became oldest player (46) to win Masters with 1986 victory...first professional win came in 1962 U.S. Open at Oakmont CC, where he defeated Arnold Palmer in a playoff...had outstanding amateur record...won five consecutive Ohio State Junior Championships, beginning at age 12...won 1959 U.S. Amateur by defeating Charles Coe, 1 up...claimed second U.S. Amateur in 1961 by defeating Dudley Wysong, 8 and 6...same year was member of victorious Walker Cup squad, Western Amateur, NCAA and Big Ten Champion and finished fourth in U.S. Open...finished runner-up to Arnold Palmer in 1960 U.S. Open at Cherry Hills by two strokes, establishing amateur record of 282...posted a 17-8-3 Ryder Cup record...owner of eight Senior TOUR victories through 1995, including two U.S. Senior Opens.

PERSONAL: One of golf's driving forces off the course...founder and host of the Memorial Tournament...one of the world's leading course designers under the aegis of his own company, Golden Bear International...at age 10, carded a 51 in first nine holes he ever played...does occasional golf commentary for ABC Sports...son Jackie was his caddie in last TOUR victory, the 1986 Masters.

JACK NICKLAUS...*continued*

PGA TOUR CAREER SUMMARY — **PLAYOFF RECORD: 13-10**

Year	Events Played	Cuts Made	1st	2nd	3rd	Top 10	Top 25	Earnings	Rank
1958(Am.)	2	2					1		
1959(Am.)	5	5					1		
1960(Am.)	3	3		1		1	2		
1961(Am.)	5	5				2	3		
1961	1	1				1	1		
1962	26	26	3	3	4	16	22	$61,869	3
1963	21	21	5	2	2	17	21	$100,040	2
1964	25	25	4	6	3	17	25	$113,285	1
1965	23	23	5	4	2	19	20	$140,752	1
1966	18	18	2	3	3	12	17	$111,419	2
1967	21	21	5	2	3	15	16	$188,998	1
1968	19	19	2	3	1	13	19	$155,286	2
1969	23	21	3	1		11	17	$140,167	3
1970	20	18	2	3	2	12	16	$142,149	4
1971	17	17	5	3	3	15	15	$244,490	1
1972	19	19	7	3		14	16	$320,542	1
1973	18	18	7	1	1	16	17	$308,362	1
1974	17	17	2	3		12	17	$238,178	2
1975	16	16	5	1	3	14	16	$298,149	1
1976	16	15	2	2	1	11	15	$266,439	1
1977	18	16	3	2	1	14	16	$284,509	2
1978	15	13	3	2		10	12	$256,672	4
1979	12	12			1	3	6	$59,434	71
1980	13	12	2	1		3	8	$172,386	13
1981	16	15		3		8	13	$178,213	16
1982	15	12	1	3	2	7	11	$232,645	12
1983	15	14		3	1	8	11	$256,158	10
1984	13	13	1	2	1	6	12	$272,595	15
1985	15	14		2	1	4	8	$165,456	43
1986	15	11	1			4	7	$226,015	34
1987	11	9				1	5	$64,686	127
1988	9	5					2	$28,845	177
1989	10	9				2	4	$96,595	129
1990	9	6				1	1	$68,045	160
1991	8	7				1	4	$123,797	122
1992	8	3						$14,868	223
1993	10	4				1	1	$51,532	182
1994	8	1						$11,514	248
1995	11	4				1	1	$68,180	179
Total	546	490	70	59	35	292	399	$5,440,357	21

SENIOR PGA TOUR CAREER SUMMARY

Year	Events Played	Cuts Made	1st	2nd	3rd	Top 10	Top 25	Earnings	Rank
1990	4		2	1	1	4	4	$340,000	15
1991	5		3			4	5	$343,734	17
1992	4			1	1	3	3	$114,548	53
1993	6		1			3	5	$206,028	42
1994	6		1			5	5	$239,278	34
1995	7		1	2	1	7	7	$538,800	22
Total	32		8	4	3	26	29	$1,782,388	37
COMBINED TOTAL MONEY								$7,164,683	

1996 PGA TOUR CHARITY TEAM: Memorial Tournament

PGA TOUR TOP TOURNAMENT SUMMARY

YEAR	58	60	61	62	63	64	65	66	67	68	69	70	71	72	73
Masters Tournament		T13	T7	T15	1	T2	1	1		T5	T23	8	T2	1	T3
U.S. Open	T41	2	T4	1		T23	T32	3	1	2	T25	T51	2	1	T4
British Open Championship				T34	3	2	T12	1	2	T2	T6	1	T5	2	4
PGA Championship				T3	1	T2	T2	T22	T3		T11	T6	1	T13	1

PGA TOUR TOP TOURNAMENT SUMMARY (cont.)

YEAR	74	75	76	77	78	79	80	81	82	83	84	85	86	87	88
Masters Tournament	T4	1	T3	2	7	4	T33	T2	T15	W/D	T18	T6	1	T7	T21
U.S. Open	T10	T7	T11	T10	T6	T9	1	T6	2	T43	T21	CUT	T8	T46	CUT
British Open Championship	3	T3	T2	2	1	T2	T4	T23	T10	T29	T31	CUT	T46	T72	T25
PGA Championship	2	1	T4	3		T65	1	T4	T16	2	T25	T32	T16	T24	CUT
THE PLAYERS Championship	1	T18	1	T5	1	T33	T14	T29	CUT	T19	T33	T17	CUT	CUT	CUT

PGA TOUR TOP TOURNAMENT SUMMARY (cont.)

YEAR	89	90	91	92	93	94	95
Masters Tournament	T18	6	T35	T42	T27	CUT	T35
U.S. Open	T43	T33	T46	CUT	T72	T28	CUT
British Open Championship	T30	T63	T44	CUT	CUT	CUT	T79
PGA Championship	T27	CUT	T23	CUT	CUT	CUT	T67
THE PLAYERS Championship	T29	CUT					CUT

SENIOR PGA TOUR TOP TOURNAMENT SUMMARY

YEAR	90	91	92	93	94	95
The Tradition	1	1	2	T9	T4	1
US Senior Open	2	1	T3	1	T7	2
PGA Seniors Championship	T3	1	T10	T9	9	8
FORD Senior PLAYERS Championship	1	T22		T22	T6	2

NATIONAL TEAMS: Walker Cup (2), 1959, 1961; World Cup (6), 1963, 1964, 1966, 1967, 1971, 1973 (medalist three times); Ryder Cup (6), 1969, 1971, 1973, 1975, 1977, 1981; Ryder Cup Captain (2), 1983, 1987.

1995 PGA TOUR STATISTICS

Scoring	72.69	(N/A)
Driving	258.8	(N/A)
Driving Accuracy	68.1	(N/A)
Greens in Regulation	58.6	(N/A)
Putting	1.789	(N/A)
Sand Saves	38.7	(N/A)
Total Driving		(N/A)
Eagles	2	(N/A)
Birdies	74	(N/A)

MISCELLANEOUS PGA TOUR STATISTICS

Scoring Avg Before Cut	73.60	(N/A)
Scoring Avg 3rd Rnd	71.25	(N/A)
Scoring Avg Final Rnd	73.00	(N/A)
Birdies Conversion %	30.1	(N/A)
Par Breakers	15.4	(N/A)

1995 Low Round: 67: 3 times, most recent 1995 Masters Tournament/1
Career Low Round: 62: 2 times, most recent 1973 Ohio Kings Island Open/3
Career Largest Paycheck: $144,000: 1986 Masters Tournament/1

1995 SENIOR PGA TOUR STATISTICS

Scoring Leaders	69.68	(N/A)
Driving Leaders	262.0	(N/A)
Driving Accuracy	69.7	(N/A)
Greens in Regulation	69.6	(N/A)
Putting Leaders	1.725	(N/A)
Sand Saves	51.4	(N/A)
Total Driving		(N/A)
Eagle Leaders	5	(N/A)
Birdie Leaders	97	(N/A)

1995 Low Round: 66: 2 times, most recent 1995 FORD SENIOR PLAYERS Championship/3
Career Low Round: 64: 2 times, most recent 1990 Mazda Senior TPC/4
Career Largest Paycheck: $150,000: 2 times, most recent 1990 Mazda Senior TPC/1

Greg Norman

EXEMPT STATUS: Winner, 1994 PLAYERS Championship
FULL NAME: Gregory John Norman
HEIGHT: 6' **WEIGHT:** 180
BIRTH DATE: February 10, 1955 **BIRTHPLACE:** Queensland, Australia
RESIDENCE: Hobe Sound, FL; plays out of Medalist
FAMILY: Wife, Laura; Morgan-Leigh (10/5/82), Gregory (9/19/85)
SPECIAL INTERESTS: Fishing, hunting, scuba diving
TURNED PROFESSIONAL: 1976 **JOINED TOUR:** 1983

TOUR VICTORIES (15): 1984 Kemper Open, Canadian Open. **1986** Panasonic-Las Vegas Invitational, Kemper Open. **1988** MCI Heritage Classic. **1989** The International, Greater Milwaukee Open. **1990** Doral-Ryder Open, The Memorial Tournament. **1992** Canadian Open. **1993** Doral-Ryder Open. **1994** THE PLAYERS Championship. **1995** Memorial Tournament, Canon Greater Hartford Open, NEC World Series of Golf.

INTERNATIONAL VICTORIES (53): 1976 Westlakes Classic (Aus). **1977** Martini International (Eur), Kuzuhz International (Jpn). **1978** New South Wales Open (Aus), Traralgon Classic (Aus), Caltex Festival of Sydney Open (Aus), South Seas Classic (Fiji). **1979** Traralgon Classic (Aus), Martini International (Eur), Hong Kong Open. **1980** Australian Open (Aus), French Open (Eur), Scandinavian Open (Eur), Suntory World Match Play Championship (Eur). **1981** Australian Masters (Aus), Martini International (Eur), Dunlop Masters (Eur). **1982** Dunlop Masters (Eur), State Express Classic (Eur), Benson & Hedges International (Eur). **1983** Australian Masters (Aus), Stefan Queensland Open (Aus), National Panasonic New South Wales Open (Aus), Hong Kong Open, Cannes Invitational (Eur), Suntory World Match Play Championship (Eur). **1984** Victorian Open (Aus), Australian Masters (Aus), Toshiba Australian PGA Championship (Aus). **1985** Toshiba Australian PGA Championship (Aus), National Panasonic Australian Open (Aus). **1986** Stefan Queensland Open (Aus), National Panasonic New South Wales Open (Aus), West End Jubilee South Australian Open (Aus), National Panasonic Western Australian Open (Aus), European Open (Eur), British Open (Eur), Suntory World Matchplay Championship (Eur). **1987** Australian Masters (Aus), National Panasonic Australian Open (Aus). **1988** Palm Meadows Cup (Aus), ESP Open (Aus), PGA National Tournament Players Championship (Aus), Panasonic New South Wales Open (Aus), Lancia Italian Open (Eur). **1989** Australian Masters (Aus), PGA National Tournament Players Championship (Aus), Chunichi Crowns (Jpn). **1990** Australian Masters (Aus). **1993** British Open (Eur), Taiheyo Masters (Jpn). **1994** Johnnie Walker Asian Classic (Eur). **1995** Australian Open (Aus).

BEST 1995 FINISHES: 1— Memorial Tournament, Canon Greater Hartford Open, NEC World Series of Golf; 2— U.S. Open; T2—Doral-Ryder Open; T3—Masters Tournament; T4—Kemper Open; T8—Sprint International; T9—THE TOUR Championship.

1995 SEASON: Won three TOUR events for the first time in his career...received first PGA TOUR Player of Year honor for his accomplishments...also earned first PGA Player of the Year award...set TOUR season record with earnings of $1,654,959...made $781,780 in June alone...matched Nick Price with three consecutive million-dollar seasons...opened and closed with 66s to claim four-stroke victory at the Memorial Tournament...in Canon Greater Hartford Open, took three-stroke lead over Fuzzy Zoeller into final round...posted final 71 for two-stroke margin in second win...claimed NEC World Series of Golf in dramatic fashion by chipping in from 66 feet to win three-way playoff with Nick Price and Billy Mayfair...recorded closing 67 to get into playoff after starting final round six strokes behind Vijay Singh...became leading money-winner in TOUR history with $360,000 World Series of Golf paycheck...raised career total at that time to $9,493,579...made usual late charge at Masters, posting three 68s after opening with a 73...after 16th-hole birdie, was tied for final-round lead with Davis Love III and eventual winner Ben Crenshaw...lost chance for victory with bogey on 17th hole after Crenshaw made birdie on 13...in the U.S. Open, held 36-hole lead and was tied with Tom Lehman for first after 54...final-round 73 in face of Corey Pavin's closing 68 produced seventh runner-up finish in a major...had earlier T2 in Doral-Ryder Open, event he has won twice...recorded nine top 10s and did not miss a cut...won Fred Meyer Challenge with Brad Faxon...Named GWAA Player of Year.

CAREER HIGHLIGHTS: Over last 13 seasons has posted 106 top-10 finishes, including 15 first victories, 28 seconds and eight third-place finishes in 206 starts...in 1983, 1987, 1994 and 1995 did not miss a cut...last cut missed was at 1993 U.S. Open...failed to earn check in only 12 events since 1983...winner of three Arnold Palmer Awards: 1986, 1990 and 1995...first TOUR player to earn $1 million four times...three-time Vardon Trophy winner (1988-89, 1994)...could have claimed two more Vardons, but missed meeting award criteria...failed to play 60 rounds in 1993 and withdrew after teeing off in Round 2 of 1995 MCI Classic...replaced 81-week fixture Nick Faldo atop Sony World Rankings after winning 1994 Johnnie Walker Classic...was, in turn, supplanted by Nick Price after Price won 1994 PGA Championship...regained top spot with his runner-up finish in 1995 U.S. Open...posted tournament-record 24-under-par 264 in winning 1994 PLAYERS Championship...captured second major championship and second British Open title at Royal St. George's in 1993...first came at Turnberry in 1986...posted British Open 18-hole record-tying 63 in Round 2 of that event...1993 PGA Championship loss to Paul Azinger gave him dubious distinction of losing playoffs in all four majors...winner of 68 individual tournaments worldwide...ended 27-month winless drought with playoff victory over Bruce Lietzke in 1992 Canadian Open...held lead going into final round of all four majors in 1986...suffered back-to-back Masters heartbreaks, finishing T2 in 1986 and losing 1987 playoff to Larry Mize's 140-foot pitch for birdie...first career victory came in 1976 West Lakes Classic in Australia...had 15-year stretch during which he won at least one tournament...has won in 13 countries.

PERSONAL: Back problems produced second-round withdrawal from 1995 MCI Classic and later at Colonial...took six weeks off following latter occurrence, returning with Memorial win...well known for charitable involvements, including annually playing host to Franklin Templeton Shark Shootout...mantra for success comes from self-help book Zen and the Martial Arts.

CAREER SUMMARY **PLAYOFF RECORD: 4-7**

Year	Events Played	Cuts Made	1st	2nd	3rd	Top 10	Top 25	Earnings	Rank
1979	2	2						$3,653	205
1981	9	8				3	5	$54,272	77
1982	4	3				1	2	$22,671	142
1983	9	9		1		2	4	$71,411	74
1984	16	15	2	2		7	10	$310,230	9
1985	16	13		2		6	9	$165,458	42
1986	19	17	2	4	1	10	12	$653,296	1
1987	18	18		2	2	9	13	$535,450	7
1988	14	12	1	2	1	7	11	$514,854	17
1989	17	16	2	1	1	8	14	$835,096	4
1990	17	16	2	2		11	15	$1,165,477	1
1991	17	15		1		6	7	$320,196	53
1992	16	15	1	2		8	10	$676,443	18
1993	15	14	1	4	2	12	13	$1,359,653	3
1994	16	16	1	3		11	14	$1,330,307	2
1995	16	15	3	2	1	9	14	$1,654,959	1
Total	221	204	15	28	8	110	153	$9,673,425	1

1996 PGA TOUR CHARITY TEAM: Freeport•McDermott Classic

TOP TOURNAMENT SUMMARY

YEAR	77	78	79	80	81	82	83	84	85	86	87	88	89	90	91
Masters Tournament					4	T36	T30	T25	T47	T2	T2	T5	T3	CUT	CUT
U.S. Open			T48		T33		T50	2	T15	T12	T51	W/D	T33	T5	W/D
British Open Championship	CUT	T29	T10	CUT	T31	T27	T19	T6	T16	1	T35	T2	T2	T6	T9
PGA Championship					T4	T5	T42	T39	CUT	2	70	T9	T12	T19	T32
THE PLAYERS Championship							T63	CUT	T49	T33	T4	T11	T4	T16	T63
THE TOUR Championship											3	30	T11	T7	

TOP TOURNAMENT SUMMARY (cont.)

YEAR	92	93	94	95
Masters Tournament	T6	T31	T18	T3
U.S. Open	18	CUT	T6	2
British Open Championship	T15	1	T11	T15
PGA Championship	T35	2	T4	T20
THE PLAYERS Championship	T7	T3	1	T37
THE TOUR Championship		T2	T13	T9

NATIONAL TEAMS: Australian Nissan Cup (2), 1985, 1986; Australian Kirin Cup, 1987; Australian Dunhill Cup (7), 1985, 1986, 1987, 1988, 1989, 1990, 1992; Australian Four Tours, 1989; Presidents Cup, 1994 (withdrew due to illnes).

1995 PGA TOUR STATISTICS

Scoring	**69.06**	**(1)**
Driving	**273.4**	**(21)**
Driving Accuracy	**73.4**	**(42T)**
Greens in Regulation	**66.5**	**(82T)**
Putting	**1.769**	**(39T)**
All Around	**426**	**(19)**
Sand Saves	**61.0**	**(9)**
Total Driving	**63**	**(4)**
Eagles	**5**	**(88T)**
Birdies	**226**	**(144T)**

MISCELLANEOUS STATISTICS

Scoring Avg Before Cut	**69.52**	**(1)**
Scoring Avg 3rd Rnd	**70.07**	**(21)**
Scoring Avg Final Rnd	**70.21**	**(18T)**
Birdies Conversion %	**35.0**	**(1)**
Par Breakers	**22.1**	**(4)**

1995 Low Round: **64:** 1995 Canon Greater Hartford Open/2
Career Low Round: **62:** 2 times, most recent 1993 Doral-Ryder Open/3
Career Largest Paycheck: **$450,000:** 1994 THE PLAYERS Championship/1

BRETT OGLE *(OH-gl)*

EXEMPT STATUS: 1994 tournament winner
FULL NAME: Brett James Ogle
HEIGHT: 6' 2" **WEIGHT:** 147
BIRTH DATE: July 14, 1964 **BIRTHPLACE:** Paddington, Australia
RESIDENCE: United Kingdom
FAMILY: Wife, Maggie; Christopher (10/1/90), Rachel Louise (11/5/93)
SPECIAL INTERESTS: Snooker, tennis, all sports
TURNED PROFESSIONAL: 1985 **Q SCHOOL:** Fall 1992

TOUR VICTORIES (2): 1993 AT&T Pebble Beach National Pro-Am. **1994** United Airlines Hawaiian Open.

INTERNATIIONAL VICTORIES (9): 1986 Tahiti Open. **1988** Tasmanian Open (Aus). **1989** Queensland Open (Aus), Equity & Law Challenge (Eur). **1990** Australian PGA Championship (Aus), AGF Open (Eur). **1991** South Australian Open (Aus). **1992** South Australian Open (Aus), World Cup (Indiv.).

BEST 1995 FINISHES: 4— Northern Telecom Open; T6— Shell Houston Open.

1995 HIGHLIGHTS: His first year without a victory was still one of his most consistent on TOUR...earned best finish with fourth at the Northern Telecom Open...started third round one stroke behind eventual winner Phil Mickelson...a 68 tied Jim Gallagher, Jr., and Mickelson for 54-hole lead...final-round 70 left him two strokes behind Mickelson...earned second and last top-10 finish in Shell Houston Open, where placed T6...followed Houston with three top-25 finishes in next four starts: 14 BellSouth Classic, T15 Colonial, T21 Memorial...put together a string of four top-25 finishes from mid-June through July: T21 U.S. Open, T14 FedEx St. Jude Classic, T13 Motorola Western Open, T11 British Open...was in contention through three rounds of Motorola Western Open and 54-hole co-leader with Steve Lowery before Sunday 74 dropped him four strokes behind winner Billy Mayfair...last top 25 finish was 25th in Sprint International...in unusual early-season incident, was forced to withdraw from United Airlines Hawaiian Open when his club shattered against a tree during a second-round shot attempt, striking him below the left eye...sunglasses may have saved him from serious injury...suffered only a bruise and arm cut, then rebounded the next week with Northern Telecom T4.

CAREER HIGHLIGHTS: Has proven himself to be a force in early-season events...had top-10 finishes in two of first four starts in 1993, including three-stroke victory in AT&T Pebble Beach National Pro-Am...opened with back-to-back 68s at Pebble Beach and Poppy Hills, closed with three-stroke decision over Billy Ray Brown...carded back-to-back 66s and a 69 in 1994 United Airlines Hawaiian Open to trail Davis Love III, who posted a second-round course-record 60, by two strokes after three rounds...closed with 68 to edge Love by one stroke and post second TOUR victory...victory in Hawaii, combined with T11 in Mercedes Championships, produced earnings of $244,250 in first two events of '94, over 80% of his total earnings for the year...qualified for TOUR as one of five co-medalists from 1992 Qualifying Tournament...of that group, was only one to retain playing privileges for 1994...qualified for 1991 NEC World Series of Golf by winning 1990 Australian PGA Championship...voiced at that time his strong desire to play PGA TOUR.

PERSONAL: Adopted at three weeks, a fact he talks about freely...was introduced to golf just after reaching his teens...his "gift for gab" has made him a gallery favorite...putting woes very nearly drove him from game...has tried putting every way imaginable: conventional, cross-handed, Langer-style and currently the long putter...because of his height and rail-thin frame, is a self-described "1-iron with ears"...as to his penchant for staying in inexpensive hotels, once said: "Maybe I'm a miser, but all I need is a toilet, bed and a TV."

CAREER SUMMARY **PLAYOFF RECORD: 0-0**

Year	Events Played	Cuts Made	1st	2nd	3rd	Top 10	Top 25	Earnings	Rank
1986	1	1					1	$6,000	216
1987	1								
1991	2	1					1	$10,175	226
1993	18	12	1			2	3	$337,374	48
1994	21	10	1			1	3	$284,495	66
1995	20	14				2	10	$326,932	56
Total	63	38	2			5	18	$964,976	187

1996 PGA TOUR CHARITY TEAM: Motorola Western Open

BRETT OGLE...continued

TOP TOURNAMENT SUMMARY

YEAR	89	90	91	93	94	95
Masters Tournament				T50	CUT	
U.S. Open					T21	
British Open Championship	T52	CUT	T73			T11
PGA Championship				CUT	CUT	CUT
THE PLAYERS Championship				T61	CUT	CUT

NATIONAL TEAMS: World Cup (2), 1992, 1995 (won individual title, 1992)

1995 PGA TOUR STATISTICS

Scoring	70.68	(49T)
Driving	278.9	(6T)
Driving Accuracy	65.3	(151T)
Greens in Regulation	68.3	(38T)
Putting	1.788	(89T)
All Around	635	(69T)
Sand Saves	53.1	(84)
Total Driving	157	(54)
Eagles	6	(69T)
Birdies	220	(149)

MISCELLANEOUS STATISTICS

Scoring Avg Before Cut	70.86	(51T)
Scoring Avg 3rd Rnd	70.36	(40T)
Scoring Avg Final Rnd	71.29	(99T)
Birdies Conversion %	30.3	(42T)
Par Breakers	19.9	(62T)

1995 Low Round: 65: 3 times, most recent 1995 FedEx St. Jude Classic/4
Career Low Round: 62: 2 times, most recent 1995 FedEx St. Jude Classic/4
Career Largest Paycheck: $225,000: 1993 AT&T Pebble Beach National Pro-Am/1

DAVID OGRIN *(OH-grin)*

EXEMPT STATUS: 123rd on 1995 money list
FULL NAME: David Allen Ogrin
HEIGHT: 6' **WEIGHT:** 220
BIRTH DATE: December 31, 1957 **BIRTHPLACE:** Waukegan, IL
RESIDENCE: Garden Ridge, TX
FAMILY: Wife, Sharon; Amy (6/20/88), Jessica (9/6/89), Dana (3/6/92), Clark Addison (10/18/93)
COLLEGE: Texas A&M (1980, Economics)
SPECIAL INTERESTS: Christianity, children, Chicago Cubs
TURNED PROFESSIONAL: 1980 **Q SCHOOL:** Fall 1982, 1992

BEST CAREER TOUR FINISH: 2--1985 St. Jude Classic (lost playoff to Hal Sutton); 2--1989 Hawaiian Open; T2--1994 GTE Byron Nelson Classic (lost playoff to Neal Lancaster)

INTERNATIONAL VICTORIES (2): 1988 Peru Open. **1994** Peru Open.

BEST 1995 FINISHES: 7— Buick Challenge; T8—Buick Invitational of California, Anheuser-Busch Golf Classic

1995 SEASON: Didn't have a stellar year, but good enough to retain exempt status...posted three top-10 finishes with earnings totaling $99,000, almost three-quarters of his yearly income...was three strokes off lead after two rounds of Buick Invitational of California...finished 74-67, good for T8...fell into slump and missed next eight cuts...broke streak with a T73 in BellSouth Classic...T8 in Anheuser-Busch Golf Classic, where he carded a third-round 66, was his second top-10...picked up final top 10 late in season with a solo seventh at the Buick Challenge, where he closed with a 67...$35,000 paycheck for that finish provided boost needed to retain playing card.

CAREER HIGHLIGHTS: Finest season came in 1989, when earned $234,196 and finished second in rain-shortened Hawaiian Open...career seemingly on upswing at that juncture, but failed to keep card after No. 167 money-list placing in 1990...reached low point with just $8,024 in 1991...rebounded slightly in 1992, followed by solid finish in 1993...lost 1985 St. Jude Classic playoff to Hal Sutton birdie on first extra hole...finished T2 at the 1994 GTE Byron Nelson Classic, where he was part of TOUR record six-man playoff won by Neal Lancaster...did record unofficial victory in 1987 Deposit Guaranty Golf Classic, edging Nick Faldo by one stroke...money won ($36,000), fashioned by closing 64, was official...made it through Qualifying Tournament on fourth try in 1982, then made it through successfully again 10 years later...winner 1980 Illinois State Open...winner of three collegiate events, including Harvey Penick Invitational...winner of 1989 Chrysler Team Championship with Ted Schulz.

DAVID OGRIN...*continued*

PERSONAL: The ultimate Chicago Cubs fan, so much so that he named his fourth child/first son "Clark Addison" for two streets adjoining Wrigley Field...golf won out over youthful dream of becoming switch-hitting catcher...father put sawed-off golf club in his hands at age of two.

PGA TOUR CAREER SUMMARY — **PLAYOFF RECORD: 0-2**

Year	Events Played	Cuts Made	1st	2nd	3rd	Top 10	Top 25	Earnings	Rank
1983	29	19					4	$36,003	121
1984	35	20					5	$45,461	113
1985	31	15		1		1	3	$76,294	95
1986	32	12				3	6	$75,245	113
1987	33	15				2	3	$80,149	110
1988	27	22			1	3	6	$138,807	86
1989	28	21		1		2	8	$234,196	59
1990	31	9			1	1	2	$64,190	167
1991	15	4						$8,024	235
1992	28	11						$33,971	193
1993	28	18				3	6	$155,016	104
1994	29	17		1		2	7	$199,199	92
1995	30	14				3	4	$151,419	123
Total	376	197		3	2	20	54	$1,297,974	154

NIKE TOUR SUMMARY

Year	Events Played	Cuts Made	1st	2nd	3rd	Top 10	Top 25	Earnings	Rank
1990	1	1					1	$1,600	172
1991	9	4					1	$3,338	152
1992	3	3					1	$3,174	160
1993	1	1			1	1	1	$9,375	110
1995	1	1					1	$2,830	184
Total	15	10			1	1	5	$20,317	
COMBINED TOTAL MONEY								$1,318,291	

1996 PGA TOUR CHARITY TEAM: Lincoln-Mercury Kapalua International

TOP TOURNAMENT SUMMARY

YEAR	83	84	85	86	87	88	89	90	94	95
Masters Tournament	45									
U.S. Open	T13	T38		T62	74		T54		CUT	
PGA Championship	CUT	T47				CUT				
THE PLAYERS Championship		CUT	CUT	T40	CUT	72	T45	T16	CUT	CUT

1995 PGA TOUR STATISTICS

Scoring	71.46	(113T)
Driving	251.2	(179T)
Driving Accuracy	73.4	(42T)
Greens in Regulation	66.6	(80T)
Putting	1.807	(145T)
All Around	732	(95T)
Sand Saves	62.5	(5)
Total Driving	221	(142T)
Eagles	5	(88T)
Birdies	285	(80T)

MISCELLANEOUS STATISTICS

Scoring Avg Before Cut	71.61	(136)
Scoring Avg 3rd Rnd	71.12	(89)
Scoring Avg Final Rnd	70.79	(54T)
Birdies Conversion %	26.1	(157T)
Par Breakers	17.7	(144T)

1995 Low Round: 66: 2 times, most recent 1995 Anheuser-Busch Golf Classic/3
Career Low Round: 64: 2 times, most recent 1994 GTE Byron Nelson Classic/1
Career Largest Paycheck: $81,000: 1989 Hawaiian Open/2

MISCELLANEOUS NIKE STATISTICS

Scoring	70.00	(N/A)
Eagles	1	(N/A)
Birdies	21	(N/A)

1995 Low Round: 68: 1995 NIKE Cleveland Open/4
Career Low Round: 66: 1993 NIKE Connecticut Open/2
Career Largest Paycheck: $9,375: 1993 NIKE Connecticut Open/T3

MARK O'MEARA *(oh-MERE-uh)*

EXEMPT STATUS: 1995 tournament winner
FULL NAME: Mark Francis O'Meara
HEIGHT: 6' **WEIGHT:** 180
BIRTH DATE: January 13, 1957 **BIRTHPLACE:** Goldsboro, NC
RESIDENCE: Windermere, FL
FAMILY: Wife, Alicia; Michelle (3/14/87), Shaun Robert (8/29/89)
COLLEGE: Long Beach State (1980, Marketing)
SPECIAL INTERESTS: Golf course consulting, hunting, fishing
TURNED PROFESSIONAL: 1980 **Q SCHOOL:** Fall 1980

TOUR VICTORIES (10): 1984 Greater Milwaukee Open. **1985** Bing Crosby Pro-Am, Hawaiian Open. **1989** AT&T Pebble Beach National Pro-Am. **1990** AT&T Pebble Beach National Pro-Am, H-E-B Texas Open. **1991** Walt Disney World/Oldsmobile Classic.**1992** AT&T Pebble Beach National Pro-Am. **1995** Honda Classic, Bell Canadian Open.

INTERNATIONAL VICTORIES (5): 1985 Fuji Sankei Classic (Jpn). **1986** Australian Masters (Aus). **1987** Lawrence Batley International (Eur). **1992** Tokai Classic (Jpn). **1994** Argentine Open.

1995 BEST FINISHES: 1—Honda Classic, Bell Canadian Open; T4--Kemper Open, Las Vegas Invitational; T6--PGA Championship; T9--AT&T Pebble Beach National Pro-Am; T10--Doral-Ryder Open, Greater Milwaukee Open.

1995 SEASON: Rebounded from frustrating 1994 to have an O'Meara-type of season...$914,129 represents his best year on TOUR...key to his 1995 success was victory in the 1994 Argentine Open, which renewed confidence in his ability to win...had three-stroke lead after 36 and 54 holes in Honda Classic...fired final-round 71 to claim first title since 1992...entered Honda event after forgetting to commit to Nissan Open...later in season, rallied from two-stroke deficit to win the Bell Canadian Open...posted 67 on the final day to land in a playoff with Bob Lohr, which he won with a par on the first extra hole...recorded a disappointing final-round 73 to finish T6 in PGA Championship after starting the day three strokes off pace...opening-round 64 was one stroke off lead at Riviera CC...131 total after 36 holes equaled PGA Championship record...at Las Vegas Invitational was one stroke back after 72 holes; finished T4...posted T10 in Greater Milwaukee Open week before Bell Canadian win...had earlier top-10 finish (T4) at Kemper Open.

CAREER HIGHLIGHTS: Had string of nine consecutive top-30 money-list finishes snapped in 1993, when failed to make TOUR Championship for first time...of 10 TOUR victories, five have come in pro-am events: four at AT&T Pebble Beach National Pro-Am, one at the 1991 Walt Disney World/Oldsmobile Classic...lost playoffs at 1990 and 1992 Bob Hope Chrysler Classics, also pro-ams...part of 1992 Hope five-man playoff won by John Cook...in 1990 Hope, matched Corey Pavin at then-TOUR record 29-under-par for 90 holes...Pavin chipped in for birdie on first extra hole to win...came from four strokes off pace with final-round 63 to capture 1990 Texas Open...winner 1979 U.S. Amateur, defeating John Cook...also winner 1979 California State and Mexican Amateurs...1981 PGA TOUR Rookie of the Year...1994 victory in Argentine Open made him one of five players (Gary Player, David Graham, Hale Irwin, Bernhard Langer the others) to win in the United States, Europe, Japan, Australia and South America.

PERSONAL: Continues fundraising efforts on behalf of longtime caddie Donny Wanstall, who was diagnosed with multiple sclerosis at 1994 PLAYERS Championship...collegiate All-American at Long Beach State...took up the game at age 13 when family moved to California with a golf course directly below their house.

CAREER SUMMARY **PLAYOFF RECORD: 2-4**

Year	Events Played	Cuts Made	1st	2nd	3rd	Top 10	Top 25	Earnings	Rank
1979(Am.)	1	1							
1981	34	22		1		4	9	$76,063	55
1982	35	19				1	4	$31,711	119
1983	32	17		1		2	6	$69,354	76
1984	32	24	1	5	3	15	19	$465,873	2
1985	25	19	2		1	6	13	$340,840	10
1986	25	22		1	4	5	12	$252,827	30
1987	26	20		2	1	7	11	$327,250	30
1988	27	20		2	1	7	12	$438,311	22
1989	26	19	1	1	1	7	13	$615,804	13
1990	25	20	2		1	6	14	$707,175	10
1991	25	15	1	1		5	12	$563,896	20
1992	23	18	1	2		9	15	$759,648	11
1993	26	18			1	4	9	$349,516	43
1994	29	17				3	8	$214,070	86
1995	27	21	2			8	12	$914,129	10
Total	418	292	10	16	13	89	169	$6,126,466	11

1996 PGA TOUR CHARITY TEAM: AT&T Pebble Beach National Pro-Am

Mark O'Meara...continued

TOP TOURNAMENT SUMMARY

YEAR	81	82	83	84	85	86	87	88	89	90	91	92	93	94	95
Masters Tournament					24	48	T24	T39	T11	CUT	T27	T4	T21	T15	T31
U.S. Open	CUT	58		T7	T15	T41	CUT	T3	CUT	CUT	CUT	CUT	CUT	CUT	
British Open Championship	T47				T3	T43	T66	27	T42	T48	T3	T12	CUT		T49
PGA Championship	T70		CUT	T25	T28	CUT	CUT	T9	CUT	T19	CUT	CUT	CUT		T6
THE PLAYERS Championship	T26	T77	T49	T5	T17	T33	3	CUT	CUT	W/D	CUT	T9	5	CUT	CUT
THE TOUR Championship							T10	29	6	T12	T16	29			T13

NATIONAL TEAMS: Ryder Cup (3), 1985, 1989, 1991; U.S. vs. Japan, 1984; Nissan Cup, 1985; Dunhill Cup (3),1985,1986, 1987.

1995 PGA TOUR STATISTICS

Scoring	70.25	(20)
Driving	268.9	(48)
Driving Accuracy	68.0	(120)
Greens in Regulation	70.5	(8)
Putting	1.763	(27T)
All Around	477	(28T)
Sand Saves	46.8	(155)
Total Driving	168	(67T)
Eagles	5	(88T)
Birdies	361	(11T)

MISCELLANEOUS STATISTICS

Scoring Avg Before Cut	70.06	(7)
Scoring Avg 3rd Rnd	69.82	(12)
Scoring Avg Final Rnd	71.09	(79T)
Birdies Conversion %	30.9	(31)
Par Breakers	21.2	(15T)

1995 Low Round: **64:** 1995 PGA Championship/1
Career Low Round: **62:** 1981 Sammy Davis Jr. Greater Hartford Open/2
Career Largest Paycheck: **$234,000:** 1995 Bell Canadian Open/1

Joe Ozaki *(oh-ZOCK-ee)*

EXEMPT STATUS: 121st on 1994 money list
FULL NAME: Naomichi Ozaki
HEIGHT: 5' 8" **WEIGHT:** 160
BIRTH DATE: May 18, 1956 **BIRTHPLACE:** Tokushima, Japan
RESIDENCE: Chiba, Japan
FAMILY: Wife, Yoshie; Takamasa
SPECIAL INTERESTS: Karaoke, fishing, family activities
TURNED PROFESSIONAL: 1977 **JOINED TOUR:** Spring 1993

BEST CAREER TOUR FINISH: T6--1991 NEC World Series of Golf; 1992 Federal Express St. Jude Classic; 1993 THE PLAYERS Championship; 1995 Northern Telecom Open.

INTERNATIONAL VICTORIES (25): 1980 Shizuoka Open, Sapporo Tokyu, KBC Augusta. **1985** Nikkei Cup. **1986** Pepsi Ube. **1987** Kantoh Pro, Hirao Masaaki Charity. **1988** Sappro Tokyu, NST Niigata Open, Zennikku Open, Nihon Series Hitachi Cup. **1989** Daiichi Fudohsan Cup, Imperial, Taylor Made Setonaikai. **1990** Nihon Match Play Unisis Hai, Jun Classic, Nihon Series Hitachi Cup. **1991** Nikkei Cup, Suntory Open, Casio World, Nihon Series Hitachi Cup. **1992** Imperial, Suntory Open, Lark Cup. **1994** Acom International (All Japan).

BEST 1995 FINISHES: T6— Northern Telecom Open; T7— Phoenix Open; T8— THE PLAYERS Championship; T10— Las Vegas Invitational

1995 HIGHLIGHTS: Four top-10 finishes highlighted his TOUR career-high $290,001 in earnings...doubled total of TOUR career top-10s to eight...finished 66th on money list to crack the top 100 for first time...started quickly with a T6 in his second event, the Northern Telecom Open...that matched his career-best finish...followed with weekend rounds of 67-67 to place T7 in Phoenix Open...marked first time in stateside career for consecutive top-10 finishes...posted T8 at THE PLAYERS Championship to earn career-best $87,000 paycheck...followed success at TPC at Sawgrass with T15 Freeport-McMoRan Classic and T16 GTE Byron Nelson Classic...recorded career-low 63 in first round of Las Vegas Invitational at Las Vegas Hilton CC...round featured back-nine 29 and brought first-round lead...went on to collect fourth top-10 (T10).

JOE OZAKI...continued

CAREER HIGHLIGHTS: Missed only one cut in 17 starts in 1994...assured retention of playing privileges for 1995 with only top-10 finish of 1994, T8 at Buick Classic worth $32,400...achieved special temporary TOUR membership with T6 finish in 1993 PLAYERS Championship, a placing worth $80,938...PLAYERS finish matched his best in TOUR event...achieved exempt status for 1994 by finishing No. 115 on money list...had 21st-place finish in '93 NEC World Series worth $26,550...closed with 69 for T25 in 1993 U.S. Open...winner of 25 events in Japan, including 1988 Japanese Series, 1989 JPGA Match Play Championship and 1990 Gene Sarazen Jun Classic...most recent victory in Japan 1994 Acom International...has earned more than $9 million during his professional career.

PERSONAL: Youngest of three golfing Ozaki brothers--Masashi (Jumbo) is 49, Tateo (Jet) is 42...1988 was "Year of the Ozakis" in Japan, when three combined for 12 victories in 35 events (Jumbo six, Joe four, Jet two)...brothers also had nine seconds and four thirds...Jumbo and Joe finished 1-2 on money list, Jet No. 7.

CAREER SUMMARY **PLAYOFF RECORD: 0-0**

Year	Events Played	Cuts Made	1st	2nd	3rd	Top 10	Top 25	Earnings	Rank
1985	2	1						$880	259
1989	2	1						$1,605	274
1990	8	5					1	$37,330	185
1991	2	1				1	1	$38,850	185
1992	7	5				1	2	$75,946	151
1993	12	8				1	3	$139,784	115
1994	17	15				1	5	$147,308	121
1995	20	13				4	8	$290,001	66
Total	70	49				8	20	$731,704	215

1996 PGA TOUR CHARITY TEAM: Sprint International

TOP TOURNAMENT SUMMARY

YEAR	84	85	89	90	92	93	94	95
Masters Tournament			T33		T45			
U.S. Open					T25			
Brtish Open Championship	T62	CUT	T46	T39	CUT	CUT		
PGA Championship			CUT	CUT	T28	T44		T31
THE PLAYERS Championship						T6	T45	T8

1995 PGA TOUR STATISTICS

Scoring	70.65	(48)
Driving	270.8	(34T)
Driving Accuracy	65.2	(154)
Greens in Regulation	67.5	(55T)
Putting	1.765	(33T)
All Around	686	(81T)
Sand Saves	50.5	(118T)
Total Driving	188	(99)
Eagles	4	(116T)
Birdies	249	(128T)

MISCELLANEOUS STATISTICS

Scoring Avg Before Cut	71.10	(79T)
Scoring Avg 3rd Rnd	69.17	(4)
Scoring Avg Final Rnd	70.58	(30T)
Birdies Conversion %	33.1	(6T)
Par Breakers	22.7	(1)

1995 Low Round: **63:** 1995 Las Vegas Invitational/1
Career Low Round: **63:** 1995 Las Vegas Invitational/1
Career Largest Paycheck: $87,000: 1995 THE PLAYERS Championship/T8

Did You Know?

PGA TOUR records show that the last time it snowed at a TOUR event was April 4, 1987, at the Greater Greensboro Open. The TOUR had a close call last year, however. Flurries greeted golfers during the Tuesday practice round of the Northern Telecom Open, but they were safely past by Thursday.

Arnold Palmer

EXEMPT STATUS: Winner, 1960 U.S. Open
FULL NAME: Arnold Daniel Palmer
HEIGHT: 5' 10" **WEIGHT:** 185
BIRTH DATE: September 10, 1929 **BIRTHPLACE:** Latrobe, PA
RESIDENCES: Latrobe, PA and Bay Hill, FL; plays out of Latrobe CC (PA), Laurel Valley GC (PA), Bay Hill Club (FL)
FAMILY: Wife, Winifred Walzer; Peggy (2/26/56); Amy (8/4/58); six grandchildren
COLLEGE: Wake Forest University
SPECIAL INTERESTS: Flying, business, club-making
TURNED PROFESSIONAL: 1954 **JOINED TOUR:** 1955

TOUR VICTORIES (60): 1955 Canadian. **1956** Insurance City, Eastern. **1957** Houston, Azalea, Rubber City, San Diego. **1958** St. Petersburg, Masters Tournament, Pepsi Golf. **1959** Thunderbird (Calif.) Invitation, Oklahoma City, West Palm Beach. **1960** Palm Springs Classic, Texas Open, Baton Rouge, Pensacola, Masters Tournament, U.S. Open, Insurance City, Mobile Sertoma. **1961** San Diego, Phoenix, Baton Rouge, Texas, Western. **1962** Palm Springs Classic, Phoenix, Masters Tournament, Texas, Tournament of Champions, Colonial National, American Golf Classic. **1963** Los Angeles, Phoenix, Pensacola, Thunderbird, Cleveland, Western, Philadelphia. **1964** Masters Tournament, Oklahoma City. **1965** Tournament of Champions. **1966** Los Angeles, Tournament of Champions, Houston Champions International, **1967** Los Angeles, Tucson, American Golf Classic, Thunderbird Classic. **1968** Hope Desert Classic, Kemper. **1969** Heritage, Danny Thomas--Diplomat. **1970** Four-Ball (with Jack Nicklaus). **1971** Hope Desert Classic, Citrus, Westchester, National Team (with Jack Nicklaus). **1973** Bob Hope Desert Classic.

SENIOR PGA TOUR VICTORIES (10): 1980 PGA Seniors'. **1981** U.S. Senior Open. **1982** Marlboro Classic, Denver Post Champions of Golf. **1983** Boca Grove Senior Classic. **1984** PGA Seniors', Senior Tournament Players Championship, Quadel Senior Classic. **1985** Senior Tournament Players Championship. **1988** Crestar Classic.

INTERNATIONAL VICTORIES (13): 1955 Panama Open, Colombia Open (South America). **1961** British Open (Eur). **1962** British Open (Eur). **1963** Australian Wills Masters (Aus). **1964** Piccadilly World Match Play Championship (Eur). **1966** Australian Open (Aus). **1967** Piccadilly World Match Play Championship (Eur), World Cup (Indiv.). **1971** Lancome Trophy (Eur). **1975** Spanish Open (Eur), British PGA Championship (Eur). **1980** Canadian PGA Championship (Can).

1995 SEASON: Played a very limited schedule...made five starts: AT&T Pebble Beach National Pro-Am, Bob Hope Chrysler Classic, Nestle Invitational, the Masters and British Open...failed to make a cut for the second consecutive year...appearances produced but two par-or-better rounds, with best being a 70 in Round 2 of the AT&T...one of the season's emotional highlights was his final appearance in a British Open...made triumphal return to St. Andrews on 35th anniversary of his first British Open in 1960...his final walk down 18th fairway was a highlight of the event.

CAREER HIGHLIGHTS: One of the most dominant figures to ever play the game...owner of 89 victories worldwide (PGA TOUR 60; International 19; Senior PGA TOUR 10)...60 PGA TOUR victories is fourth on the all-time list...tied with Jack Nicklaus for most consecutive years winning at least one tournament (17)...was first TOUR player to reach the $1 million mark in earnings (7/21/68)...named PGA Player of the Year in 1960 and 1962...led PGA TOUR in earnings 1958, 1960, 1962 and 1963...appropriately, annual award for leading money-winner on PGA TOUR and Senior TOUR named for him...four-time Vardon Trophy winner (1961-1962-1964-1967)...member of World Golf Hall of Fame, American Golf Hall of Fame, All-American Collegiate Golf Hall of Fame...named Associated Press Athlete of Decade for the 1960s, Hickok Athlete of Year (1960), Sports Illustrated Sportsman of Year (1960)...awarded PGA of America Distinguished Service Award in 1974...winner of seven professional major championships (4 Masters, 2 British Opens, 1 U.S. Open)...won Masters every other year from 1958-64...fired a final-round 65, second-lowest fourth round score in U.S. Open history, to edge amateur Jack Nicklaus by two strokes in 1960...played last U.S. Open of career in 1994, 40 years after playing his first...will play Masters as long as he feels competitive...first man to capture both the U.S. Open and U.S. Senior Open...springboard to professional fame was victory in 1954 U.S. Amateur...last TOUR victory 1973 Bob Hope Desert Classic, an event he won five times...recorded 29 of his titles during a torrid four-year stretch (1960-63)...Ryder Cup captain in 1963 and 1975...holds record for most Ryder Cup matches won with 22 (22-8-2 lifetime record)...will captain U.S. Team in second Presidents Cup Match in September.

PERSONAL: Maintains active business schedule with golf course design, construction and development...principal owner of Bay Hill Club and Lodge, which plays host to annual Bay Hill Invitational presented by Office Depot...chairman of the board of The Golf Channel...pilot of considerable renown and the holder of a number of world aviation records.

ARNOLD PALMER...continued

PGA TOUR CAREER SUMMARY **PLAYOFF RECORD: 14-10**

Year	Events Played	Cuts Made	1st	2nd	3rd	Top 10	Top 25	Earnings	Rank
1949	1	1							
1953	1	1							
1954	4	4				1	3		
1955	31	25	1		1	8	15	$7,958	32
1956	30	27	2	1		8	13	$16,145	19
1957	33	27	4		2	13	20	$27,803	5
1958	32	28	3	5	2	14	23	$42,608	1
1959	31	29	3	1	3	17	26	$32,462	5
1960	27	25	8	1	2	19	24	$75,263	1
1961	26	24	5	5	2	20	23	$61,091	2
1962	21	21	7	1		13	19	$81,448	1
1963	20	20	7	3		14	16	$128,230	1
1964	26	25	2	6	4	18	24	$113,203	2
1965	22	19	1	4		8	15	$57,770	10
1966	22	21	3	4	2	15	17	$110,467	3
1967	25	22	4	4	2	17	20	$184,065	2
1968	24	20	2	2		9	15	$114,602	7
1969	26	25	2		2	11	17	$105,128	9
1970	22	22	1	3	2	13	16	$128,853	5
1971	24	24	4	1	1	12	22	$209,603	3
1972	22	18		1	2	10	15	$84,181	25
1973	22	20	1		1	7	15	$89,457	27
1974	20	13				2	7	$36,293	72
1975	20	15			1	5	12	$59,018	36
1976	19	13					6	$17,018	115
1977	21	16					7	$21,950	101
1978	15	11				2	4	$27,073	94
1979	16	9					1	$9,276	159
1980	13	9					3	$16,589	136
1981	12	6						$4,164	204
1982	11	4					1	$6,621	199
1983	11	6				1	1	$16,904	159
1984	8	2						$2,452	218
1985	6	2						$3,327	214
1986	6								
1987	4	1						$1,650	269
1988	5								
1989	4	1						$2,290	253
1990	4								
1991	5	1					1	$7,738	237
1992	5								
1993	5	1						$1,970	316
1994	6								
1995	5								
Total	714	558	60	42	29	257	401	$1,876,317	102

SENIOR PGA TOUR CAREER SUMMARY

Year	Events Played	1st	2nd	3rd	Top 10	Top 25	Earnings	Rank
1980	1	1			1	1	$20,000	
1981	4	1	1	2	4	4	$55,100	
1982	7	2		1	5	7	$73,848	
1983	12	1	1	1	8	12	$106,590	6
1984	13	3	3		9	12	$184,582	4
1985	13	1	1	2	9	12	$137,024	11
1986	15		1	1	6	13	$99,056	21
1987	17			1	8	13	$128,910	19
1988	18	1		1	8	14	$185,373	17
1989	17				4	11	$119,907	38
1990	17					5	$66,519	65
1991	17				4	7	$143,967	46
1992	18					4	$70,815	72
1993	18				1	5	$106,232	64
1994	13					1	$34,471	91
1995	12					1	$51,526	86
Total	212	10	7	9	67	122	$1,583,920	47
COMBINED TOTAL MONEY							$3,311,289	

ARNOLD PALMER...*continued*

PGA TOUR TOP TOURNAMENT SUMMARY

YEAR	55	56	57	58	59	60	61	62	63	64	65	66	67	68	69
Masters Tournament	T10	21	T7	1	3	1	T2	1	T9	1	T2	T4	4		26
U.S. Open	T21	7		T23	T5	1	T14	2	T2	T5		2	2	T59	T6
British Open Championship						2	T1	1	T26		16	T8		T10	
PGA Championship				T40	T14	T7	T5	T17	T40	T2	T33	T6	T14	T2	

PGA TOUR TOP TOURNAMENT SUMMARY (cont.)

YEAR	70	71	72	73	74	75	76	77	78	79	80	81	82	83	84
Masters Tournament	T36	T18	T33	T24	T11	T13		T24	T37		T24	CUT	47	T36	CUT
U.S. Open	T54	T24	3	T4	T5	T9	T50	T19		T59	61	CUT	CUT	T60	
British Open Championship	12		T6	T14		T16	T55	7	T34		CUT	T23	T27	T56	CUT
PGA Championship	T2	T18	T16		T28	T33	T15	T19			T72	76	CUT	T67	CUT
THE PLAYERS Championship							T51	T40	T77	T50		T45	CUT	T54	T66

PGA TOUR TOP TOURNAMENT SUMMARY (cont.)

YEAR	85	86	87	88	89	90	91	92	93	94	95
Masters Tournament	CUT	CUT	CUT	CUT	CUT	CUT	CUT	CUT	CUT	CUT	CUT
U.S. Open										CUT	
British Open Championship			CUT		CUT	CUT					CUT
PGA Championship	T65	CUT	T65	CUT	T63	CUT	CUT	CUT	CUT	CUT	
THE PLAYERS Championship	T69	CUT									

SENIOR PGA TOUR TOP TOURNAMENT SUMMARY

YEAR	83	84	85	86	87	88	89	90	91	92	93	94	95
The Tradition							T26	T61			T57		T25
U.S. Senior Open	T11	2	T11	T25	T14	T22	T53	CUT	CUT	T32	T52	T57	T51
PGA Seniors' Championship		1			T16	T5	T11	T13	CUT	T47	T27	CUT	CUT
FORD SENIOR PLAYERS Championship	T5	1	1	T3	T5	T32	T4	T48	T43	T36	T44	T65	T46

NATIONAL TEAMS: Ryder Cup (6), 1961, 1963, 1965, 1967, 1971, 1973; Ryder Cup Captain (2), 1963, 1975; World Cup (7), 1960, 1962, 1963, 1964, 1965, 1966, 1967; Captain and member of Chrysler Cup team (5), 1986, 1987, 1988, 1989, 1990.

1995 PGA TOUR STATISTICS

Scoring	**75.67**	**(N/A)**
Driving	**237.9**	**(N/A)**
Driving Accuracy	**76.5**	**(N/A)**
Greens in Regulation	**55.6**	**(N/A)**
Putting	**1.864**	**(N/A)**
Sand Saves	**57.1**	**(N/A)**
Total Driving		**(N/A)**
Eagles		**(N/A)**
Birdies	**26**	**(N/A)**

MISCELLANEOUS STATISTICS

Scoring Avg Before Cut	**75.31**	**(N/A)**
Scoring Avg 3rd Rnd	**74.50**	**(N/A)**
Birdies Conversion %	**23.6**	**(N/A)**
Par Breakers	**11.1**	**(N/A)**

1995 Low Round: 70: 1995 AT&T Pebble Beach National Pro-Am/2
Career Low Round: 62: 1966 Los Angeles Open/3
Career Largest Paycheck: $50,000: 1971 Westchester Classic/1

1995 SENIOR PGA TOUR STATISTICS

Scoring	**73.22**	**(N/A)**
Driving	**255.7**	**(N/A)**
Driving Accuracy	**67.6**	**(N/A)**
Greens in Regulation	**63.2**	**(N/A)**
Putting	**1.824**	**(N/A)**
Sand Saves	**44.6**	**(N/A)**
Total Driving		**(N/A)**
Eagles	**1**	**(N/A)**
Birdies	**105**	**(N/A)**

MISCELLANEOUS SENIOR STATISTICS

1995 Low Round: 66: 1995 GTE Northwest Classic/3
Career Low Round: 63: 1984 PGA Seniors' Championship/2
Career Largest Paycheck: $48,750: 1988 Crestar Classic/1

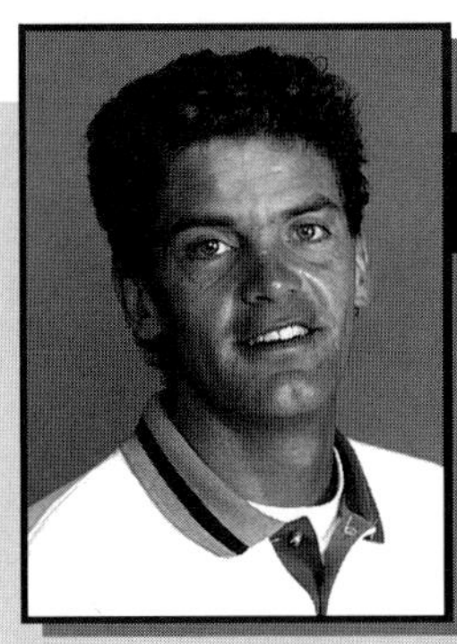

JESPER PARNEVIK *(YES-purr PAR-nuh-vick)*

EXEMPT STATUS: 84th on 1995 money list
FULL NAME: Jesper Bo Parnevik
HEIGHT: 6' **WEIGHT:** 175
BIRTH DATE: March 7, 1965 **BIRTHPLACE:** Stockholm, Sweden
RESIDENCE: South Palm Beach, FL
FAMILY: Wife, Mia; Ida Josetin Peg (9/3/95)
COLLEGE: Palm Beach Junior College
SPECIAL INTERESTS: Tennis
TURNED PROFESSIONAL: 1986 **JOINED TOUR:** 1993

BEST TOUR CAREER FINISH: 5—1994 United Airlines Hawaiian Open; T5—1995 Nestle Invitational.

INTERNATIONAL VICTORIES (5): 1988 Odense Open (Sweden), Raklosia Open (Sweden). **1990** Swedish Open. **1993** Scottish Open (Eur). **1995** Scandinavian Masters (Eur).

1995 BEST FINISHES: T5— Nestle Invitational; 6—Kmart Greater Greensboro Open

1995 SEASON: Followed TOUR rookie success with solid sophomore year...trailed first-round leader Mark Brooks by two strokes after opening with 67 at Nestle Invitational, finished T5...got into Nestle field when Tim Simpson withdrew...carded middle rounds of 68-68 en route to sixth place finish at Kmart Greater Greensboro Open...only missed four cuts in 19 events...in last four TOUR starts posted three top-25 finishes (T21 Kemper Open, T24 British Open, and T20 PGA Championship)...last TOUR event for 1995 season was Sprint International...didn't play in U.S. between British Open and PGA Championship.

CAREER HIGHLIGHTS: Turned potentially devastating 1994 British Open faux pas into semi-profitable experience...capitalized on failure to read Turnberry leaderboards (which led to 18th-hole bogey and subsequent loss to Nick Price) with commercial appearances for hotel chain...held two-stroke lead approaching 72nd hole, having birdied five of seven previous...made bogey through aggressive play, losing by stroke to Price's eagle-birdie-par finish...runner-up finish still worth $142,560 (unofficial)...joined PGA TOUR after T4 in 1993 Qualifying Tournament...first PGA European Tour win came in 1993 Bell's Scottish Open...lost to Seve Ballesteros in 1992 Turespana Open on seventh extra hole...became first Swede to win PGA European Tour event in Sweden when he captured 1995 Scandinavian Masters with a five-stroke victory over Colin Montgomerie...product of Swedish national junior program which has turned out, among others, Anders Forsbrand, Joakim Haeggman, Liselotte Neumann, Helen Alfredsson and Annika Sorenstam...played at Palm Beach (FL) Junior College from 1984-86 before qualifying for European Tour...winner 1985 Dixie Amateur.

PERSONAL: Father, Bo Parnevik, is Sweden's most famous comedian...wears golf cap in trademark fashion, with bill turned up and brand name stitched on underside...first announced intention of winning British Open at age 13...learned game by hitting floating golf balls into lake behind family home in Osterskar and putting on practice green built in backyard.

CAREER SUMMARY — **PLAYOFF RECORD: 0-0**

Year	Events Played	Cuts Made	1st	2nd	3rd	Top 10	Top 25	Earnings	Rank
1994	17	12				2	4	$148,816	120
1995	19	15				2	7	$222,458	84
Total	36	27				4	11	$371,274	292

1996 PGA TOUR CHARITY TEAM: Franklin Templeton Shark Shootout

TOP TOURNAMENT SUMMARY

YEAR	93	94	95
British Open Championship	T21	2	T24
PGA Championship		CUT	T25
THE PLAYERS Championship			T49

NATIONAL TEAMS: World Cup (2), 1994, 1995; Dunhill Cup (3), 1993, 1994, 1995.

1995 PGA TOUR STATISTICS

Scoring	70.82	(58)
Driving	265.7	(70)
Driving Accuracy	71.7	(66T)
Greens in Regulation	68.9	(28T)
Putting	1.771	(44T)
All-Around	571	(47)
Sand Saves	50.0	(126T)
Total Driving	136	(28T)
Eagles	8	(36T)
Birdies	232	(143)

MISCELLANEOUS STATISTICS

Scoring Avg. (before cut)	70.59	(33)
Scoring Avg. (3rd round)	70.93	(76T)
Scoring Avg. (4th round)	72.00	(153T)
Birdie Conversions	30.6	(38T)
Par Breakers	20.5	(35T)

1995 Low Round: 64: 1995 Buick Invitational of California/2
Career Low Round: 63: 1994 United Airlines Hawaiian Open/4
Career Largest Paycheck: $54,000: 1995 Kmart Greater Greensboro Open/6

CRAIG PARRY *(PERRY)*

EXEMPT STATUS: 46th on 1994 money list
FULL NAME: Craig David Parry
HEIGHT: 5'6" **WEIGHT:** 170
BIRTH DATE: January 12, 1966 **BIRTHPLACE:** Sunshine, Victoria, Australia
RESIDENCE: Sydney, Australia and Orlando, FL
FAMILY: Wife, Jenny; April (8/22/92), Ryan (10/20/94)
SPECIAL INTERESTS: Sailing, water sports, cricket, rugby, computers, Australian Rules Football
TURNED PROFESSIONAL: 1985 **JOINED TOUR:** April 1992

BEST CAREER TOUR FINISH: 2--1994 Honda Classic; 1995 Colonial National Invitation.

INTERNATIONAL VICTORIES (13): 1987 New South Wales Open (Aus), Canadian TPC (Can). **1989** German Open (Eur), Wang Four Stars Pro-Celebrity (Eur), Bridgestone ASO (Jpn). **1991** Italian Open (Eur), Scottish Open (Eur). **1992** Australian PGA Championship (Aus), New South Wales Open (Aus), Australian Masters (Aus). **1994** Australian Masters (Aus). **1995** Canon Challenge (Aus), Greg Norman's Holden Classic (Aus).

1995 BEST FINISHES: 2— Colonial National Invitation; 4—Freeport-McMoRan Classic.

1995 SEASON: After starting year somewhat slowly, posted fourth-place finish in Freeport-McMoRan Classic...five birdies in six holes en route to second-round 65 at Colonial National Invitation provided boost needed for two-stroke 36-hole lead...led after third round by one stroke over Woody Austin...closed with 71 to finish second, one stroke behind Tom Lehman...began Colonial week with conjunctivitis, an eye inflammation...continued solid play with three more top-25 finishes (T21 Memorial Tournament, T24 Canon Greater Hartford Open, T21 FedEx St. Jude Classic)...had chance to win rain-shortened Walt Disney World/Oldsmobile Classic...career-best 64 put him two strokes off pace after first round...third-and-final-round 72 dashed hopes of first TOUR victory...closed the season making six of seven cuts...in February carded course-record 65 to earn three-stroke victory at Canon Challenge in Sydney, Australia...won Greg Norman's Holden Classic in Australia in December.

CAREER HIGHLIGHTS: Earned a T3 in 1993 U.S. Open...shared first-round lead after opening 66...closed 69-68 to finish five strokes behind Lee Janzen...had career-best second in '94 Honda Classic, where final-round 67 left him one stroke behind Nick Price...became special temporary member of TOUR in April 1992...was one stroke off lead at midpoint of 1992 PLAYERS Championship...tied with Ian Woosnam for 36-hole lead in 1992 Masters, then held third-round lead outright at 12-under-par 204 before skying to final-round 78 and T13...member of International Team in inaugural Presidents Cup Match...teamed with Bradley Hughes to defeat Loren Roberts-Tom Lehman in Saturday Four-Ball, then edged Corey Pavin one-up in Sunday singles...winner of 13 events worldwide, including four on PGA European Tour...pair of European victories came in 1989 playoffs: Wang Four Stars National Pro-Celebrity and German Open...Bridgestone ASO victory in Japan in 1989 was his third title that year...1984-85 State Junior and State Amateur Champion, 1985 State Foursomes Champion in Australia...low amateur 1985 Australian Masters, Tasmanian and SA Opens...1988 co-recipient Epson Shooting Star Award.

PERSONAL: Nickname is "Popeye" for well-developed forearms.

CAREER SUMMARY — **PLAYOFF RECORD: 0-0**

Year	Events Played	Cuts Made	1st	2nd	3rd	Top 10	Top 25	Earnings	Rank
1987	1								
1988	1	1						$1,650	282
1990	8	6					2	$43,351	181
1991	6	6					3	$63,767	162
1992	13	11			1	4	6	$241,901	64
1993	23	16			1	6	7	$323,068	50
1994	20	15		1		3	8	$354,602	46
1995	24	16		1		2	5	$293,413	65
Total	96	71		2	2	15	31	$1,321,751	159

1996 PGA TOUR CHARITY TEAM: MasterCard Colonial

TOP TOURNAMENT SUMMARY

YEAR	88	90	91	92	93	94	95
Masters Tournament		CUT		T13	T45	T30	
U.S. Open		46	T11	T33	T3	T25	
British Open Championship	CUT	T22	8	T28	T59	T77	CUT
PGA Championship		T40	T43		T31	T19	CUT
THE PLAYERS Championship		T61	T15	T6	CUT	T14	CUT

NATIONAL TEAMS: Kirin Cup, 1988; Four Tours World Championship of Golf (3), 1989, 1990, 1991; Presidents Cup, 1994; Dunhill Cup (2), 1993, 1995.

1995 PGA TOUR STATISTICS		
Scoring	71.10	(78)
Driving	262.4	(97)
Driving Accuracy	71.7	(66T)
Greens in Regulation	66.2	(97T)
Putting	1.781	(68T)
All Around	672	(78)
Sand Saves	58.0	(29)
Total Driving	163	(62)
Eagles	4	(116T)
Birdies	254	(121T)

MISCELLANEOUS STATISTICS		
Scoring Avg Before Cut	71.26	(96T)
Scoring Avg 3rd Rnd	71.00	(80T)
Scoring Avg Final Rnd	71.33	(105T)
Birdies Conversion %	28.8	(89T)
Par Breakers	18.9	(102T)

1995 Low Round: 64: 2 times, most recent 1995 Las Vegas Invitational/1
Career Low Round: 64: 2 times, most recent 1995 Las Vegas Invitational/1
Career Largest Paycheck: $151,200: 1995 Colonial National Invitational/2

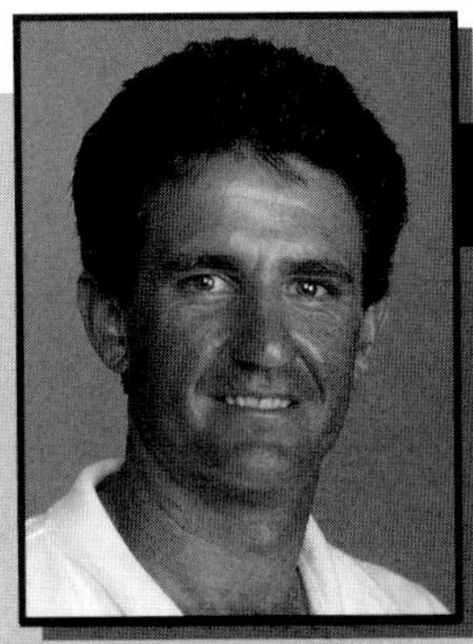

STEVE PATE

EXEMPT STATUS: Top 50 on PGA TOUR career money list
FULL NAME: Stephen Robert Pate
HEIGHT: 6' **WEIGHT:** 175
BIRTH DATE: May 26, 1961 **BIRTHPLACE:** Ventura, CA
RESIDENCE: Orlando, FL; plays out of North Ranch CC, Westlake, CA
FAMILY: Wife, Sheri; Nicole (3/12/88), Sarah (10/8/90)
COLLEGE: UCLA (1984, Psychology)
SPECIAL INTERESTS: Fishing
TURNED PROFESSIONAL: 1983 **Q SCHOOL:** Fall 1984

PGA TOUR VICTORIES (5): 1987 Southwest Classic. **1988** MONY Tournament Of Champions, Shearson Lehman Hutton-Andy Williams Open. **1991** Honda Classic. **1992** Buick Invitational of California.

BEST 1995 FINISHES: T17 -- Northern Telecom Open, Greater Milwaukee Open, B.C. Open.

1995 SEASON: After falling below top 125 for the first time in his 12-year career, Steve has taken a one-time career money exemption -- top 50 on the all-time money list -- to compete this year...his $89,758 last season bettered his rookie total by exactly $400...the year began positively enough, with a T17 in his second start at the Northern Telecom Open...the $15,813 Tucson payday was his best of the season...that was followed by T26 in the Phoenix Open, then three weeks later T28 at the Bob Hope Chrysler Classic...he closed the Hope with 65, his low round of the season...after making five cuts in his first seven starts, Steve missed 14 of 24 (plus one withdrawal) the rest of the way...there were two more top-25 finishes within a three-week September span, T17s at the Greater Milwaukee Open and the B.C. Open.

CAREER HIGHLIGHTS: Achieved lone money-list top-10 finish in 1991, when a Honda Classic victory helped produce earnings of $727,997...scored three-stroke win over Paul Azinger and Dan Halldorson at Eagle Trace...strong final-day winds allowed him to parlay closing 75 into relatively easy victory...later that season lost BellSouth Atlanta Classic playoff to Corey Pavin...fifth career victory came in 1992 Buick Invitational of California...tournament shortened to 54 holes by Saturday fog...first TOUR win came in 1987 Southwest Classic...won twice on West Coast to start 1988: MONY Tournament of Champions and Shearson Lehman Hutton-Andy Williams Open...second-place finish in 1990 International featured a double-eagle two...member 1991 Ryder Cup team, but deep hip bruise suffered when three limos collided en route to opening banquet limited play to one team match...made Santa Barbara, CA high school team as freshman, won California Interscholastic Federation title as senior...won 1983 Pac-10 Championship, along with four collegiate events...1983 All-America.

PERSONAL: Has earned nickname "Volcano" for sometimes volatile on-course temper...teammate of Corey Pavin, Duffy Waldorf and Jay Delsing at UCLA.

CAREER SUMMARY — **PLAYOFF RECORD: 0-2**

Year	Events Played	Cuts Made	1st	2nd	3rd	Top 10	Top 25	Earnings	Rank
1985	27	12		1		3	3	$89,358	86
1986	33	26			1	3	10	$176,100	51
1987	33	27	1			6	13	$335,728	26
1988	30	25	2	1	1	7	17	$582,473	12
1989	31	25			1	5	14	$306,554	35

STEVE PATE...continued

CAREER SUMMARY (cont.)

Year	Events Played	Cuts Made	1st	2nd	3rd	Top 10	Top 25	Earnings	Rank
1990	29	22		1		5	11	$334,505	39
1991	26	23	1	1	3	8	15	$727,997	6
1992	31	24	1			5	10	$472,626	30
1993	28	19				4	9	$254,841	64
1994	29	20			1	5	9	$291,651	64
1995	32	15					3	$89,758	168
Total	329	238	5	4	7	51	114	$3,661,591	40

1996 PGA TOUR CHARITY TEAM: Quad City Classic

TOP TOURNAMENT SUMMARY

YEAR	86	87	88	89	90	91	92	93	94	95
Masters Tournament			T36	T26		T3	T6	CUT		
U.S. Open		T24	T3	T51	T33	T49	CUT	T19	T21	CUT
British Open Championship				T13	T8	T63	4			
PGA Championship	T53	T61	T62	T41	T31	T7	T48	70		T58
THE PLAYERS Championship	T72	CUT	57	T34	T11	T27	T40	CUT	CUT	CUT
THE TOUR Championship		T21	T17			T26	30			

NATIONAL TEAMS: Ryder Cup,1991, Kirin Cup, 1989.

1995 PGA TOUR STATISTICS

Scoring	71.66	(132T)
Driving	260.4	(114)
Driving Accuracy	62.7	(171)
Greens in Regulation	64.5	(132T)
Putting	1.796	(117T)
All Around	971	(154)
Sand Saves	43.2	(179T)
Total Driving	285	(177T)
Eagles	7	(51T)
Birdies	288	(75)

MISCELLANEOUS STATISTICS

Scoring Avg Before Cut	71.77	(148)
Scoring Avg 3rd Rnd	71.69	(135T)
Scoring Avg Final Rnd	70.75	(50T)
Birdies Conversion %	26.1	(157T)
Par Breakers	17.3	(158T)

1995 Low Round: **65:** 1995 Bob Hope Chrysler Classic/5
Career Low Round: **62:** 1989 Bob Hope Chrysler Cl/3
Career Largest Paycheck: **$180,000:** 2 times, most recent 1991 Honda Classic/1

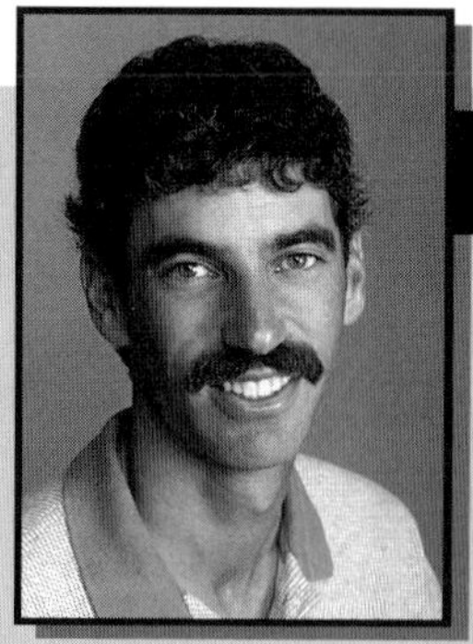

COREY PAVIN

EXEMPT STATUS: Winner, 1995 U.S. Open
FULL NAME: Corey Allen Pavin
HEIGHT: 5' 9" **WEIGHT:** 150
BIRTH DATE: November 16, 1959 **BIRTHPLACE:** Oxnard, CA
RESIDENCE: Orlando, FL
FAMILY: Wife, Shannon; Ryan (5/29/86), Austin (3/5/93)
COLLEGE: UCLA
SPECIAL INTERESTS: Fishing, basketball, skiing
TURNED PROFESSIONAL: 1982 **Q SCHOOL:** Fall 1983

TOUR VICTORIES (13): **1984** Houston Coca-Cola Open **1985** Colonial National Invitation **1986** Hawaiian Open, Greater Milwaukee Open. **1987** Bob Hope Chrysler Classic, Hawaiian Open. **1988** Texas Open presented by Nabisco. **1991** Bob Hope Chrysler Classic, BellSouth Atlanta Classic **1992** Honda Classic. **1994** Nissan Los Angeles Open. **1995** Nissan Open, U.S. Open.

INTERNATIONAL VICTORIES (9): **1983** German Open (Eur), South African PGA Championship (Afr), Calberson Classic (Eur). **1984** New Zealand Open (Aus). **1985** New Zealand Open (Aus). **1993** Toyota World Match Play Championship (Eur). **1994** Tokai Classic (Jpn). **1995** Asian Masters (Asia), Million Dollar Challenge (Afr).

BEST 1995 FINISHES: 1— Nissan Open, U.S. Open; 2—Kemper Open; T2—THE TOUR Championship; T3—THE PLAYERS Championship; T8—British Open.

1995 SEASON: Cast off mantle of "best player not to win a major" with his June victory at the U.S. Open...successfully defended 1994 Nissan Open title with three-stroke victory over Jay Don Blake...started final round one stroke off pace, but fired 67 to claim third

COREY PAVIN...continued

tournament he has won twice (Hawaiian Open and Bob Hope Chrysler Classic)...first to defend Nissan Open title since Arnold Palmer won Los Angeles Open in 1966-67...joined Ben Hogan and Palmer as only players to win consecutive events at Riviera CC...other back-to-back winners in Los Angeles (but not at Riviera) were Macdonald Smith (1928-29) and Paul Harney (1964-65)...opened with 66 and owned or shared lead for first three rounds of THE PLAYERS Championship...carded 74 to finish T3, two shots behind Lee Janzen...tied TPC at Avenel course record with third-round 63 and followed with 68 to land in playoff with Lee Janzen, which Janzen won on first extra hole...rebounded from Kemper disappointment with highlight of career...won first major title with two-stroke victory in U.S. Open...posted rounds of 72-69-71, three strokes behind third-round leader Greg Norman...closing 68 will be remembered for "The Shot"...clinging to one- stroke lead on 72nd hole, fired 228-yard 4-wood into hill 10 yards short of green, finishing within five feet of pin (two putted for par)...later said of 4-wood, "I can't think of any shot that I have hit better under pressure than that one."...finished T8 in British Open after being one shot off 36-hole lead...recorded 4-1 record for U.S. team in losing Ryder Cup effort...pumped life into team by holing 18-foot chip in Saturday's four-ball match (with Loren Roberts) to defeat Nick Faldo/Bernhard Langer...won Asian Masters by nine strokes...reached the U.S. region semifinals in Andersen Consulting World Championship of Golf before losing to Mark McCumber...T2 in TOUR Championship to end the year...earned $240,000 at Skins Game, second to Fred Couples...won Million Dollar Challenge in South Africa in December.

CAREER HIGHLIGHTS: Claimed 11th TOUR title in battle with Fred Couples at 1994 Nissan Los Angeles Open...second in 1994 PGA Championship was best finish in major prior to '95 U.S. Open...went 2-2-1 in five matches in inaugural Presidents Cup in 1994...owns an 8-5 record in three Ryder Cup Matches (1991-93-95)...holed dramatic 136-yard 8-iron for eagle on final hole of 1992 Honda Classic to force playoff with Couples, then won with birdie on second extra hole...lost playoff to Bruce Lietzke in 1992 Colonial...won Arnold Palmer Award as PGA TOUR's Official Money Leader in 1991...also honored as PGA of America's Player of Year...1991 season featured pair of playoff victories: over Mark O'Meara in Bob Hope Chrysler Classic and Steve Pate in BellSouth Atlanta Classic...also lost Canon Greater Hartford Open playoff to Billy Ray Brown...Hope finish was 29-under-par 331, then-TOUR record for 90-hole event...scored victories first five years on TOUR, beginning with Houston Open in 1984...captured 1988 Texas Open with 21-under-par 259, becoming just fifth player in TOUR history to better 260...at 17, won Junior World title and became youngest winner of Los Angeles City Men's crown...1981 winner North-South Amateur, Southwest Amateur, Maccabiah Games...won 11 college tournaments at UCLA, including 1982 PAC-10 title.

PERSONAL: Close friend of basketball star David Robinson, who named son Corey Mathew Robinson.

CAREER SUMMARY — **PLAYOFF RECORD: 5-3**

Year	Events Played	Cuts Made	1st	2nd	3rd	Top 10	Top 25	Earnings	Rank
1980(Am.)	1	1							
1983	3	1					1	$4,209	207
1984	29	26	1	2		5	14	$260,536	18
1985	27	23	1	1	1	13	19	$367,506	6
1986	28	23	2			6	14	$304,558	19
1987	26	17	2			7	10	$498,406	15
1988	26	17	1			3	7	$216,768	50
1989	28	23				1	10	$177,084	82
1990	29	26		1	1	6	13	$468,830	26
1991	25	24	2	2	2	10	18	$979,430	1
1992	25	20	1	3	2	7	13	$980,934	5
1993	24	21		2		6	13	$675,087	18
1994	20	16	1	3	1	9	11	$906,305	8
1995	22	18	2	2	1	6	11	$1,340,079	4
Total	313	256	13	16	8	79	154	$7,179,732	6

1996 PGA TOUR CHARITY TEAM: Kemper Open

TOP TOURNAMENT SUMMARY

YEAR	83	84	85	86	87	88	89	90	91	92	93	94	95
Masters Tournament			T25	T11	T27	T42	50		T22	3	T11	T8	T17
U.S. Open	CUT		T9	CUT	W/D	CUT		T24	T8	CUT	T19	CUT	1
British Open Championship		T22	T39	CUT	CUT	T38		T8	CUT	T34	T4	CUT	T8
PGA Championship		T20	T6	T21	CUT	T17	CUT	T14	T32	T12	CUT	2	CUT
THE PLAYERS Championship		CUT	CUT	T58	T50	T42	T34	CUT	T41	T46	T16	T78	T3
THE TOUR Championship					T5			21	T10	T2	T7	T10	T2

NATIONAL TEAMS: Ryder Cup (3),1991, 1993, 1995; Walker Cup, 1981; Nissan Cup, 1985; Presidents Cup, 1994.

1995 PGA TOUR STATISTICS

Scoring	70.04	(11)
Driving	254.9	(159T)
Driving Accuracy	73.6	(39T)
Greens in Regulation	66.1	(100T)
Putting	1.759	(21T)
All Around	676	(80)
Sand Saves	52.6	(92)
Total Driving	198	(112)
Eagles	2	(161T)
Birdies	278	(93T)

MISCELLANEOUS STATISTICS

Scoring Avg Before Cut	70.56	(31T)
Scoring Avg 3rd Rnd	69.67	(10)
Scoring Avg Final Rnd	71.29	(99T)
Birdies Conversion %	31.1	(26)
Par Breakers	19.7	(74T)

1995 Low Round: **63:** 1995 Kemper Open/3
Career Low Round: **62:** 1990 H.E.B. Texas Open/3
Career Largest Paycheck: **$350,000:** 1995 U.S. Open/1

Kenny Perry

EXEMPT STATUS: 1995 tournament winner
FULL NAME: James Kenneth Perry
HEIGHT: 6' 1" **WEIGHT:** 190
BIRTH DATE: August 10, 1960 **BIRTHPLACE:** Elizabethtown, KY
RESIDENCE: Franklin, KY; plays out of Franklin CC
FAMILY: Wife, Sandy; Lesslye (5/20/84), Justin (11/23/85), Lindsey (4/27/88)
COLLEGE: Western Kentucky University
SPECIAL INTERESTS: Restoring old cars, all sports
TURNED PROFESSIONAL: 1982 **Q SCHOOL:** Fall 1986

TOUR VICTORIES (3): 1991 Memorial Tournament. **1994** New England Classic. **1995** Bob Hope Chrysler Classic.

BEST 1995 FINISHES: 1—Bob Hope Chrysler Classic; T2—Nissan Open; T3—AT&T Pebble Beach National Pro-Am; T5—GTE Byron Nelson Classic; T9—Kemper Open.

1995 SEASON: Torrid start highlighted best year...with T3-1-T2 finishes in three-tournament stretch, made more money ($430,927) in first six starts than seven of eight years on TOUR...held three-stroke lead after 54 holes in AT&T Pebble Beach National Pro-Am, only to fire 72 and finish T3...the next week claimed third career title with one-stroke win over David Duval in Bob Hope Chrysler Classic...ended California assault with T2 in Nissan Open...rounds of 62-68 gave him 36- and 54-hole leads...hope for consecutive wins was dashed during closing 71 when shot on 13th hole went out of bounds...posted two other top-10 finishes (T5 GTE Byron Nelson Classic and T9 Kemper Open), plus eight more top 25s...held opening-round lead at GTE Byron Nelson Classic with 65...started PGA Championship in 10th place in Ryder Cup standings, but was bumped from U.S. team by Brad Faxon's (5) and Jeff Maggert's (T3) strong finishes in PGA Championship...topped season-long Merrill Lynch Shoot-Out money list.

CAREER HIGHLIGHTS: Claimed first TOUR victory at The Memorial in 1991...Muirfield Village course-record, nine-under-par 63 in Round 2 propelled to lead...Hale Irwin caught him on final day, forcing playoff...birdie on first extra hole provided win and $216,000 first-place check... fired closing-round 65 to take 1994 New England Classic by one stroke over David Feherty...top-30 finish on money list in '94 (No. 26) produced first trip to TOUR Championship...money-won total dropped for first time in career in 1992...rebounded slightly in 1993, but had to play catch-up late in season to save his card with back-to-back September top-10s.

PERSONAL: Encouraged by his "biggest fan," Kenny Perry, Sr., to start playing golf at age 7...father used to sit for hours teeing golf balls up for him...first competition came at 11...designed and built Country Creek GC, a public golf course which opened in hometown in April 1995...attended National Hot Road Association driving school in Gainesville, FL in Dec. 1995...played collegiately at Western Kentucky, where he is member of Sports Hall of Fame...possessor of an unusual backswing, of which he says: "It's ugly going back, but from the top down I'm as good as anyone."

CAREER SUMMARY — **PLAYOFF RECORD: 1-0**

Year	Events Played	Cuts Made	1st	2nd	3rd	Top 10	Top 25	Earnings	Rank
1984	1								
1985	1								
1987	26	15				1	5	$107,239	93
1988	32	20				3	7	$139,421	85
1989	26	15		1		3	7	$202,099	70
1990	23	17		1		2	9	$279,881	50
1991	24	16	1			3	7	$368,784	44
1992	25	17				3	9	$190,455	81
1993	29	18				3	8	$196,863	88
1994	30	22	1	1		4	10	$585,941	26
1995	25	21	1	1	1	5	13	$773,388	21
Total	242	161	3	4	1	27	75	$2,844,072	62

1996 PGA TOUR CHARITY TEAM: THE PLAYERS Championship

TOP TOURNAMENT SUMMARY

YEAR	88	89	90	91	92	93	94	95
Masters Tournament				CUT			T12	
U.S. Open	T55					T25		CUT
British Open Championship				CUT				
PGA Championship	T51	T49	77			T55	T49	
THE PLAYERS Championship	33	T21	T56	T57	W/D	T65	T62	T55
THE TOUR Championship							T26	T20

KENNY PERRY...continued

1995 PGA TOUR STATISTICS		
Scoring	70.35	(29T)
Driving	270.2	(43)
Driving Accuracy	69.5	(97T)
Greens in Regulation	67.2	(61T)
Putting	1.767	(36T)
All Around	455	(25)
Sand Saves	52.4	(93)
Total Driving	140	(34)
Eagles	6	(69T)
Birdies	339	(27)

MISCELLANEOUS STATISTICS		
Scoring Avg Before Cut	70.38	(17)
Scoring Avg 3rd Rnd	70.36	(40T)
Scoring Avg Final Rnd	70.71	(44T)
Birdies Conversion %	29.8	(56T)
Par Breakers	20.4	(38T)

1995 Low Round: **62:** 1995 Nissan Open/2
Career Low Round: **62:** 1995 Nissan Open/2
Career Largest Paycheck: **$216,000:** 2 times, most recent 1991 Memorial Tournament/1

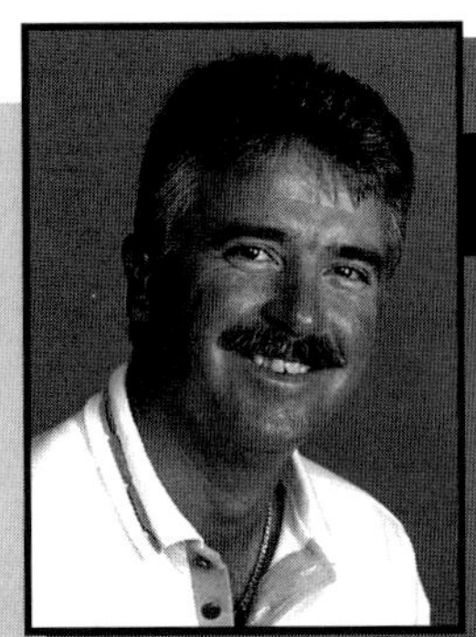

DAN POHL *(POLL)*

EXEMPT STATUS: Winner, 1986 NEC World Series of Golf
FULL NAME: Danny Joe Pohl
HEIGHT: 5' 11" **WEIGHT:** 175
BIRTH DATE: April 1, 1955 **BIRTHPLACE:** Mt. Pleasant, MI
RESIDENCE: Mt. Pleasant, MI
FAMILY: Wife, Mitzi; Michelle (2/2/78); Joshua Daniel (9/10/84); Taylor Whitney (9/10/86)
COLLEGE: University of Arizona **SPECIAL INTERESTS:** Fishing, hunting
TURNED PROFESSIONAL: 1977 **Q SCHOOL:** Spring 1978,1979

TOUR VICTORIES (2): 1986 Colonial National Invitational, NEC World Series of Golf

BEST 1995 FINISHES: T4— United Airlines Hawaiian Open; T6— Buick Invitational of California

1995 SEASON: Had best year since 1992 despite playing only 15 events...placed in top 25 four times, including two top-10 finishes...pair of closing 69s earned T4 in United Airlines Hawaiian Open, his best finish since T3 in 1992 Nestle Invitational...other top 10 was T6 in Buick Invitational of California...tied for first-round lead with a 64...later in year put together back-to-back top-25 finishes with T18 (Canon Greater Hartford Open) and T13 (Motorola Western Open)...forced to have September neck surgery after experiencing numbness in left hand...as a result, missed on-course Ryder Cup duty with NBC Sports.

CAREER HIGHLIGHTS: Has been plagued by injuries throughout his career...made strong early start in 1993 before chronic back trouble sidetracked him...later had to pull out of Kmart Greater Greensboro Open after player on son's baseball team fouled "soft toss" into his mouth, loosening his front teeth and requiring 24 stitches...spent most of 1994 season recovering from surgery on both knees...after enduring back pain for years, finally underwent surgery October 2, 1989...spent entire 1990 season in rehabilitation, returning to TOUR for 1991 campaign...considering circumstances, produced excellent year in 1991, finishing 95th on money list...made first four cuts, later finished T8 at Anheuser-Busch Golf Classic and T7 at Canon Greater Hartford Open...won twice in 1986, when captured Colonial National Invitation and NEC World Series of Golf, earning 10-year TOUR exemption...winner 1987 Vardon Trophy...winner 1987 All-Around category...winner 1988 EPSON Stats Match...TOUR driving distance leader 1980-81...playoff loser to Craig Stadler at 1982 Masters.

PERSONAL: Nickname "Pohl Cat"...pursuing career in golf course architecture...Michigan State Amateur champion 1975 and 1977...does on-course commentary for NBC when not playing.

DAN POHL...*continued*

CAREER SUMMARY — **PLAYOFF RECORD: 1-2**

Year	Events Played	Cuts Made	1st	2nd	3rd	Top 10	Top 25	Earnings	Rank
1978	11	4						$1,047	224
1979	22	11			1	3	5	$38,393	100
1980	28	20		1	1	5	11	$105,008	44
1981	28	20			1	6	8	$94,303	42
1982	31	21		1	1	4	7	$97,213	39
1983	27	20				6	8	$89,830	62
1984	28	26			1	7	15	$182,653	32
1985	27	22		1		7	17	$198,829	27
1986	25	19	2	1		5	11	$463,630	5
1987	26	24		1	2	9	19	$465,269	17
1988	27	21		2		7	13	$396,400	27
1989	19	15				4	5	$195,789	74
1991	21	16				2	8	$163,438	95
1992	19	12			1	1	5	$131,486	110
1993	19	10				2	4	$97,830	146
1994	15	6						$21,734	221
1995	15	9				2	4	$166,219	117
Total	388	276	2	7	8	70	140	$2,908,754	58

1996 PGA TOUR CHARITY TEAM: Diners Club Matches.

TOP TOURNAMENT SUMMARY

YEAR	80	81	82	83	84	85	86	87	88	89	91	92	93	94	95
Masters Tournament		2	T8	T35		T31	CUT	T16	42						
U.S. Open	CUT		T3	CUT		CUT	CUT	T9	T12	T29					
British Open Championship							CUT								
PGA Championship	3	T70	8	T39	T12	T26	T14	8	T24						
THE PLAYERS Championship	T8	T45	W/D	CUT	T8	74	CUT	T7	T8	T50	CUT	T35	W/D	CUT	T68
THE TOUR Championship							T27	23							

NATIONAL TEAMS: Nissan Cup, 1985; Ryder Cup, 1987

1995 PGA TOUR STATISTICS

Scoring	70.48	(N/A)
Driving	277.3	(N/A)
Driving Accuracy	64.8	(N/A)
Greens in Regulation	70.9	(N/A)
Putting	1.780	(N/A)
Sand Saves	45.6	(N/A)
Total Driving		(N/A)
Eagles	3	(N/A)
Birdies	173	(N/A)

MISCELLANEOUS STATISTICS

Scoring Avg Before Cut	70.54	(N/A)
Scoring Avg 3rd Rnd	70.56	(N/A)
Scoring Avg Final Rnd	71.22	(N/A)
Birdies Conversion %	29.5	(N/A)
Par Breakers	21.3	(38T)

1995 Low Round: 65: 1995 Buick Invitational of California/1
Career Low Round: 62: 1989 Honda Classic/2
Career Largest Paycheck: $126,000: 1986 NEC WSOG/1

Did You Know?

Curtis Strange is one of three players in PGA TOUR history to win three playoffs in a year -- Independent Insurance Agent Open, U.S. Open and Nabisco Championships in 1988. Lloyd Mangrum in 1948 and Arnold Palmer in 1963 are the others. There is no record of one player losing three playoffs in one year.

Don Pooley

EXEMPT STATUS: 82nd on 1995 money list
FULL NAME: Sheldon George Pooley, Jr.
HEIGHT: 6' 3" **WEIGHT:** 185
BIRTH DATE: August 27, 1951 **BIRTHPLACE:** Phoenix, AZ
RESIDENCE: Tucson, AZ; plays out of LaPaloma CC, Tucson, AZ
FAMILY: Wife, Margaret; Lynn (1/19/80), Kerri (5/19/82)
COLLEGE: University of Arizona (1973, Business Administration)
SPECIAL INTERESTS: Basketball, Lynn & Kerri's sporting events
TURNED PROFESSIONAL: 1973 **Q SCHOOL:** Fall 1975, 1976

TOUR VICTORIES (2): 1980 B.C. Open. **1987** Memorial Tournament.

INTERNATIONAL VICTORIES (1): 1989 Ebel Match Play (France).

BEST 1995 FINISHES: 3— Ideon Classic; T5— Canon Greater Hartford Open; T6—Northern Telecom Open

1995 SEASON: Was physically able to play 22 events, his most since 24 starts in 1990...began season on special medical extension...was given 23 events to earn $137,587, which was what 128th place on 1994 money list made...earned full exempt status with T20 at Motorola Western Open (15th event)...was one stroke off 54-hole lead in the Northern Telecom Open after posting rounds of 71-66-65...finished T6 after a closing 72...while he was never in contention to win, finished well on the weekend with rounds of 66-65 to earn T5 in Canon Greater Hartford Open...after opening with 70, rebounded with 64-68-68 to finish third at Ideon Classic...was in money 11 consecutive times from Nestle Invitational through Ideon Classic, including two top 10s...faded at end of year, missing four of last five cuts, including last three.

CAREER HIGHLIGHTS: While relatively healthy in 1995, was hampered the previous four seasons by various ailments, including lower back problems...suffered ruptured neck disc taking practice swing while trying to play way through back problem...underwent neck disc surgery in Jan. 1992...followed with lower back surgery in Oct. 1993...back hampered play throughout 1991 season and caused him to miss first four months of 1993...received medical extension for 12 tournaments in 1992...managed to put together enough playing time in 1993 to retain playing privileges for 1994...1993 lower back surgery prevented extensive play in '94...went from Oct. 1993-April 1994 and May-September 1994 without touching a club but still managed a late-season third in the Texas Open...first victory came in 1980 B.C. Open, where he closed with 68 for one-stroke win over Peter Jacobsen...came from four strokes behind final day of 1987 Memorial Tournament to overtake Scott Hoch...scored Million Dollar Hole-in-One at 1987 Bay Hill Classic...192-yard 4-iron hit 17th hole flagstick two feet above cup and dropped in...Arnold Palmer Children's Hospital received $500,000...winner1992 Amoco Centel Championship...won 1985 Vardon Trophy...led TOUR in putting in 1988.

PERSONAL: Made swing change in 1992 to take pressure off lower back...credits physical therapist Tom Boers with enabling him to continue playing.

CAREER SUMMARY **PLAYOFF RECORD: 0-0**

Year	Events Played	Cuts Made	1st	2nd	3rd	Top 10	Top 25	Earnings	Rank
1976	18	6					1	$2,439	208
1977	29	14				3	3	$24,507	94
1978	29	15				1	9	$31,945	84
1979	24	8					1	$6,932	170
1980	27	22	1	1	1	7	12	$157,973	18
1981	31	22				5	9	$75,730	57
1982	29	18				5	10	$87,962	49
1983	29	24		1		7	14	$145,979	36
1984	24	19		1	1	3	9	$120,699	54
1985	26	24				5	15	$162,094	46
1986	27	24		1		9	13	$268,274	22
1987	26	21	1	1		8	11	$450,005	18
1988	23	17		1		7	9	$239,534	46
1989	23	15			1	4	9	$214,662	66
1990	24	14			1	3	6	$192,570	83
1991	15	8					3	$67,549	156
1992	16	12				1	5	$135,683	107
1993	15	8			1	2	3	$123,105	122
1994	5	3			1	1	1	$76,978	171
1995	22	15			1	3	5	$226,804	82
Total	462	309	2	6	7	74	148	$2,808,097	64

1996 PGA TOUR CHARITY TEAM: Nortel Open

Don Pooley...continued

TOP TOURNAMENT SUMMARY

YEAR	80	81	82	83	84	85	86	87	88	89	90	91	92	93	95
Masters Tournament	T19	CUT				41	T45	T5	T14	T42	T46				
U.S. Open	CUT	CUT			T15	T24	T24	CUT	T26	CUT		T44			
British Open Championship									T16	T19	T39				T101
PGA Championship	T46	T19	T67	T23	T34	T62	T16	T5	T58	T34	T8	T73			CUT
THE PLAYERS Championship	T14	T66	T56	T10	CUT	T17	CUT	T41	T54	CUT	CUT	W/D		CUT	
THE TOUR Championship							T10								

1995 PGA TOUR STATISTICS

Scoring	71.07	(76)
Driving	250.6	(182T)
Driving Accuracy	73.8	(36T)
Greens in Regulation	68.4	(37)
Putting	1.759	(21T)
All Around	714	(88T)
Sand Saves	44.8	(170T)
Total Driving	218	(139T)
Eagles	5	(88T)
Birdies	268	(104T)

MISCELLANEOUS STATISTICS

Scoring Avg Before Cut	71.04	(71)
Scoring Avg 3rd Rnd	70.94	(78T)
Scoring Avg Final Rnd	71.33	(105T)
Birdies Conversion %	29.8	(56T)
Par Breakers	19.7	(74T)

1995 Low Round: 64: 1995 Ideon Classic at Pleasant Valley/2
Career Low Round: 61: 1986 Phoenix Open/2
Career Largest Paycheck: $140,000: 1987 Memorial Tournament/1

Nick Price

EXEMPT STATUS: Winner, 1994 PGA Championship
FULL NAME: Nicholas Raymond Leige Price
HEIGHT: 6' **WEIGHT:** 190
BIRTH DATE: January 28, 1957 **BIRTHPLACE:** Durban, South Africa
RESIDENCE: Hobe Sound, FL; plays out of The Medalist
FAMILY: Wife, Sue; Gregory (8/9/91); Robyn Frances (8/5/93)
SPECIAL INTERESTS: Water skiing, tennis, fishing, flying
TURNED PROFESSIONAL: 1977 **Q SCHOOL:** Fall 1982

TOUR VICTORIES (14): 1983 World Series of Golf. **1991** GTE Byron Nelson Classic, Canadian Open. **1992** PGA Championship, H-E-B Texas Open. **1993** The PLAYERS Championship, Canon Greater Hartford Open, Sprint Western Open, Federal Express St. Jude Classic. **1994** Honda Classic, Southwestern Bell Colonial, Motorola Western Open, PGA Championship, Bell Canadian Open.

INTERNATIONAL VICTORIES (16): 1979 Asseng Invitational (Afr). **1980** Canon European Masters (Eur). **1981** Italian Open (Eur), South African Masters (Afr). **1982** Vaals Reef Open (Afr). **1985** Trophee Lancome (Eur), ICL International (Afr). **1989** West End South Australian Open (Aus). **1992** Air New Zealand/Shell Open (Aus). **1993** ICL International (Afr), Sun City Million Dollar Challenge (Afr). **1994** British Open (Eur), ICL International (Afr). **1995** Alfred Dunhill Challenge (Afr), Hassan II Golf Trophy (Moracco), Zimbabwe Open (Afr).

BEST 1995 FINISHES: T2—World Series of Golf; 3—Bell Canadian Open; T7—MCI Classic; T9—Kemper Open 10—Memorial Tournament

1995 SEASON: When asked if 1995 had been a disappointing year, responded by saying: "I guess I've made around $800,000 around the world. If people want to call that a bad year, I'll take bad years from here on out."...was beaten in a three-man playoff at the NEC World Series of Golf when Greg Norman made birdie by chipping in from 66 feet on first extra hole...posted closing back-to-back 68s to finish T3 in Bell Canadian Open...started his year with a third in Dubai Classic and a second at Johnnie Walker Classic on the PGA European Tour...returned to the PGA TOUR in Florida with back-to-back top 25s at Honda Classic (T13) and Nestle Invitational (T14)...closing 65 earned a T7 at MCI Classic...after missing cut in Shell Houston Open, followed caddie Jeff "Squeeky" Medlen's advice to take time off...cited "burnout" as reason for substandard play...returned three weeks later and placed no lower than 13th in next four events (T12 Colonial National Invitation, 10 Memorial, T9 Kemper Open, T13 U.S. Open)...that stretch highlighted by opening 66 to lead the U.S. Open, plus closing rounds of 65 at the Memorial and 66 in the Colonial National...felt pain in right hip at U.S. Open...pain increased at FedEx St. Jude Classic due to inflamed tendon, but improved by Motorola Western Open...led South Africa over Australia in Alfred Dunhill Cup.

Nick Price...*continued*

CAREER HIGHLIGHTS: Captured six titles in 1994, including first British Open crown and second PGA Championship...first to win two majors in same year since Nick Faldo (1990)...one of only six players (Ben Hogan three times, Jack Nicklaus, Arnold Palmer, Lee Trevino, Tom Watson) to win back-to-back majors since World War II...third foreign player to win two PGA titles: Jim Barnes 1916, 1919; Gary Player 1962, 1972...first since Watson (1980) to win six times in year...10 victories in two years (1993-94) best since Watson won 11 in 1979-80...back-to-back winner of PGA TOUR Player of Year Award in 1993-94...also winner of 1993-94 PGA Player of Year Awards...first since Curtis Strange (1987-88) to capture consecutive Arnold Palmer Awards...winner of 1993 Vardon Trophy...named 1994 Player of Year by GWAA...ranked first in Sony World Rankings from 1994 PGA Championship through 1995 U.S. Open...from breakthrough victory in 1992 PGA Championship through end of '94 TOUR season, totaled 17 worldwide wins...captured 1993 PLAYERS Championship in then-record fashion, later that season won three consecutive TOUR starts...qualified for 1983 World Series of Golf as leader of South African Order of Merit...prior to 1994 win, was two-time runner-up in British Open (1982 and 1988).

PERSONAL: Born in South Africa, moved to Rhodesia (now Zimbabwe) at early age...served two years in Rhodesian Air Force...since parents were British citizens, carries British passport...at 17 won Junior World at Torrey Pines in LaJolla, CA...in 1975 played South African and European Tours as amateur.

CAREER SUMMARY — **PLAYOFF RECORD: 2-2**

Year	Events Played	Cuts Made	1st	2nd	3rd	Top 10	Top 25	Earnings	Rank
1983	21	14	1			2	5	$49,435	104
1984	19	15			1	4	6	$109,480	66
1985	20	14				2	5	$96,069	80
1986	25	17		1		6	11	$225,373	35
1987	25	19		1		7	14	$334,169	28
1988	24	20		1		4	10	$266,300	42
1989	27	22			1	7	12	$296,170	42
1990	28	22		2	1	6	13	$520,777	22
1991	23	18	2			9	11	$714,389	7
1992	26	24	2	1	2	13	19	$1,135,773	4
1993	18	17	4	2		8	12	$1,478,557	1
1994	19	14	5	1		8	10	$1,499,927	1
1995	18	15		1	1	5	11	$611,700	30
Total	293	231	14	10	6	81	139	$7,338,119	4

1996 PGA TOUR CHARITY TEAM: Nissan Open

TOP TOURNAMENT SUMMARY

YEAR	78	80	81	82	83	84	85	86	87	88	89	90	91
Masters Tournament						CUT		5	T22	T14	CUT		T49
U.S. Open					T48		CUT		T17	T40	CUT		T19
British Open Championship	T39	T28	T23	T2	CUT	T44	CUT		T8	2	CUT	T25	T44
PGA Championship					T67	T54	5	CUT	T10	T17	T46	T63	
THE PLAYERS Championship						7	T22	T58	T24	DQ	CUT	T16	T9
THE TOUR Championship									T5			5	T5

TOP TOURNAMENT SUMMARY

YEAR	92	93	94	95
Masters Tournament	T6	CUT	T35	CUT
U.S. Open	T4	T11	CUT	T13
British Open Championship	T51	T6	1	T40
PGA Championship	1	T31	1	T39
THE PLAYERS Championship	8	1	CUT	T37
THE TOUR Championship	T13	T18	T20	30

NATIONAL TEAMS: Dunhill Cup (3), 1993, 1994, 1995; World Cup, 1993; Presidents Cup, 1994.

1995 PGA TOUR STATISTICS

Scoring	69.81	(3T)
Driving	273.0	(23)
Driving Accuracy	76.3	(17)
Greens in Regulation	66.5	(82T)
Putting	1.760	(23T)
All Around	475	(27)
Sand Saves	51.3	(105)
Total Driving	40	(1)
Eagles	5	(88T)
Birdies	244	(134T)

MISCELLANEOUS STATISTICS

Scoring Avg Before Cut	71.21	(92T)
Scoring Avg 3rd Rnd	70.20	(29)
Scoring Avg Final Rnd	70.40	(26)
Birdies Conversion %	32.9	(10T)
Par Breakers	21.0	(19T)

1995 Low Round: **65:** 2 times, most recent 1995 Memorial Tournament/4
Career Low Round: **62:** 2 times, most recent 1992 H-E-B Texas Open/2
Career Largest Paycheck: **$450,000:** 1993 THE PLAYERS Championship/1

DICKY PRIDE

EXEMPT STATUS: 1994 tournament winner
FULL NAME: Richard Fletcher Pride III
HEIGHT: 6' **WEIGHT:** 175
BIRTH DATE: July 15, 1969 **BIRTHPLACE:** Tuscaloosa, AL
RESIDENCE: Orlando, FL
FAMILY: Wife, Kim
COLLEGE: University of Alabama
SPECIAL INTERESTS: Basketball, reading, University of Alabama football
TURNED PROFESSIONAL: 1992 **Q SCHOOL:** 1993

TOUR VICTORIES (1): 1994 Federal Express St. Jude Classic

1995 BEST FINISH: T8— Deposit Guaranty Golf Classic

1995 SEASON: Fell off significantly from superlative rookie season...failed to reach $100,000 mark, with money-won total $208,057 less than in 1994...earned paycheck in consecutive events just once: T45 Anheuser-Busch Golf Classic, followed by T8 (for the second year in a row) Deposit Guaranty Golf Classic...placed in top 25 four times...Deposit Guaranty finish featured opening-round 66, followed by a 68 to tie for the 36-hole lead...was one stroke off first- and third-round leads at Annandale GC, where finish produced top paycheck of year ($20,300)...other top finishes were T20 Mercedes Championship, T19 Shell Houston Open and T20 Sprint International, which provided second-best check ($18,750).

CAREER HIGHLIGHTS: Surprised golf world by winning 1994 FedEx St. Jude Classic...opened with 66, then followed with three consecutive 67s at TPC at Southwind...sank memorable 20-foot birdie putt on 72nd hole to tie Hal Sutton and Gene Sauers, then made 25-foot birdie putt for win on first playoff hole...was in Memphis field as third alternate...had first top-10 finish of career (T8) at weather-shortened Deposit Guaranty Golf Classic...$245,300 of rookie season earnings came during three-week span...qualified for TOUR with T24 in 1993 Qualifying Tournament...semifinalist in 1991 U.S. Amateur...two-time All-Southeastern Conference.

PERSONAL: Hole-in-one in 1994 Buick Southern Open won Buick of his choice for then-fiancee Kim (they were married the following December)...BIG University of Alabama football fan.

PGA TOUR CAREER SUMMARY — **PLAYOFF RECORD: 1-0**

Year	Events Played	Cuts Made	1st	2nd	3rd	Top 10	Top 25	Earnings	Rank
1992	1								
1994	27	12	1			2	3	$305,769	57
1995	31	12				1	4	$97,712	161
Total	59	24	1			3	7	$403,480	279

NIKE TOUR SUMMARY

Year	Events Played	Cuts Made	1st	2nd	3rd	Top 10	Top 25	Earnings	Rank
1993	1	1						$960	212
1994	2	2					2	$3,971	149
Total	3	3					2	$4,931	
COMBINED TOTAL MONEY								$408,411	

1996 PGA TOUR CHARITY TEAM: Quad City Classic

TOP TOURNAMENT SUMMARY

YEAR	92	94	95
Masters Tournament		CUT	
U.S. Open	CUT		
PGA Championship		T73	
THE PLAYERS Championship			T49

DICKY PRIDE...continued

1995 PGA TOUR STATISTICS		
Scoring	72.20	(176T)
Driving	254.8	(162)
Driving Accuracy	69.5	(97T)
Greens in Regulation	61.4	(180)
Putting	1.808	(148T)
All Around	1,247	(187)
Sand Saves	44.3	(174)
Total Driving	259	(168T)
Eagles		(184T)
Birdies	251	(126)

MISCELLANEOUS STATISTICS		
Scoring Avg Before Cut	72.21	(171T)
Scoring Avg 3rd Rnd	72.57	(174T)
Scoring Avg Final Rnd	74.33	(187)
Birdies Conversion %	27.4	(131T)
Par Breakers	16.8	(171T)

1995 Low Round: **166:** 1995 Deposit Guaranty Golf Classic/1
Career Low Round: **64:** 1994 Deposit Guaranty Golf Classic/2
Career Largest Paycheck: **$225,000:** 1994 Federal Express St. Jude Classic/1

DILLARD PRUITT

EXEMPT STATUS: 88th on 1995 money list
HEIGHT: 5' 11" **WEIGHT:** 200
BIRTH DATE: September 24, 1961 **BIRTHPLACE:** Greenville, SC
RESIDENCE: Greenville, SC
FAMILY: Wife, Fran
COLLEGE: Clemson University
SPECIAL INTERESTS: Music, Harley-Davidson motorcycles
TURNED PROFESSIONAL: 1985 **Q SCHOOL:** Fall 1988,1989,1990

TOUR VICTORIES (1): 1991 Chattanooga Classic.

1995 BEST FINISHES: T3—Bob Hope Chrysler Classic; T4—Buick Classic; T6—Buick Invitational of California

1995 SEASON: Took early giant step toward renewing exempt status by posting back-to-back top-10 finishes in his third and fourth events...closed with two consecutive 68s to record a T6 at Buick Invitational of California...followed that effort the next week by opening and closing with 65s to earn T3 in Bob Hope Chrysler Classic...those two finishes marked first time in his career he posted back-to-back top 10s...collected second-best check of the year ($47,250) for third and last top 10 of season, Buick Classic T4...logged third top-25 finish in Buick-sponsored events with T24 at Buick Open, but failed to complete "sweep" by missing cut at Buick Challenge.

CAREER HIGHLIGHTS: Fired 20-under-par 260 for two-stroke win over Lance Ten Broeck in 1991 Chattanooga Classic...$126,000 winner's share keyed career-best earnings of $271,861...other 1991 top-10 finish came at NEC World Series of Golf...was third-round leader on 30th birthday, but finished with 77 and T6 at 2-over 282...prior to Chattanooga, best previous finish had been T9 in 1990 International...long-stated dream was to play in Masters, opportunity that Chattanooga victory provided...finished T13 at Augusta National in 1992, allowing return engagement in '93 (missed cut)...played European Tour in 1986-87, posting sixth-place finishes in 1987 German Open and Benson & Hedges event in England...winner Sunnehanna Amateur...three-time All-ACC, one-time All-American...winner of two collegiate tournaments.

PERSONAL: Has various family connections to golf: Jay Haas is brother-in-law, Scott Verplank is married to his sister-in-law; Jay and brother Jerry Haas's uncle is Bob Goalby...Jay Haas has had strong influence on development of his game and career...enjoys riding Harley-Davidson motorcycles on roads around Greenville, SC home.

CAREER SUMMARY — **PLAYOFF RECORD: 0-0**

Year	Events Played	Cuts Made	1st	2nd	3rd	Top 10	Top 25	Earnings	Rank
1988	29	13					1	$33,889	164
1989	4	3						$6,831	222
1990	30	12				1	3	$76,352	150
1991	27	18	1			2	7	$271,861	63
1992	30	18				1	6	$189,604	82
1993	26	20				2	5	$168,053	98
1994	29	18				2	6	$171,866	105
1995	25	16			1	3	4	$210,453	88
Total	200	118	1		1	11	32	$1,128,909	173

DILLARD PRUITT...*continued*

1996 PGA TOUR CHARITY TEAM: MCI Classic

TOP TOURNAMENT SUMMARY

YEAR	89	91	92	93	94	95
Masters Tournament			T13	CUT		
U.S. Open	T67		T44			
PGA Championship		T66	T33			66
THE PLAYERS Championship			CUT	69	T19	CUT

1995 PGA TOUR STATISTICS

Scoring	71.12	(79T)
Driving	258.3	(132)
Driving Accuracy	73.6	(39T)
Greens in Regulation	68.1	(44)
Putting	1.794	(110T)
All Around	723	(92)
Sand Saves	54.2	(69)
Total Driving	171	(73T)
Eagles	2	(161T)
Birdies	280	(89T)

MISCELLANEOUS STATISTICS

Scoring Avg Before Cut	71.35	(105T)
Scoring Avg 3rd Rnd	71.20	(97)
Scoring Avg Final Rnd	69.87	(10)
Birdies Conversion %	29.7	(60T)
Par Breakers	20.3	(40T)

1995 Low Round: 65: 2 times, most recent 1995 Bob Hope Chrysler Classic/5
Career Low Round: 62: 2 times, most recent 1993 Anheuser-Busch Golf Classic/3
Career Largest Paycheck: $126,000: 1991 Chattanooga Classic/1

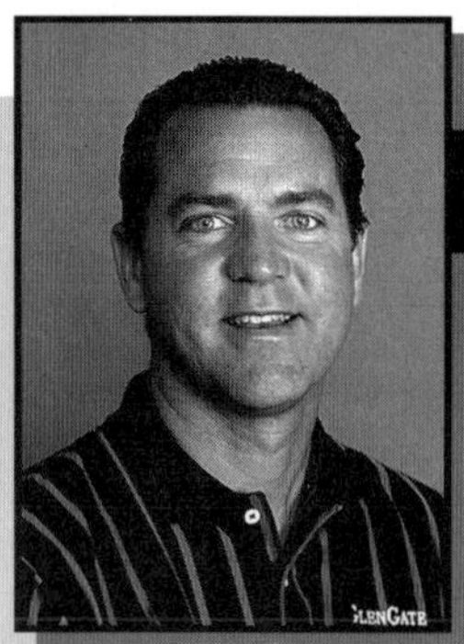

TOM PURTZER

EXEMPT STATUS: Winner, 1991 NEC World Series of Golf
FULL NAME: Thomas Warren Purtzer
HEIGHT: 6' **WEIGHT:** 180
BIRTH DATE: Dec. 5, 1951 **BIRTHPLACE:** Des Moines, IA
RESIDENCE: Scottsdale, AZ
FAMILY: Wife, Lori; Laura (7/3/80); Ashley (12/5/83), Eric (11/5/85)
COLLEGE: Arizona State University (1973, Business)
SPECIAL INTERESTS: All sports, music, auto racing
TURNED PROFESSIONAL: 1973 **Q SCHOOL:** Spring 1975

TOUR VICTORIES (5): 1977 Glen Campbell-Los Angeles Open. **1984** Phoenix Open. **1988** Gatlin Brothers-Southwest Classic. **1991** Southwestern Bell Colonial, NEC World Series of Golf

1995 BEST FINISHES: T12—Northern Telecom Open, Phoenix Open

1995 SEASON: Began year with best two starts of campaign in home state...fired an opening 65 in Northern Telecom Open to share first-round lead with Phil Mickelson...fell off the pace next two days, but a closing 69 earned T12 finish...following week claimed another T12 in the Phoenix Open...alternated 69s and 68s for 274 total...was only event of the year in which he posted four sub-70 rounds...later in season carded three rounds of 69 to finish T17 in Buick Open...other top-25 finish was T18 in Anheuser-Busch Golf Classic...No. 144 money list finish his lowest since partial first-year season of 1975...low round of the year was 65, which he carded three times (also second round GTE Byron Nelson Classic, third round Greater Milwaukee Open).

CAREER HIGHLIGHTS: Won twice in 1991, when he finished fourth on the money list...victories in that best season of his 21 on TOUR came in Southwestern Bell Colonial and NEC World Series of Golf...World Series victory came in playoff with Jim Gallagher, Jr., and Davis Love III...win at age 39 gave him 10-year TOUR exemption...victory, worth $216,000, carries him to threshold of Senior TOUR...in 1991 Northern Telecom Open tied with Bob Tway, one stroke behind amateur winner Phil Mickelson...since Mickelson could not accept prize money, runners-up collected $144,000 each...first victory came in 1977 Glen Campbell-Los Angeles Open...next win came on home turf, 1984 Phoenix Open...also captured 1988 Southwest Classic in playoff with Mark Brooks...1972 Arizona State Amateur and Southwest Open champion...winner 1986 JCPenney Mixed Team Classic (with Juli Inkster)...won 1993 Fred Meyer Challenge (with Steve Elkington).

PERSONAL: Married wife Lori on idyllic Maui during 1994 Lincoln-Mercury Kapalua International...often described as having "sweetest" swing on TOUR...played high school football before started to concentrate on golf...went to Arizona State and became one of better collegiate players...brother Paul played TOUR for a while...close friend of future baseball Hall of Famer Robin Yount.

TOM PURTZER...*continued*

CAREER SUMMARY					PLAYOFF RECORD: 2-0				
Year	**Events Played**	**Cuts Made**	**1st**	**2nd**	**3rd**	**Top 10**	**Top 25**	**Earnings**	**Rank**
1975	9	5						$2,093	194
1976	21	12			1	1	6	$26,682	82
1977	32	14	1		1	4	7	$79,337	37
1978	31	24				6	12	$58,618	55
1979	31	25		1		6	17	$113,270	30
1980	29	18		2		5	10	$118,185	34
1981	30	24			3	6	13	$122,812	27
1982	29	25				4	15	$100,118	36
1983	27	20				4	12	$103,261	55
1984	29	20	1			2	10	$164,244	39
1985	26	18					3	$49,979	119
1986	31	26				10	17	$218,280	37
1987	26	21				1	8	$123,287	85
1988	24	17	1			3	7	$197,740	57
1989	24	16				2	7	$154,868	88
1990	24	15			1	3	10	$285,176	49
1991	25	19	2	1		4	11	$750,568	4
1992	25	18				1	6	$166,722	93
1993	21	10				1	5	$107,570	136
1994	22	13			1	2	7	$187,307	94
1995	19	12					4	$120,717	144
Total	525	372	5	4	7	65	187	$3,247,596	52

1996 PGA TOUR CHARITY TEAM: Doral-Ryder Open

TOP TOURNAMENT SUMMARY

YEAR	**76**	**77**	**78**	**79**	**80**	**81**	**82**	**83**	**84**	**85**	**86**	**87**	**88**	**89**	**90**
Masters Tournament		T37		32				T25	CUT				T24	T45	
U.S. Open	T44	4	T24	8	CUT	CUT	CUT		T16			T68			
British Open Championship							T4	CUT							
PGA Championship		T54		CUT	T19	T16	CUT	CUT		CUT	T47	CUT	T53	T31	
THE PLAYERS Championship		T59			CUT	T19	CUT	T19	T41	T40	T48	T9	T45	T55	T3

TOP TOURNAMENT SUMMARY (cont.)

YEAR	**91**	**92**	**93**	**94**	**95**
Masters Tournament		T61			
U.S. Open	T37	T33			
British Open Championship		T22	T70		
PGA Championship	T32	T21			
THE PLAYERS Championship	CUT	CUT	CUT	CUT	CUT
THE TOUR Championship	29				

NATIONAL TEAMS: U.S. vs. Japan, 1979 (medalist); Four Tours Championship, 1991

1995 PGA TOUR STATISTICS		
Scoring	**70.95**	**(64T)**
Driving	**275.3**	**(13)**
Driving Accuracy	**65.5**	**(148T)**
Greens in Regulation	**70.4**	**(9T)**
Putting	**1.802**	**(133T)**
All Around	**813**	**(122)**
Sand Saves	**46.3**	**(160)**
Total Driving	**161**	**(59T)**
Eagles	**4**	**(116T)**
Birdies	**197**	**(170T)**

MISCELLANEOUS STATISTICS		
Scoring Avg Before Cut	**70.95**	**(65T)**
Scoring Avg 3rd Rnd	**70.45**	**(49T)**
Scoring Avg Final Rnd	**70.10**	**(14)**
Birdies Conversion %	**27.1**	**(136T)**
Par Breakers	**19.4**	**(85T)**

1995 Low Round: **65:** 3 times, most recent 1995 Greater Milwaukee Open/3
Career Low Round: **62:** 1988 Seiko Tucson/2
Career Largest Paycheck: $216,000: 2 times, most recent 1991 Southwestern Bell/1

Mike Reid

EXEMPT STATUS: Winner, 1988 NEC World Series of Golf
FULL NAME: Michael Daniel Reid
HEIGHT: 5' 11" **WEIGHT:** 160
BIRTH DATE: July 1, 1954 **BIRTHPLACE:** Bainbridge, MD
RESIDENCE: Provo, UT
FAMILY: Wife, Randolyn; Brendalyn (2/3/81), Lauren Michelle (8/14/83), Michael Daniel (10/2/86), Clarissa Ann (5/27/90), John William (9/29/93)
COLLEGE: Brigham Young University
SPECIAL INTERESTS: Snow skiing, family activities, fishing
TURNED PROFESSIONAL: 1976 **Q SCHOOL:** Fall 1976

TOUR VICTORIES (2): 1987 Seiko Tucson Open. **1988** NEC World Series of Golf.

INTERNATIONAL VICTORIES (1): 1990 Casio World Open (Japan).

BEST 1995 FINISHES: T4—Walt Disney World/Oldsmobile Classic; T9—Nissan Classic

1995 SEASON: Fell out of the top 125 for the first time in career, other than injury-impacted 1993 season, despite making 23 starts, his most since 1992...started slowly by missing first three cuts, but picked up pace at Nissan Open...carded four 69s to claim a T9...experienced three streaks where he was out of the money for three consecutive events...highlight of year came late in season, T4 at Walt Disney World/Oldsmobile Classic...posted rounds of 68-66-67 in rain-shortened event...lost ball for first time in career during opening round AT&T Pebble Beach National Pro-Am...low round of year was a 64 in the fourth round of the Bob Hope Chrysler Classic.

CAREER HIGHLIGHTS: Missed most of 1993 after suffering separated tendon, sustained while playing table tennis in Japan in late 1992...after resting what initially was diagnosed as chip fracture of right wrist for the early stages of '93, attempted mid-March return to action...after making just five appearances/one cut through early May, further examination revealed the separated tendon, which was surgically repaired...two career victories came in back-to-back years, with first setting up second...after 10 winless years on TOUR, finally broke through in 11th season, winning 1987 Seiko Tucson Open...Tucson triumph provided entry into 1988 NEC World Series of Golf, which he won in playoff with Tom Watson...par on first extra hole was good for title and 10-year TOUR exemption...another freak injury, this one to his back, curtailed play from late March to early June 1991...winner 1983-85 Utah Opens...teamed with Bob Goalby to win 1983 Shootout at Jeremy Ranch in Park City, UT (Senior PGA TOUR event)...one of TOUR's straightest drivers...low amateur 1976 U.S. Open...1976 Western Athletic Conference champion...winner 1976 Pacific Coast Amateur...collegiate All-American 1974-75.

PERSONAL: Earned nickname "Radar" thanks to his accuracy off the tee...brother is TPC at Sawgrass General Manager Bill Reid.

PGA TOUR CAREER SUMMARY **PLAYOFF RECORD: 1-2**

Year	Events Played	Cuts Made	1st	2nd	3rd	Top 10	Top 25	Earnings	Rank
1976(Am.)	1	1							
1977	35	23				1	7	$26,314	90
1978	27	16		1		2	4	$37,420	79
1979	31	25			1	1	13	$64,046	66
1980	28	27			4	13	16	$206,097	9
1981	26	19			1	5	12	$93,037	44
1982	26	22			1	3	9	$80,167	51
1983	24	17				4	10	$99,135	58
1984	26	22			2	4	12	$134,672	49
1985	26	22		2		3	11	$169,871	40
1986	25	20			1	3	10	$135,143	66
1987	30	20	1			6	13	$365,334	24
1988	23	18	1	1	1	5	10	$533,343	15
1989	22	17		1	1	7	9	$401,665	28
1990	19	14		1		3	5	$249,148	60
1991	20	15				2	5	$152,678	98
1992	25	15			1	1	3	$121,376	117
1993	5	1						$5,125	270
1994	22	13				2	6	$154,441	119
1995	23	9				2	2	$102,809	159
Total	464	336	2	6	13	67	157	$3,130,718	55

MIKE REID...continued

NIKE TOUR SUMMARY

Year	Events Played	Cuts Made	1st	2nd	3rd	Top 10	Top 25	Earnings	Rank
1990	1	1				1	1	$2,500	156
Total	1	1				1	1	$2,500	
COMBINED TOTAL MONEY								$3,133,218	

1996 PGA TOUR CHARITY TEAM: Walt Disney World/Oldsmobile Classic

TOP TOURNAMENT SUMMARY

YEAR	76	77	78	79	80	81	82	83	84	85	86	87	88	89	90
Masters Tournament						CUT							CUT	6	CUT
U.S. Open	T50			T25	T6	T20	CUT	T43	T52	T23	T24	CUT	CUT	CUT	T33
British Open Championship													CUT	T61	T39
PGA Championship					T55		T42	T9	T14	T70	T41	T47	64	T2	T45
THE PLAYERS Championship		T71	T57	T35	T5	CUT	T27	CUT	CUT	T40	CUT	T15	2	T29	T46
THE TOUR Championship												16	T8	30	

TOP TOURNAMENT SUMMARY (cont.)

YEAR	91	92	93	94	95
U.S. Open	T26	CUT			
British Open Championship	T26				
THE PLAYERS Championship		CUT	T67	CUT	CUT

NATIONAL TEAMS: World Cup, 1980; Kirin Cup 1988.

1995 PGA TOUR STATISTICS

Scoring	71.82	(149T)
Driving	250.0	(184T)
Driving Accuracy	73.9	(31T)
Greens in Regulation	65.1	(116T)
Putting	1.831	(185)
All Around	1,102	(173)
Sand Saves	52.9	(87T)
Total Driving	215	(134)
Eagles	1	(174T)
Birdies	182	(176T)

MISCELLANEOUS STATISTICS

Scoring Avg Before Cut	71.69	(143T)
Scoring Avg 3rd Rnd	72.90	(182)
Scoring Avg Final Rnd	71.50	(113T)
Birdies Conversion %	25.0	(174T)
Par Breakers	16.4	(177T)

1995 Low Round: **64:** 1995 Bob Hope Chrysler Classic/4
Career Low Round: **64:** 2 times, most recent 1995 Bob Hope Chrysler Classic/4
Career Largest Paycheck: **$162,000:** 1988 World Series Of Golf/1

LEE RINKER

EXEMPT STATUS: 96th on 1995 money list
FULL NAME: Lee Cross Rinker
HEIGHT: 6' **WEIGHT:** 185
BIRTH DATE: November 10, 1960 **BIRTHPLACE:** Stuart, FL
RESIDENCE: Beavercreek, OH
FAMILY: Wife, Molly; Lee, Jr. (7/21/95)
COLLEGE: Alabama
SPECIAL INTERESTS: Music, Sports
TURNED PROFESSIONAL: 1983 **Q SCHOOL:** 1994

BEST PGA TOUR CAREER FINISH: T6—1995 Greater Milwaukee Open.

BEST NIKE TOUR CAREER FINISH: T2—1994 NIKE TOUR Championship.

BEST PGA TOUR 1995 FINISHES: T6—Greater Milwaukee Open; T7—Walt Disney World/Oldsmobile Golf Classic; T9—LaCantera Texas Open.

LEE RINKER...continued

1995 SEASON: Second trip to PGA TOUR proved to be much more successful than first...three top-10 finishes highlighted 96th-place finish on the money list...middle rounds of 68-67 catalyst for first career top-10, T6 in Greater Milwaukee Open...five starts later, went 68-67-67 in rain-shortened Walt Disney World/Oldsmobile Classic to register a T7...ended season on a high note with T9 at LaCantera Texas Open...career-low 65 in closing round of Bob Hope Chrysler Classic earned T12 finish...equaled that round with 65 in Round 2 of Canon Greater Hartford Open...had one other top-25 placing, T13 in the Honda Classic...closed his year with five consecutive events in the money.

CAREER HIGHLIGHTS: Other full season on TOUR was 1984, when finished 100 places worse on money list (196) than in 1995...played 17 events, with best finish T31 in Miller High-Life Quad Cities Open...experienced success on NIKE TOUR in 1994...posted nine top-10 finishes, including T3 in the season-ending NIKE TOUR Championship...earned exemption to finals of 1994 PGA TOUR Qualifying Tournament via 12th-place finish on the NIKE TOUR money list...took advantage of opportunity, finishing T12 to earn 1995 TOUR card.

PERSONAL: Brother Larry is a PGA TOUR veteran, while sister Laurie Rinker-Graham owns several LPGA victories.

PGA TOUR CAREER SUMMARY — **PLAYOFF RECORD: 0-0**

Year	Events Played	Cuts Made	1st	2nd	3rd	Top 10	Top 25	Earnings	Rank
1983(Am.)	1								
1984	17	6						$6,002	196
1985	2	2						$3,197	216
1991	1								
1992	1	1						$3,000	282
1993	1	1						$11,052	235
1995	29	18				3	5	$187,065	96
Total	52	28				3	5	$210,316	343

NIKE TOUR SUMMARY

Year	Events Played	Cuts Made	1st	2nd	3rd	Top 10	Top 25	Earnings	Rank
1990	1	1						$581	274
1991	2	1				1	1	$3,000	161
1992	4	2				1	1	$4,456	138
1993	1								
1994	26	19		1	2	9	17	$108,229	12
1995	2	2					2	$5,696	152
Total	36	25		1	2	11	21	$121,963	
COMBINED TOTAL MONEY								$332,279	

1996 PGA TOUR CHARITY TEAM: BellSouth Classic

TOP TOURNAMENT SUMMARY

YEAR	83	85	91	92	93
U.S. Open	CUT	T58			T33
PGA Championship			CUT	T56	

1995 PGA TOUR STATISTICS

Scoring	71.20	(91T)
Driving	262.8	(94)
Driving Accuracy	75.4	(25)
Greens in Regulation	68.9	(28T)
Putting	1.816	(169T)
All Around	688	(84)
Sand Saves	46.2	(161T)
Total Driving	119	(17)
Eagles	8	(36T)
Birdies	284	(84T)

MISCELLANEOUS STATISTICS

Scoring Avg Before Cut	70.77	(42)
Scoring Avg 3rd Rnd	72.17	(158T)
Scoring Avg Final Rnd	71.29	(99T)
Birdies Conversion %	25.2	(172)
Par Breakers	17.8	(140T)

1995 Low Round: **65:** 2 times, most recent 1995 Canon Greater Hartford Open/2
Career Low Round: **65:** 2 times, most recent 1995 Canon Greater Hartford Open/2
Career Largest Paycheck: **$32,375:** 1995 Greater Milwaukee Open/T6

1995 NIKE TOUR STATISTICS

Scoring	69.88	(N/A)
Eagles	1	(N/A)
Birdies	28	(N/A)

MISCELLANEOUS NIKE STATISTICS

1995 Low Round: **68:** 1995 NIKE Louisiana Open/1
Career Low Round: **64:** 1994 NIKE Boise Open/3
Career Largest Paycheck: **$19,762:** 1994 NIKE TOUR Championship/T2

Loren Roberts

EXEMPT STATUS: 1995 tournament winner
FULL NAME: Loren Lloyd Roberts
HEIGHT: 6'2" **WEIGHT:** 190
BIRTH DATE: June 24, 1955 **BIRTHPLACE:** San Luis Obispo, CA
RESIDENCE: Germantown, TN
FAMILY: Wife, Kimberly; Alexandria (10/14/86), Addison (10/15/91)
COLLEGE: Cal Poly San Luis Obispo
SPECIAL INTERESTS: Golf
TURNED PROFESSIONAL: 1975 **Q SCHOOL:** Fall 1980, 1982, 1983, 1986, 1987

TOUR VICTORIES (2): 1994 Nestle Invitational. **1995** Nestle Invitational.

BEST 1995 FINISH: 1—Nestle Invitational; T2—Buick Challege; T3—LaCantera Texas Open; T9—GTE Byron Nelson Classic, NEC World Series of Golf.

1995 SEASON: Proved 1994 season was no fluke by having another steller year...became first to successfully defend Nestle Invitational title at Bay Hill...also the first since Calvin Peete (1979, 1982 Greater Milwaukee Open) to win same event for first two career victories...held Nestle lead from second round on, although Brad Faxon briefly did share the lead for a few holes during the final round...bogeyed the final two holes but still won by two strokes...$216,000 paychecks from 1994 and '95 Nestle Invitationals more than he earned in any of his first seven years on TOUR...came close to multi-victory season a couple times...was one stroke off 54-hole lead en route to finishing T2 at Buick Classic...opened with a 64, good for first-round lead at the LaCantera Texas Open...claimed a T3 and $57,200, enough to vault him into the Top 30 and a return to THE TOUR Championship...other top-10 finishes were a pair of T9s at the GTE Byron Nelson Classic and NEC World Series of Golf...performed admirably in first Ryder Cup, posting a 3-1 record in the losing U.S. effort...finished in the money in first 13 starts and in 19 of 23 events...made a 108-foot eagle putt on the ninth hole at Poppy Hills during the AT&T Pebble Beach National Pro-Am...withdrew after first round of U.S. Open after hurting back while marking ball...injury later diagnosed as bulging disc.

CAREER HIGHLIGHTS: Shed title of PGA TOUR money leader without a win with his victory in the 1994 Nestle Invitational...was three strokes off lead going into final day, but won by one over Nick Price, Fuzzy Zoeller and Vijay Singh...had nine top-10 finishes the remainder of the year, with three coming in majors: T5 Masters, T2 U.S. Open and T9 PGA Championship...with T24 in British Open, owned best record in '94 majors...after having chance to win U.S. Open in regulation, lost to Ernie Els on second sudden-death hole following 18-hole playoff...member of U.S. Team in inaugural Presidents Cup...first achieved exempt status in 1984-85, then lost card each of next two seasons...winner 1979 Foot-Joy National Assistant Pro Championship...lost to Fred Couples in playoff at Johnnie Walker World Championship.

PERSONAL: Nicknamed "Boss of the Moss" for his putting prowess...regarded by peers as one of hardest workers on TOUR...donated $10,000 to Arnold Palmer Hospital for Women and Children after winning '94 Nestle Invitational.

CAREER SUMMARY **PLAYOFF RECORD: 0-1**

Year	Events Played	Cuts Made	1st	2nd	3rd	Top 10	Top 25	Earnings	Rank
1981	20	8					2	$8,935	177
1982	2								
1983	24	8						$7,724	189
1984	26	14				3	7	$67,515	87
1985	32	22			1	3	5	$92,761	83
1986	33	20				2	5	$53,655	133
1987	31	13					4	$57,489	138
1988	29	19				3	13	$136,890	89
1989	30	28				5	11	$275,882	46
1990	30	26			1	7	14	$478,522	24
1991	29	23				4	12	$281,174	58
1992	28	23		1	1	3	12	$338,673	43
1993	28	19			1	4	9	$316,506	53
1994	22	19	1	3	1	9	12	$1,015,671	6
1995	23	19	1	1	1	5	10	$678,335	27
Total	387	261	2	5	6	48	116	$3,809,733	39

1996 PGA TOUR CHARITY TEAM: Quad City Classic

TOP TOURNAMENT SUMMARY

YEAR	85	86	87	88	89	90	91	92	93	94	95
Masters Tournament							CUT			T5	T24
U.S. Open	T34		CUT		CUT		T49		T11	T2	W/D
British Open Championship										T24	CUT
PGA Championship	CUT				T34	T5	T27		T28	T9	T58
THE PLAYERS Championship	CUT	T40		CUT	T14	T46	T27	T21	CUT	T14	T34
THE TOUR Championship						T14				T8	11

LOREN ROBERTS...*continued*

NATIONAL TEAMS: Presidents Cup, 1994; Ryder Cup, 1995

1995 PGA TOUR STATISTICS		
Scoring	70.21	(14)
Driving	255.3	(157T)
Driving Accuracy	76.8	(16)
Greens in Regulation	67.2	(61T)
Putting	1.773	(53)
All Around	549	(42T)
Sand Saves	51.6	(102)
Total Driving	173	(75T)
Eagles	7	(51T)
Birdies	277	(95T)

MISCELLANEOUS STATISTICS		
Scoring Avg Before Cut	70.32	(16)
Scoring Avg 3rd Rnd	70.74	(66)
Scoring Avg Final Rnd	70.74	(49)
Birdies Conversion %	28.3	(108T)
Par Breakers	19.0	(96T)

1995 Low Round: **64:** 1995 LaCantera Texas Open/1
Career Low Round: **62:** 1994 MCI Heritage Golf Classic/4
Career Largest Paycheck: $216,000: 2 times, most recent 1994 Nestle Invitational/1

CHARLIE RYMER

EXEMPT STATUS: 103rd on 1995 money list
FULL NAME: Charles Christopher Rymer
HEIGHT: 6'4" **WEIGHT:** 240
BIRTH DATE: December 18, 1967 **BIRTHPLACE:** Cleveland, TN
RESIDENCE: Atlanta, GA
FAMILY: Wife, Carol
COLLEGE: Georgia Tech
SPECIAL INTERESTS: Fly-fishing
TURNED PROFESSIONAL: 1991 **Q SCHOOL:** 1994

BEST PGA TOUR CAREER FINISH: 3— 1995 Shell Houston Open

NIKE TOUR VICTORIES (1): **1994** NIKE South Carolina Classic

BEST 1995 FINISHES: 3—Shell Houston Open; T7—Walt Disney World/Oldsmobile Classic.

1995 SEASON: In first TOUR season proved, besides having a great sense of humor, he can play some golf...burst on the scene with a third at the Shell Houston Open...claimed his best finish of year by carding rounds of 69-69-68 through Saturday...although he closed with 71, the $95,200 paycheck eased his mind about exempt status...finished one stroke out of Payne Stewart/Scott Hoch playoff...placed in the money only 11 of 28 times, but each check averaged $16,400...other top-10 finish was a T7 in the rain-shortened Walt Disney World/Oldsmobile Classic...posted a closing 66 to finish four strokes behind Brad Bryant...career low round is 66, which he recorded three other times, all in first rounds (GTE Byron Nelson, FedEx St. Jude Classic, Las Vegas Invitational)...earned two other top-25 finishes, T22 in United Airlines Hawaiian Open and T21 at the FedEx St. Jude Classic.

CAREER HIGHLIGHTS: Prior to 1995, had played in only two PGA TOUR events and missed cut both times...member of NIKE TOUR in 1994...collected first career title at the NIKE South Carolina Classic...followed victory with playoff loss the next week in NIKE Central Georgia Open...overall, posted four top-10 finishes en route to finishing 21st on NIKE Tour money list...earned PGA TOUR status by finishing T10 at 1994 PGA TOUR Qualifying Tournament...played mini-tours for 3 1/2 years...won 1985 U.S. Junior Amateur Championship.

PERSONAL: Has been known to go into gallery in search of food...was introduced to the sport at age five by his grandparents...teammate of David Duval at Georgia Tech...emceed Shoot-Outs on NIKE TOUR...has worked with sports psychologist Bob Rotella since junior year of college.

PGA TOUR CAREER SUMMARY — **PLAYOFF RECORD: 0-0**

Year	Events Played	Cuts Made	1st	2nd	3rd	Top 10	Top 25	Earnings	Rank
1992	2	1						$1,832	307
1993	1								
1995	28	11			1	2	4	$180,401	103
Total	31	12			1	2	4	$182,233	351

CHARLIE RYMER...*continued*

Year	Events Played	Cuts Made	1st	2nd	3rd	Top 10	Top 25	Earnings	Rank
1993	1	1						$255	290
1994	24	15	1	1		4	7	$75,658	21
1995	2	2				1	2	$9,060	129
Total	27	18	1	1		5	9	$84,973	
COMBINED TOTAL MONEY								$267,206	

1996 PGA TOUR CHARITY TEAM: Buick Classic

TOP TOURNAMENT SUMMARY

YEAR	92
U.S. Open	CUT

1995 PGA TOUR STATISTICS

Scoring	71.56	(121T)
Driving	274.4	(15)
Driving Accuracy	60.9	(178)
Greens in Regulation	66.1	(100T)
Putting	1.793	(105T)
All Around	854	(127)
Sand Saves	43.7	(178)
Total Driving	193	(105T)
Eagles	7	(51T)
Birdies	267	(106T)

1995 NIKE TOUR STATISTICS

Scoring	70.38	(N/A)
Eagles	3	(N/A)
Birdies	35	(N/A)

MISCELLANEOUS STATISTICS

Scoring Avg Before Cut	71.68	(142)
Scoring Avg 3rd Rnd	70.45	(49T)
Scoring Avg Final Rnd	70.80	(57)
Birdies Conversion %	29.9	(52T)
Par Breakers	20.3	(40T)

1995 Low Round: **66:** 4 times, most recent 1995 Las Vegas Invitational/1
Career Low Round: **66:** 2 times, most recent 1995 Las Vegas Invitational/1
Career Largest Paycheck: **$95,200:** 1995 Shell Houston Open/3

MISCELLANEOUS NIKE STATISTICS

1995 Low Round: **67:** 1995 NIKE Louisiana Open/2
Career Low Round: **65:** 2 times, most recent 1994 NIKE Ozarks Open/4
Career Largest Paycheck: **$31,500:** 1994 NIKE South Carolina Classic/1

GENE SAUERS *(SOURS)*

EXEMPT STATUS: 60th on 1995 money list
FULL NAME: Gene Craig Sauers
HEIGHT: 5' 8" **WEIGHT:** 150
BIRTH DATE: August 22, 1962 **BIRTHPLACE:** Savannah,GA
RESIDENCE: Savannah, GA; plays out of Haig Point Club, Daufuskie Island, SC
FAMILY: Wife, Tammy; Gene, Jr. (1/23/89), Rhett (7/16/90), Dylan Thomas (8/30/93)
COLLEGE: Georgia Southern University
SPECIAL INTERESTS: Snow skiing, hunting, sport fishing
TURNED PROFESSIONAL: 1984 **Q SCHOOL:** Fall 1983

TOUR VICTORIES (2): 1986 Bank of Boston Classic. **1989** Hawaiian Open.

1995 BEST FINISHES: T3—THE PLAYERS Championship; 4—FedEx St. Jude Classic

1995 SEASON: Was in position to win several times, but one bad round always managed to hurt his chances...opening 67 placed him one stroke behind leader Corey Pavin at THE PLAYERS Championship...followed with a 72 to tie Pavin atop the leaderboard through 36 holes...after a disappointing third-round 78, carded a closing 68 to earn a T3...$156,000 paycheck was largest of career...tied for 18- and 36-hole leads at the MCI Classic...killed chances of third TOUR victory with a closing 73...one stroke behind

GENE SAUERS...*continued*

Jim Gallagher, Jr., after 54 holes of FedEx St. Jude Classic...again fired a closing 73 to finish fourth...recorded third-round 63, which included a back-side 29, at the TPC at Southwind...put together string of six consecutive events in money from March 5-May 7...during that stretch had one top-10 (THE PLAYERS Championship) and three top-25 finishes (T24 Honda Classic, T13 MCI Classic, T18 BellSouth Classic).

CAREER HIGHLIGHTS: Best year of career, 1992, could have been even better...birdied all four holes of Bob Hope Chrysler Classic playoff, yet lost to John Cook...had share of or outright lead first three rounds of PGA Championship...finished second at Nestle Invitational, nine strokes behind Fred Couples...recorded playoff victory over Blaine McCallister in 1986 Bank of Boston Classic...won rain-shortened 1989 Hawaiian Open...captured 1990 Deposit Guaranty Golf Classic (unofficial)...lost on third playoff hole to Mark Brooks in 1991 Kmart Greater Greensboro Open...along with Hal Sutton, lost playoff to DIcky Pride at 1994 FedEx St. Jude Classic...winner Trans America Athletic Conference title at Georgia Southern.

PERSONAL: Avid sport fisherman who has won a number of fishing tournaments...winner of three Georgia State Opens, one as amateur...youngest son, Dylan Thomas, not named for the Irish poet.

CAREER SUMMARY | **PLAYOFF RECORD: 1-3**

Year	Events Played	Cuts Made	1st	2nd	3rd	Top 10	Top 25	Earnings	Rank
1984	23	13				1	4	$36,537	128
1985	21	12				1	5	$48,526	121
1986	34	28	1			4	9	$199,044	42
1987	32	22		1	1	5	12	$244,655	38
1988	30	23			1	6	11	$280,719	35
1989	24	18	1			4	7	$303,669	38
1990	27	21	1			5	13	$374,485	31
1991	25	17		1	1	5	10	$400,535	37
1992	24	16		3	1	5	9	$434,566	32
1993	28	19					3	$117,608	128
1994	26	18		1		2	4	$250,654	73
1995	23	15			1	2	5	$311,578	60
Total	317	222	3	6	5	40	92	$3,002,576	57

1996 PGA TOUR CHARITY TEAM: Memorial Tournament

TOP TOURNAMENT SUMMARY

YEAR	84	85	86	87	88	89	90	91	92	93	94	95
Masters Tournament				T33		CUT				T34		
U.S. Open	CUT	T58		T58								
British Open Championship						T52						T88
PGA Championship			T30	T24	CUT	T58	CUT	T63	T2	T22		T44
THE PLAYERS Championship		CUT	CUT	T32	T16	T55	T29	T9	CUT	CUT	T51	T3

1995 PGA TOUR STATISTICS

Scoring	71.05	(74)
Driving	262.5	(95T)
Driving Accuracy	67.7	(122T)
Greens in Regulation	65.9	(108T)
Putting	1.740	(3)
All Around	715	(90)
Sand Saves	57.3	(38T)
Total Driving	217	(137T)
Eagles		(184T)
Birdies	279	(91T)

MISCELLANEOUS STATISTICS

Scoring Avg Before Cut	70.47	(22T)
Scoring Avg 3rd Rnd	71.88	(145T)
Scoring Avg Final Rnd	71.94	(149T)
Birdies Conversion %	33.1	(6T)
Par Breakers	20.7	(30T)

1995 Low Round: 63: 1995 FedEx St. Jude Classic/3
Career Low Round: 62: 2 times, most recent 1990 S.W.Bell Colonial/4
Career Largest Paycheck: $156,000: 1995 THE PLAYERS Championship/T3

SCOTT SIMPSON

EXEMPT STATUS: Winner, 1987 U.S. Open
FULL NAME: Scott William Simpson
HEIGHT: 6' 2" **WEIGHT:** 180
BIRTH DATE: Sept. 17, 1955 **BIRTHPLACE:** San Diego, CA
RESIDENCE: San Diego, CA
FAMILY: Wife, Cheryl; Brea Yoshiko (10/10/82), Sean Tokuzo (10/14/86)
COLLEGE: University of Southern California (1978, Business Administration)
SPECIAL INTERESTS: Bible study, family activities, exercise, reading
TURNED PROFESSIONAL: 1977 **Q SCHOOL:** Fall 1978

TOUR VICTORIES (6): 1980 Western Open. **1984** Manufacturers Hanover Westchester Classic. **1987** Greater Greensboro Open, U.S. Open. **1989** BellSouth Atlanta Classic. **1993** GTE Byron Nelson Classic.

INTERNATIONAL VICTORIES (3): 1984 Chunichi Crowns (Jpn), Dunlop Phoenix (Jpn). **1990** Perrier Invitational (Eur).

BEST 1995 FINISHES: 2—Anheuser-Busch Golf Classic; T2—Northern Telecom Open, Motorola Western Open; T4—Nissan Open, TOUR Championship; T8—Freeport-McMoRan Classic.

1995 SEASON: Parlayed three runner-up paychecks and a total of six top-10 finishes into his most lucrative of 17 years on TOUR...made birdie on final hole of Northern Telecom Open, good for a closing 68 and T2 finish, one stroke behind Phil Mickelson...posted third- round 68 to begin final day one stroke off lead, and stayed there...after opening with 70 at the Nissan Open, followed with rounds of 66-68-68 to post a T4...continued solid play the next three weeks with T11s at the Nestle Invitational and THE PLAYERS Championship, followed by a T8 at the Freeport-McMoRan Classic...best two weeks of year came in early July...closed with a 68 to finish T2 in the Motorola Western Open, one stroke behind Billy Mayfair...the next week, a closing 67 left him one stroke short at the Anheuser-Busch Golf Classic...put together a streak of 15 consecutive events in the money from the Bob Hope Chrysler Classic through the A-B Classic...first-round 67 was one stroke off lead at the U.S. Open...last round of year was a 69, which earned a T4 in THE TOUR Championship.

CAREER HIGHLIGHTS: Enjoyed fine year in 1993...captured sixth title by winning GTE Byron Nelson Classic in May...also had T2 in season-ending TOUR Championship at Olympic Club, site of his 1987 U.S. Open championship...battled Tom Watson down stretch to win that Open...on final nine made three birdies and saved par three times from off green to win by one stroke...finished T6 in 1988-89 U.S. Opens...lost Open playoff to Payne Stewart at Hazeltine National in 1991 and lost another playoff to Nick Price in rare Monday finish at 1994 Southwestern Bell Colonial...defeated Bob Tway in playoff to win 1989 BellSouth Atlanta Classic...claimed first title in second year on TOUR, 1980 Western Open...winner 1976-77 NCAA Championships, 1976 Porter Cup, 1975 and 1977 PAC-8 Championships...collegiate All-American 1976-77...winner California and San Diego junior titles...winner 1979, 1981 Hawaii State Opens.

PERSONAL: Traditionally takes family time away from TOUR late in season...he and his family moved back to San Diego in 1994 after a number of years in Hawaii.

CAREER SUMMARY **PLAYOFF RECORD: 1-3**

Year	Events Played	Cuts Made	1st	2nd	3rd	Top 10	Top 25	Earnings	Rank
1976	1	1							
1978	1	1					1	$3,100	186
1979	29	21				2	6	$53,084	74
1980	30	23	1	1		4	10	$141,323	24
1981	30	21		1	1	3	14	$108,793	34
1982	26	21		2		4	12	$146,903	24
1983	26	23		1		5	12	$144,172	38
1984	27	23	1		1	8	14	$248,581	22
1985	26	23			2	5	14	$171,245	39
1986	23	18		1	1	3	9	$202,223	41
1987	25	22	2		1	10	13	$621,032	4
1988	23	13				1	6	$108,301	106
1989	22	15	1			3	7	$298,920	40
1990	20	12		1	1	3	6	$235,309	63
1991	18	14		1	1	3	9	$322,936	51
1992	22	15				1	6	$155,284	97
1993	22	20	1	1	1	5	9	$707,166	14
1994	21	15		1		2	6	$307,884	56
1995	25	19		3		6	12	$795,798	17
Total	417	320	6	13	9	68	166	$4,770,385	27

1996 PGA TOUR CHARITY TEAM: BellSouth Classic

Scott Simpson...*continued*

TOP TOURNAMENT SUMMARY

YEAR	80	81	82	83	84	85	86	87	88	89	90	91	92	93	94	95
Masters Tournament		CUT		11	40	T41	T25	T27	CUT	T38	T7	T22	T13	T11	T27	
U.S. Open	T43	T23	T15	T13	T25	T15	CUT	1	T6	T6	T14	2	T64	T46	T55	T28
British Open Championship							T65	T62		T26	T39	T57		T9	CUT	CUT
PGA Championship	T30	CUT	T32	T9	T6	T12	T41	T47	CUT	T53	T66	CUT		T6	CUT	T54
THE PLAYERS Championship	T51	CUT	T2	T61	T33	T33	CUT	T4	CUT	CUT	CUT		T17	CUT	CUT	T11
THE TOUR Championship								15						T2		T4

NATIONAL TEAMS: Ryder Cup, 1987; Kirin Cup, 1987; Walker Cup, 1977.

1995 PGA TOUR STATISTICS

Scoring	69.99	(9)
Driving	259.7	(122T)
Driving Accuracy	73.1	(44)
Greens in Regulation	70.6	(7)
Putting	1.757	(16T)
All Around	511	(35)
Sand Saves	50.4	(122T)
Total Driving	166	(64T)
Eagles	2	(161T)
Birdies	337	(30)

MISCELLANEOUS STATISTICS

Scoring Avg Before Cut	70.08	(8T)
Scoring Avg 3rd Rnd	70.50	(52T)
Scoring Avg Final Rnd	69.95	(12)
Birdies Conversion %	31.0	(27T)
Par Breakers	21.5	(10T)

1995 Low Round: **65:** 2 times, most recent 1995 FedEx St. Jude Classic/1
Career Low Round: **62:** 1991 U.A. Hawaiian Open/1
Career Largest Paycheck: **$216,000:** 1993 GTE Byron Nelson Classic/1

Joey Sindelar *(SIN-deh-lahr)*

EXEMPT STATUS: 90th on 1995 money list
FULL NAME: Joseph Paul Sindelar
HEIGHT: 5' 10" **WEIGHT:** 200
BIRTH DATE: March 30, 1958 **BIRTHPLACE:** Ft. Knox, KY
RESIDENCE: Horseheads, NY
FAMILY: Wife, Suzanne Lee; Jamison Prescott (2/2/90), Ryan Joseph (5/13/93)
COLLEGE: Ohio State University
SPECIAL INTERESTS: Fishing, electronics
TURNED PROFESSIONAL: 1981 **Q SCHOOL:** Fall 1983

TOUR VICTORIES (6): 1985 Greater Greensboro Open, B.C. Open. **1987** B.C. Open. **1988** Honda Classic, The International. **1990** Hardee's Golf Classic.

1995 BEST FINISHES: T4—Ideon Classic; T6—Greater Milwaukee Open; T7—Quad Cities Open.

1995 SEASON: Started season under a special medical extension...had eight events to earn $31,347 and regain exempt status...fell $6,480 short when he made only three cuts in those eight outings: T32 Buick Invitational, T27 Honda Classic, T27 Shell Houston Open...continued to play as past champion and under sponsor exemptions...rebounded from early disappointment to have a solid year and regain exempt status...in last 16 events placed in top 10 three times...fired 66s in the second and fourth rounds of the Ideon Classic to finish T4...carded low round of year (65) in final round of Greater Milwaukee Open for T4...opened with consecutive 68s on his way to T7 in the B.C. Open.

CAREER HIGHLIGHTS: After 10 TOUR seasons in which worst money-list finish was 94th in 1991, wound up 145th in 1994 due to injury tracing back to 1993...withdrew from 1993 PGA Championship with a wrist injury...diagnosed as fracture of hamate bone, which caused him to miss the remainder of '93...underwent surgery for removal of hook of hamate bone in Feb. 1994...career year was 1988, when he won the Honda Classic and International...has twice won the B.C. Open in front of hometown fans (lives in nearby Horseheads, NY)...first B.C. Open victory came in 1985, the second in 1987...first TOUR victory came in 1985 Greater Greensboro Open...defeated Willie Wood in playoff to win 1990 Hardee's Golf Classic...winner of 10 collegiate titles...member of 1979 NCAA Championship team at Ohio State, which included John Cook...three time All-American.

JOEY SINDELAR...continued

PERSONAL: He and Mike Hulbert have been friends since their childhood days in upstate New York. . . 1992 inductee into Ohio State University Athletic Hall of Fame.

CAREER SUMMARY				PLAYOFF RECORD: 1-1					
Year	**Events Played**	**Cuts Made**	**1st**	**2nd**	**3rd**	**Top 10**	**Top 25**	**Earnings**	**Rank**
1982	2								
1983	3	2					1	$4,696	203
1984	33	23		1		3	9	$116,528	59
1985	33	28	2		1	7	15	$282,762	12
1986	35	29		2	2	7	17	$341,231	14
1987	33	25	1	1		4	10	$235,033	40
1988	30	27	2	2	1	10	16	$813,732	3
1989	28	20				3	9	$196,092	72
1990	27	15	1			3	5	$307,207	46
1991	28	19				2	6	$168,352	94
1992	32	22			1	6	13	$395,354	35
1993	22	14		1	1	5	8	$391,649	38
1994	22	12			1	1	3	$114,563	145
1995	24	14				3	7	$202,896	90
Total	352	250	6	7	7	54	119	$3,570,095	43

1996 PGA TOUR CHARITY TEAM: Bell Canadian Open.

TOP TOURNAMENT SUMMARY												
YEAR	**82**	**84**	**85**	**86**	**87**	**88**	**89**	**90**	**91**	**92**	**93**	**94**
Masters Tournament			T31	CUT	T35	T39	CUT		T46		T27	
U.S. Open	CUT		T15	T15	T51	T17	T33			T6	CUT	
British Open Championship				CUT								
PGA Championship		T62	T28	T53	CUT	CUT	CUT		T63	T56	W/D	
THE PLAYERS Championship		CUT	T27	T17	T63	T16	T34	T46	T41	T46	T16	T35
THE TOUR Championship						T21						

NATOINAL TEAMS: Kirin Cup, 1988; World Cup, 1991.

1995 PGA TOUR STATISTICS		
Scoring	70.90	(63)
Driving	265.9	(68T)
Driving Accuracy	68.2	(113T)
Greens in Regulation	70.3	(11)
Putting	1.804	(136T)
All Around	750	(103)
Sand Saves	42.9	(181T)
Total Driving	181	(87T)
Eagles	8	(36T)
Birdies	235	(142)

MISCELLANEOUS STATISTICS		
Scoring Avg Before Cut	71.33	(101T)
Scoring Avg 3rd Rnd	71.57	(126)
Scoring Avg Final Rnd	69.92	(11)
Birdies Conversion %	26.1	(157T)
Par Breakers	19.0	(96T)

1995 Low Round: **65:** 1995 Greater Milwaukee Open/4
Career Low Round: **62:** 2 times, most recent 1987 Provident Classic/1
Career Largest Paycheck: **$180,000:** 2 times, most recent 1988 The International/1

Did You Know?

Ed Dougherty won his first PGA TOUR event at the 1995 Deposit Guaranty Classic at the age of 47 years, 8 months, 19 days, making him the second-oldest first-time winner in PGA TOUR history. Only John Barnum, who won the 1962 Cajun Classic at age 51 years, 1 month, 5 days, was older.

VIJAY SINGH *(VEE-jay SING)*

EXEMPT STATUS: 1995 tournament winner
FULL NAME: Vijay Singh
HEIGHT: 6' 2" **WEIGHT:** 198
BIRTH DATE: February 22, 1963 **BIRTHPLACE:** Lautoka, Fiji
RESIDENCE: London, England and Ponte Vedra Beach, FL
FAMILY: Wife, Ardena Seth; Qass Seth (6/19/90)
SPECIAL INTERESTS: Snooker, cricket, rugby, soccer
TURNED PROFESSIONAL: 1982 **JOINED TOUR:** Spring 1993

TOUR VICTORIES (3): 1993 Buick Classic. **1995** Phoenix Open, Buick Open.

INTERNATIONAL VICTORIES (16): 1984 Malaysian PGA Championship (Asia). **1988** Nigerian Open (Afr), Swedish PGA. **1989** Volvo Open di Firenze (Eur), Ivory Coast Open (Afr), Nigerian Open (Afr), Zimbabwe Open (Afr). **1990** El Bosque Open (Eur). **1991** King Hassan Trophy (Morocco). **1992** Turespana Masters Open de Andalucia (Eur), Malaysian Open (Asia), Volvo German Open (Eur). **1993** Bells Cup (Afr). **1994** Scandinavian Masters (Eur), Trophee Lancome (Eur). **1995** Passport Open (Asia).

BEST 1995 FINISHES: 1—Phoenix Open, Buick Classic; T4—Kemper Open, NEC World Series of Golf; 6—THE TOUR Championship; T6—British Open; T7—Kmart Greater Greensboro Open; T8—Shell Houston Open; T10—U.S. Open

1995 SEASON: Recovered strongly from back and neck problems that caused him to miss most of the second half of the 1994 season...surpassed $1 million in earnings for the first time in his career...went over that plateau with a sixth-place finish at the season-ending TOUR Championship...consecutive 66s on the weekend put him in a playoff with Billy Mayfair at the Phoenix Open...won the playoff with a par on the first extra hole...earned his second title of the year, and the third of his career, in May at the Buick Classic...defeated Doug Martin with a birdie on the fifth hole of their playoff...birdie was his first of the day, and it came on his 23rd hole...five-hole affair was the longest on TOUR since it took seven holes to determine champion at 1991 New England Classic...it was Singh's first appearance at Westchester CC since he won there as a rookie in 1993...the first player since Corey Pavin in 1991 to win two playoffs in a single season...Buick Classic win came in the midst of a streak of five top-10 finishes in six events...lost playoff to Fred Couples at Johnnie Walker World Championship.

CAREER HIGHLIGHTS: PGA TOUR Rookie of Year for 1993, when he won Buick Classic in playoff with Mark Wiebe...birdied third extra hole for win...held second-round lead in '93 PGA Championship after Inverness Club record 63...63 equaled lowest 18-hole score in PGA Championship, as well as low 18 in any major...tied PGA 36-hole record of 131 (had opened with 68)...made cut in first 11 PGA TOUR events, first seven of 1993 and four in 1992...gained special temporary membership with T2 finish in '93 Nestle Invitational...winner of 15 events outside U.S., first title came in 1984 Malaysian PGA Championship...joined PGA European Tour in 1989, winning Volvo Open in rookie season...most recent European Tour victories came in 1994 when he captured Scandinavian Masters in July and Lancome Trophy in September...opened with rounds of 65-63—128 in latter, needed birdies on two of final three holes to beat Miguel Angel Jimenez...has captured titles in Nigeria, Sweden, Zimbabwe, Spain, Germany, the Ivory Coast and Morocco...led Order of Merit of Safari Tour in Africa in 1988...only non-Swede to win Swedish PGA (1988).

PERSONAL: Only world-class golfer produced by Fiji...of Indian ancestry, name means "Victory" in Hindi...Tom Weiskopf was golfing role model...one of TOUR's hardest workers, learned basics of game from father, an airplane technician who also taught golf...left Fiji to pursue dream of becoming professional golfer, tried Australian Tour, later took club job in Malaysia.

CAREER SUMMARY **PLAYOFF RECORD: 3-0**

Year	Events Played	Cuts Made	1st	2nd	3rd	Top 10	Top 25	Earnings	Rank
1992	4	4				1	3	$70,680	156
1993	14	12	1	1		6	10	$657,831	19
1994	21	16		2		3	7	$325,959	52
1995	22	17	2			9	13	$1,018,713	9
Total	61	49	3	3		19	33	$2,073,183	97

1996 PGA TOUR CHARITY TEAM: Buick Classic.

TOP TOURNAMENT SUMMARY

YEAR	89	90	91	92	93	94	95
Masters Tournament						T27	CUT
U.S. Open					CUT		T10
British Open Championship	T23	T12	T12	T51	T59	T20	T6
PGA Championship				T48	4	CUT	CUT
THE PLAYERS Championship					T28	T55	T43
THE TOUR Championship					T16		6

VIJAY SINGH...continued

NATIONAL TEAMS: Presidents Cup, 1994

1995 PGA TOUR STATISTICS		
Scoring	69.92	(7)
Driving	283.5	(4)
Driving Accuracy	65.5	(148T)
Greens in Regulation	66.0	(106T)
Putting	1.814	(165T)
All Around	652	(72)
Sand Saves	52.1	(97)
Total Driving	152	(47)
Eagles	11	(12T)
Birdies	263	(113)

MISCELLANEOUS STATISTICS		
Scoring Avg Before Cut	70.84	(49)
Scoring Avg 3rd Rnd	70.44	(46T)
Scoring Avg Final Rnd	71.29	(99T)
Birdies Conversion %	29.5	(68T)
Par Breakers	19.3	(89T)

1995 Low Round: **65:** 3 times, most recent 1995 NEC World Series of Golf/3
Career Low Round: **63:** 1993 PGA Championship/2
Career Largest Paycheck: **$234,000:** 1995 Phoenix Open/1

JEFF SLUMAN *(SLEW-mun)*

EXEMPT STATUS: Winner, 1988 PGA Championship
FULL NAME: Jeffrey George Sluman
HEIGHT: 5' 7" **WEIGHT:** 140
BIRTH DATE: Sept. 11, 1957 **BIRTHPLACE:** Rochester, NY
RESIDENCE: Chicago, IL
FAMILY: Wife, Linda
COLLEGE: Florida State University (1980, Finance)
SPECIAL INTERESTS: Old cars, stock market, Akitas
TURNED PROFESSIONAL: 1980 **Q SCHOOL:** Fall 1982, 1984

TOUR VICTORIES (1): 1988 PGA Championship

BEST 1995 FINISHES: T2—Kmart Greater Greensboro Open; T3—Buick Open; Greater Milwaukee Open; T4—Buick Challenge; T7—B.C. Open; T8—Anheuser-Busch Golf Classic, PGA Championship.

1995 SEASON: Nearly added his second career PGA TOUR win in April at the Kmart Greater Greensboro Open...rounds of 70-65-66 gave him a two-stroke lead, but a 74 on Sunday left him and Peter Jacobsen a stroke behind winner Jim Gallagher, Jr...drove from Greensboro to Pinehurst after the third round to attend his sister-in-law's wedding reception...runner-up finish was the eighth of his career. . . next top-10 finish came in July when he tied for eighth at the Anheuser-Busch Golf Classic...another eighth-place tie at the PGA Championship was sandwiched between third-place ties at the Buick Open and the Greater Milwaukee Open...at the Buick Open, missed a spot in the Woody Austin/Mike Brisky playoff by one stroke. . . had back-to-back top-10 placings at the B.C. Open (T7) and the Buick Challenge (T4)...earnings of $563,681 surpassed only by the $729,027 he earned in 1992. . . missed qualifying for THE TOUR Championship by only $19.

CAREER HIGHLIGHTS: Recorded one of great finishing rounds in PGA Championship history to win 1988 title...started day three strokes behind Paul Azinger, fired 6-under-par 65 at Oak Tree Golf Club to win by three over Azinger...nearly won twice in 1991, losing playoff to Billy Andrade in Kemper Open and finishing second by stroke to Ted Schulz in Nissan Los Angeles Open...1992 season punctuated by remarkable accomplishments, including final-round 71 and second-place finish in U.S. Open at Pebble Beach (just one of four sub-par rounds that day)...had T4 in Masters, where became first player to ace fourth hole during opening-round 65 that produced tie for lead...held lead through first three rounds of the 1994 B.C. Open, closed with 72 to finish four strokes behind Mike Sullivan...opened with 63 at En-Joie GC, then led Sullivan through Rounds 2 and 3 before stumbling final day...first close encounter with victory came in 1987 Tournament Players Championship, where lost three-hole playoff to Sandy Lyle...had unofficial victory in 1985 Tallahassee Open, part of Tournament Players Series...winner 1980 Metro Conference Championship.

PERSONAL: Former Player Director, PGA TOUR Policy Board...is good friends with 1986 Indy 500 winner Bobby Rahal...their friendship began after they were paired together in the 1987 AT&T Pebble Beach National Pro-Am.

JEFF SLUMAN...*continued*

CAREER SUMMARY — **PLAYOFF RECORD: 0-3**

Year	Events Played	Cuts Made	1st	2nd	3rd	Top 10	Top 25	Earnings	Rank
1983	19	11					2	$13,643	171
1984	1	1						$603	282
1985	25	18				4	10	$100,523	78
1986	34	24				7	12	$154,129	60
1987	32	22		2		6	11	$335,590	27
1988	32	30	1		1	6	15	$503,321	18
1989	23	16				4	6	$154,507	89
1990	31	22		1		2	6	$264,012	56
1991	30	24		2		7	13	$552,979	23
1992	30	26		2	1	8	17	$729,027	14
1993	27	21				1	6	$187,841	93
1994	30	16		1		4	8	$301,178	59
1995	29	20		1	2	7	12	$563,681	31
Total	343	251	1	9	4	56	118	$3,861,034	36

1996 PGA TOUR CHARITY TEAM: Walt Disney World/Oldsmobile Classic

TOP TOURNAMENT SUMMARY

YEAR	86	87	88	89	90	91	92	93	94	95
Masters Tournament			T45	T8	T27	T29	T4	T17	T25	T41
U.S. Open	T62		CUT	CUT	T14	CUT	2	T11	T9	T13
British Open Championship				CUT	T25	T101	CUT	CUT		
PGA Championship	T30	T14	1	T24	T31	T61	T12	T61	T25	T8
THE PLAYERS Championship	T40	2	T45	CUT	CUT	CUT	T40	T46	CUT	T49
THE TOUR Championship		T27	T26			T10	T13			

1995 PGA TOUR STATISTICS

Statistic	Value	Rank
Scoring	70.34	(27T)
Driving	266.1	(66T)
Driving Accuracy	69.1	(102T)
Greens in Regulation	68.0	(45T)
Putting	1.768	(38)
All Around	326	(2)
Sand Saves	60.8	(10)
Total Driving	168	(67T)
Eagles	9	(20T)
Birdies	353	(18T)

MISCELLANEOUS STATISTICS

Statistic	Value	Rank
Scoring Avg Before Cut	70.50	(25T)
Scoring Avg 3rd Rnd	69.95	(18)
Scoring Avg Final Rnd	70.70	(41T)
Birdies Conversion %	28.6	(95T)
Par Breakers	19.9	(62T)

1995 Low Round: **65:** 2 times, most recent 1995 Greater Milwaukee Open/3
Career Low Round: **62:** 1992 GTE Byron Nelson Cl./3
Career Largest Paycheck: **$160,000:** 1988 PGA Championship/1

Did You Know?

By adding the 1995 Nestle Invitational title to his win there in 1994, Loren Roberts became the first player in 13 years to have his first two career victories come in the same event. In 1982, Calvin Peete earned his second TOUR win at the Greater Milwaukee Open. Three years earlier, Peete had captured his first TOUR title at the GMO.

SAM SNEAD

EXEMPT STATUS: Winner, 1942 PGA Championship
FULL NAME: Samuel Jackson Snead
HEIGHT: 5' 11" **WEIGHT:** 190
BIRTH DATE: May 27, 1912 **BIRTHPLACE:** Hot Springs, VA
RESIDENCE: Hot Springs, VA; represents The Greenbrier, White Sulphur Springs, WV
FAMILY: Sam, Jr. (6/30/44), Terrance (5/27/52), 2 grandchildren
SPECIAL INTERESTS: Hunting, fishing
TURNED PROFESSIONAL: 1934 **JOINED TOUR:** 1937

TOUR VICTORIES (81): 1936 West Virginia PGA. **1937** Oakland Open, Bing Crosby Pro-Am, St. Paul Open, Nassau Open, Miami Open. **1938** Bing Crosby Pro-Am, Greensboro Open, Inverness Four-Ball, Goodall Round Robin, Chicago Open,Canadian Open, Westchester 108 Hole Open, White Sulphur Springs Open. **1939** St. Petersburg Open, Miami Biltmore Four-Ball, Miami Open. **1940** Inverness Four-Ball, Canadian Open, Anthracite Open.**1941** Bing Crosby Pro-Am, St. Petersburg Open, North and South Open, Canadian Open, Rochester Times Union Open, Henry Hurst Invitational. **1942** St. Petersburg Open, PGA Championship. **1944** Portland Open, Richmond Open. **1945** Los Angeles Open, Gulfport Open, Pensacola Open, Jacksonville Open, Dallas Open,Tulsa Open. **1946** Jacksonville Open, Greensboro Open, Virginia Open, World Championship, Miami Open. **1948** Texas Open. **1949** Greensboro Open, Masters, PGA Championship, Washington Star Open, Dapper Dan Open, Western Open. **1950** Bing Crosby Pro-Am, Los Angeles Open, Texas Open, Miami Beach Open, Greensboro Open, Western Open, Colonial National Invitational, Inverness Four-Ball, Reading Open, Miami Open . **1951** PGA Championship, Miami Open. **1952** Masters, Palm Beach Round Robin, Inverness Four-Ball, All American, Eastern Open. **1953** Baton Rouge Open. **1954** Masters, Palm Beach Round Robin. **1955** Greensboro Open, Palm Beach Round Robin, Insurance City Open, Miami Open.**1956** Greensboro Open. **1957** Palm Beach Round Robin, Dallas Open. **1958** Dallas Open. **1960** De Soto Open, Greensboro Open. **1961** Tournament of Champions. **1965** Greensboro Open.

SENIOR VICTORIES (14): 1964, 1965, 1967, 1970, 1972, 1973 PGA Seniors'. **1964, 1965, 1970, 1972, 1973** World Seniors. **1978** Legends of Golf (with Gardner Dickinson). **1980** Golf Digest Commemorative Pro-Am. **1982** Legends of Golf (with Don January).

1995 SEASON: In his only start on the Senior PGA TOUR in 1995, teamed with Johnny Bulla to finish tied for sixth in the Demaret Division of the Liberty Mutual Legends of Golf...earned $5,000.

CAREER HIGHLIGHTS: The all-time leader with 81 career PGA TOUR victories...independent record keepers have credited him with 135 worldwide victories...won the PGA Championship three times, in 1942, 1949 and 1951...won the Masters in 1949 and 1952 and the British Open in 1946...holds the TOUR record for most victories in a single event with eight Greater Greensboro Open titles...won in Greensboro in 1938, 1946, 1949, 1950, 1955, 1956, 1960 and in 1965...when he won in 1965 he was 52 years, 10 months, 8 days old, making him the oldest player to ever win on the PGA TOUR...won the Miami Open six times...won 11 times in 1950, the third highest yearly total in TOUR history...in the 1979 Quad Cities Open he became the youngest PGA TOUR player to ever shoot his age...at age 67, he matched his age in the second round and then bettered it by one stroke in the final round...has won 14 unofficial Senior TOUR titles, including the PGA Seniors' Championship six times (1964-65, 1967, 1970, 1972-73)...won the World Seniors title five times...captured the 1980 Golf Digest Commemorative...teamed with Gardner Dickinson to win the 1978 Legends of Golf and with Don January to win the 1982 Legends...member of the 1937, 1947, 1949, 1951, 1953, 1955 and 1959 Ryder Cup teams...was Ryder Cup team captain in 1951, 1959 and 1969...member of four World Cup winning teams, 1956, 1960-62 (won individual title 1961).

CAREER SUMMARY **PLAYOFF RECORD: 10-8**

Year	Money	Postion	Year	Money	Postion	Year	Money	Postion
1937	$10,243	3	1952	$19,908	4	1966	$12,109	72
1938	$19,534	1	1953	$14,115	15	1967	$7,141	104
1939	$9,712	2	1954	$7,889	29	1968	$43,106	39
1940	$9,206	3	1955	$23,464	7	1969	$15,439	100
1941	$12,848	2	1956	$8,253	36	1970	$25,103	85
1942	$8,078	3	1957	$28,260	4	1971	$22,258	94
1944	$5,755	7	1958	$15,905	18	1972	$35,462	71
1945	$24,436	4	1959	$8,222	45	1973	$38,685	78
1946	$18,341	6	1960	$19,405	19	1974	$55,562	49
1947	$9,703	12	1961	$23,906	17	1975	$8,285	138
1948	$6,980	18	1962	$9,169	59	1976	$2,694	198
1949	$31,593	1	1963	$28,431	16	1977	$488	256
1950	$35,758	1	1964	$8,383	74	1978	$385	265
1951	$15,072	6	1965	$36,889	24	1979	$4,671	190

CAREER EARNINGS: $620,126
COMBINED CAREER EARNINGS: $726,700

Career Low Round: 60: 1957 Dallas Open/2
Career Largest Paycheck: $28,000/1968 Greater Milwaukee/2

Mike Springer

EXEMPT STATUS: 1994 tournament winner
FULL NAME: Michael Paul Springer
HEIGHT: 5'11" **WEIGHT:** 210
BIRTH DATE: Nov. 3, 1965 **BIRTHPLACE:** San Francisco, CA
RESIDENCE: Fresno, CA; plays out of Fort Washington CC
FAMILY: Wife, Crystol; Haylee Danielle (5/26/93), Cody (8/24/95)
COLLEGE: University of Arizona
SPECIAL INTERESTS: Hunting, skiing
TURNED PROFESSIONAL: 1988 **JOINED TOUR:** 1991

TOUR VICTORIES (2): 1994 Kmart Greater Greensboro Open, Greater Milwaukee Open.

NIKE TOUR VICTORIES (4): 1990 Bakersfield Open, Ben Hogan Reno Open, El Paso Open. 1992 BH Fresno Open

BEST 1995 FINISH: T20—NEC World Series of Golf

1995 SEASON: Trouble with his driver led to his lowest money list finish...fell from 13th on the money list in 1994 to 206th..."I've been putting and chipping well. But you can't play golf from where I've been driving it" is how he described his troubles...did finish the season on a positive note, making the cut in three of his final five tournaments...prior to T20 in the NEC World Series of Golf, his best finish of the year, had gone 17 tournaments without making a cut...posted his best score of the year, 66, in consecutive rounds: the final round of the B.C. Open and the first round of the Las Vegas Invitational.

CAREER HIGHLIGHTS: Truly had "Greater" season in 1994, winning both Kmart Greater Greensboro Open and Greater Milwaukee Open...final earnings total more than first three years combined...GGO win, first on TOUR, was a wire-to-wire effort...held four-stroke lead after both 36 and 54 holes, finished three in front of Ed Humenik, Hale Irwin and Brad Bryant...win was worth $270,000...GMO victory took different form, since didn't taste lead until late on final day...began Sunday three strokes behind Bob Estes, closed one in front of Loren Roberts after final-round 67...battled left elbow and wrist problems virtually entire 1993 season, missing 16 cuts and failing to either finish or even start 14 of final 19 tournaments...diagnosis: elbow and wrist out of alignment, for which had periodic chiropractic adjustment...still managed to finish 79th on money list...best placing T3 in Phoenix Open...T2 in 1992 Kemper Open, one shot behind winner Bill Glasson...trailed only John Daly, Jeff Maggert and Scott Gump in 1991 rookie earnings with $178,587...finished third in '91 BellSouth Atlanta Classic, missing eagle putt on final hole to finish stroke out of Corey Pavin-Steve Pate playoff...earned TOUR membership by finishing fourth on 1990 Ben Hogan Tour money list...won first-ever Hogan Tour event at Bakersfield, closed inaugural campaign by winning two of final three tournaments--Reno and El Paso Opens--to finish in top five...1986-88 Second-Team All-America selection at University of Arizona...Arizona teammates included Robert Gamez.

PERSONAL: Has priorities in order...was delayed arriving in Milwaukee for 1995 defense of 1994 GMO title due to birth of second child the week before.

PGA TOUR CAREER SUMMARY **PLAYOFF RECORD: 0-0**

Year	Events Played	Cuts Made	1st	2nd	3rd	Top 10	Top 25	Earnings	Rank
1987(Am.)	1	1				1	1		
1988(Am.)	1	1							
1988	1								
1991	28	17			1	3	6	$178,587	91
1992	30	13		1		2	4	$144,316	104
1993	27	14			1	4	5	$214,729	79
1994	24	17	2		1	5	9	$770,717	13
1995	28	6					1	$55,146	198
Total	140	69	2	1	3	15	26	$1,363,496	148

NIKE TOUR SUMMARY

Year	Events Played	Cuts Made	1st	2nd	3rd	Top 10	Top 25	Earnings	Rank
1990	26	12	3	1		6	9	$82,906	4
1992	1	1	1			1	1	$30,000	53
Total	27	13	4	1		7	10	$112,906	
COMBINED TOTAL MONEY								$1,476,401	

1996 PGA TOUR CHARITY TEAM: Buick Open.

MIKE SPRINGER...*continued*

TOP TOURNAMENT SUMMARY

YEAR	92	93	94	95
Masters Tournament				CUT
U.S. Open		CUT	T25	CUT
British Open Championship			T24	CUT
PGA Championship		CUT	T55	CUT
THE PLAYERS Championship	CUT	CUT	13	CUT
THE TOUR Championship			T17	

1995 PGA TOUR STATISTICS

Scoring	73.14	(188)
Driving	261.9	(102T)
Driving Accuracy	54.6	(188)
Greens in Regulation	57.4	(188)
Putting	1.812	(161T)
All Around	1,308	(188)
Sand Saves	44.8	(170T)
Total Driving	290	(181)
Eagles	3	(137T)
Birdies	189	(174)

MISCELLANEOUS STATISTICS

Scoring Avg Before Cut	73.62	(188)
Scoring Avg 3rd Rnd	74.50	(188)
Scoring Avg Final Rnd	70.67	(37)
Birdies Conversion %	28.3	(108T)
Par Breakers	16.0	(183T)

1995 Low Round: **66:** 2 times, most recent 1995 Las Vegas Invitational/1
Career Low Round: **63:** 2 times, most recent 1992 Bob Hope Chrysler/3
Career Largest Paycheck: **$270,000:** 1994 Kmart Greater Greensboro Open/1

CRAIG STADLER

EXEMPT STATUS: Winner, 1992 NEC World Series of Golf
FULL NAME: Craig Robert Stadler
HEIGHT: 5' 10" **WEIGHT:** 210
BIRTH DATE: June 2, 1953 **BIRTHPLACE:** San Diego, CA
RESIDENCE: Denver, CO
FAMILY: Wife, Sue; Kevin (2/5/80), Christopher (11/23/82)
COLLEGE: University of Southern California
SPECIAL INTERESTS: Snow skiing, hunting
TURNED PROFESSIONAL: 1975 **Q SCHOOL:** Spring 1976

TOUR VICTORIES (11): 1980 Bob Hope Desert Classic, Greater Greensboro Open. **1981** Kemper Open. **1982** Joe Garagiola-Tucson Open, Masters Tournament, Kemper Open, World Series of Golf. **1984** Byron Nelson Classic. **1991** THE TOUR Championship. **1992** NEC World Series of Golf. **1994** Buick Invitational of California

INTERNATIONAL VICTORIES (4): 1985 Canon European Masters (Eur). **1987** Dunlop Phoenix (Jpn). **1990** Scandinavian Enterprise Open (Eur). **1992** Argentine Open.

BEST 1995 FINISHES: T3—B.C. Open; 4—Mercedes Championships; T4—Nissan Open; T8—PGA Championship.

1995 SEASON: Earned more than $400,000 for the fifth consecutive season...started the year with a solo fourth-place finish in the Mercedes Championships, the first of four 1995 top-10 finishes...final round 1-under-par 71 at La Costa began a stretch of 17 consecutive rounds of par or better...finished T4 in the Nissan Open at Riviera CC...had the first hole-in-one of his PGA TOUR career at the sixth hole during the third round...added another top-10 at Riviera in August when T8 at the PGA Championship...best finish of the season was a T3 at the B.C. Open...was one-stroke back after 54 holes before he was passed by Hal Sutton's final-round 61 and Jim McGovern's 63...surpassed the $6 million mark in career earnings with $58,000 paycheck at B.C. Open.

CAREER HIGHLIGHTS: Earned his 11th career title in his hometown of San Diego in the 1994 Buick Invitational of California...trailed runner-up Steve Lowery by one stroke after 54 holes before a final-round 6-under-par 66 gave him a one-stroke victory...captured NEC World Series of Golf in 1992, 10 years after winning same event in 1982...both victories carried 10-year exemptions...start of 1992 campaign delayed by off-season skiing collision with young girl (Dec. 1991)...accident made it impossible for him to play in Tournament of Champions...qualified for '92 T of C by winning 1991 TOUR Championship...TOUR title first victory in seven years...led in earnings in 1982, when won four times, including Masters and World Series...also captured Kemper Open for second time in '82, year that began with victory in Joe Garagiola-Tucson Open...named 1982 PGA TOUR Arnold Palmer Award recipient as leading money-winner...first title came in 1980 Bob Hope Chrysler Classic...winner 1978 Magnolia Classic, 1988 Fred Meyer

CRAIG STADLER...continued

Challenge (with Joey Sindelar)...winner 1971 World Junior Championship, 1973 U.S. Amateur at Inverness...two-time All-American at USC (1974-75)...member 1975 Walker Cup team.

PERSONAL: One of game's most colorful personalities and gallery favorites...nickname "Walrus" needs no explanation...gained revenge on "Stadler Tree" at Torrey Pines in 1995, when he cut down diseased tree with a chainsaw...tournament officials thought him perfect for the job, since he was disqualified for "building a stance" under the tree when he knelt on a towel to hit a ball from underneath it in 1987.

CAREER SUMMARY — **PLAYOFF RECORD: 2-2**

Year	Events Played	Cuts Made	1st	2nd	3rd	Top 10	Top 25	Earnings	Rank
1974(Am.)	1	1				1	1		
1975(Am.)	1	1					1		
1976	9	5						$2,702	196
1977	29	19				4	10	$42,949	66
1978	27	20				5	11	$63,486	48
1979	33	24				4	11	$73,392	55
1980	24	21	2	1		7	11	$206,291	8
1981	28	21	1	2	3	8	12	$218,829	8
1982	25	23	4	2		11	18	$446,462	1
1983	27	20		2	1	11	14	$214,496	17
1984	22	20	1		3	8	16	$324,241	8
1985	24	20		3		8	14	$297,926	11
1986	26	17			1	8	10	$170,076	53
1987	22	17		1		6	11	$235,831	39
1988	21	16			2	5	11	$278,313	37
1989	22	20		1	1	4	13	$409,419	25
1990	19	16			1	5	9	$278,482	52
1991	21	16	1	1	1	7	12	$827,628	2
1992	25	18	1			4	10	$487,460	28
1993	24	17		2	1	5	7	$553,623	29
1994	22	15	1	1		4	8	$474,831	32
1995	21	15			1	4	9	$402,316	45
Total	473	362	11	16	15	119	219	$6,000,818	13

1996 PGA TOUR CHARITY TEAM: Buick Invitational.

TOP TOURNAMENT SUMMARY

YEAR	78	79	80	81	82	83	84	85	86	87	88	89	90	91	92
Masters Tournament		T7	T26	T43	1	T6	T35	T6	CUT	T17	3	CUT	T14	T12	T25
U.S. Open			T16	T26	T22	T10	W/D	CUT	T15	T24	T25		T8	T19	T33
British Open Championship			T6	CUT	T35	T12	T28	CUT	WD	T8	T61	T13	CUT	T101	T64
PGA Championship	6		T55	CUT	T16	T63	T18	T18	T30	T28	T15	T7	T57	T7	T48
THE PLAYERS Championship		T67	T67	CUT	T6	T63	T3	T13	CUT	CUT	T45	T21	T61	CUT	CUT
THE TOUR Championship												T14		1	T13

TOP TOURNAMENT SUMMARY (cont.)

YEAR	93	94	95
Masters Tournament	T34	CUT	CUT
U.S. Open	T33	CUT	
British Open Championship		T32	CUT
PGA Championship	CUT	T19	T8
THE PLAYERS Championship	CUT	CUT	T14
THE TOUR Championship	29		

NATIONAL TEAMS: Ryder Cup (2) 1983, 1985; Walker Cup, 1975; U.S. vs. Japan, 1982.

1995 PGA TOUR STATISTICS

Scoring	70.42	(37)
Driving	265.5	(72T)
Driving Accuracy	73.9	(31T)
Greens in Regulation	71.3	(3T)
Putting	1.805	(139T)
All Around	477	(28T)
Sand Saves	55.8	(45T)
Total Driving	103	(10)
Eagles	9	(20T)
Birdies	247	(130)

MISCELLANEOUS STATISTICS

Scoring Avg Before Cut	70.50	(25T)
Scoring Avg 3rd Rnd	69.64	(9)
Scoring Avg Final Rnd	70.71	(44T)
Birdies Conversion %	28.7	(92T)
Par Breakers	20.6	(34)

1995 Low Round: **65:** 1995 Mercedes Championships/2
Career Low Round: **62:** 2 times, most recent 1987 Shearson Lehman Brothers Andy Williams Open/2
Career Largest Paycheck: $360,000: 1991 TOUR Championship/1

MIKE STANDLY *(STAND-lee)*

EXEMPT STATUS: 105th on 1995 money list
FULL NAME: Michael Dean Standly
HEIGHT: 6' **WEIGHT:** 200
BIRTH DATE: May 19, 1964 **BIRTHPLACE:** Abilene, TX
RESIDENCE: Houston, TX
FAMILY: Wife, Nicole; Charles Allen(11/16/88), Suzanne Augusta (12/11/92)
COLLEGE: University of Houston
SPECIAL INTERESTS: Fishing, hunting
TURNED PROFESSIONAL: 1986 **Q-SCHOOL:** Fall 1990

TOUR VICTORIES (1): 1993 Freeport-McMoRan Classic

BEST 1995 FINISHES: T5—Freeport-McMoRan Classic; T6—LaCantera Texas Open; 7—Honda Classic.

1995 SEASON: Once again, posted his best finish of the year in New Orleans...this time he finished T5 in the Freeport-McMoRan Classic...was tied for the lead after 36 holes and trailed by one stroke after 54...New Orleans showing came two weeks after a solo seventh at the Honda Classic...final top-10 finish was a big one...final-round 4-under-par 68 at the LaCantera Texas Open earned T6 and assured PGA TOUR membership for 1996...entered the week 132nd on the money list...$38,225 paycheck vaulted him 27 positions to 105th place, his lowest finish since his rookie season of 1991...had his career-low round, a 9-under-par 62, during the first round of the FedEx St. Jude Classic.

CAREER HIGHLIGHTS: After 1992 New Orleans tie for second with Greg Norman, one stroke behind Chip Beck, broke through with a one-stroke victory over Russ Cochran and Payne Stewart in 1993 Freeport-McMoRan Classic...carded final-round 67 in coming from two strokes off Greg Kraft's 54-hole lead...best finish in nine events leading to English Turn was T24 at the Honda Classic...win provided a berth in following week's Masters, appropriate for someone whose daughter's middle name is "Augusta"...New Orleans triumph came between missed cuts in PLAYERS Championship and at Masters...made cut in 22 of 29 tournaments in 1992...medalist in the 1991 PGA TOUR Qualifying Tournament...played Ben Hogan Tour in 1990, with earnings of $10,446 in 28 events...Runnerup to Scott Verplank in the 1986 NCAA Finals...1986 All-American...winner of the 1984 Boone Links Invitational.

PERSONAL: On the advisory board for NIKE's P.L.A.Y., "Participating in the Lives of America's Youth"...wife, Nicole, spent time in Nashville last year recording a country and western album...plays host to the Mike Standly Pro-Am Benefitting the AIDS Foundation...enjoys tying his own fishing flies, has tied them for Paul Azinger.

PGA TOUR CAREER SUMMARY — **PLAYOFF RECORD: 0-0**

Year	Events Played	Cuts Made	1st	2nd	3rd	Top 10	Top 25	Earnings	Rank
1986	1								
1987	1								
1988	1	1						$800	316
1991	31	14					2	$55,846	171
1992	29	22		1		2	5	$213,712	73
1993	30	17	1			2	5	$323,886	49
1994	30	19					6	$179,850	99
1995	30	17				3	3	$177,920	105
Total	153	90	1	1		7	21	$952,014	186

NIKE TOUR SUMMARY

Year	Events Played	Cuts Made	1st	2nd	3rd	Top 10	Top 25	Earnings	Rank
1990	28	13					4	$10,446	84
1991	2	2					1	$1,700	186
1992	1								
Total	31	15					5	$12,146	
COMBINED TOTAL MONEY								$964,160	

1996 PGA TOUR CHARITY TEAM: Freeport•McDermott Classic.

TOP TOURNAMENT SUMMARY

YEAR	93	94	95
Masters Tournament	CUT	T41	
U.S. Open	T16		CUT
PGA Championship	T61		
THE PLAYERS Championship	CUT	T19	CUT

MIKE STANDLY...*continued*

1995 PGA TOUR STATISTICS		
Scoring	71.49	(117)
Driving	270.6	(38T)
Driving Accuracy	66.4	(140T)
Greens in Regulation	65.1	(116T)
Putting	1.796	(117T)
All Around	738	(99)
Sand Saves	48.6	(138T)
Total Driving	178	(82T)
Eagles	12	(5T)
Birdies	295	(67T)

MISCELLANEOUS STATISTICS		
Scoring Avg Before Cut	71.26	(96T)
Scoring Avg 3rd Rnd	72.89	(181)
Scoring Avg Final Rnd	71.38	(107)
Birdies Conversion %	27.1	(136T)
Par Breakers	18.3	(115T)

1995 Low Round: 62: 1995 FedEx St. Jude Classic/1
Career Low Round: 62: 1995 FedEx St. Jude Classic/1
Career Largest Paycheck: $180,000: 1993 Freeport-McMoRan Classic/1

PAYNE STEWART

EXEMPT STATUS: Winner, 1991 U.S. Open
FULL NAME: William Payne Stewart
HEIGHT: 6'1" **WEIGHT:** 180
BIRTH DATE: Jan. 30, 1957 **BIRTHPLACE:** Springfield, MO
RESIDENCE: Orlando, FL
FAMILY: Wife, Tracey Ferguson; Chelsea (11/13/85), Aaron (4/2/89)
COLLEGE: Southern Methodist University (1979, Business)
SPECIAL INTERESTS: Hunting, fishing, cooking
TURNED PROFESSIONAL: 1979 **Q SCHOOL:** Spring 1981

TOUR VICTORIES (9): 1982 Quad Cities Open. **1983** Walt Disney World Classic. **1987** Hertz Bay Hill Classic. **1989** MCI Heritage Classic, PGA Championship. **1990** MCI Heritage Classic, GTE Byron Nelson Classic.**1991** U.S. Open. **1995** Shell Houston Open.

INTERNATIONAL VICTORIES (6): 1981 Indonesian Open (Asia), Indian Open (Asia). **1982** Coolangatta-Tweed Head Classic (Aus). **1990** World Cup (Indiv.). **1991** Heineken Dutch Open (Eur). **1993** Hassan II Trophy (Morocco).

BEST 1995 FINISHES: 1—Shell Houston Open; T3—THE PLAYERS Championship; T4—Phoenix Open; 5—AT&T Pebble Beach National Pro-Am; 8—Buick Open; T9—Kemper Open.

1995 SEASON: After struggling with his game in 1994, he returned to prior form and won his ninth career title at the Shell Houston Open...came from seven strokes back after 54 holes to tie Scott Hoch and force a playoff...won playoff with a par on the first extra hole...win came 3 years, 10 months, 14 days after 1991 U.S. Open victory...was one of only 10 players under par as he finished T3, two strokes behind winner Lee Janzen, at THE PLAYERS Championship...finished T4 in his second start of the season at the Phoenix Open and fifth the next week at the AT&T Pebble Beach National Pro-Am...other top-10 finishes included T9 at the Kemper Open, where he was only one stroke back through 54 holes, and an eighth at the Buick Open, where he opened with a pair of 65s.

CAREER HIGHLIGHTS: Says of his year in 1994: "The reason I had such a poor year, I didn't dedicate myself."...runner-up four times in '93, including head-to-head battle with Lee Janzen in U.S. Open...placed third at Memorial, where Paul Azinger holed out from bunker on 72nd hole to supplant him as tournament leader...owns victories in two majors, 1989 PGA Championship and 1991 U.S. Open...won Open in 18-hole playoff with Scott Simpson at Hazeltine National...was eight strokes off lead after opening 74 at PGA, rebounded to win by stroke...also captured MCI Heritage Classic and lost Nabisco Championships playoff to Tom Kite in '89 to finish second on money list with $1,201,301...won Heritage Classic title in 1990 as well, year in which he also won GTE Byron Nelson Classic...missed 10 weeks of 1991 season with nerve problem in neck...winner All-Around Category, 1988 Nabisco Statistics; Scoring Leader, 1989 Nabisco Statistics...third in Asian Tour Order of Merit, 1981...third in Australian Order of Merit, 1982...winner 1982 Magnolia Classic...three-time winner of the Skins Game, 1991-93...1979 Southwest Conference co-champion...1979 All-American...1979 Missouri Amateur champion.

PERSONAL: Donated 1987 Bay Hill Classic winner's check to Florida Hospital Circle of Friends in memory of father, who died two years before...met and married Tracey Ferguson of Australia while in Malaysia...completed construction of 13,000-square-foot home in Orlando, FL in 1994.

PAYNE STEWART...*continued*

CAREER SUMMARY — **PLAYOFF RECORD: 3-5**

Year	Events Played	Cuts Made	1st	2nd	3rd	Top 10	Top 25	Earnings	Rank
1981	10	5				1	2	$13,400	160
1982	24	14	2		1	4	7	$98,686	39
1983	32	23	1		1	7	12	$178,809	25
1984	31	25		2	2	6	18	$288,795	11
1985	26	24		1		6	15	$225,729	19
1986	29	22		3	1	16	17	$535,389	3
1987	27	22	1	2	2	7	17	$511,026	12
1988	27	25		2	1	12	20	$553,571	14
1989	24	19	2	3	2	11	15	$1,201,301	2
1990	26	22	2	2	1	8	16	$976,281	3
1991	19	16	1			2	12	$476,971	31
1992	23	19			1	5	10	$334,738	44
1993	26	22		4	3	12	16	$982,875	6
1994	23	15				2	5	$145,687	123
1995	27	22	1		1	6	15	$866,219	12
Total	374	295	10	19	16	105	197	$7,389,479	3

1996 PGA TOUR CHARITY TEAM: MCI Classic.

TOP TOURNAMENT SUMMARY

YEAR	81	82	83	84	85	86	87	88	89	90	91	92	93	94	95
Masters Tournament			T32	T21	T25	T8	T42	T25	T24	T36		CUT	T9	CUT	T41
U.S. Open				CUT	T5	T6	CUT	T10	T13	CUT	1	T51	2	CUT	T21
British Open Championship	T58			CUT	2	T35	T4	T7	T8	T2	T32	T34	12	CUT	T11
PGA Championship		CUT	CUT	CUT	T12	T5	T24	T9	1	T8	T13	T69	T44	T66	T13
THE PLAYERS Championship			CUT	T64	T13	T10	CUT	T8	CUT	T11		T13	T11	CUT	T3
THE TOUR Championship							T21	T3	2	T25	T21		26		T16

NATIONAL TEAMS: Ryder Cup (4), 1987, 1989, 1991, 1993; Kirin Cup, 1987; Asahi Glass Four Tours World Championship of Golf (2), 1989, 1990. World Cup (2), 1987, 1990. Nissan Cup, 1986. Dunhill Cup, 1993.

1995 PGA TOUR STATISTICS

Scoring	**70.23**	**(17T)**
Driving	**266.1**	**(66T)**
Driving Accuracy	**66.2**	**(142T)**
Greens in Regulation	**62.6**	**(170)**
Putting	**1.750**	**(6)**
All Around	**479**	**(30)**
Sand Saves	**56.5**	**(43)**
Total Driving	**208**	**(122T)**
Eagles	**9**	**(20T)**
Birdies	**358**	**(15)**

MISCELLANEOUS STATISTICS

Scoring Avg Before Cut	**70.11**	**(11)**
Scoring Avg 3rd Rnd	**71.59**	**(127)**
Scoring Avg Final Rnd	**71.14**	**(85)**
Birdies Conversion %	**34.2**	**(3)**
Par Breakers	**21.0**	**(19T)**

1995 Low Round: **64:** 1995 Walt Disney World/Oldsmobile Classic/2
Career Low Round: **61:** 1990 WDW/OLDS Classic/3
Career Largest Paycheck: **$270,000:** 1989 Nabisco/2

Did You Know?

In 1995, Jim Gallagher, Jr., and Payne Stewart each came from seven strokes behind on the final day to win PGA TOUR events. Gallagher won the Kmart Greater Greensboro Open and, the following week, Stewart won the Shell Houston Open. Prior to 1995, the last seven-stroke, final-day comeback was by Nick Price over Scott Simpson at the 1994 Southwestern Bell Colonial.

Dave Stockton, Jr.

EXEMPT STATUS: 124th on 1995 money list
FULL NAME: David Bradley Stockton, Jr.
HEIGHT: 6'2" **WEIGHT:** 195
BIRTH DATE: July 31, 1968 **BIRTHPLACE:** Redlands, CA
RESIDENCE: La Quinta, CA; plays out of Palmilla Hotel & Golf Club, Los Cabos, Mexico
FAMILY: Wife, Diane
COLLEGE: University of Southern California
SPECIAL INTERESTS: Hunting, fishing, all sports
TURNED PROFESSIONAL: 1991 **Q-SCHOOL:** 1993

BEST TOUR CAREER FINISH: T2--1995 Canon Greater Hartford Open.

NIKE TOUR VICTORIES(2): 1993 NIKE Connecticut Open, NIKE Hawkeye Open.

BEST 1995 FINISH: T2—Canon Greater Hartford Open

1995 SEASON: Continued his fine play in the state of Connecticut...finished T2 with Grant Waite and Fuzzy Zoeller in the Canon Greater Hartford Open, two strokes behind Greg Norman...finished T3 there in 1994, and one of his two NIKE TOUR wins came in Connecticut...$89,600 paycheck was the largest of his two-year PGA TOUR career...a T15 worth $23,250 in the Las Vegas Invitational assured him PGA TOUR membership for 1996...made five consecutive cuts from the Greater Milwaukee Open through the Buick Challenge...low round of the year, and his career, was a 9-under-par 63 in the second round of the Walt Disney World/Oldsmobile Classic.

CAREER HIGHLIGHTS: Almost won a PGA TOUR tournament his father had won on the same weekend his father was winning on Senior TOUR...led or near lead for three rounds of 1994 Canon Greater Hartford Open while senior Stockton was wrapping up FORD SENIOR PLAYERS Championship...elder Stockton captured 1974 GHO...final-round 72 produced a tie for third, three strokes behind David Frost...opened with back-to-back 66s, was even with Frost going into final round, one stroke in front of Greg Norman, who finished second...Hartford heroics provided check for $57,600, which came after 10 missed cuts in first 16 starts...three weeks later had another T3, in weather-shortened Deposit Guaranty Golf Classic...final top-10 (T8) came at the Sprint International, where check for $42,000 assured playing privileges for 1995...held midpoint lead in Walt Disney World/Oldsmobile Classic after second-round 64, ultimately finished T15...64 featured three eagles, including two on the final two holes at the appropriately named Eagle Pines...added a fourth Disney eagle, doubling his season total to eight...earned playing privileges by finishing as co-medalist (with Ty Armstrong and Robin Freeman) in 1993 Qualifying Tournament...placed 23rd on 1993 NIKE TOUR money list with $64,214...won pair of NIKE TOUR events in 1993, NIKE Connecticut Open and NIKE Hawkeye Open...second to Phil Mickelson at the 1989 NCAA Championship...All-American at USC.

PERSONAL: Technically not a Junior, since father's middle name is Knapp and his is Bradley...took Jr. as part of name to show relationship to and pride in father...caddied for his dad on PGA TOUR, as brother Ron does on Senior TOUR...father repaid the favor in the final round of this year's Nissan Open, as the duo went on to record a 68 for a 288 total and T66 finish.

PGA TOUR CAREER SUMMARY — **PLAYOFF RECORD: 0-0**

Year	Events Played	Cuts Made	1st	2nd	3rd	Top 10	Top 25	Earnings	Rank
1994	31	15			2	3	4	$185,209	96
1995	32	15		1		1	2	$149,579	124
Total	63	30		1	2	4	6	$334,788	299

NIKE TOUR SUMMARY

Year	Events Played	Cuts Made	1st	2nd	3rd	Top 10	Top 25	Earnings	Rank
1993	22	11	2			2	3	$64,214	23
1994	2	2				1	1	$4,865	143
Total	24	13	2			3	4	$69,079	
COMBINED TOTAL MONEY								$403,867	

1996 PGA TOUR CHARITY TEAM: Kemper Open.

TOP TOURNAMENT SUMMARY

YEAR	95
THE PLAYERS Championship	CUT

DAVE STOCKTON, JR...continued

1995 PGA TOUR STATISTICS		
Scoring	71.89	(158)
Driving	271.4	(29T)
Driving Accuracy	65.1	(155)
Greens in Regulation	66.7	(75T)
Putting	1.800	(129)
All Around	710	(87)
Sand Saves	53.8	(74T)
Total Driving	184	(91)
Eagles	9	(20T)
Birdies	294	(70)

MISCELLANEOUS STATISTICS		
Scoring Avg Before Cut	71.55	(127T)
Scoring Avg 3rd Rnd	71.65	(129)
Scoring Avg Final Rnd	72.27	(167)
Birdies Conversion %	26.3	(155)
Par Breakers	18.1	(127T)

1995 Low Round: 63: 1995 Walt Disney World/Oldsmobile Classic/2
Career Low Round: 63: 1995 Walt Disney World/Oldsmobile Classic/2
Career Largest Paycheck: $89,600: 1995 Canon Greater Hartford Open/T2

CURTIS STRANGE

EXEMPT STATUS: Winner, 1989 U.S. Open
FULL NAME: Curtis Northrop Strange
HEIGHT: 5' 11" **WEIGHT:** 170
BIRTH DATE: January 30, 1955 **BIRTHPLACE:** Norfolk, VA
RESIDENCE: Kingsmill, VA; plays out of Kingsmill on the James
FAMILY: Wife Sarah; Thomas Wright III (8/25/82), David Clark (4/3/85)
COLLEGE: Wake Forest University
SPECIAL INTERESTS: Hunting and fishing
TURNED PROFESSIONAL: 1976 **Q SCHOOL:** Spring 1977

TOUR VICTORIES (17): 1979 Pensacola Open. **1980** Michelob-Houston Open, Manufacturers Hanover Westchester Classic. **1983** Sammy Davis, Jr.-Greater Hartford Open. **1984** LaJet Classic. **1985** Honda Classic, Panasonic-Las Vegas Invitational, Canadian Open. **1986** Houston Open. **1987** Canadian Open, Federal Express-St. Jude Classic, NEC World Series of Golf. **1988** Independent Insurance Agent Open, Memorial Tournament, U.S. Open, Nabisco Championships. **1989** U.S. Open.

INTERNATIONAL VICTORIES (3): 1988 Sanctuary Cove Classic (Aus). **1989** Palm Meadows Cup (Aus). **1993** Greg Norman's Holden Classic (Aus).

BEST 1995 FINISHES: T3—Bob Hope Chrysler Classic; T4—BellSouth Classic; T6—Anheuser-Busch Golf Classic; 9—Masters Tournament.

1995 SEASON: Named to his fifth Ryder Cup team by Captain Lanny Wadkins...struggled at Oak Hill, site of his 1988 U.S. title, going 0-3...won the Merrill Lynch Shoot-Out Championship the next week in Bermuda, earning $150,000...best finish of the year was a T3 at the Bob Hope Chrysler Classic...strong finish in Palm Springs was keyed by an 8-under-par 64 in the opening round and a 9-under 63 in the fourth round...finished T4 at the BellSouth Classic following a final-round 65...finished T6 at his home course at Kingsmill, VA in the Anheuser-Busch Golf Classic...a third-round 7-under-par 65 led to a ninth-place finish in the Masters.

CAREER HIGHLIGHTS: Two-time U.S. Open champ missed 1994 Ernie Els-Loren Roberts-Colin Montgomerie Open playoff by single stroke...posted four consecutive rounds of one-under-par 70 at Oakmont, where 280 total fell one shy...winner of back-to-back U.S. Opens in 1988 and 1989, first to do so since Ben Hogan (1950-51)...1988 Open victory at The Country Club in Brookline, MA, came in playoff with Nick Faldo...captured '89 crown at Oak Hills in Rochester, NY...three-time recipient of Arnold Palmer Award as TOUR's leading money winner (1985, 1987-88), first to win consecutively since Tom Watson in 1979-80...became first player to surpass $1 million in yearly earnings in 1988, when he won four titles...biggest payday--$360,000--came with playoff victory over Tom Kite in 1988 Nabisco Championships at Pebble Beach...had T2 in 1989 PGA Championship...had seven-year tournament victory streak (1983-89)...earned first victory since 1989 U.S. Open in Greg Norman Holden Classic in Australia in Dec. 1993...holder of Old Course record (62) at St. Andrews, Scotland in 1987 Dunhill Cup...1985-87-88 Golf Writers Player of Year...1988 PGA Player of Year...winner 1986 ABC Cup (Japan)...Member 1974 World Amateur Cup, 1975 Walker Cup teams...winner 1973 Southeastern Amateur, 1974 NCAA Championship, 1974 Western Amateur, 1975 Eastern Amateur, 1975-76 North and South Amateur, 1975-76 Virginia State Amateur...1974 College Player-of-Year.

PERSONAL: Started playing golf at seven; father owned White Sands CC in Virginia Beach, VA...identical twin, Allen, is former TOUR member.

CURTIS STRANGE...*continued*

CAREER SUMMARY — **PLAYOFF RECORD: 6-3**

Year	Events Played	Cuts Made	1st	2nd	3rd	Top 10	Top 25	Earnings	Rank
1975(Am.)	1	1							
1976(Am.)	1	1					1		
1976	1	1						$375	267
1977	18	11		1		2	3	$28,144	87
1978	28	16				3	7	$29,346	88
1979	34	24	1		1	9	16	$138,368	21
1980	30	27	2	1	2	9	21	$271,888	3
1981	28	23		1	3	12	19	$201,513	9
1982	29	26		2	3	12	19	$263,378	10
1983	28	22	1	1	1	6	14	$200,116	21
1984	26	23	1		3	9	18	$276,773	14
1985	25	22	3	2		7	12	$542,321	1
1986	25	19	1			6	12	$237,700	32
1987	26	23	3	1	1	11	16	$925,941	1
1988	24	21	4			6	12	$1,147,644	1
1989	21	20	1	1	3	9	16	$752,587	7
1990	20	17				6	10	$277,172	53
1991	20	13		2		3	5	$336,333	48
1992	17	13				2	6	$150,639	99
1993	24	16			1	5	8	$262,697	63
1994	23	18			1	5	9	$390,881	41
1995	24	17			1	4	9	$358,175	49
Total	473	374	17	12	20	126	233	$6,794,776	10

1996 PGA TOUR CHARITY TEAM: Michelob Championship at Kingsmill.

TOP TOURNAMENT SUMMARY

YEAR	76	78	80	81	82	83	84	85	86	87	88	89	90	91	92
Masters Tournament	T15		CUT	T19	T7	CUT	T46	T2	T21	T12	T21	T18	T7	T42	T31
U.S. Open			T16	T17	T39	T26	3	T31	CUT	T4	1	1	T21	CUT	T23
British Open	CUT				T15	T29			T14		T13	T61	CUT	T38	CUT
PGA Championship		T58	T5	T27	T14	86	CUT	CUT	CUT	9	T31	T2	CUT	W/D	CUT
THE PLAYERS Championship			21	T2	T51	T8	T33	T33	CUT	CUT	DQ	T34	T16	T6	W/D
THE TOUR Championship										30	1	T11			

TOP TOURNAMENT SUMMARY (cont.)

YEAR	93	94	95
Masters Tournament	W/D	T27	9
U.S. Open	T25	4	T36
British Open Championship			CUT
PGA Championship	CUT	T19	T17
THE PLAYERS Championship	CUT	CUT	T23

NATIONAL TEAMS: Ryder Cup (5) 1983, 1985, 1987, 1989, 1995. Nissan Cup, 1985. Kirin Cup (2) 1987, 1988. Four Tours Championship, 1989. Dunhill Cup (7), 1985, 1987, 1988, 1989, 1990, 1991, 1994. World Amateur Team, 1974. Walker Cup, 1975.

1995 PGA TOUR STATISTICS

Scoring	70.72	(53T)
Driving	255.8	(150T)
Driving Accuracy	77.9	(8)
Greens in Regulation	66.5	(82T)
Putting	1.775	(56)
All Around	519	(37)
Sand Saves	58.9	(19T)
Total Driving	158	(55T)
Eagles	5	(88T)
Birdies	298	(63T)

MISCELLANEOUS STATISTICS

Scoring Avg Before Cut	71.24	(94T)
Scoring Avg 3rd Rnd	70.72	(63)
Scoring Avg Final Rnd	70.18	(16)
Birdies Conversion %	30.3	(42T)
Par Breakers	20.0	(56T)

1995 Low Round: **63:** 1995 Bob Hope Chrysler Classic/4
Career Low Round: **62:** 2 times, most recent 1983 Sammy Davis-Greater Hartford/2
Career Largest Paycheck: $360,000: 1988 Nabisco Championship/1

STEVE STRICKER *(STRICK-er)*

EXEMPT STATUS: 40th on 1995 money list
FULL NAME: Steven Charles Stricker
HEIGHT: 6' **WEIGHT:** 185
BIRTH DATE: February 23, 1967 **BIRTHPLACE:** Edgerton, WI
RESIDENCE: Edgerton, WI; plays out of Cherokee CC
FAMILY: Wife, Nicki
COLLEGE: University of Illinois
SPECIAL INTERESTS: Hunting, clay target shooting
TURNED PROFESSIONAL: 1990 **Q-SCHOOL:** 1993

BEST PGA TOUR FINISH: T2--1994 Northern Telecom Open

BEST NIKE TOUR CAREER FINISH: T2— 1990 Dakota Dunes Open

INTERNATIONAL VICTORIES: 1990 Victoria Open (Can). **1993** Canadian PGA.

BEST 1995 FINISHES: 4—Nestle Invitational; T7—Kmart Greater Greensboro Open; T8—Buick Challenge; 9—Doral-Ryder Open.

1995 SEASON: Another solid season for the second-year PGA TOUR pro...missed only three cuts in 23 tournaments and posted four top-10 finishes...finished fourth, his best placing of the season, in the Nestle Invitational after opening with a 5-under-par 67...two weeks earlier had finished alone in ninth place at the Doral-Ryder Open...other top-10 finishes included a T7 at the Kmart Greater Greensboro Open and a T8 at the Buick Challenge, where he led by two strokes over Glen Day after 36 holes...had string of 26 consecutive cuts made broken at homestate GMO.

CAREER HIGHLIGHTS: After leading first two rounds of 1993 Canadian Open as a non-member and contending through three, found himself in hunt for first TOUR victory twice more in '94...established credentials early as Rookie of Year candidate...finished in four-way tie for second in Northern Telecom Open, two strokes behind Andrew Magee...in June wound up in another four-way tie, this time for third, in Canon Greater Hartford Open...fourth among rookies in earnings, behind Ernie Els, Mike Heinen and Glen Day...finished T18 in 1993 Qualifying Tournament after failing to make finals three years in a row...matriculated on Canadian Tour...placed T10 in 1990 Canadian TPC...winner 1990 Payless/Pepsi Open, Wisconsin Open...All-American 1988-89.

PERSONAL: Wife Nicki is his caddie...father-in-law Dennis Tiziani, golf coach at University of Wisconsin, also his teacher...Tiziani recruited him for Wisconsin, but instead he chose the University of Illinois...was joined by Dennis and brother-in-law Mario Tiziani in the field of last year's Greater Milwaukee Open...Mario Monday-qualified, while Dennis was a last-minute alternate.

PGA TOUR CAREER SUMMARY — **PLAYOFF RECORD: 0-0**

Year	Events Played	Cuts Made	1st	2nd	3rd	Top 10	Top 25	Earnings	Rank
1990	1	1						$3,974	255
1991	1								
1992	2	1						$5,550	261
1993	6	2				1	1	$46,171	186
1994	26	22		1	1	4	6	$334,409	50
1995	23	20				4	13	$438,931	40
Total	59	46		1	1	9	20	$829,034	207

NIKE TOUR SUMMARY

Year	Events Played	Cuts Made	1st	2nd	3rd	Top 10	Top 25	Earnings	Rank
1990	2	2		1		1	1	$10,080	86
1991	12	7				1	4	$11,298	85
1992	1	1						$1,065	227
1993	3	1						$820	226
Total	18	11		1		2	5	$23,263	
COMBINED TOTAL MONEY								$852,297	

1996 PGA TOUR CHARITY TEAM: Mercedes Championships.

TOP TOURNAMENT SUMMARY

YEAR	93	94	95
U.S. Open	83		T13
PGA Championship			T23
THE PLAYERS Championship		T23	T11

Steve Stricker...*continued*

1995 PGA TOUR STATISTICS

Statistic	Value	Rank
Scoring	70.29	(24T)
Driving	275.2	(14)
Driving Accuracy	68.8	(108)
Greens in Regulation	67.7	(51T)
Putting	1.766	(35)
All Around	441	(21)
Sand Saves	47.1	(152T)
Total Driving	122	(19)
Eagles	9	(20T)
Birdies	319	(37T)

MISCELLANEOUS STATISTICS

Statistic	Value	Rank
Scoring Avg Before Cut	70.29	(15)
Scoring Avg 3rd Rnd	70.45	(49T)
Scoring Avg Final Rnd	71.20	(92)
Birdies Conversion %	31.5	(22T)
Par Breakers	22.0	(5T)

1995 Low Round: 64: 2 times, most recent 1995 PGA Championship/2
Career Low Round: 64: 2 times, most recent 1995 PGA Championship/2
Career Largest Paycheck: $72,600: 1994 Northern Telecom Open/T2

Mike Sullivan

EXEMPT STATUS: 1994 tournament winner
FULL NAME: Michael James Sullivan
HEIGHT: 6'2"
WEIGHT: 220
BIRTH DATE: January 1, 1955
BIRTHPLACE: Gary, IN
RESIDENCE: Greeneville, TN
FAMILY: Wife, Sandy; Rebecca (6/13/85)
COLLEGE: University of Florida
SPECIAL INTERESTS: Flying, fishing, hunting
TURNED PROFESSIONAL: 1975
Q-SCHOOL: Fall, 1976, 1985

TOUR VICTORIES (3): 1980 Southern Open. **1989** Independent Insurance Agent Open. **1994** B.C. Open.

BEST 1995 FINISH: 8—NEC World Series of Golf

1995 SEASON: Followed his best year on TOUR, 1994, with another solid season...earned $167,486, the third highest total of his 19-year PGA TOUR career...made the cut in 17 of his 26 tournaments...best finish was eighth place at the NEC World Series of Golf...$62,000 paycheck earned at Firestone CC was the highest of his year...finished T19 at the Shell Houston Open, a tournament he won in 1989...low round of the year was a second round 66 in defense of his B.C. Open title...fired Bay Course record 62 during Round 2 of Lincoln-Mercury Kapalua International.

CAREER HIGHLIGHTS: Suffering from stiff neck and with problematic back giving him trouble, having missed 13 cuts in 21 starts and four of previous five, did what one might expect: went out and won the 1994 B.C. Open, his first tournament victory in five years...final-round 66 provided four-stroke victory over Jeff Sluman...two months (and six tournaments) before, lost playoff to Brian Henninger in weather-shortened Deposit Guaranty Golf Classic...second-place finish was his first top-10 since T8 in 1992 Buick Open...captured second career title as early starter in 1989 Independent Insurance Agent Open...barely made cut after opening 76-71, then carded 4-under 68 on third day at TPC at The Woodlands...began final round seven strokes off lead, proceeded to fire 65...8-under 280 total held up for one-stroke victory over Craig Stadler...first win came at 1980 Southern Open, where next year lost playoff to J.C. Snead...also lost 1978 Buick Open playoff to Australian Jack Newton...posted 7-under-par 28 for nine holes in 1988 Texas Open...teamed with Don January to win 1984 Shootout at Jeremy Ranch, then a PGA TOUR/Senior PGA TOUR event.

PERSONAL: Attended University of Florida "briefly"...emphasizes he "survived" rooming with Andy Bean in college.

CAREER SUMMARY **PLAYOFF RECORD: 0-4**

Year	Events Played	Cuts Made	1st	2nd	3rd	Top 10	Top 25	Earnings	Rank
1977	21	6				1	1	$11,170	142
1978	28	15		1		3	8	$41,184	74
1979	30	16				2	7	$38,596	97
1980	28	19	1	2	1	8	11	$147,759	22

MIKE SULLIVAN...*continued*

CAREER SUMMARY (cont.)

Year	Events Played	Cuts Made	1st	2nd	3rd	Top 10	Top 25	Earnings	Rank
1981	31	23		1	1	4	11	$94,844	41
1982	29	19				1	6	$37,957	109
1983	28	19			1	3	10	$93,437	60
1984	25	18				5	9	$111,415	63
1985	26	12				2	6	$45,032	127
1986	25	22		1		3	8	$150,407	62
1987	26	16				1	6	$79,456	112
1988	30	17				2	6	$115,994	99
1989	24	17	1			2	5	$273,962	47
1990	27	16				1	3	$80,038	147
1991	29	16					5	$106,048	133
1992	28	13				2	3	$115,441	121
1993	15	9					2	$68,587	167
1994	26	11	1	1		2	3	$298,586	60
1995	26	17				1	3	$167,486	113
Total	502	301	3	6	3	43	113	$2,076,977	94

1996 PGA TOUR CHARITY TEAM: Bob Hope Chrysler Classic.

TOP TOURNAMENT SUMMARY

YEAR	78	80	81	82	83	84	85	86	87	88	89	90	93	94	95
Masters Tournament			T35								T46				CUT
U.S. Open			CUT		T34	T25								CUT	
British Open Championship					T14	CUT									
PGA Championship	T34	T30	T56	CUT	CUT	T65		T53	T56		T12	CUT			T63
THE PLAYERS Championship		CUT	T63	W/D	DQ	T26	W/D	T40		CUT	T17	T46	CUT		CUT

1995 PGA TOUR STATISTICS

Scoring	71.70	(136T)
Driving	261.9	(102T)
Driving Accuracy	59.3	(183)
Greens in Regulation	63.5	(154T)
Putting	1.801	(130T)
All Around	1,001	(158)
Sand Saves	53.0	(85T)
Total Driving	285	(177T)
Eagles	4	(116T)
Birdies	277	(95T)

MISCELLANEOUS STATISTICS

Scoring Avg Before Cut	71.98	(158T)
Scoring Avg 3rd Rnd	72.47	(170)
Scoring Avg Final Rnd	71.59	(121T)
Birdies Conversion %	28.2	(113T)
Par Breakers	18.2	(122T)

1995 Low Round: **66:** 1995 B.C. Open/2
Career Low Round: **62:** 2 times, most recent 1992 Fed Exp St. Jude/3
Career Largest Paycheck: **$162,000:** 1994 B.C. Open/1

HAL SUTTON

EXEMPT STATUS: 1995 tournament winner
FULL NAME: Hal Evan Sutton
HEIGHT: 6' 1" **WEIGHT:** 185
BIRTH DATE: April 28, 1958 **BIRTHPLACE:** Shreveport, LA
RESIDENCE: Shreveport, LA
FAMILY: Wife, Ashley
COLLEGE: Centenary College (Business)
SPECIAL INTERESTS: Horses, hunting and fishing
TURNED PROFESSIONAL: 1981 **Q SCHOOL:** Fall 1981

TOUR VICTORIES (8): 1982 Walt Disney World Golf Classic. **1983** Tournament Players Championship, PGA Championship. **1985** St. Jude Memphis Classic, Southwest Classic. **1986** Phoenix Open, Memorial Tournament. **1995** B.C. Open.

BEST 1995 FINISHES: 1—B.C. Open; T2—Buick Invitational of California; Walt Disney World/Oldsmobile Classic; 4—Bell Canadian Open.

HAL SUTTON...*continued*

1995 SEASON: Completed comeback with the lowest final round to win a tournament in 20 years at the B.C. Open...was late entry into field, proving decision to be a fortuitous one...his 10-under-par 61 (11 birdies, one bogey) in the final round at En-Joie GC earned his eighth career title, and his first since 1986...victory came in the midst of a streak of six consecutive tournaments in which he made the cut...included in that run was a fourth the week prior to his victory at the Bell Canadian Open and a T2 a month later at the Walt Disney World/Oldsmobile Classic...had another T2 earlier in the season, finishing four strokes behind Peter Jacobsen at the Buick Invitational of California...named PGA TOUR Player of the Month for September.

CAREER HIGHLIGHTS: In 1994, authored one of season's best comeback stories, which earned him Hilton Bounceback Award...played on TOUR under one-time exemption for being Top-50 on all-time money list...returned to Top 30 for first time since 1989, after having fallen to as low as No. 185 in 1992...finished T2 in the Shell Houston Open and lost in a playoff to Dicky Pride at the Federal Express St. Jude Classic...after drastic falloff from 1991 ($346,411) to 1992 ($39,234), rebounded slightly in 1993...had encouraging early start that year with T9 in Buick Invitational, his best finish since T7 in 1991 Greater Milwaukee Open...enjoyed finest year in 1983, his second on TOUR...finished atop money list with $426,668 and victories in PGA and Tournament Players Championships...wire-to-wire PGA effort good for one-stroke win over Jack Nicklaus at Riviera CC...Tournament Players Championship victory came on TPC at Sawgrass course, just second tournament held at Ponte Vedra layout...outlasted Bob Eastwood down stretch for win...defeated Bill Britton in four-hole playoff to win first title in final event of rookie season, 1982 Walt Disney World Classic...notched pair of wins in both 1985 and 1986...won 1985 Chrysler Team Championship with Raymond Floyd...1983 Arnold Palmer Award winner...1983 PGA and Golf Writers Player of Year...winner 1980 U.S. Amateur...1980 Golf Magazine College Player of Year, Collegiate All-America...runner-up 1981 NCAA Championship...winner 1974 Louisiana State Juniors.

PERSONAL: Turn-around in his comeback effort occurred when he returned to his old teacher, Jimmy Ballard.

CAREER SUMMARY — **PLAYOFF RECORD: 3-2**

Year	Events Played	Cuts Made	1st	2nd	3rd	Top 10	Top 25	Earnings	Rank
1980(Am.)	1	1							
1981(Am.)	2	2							
1981	4								
1982	31	25	1	3	1	8	15	$237,434	11
1983	30	25	2	1	1	12	16	$426,668	1
1984	26	23		1	1	11	16	$227,949	26
1985	26	23	2	1	1	7	16	$365,340	7
1986	28	23	2	1		9	11	$429,434	6
1987	25	20		3		6	16	$477,996	16
1988	27	16				1	8	$137,296	88
1989	30	20		2		7	12	$422,703	23
1990	28	18				4	8	$207,084	75
1991	28	23			1	5	13	$346,411	47
1992	29	8					1	$39,234	185
1993	29	13				1	2	$74,144	161
1994	29	23		2		4	15	$540,162	29
1995	31	17	1	2		4	8	$554,733	32
Total	404	280	8	16	5	79	157	$4,486,587	32

1996 PGA TOUR CHARITY TEAM: B.C. Open.

TOP TOURNAMENT SUMMARY

YEAR	81	82	83	84	85	86	87	88	89	90	91	92	93	94	95
Masters Tournament	CUT		T27	CUT	T31	CUT	CUT	CUT	CUT	CUT		CUT			CUT
U.S. Open	CUT	T19	6	T16	T23	T4	T31	64	T29	CUT	CUT				T36
British Open Championship	T47	CUT	T29	CUT			T11	CUT							
PGA Championship		T29	1	T6	T65	T21	T28	T66	CUT	T49	T7	CUT	T31	T55	CUT
THE PLAYERS Championship			1	T41	T22	T7	T24	CUT	T29	CUT	T68	CUT	CUT	T19	CUT
THE TOUR Championship							T5		T22					T24	

NATIONAL TEAMS: USA vs. Japan, 1983. Ryder Cup (2), 1985, 1987. Nissan Cup, 1986. Walker Cup (2), 1979, 1981.

1995 PGA TOUR STATISTICS

Statistic	Value	Rank
Scoring	70.84	(59T)
Driving	270.1	(44)
Driving Accuracy	77.0	(14)
Greens in Regulation	70.0	(13)
Putting	1.777	(58T)
All Around	407	(14)
Sand Saves	39.7	(186)
Total Driving	58	(2)
Eagles	9	(20T)
Birdies	360	(13T)

MISCELLANEOUS STATISTICS

Statistic	Value	Rank
Scoring Avg Before Cut	70.97	(67)
Scoring Avg 3rd Rnd	70.68	(61)
Scoring Avg Final Rnd	70.35	(25)
Birdies Conversion %	30.4	(41)
Par Breakers	21.8	(7T)

1995 Low Round: **61:** 1995 B.C. Open/4
Career Low Round: **61:** 1995 B.C. Open/4
Career Largest Paycheck: $180,000: 1995 B.C. Open/1

Jim Thorpe

EXEMPT STATUS: Special Medical Extension
FULL NAME: Jimmy Lee Thorpe
HEIGHT: 6' **WEIGHT:** 200
BIRTH DATE: February 1, 1949 **BIRTHPLACE:** Roxboro, NC
RESIDENCE: Buffalo, NY
FAMILY: Wife, Carol; Sheronne (3/6/77), Chera (12/3/88)
COLLEGE: Morgan State University
SPECIAL INTERESTS: Football, basketball, hunting
TURNED PROFESSIONAL: 1972 **Q SCHOOL:** Fall, 1978

TOUR VICTORIES (3): 1985 Greater Milwaukee Open, Seiko Tucson Match Play Championship. **1986** Seiko Tucson Match Play Championship.

INTERNATIONAL VICTORIES (1): 1982 Canadian PGA Championship (Can).

1995 SEASON: Competition was limited to 15 events due to back problems...missed Buick Open cut in August was his final start of the season...he missed the cut in 10 events and had to withdraw from another two...best 1995 finish was a T32 in the Shell Houston Open...this year he is playing under a Special Medical Extension, in which he has 10 events to earn $133,414.

CAREER HIGHLIGHTS: After struggling for three seasons, he regained full exempt status by finishing 95th on the 1994 money list...earned $185,714 for his fourth-best earnings year on TOUR...he credited fellow TOUR player Vijay Singh with inspiring him to practice more...last player to win back-to-back match play championships ...capped brilliant 1985 season by defeating Jack Renner in final of Seiko-Tucson Match Play Championship...followed with repeat victory in Tucson in 1986, besting Scott Simpson...each Match Play victory was worth $150,000...unable to make it three in a row in Tucson in 1987, when the event returned to stroke play...underwent surgery on left wrist/thumb that Sept. 30...missed most of the 1988 season due to recuperation from surgery...began to return to form in 1989, when he finished tied for second in the Kemper Open...had another runner-up finish in the 1990 Phoenix Open, his second start of the year...1985 campaign also featured a victory in the Greater Milwaukee Open, as well as a playoff loss to Scott Verplank in the Western Open...co-medalist (with John Fought) in the Fall 1978 Qualifying Tournament...finished tied for second the next year in the Joe Garagiola-Tucson Open...first earned card in 1975, but returned home after making just $2,000 in 1976.

PERSONAL: Ninth of 12 children...grew up adjacent to Roxboro (NC) Golf Club, where his father was greens superintendent...earned scholarship to Morgan State as a football running back...brother Chuck played the PGA TOUR in the early 1970s.

CAREER SUMMARY **PLAYOFF RECORD: 0-1**

Year	Events Played	Cuts Made	1st	2nd	3rd	Top 10	Top 25	Earnings	Rank
1976	8	2						$1,140	227
1979	26	18		1		2	6	$48,987	80
1980	25	15				2	5	$33,671	99
1981	29	16				1	6	$43,011	93
1982	28	21				3	7	$66,379	63
1983	30	21		2		3	9	$118,197	46
1984	29	21			1	5	11	$135,818	48
1985	28	21	2	1		6	9	$379,091	4
1986	27	20	1	1		7	11	$326,087	15
1987	22	9				1	4	$57,198	139
1988	9	3						$4,028	252
1989	29	11		1		1	4	$104,704	123
1990	28	16		1		1	8	$211,297	70
1991	27	13					1	$46,039	179
1992	21	6					1	$28,235	200
1993	19	9					4	$70,376	166
1994	26	14				3	6	$185,714	95
1995	15	3						$12,945	251
Total	426	239	3	7	1	35	92	$1,872,916	104

JIM THORPE...*continued*

TOP TOURNAMENT SUMMARY

YEAR	79	80	81	82	83	84	85	86	87	88	90	91	93	94	95
Masters Tournament				CUT		CUT	T18	T45	T42	W/D					
U.S. Open			T11	T30	T13	T4	T34	CUT	T9	CUT			CUT	CUT	
British Open Championship								CUT	CUT						
PGA Championship			T39	T34	T14	T59		T7	CUT		CUT				
THE PLAYERS Championship	T28	T45	74	T32	T54	T10	CUT	T4	CUT		W/D	CUT		T62	CUT

1995 PGA TOUR STATISTICS

Scoring	72.85	(N/A)
Driving	258.0	(N/A)
Driving Accuracy	64.6	(N/A)
Greens in Regulation	63.4	(N/A)
Putting	1.844	(N/A)
Sand Saves	40.3	(N/A)
Total Driving		(N/A)
Eagles	3	(N/A)
Birdies	90	(N/A)

MISCELLANEOUS STATISTICS

Scoring Avg Before Cut	73.23	(N/A)
Scoring Avg 3rd Rnd	70.67	(N/A)
Scoring Avg Final Rnd	73.00	(N/A)
Birdies Conversion %	23.4	(N/A)
Par Breakers	15.3	(N/A)

1995 Low Round: **69:** 3 times, most recent 1995 Shell Houston Open/1
Career Low Round: **62:** 1985 Greater Milwaukee/3
Career Largest Paycheck: $150,000: 2 times, most recent 1985 Seiko-Tucson/1

TOMMY TOLLES *(TOLLS)*

EXEMPT STATUS: 116th on 1995 money list
FULL NAME: Thomas Louis Tolles, Jr.
HEIGHT: 6'1" **WEIGHT:** 195
BIRTH DATE: 10/21/66 **BIRTHPLACE:** Ft. Myers, FL
RESIDENCE: Flat Rock, NC
FAMILY: Wife, Ilse; Wiekus (3/27/93)
COLLEGE: University of Georgia
SPECIAL INTERESTS: Fishing, boating
TURNED PROFESSIONAL: 1988 **Q SCHOOL:** 1994

BEST TOUR FINISH: T3—1995 Bob Hope Chrysler Classic.

NIKE TOUR VICTORIES (2): 1993 NIKE Ozarks Open. **1994** NIKE Alabama Classic.

BEST 1995 FINISHES: T3—Bob Hope Chrysler Classic; T7—BellSouth Classic.

1995 SEASON: Enjoyed a solid rookie season on the PGA TOUR...finished T21 in his first start at the AT&T Pebble Beach National Pro-Am...after missing the cut in his next start, finished T3 in the Bob Hope Chrysler Classic...an 8-under-par 64 in the fourth round got him to within two strokes of lead, which is where he finished after a final-round, 2-under-par 70...$62,400 payday was the largest of his young TOUR career...in May had his only other top-10 finish, a T7 at the BellSouth Classic...tied for fifth on TOUR with 12 eagles...had three eagles during the second round of the Bell Canadian Open, the first player to do so since Dave Stockton, Jr. during the 1994 Walt Disney World/Oldsmobile Classic.

CAREER HIGHLIGHTS: Earned PGA TOUR membership by finishing 24th in the 1994 Qualifying Tournament...qualified for and participated in the 1988 and 1991 U.S. Opens, missing the cut in both...four-year veteran of the NIKE TOUR, where he won two tournaments...first victory came in the 1993 NIKE Ozarks Open...trailed by two strokes after 54 holes before a final-round, 6-under-

TOMMY TOLLES...*continued*

par 66 at Highland Springs CC earned a two-stroke victory over Bob Burns and Bob May...had lost in a three-way playoff to Lennie Clements there in 1992...won the 1994 NIKE Alabama Classic by one stroke over Clark Burroughs...finished 16th on the 1994 NIKE TOUR money list with $98,618...led the 1994 NIKE TOUR with 368 birdies...ranked second to David Duval on the 1994 NIKE TOUR in par breakers at 24%...also finished second in par breakers in 1993...played the South African PGA Tour in 1989-90.

PERSONAL: Met wife Ilse while playing the South African Tour.

PGA TOUR CAREER SUMMARY — **PLAYOFF RECORD: 0-0**

Year	Events Played	Cuts Made	1st	2nd	3rd	Top 10	Top 25	Earnings	Rank
1988	1								
1991	2								
1995	27	13			1	2	5	$166,431	116
Total	30	13			1	2	5	$166,431	357

NIKE TOUR SUMMARY

Year	Events Played	Cuts Made	1st	2nd	3rd	Top 10	Top 25	Earnings	Rank
1991	24	13				3	10	$20,480	61
1992	24	15		1		3	9	$43,062	33
1993	20	12	1	1		3	6	$61,391	24
1994	26	18	1		1	7	13	$98,618	16
Total	94	58	2	2	1	16	38	$223,550	4
COMBINED TOTAL MONEY								$389,980	

1996 PGA TOUR CHARITY TEAM: Greater Vancouver Open.

TOP TOURNAMENT SUMMARY

YEAR	88	91
U.S. Open	CUT	CUT

1995 PGA TOUR STATISTICS

Scoring	71.28	(99T)
Driving	271.4	(29T)
Driving Accuracy	55.0	(187)
Greens in Regulation	64.3	(138T)
Putting	1.774	(54T)
All Around	635	(69T)
Sand Saves	58.6	(24T)
Total Driving	216	(135T)
Eagles	12	(5T)
Birdies	272	(99T)

MISCELLANEOUS STATISTICS

Scoring Avg Before Cut	70.95	(65T)
Scoring Avg 3rd Rnd	70.69	(62)
Scoring Avg Final Rnd	71.00	(72T)
Birdies Conversion %	29.8	(56T)
Par Breakers	20.0	(56T)

1995 Low Round: 63: 1995 Buick Open/2
Career Low Round: 63: 1995 Buick Open/2
Career Largest Paycheck: $62,400: 1995 Bob Hope Chrysler Classic/T3

Did You Know?

When Jim McGovern scored a hole-in-one at the sixth hole at Westchester Country Club during the 1995 Buick Classic, it was the 11th ace recorded at that hole in the 1990s. No course on the PGA TOUR can boast as many.

David Toms

EXEMPT STATUS: 3rd on 1995 NIKE TOUR money list
FULL NAME: David Wayne Toms
HEIGHT: 5'10" **WEIGHT:** 160
BIRTH DATE: January 4, 1967 **BIRTHPLACE:** Monroe, LA
RESIDENCE: Bossier City, LA
FAMILY: Wife, Sonya
COLLEGE: Louisiana State University
SPECIAL INTERESTS: Hunting, fishing
TURNED PROFESSIONAL: 1989 **Q-SCHOOL:** Fall, 1991

BEST TOUR FINISH: 3—1992 Northern Telecom Open

NIKE TOUR VICTORIES (2): 1995 NIKE Greater Greenville Classic, NIKE Wichita Open.

BEST 1995 FINISHES: Did not play PGA TOUR in 1995

1995 SEASON: Earned a return trip to the PGA TOUR by finishing third on the 1995 NIKE TOUR money list...won the NIKE Greater Greenville Classic in a playoff over Tom Scherrer...added his second victory of the year at the NIKE Wichita Open, where he defeated E.J. Pfister in a playoff...among his 10 top-10 finishes were a T2 at the NIKE Inland Empire Open and T3s at the NIKE Carolina Classic and NIKE Gateway Classic...one of six multiple winners on the 1995 NIKE TOUR...had holes-in-one in the second round of the NIKE Monterrey Open and during the third round of the NIKE Ozarks Open...ranked seventh on the NIKE TOUR with a 70.28 scoring average and sixth in birdies with 348.

CAREER HIGHLIGHTS: Member of the PGA TOUR in 1992-94...first qualified for the TOUR by finishing 24th in the 1991 Qualifying Tournament...best-ever finish came in the 1992 Northern Telecom Open ...was tied for 27th place through 54 holes before a final-round 63 boosted him to a tie for third...had his best TOUR season in 1992, finishing 101st on the money list with $148,712...opened the 1992 Kemper Open with a course-record-tying 63...had never seen TPC at Avenel course before round...had been married the Saturday before, delaying arrival in the D.C. area...after retaining his membership by finishing 123rd on the 1993 money list, he lost it by dropping to 164th ($87,607) in 1994...first-team All-American at LSU in 1988-89...1988 and '89 Southeastern Conference Player of the Year...semifinalist in the 1988 U.S. Amateur.

PERSONAL: Teammates at LSU included Robert Friend, Emlyn Aubrey, Perry Moss and Greg Lesher, all of whom have played the PGA TOUR at one time or another.

PGA TOUR CAREER SUMMARY — **PLAYOFF RECORD: 0-0**

Year	Events Played	Cuts Made	1st	2nd	3rd	Top 10	Top 25	Earnings	Rank
1989	5	1						$1,463	278
1990	3								
1992	30	14			1	1	4	$148,712	101
1993	32	12				3	5	$120,952	123
1994	32	16					4	$87,607	164
Total	102	43			1	4	13	$358,734	280

NIKE TOUR SUMMARY

Year	Events Played	Cuts Made	1st	2nd	3rd	Top 10	Top 25	Earnings	Rank
1990	26	12		1		1	5	$20,943	49
1991	6	4					3	$3,372	149
1993	1								
1995	27	17	2	1	2	10	15	$174,892	3
Total	60	33	2	2	2	11	23	$199,206	
COMBINED TOTAL MONEY								$557,940	

1996 PGA TOUR CHARITY TEAM: Mercedes Championships.

TOP TOURNAMENT SUMMARY

YEAR	92	93	94
THE PLAYERS Championship	CUT	CUT	CUT

1995 NIKE TOUR STATISTICS

Scoring	70.28	(7)
Eagles	9	(21T)
Birdies	348	(6)

MISCELLANEOUS PGA TOUR STATISTICS

Career Low Round: 63: 2 times, most recent 1992 Kemper Open/1
Career Largest Paycheck: $74,800: 1992 Northern Telecom/3

Kirk Triplett

EXEMPT STATUS: 29th on 1995 money list
FULL NAME: Kirk Alan Triplett
HEIGHT: 6' 3" **WEIGHT:** 200
BIRTH DATE: March 29, 1962 **BIRTHPLACE:** Moses Lake, WA
RESIDENCE: Nashville, TN
FAMILY: Wife, Cathi
COLLEGE: University of Nevada (1985, Civil Engineering)
SPECIAL INTERESTS: Basketball, reading, computers
TURNED PROFESSIONAL: 1985 **Q SCHOOL:** Fall 1989

BEST-EVER FINISHES: 2--1992 Shell Houston Open; T2--1994 AT&T Pebble Beach National Pro-Am; T2—1995 Buick Invitational of California; T2--1995 Canon Greater Hartford Open.

BEST 1995 FINISHES: T2—Buick Invitational of California, Canon Greater Hartford Open; T3—B.C. Open; T4—Deposit Guaranty Golf Classic, Buick Challenge; T10—Freeport-McMoRan Classic, Las Vegas Invitational.

INTERNATIONAL VICTORIES (1): 1988 Alberta Open (Can).

1995 SEASON: Matched his career-best finish when he posted a pair of T2s in the Buick Invitational of California and the Canon Greater Hartford Open...in San Diego he finished four strokes back of champion Peter Jacobsen, while he finished two behind Greg Norman in Hartford...a closing 5-under-par 66 earned him a T3 at the B.C. Open...followed that with a T4 the next week at the Buick Challenge and a T10 the following week at the Las Vegas Invitational...from the second round of the Motorola Western Open through the first round of the LaCantera Texas Open, had a streak of 27 consecutive rounds of par-or-better...that was the longest streak on the PGA TOUR since Mark O'Meara had 29 in 1991...his $655,607 in earnings were a career best.

CAREER HIGHLIGHTS: Began the 1994 season with four top-10s in first six starts, including a T2 in the AT&T Pebble Beach National Pro-Am...finished in four-way tie at 6-under-par 282, one stroke behind Johnny Miller...Pebble Beach showing matched career-best finish, a second behind Fred Funk in 1992 Shell Houston Open...Houston showing produced career paycheck, $129,600...top 1993 placing came in second start, T3 at Phoenix Open...shared first-round 1993 PLAYERS Championship lead with Nick Price after opening 64...placed third in TOUR rookie earnings in 1990 with $183,464, trailing only Robert Gamez ($461,407) and Peter Persons ($218,505)...placed third in '90 Buick Classic after holding first-round lead with 6-under-par 65...fell back with second-round 74 at Westchester CC before closing 67-66...played Australian, Asian and Canadian Tours 1987-89...winner 1988 Alberta Open, Sierra Nevada Open, Ft. McMurray Classic...is second on the all-time money list among players who have yet to win, trailing only Bobby Wadkins ($2,448,213).

PERSONAL: Says of foreign tours play: "I wouldn't trade the experience for anything. I learned so much, not only about golf but about myself. I'll be telling stories about Asia until the day I die."...wife Cathi occasionally caddies for him and is very active in TOUR Wives Association.

CAREER SUMMARY — **PLAYOFF RECORD: 0-0**

Year	Events Played	Cuts Made	1st	2nd	3rd	Top 10	Top 25	Earnings	Rank
1986	1								
1987	1								
1988	1								
1990	26	13			1	2	5	$183,464	88
1991	28	18					6	$137,302	112
1992	25	10		1		1	2	$175,868	85
1993	27	19			1	2	6	$189,418	90
1994	26	19		1		8	15	$422,171	38
1995	27	24		2	1	7	17	$644,607	29
Total	162	103		4	3	20	51	$1,752,830	115

1996 PGA TOUR CHARITY TEAM: Bob Hope Chrysler Classic.

TOP TOURNAMENT SUMMARY

YEAR	86	87	90	91	92	93	94	95
U.S. Open	CUT	CUT	T33	CUT	66	T52	T23	
British Open Championship							CUT	
PGA Championship			CUT		CUT		T15	T13
THE PLAYERS Championship			T36	T68	CUT	T39	T45	67
THE TOUR Championship								T20

Kirk Triplett...continued

1995 PGA TOUR STATISTICS		
Scoring	70.22	(15T)
Driving	262.9	(93)
Driving Accuracy	74.5	(27)
Greens in Regulation	69.7	(15T)
Putting	1.752	(12)
All Around	339	(3)
Sand Saves	50.4	(122T)
Total Driving	120	(18)
Eagles	7	(51T)
Birdies	399	(4)

MISCELLANEOUS STATISTICS		
Scoring Avg Before Cut	69.89	(4)
Scoring Avg 3rd Rnd	70.09	(24)
Scoring Avg Final Rnd	71.13	(82T)
Birdies Conversion %	31.8	(20)
Par Breakers	22.6	(2)

1995 Low Round: 64: 1995 Canon Greater Hartford Open/1
Career Low Round: 63: 1994 Buick Invitational of California/2
Career Largest Paycheck: $129,600: 1992 Shell Houston Open/2

Ted Tryba *(TREE-buh)*

EXEMPT STATUS: 1995 tournament winner
FULL NAME: Ted Nickolas Tryba
HEIGHT: 6' 4" **WEIGHT:** 205
BIRTH DATE: January 15, 1967 **BIRTHPLACE:** Wilkes-Barre, PA
RESIDENCE: Orlando, FL
COLLEGE: Ohio State University (1989, Marketing)
SPECIAL INTERESTS: Basketball
TURNED PROFESSIONAL: 1989 **Q SCHOOL:** Fall 1989

TOUR VICTORIES (1): 1995 Anheuser-Busch Golf Classic.

NIKE TOUR VICTORIES (3): 1990 Gateway Open. **1991** Ben Hogan Utah Classic. **1992** BH Shreveport Open.

BEST 1995 FINISHES: 1—Anheuser-Busch Golf Classic; T2—Walt Disney World/Oldsmobile Classic; T7—Kmart Greater Greensboro Open.

1995 SEASON: Broke through with his first career title in July at the Anheuser-Busch Golf Classic...trailed by one stroke after 54 holes, but a final-round 3-under-par 68 earned a one-stroke triumph over Scott Simpson...a birdie on the 11th hole gave him a four-stroke lead, before Simpson birdied three of his final six holes to pull to within a stroke...earned $198,000 for the victory...nearly added a second win in October at the rain-shortened Walt Disney World/Oldsmobile Classic...along with Hal Sutton finished tied for second, one stroke behind Brad Bryant...due to logistics of three courses, finished his final round before Bryant even teed off...low round of the season came the next week when he fired a 63 during the third round of the Las Vegas Invitational...other top-10 finish was a T7 in the Kmart Greater Greensboro Open.

CAREER HIGHLIGHTS: Had a quick start to his 1994 season... finished T6 in United Airlines Hawaiian Open...followed that three weeks later with a T7 in AT&T Pebble Beach National Pro-Am...those two top-10s wrapped around T20 in Northern Telecom Open and a T18 at Phoenix Open...began season with earnings of $105,925 after just four outings...biggest payday rest of way was $23,800 for T15 in Sprint International...finished T3 in 1993 Walt Disney World/ Oldsmobile Classic, his third-to-last event, to retain playing privileges for 1994...$52,800 payday secured place in Top 125...earned TOUR card on first attempt in 1989, lost it after earning just $10,708 in 1990...played Ben Hogan Tour 1990-92...won 1990 Gateway Open, 1991 Utah Classic...became only player to win three consecutive years on Hogan (now NIKE) Tour by capturing 1992 Shreveport Open...earned TOUR card for 1993 by shooting 69 on final day of 1992 season to finish T3 in Fresno Open...finished No. 4 overall with earnings of $105,951...tied for first in Hogan Tour eagles with 12 in 1992...four-time All-Big Ten and three-time NCAA All-American at Ohio State...Pennsylvania State High School Champion.

PERSONAL: Troubled by neck problems from December 1994 to mid-March 1995...A-B Classic in July helped him forgot all about those earlier woes.

TED TRYBA...*continued*

PGA TOUR CAREER SUMMARY					PLAYOFF RECORD: 0-0				
Year	**Events Played**	**Cuts Made**	**1st**	**2nd**	**3rd**	**Top 10**	**Top 25**	**Earnings**	**Rank**
1987(Am.)	1								
1989	1								
1990	18	6						$10,708	226
1993	33	16			1	2	2	$136,670	116
1994	34	22				2	10	$246,481	74
1995	35	17	1	1		3	5	$451,983	39
Total	122	61	1	1	1	7	17	$845,841	197

NIKE TOUR SUMMARY									
Year	**Events Played**	**Cuts Made**	**1st**	**2nd**	**3rd**	**Top 10**	**Top 25**	**Earnings**	**Rank**
1990	7	6	1			1	2	$23,735	42
1991	27	12	1	1		5	11	$46,491	16
1992	28	21	1	2	2	9	15	$105,952	4
1993	1	1					1	$1,894	185
Total	63	40	3	3	2	15	29	$178,072	
COMBINED TOTAL MONEY								$1,023,913	

1996 PGA TOUR CHARITY TEAM: Michelob Championship at Kingsmill.

TOP TOURNAMENT SUMMARY		
YEAR	**94**	**95**
U.S. Open		T51
PGA Championship	CUT	CUT
THE PLAYERS Championship	T35	CUT

1995 PGA TOUR STATISTICS		
Scoring	71.66	(132T)
Driving	259.7	(122T)
Driving Accuracy	70.6	(79T)
Greens in Regulation	62.7	(168T)
Putting	1.793	(105T)
All Around	790	(113)
Sand Saves	54.7	(65)
Total Driving	201	(117T)
Eagles	5	(88T)
Birdies	335	(31)

MISCELLANEOUS STATISTICS		
Scoring Avg Before Cut	71.41	(108T)
Scoring Avg 3rd Rnd	71.44	(115T)
Scoring Avg Final Rnd	70.88	(62T)
Birdies Conversion %	28.8	(89T)
Par Breakers	18.3	(115T)

1995 Low Round: **63:** 1995 Las Vegas Invitational/3
Career Low Round: **63:** 1995 Las Vegas Invitational/3
Career Largest Paycheck: **$198,000:** 1995 Anheuser-Busch Golf Classic/1

BOB TWAY

EXEMPT STATUS: Winner, 1986 PGA Championship
FULL NAME: Robert Raymond Tway
HEIGHT: 6' 4" **WEIGHT:** 180
BIRTH DATE: May 4, 1959 **BIRTHPLACE:** Oklahoma City, OK
RESIDENCE: Edmond, OK; plays out of Oak Tree Golf Club
FAMILY: Wife, Tammie; Kevin (7/23/88), Carly Paige (11/8/93)
COLLEGE: Oklahoma State University
SPECIAL INTERESTS: Snow skiing, fishing, all sports
TURNED PROFESSIONAL: 1981 **Q SCHOOL:** Fall 1984

TOUR VICTORIES (7): 1986 Shearson Lehman Bros.-Andy Williams Open, Manufacturers Hanover Westchester Classic, Georgia Pacific Atlanta Classic, PGA Championship. **1989** Memorial Tournament. **1990** Las Vegas Invitational. **1995** MCI Classic.

BEST 1995 FINISHES: 1—MCI Classic; T4—Walt Disney World/Oldsmobile Classic; T5—Fedex St. Jude Classic; T6—Northern Telecom Open, Motorola Western Open; T9—GTE Byron Nelson Classic, Bell Canadian Open; T10—U.S. Open.

1995 SEASON: After three down years, returned to the level of play he exhibited in the past...opened his season with his first top-10 finish since the 1993 Las Vegas Invitational, when he finished T6 in the Northern Telecom Open...earned his first PGA TOUR victory since 1990, defeating Nolan Henke and David Frost in a playoff at the MCI Classic...after Henke was eliminated on the first extra hole, defeated Frost with a birdie on the second hole after he hit a 7-iron to within three feet...had eight top-10 finishes on the season, including three consecutively at the U.S. Open (T10), FedEx St. Jude Classic (T5) and Motorola Western Open (T6)...was tied for the U.S. Open lead through 63 holes, before bogeys on four of his final holes dropped him to T10...$787,348 in earnings were a career high...ranked seventh on the PGA TOUR with a scoring average of 69.91...received PGA TOUR Comeback Player Award in vote of TOUR membership.

CAREER HIGHLIGHTS: Struggled through worst season of 10-year career in 1992...turned things around during late stages of 1993 with pair of top-10 finishes...solo fourth in Hardee's Golf Classic highest finish since T2 behind Phil Mickelson in 1991 Northern Telecom Open...concluded 1993 campaign with T6 in Las Vegas Invitational...jumped from No. 142 to 109 on money list with that performance...made two aces at 1994 Memorial, first TOUR player in 30 years to record two holes-in-one in same event...finished as runner-up in 1994 Mexican Open...enjoyed dream sophomore season in 1986, collecting four victories, including PGA Championship...won PGA with hole-out from bunker on 72nd hole at Inverness to defeat Greg Norman...named PGA Player of Year and finished No. 2 on money list, just $516 behind Norman...defeated Fuzzy Zoeller by two strokes in 1989 Memorial Tournament, parred first playoff hole to edge John Cook in 1990 Las Vegas Invitational...member 1986 Nissan Cup...winner 1983 Sandpiper-Santa Barbara Open (TPS Series), 1987 Oklahoma State Open, 1987 Chrysler Team Championship (with Mike Hulbert) and 1988 Fred Meyer Challenge (with Paul Azinger)...member 1980 World Amateur Cup team...three-time All-American at Oklahoma State (1979-81)...winner 1981 Fred Haskins Trophy as outstanding collegiate player...member 1978, '80 NCAA Championship teams...winner 1978 Trans-Mississippi Amateur, 1979 Southern Amateur.

PERSONAL: Described MCI Classic win as "better than any other win I've ever had, because I was down so low."...played mini-tours and in Asia before joining TOUR in 1985.

CAREER SUMMARY — **PLAYOFF RECORD: 2-3**

Year	Events Played	Cuts Made	1st	2nd	3rd	Top 10	Top 25	Earnings	Rank
1981(Am.)	1	1							
1981	2	1						$582	295
1982	9	7					1	$9,039	177
1983	8	6					2	$12,089	174
1984	2	1						$1,719	237
1985	25	14		1	2	4	9	$164,023	45
1986	33	28	4			13	21	$652,780	2
1987	27	19			1	7	12	$212,362	47
1988	30	25		2	1	4	13	$381,966	29
1989	28	19	1	2		4	9	$488,340	17
1990	29	20	1			5	8	$495,862	23
1991	24	15		1		5	7	$322,931	52
1992	21	12						$47,632	179
1993	25	11				2	4	$148,120	109
1994	29	13					4	$114,176	146
1995	27	22	1			8	15	$787,348	20
Total	320	214	7	6	4	52	105	$3,838,969	38

1996 PGA TOUR CHARITY TEAM: NEC World Series of Golf.

TOP TOURNAMENT SUMMARY

YEAR	86	87	88	89	90	91	92	93	94	95
Masters Tournament	T8	CUT	T33	CUT	T36	CUT				
U.S. Open	T8	T68	T25	CUT	T33	T26		CUT	CUT	T10
British Open Championship	T46	T35	T20	T61	CUT	T5	CUT			CUT
PGA Championship	1	T47	T48	CUT	T45	T66	T56	CUT	CUT	CUT
THE PLAYERS Championship	T10	CUT	CUT	T29	CUT	T41	T70	CUT	CUT	T68
THE TOUR Championship			T8	T22	T14					15

NATIONAL TEAMS: World Amateur Cup, 1980. Nissan Cup, 1986. Asahi Glass Four Tours, 1991.

1995 PGA TOUR STATISTICS

Scoring	69.93	(8)
Driving	266.9	(62)
Driving Accuracy	70.2	(88)
Greens in Regulation	67.5	(55T)
Putting	1.754	(15)
All Around	439	(20)
Sand Saves	51.1	(106T)
Total Driving	150	(45)
Eagles	5	(88T)
Birdies	354	(17)

MISCELLANEOUS STATISTICS

Scoring Avg Before Cut	70.08	(8T)
Scoring Avg 3rd Rnd	69.38	(7)
Scoring Avg Final Rnd	70.95	(71)
Birdies Conversion %	31.7	(21)
Par Breakers	21.2	(15T)

1995 Low Round: **64:** 1995 FedEx St. Jude Classic/2
Career Low Round: **61:** 1989 Disney/Olds Classic/1
Career Largest Paycheck: $234,000: 2 times, most recent 1990 Las Vegas Invitational/1

SCOTT VERPLANK

EXEMPT STATUS: 55th on 1995 money list
FULL NAME: Scott Rachal Verplank
HEIGHT: 5'9" **WEIGHT:** 165
BIRTH DATE: July 9, 1964 **BIRTHPLACE:** Dallas, TX
RESIDENCE: Edmond, OK
FAMILY: Wife, Kim; Scottie (7/14/92), Hannah (1/26/95)
COLLEGE: Oklahoma State University (Business)
SPECIAL INTERESTS: Reading, playing with his kids, sports
TURNED PROFESSIONAL: 1986

TOUR VICTORIES (2): 1985 Western Open. **1988** Buick Open.

BEST 1995 FINISHES: T4—BellSouth Classic; T5—GTE Byron Nelson Classic: T8—Honda Classic; T10—Quad City Classic.

1995 SEASON: Showed that his comeback from past physical problems was complete by having the second-best money-won year of his career...earned $332,886 to rank 55th...best finish of the season was aT4 in the BellSouth Classic, which he followed with a T5 the next week at the GTE Byron Nelson Classic...those two tournaments came in the midst of streak where he had 17 of 18 rounds at par-or-better...first top-10 finish of the year came in the Honda Classic, where he closed with a 3-under-par 69...in September, finished T10 at the Quad City Classic...a tie for 32nd worth $6,227 in his second start of the year, at the Buick Invitational of California, pushed him over the $1 million mark in career earnings...ranked ninth in the All-Around statistical category.

CAREER HIGHLIGHTS: Penned inspiring comeback story in 1994, having battled back from physical adversity and through long-term diabetes...right elbow pain in Nov. 1990 led to Dec. 1991 surgery for the removal of bone spurs...following the 1992 season had operation to increase blood flow in joint of the elbow...missed most of 1991 and 1992 seasons, all of 1993...given special medical extension and 11 tournaments (through U.S. Open) to earn $117,608 in '94, made eight of 11 cuts but failed to earn necessary amount...playing with sponsor's exemptions or as past champion from July on, regained full privileges for 1995...struggled through first two years on TOUR, a victim of high expectations stemming from 1985 Western Open playoff victory (as an amateur) over Jim Thorpe...first amateur to win TOUR event since Gene Littler in 1954...finished well out of Top 125 in 1986 and 1987, had to go to Qualifying Tournament to regain playing privileges for 1988 (finished T6)...took the pressure off by winning 1988 Buick Open...268 total tied second-best score ever at Warwick Hills CC...had been tied with Howard Twitty and Steve Elkington entering final round...highly acclaimed amateur even before 1985 Western Open victory...winner 1984 U.S. Amateur...winner 1986 NCAA Championship...winner 1982-84-85 Texas State Amateur, 1982-83-84-85 LaJet Amateur Classic, 1984 Western Amateur (medalist 1984-85)...winner 1984-85 Sunnehanna Amateur...1984 Big Eight Conference champion...two-time All-American...member 1985 Academic All-America team...1982 AJGA Player of Year.

PERSONAL: Was youngest player on TOUR when he joined in 1986...following 1992 surgery by Dr. Frank Jobe, didn't play golf for a year or in a tournament 18 months.

PGA TOUR CAREER SUMMARY **PLAYOFF RECORD: 1-0**

Year	Events Played	Cuts Made	1st	2nd	3rd	Top 10	Top 25	Earnings	Rank
1983(Am.)	1								
1984(Am.)	1	1							
1985(Am.)	4	2	1			1	1		
1986(Am.)	5	3				1	2		
1986	13	5				1	2	$19,757	177
1987	31	12					2	$34,136	173
1988	28	19	1	1		3	9	$366,045	31
1989	28	15				1	3	$82,345	141
1990	27	18		1	1	4	7	$303,589	47
1991	26	1						$3,195	266
1992	13	1						$1,760	309
1994	19	14				1	8	$183,015	97
1995	25	20				4	10	$332,886	55
Total	222	111	2	2	1	16	44	$1,326,728	152

NIKE TOUR SUMMARY

Year	Events Played	Cuts Made	1st	2nd	3rd	Top 10	Top 25	Earnings	Rank
1992	1								
1994	1	1						$220	309
Total	2	1						$220	
COMBINED TOTAL MONEY								$1,326,948	

SCOTT VERPLANK...*continued*

1996 PGA TOUR CHARITY TEAM: NEC World Series of Golf.

TOP TOURNAMENT SUMMARY

YEAR	85	86	87	88	89	90	91	94	95
Masters Tournament	CUT	CUT	CUT		CUT				
U.S. Open	T34	T15	CUT			T61		T18	T21
British Open Championship		CUT		CUT					
PGA Championship				CUT	CUT	T31			CUT
THE PLAYERS Championship		CUT			CUT		CUT		CUT
THE TOUR Championship				T8					

NATIONAL TEAMS: Walker Cup, 1985.

1995 PGA TOUR STATISTICS

Scoring	70.23	(17T)
Driving	268.2	(53)
Driving Accuracy	69.8	(91T)
Greens in Regulation	68.0	(45T)
Putting	1.764	(30T)
All Around	378	(7)
Sand Saves	55.1	(58T)
Total Driving	144	(37T)
Eagles	8	(36T)
Birdies	309	(48)

MISCELLANEOUS STATISTICS

Scoring Avg Before Cut	70.61	(34T)
Scoring Avg 3rd Rnd	69.47	(8)
Scoring Avg Final Rnd	70.26	(21)
Birdies Conversion %	29.7	(60T)
Par Breakers	20.7	(30T)

1995 Low Round: **65:** 3 times, most recent 1995 Quad City Classic/1
Career Low Round: **62:** 1990 GMO/2
Career Largest Paycheck: **$126,000:** 1988 Buick Open/1

BOBBY WADKINS

EXEMPT STATUS: 115th on 1995 money list
FULL NAME: Robert Edwin Wadkins
HEIGHT: 6'1" **WEIGHT:** 195
BIRTH DATE: July 26, 1951 **BIRTHPLACE:** Richmond, VA
RESIDENCE: Richmond, VA
FAMILY: Wife, Linda; Casey Tanner (2/14/90)
COLLEGE: East Tennessee State University (1973, Health & Physical Education)
SPECIAL INTERESTS: Fishing, duck and goose hunting
TURNED PROFESSIONAL: 1973 **Q SCHOOL:** Fall 1974

BEST TOUR CAREER FINISH: 2—1978 IVB-Philadelphia Classic, 1985 Sea Pines Heritage Classic. T2--1994 Kemper Open.

INTERNATIONAL VICTORIES (3): 1978 European Open (Eur). **1979** Dunlop Phoenix (Jpn). **1986** Dunlop Phoenix (Jpn).

BEST 1995 FINISH: 3—Buick Classic.

1995 SEASON: Came up one stroke short in his attempt to collect his first-ever PGA TOUR title...a final-round Buick Classic 1-over-par 72 left him one shot shy of joining Vijay Singh and Doug Martin in playoff, eventually won by Singh...entered final round one stroke off Singh's lead...finished T21 the next week at the Kemper Open, site of his 1994 runner-up finish...finished T14 in September at the Bell Canadian Open...continues as TOUR's all-time leader in earnings without win...relinquished that distinction to Loren Roberts in Oct. 1993, but Roberts won Nestle Invitational in March '94...was passed by Brad Bryant at last year's Buick Open, then Bryant won the Walt Disney World/Oldsmobile Classic.

CAREER HIGHLIGHTS: Tie for second in the 1994 Kemper Open matched career bests in 1979 IVB-Philadelphia Classic and 1985 Sea Pines Heritage Classic...playoff loser in each instance, to Lou Graham in '79 and Bernhard Langer in '85...at Kemper led by two strokes over eventual champion Mark Brooks through 54 holes...lost ball and triple-bogey on the sixth hole at the TPC at Avenel led to a final-round 74 and a tie for second with D.A. Weibring, three strokes behind Brooks...Kemper finish also helped prove had come back from April 1992 neck surgery (herniated disc), which limited play that year to just 15 events, none from May to August...surgery occurred Tuesday after '92 Kmart Greater Greensboro Open, last cut made that year...returned to action for Canadian Open, missing cuts in final five starts...played under special medical extension for 1993, when on-going rehab delayed start until May...best finish that year T25 in Memorial...although has not won on TOUR, has three victories overseas: 1978 European Open in Surrey, England and two Dunlop Phoenix titles in Japan (1979 and '86)...prior to 1992 had streak of 14 consecutive years (1978-91) among top 100 money winners...winner 1971 Virginia State Amateur, 1981-82 Virginia State Open...1972-73 NCAA All-America at East Tennessee State attended University of Houston for year.

PERSONAL: Along with older brother Lanny kept Richmond, VA city junior title in family six straight years (Lanny 4, Bobby 2)...served as Lanny's "on-course eyes" during 1995 Ryder Cup.

PGA TOUR CAREER SUMMARY — **PLAYOFF RECORD: 0-2**

Year	Events Played	Cuts Made	1st	2nd	3rd	Top 10	Top 25	Earnings	Rank
1975	28	18				1	6	$23,330	90
1976	34	22					4	$23,510	93
1977	33	19					3	$20,867	103
1978	32	23		1	1	5	10	$70,426	41
1979	31	21		2	1	7	12	$121,373	28
1980	35	23				2	9	$56,728	67
1981	34	25				2	7	$58,346	73
1982	34	26				2	12	$69,400	59
1983	33	22				1	6	$56,363	92
1984	31	22			1	3	9	$108,335	67
1985	31	22		1		1	3	$84,542	90
1986	31	25			1	7	15	$226,079	33
1987	30	22		1		7	17	$342,173	25
1988	31	25				3	13	$193,022	59
1989	31	22			1	1	7	$152,184	91
1990	28	23				2	7	$190,613	85
1991	31	20				2	7	$206,503	81
1992	15	6					1	$30,382	197
1993	24	8					1	$39,153	189
1994	22	14		1		2	5	$208,358	89
1995	30	16			1	1	4	$166,527	115
Total	629	424		6	6	49	158	$2,448,213	75

NIKE TOUR SUMMARY

Year	Events Played	Cuts Made	1st	2nd	3rd	Top 10	Top 25	Earnings	Rank
1993	1								
1994	3	3						$1,953	187
Total	4	3						$1,953	
COMBINED TOTAL MONEY								$2,449,189	

1996 PGA TOUR CHARITY TEAM: Michelob Championship at Kingsmill.

TOP TOURNAMENT SUMMARY

YEAR	75	76	78	79	80	81	82	83	84	85	86	87	88	89	90
Masters Tournament						CUT						21	CUT		
U.S. Open		T35	T46		T12	T43	T60	T65		T46	T15	T4	CUT	66	T33
PGA Championship			T54	71	T59	T67	T49	T27	CUT	W/D	T41	T7	T66	CUT	T66
THE PLAYERS Championship	T8		T12		CUT	T37	T56	T49	CUT	T64	CUT	CUT	T51	CUT	T36
THE TOUR Championship												T24			

TOP TOURNAMENT SUMMARY (cont.)

YEAR	91	92	95
U.S. Open	CUT		
PGA Championship	CUT		CUT
THE PLAYERS Championship	T9	CUT	T61

BOBBY WADKINS...continued

1995 PGA TOUR STATISTICS		
Scoring	71.58	(124T)
Driving	262.3	(98)
Driving Accuracy	69.4	(99)
Greens in Regulation	67.5	(55T)
Putting	1.822	(181)
All Around	810	(120)
Sand Saves	53.8	(74T)
Total Driving	197	(110T)
Eagles	5	(88T)
Birdies	279	(91T)

MISCELLANEOUS STATISTICS		
Scoring Avg Before Cut	71.64	(138)
Scoring Avg 3rd Rnd	71.42	(114)
Scoring Avg Final Rnd	71.94	(149T)
Birdies Conversion %	23.9	(184)
Par Breakers	16.4	(177T)

1995 Low Round: 66: 2 times, most recent 1995 Las Vegas Invitational/2
Career Low Round: 64: 2 times, most recent 1991 H.E.B. Texas Open/2
Career Largest Paycheck: $114,400: 1994 Kemper Open/T2

LANNY WADKINS

EXEMPT STATUS: Life Member
FULL NAME: Jerry Lanston Wadkins
HEIGHT: 5' 9" **WEIGHT:**170
BIRTH DATE: Dec. 5, 1949 **BIRTHPLACE:** Richmond, VA
RESIDENCE: Dallas, TX; plays out of The Homestead
FAMILY: Wife, Penelope; Jessica (10/14/73), Travis (8/25/87), Tucker (8/19/92)
COLLEGE: Wake Forest University
SPECIAL INTERESTS: Fishing, hunting, snow skiing, scuba-diving
TURNED PROFESSIONAL: 1971 **Q SCHOOL:** Fall 1971

TOUR VICTORIES (21): 1972 Sahara Invitational. **1973** Byron Nelson Classic, USI Classic. **1977** PGA Championship, World Series of Golf. **1979** Glen Campbell Los Angeles Open, Tournament Players Championship. **1982** Phoenix Open, MONY-Tournament of Champions, Buick Open. **1983** Greater Greensboro Open, MONY-Tournament of Champions. **1985** Bob Hope Classic, Los Angeles Open, Walt Disney World/Oldsmobile Classic. **1987** Doral-Ryder Open. **1988** Hawaiian Open, Colonial National Invitation. **1990** Anheuser-Busch Golf Classic. **1991** United Hawaiian Open. **1992** Canon Greater Hartford Open.

INTERNATIONAL VICTORIES (4): 1978 Victorian PGA Championship (Aus), Canadian PGA Championship (Can). **1979** Bridgestone Open (Jpn). **1984** World Nissan Championship (Jpn).

BEST 1995 FINISH: T7—Nissan Open.

1995 SEASON: Was only able to play in 20 tournaments, due mainly to demands on his time as the Ryder Cup Captain... posted a pair of solid finishes in tournaments he won in the past, though...finished T7 after rounds of 66-69 on the weekend at the Nissan Open...$38,700 paycheck was his largest of the season...it was his first top-10 since a T3 in the 1993 Anheuser-Busch Golf Classic...finished T15 at the Colonial National Invitation, which he won in 1988...a final-round 4-under-par 67 earned him a T13 at the MCI Classic...went over the $6 million mark in career earnings with $20,335 paycheck at Hilton Head.

CAREER HIGHLIGHTS: Battled infection in his system part of 1993, injured back following '93 PGA Championship...latter jeopardized his chances for making eighth Ryder Cup team, but was Captain's Choice of Tom Watson...captured 21st title in 22nd year on TOUR, winning 1992 Canon Greater Hartford Open...playing 75 minutes ahead of leaders, came from five strokes off lead with final-round 65 to put 274 on board, then watched from CBS-TV tower as all contenders fell short...one of game's fiercest competitors...has won twice in season five times and three times twice (1982, 1985)...named PGA Player of Year in '85...had highest money list finish that year, No. 2...in 1977 won PGA Championship in playoff with Gene Littler, then World Series of Golf title at Firestone CC...claimed 1979 Tournament Players Championship in fierce winds on Sawgrass CC course, scoring five-stroke victory over Tom Watson...winner 1990 Fred Meyer Challenge (with Bobby Wadkins)...winner 1963-64 National Pee Wee, 1970 U.S. Amateur, 1970 Western Amateur, 1968 and '70 Southern Amateur, 1969 Eastern Amateur...1970-71 Collegiate All-America...member 1969-71 Walker Cup, 1970 World Amateur Cup teams.

PERSONAL: Inspirational leader to younger players in Ryder Cups, factor which entered into 1995 Captain selection...enjoys well-deserved reputation as fierce on-course competitor.

CAREER SUMMARY						PLAYOFF RECORD: 3-2			
Year	Events Played	Cuts Made	1st	2nd	3rd	Top 10	Top 25	Earnings	Rank
1969(Am.)	1	1							
1970(Am.)	1	1		1		1	1		
1971(Am.)	4	2					1		
1971	5	5			1	2	4	$15,291	111
1972	33	26	1	2		7	17	$116,616	10
1973	26	23	2	3	3	13	17	$20,455	5
1974	26	15		1		2	6	$51,124	54
1975	23	13			1	1	3	$23,582	88
1976	29	19			1	3	6	$42,850	64
1977	28	22	2	2		9	14	$244,882	3
1978	24	16				5	9	$53,811	61
1979	24	22	2			6	13	$195,710	10
1980	27	18				6	8	$67,778	60
1981	27	21				1	10	$51,704	83
1982	26	21	3	1		9	12	$306,827	7
1983	25	18	2	2	1	11	17	$319,271	3
1984	23	19		1		7	10	$198,996	29
1985	24	22	3	1		12	18	$446,893	2
1986	26	24		2		5	11	$264,931	23
1987	22	19	1	1	2	6	9	$501,727	13
1988	24	23	2	1		6	15	$616,596	10
1989	25	16				6	10	$233,363	60
1990	23	18	1	2	1	6	10	$673,433	13
1991	23	19	1	1	2	7	10	$651,495	12
1992	24	19	1			2	9	$366,837	40
1993	22	12			2	2	7	$244,544	68
1994	25	9					2	$54,114	185
1995	20	8				1	3	$97,485	162
Total	610	451	21	21	14	136	252	$6,009,867	12

1996 PGA TOUR CHARITY TEAM: FedEx St. Jude Classic.

TOP TOURNAMENT SUMMARY

YEAR	71	72	73	74	75	76	77	78	79	80	81	82	83	84	85
Masters Tournament		T19	T29					T18	T7	CUT	T21	T33	T8	CUT	T18
U.S. Open	T13	T25	T7	T26	T38				T19	CUT	T14	T6	7	T11	T5
British Open			T7	T22	CUT			CUT					T29	T4	CUT
PGA Championship		T16	T3				1	T34	70	T30	T33	2	CUT	T2	T10
THE PLAYERS Championship						T65	T34		1	T45	CUT	CUT	CUT	T5	CUT

TOP TOURNAMENT SUMMARY (cont.)

YEAR	86	87	88	89	90	91	92	93	94	95
The Masters Tournament	T31	T12	T11	T26	T3	T3	T48	T3	T18	CUT
U.S. Open	T2	T36	T12	CUT	T51	T63	CUT			
British Open Championship		T29	T34	T26	CUT	T73	T45	CUT		
PGA Championship	T11	2	T25	CUT	CUT	T43	T40	T14	T61	T63
THE PLAYERS Championship	T40	CUT	T6	T41	CUT	62	T29	CUT	CUT	CUT
THE TOUR Championship		29	T14		24	23				

NATIONAL TEAMS: Ryder Cup (8), 1977, 1979, 1983,1985, 1987, 1989, 1991, 1993; Captain, 1995. World Cup (3), 1977, 1984, 1985. Walker Cup (2) 1969, 1971. World Amateur Cup, 1970. U.S. vs. Japan (2), 1982, 1983. Nissan Cup, 1985. Kirin Cup 1987. Dunhill Cup, 1986. Asahi Glass Four Tours, 1991.

1995 PGA TOUR STATISTICS		
Scoring	72.20	(176T)
Driving	252.3	(176)
Driving Accuracy	65.0	(156T)
Greens in Regulation	64.5	(132T)
Putting	1.777	(58T)
All Around	974	(155)
Sand Saves	60.6	(12T)
Total Driving	332	(187)
Eagles	5	(88T)
Birdies	182	(176T)

MISCELLANEOUS STATISTICS		
Scoring Avg Before Cut	72.21	(171T)
Scoring Avg 3rd Rnd	70.40	(42)
Scoring Avg Final Rnd	72.00	(153T)
Birdies Conversion %	26.6	(147T)
Par Breakers	17.6	(147T)

1995 Low Round: 66: 1995 Nissan Open/3
Career Low Round: 62: 1989 Texas Open/1
Career Largest Paycheck: $198,000: 1991 U.A. Hawaiian Open/1

Grant Waite

EXEMPT STATUS: 76th on 1995 money list
FULL NAME: Grant Osten Waite
HEIGHT: 6' **WEIGHT:** 190
BIRTH DATE: August 11, 1964 **BIRTHPLACE:** Palmerston, NZ
RESIDENCE: Palmerston North, New Zealand
FAMILY: Wife, Lea; Osten Holland (6/1/94), Tanner Brian (6/2/95)
COLLEGE: University of Oklahoma
SPECIAL INTERESTS: Wind surfing, reading, skiing, fitness
TURNED PROFESSIONAL: 1987 **Q SCHOOL:** Fall 1989, 1992

TOUR VICTORIES (1): 1993 Kemper Open.

INTERNATIONAL VICTORIES (2): 1992 New Zealand Open (Aus), Trafalgar Capital Classic (Can).

BEST 1995 FINISHES: T2—Canon Greater Hartford Open; T10—United Airlines Hawaiian Open.

1995 SEASON: Began the season with his first top-10 finish since finishing 10th at 1993 NEC World Series of Golf with a T10 at the United Airlines Hawaiian Open...had only one more top-10, but it was a big one...finished T2 with Dave Stockton, Jr., and Kirk Triplett, two strokes behind Greg Norman at the Canon Greater Hartford Open...entered the final round four strokes behind Norman...was his second-best season from an earnings standpoint...ended his season on a positive note, making his last four cuts...low round of the year was a 7-under-par 65 during the third round of the Doral-Ryder Open...ranked tied for fourth on the PGA TOUR in Greens in Regulation (71.3) and fifth in Total Driving.

CAREER HIGHLIGHTS: Had anticipated high point of 1994 season would be defense of Kemper Open title...Kemper week still high point of that season, but for different reason...after checking in at TPC at Avenel, wound up withdrawing to be with wife Lea in Arizona as she delivered their first child, son Osten Holland born June 1, 1994...captured first TOUR title in head-to-head battle with Tom Kite in 1993 Kemper Open...held first- and second-round leads after going 66-67, then gave way to Kite at 54-hole juncture...held steady in face of pressure, carding final-round 70 for one-stroke win...posted T7 in 1993 AT&T Pebble Beach National Pro-Am for first of four top-10s...was Deposit Guaranty Golf Classic clubhouse leader following final-round 63, his career low...ultimately finished T4 in Hattiesburg, MS event...final top-10 of '93 came in NEC World Series of Golf, where made 10-stroke improvement over third-round score with closing 65...prior to 1993, best finish had been T6 in 1990 Hawaiian Open...finished three strokes behind winner David Ishii...finished 25th in 1989 and T20 in 1992 Qualifying Tournaments...three-time All-American at Oklahoma...two-time Australian Junior Champion.

PERSONAL: Selected by CBS Sports as "New Breed Player of Year" for 1993.

PGA TOUR CAREER SUMMARY — **PLAYOFF RECORD: 0-0**

Year	Events Played	Cuts Made	1st	2nd	3rd	Top 10	Top 25	Earnings	Rank
1988	3	1						$1,494	289
1990	27	11				1	1	$50,076	177
1991	4	2				1	1	$9,307	229
1992	2								
1993	30	16	1			4	6	$411,405	35
1994	25	13					2	$71,695	172
1995	26	16		1		2	5	$240,722	76
Total	117	59	1	1		8	15	$784,699	206

NIKE TOUR SUMMARY

Year	Events Played	Cuts Made	1st	2nd	3rd	Top 10	Top 25	Earnings	Rank
1991	2	2						$1,502	199
Total	2	2						$1,502	
COMBINED TOTAL MONEY								$786,201	

1996 PGA TOUR CHARITY TEAM: Freeport•McDermott Classic.

TOP TOURNAMENT SUMMARY

YEAR	93	94	95
Masters Tournament		CUT	
U.S. Open	T72		
PGA Championship	CUT		CUT
THE PLAYERS Championship		T51	

GRANT WAITE...continued

NATIONAL TEAMS: Dunhill Cup (4), 1989, 1992, 1994, 1995.

1995 PGA TOUR STATISTICS		
Scoring Average	69.28	(2)
Driving Distance	279.9	(3)
Driving Accuracy	60.1	(172)
Greens in Regulation	70.5	(12)
Putting	1.787	(73T)
All-Around	551	(46)
Sand Saves	53.8	(57T)
Total Driving	70.5	(12)
Eagles	6	(64T)
Birdies	182	(168T)

MISCELLANEOUS STATISTICS		
Scoring Avg Before Cut	70.94	(63T)
Scoring Avg 3rd Rnd	70.41	(43T)
Scoring Avg Final Rnd	71.75	(133T)
Birdies Conversion %	26.5	(150T)
Par Breakers	19.5	(80T)

1995 Low Round: 65: 1995 Doral-Ryder Open/3
Career Low Round: 63: 2 times, most recent 1993 Deposit Guaranty Golf Classic/4
Career Largest Paycheck: $234,000: 1993 Kemper Open/1

DUFFY WALDORF

EXEMPT STATUS: 1995 tournament winner
FULL NAME: James Joseph Waldorf, Jr.
HEIGHT: 5' 11" **WEIGHT:** 225
BIRTH DATE: August 20, 1962 **BIRTHPLACE:** Los Angeles, CA
RESIDENCE: Newhall, CA
FAMILY: Wife, Vicky; Tyler Lane (7/16/90), Shea Duffy (4/23/92), Kelli Ann (1/14/94)
COLLEGE: UCLA (1985, Psychology)
SPECIAL INTERESTS: Wine collecting
TURNED PROFESSIONAL: 1985 **Q SCHOOL:** Fall 1986, 1987, 1988, 1990

TOUR VICTORIES (1): 1995 LaCantera Texas Open.

BEST 1995 FINISHES: 1—LaCantera Texas Open; T2—United Airlines Hawaiian Open; T5—Nestle Invitational; T6—Greater Milwaukee Open.

1995 SEASON: After coming close twice with a pair of 1992 runner-up finishes, finally collected his first PGA TOUR title at the LaCantera Texas Open...took a two-stroke lead with a 6-under-par 66 in the second round and was never headed...led by one after 54 holes...final-round 7-under-par 65 gave him a six-stroke win over Justin Leonard...margin was largest on TOUR since Nick Price six-stroke win at 1994 PGA Championship...so complete was his domination that, with the exception of Leonard, the next closest competitors were 12 strokes back...$198,000 paycheck was his career high, and pushed his career earnings over the $2 million mark...ended the year in the midst of a streak of 18 consecutive rounds of par-or-better...started his season on a high note, finishing T2 at the United Airlines Hawaiian Open...also had top-10 finishes at the Nestle Invitational (T5) and Greater Milwaukee Open (T6)...finished the season by making his last 11 cuts...teamed with Tom Lehman to win Diners Club Matches in December.

CAREER HIGHLIGHTS: Turned potentially disastrous 1994 season into third-best of career with some late-year heroics...had earned only a little more than $70,000 through his first 18 events...turned season around with three straight top-10s, in the midst of season-ending skein of eight consecutive events in the money...opened with T10 in FedEx St. Jude Classic...followed with T8 in Buick Open, then placed third in Sprint International worth $95,200...total for those three events $155,580, raising season figure to $226,492 en route to final tally of $274,971...best shot at winning in 1993 came in Buick Classic, where had share of second- and third-round leads...final 75 dropped him to T10, four strokes out of Vijay Singh-Mark Wiebe playoff...held midpoint lead in 1992 Centel Western Open, where he finished T3...had rain-delayed 54-hole lead at Kemper Open, but dropped off to T13...also had pair of career-best second-place finishes in 1992, at Phoenix Open and in Buick Classic...finished five shots behind Phoenix winner Mark Calcavecchia after closing with three 67s...held or shared second place for last three rounds of Buick Classic, which David Frost won by eight strokes...finished two strokes behind Fulton Allem in 1991 Independent Insurance Agent Open...tied for third-round lead at Kmart Greater Greensboro Open after 63, but finished four strokes behind Mark Brooks...Qualifying Tournament medalist fourth time through in 1990...winner 1984 California State Amateur, 1984 Broadmoor Invitational, 1985 Rice Planters (Charleston, SC)...1985 College Player of Year...1985 All-American.

PERSONAL: An avid wine collector and connoisseur...celebrated LaCantera win with bottle of the finest...colorful shirt and cap combinations make him easy to spot on course.

DUFFY WALDORF...continued

CAREER SUMMARY								PLAYOFF RECORD: 0-0	
Year	Events Played	Cuts Made	1st	2nd	3rd	Top 10	Top 25	Earnings	Rank
1985(Am.)	1	1							
1985	1								
1986	3								
1987	32	17				1	4	$52,175	148
1988	29	16				1	3	$58,221	143
1989	28	16			1	3	9	$149,945	94
1990	28	16				1	2	$71,674	157
1991	29	20				2	9	$196,081	86
1992	25	19		2	2	8	12	$582,120	23
1993	25	15				4	6	$202,638	84
1994	26	14			1	4	8	$274,971	71
1995	26	21	1	1		4	9	$525,622	35
Total	253	155	1	3	4	28	62	$2,113,447	93

1996 PGA TOUR CHARITY TEAM: LaCantera Texas Open.

TOP TOURNAMENT SUMMARY								
YEAR	87	88	89	90	92	93	94	95
Masters Tournament						T39		T24
U.S. Open	T58	CUT	CUT		T57	T72	T9	T13
British Open Championship					T25	T39		
PGA Championship					T9	CUT		T20
THE PLAYERS Championship				T61	T35	T52	CUT	CUT
THE TOUR Championship					T7			

NATIONAL TEAMS: Walker Cup, 1985.

1995 PGA TOUR STATISTICS		
Scoring	70.35	(29T)
Driving	274.2	(18)
Driving Accuracy	68.9	(107)
Greens in Regulation	69.0	(26T)
Putting	1.769	(39T)
All Around	397	(10T)
Sand Saves	51.0	(110T)
Total Driving	125	(21T)
Eagles	8	(36T)
Birdies	333	(32T)

MISCELLANEOUS STATISTICS		
Scoring Avg Before Cut	70.10	(10)
Scoring Avg 3rd Rnd	70.90	(73)
Scoring Avg Final Rnd	70.70	(41T)
Birdies Conversion %	29.8	(56T)
Par Breakers	21.0	(19T)

1995 Low Round: **64:** 1995 Phoenix Open/1
Career Low Round: **63:** 2 times, most recent 1991 K-Mart GGO/3
Career Largest Paycheck: **$198,000:** 1995 LaCantera Texas Open/1

DENIS WATSON

EXEMPT STATUS: Special Medical Extension
FULL NAME: Denis Leslie Watson
HEIGHT: 6' **WEIGHT:** 165
BIRTH DATE: October 18, 1955 **BIRTHPLACE:** Salisbury, Rhodesia (Zimbabwe)
RESIDENCE: Orlando, FL
FAMILY: Wife, Hilary; Kyle (9/23/86), Paige (4/23/89), Ross (7/31/91)
COLLEGE: Rhodesia (English System)
SPECIAL INTERESTS: Golf course design, fishing, farming
TURNED PROFESSIONAL: 1976 **Q SCHOOL:** 1981

PGA TOUR VICTORIES (3): **1984** Buick Open, World Series Of Golf, Panasonic Las Vegas

1995 SEASON: Did not play in 1995 due to an injury to his left shoulder...playing under a Special Medical Extension in 1996, he will have 11 events to earn $142,109.

CAREER HIGHLIGHTS: Earned more than $100,000 in 1993 for the first time since 1987...bulk of that came at the B.C. Open, where he finished second to Blaine McCallister...that finish was his best since he tied for second in the 1987 Federal Express St. Jude Classic...after career year of 1984 and solid 1987 campaign, has been plagued by injuries and other physical problems...had wrist and elbow surgery in 1989, followed by cervical fusion in 1989...latter procedure corrected a neck problem that had existed since 1985...1984 season was the best of his career, with all three TOUR victories, earnings of $408,652 and fourth-place money-list finish...came close to winning PGA Player of the Year honors by joining Tom Watson as the season's only three-time winners...had brilliant seven-week spurt late that summer: 63-68 finish provided Buick Open win; placed 33rd in PGA Championship; shot course-record 8-under-par 62 in the second round of the NEC World Series of Golf, on his way to collecting $126,000 paycheck and 10-year exemption; three events later earned the TOUR's richest payday ($162,000) in the Las Vegas Invitational...finished tied for second in the 1985 U.S. Open, one shot behind Andy North...finished second to Roger Maltbie in 1985 defense of World Series title...winner of the 1975 World Amateur Team title with George Harvey.

PERSONAL: Named Rhodesian Sportsman of the Year in 1975...spent 1995 as an instructor on the Golf Channel Academy.

CAREER SUMMARY — **PLAYOFF RECORD: 0-1**

Year	Events Played	Cuts Made	1st	2nd	3rd	Top 10	Top 25	Earnings	Rank
1980	3	1					1	$5,750	195
1981	12	9				4	7	$49,153	89
1982	19	9		2		3	5	$59,090	75
1983	19	12		1		2	2	$59,284	88
1984	27	17	3			4	9	$408,562	4
1985	19	14		2		2	5	$155,845	48
1986	21	12					6	$59,453	129
1987	29	21		1	1	5	8	$231,074	43
1988	26	14					2	$51,239	148
1989	8	1						$3,959	240
1990	13	3				1	1	$43,013	182
1991	22	8						$17,749	213
1992	16	5						$16,105	219
1993	23	9		1		1	1	$111,977	132
1994	16	1						$4,250	285
Total	273	136	3	7	1	22	47	$1,276,503	145

TOP TOURNAMENT SUMMARY

YEAR	79	80	82	83	84	85	86	87	88	89	90	91	92	93	94
Masters Tournament						T53	CUT	T27							
U.S. Open						T2	T12	T36	CUT				W/D		
British Open Championship	T41	CUT	T15	WD		T47	CUT								
PGA Championship			CUT		33	T40	71	T40	T48						
THE PLAYERS Championship			T41	CUT	CUT	T69		CUT	CUT	CUT	CUT	CUT		T52	85

1995 PGA TOUR STATISTICS

Scoring Average ---------- N/A
Driving Distance ---------- N/A
Driving Accuracy ---------- N/A
Greens in Regulation ---------- N/A
Putting ---------- N/A
All-Around ---------- N/A
Sand Saves ---------- N/A
Total Driving ---------- N/A
Eagles ---------- N/A
Birdies ---------- N/A

MISCELLANEOUS STATISTICS

Scoring Avg. (before cut) ---------- N/A
Scoring Avg. (3rd round) ---------- N/A
Scoring Avg. (4th round) ---------- N/A
Birdie Conversions ---------- N/A
Par Breakers ---------- N/A

Career Low Round: 62: 1984 World Series Of Golf/2
Career Largest Paycheck: $162,000: 1984 Panasonic Las Vegas/1

Tom Watson

EXEMPT STATUS: Life Member
FULL NAME: Thomas Sturges Watson
HEIGHT: 5' 9" **WEIGHT:** 160
BIRTH DATE: Sept. 4, 1949 **BIRTHPLACE:** Kansas City, MO
RESIDENCE: Mission Hills, KS
FAMILY: Wife, Linda; Meg (9/13/79), Michael Barrett (12/15/82)
COLLEGE: Stanford University (1971, Psychology)
SPECIAL INTERESTS: Hunting, fishing
TURNED PROFESSIONAL: 1971 **Q SCHOOL:** Fall 1971

TOUR VICTORIES (32): 1974 Western Open. **1975** Byron Nelson Golf Classic. **1977** Bing Crosby National Pro-Am, Wickes-Andy Williams San Diego Open, Masters Tournament, Western Open. **1978** Joe Garagiola-Tucson Open, Bing Crosby National Pro-Am, Byron Nelson Golf Classic, Colgate Hall of Fame Classic, Anheuser-Busch Classic. **1979** Sea Pines Heritage Classic, Tournament of Champions, Byron Nelson Golf Classic, Memorial Tournament, Colgate Hall of Fame Classic. **1980** Andy Williams-San Diego Open, Glen Campbell-Los Angeles Open, MONY-Tournament of Champions, New Orleans Open, Byron Nelson Classic, World Series of Golf. **1981** Masters Tournament, USF&G-New Orleans Open, Atlanta Classic. **1982** Glen Campbell-Los Angeles Open, Sea Pines Heritage Classic, U.S. Open. **1984** Seiko-Tucson Match Play, MONY-Tournament of Champions, Western Open. **1987** Nabisco Championships of Golf.

INTERNATIONAL VICTORIES (8): **1975** British Open (Eur). **1977** British Open (Eur). **1980** British Open (Eur), Dunlop Phoenix (Jpn). **1982** British Open (Eur). **1983** British Open (Eur). **1984** Australian Open (Aus). **1992** Hong Kong Open.

BEST 1995 FINISHES: T5—Memorial Tournament; T6—Sprint International; T7—MCI Classic.

1995 SEASON: Went over $300,000 in earnings for the third consecutive season, and 12th overall, despite playing in only 16 events...earned $320,785 to rank 58th on the money list...ended his season by making his last 12 cuts...had three top-10 finishes, with his best being a T5 in the Memorial Tournament, an event he won in 1979...finished T6 in the Sprint International and T7 in the MCI Classic...became the fifth player in PGA TOUR history to surpass $7 million in career earnings after making $34,286 for his T13 at the Motorola Western Open...finished in a three-way tie for second, one stroke behind Peter Senior, in the Australian Masters.

CAREER HIGHLIGHTS: In 1994 had excellent early-season opportunity to win for first time since 1987 Nabisco Championships, but putter failed him during final round of AT&T Pebble Beach National Pro-Am...finished in four-way tie for second, one stroke behind Johnny Miller...winner of 1994 Skins Game and $210,000 with playoff birdie...holds PGA TOUR record for consecutive seasons with earnings over $100,000 (22)...captained United States to victory in 1993 Ryder Cup at The Belfry...numbers five British Opens (1975-77-80-82-83), two Masters and 1982 U.S. Open among his career titles...of majors, only PGA Championship has escaped him...leading money winner on TOUR five times, including 1977-80 consecutively...last player to win the same event three consecutive times when he won the Byron Nelson Classic from 1978-80...became first player to earn $500,000 in season in 1980, when won six TOUR events, plus third British Open...winner 1977-78-79 Vardon Trophies...winner 1980 Dunlop Phoenix (Japan)...six-time PGA Player of Year (1977-78-79-80-82-84)...winner of 1984 Arnold Palmer Award.

PERSONAL: Big fan of hometown Kansas City Royals...active on behalf of Children's Mercy Hospital in Kansas City.

CAREER SUMMARY — **PLAYOFF RECORD: 8-4**

Year	Events Played	Cuts Made	1st	2nd	3rd	Top 10	Top 25	Earnings	Rank
1968(Am.)	1	1							
1971	3	3						$2,185	224
1972	30	20		1		1	7	$31,081	79
1973	30	22			1	7	12	$74,973	35
1974	29	27	1	1		10	20	$135,474	10
1975	25	22	1	1	1	12	21	$153,796	7
1976	23	22		2	1	11	15	$133,202	12
1977	25	22	4	1	3	17	19	$310,653	1
1978	24	22	5	3	1	15	21	$362,429	1
1979	21	20	5	4	1	15	18	$462,636	1
1980	22	22	6	1	3	16	22	$530,808	1
1981	21	19	3	3	1	10	16	$347,660	3
1982	20	19	3	1	1	12	17	$316,483	5
1983	17	16		2		10	14	$237,519	12
1984	20	17	3	2	1	9	15	$476,260	1
1985	19	17		1	1	7	11	$226,778	18
1986	19	17			4	9	13	$278,338	20
1987	20	15	1	1		5	12	$616,351	5
1988	19	15		1		6	11	$273,216	39

CAREER SUMMARY (cont.)

Year	Events Played	Cuts Made	1st	2nd	3rd	Top 10	Top 25	Earnings	Rank
1989	18	13			1	2	7	$185,398	80
1990	17	13				5	9	$213,989	68
1991	16	12		1	1	6	10	$354,877	45
1992	15	12		1		5	7	$299,818	50
1993	16	14				4	9	$342,023	46
1994	15	14		1		5	9	$380,378	43
1995	16	14				3	7	$320,785	58
Total	501	430	32	28	21	202	322	$7,061,350	7

1996 PGA TOUR CHARITY TEAM: Greater Vancouver Open.

TOP TOURNAMENT SUMMARY

YEAR	72	73	74	75	76	77	78	79	80	81	82	83	84	85	86
Masters Tournament				T8	T33	1	T2	T2	T12	1	T5	T4	2	T10	T6
U.S. Open	T29		T5	T9	7	T7	T6		T3	T23	1	2	T11	CUT	T24
British Open Championship				1	CUT	1	T14	T26	1	T23	1	1	T2	T47	T35
PGA Championship		T12	T11	9	T15	T6	T2	T12	T10	CUT	T9	T47	T39	T6	T16
THE PLAYERS Championship				T8	T9	T5		2	T3	CUT	T6	T19	T8	T55	T58

TOP TOURNAMENT SUMMARY (cont.)

YEAR	87	88	89	90	91	92	93	94	95
Masters Tournament	T7	T9	T14	T7	T3	T48	T45	13	T14
U.S. Open	2	T36	T46	CUT	T16	CUT	T5	T6	T56
British Open Championship	7	T28	4	CUT	T26	CUT	CUT	T11	T31
PGA Championship	T14	T31	T9	T19	CUT	T62	5	T9	T58
THE PLAYERS Championship	CUT	CUT	T11	T36	T20	T2	10	T14	T29
THE TOUR Championship	1								

NATIONAL TEAMS: Ryder Cup (4), 1977, 1981, 1983, 1989; Captain, 1993. U.S. vs. Japan (2) 1982, 1984.

1995 PGA TOUR STATISTICS

Scoring	70.35	(29T)
Driving	273.2	(22)
Driving Accuracy	71.9	(65)
Greens in Regulation	69.4	(20)
Putting	1.817	(172T)
All Around	686	(81T)
Sand Saves	50.6	(115T)
Total Driving	87	(8)
Eagles	5	(88T)
Birdies	187	(175)

MISCELLANEOUS STATISTICS

Scoring Avg Before Cut	70.45	(20T)
Scoring Avg 3rd Rnd	71.15	(90T)
Scoring Avg Final Rnd	72.00	(153T)
Birdies Conversion %	28.8	(89T)
Par Breakers	19.0	(96T)

11995 Low Round: 65: 1995 AT&T Pebble Beach National Pro-Am/2
Career Low Round: 63: 2 times, most recent 1992 Buick Invitational/1
Career Largest Paycheck: $360,000: 1987 Nabisco Championship/1

Did You Know?

During 1995, 103 players either held or shared the lead at the end of a PGA TOUR event. Jim Gallagher, Jr., led most rounds, 10, followed by Greg Norman, who led at the close of nine rounds. Lee Janzen held the lead after only three rounds during 1995 -- the final round of THE PLAYERS Championship, Kemper Open and Sprint International, the three tournaments he won in 1995. Scott Simpson, the 17th-leading money-winner on the PGA TOUR, never held or shared an overnight lead in 1995. Brad Faxon led the most rounds without winning, four.

D. A. WEIBRING *(Y-bring)*

EXEMPT STATUS: 1995 tournament winner
FULL NAME: Donald Albert Weibring, Jr.
HEIGHT: 6' 1" **WEIGHT:** 190
BIRTH DATE: May 25, 1953 **BIRTHPLACE:** Quincy, IL
RESIDENCE: Plano, TX
FAMILY: Wife, Kristy; Matt (12/4/79), Katey (12/29/82), Allison Paige (10/3/87)
COLLEGE: Illinois State University
SPECIAL INTERESTS: Basketball
TURNED PROFESSIONAL: 1975 **Q SCHOOL:** Spring 1977

TOUR VICTORIES (4): 1979 Quad Cities Open. **1987** Beatrice Western Open. **1991** Hardee's Golf Classic. **1995** Quad City Classic.

INTERNATIONAL VICTORIES (2): 1985 Polaroid Cup (Jpn), Shell-Air New Zealand Open.

BEST 1995 FINISHES: 1—Quad City Classic; T2—GTE Byron Nelson Classic; 3—Colonial National Invitation; T10—Greater Milwaukee Open.

1995 SEASON: Continued unusual winning record of Illinois-only victories by capturing rain-shortened Quad City Classic...winner of that event three times in his career...birdied the 54th, and final, hole from 18-feet away on the fringe to defeat Jonathan Kaye by one stroke...led or shared the lead after each round...finished T2 in the GTE Byron Nelson Classic at the TPC at Four Seasons Resort-Las Colinas, a course he helped redesign...closed with a 65 in that event...played well despite receiving a cortisone injection prior to the tournament due to chronic wrist problems...hot play carried over to the next week as he finished third at the Colonial National Invitation...earned more than $500,000 for the second time in his career, 1991 being the other.

CAREER HIGHLIGHTS: Illinois native whose victories constitute "Illinois Slam"...all four wins have come in Illinois...finest season came in 1991, when captured Hardee's Golf Classic for second time and lost playoff to Andrew Magee in Las Vegas Invitational...finished Hardee's with sizzling 64 to win by stroke over Paul Azinger and Peter Jacobsen...in Las Vegas, tied Magee at 31-under-par 329, at that time TOUR record for low 90-hole total...won 1987 Western Open at Butler National GC by stroke over Larry Nelson and Greg Norman...captured 1979 Quad Cities Open...finished T2 twice in 1993, at GTE Byron Nelson and in Hardee's tournament...other high career finishes include second in 1985 Tournament Players Championship, fourth in 1986 PGA Championship, T3s 1987 PGA and 1988 U.S. Open...winner 1985 Polaroid Cup (Japan), 1985 Shell-Air New Zealand Open, 1989 Family House Invitational in Pittsburgh...lost Morocco Open playoff to Payne Stewart.

PERSONAL: Has own design and management company, The Golf Resources Group...responsible for "fine tuning" of several holes at TPC at Four Seasons Resort-Las Colinas...co-winner 1991 Hilton Bounceback Award, product of successful rebound from right wrist surgery in November 1989.

CAREER SUMMARY **PLAYOFF RECORD: 0-2**

Year	Events Played	Cuts Made	1st	2nd	3rd	Top 10	Top 25	Earnings	Rank
1977	9	3						$1,681	215
1978	27	17			1	4	7	$41,052	75
1979	33	20	1			2	6	$71,343	57
1980	28	20		1		4	6	$78,611	53
1981	30	21		1		6	8	$92,365	45
1982	30	26			1	7	12	$117,941	31
1983	23	14			1	3	7	$61,631	84
1984	28	21				4	11	$110,325	65
1985	24	14		1		1	8	$153,079	50
1986	24	19			1	3	11	$167,602	55
1987	26	19	1		1	5	10	$391,363	21
1988	25	17			1	5	9	$186,677	63
1989	24	17					5	$98,686	127
1990	22	13			1	2	6	$156,235	101
1991	24	20	1	1		5	8	$558,648	22
1992	24	19			1	3	9	$253,018	62
1993	22	18		2		2	6	$299,293	58
1994	20	14		1		3	4	$255,757	72
1995	24	18	1	1	1	4	8	$517,065	36
Total	467	330	4	8	9	63	141	$3,611,512	42

1996 PGA TOUR CHARITY TEAM: GTE Byron Nelson Classic.

D.A. WEIBRING...*continued*

TOP TOURNAMENT SUMMARY															
YEAR	**79**	**80**	**81**	**82**	**83**	**84**	**85**	**86**	**87**	**88**	**89**	**90**	**91**	**92**	**93**
Masters Tournament		CUT							T7	CUT	T46			T25	
U.S. Open	T19	CUT	T43		T20	T38	CUT		CUT	T3	T21		T11	CUT	CUT
British Open Championship							T8	T30							
PGA Championship		T46	T39	CUT	CUT	69	T65	4	T3	T52				CUT	T44
THE PLAYERS Championship		T64	T51	T27	CUT	CUT	2	T33	CUT	CUT	T21	T36	T41	CUT	T61
THE TOUR Championship									T24				T16		

TOP TOURNAMENT SUMMARY (cont.)		
YEAR	**94**	**95**
British Open Championship	CUT	
PGA Championship	T47	T31
THE PLAYERS Championship	T69	T43

1995 PGA TOUR STATISTICS		
Scoring	**70.64**	**(47)**
Driving	**257.4**	**(141)**
Driving Accuracy	**75.6**	**(23T)**
Greens in Regulation	**68.5**	**(35T)**
Putting	**1.762**	**(26)**
All Around	**567**	**(46)**
Sand Saves	**48.7**	**(137)**
Total Driving	**164**	**(63)**
Eagles	**4**	**(116T)**
Birdies	**315**	**(42)**

MISCELLANEOUS STATISTICS		
Scoring Avg Before Cut	**70.42**	**(19)**
Scoring Avg 3rd Rnd	**70.65**	**(58T)**
Scoring Avg Final Rnd	**71.53**	**(117)**
Birdies Conversion %	**30.8**	**(32T)**
Par Breakers	**21.4**	**(12T)**

1995 Low Round: **64:** 1995 Quad City Classic/1
Career Low Round: **64:** 2 times, most recent 1995 Quad City Classic/1
Career Largest Paycheck: $180,000: 2 times, most recent 1995 Quad City Classic/1

MARK WIEBE *(WEE-bee)*

EXEMPT STATUS: 112th on 1995 money list
FULL NAME: Mark Charles Wiebe
HEIGHT: 6' 3" **WEIGHT:** 225
BIRTH DATE: September 13, 1957 **BIRTHPLACE:** Seaside, OR
RESIDENCE: Denver, CO
FAMILY: Wife, Cathy; Taylor (9/9/86), Gunner (1/1/89), Collier (4/17/92)
COLLEGE: San Jose State University
SPECIAL INTERESTS: Fishing, skiing
TURNED PROFESSIONAL: 1980 **Q SCHOOL:** Fall 1983, 1984

TOUR VICTORIES (2): 1985 Anheuser-Busch Classic. **1986** Hardee's Golf Classic.

BEST 1995 FINISHES: T3—Sprint International; T9—LaCantera Texas Open; T10—Freeport-McMoRan Golf Classic.

1995 SEASON: A tie for ninth in the season-ending LaCantera Texas Open allowed him to finish among the top-130 money winners and ensured full-exempt status for 1996...jumped from No. 135 to 112th on money list...played the season under a 20-tournament Special Medical Extension after breaking and dislocating his shoulder in a March 7, 1994 skiing accident in Boulder, CO...first top-10 of the season came in the Freeport-McMoRan Classic, where he tied for 10th...carded middle rounds of 68-68...more than half of his earnings came in the Sprint International, where he tied for third, earning $87,000 with best finish of year...was second-round leader with 23 points.

MARK WIEBE...*continued*

CAREER HIGHLIGHTS: Waged strong comeback in 1993 from previous shoulder trouble...season earnings of $360,213 second-best of career...came close to winning third title in Buick Classic...closing rounds of 67-66 at Westchester CC produced tie with Vijay Singh at 280...Singh went on to capture first TOUR title with birdie on third playoff hole...wound up with best money-list ranking since 1989...had to rely on sponsor's exemptions to get into many tournament fields in 1992...enjoyed finest earnings season in 1988 with $392,166...lost Anheuser-Busch Golf Classic playoff that year to Tom Sieckmann...Anheuser-Busch Golf Classic provided first TOUR victory in 1985, this time with playoff win over John Mahaffey...captured second tournament title the very next year, winning 1986 Hardee's Golf Classic...winner 1986 Colorado Open, 1981 "Texas Dolly" Match Play Championship in Las Vegas...second team All-American at San Jose State...winner California junior college title at Palomar JC.

PERSONAL: Skiing an activity his family still enjoys, in spite of his 1994 accident.

CAREER SUMMARY — **PLAYOFF RECORD: 1-2**

Year	Events Played	Cuts Made	1st	2nd	3rd	Top 10	Top 25	Earnings	Rank
1981	2	1						$2,538	222
1982	1								
1983	2	2					1	$6,628	197
1984	19	8				1	1	$16,257	166
1985	29	15	1			5	5	$181,894	36
1986	30	22	1	1	1	5	7	$260,180	25
1987	33	26			1	2	5	$128,651	82
1988	32	27		1		7	16	$392,166	28
1989	29	20		1	1	4	12	$296,269	41
1990	31	21		1		2	7	$210,435	72
1991	31	14					4	$100,046	136
1992	26	17				2	6	$174,763	86
1993	27	19		1		5	9	$360,213	42
1994	9	5						$16,032	233
1995	23	11			1	3	3	$168,832	112
Total	324	208	2	5	4	36	76	$2,314,905	80

1996 PGA TOUR CHARITY TEAM: Sprint International.

TOP TOURNAMENT SUMMARY

YEAR	85	86	87	88	89	90	91	92	93
Masters Tournament	CUT	T35		CUT					
U.S. Open	CUT		T58	T25	T33	CUT			T77
PGA Championship	CUT	T47	T65	T38	T12	T19	T66		67
THE PLAYERS Championship	T54	T20	T11	T17	CUT	CUT	CUT	T61	
THE TOUR Championship			T24						

1995 PGA TOUR STATISTICS

Scoring	**71.75**	**(144T)**
Driving	**257.7**	**(137)**
Driving Accuracy	**66.2**	**(142T)**
Greens in Regulation	**61.8**	**(178)**
Putting	**1.796**	**(117T)**
All Around	**1,209**	**(185)**
Sand Saves	**42.9**	**(181T)**
Total Driving	**279**	**(174)**
Eagles	**3**	**(137T)**
Birdies	**193**	**(173)**

MISCELLANEOUS STATISTICS

Scoring Avg Before Cut	**72.18**	**(168T)**
Scoring Avg 3rd Rnd	**71.50**	**(120T)**
Scoring Avg Final Rnd	**71.91**	**(148)**
Birdies Conversion %	**27.1**	**(136T)**
Par Breakers	**17.0**	**(167T)**

1995 Low Round: **65:** 1995 Ideon Classic at Pleasant Valley/2
Career Low Round: **61:** 1988 Seiko Tucson/3
Career Largest Paycheck: **$108,000:** 1993 Buick Classic/2

John Wilson

EXEMPT STATUS: 125th on 1995 money list
FULL NAME: John Arthur Wilson
HEIGHT: 6'1" **WEIGHT:** 165
BIRTH DATE: February 23, 1959 **BIRTHPLACE:** Ceres, CA
RESIDENCE: Palm Desert, CA; plays out of PGA West
FAMILY: Wife, Kathy; Christopher (2/26/78), Shannon (4/28/79), Spencer (12/10/91), Sacher Joseph (9/21/95)
COLLEGE: College of the Desert
SPECIAL INTERESTS: Fishing, all sports, horticulture
TURNED PROFESSIONAL: 1987 **Q SCHOOL:** 1990, 1993

BEST CAREER FINISH: T4—1994 Anheuser-Busch Golf Classic.

BEST 1995 FINISHES: T8—Shell Houston Open.

1995 SEASON: Late-season T11 in the Bell Canadian Open vaulted him into the top-125, a status he was able to maintain by making three of his final four cuts...middle rounds of 67-68 at Glen Abbey put him into position to earn $31,200 payday...best finish of the season was a tie for eighth in the Shell Houston Open...earned his largest paycheck of the year, $40,600, there...had middle rounds of 69-68 at the TPC at The Woodlands...low round of the year was an 8-under-par 64 during the first round of the Las Vegas Invitational...final-round 7-under-par 65 at the Buick Invitational of California moved him into a tie for 16th, earning $15,240...was tied for 57th entering the final round.

CAREER HIGHLIGHTS: Pair of top-10 finishes, second of which came in penultimate start of 1994, were keys to retaining playing privileges for 1995...in fact, T5 in next-to-last start in Texas Open was critical...opening-round 64 at Kingsmill GC left him three strokes behind Bob Lohr's early lead in Anheuser-Busch Golf Classic...closing 67 produced T4 and largest check of season, $45,467...that came four weeks after T13 in Buick Classic, worth $24,000...going into A-B Classic had missed nine cuts in 15 outings, so hefty paycheck there lifted earnings total to $87,641...heading to San Antonio, had made $114,043 and stood No. 141 on money list...opened with 66-68-67, followed by one-under-par 70, good for 271 total and, most importantly, paycheck for $36,500 that lifted him into the top-125...played Australian Tour in 1990...qualified for 1991 PGA TOUR by placing T31 in 1990 Qualifying Tournament...tied for second in 1991 Ben Hogan Mississippi Gulf Coast Classic, losing in a playoff to Tom Lehman.

PERSONAL: Along with Jack Renner, only members of TOUR who attended College of the Desert in Palm Springs area.

PGA TOUR CAREER SUMMARY — **PLAYOFF RECORD: 0-0**

Year	Events Played	Cuts Made	1st	2nd	3rd	Top 10	Top 25	Earnings	Rank
1991	29	12					3	$43,041	180
1992	1	1						$576	318
1994	29	14				2	4	$155,058	117
1995	30	17				1	4	$149,280	125
Total	89	44				3	11	$347,956	296

NIKE TOUR SUMMARY

Year	Events Played	Cuts Made	1st	2nd	3rd	Top 10	Top 25	Earnings	Rank
1991	2	2		1		1	2	$13,630	75
1992	7	3				1	2	$4,875	134
1994	2	1			1	1	1	$13,167	93
Total	11	6		1	1	3	5	$31,672	
COMBINED TOTAL MONEY								$379,628	

1996 PGA TOUR CHARITY TEAM: Lincoln-Mercury Kapalua International.

TOP TOURNAMENT SUMMARY

YEAR	91	95
U.S. Open	CUT	
THE PLAYERS Championship		CUT

1995 PGA TOUR STATISTICS

Scoring	71.36	(106)
Driving	265.3	(77)
Driving Accuracy	65.4	(150)
Greens in Regulation	66.2	(97T)
Putting	1.757	(16T)
All Around	589	(55)
Sand Saves	51.9	(99T)
Total Driving	227	(150T)
Eagles	9	(20T)
Birdies	342	(24)

MISCELLANEOUS STATISTICS

Scoring Avg Before Cut	71.16	(85T)
Scoring Avg 3rd Rnd	71.28	(103)
Scoring Avg Final Rnd	71.59	(121T)
Birdies Conversion %	30.2	(45T)
Par Breakers	20.5	(35T)

1995 Low Round: **64:** 1995 Las Vegas Invitational/1
Career Low Round: **64:** 2 times, most recent 1995 Las Vegas Invitational/1
Career Largest Paycheck: **$45,466:** 1994 Anheuser-Busch Golf Classic/T4

FUZZY ZOELLER *(ZELL-er)*

EXEMPT STATUS: 110th on 1995 money list
FULL NAME: Frank Urban Zoeller
HEIGHT: 5' 10" **WEIGHT:** 190
BIRTH DATE: Nov. 11, 1951 **BIRTHPLACE:** New Albany, IN
RESIDENCE: New Albany, IN; plays out of Naples National, Naples, FL
FAMILY: Wife, Diane; Sunnye Noel (5/5/79), Heidi Leigh (8/23/81), Gretchen Marie (3/27/84), Miles Remington (6/1/89)
COLLEGE: Edison Junior College in Ft. Myers, FL, and University of Houston
SPECIAL INTERESTS: All sports, golf course design
TURNED PROFESSIONAL: 1973 **Q SCHOOL:** Fall 1974

TOUR VICTORIES (10): 1979 Wickes-Andy Williams San Diego Open, Masters Tournament. **1981** Colonial National Invitation. **1983** Sea Pines Heritage Classic, Las Vegas Pro-Celebrity Classic. **1984** United States Open. **1985** Hertz Bay Hill Classic. **1986** AT&T Pebble Beach National Pro-Am, Sea Pines Heritage Golf Classic, Anheuser-Busch Golf Classic.

BEST 1995 FINISH: T5—Canon Greater Hartford Open.

1995 SEASON: Once again, back problems limited his appearances on the PGA TOUR...played in just 15 events in 1995, earning money in 12 of them...consequently, money list finish was the third lowest of his career...best finish was a T5 in the Canon Greater Hartford Open...led late into the final round before he was overtaken by Greg Norman...fired a course-record 7-under-par 63 in the second round to pull to within two strokes of the lead...record lasted all of one day before Billy Andrade bettered it with an 8-under-par 62...fired a final-round 3-under-par 69 in tough conditions at the Kmart Greater Greensboro Open...only three players had lower scores in the cold and rainy conditions...had the second hole-in-one of his PGA TOUR career during the first round of the PGA Championship...oddly enough, both of his aces have come in major championships, the other happening at the 1991 U.S. Open.

CAREER HIGHLIGHTS: Owner of two major titles, 1979 Masters and 1984 U.S. Open...former came in playoff with Ed Sneed and Tom Watson on third extra hole...latter came in 18-hole playoff with Greg Norman at Winged Foot...established TOUR record in 1994 by earning $1,016,804 without winning a tournament...this non-winning was not for lack of trying, however, since he finished second five times...those five runner-up finishes most since Jack Nicklaus and Arnold Palmer recorded six apiece in 1964...concluded best year of career by losing TOUR Championship playoff to Mark McCumber, a finish that produced biggest paycheck of career—$324,000...accomplishments have come despite challenges provided by medical history, principally back trouble tracing to high school basketball...back problems became public knowledge prior to '84 PGA Championship...barely could move morning was to play first round at Shoal Creek...was rushed to hospital, where he remained for nearly a week...back condition worsened week later in Las Vegas, where he was defending Panasonic Invitational title...underwent surgery for ruptured discs, returning to TOUR in February 1985...finished T46 in Doral-Eastern Open, won Hertz Bay Hill Classic two weeks later...first TOUR victory was in 1979 Andy Williams Open...winner 1985-86 Skins Games...winner 1987 Merrill Lynch Shoot-Out Championship...winner 1973 Indiana State Amateur...1972 Florida State Junior College champion.

PERSONAL: One of game's all-time personalities and gallery favorites...wears sunglasses while he plays, enjoys "whistling while he works"...golf course design projects include TPC at Summerlin, host course for Las Vegas Invitational.

CAREER SUMMARY — **PLAYOFF RECORD: 2-2**

Year	Events Played	Cuts Made	1st	2nd	3rd	Top 10	Top 25	Earnings	Rank
1975	21	10					3	$7,318	146
1976	27	18		2		4	6	$52,557	56
1977	32	24			2	7	13	$76,417	40
1978	28	23		2	1	5	15	$109,055	20
1979	24	20	2	1		6	12	$196,951	9
1980	22	19			2	7	12	$95,531	46
1981	25	19	1	1	1	4	11	$151,571	19
1982	25	20		1	1	6	10	$126,512	28
1983	28	23	2	2		12	18	$417,597	2
1984	21	15	1			3	7	$157,460	40
1985	21	18	1			7	11	$244,003	15
1986	20	16	3			4	10	$358,115	13
1987	21	16		1	1	5	10	$222,921	44
1988	22	18			2	4	9	$209,564	51
1989	19	14		1		4	7	$217,742	65
1990	20	13		1		2	8	$199,629	79
1991	16	12		1	1	3	8	$385,139	42
1992	18	11				1	4	$125,003	114
1993	18	17		1	1	4	8	$378,175	39
1994	19	16		5		6	9	$1,016,804	5
1995	15	12				1	5	$170,706	110
Total	462	354	10	19	12	95	196	$4,918,648	25

1996 PGA TOUR CHARITY TEAM: JCPenney Classic.

TOP TOURNAMENT SUMMARY

YEAR	76	77	78	79	80	81	82	83	84	85	86	87	88	89	90
Masters Tournament				1	T19	T43	T10	T20	T31	CUT	T21	T27	T16	T26	T20
U.S. Open	T38	T44			T51		T15	CUT	1	T9	T15	CUT	T8	CUT	T8
British Open Championship				CUT	CUT		T8	T14	T14	T11	T8	T29	T53	CUT	
PGA Championship		T54	10	T54	T41	2	CUT	T6		T54	CUT	64	CUT	CUT	T14
THE PLAYERS Championship	79				CUT	CUT	T56	CUT		T27	CUT	T54	T23	T45	CUT

TOP TOURNAMENT SUMMARY (cont.)

YEAR	91	92	93	94	95
Masters Tournament	T12	T19	T11	T35	CUT
U.S. Open	5	CUT	T68	T58	T21
British Open Championship	T80		T14	3	
PGA Championship	CUT		T31	T19	69
THE PLAYERS Championship	2	T64	T34	2	T55
THE TOUR Championship				2	

NATIONAL TEAMS: Ryder Cup (3) 1979, 1983, 1985.

1995 PGA TOUR STATISTICS

Statistic	Value	Rank
Scoring	70.62	(46)
Driving	267.0	(61)
Driving Accuracy	72.5	(55T)
Greens in Regulation	69.2	(22T)
Putting	1.751	(7T)
All Around	500	(33)
Sand Saves	58.8	(21T)
Total Driving	116	(14T)
Eagles	4	(116T)
Birdies	194	(172)

MISCELLANEOUS STATISTICS

Statistic	Value	Rank
Scoring Avg Before Cut	69.84	(3)
Scoring Avg 3rd Rnd	71.69	(135T)
Scoring Avg Final Rnd	71.50	(113T)
Birdies Conversion %	28.7	(92T)
Par Breakers	20.3	(40T)

1995 Low Round: 63: 1995 Canon Greater Hartford Open/2
Career Low Round: 62: 1982 B.C. Open/2
Career Largest Paycheck: $324,000: 1994 TOUR Championship/2

Fuzzy Zoeller won more than $1 million in 1994 with five second-place finishes but nary a victory. His $1,016,804 without a win is the PGA TOUR record for a victory-less season.

OTHER PROMINENT MEMBERS OF THE PGA TOUR

A

ARMOUR III, Tommy **Birth Date** 10/8/59 **Birthplace** Denver, CO **Residence** Irving, TX **Height** 6-2 **Weight** 205 **Family** Single; Tommy (10/16/89) **College** University of New Mexico **Special Interests** Music, sports **Turned Professional** 1981 **Q School** Fall 1981, 1987 **Other Achievements** Winner 1981 New Mexico State Amateur; 1981 William Tucker Intercollegiate; 1983 Mexican Open. Won 1994 NIKE Miami Valley and NIKE Cleveland Opens in consecutive weeks to become first player to win back-to-back NIKE TOUR events. Spent most of 1994 on NIKE TOUR but still finished No. 147 on PGA TOUR money list. Played in 1994 U.S. Open at Oakmont CC, site of grandfather's 1927 U.S. Open victory.

Exempt Status: 141st on 1995 money list

TOUR Victories: 1 — 1990 Phoenix Open

Money And Position:

1982 — $ 4,254 — 208	1989 — $185,018 — 81	1992 — $ 47,218 — 180
1987 — $ 970 — 290	1990 — $348,658 — 35	1993 — $ 52,011 — 181
1988 — $175,461 — 66	1991 — $ 90,478 — 140	1994 — $112,778 — 147
		1995 — $134,407 — 141

Best 1995 Finish: T7 — Bob Hope Chrysler Classic

1995 Summary: Tournaments entered — 30; in money — 16; top-10 finishes — 1.

Career Earnings: $1,146,029

AUBREY, Emlyn (EHM-Lin OB-ree) **Birth Date** 1/28/64 **Birthplace** Reading, PA **Residence** Austin, TX **Height** 6-2 **Weight** 185 **Family** Wife, Cindy **College** Louisiana State University **Special Interest** Auto racing **Turned Professional** 1986 **Other Achievements** Played NIKE TOUR full time 1993-94. Earned $72,944 to finish 14th on NIKE TOUR money list in 1993 and regained PGA TOUR card by making $113,919 for 10th-place finish in 1994. Finished T62 in 1994 U.S. Open. Winner 1982-84 Pennsylvania State Public Links, 1984 Southeastern Conference title, 1989 Philippines Open and 1994 Indian Open. Wife Cindy serves as caddie.

Exempt Status: 140th on 1995 money list

Best-Ever Finish: T7 — 1990 H-E-B Texas Open

Money and Position:

1990 — $122,329 — 126	1992 — $ 58,087 — 167
1991 — $ 91,257 — 139	1995 — $137,020 — 140

Best 1995 Finish: T9--AT&T Pebble Beach National Pro-Am

1995 Summary: Tournaments entered — 30; in money — 5; top-10 finishes — 1.

Career Money: $412,494

B

Barr, Dave **Birth Date** 3/1/52 **Birthplace** Kelowna, British Columbia **Residence** Richmond, BC; plays out of Swan-E-Set Bay Resort & CC **Height** 6-1 **Weight** 210 **Family** Wife, Lu Ann; Brent Jason (10/11/80), Teryn Amber (4/13/83) **College** Oral Roberts University **Special Interest** Hockey **Turned Professional** 1974 **Q School** Fall 1977 **Other Achievements** Member of 13 Canadian World Cup teams (1977-78, 1982-85, 1987-91, 1993-94)...winner of 1983 World Cup individual title, 1985 team title with Dan Halldorson...nine-time member of Canadian Dunhill Cup team (1985-89, 1991,1993-95); captain of winning 1994 squad, which included Rick Gibson and Ray Stewart...member of 1972 Canadian World Amateur Cup team...four-time winner Canadian Order of Merit (1977, 1985-86, 1988)...winner of eight SCORE awards as Canada's top player...winner of 12 tournaments on Canadian Tour.

Exempt Status: 147th on 1995 money list

TOUR Victories: 2 — 1981 Quad Cities Open. 1987 Georgia-Pacific Atlanta Golf Classic.

Money And Position:

1978 — $11,897 — 133	1984 — $113,336 — 62	1990 — $197,979 — 80
1979 — $13,022 — 142	1985 — $126,177 — 65	1991 — $144,389 — 108
1980 — $14,664 — 141	1986 — $122,181 — 70	1992 — $118,859 — 119
1981 — $46,214 — 90	1987 — $202,241 — 54	1993 — $179,264 — 96
1982 — $12,474 — 166	1988 — $291,244 — 33	1994 — $314,885 — 53
1983 — $52,800 — 96	1989 — $190,480 — 75	1995 — $118,218 — 53

Best 1995 Finish: T11—Canon Greater Hartford Open

1995 Summary: Tournaments entered—27; in money—13; top-10 finishes—0.

Career Money: $2,270,323

OTHER PROMINENT MEMBERS OF THE PGA TOUR

BEAN, Andy **Birth Date** 3/13/53 **Birthplace** Lafayette, GA **Residence** Lakeland, FL **Height** 6-4 **Weight** 238 **Family** Wife, Debbie; Lauren Ashley (4/17/82), Lindsey Ann (8/10/84), Jordan Alise (11/19/85) **College** University of Florida **Special Interests** Hunting, fishing **Turned Professional** 1975 **Q School** Fall 1975 **Other Achievements** Member, 1987 Ryder Cup team. Low round of career third-round 61 en route to winning 1979 Atlanta Classic. Had outstanding amateur career, winning 1974 Eastern and Falstaff Amateurs and 1975 Dixie and Western Amateurs. All-American at University of Florida.

Exempt Status: 46th on 1995 PGA TOUR Qualifying Tournament/NIKE TOUR 6-10 List

TOUR Victories: 11 — 1977 Doral-Eastern Open. 1978 Kemper Open, Danny Thomas Memphis Classic, Western Open. 1979 Atlanta Classic. 1980 Hawaiian Open. 1981 Bay Hill Classic. 1982 Doral-Eastern Open. 1984 Greater Greensboro Open. 1986 Doral-Eastern Open, Byron Nelson Golf Classic.

Money and Position:

1976 — $ 10,761 — 139	1983 — $181,246 — 24	1990 — $129,669 — 119
1977 — $127,312 — 12	1984 — $422,995 — 3	1991 — $193,609 — 88
1978 — $268,241 — 3	1985 — $190,871 — 33	1992 — $ 30,798 — 195
1979 — $208,253 — 7	1986 — $491,938 — 4	1993 — $ 37,292 — 191
1980 — $269,033 — 4	1987 — $ 73,808 — 120	1994 — $ 8,810 — 253
1981 — $105,755 — 35	1988 — $ 48,961 — 149	1995 —$ 7,405 — 277
1982 — $208,627 — 15	1989 — $236,097 — 58	

1995 Best Finish: T47 — United Airlines Hawaiian Open

1995 Summary: Tournaments entered — 14; in money — 3; top-10 finishes — 0

Career Earnings: $3,250,480

BENEPE, Jim (BEN-ih-pee) **Birth Date** 10/24/63 **Birthplace** Sheridan, WY **Residence** Sheridan, WY; plays out of Powder Horn GC & Development **Height** 5-7 **Weight** 150 **Family** Single **College** Northwestern University (1986, Psychology) **Special Interests** Hunting, fishing, reading, music **Turned Professional** 1986 **Q School** 1990 **Other Achievements** Winner 1982 Wyoming State Amateur (stroke play); 1983 Wyoming State Amateur (medal play). Winner 1982 Western Junior Championship. Winner of four collegiate events for Northwestern, including co-champion 1986 Big Ten title. 1986 Collegiate All-American. Winner 1987 Canadian Tour Order of Merit. Named 1987 Canadian Tour Rookie of the Year. Winner 1988 Victorian (Australia) Open. 1988 PGA TOUR Rookie of Year.

Exempt Status: Past Champion

TOUR Victories: 1 — 1988 Beatrice Western Open

Money and Position:

1988 — $176,055 — 65	1990 — $105,087 — 135	1993 — $ 0
1989 — $ 38,089 — 176	1991 — $ 62,082 — 164	1994 — $ 0

Best 1995 Finish: Did not play PGA TOUR in 1995

1995 Summary: Did not play PGA TOUR in 1995

Career Money: $381,314

BERTSCH, Shane (BIRCH) **Birth Date** 3/3/70 **Birthplace** Denver, CO **Residence** Colorado Springs, CO **Height** 6-2 **Weight** 180 **Family** Single **College** Texas A&M (1993, Parks and Recreation) **Turned Professional** 1992 **Q School** 1995 **Other Achievements** Finished T72 in only PGA TOUR event, 1993 Shell Houston Open. Earned $26,099 to rank 72nd on 1995 NIKE TOUR money list. Best finish was T4 in season-opening NIKE San Jose Open. Biggest thrill in golf was first tournament win in 1994 Southwest Kansas Pro-Am. Has made four holes-in-one in his lifetime. A promising junior tennis player, he gave up game to concentrate on golf after losing a big match to future No. 1-ranked player Andre Agassi.

Exempt Status: 4th at 1995 PGA TOUR Qualifying Tournament

Best-Ever Finish: T72 — 1993 Shell Houston Open

Money & Position: 1993 — $2,548 — 300

Best 1995 Finish: Did not play PGA TOUR in 1995

1995 Summary: Did not play PGA TOUR in 1995

Career Earnings: $2,548

BLACK, Ronnie **Birth Date** 5/26/58 **Birthplace** Lovington, NM **Residence** Tucson, AZ **Height** 6-1 **Weight** 180 **Family** Wife, Sandra; Justin (12/14/86), Alex (5/11/88), Anthony (1/26/92) **College** Lamar University **Special Interests** Hunting, fishing, movies **Turned Professional** 1981 **Q School** 1981, 1982, 1990 **Other Achievements** Won 1983 Southern Open in four-hole playoff with Sam Torrance. Claimed 1984 Anheuser-Busch Classic with final-round 63 after opening final day seven strokes off lead. Winner 1976 and 1977 New Mexico State High School Championships. Winner 1981 Collegiate Conference Championship. Winner 1995 Pebble Beach Invitational.

Exempt Status: 30th on 1995 PGA TOUR Qualifying Tournament/NIKE TOUR 6-10 List

TOUR Victories: 2 — 1983 Southern Open, 1984 Anheuser-Busch Classic.

Money and Position:

1982 — $ 6,329 — 91	1987 — $144,158 — 77	1992 — $129,386 — 111
1983 — $ 87,524 — 63	1988 — $100,603 — 112	1993 — $120,041 — 125
1984 — $172,636 — 35	1989 — $264,988 — 51	1994 — $123,404 — 137
1985 — $ 61,684 — 109	1990 — $ 34,001 — 190	1995 — $122,188 — 143
1986 — $166,761 — 56	1991 — $135,865 — 113	

Best 1995 Finish: T9 — Nissan Open

1995 Summary: Tournaments entered — 29; in money — 17; top-10 finishes — 1.

Career Earnings: $1,669,567

OTHER PROMINENT MEMBERS OF THE PGA TOUR

BLACKBURN, Woody Birth Date 7/26/51 **Birthplace** Pikeville, KY **Residence** Orange Park, FL; plays out of Orange Park CC **Height** 6-2 **Weight** 185 **Family** Wife, Brenda; Todd (1/7/80), Richard (7/28/83), Brian (7/28/83) **College** University of Florida **Special Interests** Fly fishing, all sports **Turned Professional** 1974 **Other Achievements** Co-medalist 1976 Q-School. All-SEC 1973.
Exempt Status: Past Champion
TOUR Victories: 2 — 1976 Walt Disney World Team Championship (with Bill Kratzert), 1985 Isuzu Andy Williams San Diego Open.

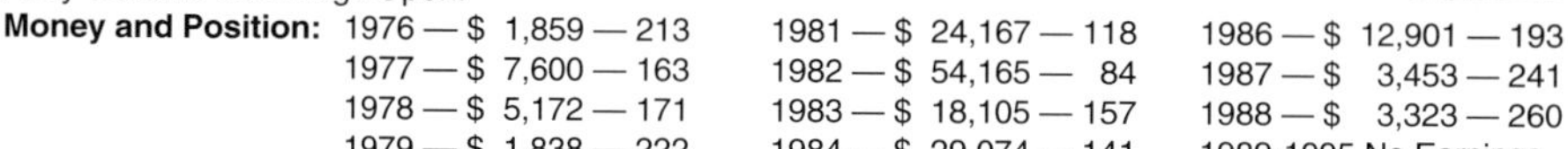

Money and Position:			
	1976 — $ 1,859 — 213	1981 — $ 24,167 — 118	1986 — $ 12,901 — 193
	1977 — $ 7,600 — 163	1982 — $ 54,165 — 84	1987 — $ 3,453 — 241
	1978 — $ 5,172 — 171	1983 — $ 18,105 — 157	1988 — $ 3,323 — 260
	1979 — $ 1,838 — 222	1984 — $ 29,074 — 141	1989-1995 No Earnings
	1980 — $ 9,319 — 166	1985 — $139,257 — 57	

Best 1995 Finish: Did not make a cut on 1995 PGA TOUR
1995 Summary: Tournaments entered--1; in money--0; top-10 finishes--0.
Career Earnings: $310,231

BRITTON, Bill Birth Date 11/13/55 **Birthplace** Staten Island, NY **Residence** Fair Haven, NJ; plays out of Shore Oaks GC **Height** 5-7 **Weight** 140 **Family** Wife, Isabelle; Kevin (1/2/90), Caitlin (2/27/91), Ashley (2/16/94) **College** University of Florida **Special Interest** Reading **Turned Professional** 1979 **Q School** Spring 1980; Fall 1986, 1987, 1994 **Other Achievements** Winner 1979 Metropolitan Open, 1975, 1976 Metropolitan Amateur Championships. Collected 1975 National Junior College Championship. Lost playoff to Hal Sutton at 1982 Walt Disney/Oldsmobile Classic. Lone TOUR victory came in rain-shortened 1989 Centel Classic. Low round of career a 63, which has posted several times.
Exempt Status: Past Champion
TOUR Victories: 1 — 1989 Centel Classic

Money and Position:			
	1980 — $ 9,022 — 171	1985 — $ 3,245 — 215	1991 — $282,894 — 57
	1981 — $39,358 — 97	1987 — $ 45,939 — 158	1992 — $391,700 — 36
	1982 — $75,328 — 57	1988 — $110,781 — 103	1993 — $ 74,748 — 159
	1983 — $20,492 — 148	1989 — $307,978 — 34	1994 — $ 68,033 — 173
	1984 — $28,149 — 142	1990 — $278,977 — 51	1995 — $ 73,574 — 175

Best 1995 Finish: 6 — Honda Classic
1995 Summary: Tournaments entered — 24; in money — 10; top-10 finishes — 1.
Career Earnings: $1,810,217

BROWN, Billy Ray Birth Date 4/5/63 **Birthplace** Missouri City, TX **Residence** Missouri City, TX; plays out of Quail Valley CC **Height** 6-3 **Weight** 205 **Family** Wife, Cindy **College** University of Houston **Special Interests** Hunting, fishing **Turned Professional** 1987 **Other Achievements** Won 1991 Canon Greater Hartford Open in playoff with Rick Fehr and Corey Pavin. Other victory came in playoff at rain-shortened 1992 GTE Byron Nelson Classic. Finished T3 in 1990 U.S. Open. Injured wrist at end of 1992 season, causing him to miss 16 weeks in 1993. Four-time All-America selection who won 1982 NCAA Championship as freshman. Along with teammate Steve Elkington, member of three NCAA championship teams. Father Charlie was a tackle for Oakland Raiders, brother Chuck played center for St. Louis Cardinals.
Exempt Status: 25th on 1995 PGA TOUR Qualifying Tournament/NIKE TOUR 6-10 List
TOUR Victories: 2 — 1991 Canon Greater Hartford Open. 1992 GTE Byron Nelson Classic

Money and Position:			
	1988 — $ 83,590 — 125	1991 — $348,082 — 46	1994 — $ 4,254 — 284
	1989 — $162,964 — 85	1992 — $485,151 — 29	1995 — $ 56,111 — 196
	1990 — $312,486 — 44	1993 — $173,662 — 97	

Best 1995 Finish: T15 — Ideon Classic at Pleasant Valley
1995 Summary: Tournaments entered — 24; in money — 9; top-10 finishes — 0.
Career Earnings: $1,626,281

BROWNE, Olin (OH-lin) Birth Date 5/22/59 **Birthplace** New York, NY **Residence** Jupiter, FL; plays out of Admirals Cove **Height** 5-9 **Weight** 175 **Family** Wife, Pam; Olin Jr. (7/9/88), Alexandra Grace (10/24/91) **College** Occidental College **Special Interests** Fly fishing, environment, some politics **Turned Professional** 1984 **Other Achievements** Winner 1991 Ben Hogan Bakersfield Open, Ben Hogan Hawkeye Open, 1993 NIKE Monterrey Open. Recorded double-eagle in 1994 Northern Telecom Open. Gave his victory speech at the 1993 Monterrey Open in Mexico in Spanish.
Exempt Status: 8th on 1995 PGA TOUR Qualifying Tournament/NIKE TOUR 6-10 List
Best Ever Finish: T4 — 1992 Northern Telecom Open

Money and Position:			
	1992 — $84,152 — 147	1993 — $2,738 — 290	1994 — $101,580 — 154

Best 1995 Finish: Did not play PGA TOUR in 1995
1995 Summary: Did not play PGA TOUR in 1995
Career Earnings: $188,470

OTHER PROMINENT MEMBERS OF THE PGA TOUR

BRYANT, Bart Birth Date 11/18/62 **Birthplace** Gatesville, TX **Residence** Winter Park, FL **Height** 6-0 **Weight** 185 **Family** Wife, Cathy; Kristin (8/11/88), Michelle (1/11/94) **College** New Mexico State University **Special Interests** Fishing, spending time with family **Turned Professional** 1985 **Q School** 1990, 1994 **Other Achievements** Winner 1984 UCLA Billy Bryant Invitational, 1983, 1984 Sun Country Amateur, 1988 Florida Open. Two-time All-American. PCAA Player of Year in 1984. Older brother Brad is PGA TOUR veteran.

Exempt Status: 33rd on 1995 PGA TOUR Qualifying Tournament/NIKE TOUR 6-10 List
Best Ever Finish: 7 — 1991 Honda Classic
Money and Position: 1991 — $119,931 — 124 1992 — $52,075 — 172 1995 — $119,201 — 146
Best 1995 Finish: T11 — LaCantera Texas Open
1995 Summary: Tournaments entered — 27; in money — 13; top-10 finishes — 0.
Career Earnings: $291,207

BURNS III, George Birth Date 7/29/49 **Birthplace** Brooklyn, NY **Residence** Boynton Beach, FL **Height** 6-2 **Weight** 200 **Family** Wife, Irene; Kelly (4/2/76), Eileen (8/25/80) **College** University of Maryland **Turned Professional** 1975 **Q School** 1975, 1990 **Other Achievements** Winner 1973 Canadian Amateur, 1974 Porter Cup, North-South Amateur, New York State Amateur. As professional, won 1975 Scandinavian Open and 1975 Kerrygold (Ireland). Member 1975 Walker Cup team and 1975 World Amateur Cup team. Winner 1988 Chrysler Team Championship with Wayne Levi.

Exempt Status: Past Champion
TOUR Victories: 4 — 1979 Walt Disney World Team Championship (with Ben Crenshaw). 1980 Bing Crosby National Pro-Am. 1985 Bank of Boston Classic. 1987 Shearson Lehman Bros.-Andy Williams Open.

Money & Position:			
	1976 — $ 85,732 — 32	1982 — $181,864 — 18	1988 — $ 30,130 — 174
	1977 — $102,026 — 26	1983 — $ 62,371 — 83	1989 — $ 5,645 — 230
	1978 — $171,498 — 38	1984 — $198,848 — 37	1990 — $ 96,443 — 139
	1979 — $107,830 — 33	1985 — $223,352 — 21	1992 — $ 6,864 — 254
	1980 — $219,928 — 7	1986 — $ 77,474 — 112	1993 — $ 2,550 — 298
	1981 — $105,395 — 37	1987 — $216,257 — 45	1994 — $ 0
			1995 — $ 2,463 — 332

Best 1995 Finish: T48 — Ideon Classic at Pleasant Valley
1995 Summary: Tournaments entered — 7; in money — 1; top-10 finishes — 0.
Career Earnings: $1,765,671

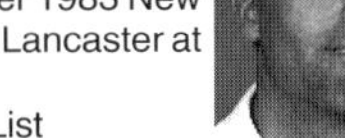

BYRUM, Tom Birth Date 9/28/60 **Birthplace** Onida,SD **Residence** Sugarland, TX; plays out of Sweetwater CC **Height** 5-10 **Weight** 175 **Family** Wife, Dana; Brittni Rene (4/2/88), Corinne (1/21/91) **College** New Mexico State University **Special Interests** Hunting, fishing, all sports **Turned Professional** 1984 **Q School** 1985, 1991, 1992 **Other Achievements** Winner 1983 New Mexico State Intercollegiate. Participant in TOUR-record six-man playoff won by Neal Lancaster at 1994 GTE Byron Nelson Classic.

Exempt Staus: 6th on 1995 PGA TOUR Qualifying Tournament/NIKE TOUR 6-10 List
TOUR Victories: 1 — 1989 Kemper Open

Money and Postion:			
	1986 — $ 89,739 — 93	1989 — $320,939 — 32	1992 — $ 94,399 — 136
	1987 — $146,384 — 76	1990 — $136,910 — 113	1993 — $ 82,354 — 154
	1988 — $174,378 — 67	1991 — $ 68,871 — 153	1994 — $112,259 — 148
			1995 — $145,427 — 132

Best 1995 Finish: T3 — Buick Open
1995 Summary: Tournaments entered — 14; in money — 10; top-10 finishes — 2.
Career Earnings: $1,371,662

C

CALDWELL, Rex Birth Date 5/5/50 **Birthplace** Everett, WA **Residence** San Antonio, TX **Height** 6-2 **Weight** 225 **Family** Wife, JoAnn **College** San Fernando Valley State **Special Interests** Basketball, jogging **Turned Professional** 1972 **Other Achievements** College Division All-American 1971-72. Winner 1978 California State Open. Winner 1983 World Cup team title with John Cook. Winner 1994 Alaska State Open.

Exempt Staus: Past Champion
TOUR Victories: 1 — 1983 LaJet Classic

Money and Position:			
	1975 — $ 3,094 — 178	1982 — $ 64,622 — 68	1989 — $ 55,066 — 161
	1976 — $ 24,912 — 87	1983 — $ 284,434 — 6	1990 — $ 0
	1977 — $ 11,693 — 137	1984 — $ 126,400 — 53	1991 — $ 0
	1978 — $ 66,451 — 42	1985 — $ 58,689 — 114	1992 — $ 3,865 — 272
	1979 — $ 96,088 — 36	1986 — $ 39,674 — 149	1993 — $ 4,350 — 276
	1980 — $ 64,859 — 62	1987 — $ 50,054 — 153	1994 — $ 0
	1981 — $ 33,945 — 102	1988 — $ 15,896 — 205	1995 — $ 8,694 — 268

Best 1995 Finish: T38 — LaCantera Texas Open
1995 Summary: Tournaments entered — 6; in money — 3; top-10 finishes — 0.
Career Earnings: $1,016,242

OTHER PROMINENT MEMBERS OF THE PGA TOUR

CARNEVALE, Mark (CAR-nuh-VALE) Birth Date 5/21/60 **Birthplace** Annapolis, MD **Residence** Ponte Vedra Beach, FL **Height** 6-2 **Weight** 238 **Family** Single **College** James Madison University **Special Interests** Jazz, travel, skiing, sailing **Turned Professional** 1983 **Q School** 1991 **Other Achievements** PGA TOUR Rookie of the Year in 1992 after winning Chattanooga Classic and earning $220,921. Winner of 1984 Virginia Open and 1990 Utah Open. Quit golf for a brief period during 1980s to work for brokerage firm. Father, Ben Carnevale, was longtime basketball coach at Navy, who also coached the University of North Carolina to its first national championship basketball game in 1945.

Exempt Status: Past Champion
TOUR Victories: 1— 1992 Chattanooga Classic.

Money & Position:			
	1992 — $220,921 — 70	1993 — $100,046 — 145	1994 — $192,653 — 93
			1995 — $ 62,206 — 185

Best 1995 Finish: T17 — Sprint International
1995 Summary: Tournaments entered — 29; in money — 11; top-10 finishes — 0.
Career Earnings: $575,827

CLAMPETT, Bobby Birth Date 4/22/60 **Birthplace** Monterey, CA **Residence** Cary, NC; plays out of Deerfield Greens Resort, Lafollette, TN **Height** 5-10 **Weight** 161 **Family** Wife, Ann; Katelyn (10/30/87), Daniel (8/11/89), Michael (12/29/91) **College** Brigham Young University **Special Interests** Bible study, flying, snow skiing **Turned Professional** 1980 **Q School** 1980, 1990 **Other Achievements** Winner 1978 and 1980 California State Amateur. Low Amateur 1978 U.S. Open. Winner 1978 World Amateur medal. Three-time All-American, 1978-80. Two-time winner Fred Haskins Award, presented to top collegiate player. Active in Children's Flight of Hope program, tied to Children's Hospital at Duke University. Host of nationally syndicated radio show ("Drive Time—The Golf Radio Show") on Capitol Sports Network; also television commentator for TBS and CBS Sports.

Exempt Status: Past Champion
TOUR Victories: 1—1982 Southern Open

Money and Position:			
	1980 — $ 10,190 — 163	1985 — $ 81,121 — 94	1990 — $ 29,268 — 194
	1981 — $184,710 — 14	1986 — $ 97,178 — 87	1991 — $127,817 — 116
	1982 — $184,600 — 17	1987 — $124,872 — 84	1992 — $ 29,175 — 199
	1983 — $ 86,575 — 64	1988 — $ 88,067 — 118	1993 — $112,293 — 131
	1984 — $ 41,837 — 117	1989 — $ 68,868 — 148	1994 — $105,710 — 152
			1995 — $ 5,472 — 299

Best 1995 Finish: T35 — Deposit Guaranty Golf Classic
1995 Summary: Tournaments entered — 9; in money — 3; top-10 finishes — 0.
Career Earnings: $1,377,755

CLEARWATER, Keith Birth Date 9/1/59 **Birthplace** Long Beach, CA **Residence** Orem, UT **Height** 6-0 **Weight** 180 **Family** Wife, Sue; Jennifer (3/8/85), Melissa (6/30/88) **College** Brigham Young University **Special Interests** Family and church activities, home building, water sports, all sports **Turned Professional** 1982 **Q School** 1986 **Other Achievements** Named MasterCard PGA TOUR Rookie of Year in 1987 after winning Colonial National Invitation and Centel Classic. Winner of 1982 North & South Amateur and 1985 Alaska State Open. Member 1981 NCAA National Championship team at Brigham Young. Teammates at BYU included Rick Fehr, Richard Zokol and Bobby Clampett.

Exempt Status: Past Champion
TOUR Victories: 2 — 1987 Colonial National Invitation, Centel Classic.

Money & Position:			
	1987 — $320,007 — 31	1990 — $130,103 — 118	1993 — $348,763 — 44
	1988 — $ 82,876 — 127	1991 — $239,727 — 69	1994 — $203,549 — 90
	1989 — $ 87,490 — 136	1992 — $609,273 — 22	1995 — $ 34,354 — 219

Best 1995 Finish: T25 — Nissan Open
1995 Summary: Tournaments entered — 28; in money — 8; top-10 finishes — 0.
Career Earnings: $2,056,142

OTHER PROMINENT MEMBERS OF THE PGA TOUR

COCHRAN, Russ **Birth Date** 10/31/58 **Birthplace** Paducah, KY **Residence** Paducah, KY **Height** 6-0 **Weight** 160 **Family** Wife, Jackie; Ryan (9/4/83), Reed (9/29/85), Case (4/5/89), Kelly Marie (2/21/92) **College** University of Kentucky **Special Interest** Basketball **Turned Professional** 1979 **Q School** Fall 1982 **Other Achievements** One of only five lefthanders to win on PGA TOUR, with Bob Charles, Sam Adams, Ernie Gonzalez and Phil Mickelson. Winner of two Tournament Players Series events in 1983, Magnolia Classic and Greater Baltimore Open. Playing in eight events, finished as leading money winner on TPS, earning PGA TOUR exemption for 1984. Son Ryan scored a hole-in-one at age six, one of youngest ever to record an ace. Started playing with a ladies' set because he couldn't find any other lefthanded clubs. Won the 1975 Kentucky State High School Championship. Ardent University of Kentucky basketball fan.

Exempt Status: 131st on 1995 money list

TOUR Victories: 1 — 1991 Centel Western Open

Money & Position:

1983 — $ 7,968 — 188	1987 — $148,110 — 74	1991 — $684,851 — 10
1984 — $133,342 — 51	1988 — $148,960 — 80	1992 — $326,290 — 46
1985 — $ 87,331 — 87	1989 — $132,678 — 107	1993 — $293,868 — 59
1986 — $ 89,817 — 92	1990 — $230,278 — 65	1994 — $239,827 — 77
		1995 — $145,663 — 131

Best 1995 Finish: T7 — Walt Disney World/Oldsmobile Classic

1995 Summary: Tournaments entered — 26; in money — 16; top-10 finishes — 1.

Career Earnings: $2,668,983

COLE, Bobby **Birth Date** 5/11/48 **Birthplace** Springs, South Africa **Residence** Orlando, FL **Height** 5-10 **Weight** 165 **Family** Wife, Laura; Chelsea (7/23/82), Eric (6/12/88), Haley (4/28/90), Robert (3/13/92), Michael (11/93) **Special Interest** Cycling **Turned Professional** 1967 **Q School** 1967 **Other Achievements** Winner 1966 British Amateur, 1974 World Cup (with Dale Hayes), 1977 and 1981 South African Open, 1985 Seattle/Everett Open. Member South African World Cup team in 1970, 1974 and 1976.

Exempt Status: Past Champion

TOUR Victories: 1 — 1977 Buick Open

Money and Position:

1968 — $13,383 — 90	1977 — $ 41,301 — 68	1985 — $ 7,871 — 187
1969 — $17,898 — 90	1978 — $ 32,541 — 83	1986 — $ 88,472 — 95
1970 — $ 8,379 — 140	1979 — $ 6,525 — 175	1987 — $ 46,309 — 156
1971 — $10,585 — 122	1980 — $ 22,202 — 158	1988 — $ 0
1972 — $19,016 — 102	1981 — $ 13,559 — 158	1989 — $ 980 — 284
1973 — $28,875 — 89	1982 — $ 39,060 — 104	1990 — $ 612 — 310
1974 — $59,617 — 43	1983 — $ 16,153 — 162	1991 — $ 1,400 — 313
1975 — $42,441 — 61	1984 — $ 0	1992-95 No Earnings
1976 — $18,902 — 107		

Best 1995 Finish: Did not make a cut on PGA TOUR in 1995.

1995 Summary: Tournaments entered — 2; in money — 0; top-10 finishes — 0.

Career Earnings: $534,049

D

DALEY, Joe **Birth Date** 10/30/60 **Birthplace** Chestnut Hill, PA **Residence** Kissimmee, FL **Height** 6-3 **Weight** 157 **Family** Wife, Carol **College** Old Dominion University (1983, Finance) **Turned Professional** 1991 **Q School** 1995 **Other Achievements** Has played in two PGA TOUR events entering 1996, finishing T31 in 1994 Anheuser-Busch Golf Classic and missing cut in last year's Kmart Greater Greensboro Open.

Exempt Status: 32nd on 1995 PGA TOUR Qualifying Tournament/NIKE TOUR 6-10 List

Best-Ever Finish: T31 — 1994 Anheuser-Busch Golf Classic

Money & Position: 1994 — $6,239 — 270 1995 — $ 0

Best 1995 Finish: Did not make a cut on PGA TOUR in 1995.

1995 Summary: Tournaments entered — 1; in money — 0; top-10 finishes — 0.

Career Earnings: $6,239

DONALD, Mike **Birth Date** 7/11/55 **Birthplace** Grand Rapids, MI **Residence** Hollywood, FL **Height** 5-11 **Weight** 200 **Family** Single **College** Broward Community College and Georgia Southern University **Turned Professional** 1978 **Q School** Fall 1979 **Other Achievements** Winner 1984 JCPenney Classic with Vicki Alvarez. Teamed with Fred Couples to win 1990 Sazale Classic. Finished second to Hale Irwin in 1990 U.S. Open. Both shot 74 in playoff; on first sudden-death playoff hole in Open history, Irwin rolled in 10-foot birdie putt for win. Former Player Director on PGA TOUR Policy Board. Winner 1974 National Junior College Championship at Broward Community College and 1973 Florida Junior Championship.

Exempt Status: Past Champion **Playoff Record:** 1-1

TOUR Victories: 1 — 1989 Anheuser Busch Golf Classic

Money and Position:

1980 — $ 12,365 — 151	1985 — $ 91,888 — 46	1990 — $ 348,328 — 36
1981 — $ 50,665 — 83	1986 — $108,772 — 82	1991 — $ 88,248 — 142
1982 — $ 39,967 — 101	1987 — $137,734 — 79	1992 — $ 117,252 — 120
1983 — $ 72,343 — 73	1988 — $118,509 — 96	1993 — $ 51,312 — 183
1984 — $ 146,324 — 46	1989 — $430,232 — 22	1994 — $ 119,065 — 141
		1995 — $ 5,760 — 297

Best 1995 Finish: T40 — Anheuser-Busch Golf Classic

1995 Summary: Tournaments entered —15; in money — 2; top-10 finishes — 0.

Career Earnings: $1,938,765

DUNLAP, Scott **Birth Date** 8/16/63 **Birthplace** Pittsburgh, PA **Residence** Sarasota, FL; plays out of Misty Creek CC **Height** 5-11 **Weight** 170 **Family** Single **College** University of Florida (1985, Finance) **Special Interests** Jazz, conservative politics **Turned Professional** 1985 **Q School** 1995 **Other Achievements** Winner of the 1995 South African Masters and 1995 Canadian Masters Championships. 1994 Manitoba Open champion. Says winning the Canadian Masters by 10 strokes was his biggest thrill in golf. Finished eighth in last year's Bell Canadian Open, and T41 the next week at B.C. Open. Only other TOUR event was 1992 U.S. Open, in which he missed cut.

Exempt Status: 31st on 1995 PGA TOUR Qualifying Tournament/NIKE TOUR 6-10 List

Best-Ever Finish: 8 — 1995 Canadian Open

Money & Position: 1992 — $ 0 1995 — $44,000 — 211

Best 1995 Finish: 8 — Bell Canadian Open

1995 Summary: Tournaments entered — 2; in money — 2; top-10 finishes — 1.

Career Earnings: $44,000

E

EASTWOOD, Bob **Birth Date** 2/9/46 **Birthplace** Providence, RI **Residence** Stockton, CA and Ft. Worth, TX **Height** 5-10 **Weight** 185 **Family** Wife, Connie; Scott (8/19/71), Steven (12/29/73) **College** San Jose State University **Special Interests** Hunting, fishing **Turned Professional** 1969 **Q School** Spring 1969 **Other Achievements** Winner 1973 mini-Kemper Open, 1976 Little Bing Crosby (both Second Tour); 1965 Sacramento City Amateur, 1966 California State Amateur, 1968 West Coast Athletic Conference, 1981 Morocco Grand Prix. Medalist Spring 1969 Qualifying School. Becomes eligible for Senior TOUR in February.

Exempt Status: Past Champion **Playoff Record:** 1-0

TOUR Victories: 3 — 1984 USF&G Classic, Danny Thomas-Memphis Classic. 1985 Byron Nelson Classic.

Money and Position:

1972 — $ 9,528	1980 — $ 36,751 — 90	1988 — $ 94,504 — 117
1973 — $ 14,918	1981 — $ 66,017 — 67	1989 — $ 84,088 — 139
1974 — $ 18,535 — 114	1982 — $ 91,633 — 44	1990 — $123,908 — 125
1975 — $ 16,812 — 110	1983 — $157,640 — 30	1991 — $ 65,215 — 157
1976 — $ 14,539 — 123	1984 — $232,742 — 24	1992 — $ 83,818 — 148
1977 — $ 19,706 — 107	1985 — $152,839 — 51	1993 — $ 24,289 — 204
1978 — $ 24,681 — 100	1986 — $ 72,449 — 117	1994 — $ 6,737 — 264
1979 — $ 29,630 — 110	1987 — $114,897 — 88	1995 — $ 0

Best 1995 Finish: Did not make a cut on the 1995 PGA TOUR

1995 Summary: Tournaments entered — 4; in money — 0; top-10 finishes — 0.

Career Earnings: $1,551,414

OTHER PROMINENT MEMBERS OF THE PGA TOUR

EDWARDS, Danny **Birth Date** 6/14/51 **Birthplace** Ketchikan, AK **Residence** Scottsdale, AZ **Height** 5-11 **Weight** 155 **Family** Single **College** Oklahoma State University **Special Interests** Car collecting and skiing **Turned Professional** 1973 **Q School** Fall 1974 **Other Achievements** Collegiate All-American, 1972 & 1973. Winner 1972 North and South Amateur; member 1973 Walker Cup team; low amateur 1973 British Open. Winner 1972 & 1973 Big Eight Conference, 1972 Southeastern Amateur, 1981 Toshiba Taiheiyo Masters. Founder, CEO, chairman and president of Royal Grip.

Exempt Status: Past Champion **Playoff Record:** 1-0

TOUR Victories: 5 — 1977 Greater Greensboro Open. 1980 Walt Disney World National Team Play (with David Edwards). 1982 Greater Greensboro Open. 1983 Miller High Life-QCO. 1985 Pensacola Open.

Money and Position:

1975	$27,301	80	1982	$124,018	29	1989	$12,917	205
1976	$25,859	85	1983	$104,942	54	1990	$ 8,343	240
1977	$96,811	28	1984	$ 54,472	102	1991	$ 5,423	253
1978	$55,343	60	1985	$206,891	25	1992	$10,852	237
1979	$21,238	120	1986	$126,139	67	1993	$ 1,557	323
1980	$73,196	57	1987	$146,688	75	1994	$ 0	
1981	$66,567	66	1988	$ 36,637	160	1995	$ 0	

Best 1995 Finish: Did not make a cut on 1995 PGA TOUR

1995 Summary: Tournaments entered — 2; in money — 0; top-10 finishes — 0.

Career Earnings: $1,205,194

EDWARDS, Joel **Birth Date** 11/22/61 **Birthplace** Dallas, TX **Residence** Irving, TX **Height** 6-0 **Weight** 165 **Family** Wife, Rhonda **College** North Texas State University **Special Interests** Music, movies **Turned Professional** 1984 **Q School** 1988, 1989, 1990 **Other Achievements** Winner of 1988 North Dakota Open. Commented after finishing T2 in 1992 B.C. Open: "Andy Warhol promised me this (15 minutes of fame), so I'm just going to enjoy it." American Junior Golf Association All-American. Named to All-Southland Conference team at North Texas State.

Exempt Status: 149th on 1995 money list

Best-Ever Finish: T2 — 1992 B.C. Open

Money & Position:

1989	$ 46,851	167	1992	$107,264	126	1995	$114,285	149
1990	$109,808	132	1993	$150,623	106			
1991	$106,820	131	1994	$139,141	127			

Best 1995 Finish: 7 — Buick Open

1995 Summary: Tournaments entered — 31; in money — 16; top-10 finishes — 1.

Career Earnings: $774,793

ELLIOTT, John **Birth Date** 9/5/63 **Birthplace** Bristol, CT **Residence** Crystal River, FL **Height** 5-11 **Weight** 195 **Family** Single **College** Central Connecticut College **Special Interests** Skiing, working out **Turned Professional** 1988 **Q School** 1991, 1992, 1995 **Other Achievements** Winner of 1991 Massachusetts State Open and 15 mini-tour events. Defeated Chris Perry in playoff to win 1994 NIKE Mississippi Gulf Coast Classic. Ranked 45th on 1995 NIKE TOUR with $46,542 and four top-10 finishes. Fired final-round 63 in posting career-best 11th-place tie in 1993 H-E-B Texas Open. Goes by nickname "Jumbo".

Exempt Status: 45th on 1995 PGA TOUR Qualifying Tournament/NIKE TOUR 6-10 List

Best-Ever Finish: T11 — 1993 H-E-B Texas Open

Money & Position:

1992	$ 9,857	246	1993	$60,378	173	1994	$ 4,480	278

Best 1995 Finish: Did not play PGA TOUR in 1995

1995 Summary: Did not play PGA TOUR in 1995

Career Earnings: $74,715

F

FABEL, Brad **Birth Date** 11/30/55 **Birthplace** Lousiville, KY **Residence** Nashville, TN **Height** 6-0 **Weight** 185 **Family** Wife, Beth; Austin (4/24/89), Morgan Scott (9/9/92) **College** Western Kentucky University (1982, Public Relations) **Special Interests** Fishing, hunting **Turned Professional** 1982 **Q School** Fall 1984 **Other Achievements** Played on NIKE TOUR in 1994 and 1995. Won 1994 NIKE Gateway Classic and 1995 NIKE Shreveport Open. Earned $115,513 to finish 10th on 1995 NIKE TOUR money list. Winner 1974 Kentucky State Amateur.

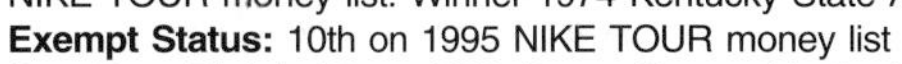

Exempt Status: 10th on 1995 NIKE TOUR money list

Best Ever Finish: T2 — 1990 Canon Greater Hartford Open

Money & Position:

1985	$ 74,425	100	1989	$ 69,823	146	1993	$ 59,672	175
1986	$ 25,634	165	1990	$165,876	96	1994	$ 33,812	205
1987	$ 90,024	104	1991	$147,562	103	1995	$ 0	
1988	$112,093	101	1992	$220,495	71			

Best 1995 Finish: Did not play PGA TOUR in 1995

1995 Summary: Did not play PGA TOUR in 1995

Career Earnings: $999,417

OTHER PROMINENT MEMBERS OF THE PGA TOUR

FEZLER, Forrest **Birth Date** 9/23/49 **Birthplace** Hayward, CA **Residence** Hampton, VA **Height** 5-9 **Weight** 165 **Family** Wife, Allison; Brooke, Jordan Jennifer **College** San Jose Community College **Special Interests** Golf course and home design **Turned Professional** 1969 **Other Achievements** Winner 1969 California Amateur, 1969 California Junior College Championship. Named 1969 Junior College Player of Year. Runner-up 1974 U.S. Open.

Exempt Status: Past Champion **Playoff Record:** 0-1

TOUR Victories: 1 — 1974 Southern Open

Money & Position

1972 — $ 26,542 — 88	1979 — $ 11,427 — 148	1986 — $ 2,080 — 244
1973 — $106,390 — 12	1980 — $ 19,269 — 127	1987 — $ 1,784 — 258
1974 — $ 90,066 — 24	1981 — $ 13,064 — 158	1988 — $ 3,477 — 207
1975 — $ 52,157 — 43	1982 — $ 38,983 — 105	1989 — $ 1,853 — 152
1976 — $ 59,793 — 44	1983 — $ 24,452 — 143	1993 — $ 2,610 — 295
1977 — $ 30,029 — 82	1984 — $ 14,152 — 150	1994 — $ 0
1978 — $ 30,812 — 85	1985 — $ 1,400 — 154	1995 — $ 0

Best 1995 Finish: Did not make a cut on 1995 PGA TOUR

1995 Summary: Tournaments entered — 1; in money — 0; top-10 finishes — 0.

Career Earnings: $527,996

FLEISHER, Bruce **Birth Date** 10/16/48 **Birthplace** Union City, TN **Residence** Ballen Isles, FL **Height** 6-3 **Weight** 205 **Family** Wife, Wendy; Jessica (3/23/80) **College** Miami Dade Junior College **Special Interests** Reading, helping others **Turned Professional** 1970 **Q School** Fall 1971 **Other Achievements** Lone PGA TOUR victory came at 1991 New England Classic, when rolled in 50-foot birdie putt on seventh playoff hole to defeat Ian Baker-Finch. Winner 1968 U.S. Amateur, 1971 Brazilian Open, 1989 Club Pro Championship, 1990 Jamaica, Bahamas and Brazilian Opens. Low amateur 1969 Masters Tournament.

Exempt Status: Past Champion **Playoff Record:** 1-0

TOUR Victories: 1 — 1991 New England Classic

Money and Position:

1972 — $ 6,035 — 144	1980 — $13,649 — 149	1988 — $ 2,198 — 268
1973 — $ 9,483 — 131	1981 — $69,221 — 64	1989 — $ 0
1974 — $ 33,975 — 77	1982 — $36,659 — 110	1990 — $ 10,626 — 227
1975 — $ 7,773 — 141	1983 — $50,285 — 102	1991 — $219,335 — 76
1976 — $ 11,295 — 137	1984 — $30,186 — 138	1992 — $236,516 — 68
1977 — $ 9,101 — 155	1985 — $ 0	1993 — $214,279 — 81
1978 — $ 8,347 — 154	1986 — $ 7,866 — 213	1994 — $ 88,680 — 163
1979 — $ 11,420 — 149	1987 — $ 2,405 — 254	1995 — $108,830 — 154

Best 1995 Finish: T8 — Buick Classic

1995 Summary: Tournaments entered — 22; in money — 13; top-10 finishes — 2.

Career Earnings: $1,201,886

G

GALLAGHER, Jeff **Birth Date** 12/29/64 **Birthplace** Marion, IN **Residence** Jacksonville, FL; plays out of Marsh Landing CC **Height** 6-0 **Weight** 185 **Family** Wife, Kim; Allison (11/18/95) **College** Ball State University (1987, Exercise Physiology) **Special Interests** Fishing, hunting **Turned Professional** 1988 **Q School** 1995 **Other Achievements** Member of NIKE TOUR since 1990. Best year was 1991, when he won the Cleveland Open and earned $56,592 to rank ninth on money list. Earned $48,085 to rank 43rd on 1995 NIKE TOUR money list. Winner of 1982 Indiana State Junior Championship. Two-time All Mid-American Conference. Brother of PGA TOUR veteran Jim Gallagher, Jr. and LPGA member Jackie Gallagher-Smith. Caddied for Jim in 1993 British Open. Entering 1996, had played in two PGA TOUR events, missing cut in 1989 Hardee's Golf Classic and 1994 Deposit Guaranty Golf Classic.

Exempt Status: 28th on 1995 PGA TOUR Qualifying Tournament/NIKE TOUR 6-10 List

Money & Position: No PGA TOUR earnings

Best 1995 Finish: Did not play PGA TOUR in 1995

1995 Summary: Did not play PGA TOUR in 1995

Career Earnings: No PGA TOUR career earnings

OTHER PROMINENT MEMBERS OF THE PGA TOUR

GARDNER, Buddy **Birth Date** 8/24/55 **Birthplace** Montgomery, AL **Residence** Birmingham, AL **Weight** 175 **Height** 5-11 **Family** Wife, Susan; Brooke Marie (2/1/87), Payton Webb (12/2/89) **College** Auburn University **Turned Professional** 1977 **Q School** Fall 1977, 1978, 1982 **Other Achievements** Winner 1974, 1975 Alabama Amateur and 1976 Dixie Amateur. 1977 All-American. Won 1990 Ben Hogan Panama City Beach Classic. Registered back-to-back eagles, second a hole-in-one, in Round 1 of 1994 Walt Disney/Oldsmobile Classic.

Exempt Status: Veteran Member **Playoff Record:** 0-2

Best Ever Finish: 2 — 1984 Houston Coca-Cola Open. 2 — 1987 Big I Houston Open. T2 — 1979 Tucson Open, 1979 Anheuser-Busch Classic.

Money and Position:

1978 — $ 5,637 — 170	1984 — $118,945 — 55	1990 — $159,737 — 99
1979 — $ 71,468 — 56	1985 — $121,809 — 67	1991 — $201,700 — 83
1980 — $ 30,907 — 102	1986 — $ 92,006 — 91	1992 — $113,394 — 124
1981 — $ 14,635 — 151	1987 — $173,047 — 60	1993 — $ 13,721 — 232
1982 — $ 6,214 — 192	1988 — $130,589 — 91	1994 — $ 37,609 — 201
1983 — $ 56,529 — 91	1989 — $135,488 — 103	1995 — $ 5,622 — 298

Best 1995 Finish: T35 — Deposit Guaranty Golf Classic

1995 Summary: Tournaments entered — 6; in money — 2; top-10 finishes — 0.

Career Earnings: $1,489,327

GILDER, Bob **Birth Date** 12/31/50 **Birthplace** Corvallis, OR **Residence** Corvallis, OR **Height** 5-9 **Weight** 165 **Family** Wife, Peggy; Bryan (3/24/75), Cammy Lynn (6/10/77), Brent (3/3/81) **College** Arizona State University (1973, Business Administration) **Special Interests** All sports, car racing **Turned Professional** 1973 **Q School** Fall 1975 **Other Achievements** Win in 1976 Phoenix Open came in only his second PGA TOUR start. Won 1974 New Zealand Open in playoff over Jack Newton and Bob Charles. Winner of 1988 Isuzu Kapalua International. Winner of three events on Japan PGA Tour: 1982 Bridgestone International, 1988 Acom Team title (with Doug Tewell) and 1990 Acom P.T. Fairway marker at Westchester CC commemorates third-round double-eagle on his way to victory in 1982 Manufacturers Hanover Westchester Classic.

Exempt Status: 138th on 1995 money list

TOUR Victories: 6 — 1976 Phoenix Open. 1980 Canadian Open. 1982 Byron Nelson Classic, Manufacturers Hanover Westchester Classic, Bank of Boston Classic. 1983 Phoenix Open.

Money & Position:

1976 — $101,262 — 24	1983 — $139,125 — 39	1990 — $154,934 — 102
1977 — $ 36,844 — 72	1984 — $ 23,313 — 147	1991 — $251,683 — 66
1978 — $ 72,515 — 36	1985 — $ 47,152 — 123	1992 — $170,761 — 91
1979 — $134,428 — 22	1986 — $ 98,181 — 85	1993 — $148,496 — 108
1980 — $152,597 — 19	1987 — $ 94,310 — 100	1994 — $154,868 — 118
1981 — $ 74,756 — 59	1988 — $144,523 — 82	1995 — $139,361 — 138
1982 — $308,648 — 6	1989 — $187,910 — 78	

Best 1995 Finish: T8 — Buick Classic, Deposit Guaranty Golf Classic, Quad City Classic

1995 Summary: Tournaments entered — 30; in money — 14; top-10 finishes — 3.

Career Earnings: $2,636,473

GONZALEZ, Ernie **Birth Date** 2/19/61 **Birthplace** San Diego, CA **Residence** Orlando, FL **Height** 5-9 **Weight** 195 **Family** Wife, Judy; David (6/2/92) **College** United States International University **Special Interest** All sports **Turned Professional** 1983 **Q School** 1984, 1985, 1989 **Other Achievements** Winner 1981, 1982 San Diego County Amateur Match Play Championships; 1983 San Diego County Open (as amateur); 1984-1985 Queen Mary Open. One of only five lefthanders to win on PGA TOUR (Sam Adams, Bob Charles, Russ Cochran, Phil Mickelson).

Exempt Status: Past Champion.

TOUR Victories: 1 — 1986 Pensacola Open.

Money & Position:

1985 — $ 12,729 — 171	1989 — $ 13,840 — 203	1993 — $ 2,175 — 310
1986 — $125,548 — 68	1990 — $ 13,540 — 221	1994 — $ 16,860 — 230
1987 — $ 60,234 — 154	1991 — $ 5,550 — 252	1995 — $ 4,227 — 309
1988 — $ 14,135 — 207	1992 — $ 5,485 — 262	

Best 1995 Finish: T44 — Quad City Classic

1995 Summary: Tournaments entered — 3; in money — 2; top-10 finishes — 0.

Career Earnings: $261,592

OTHER PROMINENT MEMBERS OF THE PGA TOUR

GORMAN, Bryan Birth Date 5/16/63 **Birthplace** San Diego, CA **Residence** San Diego, CA; plays out of Chula Vista GC **Height** 6-4 **Weight** 190 **Family** Wife, Kim; Kevin **College** United States International University (1985, Business Administration) **Special Interest** Woodworking **Turned Professional** 1987 **Q School** 1995 **Other Achievements** Member of NIKE TOUR in 1993. Prior to 1996, played in two PGA TOUR events, missing cut in 1992 U.S. Open and 1994 Buick Invitational of California. Career-best NIKE TOUR finish was T3 in 1993 Boise Open. Second leading money winner on 1991 Golden State Tour.

Exempt Status: 4th at 1995 PGA TOUR Qualifying Tournament
Money & Position: No PGA TOUR earnings
Best 1995 Finish: Did not play PGA TOUR in 1995
1995 Summary: Did not play PGA TOUR in 1995
Career Earnings: No PGA TOUR career earnings

GRAHAM, David Birth Date 5/23/46 **Birthplace** Windsor, Australia **Residence** Dallas, TX **Height** 5-10 **Weight** 162 **Family** Wife, Maureen Burdett; Andrew (11/8/74), Michael (10/8/77) **Special Interests** Hunting, golf club design, cars **Turned Professional** 1962 **Q School** Fall, 1971 **Other Achievements** Foreign victories include 1970 French Open, 1970 Thailand Open, 1971 Caracas Open, 1971 JAL Open, 1975 Wills Masters, 1976 Chunichi Crowns Invitational (Japan), 1976 Piccadilly World Match Play, 1977 Australian Open and South African PGA, 1978 Mexico Cup, 1979 Westlakes Classic (Australia), New Zealand Open, 1980 Mexican Open, Rolex Japan, Brazilian Classic, 1981-1982 Lancome (France), 1985 Queensland Open. **National Teams** Australian World Cup 1970 (won team title with Bruce Devlin), U.S. vs. Japan 1983. Australian Dunhill Cup 1985, 1986, 1988. Captain of International Team for 1994 and 1996 Presidents Cups.

Exempt Status: Past Champion **Playoff Record:** 2-1

TOUR Victories: 8—1972 Cleveland Open. 1976 Westchester Classic, American Golf Classic. 1979 PGA Championship. 1980 Memorial Tournament. 1981 Phoenix Open, U.S. Open. 1983 Houston Coca-Cola Open.

Money and Position:

Year	Money	Position	Year	Money	Position	Year	Money	Position
1971	$ 10,062	135	1980	$137,819	27	1989	$ 22,275	192
1972	$ 57,827	38	1981	$188,286	13	1990	$ 24,492	204
1973	$ 43,062	71	1982	$103,616	35	1991	$ 12,233	225
1974	$ 61,625	41	1983	$244,924	11	1992	$ 0	
1975	$ 51,642	44	1984	$116,627	58	1993	$ 0	
1976	$176,174	8	1985	$ 72,802	101	1994	$ 0	
1977	$ 72,086	44	1986	$ 95,109	88	1995	$ 3,196	315
1978	$ 66,909	43	1987	$ 58,860	142			
1979	$177,683	16	1988	$ 99,087	113			

Best 1995 Finish: 76 — Memorial Tournament
1995 Summary: Tournaments entered — 5; in money — 1; top-10 finishes — 0.
Career Earnings: $1,877,976

GREEN, Hubert Birth Date 12/28/46 **Birthplace** Birmingham, AL **Residence** Birmingham, AL **Height** 6-1 **Weight** 175 **Family** Hubert Myatt, Jr. (8/18/75), Patrick (10/17/78), J.T. (2/11/84) **College** Florida State University (1968) **Special Interests** Fishing, gardening **Turned Professional** 1970 **Q School** Fall 1970 **Other Achievements** Becomes eligible for Senior PGA TOUR in December of 1996. Claimed first of two major titles in 1977 U.S. Open at Southern Hills. Won 1985 PGA Championship at Cherry Hills. In 1976, won three consecutive events: Doral-Eastern Open, Greater Jacksonville Open and Sea Pines Heritage Classic. Was named Rookie of Year in 1971. Winner of 1975 Dunlop Phoenix tournament in Japan and 1977 Irish Open. Member 1977, 1979 and 1985 U.S. Ryder Cup teams. Won Southern Amateur in 1966 and 1969. Very active in golf course design, worked with Fuzzy Zoeller on design of TPC at Southwind.

Exempt Status: Past Champion

TOUR Victories:19 —1971 Houston Champions International. 1973 Tallahassee Open, B. C. Open. 1974 Bob Hope Classic, Greater Jacksonville Open, Philadelphia Classic, Walt Disney World National Team Play (with Mac McLendon).1975 Southern Open. 1976 Doral Eastern Open, Jacksonville Open, Sea Pines Heritage Classic. 1977 U.S. Open. 1978 Hawaiian Open, Sea Pines Heritage Classic. 1979 Hawaiian Open, New Orleans Open. 1981 Sammy Davis, Jr.-Greater Hartford Open. 1984 Southern Open. 1985 PGA Championship.

Money & Position:

Year	Money	Position	Year	Money	Position	Year	Money	Position
1970	$ 1,690	218	1979	$183,111	13	1988	$ 52,268	147
1971	$ 73,439	29	1980	$ 83,307	50	1989	$161,190	86
1972	$ 44,113	58	1981	$110,133	32	1990	$ 65,948	165
1973	$114,397	11	1982	$ 77,448	54	1991	$ 18,031	212
1974	$211,709	3	1983	$ 29,171	135	1992	$ 23,602	204
1975	$113,569	12	1984	$181,585	33	1993	$ 29,786	199
1976	$228,031	4	1985	$233,527	16	1994	$ 4,854	277
1977	$140,255	9	1986	$120,051	73			
1978	$247,406	5	1987	$ 63,349	129			

Best 1995 Finish: T59--Memorial Tournament
1995 Summary: Tournaments entered — 17; in money — 2; top-10 finishes — 0.
Career Earnings: $2,586,664

OTHER PROMINENT MEMBERS OF THE PGA TOUR

GULLION, Joey (GOOL-yun) **Birth Date** 6/9/71 **Birthplace** Gallapolis, OH **Residence** Plano, TX; plays out of Gleneagles CC **Height** 5-11 **Weight** 160 **Family** Single **College** University of Minnesota (1993, Business) **Special Interests** Skiing, basketball, reading **Turned Professional** 1993 **Q School** 1995 **Other Achievements** Member of NIKE TOUR in 1994 and 1995. Earned $36,826 to rank 52nd on 1995 NIKE TOUR money list. Best finish was T4 in season-opening NIKE San Jose Open. Biggest thrill in golf was making cut at 1995 U.S. Open at Shinnecock Hills. Tied with Nick Price for lead after making a 35-foot birdie putt on ninth hole. Went on to finish 73rd.

Exempt Status: 5th at 1995 PGA TOUR Qualifying Tournament
Best-Ever Finish: 73 — 1995 U.S. Open
Money & Position: 1995 — $2,574 — 330
Best 1995 Finish: 73 — U.S. Open
1995 Summary: Tournaments entered — 1; in money — 1; top-10 finishes — 0.
Career Earnings: $2,574

H

HALLBERG, Gary **Birth Date** 5/31/58 **Birthplace** Berwyn, IL **Residence** Castle Rock, CO **Height** 5-10 **Weight** 155 **Family** Wife, Shirley; Christina (8/19/92), Eric Anders (1/10/94) **College** Wake Forest University **Special Interests** Family, sports, TOUR Bible study **Turned Professional** July 2, 1980 **Q School** July 1980 **Other Achievements** In 1980 became first TOUR player to earn playing privileges without going through Qualifying Tournament. Won 1981 Lille Open in France and the 1982 Chunichi Crowns Invitational in Japan. Winner 1986 Chrysler Team Championship (with Scott Hoch). Was first four-time first-team All-American selection. That feat was later matched by Phil Mickelson and David Duval. Won 1979 NCAA Championship and 1978 and 1979 North & South Amateurs.

Exempt Status: Past Champion
TOUR Victories: 3 — 1983 Isuzu-Andy Williams San Diego Open. 1987 Greater Milwaukee Open. 1992 Buick Southern Open.

Money & Position:

1980 — $ 64,244 — 63	1986 — $ 68,479 — 121	1992 — $236,629 — 67
1981 — $ 45,793 — 91	1987 — $210,786 — 48	1993 — $147,706 — 111
1982 — $ 36,192 — 111	1988 — $ 28,551 — 179	1994 — $224,965 — 82
1983 — $120,140 — 45	1989 — $146,833 — 95	1995 — $ 99,332 — 160
1984 — $187,260 — 30	1990 — $128,954 — 121	
1985 — $108,872 — 75	1991 — $273,546 — 62	

Best 1995 Finish: T14 — Kmart Greater Greensboro Open
1995 Summary: Tournaments entered — 28; in money — 11; top-10 finishes — 0.
Career Earnings: $2,128,311

HALLDORSON, Dan **Birth Date** 4/2/52 **Birthplace** Winnipeg, Canada **Residence** Cambridge,IL **Height** 5-10 **Weight** 180 **Family** Wife, Pat; Angie (4/7/75) **Special Interest** Sports **Turned Professional** 1971 **Q School** 1974, 1978, 1990 **Other Achievements** Winner 1986 Deposit Guaranty Golf Classic, unofficial PGA TOUR event. Defeated Paul Azinger by two strokes in Hattiesburg, MS tournament. Member several Canadian World Cup teams. Leader 1983 Canadian Tour Order of Merit.

Exempt Status: Past Champion **Playoff Record:** 0-1
TOUR Victories: 1 — 1980 Pensacola Open

Money & Position:

1975 — $ 619 — 243	1984 — $ 55,215 — 99	1990 — $ 18,155 — 215
1979 — $ 24,559 — 116	1985 — $112,102 — 73	1991 — $ 158,743 — 97
1980 — $111,553 — 36	1986 — $ 83,876 — 101	1992 — $ 119,002 — 118
1981 — $ 90,064 — 47	1987 — $ 69,094 — 125	1993 — $ 24,284 — 205
1982 — $ 93,705 — 43	1988 — $ 96,079 — 116	1994 — $ 7,215 — 262
1983 — $ 21,458 — 146	1989 — $ 86,667 — 137	1995 — $ 0

Best 1995 Finish: Did not make a cut on 1995 PGA TOUR
1995 Summary: Tournaments entered — 3; in money — 0; top-10 finishes — 0.
Career Earnings: $1,173,134

OTHER PROMINENT MEMBERS OF THE PGA TOUR

HAMMOND, Donnie **Birth Date** 4/1/57 **Birthplace** Frederick, MD **Residence** Winter Park, FL; plays out of Marriott Ownership Resorts **Height** 5-10 **Weight** 170 **Family** Matthew William (10/22/86), Brittany Marie (3/8/89) **College** Jacksonville University (1979, Psychology) **Special Interests** Sports, cars, gardening, tennis, flying **Turned Professional** 1979 **Q School** Fall 1982, 1991 **Other Achievements** 258 total in winning 1989 Texas Open was second lowest cumulative score in PGA TOUR history, one shy of all-time record (257). Medalist in 1982 Qualifying Tournament, where he broke Ben Crenshaw's record in winning by 14 strokes. Winner of 1982 Florida Open. Got start in golf through Baltimore Colts; growing up near Colts training camp, he and his father would attend practices and then play local nine-hole course. Charter member of Jacksonville University Sports Hall of Fame.

Exempt Status: 136th on 1995 money list

TOUR Victories: 2 — 1986 Bob Hope Chrysler Classic. 1989 Texas Open presented by Nabisco.

Money & Position:

1983 — $ 41,336 — 112	1988 — $256,010 — 44	1993 — $340,432 — 47
1984 — $ 67,874 — 86	1989 — $458,741 — 20	1994 — $295,436 — 61
1985 — $102,719 — 77	1990 — $151,811 — 104	1995 — $141,150 — 136
1986 — $254,987 — 28	1991 — $102,668 — 135	
1987 — $157,480 — 64	1992 — $197,085 — 77	

Best 1995 Finish: T7 — Bob Hope Chrysler Classic

1995 Summary: Tournaments entered — 24; in money — 17; top-10 finishes — 1.

Career Earnings: $2,567,729

HART, Dudley **Birth Date** 8/4/68 **Birthplace** Rochester, NY **Residence** Ft. Lauderdale, FL **Height** 5-10 **Weight** 175 **Family** Single **College** University of Florida **Special Interest** Sports **Turned Professional** 1990 **Q School** 1990, 1994 **Other Achievements** Four-time All-American. After turning professional in 1990, won Florida Open and Louisiana Open later in year. Missed 10 weeks of 1994 season due to rib and back problems. Won pro-am portion of 1994 AT&T Pebble Beach National Pro-Am with Raymond Floyd's son Robert.

Exempt Status: 148th on 1995 money list

Best-Ever Finish: T3 — 1992 Greater Milwaukee Open; T3 — 1993 Northern Telecom Open; T3 — 1993 Kmart Greater Greensboro Open.

Money and Position:

1991 — $126,217 — 120	1993 — $316,750 — 52	1995 — $116,334 — 148
1992 — $254,903 — 61	1994 — $126,313 — 135	

Best 1995 Finish: T15 — Canon Greater Hartford Open, Ideon Classic at Pleasant Valley

1995 Summary: Tournaments entered — 30; in money — 18; top-10 finishes — 0.

Career Earnings: $940,518

HART, Jeff **Birth Date** 5/5/60 **Birthplace** Pomona, CA **Residence** Solana Beach, CA **Height** 5-9 **Weight** 150 **Family** Carmen; Sabrina Nicole (2/13/91) **College** University of Southern California (1983, Physical Education) **Special Interests** USC football, all sports **Turned Professional** 1983 **Q School** 1988, 1989, 1995 **Other Achievements** First team All-American in 1982, third team in 1981. Member of PGA TOUR in 1989 and 1990. Played NIKE TOUR in 1995 with best finish T8 in NIKE Louisiana Open. Earned $23,935 to rank 78th on NIKE TOUR money list. Best-ever NIKE TOUR finish third in 1992 South Texas Open. Winner 1994 California State Open.

Exempt Status: 44th on 1995 PGA TOUR Qualifying Tournament/NIKE TOUR 6-10 List

Best-Ever Finish: T11 — 1989 Kemper Open

Money & Position:

1988 — $ 7,875 — 223	1990 — $57,189 — 171	1992 — $ 0
1989 — $44,650 — 169	1991 — $ 1,866 — 303	1994 — $ 0

Best 1995 Finish: Did not play PGA TOUR in 1995

1995 Summary: Did not play PGA TOUR in 1995

Career Earnings: $112,305

OTHER PROMINENT MEMBERS OF THE PGA TOUR

HART, Steve **Birth Date** 9/13/59 **Birthplace** St. Paul, MN **Residence** Tequesta, FL **Height** 5-8 **Weight** 175 **Family** Wife, Pattie; Gregory (3/29/95) **College** University of Florida **Special Interests** Deep sea fishing, football **Turned Professional** 1981 **Q School** 1988, 1991, 1994, 1995 **Other Achievements** Winner, 1981 Palm Beach County Amateur Championship. Runner-up 1981 Florida State Amateur.

Exempt Status: 3rd at 1995 PGA TOUR Qualifying Tournament

Best-Ever Finish: T14 — 1992 Shell Houston Open

Money & Position:

1982 — $ 2,762 — 240	1986 — $ 1,440 — 262	1992 — $ 69,124 — 157
1983 — $19,314 — 153	1989 — $ 40,079 — 171	1993 — $ 2,175 — 310
1984 — $ 4,060 — 206	1990 — $ 28,575 — 196	1994 — $ 0
1985 — $ 0	1991 — $ 0	1995 — $ 2,748 — 326

Best 1995 Finish: T54 — Buick Invitational of California

1995 Summary: Tournaments entered — 17; in money — 1; top-10 finishes — 0.

Career Earnings: $161,603

HATALSKY, Morris **Birth Date** 11/10/51 **Birthplace** San Diego, CA **Residence** Ormond Beach, FL **Height** 5-11 **Weight** 165 **Family** Wife, Tracy; Daniel Kenneth (12/11/80), Laura Rose (2/26/83) **College** United States International University **Special Interests** Family activities, TOUR Bible study, snow skiing **Turned Professional** 1973 **Q School** Spring 1976, 1993 **Other Achievements** 1972 NAIA All-American. Captained 1972 U.S. International University NAIA Championship team. Winner 1968 Mexico National Junior Championship.

Exempt Status: Past Champion **Playoff Record:** 2-1

TOUR Victories: 4 — 1981 Hall of Fame Classic. 1983 Greater Milwaukee Open. 1988 Kemper Open. 1990 Bank of Boston Classic.

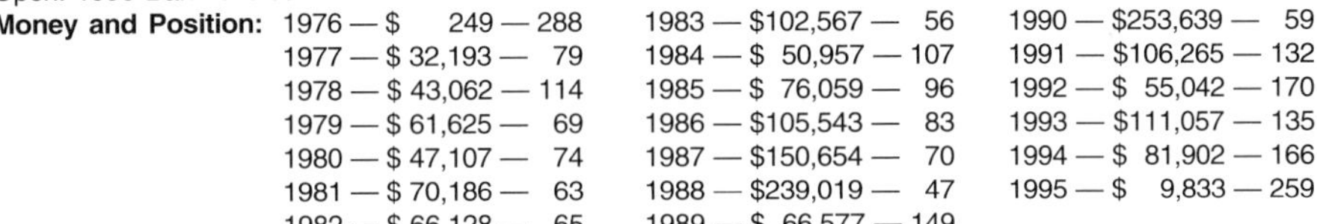

Money and Position:

1976 — $ 249 — 288	1983 — $102,567 — 56	1990 — $253,639 — 59
1977 — $ 32,193 — 79	1984 — $ 50,957 — 107	1991 — $106,265 — 132
1978 — $ 43,062 — 114	1985 — $ 76,059 — 96	1992 — $ 55,042 — 170
1979 — $ 61,625 — 69	1986 — $105,543 — 83	1993 — $111,057 — 135
1980 — $ 47,107 — 74	1987 — $150,654 — 70	1994 — $ 81,902 — 166
1981 — $ 70,186 — 63	1988 — $239,019 — 47	1995 — $ 9,833 — 259
1982 — $ 66,128 — 65	1989 — $ 66,577 — 149	

Best 1995 Finish: T20 — Deposit Guaranty Golf Classic

1995 Summary: Tournaments entered — 5; in money — 2; top-10 finishes — 0.

Career Earnings: $1,703,280

HAYES, J.P. **Birth Date** 8/2/65 **Birthplace** Appleton, WI **Residence** El Paso, TX **Height** 6-0 **Weight:** 170 **Family** Wife, Laura **College** University of Texas-El Paso **Special Interests** Fishing, skiing **Turned Professional** 1989 **Q School** 1991, 1994 **Other Achievements** Played NIKE TOUR in 1991, 1993 and 1994. Member of PGA TOUR in 1992. Posted career-low round, a 10-under-par 61, during second round of 1994 NIKE Boise Open.

Exempt Status: 153rd on 1995 money list

Best-Ever Finish: T6 — 1992 Anheuser-Busch Golf Classic

Money and Position: 1992 — $72,830 — 155 1993 — $6,650 — 253 1995— $111,696 — 153

Best 1995 Finish: T12 — Quad City Classic

1995 Summary: Tournaments entered — 27; in money — 13; top-10 finishes — 0.

Career Earnings: $184,526

HAYES, Mark **Birth Date** 7/12/49 **Birthplace** Stillwater, OK **Residence** Edmond, OK; plays out of Oak Tree GC **Height** 5-11 **Weight** 170 **Family** Wife, Jana; Kelly (12/9/79), Ryan (3/25/83) **College** Oklahoma State University **Special Interest** Sports **Turned Professional** 1973 **Q School** 1973, 1988, 1989, 1990 **Other Achievements** 1967 and 1971 Oklahoma Amateur Champion. 1970-71 Collegiate All-American.

Exempt Status: Past Champion **Playoff Record:** 0-2

TOUR Victories: 3 — 1976 Byron Nelson Classic, Pensacola Open. 1977 Tournament Players Championship.

Money and Position:

1973 — $ 8,637 — 160	1981 — $ 91,624 — 46	1989 — $ 87,689 — 134
1974 — $ 40,620 — 68	1982 — $ 47,777 — 95	1990 — $ 76,743 — 149
1975 — $ 49,297 — 47	1983 — $ 63,431 — 81	1991 — $ 36,370 — 191
1976 — $151,699 — 11	1984 — $ 42,207 — 115	1992 — $ 50,324 — 175
1977 — $115,749 — 19	1985 — $ 61,988 — 108	1993 — $ 6,942 — 249
1978 — $146,456 — 15	1986 — $117,837 — 74	1994 — $ 0
1979 — $130,878 — 23	1987 — $ 76,666 — 116	1995 — $ 7,061 — 283
1980 — $ 66,535 — 61	1988 — $ 77,072 — 131	

Best 1995 Finish: T20 — Deposit Guaranty Golf Classic

1995 Summary: Tournaments entered — 6; in money — 1; top-10 finishes — 0.

Career Earnings: $1,551,898

OTHER PROMINENT MEMBERS OF THE PGA TOUR

HEAFNER, Vance (HEF-ner) Birth Date 8/11/54 **Birthplace** Charlotte, NC **Residence** Raleigh, NC **Height** 6-0 **Weight** 185 **Family** Wife, Paige; Elizabeth (10/13/85), Allison (10/4/88) **College** North Carolina State University **Special Interests** Fishing, hunting **Turned Professional** 1978 **Q School** 1980, 1989 **Other Achievements** All American at North Carolina State 1984, 1985, 1986. Winner 1976-78 Eastern Amateur titles, 1977 Porter Cup. Member 1977 Walker Cup team. Winner 1977 Azalea Invitational, 1978 American Amateur Classic. Made 150th cut to achieve Veteran Member staus in 1994.

Exempt Status: Past Champion

TOUR Victories: 1 — 1981 Walt Disney World National Team Championship (w/Mike Holland)

Money and Position:

1980 — $ 11,398 — 156	1985 — $ 31,964 — 142	1990 — $ 6,525 — 256
1981 — $ 73,244 — 60	1986 — $ 28,763 — 159	1994 — $ 5,297 — 271
1982 — $113,717 — 33	1987 — $ 74,489 — 119	1995 — $ 1,690 — 356
1983 — $ 68,210 — 65	1988 — $ 2,117 — 170	
1984 — $ 90,702 — 71	1989 — $ 1,624 — 273	

Best 1995 Finish: T85 — Quad City Classic

1995 Summary: Tournaments entered — 2; in money — 1; top-10 finishes — 0.

Career Earnings: $527,739

HERRON, Tim (HAIR-un) Birth Date 2/16/70 **Birthplace** Minneapolis, MN **Residence** Wayzata, MN; plays out of Wayzata CC **Height** 5-10 **Weight** 210 **Family** Single **College** University of New Mexico (1993, University Studies) **Special Interests** Fishing, pool, skiing **Turned Professional** 1993 **Q School** 1995 **Other Achievements** First-team All-American in 1992 and 1993. Member of victorious 1993 United States Walker Cup team, going undefeated in three matches as U.S. won by largest margin ever, 19-5. Member of NIKE TOUR in 1995, earning $69,534 to rank 25th on money list. Best finish was T3 in NIKE Mississippi Gulf Coast Classic.

Exempt Status: 12th on 1995 PGA TOUR Qualifying Tournament/NIKE TOUR 6-10 List

Money & Position: No PGA TOUR earnings

Best 1995 Finish: Did not make a cut on PGA TOUR in 1995

1995 Summary: Tournaments entered — 1; in money — 0; top-10 finishes — 0.

Career Earnings: No PGA TOUR career earnings

HINKLE, Lon Birth Date 7/17/49 **Birthplace** Flint, MI **Residence** San Diego, CA; plays out of Eagle Bend GC **Height** 6-2 **Weight** 220 **Family** Monique (8/10/78), Danielle (3/20/82); Jake (9/6/85) **College** San Diego State University **Special Interest** Reading **Turned Professional** 1972 **Q School** 1972, 1991 **Other Achievements** Co-champion 1972 Pacific Coast Athletic Conference. Runner-up 1975 German Open and Sanpo Classic in Japan. Winner 1978 JCPenney Classic with Pat Bradley. Runner-up 1980 European Open. 1981 National Long Drive Champion.

Exempt Status: Past Champion **Playoff Record:** 1-2

TOUR Victories: 3 — 1978 New Orleans Open. 1979 Bing Crosby National Pro-Am, World Series of Golf

Money and Position:

1972 — $ 7,350 — 145	1980 — $134,913 — 29	1989 — $151,828 — 92
1973 — $ 7,539 — 164	1981 — $144,307 — 22	1990 — $ 26,052 — 201
1974 — $ 6,509 — 162	1982 — $ 55,406 — 81	1991 — $ 49,692 — 174
1975 — $ 8,420 — 136	1983 — $116,822 — 47	1992 — $ 91,854 — 139
1976 — $ 11,058 — 138	1984 — $ 89,850 — 73	1993 — $ 8,621 — 244
1977 — $ 51,494 — 60	1985 — $105,499 — 76	1994 — $ 4,411 — 281
1978 — $138,388 — 16	1986 — $ 97,610 — 86	1995 — $ 0
1979 — $247,693 — 3	1987 — $ 45,751 — 159	

Best 1995 Finish: Did not make a cut on 1995 PGA TOUR

1995 Summary: Tournaments entered — 1; in money — 0; top-10 finishes — 0.

Career Earnings: $1,600,247

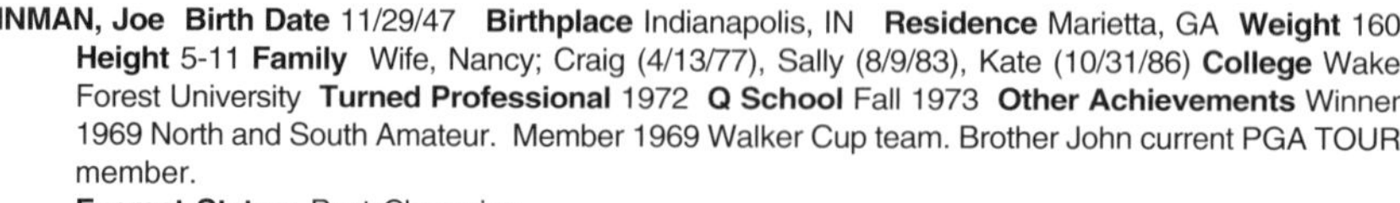

INMAN, Joe Birth Date 11/29/47 **Birthplace** Indianapolis, IN **Residence** Marietta, GA **Weight** 160 **Height** 5-11 **Family** Wife, Nancy; Craig (4/13/77), Sally (8/9/83), Kate (10/31/86) **College** Wake Forest University **Turned Professional** 1972 **Q School** Fall 1973 **Other Achievements** Winner 1969 North and South Amateur. Member 1969 Walker Cup team. Brother John current PGA TOUR member.

Exempt Status: Past Champion

TOUR Victories: 1 — 1976 Kemper Open

Money and Position:

1973 — $ 1,331 — 227	1979 — $ 75,035 — 52	1985 — $ 62,562 — 107
1974 — $ 46,645 — 61	1980 — $ 35,014 — 95	1986 — $ 23,229 — 170
1975 — $ 53,225 — 41	1981 — $ 51,068 — 82	1987 — $ 7,013 — 216
1976 — $ 69,892 — 39	1982 — $ 52,091 — 89	1988 — $ 7,400 — 229
1977 — $ 67,064 — 47	1983 — $ 59,913 — 86	1994 — $ 1,618 — 324
1978 — $ 62,034 — 51	1984 — $ 54,494 — 101	1995 — $ 0

Best 1995 Finish: Did not make a cut on 1995 PGA TOUR

1995 Summary: Tournaments entered — 1; in money — 0; top-10 finishes — 0.

Career Earnings: $749,249

OTHER PROMINENT MEMBERS OF THE PGA TOUR

J

JAECKEL, Barry (JAY-kul) Birth Date 2/14/49 **Birthplace** Los Angeles, CA **Residence** Palm Desert, CA **Height** 5-11 **Weight** 160 **Family** Wife, Evelyn **College** Santa Monica Junior College **Special Interest** All sports **Turned Professional** 1971 **Q School** Spring 1975 **Other Achievements** 1968 Southern California Amateur champion. Winner 1972 French Open. Father veteran movie character actor Richard Jaeckel.

Exempt Status: Past Champion

TOUR Victories: 1 — 1978 Tallahassee Open

Money and Position:

1975 — $ 8,883 — 133	1983 — $ 64,473 — 80	1990 — $ 63,590 — 168
1976 — $ 36,888 — 70	1984 — $ 49,308 — 110	1991 — $ 59,216 — 167
1978 — $ 72,421 — 37	1985 — $ 81,765 — 92	1992 — $ 13,351 — 226
1979 — $ 46,541 — 86	1986 — $ 80,646 — 105	1993 — $ 15,584 — 226
1980 — $ 25,501 — 116	1987 — $ 53,909 — 144	1994 — $ 15,750 — 235
1981 — $ 87,931 — 48	1988 — $ 39,227 — 173	1995 — $ 1,540 — 357
1982 — $ 62,940 — 70	1989 — $ 64,782 — 151	

Best 1995 Finish: T57 — Deposit Guaranty Golf Classic

1995 Summary: Tournaments entered — 8; in money — 1; top-10 finishes — 0.

Career Earnings: $954,749

JENKINS, Tom Birth Date 12/14/47 **Birthplace** Houston, TX **Residence** Austin, TX **Height** 5-11 **Weight** 175 **Family** Wife, Lynn; Melani (9/13/79) **College** University of Houston **Special Interests** Camping, computers **Turned Professional** 1971 **Joined TOUR** 1972 **Other Achievements** Two-time All-American. Member 1970 NCAA Championship team at Houston.

Exempt Status: Past Champion **Playoff Record:** 0-1

TOUR Victories: 1 — 1975 IVB-Philadelphia Classic

Money and Position:

1972 — $ 1,317 — 270	1979 — $ 6,689 — 171	1986 — $ 995 — 275
1973 — $ 38,241 — 80	1980 — $ 16,178 — 137	1992 — $ 6,963 — 253
1974 — $ 30,826 — 86	1981 — $ 78,127 — 54	1993 — $ 4,302 — 277
1975 — $ 45,267 — 52	1982 — $ 64,753 — 67	1994— $ 0
1976 — $ 42,740 — 65	1983 — $ 52,564 — 97	1995— $ 0
1977 — $ 15,780 — 120	1984 — $ 53,200 — 103	
1978 — $ 2,902 — 186	1985 — $ 9,347 — 183	

Best 1995 Finish: Did not make a cut on 1995 PGA TOUR

1995 Summary: Tournaments entered — 3; in money — 0; top-10 finishes — 0.

Career Earnings: $456,669

JORDAN, Pete Birth Date 6/10/64 **Birthplace** Elmhurst, IL **Residence** Valrico, FL **Height** 5-11 **Weight** 180 **Family** Wife, Kelly; Ryan (11/26/91), Peyton Ashley (7/14/94) **College** Texas Christian University **Special Interests** Sports, music **Turned Professional** 1986 **Q School** 1993, 1994 **Other Achievements** 1986 NCAA All-American. All-Southwest Conference 1985 and 1986. Member NIKE TOUR 1991-93. Played 1993 U.S. Open.

Exempt Status: 134th on 1995 PGA TOUR money list

Best-Ever Finish: 3 — 1995 Deposit Guaranty Golf Classic

Money and Position: 1994 — $128,960 — 132 1995--$143,936--134

Best 1995 Finish: 3 — Deposit Guaranty Golf Classic

1995 Summary: Tournaments entered — 18; in money — 12; top-10 finishes — 1.

Career Earnings: $272,896

JULIAN, Jeff (JEWEL-yun) Birth Date 7/29/61 **Birthplace** Portland, ME **Residence** Quechee, VT; plays out of The Quechee Club **Height** 6-2 **Weight** 200 **Family** Wife, Hillie Lutter; Keegan (9/22/90) **College** Clemson University **Special Interests** Hockey, skiing **Turned Professional** 1986 **Q School** 1995 **Other Achievements** Winner of 1995 New England Open championship. 1993 and 1995 Vermont PGA Player of the Year. Played in 1990 and 1995 U.S. Opens. Biggest thrill in golf was holing out for eagle during second round of 1995 U.S. Open at Shinnecock Hills. Golf heroes are Arnold Palmer and Seve Ballesteros. Birdied three of final four holes at 1995 Qualifying Tournament to earn TOUR membership.

Exempt Status: 44th on 1995 PGA TOUR Qualifying Tournament/NIKE TOUR 6-10 List

Money & Position: No PGA TOUR earnings

Best 1995 Finish: Did not make a cut on PGA TOUR in 1995

1995 Summary: Tournaments entered — 1; in money — 0; top-10 finishes — 0.

Career Earnings: No PGA TOUR career earnings

OTHER PROMINENT MEMBERS OF THE PGA TOUR

JURGENSEN, Steve **Birth Date** 10/27/61 **Birthplace** San Jose, CA **Residence** Newport Beach, CA; plays out of Big Canyon GC **Height** 5-10 **Weight** 160 **Family** Wife, Cheryl **College** University of Houston (1985, Business Technology) **Special Interests** Travelling, outdoors **Turned Professional** 1985 **Q School** 1995 **Other Achievements** Member of NIKE TOUR since 1993. Birdied seven of final nine holes to win 1993 NIKE Tri-Cities Open. Earned $31,847 to rank 60th on 1995 NIKE TOUR money list. Prior to 1996, had played in three PGA TOUR events.

Exempt Status: 16th on 1995 PGA TOUR Qualifying Tournament/NIKE TOUR 6-10 List

Best-Ever Finish: T63 — 1994 United Airlines Hawaiian Open

Money & Position: 1987 — $ 0 | 1991 — $ 0 | 1994 — $ 2,544 — 303

Best 1995 Finish: Did not play PGA TOUR in 1995

1995 Summary: Did not play PGA TOUR in 1995

Career Earnings: $2,544

KNOX, Kenny **Birth Date** 8/15/56 **Birthplace** Columbus,GA **Residence** Tallahassee, FL **Height** 5-10 **Weight** 190 **Family** Wife, Karen; Michelle (12/24/80) **College** Florida State University (1978 Physical Education) **Special Interests** Working with kids, Atlanta Braves **Turned Professional** 1978 **Q School** Fall 1981, 1983, 1984. **Other Achievements** 1977 and 1978 All-American. Winner 1977 Southeastern Amateur. Wife Karen one of first wives to caddy on TOUR.

Exempt Status: Past Champion **Playoff Record:** 1-1

TOUR Victories: 3-1986 Honda Classic. 1987 Hardee's Golf Classic. 1990 Buick Southern Open.

Money and Position:

1982 — $ 6,919 — 186	1987 — $200,783 — 55	1991 — $423,025 — 32
1984 — $ 15,606 — 71	1988 — $168,099 — 70	1992 — $ 24,889 — 203
1985 — $ 26,968 — 41	1989 — $230,012 — 62	1993 — $ 3,630 — 282
1986 — $261,608 — 24	1990 — $209,679 — 73	1994 — $ 23,872 — 218
		1995 — $ 9,010 — 262

Best 1995 Finish: T27 — Quad City Classic

1995 Summary: Tournaments entered — 11; in money — 2; top-10 finishes — 0.

Career Earnings: $1,604,098

KOCH, Gary (COKE) **Birth Date** 11/21/52 **Birthplace** Baton Rouge, LA **Residence** Tampa, FL **Height** 5-11 **Weight** 165 **Family** Wife, Donna; Patricia (4/1/81), Rachel (7/30/83) **College** University of Florida **Special Interests** Fishing, reading, music **Turned Professional** 1975 **Q School** Fall 1975 **Other Achievements** Winner 1968, 1969, 1970 Florida State Juniors; 1970 U.S. Juniors; 1969 Orange Bowl Juniors; 1969 Florida State Open; 1973 Trans-Mississippi Amateur; 1973, 1974 Southeastern Conference. First-team All-American 1972, 1973, 1974. Member 1973 NCAA Championship team at Florida. Winner 10 collegiate events. **National Teams** Walker Cup (2), 1973, 1975; U.S. World Amateur Cup Team 1974. Color analyst for ESPN golf coverage.

Exempt Status: Past Champion **Playoff Record:** 2-0

TOUR Victories: 6 — 1976 Tallahassee Open. 1978 Florida Citrus Open. 1983 Doral Eastern Open. 1984 Isuzu-Andy Williams San Diego Open, Bay Hill Classic. 1988 Panasonic-Las Vegas Invitational.

Money and Position:

1976 — $ 38,195 — 69	1983 — $168,330 — 27	1990 — $ 36,469 — 186
1977 — $ 58,383 — 52	1984 — $262,679 — 17	1991 — $ 7,189 — 243
1978 — $ 58,660 — 54	1985 — $121,566 — 68	1992 — $ 3,690 — 274
1979 — $ 46,809 — 84	1986 — $180,693 — 50	1993 — $ 702 — 329
1980 — $ 39,827 — 82	1987 — $ 33,727 — 175	1994 — $ 0
1981 — $ 11,999 — 162	1988 — $414,694 — 24	1995 — $ 0
1982 — $ 43,449 — 98	1989 — $ 86,348 — 138	

Best 1995 Finish: Did not make a cut on 1995 PGA TOUR

1995 Summary: Tournaments entered — 2; in money — 0; top-10 finishes — 0.

Career Earnings: $1,613,407

KRAFT, Greg **Birth Date** 4/4/64 **Birthplace** Detroit, MI **Residence** Clearwater, FL **Height** 5-11 **Weight** 170 **Family** Single **College** University of Tampa **Special Interest** Sports **Turned Professional** 1986 **Q School** 1991, 1992 **Other Achievements** Won the unofficial 1993 Deposit Guaranty Golf Classic in Hattiesburg, MS. Birdied the 72nd hole to defeat Morris Hatalsky and Tad Rhyan by one stroke. In 1992 Qualifying Tournament, birdied last two holes to make cut, then fired a 5-under-par 31 in final round at TPC at The Woodlands to earn TOUR membership. Has seven mini-tour victories to his credit. Had four top-5 finishes on 1991 Ben Hogan Tour.

Exempt Status: 139th on 1995 money list

Best-Ever Finish: 2 — 1993 Walt Disney World/Oldsmobile Classic; 1994 Motorola Western Open.

Money & Position:

1992 — $88,824 — 140	1993 — $290,581 — 60	1994 — $279,901 — 69
		1995 — $137,655 — 139

Best 1995 Finish: T8 — Ideon Classic at Pleasant Valley

1995 Summary: Tournaments entered — 35; in money — 15; top-10 finishes — 1.

Career Earnings: $796,960

OTHER PROMINENT MEMBERS OF THE PGA TOUR

KRATZERT, Bill **Birth Date** 6/29/52 **Birthplace** Quantico, VA **Residence** Ft. Wayne, IN **Height** 6-0 **Weight** 190 **Family** Wife, Janie; Rebecca Brea (9/6/78), Tyler Brennen (12/5/80), Thomas Andrew (4/29/91) **College** University of Georgia **Special Interests** Family, all sports **Turned Professional** 1974 **Q School** Spring 1976 **Other Achievements** Winner 1968 Indiana Amateur and 1969 Indiana Open. 1973 and 1974 All-American. Inducted into Indiana Golf Hall of Fame 1993.

Exempt Status: Past Champion **Playoff Record:** 1-1

TOUR Victories: 4 — 1976 Walt Disney World National Team Play (with Woody Blackburn), 1977 Greater Hartford Open. 1980 Greater Milwaukee Open. 1984 Pensacola Open

Money and Position :

1976 — $ 21,253 — 102	1983 — $ 14,744 — 166	1990 — $ 14,630 — 218
1977 — $134,758 — 10	1984 — $149,827 — 37	1991 — $ 19,819 — 209
1978 — $183,683 — 8	1985 — $180,331 — 37	1992 — $ 16,439 — 217
1979 — $101,628 — 35	1986 — $ 47,421 — 139	1993 — $ 78,992 — 156
1980 — $175,771 — 12	1987 — $ 78,232 — 114	1994 — $ 42,127 — 196
1981 — $ 55,513 — 75	1988 — $ 43,519 — 158	1995 — $ 4,548 — 308
1982 — $ 22,779 — 139	1989 — $ 7,773 — 220	

Best 1995 Finish: T59 — B.C. Open

1995 Summary: Tournaments entered — 10; in money — 2; top-10 finishes — 0.

Career Earnings: $1,393,789

L

LICKLITER, Jr., Frank (LICK-light-er) **Birth Date** 7/28/69 **Birthplace** Middletown, OH **Residence** Franklin, OH **Height** 6-1 **Weight** 180 **Family** Single **College** Wright State University (1991, Sociology) **Special Interests** Hunting, fishing, 4-wheel drives **Turned Professional** 1991 **Q School** 1995 **Other Achievements** Member of the NIKE TOUR in 1995. Finished 15th on money list with $102,227. Defeated Kevin Burton and Craig Kanada by one stroke to win NIKE Utah Classic, making clutch 15-foot par putt on final hole to preserve victory. Once made a double-eagle while playing with major league baseball player Chris Sabo. After opening 73-75, posted rounds of 65-67-67-69 at Qualifying Tournament to earn PGA TOUR membership. Prior to this year, only PGA TOUR appearance was missed cut in the 1994 U.S. Open. Winner 1994 Kansas Open.

Exempt Status: 26th on 1995 PGA TOUR Qualifying Tournament/NIKE TOUR 6-10 List

Money & Position: No PGA TOUR earnings

Best 1995 Finish: Did not play PGA TOUR in 1995

1995 Summary: Did not play PGA TOUR in 1995

Career Earnings: No PGA TOUR career earnings

LYE, Mark **Birth Date** 11/13/52 **Birthplace** Vallejo, CA **Residence** Bonita Springs, FL; plays out of Bonita Bay CC **Height** 6-2 **Weight** 185 **Family** Single **College** San Jose State University. **Special Interests** Guitar, fishing **Turned Professional** 1975 **Q School** Fall 1976 **Other Achievements** Winner 1976 Rolex Trophy in Switzerland, 1977 Australian Tour Order of Merit. Won 1976 Champion of Champions Tournament in Australia. 1975 All-American. Commentator for The Golf Channel.

Exempt Status: Special Medical Extension beyond 126-150

TOUR Victories: 1 — 1983 Bank of Boston Classic

Money and Position:

1977 — $ 22,034 — 100	1983 — $164,506 — 28	1989 — $242,884 — 56
1978 — $ 13,648 — 125	1984 — $152,356 — 43	1990 — $201,001 — 77
1979 — $ 51,184 — 75	1985 — $112,735 — 72	1991 — $147,530 — 104
1980 — $109,454 — 39	1986 — $ 78,960 — 111	1992 — $ 9,921 — 243
1981 — $ 76,044 — 56	1987 — $ 73,625 — 121	1993 — $106,935 — 139
1982 — $ 67,460 — 61	1988 — $106,972 — 108	1994 — $ 63,394 — 178
		1995 — $ 0

Best 1995 Finish: Did not make a cut on 1995 PGA TOUR

1995 Summary: Tournaments entered — 2; in money — 0; top-10 finishes — 0.

Career Earnings: $1,800,654

M

MAGINNES, John (ma-GINN-us) **Birth Date** 7/14/68 **Birthplace** Atlanta, GA **Residence** Southport, NC **Height** 6-0 **Weight** 210 **Family** Single **College** East Carolina University **Special Interests** Reading, television **Turned Professional** 1991 **Q School** 1995 **Other Achievements** Member of NIKE TOUR in 1994 and 1995. Won 1995 season-opening event, NIKE San Jose Open, by three strokes over Larry Silveira. Nearly added second title in final event of season, losing to Allen Doyle at the NIKE TOUR Championship. Finished 16th on money list with $91,125. Says biggest thrill in golf was making cut in 1995 U.S. Open.

Exempt Status: 5th at 1995 PGA TOUR Qualifying Tournament

Money & Position: 1992 — $ 0 1995 — $2,807 — 324

Best 1995 Finish: T71 — U.S. Open

1995 Summary: Tournaments entered — 1; in money — 1; top-10 finishes — 0.

Career Earnings: $2,807

OTHER PROMINENT MEMBERS OF THE PGA TOUR

MALTBIE, Roger **Birth Date** 6/30/51 **Birthplace** Modesto, CA **Residence** Los Gatos, CA **Height** 5-10 **Weight** 200 **Family** Wife, Donna; Spencer Davis (3/3/87), Parker Travis (3/12/90) **College** San Jose State University **Special Interests** Music, 49ers football **Turned Professional** 1973 **Q School** 1974 **Other Achievements** During rookie year on TOUR, won back-to-back titles at 1975 Quad Cities Open and Pleasant Valley Classic. Won unofficial 1980 Magnolia Classic in Hattiesburg, MS. Member NBC-TV golf coverage team. Big San Francsico 49ers fan and possessor of Super Bowl ring given to him by team owner Ed Debartolo, Jr. Has undergone two shoulder surgeries during playing career. Winner of 1972 and 1973 Northern California Amateurs and 1974 California State Open. Member of PGA TOUR Policy Board from 1985-87.

Exempt Status: Past Champion

TOUR Victories: 5 — 1975 Ed McMahon-Quad Cities Open, Pleasant Valley Classic. 1976 Memorial Tournament. 1985 Manufacturers Hanover Westchester Classic, NEC World Series of Golf.

Money & Position:			
	1975 — $ 81,035 — 23	1982 — $ 77,067 — 55	1989 — $134,333 — 105
	1976 — $117,736 — 18	1983 — $ 75,751 — 70	1990 — $ 58,536 — 169
	1977 — $ 51,727 — 59	1984 — $118,128 — 56	1991 — $ 37,962 — 188
	1978 — $ 12,440 — 129	1985 — $360,554 — 8	1992 — $109,742 — 125
	1979 — $ 9,796 — 155	1986 — $213,206 — 40	1993 — $155,454 — 103
	1980 — $ 38,626 — 84	1987 — $157,023 — 65	1994 — $ 67,686 — 174
	1981 — $ 75,009 — 58	1988 — $150,602 — 77	1995 — $ 61,664 — 187

Best 1995 Finish: T4 — Ideon Classic at Pleasant Valley

1995 Summary: Tournaments entered — 11; in money — 6; top-10 finishes — 1.

Career Earnings: $2,164,079

MAST, Dick **Birth Date** 3/23/51 **Birthplace** Bluffton, OH **Residence** Winter Garden, FL; plays out of Cypress Creek GC **Height** 5-11 **Weight** 180 **Family** Wife, Roberta; Richard (4/9/79), Joshua (4/1/83), Caleb (6/11/86), Jonathan (3/14/89), Jacob (12/5/90) **College** St. Petersburg Junior College **Special Interests** TOUR Bible study, fishing, water skiing**Turned Professional** 1972 **Q School** Fall 1973, 1977, 1978, 1985, 1990. **Other Achievements** Won three Ben Hogan Tour events in 1990—Mississippi Gulf Coast Classic, Pensacola Open and Fort Wayne Open—en route to finishing third on money list. Largest payday $108,000 in 1992 Greater Milwaukee Open. Noted after 1992 GMO: "I've played virtually every tour except the ladies'."

Exempt Status: Veteran Member

Best-Ever Finish: 2 — 1992 Greater Milwaukee Open

Money and Position:			
	1974 — $ 7,108 — 156	1986 — $ 79,389 — 109	1991 — $ 17,274 — 216
	1975 — $ 280 — 276	1987 — $ 90,768 — 103	1992 — $150,847 — 98
	1977 — $ 4,387 — 182	1988 — $128,568 — 56	1993 — $210,125 — 82
	1979 — $ 5,715 — 180	1989 — $ 38,955 — 173	1994 — $129,822 — 131
	1985 — $ 2,887 — 219	1990 — $ 4,200 — 252	1995 — $ 26,623 — 231

Best 1995 Finish: T12 — Quad City Classic

1995 Summary: Tournaments entered — 13; in money — 6; top-10 finishes — 0.

Career Earnings: $892,747

MATTIACE, Len (MUH-teece) **Birth Date** 10/15/67 **Birthplace** Mineola, NY **Residence** Ponte Vedra Beach, FL; plays out of the TPC at Sawgrass **Height** 6-1 **Weight** 185 **Family** Wife, Kristen **College** Wake Forest University (1990, Sociology) **Special Interests** All sports **Turned Professional** 1990 **Q School** 1992, 1995 **Other Achievements** Ranked as No. 1 Junior in the country by Golf Digest in 1985. All-American in 1987. Member of 1987 United States Walker Cup team and Wake Forest's 1986 NCAA Championship team. Member of NIKE TOUR in 1992 and 1994. Finished 69th on the 1995 NIKE TOUR money list with $27,430. Best finishes were T5s in NIKE Cleveland Open and NIKE Buffalo Open.

Exempt Status: 27th on 1995 PGA TOUR Qualifying Tournament/NIKE TOUR 6-10 List

Best-Ever Finish: T4 — 1993 Deposit Guaranty Golf Classic

Money & Position:		
	1992 — $ 0	1994 — $74,521 — 160

Best 1995 Finish: Did not play PGA TOUR in 1995

1995 Summary: Did not play PGA TOUR in 1995

Career Earnings: $74,521

OTHER PROMINENT MEMBERS OF THE PGA TOUR

McCORD, Gary **Birth Date** 5/23/48 **Birthplace** San Gabriel, CA **Residence** Scottsdale, AZ **Height** 6-2 **Weight** 185 **Family** Wife, Diane **College** University of California-Riverside (1971, Economics) **Special Interest** Enjoys spoofing people **Turned Professional** 1971 **Joined TOUR** Fall 1973; Fall 1982 **Other Achievements** Two-time All-American. 1970 NCAA Division II champion. Player Director on TOUR Policy Board 1983-1986. Color analyst on CBS golf telecasts. Winner 1991 Ben Hogan Gateway Open. Writer for America Online and Golf Digest. Has book due out on Father's Day. Opened Kostis-McCord Teaching Center in Scottsdale with Peter Kostis.

Best-Ever Finish: 2 — 1975 Greater Milwaukee Open; T2 — 1977 Greater Milwaukee Open

Exempt Status: Veteran Member

Money and Position:

1973 — $ 499 — 423	1981 — $ 20,722 — 130	1989 — $ 29,629 — 181
1974 — $ 33,640 — 78	1982 — $ 27,380 — 130	1990 — $ 32,249 — 191
1975 — $ 43,028 — 59	1983 — $ 55,756 — 94	1991 — $ 7,365 — 241
1976 — $ 26,479 — 84	1984 — $ 68,213 — 85	1992 — $ 59,061 — 160
1977 — $ 46,318 — 65	1985 — $ 32,198 — 140	1993 — $ 16,456 — 225
1978 — $ 15,280 — 117	1986 — $ 27,747 — 160	1994 — $ 25,602 — 216
1979 — $ 36,843 — 105	1987 — $ 3,689 — 240	1995 — $ 15,813 — 245
1980 — $ 13,521 — 146	1988 — $ 15,502 — 204	

Best 1995 Finish: T17 — Northern Telecom Open

1995 Summary: Tournaments entered — 5; in money — 1; top-10 finishes — 0.

Career Earnings: $656,931

McGOWAN, Pat **Birth Date** 11/27/54 **Birthplace** Grand Forks, ND **Residence** Southern Pines, NC; plays out of Pine Needles Resort **Height** 5-11 **Weight** 170 **Family** Wife, Bonnie **College** Brigham Young University **Special Interests** Reading, psycho-cybernetics, bird hunting **Turned Professional** 1977 **Q School** 1977 **Other Achievements** Winner 1971 Mexican International Junior, 1976 Air Force Academy Invitational, 1977 Pacific Coast Intercollegiate, 1984 Sacramento Classic (TPS). Member PGA TOUR Tournament Policy Board 1989-92.

Exempt Status: Veteran Member

Best-Ever Finish: 2 — 1978 Canadian Open, 1986 USF&G Classic; T2-1982 Quad Cities Open.

Money and Position:

1978 — $ 47,091 — 67	1984 — $ 53,008 — 104	1990 — $ 66,738 — 164
1979 — $ 37,018 — 104	1985 — $ 86,032 — 89	1991 — $ 21,098 — 204
1980 — $ 28,955 — 106	1986 — $137,665 — 65	1992 — $ 4,065 — 271
1981 — $ 15,387 — 147	1987 — $ 79,078 — 113	1993 — $ 6,650 — 253
1982 — $ 58,673 — 75	1988 — $ 74,156 — 135	1995 — $ 0
1983 — $100,508 — 57	1989 — $ 99,454 — 125	1995 — $ 0

Best 1995 Finish: Did not play PGA TOUR in 1995

1995 Summary: Did not play PGA TOUR in 1995

Career Earnings: $915,577

MEDLIN, Scott **Birth Date** 11/7/66 **Birthplace** Greenville, SC **Residence** Rockingham, NC; plays out of Pinehurst CC **Height** 6-2 **Weight** 190 **Family** Single **College** University of Miami, FL (1990, Speech Communications) **Turned Professional** 1990 **Q School** 1995 **Other Achievements** 1990 All-American. Winner 1992 Long Beach Open, 1993 Foxfire Open on T.C. Jordan Tour. Named Hurricane Tour Player of Year in 1992 and 1993. Made only two appearances on PGA TOUR in 1994, missing cut in Kmart Greater Greensboro Open and U.S. Open.

Exempt Status: 18th on 1995 PGA TOUR Qualifying Tournament/NIKE TOUR 6-10 List

Money & Position: No PGA TOUR earnings

Best 1995 Finish: Did not play PGA TOUR in 1995

1995 Summary: Did not play PGA TOUR in 1995

Career Earnings: No PGA TOUR earnings

MURPHY, Sean **Birth Date** 8/17/65 **Birthplace** Des Moines, IA **Residence** Lovington, NM **Height** 5-8 **Weight** 150 **Family** Single **College** University of New Mexico **Special Interests** Music, theatre, handicapped children, sports **Turned Professional** 1988 **Q School** 1989, 1990 **Other Achievements** Named NIKE TOUR Player of Year in 1993. Six career victories the most ever on NIKE TOUR, as are four wins in 1993. Donated portion of his winner's check at 1993 Utah Classic to Special Olympics. Finished eighth on 1995 NIKE TOUR money list with $118,985. Won 1995 NIKE Philadelphia Classic. Winner 1982 New Mexico High School State Championship and 1983 AJGA Southwest Championship. 1988 Western Athletic Conference Player of Year. Honorable Mention All-American 1986. All-State punter on his high school football team.

Exempt Status: 8th on 1995 NIKE TOUR money list

Best Ever Finish: T8 — 1994 Las Vegas Invitational

Money & Position:

1990 — $ 19,705--211	1993 — $ 0	1995 — $ 40,115 — 215
1991 — $ 24,187--203	1994 — $ 97,597 — 156	

Best 1995 Finish: T18 — United Airlines Hawaiian Open

1995 Summary: Tournaments entered — 3; in money — 3; top-10 finishes — 0.

Career Earnings: $181,604

OTHER PROMINENT MEMBERS OF THE PGA TOUR

N

NELFORD, Jim **Birth Date** 6/28/55 **Birthplace** Vancouver, BC **Residence** Scottsdale, AZ **Height** 5-10 **Weight** 155 **Family** Wife, Linda; Blake (7/84) **College** Brigham Young University **Special Interests** Hockey, tennis, fishing **Turned Professional** 1977 **Joined TOUR** 1977, 1987 **Other Achievements** Winner 1975 and 1976 Canadian Amateurs, 1977 Western Amateur, 1977 French Nation's Cup, 1978 Cacherel Under 25. Member 1979, 1980 and 1983 Canada World Cup teams. Winner 1980 World Cup team championship with Dan Halldorson. Winner 1983 Essex International Classic (TPS).

Exempt Status: Veteran Member **Playoff Record:** 0-1

Best-Ever Finish: 2 — 1983 Sea Pines Heritage Classic, 1984 Bing Crosby National Pro Am

Money and Position:

1978 — $ 29,959 — 87	1984 — $80,470 — 76	1990 — $4,132 — 254
1979 — $ 40,174 — 95	1985 — $60,276 — 112	1991 — $3,510 — 263
1980 — $ 33,769 — 98	1986 — $ 0	1992 — $ 0
1981 — $ 20,275 — 132	1987 — $24,097 — 182	1993 — DNP
1982 — $ 48,088 — 94	1988 — $20,209 — 200	1994 — $4,435 — 279
1983 — $111,932 — 50	1989 — $ 1,225 — 289	1995 — $ 0

Best 1995 Finish: Did not make a cut on 1995 PGA TOUR

1995 Summary: Tournaments entered — 1; in money — 0; top-10 finishes — 0.

Career Earnings: $483,251

NICOLETTE, Mike **Birth Date** 12/7/56 **Birthplace** Pittsburgh, PA **Residence** Scottsdale, AZ **Height** 5-9 **Weight** 155 **Family** Wife, Denise; Mikey, Casey, Kelly **College** Rollins College **Special Interests** Skiing, fishing **Turned Professional** 1978 **Q School** 1979, 1981,1985 **Other Achievements** Three-time Division II All-American.

Exempt Status: Veteran Member **Playoff Record:** 1-0

TOUR Victories: 1 — 1983 Bay Hill Classic

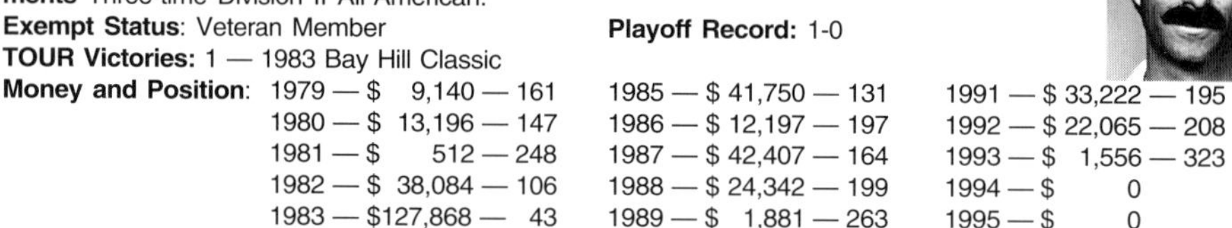

Money and Position:

1979 — $ 9,140 — 161	1985 — $ 41,750 — 131	1991 — $ 33,222 — 195
1980 — $ 13,196 — 147	1986 — $ 12,197 — 197	1992 — $ 22,065 — 208
1981 — $ 512 — 248	1987 — $ 42,407 — 164	1993 — $ 1,556 — 323
1982 — $ 38,084 — 106	1988 — $ 24,342 — 199	1994 — $ 0
1983 — $127,868 — 43	1989 — $ 1,881 — 263	1995 — $ 0
1984 — $ 61,394 — 93	1990 — $ 4,200 — 252	

Best 1995 Finish: Did not make a cut on 1995 PGA TOUR

1995 Summary: Tournaments entered — 1; in money — 0; top-10 finishes — 0.

Career Earnings: $433,816

NORTH, Andy **Birth Date** 3/9/50 **Birthplace** Thorpe, WI **Residence** Madison, WI; plays out of Beaver Creek, Vail, CO **Height** 6-4 **Weight** 200 **Family** Wife, Susan; Nichole (11/30/74), Andrea (8/22/78) **College** University of Florida (1972) **Special Interests** All sports **Turned Professional** 1972 **Q School** Fall 1972 **Other Achievements** With victories in two U.S. Opens, one of only 16 men to win that event more than once. Winner 1969 Wisconsin State Amateur and 1971 Western Amateur. Three-time All-American University of Florida. Member 1978 World Cup and 1985 Ryder Cup teams. Turned to golf in seventh grade because bone in knee stopped growing and was disentegrating, causing him to give up football and basketball. Later returned to basketball, earning all-state honors. Spent a few years assisting University of Wisconsin football staff. Golf commentator for ESPN.

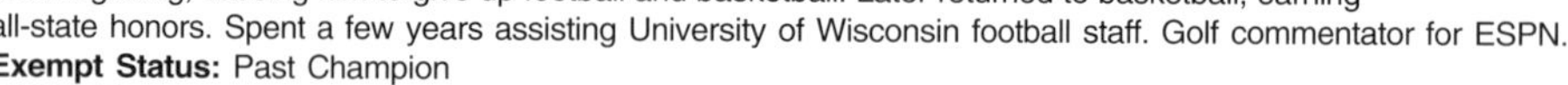

Exempt Status: Past Champion

TOUR Victories: 1977 American Express-Westchester Classic. 1978 U.S. Open. 1985 U.S. Open.

Money & Position:

1973 — $ 48,672 — 64	1981 — $111,401 — 30	1989 — $ 13,620 — 204
1974 — $ 58,409 — 64	1982 — $ 82,698 — 49	1990 — $ 99,651 — 137
1975 — $ 44,729 — 53	1983 — $ 52,416 — 98	1991 — $ 24,653 — 201
1976 — $ 71,267 — 37	1984 — $ 22,131 — 149	1992 — $ 16,360 — 218
1977 — $116,794 — 18	1985 — $212,268 — 24	1993 — $ 14,500 — 230
1978 — $150,398 — 14	1986 — $ 41,651 — 146	1994 — $ 3,165 — 292
1979 — $ 73,873 — 54	1987 — $ 42,876 — 163	1995 — $ 0
1980 — $ 55,212 — 69	1988 — $ 10,759 — 212	

Best 1995 Finish: Did not make a cut on 1995 PGA TOUR

1995 Summary: Tournaments entered — 9; in money — 0; top-10 finishes — 0.

Career Earnings: $1,364,013

OTHER PROMINENT MEMBERS OF THE PGA TOUR

O

O'GRADY, Mac **Birth Date** 4/26/51 **Birthplace** Minneapolis, MN **Residence** Palm Springs, CA **Height** 6-0 **Weight** 165 **Family** Wife, Fumiko Aoyagi **College** Santa Monica Junior College **Special Interests** Modern times, sciences, history **Turned Professional** 1972 **Q School** 1982

Exempt Status: Past Champion **Playoff Record:** 1-0

TOUR Victories: 2 — 1986 Canon-Sammy Davis Jr.-Greater Hartford Open. 1987 MONY Tournament of Champions

Money and Position:

1983 — $ 50,379 — 101	1988 — $116,153 — 98	1993 — $ 10,483 — 240
1984 — $ 41,143 — 120	1989 — $ 40,090 — 170	1994 — $ 2,404 — 306
1985 — $223,808 — 20	1990 — $ 0	1995 — $ 1,540 — 357
1986 — $256,344 — 26	1991 — $ 14,102 — 220	
1987 — $285,109 — 35	1992 — $ 2,030 — 305	

Best 1995 Finish: T57 — Deposit Guaranty Golf Classic

1995 Summary: Tournaments entered — 5; in money — 1; top-10 finishes — 0.

Career Earnings: $1,043,535

P

PARSONS, Lucas **Birth Date** 10/4/69 **Birthplace** Orange, NSW, Australia **Residence** Double Bay, NSW, Australia; plays out of Duntregy League CC **Height** 6-1 **Weight** 230 **Family** Single **Special Interests** Cooking, snow skiing, fishing, surfing **Turned Professional** 1992 **Q School** 1995 **Other Achievements** Successful player on Australasian PGA Tour with victories in each of past three seasons. Winner 1993 Victorian Open, 1994 Foodlink Queensland Open and 1995 New Zealand Open. Winner 1991 Australian Amateur and New Zealand Amateur. Won three state championships in diving and once was runner-up in Australian championships. Captained his high school Australian Rules football team. No prior PGA TOUR experience.

Exempt Status: 23rd on 1995 PGA TOUR Qualifying Tournament/NIKE TOUR 6-10 List

Money & Position: No PGA TOUR earnings

Best 1995 Finish: Did not play PGA TOUR in 1995

1995 Summary: Did not play PGA TOUR in 1995

Career Earnings: No PGA TOUR earnings

PATE, Jerry **Birth Date** 9/16/53 **Birthplace** Macon, GA **Residence** Pensacola, FL **Height** 6-0 **Weight** 175 **Family** Wife, Soozi; Jennifer (10/5/78), Wesley Nelson (9/5/80), James Kendrick (10/12/83) **College** University of Alabama **Special Interest** Water skiing **Turned Professional** 1975 **Q School** Fall 1975. **Other Achievements** Winner 1974 U.S. Amateur, 1974 Florida Amateur, 1976 Pacific Masters, 1977 Mixed Team Championship (with Hollis Stacy). Wife Soozi and Bruce Lietzke's wife Rosemarie are sisters.

Exempt Status: Past Champion **Playoff Record:** 1-2

TOUR Victories: 8 — 1976 U.S. Open, Canadian Open. 1977 Phoenix Open, Southern Open. 1978 Southern Open. 1981 Danny Thomas-Memphis Classic, Pensacola Open. 1982 Tournament Players Championship.

Money and Position:

1976 — $153,102 — 10	1983 — $ 28,890 — 136	1990 — $ 26,953 — 200
1977 — $ 98,152 — 27	1984 — $ 41,746 — 118	1991 — $ 6,249 — 248
1978 — $172,999 — 10	1985 — $ 7,792 — 188	1992 — $ 10,971 — 236
1979 — $193,707 — 11	1986 — $ 1,445 — 260	1993 — $ 0
1980 — $222,976 — 6	1987 — $ 2,116 — 265	1994 — $ 6,513 — 268
1981 — $280,627 — 6	1988 — $ 10,075 — 265	1995 — $ 62,001 — 186
1982 — $280,141 — 9	1989 — $ 9,168 — 213	

Best 1995 Finish: T15 — BellSouth Classic

1995 Summary: Tournaments entered — 22; in money — 9; top-10 finishes — 0.

Career Earnings: $1,618,874

PAULSON, Carl **Birth Date** 12/29/70 **Birthplace** Quantico, VA **Residence** Virginia Beach, VA; plays out of Cavalier GC **Height** 5-10 **Weight** 180 **Family** Single **College** University of South Carolina (1994, Marketing) **Special Interest** All sports **Turned Professional** 1993 **Q School** 1994, 1995 **Other Achievements** Southeastern Conference Player of Year and All-American in 1994. Played select level soccer until high school. Medalist at 1995 PGA TOUR Qualifying Tournament. Ranked eighth on 1995 PGA TOUR with average driving distance of 278.2 yards.

Exempt Status: 1st at 1995 PGA TOUR Qualifying Tournament

Best-Ever Finish: T7 — 1995 Walt Disney World/Oldsmobile Classic

Money & Position: 1995 — $64,501 — 183

Best 1995 Finish: T7 — Walt Disney World/Oldsmobile Classic

1995 Summary: Tournaments entered — 21; in money — 10; top-10 finishes — 1.

Career Earnings: $64,501

OTHER PROMINENT MEMBERS OF THE PGA TOUR

PEOPLES, David **Birth Date** 1/9/60 **Birthplace** Augusta, ME **Residence** Orlando, FL **Height** 5-9 **Weight** 170 **Family** Wife, Melissa; Andrew David (10/20/89), Benjamin Thomas (6/4/92), Matthew Christopher (1/28/94) **College** University of Florida **Special Interests** Fishing, Harley-Davidson motorcycles, windsurfing, hunting **Turned Professional** 1981 **Q School** Fall 1982, 1983, 1985, 1986, 1987, 1989 **Other Achievements** Winner 1979 Florida State Amateur. Entered Qualifying Tournament each year 1981-89, earning card six times. Medalist at 1989 Qualifying Tournament. Won 1990 Isuzu Kapalua International.

Exempt Status: Past Champion

TOUR Victories: 2 — 1991 Buick Southern Open; 1992 Anheuser-Busch Golf Classic

Money and Position:

1983 — $ 26,446 — 137	1988 — $ 65,537 — 139	1992 — $539,531 — 25
1984 — $ 18,124 — 160	1989 — $ 82,642 — 140	1993 — $105,309 — 142
1986 — $ 37,668 — 154	1990 — $ 59,367 — 57	1994 — $126,918 — 133
1987 — $ 31,234 — 180	1991 — $414,346 — 35	1995 — $ 86,679 — 169

Best 1995 Finish: T5 — Freeport-McMoRan Classic

1995 Summary: Tournaments entered — 15; in money — 11; top-10 finishes — 1.

Career Earnings: $1,795,783

PERRY, Chris **Birth Date** 9/27/61 **Birthplace** Edenton, NC **Residence** Powell, OH **Height** 6-1 **Weight** 195 **Family** Wife, Kathy; Andrew (3/1/93) **College** Ohio State University **Special Interests** Snow skiing, family **Turned Professional** 1984 **Q School** Fall 1984 **Other Achievements** Named 1994 NIKE TOUR Player of Year after winning NIKE Utah Classic and leading money list with $167,148. Three-time All-American in 1982-84. Named 1984 Collegiate Player of Year. Won Ohio State-record 14 tournaments and 1983 Big-10 Conference championship. Played baseball and hockey as a youngster and was captain of high school hockey team his senior year. Father, Jim Perry, pitched in the major leagues with Cleveland, Minnesota, Detroit and Oakland. Uncle, Gaylord Perry, is member of Baseball Hall of Fame. As ninth-grader, had 9-0 pitching record with 0.91 earned run average and batted .325.

Exempt Status: 150th on 1995 money list

Best-Ever Finish: T2 — 1987 Kemper Open, 1990 Canon Greater Hartford Open

Money & Position:

1985 — $ 60,801 — 110	1989 — $206,932 — 67	1993 — $ 25,332 — 202
1986 — $ 72,212 — 114	1990 — $259,108 — 58	1994 — $ 14,840 — 237
1987 — $197,593 — 56	1991 — $116,105 — 126	1995 — $113,632 — 150
1988 — $ 85,546 — 121	1992 — $ 53,943 — 171	

Best 1995 Finish: T12 — Buick Classic, Quad City Classic

1995 Summary: Tournaments entered — 30; in money — 17; top-10 finishes — 0.

Career Earnings: $1,209,045

PERSONS, Peter **Birth Date** 9/8/62 **Birthplace** Macon, GA **Residence** Macon, GA **Height** 5-7 **Weight** 155 **Family** Wife, Colyar; Pierce (8/15/91), Robert and Henry (7/19/94) **College** University of Georgia **Special Interests** Tennis, Georgia football, hunting, reading **Turned Professional** 1986 **Q School** Fall 1989 **Other Achievements** Runner-up 1985 U.S. Amateur. Three-time All-American, first team 1986. Winner 1985 Southeastern Conference championship, plus five collegiate events. Won 1979 Georgia State Junior and 1985 Georgia State Open.

Exempt Status: Past Champion

TOUR Victories: 1—1990 Chattanooga Classic

Money and Position:

1990 — $218,505 — 66	1992 — $203,625 — 75	1994 — $ 10,986 — 249
1991 — $130,447 — 114	1993 — $ 73,092 — 164	1995 — $ 0

1995 Summary: Tournaments entered — 1; in money — 0; top-10 finishes — 0.

Career Earnings: $636,655

PFEIL, Mark (FILE) **Birth Date** 7/18/51 **Birthplace** Chicago Heights, IL **Residence** La Quinta, CA **Height** 5-11 **Weight** 175 **Family** Wife, Diana; Kimberly Ann (9/19/80), Kathryn (8/23/84) **College** University of Southern California (B.S. 1974) **Special Interest** Family activities **Turned Professional** 1974 **Joined TOUR** Fall 1975 and Fall 1976 **Other Achievements** Member 1973 Walker Cup team. All-American 1973, 1974. Winner 1972, 1974 Pacific Coast Amateur, 1973 Southern California Amateur, 1974 PAC-8. Winner 1983 Anderson-Pacific Classic (TPS), 1991 Concord General Pro-Am.

Exempt Status: Past Champion

TOUR Victories: 1 — 1980 Tallahassee Open

Money and Position:

1976 — $ 198 — 276	1983 — $ 85,477 — 66	1990 — $ 3,383 — 260
1977 — $ 9,243 — 153	1984 — $101,878 — 69	1991 — $ 0
1978 — $ 13,943 — 124	1985 — $ 54,098 — 116	1992 — $ 2,495 — 287
1979 — $ 18,963 — 124	1986 — $ 67,488 — 122	1993 — $ 9,100 — 242
1980 — $ 52,704 — 73	1987 — $ 11,882 — 203	1994 — $ 1,435 — 326
1981 — $ 28,950 — 114	1988 — $ 6,057 — 235	1995 — $ 2,890 — 323
1983 — $ 62,663 — 72	1989 — $ 0	

Best 1995 Finish: T44 — Quad City Classic

1995 Summary: Tournaments entered — 4; in money — 1; top-10 finishes — 0.

Career Earnings: $533,739

OTHER PROMINENT MEMBERS OF THE PGA TOUR

POWERS, Greg **Birth Date** 3/17/46 **Birthplace** Albany, NY **Residence** Atlanta, GA **Height** 6-0 **Weight** 180 **Family** Single **College** Memphis State University **Special Interests** Fishing, bowling **Turned Professional** 1970 **Q School** 1971, 1989 **Other Achievements** Involved in near-fatal car crash in 1992. Returned to TOUR in 1994 after intense rehabilitation on shattered hip. Made 150th cut to earn Veteran Member status early in 1992. 1970 All-American.

Exempt Status: Veteran Member

Money and Position:

1976 — $ 4,164 — 180	1983 — $ 29,803 — 133	
1978 — $ 27,499 — 93	1984 — $ 31,845 — 136	1989 — $ 1,234 — 287
1979 — $ 15,749 — 136	1985 — $ 10,092 — 178	1990 — $ 3,806 — 256
1980 — $ 19,939 — 122	1986 — $ 3,329 — 238	1991 — $ 6,464 — 245
1981 — $ 82,210 — 52	1987 — $ 58,958 — 135	1992 — $ 10,473 — 241
1982 — $ 39,645 — 102	1988 — $ 30,676 — 171	1995 — $ 2,712 — 328

Best 1995 Finish: T55 — Buick Classic

1995 Summary: Tournaments entered — 4; in money — 1; top-10 finishes — 0.

Career Earnings: $328,648

R

RANDOLPH, Sam **Birth Date** 5/13/64 **Birthplace** Santa Barbara, CA **Residence** McKinney, TX **Height** 6-0 **Weight** 175 **Family** Wife, Julie **College** University of Southern California **Special Interests** All sports, fishing **Turned Professional** 1986 **Q School** 1986, 1990 **Other Achievements** 1985 U.S. Amateur Champion. Winner 1981 Junior World title, California State Amateur. Three-time first-team All-American. Winner 13 collegiate titles. Awarded 1985 Fred Haskins Trophy as outstanding collegiate player.

Exempt Status: Past Champion

TOUR Victories: 1 — 1987 Bank of Boston Classic.

Money and Position:

1987 — $180,378 — 58	1990 — $ 27,529 — 198	1993 — $ 4,460 — 275
1988 — $117,132 — 97	1991 — $ 68,668 — 154	1994 — $ 3,513 — 290
1989 — $ 35,561 — 178	1992 — $ 49,085 — 176	1995 — $ 4,956 — 303

Best 1995 Finish: T33 — Ideon Classic at Pleasant Valley

1995 Summary: Tournaments entered — 1; in money — 1; top-10 finishes — 0.

Career Earnings: $491,283

RENNER, Jack **Birth Date** 7/6/56 **Birthplace** Palm Springs, CA **Residence** San Diego, CA **Height** 6-0 **Weight** 150 **Family** Wife, Lisa; Jill Marie (6/10/90) **College** College of the Desert **Special Interests** Reading, all sports **Turned Professional** 1976 **Q School** Spring 1977 **Other Achievements** Winner 1972 World Junior, 1973 U.S Junior.

Exempt Status: Past Champion **Playoff Record:** 1-0

TOUR Victories: 3-1979-Manufacturers Hanover Westchester Classic, 1981-Pleasant Valley-Jimmy Fund Classic, 1984-Hawaiian Open

Money and Position:

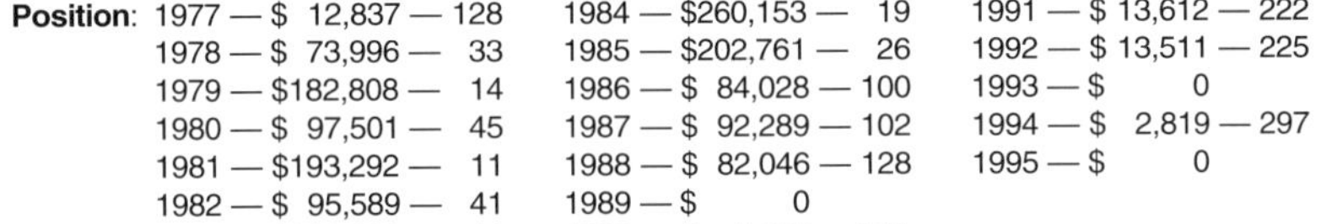

1977 — $ 12,837 — 128	1984 — $260,153 — 19	1991 — $ 13,612 — 222
1978 — $ 73,996 — 33	1985 — $202,761 — 26	1992 — $ 13,511 — 225
1979 — $182,808 — 14	1986 — $ 84,028 — 100	1993 — $ 0
1980 — $ 97,501 — 45	1987 — $ 92,289 — 102	1994 — $ 2,819 — 297
1981 — $193,292 — 11	1988 — $ 82,046 — 128	1995 — $ 0
1982 — $ 95,589 — 41	1989 — $ 0	
1983 — $133,290 — 41	1990 — $ 7,451 — 241	

1995 Best Finish: Did not make a cut on 1995 PGA TOUR

1995 Summary: Tournaments entered — 1; in money — 0; top-10 finishes — 0

Career Earnings: $1,547,984

OTHER PROMINENT MEMBERS OF THE PGA TOUR

RINKER, Larry **Birth Date** 7/20/57 **Birthplace** Stuart, FL **Residence** Winter Park, FL **Weight** 145 **Height** 5-9 **Family** Wife, Jan; Devon Lyle (11/15/88), Trevor William (2/12/91), Morgan Elizabeth (6/4/92) **College** University of Florida (1979, Finance) **Special Interests** Guitar, jazz, music, sports **Turned Professional** 1979 **Q School** 1979, 1981 **Other Achievements** Won 1985 JCPenney/ Mixed Team Classic with sister Laurie, member of LPGA Tour. Brother Lee qualified for PGA TOUR in 1995. Leading money winner on 1980 Space Coast mini-tour and named Player of the Year by Florida Golfweek Magazine the same year. Won 1978 Southeastern Conference Championship. Largest paycheck $61,200 for third at 1985 Tournament Players Championship.

Exempt Status: Veteran Member

Best-Ever Finish: 1 — 1985 JCPenney Classic (unofficial); 2 — 1984 USF&G Classic; T2 — 1985 Bing Crosby Pro-Am.

Money and Position:

1981 — $ 2,729 — 211	1986 — $ 80,635 — 106	1991 — $115,956 — 127
1982 — $ 26,993 — 132	1987 — $ 72,173 — 123	1992 — $163,954 — 94
1983 — $ 31,394 — 128	1988 — $125,471 — 95	1993 — $130,613 — 118
1984 — $116,494 — 60	1989 — $109,305 — 117	1994 — $ 47,435 — 192
1985 — $195,390 — 30	1990 — $132,442 — 117	1995 — $ 9,975 — 258

Best 1995 Finish: [1 — JCPenney Classic (unofficial)]; T36 — Buick Classic

1995 Summary: Tournaments entered — 8; in money — 2; top-10 finishes — 0.

Career Earnings: $1,360,510

RINTOUL, Steve (RIN-tool) **Birth Date** 6/7/63 **Birthplace** Bowral, Australia **Residence** Tampa, FL; plays out of Hunters Green CC **Height** 6-1 **Weight** 200 **Family** Wife, Jill **College** University of Oregon (1988, Business) **Special Interests** Water sports, music, all sports, swimming **Turned Professional** 1988 **Q School** 1993, 1995 **Other Achievements** Winner of 1987-88 Oregon Stroke Play Amateur Championship, 1988 Oregon State Amateur and 1991 Northwest Open. Member of 1982 All-Australian schoolboy team. Grew up competing with Steve Elkington, with whom he remains close friends to this day. Played NIKE TOUR for three years. In 1988 become first Australian to play in U.S. Open as an amateur.

Exempt Status: 29th on 1995 PGA TOUR Qualifying Tournament

Best-Ever Finish: 2 — 1994 Buick Southern Open

Money & Position: 1994 — $157,618 — 115 1995 — $112,877 — 152

Best 1995 Finish: T4 — Deposit Guaranty Golf Classic

1995 Summary: Tournaments entered — 33; in money — 17; top-10 finishes — 2.

Career Earnings: $270,495

ROSBURG, Bob **Birth Date** 10/21/26 **Birthplace** San Francisco, CA **Residence** La Quinta, CA **Height** 5-11 **Weight** 185 **Family** Wife, Eleanor; three children **College** Stanford University (1948) **Special Interest** All sports **Turned Professional** 1953 **Joined TOUR** 1954 **Other Achievements** 1958 Vardon Trophy winner. Member 1959 Ryder Cup team. Tournament Policy Board Player Director 1972-73. Color commentator ABC golf telecasts.

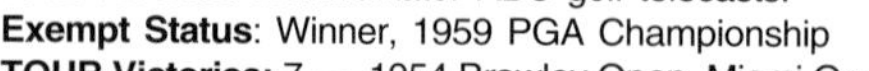

Exempt Status: Winner, 1959 PGA Championship

TOUR Victories: 7 — 1954 Brawley Open, Miami Open. 1956 Motor City Open, San Diego Open. 1959 PGA Championship. 1961 Bing Crosby Pro-Am. 1972 Bob Hope Desert Classic.

ROSE, Clarence **Birth Date** 12/8/57 **Birthplace** Goldsboro, NC **Residence** Goldsboro, NC **Height** 5-8 **Weight** 175 **Family** Wife, Jan; Clark (2/20/89), Allison (12/8/90) **College** Clemson University **Special Interests** All sports **Turned Professional** 1981 **Q School** Spring 1981 **Other Achievements** Winner 1979 North Carolina Amateur. Quarterfinalist 1986 U.S. Amateur. All-American 1980. Winner 1995 NIKE Pensacola Classic. Finished 21st on 1995 NIKE TOUR money list with $80,601.

Exempt Status: 17th on 1995 PGA TOUR Qualifying Tournament/NIKE TOUR 6-10 List

Playoff Record: 0-1

Best-Ever Finish: 2 — 1985 Southern Open; 1986 Los Angeles Open; 1987 Greater Greensboro Open; 1988 GTE Byron Nelson Classic; 1989 The International; T2 — 1986 Honda Classic.

Money and Position:

1981 — $ 965 — 233	1986 — $189,387 — 44	1991 — $ 9,564 — 228
1982 — $ 41,075 — 100	1987 — $173,154 — 59	1992 — $ 10,488 — 240
1983 — $ 45,271 — 109	1988 — $228,976 — 48	1993 — $ 6,823 — 251
1984 — $ 62,278 — 92	1989 — $267,141 — 49	1994 — $ 2,992 — 295
1985 — $133,610 — 63	1990 — $ 25,908 — 202	1995 — $ 7,061 — 283

Best 1995 Finish: T20 — Deposit Guaranty Golf Classic

1995 Summary: Tournaments entered — 2; in money — 1; top-10 finishes — 0.

Career Earnings: $1,204,695

OTHER PROMINENT MEMBERS OF THE PGA TOUR

ROYER III, Hugh **Birth Date** 2/13/64 **Birthplace** Columbus, GA **Residence** Aiken, SC **Height** 6-1 **Weight** 155 **Family** Wife, Lori; Sydney **College** Columbus College **Special Interests** Hunting, fishing, baseball **Turned Professional** 1987 **Joined TOUR** 1996 **Other Achievements** Only player in NIKE TOUR history to record two multiple-win seasons, winning twice in 1993 and 1995. In 1993 won NIKE South Carolina Classic and NIKE Texarakana Open. Last season won NIKE Dominion Open and NIKE Permian Basin Open. Finished ninth on 1995 NIKE TOUR money list with $118,804. Winner 1995 Powerbilt Tour Championship. Finished 14th on 1990 South African Tour Order of Merit after finishing as runner-up in South African Open. Father, Hugh Royer, Jr., played PGA TOUR, winning 1970 Western Open.

Exempt Status: 9th on 1995 NIKE TOUR money list
Money and Position: No PGA TOUR earnings
Best 1995 Finish: Did not play PGA TOUR in 1995
1995 Summary: Did not play PGA TOUR in 1995
Career Earnings: No PGA TOUR earnings

RUMMELLS, Dave **Birth Date** 1/26/58 **Birthplace** Cedar Rapids, IA **Residence** West Branch, IA **Height** 6-0 **Weight** 150 **Family** Wife, Ira; Melissa (12/23/89), Eric (7/1/90) **College** Iowa **Special Interests** Fishing, bowling, basketball **Turned Professional** 1981 **Q School** Fall 1985, 1990, 1992 **Other Achievements** Earned $108,000 for second at 1993 Buick Invitational of California, largest paycheck of career. Has carded four 61s in PGA TOUR events. Introduced to golf at age 5 by his father.

Exempt Status: Veteran Member
Best Ever Finish: 2 — 1993 Buick Invitational of California

Money and Position:			
	1986 — $ 83,227 — 103	1990 — $111,539 — 131	1993 — $247,963 — 67
	1987 — $154,720 — 67	1991 — $213,627 — 79	1994 — $122,872 — 138
	1988 — $274,800 — 38	1992 — $ 95,203 — 134	1995 — $ 26,095 — 232
	1989 — $419,979 — 24		

Best 1995 Finish: T20 — Deposit Guaranty Golf Classic
1995 Summary: Tournaments entered — 10; in money — 6; top-10 finishes — 0.
Career Earnings: $1,750,025

RUSNAK, Gary (RUSS-nak) **Birth Date** 11/23/62 **Birthplace** Orangeburg, SC **Residence** Painesville, OH; plays out of Quail Hollow Resort **Height** 6-0 **Weight** 155 **Family** Wife, Alma **College** Marshall University (1985, B.B.A. Marketing) **Special Interests** Travel, geography **Turned Professional** 1985 **Q School** 1995 **Other Achievements** Member of NIKE TOUR in 1990-91 and 1993-95. Last year, finished 13th on money list with $102,858. Best finish was second in NIKE Texarkana Open. Also posted runner-up finishes in 1993 NIKE White Rose Classic and 1994 NIKE Permian Basin Open. Played Canadian Tour in 1985-86 and Asian Tour in 1987-89. Met wife Alma in Manila when playing on Asian Tour. She doubled as his caddie on the NIKE TOUR. Academic All-American in 1984 and 1985, Southern Conference champion in 1985. Pitched perfect game in Little League state regional playoffs at age 12. Birdied three of final four holes to earn PGA TOUR membership at 1995 PGA TOUR Qualifying Tournament.

Exempt Status: 43rd on 1995 PGA TOUR Qualifying Tournament/NIKE TOUR 6-10 List
Best-Ever Finish: T46 — 1991 Deposit Guaranty Golf Classic

Money & Position:			
	1986 — $ 0	1988 — $1,136 — 304	1990 — $ 0
	1987 — $ 0	1989 — $ 0	1991 — $ 858 — 316

Best 1995 Finish: Did not play PGA TOUR in 1995
1995 Summary: Did not play PGA TOUR in 1995
Career Earnings: $1,994

SANDELIN, Jarmo **(YAR-mo SAN-duh-lin)** **Birth Date** 5/10/67 **Birthplace** Imatra, Finland **Residence** Monte Carlo, Monaco; plays out of Stockholm GC **Height** 6-1 **Weight** 170 **Family** Single **Special Interests** Skiing, tennis, gymnastics **Turned Professional** 1987 **Q School** 1995 **Other Achievements** Earned 1995 Sir Henry Cotton Award as top rookie on PGA European Tour. Won first European Tour title at Turespana Open Canarias. Also posted runner-up finishes in Turespana Open Mediterrania, Land of Valencia and BMW International Open.

Exempt Status: 35th on 1995 PGA TOUR Qualifying Tournament/NIKE TOUR 6-10 List
Best-Ever Finish: T79 — 1995 British Open
Money & Position: 1995 — $ 7,178 — 278
Best 1995 Finish: T79 — British Open
1995 Summary: Tournaments entered — 1; in money — 1; top-10 finishes — 0
Career Earnings: $7,178

OTHER PROMINENT MEMBERS OF THE PGA TOUR

SASAKI, Hisayuki (His-a-YOU-kee Sa-SAW-kee) Birth Date 11/27/64 **Birthplace** Gumma, Japan **Residence** Tokyo, Japan; plays out of GMG Hachioji **Height** 6-2 **Weight** 180 **Family** Wife, Mayumi; Anna (6/24/88) **Special Interests** Car collection **Turned Professional** 1986 **Q School** 1995 **Other Achievements** Lost to Davis Love III in five-hole playoff for Individual Trophy at 1995 World Cup of Golf. Opened with World Cup-record 10-under-par 62. Improved 10 strokes during second round of 1995 PGA TOUR Qualifying Tournament. After first-round 2-over-par 74, recorded an 8-under-par 64. Member of Japan PGA Tour since 1986. Won first two titles of career in 1994, Japan Series and Japan PGA Championship. Finished eighth on 1994 Japan PGA Tour money list, 33 places better than previous best placing in 1993. Has won three times on mini-tours in Japan.

Exempt Status: 22nd on 1995 PGA TOUR Qualifying Tournament/6-10 NIKE TOUR List
Best-Ever Finish: T31 — 1995 British Open
Money & Position: 1995 — $27,855 — 229
Best 1995 Finish: T31 — British Open
1995 Summary: Tournaments entered — 2; in money — 2; top-10 finishes — 0
Career Earnings: $27,855

SCHERRER, Tom (SHARE-ur) Birth Date: 7/20/70 **Birthplace** Syracuse, NY **Residence** Orlando, FL **Height** 6-1 **Weight** 205 **Family** Single **College** University of North Carolina **Special Interest** Hockey **Turned Professional** 1992 **Joined TOUR** 1996 **Other Achievements** Finished sixth on 1995 NIKE TOUR money list with $143,404. Won 1995 NIKE Knoxville Open in a playoff, one of a NIKE TOUR-record three consecutive playoff appearances. Runner-up to Justin Leonard in 1992 U.S. Amateur. Winner 1990 North & South Classic. Member 1991 Walker Cup team. Only prior PGA TOUR appearance came in 1992 B.C Open, where he missed cut.

Exempt Status: 6th on 1995 NIKE TOUR money list
Money and Position: No PGA TOUR earnings
Best 1995 Finish: Did not play PGA TOUR in 1995
1995 Summary: Did not play PGA TOUR in 1995
Career Earnings: No PGA TOUR earnings

SCHULZ, Ted Birth Date 10/29/59 **Birthplace** Louisville, KY; plays out of Lake Forest CC **Residence** Louisville, KY **Height** 6-2 **Weight** 190 **Family** Wife, Diane; Samuel Tucker (11/10/91) **College** Louisville **Special Interests** All sports, Bible study **Turned Professional** 1984 **Q School** Fall 1986, 1988 **Other Achievements** Fired 12-under-par 272 to claim one-stroke win over Jeff Sluman in 1991 Nissan Los Angeles Open. Two-time victor in 1989, in Southern Open and in Chrysler Team Championship with David Ogrin. Played Asian Tour after losing card in 1988. Won 1983 Kentucky State Amateur, 1984 and 1988 Kentucky State Opens.

Exempt Status: Past Champion
TOUR Victories: 2 — 1989 Southern Open. 1991 Nissan Los Angeles Open

Money and Position:			
	1987 — $ 17,838 — 190	1991 — $508,058 — 29	1993 — $164,260 — 100
	1989 — $391,855 — 30	1992 — $259,204 — 60	1994 — $ 37,537 — 202
	1990 — $193,126 — 82		1995 — $ 29,290 — 227

Best 1995 Finish: 16 — Greater Milwaukee Open
1995 Summary: Tournaments entered — 16; in money — 5; top-10 finishes — 0.
Career Earnings: $1,601,168

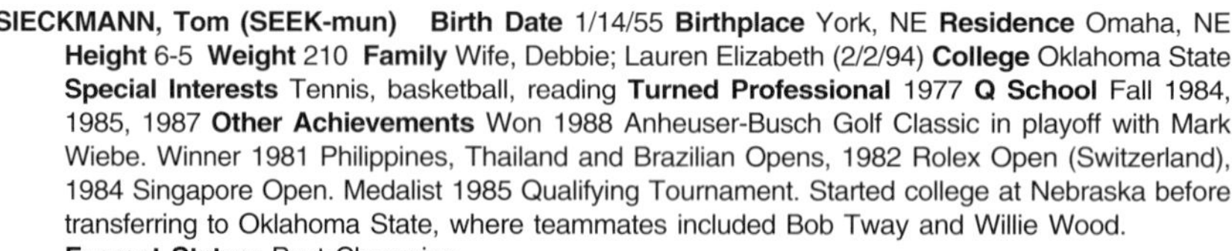

SIECKMANN, Tom (SEEK-mun) Birth Date 1/14/55 **Birthplace** York, NE **Residence** Omaha, NE **Height** 6-5 **Weight** 210 **Family** Wife, Debbie; Lauren Elizabeth (2/2/94) **College** Oklahoma State **Special Interests** Tennis, basketball, reading **Turned Professional** 1977 **Q School** Fall 1984, 1985, 1987 **Other Achievements** Won 1988 Anheuser-Busch Golf Classic in playoff with Mark Wiebe. Winner 1981 Philippines, Thailand and Brazilian Opens, 1982 Rolex Open (Switzerland), 1984 Singapore Open. Medalist 1985 Qualifying Tournament. Started college at Nebraska before transferring to Oklahoma State, where teammates included Bob Tway and Willie Wood.

Exempt Status: Past Champion
TOUR Victories: 1 — 1988 Anheuser-Busch Classic

Money and Position:			
	1985 — $ 30,052 — 143	1989 — $ 97,465 — 128	1993 — $201,429 — 87
	1986 — $ 63,395 — 125	1990 — $141,241 — 110	1994 — $ 55,304 — 184
	1987 — $ 52,259 — 146	1991 — $278,598 — 61	
	1988 — $209,151 — 54	1992 — $173,424 — 88	

Best 1995 Finish: Did not play PGA TOUR in 1995
1995 Summary: Did not play PGA TOUR in 1995
Career Money: $1,302,657

OTHER PROMINENT MEMBERS OF THE PGA TOUR

SILLS, Tony **Birth Date** 12/5/55 **Birthplace** Los Angeles, CA **Residence** Bermuda Dunes, CA **Height** 5-10 **Weight** 165 **Family** Single **College** University of Southern California **Special Interests** Running, weights, martial arts **Turned Professional** 1980 **Q School** Fall 1982, 1994 **Other Achievements** Winner 1971 Los Angeles City Junior title, 1976 Southern California Amateur, 1981 Queen Mary Open, 1982 Coors (Kansas) Open.

Exempt Status: 151st on 1995 money list **Playoff Record**: 1-0

TOUR Victories: 1—1990 Independent Insurance Agent Open

Money and Position:

1983 — $ 47,488 — 104	1988 — $ 76,689 — 132	1993 — $ 11,686 — 233
1984 — $ 90,055 — 72	1989 — $ 77,181 — 143	1994 — $ 22,807 — 219
1985 — $114,895 — 66	1990 — $243,350 — 61	1995 — $113,186 — 151
1986 — $216,881 — 38	1991 — $ 13,914 — 223	
1987 — $107,508 — 92	1992 — $ 10,574 — 238	

Best 1995 Finish: 7 — Bell Canadian Open

1995 Summary: Tournaments entered — 24; in money — 12; top-10 finishes — 1.

Career Earnings: $1,156,153

SIMPSON, Tim **Birth Date** 5/6/56 **Birthplace** Atlanta, GA **Residence** Cummings, GA **Height** 5-10 **Weight** 195 **Family** Wife, Kathy; Christopher (1/5/84), Katie (9/24/86) **College** University of Georgia **Special Interests** Bow hunting, fishing, Harley Davidsons **Turned Professional** 1977 **Q School** Spring 1977 **Other Achievements** Winner 1976 Southern Amateur, All-Southeastern Conference and All-American. Winner Georgia and Atlanta Junior titles, 1981 World Under-25 Championship. Continuing effort to come back from Chronic Fatigue Syndrome.

Exempt Status: Past Champion **Playoff Record:** 0-2

TOUR Victories: 4 — 1985 Southern Open. 1989 USF&G Classic, Walt Disney World/Oldsmobile Classic. 1990 Walt Disney World/Oldsmobile Classic.

Money and Position:

1977 — $ 2,778 — 193	1984 — $157,082 — 41	1991 — $196,582 — 85
1978 — $ 38,714 — 78	1985 — $164,702 — 44	1992 — $ 85,314 — 144
1979 — $ 36,223 — 106	1986 — $240,911 — 31	1993 — $111,435 — 134
1980 — $ 27,172 — 112	1987 — $168,261 — 62	1994 — $126,861 — 134
1981 — $ 63,063 — 70	1988 — $200,748 — 56	1995 — $ 2,688 — 329
1982 — $ 62,153 — 72	1989 — $761,597 — 6	
1983 — $ 96,419 — 59	1990 — $809.772 — 8	

Best 1995 Finish: T54 — Bob Hope Chrysler Classic

1995 Summary: Tournaments entered — 1; in money — 1; top-10 finishes — 0

Career Earnings: $3,351,476

SMITH, Chris **Birth Date** 4/15/69 **Birthplace** Indianapolis, IN **Residence** Rochester, IN **Height** 5-10 **Weight** 185 **Family** Wife, Beth; Abigail (2/28/93) **College** Ohio State University (Economics, 1991) **Special Interests** Fishing, hunting, family time **Turned Professional** 1991 **Other Achievements** Ranked sixth on 1995 NIKE TOUR money list with $143,200. Won 1995 NIKE Gateway Classic and NIKE Dakota Dunes Open. All-American selection in 1991 at Ohio State, where he was Big-10 Conference individual champion. Indiana State Amateur champion and Player of Year in 1990. All-District quarterback while in high school. Lifelong St. Louis Cardinals fan was thrilled when catcher Tom Pagnozzi followed him during his victory in NIKE Gateway Classic.

Exempt Status: 7th on 1995 NIKE TOUR money list

Best Ever Finish: T8 — 1993 B.C. Open

Money & Position: 1993 — $ 24,000 — 207 1994 — $ 3,075 — 294

1995 Summary: Did not play PGA TOUR in 1995

Career Earnings: $27,075

SMITH, Mike **Birth Date** 8/25/50 **Birthplace** Selma, AL **Residence** Titusville, FL **Height** 5-11 **Weight** 175 **Family** Wife, Monica; Christopher Michael (6/22/87), Payton (7/5/94) **College** Brevard Junior College **Turned Professional** 1973 **Q School** Spring 1973, Fall 1981, 1983, 1989 **Other Achievements** Winner 1968 Dixie Junior, 1971 National Junior College Tournament.

Exempt Status: Veteran Member

Best Ever Finish: 2 — 1985 Panasonic Invitational

Money and Position:

1980 — $ 508 — 246	1985 — $158,918 — 47	1992 — $178,964 — 84
1981 — $ 19,682 — 134	1986 — $ 19,159 — 179	1993 — $107,375 — 137
1982 — $ 13,749 — 161	1990 — $170,034 — 94	1994 — $ 57,850 — 183
1984 — $ 42,045 — 116	1991 — $149,613 — 101	1995 — $ 48,088 — 205

Best 1995 Finish: T20 — Buick Challenge

1995 Summary: Tournaments entered — 25; in money — 10; top-10 finishes — 0.

Career Earnings: $999,619

OTHER PROMINENT MEMBERS OF THE PGA TOUR

SMITH, Taylor **Birth Date** 6/28/67 **Birthplace** Pensacola, FL **Residence** Waycross, GA **Height** 6-3 **Weight** 185 **Family** Single **College** Augusta College **Special Interests** Sports, children **Turned Professional** 1987 **Q School** 1995 **Other Achievements** Member of NIKE TOUR since 1992. Best season was 1992, when he earned $71,285 to rank 12th on money list and won NIKE Permian Basin Open. Last year, he finished 57th on money list with $32,851. Winner of 10 mini-tour events. Winner 1986 Big South Conference championship. Turned pro at 19. Was an all-state selection in soccer and basketball in high school.

Exempt Status: 34th on 1995 PGA TOUR Qualifying Tournament/NIKE TOUR 6-10 List
Best-Ever Finish: 71 — 1991 BellSouth Atlanta Classic
Money & Position: 1987 — $ 0   1991 — $1,980 — 300   1992 — $2,232 — 298
Best 1995 Finish: Did not play PGA TOUR in 1995
1995 Summary: Did not play PGA TOUR in 1995
Career Earnings: $4,212

STANKOWSKI, Paul **Birth Date** 12/2/69 **Birthplace** Oxnard, CA **Residence** Flower Mound, TX **Height** 6-1 **Weight** 180 **Family** Wife, Regina **College** University of Texas-El Paso **Special Interests** All sports **Turned Professional** 1991 **Q School** 1993, 1995 **Other Achievements** Kept PGA TOUR membership at last year's Qualifying Tournament, finishing tied for 15th. In 1994, tied for fifth in final event of year, Las Vegas Invitational, to finish 106th on money list and retain TOUR membership. Winner 1992 New Mexico Open, 1992 San Juan Open. 1990 Western Athletic Conference champion. Three-time All-American at UTEP.

Exempt Status: 133rd on 1995 money list
Best-Ever Finish: T4 — 1995 Shell Houston Open
Money & Position: 1994 — $170,393 — 106   1995 — $144,558 — 133
Best 1995 Finish: T4 — Shell Houston Open
1995 Summary: Tournaments entered — 31; in money — 15; top-10 finishes — 1
Career Earnings: $314,951

STRECK, Ron **Birth Date** 7/17/54 **Birthplace** Tulsa, OK **Residence** Tulsa, OK **Height** 6-0 **Weight** 180 **College** University of Tulsa **Special Interests** Skiing, basketball **Turned Professional** 1976 **Q School** Fall 1976 **Other Achievements** Winner1993 NIKE Yuma Open. Finished 21st on 1993 NIKE TOUR money list with $65,718. Shares PGA TOUR record for low consecutive rounds, 125 (63-62 in final two rounds of 1978 Texas Open). Winner 1983 King Hassan Trophy (Morocco). Two-time All-American at University of Tulsa. Winner 1984 Chrysler Team Championship (with Phil Hancock).

Exempt Status: Past Champion   **Playoff Record:** 0-1

TOUR Victories: 2 — 1978 San Antonio-Texas Open; 1981 Michelob-Houston Open

Money and Position:

1977 — $ 11,014 — 143	1984 — $ 82,235 — 81	1991 — $ 13,914 — 221
1978 — $ 46,933 — 68	1985 — $142,848 — 55	1992 — $ 9,917 — 244
1979 — $ 39,484 — 99	1986 — $ 21,605 — 172	1993 — $ 885 — 328
1980 — $ 51,728 — 73	1987 — $ 62,289 — 133	1994 — $ 2,189 — 312
1981 — $114,895 — 29	1988 — $ 31,094 — 170	1995 — $ 0
1982 — $ 67,962 — 60	1989 — $ 50,444 — 164	
1983 — $ 68,950 — 77	1990 — $ 10,356 — 229	

Best 1995 Finish: Did not make a cut on the PGA TOUR in 1995
1995 Summary: Tournaments entered — 1; in money — 0; top-10 finishes — 0.
Career Earnings: $817,211

SUTHERLAND, Kevin **Birth Date** 7/4/64 **Birthplace** Sacramento, CA **Residence** Sacramento, CA; plays out of Northridge CC **Height** 6-1 **Weight** 185 **Family** Wife, Mary **College** Fresno State University (1987, Business) **Special Interests** Basketball, baseball **Turned Professional** 1987 **Q School** 1993, 1995 **Other Achievements** Winner of 1990 Queen Mary Open and 1994 Portland Invitational. Leading money-winner on 1990 Golden State Tour. Second-team All-American in 1987. Member of NIKE TOUR in 1991-92 and 1995. Best finishes were second in 1991 Greater Ozarks Open and 1992 Hawkeye Open. Brother David was member of PGA TOUR in 1991 and 1992.

Exempt Status: 10th on 1995 PGA TOUR Qualifying Tournament/NIKE TOUR 6-10 List
Best-Ever Finish: T68 — 1991 USF&G Classic
Money & Position: 1991 — $2,030 — 296   1995 — $ 0
Best 1995 Finish: Did not make a cut on the PGA TOUR in 1995
1995 Summary: Tournaments entered — 1; in money — 0; top-10 finishes — 0
Career Earnings: $2,030

OTHER PROMINENT MEMBERS OF THE PGA TOUR

SWARTZ, Mike **Birth Date** 7/18/64 **Birthplace** Campbell, CA **Residence** Phoenix, AZ **Height** 6-4 **Weight** 190 **Family** Single **College** University of Arkansas (1986, Personnel Management) **Special Interests** **Turned Professional** 1987 **Q School** 1995 **Other Achievements** Has played in five career PGA TOUR events entering 1996. In 1995, his only TOUR appearance was missed cut at Phoenix Open.

Exempt Status: 40th on 1995 PGA TOUR Qualifying Tournament/NIKE TOUR 6-10 List
Money & Position: No PGA TOUR earnings
Best 1995 Finish: Did not make a cut on PGA TOUR in 1995
1995 Summary: Tournaments entered — 1; in money — 0; top-10 finishes — 0
Career Earnings: No PGA TOUR earnings

T

TEN BROECK, Lance (10-BROOK) **Birth Date** 3/21/56 **Birthplace** Chicago, IL **Residence** Jupiter, FL; plays out of Ballen Isles CC **Height** 6-3 **Weight** 195 **Family** Wife, Linda; Jonathan (3/13/86) **College** University of Texas **Special Interest** All sports **Turned Professional** 1977 **Other Achievements** Winner 1984 Magnolia Classic.

Exempt Status: Veteran Member
Best Ever Finish: 2 — 1991 Chattanooga Classic
Money and Position:

1980 — $ 10,230 — 162	1986 — $ 18,165 — 181	1992 — $113,617 — 122
1981 — $ 4,464 — 202	1987 — $ 1,920 — 266	1993 — $ 88,262 — 151
1982 — $ 25,049 — 135	1988 — $ 65,987 — 138	1994 — $ 10,843 — 250
1983 — $ 19,450 — 152	1989 — $146,568 — 96	1995 — $ 0
1984 — $ 40,185 — 123	1990 — $ 72,896 — 155	
1985 — $ 23,591 — 153	1991 — $146.089 — 106	

Best 1995 Finish: Did not make a cut on PGA TOUR in 1995
1995 Summary: Tournaments entered — 3; in money — 0; top-10 finishes — 0.
Career Earnings: $742,428

TENNYSON, Brian **Birth Date** 7/10/62 **Birthplace** Evansville, IN **Residence** Evansville, IN **Height** 5-10 **Weight** 160 **Family** Wife, Jeanne; Ryan (3/27/89); Taryn (7/9/92) **College** Ball State University (1984, Business Administration) **Special Interests** Snow skiing, tennis, reading **Turned Professional** 1984 **Q School** 1987, 1995 **Other Achievements** Winner of 1987 Razorback Open on TPS Tour. Won 1987 Indian Open and Philippines Open on Asian Tour. Winner of eight collegiate events. Named 1984 NCAA Academic All-American. Biggest thrill in golf was playing in 1991 Masters Tournament. Returns to PGA TOUR for first time since 1992. Spent last five years as vice president of Papa John's national pizza chain.

Exempt Status: 24th on 1995 PGA TOUR Qualifying Tournament/NIKE TOUR 6-10 List
Best-Ever Finish: T2 — 1989 Hardee's Golf Classic, 1990 Bob Hope Chrysler Classic
Money & Position:

1987 — $ 4,694 — 229	1989 — $189,345 — 76	1991 — $110,302 — 130
1988 — $108,082 — 107	1990 — $443,508 — 29	1992 — $ 38,614 — 288

Best 1995 Finish: Did not play PGA TOUR in 1995
1995 Summary: Did not play PGA TOUR in 1995
Career Earnings: $889,851

TEWELL, Doug (TOOL) **Birth Date** 8/27/49 **Birthplace** Baton Rouge, LA **Residence** Edmond, OK; plays out of Oak Tree GC **Height** 5-10 **Weight** 190 **Family** Wife, Pam; Kristi (9/24/69), Jay (3/31/75) **College** Oklahoma State University (1971, Speech Communications) **Special Interests** Golf course management & marketing, family, automobiles, jet skis **Turned Professional** 1971 **Q School** June 1975 **Other Achievements** Winner of 1966 Oklahoma State Junior and Scholastic titles, 1971 Tulsa Intercollegiate title. Winner of 1988 Acom Team title (Japan) with Bob Gilder. Winner of 1978 South Central PGA. Led PGA TOUR in Driving Accuracy in 1992 and 1993.

Exempt Status: Past Champion
TOUR Victories: 4 — 1980 Sea Pines Heritage Classic, IVB-Philadelphia Classic. 1986 Los Angeles Open. 1987 Pensacola Open.
Money & Position:

1975 — $ 1,812 — 201	1982 — $ 78,770 — 52	1989 — $174,607 — 83
1976 — $ 3,640 — 185	1983 — $112,367 — 49	1990 — $137,795 — 112
1977 — $ 33,162 — 76	1984 — $117,988 — 57	1991 — $137,360 — 111
1978 — $ 16,629 — 113	1985 — $137,426 — 58	1992 — $159,856 — 96
1979 — $ 84,500 — 43	1986 — $310,285 — 18	1993 — $132,478 — 117
1980 — $161,684 — 17	1987 — $150,116 — 71	1994 — $177,388 — 102
1981 — $ 41,540 — 94	1988 — $209,196 — 53	1995 — $ 45,878 — 209

Best 1995 Finish: T11 — Deposit Guaranty Golf Classic
1995 Summary: Tournaments entered — 21; in money — 7; top-10 finishes — 0.
Career Earnings: $2,424,476

THOMPSON, Leonard **Birth Date** 1/1/47 **Birthplace** Laurinburg, NC **Residence** Ponte Vedra Beach, FL **Height** 6-2 **Weight** 200 **Family** Wife, Lesley; Martha (6/7/67), Stephen (4/6/74). **College** Wake Forest **Special Interest** Fishing **Turned Professional** 1970 **Q School** Fall 1971. **Other Achievements** Winner 1975 Carolinas Open.

Exempt Status: Past Champion

TOUR Victories: 3 — 1974 Jackie Gleason-Inverrary Classic. 1977 Pensacola Open. 1989 Buick Open.

Money and Position:

1971 — $ 6,556 — 153	1980 — $138,826 — 25	1989 — $261,397 — 52
1972 — $ 39,882 — 63	1981 — $ 95,517 — 40	1990 — $ 78,017 — 148
1973 — $ 91,158 — 15	1982 — $ 60,998 — 73	1991 — $114,275 — 128
1974 — $122,349 — 15	1983 — $ 76,326 — 69	1992 — $ 30,540 — 196
1975 — $ 48,748 — 48	1984 — $ 36,920 — 126	1993 — $ 15,152 — 228
1976 — $ 26,566 — 83	1985 — $ 48,395 — 122	1994 — $ 32,992 — 207
1977 — $107,293 — 23	1986 — $ 83,420 — 102	1995 — $ 0
1978 — $ 52,231 — 63	1987 — $ 52,326 — 147	
1979 — $ 90,465 — 41	1988 — $ 84,659 — 123	

Best 1995 Finish: Did not make a cut on the PGA TOUR in 1995

1995 Summary: Tournaments entered — 5; in money — 0; top-10 finishes — 0.

Career Earnings: $1,782,683

TWIGGS, Greg **Birth Date** 10/31/60 **Birthplace** Los Angeles, CA **Residence** Greensboro, NC **Height** 6-2 **Weight** 225 **Family** Wife, Teresa; Amber Alexander (10/16/87), Tianna (7/20/90) **College** San Diego State **Special Interest** Peace of mind **Turned Professional** 1984 **Q School** Fall 1984, 1986, 1988 **Other Achievements** Lone TOUR victory came in 1989 Shearson Lehman Hutton Open on Torrey Pines GC, a course near home which he had played often. 62 in 1984 Provident Classic lowest score in history of old Tournament Players Series. Lists outstanding achievement in golf as learning to enjoy the game.

Exempt Status: Past Champion

TOUR Victories: 1 — 1989 Shearson Lehman Hutton Open

Money and Position:

1985 — $33,559 — 139	1989 — $154,302 — 90	1993 — $231,823 — 72
1986 — $41,418 — 147	1990 — $ 49,696 — 178	1994 — $ 13,676 — 240
1987 — $21,443 — 186	1991 — $ 65,080 — 158	1995 — $ 42,474 — 213
1988 — $ 2,999 — 262	1992 — $ 74,761 — 153	

Best 1995 Finish: T18 — Ideon Classic at Pleasant Valley

1995 Summary: Tournaments entered — 9; in money — 6; top-10 finishes — 0.

Career Earnings: $728,234

TWITTY, Howard **Birth Date** 1/15/49 **Birthplace** Phoenix, AZ **Residence** Scottsdale, AZ **Height** 6-5 **Weight** 210 **Family** Wife, Sheree; Kevin Scott (10/2/76), Jocelyn Noel (11/20/80), Charles Barnes Burris (6/7/89), Mary Carolina Claire (9/11/90), Alicia Anne Marie (1/22/92), William Howard Hudson (2/23/94) **College** Arizona State University (1972, Business Administration) **Special Interests** All sports **Turned Professional** 1974 **Q School** Spring 1975 **Other Achievements** Collaborated with Roger Maltbie on well-received course redesign of TPC at River Highlands and Tom Weiskopf on TPC of Scottsdale. Player Director on the PGA TOUR Policy Board from1981-82. Winner of 1970 Sunnehanna Amateur and Porter Cup. All-American selection in 1970 and 1972. Winner of 1975 Thailand Open.

Exempt Status: 137th on 1995 money list

TOUR Victories: 3—1979 B. C. Open. 1980 Sammy Davis, Jr.-Greater Hartford Open. 1993 United Airlines Hawaiian Open.

Money & Position:

1975 — $ 8,211 — 139	1982 — $ 57,355 — 78	1989 — $107,200 — 119
1976 — $ 54,268 — 51	1983 — $ 20,000 — 150	1990 — $129,444 — 120
1977 — $ 60,091 — 49	1984 — $ 51,971 — 106	1991 — $226,426 — 74
1978 — $ 92,409 — 25	1985 — $ 92,958 — 82	1992 — $264,042 — 57
1979 — $179,619 — 15	1986 — $156,119 — 57	1993 — $416,833 — 34
1980 — $166,190 — 14	1987 — $169,442 — 61	1994 — $131,408 — 130
1981 — $ 52,183 — 79	1988 — $ 87,985 — 119	1995 — $140,695 — 137

Best 1995 Finish: T8 — Ideon Classic at Pleasant Valley

1995 Summary: Tournaments entered — 29; in money — 16; top-10 finishes — 1.

Career Earnings: $2,665,173

OTHER PROMINENT MEMBERS OF THE PGA TOUR

TYNER, Tray (TIE-ner) **Birth Date** 9/29/64 **Birthplace** Anchorage, AK **Residence** Humble, TX **Height** 5-10 **Weight** 175 **Family** Wife, Carrie; Derek (4/1/93) **College** Houston **Special Interests** Hunting, movies, music **Turned Professional** 1987 **Q School** 1991, 1994 **Other Achievements** Winner 1988 Malaysian Open and 1989 Texas State Open. Played NIKE TOUR in 1990, 1993, and 1994.

Exempt Status: 142nd on 1995 money list
Best Ever Finish: T4 — 1995 Shell Houston Open
Money and Position: 1992 — $ 44,153 — 182 | 1994 — $ 7,193 — 263 | 1995 — $140,695 — 137
Best 1995 Finish: T4 — Shell Houston Open
1995 Summary: Tournaments entered — 31; in money — 12; top-10 finishes — 1.
Career Earnings: $177,685

U

URESTI, Omar (OH-mar U-RES-tee) **Birth Date** 8/3/68 **Birthplace** Austin, TX **Residence** Austin, TX **Height** 5-6 **Weight** 175 **Family** Single **College** University of Texas **Special Interests** Billiards, ping pong, going to movies, Stephen King books **Turned Professional** 1991 **Q School** 1994 **Other Achievements** Won 1994 NIKE Shreveport Open en route to finishing 30th on 1994 NIKE TOUR money list. Winner 1994 Hollard Insurance Royal Swazi Sun Classic. 1985 Boys' Texas State Junior State Champion, ages 15-17. Biggest thrills in golf include nine consecutive birdies during 1994 NIKE Shreveport Open and a hole-in-one at age 8. Named for actor Omar Sharif.

Exempt Status: 156th on 1995 money list
Best Ever Finish: T12 — 1995 Shell Houston Open
Money & Position: 1995 — $104,876 — 156
Best 1995 Finish: T12 — Shell Houston Open
1995 Summary: Tournaments entered — 31; in money — 16; top-10 finishes — 0.
Career Earnings: $104,876

UTLEY, Stan (UT-lee) **Birth Date** 1/16/62 **Birthplace** Thayer, MO; plays out of CC of Missouri **Residence** Columbia, MO **Height** 6-0 **Weight** 175 **Family** Wife, Elayna; Tatum Elayne (6/29/95) **College** University of Missouri **Special Interests** Church, basketball, hunting, fishing **Turned Professional** 1984 **Q School** Fall 1988 **Other Achievements** Won 1993 NIKE Cleveland Open en route to finishing second on NIKE TOUR money list. Finished 12th on 1995 NIKE TOUR money list with $108,270 after winning NIKE Louisiana Open and NIKE Miami Valley Open. Carded rounds of 62 in each of those victories. Three-time All-Big Eight selection and twice All-American. Won 1986 Kansas Open, 1988 and 1989 Missouri Opens, 1980 Missouri Junior Championship. His annual "Go For The Gold" Skins Game in Columbia has been benefitting Rainbow House, a safe house for children, since 1991.

Exempt Status: Past Champion
TOUR Victories: 1 — 1989 Chattanooga Classic
Money and Position: 1989 — $107,400 — 118 | 1990 — $143,604 — 108 | 1991 — $127,849 — 115 | 1992 — $ 14,964 — 222 | 1993 — $ 17,371 — 223 | 1994 — $ 63,345 — 179 | 1995 — $ 0
Best 1995 Finish: Did not make a cut on 1995 PGA TOUR
1995 Summary: Tournaments entered — 1; in money — 0; top-10 finishes — 0.
Career Earnings: $474,532

V

VENTURI, Ken **Birth Date** 5/15/31 **Birthplace** San Francisco, CA **Residence** Marco Island, FL **Height** 6-0 **Weight** 175 **Family** Wife, Beau; Matthew, Timothy **College** San Jose State University (1953) **Special Interests** Hunting, fishing, cars. **Turned Professional** 1956 **Joined TOUR** 1957 **Other Achievements**1964 PGA Player of the Year. 1965 Ryder Cup team member. Color commentator for CBS golf telecasts. Named Sports Illustrated "Sportsman of Year" in 1964.

Exempt Status: 1964 U.S. Open winner
TOUR Victories: 14 — 1957 St. Paul Open, Miller Open; 1958 Thunderbird Invitational, Phoenix Open, Baton Rouge Open, Gleneagles Chicago Open; 1959 Gleneagles Chicago Open, Los Angeles Open; 1960 Bing Crosby Pro-Am, Milwaukee Open; 1964 U.S. Open, Insurance City Open, American Golf Classic; 1966 Lucky International.
Money Summary: Started in 1957 and won $18,781 for 10th place. Best year 1964 with $62,465 for sixth place. Last year won money was in 1975.
Career Earnings: $268,293

W

WADSWORTH, Fred **Birth Date** 7/17/62 **Birthplace** Munich, Germany **Residence** Columbus, GA **Height** 6-3 **Weight** 170 **Family** Wife, Juli; Fred (6/15/95) **College** University of South Carolina **Special Interests** All sports, fishing **Turned Professional** 1984 **Other Achievements**1984 Eastern Amateur champion. 1984 All-American at South Carolina. Three mini-tour wins. South African Open champion.

Exempt Status: Past Champion

TOUR Victories: 1 — 1986 Southern Open

Money and Position:

1980 — $ 24,129 — 190	1988 — $ 24,129 — 190	1993 — $ 609 — 333
1986 — $ 75,092 — 115	1989 — $ 10,587 — 208	1995 — $ 0
1987 — $ 80,585 — 109	1991 — $ 1,292 — 314	

1995 Summary: Tournaments entered — 1; in money — 0; top-10 finishes — 0.

Career Earnings: $192,977

WHITTAKER, Ron **Birth Date** 8/12/71 **Birthplace** Raleigh, NC **Residence** Little Rock, AR; plays out of Pleasant Valley CC **Height** 5-11 **Weight** 155 **Family** Single **College** Wake Forest University **Special Interests** Fishing, college basketball **Turned Professional** 1994 **Q School** 1995 **Other Achievements** Winner of 1995 FNB Players Championship on South African PGA Tour in only 10th tournament as professional. All-American and All-ACC selection at Wake Forest. Alternate on 1993 Walker Cup team. Nephew of PGA TOUR veteran Lanny Wadkins.

Exempt Status: 42nd on 1995 PGA TOUR Qualifying Tournament/NIKE TOUR 6-10 List

Best-Ever Finish: T40 — 1995 NEC World Series of Golf

Money & Position: 1995 — $14,650 — 247

Best 1995 Finish: T40 — NEC World Series of Golf

1995 Summary: Tournaments entered — 4; in money — 1; top-10 finishes — 0

Career Earnings: $14,650

WILLIAMSON, Jay **Birth Date** 2/7/67 **Birthplace** St, Louis, MO **Residence** St. Louis, MO **Height** 5-10 **Weight** 180 **Family** Single **College** Trinity College (CT) **Special Interests** Hockey, baseball, politics, stock market **Turned Professional** 1989 **Q School** 1994 **Other Achievements** Winner 1991 Kansas Open.

Exempt Status: 145th on 1995 money list

Best Ever Finish: T4 — 1995 Ideon Classic at Pleasant Valley

Money & Position: 1995 — $120,180 — 145

Best 1995 Finish: T4 — Ideon Classic at Pleasant Valley

1995 Summary: Tournaments entered — 22; in money — 11; top-10 finishes — 3.

Career Earnings: $120,180

WOOD, Willie **Birth Date** 10/1/60 **Birthplace** Kingsville, TX **Residence** Scottsdale, AZ; plays out of Desert Mountain **Height** 5-7 **Weight** 150 **Family** Wife, Wendi; William King (12/17/86), Kelly Curtis (6/15/88) **College** Oklahoma State University **Special Interests** Fishing, physical fitness **Turned Professional** 1983 **Q School** 1983, 1992 **Other Achievements** Posted all-time low score of 61 at 49ers Club in Tucson when high school senior. Won 1979 Nevada State Open, 1984 Colorado State Open, 1990 Oklahoma Open. Winner of five major junior titles, including 1977 USGA Junior, 1978 PGA National Junior and 1979 Western Junior. Medalist 1983 U.S. Walker Cup team. Claimed medalist honors at 1983 TOUR Qualifying Tournament. Sister Deanie played LPGA Tour.

Exempt Status: Veteran Member **Playoff Record:** 0-1

Best Ever Finish: 2 — 1984 Anheuser-Busch Golf Classic, 1986 Manufacturers Hanover Westchester Classic, 1990 Hardee's Golf Classic

Money and Position:

1983 — $ 8,400 — 185	1988 — $ 53,064 — 146	1993 — $146,206 — 112
1984 — $115,741 — 61	1989 — $ 9,617 — 212	1994 — $ 87,102 — 165
1985 — $153,706 — 49	1990 — $179,972— 90	1995 — $ 64,697 — 182
1986 — $172,629 — 52	1991 — $ 48,033 — 176	
1987 — $ 95,917 — 98	1992 — $ 57,748 — 168	

Best 1995 Finish: T12 — Shell Houston Open

1995 Summary: Tournaments entered — 11; in money — 8; top-10 finishes — 0.

Career Earnings: $1,126,743

OTHER PROMINENT MEMBERS OF THE PGA TOUR

WRENN, Robert **Birth Date** 9/11/59 **Birthplace** Richmond, VA **Residence** Richmond, VA **Height** 5-10 **Weight** 170 **Family** Wife, Kathy; Tucker (12/12/92), Jordan (11/9/94) **College** Wake Forest **Special Interests** Reading, family, outdoors, TV commentary, golf course design **Turned Professional** 1981 **Q School** Fall 1984, 1985, 1986 **Other Achievements** Winner 1981 Trans-Mississippi Amateur, 1983 Virginia State Open, 1983 Indonesian Open. All-Atlantic Coast Conference 1978-1981.

Exempt Status: 20th on 1995 PGA TOUR Qualifying Tournament/NIKE TOUR 6-10 List

Playoff Record: 0-1

TOUR Victories: 1 — 1987 Buick Open

Money and Position:

1985 — $ 36,396 — 135	1989 — $243,638 — 55	1993 — $103,928 — 143
1986 — $ 22,869 — 171	1990 — $174,308 — 92	1994 — $ 77,279 — 170
1987 — $203,557 — 52	1991 — $141,255 — 109	1995 — $ 0
1988 — $209,404 — 52	1992 — $127,729 — 113	

Best 1995 Finish: Did not make a cut on PGA TOUR in 1995

1995 Summary: Tournaments entered — 1; in money — 0; top-10 finishes — 0.

Career Earnings: $1,340,363

ZOKOL, Richard (ZO-kul) **Birth Date** 8/21/58 **Birthplace** Kitimat, B.C., Canada **Residence** Richmond, B.C., Canada **Height** 5-9 **Weight** 170 **Family** Wife, Joanie; Conor and Garrett (10/14/87), Hayley (6/25/90) **College** Brigham Young University **Special Interests** Hunting **Turned Professional** 1981 **Q School** Fall 1981, 1982, 1986, 1989, 1991 **Other Achievements** Won 1992 Deposit Guaranty Classic. Member 1980 Canada World Amateur and 1981 Brigham Young University NCAA Championship teams. Winner 1980 International Champions (Morocco), 1981 Canadian Amateur, 1982 British Columbia Open, 1984 Utah Open.

Exempt Status: Past Champion

TOUR Victories: 1 — 1992 Greater Milwaukee Open

Money and Position:

1982 — $ 15,110 — 156	1987 — $114,406 — 89	1992 — $311,909 — 48
1983 — $ 38,107 — 117	1988 — $142,153 — 83	1993 — $214,419 — 80
1984 — $ 56,605 — 102	1989 — $ 51,323 — 163	1994 — $78,074 — 169
1985 — $ 71,192 — 152	1990 — $191,634 — 84	1995 — $23,371 — 234
1986 — $ 37,888 — 102	1991 — $ 78,426 — 149	

Best 1995 Finish: T17 — Greater Milwaukee Open

1995 Summary: Tournaments entered — 10; in money — 4; top-10 finishes — 0.

Career Earnings: $1,424,618

Nick Faldo got his 1995 return to the PGA TOUR off to a successful start with a March win in the Doral-Ryder Open. The victory was his first in a TOUR event since the 1990 Masters Tournament.

PROMINENT INTERNATIONAL PLAYERS

Robert Allenby

HEIGHT: 6' 1" **WEIGHT:** 150 **BIRTHDATE:** July 12, 1971
BIRTHPLACE: Melbourne, Australia **RESIDENCE:** Melbourne, Australia
FAMILY: Wife, Nadina
SPECIAL INTERESTS: Fishing, golf, fast boats
TURNED PROFESSIONAL: 1991
BEST PGA TOUR FINISH: T15 -- 1995 British Open
MONEY & POSITION: 1993--$ 11,052--235 1994-- -0- 1995--$73,288--176
BEST 1995 PGA TOUR FINISH: T15 -- British Open
1995 SUMMARY: Tournaments entered--9; in money--5; top-10 finishes--0.
OTHER ACHIEVEMENTS: Led Australian Order of Merit 1992, 1994; Winner of 1992 Perak Masters, 1992 Johnnie Walker Classic, 1993 Optus Players Championship and 1994 Heineken Australian Open on Australasian Tour and 1994 Honda Open on European Tour.
NATIONAL TEAMS: World Cup (2), 1993, 1995; Dunhill Cup 1993; Presidents Cup, 1994.

Seve Ballesteros

HEIGHT: 6' **WEIGHT:** 195 **BIRTHDATE:** April 9, 1957
BIRTHPLACE: Pedrena, Spain **RESIDENCE:** Monaco
FAMILY: Wife, Carmen; Baldomero (1990), Miguel (1992), Carmen (1994)
SPECIAL INTERESTS: Cycling, fishing, hunting
TURNED PROFESSIONAL: 1974 **PGA TOUR PLAYOFF RECORD:** 1-2
TOUR VICTORIES: 6 — **1978** Greater Greensboro Open. **1980** Masters Tournament. **1983** Masters Tournament, Manufacturers Hanover Westchester Classic. **1985** USF&G Classic. **1988** Manufacturers Hanover Westchester Classic.

MONEY & POSITION:

1983--$ 210,933-- 18	1988--$ 165,202-- 71	1992--$ 39,206--184
1984--$ 132,660-- 52	1989--$ 138,094--101	1993--$ 34,850--193
1985--$ 206,638-- 26	1990--$ 84,584--144	1994--$ 49,245--189
1986--$ 45,877-- 141	1991--$ 64,320--160	1995--$ 64,345--184
1987--$ 305,058 -- 32		

BEST 1995 FINISHES: T8--Honda Classic
1995 SUMMARY: Tournaments entered--9; in money--4; top-10 finishes--1.
OTHER ACHIEVEMENTS: Winner of three British Opens, 1979, 1984, 1988. Winner of 60 tournaments worldwide, including World Match Play, 1981, 1982, 1984, 1985; Lancome Trophy, 1976, 1983, 1986, 1988; Spanish Open, 1981, 1985; French Open, 1977, 1982, 1985, 1986; Dutch Open, 1976, 1980, 1986; Swiss Open, 1977, 1978, 1989; German Open, 1978, 1988; Irish Open, 1983, 1985, 1986; British Masters, 1986, 1991; British PGA, 1983; Madrid Open, 1980, 1981, 1989; Japanese Open, 1977, 1978; Australian PGA, 1981; Dunlop Phoenix (Japan), 1977, 1981; Taiheiyo Masters (Japan), 1988; Kenya Open, 1978; Volvo PGA, 1991. Winner, 1992 Dubai Desert Classic and Turespana Open De Baleares. After not winning a tournament in 1993, he won the 1994 Benson & Hedges International and Mercedes German Masters. Won 1995 Tournoi Perrier de Pans with Jose Maria Olazabal.
NATIONAL TEAMS: European Ryder Cup (8), 1979, 1983, 1985, 1987, 1989, 1991, 1993, 1995. World Cup (4), 1975, 1976, 1977, 1991. Dunhill Cup (3), 1985, 1986, 1988. Hennessy Cognac Cup (3), 1976, 1978, 1980.

Michael Campbell

HEIGHT: 5' 10" **WEIGHT:** 185 **BIRTH DATE:** February 23, 1969
BIRTHPLACE: Hawera, New Zealand **RESIDENCE:** Wellington, New Zealand
FAMILY: Single
SPECIAL INTERESTS: Fishing, golf, fast boats
TURNED PROFESSIONAL: 1993
BEST PGA TOUR FINISH: T3 -- 1995 British Open
MONEY & POSITION: 1995--$ 141,388--135
BEST 1995 PGA TOUR FINISH: T3 -- British Open
1995 SUMMARY: Tournaments entered -- 3; in money -- 3; top-10 finishes -- 1.
OTHER ACHIEVEMENTS: Finished seventh on Australasian Tour Order of Merit in 1993 and 17th in 1994; Winner, 1993 Canon Challenge in Australia; In first full year on European Tour in 1995, finished fifth on Order of Merit; Winner, 1995 Alfred Dunhill Masters in Indonesia.
NATIONAL TEAMS: World Cup, 1995; Dunhill Cup 1995; World Amateur Team 1992.

David Gilford

HEIGHT: 5'10" **WEIGHT:** 160 **BIRTHDATE:** September 14, 1965
BIRTHPLACE: Crewe, England **RESIDENCE:** Crewe, England
BEST-EVER FINISH: T24--1995 Masters Tournament
MONEY & POSITION: 1992--$ 8,847--249 1994--$ 5,200--272 1995--$26,993--230
BEST 1995 FINISH: T24--Masters Tournament
1995 SUMMARY: Tournaments entered--3; in money--2; top-10 finishes--0.
OTHER ACHIEVEMENTS: Winner, 1994 Turespana Open de Tenerife, 1994 European Open, 1993 Moroccan Open, 1993 Portuguese Open, 1992 Moroccan Open, 1991 English Open. Finished seventh on PGA European Tour Order of Merit in 1994, the best finish of his nine-year career. Led European Tour in Fairways Hit and Greens in Regulation in 1992.
NATIONAL TEAMS: European Ryder Cup (2), 1991, 1995. Dunhill Cup, 1992. World Cup (2) 1992, 1993. Walker Cup, 1985.

Mark James

HEIGHT: 5'11" **WEIGHT:** 180 **BIRTHDATE:** October 28, 1953
BIRTHPLACE: Manchester, England **RESIDENCE:** Ilkley, England
FAMILY: Wife, Jane
SPECIAL INTERESTS: Science fiction, gardening, American football
TURNED PROFESSIONAL: 1978
BEST PGA TOUR FINISH: T8 -- 1985 British Open
MONEY & POSITION: 1979-- $2,983--212 1982--$1,580--256 1995--$53,167--202
1980 --$1,588--242 1992--$5,163--264
BEST 1995 FINISH: T8 -- British Open
1995 SUMMARY: Tournaments entered -- 1; in money -- 1; top-10 finishes -- 1
OTHER ACHIEVEMENTS: Winner of 17 events on the PGA European Tour, most recently the 1995 Moroccan Open; 1976 PGA European Tour Rookie of the Year; Winner, 1979-80 Carrolls Irish Open, 1989-90 NM English Open, 1990 Dunhill British Masters; Winner, 1988 South African TPC; Winner, 1974 English Amateur.
NATIONAL TEAMS: European Ryder Cup (6) 1977, 1979, 1981, 1989, 1991, 1993; Dunhill Cup (5), 1988, 1989, 1990, 1993, 1995; World Cup (8) 1978, 1979, 1982, 1984, 1987, 1988, 1990, 1993; Walker Cup 1975.

Miguel Angel Jimenez

HEIGHT: 5'9" **WEIGHT:** 165 **BIRTHDATE:** January 5, 1964
BIRTHPLACE: Malaga, Spain **RESIDENCE:** Malaga, Spain
FAMILY: Wife, Monserrat
SPECIAL INTERESTS: Cars
TURNED PROFESSIONAL: 1982
BEST PGA TOUR FINISH: T13 -- 1985 PGA Championship
MONEY & POSITION: 1995--$57,196--193
BEST 1995 FINISH: T8 -- British Open
1995 SUMMARY: Tournaments entered -- 5; in money -- 4; top-10 finishes -- 1
OTHER ACHIEVEMENTS: Winner, 1994 Heineken Dutch Open, 1993 PIAGET Open, 1989 Benson & Hedges Trophy (with Xonia Wunsch-Ruiz). Finished 23rd on the 1995 PGA European Tour Order of Merit.
NATIONAL TEAMS: Dunhill Cup (5), 1990, 1992, 1993, 1994, 1995; World Cup (4) 1990, 1992, 1993, 1994.

Barry Lane

HEIGHT: 5'10" **WEIGHT:** 170 **BIRTHDATE:** June 21, 1960
BIRTHPLACE: Hayes, England **RESIDENCE:** Ascot, England
FAMILY: Wife, Melanie; Benjamin (1990), Emma (1992)
SPECIAL INTERESTS: Cars, chess
TURNED PROFESSIONAL: 1976
BEST-EVER FINISH: T16-- 1993 U.S. Open
MONEY & POSITION: 1993--$24,088--206 1994--$18,105--229 1995--$33,080--223
BEST 1995 FINISH: T20-- British Open
1995 SUMMARY: Tournaments entered--3; in money--3; top 10-finishes--0.
OTHER ACHIEVEMENTS: Winner of five European Tour events: 1987 Equity & Law Challenge, 1988 Bell's Scottish Open; 1992 Mercedes German Masters; 1993 Canon European Masters; 1994 Iberia Open; 5th on 1992 European Order of Merit, 10th in 1993, 11th in 1994. Winner, 1983 Jamaica Open; 1995 European region champion at Andersen Consulting World Championship of Golf.
NATIONAL TEAMS: European Ryder Cup, 1993. Dunhill Cup (3),1988, 1994, 1995. World Cup (2), 1988, 1994.

Bernhard Langer

HEIGHT: 5'9" **WEIGHT:** 155 **BIRTHDATE:** August 27, 1957
BIRTHPLACE: Anhausen, Germany **RESIDENCE:** Anhausen, Germany
FAMILY: Wife, Vikki; Jackie (1986), Stefan (1990), Christina (1993).
SPECIAL INTERESTS: Snow skiing, soccer, tennis, cycle riding
TURNED PROFESSIONAL: 1976 **PGA TOUR PLAYOFF RECORD:** 1-1
TOUR VICTORIES: 3— **1985** Masters Tournament, Sea Pines Heritage Classic. **1993** Masters Tournament.
MONEY & POSITION:

1984--$ 82,465-- 75	1988--$100,635--111	1992--$ 41,211--181
1985--$271,044-- 13	1989--$195,973-- 73	1993--$ 626,938-- 23
1986--$379,800-- 10	1990--$ 35,150--187	1994--$ 118,241--142
1987--$366,430-- 23	1991--$112,539--129	1995--$ 394,877-- 46

BEST 1995 FINISH: 2 -- THE PLAYERS Championship
1995 SUMMARY: Tournaments entered--7; in money--7; top-10 finishes--1.
OTHER ACHIEVEMENTS: Winner of over 33 PGA European Tour tournaments including two in 1995 -- Volvo PGA Championship (his third) and Deutsche Bank Open; has won at least one tournament on the European Tour each year since 1979; has won five German Opens (1981-82-85-86-93); Winner, 1980, 1994 Volvo Masters, 1985 Australian Masters, 1983 Johnnie Walker and Casio World Open, 1986 and 1991 Million Dollar Challenge; 1993 World Cup individual title.
NATIONAL TEAMS: European Ryder Cup (8), 1981, 1983, 1985, 1987, 1989, 1991, 1993, 1995; World Cup (10), 1976, 1977, 1978, 1979, 1980, 1990, 1991, 1992, 1993, 1994; Dunhill Cup (2), 1992, 1994; Nissan Cup (2), 1985, 1986 (captain both years); Kirin Cup, 1987 (captain in 1987). Four Tours World Championship (2), 1989 (captain), 1990. Hennessy Cognac Cup (4), 1976, 1978, 1980, 1982.

Mark McNulty

HEIGHT: 5'10" **WEIGHT:** 160 **BIRTHDATE:** October 25, 1953
BIRTHPLACE: Bindwa, Zimbabwe **RESIDENCE:** Sunningdale, England
FAMILY: Wife, Sue; Matthew, Catherine
SPECIAL INTERESTS: Piano, fine arts, Koi fish
TURNED PROFESSIONAL: 1977
BEST-EVER FINISH: 4 -- 1982 Danny Thomas Memphis Classic; T4 --1982 Sammy Davis, Jr.-Greater Hartford Open
MONEY & POSITION:

1982--$ 50,322-- 90	1986--$ 6,175--225	1991--$ 34,321--194
1983--$ 40,062--115	1987--$ 4,165--243	1992--$ 46,171--181
1984--$ 5,382--198	1988--$39,481--159	1994--$157,700--114
1985--$ 3,600--217	1990--$34,375--188	1995--$ 64,795--181

BEST 1995 FINISH: T11 -- Nestle Invitational
1995 SUMMARY: Tournaments entered -- 10; in money -- 3; top-10 finishes -- 0.
OTHER ACHIEVEMENTS: Winner of 23 events on the South African Tour dating back to the 1980 Holiday Inns Invitational; Led South African Tour Order of Merit five times (1980-81-85-86-87);Winner, 1987 South African Open, 1992 Zimbabwe Open; Winner of 13 PGA European Tour events with his first win coming at 1979 Greater Manchester Open; Four-time winner of Volvo German Open (1980-87-90-91).
NATIONAL TEAMS: Presidents Cup, 1994. Dunhill Cup (3), 1993, 1994, 1995. World Cup (3), 1993, 1994, 1995.

Colin Montgomerie

HEIGHT: 6'1" **WEIGHT:** 205 **BIRTHDATE:** June 23, 1963
BIRTHPLACE: Glasgow, Scotland **RESIDENCE:** Oxshott, Surrey, England
FAMILY: Wife, Eimear; Olivia (1993)
SPECIAL INTERESTS: Music, cars, films
TURNED PROFESSIONAL: 1987 **PGA TOUR PLAYOFF RECORD:** 0-2
BEST PGA TOUR FINISH: 2 -- 1995 PGA Championship; T2--1994 U.S. Open
MONEY & POSITION:

1992--$ 98,045--132	1994--$213,828--87
1993--$ 17,992--221	1995--$335,617--53

BEST 1995 FINISH: 2 -- PGA Championship
1995 SUMMARY: Tournaments entered -- 8; in money -- 7; top-10 finishes -- 1.
OTHER ACHIEVEMENTS: Has finished first on PGA European Tour Order of Merit the last three years, the first to do so since Seve Ballesteros (1976-78). Winner, 1995 Volvo German Open, Trophee Lancome; 1994 Peugeot Open de Espana, Murphy's English Open, Volvo German Open; 1993 Heineken Dutch Open, Volvo Masters. 1989 Portuguese Open; 1991 Scandinavian Masters; 1985 Scottish Stroke Play, 1987 Scottish Amateur Championship. 1988 European Tour Rookie of the Year. Three-time All-American at Houston Baptist.
NATIONAL TEAMS: Walker Cup (2), 1985,1987; Ryder Cup (3), 1991, 1993, 1995. Dunhill Cup (5), 1988, 1991, 1992, 1993, 1994. World Cup (4), 1988, 1991, 1992, 1993. Asahi Glass Four Tours, 1991.

Frank Nobilo

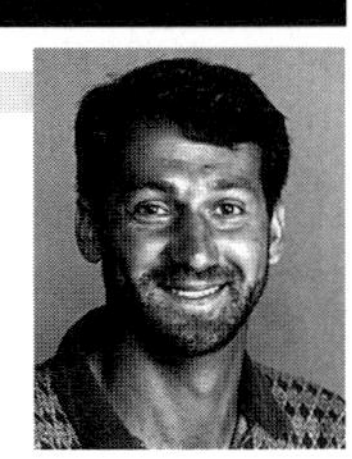

HEIGHT: 5'11" **WEIGHT:** 180 **BIRTHDATE:** May 14, 1960
BIRTHPLACE: Auckland, New Zealand **RESIDENCE:** Auckland, New Zealand
FAMILY: Daughter, Bianca
SPECIAL INTERESTS: Photography, squash, motor racing
TURNED PROFESSIONAL: 1979
BEST-EVER FINISH: T9--1994 U.S. Open
MONEY & POSITION: 1992--$ 7,000--252 1994--$41,292--138
1993--$14,500--230 1995--$ 52,119--203
BEST 1995 FINISH: T10--U.S. Open
1995 SUMMARY: Tournaments entered--5; in money--2; top-10 finishes--1.
OTHER ACHIEVEMENTS: Winner of four PGA European Tour events: 1988 PLM Open, 1991 Lancome Trophy, 1993 Turespana Mediterranean Open, 1995 BMW International. Winner, 1995 Sarazen World Open; 1994 Indonesian Open; 1985 and 1987 New Zealand PGA; 1982 New South Wales PGA; 1978 New Zealand Amateur.
NATIONAL TEAMS: Presidents Cup, 1994. Dunhill Cup (8), 1985, 1986, 1987, 1989, 1990, 1992, 1994, 1995. World Cup (9), 1982, 1987, 1988, 1990, 1991, 1992, 1993, 1994, 1995. World Amateur Team, 1978.

Jose Maria Olazabal

HEIGHT: 5'10" **WEIGHT:** 160 **BIRTHDATE:** February 5, 1966
BIRTHPLACE: Fuenterrabia, Spain **RESIDENCE:** Fuenterrabia, Spain
SPECIAL INTERESTS: Music, cinema, hunting, wildlife, ecology
TURNED PROFESSIONAL: 1985
TOUR VICTORIES: 4--**1990** NEC World Series of Golf. **1991** The International. **1994** Masters Tournament, NEC World Series of Golf.
MONEY & POSITION: 1987--$ 7,470--215 1991--$ 382,124-- 43
1989--$ 56,039--160 1992--$ 63,429--161 1994--$969,900-- 7
1990--$337,837-- 38 1993--$ 60,160--174 1995--$ 33,080--223
BEST 1995 FINISH: T20 -- British Open
1995 SUMMARY: Tournaments entered--3; in money--3; top-10 finishes--0.
OTHER ACHIEVEMENTS: Winner of 16 PGA European Tour events -- 1995 Tournoi Perrier de Paris (with Seve Ballesteros); 1994 Turespana Open Mediterrania, Volvo PGA Championship; 1992 Turespana Open de Tenerife, Open Mediterrania; 1991 Open Catalonia, Epson Grand Prix of Europe; 1990 Benson & Hedges International, Carrolls Irish Open, Lancome Trophy; 1989 Tenerife Open, KLM Dutch Open; 1988 Volvo Belgian Open, German Masters; 1986 Ebel European Masters, Sanyo Open.
NATIONAL TEAMS: European Ryder Cup (4), 1987, 1989, 1991, 1993. Kirin Cup, 1987. Four Tours World Championship (2), 1989, 1990. World Cup, 1989. Dunhill Cup (6), 1986, 1987, 1988, 1989, 1992, 1993.

Masashi "Jumbo" Ozaki

HEIGHT: 6' 2" **WEIGHT:** 200 **BIRTHDATE:** January 27, 1947
BIRTHPLACE: Tokushima, Japan **RESIDENCE:** Chiba, Japan
TURNED PROFESSIONAL: 1970
BEST-EVER FINISH: T4--1993 Memorial Tournament
MONEY & POSITION: 1987--$21,727--184 1990--$ 31,834--192 1993--$66,742--169
1988--$ 6,321--233 1991--$ 15,765--218 1994--$25,557--217
1989--$47,755--165 1992--$ 13,906--223 1995-$60,292-- 188
BEST 1995 FINISH: T28--U.S. Open
1995 SUMMARY: Tournaments entered--6; in money--5; top-10 finishes--0.
OTHER ACHIEVEMENTS: The most successful Japanese player in history with 69 career wins in Japan: Winner of 1995 Chunichi Crowns and Dunlop Phoenix; Winner of seven tournaments in 1994: Dunlop Open, Yonex Open Hiroshima, ANA Open, Japan Open, Daiwa International, Sumitomo Visa Taiheiyo Masters, Dunlop Phoenix; Winner of three events in 1993: Fuji Sankei Classic, Japan PGA Championship and Asahi Beer Golf Digest Tournament. Won six JPGA tournaments in 1992: Dunlop Open, Chunichi Crowns, Philanthropy Cup, All Nippon Airways Open, Japan Open, Visa Taiheiyo Masters. Has led the JPGA in earnings six times since 1973. WInner, 1990 Yonex Hiroshima Open, Maruman Open and Daiwa KBC Augusta.

Costantino Rocca

HEIGHT: 5' 9" **WEIGHT:** 190 **BIRTHDATE:** December 4, 1956
BIRTHPLACE: Bergamo, Italy **RESIDENCE:** Bergamo, Italy
FAMILY: Wife, Antonella; Chiara (1985), Francesco (1991)
SPECIAL INTERESTS: Fishing, soccer
TURNED PROFESSIONAL: 1981 **PGA TOUR PLAYOFF RECORD:** 0-1
BEST-EVER FINISH: 2 --1995 British Open
MONEY & POSITION: 1994--$ 16,350--232 1995--$185,500-- 98
BEST 1995 FINISH: 2 -- British Open

1995 SUMMARY: Tournaments entered -- 2; in money -- 1; top-10 finishes -- 1.
OTHER ACHIEVEMENTS: Finished fourth on 1995 PGA European Tour Order of Merit, sixth in 1993; Winner, 1993 Open V33 du Grand Lyons, 1993 Peugeot Open de France. Was first Italian winner on PGA European Tour since 1980.
NATIONAL TEAMS: European Ryder Cup (2), 1993, 1995; World Cup (7) 1988, 1990, 1991, 1992, 1993, 1994, 1995. Dunhill Cup (5) 1986, 1987, 1989, 1991, 1992. Hennessy Cognac Cup,1984.

Peter Senior

HEIGHT: 5' 6" **WEIGHT:** 170 **BIRTHDATE:** July 31, 1959
BIRTHPLACE: Singapore **RESIDENCE:** Narangba, Queensland, Australia
FAMILY: Wife, June; Krystall, Jasmine, Mitchell
SPECIAL INTERESTS: Fishing, entertaining, reading
TURNED PROFESSIONAL: 1978
BEST-EVER FINISH: T2--1990 International
MONEY & POSITION: 1986--$ 2,498--246 1991--$ 32,217--197
1988--$ 5,074--245 1992--$ 3,688--275 1994--$ 2,513--304
1990--$94,244--141 1993--$ 3,600--283 1995--$33,391--222
BEST 1995 FINISH: T42 --Sprint International, NEC World Series of Golf
1995 SUMMARY: Tournaments entered -- 4; in money -- 4; top-10 finishes -- 0.
OTHER ACHIEVEMENTS: Led the Australasian Tour Order of Merit in 1987, 1989 and 1993. Winner, 1995 Australian Masters, 1994 Canon Challenge; 1993 Heineken Classic, Chunichi Crowns; 1992 Bridgestone ASO Open, Benson & Hedges International; 1991 Pyramid Australian Masters, Johnnie Walker Classic; 1990 European Open; 1989 New South Wales PGA Championship, Australian PGA Championship, Australian Open, Johnnie Walker Classic; 1987 U-Bix Classic, Rich River Classic, PGA Championship of Queensland, Johnnie Walker Monte Carlo Open; 1986 PLM Open; 1984 Stefan Queensland Open, Honeywell Classic; 1979 Dunhill South Australian Open.
NATIONAL TEAMS: Presidents Cup 1994. World Cup (2), 1988, 1990. Dunhill Cup (2), 1987, 1993. Kirin Cup (2), 1987, 1988. Asahi Glass Four Tours (2), 1989, 1990.

Sam Torrance

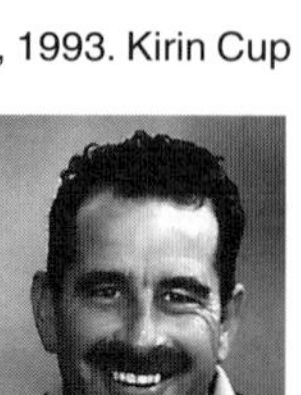

HEIGHT: 5' 11" **WEIGHT:** 190 **BIRTHDATE:** August 24, 1953
BIRTHPLACE: Largs, Scotland **RESIDENCE:** Wentworth, England
FAMILY: Wife, Suzanne; Daniel (1988), Phoebe (1992)
SPECIAL INTERESTS: Snooker, tennis, cards, family
TURNED PROFESSIONAL: 1970 **PGA TOUR PLAYOFF RECORD:** 0-1
BEST-EVER FINISH: 2--1983 Southern Open
MONEY & POSITION: 1982--$ 4,550--218 1984--$ 919--255
1983--$27,000--138 1994--$123,492--136 1995--$ 56,970--194
BEST 1995 FINISH: T11 -- British Open Championship
1995 SUMMARY: Tournaments entered --2; in money -- 2; top-10 finishes --0.
OTHER ACHIEVEMENTS: Winner of 20 PGA European Tour events: 1995 Italian Open, 1995 Murphy's Irish Open, 1995 Collingtree British Masters,1993 Kronenbourg Open, 1993 Heineken Open Catalonia, 1993 Honda Open, 1991 Jersey European Airways Open, 1990 Mercedes German Masters, 1987 Lancia Italian Open, 1985 Johnnie Walker Monte Carlo Open, 1984 Tunisian Open, 1984 Benson & Hedges International, 1984 Sanyo Open, 1983 Scandinavian Enterprise Open, 1983 Portuguese Open, 1981 Carrolls Irish Open, 1976 Piccadilly Medal, 1976 Martini International, 1972 Under-25 Match Play. Winner, 1980 Australian PGA Championship. Finished in top 10 on PGA European Tour Order of Merit 10 times, including second place in 1984 and 1995. Lost playoff to Ronnie Black 1983 Southern Open.
NATIONAL TEAMS: Ryder Cup (8) 1981, 1983, 1985, 1987, 1989, 1991, 1993, 1995. Dunhill Cup (8) 1985, 1986, 1987, 1989, 1990, 1991, 1993, 1995. World Cup (11) 1976, 1978, 1982, 1984, 1985, 1987, 1989, 1990, 1991, 1993, 1995. Nissan Cup 1985. Asahi Glass Four Tours 1991. Hennessy Cup (5) 1976, 1978, 1980, 1982, 1984. Double Diamond (3) 1973, 1976, 1977.

Ian Woosnam

HEIGHT: 5'4" **WEIGHT:** 161 **BIRTHDATE:** March 2, 1958
BIRTHPLACE: Oswestry, Wales **RESIDENCE:** Oswestry, Wales
FAMILY: Wife, Glendryth; Daniel, Rebecca, Amy
SPECIAL INTERESTS: Fishing, sports, snooker
TURNED PROFESSIONAL: 1976 **PGA TOUR PLAYOFF RECORD:** 1-0
TOUR VICTORIES: 2—**1991** USF&G Classic, Masters Tournament
MONEY & POSITION: 1986--$ 4,000--233 1990--$ 72,138--156 1993--$ 55,426--176
1987--$ 3,980--236 1991--$485,023-- 23 1994--$ 51,895--188
1988--$ 8,464--219 1992--$ 52,046--171 1995--$174,464--106
1989--$146,323-- 97
BEST 1995 FINISH: 3 --Honda Classic
1995 SUMMARY: Tournaments entered -- 8; in money -- 7; top-10 finishes --1.
OTHER ACHIEVEMENTS: Winner of 28 events on the PGA European Tour; 1982 Swiss Open; Winner of 1983 Silk Cut Masters; 1984 Scandinavian Enterprise Open; 1986 Lawrence Batley TPC; 1987 Jersey Open, Cespa Madrid Open, Bell's Scottish Open, Lancome Trophy, Suntory World Match Play Championship; 1988 Volvo PGA Championship, Carrolls Irish Open, Panasonic European Open; 1989 Carrolls Irish Open; 1990 Amex Mediterranean Open, Monte Carlo Open, Bell's Scottish Open, Epson Grand Prix, Suntory World Match Play Championship; 1991 Mediterranean Open, Monte Carlo Open; 1992 European Monte Carlo. Also has won the 1979 News of the World Under-23 Match Play Championship, 1982 Cacherel under-25 Championship; 1985 Zambian Open; 1986 '555' Kenya Open; 1987 Hong Kong Open and World Cup individual title; 1992 European Monte Carlo Open; 1993 Murphy's English Open, Lancome Trophy; 1994 Air France Cannes Open, Dunhill British Masters.
NATIONAL TEAMS: Ryder Cup (7), 1983, 1985, 1987, 1989, 1991, 1993, 1995. World Cup (11), 1980, 1982, 1983, 1984, 1985, 1987, 1990, 1991, 1992, 1993, 1994. Dunhill Cup (8), 1985, 1986, 1988, 1989, 1990, 1991, 1993, 1995. Nissan Cup (2), 1985, 1986; Kirin Cup, 1987. Four Tours World Championship of Golf (2), 1989, 1990. Hennessy Cognac Cup (2), 1982, 1984

Lee Janzen made THE PLAYERS Championship the first of his three 1995 wins, lifting his career victory total to seven in six years on TOUR.

1995 MERCEDES CHAMPIONSHIPS

La Costa Resort & Spa, Carlsbad, CA **Purse: $1,000,000**
Par: 36-36--72 Yards: 7,022 **January 5-8, 1995**

LEADERS: First Round--John Huston, at 5-under-par 67, led by two over Bob Estes and Steve Elkington. **Second Round--**Huston, at 11-under-par 133, led by two over Lee Janzen. **Third Round--**Huston, at 11-under-par 205, led by four over Fred Couples and Craig Stadler.

PRO-AM: Due to heavy rains, the pro-am was shortened to nine holes. Front Nine Individual--Andrew Magee, 35, $700. Front Nine Team--Craig Stadler, 29, $700. Back Nine Individual--Lee Janzen, 34, $700. Back Nine Team--Tom Lehman, 29, $700.

WEATHER: Thursday's round was postponed due to soggy course conditions. The players completed 36 holes on Friday starting at 7:30 a.m. with no delays. Saturday was overcast and rainy, but no delays. The start of Sunday's round was delayed two hours, due to soggy course conditions. Preferred lies were used during the four rounds of the tournament.

Winner: Steve Elkington 69-71-71-67 278 $180,000.00

(Won playoff with birdie-3 on second extra hole)

Player	Pos.	Scores	Total	Money
Bruce Lietzke	2	71-69-71-67	278	$108,000.00
Bill Glasson	3	70-69-73-67	279	$68,000.00
Craig Stadler	4	71-65-73-71	280	$48,000.00
Fred Couples	T 5	73-68-68-72	281	$35,250.00
Ben Crenshaw	T 5	71-67-75-68	281	$35,250.00
Rick Fehr	T 5	71-74-70-66	281	$35,250.00
Tom Lehman	T 5	75-68-72-66	281	$35,250.00
John Huston	T 9	67-66-72-77	282	$28,750.00
Lee Janzen	T 9	72-63-76-71	282	$28,750.00
Scott Hoch	11	74-67-73-69	283	$26,750.00
Bob Estes	T12	69-68-74-73	284	$24,750.00
Hale Irwin	T12	73-69-72-70	284	$24,750.00
Corey Pavin	T12	74-71-69-70	284	$24,750.00
Mark Brooks	15	71-71-73-70	285	$22,750.00
Mark McCumber	T16	70-72-72-72	286	$21,250.00
Kenny Perry	T16	72-70-74-70	286	$21,250.00
Greg Norman	18	74-72-72-70	288	$20,000.00
Phil Mickelson	19	72-73-71-73	289	$19,250.00
John Daly	T20	75-74-72-69	290	$18,125.00
Dicky Pride	T20	71-72-74-73	290	$18,125.00
Steve Lowery	22	71-79-70-71	291	$17,250.00
Neal Lancaster	23	72-75-70-75	292	$16,750.00
Mike Heinen	T24	72-75-71-75	293	$16,000.00
Loren Roberts	T24	71-73-75-74	293	$16,000.00
Brian Henninger	T26	75-74-70-78	297	$15,375.00
Andrew Magee	T26	75-72-75-75	297	$15,375.00
Mike Sullivan	28	71-77-75-75	298	$15,050.00
Brett Ogle	29	77-73-75-75	300	$14,850.00
Mike Springer	30	72-72-83-75	302	$14,650.00

The following players did not finish (C=cut, W=withdrew, D=disqualified)

W — 219- Johnny Miller

MERCEDES CHAMPIONSHIPS

TOURNAMENT HISTORY

Year	Winner	Score	Runner-up	Score	Location	Par/Yards
TOURNAMENT OF CHAMPIONS						
1953	Al Besselink	280	Chandler Harper	281	Desert Inn CC, Las Vegas, NV	72/7209
1954	Art Wall	278	Al Besselink	284	Desert Inn CC, Las Vegas, NV	72/7209
1955	Gene Littler	280	Lloyd Mangrum Jerry Barber Pete Cooper Bob Toski	293	Desert Inn CC, Las Vegas, NV	72/7209
1956	Gene Littler	281	Cary Middlecoff	285	Desert Inn CC, Las Vegas, NV	72/7209
1957	Gene Littler	285	Billy Casper Jimmy Demaret Dow Finsterwald Billy Maxwell	288	Desert Inn CC, Las Vegas, NV	72/7209
1958	Stan Leonard	275	Billy Casper	276	Desert Inn CC, Las Vegas, NV	72/7209
1959	Mike Souchak	281	Art Wall	283	Desert Inn CC, Las Vegas, NV	72/7209
1960	Jerry Barber	268	Jay Hebert	272	Desert Inn CC, Las Vegas, NV	72/7209
1961	Sam Snead	273	Tommy Bolt	280	Desert Inn CC, Las Vegas, NV	72/7209
1962	Arnold Palmer	276	Billy Casper	277	Desert Inn CC, Las Vegas, NV	72/7209
1963	Jack Nicklaus	273	Tony Lema	278	Desert Inn CC, Las Vegas, NV	72/7209
1964	Jack Nicklaus	279	Arnold Palmer Al Geiberger Doug Sanders	281	Desert Inn CC, Las Vegas, NV	72/7209
1965	Arnold Palmer	277	Chi Chi Rodriguez	279	Desert Inn CC, Las Vegas, NV	72/7209
1966	*Arnold Palmer	283	Gay Brewer	283	Desert Inn CC, Las Vegas, NV	72/7209
1967	Frank Beard	278	Arnold Palmer	279	Stardust CC, Las Vegas, NV	71/6725
1968	Don January	276	Julius Boros	277	Stardust CC, Las Vegas, NV	71/6725
1969	Gary Player	284	Lee Trevino	286	La Costa CC, Carlsbad, CA	72/6911
1970	Frank Beard	273	Billy Casper Tony Jacklin Gary Player	280	La Costa CC, Carlsbad, CA	72/6911
1971	Jack Nicklaus	279	Bruce Devlin Gary Player Dave Stockton	287	La Costa CC, Carlsbad, CA	72/6911
1972	*Bobby Mitchell	280	Jack Nicklaus	280	La Costa CC, Carlsbad, CA	72/6911
1973	Jack Nicklaus	276	Lee Trevino	277	La Costa CC, Carlsbad, CA	72/6911
1974	Johnny Miller	280	Bud Allin John Mahaffey	281	La Costa CC, Carlsbad, CA	72/6911
MONY TOURNAMENT OF CHAMPIONS						
1975	*Al Geiberger	277	Gary Player	277	La Costa CC, Carlsbad, CA	72/6911
1976	Don January	277	Hubert Green	282	La Costa CC, Carlsbad, CA	72/6911
1977	*Jack Nicklaus	281	Bruce Lietzke	281	La Costa CC, Carlsbad, CA	72/6911
1978	Gary Player	281	Andy North Lee Trevino	283	La Costa CC, Carlsbad, CA	72/6911
1979	Tom Watson	275	Bruce Lietzke Jerry Pate	281	La Costa CC, Carlsbad, CA	72/6911
1980	Tom Watson	276	Jim Colbert	279	La Costa CC, Carlsbad, CA	72/6911
1981	Lee Trevino	273	Ray Floyd	275	La Costa CC, Carlsbad, CA	72/6911
1982	Lanny Wadkins	280	Andy Bean David Graham Craig Stadler Ron Streck	283	La Costa CC, Carlsbad, CA	72/6911
1983	Lanny Wadkins	280	Ray Floyd	281	La Costa CC, Carlsbad, CA	72/6911
1984	Tom Watson	274	Bruce Lietzke	279	La Costa CC, Carlsbad, CA	72/7022
1985	Tom Kite	275	Mark McCumber	281	La Costa CC, Carlsbad, CA	72/7022
1986	Calvin Peete	267	Mark O'Meara	273	La Costa CC, Carlsbad, CA	72/7022
1987	Mac O'Grady	278	Rick Fehr	279	La Costa CC, Carlsbad, CA	72/7022
1988	~Steve Pate	202	Larry Nelson	203	La Costa CC, Carlsbad, CA	72/7022
1989	Steve Jones	279	David Frost Jay Haas	282	La Costa CC, Carlsbad, CA	72/7022
INFINITI TOURNAMENT OF CHAMPIONS						
1990	Paul Azinger	272	Ian Baker-Finch	273	La Costa CC, Carlsbad, CA	72/7022
1991	Tom Kite	272	Lanny Wadkins	273	La Costa CC, Carlsbad, CA	72/7022
1992	*Steve Elkington	279	Brad Faxon	279	La Costa CC, Carlsbad, CA	72/7022
1993	Davis Love III	272	Tom Kite	273	La Costa CC, Carlsbad, CA	72/7022
MERCEDES CHAMPIONSHIPS						
1994	*Phil Mickelson	276	Fred Couples	276	La Costa CC, Carlsbad, CA	72/7022
1995	*Steve Elkington	278	Bruce Lietzke	278	La Costa CC, Carlsbad, CA	72/7022

Tournament Record: 267 -- Calvin Peete, 1986
Current Course Record: 63 -- Lee Janzen, 1995

KEY: *=Playoff ~=Weather-shortened

1995 UNITED AIRLINES HAWAIIAN OPEN

Waialae CC, Honolulu, HI **Purse: $1,200,000**
Par: 36-36--72 Yards: 6,975 **January 12-15, 1995**

LEADERS: First Round--Keith Fergus and Jim Furyk, with 5-under-par 67s, led by one over Mark Brooks, Tom Lehman, Steve Jones, Clark Dennis, Yoshinori Mizumaki and Duffy Waldorf. **Second Round--**Waldorf, at 11-under-par 133, led by three over Dennis, John Morse and Dan Pohl. **Third Round--**Morse, at 15-under-par 201, led by two over Chip Beck.

CUT: 78 players at 1-over-par 145.

PRO-AM: $10,000. Individual--David Edwards, 63, $1,000. Team--Hubert Green, 53, $1,000.

WEATHER: Gusty winds every day. Showers on Saturday afternoon and Sunday morning, but no delays.

Winner: John Morse 71-65-65-68 269 $216,000.00

Player	Pos	Scores	Total	Money
Tom Lehman	T 2	68-70-67-67	272	$105,600.00
Duffy Waldorf	T 2	68-65-71-68	272	$105,600.00
Paul Azinger	T 4	72-67-69-66	274	$49,600.00
Bill Glasson	T 4	70-70-68-66	274	$49,600.00
Dan Pohl	T 4	69-67-69-69	274	$49,600.00
Mark Brooks	T 7	68-69-68-70	275	$38,700.00
John Huston	T 7	72-68-69-66	275	$38,700.00
Chip Beck	9	71-66-66-73	276	$34,800.00
David Ishii	T10	71-69-68-69	277	$31,200.00
Grant Waite	T10	71-69-66-71	277	$31,200.00
Robert Gamez	T12	72-67-67-72	278	$26,400.00
Brian Henninger	T12	72-65-74-67	278	$26,400.00
Dave Barr	T14	69-70-69-71	279	$21,000.00
Mark Calcavecchia	T14	75-69-67-68	279	$21,000.00
David Duval	T14	71-73-64-71	279	$21,000.00
Keith Fergus	T14	67-72-70-70	279	$21,000.00
Patrick Burke	T18	74-70-66-70	280	$16,200.00
Jim Furyk	T18	67-72-72-69	280	$16,200.00
Sean Murphy	T18	72-70-71-67	280	$16,200.00
Jesper Parnevik	T18	70-75-67-68	280	$16,200.00
Pat Bates	T22	75-70-70-66	281	$11,520.00
Steve Jones	T22	68-73-69-71	281	$11,520.00
Greg Kraft	T22	72-71-69-69	281	$11,520.00
Yoshi Mizumaki	T22	68-71-74-68	281	$11,520.00
Charles Rymer	T22	71-69-72-69	281	$11,520.00
David Edwards	T27	73-72-68-69	282	$7,820.00
Jim Gallagher, Jr.	T27	75-68-71-68	282	$7,820.00
Scott Gump	T27	72-73-69-68	282	$7,820.00
Jonathan Kaye	T27	73-69-68-72	282	$7,820.00
Jim McGovern	T27	69-70-71-72	282	$7,820.00
David Ogrin	T27	70-72-70-70	282	$7,820.00
Dave Rummells	T27	73-71-70-68	282	$7,820.00
Mike Sullivan	T27	69-69-74-70	282	$7,820.00
Craig Stadler	T27	71-72-68-71	282	$7,820.00
Clark Dennis	T36	68-68-71-76	283	$5,530.00
Doug Martin	T36	71-68-72-72	283	$5,530.00
Corey Pavin	T36	69-75-69-70	283	$5,530.00
Don Pooley	T36	74-70-68-71	283	$5,530.00
Steve Stricker	T36	74-70-70-69	283	$5,530.00
Mark Wurtz	T36	72-66-74-71	283	$5,530.00
Russ Cochran	T42	73-68-71-72	284	$4,200.00
Skip Kendall	T42	70-71-72-71	284	$4,200.00
Steve Lowery	T42	72-72-70-70	284	$4,200.00
Joe Ozaki	T42	70-75-68-71	284	$4,200.00
Curtis Strange	T42	70-73-69-72	284	$4,200.00
Andy Bean	T47	75-69-71-70	285	$2,960.73
Michael Bradley	T47	73-72-67-73	285	$2,960.73
Curt Byrum	T47	70-75-69-71	285	$2,960.73
Paul Goydos	T47	75-68-73-69	285	$2,960.73
Peter Jacobsen	T47	70-72-69-74	285	$2,960.73
Mark O'Meara	T47	76-69-69-71	285	$2,960.73
Vijay Singh	T47	70-73-73-69	285	$2,960.73
Richard Zokol	T47	71-72-70-72	285	$2,960.73
Kelly Gibson	T47	69-71-74-71	285	$2,960.72
Gene Sauers	T47	70-71-74-70	285	$2,960.72
Bruce Vaughan	T47	72-68-72-73	285	$2,960.72
Woody Austin	T58	73-72-71-70	286	$2,652.00
Brian Claar	T58	70-74-69-73	286	$2,652.00
Mike Heinen	T58	73-71-74-68	286	$2,652.00
Jeff Leonard	T58	72-73-69-72	286	$2,652.00
Joel Edwards	T62	76-68-71-72	287	$2,568.00
J.L. Lewis	T62	69-72-76-70	287	$2,568.00
Omar Uresti	T62	70-71-74-72	287	$2,568.00
Bob Burns	T65	74-71-71-72	288	$2,460.00
Hubert Green	T65	72-71-74-71	288	$2,460.00
Dudley Hart	T65	72-72-71-73	288	$2,460.00
Massy Kuramoto	T65	73-71-74-70	288	$2,460.00
Dennis Paulson	T65	70-72-71-75	288	$2,460.00
Scott Simpson	T65	73-70-71-74	288	$2,460.00
Bart Bryant	T71	70-73-74-72	289	$2,352.00
Kawika Cotner	T71	73-71-75-70	289	$2,352.00
Harry Taylor	T71	73-71-76-69	289	$2,352.00
Fred Funk	T74	74-71-73-72	290	$2,292.00
Ted Tryba	T74	74-70-69-77	290	$2,292.00
Scott Hoch	76	70-74-72-76	292	$2,256.00
Bill Britton	77	72-72-73-77	294	$2,232.00
John Daly	78	73-71-76-78	298	$2,208.00

The following players did not finish (C=cut, W=withdrew, D=disqualified)

C—146- Emlyn Aubrey, Keith Clearwater, David Feherty, Ken Green, John Inman, Tom Kite, Craig Parry, Chris Perry, Joey Rassett, Don Reese, Jim Thorpe, Tray Tyner, John Wilson. **147-** Ronnie Black, Jay Don Blake, Mike Brisky, Robin Freeman, Ed Humenik, Lee Rinker, Ray Stewart, Dicky Thompson. **148-** Brad Bryant, Bob Gilder, Wayne Grady, John Mahaffey, Greg Meyer, Jerry Pate, Dave Stockton, Jr., Howard Twitty. **149-** Ian Baker-Finch, Guy Boros, John Cook, Chris DiMarco, Justin Leonard, Scott McCarron, Steve Pate, Mike Standly. **150-** Joe Acosta, Jr., Jim Carter, Todd Fischer, Nolan Henke, Wayne Levi, Hajime Meshiai, Eiji Mizoguchi, Steve Rintoul, Guy Yamamoto. **151-** Marco Dawson, Dick McClean, Bill Porter. **152-** Phil Blackmar, Glen Day, Jerry Haas, Jeff Maggert, Billy Mayfair, Craig Sasada, Paul Stankowski, Bobby Wadkins. **153-** Steve Gotsche. **154-** Billy Ray Brown, John Freitas. **156-** Ron Castillo, John Flannery. **158-** Atsushi Nakajima. **W—147-**Brett Ogle, **75-** Dillard Pruitt. **D—**Lanny Wadkins.

UNITED AIRLINES HAWAIIAN OPEN

TOURNAMENT HISTORY

Year	Winner	Score	Runner-up	Score	Location	Par/Yards
HAWAIIAN OPEN						
1965	*Gay Brewer	281	Bob Goalby	281	Waialae CC, Honolulu, HI	72/7234
1966	Ted Makalena	271	Gay Brewer Billy Casper	274	Waialae CC, Honolulu, HI	72/7234
1967	*Dudley Wysong	284	Billy Casper	284	Waialae CC, Honolulu, HI	72/7234
1968	Lee Trevino	272	George Archer	274	Waialae CC, Honolulu, HI	72/7234
1969	Bruce Crampton	274	Jack Nicklaus	278	Waialae CC, Honolulu, HI	72/7234
1970	No Tournament					
1971	Tom Shaw	273	Miller Barber	274	Waialae CC, Honolulu, HI	72/7234
1972	*Grier Jones	274	Bob Murphy	274	Waialae CC, Honolulu, HI	72/7234
1973	John Schlee	273	Orville Moody	275	Waialae CC, Honolulu, HI	72/7234
1974	Jack Nicklaus	271	Eddie Pearce	274	Waialae CC, Honolulu, HI	72/7234
1975	Gary Groh	274	Al Geiberger	275	Waialae CC, Honolulu, HI	72/7234
1976	Ben Crenshaw	270	Hale Irwin Larry Nelson	274	Waialae CC, Honolulu, HI	72/7234
1977	Bruce Lietzke	273	Don January Takashi Murakami	276	Waialae CC, Honolulu, HI	72/7234
1978	*Hubert Green	274	Bill Kratzert	274	Waialae CC, Honolulu, HI	72/7234
1979	Hubert Green	267	Fuzzy Zoeller	270	Waialae CC, Honolulu, HI	72/7234
1980	Andy Bean	266	Lee Trevino	269	Waialae CC, Honolulu, HI	72/7234
1981	Hale Irwin	265	Don January	271	Waialae CC, Honolulu, HI	72/7234
1982	Wayne Levi	277	Scott Simpson	278	Waialae CC, Honolulu, HI	72/7234
1983	Isao Aoki	268	Jack Renner	269	Waialae CC, Honolulu, HI	72/7234
1984	*Jack Renner	271	Wayne Levi	271	Waialae CC, Honolulu, HI	72/7234
1985	Mark O'Meara	267	Craig Stadler	268	Waialae CC, Honolulu, HI	72/6975
1986	Corey Pavin	272	Paul Azinger	274	Waialae CC, Honolulu, HI	72/6975
1987	*Corey Pavin	270	Craig Stadler	270	Waialae CC, Honolulu, HI	72/6975
1988	Lanny Wadkins	271	Richard Zokol	272	Waialae CC, Honolulu, HI	72/6975
1989	~Gene Sauers	197	David Ogrin	198	Waialae CC, Honolulu, HI	72/6975
1990	David Ishii	279	Paul Azinger	280	Waialae CC, Honolulu, HI	72/6975
UNITED HAWAIIAN OPEN						
1991	Lanny Wadkins	270	John Cook	274	Waialae CC, Honolulu, HI	72/6975
UNITED AIRLINES HAWAIIAN OPEN						
1992	John Cook	265	Paul Azinger	267	Waialae CC, Honolulu, HI	72/6975
1993	Howard Twitty	269	Joey Sindelar	273	Waialae CC, Honolulu, HI	72/6975
1994	Brett Ogle	269	Davis Love III	270	Waialae CC, Honolulu, HI	72/6975
1995	John Morse	269	Tom Lehman Duffy Waldorf	272	Waialae CC, Honolulu, HI	72/6975

Tournament Record: 265 -- Hale Irwin, 1981; John Cook, 1992
Current Course Record: 60 -- Davis Love III, 1994

KEY: *=Playoff ~=Weather-shortened

1995 NORTHERN TELECOM OPEN

Tucson National GC, Tucson, AZ
Par: 36-36--72 Yards: 7,148
Starr Pass GC, Tucson, AZ
Par: 35-36--71 Yards: 6,942

Purse: $1,250,000
January 19-22, 1995

LEADERS: First Round--Tom Purtzer (TN) and Phil Mickelson (TN) shot 7-under-par 65 and led Howard Twitty (SP) by one stroke. **Second Round**--Mickelson (SP) shot 5-under-par 66 for 131 to lead Jim Gallagher, Jr., (TN) by one stroke and Brett Ogle (SP) and Paul Stankowski (TN) by two. **Third Round**--Mickelson, Ogle and Gallagher shared the lead at 14-under-par 201. They led Stankowski, Don Pooley and Scott Simpson by one stroke.

CUT: 79 players at 1-under-par 142.

PRO-AM: Tucson National--Individual, Bob Estes, 64, $750; Team, Steve Pate, 53, $750. Starr Pass--Individual, Curtis Strange, 66, $750; Team, Donnie Hammond, 54, $750.

WEATHER: After snow flurries Tuesday, partly cloudy and cool the remainder of the week. Temperatures in the upper 50s and low 60s.

Winner: Phil Mickelson 65-66-70-68 269 $225,000.00

Player	Pos.	Scores	Total	Money
Jim Gallagher, Jr.	T 2	68-64-69-69	270	$110,000.00
Scott Simpson	T 2	69-65-68-68	270	$110,000.00
Brett Ogle	4	68-65-68-70	271	$60,000.00
Jim Furyk	5	69-69-67-67	272	$50,000.00
Woody Austin	T 6	68-69-70-67	274	$37,812.50
David Duval	T 6	67-70-67-70	274	$37,812.50
Tom Kite	T 6	71-66-67-70	274	$37,812.50
Joe Ozaki	T 6	68-67-70-69	274	$37,812.50
Don Pooley	T 6	71-66-65-72	274	$37,812.50
Bob Tway	T 6	70-65-69-70	274	$37,812.50
Bart Bryant	T12	70-69-67-69	275	$26,250.00
Brandel Chamblee	T12	70-71-68-66	275	$26,250.00
Tom Purtzer	T12	65-71-70-69	275	$26,250.00
Nolan Henke	T15	70-67-70-69	276	$21,875.00
Hal Sutton	T15	70-71-69-66	276	$21,875.00
Tommy Armour III	T17	70-66-71-70	277	$15,812.50
Lennie Clements	T17	69-71-68-69	277	$15,812.50
Russ Cochran	T17	68-69-70-70	277	$15,812.50
John Cook	T17	74-67-70-66	277	$15,812.50
Peter Jordan	T17	68-72-69-68	277	$15,812.50
Gary McCord	T17	72-68-71-66	277	$15,812.50
Steve Pate	T17	71-69-70-67	277	$15,812.50
Paul Stankowski	T17	67-66-69-75	277	$15,812.50
Lee Janzen	T25	72-70-68-68	278	$9,339.29
Jeff Maggert	T25	68-74-68-68	278	$9,339.29
Steve Stricker	T25	70-71-69-68	278	$9,339.29
Bruce Vaughan	T25	72-69-70-67	278	$9,339.29
Dave Barr	T25	71-67-70-70	278	$9,339.28
Nick Faldo	T25	70-70-70-68	278	$9,339.28
Bobby Wadkins	T25	69-69-70-70	278	$9,339.28
Bob Estes	T32	72-70-67-70	279	$6,486.12
Mark Calcavecchia	T32	69-69-74-67	279	$6,486.11
Rick Fehr	T32	68-70-70-71	279	$6,486.11
Paul Goydos	T32	67-71-70-71	279	$6,486.11
Scott Hoch	T32	70-68-74-67	279	$6,486.11
Neal Lancaster	T32	72-67-72-68	279	$6,486.11
Rocco Mediate	T32	68-69-72-70	279	$6,486.11
Ted Tryba	T32	71-67-72-69	279	$6,486.11
Tray Tyner	T32	71-68-72-68	279	$6,486.11
Jay Don Blake	T41	67-71-71-71	280	$4,750.00
Mike Brisky	T41	71-68-71-70	280	$4,750.00
Dudley Hart	T41	72-68-69-71	280	$4,750.00
Howard Twitty	T41	66-69-72-73	280	$4,750.00
Danny Briggs	T45	70-67-74-70	281	$3,575.00
Robin Freeman	T45	69-67-76-69	281	$3,575.00
Jerry Haas	T45	71-70-71-69	281	$3,575.00
Mike Hulbert	T45	74-68-68-71	281	$3,575.00
Mark O'Meara	T45	69-71-71-70	281	$3,575.00
Lanny Wadkins	T45	67-73-69-72	281	$3,575.00
John Adams	T51	72-69-71-70	282	$2,925.00
Andrew Magee	T51	69-70-71-72	282	$2,925.00
Doug Martin	T51	70-71-72-69	282	$2,925.00
Dan Pohl	T51	71-71-71-69	282	$2,925.00
Jim Thorpe	T51	71-69-69-73	282	$2,925.00
Ronnie Black	T51	72-70-71-69	282	$2,925.00
J.B. Sneve	T51	71-71-68-72	282	$2,925.00
Mark Brooks	T58	68-70-74-71	283	$2,762.50
Gil Morgan	T58	72-69-69-73	283	$2,762.50
Loren Roberts	T58	72-67-72-72	283	$2,762.50
John Wilson	T58	70-68-73-72	283	$2,762.50
Jeff Leonard	T62	71-67-75-71	284	$2,637.50
Yoshi Mizumaki	T62	69-72-68-75	284	$2,637.50
Mike Standly	T62	72-70-72-70	284	$2,637.50
Mike Sullivan	T62	71-69-70-74	284	$2,637.50
Doug Tewell	T62	73-69-74-68	284	$2,637.50
Omar Uresti	T62	71-71-74-68	284	$2,637.50
Jim Carter	T68	67-72-74-72	285	$2,512.50
Brian Henninger	T68	68-73-71-73	285	$2,512.50
Bob Lohr	T68	71-70-76-68	285	$2,512.50
Dillard Pruitt	T68	73-69-72-71	285	$2,512.50
Kenny Perry	72	71-70-70-75	286	$2,450.00
Brian Claar	T73	70-70-74-73	287	$2,400.00
Fred Funk	T73	70-70-74-73	287	$2,400.00
Jesper Parnevik	T73	71-69-74-73	287	$2,400.00
Kirk Triplett	76	70-70-74-74	288	$2,350.00
Pat Bates	77	70-72-72-77	291	$2,325.00
Chip Beck	78	68-71-76-78	293	$2,300.00

The following players did not finish (C=cut, W=withdrew, D=disqualified)

C—143- Billy Andrade, Brad Bryant, Jay Delsing, Chris DiMarco, Bill Dodd, John Inman, Steve Jones, Bruce Lietzke, Chris Perry, Joey Rassett, Vijay Singh, Scott Watkins, Mark Wiebe. **144-** Michael Bradley, Bob Burns, Curt Byrum, R.W. Eaks, Joel Edwards, Robert Gamez, Jay Haas, Donnie Hammond, Brian Kamm, Jim McGovern, Jodie Mudd, Steve Rintoul, Jeff Sluman, Mike Springer, D.A. Weibring. **145-** Emlyn Aubrey, Andy Bean, Guy Boros, Scott Gump, Jim Lemon, Craig Parry, Dicky Pride, Rocky Walcher. **146-** Ian Baker-Finch, Keith Clearwater, Mike Heinen, Ed Humenik, Skip Kendall, Greg Kraft, John Morse, Christian Pena, Dave Powell, Mike Reid, Charlie Rymer, Payne Stewart, Scott Verplank, Richard Zokol. **147-** Mark Carnevale, Clark Dennis, Bob Gilder, Bill Porter, Don Reese. **148-** Mike Cunning, John Daly, Glen Day, Dan Forsman, Gary Hallberg, Larry Nelson, Duffy Waldorf. **149-** Phil Blackmar, Hubert Green, Mark Gurnow, Justin Leonard. **150-** Carlton Blewett, David Ishii, Dennis Paulson, Harry Taylor. **151-** Ken Green, Billy Mayfair, Dave Stockton, Jr. **152-** David Feherty, Grant Waite. **153-** Curtis Strange. **W—294-** Wayne Grady, **80-** Gene Sauers.

NORTEL OPEN

TOURNAMENT HISTORY

Year	Winner	Score	Runner-up	Score	Location	Par/Yards
TUCSON OPEN						
1945	Ray Mangrum	268	Byron Nelson	269	El Rio G&CC, Tucson, AZ	70/6418
1946	Jimmy Demaret	268	Herman Barron	272	El Rio G&CC, Tucson, AZ	70/6418
1947	Jimmy Demaret	264	Ben Hogan	267	El Rio G&CC, Tucson, AZ	70/6418
1948	Skip Alexander	264	Johnny Palmer	265	El Rio G&CC, Tucson, AZ	70/6418
1949	Lloyd Mangrum	263	Al Smith	268	El Rio G&CC, Tucson, AZ	70/6418
1950	Chandler Harper	267	Sam Snead	269	El Rio G&CC, Tucson, AZ	70/6418
1951	Lloyd Mangrum	269	Jack Burke, Jr. Jim Turnesa Lew Worsham	271	El Rio G&CC, Tucson, AZ	70/6418
1952	Henry Williams	274	Cary Middlecoff	276	El Rio G&CC, Tucson, AZ	70/6418
1953	Tommy Bolt	265	Chandler Harper	266	El Rio G&CC, Tucson, AZ	70/6418
1954	No Tournament					
1955	Tommy Bolt	265	Bud Holscher Art Wall	269	El Rio G&CC, Tucson, AZ	70/6418
1956	Ted Kroll	264	Dow Finsterwald	267	El Rio G&CC, Tucson, AZ	70/6418
1957	*Dow Finsterwald	269	Don Whitt	269	El Rio G&CC, Tucson, AZ	70/6418
1958	Lionel Hebert	265	Don January	267	El Rio G&CC, Tucson, AZ	70/6418
1959	Gene Littler	266	Joe Campbell Art Wall	267	El Rio G&CC, Tucson, AZ	70/6418
1960	Don January	271	Bob Harris	274	El Rio G&CC, Tucson, AZ	70/6418
HOME OF THE SUN INVITATIONAL						
1961	*Dave Hill	269			El Rio G&CC, Tucson, AZ	70/6418
TUCSON OPEN						
1962	Phil Rodgers	263	Jim Ferrier	266	El Rio G&CC, Tucson, AZ	70/6418
1963	Don January	266	Gene Littler Phil Rodgers	277	49er CC, Tucson, AZ	72/6722
1964	Jack Cupit	274	Rex Baxter	276	49er CC, Tucson, AZ	72/6722
1965	Bob Charles	271	Al Geiberger	275	Tucson National GC, Tucson, AZ	72/7305
1966	*Joe Campbell	278	Gene Littler	278	Tucson National GC, Tucson, AZ	72/7305
1967	Arnold Palmer	273	Chuck Courtney	274	Tucson National GC, Tucson, AZ	72/7305
1968	George Knudson	273	Frank Beard Frank Boynton	274	Tucson National GC, Tucson, AZ	72/7305
1969	Lee Trevino	271	Miller Barber	278	Tucson National GC, Tucson, AZ	72/7305
1970	*Lee Trevino	275	Bob Murphy	275	Tucson National GC, Tucson, AZ	72/7305
1971	J.C. Snead	273	Dale Douglass	274	Tucson National GC, Tucson, AZ	72/7305
1972	*Miller Barber	273	George Archer	273	Tucson National GC, Tucson, AZ	72/7305
DEAN MARTIN TUCSON OPEN						
1973	Bruce Crampton	277	George Archer Gay Brewer Labron Harris, Jr.	282	Tucson National GC, Tucson, AZ	72/7305
1974	Johnny Miller	272	Ben Crenshaw	275	Tucson National GC, Tucson, AZ	72/7305
1975	Johnny Miller	263	John Mahaffey	272	Tucson National GC, Tucson, AZ	72/7305
NBC TUCSON OPEN						
1976	Johnny Miller	274	Howard Twitty	277	Tucson National GC, Tucson, AZ	72/7305
JOE GARAGIOLA TUCSON OPEN						
1977	*Bruce Lietzke	275	Gene Littler	275	Tucson National GC, Tucson, AZ	72/7305
1978	Tom Watson	276	Bobby Wadkins	277	Tucson National GC, Tucson, AZ	72/7305
1979	Bruce Lietzke	265	Buddy Gardner Jim Thorpe Tom Watson	267	Randolph Park Municpal GC, Tucson, AZ	70/6860
1980	Jim Colbert	270	Dan Halldorson	274	Tucson National GC, Tucson, AZ	72/7305
1981	Johnny Miller	265	Lon Hinkle	267	Randolph Park Municipal GC, Tucson, AZ	70/6860
1982	Craig Stadler	266	Vance Heafner John Mahaffey	269	Randolph Park Municipal GC, Tucson, AZ	70/6860
1983	*Gil Morgan	271	Curtis Strange Lanny Wadkins	271	Randolph Park Municipal GC, Tucson, AZ	70/6860
SEIKO-TUCSON MATCH PLAY CHAMPIONSHIPS						
1984	Tom Watson	2&1	Gil Morgan		Randolph Park Municipal GC, Tucson, AZ	70/6860

NORTEL OPEN

TOURNAMENT HISTORY

Year	Winner	Score	Runner-up	Score	Location	Par/Yards
1985	Jim Thorpe	4&3	Jack Renner		Randolph Park Municipal GC, Tucson, AZ	70/6860
1986	Jim Thorpe	67	Scott Simpson		Randolph Park Municipal GC, Tucson, AZ	70/6860
SEIKO-TUCSON OPEN						
1987	Mike Reid	268	Chip Beck	272	TPC at StarPass, Tucson, AZ	72/7010
			Mark Calcavecchia			
			Hal Sutton			
			Fuzzy Zoeller			
NORTHERN TELECOM TUCSON OPEN						
1988	David Frost	266	Mark Calcavecchia	271	TPC at StarPass, Tucson, AZ	72/7010
			Mark O'Meara			
1989	No tournament held due to schedule change from end of year to beginning of year.					
1990	Robert Gamez	270	Mark Calcavecchia	274	TPC at StarPass, Tucson, AZ	72/7010
			Jay Haas		Randolph Park Municipal GC, Tucson, AZ	72/6902
NORTHERN TELECOM OPEN						
1991	#Phil Mickelson	272	Tom Purtzer	273	TPC at StarPass, Tucson, AZ	72/7010
			Bob Tway		Tucson National GC, Tucson, AZ	72/7305
1992	Lee Janzen	270	Bill Britton	271	TPC at StarPass, Tucson, AZ	72/7010
					Tucson National GC, Tucson, AZ	72/7305
1993	Larry Mize	271	Jeff Maggert	273	Tucson National GC, Tucson, AZ	72/7148
					Starr Pass GC, Tucson, AZ	72/7010
1994	Andrew Magee	270	Jay Don Blake	272	Tucson National GC, Tucson, AZ	72/7148
			Loren Roberts		Starr Pass GC, Tucson, AZ	72/7010
			Vijay Singh			
			Steve Stricker			
1995	Phil Mickelson	269	Jim Gallagher, Jr.	270	Tucson National GC, Tucson, AZ	72/7148
			Scott Simpson		Starr Pass GC, Tucson, AZ	72/7010

Tournament Record: 263 -- Lloyd Mangrum, 1949 (El Rio G&CC); Phil Rodgers, 1962 (El Rio G&CC); Johnny Miller, 1975 (Tucson National)

Current Course Records: Tucson National GC 61 -- Johnny Miller, 1975
Starr Pass GC 61 -- Mark Wiebe, 1988

KEY: *=Playoff #=Amateur

1995 PHOENIX OPEN

TPC of Scottsdale, Scottsdale, AZ **Purse: $1,300,000**
Par: 35-36--71 **Yards: 6,992** **January 26-29, 1995**

LEADERS: First Round--Duffy Waldorf shot a 7-under-par 64 to lead Hale Irwin by two strokes. **Second Round--**Irwin and Ben Crenshaw shared the lead at 10-under-par 132, two strokes ahead of Jim Carter and Tom Watson. **Third Round--**Crenshaw, at 11-under-par 202, held a one-stroke lead over Steve Lowery, John Adams, Vijay Singh, Billy Mayfair and Jim Furyk.

CUT: 70 players at 1-under-par 141.

PRO-AM: Rain caused the cancellation of the pro-am after nine holes. Each of the 32 professionals received $234.38.

WEATHER: After rain on Wednesday, Thursday was overcast and chilly with high winds and temperatures in the 50s. Partly cloudy and in the 60s Friday. Saturday and Sunday were magnificent.

Winner: Vijay Singh 70-67-66-66 269 $234,000.00

(Won playoff with par-4 on first extra hole)

Player	Pos	Scores	Total	Money
Billy Mayfair	2	69-67-67-66	269	$140,400.00
Ben Crenshaw	3	68-64-70-69	271	$88,400.00
Bruce Lietzke	T 4	72-65-69-66	272	$53,733.34
Steve Jones	T 4	68-69-68-67	272	$53,733.33
Payne Stewart	T 4	71-68-67-66	272	$53,733.33
John Adams	T 7	71-66-66-70	273	$37,830.00
Mark Calcavecchia	T 7	72-67-66-68	273	$37,830.00
Hale Irwin	T 7	66-66-72-69	273	$37,830.00
Steve Lowery	T 7	70-68-65-70	273	$37,830.00
Joe Ozaki	T 7	68-71-67-67	273	$37,830.00
Jim Carter	T12	70-64-73-67	274	$24,700.00
Jim Furyk	T12	67-68-68-71	274	$24,700.00
Donnie Hammond	T12	70-68-68-68	274	$24,700.00
Tom Purtzer	T12	69-68-69-68	274	$24,700.00
Steve Stricker	T12	70-68-67-69	274	$24,700.00
Tom Watson	T12	67-67-71-69	274	$24,700.00
Rick Fehr	T18	71-70-65-69	275	$17,550.00
Blaine McCallister	T18	68-69-71-67	275	$17,550.00
John Morse	T18	72-69-66-68	275	$17,550.00
John Wilson	T18	69-66-69-71	275	$17,550.00
Paul Azinger	T22	72-68-69-67	276	$13,000.00
Dan Forsman	T22	71-67-71-67	276	$13,000.00
Tom Lehman	T22	70-71-66-69	276	$13,000.00
Doug Tewell	T22	69-69-70-68	276	$13,000.00
Joel Edwards	T26	71-70-69-67	277	$10,010.00
Steve Elkington	T26	68-71-68-70	277	$10,010.00
Steve Pate	T26	71-69-71-66	277	$10,010.00
Bob Estes	T29	69-71-71-67	278	$8,265.84
Loren Roberts	T29	72-67-67-72	278	$8,265.84
Ronnie Black	T29	69-70-69-70	278	$8,265.83
David Edwards	T29	73-67-68-70	278	$8,265.83
Gil Morgan	T29	70-67-71-70	278	$8,265.83
Grant Waite	T29	69-71-71-67	278	$8,265.83
Woody Austin	T35	71-68-69-71	279	$6,272.50
David Feherty	T35	73-66-69-71	279	$6,272.50
Bob Lohr	T35	67-72-69-71	279	$6,272.50
Andrew Magee	T35	69-71-69-70	279	$6,272.50
Phil Mickelson	T35	70-66-70-73	279	$6,272.50
Kirk Triplett	T35	74-65-67-73	279	$6,272.50
Jay Don Blake	T41	68-70-70-72	280	$4,426.50
Bill Glasson	T41	69-70-69-72	280	$4,426.50
Yoshi Mizumaki	T41	70-69-72-69	280	$4,426.50
Kenny Perry	T41	73-68-67-72	280	$4,426.50
Dillard Pruitt	T41	71-68-71-70	280	$4,426.50
Gene Sauers	T41	72-65-70-73	280	$4,426.50
Bob Tway	T41	73-67-69-71	280	$4,426.50
Fuzzy Zoeller	T41	70-71-67-72	280	$4,426.50
Mark Carnevale	T49	72-68-67-74	281	$3,328.00
Bobby Wadkins	T49	69-68-75-69	281	$3,328.00
Skip Kendall	T51	69-69-71-73	282	$3,128.67
Jim McGovern	T51	71-70-70-71	282	$3,128.67
Pat Bates	T51	69-70-72-71	282	$3,128.66
Nick Faldo	T54	71-69-76-67	283	$2,964.00
Paul Goydos	T54	72-68-73-70	283	$2,964.00
Mike Hulbert	T54	73-68-75-67	283	$2,964.00
Howard Twitty	T54	72-69-70-72	283	$2,964.00
Duffy Waldorf	T54	64-72-72-75	283	$2,964.00
Brian Claar	T59	69-72-69-74	284	$2,847.00
Jay Delsing	T59	72-67-70-75	284	$2,847.00
Davis Love III	T59	72-67-76-69	284	$2,847.00
Dave Stockton, Jr.	T59	72-68-74-70	284	$2,847.00
Lee Janzen	63	68-71-75-71	285	$2,782.00
Michael Bradley	T64	68-69-73-76	286	$2,743.00
David Ogrin	T64	71-70-74-71	286	$2,743.00
Bob Burns	T66	68-72-73-74	287	$2,652.00
Brandel Chamblee	T66	73-68-73-73	287	$2,652.00
Neal Lancaster	T66	68-70-72-77	287	$2,652.00
Mike Standly	T66	69-72-77-69	287	$2,652.00
Mike Sullivan	T66	72-69-73-73	287	$2,652.00

The following players did not finish (C=cut, W=withdrew, D=disqualified)

C—142- Alan Bratton, Brad Bryant, Mike Heinen, John Huston, Peter Jacobsen, Justin Leonard, Jeff Maggert, Rocco Mediate, Chris Perry, Dan Pohl, Jeff Sluman, Curtis Strange, Lanny Wadkins. **143-** Billy Andrade, Keith Clearwater, John Daly, Brad Faxon, Fred Funk, Gary McCord, Don Pooley. **144-** Dave Barr, Guy Boros, Russ Cochran, Nolan Henke, Mike Springer. **145-** Kelly Gibson, Ed Humenik, Jerry Pate, Dennis Paulson, Steve Rintoul. **146-** Andy Bean, Chris DiMarco, Robert Gamez, Jay Haas, Hal Sutton, Mark Wiebe. **147-** Fulton Allem, Bob Gilder, Jesper Parnevik, Paul Stankowski, Ted Tryba. **148-** Scott Gump, Mark Gurnow, Gary Hallberg, Brian Kamm, Chris Stutts. **149-**Tommy Armour III, Glen Day, Clark Dennis, Robin Freeman, Dicky Pride. **150-** Curt Byrum, Brian Henninger. **151-** Greg Kraft. **152-** Joey Sindelar, Mike Swartz. **153-** Jim Gallagher, Jr. **154-** Ron Faria. **157-** Kim Dolan. **W—149-**Ken Green, **76-** Jodie Mudd, **80-** John Inman.

PHOENIX OPEN

PHOENIX OPEN

TOURNAMENT HISTORY

Year	Winner	Score	Runner-up	Score	Location	Par/Yards
PHOENIX OPEN INVITATIONAL						
1935	Ky Laffoon	281	Craig Wood	285	Phoenix CC, Phoenix, AZ	71/6726
1936-1938	No Tournaments					
1939	Byron Nelson	198	Ben Hogan	210	Phoenix CC, Phoenix, AZ	71/6726
1940	Ed Oliver	205	Ben Hogan	206	Phoenix CC, Phoenix, AZ	71/6726
1941-1943	No Tournaments					
1944	*Harold McSpaden	273	Byron Nelson	273	Phoenix CC, Phoenix, AZ	71/6726
1945	Byron Nelson	274	Denny Shute	276	Phoenix CC, Phoenix, AZ	71/6726
1946	*Ben Hogan	273	Herman Keiser	273	Phoenix CC, Phoenix, AZ	71/6726
1947	Ben Hogan	270	Lloyd Mangrum Ed Oliver	277	Phoenix CC, Phoenix, AZ	71/6726
1948	Bobby Locke	268	Jimmy Demaret	269	Phoenix CC, Phoenix, AZ	71/6726
1949	*Jimmy Demaret	278	Ben Hogan	278	Phoenix CC, Phoenix, AZ	71/6726
1950	Jimmy Demaret	269	Sam Snead	270	Phoenix CC, Phoenix, AZ	71/6726
1951	Lew Worsham	272	Lawson Little	273	Phoenix CC, Phoenix, AZ	71/6726
1952	Lloyd Mangrum	274	E. J. Harrison	279	Phoenix CC, Phoenix, AZ	71/6726
1953	Lloyd Mangrum	272	Johnny Bulla Ted Kroll Bo Wininger	278	Phoenix CC, Phoenix, AZ	71/6726
1954	*Ed Furgol	272	Cary Middlecoff	272	Phoenix CC, Phoenix, AZ	71/6726
1955	Gene Littler	275	Billy Maxwell Johnny Palmer	276	Arizona CC, Phoenix, AZ	70/6216
1956	Cary Middlecoff	276	Mike Souchak	279	Phoenix CC, Phoenix, AZ	71/6726
1957	Billy Casper	271	Cary Middlecoff Mike Souchak	274	Arizona CC, Phoenix, AZ	70/6216
1958	Ken Venturi	274	Walter Burkemo Jay Hebert	275	Phoenix CC, Phoenix, AZ	71/6726
1959	Gene Littler	268	Art Wall	269	Arizona CC, Phoenix, AZ	70/6216
1960	*Jack Fleck	273	Bill Collins	273	Phoenix CC, Phoenix, AZ	71/6726
1961	*Arnold Palmer	270	Doug Sanders	270	Arizona CC, Phoenix, AZ	70/6216
1962	Arnold Palmer	269	Billy Casper Don Fairfield Bob McCallister Jack Nicklaus	281	Phoenix CC, Phoenix, AZ	71/6726
1963	Arnold Palmer	273	Gary Player	274	Arizona CC, Phoenix, AZ	70/6216
1964	Jack Nicklaus	271	Bob Brue	274	Phoenix CC, Phoenix, AZ	71/6726
1965	Rod Funseth	274	Bert Yancey	277	Arizona CC, Phoenix, AZ	70/6216
1966	Dudley Wysong	278	Gardner Dickinson	279	Phoenix CC, Phoenix, AZ	71/6726
1967	Julius Boros	272	Ken Still	273	Arizona CC, Phoenix, AZ	70/6216
1968	George Knudson	272	Julius Boros Sam Carmichael Jack Montgomery	275	Phoenix CC, Phoenix, AZ	71/6726
1969	Gene Littler	263	Miller Barber Don January Billy Maxwell	265	Arizona CC, Phoenix, AZ	70/6216
1970	Dale Douglass	271	Howie Johnson Gene Littler	272	Phoenix CC, Phoenix, AZ	71/6726
1971	Miller Barber	261	Billy Casper Dan Sikes	263	Arizona CC, Phoenix, AZ	70/6216
1972	*Homero Blancas	273	Lanny Wadkins	273	Phoenix CC, Phoenix, AZ	71/6726
1973	Bruce Crampton	268	Steve Melnyk Lanny Wadkins	269	Arizona CC, Phoenix, AZ	70/6216
1974	Johnny Miller	271	Lanny Wadkins	272	Phoenix CC, Phoenix, AZ	71/6726
1975	Johnny Miller	260	Jerry Heard	274	Phoenix CC, Phoenix, AZ	71/6726
1976	Bob Gilder	268	Roger Maltbie	270	Phoenix CC, Phoenix, AZ	71/6726
1977	*Jerry Pate	277	Dave Stockton	277	Phoenix CC, Phoenix, AZ	71/6726
1978	Miller Barber	272	Jerry Pate Lee Trevino	273	Phoenix CC, Phoenix, AZ	71/6726

PHOENIX OPEN

TOURNAMENT HISTORY

Year	Winner	Score	Runner-up	Score	Location	Par/Yards
1979	~Ben Crenshaw	199	Jay Haas	200	Phoenix CC, Phoenix, AZ	71/6726
1980	Jeff Mitchell	272	Rik Massengale	276	Phoenix CC, Phoenix, AZ	71/6726
1981	David Graham	268	Lon Hinkle	269	Phoenix CC, Phoenix, AZ	71/6726
1982	Lanny Wadkins	263	Jerry Pate	269	Phoenix CC, Phoenix, AZ	71/6726
1983	*Bob Gilder	271	Rex Caldwell Johnny Miller Mark O'Meara	271	Phoenix CC, Phoenix, AZ	71/6726
1984	Tom Purtzer	268	Corey Pavin	269	Phoenix CC, Phoenix, AZ	71/6726
1985	Calvin Peete	270	Morris Hatalsky Doug Tewell	272	Phoenix CC, Phoenix, AZ	71/6726
1986	Hal Sutton	267	Calvin Peete Tony Sills	269	Phoenix CC, Phoenix, AZ	71/6726
1987	Paul Azinger	268	Hal Sutton	269	TPC of Scottsdale, Scottsdale, AZ	71/6992
1988	*Sandy Lyle	269	Fred Couples	269	TPC of Scottsdale, Scottsdale, AZ	71/6992
1989	Mark Calcavecchia	263	Chip Beck	270	TPC of Scottsdale, Scottsdale, AZ	71/6992
1990	Tommy Armour III	267	Jim Thorpe	272	TPC of Scottsdale, Scottsdale, AZ	71/6992
1991	Nolan Henke	268	Gil Morgan Curtis Strange Tom Watson	269	TPC of Scottsdale, Scottsdale, AZ	71/6992
1992	Mark Calcavecchia	264	Duffy Waldorf	269	TPC of Scottsdale, Scottsdale, AZ	71/6992
1993	Lee Janzen	273	Andrew Magee	275	TPC of Scottsdale, Scottsdale, AZ	71/6992
1994	Bill Glasson	268	Bob Estes	271	TPC of Scottsdale, Scottsdale, AZ	71/6992
1995	*Vijay Singh	269	Billy Mayfair	269	TPC of Scottsdale, Scottsdale, AZ	71/6992

Tournament Record: 260 -- Johnny Miller, 1975 (Phoenix CC)
Current Course Record: 62 -- Doug Tewell, 1987

KEY: *=Playoff ~=Weather-shortened

1995 AT&T PEBBLE BEACH NATIONAL PRO-AM

Pebble Beach GL, Pebble Beach, CA **Purse: $1,400,000**
(Host Course) Par: 72 Yards: 6,799
Spyglass Hill GC Par: 72 Yards: 6,810 **February 2-5, 1995**
Poppy Hills CC Par: 72 Yards: 6,865

LEADERS: First Round--Davis Love III (PH) shot a 7-under-par 65 and led Nick Faldo (PH) by one stroke. **Second Round--**Brad Faxon (PH), at 10-under-par 134, led by one over Guy Boros (PB), Fuzzy Zoeller (PB) and Tom Watson (SH). **Third Round--**Kenny Perry (PB), at 13-under-par 203, led by three over Boros (SH), Faxon (PB), David Duval (PB) and Peter Jacobsen (PB).

CUT: 75 players at 1-under-par 215; one player (Jim McGovern) withdrew after making the cut. 64 played on Sunday at 2-under-par 214. Team cut was 20-under-par 196.

PRO-AM: $70,000. David Duval-Hughes Norton, 254, $7,000.

WEATHER: Sunny and warm on Thursday and Friday. Saturday and Sunday were overcast with some fog.

Winner: Peter Jacobsen 67-73-66-65 271 $252,000.00

Player	Pos	Scores	Total	Money
David Duval	2	72-67-67-67	273	$151,200.00
Davis Love III	T 3	65-71-71-68	275	$81,200.00
Kenny Perry	T 3	68-68-67-72	275	$81,200.00
Payne Stewart	5	71-67-69-70	277	$56,000.00
Guy Boros	T 6	69-66-71-72	278	$46,900.00
Brad Faxon	T 6	70-64-72-72	278	$46,900.00
Jack Nicklaus	T 6	71-70-67-70	278	$46,900.00
John Adams	T 9	72-66-71-70	279	$36,400.00
Emlyn Aubrey	T 9	70-69-68-72	279	$36,400.00
Nick Faldo	T 9	66-72-69-72	279	$36,400.00
Mark O'Meara	T 9	73-68-70-68	279	$36,400.00
Mark Calcavecchia	T13	72-70-69-69	280	$24,733.34
Fuzzy Zoeller	T13	68-67-76-69	280	$24,733.34
Ben Crenshaw	T13	73-72-69-66	280	$24,733.33
Andrew Magee	T13	70-69-70-71	280	$24,733.33
Steve Stricker	T13	74-72-64-70	280	$24,733.33
Tom Watson	T13	70-65-73-72	280	$24,733.33
Steve Elkington	T19	74-70-68-69	281	$18,900.00
Blaine McCallister	T19	70-72-67-72	281	$18,900.00
Mark Brooks	T21	70-69-74-69	282	$12,460.00
Jim Carter	T21	70-70-69-73	282	$12,460.00
Fred Funk	T21	69-71-72-70	282	$12,460.00
Jim Furyk	T21	70-68-74-70	282	$12,460.00
Bob Lohr	T21	71-69-73-69	282	$12,460.00
Steve Lowery	T21	76-74-64-68	282	$12,460.00
Jeff Maggert	T21	71-68-70-73	282	$12,460.00
Hal Sutton	T21	69-69-70-74	282	$12,460.00
Kirk Triplett	T21	71-70-70-71	282	$12,460.00
Tommy Tolles	T21	74-66-73-69	282	$12,460.00
Robin Freeman	T31	72-72-69-70	283	$7,140.00
Steve Gotsche	T31	70-70-72-71	283	$7,140.00
Mike Heinen	T31	72-67-70-74	283	$7,140.00
Ed Humenik	T31	70-69-74-70	283	$7,140.00
Brian Kamm	T31	76-70-68-69	283	$7,140.00
Tom Purtzer	T31	72-68-73-70	283	$7,140.00
Loren Roberts	T31	68-72-69-74	283	$7,140.00
Charlie Rymer	T31	71-70-71-71	283	$7,140.00
Craig Stadler	T31	72-71-70-70	283	$7,140.00
Ray Stewart	T31	72-70-70-71	283	$7,140.00
Duffy Waldorf	T31	70-71-69-73	283	$7,140.00
Willie Wood	T31	70-74-70-69	283	$7,140.00
Billy Andrade	T43	71-70-72-71	284	$4,368.00
Rick Fehr	T43	72-73-68-71	284	$4,368.00
Keith Fergus	T43	72-71-71-70	284	$4,368.00
Bob Gilder	T43	72-68-74-70	284	$4,368.00
Peter Jordan	T43	74-68-70-72	284	$4,368.00
Justin Leonard	T43	71-71-71-71	284	$4,368.00
Rocco Mediate	T43	70-69-70-75	284	$4,368.00
John Cook	T50	74-69-70-72	285	$3,376.80
David Frost	T50	71-72-68-74	285	$3,376.80
Mike Hulbert	T50	71-72-68-74	285	$3,376.80
Gil Morgan	T50	73-69-68-75	285	$3,376.80
Jay Williamson	T50	70-71-71-73	285	$3,376.80
Chris Perry	55	73-69-69-75	286	$3,220.00
Kawika Cotner	56	67-73-72-75	287	$3,192.00
Paul Azinger	T57	74-70-70-74	288	$3,122.00
Larry Mize	T57	72-69-72-75	288	$3,122.00
Jeff Sluman	T57	73-71-68-76	288	$3,122.00
Dave Stockton	T57	69-72-71-76	288	$3,122.00
Howard Twitty	61	69-72-73-75	289	$3,052.00
Don Reese	62	72-70-69-79	290	$3,024.00
Brad Bryant	T63	71-73-70-77	291	$2,982.00
Steve Rintoul	T63	72-70-69-80	291	$2,982.00

The following players did not finish **(C=cut, W=withdrew, D=disqualified)**

T65 ($2,800.00 each)—215- Ronnie Black, Bill Britton, Patrick Burke, Dan Forsman, Scott Gump, Jerry Haas, Hale Irwin, Corey Pavin, Paul Stankowski, Dave Stockton, Jr. **C—216-** Joe Acosta, Jr., Keith Clearwater, Lennie Clements, Clark Dennis, Paul Goydos, Dudley Hart, Eduardo Romero, Mark Wiebe. **217-** Tommy Armour III, Woody Austin, Phil Blackmar, Steve Haskins, Jonathan Kaye, Shawn McEntee, John Morse, Jim Nelford, Scott Simpson, Vijay Singh, Bobby Wadkins. **218-** Bob Borowicz, Jim Gallagher, Jr., Lee Janzen, Bill Kratzert, Tom Lehman, Larry Nelson, Carl Paulson, David Sutherland, D.A. Weibring. **219-** J.L. Lewis, Doug Martin, Johnny Miller, David Ogrin, Jesper Parnevik, Joey Rassett, Larry Rinker, Lee Rinker, Grant Waite, Jeff Wilson. **220-** Brian Claar, Greg Kraft, Phil Mickelson, Jack Nicklaus II, Mike Springer, Ted Tryba. **221-** Pat Bates, Chip Beck, George Burns, Jay Delsing, Chris DiMarco, Gary Hallberg, Steve Hart, Roger Maltbie, Arnold Palmer, Jerry Pate, Dennis Paulson. **222-** Jeff Leonard, Dick Mast, Scott McCarron, Dicky Pride, Mike Reid, Mike Smith, Dicky Thompson, John Wilson. **223-** Bobby Clampett, Mike Donald, Joel Edwards, Scott Ford, J.P. Hayes, Tom Hearn, Ryan Howison, Mick Soli, Omar Uresti, Mark Wurtz. **224-** Michael Allen, Mark Hayes, Brian Henninger, Barry Jaeckel, Bill Porter. **225-** Mark Carnevale, Kelly Gibson, Skip Kendall, Tim Loustalot, Laird Small, Mike Standly, Tray Tyner, Bruce Vaughan. **226-** Marco Dawson, Dave Eichelberger, John Flannery. **227-** Billy Ray Brown, Ted Schulz. **228-** Clark Burroughs, Charlie Gibson, Lon Hinkle, John Miller, Jr., Tony Sills, Kevin Sutherland. **229-** Bart Bryant, David Graham, Greg Powers. **230-** Dennis Trixler. **232-** Mike Steiner. **233-** Ian Baker-Finch. **234-** Mike Brisky, Bill McKinney. **W—213-**Jim McGovern.

AT&T PEBBLE BEACH NATIONAL PRO-AM

TOURNAMENT HISTORY

Year	Winner	Score	Runner-up	Score	Location	Par/Yards
BING CROSBY PROFESSIONAL-AMATEUR						
1937	Sam Snead	68	George Von Elm	72	Rancho Santa Fe CC, San Diego, CA	73/6769
1938	Sam Snead	139	Jimmy Hines	141	Rancho Santa Fe CC, San Diego, CA	73/6769
1939	Dutch Harrison	138	Byron Nelson	139	Rancho Santa Fe CC, San Diego, CA	73/6769
			Horton Smith			
1940	Ed Oliver	135	Victor Ghezzi	138	Rancho Santa Fe CC, San Diego, CA	73/6769
1941	Sam Snead	136	Craig Wood	137	Rancho Santa Fe CC, San Diego, CA	73/6769
1942	# John Dawson	133	Leland Gibson	136		
			Lloyd Mangrum		Rancho Santa Fe CC, San Diego, CA	73/6769
1943—1946 No Tournaments						
1947	Tie-Ed Furgol	213			Cypress Point CC, Monterey Peninsula, CA	72/6506
	George Fazio				Monterey Peninsula CC, Monterey Peninsula, CA	71/6356
					Pebble Beach GL, Monterey Peninsula, CA	72/6815
1948	Lloyd Mangrum	205	Stan Leonard	210	Cypress Point CC, Monterey Peninsula, CA	72/6506
					Monterey Peninsula CC, Monterey Peninsula, CA	71/6356
					Pebble Beach GL, Monterey Peninsula, CA	72/6815
1949	Ben Hogan	208	Jim Ferrier	210	Cypress Point CC, Monterey Peninsula, CA	72/6506
					Monterey Peninsula CC, Monterey Peninsula, CA	71/6356
					Pebble Beach GL, Monterey Peninsula, CA	72/6815
1950	Tie-Sam Snead	214			Cypress Point CC, Monterey Peninsula, CA	72/6506
	Jack Burke, Jr				Monterey Peninsula CC, Monterey Peninsula, CA	71/6356
	Smiley Quick				Pebble Beach GL, Monterey Peninsula, CA	72/6815
	Dave Douglas					
1951	Byron Nelson	209	Cary Middlecoff	212	Cypress Point CC, Monterey Peninsula, CA	72/6506
					Monterey Peninsula CC, Monterey Peninsula, CA	71/6356
					Pebble Beach GL, Monterey Peninsula, CA	72/6815
1952	Jimmy Demaret	145	Art Bell	147	Cypress Point CC, Monterey Peninsula, CA	72/6506
					Monterey Peninsula CC, Monterey Peninsula, CA	71/6356
					Pebble Beach GL, Monterey Peninsula, CA	72/6815
THE BING CROSBY PROFESSIONAL-AMATEUR INVITATIONAL						
1953	Lloyd Mangrum	204	Julius Boros	208	Cypress Point CC, Monterey Peninsula, CA	72/6506
					Pebble Beach GL, Monterey Pennsula, CA	72/6815
1954	Dutch Harrison	210	Jimmy Demaret	211	Cypress Point CC, Monterey Peninsula, CA	72/6506
					Monterey Peninsula CC, Monterey Peninsula, CA	71/6356
					Pebble Beach GL, Monterey Peninsula, CA	72/6815
1955	Cary Middlecoff	209	Julius Boros	213	Cypress Point CC, Monterey Peninsula, CA	72/6506
			Paul McGuire		Monterey Peninsula CC, Monterey Peninsula, CA	71/6356
					Pebble Beach GL, Monterey Peninsula, CA	72/6815
BING CROSBY NATIONAL PROFESSIONAL-AMATEUR GOLF CHAMPIONSHIP						
1956	Cary Middlecoff	202	Mike Souchak	207	Cypress Point CC, Monterey Peninsula, CA	72/6506
					Monterey Peninsula CC, Monterey Peninsula, CA	71/6356
					Pebble Beach GL, Monterey Peninsula, CA	72/6815
1957	Jay Hebert	213	Cary Middlecoff	215	Cypress Point CC, Monterey Peninsula, CA	72/6506
					Monterey Peninsula CC, Monterey Peninsula, CA	71/6356
					Pebble Beach GL, Monterey Peninsula, CA	72/6815
1958	Billy Casper	277	Dave Marr	281	Cypress Point CC, Monterey Peninsula, CA	72/6506
					Monterey Peninsula CC, Monterey Peninsula, CA	71/6356
					Pebble Beach GL, Monterey Peninsula, CA	72/6815
BING CROSBY NATIONAL						
1959	Art Wall	279	Jimmy Demaret	281	Cypress Point CC, Monterey Peninsula, CA	72/6506
			Gene Littler		Monterey Peninsula CC, Monterey Peninsula, CA	71/6356
					Pebble Beach GL, Monterey Peninsula, CA	72/6815
1960	Ken Venturi	286	Julius Boros	289	Cypress Point CC, Monterey Peninsula, CA	72/6506
			Tommy Jacobs		Monterey Peninsula CC, Monterey Peninsula, CA	71/6356
					Pebble Beach GL, Monterey Peninsula, CA	72/6815
1961	Bob Rosburg	282	Roberto De Vicenzo	283	Cypress Point CC, Monterey Peninsula, CA	72/6506
			Dave Ragan		Monterey Peninsula CC, Monterey Peninsula, CA	71/6356
					Pebble Beach GL, Monterey Peninsula, CA	72/6815

AT&T PEBBLE BEACH NATIONAL PRO-AM

TOURNAMENT HISTORY

Year	Winner	Score	Runner-up	Score	Location	Par/Yards
1962	*Doug Ford	286	Joe Campbell	286	Cypress Point CC, Monterey Peninsula, CA Monterey Peninsula CC, Monterey Peninsula, CA Pebble Beach GL, Monterey Peninsula, CA	72/6506 71/6356 72/6815
1963	Billy Casper	285	Dave Hill Jack Nicklaus Gary Player Bob Rosburg Art Wall	286	Cypress Point CC, Monterey Peninsula, CA Monterey Peninsula CC, Monterey Peninsula, CA Pebble Beach GL, Monterey Peninsula, CA	72/6506 71/6356 72/6815
BING CROSBY NATIONAL PROFESSIONAL-AMATEUR						
1964	Tony Lema	284	Gay Brewer Bo Wininger	287	Cypress Point CC, Monterey Peninsula, CA Monterey Peninsula CC, Monterey Peninsula, CA Pebble Beach GL, Monterey Peninsula, CA	72/6506 71/6356 72/6815
1965	Bruce Crampton	284	Tony Lema	287	Cypress Point CC, Monterey Peninsula, CA Monterey Peninsula CC, Monterey Peninsula, CA Pebble Beach GL, Monterey Peninsula, CA	72/6506 71/6356 72/6815
1966	Don Massengale	283	Arnold Palmer	284	Cypress Point CC, Monterey Peninsula, CA Monterey Peninsula CC, Monterey Peninsula, CA Pebble Beach GL, Monterey Peninsula, CA	72/6506 71/6356 72/6815
1967	Jack Nicklaus	284	Billy Casper	289	Pebble Beach GL, Monterey Peninsula, CA Cypress Point CC, Monterey Peninsula, CA Spyglass Hill GC, Monterey Peninsula, CA	72/6815 72/6506 72/6810
1968	*Johnny Pott	285	Billy Casper Bruce Devlin	285	Pebble Beach GL, Monterey Peninsula, CA Cypress Point CC, Monterey Peninsula, CA Spyglass Hill GC, Monterey Peninsula, CA	72/6815 72/6506 72/6810
1969	George Archer	283	Bob Dickson Dale Douglass Howie Johnson	284	Pebble Beach GL, Monterey Peninsula, CA Cypress Point CC, Monterey Peninsula, CA Spyglass Hill GC, Monterey Peninsula, CA	72/6815 72/6506 72/6810
1970	Bert Yancey	278	Jack Nicklaus	279	Pebble Beach GL, Monterey Peninsula, CA Cypress Point CC, Monterey Peninsula, CA Spyglass Hill GC, Monterey Peninsula, CA	72/6815 72/6506 72/6810
1971	Tom Shaw	278	Arnold Palmer	280	Pebble Beach GL, Monterey Peninsula, CA Cypress Point CC, Monterey Peninsula, CA Spyglass Hill GC, Monterey Peninsula, CA	72/6815 72/6506 72/6810
1972	*Jack Nicklaus	284	Johnny Miller	284	Pebble Beach GL, Monterey Peninsula, CA Cypress Point CC, Monterey Peninsula, CA Spyglass Hill GC, Monterey Peninsula, CA	72/6815 72/6506 72/6810
1973	*Jack Nicklaus	282	Ray Floyd Orville Moody	282	Pebble Beach GL, Monterey Peninsula, CA Cypress Point CC, Monterey Peninsula, CA Spyglass Hill GC, Monterey Peninsula, CA	72/6815 72/6506 72/6810
1974	~Johnny Miller	208	Grier Jones	212	Pebble Beach GL, Monterey Peninsula, CA Cypress Point CC, Monterey Peninsula, CA Spyglass Hill GC, Monterey Peninsula, CA	72/6815 72/6506 72/6810
1975	Gene Littler	280	Hubert Green	284	Pebble Beach GL, Monterey Peninsula, CA Cypress Point CC, Monterey Peninsula, CA Spyglass Hill GC, Monterey Peninsula, CA	72/6815 72/6506 72/6810
1976	Ben Crenshaw	281	Mike Morley	283	Pebble Beach GL, Monterey Peninsula, CA Cypress Point CC, Monterey Peninsula, CA Spyglass Hill GC, Monterey Peninsula, CA	72/6815 72/6506 72/6810
1977	Tom Watson	273	Tony Jacklin	274	Pebble Beach GL, Monterey Peninsula, CA Cypress Point CC, Monterey Peninsula, CA Monterey Peninsula CC, Monterey Peninsula, CA	72/6815 72/6506 71/6400
1978	*Tom Watson	280	Ben Crenshaw	280	Pebble Beach GL, Monterey Peninsula, CA Cypress Point CC, Monterey Peninsula, CA Spyglass Hill GC, Monterey Peninsula, CA	72/6815 72/6506 72/6810
1979	*Lon Hinkle	284	Andy Bean Mark Hayes	284	Pebble Beach GL, Monterey Peninsula, CA Cypress Point CC, Monterey Peninsula, CA Spyglass Hill GC, Monterey Peninsula, CA	72/6815 72/6506 72/6810

AT&T PEBBLE BEACH NATIONAL PRO-AM

TOURNAMENT HISTORY

Year	Winner	Score	Runner-up	Score	Location	Par/Yards
1980	George Burns	280	Dan Pohl	281	Pebble Beach GL, Monterey Peninsula, CA	72/6815
					Cypress Point CC, Monterey Peninsula, CA	72/6506
					Spyglass Hill GC, Monterey Peninsula, CA	72/6810
1981	~*John Cook	209	Bobby Clampett	209	Pebble Beach GL, Monterey Peninsula, CA	72/6815
			Ben Crenshaw		Cypress Point CC, Monterey Peninsula, CA	72/6506
			Hale Irwin		Spyglass Hill GC, Monterey Peninsula, CA	72/6810
			Barney Thompson			
1982	Jim Simons	274	Craig Stadler	276	Pebble Beach GL, Monterey Peninsula, CA	72/6815
					Cypress Point CC, Monterey Peninsula, CA	72/6506
					Spyglass Hill GC, Monterey Peninsula, CA	72/6810
1983	Tom Kite	276	Rex Caldwell	278	Pebble Beach GL, Monterey Peninsula, CA	72/6815
			Calvin Peete		Cypress Point CC, Monterey Peninsula, CA	72/6506
					Spyglass Hill GC, Monterey Peninsula CA	72/6810
1984	*Hale Irwin	278	Jim Nelford	278	Pebble Beach GL, Monterey Peninsula, CA	72/6815
					Cypress Point CC, Monterey Peninsula, CA	72/6506
					Spyglass Hill GC, Monterey Peninsula, CA	72/6810
1985	Mark O'Meara	283	Kikuo Arai	284	Pebble Beach GL, Monterey Peninsula, CA	72/6815
			Larry Rinker		Cypress Point CC, Monterey Peninsula, CA	72/6506
			Curtis Strange		Spyglass Hill GC, Monterey Peninsula, CA	72/6810
AT&T PEBBLE BEACH NATIONAL PRO-AM						
1986	~Fuzzy Zoeller	205	Payne Stewart	210	Pebble Beach GL, Monterey Peninsula, CA	72/6815
					Cypress Point CC, Monterey Peninsula, CA	72/6506
					Spyglass Hill GC, Monterey Peninsula, CA	72/6810
1987	Johnny Miller	278	Payne Stewart	279	Pebble Beach GL, Monterey Peninsula, CA	72/6815
					Cypress Point CC, Monterey Peninsula, CA	72/6506
					Spyglass Hill GC, Monterey Peninsula, CA	72/6810
1988	*Steve Jones	280	Bob Tway	280	Pebble Beach GL, Monterey Peninsula, CA	72/6815
					Cypress Point CC, Monterey Peninsula, CA	72/6506
					Spyglass Hill GC, Monterey Peninsula, CA	72/6810
1989	Mark O'Meara	277	Tom Kite	278	Pebble Beach GL, Monterey Peninsula, CA	72/6815
					Cypress Point CC, Monterey Peninsula, CA	72/6506
					Spyglass Hill GC, Monterey Peninsula, CA	72/6810
1990	Mark O'Meara	281	Kenny Perry	283	Pebble Beach GL, Monterey Peninsula, CA	72/6815
					Cypress Point CC, Monterey Peninsula, CA	72/6506
					Spyglass Hill GC, Monterey Peninsula, CA	72/6810
1991	Paul Azinger	274	Brian Claar	278	Pebble Beach GL, Monterey Peninsula, CA	72/6815
			Corey Pavin		Spyglass Hill GC, Monterey Peninsula, CA	72/6810
					Poppy Hills GC, Monterey Peninsula, CA	72/6865
1992	*Mark O'Meara	275	Jeff Sluman	275	Pebble Beach GL, Monterey Peninsula, CA	72/6815
					Spyglass Hill GC, Monterey Peninsula, CA	72/6810
					Poppy Hills GC, Monterey Peninsula, CA	72/6865
1993	Brett Ogle	276	Billy Ray Brown	279	Pebble Beach GL, Monterey Peninsula, CA	72/6815
					Spyglass Hill GC, Monterey Peninsula, CA	72/6810
					Poppy Hills GC, Monterey Peninsula, CA	72/6865
1994	Johnny Miller	281	Jeff Maggert	282	Pebble Beach GL, Monterey Peninsula, CA	72/6815
			Corey Pavin		Spyglass Hill GC, Monterey Peninsula, CA	72/6810
			Kirk Triplett		Poppy Hills GC, Monterey Peninsula, CA	72/6865
			Tom Watson			
1995	Peter Jacobsen	271	David Duval	273	Pebble Beach GL, Monterey Peninsula, CA	72/6815
					Spyglass Hill GC, Monterey Peninsula, CA	72/6810
					Poppy Hills GC, Monterey Peninsula, CA	72/6865

Tournament Record:	271--Peter Jacobsen, 1995	
Current Course Records:	Pebble Beach GL	62 -- Tom Kite, 1983
	Poppy Hills GC	64 -- Brad Faxon, 1995
	Spyglass Hill GC	64 -- Dan Forsman, 1993; Steve Lowery, 1995

KEY: *=Playoff ~=Weather shortened #=Amateur

1995 BUICK INVITATIONAL OF CALIFORNIA

BUICK INVITATIONAL

Torrey Pines GC, La Jolla, CA **Purse: $1,200,000**
South Course Par: 36-36--72 **Yards: 7,000**
(Host Course)
North Course: Par: 36-36--72 **Yards: 6,592** **February 9-12, 1995**

LEADERS: First Round--Jerry Haas (NC), Joel Edwards (SC), Chris DiMarco (NC), Dan Pohl (SC) and Phil Mickelson (NC), with 7-under-par 65s, led by one over Bob Burns (SC), Brandel Chamblee (SC), David Ogrin (NC), Payne Stewart (NC) and Brad Faxon (NC). **Second Round--**Chamblee (NC), at 12-under-par 132, led by one over Steve Stricker (NC) and Peter Jacobsen (SC). **Third Round--**Jacobsen (SC), at 15-under-par 201, led by three over Kirk Triplett (SC) and Hal Sutton (SC).

CUT: 85 players at 3-under-par 141.

PRO-AM: $15,000. South Individual--Loren Roberts, 67, $750. South Team --Loren Roberts, 56, $750. North Individual--Nick Faldo, Guy Boros, 66, $675 each. North Team--Steve Stricker, 53, $750.

WEATHER: Sunny and breezy every day.

Winner : Peter Jacobsen 68-65-68-68 269 $216,000.00

Player	Pos	Scores	Total	Money
Mark Calcavecchia	T 2	71-67-67-68	273	$79,200.00
Mike Hulbert	T 2	70-65-70-68	273	$79,200.00
Hal Sutton	T 2	67-69-68-69	273	$79,200.00
Kirk Triplett	T 2	69-69-66-69	273	$79,200.00
Dan Pohl	T 6	65-74-66-70	275	$41,700.00
Dillard Pruitt	T 6	69-70-68-68	275	$41,700.00
Brandel Chamblee	T 8	66-66-74-70	276	$33,600.00
Nolan Henke	T 8	68-66-73-69	276	$33,600.00
John Huston	T 8	69-71-67-69	276	$33,600.00
David Ogrin	T 8	66-69-74-67	276	$33,600.00
Brad Bryant	T12	72-67-69-69	277	$24,300.00
Brian Kamm	T12	69-71-70-67	277	$24,300.00
Davis Love III	T12	69-71-72-65	277	$24,300.00
Craig Stadler	T12	67-69-72-69	277	$24,300.00
Chip Beck	T16	70-70-71-67	278	$15,240.00
Danny Briggs	T16	69-69-70-70	278	$15,240.00
Bob Estes	T16	69-69-71-69	278	$15,240.00
J.P. Hayes	T16	67-71-72-68	278	$15,240.00
Ed Humenik	T16	69-71-69-69	278	$15,240.00
Bob Lohr	T16	72-69-67-70	278	$15,240.00
Phil Mickelson	T16	65-69-75-69	278	$15,240.00
Payne Stewart	T16	66-73-67-72	278	$15,240.00
John Wilson	T16	71-69-73-65	278	$15,240.00
Jay Don Blake	T16	69-72-69-68	278	$15,240.00
Fred Funk	T26	69-70-72-68	279	$8,700.00
Scott Gump	T26	70-68-70-71	279	$8,700.00
Steve Lowery	T26	68-69-70-72	279	$8,700.00
Blaine McCallister	T26	68-70-72-69	279	$8,700.00
Dennis Paulson	T26	67-68-72-72	279	$8,700.00
Loren Roberts	T26	72-69-72-66	279	$8,700.00
John Adams	T32	70-67-71-72	280	$6,226.67
Ronnie Black	T32	69-71-67-73	280	$6,226.67
Brad Faxon	T32	66-73-70-71	280	$6,226.67
Kelly Gibson	T32	67-73-68-72	280	$6,226.67
Jerry Haas	T32	65-73-71-71	280	$6,226.67
Chris Perry	T32	73-66-69-72	280	$6,226.67
Joey Sindelar	T32	68-67-74-71	280	$6,226.66
Mike Smith	T32	73-68-71-68	280	$6,226.66
Scott Verplank	T32	67-74-70-69	280	$6,226.66
Jim Carter	T41	69-72-69-71	281	$4,200.00
Ben Crenshaw	T41	73-64-69-75	281	$4,200.00
Keith Fergus	T41	69-68-75-69	281	$4,200.00
Tom Kite	T41	75-66-67-73	281	$4,200.00
Jesper Parnevik	T41	72-64-74-71	281	$4,200.00
Steve Stricker	T41	67-66-75-73	281	$4,200.00
Howard Twitty	T41	68-67-74-72	281	$4,200.00
Tommy Armour III	T48	69-67-71-75	282	$3,204.00
Billy Mayfair	T48	69-72-70-71	282	$3,204.00
Billy Andrade	T50	71-68-73-71	283	$2,922.00
Donnie Hammond	T50	68-72-70-73	283	$2,922.00
Tom Hearn	T50	69-72-73-69	283	$2,922.00
Scott McCarron	T50	71-68-71-73	283	$2,922.00
Bob Burns	T54	66-69-74-75	284	$2,748.00
Curt Byrum	T54	68-70-76-70	284	$2,748.00
Chris DiMarco	T54	65-72-79-68	284	$2,748.00
Steve Hart	T54	71-68-74-71	284	$2,748.00
Lennie Clements	T58	74-66-72-73	285	$2,640.00
John Cook	T58	71-70-72-72	285	$2,640.00
Joel Edwards	T58	65-70-76-74	285	$2,640.00
Steve Gotsche	T58	68-71-76-70	285	$2,640.00
Mark O'Meara	T58	68-70-76-71	285	$2,640.00
Joe Acosta, Jr.	T63	69-72-70-75	286	$2,508.00
David Duval	T63	69-70-76-71	286	$2,508.00
John Mahaffey	T63	69-71-74-72	286	$2,508.00
Dave Stockton, Jr.	T63	73-68-72-73	286	$2,508.00
Bobby Wadkins	T63	68-68-76-74	286	$2,508.00
Curtis Strange	T63	71-70-75-70	286	$2,508.00
Emlyn Aubrey	T69	69-69-76-73	287	$2,352.00
Dan Forsman	T69	70-70-76-71	287	$2,352.00
Robin Freeman	T69	71-68-75-73	287	$2,352.00
J.L. Lewis	T69	71-70-73-73	287	$2,352.00
Yoshi Mizumaki	T69	68-70-73-76	287	$2,352.00
Lee Rinker	T69	67-73-73-74	287	$2,352.00
Brad Sherfy	T69	72-69-75-71	287	$2,352.00
Mike Brisky	76	67-69-82-70	288	$2,256.00
Craig Kanada	T77	68-73-74-74	289	$2,220.00
Steve Rintoul	T77	71-70-76-72	289	$2,220.00
Larry Nelson	T79	67-72-76-75	290	$2,172.00
Doug Tewell	T79	70-71-77-72	290	$2,172.00
Keith Clearwater	T81	70-67-82-72	291	$2,112.00
Paul Goydos	T81	68-71-75-77	291	$2,112.00
John Morse	T81	71-68-77-75	291	$2,112.00
Mark Wurtz	84	69-71-78-74	292	$2,064.00
Bruce Vaughan	85	73-68-75-77	293	$2,040.00

The following players did not finish (C=cut, W=withdrew, D=disqualified)

C—142- Bart Bryant, Russ Cochran, Nick Faldo, Dudley Hart, Steve Jones, Jonathan Kaye, Cliff Kresge, Scott Mahlberg, Jodie Mudd, Joe Ozaki, Tom Purtzer, Mike Reid, Scott Simpson, Duffy Waldorf. **143-** Guy Boros, Bill Britton, Steve Elkington, Scott Ford, Wayne Levi, Larry Mize, Carl Paulson, Dicky Pride, John Schroeder, Tony Sills, Harry Taylor, Greg Twiggs, Tray Tyner, Omar Uresti. **144-** Michael Bradley, Patrick Burke, Mark Carnevale, Kawika Cotner, Glen Day, Bill Glasson, Jay Haas, Jeff Leonard, Tim Loustalot, Gary McCord, Toshi Odate, Dicky Thompson, Bob Tway. **145-** George Burns, Gary Griggs, Eduardo Romero, Charlie Rymer, Tommy Tolles. **146-** David Feherty, Bill Porter, Ray Stewart, Ted Tryba. **147-** Marco Dawson, Paul Stankowski, Jay Williamson. **148-** Clark Burroughs. **149-** Woody Austin. **150-** Woody Blackburn, Ed Cuff, Greg Kraft. **151-** Pat Bates, Doug Martin, John Mason, Don Reese, Chris Riley. **152-** Paul Dietsche, Kenny Knox, Steve Pate, Joey Rassett. **153-** Hank Woodrome. **157-** Joey Sugar. **W— 73-** Rocco Mediate, **78-** Phil Blackmar.

BUICK INVITATIONAL

TOURNAMENT HISTORY

Year	Winner	Score	Runner-up	Score	Location	Par/Yards
SAN DIEGO OPEN						
1952	Ted Kroll	276	Jimmy Demaret	279	San Diego CC, San Diego, CA	72/6931
1953	Tommy Bolt	274	Doug Ford	277	San Diego CC, San Diego, CA	72/6931
1954	#Gene Littler	274	E. J. Harrison	278	Rancho Santa Fe GC, San Diego, CA	72/6797
CONVAIR-SAN DIEGO OPEN						
1955	Tommy Bolt	274	Johnny Palmer	276	Mission Valley CC, San Diego, CA	72/6619
1956	Bob Rosburg	270	Dick Mayer	272	Singing Hills GC, San Diego, CA	72/6573
SAN DIEGO OPEN INVITATIONAL						
1957	Arnold Palmer	271	Al Balding	272	Mission Valley CC, San Diego, CA	72/6619
1958	No Tournament					
1959	Marty Furgol	274	Joe Campbell Billy Casper Dave Ragan Mike Souchak Bo Wininger	275	Mission Valley CC, San Diego, CA	72/6619
1960	Mike Souchak	269	Johnny Pott	270	Mission Valley CC, San Diego, CA	72/6619
1961	*Arnold Palmer	271	Al Balding	271	Mission Valley CC, San Diego, CA	72/6619
1962	*Tommy Jacobs	277	Johnny Pott	277	Stardust CC, San Diego, CA	71/6725
1963	Gary Player	270	Tony Lema	271	Stardust CC, San Diego, CA	71/6725
1964	Art Wall	274	Tony Lema Bob Rosburg	276	Rancho Bernardo CC, San Diego, CA	72/6455
1965	*Wes Ellis	267	Billy Casper	267	Stardust CC, San Diego, CA	71/6725
1966	Billy Casper	268	Tommy Aaron Tom Weiskopf	272	Stardust CC, San Diego, CA	71/6725
1967	Bob Goalby	269	Gay Brewer	270	Stardust CC, San Diego, CA	71/6725
ANDY WILLIAMS-SAN DIEGO OPEN INVITATIONAL						
1968	Tom Weiskopf	273	Al Geiberger	274	Torrey Pines GC, San Diego, CA	72/N-6659, S-7021
1969	Jack Nicklaus	284	Gene Littler	285	Torrey Pines GC, San Diego, CA	72/N-6659, S-7021
1970	*Pete Brown	275	Tony Jacklin	275	Torrey Pines GC, San Diego, CA	72/N-6659, S-7021
1971	George Archer	272	Dave Eichelberger	275	Torrey Pines GC, San Diego, CA	72/N-6659, S-7021
1972	Paul Harney	275	Hale Irwin	276	Torrey Pines GC, San Diego, CA	72/N-6659, S-7021
1973	Bob Dickson	278	Billy Casper Bruce Crampton Grier Jones Phil Rodgers	281	Torrey Pines GC, San Diego, CA	72/N-6659, S-7021
1974	Bobby Nichols	275	Rod Curl Gene Littler	276	Torrey Pines GC, San Diego, CA	72/N-6659, S-7021
1975	*J.C. Snead	279	Ray Floyd Bobby Nichols	279	Torrey Pines GC, San Diego, CA	72/N-6659, S-7021
1976	J.C. Snead	272	Don Bies	273	Torrey Pines GC, San Diego, CA	72/N-6659, S-7021
1977	Tom Watson	269	Larry Nelson John Schroeder	274	Torrey Pines GC, San Diego, CA	72/N-6659, S-7021
1978	Jay Haas	278	Andy Bean Gene Littler John Schroeder	281	Torrey Pines GC, San Diego, CA	72/N-6659, S-7021
1979	Fuzzy Zoeller	282	Bill Kratzert Wayne Levi Artie McNickle Tom Watson	287	Torrey Pines GC, San Diego, CA	72/N-6659, S-7021
1980	*Tom Watson	275	D.A. Weibring	275	Torrey Pines GC, San Diego, CA	72/N-6659, S-7021
WICKES/ANDY WILLIAMS SAN DIEGO OPEN						
1981	*Bruce Lietzke	278	Ray Floyd Tom Jenkins	278	Torrey Pines GC, San Diego, CA	72/N-6659, S-7021
1982	Johnny Miller	270	Jack Nicklaus	271	Torrey Pines GC, San Diego, CA	72/N-6659, S-7021
ISUZU/ANDY WILLIAMS SAN DIEGO OPEN						
1983	Gary Hallberg	271	Tom Kite	272	Torrey Pines GC, San Diego, CA	72/N-6659, S-7021
1984	*Gary Koch	272	Gary Hallberg	272	Torrey Pines GC, San Diego, CA	72/N-6659, S-7021
1985	*Woody Blackburn	269	Ron Streck	269	Torrey Pines GC, San Diego, CA	72/N-6659, S-7021
SHEARSON LEHMAN BROTHERS ANDY WILLIAMS OPEN						
1986	~*Bob Tway	204	Bernhard Langer	204	Torrey Pines GC, San Diego, CA	72/N-6659, S-7021
1987	George Burns	266	J.C. Snead Bobby Wadkins	270	Torrey Pines GC, San Diego, CA	72/N-6659, S-7021

BUICK INVITATIONAL

TOURNAMENT HISTORY

Year	Winner	Score	Runner-up	Score	Location	Par/Yards
SHEARSON LEHMAN HUTTON ANDY WILLIAMS OPEN						
1988	Steve Pate	269	Jay Haas	270	Torrey Pines GC, San Diego, CA	72/N-6659, S-7021
SHEARSON LEHMAN HUTTON OPEN						
1989	Greg Twiggs	271	Steve Elkington Brad Faxon Mark O'Meara Mark Wiebe	273	Torrey Pines GC, San Diego, CA	72/N-6659, S-7021
1990	Dan Forsman	275	Tommy Armour III	277	Torrey Pines GC, San Diego, CA	72/N-6659, S-7021
SHEARSON LEHMAN BROTHERS OPEN						
1991	Jay Don Blake	268	Bill Sander	270	Torrey Pines GC, San Diego, CA	72/N-6659, S-7021
BUICK INVITATIONAL OF CALIFORNIA						
1992	~Steve Pate	200	Chip Beck	201	Torrey Pines GC, San Diego, CA	72/N-6659, S-7021
1993	Phil Mickelson	278	Dave Rummells	282	Torrey Pines GC, San Diego, CA	72/N-6659, S-7021
1994	Craig Stadler	268	Steve Lowery	269	Torrey Pines GC, San Diego, CA	72/N-6592, S-7000
1995	Peter Jacobsen	269	Mark Calcavecchia Mike Hulbert Hal Sutton Kirk Triplett	273	Torrey Pines GC, San Diego, CA	72/N-6592, S-7000

Tournament Record:	266--George Burns, 1987	
Current Course Record:	Torrey Pines North	61 -- Mark Brooks, 1990
	Torrey Pines South	63 -- Tommy Nakajima, 1984; Tom Watson, 1992

KEY: *=Playoff N=North S=South ~=Weather-shortened #=Amateur

1995 BOB HOPE CHRYSLER CLASSIC

Bermuda Dunes CC (Host Course)
Palm Desert, CA Par: 72 Yards: 6,927
Indian Wells CC Par: 72 Yards: 6,478
LaQuinta CC Par: 72 Yards: 6,901
Indian Ridge CC Par: 72 Yards: 7,037

Purse: $1,200,000
February 16-19, 1995

LEADERS: First Round--Kenny Perry (IR), with a course record 9-under-par 63, led by one over Curtis Strange (IW), Marco Dawson (IR), Robin Freeman (IW) and Jim Gallagher, Jr. (IW). **Second Round--**Harry Taylor (IR), at 14-under-par 130, led by three over Tommy Armour III (BD) and Chris Perry (IR). **Third Round--**Taylor (BD), at 20-under-par 196, led by two over K. Perry (IW). **Fourth Round--**K. Perry (LQ) led by two over Taylor (IW), Strange (BD), Tommy Tolles (IR) and David Duval (BD).

CUT: 74 players at 9-under-par 279.

PRO-AM: $5,000. Individual--Tommy Armour III, 228, $2,500.

WEATHER: Beautiful for all five days of the tournament.

Winner: Kenny Perry 63-71-64-67-70 335 $216,000.00

Player	Pos.	Scores	Total	Money
David Duval	2	67-68-65-67-69	336	$129,600.00
Dillard Pruitt	T 3	65-70-69-68-65	337	$62,400.00
Curtis Strange	T 3	64-73-67-63-70	337	$62,400.00
Tommy Tolles	T 3	66-69-68-64-70	337	$62,400.00
Robert Gamez	6	70-68-66-68-66	338	$43,200.00
Tommy Armour III	T 7	66-67-69-68-69	339	$34,920.00
Mark Brooks	T 7	67-68-69-65-70	339	$34,920.00
Kelly Gibson	T 7	65-71-67-67-69	339	$34,920.00
Donnie Hammond	T 7	67-69-66-69-68	339	$34,920.00
Harry Taylor	T 7	66-64-66-71-72	339	$34,920.00
Lee Rinker	T12	67-69-71-68-65	340	$26,400.00
Tray Tyner	T12	67-68-70-65-70	340	$26,400.00
Jim Gallagher, Jr.	T14	64-72-70-69-66	341	$22,200.00
Justin Leonard	T14	68-68-67-71-67	341	$22,200.00
Brandel Chamblee	T16	70-68-68-67-69	342	$15,760.00
Jim Furyk	T16	70-65-68-68-71	342	$15,760.00
Larry Mize	T16	67-69-69-69-68	342	$15,760.00
Mark O'Meara	T16	69-68-65-67-73	342	$15,760.00
Brad Sherfy	T16	71-67-69-66-69	342	$15,760.00
Scott Simpson	T16	66-69-69-68-70	342	$15,760.00
Paul Stankowski	T16	71-64-66-69-72	342	$15,760.00
Bob Tway	T16	70-67-67-69-69	342	$15,760.00
Kirk Triplett	T16	70-68-67-69-68	342	$15,760.00
Keith Fergus	T25	65-69-69-69-71	343	$9,800.00
Dennis Paulson	T25	69-69-70-66-69	343	$9,800.00
Fuzzy Zoeller	T25	68-68-66-70-71	343	$9,800.00
Chris DiMarco	T28	72-73-66-66-67	344	$8,160.00
Fred Funk	T28	66-69-70-69-70	344	$8,160.00
Steve Gotsche	T28	67-72-68-69-68	344	$8,160.00
John Huston	T28	67-70-68-70-69	344	$8,160.00
Steve Pate	T28	68-68-72-71-65	344	$8,160.00
Patrick Burke	T33	68-67-67-74-69	345	$6,205.72
Bob Burns	T33	68-69-65-73-70	345	$6,205.72
Tom Kite	T33	71-71-64-70-69	345	$6,205.72
Joe Acosta, Jr.	T33	66-68-72-72-67	345	$6,205.71
Marco Dawson	T33	64-70-70-70-71	345	$6,205.71
Neal Lancaster	T33	68-72-69-68-68	345	$6,205.71
Chris Perry	T33	66-67-71-69-72	345	$6,205.71
Yoshinori Kaneko	T40	70-66-69-71-70	346	$4,205.34
J.L. Lewis	T40	67-70-68-71-70	346	$4,205.34
Robin Freeman	T40	64-70-72-69-71	346	$4,205.33
Skip Kendall	T40	71-73-65-69-68	346	$4,205.33
Bob Lohr	T40	72-73-64-69-68	346	$4,205.33
John Mahaffey	T40	70-72-66-70-68	346	$4,205.33
Gil Morgan	T40	70-68-71-68-69	346	$4,205.33
Tony Sills	T40	71-71-67-70-67	346	$4,205.33
Mike Reid	T40	71-75-66-64-70	346	$4,205.34
Guy Boros	T49	67-72-68-70-70	347	$2,961.60
Bob Estes	T49	72-72-65-69-69	347	$2,961.60
Bob Gilder	T49	71-70-66-71-69	347	$2,961.60
Andrew Magee	T49	67-71-69-68-72	347	$2,961.60
Steve Rintoul	T49	73-67-69-69-69	347	$2,961.60
Emlyn Aubrey	T54	71-71-65-71-70	348	$2,688.00
Curt Byrum	T54	69-73-66-68-72	348	$2,688.00
Joel Edwards	T54	70-65-72-70-71	348	$2,688.00
Dan Forsman	T54	70-69-70-70-69	348	$2,688.00
Scott Hoch	T54	70-69-68-72-69	348	$2,688.00
Yoshi Mizumaki	T54	69-69-70-71-69	348	$2,688.00
Tim Simpson	T54	67-68-71-67-75	348	$2,688.00
Ted Tryba	T54	69-69-71-68-71	348	$2,688.00
John Wilson	T54	69-73-66-71-69	348	$2,688.00
Bart Bryant	T63	70-70-70-69-70	349	$2,532.00
Nolan Henke	T63	69-69-70-71-70	349	$2,532.00
Brian Henninger	T63	71-68-69-70-71	349	$2,532.00
Mike Springer	T63	69-68-72-68-72	349	$2,532.00
Woody Austin	T67	68-71-70-68-73	350	$2,448.00
J.P. Hayes	T67	71-70-69-69-71	350	$2,448.00
Mark Wurtz	T67	67-68-70-72-73	350	$2,448.00
Gary Hallberg	T70	70-71-69-68-73	351	$2,376.00
Corey Pavin	T70	69-70-72-68-72	351	$2,376.00
Grant Waite	T70	68-68-70-72-73	351	$2,376.00
Lanny Wadkins	73	69-74-68-68-73	352	$2,328.00
Ikuo Shirahama	74	71-67-68-71-80	357	$2,304.00

The following players did not finish (C=cut, W=withdrew, D=disqualified)

C— 280- Jay Don Blake, David Edwards, Steve Jones, Hal Sutton, Omar Uresti. **281-** Michael Bradley, Don Pooley, John Schroeder, D.A. Weibring. **282-** Lennie Clements, Glen Day, Blaine McCallister, David Ogrin, Charlie Rymer. **283-** John Adams, Brian Claar, Keith Clearwater, Russ Cochran, Rick Fehr, Jeff Leonard, Scott McCarron, Bruce Vaughan. **284-** Paul Goydos, Jay Haas, Joey Rassett, Gene Sauers, Jeff Sluman, Mike Standly, Dave Stockton,Jr., Doug Tewell. **285-** Jay Delsing, Clark Dennis, Jerry Haas, Mark Hayes, Ed Humenik, Doug Martin, Mark Pfeil. **286-** Dave Barr, Kawika Cotner, Eduardo Romero, Ted Schulz, Ray Stewart, Dicky Thompson. **287-** Ronnie Black, Barry Jaeckel. **288-** John Cook, Don Reese. **289-** Gary McCord, Bobby Wadkins. **291**-Dudley Hart. **293-** Jerry Pate. **294-** Hubert Green. **297-** Arnold Palmer. **298-** Rik Massengale.

BOB HOPE CHRYSLER CLASSIC

TOURNAMENT HISTORY

Year	Winner	Score	Runner-up	Score	Location	Par/Yards
PALM SPRINGS GOLF CLASSIC						
1960	Arnold Palmer	338	Fred Hawkins	341	Bermuda Dunes CC, Palm Springs, CA	72/6837
					Indian Wells CC, Indian Wells, CA	72/6478
					Tamarisk CC, Palm Springs, CA	72/6869
					Thunderbird CC, Palm Springs, CA	N/A
1961	Billy Maxwell	345	Doug Sanders	347	Bermuda Dunes CC, Palm Springs, CA	72/6837
					Indian Wells CC, Indian Wells, CA	72/6478
					Tamarisk CC, Palm Springs, CA	72/6869
					Thunderbird CC, Palm Springs, CA	N/A
					Eldorado CC, Palm Springs, CA	72/6708
1962	Arnold Palmer	342	Jay Hebert Gene Littler	345	Bermuda Dunes CC, Palm Springs, CA	72/6837
					Indian Wells CC, Indian Wells, CA	72/6478
					Tamarisk CC, Palm Springs, CA	72/6869
					Thunderbird CC, Palm Springs, CA	N/A
					Eldorado CC, Palm Springs, CA	72/6708
1963	*Jack Nicklaus	345	Gary Player	345	Bermuda Dunes CC, Palm Springs, CA	72/6837
					Indian Wells CC, Indian Wells, CA	72/6478
					Tamarisk CC, Palm Springs, CA	72/6869
					Eldorado CC, Palm Springs, CA	72/6708
1964	*Tommy Jacobs	353	Jimmy Demaret	353	Bermuda Dunes CC, Palm Springs, CA	72/6837
					Indian Wells CC, Indian Wells, CA	72/6478
					Eldorado CC, Palm Springs, CA	72/6708
					La Quinta CC, La Quinta, CA	72/6911
BOB HOPE DESERT CLASSIC						
1965	Billy Casper	348	Tommy Aaron Arnold Palmer	349	Bermuda Dunes CC, Palm Springs, CA	72/6837
					Indian Wells CC, Indian Wells, CA	72/6478
					Eldorado CC, Palm Springs, CA	72/6708
					La Quinta CC, La Quinta, CA	72/6911
1966	*Doug Sanders	349	Arnold Palmer	349	Bermuda Dunes CC, Palm Springs, CA	72/6837
					Indian Wells CC, Indian Wells, CA	72/6478
					Eldorado CC, Palm Springs, CA	72/6708
					La Quinta CC, La Quinta. CA	72/6911
1967	Tom Nieporte	349	Doug Sanders	350	Bermuda Dunes CC, Palm Springs, CA	72,6837
					Indian Wells CC, Indian Wells, CA	72/6478
					Eldorado CC, Palm Springs, CA	72/6708
					La Quinta CC, La Quinta, CA	72/6911
1968	*Arnold Palmer	348	Deane Beman	348	Bermuda Dunes CC, Palm Springs, CA	72/6837
					Indian Wells CC, Indian Wells, CA	72/6478
					Eldorado CC, Pa!m Springs, CA	72/6708
					La Quinta CC, La Quinta, CA	72/6911
1969	Billy Casper	345	Dave Hill	348	Bermuda Dunes CC, Palm Springs, CA	72/6837
					Indian Wells CC, Indian Wells, CA	72/6478
					Tamarisk CC, Palm Springs, CA	72/6869
					La Quinta CC, La Quinta, CA	72/6911
1970	Bruce Devlin	339	Larry Ziegler	343	Bermuda Dunes CC, Palm Springs, CA	72/6837
					Indian Wells CC, Indian Wells, CA	72/6478
					Eldorado CC, Palm Springs, CA	72/6708
					La Quinta CC, La Quinta, CA	72/6911
1971	*Arnold Palmer	342	Ray Floyd	342	Bermuda Dunes CC, Palm Springs, CA	72/6837
					Indian Wells CC, Indian Wells, CA	72/6478
					Tamarisk CC, Palm Springs, CA	72/6869
					La Quinta CC, La Quinta, CA	72/6911
1972	Bob Rosburg	344	Lanny Wadkins	345	Bermuda Dunes CC, Palm Springs, CA	72/6837
					Indian Wells CC, Indian Wells, CA	72/6478
					Eldorado CC, Palm Springs, CA	72/6708
					La Quinta CC, La Quinta, CA	72/6911

BOB HOPE CHRYSLER CLASSIC

TOURNAMENT HISTORY

Year	Winner	Score	Runner-up	Score	Location	Par/Yards
1973	Arnold Palmer	343	Johnny Miller	345	Bermuda Dunes CC, Palm Springs, CA	72/6837
			Jack Nicklaus		Indian Wells CC, Indian Wells, CA	72/6478
					Tamarisk CC, Palm Springs, CA	72/6869
					La Quinta CC, La Quinta, CA	72/6911
1974	Hubert Green	341	Bert Yancey	343	Bermuda Dunes CC, Palm Springs, CA	72/6837
					Indian Wells CC, Indian Wells, CA	72/6478
					Eldorado CC, Palm Springs, CA	72/6708
					La Quinta CC, La Quinta, CA	72/6911
1975	Johnny Miller	339	Bob Murphy	342	Bermuda Dunes CC, Palm Springs, CA	72/6837
					Indian Wells CC, Indian Wells, CA	72/6478
					Tamarisk CC, Palm Springs, CA	72/6869
					La Quinta CC, La Quinta, CA	72/6911
1976	Johnny Miller	344	Rik Massengale	347	Bermuda Dunes CC, Palm Springs, CA	72/6837
					Indian Wells CC, Indian Wells, CA	72/6478
					Eldorado CC, Palm Springs, CA	72/6708
					La Quinta CC, La Quinta, CA	72/6911
1977	Rik Massengale	337	Bruce Lietzke	343	Bermuda Dunes CC, Palm Springs, CA	72/6837
					Indian Wells CC, Indian Wells, CA	72/6478
					Tamarisk CC, Palm Springs, CA	72/6869
					La Quinta CC, La Quinta, CA	72/6911
1978	Bill Rogers	339	Jerry McGee	341	Bermuda Dunes CC, Palm Springs, CA	72/6837
					Indian Wells CC, Indian Wells, CA	72/6478
					Eldorado CC, Palm Springs, CA	72/6708
					La Quinta CC, La Quinta, CA	72/6911
1979	John Mahaffey	343	Lee Trevino	344	Bermuda Dunes CC, Palm Springs, CA	72/6837
					Indian Wells CC, Indian Wells, CA	72/6478
					Tamarisk CC, Palm Springs, CA	72/6869
					La Quinta CC, La Quinta, CA	72/6911
1980	Craig Stadler	343	Tom Purtzer	345	Bermuda Dunes CC, Palm Springs, CA	72/6837
			Mike Sullivan		Indian Wells CC, Indian Wells, CA	72/6478
					Eldorado CC, Palm Springs, CA	72/6708
					La Quinta CC, La Quinta, CA	72/6911
1981	Bruce Lietzke	335	Jerry Pate	337	Bermuda Dunes CC, Palm Springs, CA	72/6837
					Indian Wells CC, Indian Wells, CA	72/6478
					Tamarisk CC, Palm Springs, CA	72/6869
					La Quinta CC, La Quinta, CA	72/6911
1982	*Ed Fiori	335	Tom Kite	335	Bermuda Dunes CC, Palm Springs, CA	72/6837
					Indian Wells CC, Indian Wells, CA	72/6478
					Eldorado CC, Palm Springs, CA	72/6708
					La Quinta CC, La Quinta, CA	72/6911
1983	*Keith Fergus	335	Rex Caldwell	335	Bermuda Dunes CC, Palm Springs, CA	72/6837
					Indian Wells CC, Indian Wells, CA	72/6478
					Tamarisk CC, Palm Springs, CA	72/6869
					La Quinta CC, La Quinta, CA	72/6911
BOB HOPE CLASSIC						
1984	*John Mahaffey	340	Jim Simons	340	Bermuda Dunes CC, Palm Springs, CA	72/6837
					Indian Wells CC, Indian Wells, CA	72/6478
					Eldorado CC, Palm Springs, CA	72/6708
					La Quinta CC, La Quinta, CA	72/6911
1985	*Lanny Wadkins	333	Craig Stadler	333	Bermuda Dunes CC, Palm Springs, CA	72/6837
					Indian Wells CC, Indian Wells, CA	72/6478
					Tamarisk CC, Palm Springs, CA	72/6869
					La Quinta CC, La Quinta, CA	72/6911

BOB HOPE CHRYSLER CLASSIC

TOURNAMENT HISTORY

BOB HOPE CHRYSLER CLASSIC

Year	Winner	Score	Runner-up	Score	Location	Par/Yards
1986	*Donnie Hammond	335	John Cook	335	Bermuda Dunes CC, Palm Springs, CA	72/6837
					Indian Wells CC, Indian Wells, CA	72/6478
					Eldorado CC, Palm Springs, CA	72/6708
					La Quinta CC, La Quinta, CA	72/6911
1987	Corey Pavin	341	Bernhard Langer	342	Bermuda Dunes CC, Palm Springs, CA	72/6837
					Indian Wells CC, Indian Wells, CA	72/6478
					Indian Wells CC, Indian Wells, CA	72/6478
					Eldorado CC, Palm Springs, CA	72/6708
1988	Jay Haas	338	David Edwards	340	Bermuda Dunes CC, Palm Springs, CA	72/6837
					Indian Wells CC, Indian Wells, CA	72/6478
					La Quinta CC, La Quinta, CA	72/6911
					Palmer Course at PGA West, La Quinta, CA	72/6924
1989	*Steve Jones	343	Paul Azinger	343	Bermuda Dunes CC, Palm Springs, CA	72/6837
			Sandy Lyle		Indian Wells CC, Indian Wells, CA	72/6478
					Eldorado CC, Palm Springs, CA	72/6708
					PGA West/Palmer Course, La Quinta, CA	72/6924
1990	Peter Jacobsen	339	Scott Simpson	340	PGA West/Palmer Course, La Quinta, CA	72/6924
			Brian Tennyson		Bermuda Dunes CC, Palm Springs, CA	72/6927
					Indian Wells CC, Indian Wells, CA	72/6478
					Tamarisk CC, Palm Springs, CA	72/6875
1991	*Corey Pavin	331	Mark O'Meara	331	PGA West/Palmer Course, La Quinta, CA	72/6924
					Bermuda Dunes CC, Palm Springs, CA	72/6927
					Indian Wells CC, Indian Wells, CA	72/6478
					La Quinta CC, La Quinta, CA	72/6911
1992	*John Cook	336	Rick Fehr	336	PGA West/Palmer Course, La Quinta, CA	72/6924
			Tom Kite		Bermuda Dunes CC, Palm Springs, CA	72/6927
			Mark O'Meara		Indian Wells CC, Indian Wells, CA	72/6478
			Gene Sauers		La Quinta CC, La Quinta, CA	72/6911
1993	Tom Kite	325	Rick Fehr	331	PGA West/Palmer Course, La Quinta, CA	72/6924
					Bermuda Dunes CC, Palm Springs, CA	72/6927
					Indian Wells CC, Indian Wells, CA	72/6478
					Tamarisk CC, La Quinta, CA	72/6881
1994	Scott Hoch	334	Lennie Clements	337	PGA West/Palmer Course, La Quinta, CA	72/6924
			Jim Gallagher, Jr.		Bermuda Dunes CC, Palm Springs, CA	72/6927
			Fuzzy Zoeller		Indian Wells CC, Indian Wells, CA	72/6478
					La Quinta CC, La Quinta, CA	72/6888
1995	Kenny Perry	335	David Duval	336	Bermuda Dunes CC, Palm Springs, CA	72/6927
					Indian Wells CC, Indian Wells, CA	72/6478
					La Quinta CC, La Quinta, CA	72/6901
					Indian Ridge CC, Palm Desert, CA	72/7037

Tournament Record:	325 -- Tom Kite, 1993	
Current Course Record:	Bermuda Dunes CC	62 -- Jim Gallagher, Jr., 1994
	Indian Ridge CC	63 -- Kenny Perry, 1995
	Indian Wells CC	61 -- Bert Yancey, 1974; David Edwards, 1987
	La Quinta CC	61 -- Lennie Clements, 1994
	Tamarisk CC	63 -- Johnny Miller, 1973; Bob Estes, 1993

KEY: *=Playoff

1995 NISSAN OPEN

Riviera CC, Pacific Palisades, CA **Purse: $1,200,000**
Par: 35-36--71 **Yards: 6,946** **February 23-26, 1995**

LEADERS: First Round--Billy Mayfair and Jodie Mudd, each at 5-under-par 66, led by one over seven players. **Second Round**--Kenny Perry, at 10-under-par 132, led by one over Corey Pavin. **Third Round**--Perry, at 13-under par 200, led by one over Pavin and two over Craig Stadler and Jay Don Blake.

CUT: A total of 79 players at 1-over-par 143.

PRO-AM: $7,500. Team--Paul Azinger and Fred Couples, 55, $675 each. Individual--Bob Estes, Davis Love III, Fred Couples, Blaine McCallister and Lennie Clements, 67, $540 each.

WEATHER: Pleasant, with overcast burning off in the afternoon each day.

Winner: Corey Pavin 67-66-68-67 268 $216,000.00

Player	Pos	Scores	Total	Money
Jay Don Blake	T 2	69-67-66-69	271	$105,600.00
Kenny Perry	T 2	70-62-68-71	271	$105,600.00
Scott Simpson	T 4	70-66-68-68	272	$52,800.00
Craig Stadler	T 4	67-68-67-70	272	$52,800.00
Jodie Mudd	6	66-71-69-67	273	$43,200.00
Jay Haas	T 7	69-70-68-67	274	$38,700.00
Lanny Wadkins	T 7	67-72-66-69	274	$38,700.00
Ronnie Black	T 9	72-68-66-70	276	$30,000.00
Jim Furyk	T 9	67-74-65-70	276	$30,000.00
Mike Hulbert	T 9	71-66-68-71	276	$30,000.00
Brian Kamm	T 9	67-74-67-68	276	$30,000.00
Mike Reid	T 9	69-69-69-69	276	$30,000.00
Guy Boros	T14	73-70-65-69	277	$20,400.00
Steve Elkington	T14	68-72-68-69	277	$20,400.00
Bob Estes	T14	68-66-70-73	277	$20,400.00
Steve Lowery	T14	69-70-68-70	277	$20,400.00
Jeff Sluman	T14	72-67-69-69	277	$20,400.00
Fred Couples	T19	69-69-68-72	278	$15,060.00
David Feherty	T19	69-68-72-69	278	$15,060.00
Blaine McCallister	T19	72-70-69-67	278	$15,060.00
Bob Tway	T19	70-72-69-67	278	$15,060.00
Lennie Clements	T23	71-70-68-70	279	$12,000.00
Scott Hoch	T23	70-69-69-71	279	$12,000.00
Emlyn Aubrey	T25	70-69-72-69	280	$8,406.00
Brandel Chamblee	T25	70-72-71-67	280	$8,406.00
Keith Clearwater	T25	70-73-69-68	280	$8,406.00
Jerry Haas	T25	71-70-71-68	280	$8,406.00
Donnie Hammond	T25	68-73-70-69	280	$8,406.00
Mike Heinen	T25	70-72-71-67	280	$8,406.00
Dennis Paulson	T25	70-73-69-68	280	$8,406.00
Don Pooley	T25	72-68-71-69	280	$8,406.00
Kirk Triplett	T25	71-69-70-70	280	$8,406.00
Omar Uresti	T25	68-72-67-73	280	$8,406.00
Peter Jacobsen	T35	69-71-69-72	281	$5,790.00
Davis Love III	T35	69-74-68-70	281	$5,790.00
Billy Mayfair	T35	66-72-68-75	281	$5,790.00
Dan Pohl	T35	70-67-70-74	281	$5,790.00
Scott Verplank	T35	74-67-70-70	281	$5,790.00
John Wilson	T35	72-70-71-68	281	$5,790.00
Mark Calcavecchia	T41	73-69-72-68	282	$4,440.00
John Daly	T41	67-69-71-75	282	$4,440.00
David Edwards	T41	70-72-71-69	282	$4,440.00
Tom Kite	T41	71-67-74-70	282	$4,440.00
Bobby Wadkins	T41	71-71-69-71	282	$4,440.00
Patrick Burke	T46	70-73-69-71	283	$3,264.00
Dudley Hart	T46	73-68-69-73	283	$3,264.00
Lee Janzen	T46	77-66-67-73	283	$3,264.00
Skip Kendall	T46	73-67-72-71	283	$3,264.00
Bruce Vaughan	T46	71-69-72-71	283	$3,264.00
Duffy Waldorf	T46	71-72-70-70	283	$3,264.00
Jim Carter	T52	68-73-70-73	284	$2,784.00
Brad Faxon	T52	67-75-68-74	284	$2,784.00
Rick Fehr	T52	72-71-71-70	284	$2,784.00
Justin Leonard	T52	69-70-74-71	284	$2,784.00
Scott McCarron	T52	70-69-73-72	284	$2,784.00
Tony Sills	T52	73-70-68-73	284	$2,784.00
Robin Freeman	T58	69-72-71-73	285	$2,664.00
Doug Martin	T58	73-67-71-74	285	$2,664.00
Mark Wiebe	T58	69-72-73-71	285	$2,664.00
Tommy Armour III	T61	73-69-73-71	286	$2,592.00
Brian Claar	T61	71-71-73-71	286	$2,592.00
Ben Crenshaw	T61	71-71-71-73	286	$2,592.00
Kelly Gibson	T64	72-66-79-70	287	$2,532.00
Tray Tyner	T64	72-71-73-71	287	$2,532.00
Hale Irwin	T66	69-72-76-71	288	$2,448.00
Steve Pate	T66	68-72-73-75	288	$2,448.00
Paul Stankowski	T66	71-72-73-72	288	$2,448.00
Dave Stockton, Jr.	T66	73-70-73-72	288	$2,448.00
D.A. Weibring	T66	68-70-77-73	288	$2,448.00
Marco Dawson	T71	71-72-74-72	289	$2,328.00
Glen Day	T71	72-69-74-74	289	$2,328.00
J.P. Hayes	T71	71-71-72-75	289	$2,328.00
Tim Loustalot	T71	69-72-72-76	289	$2,328.00
Kazuhiro Takami	T71	72-71-72-74	289	$2,328.00
Bill Porter	76	71-72-75-72	290	$2,256.00
Kevin Burton	77	74-69-76-72	291	$2,232.00
Jeff Leonard	T78	71-72-74-77	294	$2,196.00
Mike Standly	T78	69-74-80-71	294	$2,196.00

The following players did not finish (C=cut, W=withdrew, D=disqualified)

C—144- Curt Byrum, John Cook, Chris DiMarco, Yoshinori Kaneko, Neal Lancaster, Harry Taylor. **145-** Pat Bates, Mark Brooks, Kawika Cotner, Todd Gleaton, Jonathan Kaye, Phil Mickelson, Tom Purtzer, Joey Rassett, Eduardo Romero, Brad Sherfy, Ray Stewart, Doug Tewell. **146-** Michael Allen, Billy Andrade, Woody Austin, Paul Azinger, Bob Burns, Russ Cochran, Lee Rinker, Gene Sauers, Ted Tryba, Howard Twitty. **147-** Steve Jones, John Mason, Jim McGovern, Mike Smith, Chris Tidland, Tommy Tolles, Grant Waite. **148-** Joe Acosta, Jr., Chip Beck, Mike Brisky, Bob Gilder, Johnny Gonzales, Paul Goydos, Scott Gump. **149-** Clark Dennis, Mike Donald, Scott Ford, Satoshi Higashi, Kevin Leach, Rocco Mediate, Gil Morgan, Mark Wurtz. **151-** J.L. Lewis, Ted Schulz. **152-** Jay Delsing, John Hughes, Ted Oh, Dicky Thompson. **153-** Billy Ray Brown, Carl Paulson. **154-** Steve Gotsche, Robert Huxtable, Shigeki Maruyama. **155-** Don Reese. **156-** Stephen Heeney. **W—76-** Charlie Rymer, **79-** Mike Springer.

NISSAN OPEN

TOURNAMENT HISTORY

Year	Winner	Score	Runner-up	Score	Location	Par/Yards
LOS ANGELES OPEN						
1926	Harry Cooper	279	George Von Elm	282	Los Angeles CC, Los Angeles, CA	71/6895 (North)
1927	Bobby Cruickshank	282	Ed Dudley	288	El Caballero CC, Los Angeles, CA	71/6830
			Charles Guest			
1928	Mac Smith	284	Harry Cooper	287	Wilshire CC, Los Angeles, CA	71/6442
1929	Mac Smith	285	Tommy Armour	291	Riviera CC, Pacific Palisades, CA	71/7029
1930	Densmore Shute	296	Bobby Cruickshank	300	Riviera CC, Pacific Palisades, CA	71/7029
			Horton Smith			
1931	Ed Dudley	285	Al Espinosa	287	Wilshire CC, Los Angeles, CA	71/6442
			Eddie Loos			
1932	Mac Smith	281	Leo Diegel	285	Hillcrest CC, Los Angeles, CA	71/6911
			Olin Dutra			
			Joe Kirkwood, Sr.			
			Dick Metz			
1933	Craig Wood	281	Leo Diegel	285	Wilshire CC, Los Angeles, CA	71/6442
			Willie Hunter			
1934	Mac Smith	280	Willie Hunter	288	Los Angeles CC, Los Angeles, CA	71/6895 (North)
			Bill Mehlhorn			
1935	*Vic Ghezzi	285	Johnny Revolta	285	Los Angeles CC, Los Angeles, CA	71/6895 (North)
1936	Jimmy Hines	280	Henry Picard	284	Los Angeles CC, Los Angeles, CA	71/6895 (North)
			Jimmy Thomson			
1937	Harry Cooper	274	Ralph Guldahl	279	Griffith Park, Los Angeles, CA	
			Horton Smith		Wilson-72/6802, Harding-72/6488	
1938	Jimmy Thomson	273	Johnny Revolta	277	Griffith Park, Los Angeles, CA	
					Wilson-72/6802, Harding-72/6488	
1939	Jimmy Demaret	274	Harold McSpaden	281	Griffith Park, Los Angeles, CA	
					Wilson-72/6802, Harding-72/6488	
1940	Lawson Little	282	Clayton Heafner	283	Los Angeles CC, Los Angeles, CA	71/6895 (North)
1941	Johnny Bulla	281	Craig Wood	283	Riviera CC, Pacific Palisades, CA	71/7029
1942	*Ben Hogan	282	Jimmy Thomson	282	Hillcrest CC, Los Angeles, CA	71/6911
1943	No Tournament					
1944	Harold McSpaden	278	Johnny Bulla	281	Wilshire CC, Los Angeles, CA	71/6442
1945	Sam Snead	283	Harold McSpaden	284	Riviera CC, Pacific Palisades, CA	71/7029
			Byron Nelson			
1946	Byron Nelson	284	Ben Hogan	289	Riviera CC, Pacific Palisades, CA	71/7029
1947	Ben Hogan	280	Toney Penna	283	Riviera CC, Pacific Palisades, CA	71/7029
1948	Ben Hogan	275	Lloyd Mangrum	279	Riviera CC, Pacific Palisades, CA	71/7029
1949	Lloyd Mangrum	284	E. J. Harrison	287	Riviera CC, Pacific Palisades, CA	71/7029
1950	*Sam Snead	280	Ben Hogan	280	Riviera CC, Pacific Palisades, CA	71/7029
1951	Lloyd Mangrum	280	Henry Ransom	281	Riviera CC, Pacific Palisades, CA	71/7029
1952	*Tommy Bolt	289	Jack Burke, Jr.	289	Riviera CC, Pacific Palisades, CA	71/7029
1953	Lloyd Mangrum	280	Jack Burke, Jr.	285	Riviera CC, Pacific Palisades, CA	71/7029
1954	Fred Wampler	281	Jerry Barber	282	Fox Hills CC, Culver City, CA	N/A
			Chick Harbert			
1955	Gene Littler	276	Ted Kroll	278	Inglewood CC, Inglewood, CA	N/A
1956	Lloyd Mangrum	272	Jerry Barber	275	Rancho Municipal GC, Los Angeles, CA	71/6827
1957	Doug Ford	280	Jay Hebert	281	Rancho Municipal GC, Los Angeles, CA	71/6827
1958	Frank Stranahan	275	E. J. Harrison	278	Rancho Municipal GC, Los Angeles, CA	71/6827
1959	Ken Venturi	278	Art Wall	280	Rancho Municipal GC, Los Angeles, CA	71/6827
1960	Dow Finsterwald	280	Bill Collins	283	Rancho Municipal GC, Los Angeles, CA	71/6827
			Jay Hebert			
			Dave Ragan			
1961	Bob Goalby	275	Eric Brown	278	Rancho Municipal GC, Los Angeles, CA	71/6827
			Art Wall			
1962	Phil Rodgers	268	Bob Goalby	277	Rancho Municipal GC, Los Angeles, CA	71/6827
			Fred Hawkins			
1963	Arnold Palmer	274	Al Balding	277	Rancho Municipal GC, Los Angeles, CA	71/6827
			Gary Player			
1964	Paul Harney	280	Bobby Nichols	281	Rancho Municipal GC, Los Angeles, CA	71/6827
1965	Paul Harney	276	Dan Sikes	279	Rancho Municipal GC, Los Angeles, CA	71/6827

NISSAN OPEN

TOURNAMENT HISTORY

Year	Winner	Score	Runner-up	Score	Location	Par/Yards
1966	Arnold Palmer	273	Miller Barber	276	Rancho Municipal GC, Los Angeles, CA	71/6827
			Paul Harney			
1967	Arnold Palmer	269	Gay Brewer	274	Rancho Municipal GC, Los Angeles, CA	71/6827
1968	Billy Casper	274	Arnold Palmer	277	Brookside GC, Pasadena, CA	71/7021
1969	*Charles Sifford	276	Harold Henning	276	Rancho Municipal GC, Los Angeles, CA	71/6827
1970	*Billy Casper	276	Hale Irwin	276	Rancho Municipal GC. Los Angeles, CA	71/6827
GLEN CAMPBELL LOS ANGELES OPEN						
1971	*Bob Lunn	274	Billy Casper	274	Rancho Municipal GC, Los Angeles, CA	71/6827
1972	*George Archer	270	Tommy Aaron	270	Rancho Municipal GC, Los Angeles, CA	71/6827
			Dave Hill			
1973	Rod Funseth	276	Don Bies	279	Riviera CC, Pacific Palisades, CA	71/7029
			David Graham			
			Dave Hill			
			Tom Weiskopf			
1974	Dave Stockton	276	John Mahaffey	278	Riviera CC, Pacific Palisades, CA	71/7029
			Sam Snead			
1975	Pat Fitzsimons	275	Tom Kite	279	Riviera CC, Pacific Palisades, CA	71/7029
1976	Hale Irwin	272	Tom Watson	274	Riviera CC, Pacific Palisades, CA	71/7029
1977	Tom Purtzer	273	Lanny Wadkins	274	Riviera CC, Pacific Palisades, CA	71/7029
1978	Gil Morgan	278	Jack Nicklaus	280	Riviera CC, Pacific Palisades, CA	71/7029
1979	Lanny Wadkins	276	Lon Hinkle	277	Riviera CC, Pacific Palisades, CA	71/7029
1980	Tom Watson	276	Bob Gilder	277	Riviera CC, Pacific Palisades, CA	71/7029
			Don January			
1981	Johnny Miller	270	Tom Weiskopf	272	Riviera CC, Pacific Palisades, CA	71/7029
1982	*Tom Watson	271	Johnny Miller	271	Riviera CC, Pacific Palisades, CA	71/7029
1983	Gil Morgan	270	Gibby Gilbert	272	Rancho Municipal GC, Los Angeles, CA	71/6827
			Mark McCumber			
LOS ANGELES OPEN			Lanny Wadkins			
1984	David Edwards	279	Jack Renner	282	Riviera CC, Pacific Palisades, CA	71/7029
1985	Lanny Wadkins	264	Hal Sutton	271	Riviera CC, Pacific Palisades, CA	71/7029
1986	Doug Tewell	270	Clarence Rose	277	Riviera CC, Pacific Palisades, CA	71/7029
LOS ANGELES OPEN PRESENTED BY NISSAN						
1987	*Tze-Chung Chen	275	Ben Crenshaw	275	Riviera CC, Pacific Palisades, CA	71/7029
1988	Chip Beck	267	Mac O'Grady	271	Riviera CC, Pacific Palisades, CA	71/7029
			Bill Sander			
NISSAN LOS ANGELES OPEN						
1989	Mark Calcavecchia	272	Sandy Lyle	273	Riviera CC, Pacific Palisades, CA	71/7029
1990	Fred Couples	266	Gil Morgan	269	Riviera CC, Pacific Palisades, CA	71/7029
1991	Ted Schulz	272	Jeff Sluman	273	Riviera CC, Pacific Palisades, CA	71/7029
1992	*Fred Couples	269	Davis Love III	269	Riviera CC, Pacific Palisades, CA	71/7029
1993	~Tom Kite	206	Dave Barr	209	Riviera CC, Pacific Palisades, CA	71/7029
			Fred Couples			
			Donnie Hammond			
			Payne Stewart			
1994	Corey Pavin	271	Fred Couples	273	Riviera CC, Pacific Palisades, CA	71/6946
1995	Corey Pavin	268	Jay Don Blake	271	Riviera CC, Pacific Palisades, CA	71/6946
			Kenny Perry			

Tournament Record: 264 -- Lanny Wadkins, 1985
Current Course Record: 62 -- Larry Mize, 1985; Kenny Perry, 1995

KEY: *=Playoff ~=Weather-shortened

1995 DORAL-RYDER OPEN

Doral Resort & CC, Miami, FL **Purse: $1,500,000**
Par: 36-36--72 **Yards: 6,939** **March 2-5, 1995**

LEADERS: First Round--Davis Love III, Steve Lowery and Scott Verplank, with 7-under-par 65s, led by one over Fulton Allem and Tom Kite. **Second Round--**Love III, at 10-under-par 134, led by one over Russ Cochran. **Third Round--**Peter Jacobsen and Greg Norman, at 15-under 201, led by three over Nick Faldo and Love III.

CUT: 78 players at 1-under-par 143.

PRO-AM: Individual--Jay Haas, 65, $750. Team--Steve Lowery, Billy Andrade, 53, $675 each.

WEATHER: Sunny, breezy and warm each day. More of a breeze on Sunday than any other day.

Winner: Nick Faldo 67-71-66-69 273 $270,000.00

Player	Pos.	Scores	Total	Money
Peter Jacobsen	T 2	68-69-64-73	274	$132,000.00
Greg Norman	T 2	68-68-65-73	274	$132,000.00
Steve Elkington	T 4	67-72-67-69	275	$62,000.00
Justin Leonard	T 4	68-68-71-68	275	$62,000.00
Davis Love III	T 4	65-69-70-71	275	$62,000.00
Woody Austin	T 7	66-71-68-71	276	$48,375.00
Hale Irwin	T 7	70-70-67-69	276	$48,375.00
Steve Stricker	9	70-68-71-68	277	$43,500.00
Steve Lowery	T10	65-72-73-68	278	$39,000.00
Mark O'Meara	T10	69-72-66-71	278	$39,000.00
Fulton Allem	T12	66-71-68-74	279	$29,400.00
Michael Bradley	T12	70-73-67-69	279	$29,400.00
Mark McCumber	T12	70-71-69-69	279	$29,400.00
Vijay Singh	T12	70-70-67-72	279	$29,400.00
Jeff Sluman	T12	69-67-70-73	279	$29,400.00
Lennie Clements	T17	70-70-67-73	280	$17,700.00
David Duval	T17	67-72-68-73	280	$17,700.00
Ernie Els	T17	74-67-70-69	280	$17,700.00
Ray Floyd	T17	72-71-68-69	280	$17,700.00
Bill Glasson	T17	68-68-70-74	280	$17,700.00
Jay Haas	T17	69-69-70-72	280	$17,700.00
Dudley Hart	T17	71-67-68-74	280	$17,700.00
Colin Montgomerie	T17	72-68-68-72	280	$17,700.00
Joe Ozaki	T17	68-68-72-72	280	$17,700.00
Scott Verplank	T17	65-76-70-69	280	$17,700.00
Jim Carter	T27	72-65-70-74	281	$10,425.00
Russ Cochran	T27	71-64-71-75	281	$10,425.00
Mike Hulbert	T27	71-70-70-70	281	$10,425.00
John Huston	T27	73-69-65-74	281	$10,425.00
Jesper Parnevik	T27	71-66-74-70	281	$10,425.00
Harry Taylor	T27	71-67-69-74	281	$10,425.00
Mark Calcavecchia	T33	69-74-70-69	282	$7,757.15
Brian Claar	T33	68-75-69-70	282	$7,757.15
Fred Funk	T33	70-72-70-70	282	$7,757.14
Jim Gallagher, Jr.	T33	71-68-71-72	282	$7,757.14
Hal Sutton	T33	68-71-66-77	282	$7,757.14
Tray Tyner	T33	69-68-73-72	282	$7,757.14
D.A. Weibring	T33	71-70-67-74	282	$7,757.14
Bernhard Langer	T40	69-71-71-72	283	$6,150.00
Dillard Pruitt	T40	70-69-71-73	283	$6,150.00
Bruce Vaughan	T40	70-69-71-73	283	$6,150.00
Curt Byrum	T43	71-69-72-72	284	$4,383.00
Chris DiMarco	T43	71-71-70-72	284	$4,383.00
David Edwards	T43	73-69-68-74	284	$4,383.00
Scott Gump	T43	71-69-68-76	284	$4,383.00
Skip Kendall	T43	69-73-69-73	284	$4,383.00
Billy Mayfair	T43	70-71-71-72	284	$4,383.00
Jim McGovern	T43	72-71-66-75	284	$4,383.00
Loren Roberts	T43	70-71-70-73	284	$4,383.00
Curtis Strange	T43	72-71-67-74	284	$4,383.00
Grant Waite	T43	71-71-65-77	284	$4,383.00
Bruce Fleisher	T53	73-69-71-72	285	$3,456.00
Mike Heinen	T53	68-75-73-69	285	$3,456.00
Andrew Magee	T53	70-68-74-73	285	$3,456.00
Paul Stankowski	T53	70-73-71-71	285	$3,456.00
Bobby Wadkins	T53	70-72-67-76	285	$3,456.00
Paul Azinger	T58	70-72-72-72	286	$3,240.00
Jay Don Blake	T58	72-67-70-77	286	$3,240.00
John Daly	T58	71-69-72-74	286	$3,240.00
Jim Furyk	T58	70-71-71-74	286	$3,240.00
Neal Lancaster	T58	71-72-69-74	286	$3,240.00
Chris Perry	T58	71-71-72-72	286	$3,240.00
Gene Sauers	T58	70-70-74-72	286	$3,240.00
Lanny Wadkins	T58	72-71-67-76	286	$3,240.00
Mark Wiebe	T58	70-73-71-72	286	$3,240.00
Clark Dennis	T67	71-72-71-73	287	$3,045.00
John Morse	T67	70-70-72-75	287	$3,045.00
Mike Standly	T67	73-67-71-76	287	$3,045.00
Bob Tway	T67	74-67-70-76	287	$3,045.00
Tom Kite	71	66-73-71-78	288	$2,970.00
Robert Gamez	T72	70-69-73-77	289	$2,910.00
Brian Henninger	T72	71-72-70-76	289	$2,910.00
Dave Stockton, Jr.	T72	71-70-71-77	289	$2,910.00
Billy Andrade	75	69-70-75-76	290	$2,850.00
Payne Stewart	76	68-74-76-74	292	$2,820.00
Richard Sadler	77	72-69-76-77	294	$2,790.00

The following players did not finish (C=cut, W=withdrew, D=disqualified)

C—144- Keith Clearwater, Ben Crenshaw, Ed Humenik, Steve Jones, Brian Kamm, Bob Lohr, Jack Nicklaus, Jerry Pate, Kenny Perry, Steve Rintoul, Eduardo Romero, Howard Twitty. **145-** Dave Barr, Pat Bates, Andy Bean, Steve Hart, Steve Lamontagne, Rocco Mediate, Dicky Pride, Tom Watson. **146-** Mark Brooks, Billy Ray Brown, Bob Burns, Jay Delsing, Scott Hoch, Bruce Lietzke, Gil Morgan, Craig Stadler, Doug Tewell, Ted Tryba. **147-** Guy Boros, Brad Faxon, David Feherty, Ken Green, Gary Hallberg, Greg Kraft, John Mahaffey, Hiroshi Matsuo, Gary Nicklaus, Mike Sullivan. **148-** Seve Ballesteros, Joel Edwards, Wayne Levi. **149-** Mike Brisky, Patrick Burke, Mark Carnevale, Glen Day, Take Koyama, John Lee, Jodie Mudd, Larry Nelson, David Ogrin. **150-** Chip Beck, Lee Janzen. **151-** Robert Floyd, Paul Goydos. **152-** Joe Donnelly, Hubert Green, Yoshinori Mizumaki, Jim Thorpe. **153-** Bob Gilder, Nolan Henke, Wes Smith. **155-** Bill Kennedy, Dean Prowse. **156-** Billy Casper. **W—143-** Brad Bryant, **77-** Joey Sindelar.

DORAL-RYDER OPEN

TOURNAMENT HISTORY

Year	Winner	Score	Runner-up	Score	Location	Par/Yards
DORAL CC OPEN INVITATIONAL						
1962	Billy Casper	283	Paul Bondeson	284	Doral CC (Blue), Miami, FL	72/6939
1963	Dan Sikes	283	Sam Snead	284	Doral CC (Blue), Miami, FL	72/6939
1964	Billy Casper	277	Jack Nicklaus	278	Doral CC (Blue), Miami, FL	72/6939
1965	Doug Sanders	274	Bruce Devlin	275	Doral CC (Blue), Miami, FL	72/6939
1966	Phil Rodgers	278	Jay Dolan Kermit Zarley	279	Doral CC (Blue), Miami, FL	72/6939
1967	Doug Sanders	275	Harold Henning Art Wall	276	Doral CC (Blue), Miami, FL	72/6939
1968	Gardner Dickinson	275	Tom Weiskopf	276	Doral CC (Blue), Miami, FL	72/6939
1969	Tom Shaw	276	Tommy Aaron	277	Doral CC (Blue), Miami, FL	72/6939
DORAL-EASTERN OPEN INVITATIONAL						
1970	Mike Hill	279	Jim Colbert	283	Doral CC (Blue), Miami, FL	72/6939
1971	J.C. Snead	275	Gardner Dickinson	276	Doral CC (Blue), Miami, FL	72/6939
1972	Jack Nicklaus	276	Bob Rosburg Lee Trevino	278	Doral CC (Blue), Miami, FL	72/6939
1973	Lee Trevino	276	Bruce Crampton Tom Weiskopf	277	Doral CC (Blue), Miami, FL	72/6939
1974	Brian Allin	272	Jerry Heard	273	Doral CC (Blue), Miami, FL	72/6939
1975	Jack Nicklaus	276	Forrest Fezler Bert Yancey	279	Doral CC (Blue), Miami, FL	72/6939
1976	Hubert Green	270	Mark Hayes Jack Nicklaus	276	Doral CC (Blue), Miami, FL	72/6939
1977	Andy Bean	277	David Graham	278	Doral CC (Blue), Miami, FL	72/6939
1978	Tom Weiskopf	272	Jack Nicklaus	273	Doral CC (Blue), Miami, FL	72/6939
1979	Mark McCumber	279	Bill Rogers	280	Doral CC (Blue), Miami, FL	72/6939
1980	*Raymond Floyd	279	Jack Nicklaus	279	Doral CC (Blue), Miami, FL	72/6939
1981	Raymond Floyd	273	Keith Fergus David Graham	274	Doral CC (Blue), Miami, FL	72/6939
1982	Andy Bean	278	Scott Hoch Mike Nicolette Jerry Pate	279	Doral CC (Blue), Miami, FL	72/6939
1983	Gary Koch	271	Ed Fiori	276	Doral CC (Blue), Miami, FL	72/6939
1984	Tom Kite	272	Jack Nicklaus	274	Doral CC (Blue), Miami, FL	72/6939
1985	Mark McCumber	284	Tom Kite	285	Doral CC (Blue), Miami, FL	72/6939
1986	*Andy Bean	276	Hubert Green	276	Doral CC (Blue), Miami, FL	72/6939
DORAL-RYDER OPEN						
1987	Lanny Wadkins	277	Seve Ballesteros Tom Kite Don Pooley	280	Doral CC (Blue), Miami, FL	72/6939
1988	Ben Crenshaw	274	Chip Beck Mark McCumber	275	Doral CC (Blue), Miami, FL	72/6939
1989	Bill Glasson	275	Fred Couples	276	Doral CC (Blue), Miami, FL	72/6939
1990	*Greg Norman	273	Paul Azinger Mark Calcavecchia Tim Simpson	273	Doral CC (Blue), Miami, FL	72/6939
1991	*Rocco Mediate	276	Curtis Strange	276	Doral CC (Blue), Miami, FL	72/6939
1992	Raymond Floyd	271	Keith Clearwater Fred Couples	273	Doral CC (Blue), Miami, FL	72/6939
1993	Greg Norman	265	Paul Azinger Mark McCumber	269	Doral CC (Blue), Miami, FL	72/6939
1994	John Huston	274	Billy Andrade Brad Bryant	277	Doral CC (Blue), Miami, FL	72/6939
1995	Nick Faldo	273	Peter Jacobsen Greg Norman	274	Doral CC (Blue), Miami, FL	72/6939

Tournament Record: 265 -- Greg Norman, 1993
Current Course Record: 62 -- Greg Norman, 1990 and 1993

KEY: *=Playoff

1995 HONDA CLASSIC

The Honda Classic

Weston Hills CC, Ft. Lauderdale, FL
Par: 35-36--71 Yards: 6,964

Purse: $1,200,000
March 9-12, 1995

LEADERS: First Round--Jim McGovern shot a 6-under-par 65 to lead Mark Calcavecchia by one stroke and Nick Faldo and Dave Barr by two. **Second Round--**Mark O'Meara shot 65 for 9-under-par 143, three strokes better than Blaine McCallister and Andrew Magee. **Third Round--**O'Meara shot an even-par 71 to retain his three-stroke lead. Faldo, with a 69, moved into second place at 6-under-par 207.

CUT: 83 players at 2-over-par 144.

PRO-AM: Rain and high winds forced cancellation of the pro-am. Each professional scheduled to compete received $144.24.

WEATHER: After Wednesday's rain and high winds, overcast and windy Thursday with temperatures in the 60s. Partly cloudy, more windy and warmer Friday, Saturday and Sunday. Rain greeted the final groups on 18 Sunday.

Winner: Mark O'Meara 68-65-71-71 275 $216,000.00

Player	Pos	Scores	Total	Money
Nick Faldo	2	67-71-69-69	276	$129,600.00
Ian Woosnam	3	68-72-69-68	277	$81,600.00
Andrew Magee	4	69-67-76-67	279	$57,600.00
Blaine McCallister	5	70-66-73-71	280	$48,000.00
Bill Britton	6	71-69-72-69	281	$43,200.00
Mike Standly	7	71-66-75-70	282	$40,200.00
Seve Ballesteros	T 8	70-68-76-69	283	$32,400.00
Michael Bradley	T 8	73-69-73-68	283	$32,400.00
Brian Claar	T 8	69-70-72-72	283	$32,400.00
Keith Fergus	T 8	69-72-71-71	283	$32,400.00
Scott Verplank	T 8	74-67-73-69	283	$32,400.00
Bernhard Langer	T13	70-71-73-70	284	$18,174.55
Mark McCumber	T13	71-67-76-70	284	$18,174.55
Jim McGovern	T13	65-74-75-70	284	$18,174.55
Nick Price	T13	71-70-69-74	284	$18,174.55
Lee Rinker	T13	68-72-76-68	284	$18,174.55
Steve Stricker	T13	69-72-71-72	284	$18,174.55
Woody Austin	T13	73-69-70-72	284	$18,174.54
Patrick Burke	T13	73-71-67-73	284	$18,174.54
Scott Gump	T13	73-69-70-72	284	$18,174.54
Mike Hulbert	T13	70-74-69-71	284	$18,174.54
Bob Tway	T13	71-72-70-71	284	$18,174.54
Glen Day	T24	70-69-72-74	285	$10,560.00
Eduardo Romero	T24	70-72-73-70	285	$10,560.00
Gene Sauers	T24	69-72-74-70	285	$10,560.00
Ronnie Black	T27	73-71-70-72	286	$8,700.00
Lee Janzen	T27	69-73-70-74	286	$8,700.00
Joey Sindelar	T27	75-69-71-71	286	$8,700.00
Paul Stankowski	T27	70-71-73-72	286	$8,700.00
Robin Freeman	T31	70-70-74-73	287	$6,520.00
Brian Henninger	T31	72-71-71-73	287	$6,520.00
Tom Lehman	T31	74-67-72-74	287	$6,520.00
Justin Leonard	T31	71-70-76-70	287	$6,520.00
Bob Lohr	T31	69-71-75-72	287	$6,520.00
Doug Martin	T31	71-68-75-73	287	$6,520.00
Vijay Singh	T31	69-72-77-69	287	$6,520.00
Curtis Strange	T31	72-72-71-72	287	$6,520.00
Bobby Wadkins	T31	73-70-70-74	287	$6,520.00
Donnie Hammond	T40	71-69-74-74	288	$4,440.00
Dudley Hart	T40	71-69-76-72	288	$4,440.00
Pete Jordan	T40	72-71-72-73	288	$4,440.00
Joey Rassett	T40	73-67-74-74	288	$4,440.00
Steve Rintoul	T40	69-74-70-75	288	$4,440.00
Mike Smith	T40	72-67-77-72	288	$4,440.00
Dicky Thompson	T40	74-70-71-73	288	$4,440.00
Tommy Armour III	T47	70-71-74-74	289	$3,124.00
Mark Calcavecchia	T47	66-77-74-72	289	$3,124.00
Bob Gilder	T47	71-73-74-71	289	$3,124.00
Craig Parry	T47	72-71-74-72	289	$3,124.00
Jerry Pate	T47	71-72-72-74	289	$3,124.00
Tray Tyner	T47	70-74-72-73	289	$3,124.00
Billy Andrade	T53	70-74-73-73	290	$2,752.00
Mike Brisky	T53	71-72-71-76	290	$2,752.00
Curt Byrum	T53	72-71-72-75	290	$2,752.00
Colin Montgomerie	T53	69-75-71-75	290	$2,752.00
Steve Pate	T53	73-70-76-71	290	$2,752.00
Howard Twitty	T53	73-71-72-74	290	$2,752.00
Dave Barr	T59	67-74-76-74	291	$2,592.00
Bob Burns	T59	71-73-76-71	291	$2,592.00
Brandel Chamblee	T59	70-74-74-73	291	$2,592.00
Marco Dawson	T59	69-71-79-72	291	$2,592.00
Jim Gallagher, Jr.	T59	72-68-74-77	291	$2,592.00
Jerry Haas	T59	69-75-72-75	291	$2,592.00
Mike Sullivan	T59	68-74-74-75	291	$2,592.00
Chip Beck	T66	73-69-75-75	292	$2,436.00
Chris DiMarco	T66	71-70-78-73	292	$2,436.00
Bruce Fleisher	T66	73-71-73-75	292	$2,436.00
Brian Kamm	T66	73-71-78-70	292	$2,436.00
Mark Wiebe	T66	68-76-71-77	292	$2,436.00
Chris Perry	T66	73-69-76-74	292	$2,436.00
Mark Carnevale	T72	71-72-75-75	293	$2,328.00
David Feherty	T72	71-73-76-73	293	$2,328.00
Grant Waite	T72	74-67-77-75	293	$2,328.00
Joel Edwards	T75	72-72-71-79	294	$2,232.00
Dan Forsman	T75	70-71-79-74	294	$2,232.00
Bruce Lietzke	T75	71-72-77-74	294	$2,232.00
Yoshi Mizumaki	T75	71-68-82-73	294	$2,232.00
Dicky Pride	T75	72-69-78-75	294	$2,232.00
John Daly	T80	71-70-77-77	295	$2,148.00
Neal Lancaster	T80	72-71-73-79	295	$2,148.00
Keith Clearwater	82	69-74-79-76	298	$2,112.00
Bobby Tracy	83	71-73-77-80	301	$2,088.00

The following players did not finish (C=cut, W=withdrew, D=disqualified)

C—145- Joe Acosta, Jr., Michael Allen, Guy Boros, Russ Cochran, Kawika Cotner, Kelly Gibson, John Huston, Skip Kendall, Tim Loustalot, Gary McCord, Jesper Parnevik, Mark Wurtz. **146-** Fulton Allem, Emlyn Aubrey, Pat Bates, Bart Bryant, Steve Gotsche, Kenny Knox, Phil Mickelson, Larry Nelson, Don Pooley, Payne Stewart, Omar Uresti. **147-** Paul Azinger, Jay Delsing, Clark Dennis, Paul Goydos, Guy Hill, Bill Porter. **148-** Mike Donald, David Ishii, Jeff Leonard, J.L. Lewis, Larry Mize, Joe Ozaki, Tommy Tolles, Ted Tryba, Bruce Vaughan. **149-** Robert Gamez, Greg Kraft, Charlie Rymer. **150-** Andy Bean, Ed Humenik, Don Reese, Tony Sills, Heath Wassem. **151-** J.P. Hayes, David Ogrin, Harry Taylor. **152-** Gary Hallberg. **153-** Fred Funk, Carl Paulson. **156-** Brigham Gibbs, Blair Gibson. **157-** Gary Keating. **159-** Scott Ford, Buddy Goodwin. **W—158-** Jonathan Kaye, **76-** Ken Green, **77-** Scott McCarron, **80-** Jim Thorpe.

HONDA CLASSIC

TOURNAMENT HISTORY

Year	Winner	Score	Runner-up	Score	Location	Par/Yards
JACKIE GLEASON'S INVERRARY CLASSIC						
1972	Tom Weiskopf	278	Jack Nicklaus	279	Inverrary G&CC (East), Lauderhill, FL	72/7128
JACKIE GLEASON'S INVERRARY NATIONAL AIRLINES CLASSIC						
1973	Lee Trevino	279	Forrest Fezler	280	Inverrary G&CC (East), Lauderhill, FL	72/7128
JACKIE GLEASON'S INVERRARY CLASSIC						
1974	Leonard Thompson	278	Hale Irwin	279	Inverrary G&CC (East), Lauderhill, FL	72/7128
1975	Bob Murphy	273	Eddie Pearce	274	Inverrary G&CC (East), Lauderhill, FL	72/7128
1976	Hosted Tournament Players Championship					
1977	Jack Nicklaus	275	Gary Player	280	Inverrary G&CC (East), Lauderhill, FL	72/7128
1978	Jack Nicklaus	276	Grier Jones	277	Inverrary G&CC (East), Lauderhill, FL	72/7128
1979	Larry Nelson	274	Grier Jones	277	Inverrary G&CC (East), Lauderhill, FL	72/7128
1980	Johnny Miller	274	Charles Coody Bruce Lietzke	276	Inverrary G&CC (East), Lauderhill, FL	72/7128
AMERICAN MOTORS INVERRARY CLASSIC						
1981	Tom Kite	274	Jack Nicklaus	275	Inverrary G&CC (East), Lauderhill, FL	72/7128
HONDA INVERRARY CLASSIC						
1982	Hale Irwin	269	Jack Nicklaus Denis Watson	278	Inverrary G&CC (East), Lauderhill, FL	72/7128
1983	Johnny Miller	278	Jack Nicklaus	280	Inverrary G&CC (East), Lauderhill, FL	72/7128
HONDA CLASSIC						
1984	*Bruce Lietzke	280	Andy Bean	280	TPC at Eagle Trace, Coral Springs, FL	72/7030
1985	*Curtis Strange	275	Peter Jacobsen	275	TPC at Eagle Trace, Coral Springs, FL	72/7030
1986	Kenny Knox	287	Andy Bean John Mahaffey Jodie Mudd Clarence Rose	288	TPC at Eagle Trace, Coral Springs, FL	72/7030
1987	Mark Calcavecchia	279	Bernhard Langer Payne Stewart	282	TPC at Eagle Trace, Coral Springs, FL	72/7030
1988	Joey Sindelar	276	Ed Fiori Sandy Lyle Payne Stewart	278	TPC at Eagle Trace, Coral Springs, FL	72/7030
1989	Blaine McCallister	266	Payne Stewart	270	TPC at Eagle Trace, Coral Springs, FL	72/7030
1990	John Huston	282	Mark Calcavecchia	284	TPC at Eagle Trace, Coral Springs, FL	72/7030
1991	Steve Pate	279	Paul Azinger Dan Halldorson	282	TPC at Eagle Trace, Coral Springs, FL	72/7030
1992	*Corey Pavin	273	Fred Couples	273	Weston Hills G&CC, Ft. Lauderdale, FL	72/7069
1993	~*Fred Couples	207	Robert Gamez	207	Weston Hills G&CC, Ft. Lauderdale, FL	72/7069
1994	Nick Price	276	Craig Parry	277	Weston Hills G&CC, Ft. Lauderdale, FL	71/6964
1995	Mark O'Meara	275	Nick Faldo	276	Weston Hills G&CC, Ft. Lauderdale, FL	71/6964

Tournament Record: 266 -- Blaine McCallister, 1989 (TPC at Eagle Trace)
Current Course Record: 62 -- Dan Pohl, 1989

KEY: *=Playoff ~=Weather-shortened

1995 NESTLE INVITATIONAL

BAY HILL INVITATIONAL
presented by
Office DEPOT

Bay Hill Club, Orlando, FL | **Purse: $1,200,000**
Par: 36-36--72 Yards: 7,114 | **March 16-19, 1995**

LEADERS: First Round--Mark Brooks, at 7-under-par 65, held a two-stroke lead over Rick Fehr, Steve Stricker, Billy Andrade and Jesper Parnevik. **Second Round--**Loren Roberts, at 11-under-par 133, was two strokes in front of Davis Love III. **Third Round--**Roberts, at 15-under-par 201, led Brad Faxon by two strokes.

CUT: 76 players at 1-over-par 145.

PRO-AM: $7,500. Individual--Greg Norman, 68, $750. Team--Seve Ballesteros, Craig Parry, 56, $675 each.

WEATHER: Ideal playing conditions most of Thursday gave way to cloudy, threatening skies later afternoon, along with a race against darkness to conclude play. A sunny start Friday was replaced by afternoon rain and lightning. Play was suspended initially at 2:30 p.m., then for the day at 4:15 p.m. with 68 players still on the course. Round 2 resumed with a 7:30 a.m. shotgun start Saturday. Round 3, in threesomes off two tees, got underway at 11:54 a.m. Threatening weather caused yet another suspension from 1:38-3:17 p.m.; darkness produced suspension of play for the day at 6:20 p.m. with 40 players on the course. Completion of Round 3 began at 8:30 a.m. Sunday; the round ended at 9:57 a.m. Round 4 (threesomes/two tees) got underway at 11:40 a.m. Sunday was partly sunny and windy.

Winner: Loren Roberts 68-65-68-71 272 $216,000.00

Player	Pos.	Scores	Total	Money
Brad Faxon	2	69-70-64-71	274	$129,600.00
Peter Jacobsen	3	70-68-68-69	275	$81,600.00
Steve Stricker	4	67-72-69-69	277	$57,600.00
Nick Faldo	T 5	71-73-66-68	278	$39,300.00
Jay Haas	T 5	72-69-69-68	278	$39,300.00
Bob Lohr	T 5	69-70-67-72	278	$39,300.00
Mark McCumber	T 5	69-70-69-70	278	$39,300.00
Jesper Parnevik	T 5	67-72-67-72	278	$39,300.00
Duffy Waldorf	T 5	71-72-70-65	278	$39,300.00
Mark McNulty	T11	68-72-67-72	279	$27,600.00
Greg Norman	T11	71-69-70-69	279	$27,600.00
Scott Simpson	T11	70-71-70-68	279	$27,600.00
Patrick Burke	T14	71-73-70-66	280	$22,200.00
Nick Price	T14	71-70-68-71	280	$22,200.00
Fred Funk	T16	70-71-68-72	281	$18,600.00
Davis Love III	T16	69-66-73-73	281	$18,600.00
Jeff Maggert	T16	73-69-69-70	281	$18,600.00
Curtis Strange	T16	71-70-70-70	281	$18,600.00
Billy Andrade	T20	67-69-74-72	282	$13,000.00
Emlyn Aubrey	T20	74-67-68-73	282	$13,000.00
Mark Brooks	T20	65-73-73-71	282	$13,000.00
Dan Forsman	T20	70-72-67-73	282	$13,000.00
Bill Glasson	T20	69-75-70-68	282	$13,000.00
Vijay Singh	T20	73-70-66-73	282	$13,000.00
Kelly Gibson	T26	74-70-65-74	283	$8,880.00
Paul Goydos	T26	73-67-72-71	283	$8,880.00
Mike Heinen	T26	69-71-70-73	283	$8,880.00
Jeff Sluman	T26	71-70-70-72	283	$8,880.00
Fuzzy Zoeller	T26	68-71-72-72	283	$8,880.00
Paul Azinger	T31	71-70-71-72	284	$6,960.00
Mike Hulbert	T31	75-69-72-68	284	$6,960.00
Bernhard Langer	T31	71-69-75-69	284	$6,960.00
Jumbo Ozaki	T31	71-73-72-68	284	$6,960.00
Dan Pohl	T31	72-67-69-76	284	$6,960.00
Payne Stewart	T31	69-70-73-72	284	$6,960.00
Chip Beck	T37	72-70-72-71	285	$5,400.00
Fred Couples	T37	68-71-70-76	285	$5,400.00
Jim Gallagher, Jr.	T37	70-75-70-70	285	$5,400.00
Tom Lehman	T37	70-75-73-67	285	$5,400.00
Corey Pavin	T37	71-70-71-73	285	$5,400.00
Brandel Chamblee	T42	71-73-69-73	286	$3,966.86
Ben Crenshaw	T42	71-70-70-75	286	$3,966.86
Ernie Els	T42	74-67-77-68	286	$3,966.86
Colin Montgomerie	T42	73-70-70-73	286	$3,966.86
Mark O'Meara	T42	70-73-71-72	286	$3,966.86
Jose Maria Olazabal	T42	75-69-66-76	286	$3,966.85
Mike Sullivan	T42	73-72-70-71	286	$3,966.85
Jim Carter	T49	68-70-76-73	287	$2,994.00
Steve Jones	T49	74-69-74-70	287	$2,994.00
Larry Nelson	T49	70-73-71-73	287	$2,994.00
Ian Woosnam	T49	71-74-70-72	287	$2,994.00
Mark Calcavecchia	T53	73-68-73-74	288	$2,739.43
John Cook	T53	72-71-71-74	288	$2,739.43
David Duval	T53	71-72-70-75	288	$2,739.43
Bob Estes	T53	71-72-69-76	288	$2,739.43
Chris Perry	T53	71-72-73-72	288	$2,739.43
Kenny Perry	T53	74-70-68-76	288	$2,739.43
Larry Mize	T53	71-73-68-76	288	$2,739.42
Andy Bean	T60	72-73-73-72	290	$2,604.00
Rick Fehr	T60	67-77-74-72	290	$2,604.00
Donnie Hammond	T60	75-67-72-76	290	$2,604.00
Greg Kraft	T60	74-69-74-73	290	$2,604.00
D.A. Weibring	64	74-71-72-74	291	$2,544.00
Lee Janzen	T65	73-70-72-77	292	$2,508.00
Tom Kite	T65	72-72-72-76	292	$2,508.00
John Morse	T67	71-74-73-75	293	$2,460.00
David Peoples	T67	74-70-76-73	293	$2,460.00
Neal Lancaster	69	74-70-72-78	294	$2,424.00
Brian Kamm	T70	71-71-76-77	295	$2,388.00
Bill Kratzert	T70	72-72-73-78	295	$2,388.00
John Daly	T72	68-74-73-81	296	$2,340.00
John Mahaffey	T72	72-73-73-78	296	$2,340.00
Don Pooley	74	70-75-78-75	298	$2,304.00
Eddie Pearce	75	76-69-76-79	300	$2,280.00

The following players did not finish (C=cut, W=withdrew, D=disqualified)

C—146- Fulton Allem, Billy Ray Brown, Robert Gamez, Dudley Hart, Steve Lowery, Sandy Lyle, Phil Mickelson, Gil Morgan, Joe Ozaki. **147-** Dave Barr, John Huston, Justin Leonard, Billy Mayfair, Jerry Pate. **148-** John Adams, David Edwards, Jim Furyk, Scott Hoch, Andrew Magee, Yoshinori Mizumaki, Steve Pate, Kirk Triplett. **149-** Jay Don Blake, Chris DiMarco, Jerry Haas, Tom Watson. **150-**Tommy Armour III, Seve Ballesteros, Brad Bryant, Clark Dennis, Brian Henninger, Dillard Pruitt, Walter Smith, Hal Sutton. **151-** David Frost, Gary Koch, Arnold Palmer, Craig Parry, Dicky Pride, Joey Sindelar. **153-** Guy Boros. **154-**Nolan Henke, Mike Nicolette. **155-** Mike Springer. **158-** Ian Baker-Finch. **W—149-**Glen Day, **153-**Rocco Mediate, **154-**Woody Austin, **154-**Tommy Tolles, **157-** Jack Nicklaus, **75-** Blaine McCallister. **D—219-** Ronnie Black.

BAY HILL INVITATIONAL presented by Office Depot

BAY HILL INVITATIONAL
presented by
Office DEPOT

TOURNAMENT HISTORY

Year	Winner	Score	Runner-up	Score	Location	Par/Yards
FLORIDA CITRUS OPEN INVITATIONAL						
1966	Lionel Hebert	279	Charles Coody	281	Rio Pinar CC, Orlando, FL	72/7012
			Dick Lytle			
			Jack Nicklaus			
1967	Julius Boros	274	George Knudson	275	Rio Pinar CC, Orlando, FL	72/7012
			Arnold Palmer			
1968	Dan Sikes	274	Tom Weiskopf	275	Rio Pinar CC, Orlando, FL	72/7012
1969	Ken Still	278	Miller Barber	279	Rio Pinar CC, Orlando, FL	72/7012
1970	Bob Lunn	271	Rives McBee	282	Rio Pinar CC, Orlando, FL	72/7012
1971	Arnold Palmer	270	Julius Boros	271	Rio Pinar CC, Orlando, FL	72/7012
1972	Jerry Heard	276	Bobby Mitchell	278	Rio Pinar CC, Orlando, FL	72/7012
1973	Brian Allin	265	Charles Coody	273	Rio Pinar CC, Orlando, FL	72/7012
1974	Jerry Heard	273	Homero Blancas	276	Rio Pinar CC, Orlando, FL	72/7012
			Jim Jamieson			
1975	Lee Trevino	276	Hale Irwin	277	Rio Pinar CC, Orlando, FL	72/7012
1976	*Hale Irwin	270	Kermit Zarley	270	Rio Pinar CC, Orlando, FL	72/7012
1977	Gary Koch	274	Dale Hayes	276	Rio Pinar CC, Orlando, FL	72/7012
			Joe Inman			
1978	Mac McLendon	271	David Graham	273	Rio Pinar CC, Orlando, FL	72/7012
BAY HILL CITRUS CLASSIC						
1979	*Bob Byman	278	John Schroeder	278	Bay Hill Club, Orlando, FL	71/7103
BAY HILL CLASSIC						
1980	Dave Eichelberger	279	Leonard Thompson	282	Bay Hill Club, Orlando, FL	71/7103
1981	Andy Bean	266	Tom Watson	273	Bay Hill Club, Orlando, FL	71/7103
1982	*Tom Kite	278	Jack Nicklaus	278	Bay Hill Club, Orlando, FL	71/7103
			Denis Watson			
1983	*Mike Nicolette	283	Greg Norman	283	Bay Hill Club, Orlando, FL	71/7103
1984	*Gary Koch	272	George Burns	272	Bay Hill Club, Orlando, FL	71/7103
HERTZ BAY HILL CLASSIC						
1985	Fuzzy Zoeller	275	Tom Watson	277	Bay Hill Club, Orlando, FL	71/7103
1986	~Dan Forsman	202	Ray Floyd	203	Bay Hill Club, Orlando, FL	71/7103
			Mike Hulbert			
1987	Payne Stewart	264	David Frost	267	Bay Hill Club, Orlando, FL	71/7103
1988	Paul Azinger	271	Tom Kite	276	Bay Hill Club, Orlando, FL	71/7103
THE NESTLE INVITATIONAL						
1989	*Tom Kite	278	Davis Love III	278	Bay Hill Club, Orlando, FL	71/7103
1990	Robert Gamez	274	Greg Norman	275	Bay Hill Club, Orlando, FL	72/7114
1991	~Andrew Magee	203	Tom Sieckmann	205	Bay Hill Club, Orlando, FL	72/7114
1992	Fred Couples	269	Gene Sauers	278	Bay Hill Club, Orlando, FL	72/7114
1993	Ben Crenshaw	280	Davis Love III	282	Bay Hill Club, Orlando, FL	72/7114
			Rocco Mediate			
			Vijay Singh			
1994	Loren Roberts	275	Nick Price	276	Bay Hill Club, Orlando, FL	72/7114
			Vijay Singh			
			Fuzzy Zoeller			
1995	Loren Roberts	272	Brad Faxon	274	Bay Hill Club, Orlando, FL	72/7114

Tournament Record: 264 -- Payne Stewart, 1987
Current Course Record: 62 -- Andy Bean, 1981; Greg Norman, 1984

KEY: *=Playoff ~=Weather-shortened

1995 PLAYERS CHAMPIONSHIP

TPC at Sawgrass, Ponte Vedra Beach, FL **Purse: $3,000,000**
Par: 36-36--72 **Yards: 6,896** **March 23-26, 1995**

LEADERS: First Round--Corey Pavin, at 6-under-par 66, held a one-stroke lead over Gene Sauers. **Second Round--**Sauers and Pavin, tied at 5-under par 139, were one stroke ahead of Steve Stricker, Davis Love III and Bernhard Langer. **Third Round--**Langer and Pavin, deadlocked at 5-under-par 211, were one stroke in front of Lee Janzen.

CUT: 74 players at 5-over-par 149.

WEATHER: Sunny and warm Thursday, with winds gusting to 30 mph. Continued sunny, mild and windy Friday, Saturday and Sunday.

Winner : Lee Janzen 69-74-69-71 283 $540,000.00

Player	Pos.	Scores	Total	Money
Bernhard Langer	2	69-71-71-73	284	$324,000.00
Corey Pavin	T 3	66-73-72-74	285	$156,000.00
Gene Sauers	T 3	67-72-78-68	285	$156,000.00
Payne Stewart	T 3	69-73-71-72	285	$156,000.00
Brad Bryant	T 6	72-71-72-71	286	$104,250.00
Davis Love III	T 6	73-67-74-72	286	$104,250.00
Billy Andrade	T 8	74-69-73-71	287	$87,000.00
Larry Mize	T 8	69-77-72-69	287	$87,000.00
Joe Ozaki	T 8	74-70-72-71	287	$87,000.00
Brian Claar	T11	74-70-71-73	288	$69,000.00
Scott Simpson	T11	71-72-73-72	288	$69,000.00
Steve Stricker	T11	69-71-74-74	288	$69,000.00
Tom Lehman	T14	71-72-72-74	289	$52,500.00
Phil Mickelson	T14	78-66-75-70	289	$52,500.00
Colin Montgomerie	T14	79-70-71-69	289	$52,500.00
Craig Stadler	T14	73-73-75-68	289	$52,500.00
Curt Byrum	T18	73-71-76-70	290	$39,120.00
Mark Calcavecchia	T18	74-75-71-70	290	$39,120.00
Lennie Clements	T18	71-71-76-72	290	$39,120.00
Jeff Maggert	T18	71-72-72-75	290	$39,120.00
Billy Mayfair	T18	71-77-70-72	290	$39,120.00
Jim Gallagher, Jr.	T23	74-72-73-72	291	$25,950.00
Mark McCumber	T23	71-73-72-75	291	$25,950.00
Mark Mcnulty	T23	76-72-71-72	291	$25,950.00
Jose Maria Olazabal	T23	78-70-74-69	291	$25,950.00
Curtis Strange	T23	76-71-72-72	291	$25,950.00
Ian Woosnam	T23	74-69-73-75	291	$25,950.00
Michael Bradley	T29	75-70-74-73	292	$19,500.00
Fred Couples	T29	73-72-73-74	292	$19,500.00
Peter Jacobsen	T29	74-69-71-78	292	$19,500.00
Jumbo Ozaki	T29	72-72-75-73	292	$19,500.00
Tom Watson	T29	72-71-75-74	292	$19,500.00
Bob Estes	T34	76-73-75-69	293	$16,200.00
Loren Roberts	T34	73-72-72-76	293	$16,200.00
Justin Leonard	T34	73-74-72-74	293	$16,200.00
Seve Ballesteros	T37	75-68-73-78	294	$13,200.00
David Frost	T37	72-74-75-73	294	$13,200.00
Mike Heinen	T37	74-75-67-78	294	$13,200.00
Andrew Magee	T37	70-75-72-77	294	$13,200.00
Greg Norman	T37	70-74-73-77	294	$13,200.00
Nick Price	T37	73-71-75-75	294	$13,200.00
Bob Gilder	T43	73-76-75-71	295	$9,620.00
Tom Kite	T43	71-74-76-74	295	$9,620.00
Wayne Levi	T43	73-74-74-74	295	$9,620.00
Bruce Lietzke	T43	78-70-75-72	295	$9,620.00
Vijay Singh	T43	74-72-73-76	295	$9,620.00
D.A. Weibring	T43	71-70-73-81	295	$9,620.00
Brad Faxon	T49	73-74-76-73	296	$7,330.00
Robert Gamez	T49	74-69-78-75	296	$7,330.00
Paul Goydos	T49	75-74-75-72	296	$7,330.00
Jesper Parnevik	T49	74-74-72-76	296	$7,330.00
Dicky Pride	T49	74-73-74-75	296	$7,330.00
Jeff Sluman	T49	74-74-78-70	296	$7,330.00
Bob Lohr	T55	74-75-73-75	297	$6,750.00
John Mahaffey	T55	76-73-72-76	297	$6,750.00
Rocco Mediate	T55	71-74-80-72	297	$6,750.00
Kenny Perry	T55	76-73-73-75	297	$6,750.00
Fuzzy Zoeller	T55	72-73-77-75	297	$6,750.00
Hale Irwin	T55	73-68-78-78	297	$6,750.00
Chip Beck	T61	72-75-76-75	298	$6,390.00
Clark Dennis	T61	78-71-77-72	298	$6,390.00
Fred Funk	T61	73-73-74-78	298	$6,390.00
Ken Green	T61	77-71-74-76	298	$6,390.00
Nolan Henke	T61	74-75-72-77	298	$6,390.00
Bobby Wadkins	T61	75-74-77-72	298	$6,390.00
Kirk Triplett	67	71-75-78-75	299	$6,180.00
Ernie Els	T68	72-72-78-78	300	$6,032.25
Gil Morgan	T68	74-74-75-77	300	$6,032.25
Dan Pohl	T68	72-74-76-78	300	$6,032.25
Bob Tway	T68	78-71-74-77	300	$6,032.25
Donnie Hammond	72	73-76-81-72	302	$5,880.00
Robert Allenby	73	77-72-78-79	306	$5,820.00

The following players did not finish (C=cut, W=withdrew, D=disqualified)

C—150- Guy Boros, Rick Fehr, Bill Glasson, John Morse, Larry Nelson, Frank Nobilo, David Ogrin, Mike Reid, Steve Rintoul, Mike Standly, Doug Tewell, Duffy Waldorf. **151-** Jay Don Blake, Mark Brooks, Ben Crenshaw, Yoshinori Mizumaki, Brett Ogle, Steve Pate, Hal Sutton. **152-** Dave Barr, Russ Cochran, Dan Forsman, Wayne Grady, Mike Hulbert, Greg Kraft, Roger Maltbie, Blaine McCallister, Jim McGovern, Ted Tryba. **153-** Fulton Allem, Glen Day, Joel Edwards, Nick Faldo, Robin Freeman, Jay Haas, Dennis Paulson, Mike Sullivan. **154-** Jay Delsing, David Edwards, Jim Furyk, John Huston, Scott Verplank. **155-** Mark Carnevale, David Feherty, Sandy Lyle, Jack Nicklaus, Mark O'Meara, Craig Parry, Dave Stockton, Jr. **156-** David Duval, Dillard Pruitt, Tom Purtzer, Paul Stankowski, John Wilson. **157-** Ed Humenik, Brian Kamm, Neal Lancaster, Andy North, Jim Thorpe. **158-** Bob Burns, Chris DiMarco, Mike Springer. **159-** Paul Azinger, Brandel Chamblee, Hubert Green, Gary Hallberg, Lanny Wadkins. **161-** Keith Clearwater, Brian Henninger, Jodie Mudd. **W—222-** John Cook, **76-** Steve Elkington, **82-** Scott Hoch, **85-** Ian Baker-Finch, Calvin Peete. **D—81-** Steve Lowery.

THE PLAYERS CHAMPIONSHIP

TOURNAMENT HISTORY

Year	Winner	Score	Runner-up	Score	Location	Par/Yards
TOURNAMENT PLAYERS CHAMPIONSHIP						
1974	Jack Nicklaus	272	J.C. Snead	274	Atlanta CC, Atlanta, GA	72/6883
1975	Al Geiberger	270	Dave Stockton	273	Colonial CC, Fort Worth, TX	70/7160
1976	Jack Nicklaus	269	J.C. Snead	272	Inverrary G&CC, Lauderhill, FL	72/7127
1977	Mark Hayes	289	Mike McCullough	291	Sawgrass, Ponte Vedra, FL	72/7174
1978	Jack Nicklaus	289	Lou Graham	290	Sawgrass, Ponte Vedra, FL	72/7174
1979	Lanny Wadkins	283	Tom Watson	288	Sawgrass, Ponte Vedra, FL	72/7174
1980	Lee Trevino	278	Ben Crenshaw	279	Sawgrass, Ponte Vedra, FL	72/7174
1981	*Raymond Floyd	285	Barry Jaeckel	285	Sawgrass, Ponte Vedra, FL	72/7174
			Curtis Strange			
	(Won playoff with par on first extra hole)					
1982	Jerry Pate	280	Brad Bryant	282	TPC at Sawgrass, Ponte Vedra, FL	72/6857
			Scott Simpson			
1983	Hal Sutton	283	Bob Eastwood	284	TPC at Sawgrass, Ponte Vedra, FL	72/6857
1984	Fred Couples	277	Lee Trevino	278	TPC at Sawgrass, Ponte Vedra, FL	72/6857
1985	Calvin Peete	274	D.A. Weibring	277	TPC at Sawgrass, Ponte Vedra, FL	72/6857
1986	John Mahaffey	275	Larry Mize	276	TPC at Sawgrass, Ponte Vedra, FL	72/6857
1987	*Sandy Lyle	274	Jeff Sluman	274	TPC at Sawgrass, Ponte Vedra, FL	72/6857
	(Won playoff with par on third extra hole)					
THE PLAYERS CHAMPIONSHIP						
1988	Mark McCumber	273	Mike Reid	277	TPC at Sawgrass, Ponte Vedra, FL	72/6857
1989	Tom Kite	279	Chip Beck	280	TPC at Sawgrass, Ponte Vedra, FL	72/6857
1990	Jodie Mudd	278	Mark Calcavecchia	279	TPC at Sawgrass, Ponte Vedra, FL	72/6857
1991	Steve Elkington	276	Fuzzy Zoeller	277	TPC at Sawgrass, Ponte Vedra, FL	72/6857
1992	Davis Love III	273	Ian Baker-Finch	277	TPC at Sawgrass, Ponte Vedra, FL	72/6857
			Phil Blackmar			
			Nick Faldo			
			Tom Watson			
1993	Nick Price	270	Bernhard Langer	275	TPC at Sawgrass, Ponte Vedra, FL	72/6857
1994	Greg Norman	264	Fuzzy Zoeller	268	TPC at Sawgrass, Ponte Vedra, FL	72/6857
1995	Lee Janzen	283	Bernhard Langer	284	TPC at Sawgrass, Ponte Vedra, FL	72/6857

Eligibility Requirements for the 1996 PLAYERS Championship

The starting field for the 1996 PLAYERS Championship shall consist of the following players:

1) The top 125 PGA TOUR members from Final 1995 Official Money List.
2) All winners of PGA TOUR events awarding official money and official victory status in the preceding 12 months, concluding with the Freeport•McDermott Classic and dating from the 1995 PLAYERS Championship.
3) Winners in the last 10 calendar years of THE PLAYERS Championship, Masters, U.S. Open, PGA Championship and NEC World Series of Golf.
4) British Open winners since 1990.
5) Six players, not otherwise eligible, designated by THE PLAYERS Championship Committee as "special selections."
6) Any players, not otherwise eligible, who are among the top-10 money-winners from the 1996 Official Money List through the Freeport•McDermott Classic.
7) To complete a field of 144 players, those players in order, not otherwise eligible, from the 1996 Official Money List through the Freeport•McDermott Classic.

Tournament Record: 264 -- Greg Norman, 1994
Current Course Record: 63 -- Fred Couples, 1992; Greg Norman, 1994

KEY: *= Playoff

1995 FREEPORT-MCMORAN CLASSIC

English Turn G&CC, New Orleans, LA **Purse: $1,200,000**
Par: 36-36--72 **March 30-April 2, 1995**

LEADERS: First Round--J.L. Lewis shot 8-under-par 64 to lead Brad Bryant by one stroke. **Second Round** --Dave Barr, Mike Standly and David Duval shared the lead at 9-under-par 135. They led Lewis and Omar Uresti by one stroke.**Third Round--**Davis Love III, at 13-under-par 203, led Standly and Steve Jones by one stroke.

CUT: 77 players at 1-under-par 143.

PRO-AM: Thunderstorms with heavy rain forced cancellation of the pro-am. Each professional scheduled to compete received $144.24.

WEATHER: Thursday's round was delayed 30 minutes due to wet conditions. Thursday was overcast with periods of light rain. Rain delayed Friday's round until 11:50 a.m. Play was suspended at 6 p.m. due to darkness, with 71 players left on the course. The second round resumed Saturday at 7:30 a.m. and was completed at 11:58 a.m., when it was sunny and in the 60s. The third round was suspended at 6:27 p.m., with six players left on the course. Play resumed Sunday at 8:30 a.m. Sunday was sunny and breezy with temperatures in the 70s.

Winner: Davis Love III 68-69-66-71 274 $216,000.00

(Won playoff with birdie-2 on second extra hole)

Player	Pos	Scores	Total	Money
Mike Heinen	2	66-71-71-66	274	$129,600.00
David Duval	3	67-68-71-69	275	$81,600.00
Craig Parry	4	71-69-66-70	276	$57,600.00
Jeff Maggert	T 5	72-66-70-69	277	$43,800.00
David Peoples	T 5	70-69-66-72	277	$43,800.00
Mike Standly	T 5	70-65-69-73	277	$43,800.00
Brad Bryant	T 8	65-74-69-70	278	$36,000.00
Scott Simpson	T 8	68-70-71-69	278	$36,000.00
Danny Briggs	T10	69-71-73-66	279	$27,600.00
Brian Claar	T10	68-70-71-70	279	$27,600.00
Lennie Clements	T10	69-68-70-72	279	$27,600.00
Kirk Triplett	T10	66-73-71-69	279	$27,600.00
Mark Wiebe	T10	70-68-68-73	279	$27,600.00
Woody Austin	T15	68-71-70-71	280	$16,880.00
Michael Bradley	T15	68-71-67-74	280	$16,880.00
Fred Couples	T15	73-68-68-71	280	$16,880.00
Steve Jones	T15	69-69-66-76	280	$16,880.00
Greg Kraft	T15	70-71-67-72	280	$16,880.00
Billy Mayfair	T15	67-71-70-72	280	$16,880.00
Joe Ozaki	T15	73-70-67-70	280	$16,880.00
Jesper Parnevik	T15	71-67-70-72	280	$16,880.00
Tony Sills	T15	71-71-70-68	280	$16,880.00
John Adams	T24	69-69-71-72	281	$10,560.00
Steve Lowery	T24	73-68-72-68	281	$10,560.00
Scott Verplank	T24	70-67-70-74	281	$10,560.00
Dave Barr	T27	67-68-74-73	282	$8,520.00
Pete Jordan	T27	72-67-75-68	282	$8,520.00
Mike Reid	T27	68-69-73-72	282	$8,520.00
Omar Uresti	T27	70-66-74-72	282	$8,520.00
Grant Waite	T27	68-72-72-70	282	$8,520.00
Tim Loustalot	T32	71-71-70-71	283	$6,497.15
John Mahaffey	T32	70-70-73-70	283	$6,497.15
Keith Clearwater	T32	74-69-70-70	283	$6,497.14
Sandy Lyle	T32	69-72-71-71	283	$6,497.14
Andrew Magee	T32	69-73-72-69	283	$6,497.14
Doug Martin	T32	69-71-72-71	283	$6,497.14
Don Pooley	T32	67-75-71-70	283	$6,497.14
Ronnie Black	T39	66-75-72-71	284	$4,920.00
Fred Funk	T39	70-72-68-74	284	$4,920.00
Steve Gotsche	T39	73-69-71-71	284	$4,920.00
Justin Leonard	T39	69-73-71-71	284	$4,920.00
Ian Woosnam	T39	70-69-71-74	284	$4,920.00
J.L. Lewis	T44	64-72-72-77	285	$4,080.00
Mark Wurtz	T44	68-70-74-73	285	$4,080.00
Emlyn Aubrey	T46	69-74-73-70	286	$3,496.00
Jim Carter	T46	72-70-73-71	286	$3,496.00
Mike Smith	T46	70-72-72-72	286	$3,496.00
Patrick Burke	T49	69-71-80-67	287	$2,932.00
Russ Cochran	T49	68-74-72-73	287	$2,932.00
Glen Day	T49	69-74-69-75	287	$2,932.00
Jerry Pate	T49	71-72-73-71	287	$2,932.00
Steve Rintoul	T49	73-70-71-73	287	$2,932.00
John Wilson	T49	72-68-72-75	287	$2,932.00
Michael Allen	T55	72-67-74-75	288	$2,712.00
Marco Dawson	T55	73-69-74-72	288	$2,712.00
Wayne Grady	T55	70-69-75-74	288	$2,712.00
Scott Gump	T55	70-71-74-73	288	$2,712.00
Jerry Haas	T55	73-69-74-72	288	$2,712.00
Chris DiMarco	T60	70-71-73-75	289	$2,616.00
David Frost	T60	74-69-74-72	289	$2,616.00
Skip Kendall	T60	69-71-75-74	289	$2,616.00
Bobby Doolittle	T63	71-70-73-76	290	$2,508.00
Jim Furyk	T63	70-72-72-76	290	$2,508.00
Dudley Hart	T63	71-72-71-76	290	$2,508.00
Bob Lohr	T63	69-74-76-71	290	$2,508.00
Doug Tewell	T63	68-72-77-73	290	$2,508.00
Bruce Vaughan	T63	70-72-74-74	290	$2,508.00
Kelly Gibson	T69	70-68-75-78	291	$2,412.00
Jay Williamson	T69	68-75-75-73	291	$2,412.00
Duffy Waldorf	71	70-68-77-77	292	$2,376.00
Brett Ogle	T72	71-71-73-78	293	$2,340.00
Don Reese	T72	69-70-75-79	293	$2,340.00
Robert Gamez	74	71-71-71-81	294	$2,304.00
Kawika Cotner	T75	71-69-78-77	295	$2,268.00
Pete Mathews	T75	69-74-79-73	295	$2,268.00
David Feherty	77	70-73-77-80	300	$2,232.00

The following players did not finish (C=cut, W=withdrew, D=disqualified)

C—144- Bob Burns, Curt Byrum, Robin Freeman, Gary Hallberg, Donnie Hammond, Jonathan Kaye, Dick Mast, Scott McCarron, David Ogrin, Jose Maria Olazabal, Larry Rinker, Joey Sindelar. **145-** Robert Allenby, Mark Brooks, Joel Edwards, Kiyoshi Murota, Steve Pate, Sammy Rachels, Dicky Thompson. **146-** Mike Brisky, Bill Britton, Bart Bryant, Clark Burroughs, Keith Fergus, Bruce Fleisher, Jim Gallagher, Jr., Carl Paulson, Chris Perry, Bill Porter, Lee Rinker, Charlie Rymer, Ted Schulz, Ray Stewart, Howard Twitty. **147-** Pat Bates, Ben Crenshaw, Ed Humenik, Dave Stockton, Jr., Jim Thorpe, Jeff Woodland. **148-** Joe Acosta, Jr., Phil Blackmar, Mark Carnevale, Scott Ford, Paul Goydos, Hal Sutton, Tray Tyner, Lanny Wadkins. **149-** Billy Ray Brown, Jay Delsing, Bob Eastwood, J.P. Hayes, Tom Hearn, Jeff Leonard, David Marchand, Harry Taylor. **150-** Alan Pate. **151-** Tommy Armour III, Andy Bean, Ryan Howison. **152-** Dennis Paulson, Carl Poche. **154-** Leigh Brannan. **157-** Jay Mclelland. **W—157-**Ted Tryba, **73-** Wayne Levi, **81-** Joey Rassett.

FREEPORT•McDERMOTT CLASSIC

TOURNAMENT HISTORY

Year	Winner	Score	Runner-up	Score	Location	ParYards
GREATER NEW ORLEANS OPEN INVITATIONAL						
1938	Harry Cooper	285	Harold McSpaden	289	City Park GC, New Orleans, LA	72/6656
1939	Henry Picard	284	Dick Metz	289	City Park GC, New Orleans, LA	72/6656
1940	Jimmy Demaret	286	Ralph Guldahl	287	City Park GC, New Orleans, LA	72/6656
			Harold McSpaden			
			Sam Snead			
1941	Henry Picard	276	Ben Hogan	278	City Park GC, New Orleans, LA	72/6656
1942	Lloyd Mangrum	281	Lawson Little	282	City Park GC, New Orleans, LA	72/6656
			Sam Snead			
1943	No Tournament					
1944	Sammy Byrd	285	Byron Nelson	290	City Park GC, New Orleans, LA	72/6656
1945	*Byron Nelson	284	Harold McSpaden	284	City Park GC, New Orleans, LA	72/6656
1946	Byron Nelson	277	Ben Hogan	282	City Park GC, New Orleans, LA	72/6656
1947	No Tournament					
1948	Bob Hamilton	280	Roberto De Vicenzo	281	City Park GC. New Orleans, LA	72/6656
			Fred Haas			
1949-			Lawson Little			
1957	No Tournaments					
1958	*Billy Casper	278	Ken Venturi	278	City Park GC, New Orleans, LA	72/6656
1959	Bill Collins	280	Jack Burke, Jr.	283	City Park GC, New Orleans, LA	72/6656
			Tom Nieporte			
1960	Dow Finsterwald	270	Al Besselink	276	City Park GC, New Orleans, LA	72/6656
1961	Doug Sanders	272	Gay Brewer	277	City Park GC, New Orleans, LA	72/6656
			Mac Main			
1962	Bo Wininger	281	Bob Rosburg	283	City Park GC, New Orleans, LA	72/6656
1963	Bo Wininger	279	Tony Lema	282	Lakewood CC, New Orleans, LA	72/7080
			Bob Rosburg			
1964	Mason Rudolph	283	Jack Nicklaus	284	Lakewood CC, New Orleans, LA	72/7080
			Chi Chi Rodriguez			
			Glenn Stuart			
1965	Dick Mayer	273	Bruce Devlin	274	Lakewood CC, New Orleans, LA	72/7080
			Bill Martindale			
1966	Frank Beard	276	Gardner Dickinson	278	Lakewood CC, New Orleans, LA	72/7080
1967	George Knudson	277	Jack Nicklaus	278	Lakewood CC, New Orleans, LA	72/7080
1968	George Archer	271			Lakewood CC, New Orleans, LA	72/7080
1969	*Larry Hinson	275	Frank Beard	275	Lakewood CC, New Orleans, LA	72/7080
1970	*Miller Barber	278	Bob Charles	278	Lakewood CC, New Orleans, LA	72/7080
			Howie Johnson			
1971	Frank Beard	276	Hubert Green	277	Lakewood CC, New Orleans, LA	72/7080
1972	Gary Player	279	Dave Eichelberger	280	Lakewood CC, New Orleans, LA	72/7080
			Jack Nicklaus			
1973	*Jack Nicklaus	280	Miller Barber	280	Lakewood CC, New Orleans, LA	72/7080
1974	Lee Trevino	267	Bobby Cole	275	Lakewood CC, New Orleans, LA	72/7080
			Ben Crenshaw			
FIRST NBC NEW ORLEANS OPEN						
1975	Billy Casper	271	Peter Oosterhuis	273	Lakewood CC, New Orleans, LA	72/7080
1976	Larry Ziegler	274	Victor Regalado	275	Lakewood CC, New Orleans, LA	72/7080
1977	Jim Simons	273	Stan Lee	276	Lakewood CC, New Orleans, LA	72/7080
1978	Lon Hinkle	271	Gibby Gilbert	272	Lakewood CC, New Orleans, LA	72/7080
			Fuzzy Zoeller			
1979	Hubert Green	273	Frank Conner	274	Lakewood CC, New Orleans, LA	72/7080
			Bruce Lietzke			
			Steve Melnyk			
			Lee Trevino			
GREATER NEW ORLEANS OPEN						
1980	Tom Watson	273	Lee Trevino	275	Lakewood CC, New Orleans, LA	72/7080
USF&G NEW ORLEANS OPEN						
1981	Tom Watson	270	Bruce Fleisher	272	Lakewood CC, New Orleans, LA	72/7080

FREEPORT•McDERMOTT CLASSIC

TOURNAMENT HISTORY

Year	Winner	Score	Runner-up	Score	Location	ParYards
USF&G CLASSIC						
1982	~Scott Hoch	206	Bob Shearer Tom Watson	208	Lakewood CC, New Orleans, LA	72/7080
1983	Bill Rogers	274	David Edwards Jay Haas Vance Heafner	277	Lakewood CC, New Orleans, LA	72/7080
1984	Bob Eastwood	272	Larry Rinker	275	Lakewood CC, New Orleans, LA	72/7080
1985	~Seve Ballesteros	205	Peter Jacobsen John Mahaffey	207	Lakewood CC, New Orleans, LA	72/7080
1986	Calvin Peete	269	Pat McGowan	274	Lakewood CC, New Orleans, LA	72/7080
1987	Ben Crenshaw	268	Curtis Strange	271	Lakewood CC, New Orleans, LA	72/7080
1988	Chip Beck	262	Lanny Wadkins	269	Lakewood CC, New Orleans, LA	72/7080
1989	Tim Simpson	274	Greg Norman Hal Sutton	276	English Turn G&CC, New Orleans, LA	72/7106
1990	David Frost	276	Greg Norman	277	English Turn G&CC, New Orleans, LA	72/7106
1991	*Ian Woosnam	275	Jim Hallet	275	English Turn G&CC, New Orleans, LA	72/7106
FREEPORT-McMORAN CLASSIC						
1992	Chip Beck	276	Greg Norman Mike Standly	277	English Turn G&CC, New Orleans, LA	72/7106
1993	Mike Standly	281	Russ Cochran Payne Stewart	282	English Turn G&CC, New Orleans, LA	72/7106
1994	Ben Crenshaw	273	Jose Maria Olazabal	276	English Turn G&CC, New Orleans, LA	72/7106
1995	*Davis Love III	274	Mike Heinen	274	English Turn G&CC, New Orleans, LA	72/7106

Tournament Record: 262 -- Chip Beck, 1988 (Lakewood CC)
Current Course Record: 62 -- Dennis Paulson, 1994

KEY: * = Playoff ~ = Weather-shortened

1995 MASTERS TOURNAMENT

Augusta National GC, Augusta, GA **Purse: $2,200,000**
Par: 36-36--72 **Yards: 6,925** **April 6-9, 1995**

LEADERS: First Round--David Frost, Phil Mickelson, Jose Maria Olazabal, at 6-under-par 66, led by one over Jack Nicklaus, David Gilford and Corey Pavin. **Second Round--**Jay Haas, at 9-under-par 135, led by one over Scott Hoch and John Huston. **Third Round--**Ben Crenshaw and Brian Henninger led by one over Hoch, Haas, Steve Elkington, Phil Mickelson and Fred Couples.

CUT: 47 players at 1-over-par 145 from a field of 86.

WEATHER: Thursday was cool and rainy, but no delays. Friday there was a 45-minute delay at the start of play due to fog. The rest of Friday, Saturday and Sunday were warm and sunny, with some light wind in the afternoon.

Winner: Ben Crenshaw 70-67-69-68 274 $396,000.00

Player	Pos.	Scores	Total	Money
Davis Love III	2	69-69-71-66	275	$237,600.00
Jay Haas	T3	71-64-72-70	277	$127,600.00
Greg Norman	T3	73-68-68-68	277	$127,600.00
Steve Elkington	T5	73-67-67-72	279	$83,600.00
David Frost	T5	66-71-71-71	279	$83,600.00
Scott Hoch	T7	69-67-71-73	280	$70,950.00
Phil Mickelson	T7	66-71-70-73	280	$70,950.00
Curtis Strange	9	72-71-65-73	281	$63,800.00
Fred Couples	T10	71-69-67-75	282	$57,200.00
Brian Henninger	T10	70-68-68-76	282	$57,200.00
Lee Janzen	T12	69-69-74-71	283	$48,400.00
Kenny Perry	T12	73-70-71-69	283	$48,400.00
Hale Irwin	T14	69-72-71-72	284	$39,600.00
Tom Watson	T14	73-70-69-72	284	$39,600.00
Jose Maria Olazabal	T14	66-74-72-72	284	$39,600.00
Paul Azinger	T17	70-72-73-70	285	$28,786.00
Brad Faxon	T17	76-69-69-71	285	$28,786.00
Ray Floyd	T17	71-70-70-74	285	$28,786.00
John Huston	T17	70-66-72-77	285	$28,786.00
Colin Montgomerie	T17	71-69-76-69	285	$28,786.00
Corey Pavin	T17	67-71-72-75	285	$28,786.00
Ian Woosnam	T17	69-72-71-73	285	$28,786.00
David Edwards	T24	69-73-73-71	286	$18,260.00
Nick Faldo	T24	70-70-71-75	286	$18,260.00
David Gilford	T24	67-73-75-71	286	$18,260.00
Loren Roberts	T24	72-69-72-73	286	$18,260.00
Duffy Waldorf	T24	74-69-67-76	286	$18,260.00
Bob Estes	T29	73-70-76-68	287	$15,300.00
Jumbo Ozaki	T29	70-74-70-73	287	$15,300.00
Peter Jacobsen	T31	72-73-69-74	288	$13,325.00
Bernhard Langer	T31	71-69-73-75	288	$13,325.00
Bruce Lietzke	T31	72-71-71-74	288	$13,325.00
Mark O'Meara	T31	68-72-71-77	288	$13,325.00
Chip Beck	T35	68-76-69-77	290	$10,840.00
Dan Forsman	T35	71-74-74-71	290	$10,840.00
Wayne Grady	T35	69-73-74-74	290	$10,840.00
Mark McCumber	T35	73-69-69-79	290	$10,840.00
Jack Nicklaus	T35	67-78-70-75	290	$10,840.00
Tom Lehman	40	71-72-74-75	292	$9,500.00
Mark Calcavecchia	T41	70-72-78-73	293	$8,567.00
Jeff Sluman	T41	73-72-71-77	293	$8,567.00
Payne Stewart	T41	71-72-72-78	293	$8,567.00
Tiger Woods	T41	72-72-77-72	293	Amateur
Seve Ballesteros	T45	75-68-78-75	296	$7,500.00
John Daly	T45	75-69-71-81	296	$7,500.00
Rick Fehr	47	76-69-69-83	297	$6,800.00

The following players did not finish (C=cut, W=withdrew, D=disqualified)

C—146- Clark Dennis, Miguel Jimenez, Sandy Lyle, Tsuneyuki Nakajima, Craig Stadler, Hal Sutton, Fuzzy Zoeller. **147-** Brad Bryant, Charles Coody, John Cook, Ernie Els, Mike Heinen, Tom Kite, Larry Mize, Mike Sullivan. **148-** Steve Lowery, Jeff Maggert, Mark McNulty, John Morse, Vijay Singh. **149-** Gay Brewer, Gary Player, Nick Price, Lanny Wadkins. **150-** Jim McGovern. **151-** Bill Glasson, Neal Lancaster. **152-** Arnold Palmer, Dicky Pride. **153-** Mark Brooks. **154-** Frank Nobilo. **155-** Tim Jackson, Trip Kuehne. **157-** Lee James, Mike Springer. **160-** Ian Baker-Finch. **161-** Guy Yamamoto. **168-**Billy Casper. **W—88-** Doug Ford.

MASTERS TOURNAMENT

TOURNAMENT HISTORY

Year	Winner	Score	Runner-up	Score
1934	Horton Smith	284	Craig Wood	285
1935	*Gene Sarazen (144)	282	Craig Wood (149)	282
1936	Horton Smith	285	Harry Cooper	286
1937	Byron Nelson	283	Ralph Guldahl	285
1938	Henry Picard	285	Ralph Guldahl	287
			Harry Cooper	
1939	Ralph Guldahl	279	Sam Snead	280
1940	Jimmy Demaret	280	Lloyd Mangrum	284
1941	Craig Wood	280	Byron Nelson	283
1942	*Byron Nelson (69)	280	Ben Hogan (70)	280
1943	No Tournament—World War II			
1944	No Tournament—World War II			
1945	No Tournament—World War II			
1946	Herman Keiser	282	Ben Hogan	283
1947	Jimmy Demaret	281	Byron Nelson	283
			Frank Stranahan	
1948	Claude Harmon	279	Cary Middlecoff	284
1949	Sam Snead	282	Johnny Bulla	285
			Lloyd Mangrum	
1950	Jimmy Demaret	283	Jim Ferrier	285
1951	Ben Hogan	280	Skee Riegel	282
1952	Sam Snead	286	Jack Burke, Jr.	290
1953	Ben Hogan	274	Ed Oliver, Jr.	279
1954	*Sam Snead (70)	289	Ben Hogan (71)	289
1955	Cary Middlecoff	279	Ben Hogan	286
1956	Jack Burke, Jr.	289	Ken Venturi	290
1957	Doug Ford	282	Sam Snead	286
1958	Arnold Palmer	284	Doug Ford	285
			Fred Hawkins	
1959	Art Wall, Jr.	284	Cary Middlecoff	285
1960	Arnold Palmer	282	Ken Venturi	283
1961	Gary Player	280	Charles R. Coe	281
			Arnold Palmer	
1962	*Arnold Palmer (68)	280	Gary Player (71)	280
			Dow Finsterwald (77)	
1963	Jack Nicklaus	286	Tony Lema	287
1964	Arnold Palmer	276	Dave Marr	282
			Jack Nicklaus	
1965	Jack Nicklaus	271	Arnold Palmer	280
			Gary Player	
1966	*Jack Nicklaus (70)	288	Tommy Jacobs (72)	288
			Gay Brewer, Jr. (78)	
1967	Gay Brewer, Jr.	280	Bobby Nichols	281
1968	Bob Goalby	277	Roberto De Vicenzo	278
1969	George Archer	281	Billy Casper	282
			George Knudson	
			Tom Weiskopf	
1970	*Billy Casper (69)	279	Gene Littler (74)	279
1971	Charles Coody	279	Johnny Miller	281
			Jack Nicklaus	
1972	Jack Nicklaus	286	Bruce Crampton	289
			Bobby Mitchell	
			Tom Weiskopf	
1973	Tommy Aaron	283	J. C. Snead	284
1974	Gary Player	278	Tom Weiskopf	280
			Dave Stockton	

MASTERS TOURNAMENT

TOURNAMENT HISTORY

Year	Winner	Score	Runner-up	Score
1975	Jack Nicklaus	276	Johnny Miller Tom Weiskopf	277
1976	Ray Floyd	271	Ben Crenshaw	279
1977	Tom Watson	276	Jack Nicklaus	278
1978	Gary Player	277	Hubert Green Rod Funseth Tom Watson	278
1979	*Fuzzy Zoeller	280	Ed Sneed Tom Watson	280
1980	Seve Ballesteros	275	Gibby Gilbert Jack Newton	279
1981	Tom Watson	280	Johnny Miller Jack Nicklaus	282
1982	*Craig Stadler	284	Dan Pohl	284
1983	Seve Ballesteros	280	Ben Crenshaw Tom Kite	284
1984	Ben Crenshaw	277	Tom Watson	279
1985	Bernhard Langer	282	Curtis Strange Seve Ballesteros Ray Floyd	284
1986	Jack Nicklaus	279	Greg Norman Tom Kite	280
1987	*Larry Mize	285	Seve Ballesteros Greg Norman	285
1988	Sandy Lyle	281	Mark Calcavecchia	282
1989	*Nick Faldo	283	Scott Hoch	283
1990	*Nick Faldo	278	Ray Floyd	278
1991	Ian Woosnam	277	Jose Maria Olazabal	278
1992	Fred Couples	275	Ray Floyd	277
1993	Bernhard Langer	277	Chip Beck	281
1994	Jose Maria Olazabal	279	Tom Lehman	281
1995	Ben Crenshaw	274	Davis Love III	275

Tournament Record: 271 -- Jack Nicklaus, 1965; Raymond Floyd, 1976
Current Course Record: 63 -- Nick Price, 1986

KEY: *=Playoff *Figures in parentheses indicate playoff scores*

1995 MCI CLASSIC

Harbour Town GL, Hilton Head Island, SC **Purse: $1,300,000**
Par: 36-36--72 Yards: 6,916 **April 13-16, 1995**

LEADERS: First Round--Gene Sauers and Nolan Henke, at 5-under-par 66, led Brian Kamm, Bob Tway and Tom Lehman by one stroke. **Second Round**--Lehman, at 10-under-par 132, led by four over Tway, Sauers, Jesper Parnevik, Payne Stewart and John Daly. **Third Round**--Mark McCumber, David Edwards, David Frost and Sauers, at 8-under-par 205, led by one over Gil Morgan, Tom Watson, Scott Hoch and Stewart.

CUT: 79 players at 2-over-par 144.

PRO-AM: $7,500. Individual--Scott Hoch, 64, $750. Team--Mark Brooks, Dicky Pride, 53, $675 each.

WEATHER: Brief shower on Thursday morning, but no delays. The rest of the week was sunny, warm and breezy.

Winner: Bob Tway 67-69-72-67 275 $234,000.00

(Won playoff with par-3 on second extra hole)

Player	Pos.	Scores	Total	Money
David Frost	T 2	71-68-66-70	275	$114,400.00
Nolan Henke	T 2	66-72-70-67	275	$114,400.00
Woody Austin	T 4	71-72-69-64	276	$53,733.34
Nick Faldo	T 4	74-64-70-68	276	$53,733.33
Mark McCumber	T 4	70-71-64-71	276	$53,733.33
Ernie Els	T 7	73-70-64-70	277	$36,508.34
Nick Price	T 7	69-72-71-65	277	$36,508.34
David Edwards	T 7	70-69-66-72	277	$36,508.33
Steve Lowery	T 7	68-73-66-70	277	$36,508.33
Gil Morgan	T 7	73-71-62-71	277	$36,508.33
Tom Watson	T 7	70-68-68-71	277	$36,508.33
Kelly Gibson	T13	74-69-68-67	278	$22,285.72
Blaine McCallister	T13	73-69-71-65	278	$22,285.72
Lanny Wadkins	T13	73-67-71-67	278	$22,285.72
John Daly	T13	68-68-71-71	278	$22,285.71
Phil Mickelson	T13	68-69-71-70	278	$22,285.71
Loren Roberts	T13	72-65-70-71	278	$22,285.71
Gene Sauers	T13	66-70-69-73	278	$22,285.71
Scott Hoch	T20	70-67-69-73	279	$15,145.00
Peter Jacobsen	T20	69-70-68-72	279	$15,145.00
Wayne Levi	T20	71-71-66-71	279	$15,145.00
Mike Sullivan	T20	70-71-69-69	279	$15,145.00
Paul Goydos	T24	71-69-68-72	280	$9,836.67
Hale Irwin	T24	71-73-69-67	280	$9,836.67
Brian Kamm	T24	67-71-72-70	280	$9,836.67
Steve Stricker	T24	71-69-70-70	280	$9,836.67
Scott Verplank	T24	72-68-70-70	280	$9,836.67
D.A. Weibring	T24	69-70-69-72	280	$9,836.67
Tom Lehman	T24	67-65-75-73	280	$9,836.66
Kenny Perry	T24	72-69-67-72	280	$9,836.66
Payne Stewart	T24	70-66-70-74	280	$9,836.66
Neal Lancaster	T33	69-69-74-69	281	$7,182.50
Jim McGovern	T33	73-69-66-73	281	$7,182.50
Dillard Pruitt	T33	69-72-72-68	281	$7,182.50
Mike Standly	T33	73-70-70-68	281	$7,182.50
Jay Delsing	T37	69-68-72-73	282	$5,590.00
Chris DiMarco	T37	70-73-68-71	282	$5,590.00
Steve Jones	T37	68-72-67-75	282	$5,590.00
Tom Kite	T37	74-68-68-72	282	$5,590.00
Steve Rintoul	T37	73-70-70-69	282	$5,590.00
Tommy Tolles	T37	69-68-73-72	282	$5,590.00
Duffy Waldorf	T37	70-70-72-70	282	$5,590.00
Clark Dennis	T44	69-75-70-69	283	$3,686.23
Dan Forsman	T44	70-72-71-70	283	$3,686.23
Robin Freeman	T44	70-72-71-70	283	$3,686.22
Fred Funk	T44	72-72-69-70	283	$3,686.22
Greg Kraft	T44	68-71-71-73	283	$3,686.22
Justin Leonard	T44	71-68-70-74	283	$3,686.22
Brett Ogle	T44	68-74-67-74	283	$3,686.22
Jesper Parnevik	T44	70-66-72-75	283	$3,686.22
Kirk Triplett	T44	69-73-70-71	283	$3,686.22
Corey Pavin	T53	68-72-73-71	284	$3,024.67
Bobby Wadkins	T53	74-69-69-72	284	$3,024.67
Keith Fergus	T53	70-73-69-72	284	$3,024.66
Chip Beck	T56	73-71-71-70	285	$2,912.00
Brad Faxon	T56	74-70-66-75	285	$2,912.00
Jim Furyk	T56	72-71-69-73	285	$2,912.00
Billy Mayfair	T56	73-71-71-70	285	$2,912.00
John Morse	T56	73-71-66-75	285	$2,912.00
Michael Bradley	T61	75-69-74-68	286	$2,756.00
Wayne Grady	T61	75-69-71-71	286	$2,756.00
Mark O'Meara	T61	73-71-70-72	286	$2,756.00
Craig Parry	T61	70-71-73-72	286	$2,756.00
Steve Pate	T61	74-69-73-70	286	$2,756.00
Dicky Pride	T61	72-68-68-78	286	$2,756.00
Jim Thorpe	T61	70-72-72-72	286	$2,756.00
Paul Azinger	T68	73-70-70-74	287	$2,613.00
Robert Gamez	T68	71-73-71-72	287	$2,613.00
Davis Love III	T68	70-73-73-71	287	$2,613.00
Paul Stankowski	T68	70-74-72-71	287	$2,613.00
Gary Hallberg	T72	73-71-68-76	288	$2,522.00
John Huston	T72	70-67-72-79	288	$2,522.00
Larry Nelson	T72	73-71-78-66	288	$2,522.00
Fulton Allem	T75	69-75-76-70	290	$2,457.00
Ken Green	T75	70-73-76-71	290	$2,457.00
Mark Carnevale	77	75-69-72-75	291	$2,418.00
Billy Andrade	78	74-67-73-78	292	$2,392.00

The following players did not finish (C=cut, W=withdrew, D=disqualified)

C—145- Guy Boros, David Duval, David Feherty, Mike Hulbert, Barry Jaeckel, Lee Janzen, David Ogrin, Jeff Sluman, Ted Tryba. **146-**Jay Don Blake, Bob Boyd, Bob Estes, Brian Henninger, David Thore, John Wilson. **147-**Andy Bean, Russ Cochran, Fred Couples, Joel Edwards, Jay Haas, Jodie Mudd, Dennis Paulson. **148-** Pat Bates, Glen Day, J.L. Lewis. **149-** Mark Brooks, Brandel Chamblee, Brian Claar, Mark McNulty, Larry Mize, Mike Springer, Grant Waite. **150-** Dave Barr, Curt Byrum, Keith Clearwater, Bob Gilder, Andy North, Jerry Pate, Dave Stockton, Jr. **151-** Patrick Burke, Vijay Singh. **152-** Bob Burns, Mike Reid. **153-** Ed Humenik. **154-**Buddy Gardner, Billy Lewis. **W—213-** Robert Allenby,**140-** Greg Norman, **69-** Doug Tewell.

MCI CLASSIC

TOURNAMENT HISTORY

Year	Winner	Score	Runner-up	Score	Location	Par/Yards
HERITAGE CLASSIC						
1969	Arnold Palmer	283	Richard Crawford Bert Yancey	286	Harbour Town GL, Hilton Head, SC	71/6657
1970	Bob Goalby	280	Lanny Wadkins	284	Harbour Town GL, Hilton Head, SC	71/6657
SEA PINES HERITAGE CLASSIC						
1971	Hale Irwin	279	Bob Lunn	280	Harbour Town GL, Hilton Head, SC	71/6657
1972	Johnny Miller	281	Tom Weiskopf	282	Ocean Course, Hilton Head, SC (first two rounds) Harbour Town GL, Hilton Head, SC (second two rounds)	72/6600 71/6657
1973	Hale Irwin	272	Jerry Heard Grier Jones	277	Harbour Town GL, Hilton Head, SC	71/6657
1974	Johnny Miller	276	Gibby Gilbert	279	Harbour Town GL, Hilton Head, SC	71/6657
1975	Jack Nicklaus	271	Tom Weiskopf	274	Harbour Town GL, Hilton Head, SC	71/6657
1976	Hubert Green	274	Jerry McGee	279	Harbour Town GL, Hilton Head, SC	71/6657
1977	Graham Marsh	273	Tom Watson	274	Harbour Town GL, Hilton Head, SC	71/6657
1978	Hubert Green	277	Hale Irwin	280	Harbour Town GL, Hilton Head, SC	71/6657
1979	Tom Watson	270	Ed Sneed	275	Harbour Town GL, Hilton Head, SC	71/6657
1980	*Doug Tewell	280	Jerry Pate	280	Harbour Town GL, Hilton Head, SC	71/6657
1981	Bill Rogers	278	Bruce Devlin Hale Irwin Gil Morgan Craig Stadler	279	Harbour Town GL, Hilton Head, SC	71/6657
1982	*Tom Watson	280	Frank Conner	280	Harbour Town GL, Hilton Head, SC	71/6657
1983	Fuzzy Zoeller	275	Jim Nelford	277	Harbour Town GL, Hilton Head, SC	71/6657
1984	Nick Faldo	270	Tom Kite	271	Harbour Town GL, Hilton Head, SC	71/6657
1985	*Bernhard Langer	273	Bobby Wadkins	273	Harbour Town GL, Hilton Head, SC	71/6657
1986	Fuzzy Zoeller	276	Chip Beck Roger Maltbie Greg Norman	277	Harbour Town GL, Hilton Head, SC	71/6657
MCI HERITAGE CLASSIC						
1987	Davis Love III	271	Steve Jones	272	Harbour Town GL, Hilton Head, SC	71/6657
1988	Greg Norman	271	David Frost Gil Morgan	272	Harbour Town GL, Hilton Head, SC	71/6657
1989	Payne Stewart	268	Kenny Perry	273	Harbour Town GL, Hilton Head, SC	71/6657
1990	*Payne Stewart	276	Steve Jones Larry Mize	276	Harbour Town GL, Hilton Head, SC	71/6657
1991	Davis Love III	271	Ian Baker-Finch	273	Harbour Town GL, Hilton Head, SC	71/6657
1992	Davis Love III	269	Chip Beck	273	Harbour Town GL, Hilton Head, SC	71/6657
1993	David Edwards	273	David Frost	275	Harbour Town GL, Hilton Head, SC	71/6657
1994	Hale Irwin	266	Greg Norman	268	Harbour Town GL, Hilton Head, SC	71/6657
1995	*Bob Tway	275	David Frost Nolan Henke	275	Harbour Town GL, Hilton Head, SC	71/6657

Tournament Record: 266 -- Hale Irwin, 1994
Current Course Record: 61 -- David Frost, 1994

KEY: *=Playoff

1995 KMART GREATER GREENSBORO OPEN

Forest Oaks CC, Greensboro, NC **Purse: $1,500,000**
Par: 36-36--72 Yards: 7,062 **April 20-23, 1995**

LEADERS: First Round--Vijay Singh, Brad Faxon and Steve Lowery each shot 7-under-par 65 and led Davis Love III by one stroke. **Second Round--**Kirk Triplett, after a second-round 65, stood at 11-under-par 133, one stroke ahead of Peter Jacobsen. **Third Round--**Jeff Sluman shot a 66 for 15-under-par 201, two strokes ahead of Jacobsen.

CUT: 73 players at 1-under-par 143.

PRO-AM: Individual--Billy Mayfair, 65, $750. Team--Clark Dennis, 50, $750.

WEATHER: Thursday was sunny and warm until a few afternoon showers moved in. Friday was cooler and overcast with gusty winds. Sunny and back into the 80s on Saturday. Much cooler Sunday with periods of rain.

Winner: Jim Gallagher, Jr. 69-70-69-66 274 $270,000.00

Player	Pos.	Scores	Total	Money
Peter Jacobsen	T 2	69-65-69-72	275	$132,000.00
Jeff Sluman	T 2	70-65-66-74	275	$132,000.00
John Adams	4	70-66-70-70	276	$72,000.00
Mark Calcavecchia	5	68-73-67-69	277	$60,000.00
Jesper Parnevik	6	70-68-68-72	278	$54,000.00
Guy Boros	T 7	73-67-70-69	279	$43,650.00
Brad Faxon	T 7	65-71-71-72	279	$43,650.00
Vijay Singh	T 7	65-72-69-73	279	$43,650.00
Steve Stricker	T 7	68-73-66-72	279	$43,650.00
Ted Tryba	T 7	69-70-69-71	279	$43,650.00
Hal Sutton	T12	67-68-74-71	280	$33,000.00
Fuzzy Zoeller	T12	70-71-70-69	280	$33,000.00
David Duval	T14	72-68-70-71	281	$25,500.00
Gary Hallberg	T14	69-71-69-72	281	$25,500.00
Justin Leonard	T14	70-71-72-68	281	$25,500.00
Loren Roberts	T14	71-70-71-69	281	$25,500.00
Kirk Triplett	T14	68-65-71-77	281	$25,500.00
Chris DiMarco	T19	68-73-71-70	282	$17,550.00
Robert Gamez	T19	69-72-70-71	282	$17,550.00
Steve Gotsche	T19	71-70-69-72	282	$17,550.00
Ed Humenik	T19	73-70-68-71	282	$17,550.00
Brian Kamm	T19	71-71-68-72	282	$17,550.00
Davis Love III	T19	66-71-75-70	282	$17,550.00
Dave Barr	T25	71-68-72-72	283	$11,962.50
Jay Don Blake	T25	71-71-70-71	283	$11,962.50
Brad Bryant	T25	69-66-72-76	283	$11,962.50
Howard Twitty	T25	68-70-77-68	283	$11,962.50
Michael Bradley	T29	69-74-72-69	284	$9,332.15
Chris Perry	T29	73-69-70-72	284	$9,332.15
Billy Andrade	T29	72-68-72-72	284	$9,332.14
Trevor Dodds	T29	68-73-73-70	284	$9,332.14
David Edwards	T29	67-74-71-72	284	$9,332.14
Scott Simpson	T29	67-72-70-75	284	$9,332.14
Mike Sullivan	T29	69-72-70-73	284	$9,332.14
Bob Burns	T36	68-74-72-71	285	$7,065.00
Lennie Clements	T36	68-72-73-72	285	$7,065.00
Bob Lohr	T36	71-71-74-69	285	$7,065.00
Kenny Perry	T36	68-72-74-71	285	$7,065.00
Scott Verplank	T36	72-71-69-73	285	$7,065.00
Bob Boyd	T41	69-72-72-73	286	$5,400.00
Billy Ray Brown	T41	72-70-70-74	286	$5,400.00
Curt Byrum	T41	68-73-72-73	286	$5,400.00
Glen Day	T41	72-70-74-70	286	$5,400.00
Lee Janzen	T41	70-67-76-73	286	$5,400.00
Ted Schulz	T41	72-70-70-74	286	$5,400.00
Keith Fergus	T47	73-70-72-72	287	$4,035.00
Jeff Maggert	T47	72-66-75-74	287	$4,035.00
Gene Sauers	T47	70-71-74-72	287	$4,035.00
Mike Taylor	T47	70-73-73-71	287	$4,035.00
Phil Blackmar	T51	68-73-73-74	288	$3,577.50
Jim Furyk	T51	69-73-70-76	288	$3,577.50
J.P. Hayes	T51	70-70-75-73	288	$3,577.50
Steve Lowery	T51	65-71-74-78	288	$3,577.50
David Peoples	55	68-72-77-72	289	$3,450.00
Ronnie Black	T56	68-70-78-74	290	$3,360.00
Kelly Gibson	T56	71-72-72-75	290	$3,360.00
Nolan Henke	T56	72-71-75-72	290	$3,360.00
Blaine McCallister	T56	71-72-73-74	290	$3,360.00
Tommy Tolles	T56	68-72-73-77	290	$3,360.00
Ed Fiori	T61	70-71-76-74	291	$3,225.00
Mike Heinen	T61	67-75-71-78	291	$3,225.00
Neal Lancaster	T61	70-72-73-76	291	$3,225.00
Paul Stankowski	T61	70-70-79-72	291	$3,225.00
Bob Gilder	T65	74-69-75-74	292	$3,075.00
Skip Kendall	T65	73-69-73-77	292	$3,075.00
Doug Martin	T65	72-69-75-76	292	$3,075.00
Katsumasa Miyamoto	T65	70-72-74-76	292	$3,075.00
Jerry Pate	T65	74-68-73-77	292	$3,075.00
Mike Standly	T65	71-70-75-76	292	$3,075.00
Joel Edwards	71	71-72-76-74	293	$2,970.00
Omar Uresti	72	75-68-72-79	294	$2,940.00
David Feherty	73	69-73-76-77	295	$2,910.00

The following players did not finish (C=cut, W=withdrew, D=disqualified)

C—144- Chip Beck, Danny Briggs, Bart Bryant, Mark Carnevale, Jay Haas, Jerry Haas, John Huston, Steve Jones, Jim McGovern, Lee Porter, Lee Rinker, Steve Rintoul, Payne Stewart, Doug Tewell, Jim Thorpe, Bruce Vaughan. **145-** Pat Bates, Clark Dennis, Mike Hulbert, Andrew Magee, John Morse, Mark O'Meara, Brett Ogle, Dan Pohl, John Wilson. **146-** Mike Brisky, Bill Britton, Brandel Chamblee, Brian Claar, Dudley Hart, Billy Mayfair, David Ogrin, Dennis Paulson, Mike Reid, Joey Sindelar, Craig Stadler, Bob Tway. **147-** Emlyn Aubrey, Keith Clearwater, Joe Daley, Marco Dawson, Steve Elkington, Greg Kraft, Craig Parry, Dicky Pride, Greg Twiggs. **148-** Woody Austin, Patrick Burke, Jim Carter, Jay Delsing, Steve Pate, Charlie Rymer, Dave Stockton, Jr., Harry Taylor, Bobby Wadkins. **149-** John Cook, Rick Fehr, Robin Freeman, Brian Henninger, Stiles Mitchell, Gil Morgan. **150-** Bobby Clampett, Scott Gump, Ryan Howison, J.L. Lewis, Roger Maltbie, Larry Nelson. **151-** Tommy Armour III, Mark Wurtz. **152-** Andy North, Mike Smith, Lanny Wadkins. **153-** Rocco Mediate, Mike Springer, Mark Wiebe. **154-** Fulton Allem, Rusty Cummings, Grant Waite. **156-**Gene Holland. **W—152-** Rick Lewallen, **155-** Ken Green, **74-** Paul Goydos, **78-** Tray Tyner.

KMART GREATER GREENSBORO OPEN

TOURNAMENT HISTORY

Year	Winner	Score	Runner-up	Score	Location	Par/Yards
1938	Sam Snead	272	Johnny Revolta	276	Starmount Forest CC, Greensboro, NC	71/6630
					Sedgefield CC, Greensboro, NC	70/6680
1939	Ralph Guldahl	280	Clayton Heafner	283	Starmount Forest CC, Greensboro, NC	71/6630
			Lawson Little		Sedgefield CC, Greensboro, NC	70/6680
1940	Ben Hogan	270	Craig Wood	279	Starmount Forest CC, Greensboro, NC	71/6630
					Sedgefield CC, Greensboro, NC	70/6680
1941	Byron Nelson	276	Victor Ghezzi	278	Starmount Forest CC, Greensboro, NC	71/6630
					Sedgefield CC, Greensboro, NC	70/6680
1942	Sam Byrd	279	Ben Hogan	281	Starmount Forest CC, Greensboro, NC	71/6630
1943-			Lloyd Mangrum			
1944	No Tournaments					
1945	Byron Nelson	271	Sam Byrd	279	Starmount Forest CC, Greensboro, NC	71/6630
1946	Sam Snead	270	Herman Keiser	276	Sedgefield CC, Greensboro, NC	70/6680
1947	Vic Ghezzi	286	Frank Stranahan	288	Starmount Forest CC, Greensboro, NC	71/6630
1948	Lloyd Mangrum	278	Lew Worsham	279	Sedgefield CC, Greensboro, NC	70/6680
1949	*Sam Snead	276	Lloyd Mangrum	276	Starmount Forest CC, Greensboro, NC	71/6630
1950	Sam Snead	269	Jimmy Demaret	279	Sedgefield CC, Greensboro, NC	70/6680
1951	Art Doering	279	Jim Ferrier	284	Starmount Forest CC, Greensboro, NC	71/6630
1952	Dave Douglas	277	Bobby Locke	278	Starmount Forest CC, Greensboro, NC	71/6630
1953	*Earl Stewart	275	Sam Snead	275	Sedgefield CC, Greensboro, NC	70/6680
1954	*Doug Ford	283	Marty Furgol	283	Starmount Forest CC, Greensboro, NC	71/6630
1955	Sam Snead	273	Julius Boros	274	Sedgefield CC, Greensboro, NC	70/6680
			Art Wall			
1956	*Sam Snead	279	Fred Wampler	279	Starmount Forest CC, Greensboro, NC	71/6630
1957	Stan Leonard	276	Mike Souchak	279	Sedgefield CC, Greensboro, NC	70/6680
1958	Bob Goalby	275	Dow Finsterwald	277	Starmount Forest CC, Greensboro, NC	71/6630
			Don January			
			Tony Lema			
			Sam Snead			
			Art Wall			
1959	Dow Finsterwald	278	Art Wall	280	Starmount Forest CC, Greensboro, NC	71/6630
1960	Sam Snead	270	Dow Finsterwald	272	Starmount Forest CC, Greensboro, NC	71/6630
1961	Mike Souchak	276	Sam Snead	283	Sedgefield CC, Greensboro, NC	70/6680
1962	Billy Casper	275	Mike Souchak	276	Sedgefield CC, Greensboro, NC	70/6680
1963	Doug Sanders	270	Jimmy Clark	274	Sedgefield CC, Greensboro, NC	70/6680
1964	*Julius Boros	277	Doug Sanders	277	Sedgefield CC, Greensboro, NC	70/6680
1965	Sam Snead	273	Billy Casper	278	Sedgefield CC, Greensboro, NC	70/6680
			Jack McGowan			
			Phil Rodgers			
1966	*Doug Sanders	276	Tom Weiskopf	276	Sedgefield CC, Greensboro, NC	70/6680
1967	George Archer	267	Doug Sanders	269	Sedgefield CC, Greensboro, NC	70/6680
1968	Billy Casper	267	George Archer	271	Sedgefield CC, Greensboro, NC	70/6680
			Gene Littler			
			Bobby Nichols			
1969	*Gene Littler	274	Julius Boros	274	Sedgefield CC, Greensboro, NC	70/6680
			Orville Moody			
			Tom Weiskopf			
1970	Gary Player	271	Miller Barber	273	Sedgefield CC, Greensboro, NC	71/7034
1971	*Bud Allin	275	Dave Eichelberger	275	Sedgefield CC, Greensboro, NC	71/7034
			Rod Funseth			
1972	*George Archer	272	Tommy Aaron	272	Sedgefield CC, Greensboro, NC	71/7034
1973	Chi Chi Rodriguez	267	Lou Graham	268	Sedgefield CC, Greensboro, NC	71/7012
			Ken Still			
1974	Bob Charles	270	Ray Floyd	271	Sedgefield CC, Greensboro, NC	71/7012
			Lee Trevino			
1975	Tom Weiskopf	275	Al Geiberger	278	Sedgefield CC, Greensboro, NC	71/6643
1976	Al Geiberger	268	Lee Trevino	270	Sedgefield CC, Greensboro, NC	71/6643

KMART GREATER GREENSBORO OPEN

TOURNAMENT HISTORY

Year	Winner	Score	Runner-up	Score	Location	Par/Yards
1977	Danny Edwards	276	George Burns Larry Nelson	280	Forest Oaks CC, Greensboro, NC	72/7075
1978	Seve Ballesteros	282	Jack Renner Fuzzy Zoeller	283	Forest Oaks CC, Greensboro, NC	72/6958
1979	Raymond Floyd	282	George Burns Gary Player	283	Forest Oaks CC, Greensboro, NC	72/6958
1980	Craig Stadler	275	George Burns Bill Kratzert Jack Newton Jerry Pate	281	Forest Oaks CC, Greensboro, NC	72/6958
1981	*Larry Nelson	281	Mark Hayes	281	Forest Oaks CC, Greensboro, NC	72/6984
1982	Danny Edwards	285	Bobby Clampett	286	Forest Oaks CC, Greensboro, NC	72/6984
1983	Lanny Wadkins	275	Craig Stadler Denis Watson	280	Forest Oaks CC, Greensboro, NC	72/6984
1984	Andy Bean	280	George Archer	282	Forest Oaks CC, Greensboro, NC	72/6984
1985	Joey Sindelar	285	Isao Aoki Craig Stadler	286	Forest Oaks CC, Greensboro, NC	72/6984
1986	Sandy Lyle	275	Andy Bean	277	Forest Oaks CC, Greensboro, NC	72/6984
1987	Scott Simpson	282	Clarence Rose	284	Forest Oaks CC, Greensboro, NC	72/6984
KMART GREATER GREENSBORO OPEN						
1988	*Sandy Lyle	271	Ken Green	271	Forest Oaks CC, Greensboro, NC	72/6984
1989	Ken Green	277	John Huston	279	Forest Oaks CC, Greensboro, NC	72/6984
1990	Steve Elkington	282	Mike Reid Jeff Sluman	284	Forest Oaks CC, Greensboro, NC	72/6984
1991	*Mark Brooks	275	Gene Sauers	275	Forest Oaks CC, Greensboro, NC	72/6984
1992	Davis Love III	272	John Cook	278	Forest Oaks CC, Greensboro, NC	72/6984
1993	*Rocco Mediate	281	Steve Elkington	281	Forest Oaks CC, Greensboro, NC	72/6984
1994	Mike Springer	275	Brad Bryant Ed Humenik Hale Irwin	278	Forest Oaks CC, Greensboro, NC	72/6984
1995	*Jim Gallagher, Jr.	274	Peter Jacobsen Jeff Sluman	275	Forest Oaks CC, Greensboro, NC	72/6984

Tournament Record: 267 -- George Archer, 1967; Billy Casper, 1968; Chi Chi Rodriguez, 1973 (all Sedgefield CC)

Current Course Record: 62 -- Davis Love III, 1992

KEY: *=Playoff

1995 SHELL HOUSTON OPEN

TPC at The Woodlands, The Woodlands, TX **Purse: $1,400,000**
Par: 36-36--72 **Yards: 7,042** **April 27-30, 1995**

LEADERS: First Round--Steve Rintoul, at 6-under par 66, led by one over Wayne Levi, Jim Furyk, Billy Ray Brown, Peter Jacobsen and John Cook. **Second Round--**Scott Hoch, at 12-under-par 132, led by two over Willie Wood. **Third Round--**Hoch, at 15-under-par 201, led by five over Cook and Charlie Rymer.

CUT: 87 players at 1-under-par 143.

PRO-AM: $7,500. Individual--Blaine McCallister, 64, $750. Team--Lennie Clements, D.A. Weibring, Craig Parry, Clark Dennis, 54, $581.25 each.

WEATHER: Beautiful every day.

Winner : Payne Stewart 73-65-70-68 276 $252,000.00

(Won playoff with par-4 on first extra hole)

Player	Pos.	Scores	Total	Money
Scott Hoch	2	68-64-69-75	276	$151,200.00
Charlie Rymer	3	69-69-68-71	277	$95,200.00
Paul Stankowski	T 4	71-68-71-68	278	$61,600.00
Tray Tyner	T 4	70-69-68-71	278	$61,600.00
Brian Claar	T 6	73-68-67-71	279	$48,650.00
Brett Ogle	T 6	68-69-71-71	279	$48,650.00
Steve Rintoul	T 8	66-70-71-73	280	$40,600.00
Vijay Singh	T 8	70-70-70-70	280	$40,600.00
John Wilson	T 8	71-69-68-72	280	$40,600.00
John Cook	11	67-70-69-75	281	$35,000.00
Curt Byrum	T12	72-69-70-71	282	$25,800.00
Clark Dennis	T12	74-68-69-71	282	$25,800.00
Fred Funk	T12	71-70-72-69	282	$25,800.00
Kirk Triplett	T12	73-66-72-71	282	$25,800.00
Omar Uresti	T12	73-68-68-73	282	$25,800.00
Willie Wood	T12	68-66-75-73	282	$25,800.00
Ed Fiori	T12	71-70-71-70	282	$25,800.00
Phil Blackmar	T19	70-72-69-72	283	$15,225.00
Brad Bryant	T19	69-72-72-70	283	$15,225.00
Jeff Maggert	T19	76-66-74-67	283	$15,225.00
Gil Morgan	T19	73-70-67-73	283	$15,225.00
Dicky Pride	T19	71-68-71-73	283	$15,225.00
Scott Simpson	T19	68-71-75-69	283	$15,225.00
Mike Sullivan	T19	72-70-70-71	283	$15,225.00
Greg Twiggs	T19	71-69-73-70	283	$15,225.00
Lennie Clements	T27	71-72-66-75	284	$9,940.00
David Duval	T27	71-70-72-71	284	$9,940.00
John Mahaffey	T27	68-71-70-75	284	$9,940.00
Joey Sindelar	T27	73-67-72-72	284	$9,940.00
Harry Taylor	T27	69-72-69-74	284	$9,940.00
Mark Brooks	T32	70-70-71-74	285	$7,264.45
J.P. Hayes	T32	72-69-71-73	285	$7,264.45
Andrew Magee	T32	69-72-69-75	285	$7,264.45
Curtis Strange	T32	72-70-75-68	285	$7,264.45
Scott Gump	T32	72-67-74-72	285	$7,264.44
Justin Leonard	T32	69-67-73-76	285	$7,264.44
Blaine McCallister	T32	69-71-68-77	285	$7,264.44
Doug Tewell	T32	75-68-69-73	285	$7,264.44
Jim Thorpe	T32	69-71-71-74	285	$7,264.44
Dan Forsman	T41	70-70-69-77	286	$5,180.00
Craig Stadler	T41	70-69-73-74	286	$5,180.00
Ray Stewart	T41	70-73-69-74	286	$5,180.00
Hal Sutton	T41	69-73-68-76	286	$5,180.00
Howard Twitty	T41	70-69-73-74	286	$5,180.00
Billy Ray Brown	T46	67-74-74-72	287	$3,640.00
Brandel Chamblee	T46	72-69-67-79	287	$3,640.00
David Feherty	T46	68-74-72-73	287	$3,640.00
Jim Furyk	T46	67-76-73-71	287	$3,640.00
Brian Kamm	T46	71-66-71-79	287	$3,640.00
Skip Kendall	T46	71-71-71-74	287	$3,640.00
Doug Martin	T46	71-72-75-69	287	$3,640.00
Craig Parry	T46	70-70-69-78	287	$3,640.00
Joey Rassett	T46	72-70-73-72	287	$3,640.00
Dudley Hart	T55	68-72-71-77	288	$3,178.00
Steve Jones	T55	69-71-70-78	288	$3,178.00
Tom Kite	T55	72-69-74-73	288	$3,178.00
Lee Rinker	T55	72-71-69-76	288	$3,178.00
Tommy Armour III	T59	70-71-77-71	289	$2,996.00
Mark Calcavecchia	T59	69-71-72-77	289	$2,996.00
Ben Crenshaw	T59	70-73-73-73	289	$2,996.00
Steve Gotsche	T59	71-72-72-74	289	$2,996.00
Peter Jacobsen	T59	67-75-78-69	289	$2,996.00
Lee Janzen	T59	72-68-73-76	289	$2,996.00
Mike Smith	T59	69-73-73-74	289	$2,996.00
Mike Standly	T59	72-71-73-73	289	$2,996.00
Grant Waite	T59	68-73-70-78	289	$2,996.00
John Adams	T68	71-68-74-77	290	$2,842.00
Don Pooley	T68	70-72-73-75	290	$2,842.00
Clark Burroughs	T70	71-71-74-75	291	$2,758.00
Joel Edwards	T70	69-72-75-75	291	$2,758.00
Bob Lohr	T70	70-73-77-71	291	$2,758.00
Bill Porter	T70	73-70-74-74	291	$2,758.00
Kawika Cotner	T74	71-72-74-75	292	$2,632.00
Chris Perry	T74	69-71-77-75	292	$2,632.00
Dave Rummells	T74	73-70-77-72	292	$2,632.00
Bruce Vaughan	T74	73-70-75-74	292	$2,632.00
Bobby Wadkins	T74	72-69-72-79	292	$2,632.00
Guy Boros	T79	73-70-76-74	293	$2,520.00
Bart Bryant	T79	69-71-75-78	293	$2,520.00
Tom Hearn	T79	69-74-78-72	293	$2,520.00
Robin Freeman	82	72-69-81-73	295	$2,464.00
Keith Clearwater	T83	70-73-75-78	296	$2,422.00
Bruce Fleisher	T83	71-72-76-77	296	$2,422.00
Jeff Leonard	85	72-71-77-84	304	$2,380.00

The following players did not finish (C=cut, W=withdrew, D=disqualified)

C—144- Ronnie Black, Michael Bradley, Tom Byrum, John Daly, Pete Jordan, Shingo Katayama, Jim McGovern, David Peoples, Mike Springer, Dave Stockton, Jr., Tommy Tolles, Ted Tryba. **145-** Andy Bean, Mike Brisky, Bob Burns, Bob Gilder, Wayne Grady, Steve Hart, Wayne Levi, David Ogrin, Carl Paulson, Don Reese, Zoran Zorkic. **146-** John Dowdall, J.L. Lewis, Tim Loustalot, Phil Mickelson, Nick Price. **147-** Pat Bates, Bill Britton, Jim Carter, Jerry Haas, Greg Kraft, D.A. Weibring. **148-** Emlyn Aubrey, Dave Barr, Mike Donald, Keith Fergus, Kelly Gibson, Mike Heinen, Ryan Howison, Ed Humenik, Scott McCarron. **149-** Michael Allen, Marco Dawson, Mike Hulbert, Dicky Thompson. **150-** Steve Brodie, Bob Eastwood, Steve Elkington, Mark Wurtz. **151-** Joe Acosta, Jr., Tony Sills. **152-** Woody Austin, Gary Hallberg, Rocco Mediate, Dennis Paulson, Jay Williamson. **153-** Charlie Epps, Jonathan Kaye, Steve Parker. **154-** Scott Ford, Garry Rippy. **155-** Jean-Paul Hebert. **158-** Billy Sitton. **163-** Jay Michals. **73-** John Morse. **75-** Mark Wiebe. **W—148-**Bobby Clampett. **D—217-** Dick Mast, **220-** Fulton Allem.

SHELL HOUSTON OPEN

TOURNAMENT HISTORY

Year	Winner	Score	Runner-up	Score	Location	Par/Yards
TOURNAMENT OF CHAMPIONS						
1946	Byron Nelson	274	Ben Hogan	276	River Oaks CC, Houston, TX	71/6588
1947	Bobby Locke	277	Johnny Palmer	282	Memorial Park GC, Houston, TX	72/7421
			Ellsworth Vines			
1948	No Tournament					
1949	John Palmer	272	Cary Middlecoff	273	Pine Forest CC, Houston, TX	72/6510
HOUSTON OPEN						
1950	Cary Middlecoff	277	Pete Cooper	280	Brae Burn CC, Houston, TX	72/6725
1951	Marty Furgol	277	Jack Burke, Jr.	278	Memorial Park GC, Houston, TX	70/7212
1952	Jack Burke, Jr.	277	Frank Stranahan	283	Memorial Park GC, Houston, TX	70/7212
1953	*Cary Middlecoff	283	Jim Ferrier	283	Memorial Park GC, Houston, TX	70/7212
			Shelley Mayfield			
1954	Dave Douglas	277	Cary Middlecoff	279	Memorial Park GC, Houston, TX	70/7212
1955	Mike Souchak	273	Jerry Barber	275	Memorial Park GC, Houston, TX	70/7212
1956	Ted Kroll	277	Jack Burke, Jr.	280	Memorial Park GC, Houston, TX	70/7212
			Dave Douglas			
1957	Arnold Palmer	279	Doug Ford	280	Memorial Park GC, Houston, TX	70/7212
1958	Ed Oliver	281	Roberto De Vicenzo	282	Memorial Park GC, Houston, TX	70/7212
			Jay Hebert			
HOUSTON CLASSIC						
1959	*Jack Burke, Jr.	277	Julius Boros	277	Memorial Park GC, Houston, TX	70/7212
1960	*Bill Collins	280	Arnold Palmer	280	Memorial Park GC, Houston, TX	70/7212
1961	*Jay Hebert	276	Ken Venturi	276	Memorial Park GC, Houston, TX	72/7122
1962	*Bobby Nichols	278	Jack Nicklaus	278	Memorial Park GC, Houston, TX	72/7021
			Dan Sikes			
1963	Bob Charles	268	Fred Hawkins	269	Memorial Park GC, Houston, TX	72/7021
1964	Mike Souchak	278	Jack Nicklaus	279	Sharpstown CC, Houston, TX	71/7021
1965	Bobby Nichols	273	Bruce Devlin	274	Sharpstown CC, Houston, TX	71/7021
			Chi Chi Rodriguez			
HOUSTON CHAMPION INTERNATIONAL						
1966	Arnold Palmer	275	Gardner Dickinson	276	Champions GC, Houston, TX	71/7166
1967	Frank Beard	274	Arnold Palmer	275	Champions GC, Houston, TX	71/7166
1968	Roberto De Vicenzo	274	Lee Trevino	275	Champions GC, Houston, TX	71/7166
1969	Hosted U.S. Open					70/6967
1970	*Gibby Gilbert	282	Bruce Crampton	282	Champions GC, Houston, TX	70/7166
1971	*Hubert Green	280	Don January	280	Champions GC, Houston, TX	70/7166
HOUSTON OPEN						
1972	Bruce Devlin	278	Tommy Aaron	280	Westwood CC, Houston, TX	72/6998
			Lou Graham			
			Doug Sanders			
1973	Bruce Crampton	277	Dave Stockton	278	Quail Valley GC, Houston, TX	72/6905
1974	Dave Hill	276	Rod Curl	277	Quail Valley GC, Houston, TX	72/6905
			Steve Melnyk			
			Andy North			
1975	Bruce Crampton	273	Gil Morgan	275	Woodlands CC, The Woodlands, TX	72/6929
1976	Lee Elder	278	Forrest Fezler	279	Woodlands CC, The Woodlands, TX	72/6997
1977	Gene Littler	276	Lanny Wadkins	279	Woodlands CC, The Woodlands, TX	72/6997
1978	Gary Player	270	Andy Bean	271	Woodlands CC, The Woodlands, TX	72/6997
1979	Wayne Levi	268	Michael Brannan	270	Woodlands CC, The Woodlands, TX	71/6918
MICHELOB HOUSTON OPEN						
1980	*Curtis Strange	266	Lee Trevino	266	Woodlands CC, The Woodlands, TX	71/6918
1981	~Ron Streck	198	Hale Irwin	201	Woodlands CC, The Woodlands, TX	71/7071
			Jerry Pate			
1982	*Ed Sneed	275	Bob Shearer	275	Woodlands CC, The Woodlands, TX	71/7031
HOUSTON COCA-COLA OPEN						
1983	David Graham	275	Lee Elder	280	Woodlands CC, The Woodlands, TX	71/7031
			Jim Thorpe			
			Lee Trevino			

SHELL HOUSTON OPEN

TOURNAMENT HISTORY

Year	Winner	Score	Runner-up	Score	Location	Par/Yards
1984	Corey Pavin	274	Buddy Gardner	275	Woodlands CC, The Woodlands, TX	71/7031
HOUSTON OPEN						
1985	Raymond Floyd	277	David Frost Bob Lohr	278	TPC at The Woodlands, The Woodlands, TX	72/7042
1986	*Curtis Strange	274	Calvin Peete	274	TPC at The Woodlands, The Woodlands, TX	72/7045
BIG I HOUSTON OPEN						
1987	*Jay Haas	276	Buddy Gardner	276	TPC at The Woodlands, The Woodlands, TX	72/7042
INDEPENDENT INSURANCE AGENT OPEN						
1988	*Curtis Strange	270	Greg Norman	270	TPC at The Woodlands, The Woodlands, TX	72/7045
1989	Mike Sullivan	280	Craig Stadler	281	TPC at The Woodlands, The Woodlands, TX	72/7042
1990	~*Tony Sills	204	Gil Morgan	204	TPC at The Woodlands, The Woodlands, TX	72/7042
1991	Fulton Allem	273	Billy Ray Brown Mike Hulbert Tom Kite	274	TPC at The Woodlands, The Woodlands, TX	72/7042
SHELL HOUSTON OPEN						
1992	Fred Funk	272	Kirk Triplett	274	TPC at The Woodlands, The Woodlands, TX	72/7042
1993	~*Jim McGovern	199	John Huston	199	TPC at The Woodlands, The Woodlands, TX	72/7042
1994	Mike Heinen	272	Tom Kite Jeff Maggert Hal Sutton	275	TPC at The Woodlands, The Woodlands, TX	72/7042
1995	*Payne Stewart	276	Scott Hoch	276	TPC at The Woodlands, The Woodlands, TX	72/7042

Tournament Record: 266 -- Curtis Strange/Lee Trevino, 1980 (Woodlands CC)
Current Course Record: 62 -- Fred Funk, 1992

KEY: *=Playoff ~=Weather-shortened

1995 BELLSOUTH CLASSIC

Atlanta CC, Marietta, GA **Purse: $1,300,000**
Par: 36-36--72 **Yards: 7,018** **May 4-7, 1995**

LEADERS: First Round--Bill Porter and Jim Gallagher, Jr., at 7-under-par 65, led by one over Tom Kite and Phil Blackmar. **Second Round--**John Daly, at 10-under par 134, led by one over Michael Bradley and Gallagher. **Third Round--**Stephen Keppler and Gallagher, at 13-under-par 205, led by two over Guy Boros, Mark Calcavecchia and Daly.

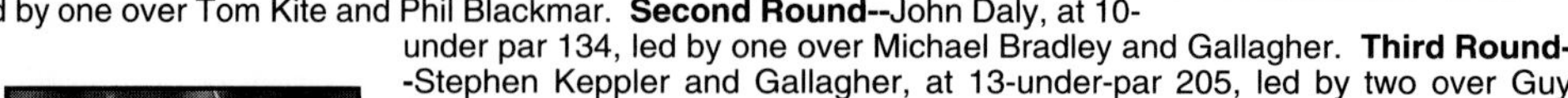

CUT: 75 players at 1-under-par 143.

PRO-AM: $7,500. Individual, Craig Parry, 64, $750. Team, Tom Kite, 54, $750.

WEATHER: Thursday's round was delayed from 1:08 p.m. to 3:48 p.m. due to rain and lightning in the area. Play was suspended for the day at 8:17 p.m. The conclusion of the first round and the start of the second round started simultaneously at 7:15 a.m. on Friday morning. Beautiful the rest of the week.

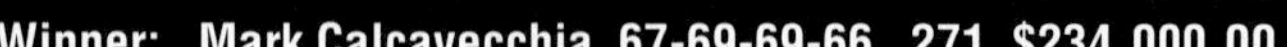

Winner: Mark Calcavecchia 67-69-69-66 271 $234,000.00

Player	Pos	Scores	Total	Money
Jim Gallagher, Jr.	2	65-70-68-70	273	$140,400.00
Stephen Keppler	3	67-69-67-71	274	$88,400.00
Curtis Strange	T 4	70-71-69-65	275	$53,733.34
Guy Boros	T 4	71-67-67-70	275	$53,733.33
Scott Verplank	T 4	72-67-67-69	275	$53,733.33
Billy Andrade	T 7	72-68-69-67	276	$37,830.00
Brandel Chamblee	T 7	68-70-69-69	276	$37,830.00
Lennie Clements	T 7	70-66-72-68	276	$37,830.00
Scott Hoch	T 7	69-71-71-65	276	$37,830.00
Tommy Tolles	T 7	70-69-68-69	276	$37,830.00
John Daly	T12	67-67-71-72	277	$28,600.00
Steve Stricker	T12	71-69-67-70	277	$28,600.00
Brett Ogle	14	71-71-70-66	278	$24,700.00
Emlyn Aubrey	T15	71-70-70-68	279	$22,100.00
David Duval	T15	69-71-73-66	279	$22,100.00
Jerry Pate	T15	69-71-71-68	279	$22,100.00
Phil Blackmar	T18	66-74-72-68	280	$17,550.00
Bill Porter	T18	65-73-68-74	280	$17,550.00
Gene Sauers	T18	71-69-71-69	280	$17,550.00
Joey Sindelar	T18	69-70-72-69	280	$17,550.00
Harry Taylor	T22	68-75-69-69	281	$11,718.58
Ronnie Black	T22	72-69-68-72	281	$11,718.57
Marco Dawson	T22	71-72-70-68	281	$11,718.57
Bob Estes	T22	67-72-68-74	281	$11,718.57
J.P. Hayes	T22	70-71-71-69	281	$11,718.57
Greg Kraft	T22	71-72-70-68	281	$11,718.57
Davis Love III	T22	67-69-70-75	281	$11,718.57
Ed Fiori	T29	72-69-71-70	282	$8,645.00
Dan Forsman	T29	71-71-70-70	282	$8,645.00
Billy Mayfair	T29	72-70-70-70	282	$8,645.00
Larry Mize	T29	73-69-72-68	282	$8,645.00
Tom Kite	T33	66-77-68-72	283	$6,442.23
Mark Wurtz	T33	72-70-70-71	283	$6,442.23
Tommy Armour III	T33	67-73-70-73	283	$6,442.22
Mike Hulbert	T33	69-72-68-74	283	$6,442.22
Neal Lancaster	T33	68-70-70-75	283	$6,442.22
J.L. Lewis	T33	69-73-71-70	283	$6,442.22
David Peoples	T33	70-71-75-67	283	$6,442.22
Ray Stewart	T33	68-74-73-68	283	$6,442.22
Hal Sutton	T33	71-70-73-69	283	$6,442.22
Clark Dennis	T42	71-69-72-72	284	$4,810.00
Keith Fergus	T42	70-73-67-74	284	$4,810.00
David Frost	T42	70-71-70-73	284	$4,810.00
Dave Barr	T45	70-70-75-70	285	$3,471.00
Jay Don Blake	T45	69-71-74-71	285	$3,471.00
Kawika Cotner	T45	71-69-71-74	285	$3,471.00
Wayne Grady	T45	68-71-72-74	285	$3,471.00
Scott Gump	T45	71-71-69-74	285	$3,471.00
Hale Irwin	T45	70-72-70-73	285	$3,471.00
Blaine McCallister	T45	70-72-75-68	285	$3,471.00
Jim McGovern	T45	70-72-69-74	285	$3,471.00
Craig Parry	T45	70-72-74-69	285	$3,471.00
Don Pooley	T45	74-69-69-73	285	$3,471.00
Michael Bradley	T55	70-65-73-78	286	$2,964.00
Rick Fehr	T55	74-68-68-76	286	$2,964.00
John Wilson	T55	69-68-74-75	286	$2,964.00
Scott Ford	T58	74-69-71-73	287	$2,899.00
Wayne Levi	T58	73-70-72-72	287	$2,899.00
Dudley Hart	T60	73-70-72-73	288	$2,834.00
Tim Loustalot	T60	70-73-74-71	288	$2,834.00
Lee Rinker	T60	70-72-72-74	288	$2,834.00
John Adams	T63	71-71-70-77	289	$2,756.00
Bob Lohr	T63	69-71-72-77	289	$2,756.00
Don Reese	T63	72-71-69-77	289	$2,756.00
Mark Brooks	T66	67-71-75-77	290	$2,691.00
Fred Funk	T66	71-71-77-71	290	$2,691.00
Michael Allen	T68	74-69-75-73	291	$2,613.00
Nolan Henke	T68	70-73-73-75	291	$2,613.00
Kirk Triplett	T68	69-72-70-80	291	$2,613.00
Ted Tryba	T68	68-74-81-68	291	$2,613.00
Stewart Cink	T68	71-72-78-70	291	Amateur
Keith Clearwater	T73	72-71-73-76	292	$2,535.00
David Ogrin	T73	72-70-79-71	292	$2,535.00
Tony Sills	75	71-72-77-74	294	$2,496.00

The following players did not finish (C=cut, W=withdrew, D=disqualified)

C—144- Curt Byrum, Jim Carter, Donnie Hammond, Brian Kamm, Mark McCumber, Steve Pate, Corey Pavin, Chris Perry, Jeff Sluman, Mike Standly, Omar Uresti. **145-** Joel Edwards, Jim Furyk, Kelly Gibson, Paul Goydos, Brian Henninger, Cliff Kresge, Andrew Magee, Phil Mickelson, Doug Tewell, Bobby Wadkins. **146-** Bruce Fleisher, Bill Glasson, Steve Gotsche, Steve Hart, Tom Hearn, Mark McNulty, Jesper Parnevik, Eduardo Romero, Paul Stankowski, Jim Thorpe, Bob Tway, Bruce Vaughan, Willie Wood. **147-** Joe Acosta, Jr., Fulton Allem, Bart Bryant, Bob Burns, Clark Burroughs, Glen Day, Chris DiMarco, Robin Freeman, John Mahaffey, Scott McCarron, Larry Nelson, Dennis Paulson, Dillard Pruitt, Jay Williamson. **148-** Woody Austin, Bill Britton, Ed Humenik, Skip Kendall, Doug Martin, Joey Rassett, Charlie Rymer. **149-** Mike Brisky, David Feherty, Jerry Haas, Jonathan Kaye, Hicks Malonson, Dave Stockton, Jr. **150-**John Cook, Gary Hallberg, Phil Taylor. **151-** Mike Smith, Dicky Thompson. **152-** Andy Bean, Mike Malone. **153-** Allen Doyle, Bob Gilder, John Godwin. **154-** Pat Bates. **158-**Jeff Leonard. **161-** Danny St. Louis. **162-** Jeff Gotham. **W—158-**Howard Twitty, **160-** Mark Carnevale, **161-** Hubert Green,**162-** Jay Delsing, **79-** Tray Tyner.

BELLSOUTH CLASSIC

TOURNAMENT HISTORY

Year	Winner	Score	Runner-up	Score	Location	Par/Yards
ATLANTA CLASSIC						
1967	Bob Charles	282	Tommy Bolt Richard Crawford Gardner Dickinson	284	Atlanta CC, Atlanta, GA	72/7007
1968	Bob Lunn	280	Lee Trevino	283	Atlanta CC, Atlanta, GA	72/7007
1969	*Bert Yancey	277	Bruce Devlin	277	Atlanta CC, Atlanta, GA	72/7007
1970	Tommy Aaron	275	Dan Sikes	276	Atlanta CC, Atlanta, GA	72/7007
1971	*Gardner Dickinson	275	Jack Nicklaus	275	Atlanta CC, Atlanta, GA	72/7007
1972	Bob Lunn	275	Gary Player	277	Atlanta CC, Atlanta, GA	72/7007
1973	Jack Nicklaus	272	Tom Weiskopf	274	Atlanta CC, Atlanta, GA	72/7007
1974	Hosted TPC					
1975	Hale Irwin	271	Tom Watson	275	Atlanta CC, Atlanta, GA	72/7007
1976	Hosted U.S. Open					
1977	Hale Irwin	273	Steve Veriato	274	Atlanta CC, Atlanta, GA	72/7007
1978	Jerry Heard	269	Lou Graham Bob Murphy Tom Watson	271	Atlanta CC, Atlanta, GA	72/7007
1979	Andy Bean	265	Joe Inman	273	Atlanta CC, Atlanta, GA	72/7007
1980	Larry Nelson	270	Andy Bean Don Pooley	277	Atlanta CC, Atlanta, GA	72/7007
1981	*Tom Watson	277	Tommy Valentine	277	Atlanta CC, Atlanta, GA	72/7007
GEORGIA-PACIFIC ATLANTA GOLF CLASSIC						
1982	*Keith Fergus	273	Ray Floyd	273	Atlanta CC, Atlanta, GA	72/7007
1983	~Calvin Peete	206	Chip Beck Jim Colbert Don Pooley	208	Atlanta CC, Atlanta, GA	72/7007
1984	Tom Kite	269	Don Pooley	274	Atlanta CC, Atlanta, GA	72/7007
1985	*Wayne Levi	273	Steve Pate	273	Atlanta CC, Atlanta, GA	72/7007
1986	Bob Tway	269	Hal Sutton	271	Atlanta CC, Atlanta, GA	72/7007
1987	Dave Barr	265	Larry Mize	269	Atlanta CC, Atlanta, GA	72/7007
1988	Larry Nelson	268	Chip Beck	269	Atlanta CC, Atlanta, GA	72/7007
BELLSOUTH ATLANTA GOLF CLASSIC						
1989	*Scott Simpson	278	Bob Tway	278	Atlanta CC, Atlanta, GA	72/7007
1990	Wayne Levi	275	Keith Clearwater Larry Mize Nick Price	276	Atlanta CC, Atlanta, GA	72/7007
1991	*Corey Pavin	272	Steve Pate	272	Atlanta CC, Atlanta, GA	72/7007
BELLSOUTH CLASSIC						
1992	Tom Kite	272	Jay Don Blake	275	Atlanta CC, Atlanta, GA	72/7007
1993	Nolan Henke	271	Mark Calcavecchia Nick Price Tom Sieckmann	273	Atlanta CC, Atlanta, GA	72/7007
1994	John Daly	274	Nolan Henke Brian Henninger	275	Atlanta CC, Marietta, GA	72/7007
1995	Mark Calcavecchia	271	Jim Gallagher, Jr.	273	Atlanta CC, Marietta, GA	72/7007

Tournament Record: 265 -- Andy Bean, 1979; Dave Barr, 1987
Current Course Record: 61 -- Andy Bean, 1979

KEY: *=Playoff ~=Weather-shortened

1995 GTE BYRON NELSON CLASSIC

GTE Byron Nelson Classic

TPC at Four Seasons Resort-Las Colinas, Irving, TX
Par: 35-35--70 Yards: 6,899 Purse: $1,300,000
Cottonwood Valley May 11-14, 1995
Par: 34-36--70 Yards: 6,845

LEADERS: First Round--Glen Day (CV), with a 7-under-par 63, led by one over Jay Don Blake (TPC) and Mark Calcavecchia (CV). **Second Round--**Robin Freeman (CV) and Ernie Els (CV), at 10-under-par 130, led by one over Kenny Perry (TPC) and Doug Martin (TPC). **Third Round--**Els, at 15-under-par 195, led by three over Freeman.

PRO-AM: $15,000. TPC Individual--David Edwards, 67, $1,500. TPC Team--Jerry Pate, Paul Goydos, Bruce Vaughan, Loren Roberts, 52, $1,162.50 each. Cottonwood Valley Individual--Donnie Hammond, 64, $1,500. Cottonwood Valley Team--Ernie Els, Corey Pavin, John Mahaffey, Wayne Levi, Hale Irwin, Tom Byrum, Brandel Chamblee, $921.43 each.

WEATHER: Sunny, hot and humid every day.

Winner: Ernie Els 69-61-65-68 263 $234,000.00

Player	Pos.	Scores	Total	Money
Mike Heinen	T 2	67-66-67-66	266	$97,066.67
D.A. Weibring	T 2	65-69-67-65	266	$97,066.67
Robin Freeman	T 2	65-65-68-68	266	$97,066.66
Jay Don Blake	T 5	64-69-69-66	268	$45,662.50
Gil Morgan	T 5	68-66-68-66	268	$45,662.50
Kenny Perry	T 5	65-66-70-67	268	$45,662.50
Scott Verplank	T 5	67-69-67-65	268	$45,662.50
Loren Roberts	T 9	68-67-69-65	269	$36,400.00
Bob Tway	T 9	68-66-69-66	269	$36,400.00
Mark Brooks	T11	68-66-69-67	270	$27,560.00
Glen Day	T11	63-69-67-71	270	$27,560.00
Keith Fergus	T11	67-66-71-66	270	$27,560.00
Steve Lowery	T11	72-67-69-62	270	$27,560.00
Craig Stadler	T11	66-67-68-69	270	$27,560.00
Mark Calcavecchia	T16	64-70-69-68	271	$19,500.00
Brandel Chamblee	T16	67-68-66-70	271	$19,500.00
Mark O'Meara	T16	68-66-71-66	271	$19,500.00
Joe Ozaki	T16	65-71-68-67	271	$19,500.00
Corey Pavin	T16	70-65-70-66	271	$19,500.00
Bart Bryant	T21	69-69-70-64	272	$13,520.00
Nick Faldo	T21	66-71-69-66	272	$13,520.00
Scott Hoch	T21	70-64-71-67	272	$13,520.00
Howard Twitty	T21	67-68-71-66	272	$13,520.00
Mark Wurtz	T21	66-69-69-68	272	$13,520.00
Emlyn Aubrey	T26	68-66-70-69	273	$9,425.00
Tom Byrum	T26	69-68-69-67	273	$9,425.00
Jim Carter	T26	68-71-69-65	273	$9,425.00
Justin Leonard	T26	70-66-68-69	273	$9,425.00
John Mahaffey	T26	71-68-66-68	273	$9,425.00
Jeff Sluman	T26	67-67-70-69	273	$9,425.00
John Cook	T32	71-66-70-67	274	$6,745.56
Jeff Maggert	T32	71-66-66-71	274	$6,745.56
Brett Ogle	T32	70-65-69-70	274	$6,745.56
Charlie Rymer	T32	66-71-67-70	274	$6,745.56
Fuzzy Zoeller	T32	68-67-64-75	274	$6,745.56
Brad Bryant	T32	70-69-69-66	274	$6,745.55
Steve Elkington	T32	71-68-68-67	274	$6,745.55
Jesper Parnevik	T32	68-66-70-70	274	$6,745.55
Payne Stewart	T32	68-66-71-69	274	$6,745.55
John Daly	T41	68-65-73-69	275	$4,550.00
Robert Hoyt	T41	66-69-74-66	275	$4,550.00
Steve Jones	T41	68-64-73-70	275	$4,550.00
J.L. Lewis	T41	67-68-69-71	275	$4,550.00
David Ogrin	T41	72-67-67-69	275	$4,550.00
Dillard Pruitt	T41	69-70-68-68	275	$4,550.00
Ray Stewart	T41	65-69-72-69	275	$4,550.00
Curt Byrum	T48	67-72-66-71	276	$3,231.43
Ben Crenshaw	T48	70-67-71-68	276	$3,231.43
Bob Gilder	T48	70-67-73-66	276	$3,231.43
Steve Gotsche	T48	66-69-72-69	276	$3,231.43
Billy Mayfair	T48	68-70-70-68	276	$3,231.43
Omar Uresti	T48	71-66-71-68	276	$3,231.43
Tom Purtzer	T48	68-65-71-72	276	$3,231.42
Bob Estes	T55	67-68-72-70	277	$2,912.00
Donnie Hammond	T55	70-69-70-68	277	$2,912.00
Ed Humenik	T55	69-67-73-68	277	$2,912.00
Doug Martin	T55	65-66-72-74	277	$2,912.00
Dennis Paulson	T55	68-67-73-69	277	$2,912.00
Scott Simpson	T55	69-69-69-70	277	$2,912.00
Mike Smith	T55	70-67-72-68	277	$2,912.00
Brian Claar	T62	67-70-73-68	278	$2,795.00
Harry Taylor	T62	70-69-68-71	278	$2,795.00
Brian Henninger	T64	67-72-69-71	279	$2,730.00
Roger Salazar	T64	69-70-68-72	279	$2,730.00
Mike Standly	T64	66-71-68-74	279	$2,730.00
Ronnie Black	T67	69-70-72-69	280	$2,626.00
Chris DiMarco	T67	65-69-76-70	280	$2,626.00
Tim Loustalot	T67	69-67-71-73	280	$2,626.00
Jerry Pate	T67	72-66-70-72	280	$2,626.00
Dave Stockton, Jr.	T67	71-67-69-73	280	$2,626.00
Tony Sills	T72	67-66-72-76	281	$2,535.00
Tom Watson	T72	68-71-67-75	281	$2,535.00
Woody Austin	T74	67-69-72-74	282	$2,457.00
Kawika Cotner	T74	69-69-73-71	282	$2,457.00
Mark Wiebe	T74	70-67-73-72	282	$2,457.00
Jay Williamson	T74	66-68-72-76	282	$2,457.00
Mark Carnevale	T78	67-72-73-71	283	$2,366.00
Paul Goydos	T78	69-67-73-74	283	$2,366.00
J.P. Hayes	T78	68-71-76-68	283	$2,366.00
Larry Nelson	T81	70-69-70-75	284	$2,301.00
Steve Pate	T81	70-68-73-73	284	$2,301.00
Lee Rinker	83	68-71-75-71	285	$2,262.00
John Sikes	84	68-69-74-77	288	$2,236.00

The following players did not finish (C=cut, W=withdrew, D=disqualified)

C—140- Tommy Armour III, David Feherty, Bruce Fleisher, Skip Kendall, Andrew Magee, Mark McNulty, Joey Rassett, Mike Reid, Eduardo Romero, Ted Tryba, Bobby Wadkins. **141-** Bill Britton, Bob Burns, Rick Fehr, Jerry Haas, Tom Hearn, Hale Irwin, Neal Lancaster, Dan Pohl, Steve Rintoul, Doug Tewell, Bruce Vaughan, Lanny Wadkins, Grant Waite. **142-** Joe Acosta, Jr., Chip Beck, Guy Boros, Billy Ray Brown, David Edwards, David Frost, Scott Gump, Jay Haas, Chris Perry, Tray Tyner, Richard Zokol. **143-** Mike Brisky, Marco Dawson, Clark Dennis, Scott Deserrano, Joel Edwards, Ed Fiori, Dan Forsman, Hubert Green, Gary Hallberg, Dudley Hart, Trip Kuehne, Jeff Leonard, Mike Sullivan, John Wilson. **144-** Keith Clearwater, Kelly Grunewald, Stephen Keppler, Dave Rummells, Paul Stankowski. **145-** John Adams, Andy Bean, Bruce Lietzke, Chad Magee. **146-** Phil Blackmar. **147-** Pat Bates, Scott McCarron. **148-** Kelly Gibson, Joe Hager, Jonathan Kaye. **150-** Bob Eastwood, Antonio Serrano. **157-** Michael Henderson. **158-** Mike Hurley. **W—70-** Hal Sutton. **D—71-** Tommy Tolles.

GTE BYRON NELSON CLASSIC

TOURNAMENT HISTORY

Year	Winner	Score	Runner-up	Score	Location	Par/Yards
DALLAS OPEN						
1944	Byron Nelson	276	Harold McSpaden	286	Lakewood CC, Dallas, TX	N/A
1945	Sam Snead	276	Harold McSpaden	280	Dallas CC, Dallas, TX	N/A
1946	Ben Hogan	284	Herman Keiser Paul Runyan	286	Brook Hollow CC, Dallas, TX	N/A
1947- 1955	No Tournaments					
1956	Don January	268	Dow Finsterwald Doug Ford	269	Preston Hollow CC, Dallas, TX	N/A
1956A	*Peter Thomson	267			Preston Hollow CC, Dallas, TX	N/A
1957	Sam Snead	264	Bob Inman Billy Maxwell Cary Middlecoff	274	Glen Lakes CC, Dallas, TX	N/A
1958	*Sam Snead	272	Julius Boros John McMullen Gary Player	272	Oak Cliffs CC, Dallas, TX	71/6836
1959	Julius Boros	274	Dow Finsterwald Earl Stewart Bo Wininger	275	Oak Cliffs CC, Dallas, TX	71/6836
1960	*Johnny Pott	275	Ted Kroll Bo Wininger	275	Oak Cliffs CC, Dallas, TX	71/6836
1961	Earl Stewart, Jr.	278	Gay Brewer Arnold Palmer Doug Sanders	279	Oak Cliffs CC, Dallas, TX	71/6836
1962	Billy Maxwell	277	Johnny Pott	281	Oak Cliffs CC, Dallas, TX	71/6836
1963	No Tournament					
1964	Charles Coody	271	Jerry Edwards	272	Oak Cliffs CC, Dallas, TX	71/6836
1965	No Tournament					
1966	Roberto De Vicenzo	276	Joe Campbell Ray Floyd Harold Henning	277	Oak Cliffs CC, Dallas, TX	71/6836
1967	Bert Yancey	274	Roberto De Vicenzo Kermit Zarley	275	Oak Cliffs CC, Dallas, TX	71/6836
BYRON NELSON GOLF CLASSIC						
1968	Miller Barber	270	Kermit Zarley	271	Preston Trail Golf Club, Dallas, TX	70/6993
1969	Bruce Devlin	277	Frank Beard Bruce Crampton	278	Preston Trail Golf Club, Dallas, TX	70/6993
1970	*Jack Nicklaus	274	Arnold Palmer	274	Preston Trail Golf Club, Dallas, TX	70/6993
1971	Jack Nicklaus	274	Frank Beard Jerry McGee	276	Preston Trail Golf Club, Dallas, TX	70/6993
1972	*Chi Chi Rodriguez	273	Billy Casper	273	Preston Trail Golf Club, Dallas, TX	70/6993
1973	*Lanny Wadkins	277	Dan Sikes	277	Preston Trail Golf Club, Dallas, TX	70/6993
1974	Brian Allin	269	Homero Blancas Charles Coody Lee Trevino Tom Watson	273	Preston Trail Golf Club, Dallas, TX	70/6993
1975	Tom Watson	269	Bob E. Smith	271	Preston Trail Golf Club, Dallas, TX	70/6993
1976	Mark Hayes	273	Don Bies	275	Preston Trail Golf Club, Dallas, TX	70/6993
1977	Raymond Floyd	276	Ben Crenshaw	278	Preston Trail Golf Club, Dallas, TX	70/6993
1978	Tom Watson	272	Lee Trevino	273	Preston Trail Golf Club, Dallas, TX	70/6993
1979	*Tom Watson	275	Bill Rogers	275	Preston Trail Golf Club, Dallas, TX	70/6993
1980	Tom Watson	274	Bill Rogers	275	Preston Trail Golf Club, Dallas, TX	70/6993
1981	*Bruce Lietzke	281	Tom Watson	281	Preston Trail Golf Club, Dallas, TX	70/6993
1982	Bob Gilder	266	Curtis Strange	271	Preston Trail Golf Club, Dallas, TX	70/6993
1983	Ben Crenshaw	273	Brad Bryant Hal Sutton	274	Las Colinas Sports Club, Irving, TX	71/6982
1984	Craig Stadler	276	David Edwards	277	Las Colinas Sports Club, Irving, TX	71/6982
1985	*Bob Eastwood	272	Payne Stewart	272	Las Colinas Sports Club, Irving, TX	71/6982

GTE BYRON NELSON CLASSIC

TOURNAMENT HISTORY

Year	Winner	Score	Runner-up	Score	Location	Par/Yards
1986	Andy Bean	269	Mark Wiebe	270	TPC at Las Colinas, Irving, TX	70/6767
1987	*Fred Couples	266	Mark Calcavecchia	266	TPC at Las Colinas, Irving, TX	70/6767
GTE BYRON NELSON GOLF CLASSIC						
1988	*Bruce Lietzke	271	Clarence Rose	271	TPC at Las Colinas, Irving, TX	70/6767
1989	*Jodie Mudd	265	Larry Nelson	265	TPC at Las Colinas, Irving, TX	70/6767
1990	~Payne Stewart	202	Lanny Wadkins	204	TPC at Las Colinas, Irving, TX	70/6767
1991	Nick Price	270	Craig Stadler	271	TPC at Las Colinas, Irving, TX	70/6767
1992	*~Billy Ray Brown	199	Ben Crenshaw Ray Floyd Bruce Lietzke	199	TPC at Las Colinas, Irving, TX	70/6850
1993	Scott Simpson	270	Billy Mayfair Corey Pavin D.A. Weibring	271	TPC at Las Colinas, Irving, TX	70/6850
1994	*~Neal Lancaster	132	Tom Byrum Mark Carnevale David Edwards Yoshinori Mizumaki David Ogrin	132	TPC at Las Colinas, Irving, TX Cottonwood Valley Course, Irving, TX	70/6850 71/6862
1995	Ernie Els	263	Mike Heinen D.A. Weibring Robin Freeman	266	TPC at Four Seasons Resort-Las Colinas, Irving, TX Cottonwood Valley Course, Irving, TX	70/6850 71/6862

Tournament Record:	263--Ernie Els, 1995	
Current Course Record:	Cottonwood Valley	61 -- Ernie Els, 1995
	TPC at Four Seasons Resort-Las Colinas	61 -- Billy Mayfair, 1993

KEY: *=Playoff ~=Weather-shortened

1995 BUICK CLASSIC

Westchester CC, Harrison, NY **Purse: $1,200,000**
Par: 36-35--71 **Yards: 6,779** **May 18-21, 1995**

LEADERS: First Round--Doug Martin shot a 4-under-par 67 to lead Grant Waite, Ernie Els, Mike McCullough, Bruce Fleisher and Mike Hulbert by one stroke. **Second Round**--Hulbert and Chris Perry shared the lead at 6-under-par 136, one stroke ahead of Doug Martin and Els. **Third Round**--Vijay Singh, after a round of 67, was at 7-under-par 206, one stroke ahead of Bobby Wadkins.

CUT: 78 players at 3-over-par 145 or better.

PRO-AM: Individual--Wayne Levi, 67, $750. Team--Brad Faxon, 56, $750.

WEATHER: Thursday was mostly cloudy and mild. Cooler with intermittent rain Friday. Saturday and Sunday were glorious.

Winner: Vijay Singh 70-69-67-72 278 $216,000.00

(Won playoff with birdie-4 on fifth extra hole)

Player	Pos	Scores	Total	Money
Doug Martin	2	67-70-72-69	278	$129,600.00
Bobby Wadkins	3	72-66-69-72	279	$81,600.00
Ernie Els	T 4	68-69-75-68	280	$47,250.00
Nick Faldo	T 4	70-70-68-72	280	$47,250.00
Fred Funk	T 4	71-68-71-70	280	$47,250.00
Dillard Pruitt	T 4	72-69-70-69	280	$47,250.00
David Duval	T 8	69-75-67-70	281	$33,600.00
Bruce Fleisher	T 8	68-71-69-73	281	$33,600.00
Bob Gilder	T 8	73-70-68-70	281	$33,600.00
Blaine McCallister	T 8	69-71-69-72	281	$33,600.00
Chris Perry	T12	69-67-74-72	282	$26,400.00
Craig Stadler	T12	70-72-71-69	282	$26,400.00
Tom Lehman	T14	70-72-73-68	283	$21,000.00
Steve Lowery	T14	73-70-66-74	283	$21,000.00
Jim McGovern	T14	74-70-65-74	283	$21,000.00
Bob Tway	T14	73-70-68-72	283	$21,000.00
Chip Beck	T18	69-70-72-73	284	$14,100.00
Mike Brisky	T18	70-72-67-75	284	$14,100.00
Steve Elkington	T18	71-69-70-74	284	$14,100.00
Jerry Haas	T18	70-72-70-72	284	$14,100.00
J.P. Hayes	T18	73-71-69-71	284	$14,100.00
Mike Hulbert	T18	68-68-73-75	284	$14,100.00
Lee Janzen	T18	73-71-69-71	284	$14,100.00
David Ogrin	T18	73-68-68-75	284	$14,100.00
Bart Bryant	T26	70-71-73-71	285	$9,240.00
Mark Carnevale	T26	74-71-69-71	285	$9,240.00
Ben Crenshaw	T26	74-70-71-70	285	$9,240.00
Brad Bryant	T29	71-71-71-73	286	$7,465.72
Jim Carter	T29	69-72-74-71	286	$7,465.72
Marco Dawson	T29	69-72-73-72	286	$7,465.72
Steve Brodie	T29	72-69-70-75	286	$7,465.71
Billy Ray Brown	T29	75-69-68-74	286	$7,465.71
Brad Faxon	T29	72-68-70-76	286	$7,465.71
Grant Waite	T29	68-73-72-73	286	$7,465.71
Tom Hearn	T36	73-68-77-69	287	$5,775.00
Ed Humenik	T36	71-74-69-73	287	$5,775.00
Wayne Levi	T36	73-69-70-75	287	$5,775.00
Larry Rinker	T36	69-74-73-71	287	$5,775.00
Michael Allen	T40	74-70-69-75	288	$4,320.00
Paul Azinger	T40	69-74-72-73	288	$4,320.00
Jim Furyk	T40	69-72-73-74	288	$4,320.00
Jim Gallagher, Jr.	T40	72-69-72-75	288	$4,320.00
Joe Ozaki	T40	72-71-68-77	288	$4,320.00
Don Pooley	T40	70-74-71-73	288	$4,320.00
John Wilson	T40	70-74-71-73	288	$4,320.00
Richard Zokol	T40	71-72-73-72	288	$4,320.00
David Feherty	T48	74-71-70-74	289	$3,204.00
Charlie Rymer	T48	71-69-74-75	289	$3,204.00
David Frost	T50	71-73-75-71	290	$2,894.40
Bill Porter	T50	71-72-68-79	290	$2,894.40
Ray Stewart	T50	73-72-73-72	290	$2,894.40
Harry Taylor	T50	73-69-73-75	290	$2,894.40
Greg Twiggs	T50	73-71-75-71	290	$2,894.40
Tom Byrum	T55	74-70-71-76	291	$2,712.00
Rocco Mediate	T55	73-71-77-70	291	$2,712.00
Greg Powers	T55	72-73-72-74	291	$2,712.00
Duffy Waldorf	T55	73-70-75-73	291	$2,712.00
Willie Wood	T55	72-69-77-73	291	$2,712.00
Bob Burns	T60	72-71-71-78	292	$2,592.00
J.L. Lewis	T60	73-71-71-77	292	$2,592.00
Mike Reid	T60	70-73-75-74	292	$2,592.00
Steve Stricker	T60	72-70-73-77	292	$2,592.00
Omar Uresti	T60	70-75-75-72	292	$2,592.00
Fulton Allem	T65	69-70-81-73	293	$2,448.00
Bill Britton	T65	74-69-75-75	293	$2,448.00
Clark Burroughs	T65	69-76-73-75	293	$2,448.00
Curt Byrum	T65	70-73-73-77	293	$2,448.00
Bobby Clampett	T65	70-74-72-77	293	$2,448.00
Buddy Gardner	T65	75-70-77-71	293	$2,448.00
Mike Smith	T65	72-73-74-74	293	$2,448.00
Mike McCullough	72	68-71-73-82	294	$2,352.00
Bruce Vaughan	T73	74-71-74-77	296	$2,316.00
Mark Wurtz	T73	72-72-77-75	296	$2,316.00
Phil Blackmar	T75	71-74-73-79	297	$2,256.00
Brian Kamm	T75	70-75-74-78	297	$2,256.00
Jay Williamson	T75	72-73-75-77	297	$2,256.00
Dennis Paulson	78	70-74-78-79	301	$2,208.00

The following players did not finish (C=cut, W=withdrew, D=disqualified)

C—146- Rob Boldt, Mike Donald, Rick Fehr, Paul Goydos, Vance Heafner, Barry Jaeckel, Steve Rintoul, Jim Thorpe, Ted Tryba. **147-** Tommy Armour III, Ronnie Black, Scott Ford, Steve Gotsche, Ken Green, Jay Haas, Dudley Hart, Jonathan Kaye, Dick Mast, Lee Rinker, John Schroeder, Dicky Thompson, Jeff Woodland. **148-**Woody Austin, Kelly Gibson, Pete Jordan, Greg Kraft, Jeff Leonard, Tim Loustalot, Roger Maltbie, David Peoples, Jack Renner, Joey Sindelar. **149-** David Graham, Scott Gump, Kenny Knox, Bob Lohr. **150-** Rex Caldwell, Brian Claar, Bill Kratzert, Scott McCarron, Howard Twitty. **151-** Jay Delsing, Robin Freeman, Steve Hart, Ryan Howison, Tony Sills, Leonard Thompson, Tray Tyner, Stan Utley. **152-** Pat Bates, Darrell Kestner, Carl Paulson, Don Reese, Ted Schulz, Ronnie Springer, Lance Ten Broeck. **153-** Billy Andrade, Paul Stankowski. **154-** Kawika Cotner, P.H. Horgan III. **155-** Emlyn Aubrey. **156-** Andy North. **157-** Tony Destefano, Chris Dimarco, Ed Dougherty, Nolan Henke, Rick Vershure, Mark Wiebe. **158-** Paul Antonucci. **160-** Skip Kendall, Bill Van Orman. **164-** Joe Felder. **171-** Sal Silvestrone. **W—154-** Joe Acosta, Jr , **155-**Ed Fiori, **78-** Joey Rassett, **84-** Keith Clearwater, Rick Meskell.

BUICK CLASSIC

TOURNAMENT HISTORY

Year	Winner	Score	Runner-up	Score	Location	Par/Yards
WESTCHESTER CLASSIC						
1967	Jack Nicklaus	272	Dan Sikes	273	Westchester CC, Harrison, NY	72/6573
1968	Julius Boros	272	Bob Murphy Jack Nicklaus Dan Sikes	273	Westchester CC, Harrison, NY	72/6648
1969	Frank Beard	275	Bert Greene	276	Westchester CC, Harrison, NY	72/6677
1970	Bruce Crampton	273	Larry Hinson Jack Nicklaus	274	Westchester CC, Harrison, NY	72/6700
1971	Arnold Palmer	270	Gibby Gilbert Hale Irwin	275	Westchester CC, Harrison, NY	72/6700
1972	Jack Nicklaus	270	Jim Colbert	273	Westchester CC, Harrison, NY	72/6700
1973	*Bobby Nichols	272	Bob Murphy	272	Westchester CC, Harrison, NY	72/6614
1974	Johnny Miller	269	Don Bies	271	Westchester CC, Harrison, NY	72/6614
1975	*Gene Littler	271	Julius Boros	271	Westchester CC, Harrison, NY	72/6614
AMERICAN EXPRESS WESTCHESTER CLASSIC						
1976	David Graham	272	Ben Crenshaw Tom Watson Fuzzy Zoeller	275	Westchester CC, Harrison, NY	71/6603
1977	Andy North	272	George Archer	274	Westchester CC, Harrison, NY	71/6603
1978	Lee Elder	274	Mark Hayes	275	Westchester CC, Harrison, NY	71/6603
MANUFACTURERS HANOVER WESTCHESTER CLASSIC						
1979	Jack Renner	277	David Graham Howard Twitty	278	Westchester CC, Harrison, NY	71/6603
1980	Curtis Strange	273	Gibby Gilbert	275	Westchester CC, Harrison, NY	71/6603
1981	Raymond Floyd	275	Bobby Clampett Gibby Gilbert Craig Stadler	277	Westchester CC, Harrison, NY	71/6603
1982	Bob Gilder	261	Peter Jacobsen Tom Kite	266	Westchester CC, Harrison, NY	70/6329
1983	Seve Ballesteros	276	Andy Bean Craig Stadler	278	Westchester CC, Harrison, NY	71/6687
1984	Scott Simpson	269	David Graham Jay Haas Mark O'Meara	274	Westchester CC, Harrison, NY	71/6687
1985	*Roger Maltbie	275	George Burns Ray Floyd	275	Westchester CC, Harrison, NY	71/6722
1986	Bob Tway	272	Willie Wood	273	Westchester CC, Harrison, NY	71/6723
1987	*J.C. Snead	276	Seve Ballesteros	276	Westchester CC, Harrison, NY	71/6769
1988	*Seve Ballesteros	276	David Frost Ken Green Greg Norman	276	Westchester CC, Harrison, NY	71/6779
1989	*Wayne Grady	277	Ronnie Black	277	Westchester CC, Harrison, NY	71/6779
BUICK CLASSIC						
1990	Hale Irwin	269	Paul Azinger	271	Westchester CC, Harrison, NY	71/6779
1991	Billy Andrade	273	Brad Bryant	275	Westchester CC, Harrison, NY	71/6779
1992	David Frost	268	Duffy Waldorf	276	Westchester CC, Harrison, NY	71/6779
1993	*Vijay Singh	280	Mark Wiebe	280	Westchester CC, Harrison, NY	71/6779
1994	Lee Janzen	268	Ernie Els	271	Westchester CC, Harrison, NY	71/6779
1995	*Vijay Singh	278	Doug Martin	278	Westchester CC, Harrison, NY	71/6779

Tournament Record: 261 -- Bob Guilder, 1982
Current Course Record: 62 -- Dan Sikes, 1967; Jim Wright, 1976; Peter Jacobsen, 1982

KEY: *=Playoff

1995 COLONIAL NATIONAL INVITATION

Colonial CC, Fort Worth, TX **Purse: $1,400,000**
Par: 35-35--70 **Yards: 7,010** **May 25-28, 1995**

LEADERS: First Round--Lennie Clements and Clark Dennis, at 6-under-par 64, led by one over Billy Andrade. **Second Round--**Craig Parry, at 9-under-par 131, led by two over Clements. **Third Round--**Parry, at 9-under-par 201, led by one over Woody Austin.

CUT: 71 players at 2-over 142.

PRO-AM: $7,500. Due to inclement weather, the afternoon portion of the pro-am was divided into two nine-hole competitions. Morning Individual--Mark Calcavecchia, 64, $450. Morning Team--Loren Roberts, Peter Jacobsen, Mark Calcavecchia, $412.50 each. Afternoon Front Nine Individual--Mark McCumber, Tom Purtzer, Curtis Strange, 33, $312.50. Back Nine Individual--Larry Mize, 30, $375. Back Nine Team--Lennie Clements, Larry Mize, Craig Parry, 26, $312.50.

WEATHER: Sunny, warm and windy all week.

Winner: Tom Lehman 67-68-68-68 271 $252,000.00

Player	Pos	Scores	Total	Money
Craig Parry	2	66-65-70-71	272	$151,200.00
D.A. Weibring	3	66-72-69-67	274	$95,200.00
Woody Austin	4	67-69-66-73	275	$67,200.00
Brad Faxon	T 5	67-70-75-64	276	$51,100.00
Justin Leonard	T 5	68-72-68-68	276	$51,100.00
Mark McCumber	T 5	67-73-68-68	276	$51,100.00
Mark Calcavecchia	T 8	70-67-68-72	277	$39,200.00
Jeff Maggert	T 8	66-68-74-69	277	$39,200.00
Billy Mayfair	T 8	68-71-67-71	277	$39,200.00
Rocco Mediate	T 8	69-68-70-70	277	$39,200.00
David Duval	T12	67-71-76-64	278	$29,400.00
Nick Price	T12	73-69-70-66	278	$29,400.00
Scott Verplank	T12	69-68-70-71	278	$29,400.00
Billy Andrade	T15	65-71-72-71	279	$20,335.00
Jay Don Blake	T15	70-72-73-64	279	$20,335.00
Steve Elkington	T15	68-68-77-66	279	$20,335.00
David Frost	T15	69-72-70-68	279	$20,335.00
Mike Hulbert	T15	66-70-68-75	279	$20,335.00
Larry Mize	T15	72-70-69-68	279	$20,335.00
Brett Ogle	T15	67-72-72-68	279	$20,335.00
Lanny Wadkins	T15	69-73-67-70	279	$20,335.00
Dave Barr	T23	68-72-71-69	280	$12,110.00
Lennie Clements	T23	64-69-74-73	280	$12,110.00
Peter Jacobsen	T23	69-71-69-71	280	$12,110.00
Jeff Sluman	T23	69-67-76-68	280	$12,110.00
Brad Bryant	T23	67-74-72-67	280	$12,110.00
Tom Kite	T23	70-68-71-71	280	$12,110.00
Bruce Lietzke	T29	67-70-74-70	281	$9,310.00
Gil Morgan	T29	73-68-70-70	281	$9,310.00
Mike Standly	T29	70-72-71-68	281	$9,310.00
Bob Tway	T29	70-69-70-72	281	$9,310.00
Glen Day	T33	70-72-69-71	282	$7,087.50
Fred Funk	T33	69-71-71-71	282	$7,087.50
Neal Lancaster	T33	71-71-70-70	282	$7,087.50
Steve Lowery	T33	73-69-71-69	282	$7,087.50
Phil Mickelson	T33	69-71-73-69	282	$7,087.50
Kenny Perry	T33	73-68-74-67	282	$7,087.50
Scott Simpson	T33	74-68-70-70	282	$7,087.50
Kirk Triplett	T33	69-72-71-70	282	$7,087.50
David Edwards	T41	67-71-75-70	283	$5,180.00
Robin Freeman	T41	72-69-68-74	283	$5,180.00
Mike Sullivan	T41	70-71-72-70	283	$5,180.00
Tom Watson	T41	68-69-70-76	283	$5,180.00
Fuzzy Zoeller	T41	66-72-74-71	283	$5,180.00
Keith Fergus	T46	69-70-76-69	284	$3,808.00
John Mahaffey	T46	69-72-71-72	284	$3,808.00
Jim McGovern	T46	67-75-77-65	284	$3,808.00
Steve Pate	T46	72-69-70-73	284	$3,808.00
Dan Pohl	T46	68-72-75-69	284	$3,808.00
Loren Roberts	T46	70-70-71-73	284	$3,808.00
Guy Boros	T52	73-69-75-68	285	$3,248.00
Clark Dennis	T52	64-74-76-71	285	$3,248.00
Robert Gamez	T52	68-69-75-73	285	$3,248.00
Scott Hoch	T52	69-70-74-72	285	$3,248.00
Payne Stewart	T52	66-72-74-73	285	$3,248.00
Tray Tyner	T52	68-70-74-73	285	$3,248.00
Davis Love III	T58	70-68-74-74	286	$3,108.00
Charlie Rymer	T58	72-70-75-69	286	$3,108.00
Curtis Strange	T58	66-72-71-77	286	$3,108.00
Paul Goydos	T61	69-68-73-77	287	$3,038.00
Bob Lohr	T61	68-74-73-72	287	$3,038.00
Gary Hallberg	T63	70-71-74-73	288	$2,968.00
Joe Ozaki	T63	68-74-73-73	288	$2,968.00
Jerry Pate	T63	67-73-76-72	288	$2,968.00
Chip Beck	T66	68-71-77-74	290	$2,884.00
Joey Sindelar	T66	67-72-76-75	290	$2,884.00
Paul Stankowski	T66	70-71-74-75	290	$2,884.00
Michael Bradley	69	68-70-75-80	293	$2,828.00
Mike Reid	70	68-73-80-73	294	$2,800.00

The following players did not finish (C=cut, W=withdrew, D=disqualified)

C—143- Ernie Els, Kelly Gibson, Bill Glasson, Greg Kraft, Blaine McCallister, Mark McNulty, Mark O'Meara, Corey Pavin, Duffy Waldorf. **144-** Fulton Allem, Mark Brooks, Brian Claar, Jim Furyk, Jim Gallagher, Jr., Hale Irwin, Pete Jordan, Jodie Mudd, Dave Stockton, Jr. **145-** Brandel Chamblee, Keith Clearwater, Donnie Hammond, Mike Heinen, Brian Henninger, Dicky Pride, Gene Sauers, Ted Tryba. **146-** John Cook, Wayne Grady, Nolan Henke, Larry Nelson, Dillard Pruitt. **147-** Lee Janzen, Trip Kuehne, Andy North, Tom Purtzer. **148-** John Daly, Dan Forsman, Andrew Magee, Tommy Tolles. **149-** Anthony Rodriguez. **150-** Ben Crenshaw. **152-** Ian Baker-Finch, Bob Estes. **154-** Rod Curl. **W—218-** John Huston, **77-** Mike Springer.

MASTERCARD COLONIAL

TOURNAMENT HISTORY

Year	Winner	Score	Runner-up	Score	Location	Par/Yards
COLONIAL NATIONAL INVITATION TOURNAMENT						
1946	Ben Hogan	279	Harry Todd	280	Colonial CC, Fort Worth, TX	70/7035
1947	Ben Hogan	279	Toney Penna	280	Colonial CC, Fort Worth, TX	70/7035
1948	Clayton Heafner	272	Skip Alexander Ben Hogan	278	Colonial CC, Fort Worth, TX	70/7035
1949	No Tournament					
1950	Sam Snead	277	Skip Alexander	280	Colonial CC, Fort Worth, TX	70/7035
1951	Cary Middlecoff	282	Jack Burke, Jr.	283	Colonial CC, Fort Worth, TX	70/7035
1952	Ben Hogan	279	Lloyd Mangrum	283	Colonial CC, Fort Worth, TX	70/7035
1953	Ben Hogan	282	Doug Ford Cary Middlecoff	287	Colonial CC, Fort Worth, TX	70/7035
1954	Johnny Palmer	280	Fred Haas	282	Colonial CC, Fort Worth, TX	70/7035
1955	Chandler Harper	276	Dow Finsterwald	284	Colonial CC, Fort Worth, TX	70/7035
1956	Mike Souchak	280	Tommy Bolt	281	Colonial CC, Fort Worth, TX	70/7035
1957	Roberto De Vicenzo	284	Dick Mayer	285	Colonial CC, Fort Worth, TX	70/7021
1958	Tommy Bolt	282	Ken Venturi	283	Colonial CC, Fort Worth, TX	70/7021
1959	*Ben Hogan	285	Fred Hawkins	285	Colonial CC, Fort Worth, TX	70/7021
1960	Julius Boros	280	Gene Littler Kel Nagle	281	Colonial CC, Fort Worth, TX	70/7021
1961	Doug Sanders	281	Kel Nagle	282	Colonial CC, Fort Worth, TX	70/7021
1962	*Arnold Palmer	281	Johnny Pott	281	Colonial CC, Fort Worth, TX	70/7021
1963	Julius Boros	279	Gary Player	283	Colonial CC, Fort Worth, TX	70/7021
1964	Billy Casper	279	Tommy Jacobs	283	Colonial CC, Fort Worth, TX	70/7021
1965	Bruce Crampton	276	George Knudson	279	Colonial CC, Fort Worth, TX	70/7021
1966	Bruce Devlin	280	R.H. Sikes	281	Colonial CC, Fort Worth, TX	70/7021
1967	Dave Stockton	278	Charles Coody	280	Colonial CC, Fort Worth, TX	70/7021
1968	Billy Casper	275	Bert Yancey	273	Colonial CC, Fort Worth, TX	70/7021
1969	Gardner Dickinson	278	Gary Player	279	Colonial CC, Fort Worth, TX	70/7142
1970	Homero Blancas	273	Gene Littler Lee Trevino	274	Colonial CC, Fort Worth, TX	70/7142
1971	Gene Littler	283	Bert Yancey	284	Colonial CC, Fort Worth, TX	70/7142
1972	Jerry Heard	275	Fred Marti	277	Colonial CC, Fort Worth, TX	70/7142
1973	Tom Weiskopf	276	Bruce Crampton Jerry Heard	277	Colonial CC, Fort Worth, TX	70/7142
1974	Rod Curl	276	Jack Nicklaus	277	Colonial CC, Fort Worth, TX	70/7142
1975	Hosted Tournament Players Championship (now THE PLAYERS Championship)					
1976	Lee Trevino	273	Mike Morley	274	Colonial CC, Fort Worth, TX	70/7142
1977	Ben Crenshaw	272	John Schroeder	273	Colonial CC, Fort Worth, TX	70/7142
1978	Lee Trevino	268	Jerry Heard Jerry Pate	272	Colonial CC, Fort Worth, TX	70/7142
1979	Al Geiberger	274	Don January Gene Littler	275	Colonial CC, Fort Worth, TX	70/7096
1980	Bruce Lietzke	271	Ben Crenshaw	272	Colonial CC, Fort Worth, TX	70/7096
1981	Fuzzy Zoeller	274	Hale Irwin	278	Colonial CC, Fort Worth, TX	70/7096
1982	Jack Nicklaus	273	Andy North	276	Colonial CC, Fort Worth, TX	70/7096
1983	*Jim Colbert	278	Fuzzy Zoeller	278	Colonial CC, Fort Worth, TX	70/7096
1984	*Peter Jacobsen	270	Payne Stewart	270	Colonial CC, Fort Worth, TX	70/7096
1985	Corey Pavin	266	Bob Murphy	270	Colonial CC, Fort Worth, TX	70/7096
1986	*~Dan Pohl	205	Payne Stewart	205	Colonial CC, Fort Worth, TX	70/7096
1987	Keith Clearwater	266	Davis Love III	269	Colonial CC, Fort Worth, TX	70/7096
1988	Lanny Wadkins	270	Mark Calcavecchia Ben Crenshaw Joey Sindelar	271	Colonial CC, Fort Worth, TX	70/7096
SOUTHWESTERN BELL COLONIAL						
1989	Ian Baker-Finch	270	David Edwards	274	Colonial CC, Fort Worth, TX	70/7096
1990	Ben Crenshaw	272	John Mahaffey Corey Pavin Nick Price	275	Colonial CC, Fort Worth, TX	70/7096

MASTERCARD COLONIAL

TOURNAMENT HISTORY

Year	Winner	Score	Runner-up	Score	Location	Par/Yards
1991	Tom Purtzer	267	David Edwards Scott Hoch Bob Lohr	270	Colonial CC, Fort Worth, TX	70/7096
1992	*Bruce Lietzke	267	Corey Pavin	267	Colonial CC, Fort Worth, TX	70/7096
1993	Fulton Allem	264	Greg Norman	265	Colonial CC, Fort Worth, TX	70/7096
1994	*Nick Price	266	Scott Simpson	266	Colonial CC, Fort Worth, TX	70/7096
1995	Tom Lehman	271	Craig Parry	272	Colonial CC, Fort Worth, TX	70/7096

Tournament Record: 264 -- Fulton Allem, 1993
Current Course Record: 61 -- Keith Clearwater/Lee Janzen, 1993

KEY: *=Playoff ~=Weather-shortened

1995 MEMORIAL TOURNAMENT

Muirfield Village GC, Dublin, OH **Purse: $1,700,000**
Par: 36-36--72 **Yards: 7,104** **June 1-4, 1995**

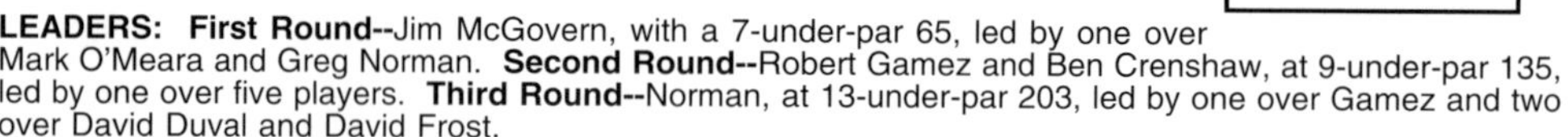

LEADERS: First Round--Jim McGovern, with a 7-under-par 65, led by one over Mark O'Meara and Greg Norman. **Second Round--**Robert Gamez and Ben Crenshaw, at 9-under-par 135, led by one over five players. **Third Round--**Norman, at 13-under-par 203, led by one over Gamez and two over David Duval and David Frost.

CUT: A total of 76 players at 1-over-par 145.

WEATHER: Play was suspended on Thursday at 8:35 a.m. due to rain and lightning with 16 players on the course. Morning play was cancelled and the round was restarted at 1 p.m. going off both tees with lift, clean and place rules. Play was suspended for the day at 8:30 p.m. with 55 players still on the course. The first round was completed on Friday morning with play beginning at 8 a.m. The second round followed immediately after. Saturday's third round was suspended due to dangerous weather conditions at 12:40 p.m. and was resumed at 4:50 p.m. Play was suspended for the day at 8:20 p.m. with 22 players still on the course. The third round was completed on Sunday morning beginning at 8:20 a.m., with the final round starting at 11:10 a.m. off both tees.

Winner: Greg Norman 66-70-67-66 269 $306,000.00

Player	Pos.	Scores	Total	Money
David Duval	T 2	70-71-64-68	273	$126,933.34
Mark Calcavecchia	T 2	69-71-66-67	273	$126,933.33
Steve Elkington	T 2	69-68-69-67	273	$126,933.33
Ben Crenshaw	T 5	67-68-71-69	275	$57,630.00
David Frost	T 5	68-72-65-70	275	$57,630.00
Robert Gamez	T 5	68-67-69-71	275	$57,630.00
Jay Haas	T 5	72-72-66-65	275	$57,630.00
Tom Watson	T 5	67-71-68-69	275	$57,630.00
Nick Price	10	71-71-69-65	276	$45,900.00
Kenny Perry	T11	68-74-68-67	277	$40,800.00
Vijay Singh	T11	69-67-71-70	277	$40,800.00
Ernie Els	T13	72-68-70-68	278	$30,033.34
Fred Funk	T13	72-69-67-70	278	$30,033.34
Nick Faldo	T13	68-72-70-68	278	$30,033.33
Bill Glasson	T13	72-66-71-69	278	$30,033.33
Peter Jacobsen	T13	68-68-70-72	278	$30,033.33
Bruce Lietzke	T13	69-67-70-72	278	$30,033.33
Jeff Sluman	T19	72-70-70-67	279	$22,950.00
Lee Janzen	T19	69-73-69-68	279	$22,950.00
Robert Allenby	T21	71-71-69-69	280	$15,958.75
Brad Bryant	T21	69-71-69-71	280	$15,958.75
Lennie Clements	T21	71-69-66-74	280	$15,958.75
David Edwards	T21	72-71-68-69	280	$15,958.75
Mark McCumber	T21	68-73-68-71	280	$15,958.75
Brett Ogle	T21	70-71-66-73	280	$15,958.75
Craig Parry	T21	69-71-69-71	280	$15,958.75
Scott Simpson	T21	68-70-74-68	280	$15,958.75
Jay Don Blake	T29	68-71-69-73	281	$11,050.00
Hale Irwin	T29	70-70-72-69	281	$11,050.00
Tom Lehman	T29	71-69-71-70	281	$11,050.00
Bob Tway	T29	72-66-70-73	281	$11,050.00
Scott Verplank	T29	74-69-71-67	281	$11,050.00
Chip Beck	T34	69-70-74-69	282	$8,967.50
Donnie Hammond	T34	72-72-70-68	282	$8,967.50
Doug Martin	T34	71-73-70-68	282	$8,967.50
Gil Morgan	T34	70-70-73-69	282	$8,967.50
Woody Austin	T38	67-76-68-72	283	$6,630.00
Mark Brooks	T38	69-75-69-70	283	$6,630.00
Clark Dennis	T38	70-71-74-68	283	$6,630.00
Jim Gallagher, Jr.	T38	67-75-73-68	283	$6,630.00
Scott Hoch	T38	67-72-72-72	283	$6,630.00
Mike Hulbert	T38	68-68-75-72	283	$6,630.00
Tom Kite	T38	72-72-67-72	283	$6,630.00
Jim McGovern	T38	65-73-73-72	283	$6,630.00
Mark O'Meara	T38	66-71-72-74	283	$6,630.00
Brad Faxon	T47	72-72-71-69	284	$4,494.80
Lee Rinker	T47	70-70-72-72	284	$4,494.80
Craig Stadler	T47	68-74-68-74	284	$4,494.80
Duffy Waldorf	T47	71-71-73-69	284	$4,494.80
D.A. Weibring	T47	70-73-68-73	284	$4,494.80
Fuzzy Zoeller	52	70-67-75-73	285	$4,080.00
Steve Jones	T53	72-70-71-73	286	$3,898.67
Davis Love III	T53	73-70-70-73	286	$3,898.67
John Mahaffey	T53	72-72-72-70	286	$3,898.67
Larry Mize	T53	72-72-73-69	286	$3,898.67
Jim Furyk	T53	71-71-68-76	286	$3,898.66
Wayne Grady	T53	69-71-72-74	286	$3,898.66
Hubert Green	T59	71-74-71-71	287	$3,740.00
Phil Mickelson	T59	70-73-71-73	287	$3,740.00
Payne Stewart	T59	70-75-71-71	287	$3,740.00
Don Pooley	T62	72-72-72-72	288	$3,621.00
Dillard Pruitt	T62	70-74-72-72	288	$3,621.00
Curtis Strange	T62	73-72-73-70	288	$3,621.00
Lanny Wadkins	T62	69-72-73-74	288	$3,621.00
Brian Claar	T66	71-71-73-75	290	$3,451.00
Keith Fergus	T66	72-70-74-74	290	$3,451.00
Jesper Parnevik	T66	73-70-73-74	290	$3,451.00
Gene Sauers	T66	70-73-74-73	290	$3,451.00
Steve Stricker	T66	73-72-72-73	290	$3,451.00
Hal Sutton	T66	69-73-73-75	290	$3,451.00
Mike Sullivan	72	67-76-77-72	292	$3,332.00
Bob Estes	73	71-72-74-77	294	$3,298.00
Allen Doyle	74	73-72-76-74	295	$3,264.00
Nolan Henke	75	75-70-73-78	296	$3,230.00
David Graham	76	73-72-78-79	302	$3,196.00

The following players did not finish (C=cut, W=withdrew, D=disqualified)

C—146- Brandel Chamblee, Mike Heinen, Andrew Magee, Jeff Maggert, Roger Maltbie, Billy Mayfair, Charlie Rymer. **147-** John Adams, John Cook, John Harris, Greg Kraft, Joe Ozaki, Steve Pate, Corey Pavin, Eduardo Romero. **148-** Dave Barr, Gary Hallberg, Justin Leonard, Kirk Triplett. **149-** Rick Fehr. **150-** Paul Azinger, John Huston, Brandt Jobe, Mark McNulty, Mike Springer. **151-** Guy Boros, Mike Donald, Brian Henninger, Larry Nelson. **152-** Billy Andrade, Glen Day. **153-** Jack Nicklaus. **154-** Andy North, Dicky Pride. **156-** Neal Lancaster. **W—72-** Chris Perry. **84-** Ian Baker-Finch.

THE MEMORIAL TOURNAMENT

TOURNAMENT HISTORY

Year	Winner	Score	Runner-up	Score	Location	Par/Yards
THE MEMORIAL TOURNAMENT						
1976	*Roger Maltbie	288	Hale Irwin	288	Muirfield Village GC, Dublin, OH	72/7027
1977	Jack Nicklaus	281	Hubert Green	283	Muirfield Village GC, Dublin, OH	72/7101
1978	Jim Simons	284	Bill Kratzert	285	Muirfield Village GC, Dublin, OH	72/7101
1979	Tom Watson	285	Miller Barber	288	Muirfield Village GC, Dublin, OH	72/7101
1980	David Graham	280	Tom Watson	281	Muirfield Village GC, Dublin, OH	72/7116
1981	Keith Fergus	284	Jack Renner	285	Muirfield Village GC, Dublin, OH	72/7116
1982	Raymond Floyd	281	Peter Jacobsen	283	Muirfield Village GC, Dublin, OH	72/7116
			Wayne Levi			
			Roger Maltbie			
			Gil Morgan			
1983	Hale Irwin	281	Ben Crenshaw	282	Muirfield Village GC, Dublin, OH	72/7116
			David Graham			
1984	*Jack Nicklaus	280	Andy Bean	280	Muirfield Village GC, Dublin, OH	72/7116
1985	Hale Irwin	281	Lanny Wadkins	282	Muirfield Village GC, Dublin, OH	72/7106
1986	Hal Sutton	271	Don Pooley	275	Muirfield Village GC, Dublin, OH	72/7106
1987	Don Pooley	272	Curt Byrum	275	Muirfield Village GC, Dublin, OH	72/7104
1988	Curtis Strange	274	David Frost	276	Muirfield Village GC, Dublin, OH	72/7104
			Hale Irwin			
1989	Bob Tway	277	Fuzzy Zoeller	279	Muirfield Village GC, Dublin, OH	72/7104
1990	~Greg Norman	216	Payne Stewart	217	Muirfield Village GC, Dublin, OH	72/7104
1991	*Kenny Perry	273	Hale Irwin	273	Muirfield Village GC, Dublin, OH	72/7104
1992	*David Edwards	273	Rick Fehr	273	Muirfield Village GC, Dublin, OH	72/7104
1993	Paul Azinger	274	Corey Pavin	275	Muirfield Village GC, Dublin, OH	72/7104
1994	Tom Lehman	268	Greg Norman	273	Muirfield Village GC, Dublin, OH	72/7104
1995	Greg Norman	269	David Duval	273	Muirfield Village GC, Dublin, OH	72/7104
			Mark Calcavecchia			
			Steve Elkington			

Tournament Record: 268 -- Tom Lehman, 1994
Current Course Record: 63 -- Kenny Perry, 1991

KEY: *=Playoff ~=Weather-shortened

1995 KEMPER OPEN

KEMPER OPEN

TPC at Avenel, Potomac, MD **Purse: $1,400,000**
Par: 36-35--71 **Yards: 7,005** **June 8-11, 1995**

LEADERS: First Round--Vijay Singh and Robert Gamez shot 6-under-par 65 to lead Jeff Maggert, Mark O'Meara, Steve Lowery and Wayne Grady by one stroke. **Second Round--**Davis Love III, at 11-under-par 131, led by one stroke over Scott Hoch. **Third Round--**Love was at 11-under-par 202 after a round of 71, one stroke ahead of Payne Stewart.

CUT: 71 players at even-par 142.

PRO-AM: Individual--Brad Bryant, Vijay Singh, Jeff Sluman, 66, $625 each. Team--Blaine McCallister, Lee Janzen, 53, $675 each.

WEATHER: Hot, humid and occasionally windy Thursday. Cooler Friday and Saturday with a threat of rain Saturday afternoon. Hot and humid Sunday.

Winner: Lee Janzen 68-69-68-67 272 $252,000.00

(Won playoff with birdie-3 on first extra hole)

Player	Pos	Scores	Total	Money
Corey Pavin	2	73-68-63-68	272	$151,200.00
Robin Freeman	3	70-69-66-68	273	$95,200.00
Justin Leonard	T 4	71-67-70-67	275	$52,780.00
Davis Love III	T 4	68-63-71-73	275	$52,780.00
Greg Norman	T 4	72-66-69-68	275	$52,780.00
Mark O'Meara	T 4	66-70-69-70	275	$52,780.00
Vijay Singh	T 4	65-71-71-68	275	$52,780.00
John Mahaffey	T 9	72-69-65-70	276	$35,000.00
Larry Mize	T 9	67-70-70-69	276	$35,000.00
Kenny Perry	T 9	72-68-69-67	276	$35,000.00
Nick Price	T 9	70-68-70-68	276	$35,000.00
Payne Stewart	T 9	69-69-65-73	276	$35,000.00
Marco Dawson	T14	67-69-73-68	277	$25,900.00
Scott Simpson	T14	72-69-68-68	277	$25,900.00
John Adams	T16	69-69-71-69	278	$21,000.00
Billy Andrade	T16	71-71-65-71	278	$21,000.00
Bill Glasson	T16	72-70-66-70	278	$21,000.00
Steve Jones	T16	69-68-69-72	278	$21,000.00
Neal Lancaster	T16	70-70-65-73	278	$21,000.00
Fulton Allem	T21	73-69-65-72	279	$12,460.00
Phil Blackmar	T21	67-68-72-72	279	$12,460.00
Paul Goydos	T21	76-66-68-69	279	$12,460.00
Wayne Grady	T21	66-69-75-69	279	$12,460.00
Tom Hearn	T21	70-71-73-65	279	$12,460.00
Scott Hoch	T21	68-65-72-74	279	$12,460.00
Tom Kite	T21	67-68-73-71	279	$12,460.00
Jesper Parnevik	T21	67-70-69-73	279	$12,460.00
Hal Sutton	T21	71-66-72-70	279	$12,460.00
Bobby Wadkins	T21	71-71-69-68	279	$12,460.00
Bart Bryant	T31	70-69-71-70	280	$7,940.00
Brad Faxon	T31	71-71-71-67	280	$7,940.00
Scott Gump	T31	69-73-68-70	280	$7,940.00
Jay Haas	T31	71-70-67-72	280	$7,940.00
Mike Hulbert	T31	72-70-70-68	280	$7,940.00
Jeff Maggert	T31	66-72-73-69	280	$7,940.00
Don Pooley	T31	68-72-70-70	280	$7,940.00
Ken Green	T38	71-68-71-71	281	$6,160.00
Skip Kendall	T38	72-70-69-70	281	$6,160.00
Jeff Sluman	T38	72-67-69-73	281	$6,160.00
Paul Stankowski	T38	69-70-71-71	281	$6,160.00
Tom Byrum	T42	71-70-73-68	282	$4,396.00
Mark Carnevale	T42	73-68-71-70	282	$4,396.00
Joel Edwards	T42	72-70-73-67	282	$4,396.00
Dan Forsman	T42	69-72-70-71	282	$4,396.00
Robert Gamez	T42	65-70-77-70	282	$4,396.00
Steve Lowery	T42	66-74-70-72	282	$4,396.00
Billy Mayfair	T42	72-67-74-69	282	$4,396.00
Scott McCarron	T42	69-71-71-71	282	$4,396.00
Doug Tewell	T42	68-72-74-68	282	$4,396.00
Chris DiMarco	T51	70-71-70-72	283	$3,315.20
Steve Gotsche	T51	73-69-69-72	283	$3,315.20
Dudley Hart	T51	72-68-72-71	283	$3,315.20
Andrew Magee	T51	67-70-71-75	283	$3,315.20
Lee Rinker	T51	69-69-76-69	283	$3,315.20
Bill Britton	T56	71-71-72-70	284	$3,136.00
Jerry Haas	T56	71-66-68-79	284	$3,136.00
J.L. Lewis	T56	72-68-71-73	284	$3,136.00
Doug Martin	T56	68-72-73-71	284	$3,136.00
Steve Pate	T56	69-73-72-70	284	$3,136.00
Bruce Fleisher	T61	69-73-76-67	285	$3,024.00
Kelly Gibson	T61	67-75-71-72	285	$3,024.00
Rocco Mediate	T61	69-71-73-72	285	$3,024.00
Miguel Jimenez	T64	68-74-72-72	286	$2,954.00
Blaine McCallister	T64	73-69-73-71	286	$2,954.00
Jay Don Blake	T66	70-70-73-74	287	$2,884.00
Donnie Hammond	T66	69-72-72-74	287	$2,884.00
Jerry Pate	T66	73-69-76-69	287	$2,884.00
Ray Stewart	69	71-71-76-71	289	$2,828.00
Craig Parry	70	73-69-75-73	290	$2,800.00
Morris Hatalsky	71	72-68-78-77	295	$2,772.00

The following players did not finish (C=cut, W=withdrew, D=disqualified)

C—143- Michael Allen, Seve Ballesteros, Pat Bates, Ronnie Black, Jim Carter, Jay Delsing, Brian Henninger, Pete Jordan, Dicky Pride, Joey Rassett, Howard Twitty, Tray Tyner, Duffy Waldorf, D.A. Weibring, Mark Wiebe. **144-** Rob Boldt, Mark Brooks, Brad Bryant, Wayne Defrancesco, Fred Funk, Bob Lohr, Phil Mickelson, Gil Morgan, Joey Sindelar, Harry Taylor. **145-** Kawika Cotner, Clark Dennis, Bob Gilder, Jeff Leonard, John Morse, Jose Maria Olazabal, Mike Reid, Dicky Thompson, Grant Waite, John Wilson. **146-** Tommy Armour III, Emlyn Aubrey, Michael Bradley, Fred Couples, Rick Fehr, Jonathan Kaye, Tim Loustalot, David Ogrin, Ted Schulz, Bruce Vaughan. **147-** Ed Humenik, Brian Kamm, Greg Kraft, Dennis Paulson, Bill Porter, Mike Smith, Mike Sullivan. **148-** Guy Boros, Ed Fiori, Wayne Levi, Rocky Walcher, Mark Wurtz. **149-** JC Anderson, Jim Furyk, J.P. Hayes, John Huston, Omar Uresti. **150-** Curt Byrum, Bobby Clampett, Eric Egloff, Jim Fitzgerald, Dave Stockton, Jr. **151-** Robert Allenby, Mike Springer. **152-** Woody Austin, Don Reese, Steve Rintoul, Eduardo Romero. **154-** Ted Tryba. **155-** Joe Acosta, Jr. **156-** Mike McGinnis. **159-** Mike Brisky. **160-** Jack Skilling, Jay Williamson, Lyle Williams. **W—74-** Brett Ogle, **75-** Dave Barr, **77-** Glen Day, **82-** Hubert Green, **85-** David Quelland.

KEMPER OPEN

TOURNAMENT HISTORY

Year	Winner	Score	Runner-up	Score	Location	Par/Yards
KEMPER OPEN						
1968	Arnold Palmer	276	Bruce Crampton	280	Pleasant Valley CC, Sutton, MA	71/7205
			Art Wall			
1969	Dale Douglass	274	Charles Coody	278	Quail Hollow CC, Charlotte, NC	72/7205
1970	Dick Lotz	278	Lou Graham	280	Quail Hollow CC, Charlotte, NC	72/7205
			Larry Hinson			
			Grier Jones			
			Tom Weiskopf			
1971	*Tom Weiskopf	277	Dale Douglass	277	Quail Hollow CC, Charlotte, NC	72/7205
			Gary Player			
			Lee Trevino			
1972	Doug Sanders	275	Lee Trevino	276	Quail Hollow CC, Charlotte, NC	72/7205
1973	Tom Weiskopf	271	Lanny Wadkins	274	Quail Hollow CC, Charlotte, NC	72/7205
1974	*Bob Menne	270	Jerry Heard	270	Quail Hollow CC, Charlotte, NC	72/7205
1975	Raymond Floyd	278	John Mahaffey	281	Quail Hollow CC, Charlotte, NC	72/7205
			Gary Player			
1976	Joe Inman	277	Grier Jones	278	Quail Hollow CC, Charlotte, NC	72/7205
			Tom Weiskopf			
1977	Tom Weiskopf	277	George Burns	279	Quail Hollow CC, Charlotte, NC	72/7205
			Bill Rogers			
1978	Andy Bean	273	Mark Hayes	278	Quail Hollow CC, Charlotte, NC	72/7205
			Andy North			
1979	Jerry McGee	272	Jerry Pate	273	Quail Hollow CC, Charlotte, NC	72/7205
1980	John Mahaffey	275	Craig Stadler	278	Congressional CC, Bethesda, MD	72/7173
1981	Craig Stadler	270	Tom Watson	276	Congressional CC, Bethesda, MD	72/7173
			Tom Weiskopf			
1982	Craig Stadler	275	Seve Ballesteros	282	Congressional CC, Bethesda, MD	72/7173
1983	*Fred Couples	287	T.C. Chen	287	Congressional CC, Bethesda, MD	72/7173
			Barry Jaeckel			
			Gil Morgan			
			Scott Simpson			
1984	Greg Norman	280	Mark O'Meara	285	Congressional CC, Bethesda, MD	72/7173
1985	Bill Glasson	278	Larry Mize	279	Congressional CC, Bethesda, MD	72/7173
			Corey Pavin			
1986	*Greg Norman	277	Larry Mize	277	Congressional CC, Bethesda, MD	72/7173
1987	Tom Kite	270	Chris Perry	277	TPC at Avenel, Potomac, MD	71/6864
			Howard Twitty			
1988	*Morris Hatalsky	274	Tom Kite	274	TPC at Avenel, Potomac, MD	71/6867
1989	Tom Byrum	268	Tommy Armour III	273	TPC at Avenel, Potomac, MD	71/6917
			Billy Ray Brown			
			Jim Thorpe			
1990	Gil Morgan	274	Ian Baker-Finch	275	TPC at Avenel, Potomac, MD	71/6917
1991	*Billy Andrade	263	Jeff Sluman	263	TPC at Avenel, Potomac, MD	71/6904
1992	Bill Glasson	276	John Daly	277	TPC at Avenel, Potomac, MD	71/7005
			Ken Green			
			Mike Springer			
			Howard Twitty			
1993	Grant Waite	275	Tom Kite	276	TPC at Avenel, Potomac, MD	71/7005
1994	Mark Brooks	271	Bobby Wadkins	274	TPC at Avenel, Potomac, MD	71/7005
			D.A. Weibring			
1995	*Lee Janzen	272	Corey Pavin	272	TPC at Avenel, Potomac, MD	71/7005

Tournament Record: 263 -- Billy Andrade/Jeff Sluman, 1991
Current Course Record: 63 -- Ted Schulz, 1991; David Toms, 1992; Corey Pavin, 1995; Davis Love III, 1995

KEY: *=Playoff ~=Weather-shortened

1995 U.S. OPEN

Shinnecock Hills GC, Southampton, NY **Purse: $2,000,000**
Par: 35-35--70 Yards: 6,944 **June 15-18, 1995**

LEADERS: First Round--Nick Price, with a 4-under-par 66, led by one over Scott Simpson. **Second Round--**Greg Norman, at 5-under-par 135, led by two over Jumbo Ozaki. **Third Round--**Tom Lehman and Norman, at 1-under-par 209, led by one over Phil Mickelson and Bob Tway.

CUT: 73 players at 6-over-par 146. Cut was low 60 and ties and anyone within 10 strokes of the lead.

WEATHER: Rainy conditions early in the week. Sunny, windy and warm during the four tournament rounds.

Winner: Corey Pavin 72-69-71-68 280 $350,000.00

Player	Pos	Scores	Total	Money
Greg Norman	2	68-67-74-73	282	$207,000.00
Tom Lehman	3	70-72-67-74	283	$131,974.00
Bill Glasson	T 4	69-70-76-69	284	$66,633.67
Neal Lancaster	T 4	70-72-77-65	284	$66,633.67
Jeff Maggert	T 4	69-72-77-66	284	$66,633.67
Phil Mickelson	T 4	68-70-72-74	284	$66,633.67
Jay Haas	T 4	70-73-72-69	284	$66,633.66
Davis Love III	T 4	72-68-73-71	284	$66,633.66
Bob Tway	T10	69-69-72-75	285	$44,184.34
Frank Nobilo	T10	72-72-70-71	285	$44,184.33
Vijay Singh	T10	70-71-72-72	285	$44,184.33
Brad Bryant	T13	71-75-70-70	286	$30,934.00
Lee Janzen	T13	70-72-72-72	286	$30,934.00
Mark McCumber	T13	70-71-77-68	286	$30,934.00
Nick Price	T13	66-73-73-74	286	$30,934.00
Mark Roe	T13	71-69-74-72	286	$30,934.00
Jeff Sluman	T13	72-69-74-71	286	$30,934.00
Steve Stricker	T13	71-70-71-74	286	$30,934.00
Duffy Waldorf	T13	72-70-75-69	286	$30,934.00
Billy Andrade	T21	72-69-74-72	287	$20,085.43
Pete Jordan	T21	74-71-71-71	287	$20,085.43
Brett Ogle	T21	71-75-72-69	287	$20,085.43
Payne Stewart	T21	74-71-73-69	287	$20,085.43
Scott Verplank	T21	72-69-71-75	287	$20,085.43
Fuzzy Zoeller	T21	69-74-76-68	287	$20,085.43
Ian Woosnam	T21	72-71-69-75	287	$20,085.42
Miguel Jimenez	T28	72-72-75-69	288	$13,912.13
Colin Montgomerie	T28	71-74-75-68	288	$13,912.13
Scott Simpson	T28	67-75-74-72	288	$13,912.13
David Duval	T28	70-73-73-72	288	$13,912.12
Jose Maria Olazabal	T28	73-70-72-73	288	$13,912.12
Jumbo Ozaki	T28	69-68-80-71	288	$13,912.12
Mike Hulbert	T28	74-72-72-70	288	$13,912.13
Gary Hallberg	T28	70-76-69-73	288	$13,912.12
Guy Boros	T36	73-71-74-71	289	$9,812.38
Steve Elkington	T36	72-73-73-71	289	$9,812.38
Ray Floyd	T36	74-72-76-67	289	$9,812.38
Curtis Strange	T36	70-72-76-71	289	$9,812.38
Curt Byrum	T36	70-70-76-73	289	$9,812.37
Bernhard Langer	T36	74-67-74-74	289	$9,812.37
Bill Porter	T36	73-70-79-67	289	$9,812.37
Hal Sutton	T36	71-74-76-68	289	$9,812.37
Barry Lane	44	74-72-71-73	290	$8,147.00
John Daly	T45	71-75-74-71	291	$7,146.00
Nick Faldo	T45	72-68-79-72	291	$7,146.00
Bradley Hughes	T45	72-71-75-73	291	$7,146.00
Jim McGovern	T45	73-69-81-68	291	$7,146.00
Christian Pena	T45	74-71-76-70	291	$7,146.00
Omar Uresti	T45	71-74-75-71	291	$7,146.00
Bob Burns	T51	73-72-75-72	292	$5,842.60
Matt Gogel	T51	73-70-73-76	292	$5,842.60
Peter Jacobsen	T51	72-72-74-74	292	$5,842.60
Eduardo Romero	T51	73-71-75-73	292	$5,842.60
Ted Tryba	T51	71-75-73-73	292	$5,842.60
Brad Faxon	T56	71-73-77-72	293	$4,833.84
Steve Lowery	T56	69-72-75-77	293	$4,833.84
Greg Bruckner	T56	70-72-73-78	293	$4,833.83
Scott Hoch	T56	74-72-70-77	293	$4,833.83
Chris Perry	T56	70-74-75-74	293	$4,833.83
Tom Watson	T56	70-73-77-73	293	$4,833.83
John Cook	T62	70-75-76-73	294	$3,969.00
David Edwards	T62	72-74-72-76	294	$3,969.00
Jim Gallagher, Jr.	T62	71-75-77-71	294	$3,969.00
Paul Goydos	T62	73-73-70-78	294	$3,969.00
Brandt Jobe	T62	71-72-76-75	294	$3,969.00
Tommy Armour III	T67	77-69-74-75	295	$3,349.00
Mike Brisky	T67	71-72-77-75	295	$3,349.00
Tom Kite	T67	70-72-82-71	295	$3,349.00
John Connelly	70	75-71-74-76	296	$3,039.00
Ben Crenshaw	T71	72-71-79-75	297	$2,806.50
John Maginnes	T71	75-71-74-77	297	$2,806.50
Joey Gullion	73	70-74-81-76	301	$2,574.00

The following players did not finish (C=cut, W=withdrew, D=disqualified)

C—147- Fulton Allem, Seve Ballesteros, Ernie Els, Bob Estes, John Huston, Hale Irwin, Doug Martin, Blaine McCallister, Larry Mize, Pat Moore, Dana Quigley, Mike Standly, Bruce Vaughan. **148-** Paul Azinger, Robert Gamez, Tim Hobby, Per-Ulrik Johansson, Darrell Kestner, Mark McNulty, Eric Meeks, Olle Nordberg, Mike San Filippo. **149-**Chip Beck, Billy Ray Brown, Fred Couples, Jerry Courville, Wayne Grady, Mike Heinen, Jeff Julian, John Mahaffey, David Morland, Chris Tidland, Kim Young. **150-** Mark Calcavecchia, Rick Fehr, David Gilford, Tim Herron, Gary Koch, Andrew Magee, Brian Mogg, Andy North, Tommy Roddy, Don Walsworth. **151-** Ian Baker-Finch, David Frost, Fred Funk, Simon Hobday, Kenny Perry, Mike Schuchart, Chris Zambri. **152-** Bill Britton, Glen Day, Craig Marseilles, Jack Nicklaus, Todd White. **153-** Bob Elliott, Fran Marrello, Bill Murchison, Steve Pate. **154-** Rafael Alarcon, Jon Chaffee, Rick Cramer, Geoffrey Sisk. **155-** D.J. Holland, Mike Muehr, John Snyder. **156-** John Calabria, Clark Dennis, Jim Estes, Mike Springer, Collin Stoops. **157-** Adam Armagost, Kelly Mitchum, Javier Sanchez, Larry Tedesco. **158-** Chris Kaufman. **159-** John Hulbert, Scott Tyson, Tiger Woods. **161-** Dustin Phillips, John Reeves. **164-** Brad Bell. **W—**73- Loren Roberts.

U.S. OPEN

TOURNAMENT HISTORY

Year	Winner	Score	Runner-up	Score	Location
1895	Horace Rawlins	173-36 Holes	Willie Dunn		Newport GC, Newport, RI
1896	James Foulis	152-36 Holes	Horace Rawlins		Shinnecock Hills GC, Southhampton, NY
1897	Joe Lloyd	162-36 Holes	Willie Anderson		Chicago GC, Wheaton, IL
1898	Fred Herd	328-72 Holes	Alex Smith		Myopia Hunt Club, Hamilton, MA
1899	Willie Smith	315	George Low		Baltimore CC, Baltimore, MD
			Val Fitzjohn		
			W. H. Way		
1900	Harry Vardon	313	J. H. Taylor		Chicago GC, Wheaton, IL
1901	*Willie Anderson (85)	331	Alex Smith	(86)	Myopia Hunt Club, Hamilton, MA
1902	Laurie Auchterlonie	307	Stewart Gardner		Garden City GC, Garden City, LI, NY
1903	*Willie Anderson (82)	307	David Brown	(84)	Baltusrol GC, Short Hills, NJ
1904	Willie Anderson	303	Gil Nicholls		Glen View Club, Golf, IL
1905	Willie Anderson	314	Alex Smith		Myopia Hunt Club, Hamilton, MA
1906	Alex Smith	295	Willie Smith		Onwentsia Club Lake Forest, IL
1907	Alex Ross	302	Gil Nicholls		Philadelphia Cricket Club, Chestnut Hill,PA
1908	*Fred McLeod (77)	322	Willie Smith	(83)	Myopia Hunt Club, Hamilton, MA
1909	George Sargent	290	Tom McNamara		Englewood GC Englewood, NJ
1910	*Alex Smith (71)	298	John McDermott	(75)	Philadelphia Cricket Club, Chestnut Hill, PA
			Macdonald Smith	(77)	
1911	*John McDermott (80)	307	Mike Brady	(82)	Chicago GC, Wheaton, IL.
			George Simpson	(85)	
1912	John McDermott	294	Tom McNamara		CC of Buffalo, Buffalo, NY
1913	*Francis Ouimet (72)	304	Harry Vardon	(77)	The Country Club, Brookline, MA
			Edward Ray	(78)	
1914	Walter Hagen	290	Charles Evans, Jr.		Midlothian CC, Blue Island, IL
1915	Jerome Travers	297	Tom McNamara		Baltusrol GC, Short Hills, NJ
1916	Charles Evans, Jr.	286	Jock Hutchison	288	Minikahda Club, Minneapolis, MN
1917—1918 No Championships Played—World War I					
1919	*Walter Hagen (77)	301	Mike Brady	(78)	Brae Burn CC, West Newton, MA
1920	Edward Ray	295	Harry Vardon	296	Inverness CC, Toledo, OH
			Jack Burke		
			Leo Diegel		
			Jock Hutchison		
1921	James M. Barnes	289	Walter Hagen	298	Columbia CC, Chevy Chase, MD
			Fred McLeod		
1922	Gene Sarazen	288	John L. Black	289	Skokie CC, Glencoe, IL
			Robert T. Jones, Jr.		
1923	*Robert. T. Jones, Jr. (76)	296	Bobby Cruickshank	(78)	Inwood CC, Inwood, LI, NY
1924	Cyril Walker	297	Robert T. Jones, Jr.	300	Oakland Hills CC, Birmingham, MI
1925	*W. Macfarlane (147)	291	Robert T. Jones, Jr.	(148)	Worcester CC, Worcester, MA
1926	Robert T. Jones, Jr.	293	Joe Turnesa	294	Scioto CC, Columbus, OH
1927	*Tommy Armour (76)	301	Harry Cooper	(79)	Oakmont CC, Oakmont, PA
1928	*Johnny Farrell (143)	294	Robert T. Jones, Jr.	(144)	Olympia Fields CC, Matteson, IL
1929	*Robert.T. Jones, Jr. (141)	294	Al Espinosa	(164)	Winged Foot GC, Marmaroneck, NY
1930	Robert T. Jones, Jr.	287	Macdonald Smith	289	Interlachen CC, Hopkins, MN
1931	*Billy Burke (149-148)	292	George Von Elm (149-149)		Inverness Club, Toledo, OH
1932	Gene Sarazen	286	Phil Perkins	289	Fresh Meadows CC, Flushing, NY
			Bobby Cruickshank		
1933	Johnny Goodman	287	Ralph Guldahl	288	North Shore CC, Glenview, IL
1934	Olin Dutra	293	Gene Sarazen	294	Merion Cricket Club, Ardmore, PA
1935	Sam Parks, Jr.	299	Jimmy Thomson	301	Oakmont CC, Oakmont, PA
1936	Tony Manero	282	Harry Cooper	284	Baltusrol GC, Springfield, NJ
1937	Ralph Guldahl	281	Sam Snead	283	Oakland Hills CC, Birmingham, MI
1938	Ralph Guldahl	284	Dick Metz	290	Cherry Hills CC, Denver, CO
1939	*Byron Nelson (68-70)	284	Craig Wood	(68-73)	Philadelphia CC, Philadelphia, PA
			Denny Shute	(76)	
1940	*Lawson Little (70)	287	Gene Sarazen	(73)	Canterbury GC, Cleveland, OH

U.S. OPEN

TOURNAMENT HISTORY

Year	Winner	Score	Runner-up	Score	Location
1941	Craig Wood	284	Denny Shute	287	Colonial Club, Fort Worth, TX
1942—1945 No Championships Played—World War II					
1946	*Lloyd Mangrum (72-72)	284	Vic Ghezzi	(72-73)	Canterbury GC, Cleveland, OH
			Byron Nelson	(72-73)	
1947	*Lew Worsham (69)	282	Sam Snead	(70)	St. Louis CC, Clayton, MO
1948	Ben Hogan	276	Jimmy Demaret	278	Riviera CC, Los Angeles, CA
1949	Cary Middlecoff	286	Sam Snead	287	Medinah CC, Medinah, IL
			Clayton Heafner		
1950	*Ben Hogan (69)	287	Lloyd Mangrum	(73)	Merion Golf Club, Ardmore, PA
			George Fazio	(75)	
1951	Ben Hogan	287	Clayton Heafner	289	Oakland Hills CC, Birmingham, MI
1952	Julius Boros	281	Ed Oliver	285	Northwood CC, Dallas, TX
1953	Ben Hogan	283	Sam Snead	289	Oakmont CC, Oakmont, PA
1954	Ed Furgol	284	Gene Littler	285	Baltusrol GC, Springfield, NJ
1955	*Jack Fleck (69)	287	Ben Hogan	(72)	Olympic Club, San Francisco, CA
1956	Cary Middlecoff	281	Ben Hogan	282	Oak Hill CC, Rochester, NY
			Julius Boros		
1957	*Dick Mayer (72)	282	Cary Middlecoff	(79)	Inverness Club, Toledo, OH
1958	Tommy Bolt	283	Gary Player	287	Southern Hills CC, Tulsa, OK
1959	Billy Casper	282	Bob Rosburg	283	Winged Foot GC, Mamaroneck, NY
1960	Arnold Palmer	280	Jack Nicklaus	282	Cherry Hills CC, Denver, CO
1961	Gene Littler	281	Bob Goalby	282	Oakland Hills CC, Birmingham, MI
			Doug Sanders		
1962	*Jack Nicklaus (71)	283	Arnold Palmer	(74)	Oakmont CC, Oakmont PA
1963	*Julius Boros (70)	293	Jacky Cupit	(73)	The Country Club, Brookline, MA
			Arnold Palmer	(76)	
1964	Ken Venturi	278	Tommy Jacobs	282	Congressional CC, Washington, DC
1965	*Gary Player (71)	282	Kel Nagle	(74)	Bellerive CC, St Louis, MO
1966	*Billy Casper (69)	278	Arnold Palmer	(73)	Olympic Club, San Francisco, CA
1967	Jack Nicklaus	275	Arnold Palmer	279	Baltusrol GC, Springfield, NJ
1968	Lee Trevino	275	Jack Nicklaus	279	Oak Hill CC, Rochester NY
1969	Orville Moody	281	Deane Beman	282	Champions GC, Houston, TX
			Al Geiberger		
			Bob Rosburg		
1970	Tony Jacklin	281	Dave Hill	288	Hazeltine GC, Chaska, MN
1971	*Lee Trevino (68)	280	Jack Nicklaus	(71)	Merion Golf Club, Ardmore, PA
1972	Jack Nicklaus	290	Bruce Crampton	293	Pebble Beach GL, Pebble Beach, CA
1973	Johnny Miller	279	John Schlee	280	Oakmont CC, Oakmont, PA
1974	Hale Irwin	287	Forrest Fezler	289	Winged Foot GC, Mamaroneck, NY
1975	*Lou Graham (71)	287	John Mahaffey	(73)	Medinah CC, Medinah, IL.
1976	Jerry Pate	277	Tom Weiskopf	279	Atlanta Athletic Club, Duluth, GA
			Al Geiberger		
1977	Hubert Green	278	Lou Graham	279	Southern Hills CC, Tulsa, OK
1978	Andy North	285	Dave Stockton	286	Cherry Hills CC, Denver, CO
			J. C. Snead		
1979	Hale Irwin	284	Gary Player	286	Inverness Club, Toledo, OH
			Jerry Pate		
1980	Jack Nicklaus	272	Isao Aoki	274	Baltusrol GC, Springfield NJ
1981	David Graham	273	George Burns	276	Merion GC, Ardmore, PA
			Bill Rogers		
1982	Tom Watson	282	Jack Nicklaus	284	Pebble Beach GL, Pebble Beach, CA
1983	Larry Nelson	280	Tom Watson	281	Oakmont CC, Oakmont, PA
1984	*Fuzzy Zoeller (67)	276	Greg Norman	(75)	Winged Foot GC, Mamaroneck, NY
1985	Andy North	279	Dave Barr	280	Oakland Hills CC, Birmingham, MI
			T.C. Chen		
			Denis Watson		

U.S. OPEN

TOURNAMENT HISTORY

Year	Winner	Score	Runner-up	Score	Location
1986	Ray Floyd	279	Lanny Wadkins Chip Beck	281	Shinnecock Hills GC, Southampton, NY
1987	Scott Simpson	277	Tom Watson	278	Olympic Club Lake Course, San Francisco,CA
1988	*Curtis Strange (71)	278	Nick Faldo	(75)	The Country Club, Brookline, MA
1989	Curtis Strange	278	Chip Beck Mark McCumber Ian Woosnam	279	Oak Hill CC, Rochester, NY
1990	*Hale Irwin (74-3)	280	Mike Donald	(74-4)	Medinah CC, Medinah, IL
1991	*Payne Stewart (75)	282	Scott Simpson	(77)	Hazeltine National GC, Chaska, MN
1992	Tom Kite	285	Jeff Sluman	287	Pebble Beach GL, Pebble Beach, CA
1993	Lee Janzen	272	Payne Stewart	274	Baltusrol GC, Springfield, NJ
1994	*Ernie Els (74-4-4)	279	Loren Roberts Colin Montgomerie	(74-4-5) (78)	Oakmont CC, Oakmont, PA
1995	Corey Pavin	280	Greg Norman	282	Shinnecock Hills GC, Southampton, NY

Tournament Record: 272 -- Jack Nicklaus, 1980; Lee Janzen, 1993 (both Baltusrol GC)
18-Hole Record: 63 -- Johnny Miller, 1973 (Oakmont CC); Tom Weiskopf, 1980 (Baltusrol GC); Jack Nicklaus, 1980 (Baltusrol GC)

KEY: *=Playoff *Figures in parentheses indicate playoff scores*

1995 CANON GREATER HARTFORD OPEN

TPC at River Highlands, Cromwell, CT **Purse: $1,200,000**
Par: 35-35--70 Yards: 6,820 **June 22-25, 1995**

LEADERS: First Round--Kirk Triplett and Bob Estes, at 6-under-par 64, led by one over Dave Stockton, Jr. **Second Round--**Triplett and Greg Norman, at 9-under-par 131, led by two over Grant Waite, Fuzzy Zoeller, Lee Rinker, Michael Bradley, Stockton, Brian Henninger, Ronnie Black and Jerry Haas. **Third Round--**Norman, at 14-under par 196, led by three over Zoeller.

CUT: 78 players at 1-over-par 141.

PRO-AM: $7,500. Individual--Steve Stricker, 64, $750. Team--Corey Pavin, 53, $750.

WEATHER: Hot early in the week. Wednesday through Saturday were sunny and mild. Sunday was overcast and humid.

Winner: Greg Norman 67-64-65-71 267 $216,000.00

Player	Pos.	Scores	Total	Money
Dave Stockton,Jr.	T 2	65-68-68-68	269	$89,600.00
Kirk Triplett	T 2	64-67-69-69	269	$89,600.00
Grant Waite	T 2	66-67-67-69	269	$89,600.00
Brian Henninger	T 5	66-67-72-65	270	$43,800.00
Don Pooley	T 5	67-72-66-65	270	$43,800.00
Fuzzy Zoeller	T 5	70-63-66-71	270	$43,800.00
Billy Andrade	T 8	74-65-62-70	271	$34,800.00
Michael Bradley	T 8	67-66-69-69	271	$34,800.00
Bob Estes	T 8	64-72-68-67	271	$34,800.00
Dave Barr	T11	68-71-68-65	272	$26,400.00
Guy Boros	T11	68-70-64-70	272	$26,400.00
David Edwards	T11	69-67-67-69	272	$26,400.00
Corey Pavin	T11	70-67-66-69	272	$26,400.00
Paul Azinger	T15	67-70-66-70	273	$20,400.00
Dudley Hart	T15	72-67-68-66	273	$20,400.00
Vijay Singh	T15	68-66-68-71	273	$20,400.00
Emlyn Aubrey	T18	66-72-68-68	274	$15,120.00
Pat Bates	T18	70-66-67-71	274	$15,120.00
Stewart Cink	T18	71-67-67-69	274	$15,120.00
Jerry Haas	T18	68-65-71-70	274	$15,120.00
Dan Pohl	T18	69-69-70-66	274	$15,120.00
Tony Sills	T18	67-70-67-70	274	$15,120.00
Steve Jones	T24	68-68-68-71	275	$10,230.00
Pete Jordan	T24	71-68-66-70	275	$10,230.00
Craig Parry	T24	70-69-68-68	275	$10,230.00
David Peoples	T24	73-68-67-67	275	$10,230.00
Chip Beck	T28	67-68-71-70	276	$8,160.00
Ronnie Black	T28	67-66-70-73	276	$8,160.00
Gary Hallberg	T28	71-69-65-71	276	$8,160.00
Andrew Magee	T28	69-66-72-69	276	$8,160.00
Mark O'Meara	T28	68-70-67-71	276	$8,160.00
Brian Claar	T33	70-71-65-71	277	$6,480.00
Bruce Fleisher	T33	71-67-66-73	277	$6,480.00
Steve Gotsche	T33	70-68-69-70	277	$6,480.00
Don Reese	T33	71-68-71-67	277	$6,480.00
Lee Rinker	T33	68-65-73-71	277	$6,480.00
Tommy Armour III	T38	71-68-69-70	278	$4,920.00
Ken Green	T38	73-66-68-71	278	$4,920.00
Scott Gump	T38	70-71-68-69	278	$4,920.00
Nolan Henke	T38	73-68-67-70	278	$4,920.00
Ryan Howison	T38	73-67-67-71	278	$4,920.00
Doug Martin	T38	70-71-69-68	278	$4,920.00
David Ogrin	T38	68-72-71-67	278	$4,920.00
Mike Brisky	T45	72-69-65-73	279	$3,432.00
John Cook	T45	66-72-71-70	279	$3,432.00
Ed Fiori	T45	70-68-67-74	279	$3,432.00
Donnie Hammond	T45	68-73-71-67	279	$3,432.00
Blaine McCallister	T45	72-67-71-69	279	$3,432.00
Joey Sindelar	T45	70-71-70-68	279	$3,432.00
Billy Ray Brown	T51	71-70-67-72	280	$2,824.00
Mike Heinen	T51	70-69-73-68	280	$2,824.00
Billy Mayfair	T51	73-68-72-67	280	$2,824.00
Steve Rintoul	T51	68-68-71-73	280	$2,824.00
Bobby Wadkins	T51	70-71-71-68	280	$2,824.00
Mark Wurtz	T51	71-66-71-72	280	$2,824.00
Lennie Clements	T57	76-65-69-71	281	$2,700.00
Steve Stricker	T57	69-71-70-71	281	$2,700.00
Fulton Allem	T59	69-69-74-70	282	$2,592.00
Mark Carnevale	T59	68-73-68-73	282	$2,592.00
Skip Kendall	T59	70-71-68-73	282	$2,592.00
Greg Kraft	T59	67-72-70-73	282	$2,592.00
Bill Porter	T59	74-67-69-72	282	$2,592.00
Mike Smith	T59	70-71-73-68	282	$2,592.00
Mike Standly	T59	71-69-72-70	282	$2,592.00
Brad Faxon	T66	74-67-71-71	283	$2,448.00
Scott McCarron	T66	70-67-72-74	283	$2,448.00
Carl Paulson	T66	72-68-69-74	283	$2,448.00
Dicky Pride	T66	71-69-72-71	283	$2,448.00
Willie Wood	T66	71-70-68-74	283	$2,448.00
Scott Ford	T71	69-70-75-70	284	$2,364.00
Jay Williamson	T71	71-70-74-69	284	$2,364.00
Dick Mast	73	72-68-72-73	285	$2,328.00
Dave Rummells	T74	67-72-72-75	286	$2,292.00
Ted Tryba	T74	72-69-72-73	286	$2,292.00
Harry Taylor	76	70-71-71-75	287	$2,256.00
Roger Maltbie	77	73-68-78-70	289	$2,232.00
Tom Sullivan	78	69-71-74-77	291	$2,208.00

The following players did not finish (C=cut, W=withdrew, D=disqualified)

C—142- Curt Byrum, Tom Hearn, Justin Leonard, Wayne Levi, Gene Sauers, Ray Stewart, Dicky Thompson, Omar Uresti. **143-** Michael Allen, Phil Blackmar, Mark Brooks, John Daly, Jay Delsing, Paul Goydos, Neal Lancaster, Kenny Perry. **144-** Clark Burroughs, Glen Day, David Frost, Steve Hart, Bradley Hughes, Ed Humenik, Jonathan Kaye, Rocco Mediate, Charlie Rymer, Tommy Tolles, Howard Twitty, Bruce Vaughan, John Wilson. **145-** Bart Bryant, Mark Calcavecchia, Jim Carter, Marco Dawson, Robin Freeman, J.L. Lewis, Dennis Paulson. **146-** Bill Britton, Keith Fergus, Mike Gilmore, Brian Kamm, Larry Nelson, Jeff Sluman, Tray Tyner. **147-** Kawika Cotner, Clark Dennis, Chris DiMarco, Tim Elliott, Robert Floyd, Hubert Green, Jim Hallet, Jeff Leonard, Doug Tewell, Lanny Wadkins. **148-** Joe Acosta, Jr., Keith Clearwater, Joel Edwards, Kelly Gibson, John Morse. **149-** Bob Burns, Mike Donald, David Duval, Bill Kratzert, Joe Ozaki, Larry Rinker, Ted Schulz. **150-** Dennis Coscina, J.P. Hayes. **151-** Tim Loustalot. **152-** Joey Rassett. **153-** Mickey Hawkes. **154-** Jon Chaffee. **155-** Tom Sutter. **156-** Tim Gavronski. **160-** Chris Tremblay. **W—77-** Ian Baker-Finch, **82-** Brandel Chamblee, Mac O'Grady. **D—78-** Ron Dellostritto.

CANON GREATER HARTFORD OPEN

TOURNAMENT HISTORY

Year	Winner	Score	Runner-up	Score	Location	Par/Yards
INSURANCE CITY OPEN						
1952	Ted Kroll	273	Lawson Little Skee Riegel Earl Stewart	277	Wethersfield CC, Hartford, CT	71/6568
1953	Bob Toski	269	Jim Ferrier	270	Wethersfield CC, Hartford, CT	71/6568
1954	*Tommy Bolt	271	Earl Stewart	271	Wethersfield CC, Hartford, CT	71/6568
1955	Sam Snead	269	Fred Hawkins Mike Souchak	276	Wethersfield CC, Hartford, CT	71/6568
1956	*Arnold Palmer	274	Ted Kroll	274	Wethersfield CC, Hartford, CT	71/6568
1957	Gardner Dickinson	272	George Bayer	274	Wethersfield CC, Hartford, CT	71/6568
1958	Jack Burke, Jr.	268	Dow Finsterwald Art Wall	271	Wethersfield CC, Hartford, CT	71/6568
1959	Gene Littler	272	Tom Nieporte	273	Wethersfield CC, Hartford, CT	71/6568
1960	*Arnold Palmer	270	Bill Collins Jack Fleck	270	Wethersfield CC, Hartford, CT	71/6568
1961	*Billy Maxwell	271	Ted Kroll	271	Wethersfield CC, Hartford, CT	71/6568
1962	*Bob Goalby	271	Art Wall	271	Wethersfield CC, Hartford, CT	71/6568
1963	Billy Casper	271	George Bayer	272	Wethersfield CC, Hartford, CT	71/6568
1964	Ken Venturi	273	Al Besselink Paul Bondeson Sam Carmichael Jim Grant	274	Wethersfield CC, Hartford, CT	71/6568
1965	*Billy Casper	274	Johnny Pott	274	Wethersfield CC, Hartford, CT	71/6568
1966	Art Wall	266	Wes Ellis	268	Wethersfield CC, Hartford, CT	71/6568
GREATER HARTFORD OPEN INVITATIONAL						
1967	Charlie. Sifford	272	Steve Oppermann	273	Wethersfield CC, Hartford, CT	71/6568
1968	Billy Casper	266	Bruce Crampton	269	Wethersfield CC, Hartford, CT	71/6568
1969	*Bob Lunn	268	Dave Hill	268	Wethersfield CC, Hartford, CT	71/6568
1970	Bob Murphy	267	Paul Harney	271	Wethersfield CC, Hartford, CT	71/6568
1971	*George Archer	268	Lou Graham J.C. Snead	268	Wethersfield CC, Hartford, CT	71/6568
1972	*Lee Trevino	269	Lee Elder	269	Wethersfield CC, Hartford, CT	71/6568
SAMMY DAVIS JR. GREATER HARTFORD OPEN						
1973	Billy Casper	264	Bruce Devlin	265	Wethersfield CC, Hartford, CT	71/6568
1974	Dave Stockton	268	Ray Floyd	272	Wethersfield CC, Hartford, CT	71/6568
1975	*Don Bies	267	Hubert Green	267	Wethersfield CC, Hartford, CT	71/6568
1976	Rik Massengale	266	Al Geiberger J.C. Snead	268	Wethersfield CC, Hartford, CT	71/6568
1977	Bill Kratzert	265	Grier Jones Larry Nelson	268	Wethersfield CC, Hartford, CT	71/6568
1978	Rod Funseth	264	Dale Douglass Lee Elder Bill Kratzert	268	Wethersfield CC, Hartford, CT	71/6568
1979	Jerry McGee	267	Jack Renner	268	Wethersfield CC, Hartford, CT	71/6568
1980	*Howard Twitty	266	Jim Simons	266	Wethersfield CC, Hartford, CT	71/6568
1981	Hubert Green	264	Bobby Clampett Fred Couples Roger Maltbie	265	Wethersfield CC, Hartford, CT	71/6568
1982	Tim Norris	259	Ray Floyd Hubert Green	265	Wethersfield CC, Hartford, CT	71/6568
1983	Curtis Strange	268	Jay Haas Jack Renner	269	Wethersfield CC, Hartford, CT	71/6568
1984	Peter Jacobsen	269	Mark O'Meara	271	TPC of Connecticut, Cromwell, CT	71/6786
1985	*Phil Blackmar	271	Jodie Mudd Dan Pohl	271	TPC of Connecticut, Cromwell, CT	71/6786
CANON SAMMY DAVIS JR.GREATER HARTFORD OPEN						
1986	*Mac O'Grady	269	Roger Maltbie	269	TPC of Connecticut, Cromwell, CT	71/6786
1987	Paul Azinger	269	Dan Forsman Wayne Levi	270	TPC of Connecticut, Cromwell, CT	71/6786

CANON GREATER HARTFORD OPEN

TOURNAMENT HISTORY

Year	Winner	Score	Runner-up	Score	Location	Par/Yards
1988	*Mark Brooks	269	Dave Barr Joey Sindelar	269	TPC of Connecticut, Cromwell, CT	71/6786
CANON GREATER HARTFORD OPEN						
1989	Paul Azinger	267	Wayne Levi	268	TPC of Connecticut, Cromwell, CT	71/6786
1990	Wayne Levi	267	Mark Calcavecchia Brad Fabel Rocco Mediate Chris Perry	269	TPC of Connecticut, Cromwell, CT	70/6531
1991	*Billy Ray Brown	271	Rick Fehr Corey Pavin	271	TPC at River Highlands, Cromwell, CT	70/6820
1992	Lanny Wadkins	274	Dan Forsman Donnie Hammond Nick Price	276	TPC at River Highlands, Cromwell, CT	70/6820
1993	Nick Price	271	Dan Forsman Roger Maltbie	272	TPC at River Highlands, Cromwell, CT	70/6820
1994	David Frost	268	Greg Norman	269	TPC at River Highlands, Cromwell, CT	70/6820
1995	Greg Norman	267	Dave Stockton, Jr. Kirk Triplett Grant Waite	269	TPC at River Highlands, Cromwell, CT	70/6820

Tournament Record: 259 -- Tim Norris, 1982 (Wethersfield CC)
Current Course Record: 62 -- Billy Andrade, 1995

KEY: *=Playoff

1995 FEDEX ST. JUDE CLASSIC

FEDERAL EXPRESS ST. JUDE CLASSIC

TPC at Southwind, Memphis, TN **Purse: $1,250,000**
Par: 36-36--71 **Yards: 7,006** **June 29-July 2, 1995**

LEADERS: First Round--Glen Day and Mike Standly, with 9-under-par 62s, led by two over Dennis Paulson. **Second Round--**Jim Gallagher, Jr., at 15-under-par 127, led by two over Standly and Bob Tway. **Third Round--**Gallagher, at 18-under-par 198, led by one over Gene Sauers.

CUT: 71 players at 3-under-par 139.

PRO-AM: $7,500. Individual--Justin Leonard, 67, $750. Team--John Cook, 48, $750.

WEATHER: Hot and humid on Thursday. Friday's play was suspended at 12:13 p.m. and postponed at 3:20 p.m. The second round resumed at 7:45 a.m. Saturday. The third round started at 2:30 p.m. with the leaders going off the 10th tee. The round was completed in near darkness. Sunny and warm on Sunday.

Winner: Jim Gallagher, Jr. 65-62-68-72 267 $225,000.00

Player	Pos.	Scores	Total	Money
Jay Delsing	T 2	69-63-69-67	268	$110,000.00
Ken Green	T 2	68-67-65-68	268	$110,000.00
Gene Sauers	4	68-65-63-73	269	$60,000.00
Brandel Chamblee	T 5	69-70-65-66	270	$40,937.50
John Cook	T 5	65-70-67-68	270	$40,937.50
Steve Jones	T 5	68-69-65-68	270	$40,937.50
Rocco Mediate	T 5	65-71-67-67	270	$40,937.50
Larry Mize	T 5	69-66-67-68	270	$40,937.50
Bob Tway	T 5	65-64-70-71	270	$40,937.50
Mark Brooks	T11	69-65-68-69	271	$28,750.00
Jay Haas	T11	68-70-67-66	271	$28,750.00
John Huston	T11	67-65-68-71	271	$28,750.00
Bob Estes	T14	69-67-67-69	272	$20,625.00
Brett Ogle	T14	67-70-70-65	272	$20,625.00
Kirk Triplett	T14	68-68-67-69	272	$20,625.00
Ted Tryba	T14	68-68-67-69	272	$20,625.00
Howard Twitty	T14	67-70-68-67	272	$20,625.00
D.A. Weibring	T14	65-70-69-68	272	$20,625.00
Curtis Strange	20	67-70-69-67	273	$16,250.00
Glen Day	T21	62-74-70-68	274	$13,000.00
Craig Parry	T21	67-72-67-68	274	$13,000.00
Charlie Rymer	T21	66-71-67-70	274	$13,000.00
Omar Uresti	T21	66-67-70-71	274	$13,000.00
Duffy Waldorf	T21	72-65-67-70	274	$13,000.00
Jim Carter	T26	73-64-69-69	275	$8,331.50
Lennie Clements	T26	70-67-69-69	275	$8,331.50
Ernie Els	T26	67-67-71-70	275	$8,331.50
Paul Goydos	T26	67-68-69-71	275	$8,331.50
Peter Jacobsen	T26	66-69-70-70	275	$8,331.50
Craig Stadler	T26	66-69-68-72	275	$8,331.50
Mike Standly	T26	62-67-75-71	275	$8,331.50
Mike Sullivan	T26	70-68-68-69	275	$8,331.50
Grant Waite	T26	69-66-67-73	275	$8,331.50
Mark Wurtz	T26	68-69-70-68	275	$8,331.50
Guy Boros	T36	71-68-69-68	276	$6,145.00
Gil Morgan	T36	68-71-66-71	276	$6,145.00
Jerry Pate	T36	71-65-71-69	276	$6,145.00
Tommy Armour III	T39	67-71-67-72	277	$5,000.00
Bob Lohr	T39	68-68-70-71	277	$5,000.00
Tom Purtzer	T39	67-68-72-70	277	$5,000.00
Scott Simpson	T39	65-74-68-70	277	$5,000.00
Bruce Vaughan	T39	68-71-68-70	277	$5,000.00
Scott Verplank	T39	66-69-68-74	277	$5,000.00
Bill Glasson	T45	68-69-72-69	278	$3,660.00
Brian Henninger	T45	74-64-74-66	278	$3,660.00
Lee Janzen	T45	69-70-70-69	278	$3,660.00
Dennis Paulson	T45	64-71-72-71	278	$3,660.00
Jay Williamson	T45	65-68-69-76	278	$3,660.00
Chip Beck	T50	70-67-69-73	279	$3,075.00
Bob Gilder	T50	67-71-71-70	279	$3,075.00
Mike Hulbert	T50	68-67-69-75	279	$3,075.00
Mike Brisky	T53	71-67-73-69	280	$2,880.00
Kawika Cotner	T53	68-70-73-69	280	$2,880.00
Ed Fiori	T53	67-69-74-70	280	$2,880.00
Justin Leonard	T53	67-69-72-72	280	$2,880.00
Tony Sills	T53	71-68-72-69	280	$2,880.00
John Mahaffey	T58	69-69-74-69	281	$2,775.00
Dillard Pruitt	T58	68-70-74-69	281	$2,775.00
Dave Stockton, Jr.	T58	68-68-68-77	281	$2,775.00
Emlyn Aubrey	T61	70-69-72-71	282	$2,700.00
Donnie Hammond	T61	71-67-70-74	282	$2,700.00
Larry Nelson	T61	73-64-71-74	282	$2,700.00
Carl Paulson	T64	67-70-75-71	283	$2,637.50
Lee Rinker	T64	69-70-71-73	283	$2,637.50
Greg Kraft	T66	69-69-75-71	284	$2,575.00
Harry Taylor	T66	70-68-72-74	284	$2,575.00
Dicky Thompson	T66	70-68-72-74	284	$2,575.00
Fulton Allem	69	70-69-71-75	285	$2,525.00
Ray Stewart	70	71-68-77-72	288	$2,500.00
Brian Kamm	71	66-73-74-76	289	$2,475.00

The following players did not finish (C=cut, W=withdrew, D=disqualified)

C—140- Joe Acosta, Jr., Michael Bradley, Bart Bryant, Bob Burns, Curt Byrum, Joel Edwards, Scott Ford, Robin Freeman, Steve Gotsche, Jerry Haas, Mike Heinen, Skip Kendall, Tim Loustalot, Scott McCarron, David Ogrin, Nick Price, Doug Tewell. **141-**Woody Austin, Rusty Brown, Keith Clearwater, Chris DiMarco, Bruce Fleisher, Doug Martin, Chris Perry, Don Reese, Mike Reid, Payne Stewart, Ron Whittaker. **142-** Ian Baker-Finch, Pat Bates, Rob Boldt, Walt Chapman, Brian Claar, Robert Gamez, J.L. Lewis, Jim McGovern, Bobby Wadkins, John Wilson. **143-** Russ Cochran, Packard Dewitt, Kelly Gibson, Hubert Green, Scott Gump, Steve Hart, J.P. Hayes, Ryan Howison, Bradley Hughes, Billy Mayfair, Joe Ozaki, Joey Rassett, Mark Wiebe. **144-** Zac Courtenay, Jonathan Kaye, Dicky Pride, Hal Sutton. **145-** Mike Donald, Keith Fergus, Ed Humenik, Jeff Leonard, Steve Rintoul, Paul Stankowski. **146-** Dudley Hart, Mike Springer, Tray Tyner. **147-** Tim Jackson. **148-**Bob Ralston. **149-** Clark Burroughs, Tom Hearn. **150-** Mike Bennett, Bob Eastwood. **151-**Tommy Tolles. **152-** Kip Henley, Bill Porter. **157-** Keith Kail. **W—146-** Patrick Burke, Steve Pate **147-**Jeff Maggert, **156-** Craig Lee, **74-**Michael Allen, **75-** Mark Carnevale, Mike Smith, **78-** Todd Baker, Jodie Mudd, **79-**Phil Blackmar, **83-** Fuzzy Zoeller.

1995 FEDEX ST. JUDE CLASSIC

TOURNAMENT HISTORY

Year	Winner	Score	Runner-up	Score	Location	Par/Yards
MEMPHIS INVITATIONAL OPEN						
1958	Billy Maxwell	267	Cary Middlecoff	268	Colonial CC, Memphis, TN	70/6466
1959	*Don Whitt	272	Al Balding Gary Player	272	Colonial CC, Memphis, TN	70/6466
1960	*Tommy Bolt	273	Ben Hogan Gene Littler	273	Colonial CC, Memphis, TN	70/6466
1961	Cary Middlecoff	266	Gardner Dickinson Mike Souchak	271	Colonial CC, Memphis, TN	70/6466
1962	*Lionel Hebert	267	Gene Littler Gary Player	267	Colonial CC, Memphis, TN	70/6466
1963	*Tony Lema	270	Tommy Aaron	270	Colonial CC, Memphis, TN	70/6466
1964	Mike Souchak	270	Billy Casper Tommy Jacobs	271	Colonial CC, Memphis, TN	70/6466
1965	*Jack Nicklaus	271	Johnny Pott	271	Colonial CC, Memphis, TN	70/6466
1966	Bert Yancey	265	Gene Littler	270	Colonial CC, Memphis, TN	70/6466
1967	Dave Hill	272	Johnny Pott	274	Colonial CC, Memphis, TN	70/6466
1968	Bob Lunn	268	Monty Kaser	269	Colonial CC, Memphis, TN	70/6466
1969	Dave Hill	265	Lee Elder	267	Colonial CC, Memphis, TN	70/6466
DANNY THOMAS MEMPHIS CLASSIC						
1970	Dave Hill	267	Frank Beard Homero Blancas Bob Charles	268	Colonial CC, Memphis, TN	70/6466
1971	Lee Trevino	268	Lee Elder Jerry Heard Hale Irwin Randy Wolff	272	Colonial CC, Memphis, TN	70/6466
1972	Lee Trevino	281	John Mahaffey	285	Colonial CC, Cordova, TN	S-72/6883
1973	Dave Hill	283	Allen Miller Lee Trevino	284	Colonial CC, Cordova, TN	S-72/7282
1974	Gary Player	273	Lou Graham Hubert Green	275	Colonial CC, Cordova, TN	S-72/7282
1975	Gene Littler	270	John Mahaffey	275	Colonial CC, Cordova, TN	S-72/7282
1976	Gibby Gilbert	273	Forrest Fezler John Lister Gil Morgan	277	Colonial CC, Cordova, TN	S-72/7282
1977	Al Geiberger	273	Jerry McGee Gary Player	276	Colonial CC, Cordova, TN	S-72/7282
1978	*Andy Bean	277	Lee Trevino	277	Colonial CC, Cordova, TN	S-72/7282
1979	*Gil Morgan	278	Larry Nelson	278	Colonial CC, Cordova, TN	S-72/7282
1980	Lee Trevino	272	Tom Purtzer	273	Colonial CC, Cordova, TN	S-72/7282
1981	Jerry Pate	274	Tom Kite Bruce Lietzke	276	Colonial CC, Cordova, TN	S-72/7282
1982	Raymond Floyd	271	Mike Holland	277	Colonial CC, Cordova, TN	S-72/7282
1983	Larry Mize	274	Chip Beck Sammy Rachels Fuzzy Zoeller	275	Colonial CC, Cordova, TN	S-72/7282
1984	Bob Eastwood	280	Ralph Landrum Mark O'Meara Tim Simpson	282	Colonial CC, Cordova, TN	S-72/7282
ST. JUDE MEMPHIS CLASSIC						
1985	*Hal Sutton	279	David Ogrin	279	Colonial CC, Cordova, TN	S-72/7282
FEDERAL EXPRESS ST. JUDE CLASSIC						
1986	Mike Hulbert	280	Joey Sindelar	281	Colonial CC, Cordova, TN	S-72/7282
1987	Curtis Strange	275	Russ Cochran Mike Donald Tom Kite Denis Watson	276	Colonial CC, Cordova, TN	S-72/7282

1995 FEDEX ST. JUDE CLASSIC

TOURNAMENT HISTORY

Year	Winner	Score	Runner-up	Score	Location	Par/Yards
1988	Jodie Mudd	273	Peter Jacobsen Nick Price	274	Colonial CC, Cordova, TN	S-72/7282
1989	John Mahaffey	272	Bob Gilder Hubert Green Bernhard Langer Bob Tway	275	TPC at Southwind, Germantown, TN	71/7006
1990	*Tom Kite	269	John Cook	269	TPC at Southwind, Germantown, TN	71/7006
1991	Fred Couples	269	Rick Fehr	272	TPC at Southwind, Germantown, TN	71/7006
1992	Jay Haas	263	Dan Forsman Robert Gamez	266	TPC at Southwind, Germantown, TN	71/7006
1993	Nick Price	266	Rick Fehr Jeff Maggert	269	TPC at Southwind, Germantown, TN	71/7006
1994	*Dicky Pride	267	Gene Sauers Hal Sutton	267	TPC at Southwind, Germantown, TN	71/7006
1995	Jim Gallagher, Jr.	267	Jay Delsing Ken Green	268	TPC at Southwind, Germantown, TN	71/7006

Tournament Record: 263 -- Jay Haas, 1992
Current Course Record: 61 -- Jay Delsing, 1993

KEY: *=Playoff

1995 MOTOROLA WESTERN OPEN

Cog Hill G&CC, Lemont, IL **Purse: $2,000,000**
Par: 36-36--72 **Yards: 7,073** **July 6-9, 1995**

LEADERS: First Round--Tom Watson, with a 4-under-par 68, led Ed Fiori, Jay Haas, Brett Ogle, Joel Edwards and Steve Lowery by one. **Second Round--**Haas, at 7-under-par 137, led by two over Watson and Lowery. **Third Round--**Ogle and Lowery, at 7-under-par 209, led Haas by one and Bob Estes and Grant Waite by two.

CUT: 71 players (70 professionals) at 3-over-par 147.

PRO-AM: $7,500. Individual--Steve Lowery, Tom Watson, 68, $675 each. Team--Vijay Singh, 52, $750.

WEATHER: Very windy all day Thursday. Beautiful Friday and Saturday. Occasional rain on Sunday.

Winner: Billy Mayfair 73-70-69-67 279 $360,000.00

Player	Pos.	Scores	Total	Money
Jay Haas	T 2	69-68-73-70	280	$132,000.00
Justin Leonard	T 2	70-71-72-67	280	$132,000.00
Jeff Maggert	T 2	74-73-69-64	280	$132,000.00
Scott Simpson	T 2	71-72-69-68	280	$132,000.00
Bob Estes	T 6	72-73-66-70	281	$64,750.00
John Huston	T 6	73-68-72-68	281	$64,750.00
Steve Lowery	T 6	69-70-70-72	281	$64,750.00
Bob Tway	T 6	76-69-68-68	281	$64,750.00
Woody Austin	T10	74-70-69-69	282	$50,000.00
Scott Gump	T10	74-70-72-66	282	$50,000.00
Scott Hoch	T10	73-69-70-70	282	$50,000.00
Bill Glasson	T13	77-70-66-70	283	$34,285.72
Dan Pohl	T13	73-71-69-70	283	$34,285.72
Nick Price	T13	75-71-68-69	283	$34,285.72
Larry Mize	T13	72-72-68-71	283	$34,285.71
Brett Ogle	T13	69-71-69-74	283	$34,285.71
Grant Waite	T13	72-72-67-72	283	$34,285.71
Tom Watson	T13	68-71-73-71	283	$34,285.71
Jay Don Blake	T20	74-72-69-69	284	$22,480.00
Mark Brooks	T20	73-71-70-70	284	$22,480.00
Greg Kraft	T20	71-71-75-67	284	$22,480.00
Sean Murphy	T20	77-66-72-69	284	$22,480.00
Don Pooley	T20	76-67-70-71	284	$22,480.00
Chip Beck	T25	74-70-72-69	285	$15,950.00
Guy Boros	T25	71-73-69-72	285	$15,950.00
Mark Calcavecchia	T25	71-73-73-68	285	$15,950.00
Robin Freeman	T25	74-70-71-70	285	$15,950.00
Patrick Burke	T29	75-72-68-71	286	$11,418.19
Jay Delsing	T29	77-70-69-70	286	$11,418.19
Paul Azinger	T29	74-67-73-72	286	$11,418.18
Michael Bradley	T29	73-73-73-67	286	$11,418.18
Jim Carter	T29	73-68-77-68	286	$11,418.18
Fred Couples	T29	70-73-71-72	286	$11,418.18
Steve Elkington	T29	76-70-69-71	286	$11,418.18
David Frost	T29	75-70-72-69	286	$11,418.18
Donnie Hammond	T29	72-72-73-69	286	$11,418.18
Nolan Henke	T29	73-72-70-71	286	$11,418.18
Tom Purtzer	T29	74-71-70-71	286	$11,418.18
Ronnie Black	T40	71-72-71-73	287	$8,200.00
Paul Stankowski	T40	74-73-70-70	287	$8,200.00
Duffy Waldorf	T40	73-69-75-70	287	$8,200.00
Mark Carnevale	T43	72-74-72-70	288	$6,240.00
John Cook	T43	76-70-69-73	288	$6,240.00
Ed Fiori	T43	69-75-71-73	288	$6,240.00
Ken Green	T43	72-71-71-74	288	$6,240.00
Doug Martin	T43	75-72-70-71	288	$6,240.00
Phil Mickelson	T43	72-73-70-73	288	$6,240.00
Steve Stricker	T43	78-67-74-69	288	$6,240.00
Billy Ray Brown	T50	72-70-73-74	289	$4,980.00
Joel Edwards	T50	69-74-75-71	289	$4,980.00
Brian Claar	T52	72-72-73-73	290	$4,664.00
Glen Day	T52	74-71-70-75	290	$4,664.00
Ed Humenik	T52	76-71-71-72	290	$4,664.00
Chris Perry	T52	73-72-71-74	290	$4,664.00
D.A. Weibring	T52	72-72-74-72	290	$4,664.00
Pat Bates	T57	74-70-75-72	291	$4,500.00
Brad Bryant	T57	73-73-73-72	291	$4,500.00
Tiger Woods	T57	74-71-77-69	291	AMATEUR
Peter Jacobsen	T60	75-71-72-74	292	$4,380.00
Davis Love III	T60	73-74-76-69	292	$4,380.00
Corey Pavin	T60	74-73-69-76	292	$4,380.00
Ted Tryba	T60	72-72-76-72	292	$4,380.00
Bob Gilder	T64	71-76-77-69	293	$4,260.00
Bobby Wadkins	T64	73-72-77-71	293	$4,260.00
Vijay Singh	66	73-73-75-73	294	$4,200.00
Alan Pate	67	80-66-71-78	295	$4,160.00
Russ Cochran	T68	73-74-71-78	296	$4,080.00
David Duval	T68	74-73-74-75	296	$4,080.00
Blaine McCallister	T68	75-72-70-79	296	$4,080.00
Dudley Hart	71	73-74-75-75	297	$4,000.00

The following players did not finish (C=cut, W=withdrew, D=disqualified)

C—148- John Adams, Ernie Els, Paul Goydos, Lee Janzen, Steve Jones, Peter Persons, Mike Reid, Hal Sutton, Tommy Tolles. **149-** Billy Andrade, Tommy Armour III, Bart Bryant, Clark Dennis, Andrew Magee, Mark McCumber, Gil Morgan, Dennis Paulson, Dillard Pruitt, Steve Rintoul, Charlie Rymer, Curtis Strange, Kirk Triplett, Mark Wiebe. **150-** Dave Barr, Lennie Clements, Jim Gallagher, Jr., Robert Gamez, Kelly Gibson, Brian Henninger, Jerry Kelly, Larry Nelson, Andy North, Mike Springer, Jim Thorpe. **151-** Steve Benson, David Edwards, Jim Estes, Keith Fergus, Steve Hart, Mike Heinen, Neal Lancaster, Bob Lohr, John Morse, David Ogrin, Lee Rinker, Jeff Sluman, Howard Twitty, Omar Uresti, Mark Wurtz. **152-** Emlyn Aubrey, Bob Burns, Brandel Chamblee, Brian Kamm, Joe Ozaki, John Wilson. **153-**Keith Clearwater, Mike Hulbert, John Mahaffey, Jerry Pate, Steve Pate, Mike Standly, Ed Terasa, Scott Verplank. **154-** Ian Baker-Finch, Curt Byrum, Gary Hallberg, Yoshinori Mizumaki, Dave Stockton, Jr. **156-** Ben Crenshaw, Fred Funk, Jim McGovern, Mike Sullivan, Tray Tyner. **157-** Skip Kendall. **159-** Chris DiMarco, Ryan Howison. **161-**Brian King. **162-** Dave Bemis. **171-** Dino Lucchesi. **174-** Jim Holmes. **W—152-**Rocco Mediate, **79-** Harry Taylor, **82-** Jim Furyk, Mark O'Meara. **D—148-**Doug Tewell, **78-** Dicky Pride.

MOTOROLA WESTERN OPEN

TOURNAMENT HISTORY

Year	Winner	Score	Runner-up	Score	Location	Par/Yards
WESTERN OPEN						
1899	*Willie Smith	156	Laurie Auchterlonie	156	Glen View GC, Chicago, IL	72/6362
1900	No Tournament					
1901	Laurie Auchterlonie	160	David Bell	162	Midlothian CC, Chicago, IL	71/6654
1902	Willie Anderson	299	Willie Smith	304	Euclid Club, Cleveland, OH	N/A
1903	Alex Smith	318	Laurie Auchterlonie	320	Milwaukee CC, Milwaukee, WI	72/6867
			David Brown			
1904	Willie Anderson	304	Alex Smith	308	Kent CC, Grand Rapids, MI	71/6514
1905	Arthur Smith	278	James Maiden	280	Cincinnati GC, Cincinnati, OH	71/6231
1906	Alex Smith	306	Jack Hobens	309	Homewood CC, Chicago, IL	70/6311
1907	Robert Simpson	307	Willie Anderson	309	Hinsdale GC, Hinsdale, IL	71/6475
			Fred McCloud			
1908	Willie Anderson	299	Fred McCloud	300	Normandie GC, St. Louis, MO	71/6534
1909	Willie Anderson	288	Stewart Gardner	297	Skokie CC, Chicago, IL	72/6913
1910	#Chick Evans, Jr.	6&5	George Simpson		Beverly CC, Chicago, IL	72/6754
1911	Robert Simpson	2&1	Tom MacNamara		Kent CC, Grand Rapids, MI	71/6514
1912	Mac Smith	299	Alex Robertson	302	Idlewild CC, Chicago, IL	72/6754
1913	John McDermott	295	Mike Brady	302	Memphis CC, Memphis, TN	70/6695
1914	Jim Barnes	293	Willie Kidd	294	Interlachen CC, Minneapolis, MN	73/6733
1915	Tom McNamara	304	Alex Cunningham	306	Glen Oak CC, Chicago, IL	72/6503
1916	Walter Hagen	286	Walter Hagen	285	Blue Mound CC, Chicago, IL	N/A
1917	Jim Barnes	283	Leo Diegel	286	Westmoreland CC, Chicago, IL	72/6798
1918	No Tournament					
1919	Jim Barnes	283	James Barnes	297	Mayfield CC, Cleveland, OH	72/6609
1920	Jock Hutchison	296	Clarence Hackney		Olympia Fields CC, Chicago, IL	71/6749
			Harry Hampton			
			Jock Hutchison	292		
1921	Walter Hagen	287	Laurie Ayton	301	Oakwood Club, Cleveland, OH	71/6709
1922	Mike Brady	291	Jock Hutchison		Oakland Hills CC, Detroit, MI	72/7052
			Bobby Cruickshank	287		
1923	Jock Hutchison	281	Leo Diegel		Colonial CC, Memphis, TN	70/7116
			Walter Hagen			
			Joe Kirkwood, Sr.			
			Al Watrous	301		
1924	Bill Mehlhorn	293	Leo Diegel	287	Calumet CC, Chicago, IL	72/6524
1925	Mac Smith	281	Johnny Farrell		Youngstown CC, Youngstown, OH	71/6597
			Emmet French			
			Walter Hagen			
			Bill Mehlhorn			
			Harry Cooper	288		
1926	Walter Hagen	279	Gene Sarazen		Highland G&CC, Indianapolis, IN	70/6501
			Al Espinosa	285		
1927	Walter Hagen	281	Bill Mehlhorn		Olympia Fields CC, Chicago, IL	71/6749
			Johnny Farrell	294		
1928	Abe Espinosa	291	Horton Smith	281	North Shore GC, Chicago, IL	72/7024
1929	Tommy Armour	273	Al Espinosa	285	Ozaukee CC, Milwaukee, WI	70/6553
1930	Gene Sarazen	278	Walter Hagen	284	Indianwood G&CC, Detroit, MI	N/A
1931	Ed Dudley	280	Olin Dutra	288	Miami Valley GC, Dayton, OH	71/6589
1932	Walter Hagen	287	Tommy Armour	288	Canterbury GC, Cleveland, OH	72/6877
1933	Mac Smith	282	Ky Laffoon	274	Olympia Fields CC, Chicago, IL	71/6749
1934	*Harry Cooper	274	Willie Goggin	294	Country Club of Peoria, Peoria, IL	70/6068
1935	John Revolta	290	Ray Mangrum	277	South Bend CC, South Bend, IN	71/6455
1936	Ralph Guldahl	274	Horton Smith	288	Davenport CC, Davenport, IA	71/6458
1937	*Ralph Guldahl	288	Sam Snead	286	Canterbury CC, Cleveland, OH	72/6877
1938	Ralph Guldahl	279	Lloyd Mangrum	282	Westwood CC, St. Louis, MO	72/6785
1939	Byron Nelson	281	Toney Penna	293	Medinah CC, Chicago, IL	71/7104
1940	*Jimmy Demaret	293	Ben Hogan	278	River Oaks CC, Houston, TX	72/6868
			Byron Nelson			

MOTOROLA WESTERN OPEN

TOURNAMENT HISTORY

Year	Winner	Score	Runner-up	Score	Location	Par/Yards
1941	Ed Oliver	275	Henry Picard	278	Phoenix GC, Phoenix, AZ	71/6726
1942	Herman Barron	276			Phoenix GC, Phoenix, AZ	71/6726
1943-						
1945	No Tournaments		Lloyd Mangrum	275		
1946	Ben Hogan	271	Bobby Locke	271	Sunset CC, St. Louis, MO	72/6323
1947	Johnny Palmer	270	Ed Oliver		Salt Lake City CC, Salt Lake City, UT	72/6891
			Ed Oliver	281		
1948	*Ben Hogan	281	Cary Middlecoff	272	Brookfield CC, Buffalo, NY	72/6813
1949	Sam Snead	268	Jim Ferrier	283	Keller GC, St. Paul, MN	72/6542
1950	Sam Snead	282	E. J. Harrison		Brentwood CC, Los Angeles, CA	72/6729
			Cary Middlecoff	271		
1951	Marty Furgol	270	Bobby Locke	282	Davenport CC, Davenport, IA	71/6450
1952	Lloyd Mangrum	274	Ed Furgol	282	Westwood CC, St. Louis, MO	72/6785
1953	Dutch Harrison	278	Fred Haas		Bellerive CC, St. Louis, MO	71/7305
			Lloyd Mangrum			
			Ted Kroll	277		
1954	*Lloyd Mangrum	277	Mike Souchak	274	Kenwood CC, Cincinnati, OH	72/6950
1955	Cary Middlecoff	272	Doug Ford	284	Portland GC, Portland, OR	72/6564
1956	*Mike Fetchick	284	Jay Hebert		Presidio CC, San Francisco, CA	72/6488
			Don January			
			George Bayer	279		
1957	*Doug Ford	279	Gene Littler		Plum Hollow GC, Detroit, MI	72/6854
			Billy Maxwell			
			Dow Finsterwald	276		
1958	Doug Sanders	275	Arnold Palmer	273	Red Run GC, Royal Oak, MI	72/6801
1959	Mike Souchak	272	Art Wall	278	Pittsburgh Field Club, Fox Chapel, PA	71/6586
1960	*Stan Leonard	278	Sam Snead	273	Western G & CC, Detroit, MI	72/6808
1961	Arnold Palmer	271	Billy Casper	283	Blythefield CC, Grand Rapids, MI	71/6730
1962	Jacky Cupit	281	Julius Boros	280	Medinah CC, Medinah, IL	71/7014
1963	*Arnold Palmer	280	Jack Nicklaus		Beverly CC, Chicago, IL	71/6923
			Arnold Palmer	269		
1964	Chi Chi Rodriguez	268	Jack McGowan	272	Tam O'Shanter CC, Niles, IL	71/6686
1965	Billy Casper	270	Chi Chi Rodriguez		Tam O'Shanter CC, Niles, IL	71/6686
			Gay Brewer	286		
1966	Billy Casper	283	Doug Sanders	276	Medinah CC, Medinah, IL	71/7014
1967	Jack Nicklaus	274	Miller Barber	276	Beverly CC, Chicago, IL	71/6923
1968	Jack Nicklaus	273	Rocky Thompson	280	Olympia Fields CC, Olympia Fields, IL	71/6749
1969	Billy Casper	276	Dale Douglass	274	Midlothian CC, Midlothian, IL	71/6654
1970	Hugh Royer	273	Bobby Nichols	281	Beverly CC, Chicago, IL	71/6923
1971	Bruce Crampton	279	Labron Harris, Jr.	277	Olympia Fields CC, Olympia Fields, IL	71/6749
1972	Jim Jamieson	271	Larry Hinson	273	Sunset Ridge, Winnetka, IL	71/6716
1973	Billy Casper	272	Hale Irwin		Midlothian CC, Midlothian, IL	71/6654
			J.C. Snead	289		
1974	Tom Watson	287	Tom Weiskopf		Butler National GC, Oak Brook, IL	71/7002
			Bobby Cole	284		
1975	Hale Irwin	283	Joe Porter	289	Butler National GC, Oak Brook, IL	71/7002
1976	Al Geiberger	288	Wally Armstrong	284	Butler National GC, Oak Brook, IL	71/7002
1977	Tom Watson	283	Johnny Miller		Butler National GC, Oak Brook, IL	72/7097
			Bill Rogers	282		
1978	*Andy Bean	282	Ben Crenshaw	286	Butler National GC, Oak Brook, IL	72/7097
1979	*Larry Nelson	286	Andy Bean	286	Butler National GC, Oak Brook, IL	72/7097
1980	Scott Simpson	281	Jim Colbert	281	Butler National GC, Oak Brook, IL	72/7097
1981	Ed Fiori	277	Greg Powers		Butler National GC, Oak Brook, IL	72/7097
			Jim Simons			
			Larry Nelson	277		
1982	Tom Weiskopf	276	Tom Watson	285	Butler National GC, Oak Brook, IL	72/7097
1983	Mark McCumber	284	Greg Norman	280	Butler National GC, Oak Brook, IL	72/7097
1984	*Tom Watson	280	Jim Thorpe	279	Butler National GC, Oak Brook, IL	72/7097
1985	*#Scott Verplank	279	Fred Couples	286	Butler National GC, Oak Brook, IL	72/7097
1986	*Tom Kite	286	David Frost		Butler National GC, Oak Brook, IL	72/7097
			Nick Price			

MOTOROLA WESTERN OPEN

TOURNAMENT HISTORY

Year	Winner	Score	Runner-up	Score	Location	Par/Yards
BEATRICE WESTERN OPEN			Larry Nelson	208		
1987	~D. A. Weibring	207	Greg Norman		Butler National GC, Oak Brook, IL**	72/6752
** Rain forced play to be held on nine holes of Butler National and nine holes at adjacent Oak Brook Village course.			Peter Jacobsen	279		
1988	Jim Benepe	278	Peter Jacobsen	275	Butler National GC, Oak Brook, IL	72/7097
1989	*Mark McCumber	275			Butler National GC, Oak Brook, IL	72/7097
CENTEL WESTERN OPEN			Payne Stewart	279		
1990	Wayne Levi	275	Greg Norman	277	Butler National GC, Oak Brook, IL	72/7097
1991	Russ Cochran	275	Greg Norman	277	Cog Hill CC (Dubsdread), Lemont, IL	72/7040
1992	Ben Crenshaw	276			Cog Hill CC (Dubsdread), Lemont, IL	72/7040
SPRINT WESTERN OPEN			Greg Norman	274		
1993	Nick Price	269			Cog Hill CC (Dubsdread), Lemont, IL	72/7040
MOTOROLA WESTERN OPEN			Greg Kraft	278		
1994	Nick Price	277			Cog Hill CC (Dubsdread), Lemont, IL	72/7040
1995	Billy Mayfair	279	Jay Haas	280	Cog Hill CC (Dubsdread), Lemont, IL	72/7040
			Justin Leonard		Cog Hill CC (Dubsdread), Lemont, IL	72/7040
			Jeff Maggert			
			Scott Simpson			

Tournament Record: 268 -- Sam Snead, 1949 (Keller GC); Chi Chi Rodriguez, 1964 (Tam O'Shanter CC)
Current Course Record: 63 -- Jeff Sluman, 1992; John Adams, 1993

KEY: *=Playoff ~=Weather shortened #=Amateur

1995 ANHEUSER-BUSCH GOLF CLASSIC

Kingsmill GC, Williamsburg, VA **Purse: $1,100,000**
Par: 36-35--71 **Yards: 6,797** **July 13-16, 1995**

LEADERS: First Round--Richard Zokol, Robin Freeman and Dudley Hart, with 6-under-par 65s, led by one over Kirk Triplett, Scott McCarron, Duffy Waldorf and Jim Carter. **Second Round**–Jim Gallagher, Jr., at 8-under-par 134, led by one over Blaine McCallister and Carter. **Third Round--**Carter, at 10-under-par 203, led by one over Ted Tryba, Gallagher and McCallister.

CUT: 73 players at even-par 142.

PRO-AM: $20,000. Individual--Dicky Pride, Jay Haas, 65, $1,800 each. Team--Neal Lancaster, Scott Simpson, 51, $1,800 each.

WEATHER: Hot and humid every day.

Winner: Ted Tryba 69-67-68-68 272 $198,000.00

Player	Pos.	Scores	Total	Money
Scott Simpson	2	69-69-68-67	273	$118,800.00
Jim Carter	T 3	66-69-68-71	274	$57,200.00
Lennie Clements	T 3	68-69-69-68	274	$57,200.00
Scott Hoch	T 3	67-69-71-67	274	$57,200.00
Marco Dawson	T 6	68-71-73-63	275	$38,225.00
Curtis Strange	T 6	72-70-65-68	275	$38,225.00
Fred Funk	T 8	68-68-70-71	277	$31,900.00
David Ogrin	T 8	71-71-66-69	277	$31,900.00
Jeff Sluman	T 8	72-69-67-69	277	$31,900.00
Michael Bradley	T11	67-71-71-69	278	$21,842.86
Mark McCumber	T11	74-68-69-67	278	$21,842.86
Joey Rassett	T11	71-70-69-68	278	$21,842.86
Payne Stewart	T11	70-68-71-69	278	$21,842.86
Kelly Gibson	T11	71-70-66-71	278	$21,842.85
Kirk Triplett	T11	66-71-70-71	278	$21,842.85
Glen Day	T11	70-72-69-67	278	$21,842.86
Joe Acosta, Jr.	T18	70-71-67-71	279	$12,466.67
Jim McGovern	T18	69-67-71-72	279	$12,466.67
Tom Purtzer	T18	72-69-68-70	279	$12,466.67
Joey Sindelar	T18	68-69-71-71	279	$12,466.67
Howard Twitty	T18	70-70-71-68	279	$12,466.67
Willie Wood	T18	69-69-70-71	279	$12,466.67
Jim Gallagher, Jr.	T18	69-65-70-75	279	$12,466.66
Paul Goydos	T18	71-70-65-73	279	$12,466.66
Blaine McCallister	T18	68-67-69-75	279	$12,466.66
John Adams	T27	73-68-68-71	280	$7,480.00
Woody Austin	T27	70-69-74-67	280	$7,480.00
Bill Britton	T27	71-71-68-70	280	$7,480.00
Jonathan Kaye	T27	68-72-72-68	280	$7,480.00
Tony Sills	T27	71-67-70-72	280	$7,480.00
Scott Verplank	T27	72-69-66-73	280	$7,480.00
John Wilson	T27	68-70-72-70	280	$7,480.00
Robin Freeman	T34	65-72-72-72	281	$5,555.00
Scott Gump	T34	69-68-71-73	281	$5,555.00
Jay Haas	T34	72-69-69-71	281	$5,555.00
Jerry Pate	T34	68-71-73-69	281	$5,555.00
Don Reese	T34	72-65-71-73	281	$5,555.00
Scott McCarron	T34	66-73-71-71	281	$5,555.00
Tom Byrum	T40	69-69-71-73	282	$4,290.00
Mark Carnevale	T40	72-68-68-74	282	$4,290.00
Mike Donald	T40	68-69-72-73	282	$4,290.00
Rick Fehr	T40	70-72-67-73	282	$4,290.00
Richard Zokol	T40	65-75-72-70	282	$4,290.00
Stewart Cink	T45	68-70-71-74	283	$3,146.00
Bob Gilder	T45	73-67-70-73	283	$3,146.00
J.P. Hayes	T45	71-68-75-69	283	$3,146.00
David Peoples	T45	70-72-70-71	283	$3,146.00
Dicky Pride	T45	69-69-70-75	283	$3,146.00
Duffy Waldorf	T45	66-71-73-73	283	$3,146.00
Mike Brisky	T51	70-71-73-70	284	$2,604.80
Ed Dougherty	T51	70-71-74-69	284	$2,604.80
Ken Green	T51	68-70-72-74	284	$2,604.80
John Mahaffey	T51	73-68-74-69	284	$2,604.80
Tommy Tolles	T51	74-66-74-70	284	$2,604.80
Phil Blackmar	T56	68-71-74-72	285	$2,453.00
Rex Caldwell	T56	69-69-78-69	285	$2,453.00
Russ Cochran	T56	71-69-76-69	285	$2,453.00
Dudley Hart	T56	65-72-78-70	285	$2,453.00
Jeff Leonard	T56	70-69-75-71	285	$2,453.00
Dave Stockton, Jr.	T56	68-71-76-70	285	$2,453.00
Steve Pate	62	70-66-73-77	286	$2,376.00
Ronnie Black	T63	70-71-70-76	287	$2,310.00
Bobby Clampett	T63	70-71-75-71	287	$2,310.00
Mike Reid	T63	70-69-76-72	287	$2,310.00
Harry Taylor	T63	68-71-74-74	287	$2,310.00
Mark Wiebe	T63	70-71-74-72	287	$2,310.00
Chris Van Der Velde	68	67-72-77-72	288	$2,244.00
Pat Bates	T69	76-66-75-73	290	$2,211.00
Roger Maltbie	T69	70-71-74-75	290	$2,211.00
Carl Paulson	T71	70-69-74-79	292	$2,167.00
Dicky Thompson	T71	71-70-75-76	292	$2,167.00

The following players did not finish (C=cut, W=withdrew, D=disqualified)

C—143- Chip Beck, Steve Brodie, Chris DiMarco, Bruce Fleisher, Robert Gamez, Steve Hart, Morris Hatalsky, Tom Hearn, Mike Hulbert, Mac O'Grady, Bill Porter, Lee Rinker. **144-** Michael Allen, Emlyn Aubrey, Bart Bryant, George Burns, Pete Jordan, Skip Kendall, Greg Kraft, Bill Malley, Rob McNamara, Dillard Pruitt, Clarence Rose, Ted Schulz, Hal Sutton, Jay Williamson. **145-** Clark Dennis, Robert Floyd, Mark Hayes, Ed Humenik, Barry Jaeckel, Bill Kratzert, J.L. Lewis, Tim Loustalot, Chris Perry, Mike Smith, Tray Tyner, Robert Wrenn, Mark Wurtz. **146-** Billy Ray Brown, Bob Burns, Scott Ford, Larry Rinker, John Schroeder, Marty Stanovich, Bruce Vaughan. **147-** Steve Gotsche, Steve Rintoul, Dave Rummells, Warren Schutte. **148-** Hubert Green, Tom Jenkins, Neal Lancaster, Gene Sauers, Ray Stewart, Lanny Wadkins. **149-** Kawika Cotner, Forrest Fezler, Scott Inman, Yoshinori Mizumaki, Paul Stankowski, Leonard Thompson, Bobby Wadkins. **150-** Frank Ferguson, Jerry Haas, Dick Mast, Josh McCumber. **151-** Jay Don Blake, Kevin Boynton, Bunky Henry, Kenny Knox, Jeff Woodland. **152-** Jim Furyk. **153-** David Quelland, Dennis Winters. **154-** Omar Uresti. **155-** Dan Halldorson. **157-** Tom Dyer. **158-** Ernie Gonzalez. **159-** Mike Hayes. **W—211-** Clark Burroughs, **74-** Jim Thorpe, **76-** Andrew Magee. **D—71-** Ryan Howison.

MICHELOB CHAMPIONSHIP AT KINGSMILL

TOURNAMENT HISTORY

Year	Winner	Score	Runner-up	Score	Location	Par/Yards
KAISER INTERNATIONAL OPEN INVITATIONAL						
1968	Kermit Zarley	273	Dave Marr	274	Silverado CC, Napa, CA	N-72/6849, S-71/6602
1969	~Miller Barber	135	Bruce Devlin	136	Silverado CC, Napa, CA	N-72/6849, S-71/6602
1969A	*Jack Nicklaus	273	George Archer Billy Casper Don January	273	Silverado CC, Napa, CA	N-72/6849, S-71/6602
1970	*Ken Still	278	Lee Trevino Bert Yancey	278	Silverado CC, Napa, CA	N-72/6849, S-71/6602
1971	Billy Casper	269	Fred Marti	273	Silverado CC, Napa, CA	N-72/6849, S-71/6602
1972	George Knudson	271	Hale Irwin Bobby Nichols	274	Silverado CC, Napa, CA	N-72/6849, S-71/6602
1973	*Ed Sneed	275	John Schlee	275	Silverado CC, Napa, CA	N-72/6849, S-71/6602
1974	Johnny Miller	271	Billy Casper Lee Trevino	279	Silverado CC, Napa, CA	N-72/6849, S-71/6602
1975	Johnny Miller	272	Rod Curl	275	Silverado CC, Napa, CA	N-72/6849, S-71/6602
1976	J. C. Snead	274	Gibby Gilbert Johnny Miller	276	Silverado CC, Napa, CA	N-72/6849, S-71/6602
ANHEUSER-BUSCH GOLF CLASSIC						
1977	Miller Barber	272	George Archer	274	Silverado CC, Napa, CA	N-72/6849, S-71/6602
1978	Tom Watson	270	Ed Sneed	273	Silverado CC, Napa, CA	N-72/6849, S-71/6602
1979	John Fought	277	Buddy Gardner Alan Tapie Bobby Wadkins	278	Silverado CC, Napa, CA	N-72/6849, S-72/6619
1980	Ben Crenshaw	272	Jack Renner	276	Silverado CC, Napa, CA	N-72/6849, S-72/6619
1981	John Mahaffey	276	Andy North	278	Kingsmill GC, Kingsmill, VA	71/6776
1982	~Calvin Peete	203	Bruce Lietzke	205	Kingsmill GC, Kingsmill, VA	71/6776
1983	Calvin Peete	276	Tim Norris	277	Kingsmill GC, Kingsmill, VA	71/6776
1984	Ronnie Black	267	Willie Wood	268	Kingsmill GC, Kingsmill, VA	71/6776
1985	*Mark Wiebe	273	John Mahaffey	273	Kingsmill GC, Kingsmill, VA	71/6776
1986	Fuzzy Zoeller	274	Jodie Mudd	276	Kingsmill GC, Kingsmill, VA	71/6776
1987	Mark McCumber	267	Bobby Clampett	268	Kingsmill GC, Kingsmill, VA	71/6776
1988	*Tom Sieckmann	270	Mark Wiebe	270	Kingsmill GC, Kingsmill, VA	71/6776
1989	*Mike Donald	268	Tim Simpson Hal Sutton	268	Kingsmill GC, Kingsmill, VA	71/6776
1990	Lanny Wadkins	266	Larry Mize	271	Kingsmill GC, Kingsmill, VA	71/6776
1991	*Mike Hulbert	266	Kenny Knox	266	Kingsmill GC, Kingsmill, VA	71/6776
1992	David Peoples	271	Bill Britton Ed Dougherty Jim Gallagher, Jr.	272	Kingsmill GC, Kingsmill, VA	71/6776
1993	Jim Gallagher, Jr.	269	Chip Beck	271	Kingsmill GC, Kingsmill, VA	71/6776
1994	Mark McCumber	267	Glen Day	270	Kingsmill GC, Kingsmill, VA	71/6776
1995	Ted Tryba	272	Scott Simpson	273	Kingsmill GC, Kingsmill, VA	71/6776

Tournament Record: 266 -- Lanny Wadkins, 1990; Mike Hulbert/Kenny Knox, 1991
Current Course Record: 61 -- Bob Lohr, 1994

KEY: *=Playoff ~=Weather-shortened A=2nd tournament same year

1995 BRITISH OPEN

Old Course at St. Andrews, St. Andrews, Scotland **Purse: $2,000,000**
Par: 36-36--72 **Yards: 6,933** **July 20-23, 1995**

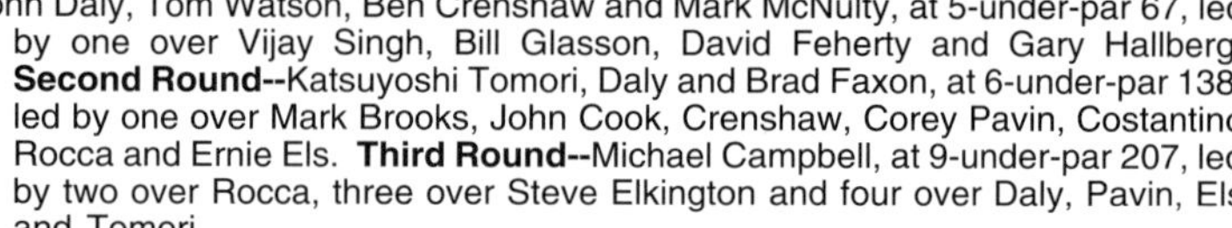

LEADERS: First Round--John Daly, Tom Watson, Ben Crenshaw and Mark McNulty, at 5-under-par 67, led by one over Vijay Singh, Bill Glasson, David Feherty and Gary Hallberg. **Second Round--**Katsuyoshi Tomori, Daly and Brad Faxon, at 6-under-par 138, led by one over Mark Brooks, John Cook, Crenshaw, Corey Pavin, Costantino Rocca and Ernie Els. **Third Round--**Michael Campbell, at 9-under-par 207, led by two over Rocca, three over Steve Elkington and four over Daly, Pavin, Els and Tomori.

CUT: 103 players at 4-over-par 148.

WEATHER: Cool and windy all four days. Light rain on Thursday.

Winner: John Daly 67-71-73-71 282 $199,375.00

(Won four-hole playoff 15-19)

Player	Pos.	Scores	Total	Money
Costantino Rocca	2	69-70-70-73	282	$159,500.00
Steven Bottomley	T 3	70-72-72-69	283	$104,738.33
Mark Brooks	T 3	70-69-73-71	283	$104,738.33
Michael Campbell	T 3	71-71-65-76	283	$104,738.33
Steve Elkington	T 6	72-69-69-74	284	$64,597.50
Vijay Singh	T 6	68-72-73-71	284	$64,597.50
Bob Estes	T 8	72-70-71-72	285	$53,166.66
Mark James	T 8	72-75-68-70	285	$53,166.66
Corey Pavin	T 8	69-70-72-74	285	$53,166.66
Ernie Els	T11	71-68-72-75	286	$41,470.00
Brett Ogle	T11	73-69-71-73	286	$41,470.00
Payne Stewart	T11	72-68-75-71	286	$41,470.00
Sam Torrance	T11	71-70-71-74	286	$41,470.00
Robert Allenby	T15	71-74-71-71	287	$29,029.00
Ben Crenshaw	T15	67-72-76-72	287	$29,029.00
Brad Faxon	T15	71-67-75-74	287	$29,029.00
Per-Ulrik Johansson	T15	69-78-68-72	287	$29,029.00
Greg Norman	T15	71-74-72-70	287	$29,029.00
Andrew Coltart	T20	70-74-71-73	288	$21,532.50
David Duval	T20	71-75-70-72	288	$21,532.50
Barry Lane	T20	72-73-68-75	288	$21,532.50
Peter Mitchell	T20	73-74-71-70	288	$21,532.50
Lee Janzen	T24	73-73-71-72	289	$16,544.08
Mark Calcavecchia	T24	71-72-72-74	289	$16,455.08
Bill Glasson	T24	68-74-72-75	289	$16,455.08
Bernhard Langer	T24	72-71-73-73	289	$16,455.08
Jesper Parnevik	T24	75-71-70-73	289	$16,455.08
Katsuyoshi Tomori	T24	70-68-73-78	289	$16,455.08
Steve Webster	T24	70-72-74-73	289	Amateur
Darren Clarke	T31	69-77-70-74	290	$12,954.94
Ross Drummond	T31	74-68-77-71	290	$12,954.94
David Feherty	T31	68-75-71-76	290	$12,954.94
David Frost	T31	72-72-74-72	290	$12,954.94
John Huston	T31	71-74-72-73	290	$12,954.94
Peter Jacobsen	T31	71-76-70-73	290	$12,954.94
Jose Maria Olazabal	T31	72-72-74-72	290	$12,954.94
Hisayuki Sasaki	T31	74-71-72-73	290	$12,954.94
Tom Watson	T31	67-76-70-77	290	$12,954.94
Seve Ballesteros	T40	75-69-76-71	291	$11,244.75
Warren Bennett	T40	72-74-73-72	291	$11,244.75
John Cook	T40	69-70-75-77	291	$11,244.75
Nick Faldo	T40	74-67-75-75	291	$11,244.75
Mark McNulty	T40	67-76-74-74	291	$11,244.75
Phil Mickelson	T40	70-71-77-73	291	$11,244.75
Nick Price	T40	70-74-70-77	291	$11,244.75
Brian Watts	T40	72-71-73-75	291	$11,244.75
Gordon Sherry	T40	70-71-74-76	291	Amateur
Brian Claar	T49	71-75-71-75	292	$10,128.25
Anders Forsbrand	T49	70-74-75-73	292	$10,128.25
Ken Green	T49	71-72-73-76	292	$10,128.25
Tommy Nakajima	T49	73-72-72-75	292	$10,128.25
Mark O'Meara	T49	72-72-75-73	292	$10,128.25
Ian Woosnam	T49	71-74-76-71	292	$10,128.25
Russell Claydon	T55	70-74-71-78	293	$9,410.50
Jim Gallagher, Jr.	T55	69-76-75-73	293	$9,410.50
Peter O'Malley	T55	71-73-74-75	293	$9,410.50
Paul Broadhurst	T58	73-72-76-73	294	$8,732.62
Derrick Cooper	T58	71-76-74-73	294	$8,732.62
Ray Floyd	T58	72-74-72-76	294	$8,732.62
Martin Gates	T58	73-73-72-76	294	$8,732.62
David Gilford	T58	69-72-75-78	294	$8,732.62
Eduardo Herrera	T58	74-72-73-75	294	$8,732.62
Tom Kite	T58	72-76-71-75	294	$8,732.62
Paul Lawrie	T58	73-71-74-76	294	$8,732.62
Justin Leonard	T58	73-67-77-77	294	$8,732.62
Peter Senior	T58	71-75-78-70	294	$8,732.62
Peter Baker	T68	70-74-81-70	295	$7,935.12
Gary Hallberg	T68	72-74-72-77	295	$7,935.12
Mats Hallberg	T68	68-76-75-76	295	$7,935.12
Scott Hoch	T68	74-72-73-76	295	$7,935.12
Olle Karlsson	T68	71-76-73-75	295	$7,935.12
Jonathan Lomas	T68	74-73-75-73	295	$7,935.12
Jeff Maggert	T68	75-70-78-72	295	$7,935.12
Frank Nobilo	T68	70-71-80-74	295	$7,935.12
Gary Player	T68	71-73-77-74	295	$7,935.12
Jose Rivero	T68	70-72-75-78	295	$7,935.12
Tiger Woods	T68	74-71-72-78	295	Amateur
Patrick Burke	T79	75-72-78-71	296	$7,177.50
Jay Haas	T79	76-72-70-78	296	$7,177.50
Ryoken Kawagishi	T79	72-76-80-68	296	$7,177.50
Bob Lohr	T79	76-68-79-73	296	$7,177.50
Steve Lowery	T79	69-74-76-77	296	$7,177.50
Sandy Lyle	T79	71-71-79-75	296	$7,177.50
Jack Nicklaus	T79	78-70-77-71	296	$7,177.50
Dean Robertson	T79	71-73-74-78	296	$7,177.50
Jarmo Sandelin	T79	75-71-77-73	296	$7,177.50
Mark Davis	T88	74-71-76-76	297	$6,579.37
Jay Delsing	T88	72-75-73-77	297	$6,579.37
Miguel Jimenez	T88	75-73-76-73	297	$6,579.37
Wayne Riley	T88	70-72-75-80	297	$6,579.37
Eduardo Romero	T88	74-74-72-77	297	$6,579.37
Gene Sauers	T88	69-73-75-80	297	$6,579.37
John Hawksworth	T94	73-74-75-76	298	$6,380.00
Bill Longmuir	T94	72-76-72-78	298	$6,380.00
Jose Coceres	T96	71-76-78-74	299	$6,380.00
Lee Westwood	T96	71-72-82-74	299	$6,380.00
Simon Burnell	T98	72-76-75-77	300	$6,380.00
Davis Love III	T98	70-78-74-78	300	$6,380.00
Gary Clark	100	71-76-80-74	301	Amateur
Mark Nichols	T01	75-68-78-81	302	$6,380.00
Don Pooley	T01	76-71-80-75	302	$6,380.00
Pedro Linhart	103	72-75-77-79	303	$6,380.00

The following players did not finish (C=cut, W=withdrew, D=disqualified)

C—149- Paul Azinger, Bob Charles, Howard Clark, Peter Fowler, Nigel Graves, John Morse, Jumbo Ozaki, Scott Simpson, Mike Springer, Curtis Strange, Bob Tway, John Watson. **150-** Michel Besanceney, Wayne Grady, Brandt Jobe, Tony Johnstone, Stephen Leaney, Miguel Martin, Mark McCumber, Colin Montgomerie, Loren Roberts, Mark Roe, Jaime Spence, Craig Stadler. **151-** John Bickerton, Paul Carman, Mike Clayton, Andrew Crerar, Stephen Gallacher, Robert Karlsson, Larry Mize, Tom Wargo, Tom Weiskopf. **152-** Billy Andrade, Brad Bryant, Carl Mason, Lee Trevino. **153-** Fredrik Andersson, Ian Baker-Finch, Richard Boxall, Mathias Gronberg, Craig Parry, Ronan Rafferty, Neil Roderick, Tohru Suzuki, Kazuhiro Takami, Adam Tillman, Russell Weir, John Wither. **155-** Martyn Thompson. **158-** Brandel Chamblee, Arnold Palmer. **159-** Paul Mayo. **162-**Gary Stafford. **W—73-** Andy Oldcorn, **75-** Philip Walton.

BRITISH OPEN

TOURNAMENT HISTORY

Year	Winner	Score	Runner-up	Score	Location
1860	Willie Park	174	Tom Morris, Sr.	176	Prestwick, Scotland
	(The first event was open only to professional golfers)				
1861	Tom Morris, Sr.,	163	Willie Park	167	Prestwick, Scotland
	(The second annual Open was open to amateurs also)				
1862	Tom Morris, Sr.	163	Willie Park	176	Prestwick, Scotland
1863	Willie Park	168	Tom Morris, Sr.	170	Prestwick, Scotland
1864	Tom Morris, Sr.	167	Andrew Strath	169	Prestwick, Scotland
1865	Andrew Strath	162	Willie Park	164	Prestwick, Scotland
1866	Willie Park	169	David Park	171	Prestwick, Scotland
1867	Tom Morris, Sr.	170	Willie Park	172	Prestwick, Scotland
1868	Tom Morris, Jr.	157	Robert Andrew	159	Prestwick, Scotland
1869	Tom Morris, Jr.	154	Tom Morris, Sr.	157	Prestwick, Scotland
1870	Tom Morris, Jr.	149	David Strath	161	Prestwick, Scotland
			Bob Kirk		
1871	No Championship played				
1872	Tom Morris, Jr.	166	David Strath	169	Prestwick, Scotland
1873	Tom Kidd	179	Jamie Anderson	180	St. Andrews, Scotland
1874	Mungo Park	159	Tom Morris, Jr.	161	Musselburgh, Scotland
1875	Willie Park	166	Bob Martin	168	Prestwick, Scotland
1876	Bob Martin	176	David Strath	176	St. Andrews, Scotland
			(Tied, but refused playoff)		
1877	Jamie Anderson	160	Robert Pringle	162	Musselburgh, Scotland
1878	Jamie Anderson	157	Bob Kirk	159	Prestwick, Scotland
1879	Jamie Anderson	169	Andrew Kirkaldy	172	St. Andrews, Scotland
			James Allan		
1880	Robert Ferguson	162	Peter Paxton	167	Musselburgh, Scotland
1881	Robert Ferguson	170	Jamie Anderson	173	Prestwick, Scotland
1882	Robert Ferguson	171	Willie Fernie	174	St. Andrews, Scotland
1883	*Willie Fernie	159 (158)	Robert Ferguson	159 (159)	Musselburgh, Scotland
1884	Jack Simpson	160	Douglas Rolland	164	Prestwick, Scotland
			Willie Fernie		
1885	Bob Martin	171	Archie Simpson	172	St. Andrews, Scotland
1886	David Brown	157	Willie Campbell	159	Musselburgh, Scotland
1887	Willie Park, Jr.	161	Bob Martin	162	Prestwick, Scotland
1888	Jack Burns	171	Ben Sayers	172	St. Andrews, Scotland
			David Anderson		
1889	*Willie Park, Jr.	155 (158)	Andrew Kirkaldy	155 (163)	Musselburgh, Scotland
1890	John Ball, Jr.	164	Willie Fernie	167	Prestwick, Scotland
			Archie Simpson		
1891	Hugh Kirkaldy	166	Andrew Kirkaldy	168	St. Andrews, Scotland
			Willie Fernie		
	(Championship extended from 36 to 72 holes)				
1892	Harold H. Hilton	305	John Ball, Jr.	308	Muirfield, Scotland
			Hugh Kirkaldy		
			Alexander Herd		
1893	William Auchterlonie	322	John E. Laidlay	324	Prestwick, Scotland
1894	John H. Taylor	326	Douglas Rolland	331	Royal St. George's, England
1895	John H. Taylor	322	Alexander Herd	326	St. Andrews, Scotland
1896	*Harry Vardon	316 (157)	John H. Taylor	316 (161)	Muirfield, Scotland
1897	Harold H. Hilton	314	James Braid	315	Hoylake, England
1898	Harry Vardon	307	Willie Park, Jr.	308	Prestwick, Scotland
1899	Harry Vardon	310	Jack White	315	Royal St. George's, England
1900	John H. Taylor	309	Harry Vardon	317	St Andrews, Scotland
1901	James Braid	309	Harry Vardon	312	Muirfield, Scotland
1902	Alexander Herd	307	Harry Vardon	308	Hoylake, England
			James Braid		
1903	Harry Vardon	300	Tom Vardon	306	Prestwick, Scotland
1904	Jack White	296	John H. Taylor	297	Royal St. George's, England
			James Braid		

BRITISH OPEN

Year	Winner	Score	Runner-up	Score	Location
1905	James Braid	318	John H. Taylor Rowland Jones	323	St. Andrews, Scotland
1906	James Braid	300	John H. Taylor	304	Muirfield, Scotland
1907	Arnaud Massy	312	John H. Taylor	314	Hoylake, England
1908	James Braid	291	Tom Ball	299	Prestwick, Scotland
1909	John H. Taylor	295	James Braid Tom Ball	301	Deal, England
1910	James Braid	299	Alexander Herd	303	St. Andrews, Scotland
1911	*Harry Vardon	303 (143 for 35 holes)	Arnaud Massy	303 (148 for 34 holes)	Royal St. George's, England
1912	Edward (Ted) Ray	295	Harry Vardon	299	Muirfield, Scotland
1913	John H. Taylor	304	Edward (Ted) Ray	312	Hoylake, England
1914	Harry Vardon	306	John H. Taylor	309	Prestwick, Scotland
1915—1919 No Championships played—World War I					
1920	George Duncan	303	Alexander Herd	305	Deal, England
1921	*Jock Hutchison	296 (150)	Roger Wethered	296 (159)	St Andrews, Scotland
1922	Walter Hagen	300	George Duncan James M. Barnes	301	Royal St. George's, England
1923	Arthur G. Havers	295	Walter Hagen	296	Troon, Scotland
1924	Walter Hagen	301	Ernest Whitcombe	302	Hoylake, England
1925	James M. Barnes	300	Archie Compston Edward (Ted) Ray	301	Prestwick, Scotland
1926	Robert T. Jones, Jr.	291	Al Watrous	293	Royal Lytham, England
1927	Robert T. Jones, Jr.	285	Aubrey Boomer Fred Robson	291	St. Andrews, Scotland
1928	Walter Hagen	292	Gene Sarazen	294	Royal St. George's, England
1929	Walter Hagen	292	Johnny Farrell	298	Muirfield, Scotland
1930	Robert T. Jones, Jr.	291	Macdonald Smith Leo Diegel	293	Hoylake, England
1931	Tommy D. Armour	296	Jose Jurado	297	Carnoustie, Scotland
1932	Gene Sarazen	283	Macdonald Smith	288	Prince's, England
1933	*Denny Shute	292 (149)	Craig Wood	292 (154)	St. Andrews, Scotland
1934	Henry Cotton	283	Sidney F. Brews	288	Royal St. George's, England
1935	Alfred Perry	283	Alfred Padgham	287	Muirfield, Scotland
1936	Alfred Padgham	287	James Adams	288	Hoylake, England
1937	Henry Cotton	290	R. A. Whitcombe	292	Carnoustie, Scotland
1938	R. A. Whitcombe	295	James Adams	297	Royal St. George's, England
1939	Richard Burton	290	Johnny Bulla	292	St. Andrews, Scotland
1940—1945 No Championships played—World War II					
1946	Sam Snead	290	Bobby Locke Johnny Bulla	294	St. Andrews, Scotland
1947	Fred Daly	293	R. W. Horne Frank Stranahan	294	Hoylake, England
1948	Henry Cotton	284	Fred Daly	289	Muirfield, Scotland
1949	*Bobby Locke	283 (135)	Harry Bradshaw	283 (147)	Royal St. George's, England
1950	Bobby Locke	279	Roberto De Vicenzo	281	Troon, Scotland
1951	Max Faulkner	285	Antonio Cerda	287	Portrush, Ireland
1952	Bobby Locke	287	Peter Thomson	288	Royal Lytham, England
1953	Ben Hogan	282	Frank Stranahan Dai Rees Peter Thomson Antonio Cerda	286	Carnoustie, Scotland
1954	Peter Thomson	283	Sidney S. Scott Dai Rees Bobby Locke	284	Royal Birkdale, England
1955	Peter Thomson	281	John Fallon	283	St. Andrews, Scotland
1956	Peter Thomson	286	Flory Van Donck	289	Hoylake, England
1957	Bobby Locke	279	Peter Thomson	282	St Andrews, Scotland
1958	*Peter Thomson	278 (139)	Dave Thomas	278 (143)	Royal Lytham, England

BRITISH OPEN

Year	Winner	Score	Runner-up	Score	Location
1959	Gary Player	284	Fred Bullock	286	Muirfield, Scotland
			Flory Van Donck		
1960	Kel Nagle	278	Arnold Palmer	279	St. Andrews, Scotland
1961	Arnold Palmer	284	Dai Rees	285	Royal Birkdale, England
1962	Arnold Palmer	276	Kel Nagle	282	Troon, Scotland
1963	*Bob Charles	277 (140)	Phil Rodgers	277 (148)	Royal Lytham, England
1964	Tony Lema	279	Jack Nicklaus	284	St. Andrews, Scotland
1965	Peter Thomson	285	Brian Huggett	287	Southport, England
			Christy O'Connor		
1966	Jack Nicklaus	282	Doug Sanders	283	Muirfield, Scotland
			Dave Thomas		
1967	Roberto DeVicenzo	278	Jack Nicklaus	280	Hoylake, England
1968	Gary Player	289	Jack Nicklaus	291	Carnoustie, Scotland
			Bob Charles		
1969	Tony Jacklin	280	Bob Charles	282	Royal Lytham, England
1970	*Jack Nicklaus	283 (72)	Doug Sanders	283 (73)	St. Andrews, Scotland
1971	Lee Trevino	278	Lu Liang Huan	279	Royal Birkdale, England
1972	Lee Trevino	278	Jack Nicklaus	279	Muirfield, Scotland
1973	Tom Weiskopf	276	Johnny Miller	279	Troon, Scotland
			Neil Coles		
1974	Gary Player	282	Peter Oosterhuis	286	Royal Lytham, England
1975	*Tom Watson	279 (71)	Jack Newton	279 (72)	Carnoustie, Scotland
1976	Johnny Miller	279	Jack Nicklaus	285	Royal Birkdale, England
			Seve Ballesteros		
1977	Tom Watson	268	Jack Nicklaus	269	Turnberry, Scotland
1978	Jack Nicklaus	281	Ben Crenshaw	283	St. Andrews, Scotland
			Simon Owen		
			Tom Kite		
			Raymond Floyd		
1979	Seve Ballesteros	283	Ben Crenshaw	286	Royal Lytham, England
			Jack Nicklaus		
1980	Tom Watson	271	Lee Trevino	275	Muirfield, Scotland
1981	Bill Rogers	276	Bernhard Langer	280	Royal St George's, England
1982	Tom Watson	284	Nick Price	285	Royal Troon, Scotland
			Peter Oosterhuis		
1983	Tom Watson	275	Andy Bean	276	Royal Birkdale, England
			Hale Irwin		
1984	Seve Ballesteros	276	Tom Watson	278	St. Andrews, Scotland
			Bernhard Langer		
1985	Sandy Lyle	282	Payne Stewart	283	Royal St. George's, England
1986	Greg Norman	280	Gordon Brand	285	Turnberry GL, Scotland
1987	Nick Faldo	279	Paul Azinger	280	Muirfield, Gullane, Scotland
			Rodger Davis		
1988	Seve Ballesteros	273	Nick Price	275	Royal Lytham and St. Annes, St. Annes-On-The-Sea, England
1989	*Mark Calcavecchia	275	Wayne Grady	275	Royal Troon GC, Troon, Scotland
			Greg Norman		
1990	Nick Faldo	270	Payne Stewart	275	St. Andrews, Scotland
			Mark McNulty		
1991	Ian Baker-Finch	272	Mike Harwood	274	Royal Birkdale, England
1992	Nick Faldo	272	John Cook	273	Muirfield, Gullane, Scotland
1993	Greg Norman	267	Nick Faldo	269	Royal St. George's, England
1994	Nick Price	268	Jesper Parnevik	269	Turnberry GL, Scotland
1995	*John Daly	282 (15)	Costantino Rocca	282 (19)	St. Andrews, Scotland

Tournament Record: 267 -- Greg Norman, 1993 (Royal St. George's)

18-Hole Record 63 -- Mark Hayes, 1977 (Turnberry); Isao Aoki, 1980 (Muirfield); Greg Norman, 1986 (Turnberry); Paul Broadhurst, 1990 (St. Andrews); Jodie Mudd, 1991 (Royal Birkdale); Nick Faldo, 1993 (Royal St. George's); Payne Stewart, 1993 (Royal St. George's)

KEY: *= Playoff *Figures in parentheses indicate playoff scores*

1995 DEPOSIT GUARANTY GOLF CLASSIC

Annandale GC, Madison, MS **Purse: $700,000**
Par: 36-36--72 **Yards: 7,157** **July 20-23, 1995**

LEADERS: First Round--David Peoples, who shot a 7-under-par 65, led Kirk Triplett and Dicky Pride by one stroke. **Second Round--**Pride and Paul Stankowski shared the lead at 10-under-par 134, one stroke ahead of Bob Gilder, Jay Williamson and Dicky Thompson. **Third Round--**Thompson, at 13-under-par 203, led Pride and Gilder by one stroke.

CUT: 75 professionals at 2-under-par 142 or better.

PRO-AM: Individual--John Wilson, Ted Schulz, 65, $675 each. Team--Robert Gamez, 53, $750.

WEATHER: Hot and humid each day. Thursday play was suspended for 43 minutes at 5:42 p.m. due to lightning.

Winner: Ed Dougherty 68-68-70-66 272 $126,000.00

Player	Pos.	Scores	Total	Money
Gil Morgan	2	69-69-67-69	274	$75,600.00
Pete Jordan	3	71-67-69-68	275	$47,600.00
Tom Byrum	T 4	69-69-68-70	276	$27,562.50
Steve Rintoul	T 4	73-68-67-68	276	$27,562.50
Dicky Thompson	T 4	67-68-68-73	276	$27,562.50
Kirk Triplett	T 4	66-70-69-71	276	$27,562.50
Bob Gilder	T 8	69-66-69-73	277	$20,300.00
Dicky Pride	T 8	66-68-70-73	277	$20,300.00
Rocky Walcher	T 8	70-68-73-66	277	$20,300.00
John Adams	T11	70-67-72-69	278	$13,900.00
Marco Dawson	T11	68-72-70-68	278	$13,900.00
Fred Funk	T11	67-71-70-70	278	$13,900.00
Ed Humenik	T11	69-73-71-65	278	$13,900.00
Jonathan Kaye	T11	70-72-63-73	278	$13,900.00
Bill Porter	T11	68-69-70-71	278	$13,900.00
Doug Tewell	T11	68-70-70-70	278	$13,900.00
Glen Day	T18	72-70-68-69	279	$10,150.00
Willie Wood	T18	67-71-68-73	279	$10,150.00
Kelly Gibson	T20	67-72-70-71	280	$7,061.25
Jerry Haas	T20	69-69-73-69	280	$7,061.25
Morris Hatalsky	T20	70-69-72-69	280	$7,061.25
Mark Hayes	T20	68-71-70-71	280	$7,061.25
Don Reese	T20	70-71-69-70	280	$7,061.25
Clarence Rose	T20	71-70-66-73	280	$7,061.25
Dave Rummells	T20	69-73-70-68	280	$7,061.25
Tommy Tolles	T20	69-67-71-73	280	$7,061.25
Mike Brisky	T28	70-70-73-68	281	$4,555.00
Joel Edwards	T28	70-67-74-70	281	$4,555.00
Dudley Hart	T28	69-71-70-71	281	$4,555.00
Skip Kendall	T28	70-69-71-71	281	$4,555.00
David Peoples	T28	65-74-73-69	281	$4,555.00
Dillard Pruitt	T28	70-68-70-73	281	$4,555.00
Paul Stankowski	T28	68-66-72-75	281	$4,555.00
Bobby Clampett	T35	71-68-72-71	282	$3,161.67
Carl Paulson	T35	70-69-67-76	282	$3,161.67
John Schroeder	T35	71-70-70-71	282	$3,161.67
Harry Taylor	T35	70-72-72-68	282	$3,161.67
Greg Twiggs	T35	72-68-71-71	282	$3,161.67
John Wilson	T35	71-69-73-69	282	$3,161.67
Buddy Gardner	T35	69-69-72-72	282	$3,161.66
Jimmy Green	T35	68-70-71-73	282	$3,161.66
Mike Standly	T35	68-69-71-74	282	$3,161.66
Bill Britton	T44	68-69-72-74	283	$2,175.60
Steve Lamontagne	T44	67-72-73-71	283	$2,175.60
John Mahaffey	T44	73-69-70-71	283	$2,175.60
Scott McCarron	T44	68-69-73-73	283	$2,175.60
David Ogrin	T44	70-70-69-74	283	$2,175.60
Keith Fergus	T49	69-70-72-73	284	$1,746.50
Dick Mast	T49	68-69-74-73	284	$1,746.50
Joey Rassett	T49	73-69-68-74	284	$1,746.50
Joey Sindelar	T49	69-73-72-70	284	$1,746.50
Pat Bates	T53	72-69-70-74	285	$1,620.50
Curt Byrum	T53	70-71-71-73	285	$1,620.50
Rex Caldwell	T53	70-70-73-72	285	$1,620.50
Brian Kamm	T53	68-73-68-76	285	$1,620.50
J.P. Hayes	T57	71-70-70-75	286	$1,540.00
Tom Hearn	T57	71-71-76-68	286	$1,540.00
Barry Jaeckel	T57	72-70-72-72	286	$1,540.00
Mac O'Grady	T57	72-67-78-69	286	$1,540.00
Mike Tschetter	T57	71-66-72-77	286	$1,540.00
Jay Williamson	T57	68-67-78-73	286	$1,540.00
Mark Wurtz	T57	72-68-71-75	286	$1,540.00
Tommy Armour III	T64	70-66-73-78	287	$1,470.00
Phil Blackmar	T64	71-71-68-77	287	$1,470.00
Mike Donald	T64	70-72-72-73	287	$1,470.00
Sean Murphy	T67	74-68-69-77	288	$1,435.00
Bobby Wadkins	T67	71-69-72-76	288	$1,435.00
Bruce Vaughan	69	70-72-78-69	289	$1,414.00
Michael Allen	T70	71-70-74-76	291	$1,393.00
Omar Uresti	T70	68-73-76-74	291	$1,393.00
Tray Tyner	72	71-67-79-75	292	$1,372.00
Joe Acosta, Jr.	73	69-72-75-77	293	$1,358.00
Kawika Cotner	T74	69-71-77-77	294	$1,337.00
Ernie Gonzalez	T74	71-70-74-79	294	$1,337.00

The following players did not finish (C=cut, W=withdrew, D=disqualified)

C—143- Billy Ray Brown, Russ Cochran, Chris DiMarco, Robert Gamez, Brian Henninger, Tico Hoffman, Jeff Leonard, Steve Pate, Mike Smith. **144-** Leigh Brannan, Jim Carter, Chad Ginn, Mike Holland, Bill Kratzert, Yoshinori Mizumaki, Mike Sullivan, Ron Whittaker. **145-** Rob Boldt, Bart Bryant, Frank Conner, Scott Ford, Steve Hart, Ryan Howison, Greg Kraft, Tim Loustalot, Charlie Rymer. **146-** Joey Davis, John Flannery, Bruce Fleisher, Steve Gotsche, J.L. Lewis, Jerry Pate, Chris Perry. **147-** JC Anderson, Steve Brodie, Jim Furyk, Tom Jenkins, Mark Pfeil, Ted Schulz. **148-** Joe Inman, Patrick Lee, Leonard Thompson, Esteban Toledo. **149-** George Burns, Pete Mathews, Chris Popp. **150-** Dwight Nevil, Jeff Woodland, Richard Zokol. **151-** David Graham, Greg Powers. **152-** Bobby Cole, Ray Stewart. **153-** Andy Bean, Lance Ten Broeck. **154-** Bunky Henry, Rik Massengale. **155-** Kenny Knox, Ernest Ross. **156-** Jay McLelland. **157-** Kent Smith. **160-** Bert Greene. **W—77-** Charles Raulerson, **83-** Mike McCullough.

DEPOSIT GUARANTY GOLF CLASSIC

TOURNAMENT HISTORY

Year	Winner	Score	Runner-up	Score	Location	Par/Yards
MAGNOLIA STATE CLASSIC						
1968	*B.R. McLendon	269	Pete Fleming	269	Hattiesburg CC, Hattiesburg, MS	70/6280
1969	Larry Mowry	272	Larry Hinson Alvin Odom	273	Hattiesburg CC, Hattlesburg, MS	70/6280
1970	Chris Blocker	271	Roy Pace Martin Roesink	272	Hattiesburg CC, Hattiesburg, MS	70/6280
1971	Roy Pace	270	Jack Lewis, Jr.	271	Hattiesburg CC, Hattiesburg, MS	70/6280
1972	Mike Morley	269	Rick Rhoads	272	Hattiesburg CC, Hattiesburg, MS	70/6280
1973	Dwight Nevil	268	Bert Greene	271	Hattiesburg CC, Hattiesburg, MS	70/6280
1974	~Dwight Nevil	133	Bunky Henry Gil Morgan	135	Hattiesburg CC, Hattiesburg, MS	70/6280
1975	Bob Wynn	270	Mike Morley	272	Hattiesburg CC, Hattiesburg, MS	70/6280
1976	Dennis Meyer	271	Artie McNickle Tom Purtzer	273	Hattiesburg CC, Hattiesburg, MS	70/6280
1977	Mike McCullough	269	Orville Moody Gary Groh	272	Hattiesburg CC, Hattiesburg, MS	70/6280
1978	Craig Stadler	268	Bob Eastwood Bruce Fleisher	269	Hattiesburg CC, Hattiesburg, MS	70/6280
1979	*Bobby Walzel	272	Buddy Gardner	272	Hattiesburg CC, Hattiesburg, MS	70/6280
1980	~Roger Maltbie	65	Lee Carter	66	Hattiesburg CC, Hattiesburg, MS	70/6280
1981	*Tom Jones	268	Mike Smith	268	Hattiesburg CC, Hattiesburg, MS	70/6280
1982	Payne Stewart	270	Jay Cudd Bruce Douglass	273	Hattiesburg CC, Hattiesburg, MS	70/6280
1983	~Russ Cochran	203	Sammy Rachels	205	Hattiesburg CC, Hattiesburg, MS	70/6280
1984	~*Lance Ten Broeck	201	Mike Smith	201	Hattiesburg CC, Hattiesburg, MS	70/6280
1985	~*Jim Gallagher, Jr.	131	Paul Azinger	131	Hattiesburg CC, Hattiesburg, MS	70/6280
DEPOSIT GUARANTY GOLF CLASSIC						
1986	Dan Halldorson	263	Paul Azinger	265	Hattiesburg CC, Hattiesburg, MS	72/6594
1987	David Ogrin	267	Nick Faldo		Hattiesburg CC, Hattiesburg, MS	72/6594
1988	Frank Conner	267	Brian Mogg	272	Hattiesburg CC, Hattiesburg, MS	72/6594
1989	~*Jim Booros	199	Mike Donald	199	Hattiesburg CC, Hattiesburg, MS	72/6594
1990	Gene Sauers	268	Jack Ferenz	270	Hattiesburg CC, Hattiesburg, MS	72/6594
1991	*Larry Silveira	266	Russ Cochran Mike Nicolette	266	Hattiesburg CC, Hattiesburg, MS	72/6594
1992	Richard Zokol	267	Mike Donald Bob Eastwood Mike Nicolette Greg Twiggs	268	Hattiesburg CC, Hattiesburg, MS	72/6594
1993	Greg Kraft	267	Morris Hatalsky Tad Rhyan	268	Hattiesburg CC, Hattiesburg, MS	72/6594
1994	~*Brian Henninger	135	Mike Sullivan	135	Annandale GC, Jackson, MS	72/7157
1995	Ed Dougherty	272	Gil Morgan	274	Annandale GC, Jackson, MS	72/7157

NOTE: 1983-85 TPS Event
1994 first year as official event

Tournament Record: 263 -- Dan Halldorson, 1986 (Hattiesburg CC)
Current Course Record: 63 -- Jonathan Kaye, 1995

KEY: *=Playoff ~=Weather-shortened

1995 IDEON CLASSIC AT PLEASANT VALLEY

Pleasant Valley CC, Sutton, MA **Purse: $1,000,000**
Par: 36-35--71 **Yards: 7,110** **July 27-30, 1995**

LEADERS: First Round--Ronnie Black, at 6-under-par 65, led 10 players by one stroke. **Second Round**--Fred Funk, with a tournament record 13-under-par 129, led by three strokes over Jim McGovern. **Third Round**--Funk, with a tournament record 18-under-par 195, led McGovern by four and Dan Forsman by six.

CUT: 80 players at 2-under-par 140.

PRO-AM: $7,500. Individual--Steve Pate, 62, $750. Team--Nolan Henke, 51, $750.

WEATHER: Hot and muggy all week. Play was suspended Friday from 2:45 to 4:40 p.m. due to lightning followed by heavy rains.

Winner: Fred Funk 66-63-66-73 268 $180,000.00

Player	Pos.	Scores	Total	Money
Jim McGovern	2	66-66-67-70	269	$108,000.00
Don Pooley	3	70-64-68-68	270	$68,000.00
Lennie Clements	T 4	67-68-69-67	271	$39,375.00
Roger Maltbie	T 4	68-67-69-67	271	$39,375.00
Joey Sindelar	T 4	69-66-70-66	271	$39,375.00
Jay Williamson	T 4	67-67-68-69	271	$39,375.00
Dan Forsman	T 8	69-65-67-71	272	$29,000.00
Greg Kraft	T 8	70-67-66-69	272	$29,000.00
Howard Twitty	T 8	67-67-68-70	272	$29,000.00
Woody Austin	T11	68-66-68-71	273	$22,000.00
Marco Dawson	T11	69-68-68-68	273	$22,000.00
Steve Lowery	T11	68-66-68-71	273	$22,000.00
Kenny Perry	T11	70-70-66-67	273	$22,000.00
Billy Ray Brown	T15	69-65-69-71	274	$17,000.00
Dudley Hart	T15	68-69-70-67	274	$17,000.00
D.A. Weibring	T15	71-67-68-68	274	$17,000.00
Billy Andrade	T18	68-66-72-69	275	$13,500.00
Tommy Armour III	T18	70-66-69-70	275	$13,500.00
Bob Estes	T18	73-67-68-67	275	$13,500.00
Greg Twiggs	T18	69-68-72-66	275	$13,500.00
Guy Boros	T22	69-66-70-71	276	$9,600.00
Michael Bradley	T22	69-71-71-65	276	$9,600.00
Brian Claar	T22	68-66-70-72	276	$9,600.00
Peter Jacobsen	T22	70-67-69-70	276	$9,600.00
Scott Gump	T22	68-68-71-69	276	$9,600.00
Ronnie Black	T27	65-70-69-73	277	$6,950.00
Curt Byrum	T27	68-69-70-70	277	$6,950.00
Mark Calcavecchia	T27	68-67-70-72	277	$6,950.00
Jim Furyk	T27	69-68-71-69	277	$6,950.00
Gene Sauers	T27	66-68-69-74	277	$6,950.00
Ted Tryba	T27	71-65-74-67	277	$6,950.00
Joe Acosta, Jr.	T33	71-68-70-69	278	$4,955.56
Rick Fehr	T33	67-71-70-70	278	$4,955.56
Jim Hallet	T33	71-65-73-69	278	$4,955.56
Billy Mayfair	T33	70-68-71-69	278	$4,955.56
Don Reese	T33	70-68-71-69	278	$4,955.56
Tom Byrum	T33	67-70-70-71	278	$4,955.55
Jim Carter	T33	66-69-74-69	278	$4,955.55
Sam Randolph	T33	73-67-70-68	278	$4,955.55
Jay Delsing	T33	68-68-71-71	278	$4,955.55
Paul Azinger	T42	71-68-73-67	279	$3,400.00
Russ Cochran	T42	70-67-71-71	279	$3,400.00
Paul Goydos	T42	72-68-68-71	279	$3,400.00
Carl Paulson	T42	69-69-70-71	279	$3,400.00
Tom Purtzer	T42	71-68-70-70	279	$3,400.00
Harry Taylor	T42	70-65-73-71	279	$3,400.00
John Adams	T48	67-72-72-69	280	$2,462.50
George Burns	T48	66-69-73-72	280	$2,462.50
P.H. Horgan III	T48	66-73-70-71	280	$2,462.50
Ryan Howison	T48	68-71-71-70	280	$2,462.50
Jonathan Kaye	T48	69-70-73-68	280	$2,462.50
Skip Kendall	T48	68-69-71-72	280	$2,462.50
Joey Rassett	T48	66-70-75-69	280	$2,462.50
David Feherty	T48	70-68-68-74	280	$2,462.50
Richard Backwell	T56	69-68-71-73	281	$2,250.00
Dave Barr	T56	70-69-70-72	281	$2,250.00
Pete Jordan	T56	68-68-73-72	281	$2,250.00
Jeff Sluman	T56	73-67-70-71	281	$2,250.00
Steve Gotsche	T60	71-68-73-70	282	$2,140.00
Jeff Leonard	T60	69-70-68-75	282	$2,140.00
Scott McCarron	T60	66-69-76-71	282	$2,140.00
Rocco Mediate	T60	70-69-73-70	282	$2,140.00
David Peoples	T60	70-67-72-73	282	$2,140.00
Mark Wiebe	T60	73-65-75-69	282	$2,140.00
Mark Wurtz	T60	66-70-74-72	282	$2,140.00
Clark Dennis	T67	73-65-72-73	283	$2,030.00
J.L. Lewis	T67	71-69-71-72	283	$2,030.00
Dicky Thompson	T67	68-71-70-74	283	$2,030.00
Tray Tyner	T67	68-71-74-70	283	$2,030.00
Joel Edwards	T71	70-70-74-70	284	$1,960.00
Eduardo Romero	T71	72-63-76-73	284	$1,960.00
John Wilson	T71	72-66-73-73	284	$1,960.00
Kenny Knox	T74	69-70-74-73	286	$1,910.00
Jeff Maggert	T74	69-71-69-77	286	$1,910.00
Bob Burns	76	70-70-75-72	287	$1,880.00
Rodney Butcher	77	68-72-76-75	291	$1,860.00
Andy Bean	78	68-72-77-76	293	$1,840.00

The following players did not finish (C=cut, W=withdrew, D=disqualified)

C—141- Bobby Clampett, Keith Clearwater, Scott Ford, Buddy Gardner, Jerry Haas, Tim Loustalot, Mark Lye, Doug Martin, Bill Porter, Dana Quigley, Mike Smith, Mike Standly, Lanny Wadkins, Rocky Walcher. **142-** Steve Brodie, Chris DiMarco, Brad Faxon, Steve Hart, Mike Heinen, Richard Karbowski, Bill Kratzert, Dave Rummells, Mike San Filippo, Tommy Tolles, Heath Wassem. **143-** Michael Allen, Emlyn Aubrey, Mike Brisky, Bill Britton, Clark Burroughs, Kawika Cotner, Bob Gilder, Tom Hearn, Dennis Paulson, Dave Stockton, Jr., Bruce Vaughan, Jeff Woodland. **144-** Mike Donald, Hubert Green, Nolan Henke, Bradley Hughes, Lee Rinker, Ted Schulz. **145-** Ed Fiori, Morris Hatalsky, Bob Lohr, Dick Mast, Steve Pate, Larry Rinker, Ray Stewart, Omar Uresti, Grant Waite. **146-** Mark Carnevale, Wayne Levi, Yoshinori Mizumaki, Charlie Rymer, Tony Sills, Leonard Thompson. **147-** Kelly Gibson, Dan Gillis, Wayne Grady, J.P. Hayes, Mark Hayes, Brian Henninger, Brian Kamm, Jim Thorpe, Chris Van Der Velde. **148-** Rob Boldt, Ed Dougherty. **149-** Paul Parajeckas, Steve Rintoul, Phil Smith. **151-** Pat Bates, Bruce Fleisher.**W—291-** Ken Green, **211-** Bill Glasson, **77-** Fulton Allem. **D— 80-**Tom Dyer.

CVS CHARITY CLASSIC

TOURNAMENT HISTORY

Year	Winner	Score	Runner-up	Score	Location	Par/Yards
CARLING WORLD OPEN						
1965	Tony Lema	279	Arnold Palmer	281	Pleasant Valley CC, Sutton, MA	71/7110
AVCO GOLF CLASSIC						
1969	Tom Shaw	280	Bob Stanton	281	Pleasant Valley CC, Sutton, MA	71/7110
1970	Billy Casper	277	Rod Funseth Tom Weiskopf	280	Pleasant Valley CC, Sutton, MA	71/7110
MASSACHUSETTS CLASSIC						
1971	Dave Stockton	275	Ray Floyd	276	Pleasant Valley CC, Sutton, MA	72/7241
USI CLASSIC						
1972	Bruce Devlin	275	Lee Elder	278	Pleasant Valley CC, Sutton, MA	72/7241
1973	Lanny Wadkins	279	Lee Elder Tom Jenkins Rik Massengale	281	Pleasant Valley CC, Sutton, MA	72/7241
PLEASANT VALLEY CLASSIC						
1974	Victor Regalado	278	Tom Weiskopf	279	Pleasant Valley CC, Sutton, MA	71/7110
1975	Roger Maltbie	276	Mac McLendon	277	Pleasant Valley CC, Sutton, MA	71/7110
1976	Bud Allin	277	Ben Crenshaw	278	Pleasant Valley CC, Sutton, MA	71/7110
1977	Raymond Floyd	271	Jack Nicklaus	272	Pleasant Valley CC, Sutton, MA	71/7110
AMERICAN OPTICAL CLASSIC						
1978	John Mahaffey	270	Ray Floyd Gil Morgan	272	Pleasant Valley CC, Sutton, MA	71/7110
1979	Lou Graham	275	Ben Crenshaw	276	Pleasant Valley CC, Sutton, MA	71/7110
PLEASANT VALLEY JIMMY FUND CLASSIC						
1980	*Wayne Levi	273	Gil Morgan	273	Pleasant Valley CC, Sutton, MA	71/7110
1981	Jack Renner	273	Scott Simpson	275	Pleasant Valley CC, Sutton, MA	71/7110
BANK OF BOSTON CLASSIC						
1982	Bob Gilder	271	Fuzzy Zoeller	273	Pleasant Valley CC, Sutton, MA	71/7110
1983	Mark Lye	273	John Mahaffey Sammy Rachels Jim Thorpe	274	Pleasant Valley CC, Sutton, MA	71/7110
1984	George Archer	270	Frank Conner Joey Sindelar	276	Pleasant Valley CC, Sutton, MA	71/7110
1985	George Burns	267	John Mahaffey Jodie Mudd Greg Norman Leonard Thompson	273	Pleasant Valley CC, Sutton, MA	71/7110
1986	*Gene Sauers	274	Blaine McCallister	274	Pleasant Valley CC, Sutton, MA	71/7110
1987	~Sam Randolph	199	Wayne Grady Gene Sauers Ray Stewart	203	Pleasant Valley CC, Sutton, MA	71/7110
1988	Mark Calcavecchia	274	Don Pooley	275	Pleasant Valley CC, Sutton, MA	71/7110
1989	Blaine McCallister	271	Brad Faxon	272	Pleasant Valley CC, Sutton, MA	71/7110
1990	Morris Hatalsky	275	Scott Verplank	276	Pleasant Valley CC, Sutton, MA	71/7110
NEW ENGLAND CLASSIC						
1991	*Bruce Fleisher	268	Ian Baker-Finch	268	Pleasant Valley CC, Sutton, MA	71/7110
1992	Brad Faxon	268	Phil Mickelson	270	Pleasant Valley CC, Sutton, MA	71/7110
1993	Paul Azinger	268	Jay Delsing Bruce Fleisher	272	Pleasant Valley CC, Sutton, MA	71/7110
1994	Kenny Perry	268	David Feherty	269	Pleasant Valley CC, Sutton, MA	71/7110
IDEON CLASSIC AT PLEASANT VALLEY						
1995	Fred Funk	268	Jim McGovern	269	Pleasant Valley CC, Sutton, MA	71/7110

Tournament Record: 267 -- George Burns, 1985
Current Course Record: 62 -- Nick Price, 1989; David Peoples, 1993

KEY: * = Playoff ~ = Weather-shortened

1995 BUICK OPEN

Warwick Hills G&CC, Grand Blanc, MI **Purse: $1,200,000**
Par: 36-36--72 **Yards: 7,105** **August 3-6, 1995**

LEADERS: First Round--Woody Austin, with a 9-under-par 63, led by two over Paul Goydos, Payne Stewart, J.L. Lewis and Bruce Vaughan. **Second Round--**Stewart, at 14-under-par 130, led by one over Austin. **Third Round--**Jeff Sluman, at 16-under-par 200, led by one over Tom Byrum.

CUT: 72 players at 4-under-par 140.

PRO-AM: Due to an afternoon storm, the pro-am was divided into three separate competitions. $7,500. Morning Individual--Mike Heinen, 67, $450. Morning Team--Mike Heinen, Ernie Els, Justin Leonard, 53, $412.50 each. Afternoon Front Nine Individual--Russ Cochran, 33, $375. Team--Robin Freeman, Scott Verplank, 26, $337.50 each. Afternoon Back Nine Individual--Gil Morgan, 33, $375. Team--David Ogrin, Billy Mayfair, 26, $337.50.

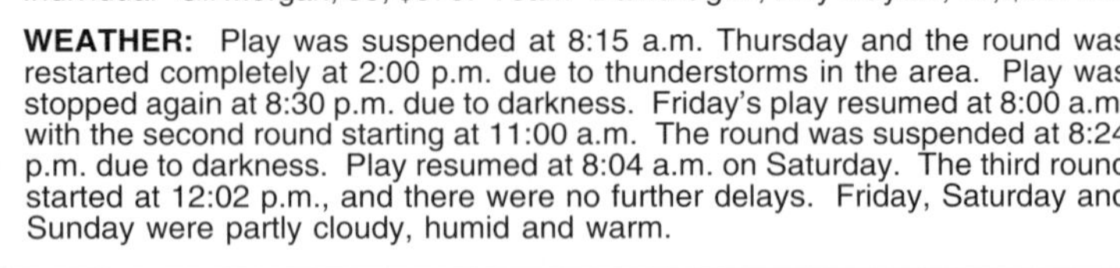

WEATHER: Play was suspended at 8:15 a.m. Thursday and the round was restarted completely at 2:00 p.m. due to thunderstorms in the area. Play was stopped again at 8:30 p.m. due to darkness. Friday's play resumed at 8:00 a.m. with the second round starting at 11:00 a.m. The round was suspended at 8:24 p.m. due to darkness. Play resumed at 8:04 a.m. on Saturday. The third round started at 12:02 p.m., and there were no further delays. Friday, Saturday and Sunday were partly cloudy, humid and warm.

Winner: Woody Austin 63-68-72-67 270 $216,000.00

(Won playoff with par-4 on second extra hole)

Player	Pos.	Scores	Total	Money
Mike Brisky	2	67-68-67-68	270	$129,600.00
Tom Byrum	T 3	69-67-65-70	271	$62,400.00
Ernie Els	T 3	69-68-66-68	271	$62,400.00
Jeff Sluman	T 3	66-67-67-71	271	$62,400.00
Fred Couples	6	68-67-67-70	272	$43,200.00
Joel Edwards	7	69-65-68-71	273	$40,200.00
Payne Stewart	8	65-65-73-71	274	$37,200.00
Jonathan Kaye	T 9	69-67-69-70	275	$33,600.00
Tom Lehman	T 9	71-66-70-68	275	$33,600.00
Brad Bryant	T11	68-67-68-73	276	$24,600.00
Fred Funk	T11	70-68-70-68	276	$24,600.00
Jim Furyk	T11	72-62-71-71	276	$24,600.00
Gil Morgan	T11	69-70-67-70	276	$24,600.00
Kenny Perry	T11	67-69-72-68	276	$24,600.00
Scott Verplank	T11	67-70-67-72	276	$24,600.00
Tommy Armour III	T17	67-71-70-69	277	$15,702.86
Russ Cochran	T17	66-70-70-71	277	$15,702.86
Justin Leonard	T17	66-71-72-68	277	$15,702.86
Larry Mize	T17	69-70-68-70	277	$15,702.86
Tom Purtzer	T17	70-69-69-69	277	$15,702.86
J.L. Lewis	T17	65-69-71-72	277	$15,702.85
Nick Price	T17	69-66-69-73	277	$15,702.85
Joe Acosta, Jr.	T24	71-67-68-72	278	$9,080.00
Bart Bryant	T24	69-68-70-71	278	$9,080.00
Clark Dennis	T24	71-68-67-72	278	$9,080.00
Chris DiMarco	T24	70-69-73-66	278	$9,080.00
Dan Forsman	T24	69-70-67-72	278	$9,080.00
Wayne Grady	T24	67-73-67-71	278	$9,080.00
Greg Kraft	T24	71-68-68-71	278	$9,080.00
Bruce Vaughan	T24	65-69-75-69	278	$9,080.00
Dillard Pruitt	T24	70-68-72-68	278	$9,080.00
Bob Burns	T33	68-72-71-68	279	$6,205.72
Jim McGovern	T33	68-71-67-73	279	$6,205.72
Tony Sills	T33	69-67-73-70	279	$6,205.72
Jim Carter	T33	67-71-68-73	279	$6,205.71
Jay Haas	T33	70-67-68-74	279	$6,205.71
Scott Hoch	T33	69-70-67-73	279	$6,205.71
Mark Wurtz	T33	71-65-70-73	279	$6,205.71
Dave Barr	T40	70-69-70-71	280	$4,560.00
Paul Goydos	T40	65-69-73-73	280	$4,560.00
Skip Kendall	T40	69-68-69-74	280	$4,560.00
Tom Kite	T40	72-67-74-67	280	$4,560.00
Tommy Tolles	T40	72-63-71-74	280	$4,560.00
Grant Waite	T40	69-68-74-69	280	$4,560.00
Harry Taylor	T46	68-72-73-68	281	$3,209.15
Howard Twitty	T46	72-68-69-72	281	$3,209.15
Brad Faxon	T46	72-65-72-72	281	$3,209.14
Robin Freeman	T46	73-66-70-72	281	$3,209.14
Nolan Henke	T46	68-70-70-73	281	$3,209.14
Pete Jordan	T46	71-69-67-74	281	$3,209.14
Doug Martin	T46	68-72-67-74	281	$3,209.14
Tim Loustalot	T53	69-69-75-69	282	$2,792.00
Bill Porter	T53	69-69-72-72	282	$2,792.00
J.P. Hayes	T53	66-72-73-71	282	$2,792.00
Marco Dawson	56	71-69-73-70	283	$2,736.00
Nick Faldo	T57	72-68-75-69	284	$2,664.00
Scott Gump	T57	70-69-72-73	284	$2,664.00
Steve Rintoul	T57	68-72-71-73	284	$2,664.00
Ted Tryba	T57	68-69-73-74	284	$2,664.00
D.A. Weibring	T57	70-70-72-72	284	$2,664.00
Michael Allen	T62	71-69-76-69	285	$2,556.00
Chip Beck	T62	70-68-72-75	285	$2,556.00
David Peoples	T62	67-71-73-74	285	$2,556.00
Mike Sullivan	T62	70-70-76-69	285	$2,556.00
Dick Mast	T66	71-69-72-74	286	$2,484.00
John Wilson	T66	69-71-70-76	286	$2,484.00
Yoshi Mizumaki	T68	67-72-74-74	287	$2,436.00
David Ogrin	T68	68-72-78-69	287	$2,436.00
Jeff Maggert	T70	69-71-74-74	288	$2,388.00
Jerry Pate	T70	69-70-74-75	288	$2,388.00
Phil Blackmar	72	71-69-75-75	290	$2,352.00

The following players did not finish (C=cut, W=withdrew, D=disqualified)

C—141- Eric Booker, Billy Ray Brown, Curt Byrum, Mark Carnevale, Keith Clearwater, John Connelly, Kawika Cotner, Keith Fergus, Scott Ford, Tom Gillis, Steve Gotsche, Ken Green, Dudley Hart, Steve Hart, John Morse, Dan Pohl, Dicky Pride, Don Reese, Loren Roberts, Joey Sindelar, Dave Stockton, Jr., Dicky Thompson. **142-** Ed Dougherty, David Duval, Kelly Gibson, Ryan Howison, Ed Humenik, Billy Mayfair, Eduardo Romero, Mike Smith, Mike Springer, Doug Tewell, Bobby Wadkins. **143-** Ronnie Black, Jay Don Blake, Guy Boros, Bruce Fleisher, Jerry Haas, Gary Hallberg, Kenny Knox, Bob Lohr, Rocco Mediate, Mike Standly, Curtis Strange, Omar Uresti, Jay Williamson. **144-** Emlyn Aubrey, Steve Brady, Bill Britton, Ben Crenshaw, Larry Nelson, Willie Wood. **145-**Clark Burroughs, John Cook, Jeff Leonard, Joey Rassett, Mike Reid, Hal Sutton. **146-**Pat Bates, Mike Heinen, Mike Hulbert, Carl Paulson, Lee Rinker, Paul Stankowski, Lanny Wadkins. **147-** David Feherty, Bradley Hughes, Wayne Levi, Bob Makoski, Charlie Rymer, Jim Thorpe. **148-** Patrick Burke, Tom Hearn. **149-** Dennis Paulson, Richard Zokol. **151-** Brian Kamm. **152-** Evan "Big Cat" Williams. **154-** Richard Stallings. **155-**Tom Gieselman, Andrew Mogg, Jeff Stalcup. **W—70-**Chris Perry, **71-**Leonard Thompson. **D—70-** Neal Lancaster.

BUICK OPEN

TOURNAMENT HISTORY

Year	Winner	Score	Runner-up	Score	Location	Par/Yards
BUICK OPEN INVITATIONAL						
1958	Billy Casper	285	Ted Kroll Arnold Palmer	286	Warwick Hills CC, Grand Blanc, MI	72/7014
1959	*Art Wall	282	Dow Finsterwald	282	Warwick Hills CC, Grand Blanc, MI	72/7014
1960	Mike Souchak	282	Gay Brewer Art Wall	283	Warwick Hills CC, Grand Blanc, MI	72/7014
1961	*Jack Burke, Jr.	284	Billy Casper Johnny Pott	284	Warwick Hills CC, Grand Blanc, MI	72/7014
1962	Bill Collins	284	Dave Ragan	285	Warwick Hills CC, Grand Blanc, MI	72/7014
1963	Julius Boros	274	Dow Finsterwald	279	Warwick Hills CC, Grand Blanc, MI	72/7014
1964	Tony Lema	277	Dow Finsterwald	280	Warwick Hills CC, Grand Blanc, MI	72/7014
1965	Tony Lema	280	Johnny Pott	282	Warwick Hills CC, Grand Blanc, MI	72/7014
1966	Phil Rodgers	284	Johnny Pott Kermit Zarley	286	Warwick Hills CC, Grand Blanc, MI	72/7014
1967	Julius Boros	283	Bob Goalby R.H. Sikes Bert Yancey	286	Warwick Hills CC, Grand Blanc, MI	72/7014
1968	Tom Weiskopf	280	Mike Hill	281	Warwick Hills CC, Grand Blanc, MI	72/7014
1969	Dave Hill	277	Frank Beard	279	Warwick Hills CC, Grand Blanc, MI	72/7014
VERN PARSELL BUICK OPEN						
1972	Gary Groh	273	John Mahaffey	275	Flint Elks CC, Flint, MI	72/6902
LAKE MICHIGAN CLASSIC						
1973	*(2T) Wilf Homenuik	215	Jim Ferriell	215	Benton Harbor Elks CC, Benton Harbor, MI	71/6690
FLINT ELKS OPEN						
1974	(2T) Bryan Abbott	135	Joe Porter	136	Flint Elks CC, Flint, MI	72/6902
1975	(2T) Spike Kelley	208	Randy Erskine Jim Marshall Mike McCullough	209	Flint Elks CC, Flint, MI	72/6902
1976	*(2T) Ed Sabo	279	Randy Erskine	279	Flint Elks CC, Flint, MI	72/6902
1977	Bobby Cole	271	Fred Marti	272	Flint Elks CC, Flint, MI	72/6902
BUICK GOODWRENCH OPEN						
1978	*Jack Newton	280	Mike Sullivan	280	Warwick Hills CC, Grand Blanc, MI	72/7014
1979	*John Fought	280	Jim Simons	280	Warwick Hills CC, Grand Blanc, MI	72/7014
1980	Peter Jacobsen	276	Bill Kratzert Mark Lye	277	Warwick Hills CC, Grand Blanc, MI	72/7014
BUICK OPEN						
1981	*Hale Irwin	277	Bobby Clampett Peter Jacobsen Gil Morgan	277	Warwick Hills CC, Grand Blanc, MI	72/7014
1982	Lanny Wadkins	273	Tom Kite	274	Warwick Hills CC, Grand Blanc, MI	72/7014
1983	Wayne Levi	272	Isao Aoki Calvin Peete	273	Warwick Hills CC, Grand Blanc, MI	72/7014
1984	Denis Watson	271	Payne Stewart	272	Warwick Hills CC, Grand Blanc, MI	72/7014
1985	Ken Green	268	Wayne Grady	272	Warwick Hills CC, Grand Blanc, MI	72/7014
1986	Ben Crenshaw	270	J.C. Snead Doug Tewell	271	Warwick Hills CC, Grand Blanc, MI	72/7014
1987	Robert Wrenn	262	Dan Pohl	269	Warwick Hills CC, Grand Blanc, MI	72/7014
1988	Scott Verplank	268	Doug Tewell	270	Warwick Hills CC, Grand Blanc, MI	72/7014
1989	Leonard Thompson	273	Billy Andrade Payne Stewart Doug Tewell	274	Warwick Hills CC, Grand Blanc, MI	72/7014
1990	Chip Beck	272	Mike Donald Hale Irwin Fuzzy Zoeller	273	Warwick Hills CC, Grand Blanc, MI	72/7014
1991	*Brad Faxon	271	Chip Beck	271	Warwick Hills CC, Grand Blanc, MI	72/7014
1992	*Dan Forsman	276	Steve Elkington Brad Faxon	276	Warwick Hills CC, Grand Blanc, MI	72/7014
1993	Larry Mize	272	Fuzzy Zoeller	273	Warwick Hills CC, Grand Blanc, MI	72/7014
1994	Fred Couples	270	Corey Pavin	272	Warwick Hills CC, Grand Blanc, MI	72/7014
1995	*Woody Austin	270	Mike Brisky	270	Warwick Hills CC, Grand Blanc, MI	72/7014

NOTE: Tournaments unofficial 1972 through 1976.

Tournament Record: 262 -- Robert Wrenn, 1987
Current Course Record: 62 -- Jim Furyk, 1995

KEY: *=Playoff 2T=Second TOUR

1995 PGA CHAMPIONSHIP

Riviera CC, Pacific Palisades, CA
Par: 35-36--71 Yards: 6,949

Purse: $2,000,000
August 10-13, 1995

LEADERS: First Round--Michael Bradley shot a tournament-record-tying 8-under-par 63, one stroke ahead of Mark O'Meara and Jim Gallagher, Jr. **Second Round--**O'Meara and Ernie Els, at a tournament-record-tying 11-under-par 131, led Justin Leonard by three strokes. **Third Round--**Els shot 66 for a tournament record 16-under-par 197, three strokes ahead of O'Meara and Jeff Maggert.

CUT: 72 players at even-par 142.

WEATHER: Sunny and warm each day. Sunday's round was delayed five minutes due to fog.

Winner: Steve Elkington 68-67-68-64 267 $360,000.00

(Won playoff with birdie-3 on first extra hole)

Player	Pos	Scores	Total	Money
Colin Montgomerie	2	68-67-67-65	267	$216,000.00
Ernie Els	T 3	66-65-66-72	269	$116,000.00
Jeff Maggert	T 3	66-69-65-69	269	$116,000.00
Brad Faxon	5	70-67-71-63	271	$80,000.00
Bob Estes	T 6	69-68-68-68	273	$68,500.00
Mark O'Meara	T 6	64-67-69-73	273	$68,500.00
Jay Haas	T 8	69-71-64-70	274	$50,000.00
Justin Leonard	T 8	68-66-70-70	274	$50,000.00
Steve Lowery	T 8	69-68-68-69	274	$50,000.00
Jeff Sluman	T 8	69-67-68-70	274	$50,000.00
Craig Stadler	T 8	71-66-66-71	274	$50,000.00
Jim Furyk	T13	68-70-69-68	275	$33,750.00
Miguel Jimenez	T13	69-69-67-70	275	$33,750.00
Payne Stewart	T13	69-70-69-67	275	$33,750.00
Kirk Triplett	T13	71-69-68-67	275	$33,750.00
Michael Campbell	T17	71-65-71-69	276	$26,000.00
Costantino Rocca	T17	70-69-68-69	276	$26,000.00
Curtis Strange	T17	72-68-68-68	276	$26,000.00
Greg Norman	T20	66-69-70-72	277	$21,000.00
Jesper Parnevik	T20	69-69-70-69	277	$21,000.00
Duffy Waldorf	T20	69-69-67-72	277	$21,000.00
Woody Austin	T23	70-70-70-68	278	$15,500.00
Nolan Henke	T23	68-73-67-70	278	$15,500.00
Peter Jacobsen	T23	69-67-71-71	278	$15,500.00
Lee Janzen	T23	66-70-72-70	278	$15,500.00
Bruce Lietzke	T23	73-68-67-70	278	$15,500.00
Billy Mayfair	T23	68-68-72-70	278	$15,500.00
Steve Stricker	T23	75-64-69-70	278	$15,500.00
Sam Torrance	T23	69-69-69-71	278	$15,500.00
Paul Azinger	T31	70-70-72-67	279	$8,906.25
Mark Brooks	T31	67-74-69-69	279	$8,906.25
Fred Couples	T31	70-69-74-66	279	$8,906.25
Nick Faldo	T31	69-73-70-67	279	$8,906.25
Gil Morgan	T31	66-73-74-66	279	$8,906.25
Jose Maria Olazabal	T31	72-66-70-71	279	$8,906.25
Joe Ozaki	T31	71-70-65-73	279	$8,906.25
D.A. Weibring	T31	74-68-69-68	279	$8,906.25
Lennie Clements	T39	67-71-72-70	280	$6,750.00
Fred Funk	T39	70-72-68-70	280	$6,750.00
Sandy Lyle	T39	67-73-69-71	280	$6,750.00
Nick Price	T39	71-71-70-68	280	$6,750.00
Philip Walton	T39	71-70-71-68	280	$6,750.00
Chip Beck	T44	66-74-73-68	281	$5,600.00
Ben Crenshaw	T44	68-73-73-67	281	$5,600.00
Jim Gallagher, Jr.	T44	64-72-73-72	281	$5,600.00
Gene Sauers	T44	69-71-68-73	281	$5,600.00
Peter Senior	T44	68-71-74-68	281	$5,600.00
John Adams	T49	65-76-71-70	282	$4,620.00
Brian Claar	T49	68-67-73-74	282	$4,620.00
Robin Freeman	T49	71-69-70-72	282	$4,620.00
Jumbo Ozaki	T49	73-68-69-72	282	$4,620.00
Kenny Perry	T49	75-67-70-70	282	$4,620.00
Michael Bradley	T54	63-73-73-74	283	$4,050.00
Hale Irwin	T54	71-68-71-73	283	$4,050.00
Tom Kite	T54	70-69-70-74	283	$4,050.00
Scott Simpson	T54	71-67-71-74	283	$4,050.00
Ed Dougherty	T58	68-72-74-70	284	$3,630.00
Per-Ulrik Johansson	T58	72-69-71-72	284	$3,630.00
Steve Pate	T58	71-71-71-71	284	$3,630.00
Loren Roberts	T58	74-68-71-71	284	$3,630.00
Tom Watson	T58	71-71-72-70	284	$3,630.00
Barry Lane	T63	74-68-75-68	285	$3,400.00
Mike Sullivan	T63	72-69-71-73	285	$3,400.00
Lanny Wadkins	T63	73-69-71-72	285	$3,400.00
Dillard Pruitt	66	73-69-72-72	286	$3,300.00
David Frost	T67	69-73-72-73	287	$3,262.50
Jack Nicklaus	T67	69-71-71-76	287	$3,262.50
Fuzzy Zoeller	69	72-69-75-72	288	$3,225.00
Brian Kamm	70	71-66-74-78	289	$3,200.00
Curt Byrum	T71	71-71-78-71	291	$3,162.50
Wayne Defrancesco	T71	69-73-74-75	291	$3,162.50

The following players did not finish (C=cut, W=withdrew, D=disqualified)

C—143- Billy Andrade, Brad Bryant, John Cook, Glen Day, David Duval, Brian Henninger, Darrell Kestner, Davis Love III, Ron McDougal, Brett Ogle, Don Pooley, Mike Springer, Bob Tway, Ian Woosnam. **144-** Robert Allenby, Frank Dobbs, Scott Hoch, Mike Hulbert, Massy Kuramoto, Jim McGovern, Larry Mize, John Morse, Frank Nobilo, Pete Oakley, Steve Rintoul, Hal Sutton, Scott Verplank, Grant Waite. **145-** Mark Calcavecchia, Wayne Grady, Hubert Green, Mike Heinen, Doug Martin, Mark Mielke, Larry Nelson, John Reeves, Brian Watts, Bruce Zabriski. **146-** Bill Glasson, David Graham, Stephen Keppler, Blaine McCallister. **147-** Guy Boros, Steve Brady, Brandel Chamblee, Tom Dolby, Greg Kraft, Tom Lehman, John Mahaffey, Bob Makoski, Mark McCumber, Craig Parry, Corey Pavin, Paul Stankowski. **148-** Phil Mickelson, Tommy Nakajima, Vijay Singh, Jim Sobb, Gary Trivisonno. **149-** John Daly, Dana Quigley, Ted Tryba. **150-** Larry Emery. **151-** Seve Ballesteros, Bobby Wadkins. **152-** Rick Acton, Ian Baker-Finch, Jay Don Blake, Drue Johnson. **153-** Robert Gamez. **154-** Michael Burke Jr.. **155-** Kent Dinsdale, Benny Passons. **156-** Phil Bland. **157-** Denny Hepler. **160-** Mike Lawrence. **W—76-** Bob Lendzion. **D—78-** John Huston.

PGA CHAMPIONSHIP

TOURNAMENT HISTORY

Year	Winner	Score	Runner-up	Score	Location
1916	James M. Barnes	1 up	Jock Hutchison		Siwanoy CC, Bronxville, NY
1917—1918 No Championships Played—World War I					
1919	James M. Barnes	6 & 5	Fred McLeod		Engineers CC, Roslyn, LI, NY
1920	Jock Hutchison	1 up	J. Douglas Edgar		Flossmoor CC, Flossmoor, IL
1921	Walter Hagen	3 & 2	James M. Barnes		Inwood CC, Far Rockaway, NY
1922	Gene Sarazen	4 & 3	Emmet French		Oakmont CC, Oakmont, PA
1923	*Gene Sarazen	1 up (38)	Walter Hagen		Pelham CC, Pelham N Y
1924	Walter Hagen	2 up	James M. Barnes		French Lick CC, French Lick, IN
1925	Walter Hagen	6 & 5	William Mehlhorn		Olympia Fields, Olympia Fields, IL
1926	Walter Hagen	5 & 3	Leo Diegel		Salisbury GC, Westbury, LI, NY
1927	Walter Hagen	1 up	Joe Turnesa		Cedar Crest C C, Dallas TX
1928	Leo Diegel	6 & 5	Al Espinosa		Five Farms CC Baltimore, MD
1929	Leo Diegel	6 & 4	Johnny Farrell		Hillcrest CC Los Angeles, CA
1930	Tommy Armour	1 up	Gene Sarazen		Fresh Meadow CC, Flushing, NY
1931	Tom Creavy	2 & 1	Denny Shute		Wannamoisett CC Rumford, RI
1932	Olin Dutra	4 & 3	Frank Walsh		Keller GC, St. Paul MN
1933	Gene Sarazen	5 & 4	Willie Goggin		Blue Mound CC, Milwaukee, WI
1934	*Paul Runyan	1 up (38)	Craig Wood		Park CC, Williamsville NY
1935	Johnny Revolta	5 & 4	Tommy Armour		Twin Hills CC, Oklahoma City, OK
1936	Denny Shute	3 & 2	Jimmy Thomson		Pinehurst CC, Pinehurst NC
1937	*Denny Shute	1 up (37)	Harold McSpaden		Pittsburgh Field Club, Aspinwall, PA
1938	Paul Runyan	8 & 7	Sam Snead		Shawnee CC, Shawnee-on-Delaware,
1939	*Henry Picard	1 up (37)	Byron Nelson		Pomonok CC, Flushing LI, NY
1940	Byron Nelson	1 up	Sam Snead		Hershey CC, Hershey, PA
1941	*Vic Ghezzi	1 up (38)	Byron Nelson		Cherry Hills CC Denver CO
1942	Sam Snead	2 & 1	Jim Turnesa		Seaview CC, Atlantic City, NJ
1943—No Championship Played—World War II					
1944	Bob Hamilton	1 up	Byron Nelson		Manito G & CC, Spokane WA
1945	Byron Nelson	4 & 3	Sam Byrd		Moraine CC, Dayton, OH
1946	Ben Hogan	6 & 4	Ed Oliver		Portland GC, Portland, OR
1947	Jim Ferrier	2 & 1	Chick Harbert		Plum Hollow CC, Detroit, MI
1948	Ben Hogan	7 & 6	Mike Turnesa		Norwood Hills CC St. Louis MO
1949	Sam Snead	3 & 2	Johnny Palmer		Hermitage CC, Richmond, VA
1950	Chandler Harper	4 & 3	Henry Williams, Jr.		Scioto CC, Columbus, OH
1951	Sam Snead	7 & 6	Walter Burkemo		Oakmont CC Oakmont PA
1952	Jim Turnesa	1 up	Chick Harbert		Big Spring CC, Louisvillie, KY
1953	Walter Burkemo	2 & 1	Felice Torza		Birmingham CC, Birmingham, MI
1954	Chick Harbert	4 & 3	Walter Burkemo		Keller GC, St. Paul, MN
1955	Doug Ford	4 & 3	Cary Middlecoff		Meadowbrook CC Detroit MI
1956	Jack Burke	3 & 2	Ted Kroll		Blue Hill CC, Boston, MA
1957	Lionel Hebert	2 & 1	Dow Finsterwald		Miami Valley CC, Dayton, OH
1958	Dow Finsterwald	276	Billy Casper	278	Llanerch CC, Havertown, PA
1959	Bob Rosburg	277	Jerry Barber Doug Sanders	278	Minneapolis GC, St. Louis Park, MN
1960	Jay Hebert	281	Jim Ferrier	282	Firestone CC, Akron, OH
1961	*Jerry Barber (67)	277	Don January (68)	277	Olympia Fields CC, Olympia Fields, IL
1962	Gary Player	278	Bob Goalby	279	Aronomink GC, Newtown Square, PA
1963	Jack Nicklaus	279	Dave Ragan, Jr.	281	Dallas Athletic Club, Dallas, TX
1964	Bobby Nichols	271	Jack Nicklaus Arnold Palmer	274	Columbus CC, Columbus, OH
1965	Dave Marr	280	Billy Casper Jack Nicklaus	282	Laurel Valley CC, Ligonier, PA
1966	Al Geiberger	280	Dudley Wysong	284	Firestone CC Akron OH
1967	*Don January (69)	281	Don Massengale (71)	281	Columbine CC, Littleton, CO
1968	Julius Boros	281	Bob Charles Arnold Palmer	282	Pecan Valley CC, San Antonio, TX

PGA CHAMPIONSHIP

TOURNAMENT HISTORY

Year	Winner	Score	Runner-up	Score	Location
1969	Ray Floyd	276	Gary Player	277	NCR CC, Dayton, OH
1970	Dave Stockton	279	Arnold Palmer	281	Southern Hills CC, Tulsa, OK
			Bob Murphy		
1971	Jack Nicklaus	281	Billy Casper	283	PGA National GC, Palm Beach Gardens, FL
1972	Gary Player	281	Tommy Aaron	283	Oakland Hills CC, Birmingham, MI
			Jim Jamieson		
1973	Jack Nicklaus	277	Bruce Crampton	281	Canterbury GC, Cleveland, OH
1974	Lee Trevino	276	Jack Nicklaus	277	Tanglewood GC, Winston-Salem, NC
1975	Jack Nicklaus	276	Bruce Crampton	278	Firestone CC, Akron OH
1976	Dave Stockton	281	Ray Floyd	282	Congressional CC, Bethesda, MD
			Don January		
1977	*Lanny Wadkins	282	Gene Littler	282	Pebble Beach GL, Pebble Beach, CA
1978	*John Mahaffey	276	Jerry Pate	276	Oakmont CC, Oakmont, PA
			Tom Watson		
1979	*David Graham	272	Ben Crenshaw	272	Oakland Hills CC, Birmingham, MI
1980	Jack Nicklaus	274	Andy Bean	281	Oak Hill CC, Rochester NY
1981	Larry Nelson	273	Fuzzy Zoeller	277	Atlanta Athletic Club, Duluth, GA
1982	Raymond Floyd	272	Lanny Wadkins	275	Southern Hills CC, Tulsa, OK
1983	Hal Sutton	274	Jack Nicklaus	275	Riviera CC, Pacific Palisades, CA
1984	Lee Trevino	273	Gary Player	277	Shoal Creek, Birmingham, AL
			Lanny Wadkins		
1985	Hubert Green	278	Lee Trevino	280	Cherry Hills CC, Denver CO
1986	Bob Tway	276	Greg Norman	278	Inverness Club, Toledo OH
1987	*Larry Nelson	287	Lanny Wadkins	287	PGA National, Palm Beach Gardens, FL
1988	Jeff Sluman	272	Paul Azinger	275	Oak Tree GC, Edmond, OK
1989	Payne Stewart	276	Andy Bean	277	Kemper Lakes GC, Hawthorn Woods, IL
			Mike Reid		
			Curtis Strange		
1990	Wayne Grady	282	Fred Couples	285	Shoal Creek, Birmingham, AL
1991	John Daly	276	Bruce Lietzke	279	Crooked Stick GC, Carmel, IN
1992	Nick Price	278	John Cook	281	Bellerive CC, St. Louis, MO
			Jim Gallagher, Jr.		
			Gene Sauers		
			Nick Faldo		
1993	*Paul Azinger	272	Greg Norman	272	Inverness Club, Toledo, OH
1994	Nick Price	269	Corey Pavin	275	Southern Hills CC, Tulsa, OK
1995	*Steve Elkington	267	Colin Montgomerie	267	Riviera CC, Pacific Palisades, CA

Tournament Record: 267 -- Steve Elkington/Colin Montgomerie, 1995
18-Hole Record: 63 -- Bruce Crampton, 1975 (Firestone CC); Raymond Floyd, 1982 (Southern Hills CC); Gary Player, 1984 (Shoal Creek); Vijay Singh, 1993 (Inverness)

KEY: *=Playoff *Figures in parentheses indicate playoff scores*

1995 SPRINT INTERNATIONAL

Castle Pines GC, Castle Rock, CO **Purse: $1,500,000**
Par: 36-36--72 **Yards: 7,559** **August 17-20, 1995**

FORMAT: Modified Stableford scoring system with points awarded as follows: double eagle +8; eagle +5; birdie +2; par 0; bogey -1; double bogey or worse -3.

LEADERS: First Round--Ernie Els, with 17 points, led by three points over Greg Norman. **Second Round --**Mark Wiebe, with 23 points, led by four over David Duval and Lee Janzen. **Third Round--**Jay Haas, with 28 points, led by three over Duval and Janzen.

CUT: Starting field of 144 players cut to 72 after 36 holes. Paul Stankowski, Keith Fergus, Mike Reid, Steve Pate, Fred Funk, Chris Perry, Tommy Armour III, Dillard Pruitt, Jesper Parnevik, Retief Goosen and Marco Gortana played for seven spots. Stankowski, Armour and Reid were eliminated on the first extra hole. Pate was eliminated on the third extra hole. After 54 holes, the field was reduced to 24 players. There was no playoff.

PRO-AM: $10,000. Individual--Greg Norman, 12 points, $1,000. Team--Tom Purtzer, 43 points, $1,000.

WEATHER: Play was suspended on Thursday from 3:21 p.m. to 3:53 p.m. due to lightning in the area. The playoff on Friday was suspended at 7:45 p.m. due to darkness. The rest of the week was sunny and warm.

Lee Janzen: 10-9-6-9 +34 points $270,000

Player	Pos.	Scores	Points	Money
Ernie Els	2	17-0-7-9	+33	$162,000
Mark Wiebe	T3	8-15-(-1)-6	+28	$87,000
Jay Haas	T3	3-12-13-0	+28	$87,000
David Duval	5	10-9-6-2	+27	$60,000
Jose Maria Olazabal	T6	7-5-6-8	+26	$52,125
Tom Watson	T6	7-8-9-2	+26	$52,125
Greg Norman	T8	14-3-(-2)-9	+24	$43,500
Dan Forsman	T8	3-10-7-4	+24	$43,500
Davis Love III	T8	11-6-6-1	+24	$43,500
Kirk Triplett	T11	5-2-10-5	+22	$34,500
David Feherty	T11	2-11-7-2	+22	$34,500
Tom Kite	T11	11-(-1)-10-2	+22	$34,500
D.A. Weibring	T14	3-10-6-1	+20	$27,000
Craig Stadler	T14	11-(-4)-11-2	+20	$27,000
Tom Lehman	T14	8-7-7-(-2)	+20	$27,000
Mark Carnevale	T17	7-4-5-3	+19	$22,500
Glen Day	T17	5-2-9-3	+19	$22,500
Mike Hulbert	T17	1-10-10-(-2)	+19	$22,500
Wayne Westner	T20	5-6-5-0	+16	$18,750
Dicky Pride	T20	3-9-6-(-2)	+16	$18,750
Joey Sindelar	22	8-(-1)-9-(-2)	+14	$16,800
Kelly Gibson	23	5-2-9-(-4)	+12	$15,600
Joe Ozaki	24	6-6-5-(-6)	+11	$14,400
Brett Ogle	25	9-7-(-2)	+14	$13,200
Mark Calcavecchia	T26	(-5)-10-8	+13	$10,650
Michael Campbell	T26	(-1)-7-7	+13	$10,650
Russ Cochran	T26	4-3-6	+13	$10,650
Duffy Waldorf	T26	(-1)-8-6	+13	$10,650
Brad Bryant	T26	4-5-4	+13	$10,650
Howard Twitty	T26	6-4-3	+13	$10,650
Steve Stricker	T26	7-4-2	+13	$10,650
Jesper Parnevik	T33	(-3)-7-8	+12	$7,925
Keith Clearwater	T33	5-3-4	+12	$7,925
Paul Goydos	T33	3-6-3	+12	$7,925
Bob Lohr	T33	3-8-1	+12	$7,925
Doug Martin	T33	4-7-1	+12	$7,925
Lee Rinker	T33	9-4-(-1)	+12	$7,925
Larry Mize	T39	3-8-0	+11	$6,450
Scott Verplank	T39	2-9-0	+11	$6,450
Chip Beck	T39	2-10-(-1)	+11	$6,450
Patrick Burke	T42	3-2-5	+10	$4,608
Anthony Rodriguez	T42	0-5-5	+10	$4,608
Tom Purtzer	T42	(-3)-8-5	+10	$4,608
Michael Bradley	T42	2-4-4	+10	$4,608
Chris DiMarco	T42	5-1-4	+10	$4,608
Bob Tway	T42	10-(-3)-3	+10	$4,608
Bruce Lietzke	T42	5-2-3	+10	$4,608
Peter Senior	T42	8-0-2	+10	$4,608
Jim Furyk	T42	3-5-2	+10	$4,608
Dudley Hart	T42	8-7-(-5)	+10	$4,608
Craig Parry	52	2-4-3	+9	$3,600
John Cook	T53	5-1-2	+8	$3,510
Emlyn Aubrey	T53	7-6-(-5)	+8	$3,510
Retief Goosen	T55	0-4-3	+7	$3,360
Fred Funk	T55	3-1-3	+7	$3,360
Chris Perry	T55	(-5)-9-3	+7	$3,360
Neal Lancaster	T55	1-5-1	+7	$3,360
Roger Maltbie	T55	5-1-1	+7	$3,360
Jim Carter	T55	7-(-1)-1	+7	$3,360
Andrew Magee	T55	9-0-(-2)	+7	$3,360
Charlie Rymer	T62	6-0-0	+6	$3,180
Dave Barr	T62	(-1)-7-0	+6	$3,180
Steve Rintoul	T62	3-5-(-2)	+6	$3,180
Justin Leonard	T62	8-1-(-3)	+6	$3,180
Jerry Haas	T62	0-9-(-3)	+6	$3,180
Keith Fergus	T67	(-2)-6-(-1)	+3	$3,075
Mike Brisky	T67	6-(-1)-(-2)	+3	$3,075
Dillard Pruitt	69	3-1-(-2)	+2	$3,030
Mike Standly	70	3-2-(-4)	+1	$3,000
Skip Kendall	71	0-6-(-6)	0	$2,970
Marco Gortana	72	4-0-(-8)	-4	$2,940

The following players did not finish (C=cut, W=withdrew, D=disqualified)

C—John Adams, Fulton Allem, Robert Allenby, Billy Andrade, Tommy Armour III, Woody Austin, Ian Baker-Finch, Pat Bates, Ronnie Black, Jay Don Blake, Guy Boros, Bill Britton, Billy Ray Brown, Bart Bryant, Bob Burns, Curt Byrum, Tom Byrum, Brandel Chamblee, Brian Claar, Jay Delsing, Clark Dennis, Ed Dougherty, David Edwards, Joel Edwards, Brad Faxon, Rick Fehr, Robin Freeman, Bob Gilder, Anthony Gilligan, Steve Gotsche, Ken Green, Scott Gump, Gary Hallberg, Donnie Hammond, J.P. Hayes, Mike Heinen, Brian Henninger, Ed Humenik, John Huston, Peter Jacobsen, Brandt Jobe, Steve Jones, Brian Kamm, Jonathan Kaye, Greg Kraft, Steve Lowery, Jim McGovern, Phil Mickelson, Yoshinori Mizumaki, Gary Nicklaus, Jack Nicklaus, Mark O'Meara, Steve Pate, Dennis Paulson, Dan Pohl, Mike Reid, Eduardo Romero, Gene Sauers, Tony Sills, Scott Simpson, Mike Springer, Paul Stankowski, Dave Stockton, Jr., Hal Sutton, Harry Taylor, Doug Tewell, Ted Tryba, Tray Tyner, Omar Uresti, Grant Waite, John Wilson, Richard Zokol.

THE SPRINT INTERNATIONAL

TOURNAMENT HISTORY

Year	Winner	Score	Runner-up	Location	Par/Yards
1986	Ken Green	Plus 12	Bernhard Langer	Castle Pines GC, Castle Rock, CO	72/7559
1987	John Cook	Plus 11	Ken Green	Castle Pines GC, Castle Rock, CO	72/7559
1988	Joey Sindelar	Plus 17	Steve Pate Dan Pohl	Castle Pines GC, Castle Rock, CO	72/7559
1989	Greg Norman	Plus 13	Clarence Rose	Castle Pines GC, Castle Rock, CO	72/7559
1990	Davis Love III	Plus 14	Steve Pate Eduardo Romero Peter Senior	Castle Pines GC, Castle Rock, CO	72/7559
1991	Jose Maria Olazabal	Plus 10	Ian Baker-Finch Scott Gump Bob Lohr	Castle Pines GC, Castle Rock, CO	72/7559
1992	Brad Faxon	Plus 14	Lee Janzen	Castle Pines GC, Castle Rock, CO	72/7559
1993	Phil Mickelson	Plus 45	Mark Calcavecchia	Castle Pines GC, Castle Rock, CO	72/7559
THE SPRINT INTERNATIONAL					
1994	*Steve Lowery	Plus 35	Rick Fehr	Castle Pines GC, Castle Rock, CO	72/7559
1995	Lee Janzen	Plus 34	Ernie Els	Castle Pines GC, Castle Rock, CO	72/7559

(Note: Prior to 1993, winning score was for fourth round only. Beginning in 1993, winning score was total for four rounds.)

Tournament Record: 45 points -- Phil Mickelson, 1993
Current Course Record: 20 points -- Greg Whisman, 1992

KEY: *=Playoff

1995 NEC WORLD SERIES OF GOLF

Firestone CC (South Course), Akron, OH **Purse: $2,000,000**
Par: 35-35--70 **Yards: 7,149** **August 24-27, 1995**

LEADERS: First Round--Jim Gallagher, Jr., with a 4-under-par 66, led by one over Payne Stewart. **Second Round--**Gallagher, at 3-under par 137, led by one over Mike Sullivan, Billy Mayfair and defending champion Jose Maria Olazabal. **Third Round--**Vijay Singh, at 5-under-par 205, led by two over Olazabal and Gallagher.

PRO-AM: $10,000. Individual--Davis Love III, 65, $1,000. Team--Nick Price, Peter Jacobsen, 55, $900 each.

WEATHER: Warm and pleasant every day.

Winner: Greg Norman 73-68-70-67 278 $360,000.00

(Won playoff with birdie-3 on first extra hole)

Player	Pos.	Scores	Total	Money
Billy Mayfair	T 2	70-68-70-70	278	$176,000.00
Nick Price	T 2	72-69-69-68	278	$176,000.00
Phil Mickelson	T 4	69-74-70-66	279	$88,000.00
Vijay Singh	T 4	71-69-65-74	279	$88,000.00
Fred Couples	T 6	68-76-68-68	280	$69,500.00
Jim Gallagher, Jr.	T 6	66-71-70-73	280	$69,500.00
Mike Sullivan	8	71-67-74-69	281	$62,000.00
Jose Maria Olazabal	T 9	68-70-69-75	282	$56,000.00
Loren Roberts	T 9	72-74-70-66	282	$56,000.00
Bob Tway	11	73-72-68-70	283	$50,000.00
Nick Faldo	T12	71-71-70-72	284	$39,200.00
Davis Love III	T12	70-73-74-67	284	$39,200.00
Mark McCumber	T12	68-76-68-72	284	$39,200.00
Ted Tryba	T12	68-72-73-71	284	$39,200.00
Tom Lehman	T12	68-75-69-72	284	$39,200.00
Peter Jacobsen	17	74-68-72-71	285	$32,000.00
Fred Funk	T18	75-72-66-73	286	$29,000.00
Lee Janzen	T18	71-71-72-72	286	$29,000.00
Robert Allenby	T20	72-73-67-75	287	$22,480.00
Mark O'Meara	T20	72-74-70-71	287	$22,480.00
Corey Pavin	T20	71-73-66-77	287	$22,480.00
Mike Springer	T20	70-75-73-69	287	$22,480.00

Player	Pos.	Scores	Total	Money
Brian Watts	T20	72-73-73-69	287	$22,480.00
Mark Calcavecchia	T25	69-72-74-73	288	$17,100.00
Bruce Lietzke	T25	71-77-73-67	288	$17,100.00
Payne Stewart	T25	67-74-75-72	288	$17,100.00
Bob Estes	T28	71-75-70-73	289	$16,000.00
Ernie Els	T28	73-67-73-76	289	$16,000.00
John Daly	30	78-73-71-68	290	$15,700.00
Kenny Perry	31	70-76-74-72	292	$15,600.00
Rick Fehr	32	75-74-75-69	293	$15,500.00
Ed Dougherty	T33	74-71-75-74	294	$15,350.00
Anthony Gilligan	T33	74-75-73-72	294	$15,350.00
Andrew Coltart	T35	79-78-67-71	295	$15,150.00
Robert Gamez	T35	70-74-76-75	295	$15,150.00
Woody Austin	T37	68-79-76-73	296	$14,900.00
Retief Goosen	T37	73-79-68-76	296	$14,900.00
Hisayuki Sasaki	T37	77-73-69-77	296	$14,900.00
Eiji Mizoguchi	T40	77-77-72-71	297	$14,650.00
Ron Whittaker	T40	70-78-71-78	297	$14,650.00
Ben Crenshaw	T42	79-72-75-72	298	$14,450.00
Peter Senior	T42	72-75-75-76	298	$14,450.00
John Morse	44	76-77-79-71	303	$14,300.00

The following players did not finish (C=cut, W=withdrew, D=disqualified)

W—228- Wayne Riley,**155-** Sammy Rachels. **D—211-** Steve Elkington.

NEC WORLD SERIES OF GOLF

TOURNAMENT HISTORY

From 1962 through 1975, the World Series of Golf was played as a four-man, 36-hole exhibition. All monies won in the tournament were unofficial. The winners in those years (with winning totals in parentheses):

1962—Jack Nicklaus (135)
1963—Jack Nicklaus (140)
1964—Tony Lema (138)
1965—Gary Player (139)
1966—Gene Littler (143)
1967—Jack Nicklaus (144)
1968—Gary Player (143)
1969—Orville Moody (141)
1970—Jack Nicklaus (136)
1971—Charles Coody (141)
1972—Gary Player (142)
1973—Tom Weiskopf (137)
1974—Lee Trevino (139)
1975—Tom Watson (140)

Year	Winner	Score	Runner-up	Score	Location	Par/Yards
WORLD SERIES OF GOLF						
1976	Jack Nicklaus	275	Hale Irwin	279	Firestone CC (South Course), Akron, OH	70/7149
1977	Lanny Wadkins	267	Hale Irwin Tom Weiskopf	272	Firestone CC (South Course), Akron, OH	70/7149
1978	*Gil Morgan (Won playoff with par on first extra hole)	278	Hubert Green	278	Firestone CC (South Course), Akron, OH	70/7149
1979	Lon Hinkle	272	Larry Nelson Bill Rogers Lee Trevino	273	Firestone CC (South Course), Akron, OH	70/7149
1980	Tom Watson	270	Ray Floyd	272	Firestone CC (South Course), Akron, OH	70/7149
1981	Bill Rogers	275	Tom Kite	276	Firestone CC (South Course), Akron, OH	70/7149
1982	*Craig Stadler (Won playoff with par on fourth extra hole)	278	Ray Floyd	278	Firestone CC (South Course), Akron, OH	70/7149
1983	Nick Price	270	Jack Nicklaus	274	Firestone CC (South Course), Akron, OH	70/7149
NEC WORLD SERIES OF GOLF						
1984	Denis Watson	271	Bruce Lietzke	273	Firestone CC (South Course), Akron, OH	70/7149
1985	Roger Maltbie	268	Denis Watson	272	Firestone CC (South Course), Akron, OH	70/7149
1986	Dan Pohl	277	Lanny Wadkins	278	Firestone CC (South Course), Akron, OH	70/7149
1987	Curtis Strange	275	Fulton Allem	278	Firestone CC (South Course), Akron, OH	70/7149
1988	*Mike Reid (Won playoff with par on first extra hole)	275	Tom Watson	275	Firestone CC (South Course), Akron, OH	70/7149
1989	*David Frost (Won playoff with par on second extra hole)	276	Ben Crenshaw	276	Firestone CC (South Course), Akron, OH	70/7149
1990	Jose Maria Olazabal	262	Lanny Wadkins	274	Firestone CC (South Course), Akron, OH	70/7149
1991	*Tom Purtzer (Won playoff with par on second extra hole)	279	Jim Gallagher, Jr. Davis Love III	279	Firestone CC (South Course), Akron, OH	70/7149
1992	Craig Stadler	273	Corey Pavin	274	Firestone CC (South Course), Akron, OH	70/7149
1993	Fulton Allem	270	Jim Gallagher, Jr. Nick Price Craig Stadler	275	Firestone CC (South Course), Akron, OH	70/7149
1994	Jose Maria Olazabal	269	Scott Hoch	270	Firestone CC (North Course), Akron, OH	70/6918
1995	*Greg Norman (Won playoff with birdie on first extra hole)	278	Billy Mayfair Nick Price	278	Firestone CC (South Course), Akron, OH	70/7149

Tournament Record: 262 -- Jose Maria Olazabal, 1990
Current Course Record: 61 -- Jose Maria Olazabal, 1990

KEY: *=Playoff

NEC WORLD SERIES OF GOLF

NEC WORLD SERIES OF GOLF FIRESTONE C.C.

Eligibility Requirements for the 1996 NEC World Series of Golf

1) The defending champion, Greg Norman
2) Winner, 1996 PLAYERS Championship
3) Winner, 1996 Masters Tournament
4) Winner, 1996 United States Open
5) Winner, 1996 British Open
6) Winner, 1996 PGA Championship
7) Winner, 1995 PGA National Club Pro Championship
8) All winners of PGA TOUR cosponsored events since the preceding year's WSOG.
9) Winners of the following overseas events:

PGA European Tour

a. Volvo European PGA Championship
b. Johnnie Walker World Championship
c. Scottish Open
d. Collingtree British Masters
e. Trophee Lancome
f. Volvo Masters
g. Mercedes German Masters
h. Toyota World Match Play
i. Murphy's Irish Open
j. Smurfit European Open

PGA Tour of Japan

a. Visa Taiheyo Club Masters
b. Dunlop Phoenix
c. Bridgestone Open
d. Chunichi Crowns
e. Japan Open
f. ANA Open
g. Casio World Open
h. Asahi Beer/Golf Digest Open
i. Japan PGA Championship
j. Japan Series of Golf
k. Phillip Morris Championship

Australasian PGA Tour

a. Microsoft Australian Masters
b. Heineken Australian Open
c. Greg Norman's Holden Classic
d. Johnny Walker Asian Championship

South African Tour

a. Sun City $1,000,000 Challenge
b. FNB Players Championship
c. Dunhill South African PGA Championship
d. Philips South African Open

10) Individual winner, 1995 World Cup

1995 GREATER MILWAUKEE OPEN

Brown Deer Park GC, Milwaukee, WI **Purse: $1,000,000**
Par: 35-36--71 **Yards: 6,739** **August 31-September 3, 1995**

LEADERS: First Round--Richard Zokol shot a 6-under-par 65 and led Billy Mayfair by one stroke. **Second Round--**Zokol and Marco Dawson shared the lead at 7-under-par 135, one stroke ahead of Robert Gamez. **Third Round--**Scott Hoch, at 9-under-par 204, led Dawson and Lee Rinker by one stroke.

CUT: 71 players at 1-over-par 143.

PRO-AM: Front nine: Individual--Tom Kite and Steve Stricker, 31, $431.25 each. Team--Tom Kite, 26, $450. Back nine: Individual--Justin Leonard, 31, $450. Team--Gary Hallberg, 25, $450.

WEATHER: Sunny and breezy Thursday and Friday. Less wind Saturday and Sunday.

Winner: Scott Hoch 68-71-65-65 269 $180,000.00

Player	Pos.	Scores	Total	Money
Marco Dawson	2	70-65-70-67	272	$108,000.00
Joe Acosta, Jr.	T 3	68-69-69-68	274	$52,000.00
Jim Gallagher, Jr.	T 3	68-71-68-67	274	$52,000.00
Jeff Sluman	T 3	72-71-65-66	274	$52,000.00
Steve Lowery	T 6	70-69-71-65	275	$32,375.00
Lee Rinker	T 6	70-68-67-70	275	$32,375.00
Joey Sindelar	T 6	74-68-68-65	275	$32,375.00
Duffy Waldorf	T 6	69-73-65-68	275	$32,375.00
Bob Estes	T10	71-70-71-64	276	$22,166.67
Jay Haas	T10	74-68-67-67	276	$22,166.67
Andrew Magee	T10	69-72-69-66	276	$22,166.67
Mark O'Meara	T10	69-71-68-68	276	$22,166.67
Robert Gamez	T10	67-69-70-70	276	$22,166.66
D.A. Weibring	T10	70-69-71-66	276	$22,166.66
Ted Schulz	16	69-72-68-68	277	$17,000.00
Lennie Clements	T17	70-72-69-67	278	$11,800.00
Ed Fiori	T17	70-70-69-69	278	$11,800.00
Nolan Henke	T17	75-66-69-68	278	$11,800.00
Mike Hulbert	T17	69-73-67-69	278	$11,800.00
Pete Jordan	T17	68-69-71-70	278	$11,800.00
Justin Leonard	T17	71-70-72-65	278	$11,800.00
Steve Pate	T17	70-68-69-71	278	$11,800.00
Curtis Strange	T17	71-66-75-66	278	$11,800.00
Richard Zokol	T17	65-70-73-70	278	$11,800.00
Howard Twitty	T17	71-67-71-69	278	$11,800.00
Russ Cochran	T27	74-68-71-66	279	$6,800.00
Greg Kraft	T27	70-72-65-72	279	$6,800.00
Tom Purtzer	T27	73-69-65-72	279	$6,800.00
Loren Roberts	T27	72-69-71-67	279	$6,800.00
Ray Stewart	T27	68-71-68-72	279	$6,800.00
Hal Sutton	T27	68-71-70-70	279	$6,800.00
Dicky Thompson	T27	74-67-67-71	279	$6,800.00
Tom Byrum	T34	70-72-69-69	280	$4,733.34
John Huston	T34	72-69-73-66	280	$4,733.34
J.L. Lewis	T34	72-69-66-73	280	$4,733.34
Dave Barr	T34	73-70-71-66	280	$4,733.33
Lee Janzen	T34	70-72-67-71	280	$4,733.33
Jerry Kelly	T34	72-68-71-69	280	$4,733.33
Bob Lohr	T34	69-71-67-73	280	$4,733.33
Billy Mayfair	T34	66-72-68-74	280	$4,733.33
Jerry Pate	T34	70-70-71-69	280	$4,733.33
Phil Blackmar	T43	73-70-73-65	281	$3,400.00
Patrick Burke	T43	73-68-73-67	281	$3,400.00
Don Pooley	T43	68-71-71-71	281	$3,400.00
Dave Rummells	T43	68-73-74-66	281	$3,400.00
Brian Kamm	T47	69-72-70-71	282	$2,568.58
Bart Bryant	T47	72-70-70-70	282	$2,568.57
Bruce Fleisher	T47	74-68-70-70	282	$2,568.57
Scott Gump	T47	71-71-70-70	282	$2,568.57
Wayne Levi	T47	71-72-68-71	282	$2,568.57
Doug Martin	T47	69-73-70-70	282	$2,568.57
Tom Watson	T47	71-72-72-67	282	$2,568.57
Woody Austin	T54	70-72-72-69	283	$2,290.00
Paul Goydos	T54	71-72-72-68	283	$2,290.00
John Morse	T54	71-70-75-67	283	$2,290.00
Don Reese	T54	71-70-70-72	283	$2,290.00
Tommy Armour III	T58	69-71-74-70	284	$2,200.00
Bill Britton	T58	69-74-72-69	284	$2,200.00
Kawika Cotner	T58	69-73-72-70	284	$2,200.00
Robin Freeman	T58	73-70-70-71	284	$2,200.00
Jim Furyk	T58	71-72-72-69	284	$2,200.00
Jay Don Blake	T63	72-70-72-71	285	$2,110.00
Gary Hallberg	T63	67-74-74-70	285	$2,110.00
Ed Humenik	T63	71-67-76-71	285	$2,110.00
Craig Parry	T63	69-72-74-70	285	$2,110.00
John Daly	T67	67-75-76-68	286	$2,050.00
Neal Lancaster	T67	72-71-76-67	286	$2,050.00
Kelly Gibson	T69	73-69-70-75	287	$2,010.00
Dave Stockton, Jr.	T69	69-70-72-76	287	$2,010.00
Skip Kendall	71	72-71-77-71	291	$1,980.00

The following players did not finish (C=cut, W=withdrew, D=disqualified)

C—144- Michael Allen, Emlyn Aubrey, Ronnie Black, Mark Brooks, Billy Ray Brown, Brandel Chamblee, Brian Claar, Glen Day, Jay Delsing, Ed Dougherty, Joel Edwards, Steve Gotsche, Ryan Howison, Tom Kite, Dick Mast, Andy North, David Ogrin, Carl Paulson, Charlie Rymer, Mike Smith, Paul Stankowski, Harry Taylor, John Wilson. **145-** Bob Burns, Andrew Coltart, Bob Gilder, Stephen Keppler, Tim Loustalot, Jim McGovern, Dan Pohl, Steve Rintoul, Doug Tewell. **146-** Clark Burroughs, Mike Donald, Gil Morgan, Michael Muranyi, David Peoples, Mike Small, Ed Terasa, Dennis Tiziani, Tray Tyner, Bruce Vaughan. **147-** Brad Bryant, Mark Carnevale, John Connelly, Keith Fergus, Scott Ford, Jerry Haas, Mark Hensby, Bill Kratzert, Dennis Paulson, Jim Schuman, Tony Sills, Steve Stricker, Omar Uresti, Jay Williamson. **148-** Pat Bates, J.P. Hayes, Dicky Pride, Tommy Tolles, Bobby Wadkins. **149-** Mark Calcavecchia, Clark Dennis, Chris DiMarco, David Feherty, Chris Perry, Bill Porter, Mario Tiziani. **150-** Jim Carter, Steve Hart, Tom Hearn, Jonathan Kaye, Dillard Pruitt, Mike Springer, Mark Wiebe, Mark Wurtz. **151-** Mike Brisky, Dan Forsman, Scott McCarron. **157-** Jeff Leonard. **161-** Charlie Brown. **W—144-** Brad Faxon, **153-** Fulton Allem, **82-** Bill Brodell. **D— 78-** Jeff Woodland.

GREATER MILWAUKEE OPEN
presented by Lite Beer

TOURNAMENT HISTORY

Year	Winner	Score	Runner-up	Score	Location	Par/Yards
GREATER MILWAUKEE OPEN						
1968	Dave Stockton	275	Sam Snead	279	Northshore CC, Mequon, WI	71/7075
1969	Ken Still	277	Gary Player	279	Northshore CC, Mequon, WI	71/7075
1970	Deane Beman	276	Richard Crawford	279	Northshore CC, Mequon, WI	71/7075
			Ted Hayes			
			Don Massengale			
1971	Dave Eichelberger	270	Ralph Johnston	271	Tripoli GC, Milwaukee, WI	71/6514
			Bob Shaw			
1972	Jim Colbert	271	Bud Allin	272	Tripoli GC, Milwaukee, WI	71/6514
			Chuck Courtney			
			George Johnson			
			Grier Jones			
1973	Dave Stockton	276	Homero Blancas	277	Tuckaway CC, Franklin, WI	72/7030
			Hubert Green			
1974	Ed Sneed	276	Grier Jones	280	Tuckaway CC, Franklin, WI	72/7030
1975	Art Wall	271	Gary McCord	272	Tuckaway CC, Franklin, WI	72/7030
1976	Dave Hill	270	John Jacobs	273	Tuckaway CC, Franklin, WI	72/7030
1977	Dave Eichelberger	278	Morris Hatalsky	280	Tuckaway CC, Franklin, WI	72/7030
			Gary McCord			
			Mike Morley			
1978	*Lee Elder	275	Lee Trevino	275	Tuckaway CC, Franklin, WI	72/7030
1979	Calvin Peete	269	Victor Regalado	274	Tuckaway CC, Franklin, WI	72/7030
			Jim Simons			
			Lee Trevino			
1980	Bill Kratzert	266	Howard Twitty	270	Tuckaway CC, Franklin, WI	72/7030
1981	Jay Haas	274	Chi Chi Rodriguez	277	Tuckaway CC, Franklin, WI	72/7030
1982	Calvin Peete	274	Victor Regalado	276	Tuckaway CC, Franklin, WI	72/7030
1983	*Morris Hatalsky	275	George Cadle	275	Tuckaway CC, Franklin, WI	72/7030
1984	Mark O'Meara	272	Tom Watson	277	Tuckaway CC, Franklin, WI	72/7030
1985	Jim Thorpe	274	Jack Nicklaus	277	Tuckaway CC, Franklin, WI	72/7030
1986	*Corey Pavin	272	Dave Barr	272	Tuckaway CC, Franklin, WI	72/7030
1987	Gary Hallberg	269	Wayne Levi	271	Tuckaway CC, Franklin, WI	72/7030
			Robert Wrenn			
1988	Ken Green	268	Mark Calcavecchia	274	Tuckaway CC, Franklin, WI	72/7030
			Jim Gallagher, Jr.			
			Donnie Hammond			
			Dan Pohl			
1989	Greg Norman	269	Andy Bean	272	Tuckaway CC, Franklin, WI	72/7030
1990	*Jim Gallagher, Jr.	271	Ed Dougherty	271	Tuckaway CC, Franklin, WI	72/7030
			Billy Mayfair			
1991	Mark Brooks	270	Robert Gamez	271	Tuckaway CC, Franklin, WI	72/7030
1992	Richard Zokol	269	Dick Mast	271	Tuckaway CC, Franklin, WI	72/7030
1993	*Billy Mayfair	270	Mark Calcavecchia	270	Tuckaway CC, Franklin, WI	72/7030
			Ted Schulz			
1994	Mike Springer	268	Loren Roberts	269	Brown Deer Park GC, Milwaukee, WI	71/6716
1995	Scott Hoch	269	Marco Dawson	272	Brown Deer Park GC, Milwaukee, WI	71/6716

Tournament Record: 266 -- Bill Kratzert, 1980 (Tuckaway CC)
Current Course Record: 63 -- Loren Roberts, 1994

KEY: *=Playoff

1995 BELL CANADIAN OPEN

Glen Abbey GC, Oakville, Ontario, Canada **Purse: $1,300,000**
Par: 35-37--72 **Yards: 7,112** **September 7-10, 1995**

LEADERS: First Round--Russ Cochran, at 6-under-par 66, led by one over Grant Waite. **Second Round --**Bob Lohr, at 9-under-par 135, led by one over Andrew Magee and by two over Jim Gallagher, Jr. **Third Round--**Lohr, at 12-under-par 204, led Mark O'Meara by two and four players by five.

CUT: 81 players at 3-over-par 147.

PRO-AM: $7,500. Individual--Lee Janzen, Paul Azinger, 67, $675 each. Team--Dave Barr, 53, $750.

WEATHER: Wet, cold and windy on Thursday. Strong winds early Friday. Cool and clear the remainder of the week.

Winner: Mark O'Meara 72-67-68-67 274 $234,000.00

(Won playoff with par-5 on first extra hole)

Player	Pos	Scores	Total	Money
Bob Lohr	2	68-67-69-70	274	$140,400.00
Nick Price	3	72-69-68-68	277	$88,400.00
Hal Sutton	4	69-72-68-69	278	$62,400.00
Bill Glasson	T 5	68-74-68-70	280	$49,400.00
Andrew Magee	T 5	68-68-73-71	280	$49,400.00
Tony Sills	7	72-68-73-69	282	$43,550.00
Scott Dunlap	8	71-67-73-72	283	$40,300.00
Brian Kamm	T 9	74-71-70-69	284	$36,400.00
Bob Tway	T 9	69-72-68-75	284	$36,400.00
Dan Forsman	T11	69-72-69-75	285	$31,200.00
John Wilson	T11	76-67-68-74	285	$31,200.00
J.P. Hayes	13	68-71-74-73	286	$27,300.00
Phil Blackmar	T14	70-73-74-70	287	$20,150.00
Jay Don Blake	T14	74-73-67-73	287	$20,150.00
Mark Brooks	T14	68-73-69-77	287	$20,150.00
Brad Bryant	T14	71-71-72-73	287	$20,150.00
Kawika Cotner	T14	70-71-74-72	287	$20,150.00
David Frost	T14	72-71-72-72	287	$20,150.00
Joey Sindelar	T14	75-67-72-73	287	$20,150.00
Bobby Wadkins	T14	69-76-71-71	287	$20,150.00
Gary Hallberg	T22	68-74-70-76	288	$14,040.00
Mark McCumber	T22	72-75-68-73	288	$14,040.00
Jay Delsing	T24	72-73-71-73	289	$10,790.00
Trevor Dodds	T24	72-73-72-72	289	$10,790.00
Bruce Fleisher	T24	72-69-72-76	289	$10,790.00
Jim Gallagher, Jr.	T24	69-68-75-77	289	$10,790.00
Grant Waite	T24	67-72-77-73	289	$10,790.00
Brandel Chamblee	T29	72-71-71-76	290	$8,450.00
Justin Leonard	T29	70-72-75-73	290	$8,450.00
Scott McCarron	T29	72-75-70-73	290	$8,450.00
John Morse	T29	70-70-71-79	290	$8,450.00
Tommy Tolles	T29	74-67-76-73	290	$8,450.00
Fred Couples	T34	71-71-72-77	291	$6,857.50
Dudley Hart	T34	71-76-68-76	291	$6,857.50
Billy Mayfair	T34	72-73-70-76	291	$6,857.50
Dave Stockton, Jr.	T34	72-75-71-73	291	$6,857.50
Pat Bates	T38	73-73-69-77	292	$5,330.00
Scott Gump	T38	70-71-71-80	292	$5,330.00
Blaine McCallister	T38	70-70-72-80	292	$5,330.00
David Ogrin	T38	69-75-69-79	292	$5,330.00
Craig Parry	T38	74-70-73-75	292	$5,330.00
Mike Springer	T38	74-73-73-72	292	$5,330.00
Scott Verplank	T38	72-72-77-71	292	$5,330.00
Joe Acosta, Jr.	T45	74-70-71-78	293	$3,471.00
Curt Byrum	T45	73-73-75-72	293	$3,471.00
Mark Calcavecchia	T45	74-71-71-77	293	$3,471.00
Brian Claar	T45	71-74-72-76	293	$3,471.00
Glen Day	T45	72-75-72-74	293	$3,471.00
Steve Lowery	T45	69-77-74-73	293	$3,471.00
Jim McGovern	T45	74-72-71-76	293	$3,471.00
Jerry Pate	T45	74-69-73-77	293	$3,471.00
Dennis Paulson	T45	69-70-76-78	293	$3,471.00
Bruce Vaughan	T45	73-69-74-77	293	$3,471.00
Bart Bryant	T55	74-72-75-73	294	$2,938.00
Jim Carter	T55	71-74-73-76	294	$2,938.00
Russ Cochran	T55	66-80-69-79	294	$2,938.00
Charlie Rymer	T55	70-77-72-75	294	$2,938.00
D.A. Weibring	T55	75-72-70-77	294	$2,938.00
Mike Brisky	60	75-71-73-76	295	$2,860.00
Joel Edwards	T61	71-73-77-75	296	$2,782.00
Greg Kraft	T61	72-72-77-75	296	$2,782.00
Neal Lancaster	T61	75-72-74-75	296	$2,782.00
Mike Reid	T61	78-69-74-75	296	$2,782.00
Mike Smith	T61	76-69-74-77	296	$2,782.00
Dicky Pride	66	70-75-71-81	297	$2,704.00
Woody Austin	T67	72-73-72-81	298	$2,652.00
Lee Rinker	T67	70-75-75-78	298	$2,652.00
Mark Wiebe	T67	74-73-73-78	298	$2,652.00
Keith Fergus	T70	70-72-75-82	299	$2,587.00
Steve Jones	T70	70-75-73-81	299	$2,587.00
Steve Rintoul	T72	74-71-79-76	300	$2,535.00
Mike Sullivan	T72	70-76-78-76	300	$2,535.00
John Huston	T74	71-74-73-83	301	$2,483.00
Sandy Lyle	T74	74-72-77-78	301	$2,483.00
David Feherty	76	71-75-75-81	302	$2,444.00
Ed Dougherty	T77	72-73-81-77	303	$2,392.00
Retief Goosen	T77	73-74-79-77	303	$2,392.00
Paul Stankowski	T77	73-74-76-80	303	$2,392.00
Jay Williamson	80	78-69-75-82	304	$2,340.00
Ray Freeman	81	73-74-78-83	308	$2,314.00

The following players did not finish:

C—148-John Adams, Nick Goetze, Mike Hulbert, Bruce Lietzke, John Mahaffey, Jack Nicklaus, Steve Pate, Craig Stadler, Greg Twiggs. **149-** Billy Andrade, Dave Barr, Ronnie Black, Billy Ray Brown, Patrick Burke, Marco Dawson, Paul Goydos, Lee Janzen, J.L. Lewis, Tim Loustalot, Bill Porter, Jeff Sluman, Payne Stewart, Curtis Strange, Mike Weir. **150-**Paul Azinger, Chip Beck, Guy Boros, Mark Carnevale, Don Reese, Mike Standly, Howard Twitty. **151-**Emlyn Aubrey, Clark Dennis, Steve Gotsche, Dan Halldorson, Brian Henninger, Ed Humenik, Carl Paulson, Steve Stricker, Omar Uresti. **152-**Tommy Armour III, Michael Bradley, Bob Gilder, Tom Hearn, Ryan Howison, Dicky Thompson, Mark Wurtz, Richard Zokol. **153-**Fulton Allem, Kelly Gibson, Ken Green, Ian Hutchings, Skip Kendall, Ian Leggatt, Ray Stewart. **154-**Jim Furyk, Stu Hamilton. **155-**Bob Burns, David Edwards, Jeff Leonard, Davidson Matyczuk. **156-**Bradley Hughes. **157-**Chris DiMarco, Jonathan Kaye, Jean-Louis Lamarre. **159-**Remi Bouchard, Tray Tyner. **163-**Garrett Willis. **164-**Doug Warner. **168-** Edward Reevey. **W—155-**Wayne Levi, **163-**Ted Tryba, **76-**Joey Rassett, **77-**Chris Perry, **80-**Keith Clearwater.

BELL CANADIAN OPEN

TOURNAMENT HISTORY

Year	Winner	Score	Runner-up	Score	Location	Par/Yards
BELL CANADIAN OPEN						
1904	John H. Oke	156	Percy Barrett	158	Royal Montreal GC, Montreal, Quebec	N/A
1905	George Cumming	148	Percy Barrett	151	Toronto GC, Toronto, Ontario	N/A
1906	Charles Murray	170	George Cumming	171	Royal Ottawa GC, Ottawa, Ontario	N/A
			Alex Robertson			
			Tom Reith			
1907	Percy Barrett	306	George Cumming	308	Lambton GC, Toronto, Ontario	N/A
1908	Albert Murray	300	George Sargent	304	Royal Montreal GC, Montreal, Quebec	N/A
1909	Karl Keffer	309	George Cumming	312	Toronto GC, Toronto, Ontario	N/A
1910	Daniel Kenny	303	George S. Lyon	307	Lambton GC, Toronto, Ontario	70/N/A
1911	Charles Murray	314	Davie Black	316	Royal Ottawa GC, Ottawa, Ontario	N/A
1912	George Sargent	299	James M. Barnes	302	Rosedale GC, Toronto, Ontario	N/A
1913	Albert Murray	295	Nicol Thompson	301	Royal Montreal GC, Montreal, Quebec	N/A
			Jack Burke, Sr.			
1914	Karl Keffer	300	George Cumming	301	Toronto GC, Toronto, Ontario	N/A
1915—1918 No Tournaments						
1919	J. Douglas Edgar	278	James Barnes	294	Hamilton GC, Hamilton, Ontario	N/A
			Robert T. Jones, Jr.			
			Karl Keffer			
1920	*J. Douglas Edgar	298	Tommy Armour	298	Rivermead GC, Ottawa, Ontario	N/A
			Charles R. Murray			
1921	W. H. Trovinger	293	Mike Brady	296	Toronto GC, Toronto, Ontario	N/A
1922	Al Watrous	303	Tom Kerrigan	304	Mt. Bruno GC, Montreal, Quebec	72/6643
1923	C. W. Hackney	295	Tom Kerrigan	300	Lakeview CG, Toronto, Ontario	N/A
1924	Leo Diegel	285	Gene Sarazen	287	Mt. Bruno GC, Montreal, Quebec	72/6643
1925	Leo Diegel	295	Mike Brady	297	Lambton GC, Toronto, Ontario	N/A
1926	Mac Smith	283	Gene Sarazen	286	Royal Montreal GC, Montreal, Quebec	N/A
1927	Tommy Armour	288	Macdonald Smith	289	Toronto GC, Toronto, Ontario	N/A
1928	Leo Diegel	282	Archie Compston	284	Rosedale GC, Toronto, Ontario	N/A
			Walter Hagen			
			Macdonald Smith			
1929	Leo Diegel	274	Tommy Armour	277	Kanawaki GC, Montreal, Quebec	N/A
1930	*Tommy Armour	273	Leo Diegel	277	Hamilton GC, Hamilton, Ontario	N/A
1931	*Walter Hagen	292	Percy Alliss	282	Mississaugua G & CC, Toronto, Ontario	N/A
1932	Harry Cooper	290	Al Watrous	293	Ottawa Hunt Club, Ottawa, Ontario	N/A
1933	Joe Kirkwood	282	Harry Cooper	290	Royal York CG, Toronto, Ontario	N/A
			Lex Robson			
1934	Tommy Armour	287	Ky Laffoon	289	Lakeview CG, Toronto, Ontario	N/A
1935	Gene Kunes	280	Victor Ghezzi	282	Summerlea GC, Montreal, Quebec	N/A
1936	Lawson Little	271	Jimmy Thomson	279	St. Andrews GC, Toronto, Ontario	70/N/A
1937	Harry Cooper	285	Ralph Guldahl	287	St. Andrews GC, Toronto, Ontario	70/N/A
1938	*Sam Snead	277	Harry Cooper	277	Mississaugua G&CC, Toronto, Ontario	N/A
1939	Harold McSpaden	282	Ralph Guldahl	287	Riverside GC, St. John, New Brunswick	70/6231
1940	*Sam Snead	281	Harold McSpaden	281	Scarborough G&CC, Toronto, Ontario	/6685
1941	Sam Snead	274	Bob Gray, Jr.	276	Lambton GC, Toronto, Ontario	70/N/A
1942	Craig Wood	275	Mike Turnesa	279	Mississaugua G&CC, Toronto, Ontario	N/A
1943-1944	No Tournaments					
1945	Byron Nelson	280	Herman Barron	284	Thornhill GC, Toronto, Ontario	N/A
1946	*George Fazio	278	Dick Metz	278	Beaconsfield GC, Montreal, Quebec	N/A
1947	Bobby Locke	268	Ed Oliver	270	Scarborough G&CC, Toronto, Ontario	N/A
1948	C. W. Congdon	280	Victor Ghezzi	283	Shaughnessy Heights GC, Vancouver, B.C.	N/A
			Ky Laffoon			
			Dick Metz			
1949	Dutch Harrison	271	Jim Ferrier	275	St. Georges G&CC, Toronto, Ontario	N/A
1950	Jim Ferrier	271	Ted Kroll	274	Royal Montreal GC, Montreal, Quebec	N/A
1951	Jim Ferrier	273	Fred Hawkins	275	Mississaugua G & CC, Toronto, Ontario	N/A
			Ed Oliver			

BELL CANADIAN OPEN

TOURNAMENT HISTORY

Year	Winner	Score	Runner-up	Score	Location	Par/Yards
1952	John Palmer	263	Fred Haas Dick Mayer	274	St. Charles CC, Winnipeg, Manitoba	N/A
1953	Dave Douglas	273	Wally Ulrich	274	Scarborough G&CC, Toronto, Ontario	N/A
1954	Pat Fletcher	280	Gordon Brydson Bill Welch	284	Point Grey GC, Vancouver, B.C.	N/A
1955	Arnold Palmer	265	Jack Burke, Jr.	269	Weston GC, Toronto, Ontario	N/A
1956	*#Doug Sanders	273	Dow Finsterwald	273	Beaconsfield GC, Montreal, Quebec	N/A
1957	George Bayer	271	Bo Wininger	273	Westmount G&CC, Kitchener, Ontario	N/A
1958	Wesley Ellis, Jr.	267	Jay Hebert	268	Mayfair G&CC, Edmonton, Alberta	N/A
1959	Doug Ford	276	Dow Finsterwald Art Wall Bo Wininger	278	Islesmere G&CC, Montreal, Quebec	N/A
1960	Art Wall, Jr.	269	Bob Goalby Jay Hebert	275	St. Georges G&CC, Toronto, Ontario	N/A
1961	Jacky Cupit	270	Buster Cupit Dow Finsterwald Bobby Nichols	275	Niakwa GC, Winnipeg, Manitoba	N/A
1962	Ted Kroll	278	Charles Sifford	280	Laval sue-le-Lac, Montreal, Quebec	N/A
1963	Doug Ford	280	Al Geiberger	281	Scarborough G&CC, Toronto, Ontario	N/A
1964	Kel Nagle	277	Arnold Palmer	279	Pinegrove CC, St. Luc, Quebec	N/A
1965	Gene Littler	273	Jack Nicklaus	274	Mississaugua G&CC, Toronto, Ontario	N/A
1966	Don Massengale	280	Chi Chi Rodriguez	283	Shaughnessy G&CC, Toronto, Ontario	N/A
1967	*Billy Casper	279	Art Wall	279	Montreal Municipal GC, Montreal, Quebec	N/A
1968	Bob Charles	274	Jack Nicklaus	276	St. Georges G&CC, Toronto, Ontario	70/6792
1969	*Tommy Aaron	275	Sam Snead	275	Pinegrove G&CC, St. Luc, Quebec	72/7076
1970	Kermit Zarley	279	Gibby Gilbert	282	London Hunt & CC, London, Ontario	72/7168
1971	*Lee Trevino	275	Art Wall	275	Richelieu Valley GC, Montreal, Quebec	72/6920
1972	Gay Brewer	275	Sam Adams Dave Hill	276	Cherry Hill Club, Ridgeway, Ontario	71/6751
1973	Tom Weiskopf	278	Forrest Fezler	280	Richelieu Valley G&CC, Ste. Julie de Vercheres, Que.	72/6905
1974	Bobby Nichols	270	John Schlee Larry Ziegler	274	Mississaugua G&CC, Mississaugua, Ontario	70/6788
1975	*Tom Weiskopf	274	Jack Nicklaus	274	Royal Montreal GC, Ile Bizard, Quebec	70/6628
1976	Jerry Pate	267	Jack Nicklaus	271	Essex G&CC,Windsor, Ontario.	70/6696
1977	Lee Trevino	280	Peter Oosterhuis	284	Glen Abbey GC, Oakville, Ontario	72/7096
1978	Bruce Lietzke	283	Pat McGowan	284	Glen Abbey GC, Oakville, Ontario	71/7050
1979	Lee Trevino	281	Ben Crenshaw	284	Glen Abbey GC, Oakville, Ontario	71/7059
1980	Bob Gilder	274	Jerry Pate Leonard Thompson	276	Royal Montreal GC, Ile Bizard, Quebec	70/6628
1981	Peter Oosterhuis	280	Bruce Lietzke Jack Nicklaus Andy North	281	Glen Abbey GC, Oakville, Ontario	71/7060
1982	Bruce Lietzke	277	Hal Sutton	279	Glen Abbey GC, Oakville, Ontario	71/7060
1983	*John Cook	277	Johnny Miller	277	Glen Abbey GC, Oakville, Ontario	71/7055
1984	Greg Norman	278	Jack Nicklaus	280	Glen Abbey GC, Oakville, Ontario	72/7102
1985	Curtis Strange	279	Jack Nicklaus Greg Norman	281	Glen Abbey GC, Oakville, Ontario	72/7102
1986	Bob Murphy	280	Greg Norman	283	Glen Abbey GC, Oakville, Ontario	72/7102
1987	Curtis Strange	276	David Frost Jodie Mudd Nick Price	279	Glen Abbey GC, Oakville, Ontario	72/7102
1988	Ken Green	275	Bill Glasson Scott Verplank	276	Glen Abbey GC, Oakville, Ontario	72/7102
1989	Steve Jones	271	Clark Burroughs Mark Calcavecchia Mike Hulbert	273	Glen Abbey GC, Oakville, Ontario	72/7102

BELL CANADIAN OPEN

TOURNAMENT HISTORY

Year	Winner	Score	Runner-up	Score	Location	Par/Yards
1990	Wayne Levi	278	Ian Baker-Finch Jim Woodward	279	Glen Abbey GC, Oakville, Ontario	72/7102
1991	Nick Price	273	David Edwards	274	Glen Abbey GC, Oakville, Ontario	72/7102
1992	*Greg Norman	280	Bruce Lietzke	280	Glen Abbey GC, Oakville, Ontario	72/7102
1993	David Frost	279	Fred Couples	280	Glen Abbey GC, Oakville, Ontario	72/7102
BELL CANADIAN OPEN						
1994	Nick Price	275	Mark Calcavecchia	276	Glen Abbey GC, Oakville, Ontario	72/7102
1995	*Mark O'Meara	274	Bob Lohr	274	Glen Abbey GC, Oakville, Ontario	72/7102

Tournament Record: 263 -- John Palmer, 1952 (St. Charles CC)
Current Course Record: 62 -- Leonard Thompson, 1981; Andy Bean, 1983 (par 71); Greg Norman, 1986 (par 72)

KEY: *=Playoff #=Amateur

1995 B.C. OPEN

En-Joie GC, Endicott, NY **Purse: $1,000,000**
Par: 37-34--71 **Yards: 6,920** **September 14-17, 1995**

LEADERS: First Round--Steve Lowery and Skip Kendall, at 5-under-par 66, led by one over 12 other players. **Second Round--**Guy Boros, Brad Faxon, Jay Williamson, Jeff Leonard and Kendall, at 7-under-par 135, led by one over nine others. **Third Round--**Kendall, at 10-under-par 203, led by one over Craig Stadler, Gary Hallberg, David Edwards, Jeff Sluman and Williamson.

CUT: 73 players at 1-under-par 141.

PRO-AM: $7,500. Individual--Fred Funk, 65, $750. Team--Peter Jacobsen, 51, $750.

WEATHER: There was a delay from 11:40 a.m. to 12:20 p.m. Thursday due to lightning in the area. Friday, Saturday and Sunday were cool and windy. There were some sprinkles on Sunday.

Winner: Hal Sutton 71-69-68-61 269 $180,000.00

Player	Pos.	Scores	Total	Money
Jim McGovern	2	71-67-69-63	270	$108,000.00
Craig Stadler	T 3	67-69-68-67	271	$58,000.00
Kirk Triplett	T 3	69-67-69-66	271	$58,000.00
Stewart Cink	T 5	71-70-66-65	272	$38,000.00
Jay Haas	T 5	68-69-71-64	272	$38,000.00
Skip Kendall	T 7	66-69-68-70	273	$29,100.00
Jeff Leonard	T 7	69-66-71-67	273	$29,100.00
Joey Sindelar	T 7	68-68-70-67	273	$29,100.00
Jeff Sluman	T 7	67-69-68-69	273	$29,100.00
Jay Williamson	T 7	67-68-69-69	273	$29,100.00
Guy Boros	T12	68-67-70-69	274	$21,000.00
Tom Byrum	T12	71-68-71-64	274	$21,000.00
David Edwards	T12	70-66-68-70	274	$21,000.00
Gary Hallberg	T15	73-63-68-71	275	$17,500.00
Neal Lancaster	T15	70-70-67-68	275	$17,500.00
Ed Fiori	T17	67-70-71-68	276	$15,000.00
Jim Furyk	T17	70-69-73-64	276	$15,000.00
Steve Pate	T17	67-69-72-68	276	$15,000.00
Fred Couples	T20	68-69-72-68	277	$10,087.50
Brad Faxon	T20	67-68-71-71	277	$10,087.50
Bruce Fleisher	T20	71-69-67-70	277	$10,087.50
Peter Jacobsen	T20	71-65-71-70	277	$10,087.50
Pete Jordan	T20	69-69-74-65	277	$10,087.50
Jonathan Kaye	T20	70-69-71-67	277	$10,087.50
Wayne Levi	T20	68-70-69-70	277	$10,087.50
Billy Ray Brown	T20	69-70-71-67	277	$10,087.50
Michael Allen	T28	69-69-74-66	278	$5,730.77
Kawika Cotner	T28	71-70-69-68	278	$5,730.77
Marco Dawson	T28	68-71-73-66	278	$5,730.77
Joel Edwards	T28	72-69-69-68	278	$5,730.77
Rick Fehr	T28	71-70-70-67	278	$5,730.77
Fred Funk	T28	69-72-69-68	278	$5,730.77
Steve Lowery	T28	66-74-69-69	278	$5,730.77
Andrew Magee	T28	67-70-69-72	278	$5,730.77
Anthony Rodriguez	T28	71-70-69-68	278	$5,730.77
Ray Stewart	T28	72-69-67-70	278	$5,730.77
Mike Sullivan	T28	73-66-71-68	278	$5,730.77
Tommy Tolles	T28	70-70-68-70	278	$5,730.77
Bill Britton	T28	68-68-74-68	278	$5,730.76
Phil Blackmar	T41	67-72-69-71	279	$3,700.00
Scott Dunlap	T41	69-71-74-65	279	$3,700.00
Ken Green	T41	67-72-71-69	279	$3,700.00
Mike Hulbert	T41	69-69-73-68	279	$3,700.00
David Peoples	T41	70-69-72-68	279	$3,700.00
Kelly Gibson	T46	68-72-69-71	280	$2,674.29
Mike Springer	T46	70-70-74-66	280	$2,674.29
Dicky Thompson	T46	68-72-70-70	280	$2,674.29
John Wilson	T46	69-70-68-73	280	$2,674.29
Tommy Armour III	T46	69-69-69-73	280	$2,674.28
Steve Rintoul	T46	67-70-74-69	280	$2,674.28
Dave Stockton, Jr.	T46	70-68-72-70	280	$2,674.28
Pat Bates	T53	72-69-68-72	281	$2,293.34
Don Reese	T53	73-68-71-69	281	$2,293.34
Patrick Burke	T53	69-68-76-68	281	$2,293.33
Curt Byrum	T53	74-67-69-71	281	$2,293.33
Nolan Henke	T53	70-71-71-69	281	$2,293.33
Howard Twitty	T53	71-68-74-68	281	$2,293.33
Jay Delsing	T59	69-69-75-69	282	$2,160.00
Bill Kratzert	T59	71-70-71-70	282	$2,160.00
Carl Paulson	T59	68-72-73-69	282	$2,160.00
Ted Schulz	T59	75-65-74-68	282	$2,160.00
Ted Tryba	T59	67-71-76-68	282	$2,160.00
Greg Twiggs	T59	72-69-73-68	282	$2,160.00
Bobby Wadkins	T59	68-72-74-68	282	$2,160.00
Ed Dougherty	T66	71-70-73-69	283	$2,070.00
Omar Uresti	T66	69-72-72-70	283	$2,070.00
Dennis Paulson	T68	71-69-75-69	284	$2,020.00
Bill Porter	T68	69-69-74-72	284	$2,020.00
Willie Wood	T68	70-71-76-67	284	$2,020.00
Ed Humenik	71	69-69-76-71	285	$1,980.00
John Schroeder	72	68-73-73-73	287	$1,960.00
Billy Andrade	73	71-69-73-76	289	$1,940.00

The following players did not finish (C=cut, W=withdrew, D=disqualified)

C—142-Joe Acosta, Jr., Dave Barr, Mike Brisky, Mark Carnevale, John Daly, Glen Day, Mike Donald, Steve Gotsche, Paul Goydos, Ryan Howison, Scott McCarron, Craig Parry, Larry Rinker, Mike Standly. **143-**Rex Caldwell, Russ Cochran, Buddy Gardner, Tom Hearn, J.L. Lewis, Tim Loustalot, Davis Love III, John Mahaffey, Dick Mast, Lee Rinker, Harry Taylor. **144-**Emlyn Aubrey, Brad Bryant, Clark Burroughs, Jim Carter, Trevor Dodds, David Frost, Bob Gilder, Jerry Haas, Tom Kite, Greg Kraft, Mark Lye, Rik Massengale, Don Pooley, Charlie Rymer, Jeff Woodland. **145-**Ronnie Black, Steve Brodie, George Burns, Bobby Cole, Danny Edwards, Barry Jaeckel, Mac O'Grady, John Riegger, Tony Sills, Mike Smith, Bruce Vaughan. **146-**Scott Ford, Donnie Hammond, Jay McWilliams, Loren Roberts, Tony Saraceno. **147-**Robert Gamez, Jim Hallet, Mark Pfeil, Mark Wiebe. **148-**Steve Hart, Alan Pate, Dicky Pride, Dave Rummells, Kevin Savage, Tray Tyner. **149-**Bob Burns, Bobby Clampett, J.P. Hayes, David Ogrin, Nick Serafino. **150-**Tim Duignan, Blaine McCallister. **151-**Kevin Roman. **152-**Chris DiMarco, Mark Wurtz. **153-**Stan Gorman, Kenny Knox. **W—73-**Bill Glasson, **75-**David Feherty, **77-**John Adams.

B.C. OPEN

TOURNAMENT HISTORY

Year	Winner	Score	Runner-up	Score	Location	Par/Yards
BROOME COUNTY OPEN						
1971	*Claude Harmon, Jr.	69	Chuck Courtney	69	En Joie GC, Endicott, NY	71/6966
			Norman Rack			
			Hal Underwood			
B. C. OPEN						
1972	Bob Payne	136	Dave Marad	137	En Joie GC, Endicott, NY	71/6966
1973	Hubert Green	266	Dwight Nevil	272	En Joie GC, Endicott, NY	71/6966
1974	*Richie Karl	273	Bruce Crampton	273	En Joie GC, Endicott, NY	71/6966
1975	Don Iverson	274	Jim Colbert	275	En Joie GC, Endicott, NY	71/6966
			David Graham			
1976	Bob Wynn	271	Bob Gilder	272	En Joie GC, Endicott, NY	71/6966
1977	Gil Morgan	270	Lee Elder	275	En Joie GC, Endicott, NY	71/6966
1978	Tom Kite	267	Mark Hayes	272	En Joie GC, Endicott, NY	71/6966
1979	Howard Twitty	270	Tom Purtzer	271	En Joie GC, Endicott, NY	71/6966
1980	Don Pooley	271	Peter Jacobsen	272	En Joie GC, Endicott, NY	71/6966
1981	Jay Haas	270	Tom Kite	273	En Joie GC, Endicott, NY	71/6966
1982	Calvin Peete	265	Jerry Pate	272	En Joie GC, Endicott, NY	71/6966
1983	Pat Lindsey	268	Gil Morgan	272	En Joie GC, Endicott, NY	71/6966
1984	Wayne Levi	275	Russ Cochran	276	En Joie GC, Endicott, NY	71/6966
			Hal Sutton			
1985	Joey Sindelar	274	Mike Reid	275	En Joie GC, Endicott, NY	71/6966
1986	Rick Fehr	267	Larry Mize	269	En Joie GC, Endicott, NY	71/6966
1987	Joey Sindelar	266	Jeff Sluman	270	En Joie GC, Endicott, NY	71/6966
1988	Bill Glasson	268	Wayne Levi	270	En Joie GC, Endicott, NY	71/6966
			Bruce Lietzke			
1989	*Mike Hulbert	268	Bob Estes	268	En Joie GC, Endicott, NY	71/6966
1990	Nolan Henke	268	Mark Wiebe	271	En Joie GC, Endicott, NY	71/6966
1991	Fred Couples	269	Peter Jacobsen	272	En Joie GC, Endicott, NY	71/6966
1992	John Daly	266	Joel Edwards	272	En Joie GC, Endicott, NY	71/6966
			Ken Green			
			Jay Haas			
			Nolan Henke			
1993	Blaine McCallister	271	Denis Watson	272	En Joie GC, Endicott, NY	71/6966
1994	Mike Sullivan	266	Jeff Sluman	270	En Joie GC, Endicott, NY	71/6966
1995	Hal Sutton	269	Jim McGovern	270	En Joie GC, Endicott, NY	71/6966

NOTE: 1971 and 1972 tournaments unofficial.

Tournament Record: 265 -- Calvin Peete, 1982
Current Course Record: 61 -- Hal Sutton, 1995

KEY: *=Playoff

1995 QUAD CITY CLASSIC

QUAD CITY QC CLASSIC

Oakwood GC, Coal Valley, IL **Purse: $1,000,000**
Par: 35-35—70 **Yards: 6,796** **September 21-24, 1995**

LEADERS: First Round—D.A. Weibring, Jim McGovern and Russ Cochran each shot 6-under-par 64 to lead Scott Verplank by one stroke. **Second Round**—Weibring shot a 65 for 11-under-par 129, four strokes ahead of Jay Delsing and Jonathan Kaye.

CUT: 88 players at 3-over-par 143.

PRO-AM: Individual—Andrew Magee, 65, $750. Team—Jim McGovern, 50, $750.

WEATHER: Cold and rainy Thursday. Play was suspended at 10:38 a.m. and called for the day at 1:20 p.m. The tournament was reduced to 54 holes. The first round resumed Friday at 9:30 a.m. under partly cloudy skies with temperatures in the 40s. Frost delayed play on Saturday for one hour and 15 minutes before temperatures rose to the upper 50s. Play was suspended because of darkness at 6:53 p.m. with seven players left on the course. The second round resumed at 9:00 a.m. Sunday, which was sunny and in the 60s.

Winner: D.A. Weibring 64-65-68 197 $180,000.00

Player	Pos	Scores	Total	Money
Jonathan Kaye	2	67-66-65	198	$108,000.00
Jay Delsing	3	69-64-67	200	$68,000.00
Jim McGovern	4	64-71-66	201	$48,000.00
Michael Allen	T 5	66-70-66	202	$36,500.00
Scott Hoch	T 5	71-65-66	202	$36,500.00
Dennis Paulson	T 5	71-66-65	202	$36,500.00
Curt Byrum	T 8	66-68-69	203	$30,000.00
Bob Gilder	T 8	68-69-66	203	$30,000.00
Bruce Fleisher	T10	72-66-66	204	$26,000.00
Scott Verplank	T10	65-73-66	204	$26,000.00
Russ Cochran	T12	64-72-69	205	$17,875.00
Clark Dennis	T12	73-65-67	205	$17,875.00
Joel Edwards	T12	66-70-69	205	$17,875.00
Robin Freeman	T12	68-68-69	205	$17,875.00
J.P. Hayes	T12	67-69-69	205	$17,875.00
Dick Mast	T12	70-69-66	205	$17,875.00
Chris Perry	T12	66-72-67	205	$17,875.00
Mike Small	T12	70-67-68	205	$17,875.00
David Edwards	T20	69-68-69	206	$11,650.00
Steve Jones	T20	71-66-69	206	$11,650.00
Greg Kraft	T20	67-75-64	206	$11,650.00
Carl Paulson	T20	70-67-69	206	$11,650.00
Chris DiMarco	T24	71-68-68	207	$8,800.00
Paul Goydos	T24	73-65-69	207	$8,800.00
Tommy Tolles	T24	69-71-67	207	$8,800.00
Kenny Knox	T27	70-67-71	208	$7,100.00
Jeff Leonard	T27	71-66-71	208	$7,100.00
Andrew Magee	T27	71-65-72	208	$7,100.00
Bill Porter	T27	68-69-71	208	$7,100.00
Bob Tway	T27	70-71-67	208	$7,100.00
Keith Fergus	T32	68-70-71	209	$5,533.34
Dillard Pruitt	T32	72-69-68	209	$5,533.34
Patrick Burke	T32	73-69-67	209	$5,533.33
Pete Jordan	T32	73-69-67	209	$5,533.33
Greg Twiggs	T32	68-70-71	209	$5,533.33
Mark Wiebe	T32	71-69-69	209	$5,533.33
Joe Acosta, Jr.	T38	72-70-68	210	$4,200.00
Tom Hearn	T38	73-67-70	210	$4,200.00
Ed Humenik	T38	69-71-70	210	$4,200.00
Mark McCumber	T38	69-74-67	210	$4,200.00
David Peoples	T38	70-69-71	210	$4,200.00
Larry Rinker	T38	69-70-71	210	$4,200.00
Phil Blackmar	T44	71-71-69	211	$2,890.00
Ernie Gonzalez	T44	71-70-70	211	$2,890.00
Donnie Hammond	T44	70-70-71	211	$2,890.00
Mark Pfeil	T44	72-71-68	211	$2,890.00
Lee Rinker	T44	73-66-72	211	$2,890.00
Dave Rummells	T44	71-71-69	211	$2,890.00
Gene Sauers	T44	71-69-71	211	$2,890.00
Ted Schulz	T44	67-72-72	211	$2,890.00
Emlyn Aubrey	T52	72-71-69	212	$2,308.58
Doug Dunakey	T52	72-69-71	212	$2,308.57
Gary Hallberg	T52	71-71-70	212	$2,308.57
J.L. Lewis	T52	68-71-73	212	$2,308.57
Dicky Pride	T52	68-73-71	212	$2,308.57
Hal Sutton	T52	70-71-71	212	$2,308.57
Harry Taylor	T52	73-70-69	212	$2,308.57
John Cook	T59	69-72-72	213	$2,150.00
Jerry Haas	T59	71-71-71	213	$2,150.00
Tom Kite	T59	70-70-73	213	$2,150.00
Don Reese	T59	69-71-73	213	$2,150.00
Joey Sindelar	T59	71-71-71	213	$2,150.00
Tray Tyner	T59	70-72-71	213	$2,150.00
Omar Uresti	T59	68-73-72	213	$2,150.00
Bruce Vaughan	T59	72-71-70	213	$2,150.00
Steve Brodie	T67	70-71-73	214	$1,960.00
Barry Cheesman	T67	73-70-71	214	$1,960.00
Lennie Clements	T67	74-69-71	214	$1,960.00
Ed Dougherty	T67	72-71-71	214	$1,960.00
David Frost	T67	71-70-73	214	$1,960.00
Kelly Gibson	T67	70-73-71	214	$1,960.00
Steve Gotsche	T67	73-70-71	214	$1,960.00
John Huston	T67	70-73-71	214	$1,960.00
Ken Schall	T67	70-72-72	214	$1,960.00
Ray Stewart	T67	71-67-76	214	$1,960.00
Willie Wood	T67	73-69-72	214	$1,960.00
Kawika Cotner	T78	74-65-76	215	$1,780.00
Bob Lohr	T78	70-73-72	215	$1,780.00
Scott McCarron	T78	70-73-72	215	$1,780.00
Steve Rintoul	T78	68-75-72	215	$1,780.00
Dave Rueter	T78	70-70-75	215	$1,780.00
Dave Stockton,Jr.	T78	73-70-72	215	$1,780.00
Mike Heinen	T78	69-74-72	215	$1,780.00
Robert Gamez	T85	69-74-73	216	$1,690.00
Vance Heafner	T85	72-71-73	216	$1,690.00
Ryan Howison	87	71-72-74	217	$1,660.00
Stephen Keppler	88	75-68-76	219	$1,640.00

The following players did not finish (C=cut, W=withdrew, D=disqualified)

C—144-Billy Ray Brown, Tom Byrum, Rex Caldwell, Kevin Denike, Buddy Gardner, Mark Hayes, Skip Kendall, Blaine McCallister, Ben Peters. **145-**Guy Boros, Bart Bryant, Mike Donald, David Feherty, David Ogrin, Tom Purtzer, Ron Whittaker, Jeff Woodland. **146-**Michael Bradley, Mike Brisky, George Burns, Ed Fiori, Steve Hart, Mac O'Grady, Mike Smith, Lance Ten Broeck. **147-**Chip Beck, Bob Burns, Stewart Cink, Scott Ford, Nolan Henke, Richie Karl, Ben Weir. **148-**Clark Burroughs, Brian Claar, Scott Gump, Bill Kratzert, Tim Loustalot, Doug Martin, Tony Sills, Jay Williamson. **149-**Mike Blackburn, Morris Hatalsky, Joey Rassett. **150-**Curt Schnell, Mark Wurtz. **151-**Bill Britton, Danny Edwards, Dan Halldorson, Gary March. **152-**Mark Egly, Barry Jaeckel, Greg Powers. **154-**Mark Carnevale, Mel McIntyre. **155-**Tom Jenkins.
W—146-Hubert Green,**160-**Bunky Henry, **75-**Dicky Thompson, **78-**Dudley Hart.

QUAD CITY CLASSIC

TOURNAMENT HISTORY

Year	Winner	Score	Runner-up	Score	Location	Par/Yards
QUAD CITIES OPEN						
1972	Deane Beman	279	Tom Watson	280	Crow Valley CC, Bettendorf, IA	71/6501
1973	Sam Adams	268	Dwight Nevil Kermit Zarley	271	Crow Valley CC, Bettendorf, IA	71/6501
1974	Dave Stockton	271	Bruce Fleisher	272	Crow Valley CC, Bettendorf, IA	71/6501
ED McMAHON-JAYCEES QUAD CITY OPEN						
1975	Roger Maltbie	275	Dave Eichelberger	276	Oakwood CC, Coal Valley, IL	70/6602
1976	John Lister	268	Fuzzy Zoeller	270	Oakwood CC, Coal Valley, IL	70/6602
1977	Mike Morley	267	Bob Murphy Victor Regalado	269	Oakwood CC, Coal Valley, IL	70/6602
1978	Victor Regalado	269	Fred Marti	270	Oakwood CC, Coal Valley, IL	70/6602
1979	D. A. Weibring	266	Calvin Peete	268	Oakwood CC, Coal Valley, IL	70/6602
QUAD CITIES OPEN						
1980	Scott Hoch	266	Curtis Strange	269	Oakwood CC, Coal Valley, IL	70/6602
1981	*Dave Barr	270	Woody Blackburn Frank Conner Dan Halldorson Victor Regalado	270	Oakwood CC, Coal Valley, IL	70/6602
MILLER HIGH-LIFE QUAD CITIES OPEN						
1982	Payne Stewart	268	Brad Bryant Pat McGowan	270	Oakwood CC, Coal Valley, IL	70/6602
1983	*Danny Edwards	266	Morris Hatalsky	266	Oakwood CC, Coal Valley, IL	70/6602
1984	Scott Hoch	266	George Archer Vance Heafner Dave Stockton	271	Oakwood CC, Coal Valley, IL	70/6602
LITE QUAD CITIES OPEN						
1985	Dan Forsman	267	Bob Tway	268	Oakwood CC, Coal Valley, IL	70/6602
HARDEE'S GOLF CLASSIC						
1986	Mark Wiebe	268	Curt Byrum	269	Oakwood CC, Coal Valley, IL	70/6602
1987	Kenny Knox	265	Gil Morgan	266	Oakwood CC, Coal Valley, IL	70/6606
1988	Blaine McCallister	261	Dan Forsman	264	Oakwood CC, Coal Valley, IL	70/6606
1989	Curt Byrum	268	Bill Britton Brian Tennyson	269	Oakwood CC, Coal Valley, IL	70/6606
1990	*Joey Sindelar	268	Willie Wood	268	Oakwood CC, Coal Valley, IL	70/6606
1991	D. A. Weibring	267	Paul Azinger Peter Jacobsen	268	Oakwood CC, Coal Valley, IL	70/6796
1992	David Frost	266	Tom Lehman Loren Roberts	269	Oakwood CC, Coal Valley, IL	70/6796
1993	David Frost	259	Payne Stewart D.A. Weibring	266	Oakwood CC, Coal Valley, IL	70/6796
1994	Mark McCumber	265	Kenny Perry	266	Oakwood CC, Coal Valley, IL	70/6796
QUAD CITY CLASSIC						
1995	~D.A. Weibring	197	Jonathan Kaye	198	Oakwood CC, Coal Valley, IL	70/6796

Tournament Record: 259 -- David Frost, 1993
Current Course Record: 61 -- Mike Smith, 1987

KEY: *=Playoff ~=Weather-shortened

1995 BUICK CHALLENGE

Callaway Gardens Resort, Pine Mountain, GA Purse: $1,000,000
Par: 36-36—72 Yards: 7,057 September 28-October 1, 1995

LEADERS: First Round—Bill Porter, at 7-under-par 65, led by one over Larry Mize, Steve Lowery and Steve Stricker. **Second Round**—Stricker, at 11-under-par 133, led by two over Glen Day. **Third Round**—Fred Funk and Stricker, at 11-under-par 205, led by one over John Morse, Loren Roberts, Kirk Triplett, Larry Nelson and Jeff Sluman.

CUT: 81 players at 1-under-par 143.

PRO-AM: $7,500. Individual—Brad Bryant, Steve Lowery, Jeff Sluman, Paul Azinger, Greg Kraft, Duffy Waldorf, 67, $500 each. Team—Bill Glasson, Larry Nelson, $675 each.

WEATHER: There was a fog delay from 7:56 a.m. to 8:45 a.m. on Thursday. Friday and Saturday were sunny and warm. Sunday was partly sunny and warm.

Winner: Fred Funk 69-67-69-67 272 $180,000.00

Player	Pos.	Scores	Total	Money
John Morse	T 2	71-68-67-67	273	$88,000.00
Loren Roberts	T 2	70-69-67-67	273	$88,000.00
Kirk Triplett	T 4	71-66-69-68	274	$41,333.34
Guy Boros	T 4	68-69-72-65	274	$41,333.33
Jeff Sluman	T 4	67-69-70-68	274	$41,333.33
David Ogrin	7	70-68-70-67	275	$33,500.00
Scott Hoch	T 8	70-70-69-67	276	$28,000.00
John Huston	T 8	67-71-70-68	276	$28,000.00
Larry Nelson	T 8	71-65-70-70	276	$28,000.00
Steve Stricker	T 8	66-67-72-71	276	$28,000.00
Brad Bryant	T12	70-69-70-68	277	$19,000.00
Bob Burns	T12	71-71-68-67	277	$19,000.00
Glen Day	T12	68-67-74-68	277	$19,000.00
Scott Gump	T12	69-73-67-68	277	$19,000.00
Mike Heinen	T12	68-73-73-63	277	$19,000.00
Bob Lohr	T12	74-68-65-70	277	$19,000.00
Steve Jones	T18	70-69-69-70	278	$14,500.00
Justin Leonard	T18	69-67-71-71	278	$14,500.00
John Adams	T20	68-68-72-71	279	$11,650.00
Jim Gallagher, Jr.	T20	71-70-69-69	279	$11,650.00
Greg Norman	T20	71-68-72-68	279	$11,650.00
Mike Smith	T20	69-73-66-71	279	$11,650.00
Emlyn Aubrey	T24	70-73-70-67	280	$8,100.00
Woody Austin	T24	68-69-70-73	280	$8,100.00
Dave Barr	T24	70-70-70-70	280	$8,100.00
Steve Lowery	T24	66-70-72-72	280	$8,100.00
Scott McCarron	T24	70-72-71-67	280	$8,100.00
Duffy Waldorf	T24	68-71-71-70	280	$8,100.00
Russ Cochran	T30	72-67-73-69	281	$6,350.00
Ben Crenshaw	T30	70-70-69-72	281	$6,350.00
Jay Delsing	T30	68-69-73-71	281	$6,350.00
Tony Sills	T30	70-69-70-72	281	$6,350.00
Dan Forsman	T34	68-73-69-72	282	$5,050.00
David Frost	T34	72-68-71-71	282	$5,050.00
Brian Kamm	T34	70-69-72-71	282	$5,050.00
Neal Lancaster	T34	71-72-66-73	282	$5,050.00
J.L. Lewis	T34	68-71-73-70	282	$5,050.00
Gene Sauers	T34	70-68-74-70	282	$5,050.00
Michael Bradley	T40	69-70-73-71	283	$3,600.00
Lennie Clements	T40	70-71-71-71	283	$3,600.00
Larry Mize	T40	66-72-71-74	283	$3,600.00
Carl Paulson	T40	70-70-72-71	283	$3,600.00
Lee Rinker	T40	70-71-75-67	283	$3,600.00
Hal Sutton	T40	73-68-70-72	283	$3,600.00
Ted Tryba	T40	69-67-73-74	283	$3,600.00
Grant Waite	T40	71-71-71-70	283	$3,600.00
Billy Ray Brown	T48	69-71-70-74	284	$2,580.00
Curt Byrum	T48	68-72-71-73	284	$2,580.00
Mike Hulbert	T48	71-72-71-70	284	$2,580.00
Craig Parry	T48	72-71-70-71	284	$2,580.00
Fulton Allem	T52	71-72-72-70	285	$2,345.00
Keith Clearwater	T52	69-71-72-73	285	$2,345.00
Scott Ford	T52	71-72-75-67	285	$2,345.00
Dicky Thompson	T52	72-71-73-69	285	$2,345.00
Jim Furyk	T56	68-73-70-75	286	$2,270.00
Howard Twitty	T56	68-70-74-74	286	$2,270.00
Mike Brisky	T58	70-71-70-76	287	$2,160.00
Bill Britton	T58	71-72-72-72	287	$2,160.00
Bart Bryant	T58	71-70-75-71	287	$2,160.00
Patrick Burke	T58	71-72-73-71	287	$2,160.00
Stewart Cink	T58	70-73-70-74	287	$2,160.00
Robin Freeman	T58	70-71-77-69	287	$2,160.00
Kelly Gibson	T58	70-73-78-66	287	$2,160.00
Billy Mayfair	T58	68-74-74-71	287	$2,160.00
Tray Tyner	T58	69-74-74-70	287	$2,160.00
John Daly	T67	71-70-74-73	288	$2,040.00
John Godwin	T67	70-73-75-70	288	$2,040.00
Dave Stockton, Jr.	T67	71-68-79-70	288	$2,040.00
Bruce Fleisher	T70	69-74-79-67	289	$1,970.00
Chris Perry	T70	70-73-72-74	289	$1,970.00
Bill Porter	T70	65-76-74-74	289	$1,970.00
Omar Uresti	T70	71-70-73-75	289	$1,970.00
Joe Acosta, Jr.	T74	72-71-75-72	290	$1,900.00
Bill Glasson	T74	68-73-78-71	290	$1,900.00
Greg Kraft	T74	72-70-76-72	290	$1,900.00
Blaine McCallister	77	69-73-76-73	291	$1,860.00
Ted Schulz	78	71-72-78-71	292	$1,840.00
Steve Rintoul	79	71-70-75-77	293	$1,820.00
Dudley Hart	80	70-72-76-76	294	$1,800.00

The following players did not finish (C=cut, W=withdrew, D=disqualified)

C—144-Michael Allen, Ronnie Black, Robert Gamez, Jerry Haas, Donnie Hammond, Ed Humenik, Skip Kendall, Jeff Leonard, Wayne Levi, Jim McGovern, Steve Pate, Dennis Paulson, Don Pooley, Scott Simpson, Paul Stankowski, Tommy Tolles. **145-**Paul Azinger, Pat Bates, Rick Beck, Mark Carnevale, Jim Carter, Clark Dennis, David Duval, Steve Elkington, Jonathan Kaye, Dillard Pruitt, Charlie Rymer, Bobby Wadkins, John Wilson. **146-**Kawika Cotner, Marco Dawson, Craig Hartle, Tom Hearn, Ryan Howison, Cliff Kresge, Bruce Vaughan. **147-**Billy Andrade, Mark Brooks, Joel Edwards, David Feherty, Keith Fergus, Gary Hallberg, Kenny Knox, John Mahaffey, David Peoples, Don Reese, Mike Reid, Mike Sullivan, Fred Wadsworth, Jay Williamson. **148-**Paul Goydos, Hubert Green, Doug Martin, Dicky Pride, Harry Taylor. **149-**Mark Anderson, Phil Blackmar. **150-**Bob Gilder, Steve Gotsche, J.P. Hayes, Mark Wurtz. **151-**Rob Butler, Ed Dougherty, Stephen Keppler. **152-**Mike Standly. **156-**Joey Sadowski, Eric Westemeier. **158-**Brigham Gibbs. **159-**Brad Nycun. **162-**Ian Baker-Finch. **173-**Evan Johnson. **W—219-**Tom Purtzer, **73-**Jerry Pate. **D—73-**Tommy Armour II.

BUICK CHALLENGE

TOURNAMENT HISTORY

Year	Winner	Score	Runner-up	Score	Location	Par/Yards
GREEN ISLAND OPEN INVITATIONAL						
1970	Mason Rudolph	274	Chris Blocker	276	Green Island CC, Columbus, GA	70/6791
SOUTHERN OPEN INVITATIONAL						
1971	Johnny Miller	267	Deane Beman	272	Green Island CC, Columbus, GA	70/6791
1972	*DeWitt Weaver	276	Chuck Courtney	276	Green Island CC, Columbus, GA	70/6791
1973	Gary Player	270	Forrest Fezler	271	Green Island CC, Columbus, GA	70/6791
1974	Forrest Fezler	271	Bruce Crampton J.C. Snead	272	Green Island CC, Columbus, GA	70/6791
1975	Hubert Green	264	John Schroeder	267	Green Island CC, Columbus, GA	70/6791
1976	Mac McLendon	274	Hubert Green	276	Green Island CC, Columbus, GA	70/6791
1977	Jerry Pate	266	Phil Hancock Mac McLendon Johnny Miller Steve Taylor	273	Green Island CC, Columbus, GA	70/6791
1978	Jerry Pate	269	Phil Hancock	270	Green Island CC, Columbus, GA	70/6791
1979	*Ed Fiori	274	Tom Weiskopf	274	Green Island CC, Columbus, GA	70/6791
1980	Mike Sullivan	269	Dave Eichelberger Johnny Miller	274	Green Island CC, Columbus, GA	70/6791
1981	*J. C. Snead	271	Mike Sullivan	271	Green Island CC, Columbus, GA	70/6791
1982	Bobby Clampett	266	Hale Irwin	268	Green Island CC, Columbus, GA	70/6791
1983	*Ronnie Black	271	Sam Torrance	271	Green Island CC, Columbus, GA	70/6791
1984	Hubert Green	265	Rex Caldwell Scott Hoch Corey Pavin	271	Green Island CC, Columbus, GA	70/6791
1985	Tim Simpson	264	Clarence Rose	266	Green Island CC, Columbus, GA	70/6791
1986	Fred Wadsworth	269	George Archer John Cook Tim Simpson Jim Thorpe	271	Green Island CC, Columbus, GA	70/6791
1987	Ken Brown	266	David Frost Mike Hulbert Larry Mize	273	Green Island CC, Columbus, GA	70/6791
1988	*David Frost	270	Bob Tway	270	Green Island CC, Columbus, GA	70/6791
1989	Ted Schulz	266	Jay Haas Tim Simpson	267	Green Island CC, Columbus, GA	70/6791
BUICK SOUTHERN OPEN						
1990	*Kenny Knox	265	Jim Hallet	265	Green Island CC, Columbus, GA	70/6791
1991	David Peoples	276	Robert Gamez	277	Callaway Gardens Resort, Pine Mountain, GA	72/7057
1992	~Gary Hallberg	206	Jim Gallagher, Jr.	207	Callaway Gardens Resort, Pine Mountain, GA	72/7057
1993	*John Inman	278	Billy Andrade Mark Brooks Brad Bryant Bob Estes	278	Callaway Gardens Resort, Pine Mountain, GA	72/7057
1994	~Steve Elkington	200	Steve Rintoul	205	Callaway Gardens Resort, Pine Mountain, GA	72/7057
BUICK CHALLENGE						
1995	Fred Funk	272	John Morse Loren Roberts	273	Callaway Gardens Resort, Pine Mountain, GA	72/7057

Tournament Record: 264 -- Hubert Green, 1975; Tim Simpson, 1984 (both Green Island CC)
Current Course Record: 63 -- Mike Heinen, 1995

KEY: *=Playoff ~=Weather-shortened

WALT DISNEY WORLD/ OLDSMOBILE GOLF CLASSIC

Three Walt Disney World Resort Courses
Magnolia (Host) Yards: 7,190
Palm Yards: 6,957
Lake Buena Vista Yards: 6,819

Purse: $1,200,000
October 5-8, 1995
All Par: 36-36—72

LEADERS: First Round—Carl Paulson (P), after a 10-under-par 62, led by two strokes over Craig Parry (LBV) and Keith Fergus (P). **Second Round**—Brad Bryant (LBV), after a 9-under-par 63, and Paulson (LBV), after a 4-under-par 68, were tied at 14-under-par 130. They led by one stroke over Patrick Burke (LBV) and by two over Bob Gilder (LBV).

CUT: 70 players at 8-under-par 208.

WEATHER: The start of play was delayed for an hour due to rain on Thursday. Second-round play was suspended at 11:25 a.m. due to heavy rains, and finally called for the day at 2:30 p.m. The decision was made to shorten the tournament to 54 holes. The second round resumed at 8:30 a.m. Saturday. There were brief periods of rain, but no delays. Sunday was cloudy with intermittent rain, but no more delays.

Winner: Brad Bryant 67-63-68 198 $216,000.00

Player	Pos.	Scores	Total	Money
Hal Sutton	T 2	67-66-66	199	$105,600.00
Ted Tryba	T 2	69-65-65	199	$105,600.00
Joe Acosta, Jr.	T 4	68-67-66	201	$49,600.00
Mike Reid	T 4	68-66-67	201	$49,600.00
Bob Tway	T 4	65-70-66	201	$49,600.00
Patrick Burke	T 7	66-65-71	202	$31,275.00
Russ Cochran	T 7	66-67-69	202	$31,275.00
Mike Heinen	T 7	65-68-69	202	$31,275.00
Mike Hulbert	T 7	68-66-68	202	$31,275.00
Lee Rinker	T 7	68-67-67	202	$31,275.00
Charlie Rymer	T 7	68-68-66	202	$31,275.00
Jay Williamson	T 7	69-65-68	202	$31,275.00
Carl Paulson	T 7	62-68-72	202	$31,275.00
Chip Beck	T15	70-66-67	203	$18,600.00
John Cook	T15	66-68-69	203	$18,600.00
Bob Gilder	T15	68-64-71	203	$18,600.00
Scott Gump	T15	69-64-70	203	$18,600.00
Doug Martin	T15	69-68-66	203	$18,600.00
Grant Waite	T15	67-67-69	203	$18,600.00
Ronnie Black	T21	67-68-69	204	$11,605.72
Lee Janzen	T21	69-67-68	204	$11,605.72
Brian Kamm	T21	68-66-70	204	$11,605.72
Curt Byrum	T21	71-68-65	204	$11,605.71
Scott Hoch	T21	72-64-68	204	$11,605.71
Bob Lohr	T21	67-67-70	204	$11,605.71
Steve Lowery	T21	65-70-69	204	$11,605.71
Paul Azinger	T28	68-70-67	205	$7,480.00
Keith Fergus	T28	64-69-72	205	$7,480.00
Ken Green	T28	68-68-69	205	$7,480.00
Tom Hearn	T28	71-69-65	205	$7,480.00
John Mahaffey	T28	71-67-67	205	$7,480.00
Larry Mize	T28	70-66-69	205	$7,480.00
Craig Parry	T28	64-69-72	205	$7,480.00
Payne Stewart	T28	70-64-71	205	$7,480.00
Tray Tyner	T28	67-69-69	205	$7,480.00
John Adams	T37	68-68-70	206	$4,564.00
Emlyn Aubrey	T37	68-68-70	206	$4,564.00
Jay Don Blake	T37	69-67-70	206	$4,564.00
Mark Brooks	T37	67-70-69	206	$4,564.00
Glen Day	T37	67-71-68	206	$4,564.00
Ed Fiori	T37	66-71-69	206	$4,564.00
Dan Forsman	T37	66-69-71	206	$4,564.00
Fred Funk	T37	66-67-73	206	$4,564.00
Skip Kendall	T37	70-69-67	206	$4,564.00
Tom Kite	T37	67-71-68	206	$4,564.00
Scott Verplank	T37	71-66-69	206	$4,564.00
Duffy Waldorf	T37	70-66-70	206	$4,564.00
Michael Bradley	T49	68-72-67	207	$2,785.72
Chris DiMarco	T49	67-67-73	207	$2,785.72
Kelly Gibson	T49	66-71-70	207	$2,785.72
Paul Goydos	T49	69-67-71	207	$2,785.72
Jeff Leonard	T49	70-68-69	207	$2,785.72
Steve Rintoul	T49	67-69-71	207	$2,785.72
Phil Blackmar	T49	66-70-71	207	$2,785.71
Bruce Fleisher	T49	69-68-70	207	$2,785.71
Jim Furyk	T49	66-69-72	207	$2,785.71
Jim Gallagher, Jr.	T49	69-66-72	207	$2,785.71
Roger Maltbie	T49	69-72-66	207	$2,785.71
Corey Pavin	T49	69-69-69	207	$2,785.71
Mike Standly	T49	71-65-71	207	$2,785.71
Dicky Thompson	T49	72-68-67	207	$2,785.71
Rick Fehr	T63	67-72-69	208	$2,484.00
Donnie Hammond	T63	71-67-70	208	$2,484.00
John Morse	T63	68-72-68	208	$2,484.00
David Ogrin	T63	71-68-69	208	$2,484.00
Joe Ozaki	T63	71-68-69	208	$2,484.00
Chris Perry	T63	66-70-72	208	$2,484.00
Tommy Tolles	T63	69-70-69	208	$2,484.00
Mark Wurtz	T63	70-66-72	208	$2,484.00

The following players did not finish (C=cut, W=withdrew, D=disqualified)

C—209-Michael Allen, Billy Andrade, Dave Barr, Jay Delsing, Clark Dennis, Ed Dougherty, Larry Nelson, Dave Stockton, Jr. **210-**Fulton Allem, Andy Bean, Marco Dawson, Dudley Hart, Nolan Henke, Ed Humenik, J.L. Lewis, Mark O'Meara, Steve Pate, Joey Rassett, Steve Stricker, Mark Wiebe. **211-**Guy Boros, Brian Claar, Ryan Howison, Greg Kraft, Don Reese, Gene Sauers, Tony Sills, Howard Twitty. **212-**Mike Brisky, J.P. Hayes, Wayne Levi, Bill Porter, Mike Smith, Omar Uresti. **213-**Woody Austin, Pat Bates, Bart Bryant, Jim Carter, Gary Hallberg. **214-**Dicky Pride. **215-**Joel Edwards, Mark McCumber, Harry Taylor. **216-**Bill Britton, Brett Ogle. **217-**Scott McCarron, Paul Stankowski. **218-**Robert Gamez. **219-**Lanny Wadkins. **W—137-**Scott Simpson, **139-**Steve Gotsche, Tom Purtzer, **140-**Dennis Paulson, **142-**Bruce Vaughan, **143-**Tommy Armour III, **144-**Mark Carnevale, **145-**John Huston, **147-**Keith Clearwater, Kawika Cotner, **76-**Jerry Haas. **D—147-**David Feherty, **84-**Ian Baker-Finch.

WALT DISNEY WORLD/ OLDSMOBILE GOLF CLASSIC

TOURNAMENT HISTORY

Year	Winner	Score	Runner-up	Score	Location	Par/Yards
WALT DISNEY WORLD OPEN INVITATIONAL						
1971	Jack Nicklaus	273	Deane Beman	276	Magnolia, Walt Disney World, Lake Buena Vista, FL	72/7190
1972	Jack Nicklaus	267	Jim Dent	276	Palm, Walt Disney World, Lake Buena Vista, FL	72/6941
			Bobby Mitchell		Magnolia, Walt Disney World, Lake Buena Vista, FL	72/7190
			Larry Wood			
1973	Jack Nicklaus	275	Mason Rudolph	276	Palm, Walt Disney World, Lake Buena Vista, FL	72/6941
					Magnolia, Walt Disney World, Lake Buena Vista, FL	72/7190
WALT DISNEY WORLD NATIONAL TEAM CHAMPIONSHIP						
1974	Hubert Green/	255	J.C. Snead/	256	Palm, Walt Disney World, Lake Buena Vista, FL	72/6941
	Mac McLendon		Sam Snead		Magnolia, Walt Disney World, Lake Buena Vista, FL	72/7190
			Ed Sneed/			
			Bert Yancey			
1975	Jim Colbert/	252	Bobby Cole/	255	Palm, Walt Disney World, Lake Buena Vista, FL	72/6941
	Dean Refram		Victor Regalado		Magnolia, Walt Disney World, Lake Buena Vista, FL	72/7190
			John Schlee/			
			Curtis Sifford			
1976	*Woody Blackburn/	260	Gay Brewer/	260	Palm, Walt Disney World, Lake Buena Vista, FL	72/6941
	Bill Kratzert		Bobby Nichols		Magnolia, Walt Disney World, Lake Buena Vista, FL	72/7190
1977	Gibby Gilbert/	253	Steve Melnyk/	254	Palm, Walt Disney World, Lake Buena Vista, FL	72/6941
	Grier Jones		Andy North		Magnolia, Walt Disney World, Lake Buena Vista, FL	72/7190
1978	Wayne Levi/	254	Bobby Wadkins/	257	Palm, Walt Disney World, Lake Buena Vista, FL	72/6941
	Bob Mann		Lanny Wadkins		Magnolia, Walt Disney World, Lake Buena Vista, FL	72/7190
1979	George Burns/	255	Scott Bess/	258	Palm, Walt Disney World, Lake Buena Vista, FL	72/6941
	Ben Crenshaw		Dan Halldorson		Magnolia, Walt Disney World, Lake Buena Vista, FL	72/7190
			Jeff Hewes/			
			Peter Jacobsen			
			Sammy Rachels/			
			D.A. Weibring			
1980	Danny Edwards/	253	Gibby Gilbert/	255	Palm, Walt Disney World, Lake Buena Vista, FL	72/6941
	David Edwards		Dan Halldorson		Magnolia, Walt Disney World, Lake Buena Vista, FL	72/7190
			Mike Harmon/			
			Barry Harwell			
			Grier Jones/			
			Dana Quigley			
1981	Vance Heafner/	246	Chip Beck/	251	Palm, Walt Disney World, Lake Buena Vista, FL	72/6941
	Mike Holland		Rex Caldwell		Magnolia, Walt Disney World, Lake Buena Vista, FL	72/7190
WALT DISNEY WORLD GOLF CLASSIC						
1982	*Hal Sutton	269	Bill Britton	269	Palm, Walt Disney World, Lake Buena Vista, FL	72/6941
					Magnolia, Walt Disney World, Lake Buena Vista, FL	72/7190
					Lake Buena Vista CC, Lake Buena Vista, FL	72/6706
1983	Payne Stewart	269	Nick Faldo	271	Palm, Walt Disney World, Lake Buena Vista, FL	72/6941
			Mark McCumber		Magnolia, Walt Disney World, Lake Buena Vista, FL	72/7190
					Lake Buena Vista CC, Lake Buena Vista, FL	72/6706
1984	Larry Nelson	266	Hubert Green	267	Palm, Walt Disney World, Lake Buena Vista, FL	72/6941
					Magnolia, Walt Disney World, Lake Buena Vista, FL	72/7190
					Lake Buena Vista CC, Lake Buena Vista, FL	72/6706
WALT DISNEY WORLD/OLDSMOBILE CLASSIC						
1985	Lanny Wadkins	267	Mike Donald	268	Palm, Walt Disney World, Lake Buena Vista, FL	72/6941
			Scott Hoch		Magnolia, Walt Disney World, Lake Buena Vista, FL	72/7190
					Lake Buena Vista CC, Lake Buena Vista, FL	72/6706
1986	*Ray Floyd	275	Lon Hinkle	275	Palm, Walt Disney World, Lake Buena Vista, FL	72/6941
			Mike Sullivan		Magnolia, Walt Disney World, Lake Buena Vista, FL	72/7190
					Lake Buena Vista CC, Lake Buena Vista, FL	72/6706
1987	Larry Nelson	268	Morris Hatalsky	269	Palm, Walt Disney World, Lake Buena Vista, FL	72/6941
			Mark O'Meara		Magnolia, Walt Disney World, Lake Buena Vista, FL	72/7190
					Lake Buena Vista CC, Lake Buena Vista, FL	72/6706

WALT DISNEY WORLD/ OLDSMOBILE GOLF CLASSIC

TOURNAMENT HISTORY

Year	Winner	Score	Runner-up	Score	Location	Par/Yards
1988	*Bob Lohr	263	Chip Beck	263	Palm, Walt Disney World, Lake Buena Vista, FL	72/6941
					Magnolia, Walt Disney World, Lake Buena Vista, FL	72/7190
					Lake Buena Vista CC, Lake Buena Vista, FL	72/6706
1989	Tim Simpson	272	Donnie Hammond	273	Palm, Walt Disney World, Lake Buena Vista, FL	72/6941
					Magnolia, Walt Disney World, Lake Buena Vista, FL	72/7190
					Lake Buena Vista CC, Lake Buena Vista, FL	72/6706
1990	Tim Simpson	264	John Mahaffey	265	Palm, Walt Disney World, Lake Buena Vista, FL	72/6941
					Magnolia, Walt Disney World, Lake Buena Vista, FL	72/7190
					Lake Buena Vista CC, Lake Buena Vista, FL	72/6706
1991	Mark O'Meara	267	David Peoples	268	Palm, Walt Disney World, Lake Buena Vista, FL	72/6941
					Magnolia, Walt Disney World, Lake Buena Vista, FL	72/7190
					Lake Buena Vista CC, Lake Buena Vista, FL	72/6706
1992	John Huston	262	Mark O'Meara	265	Palm, Walt Disney World, Lake Buena Vista, FL	72/6941
					Magnolia, Walt Disney World, Lake Buena Vista, FL	72/7190
					Lake Buena Vista CC, Lake Buena Vista, FL	72/6706
1993	Jeff Maggert	265	Greg Kraft	268	Palm, Walt Disney World, Lake Buena Vista, FL	72/6941
					Magnolia, Walt Disney World, Lake Buena Vista, FL	72/7190
					Lake Buena Vista CC, Lake Buena Vista, FL	72/6706
1994	Rick Fehr	265	Craig Stadler	271	Palm, Walt Disney World, Lake Buena Vista, FL	72/6941
			Fuzzy Zoeller		Magnolia, Walt Disney World, Lake Buena Vista, FL	72/7190
					Eagle Pines, Lake Buena Vista, FL	72/6772
1995	~Brad Bryant	198	Hal Sutton	199	Palm, Walt Disney World, Lake Buena Vista, FL	72/6941
			Ted Tryba		Magnolia, Walt Disney World, Lake Buena Vista, FL	72/7190
					Lake Buena Vista CC, Lake Buena Vista, FL	72/6819

Tournament Record:	262 -- John Huston, 1992	
Current Course Record:	Palm	61 -- Mark Lye, 1984
	Lake Buena Vista	61 -- Bob Tway, 1989
	Magnolia	61 -- Payne Stewart, 1990

KEY: * = Playoff ~ = Weather-shortened

1995 LAS VEGAS INVITATIONAL

LAS VEGAS INVITATIONAL

TPC at Summerlin, Las Vegas, NV
Par: 36-36—72 Yards: 7,243
Las Vegas CC
Par: 36-36—72 Yards: 7,164
Las Vegas Hilton CC
Par: 36-35—72 Yards: 6,815

Purse: $1,500,000
October 11-15, 1995

LEADERS: First Round—Joe Ozaki (LVH) shot an 8-under-par 63 to lead Keith Fergus (LVH), Craig Parry (LVH), Rick Fehr (LVCC) and John Wilson (LVH) by one stroke. **Second Round**—Bob Tway (TPC) shot a 7-under-par 65 for a 130 total, one stroke ahead of John Cook (LVCC), Billy Mayfair (TPC), Kelly Gibson (TPC) and Curt Byrum (TPC). **Third Round**—David Edwards (LVH), who shot 64, and Jim Furyk (TPC), who shot 65, shared the lead at 18-under-par 197, one stroke ahead of Billy Mayfair. **Fourth Round**—Mayfair and Furyk shared the lead at 23-under-par 264 and led Mark O'Meara by one stroke.

CUT: 80 players at 7-under-par 208.

WEATHER: Sunny and warm each day.

Player	Pos	Scores	Total	Money
Billy Mayfair	2	66-65-67-66-68	332	$162,000.00
Scott McCarron	3	71-65-69-64-65	334	$102,000.00
Phil Blackmar	T 4	69-66-71-64-65	335	$62,000.00
Brad Bryant	T 4	65-68-67-69-66	335	$62,000.00
Mark O'Meara	T 4	67-67-66-65-70	335	$62,000.00
Glen Day	T 7	70-67-65-68-66	336	$46,750.00
David Edwards	T 7	67-66-64-69-70	336	$46,750.00
Davis Love III	T 7	67-67-68-67-67	336	$46,750.00
Rick Fehr	T10	64-68-71-67-67	337	$36,000.00
Bill Glasson	T10	68-68-71-65-65	337	$36,000.00
Joe Ozaki	T10	63-69-71-66-68	337	$36,000.00
Kirk Triplett	T10	66-67-69-68-67	337	$36,000.00
John Cook	14	67-64-69-67-71	338	$28,500.00
Patrick Burke	T15	66-67-69-68-69	339	$23,250.00
Lennie Clements	T15	70-68-68-66-67	339	$23,250.00
Kelly Gibson	T15	66-65-74-65-69	339	$23,250.00
Paul Goydos	T15	72-65-68-66-68	339	$23,250.00
Dennis Paulson	T15	68-67-65-71-68	339	$23,250.00
Dave Stockton, Jr.	T15	68-65-70-67-69	339	$23,250.00
Jay Don Blake	T21	72-66-68-69-65	340	$17,400.00
Andrew Magee	T21	70-67-67-67-69	340	$17,400.00
Justin Leonard	T23	70-69-67-69-66	341	$15,000.00
Bruce Vaughan	T23	70-69-68-67-67	341	$15,000.00
Bart Bryant	T25	69-68-69-67-69	342	$11,700.00
Marco Dawson	T25	68-64-73-66-71	342	$11,700.00
Roger Maltbie	T25	70-65-70-69-68	342	$11,700.00
Jim McGovern	T25	68-65-70-70-69	342	$11,700.00
Bob Tway	T25	65-65-69-71-72	342	$11,700.00
Mark Brooks	T30	66-66-71-71-69	343	$8,533.34
Phil Mickelson	T30	71-65-70-69-68	343	$8,533.34
Mike Smith	T30	69-69-67-69-69	343	$8,533.34
Curt Byrum	T30	66-65-70-72-70	343	$8,533.33
Jonathan Kaye	T30	67-66-67-69-74	343	$8,533.33
Doug Martin	T30	65-72-69-67-70	343	$8,533.33
Blaine McCallister	T30	67-67-67-68-74	343	$8,533.33
Craig Parry	T30	64-70-71-68-70	343	$8,533.33
Chris Perry	T30	71-68-67-68-69	343	$8,533.33
John Adams	T39	70-70-68-68-68	344	$6,150.00
Mark Calcavecchia	T39	66-69-69-72-68	344	$6,150.00
Russ Cochran	T39	68-69-67-69-71	344	$6,150.00
Mike Hulbert	T39	68-69-71-68-68	344	$6,150.00
Skip Kendall	T39	67-67-69-68-73	344	$6,150.00
Steve Jones	T44	65-70-69-66-75	345	$5,100.00
Tommy Tolles	T44	68-70-68-69-70	345	$5,100.00
Tom Byrum	T46	66-67-67-73-73	346	$3,952.50
Clark Dennis	T46	69-68-70-67-72	346	$3,952.50
Steve Gotsche	T46	69-67-70-68-72	346	$3,952.50
Bruce Lietzke	T46	68-70-69-68-71	346	$3,952.50
Omar Uresti	T46	72-68-67-70-69	346	$3,952.50
Scott Verplank	T46	66-68-69-74-69	346	$3,952.50
Duffy Waldorf	T46	67-68-68-72-71	346	$3,952.50
Paul Stankowski	T46	69-66-70-69-72	346	$3,952.50
Chip Beck	T54	69-67-72-68-71	347	$3,420.00
Ronnie Black	T54	68-68-67-77-67	347	$3,420.00
Jeff Sluman	T54	67-68-71-70-71	347	$3,420.00
Grant Waite	T54	69-70-69-70-69	347	$3,420.00
Lee Rinker	T54	67-69-71-70-70	347	$3,420.00
Jim Carter	T59	69-69-67-70-73	348	$3,285.00
Ken Green	T59	67-69-71-73-68	348	$3,285.00
Steve Lowery	T59	66-67-72-72-71	348	$3,285.00
John Wilson	T59	64-73-69-73-69	348	$3,285.00
Bruce Fleisher	63	70-67-71-67-74	349	$3,210.00
Brad Faxon	T64	67-69-72-74-68	350	$3,090.00
Jerry Haas	T64	66-69-73-70-72	350	$3,090.00
Donnie Hammond	T64	68-68-70-75-69	350	$3,090.00
Mike Heinen	T64	68-67-72-73-70	350	$3,090.00
Brian Henninger	T64	69-69-69-73-70	350	$3,090.00
Steve Pate	T64	72-68-68-69-73	350	$3,090.00
Charlie Rymer	T64	66-72-69-71-72	350	$3,090.00
Woody Austin	T71	66-73-69-73-70	351	$2,940.00
Ray Stewart	T71	69-68-71-74-69	351	$2,940.00
Ted Tryba	T71	70-72-63-71-75	351	$2,940.00
Emlyn Aubrey	T74	67-68-71-73-73	352	$2,850.00
Paul Azinger	T74	67-67-67-77-74	352	$2,850.00
Kawika Cotner	T74	72-67-68-74-71	352	$2,850.00
Craig Stadler	77	69-69-68-73-75	354	$2,790.00
Brian Kamm	T78	67-71-68-78-76	360	$2,745.00
Bill Porter	T78	69-68-71-75-77	360	$2,745.00
Tony Sills	80	73-64-71-76-84	368	$2,700.00

The following players did not finish (C=cut, W=withdrew, D=disqualified)

C—209-Bill Britton, Brandel Chamblee, David Frost, Jeff Leonard, Carl Paulson, Dicky Pride, Bobby Wadkins. **210-**Billy Andrade, Michael Bradley, Robin Freeman, Bob Gilder, Tim Loustalot, John Mahaffey, Steve Rintoul, Harry Taylor, Howard Twitty, D.A. Weibring. **211-**Joe Acosta, Jr., Mike Brisky, Chris DiMarco, Keith Fergus, Mike Springer, Hal Sutton. **212-**Brian Claar, Scott Gump, Nolan Henke, Jeff Maggert, Mark Wurtz. **213-**Guy Boros, Bob Burns, John Huston, Greg Kraft, Wayne Levi, David Ogrin, Mike Standly, Fuzzy Zoeller. **214-**Ed Humenik, Dicky Thompson. **215-**Michael Allen, Dave Barr, Robert Gamez, Peter Jacobsen, Don Pooley, Curtis Strange. **216-**Tommy Armour III, Pat Bates, Neal Lancaster, Jay Williamson. **217-**Dudley Hart, Mike Reid. **218-**Joey Sindelar. **219-**Joel Edwards. **220-**Kenny Perry, Tom Purtzer, Don Reese. **221-**J.L. Lewis. **222-**J.P. Hayes, Heinz Thul, Lanny Wadkins. **224-**Ian Baker-Finch. **225-**Mark Carnevale. **227-**Ed Dougherty. **W—148-**Tray Tyner. **D—142-**Keith Clearwater.

LAS VEGAS INVITATIONAL

TOURNAMENT HISTORY

Year	Winner	Score	Runner-up	Score	Location	Par/Yards
PANASONIC LAS VEGAS PRO-CELEBRITY CLASSIC						
1983	Fuzzy Zoeller	340	Rex Caldwell	344	Las Vegas CC, Las Vegas, NV	72/7164
					Desert Inn CC, Las Vegas, NV	72/7111
					Dunes CC, Las Vegas, NV	72/7240
					Showboat CC, Las Vegas, NV	72/7045
PANASONIC LAS VEGAS INVITATIONAL						
1984	Denis Watson	341	Andy Bean	342	Las Vegas CC, Las Vegas, NV	72/7164
					Desert Inn CC, Las Vegas, NV	72/7111
					Showboat CC, Las Vegas, NV	72/7045
					Tropicana CC, Las Vegas, NV	71/6481
1985	Curtis Strange	338	Mike Smith	339	Las Vegas CC, Las Vegas, NV	72/7164
					Desert Inn CC, Las Vegas, NV	72/7111
					Tropicana CC, Las Vegas, NV	71/6481
1986	Greg Norman	333	Dan Pohl	340	Las Vegas CC, Las Vegas, NV	72/7164
					Desert Inn CC, Las Vegas, NV	72/7111
					Spanish Trail G&CC, Las Vegas, NV	72/7088
1987	~Paul Azinger	271	Hal Sutton	272	Las Vegas CC, Las Vegas, NV	72/7164
					Desert Inn CC, Las Vegas, NV	72/7111
					Spanish Trail G&CC, Las Vegas, NV	72/7088
1988	~Gary Koch	274	Peter Jacobsen	275	Las Vegas CC, Las Vegas, NV	72/7164
			Mark O'Meara		Desert Inn CC, Las Vegas, NV	72/7111
					Spanish Trail G&CC, Las Vegas, NV	72/7088
LAS VEGAS INVITATIONAL						
1989	*Scott Hoch	336	Robert Wrenn	336	Las Vegas CC, Las Vegas, NV	72/7164
					Desert Inn CC, Las Vegas, NV	72/7111
					Spanish Trail G&CC, Las Vegas, NV	72/7088
1990	*Bob Tway	334	John Cook	334	Las Vegas CC, Las Vegas, NV	72/7164
					Desert Inn CC, Las Vegas, NV	72/7111
					Spanish Trail G&CC, Las Vegas, NV	72/7088
1991	*Andrew Magee	329	D.A. Weibring	329	Las Vegas CC, Las Vegas, NV	72/7164
					Desert Inn CC, Las Vegas, NV	72/7111
					Sunrise GC, Las Vegas, NV	72/6914
1992	John Cook	334	David Frost	336	Las Vegas CC, Las Vegas, NV	72/7164
					Desert Inn CC, Las Vegas, NV	72/7111
					TPC at Summerlin, Las Vegas, NV	72/7243
1993	Davis Love III	331	Craig Stadler	339	Las Vegas CC, Las Vegas, NV	72/7164
					Desert Inn CC, Las Vegas, NV	72/7111
					TPC at Summerlin, Las Vegas, NV	72/7243
1994	Bruce Lietzke	332	Robert Gamez	333	Las Vegas CC, Las Vegas, NV	72/7164
					Las Vegas Hilton CC, Las Vegas, NV	71/6815
					TPC at Summerlin, Las Vegas, NV	72/7243
1995	Jim Furyk	331`	Billy Mayfair	332	Las Vegas CC, Las Vegas, NV	72/7162
					Las Vegas Hilton CC, Las Vegas, NV	71/6815
					TPC at Summerlin, Las Vegas, NV	72/7243

Tournament Record:	329 -- Andrew Magee/D.A. Weibring, 1991	
Current Course Record:	TPC at Summerlin	62 -- John Cook, 1992
	Las Vegas CC	61 -- Jim Gallagher, Jr., Dicky Thompson (both 1991)
	Las Vegas Hilton CC	63 -- Guy Boros, Scott Hoch (both 1994) Joe Ozaki, Ted Tryba (both 1995)

KEY: *=Playoff ~=Weather-shortened

1995 LACANTERA TEXAS OPEN

LaCantera GC, San Antonio, TX
Par: 36-36—72 **Yards: 6,899**

Purse: $1,100,000
October 19-22, 1995

LEADERS: First Round—Loren Roberts shot an 8-under-par 64 to lead Donnie Hammond and Chris Perry by one stroke. **Second Round**—Duffy Waldorf shot 66 for 12-under-par 132 and led Jay Don Blake by two strokes. **Third Round**—Waldorf, after a 71, was at 13-under-par 203, one stroke ahead of Blake.

CUT: 82 players at 1-over-par 145.

PRO-AM: $7,500. Individual—Bob Estes and Mike Heinen, 66, $675 each. Team—Justin Leonard, 51, $750.

WEATHER: Sunny and warm all week. Windy Friday morning and all day Saturday.

Winner: Duffy Waldorf 66-66-71-65 268 $198,000.00

Player	Pos.	Scores	Total	Money
Justin Leonard	2	67-70-69-68	274	$118,800.00
John Mahaffey	T 3	67-71-71-71	280	$57,200.00
John Morse	T 3	70-69-71-70	280	$57,200.00
Loren Roberts	T 3	64-72-73-71	280	$57,200.00
Jay Don Blake	T 6	67-67-70-77	281	$38,225.00
Mike Standly	T 6	68-71-74-68	281	$38,225.00
Jay Haas	8	68-68-74-72	282	$34,100.00
Lee Rinker	T 9	70-66-72-75	283	$30,800.00
Mark Wiebe	T 9	74-69-70-70	283	$30,800.00
Bart Bryant	T11	67-72-73-72	284	$26,400.00
Steve Jones	T11	70-73-73-68	284	$26,400.00
Blaine McCallister	T13	68-73-73-71	285	$22,000.00
Jim McGovern	T13	72-70-71-72	285	$22,000.00
Tommy Armour III	T15	69-71-75-71	286	$16,500.00
Paul Azinger	T15	68-74-76-68	286	$16,500.00
Mike Brisky	T15	74-65-77-70	286	$16,500.00
Donnie Hammond	T15	65-76-74-71	286	$16,500.00
Kenny Perry	T15	69-72-74-71	286	$16,500.00
Payne Stewart	T15	69-71-78-68	286	$16,500.00
Omar Uresti	T15	72-70-71-73	286	$16,500.00
Brandel Chamblee	T22	69-74-74-70	287	$10,211.67
Bob Estes	T22	68-73-74-72	287	$10,211.67
Paul Goydos	T22	69-72-75-71	287	$10,211.67
Bruce Vaughan	T22	72-72-75-68	287	$10,211.67
Ken Green	T22	71-69-74-73	287	$10,211.66
Dudley Hart	T22	69-72-72-74	287	$10,211.66
Frank Conner	T28	68-72-75-73	288	$7,480.00
Keith Fergus	T28	68-72-74-74	288	$7,480.00
Kelly Gibson	T28	67-71-73-77	288	$7,480.00
Chris Perry	T28	65-76-75-72	288	$7,480.00
Mike Springer	T28	69-74-75-70	288	$7,480.00
David Edwards	T33	73-71-71-74	289	$5,940.00
Joel Edwards	T33	73-71-70-75	289	$5,940.00
Steve Gotsche	T33	68-72-72-77	289	$5,940.00
Mike Hulbert	T33	72-72-71-74	289	$5,940.00
Bob Lohr	T33	70-73-73-73	289	$5,940.00
Rex Caldwell	T38	68-76-73-73	290	$4,620.00
Russ Cochran	T38	70-74-72-74	290	$4,620.00
Jerry Haas	T38	70-75-71-74	290	$4,620.00
Jeff Maggert	T38	68-77-71-74	290	$4,620.00
Scott McCarron	T38	71-74-73-72	290	$4,620.00
Larry Mize	T38	72-71-70-77	290	$4,620.00
Kawika Cotner	T44	72-72-75-72	291	$3,325.67
Mike Heinen	T44	70-73-73-75	291	$3,325.67
David Ogrin	T44	71-70-76-74	291	$3,325.67
Steve Rintoul	T44	76-68-76-71	291	$3,325.67
Dan Forsman	T44	67-77-71-76	291	$3,325.66
Scott Gump	T44	69-75-69-78	291	$3,325.66
David Duval	T50	70-75-74-73	292	$2,678.50
Ed Humenik	T50	68-71-74-79	292	$2,678.50
Steve Pate	T50	73-71-75-73	292	$2,678.50
Kirk Triplett	T50	69-74-76-73	292	$2,678.50
Phil Blackmar	T54	73-70-75-75	293	$2,508.00
Mark Carnevale	T54	70-73-75-75	293	$2,508.00
Jim Carter	T54	68-73-71-81	293	$2,508.00
Tom Kite	T54	72-66-79-76	293	$2,508.00
Anthony Rodriguez	T54	67-73-76-77	293	$2,508.00
Billy Andrade	T59	72-73-75-74	294	$2,387.00
Lennie Clements	T59	70-72-76-76	294	$2,387.00
Greg Kraft	T59	72-71-77-74	294	$2,387.00
Dicky Pride	T59	71-74-76-73	294	$2,387.00
Dillard Pruitt	T59	69-72-79-74	294	$2,387.00
Hal Sutton	T59	67-76-79-72	294	$2,387.00
Curt Byrum	T65	73-69-79-74	295	$2,266.00
David Feherty	T65	71-73-75-76	295	$2,266.00
Ed Fiori	T65	71-71-76-77	295	$2,266.00
Tom Hearn	T65	71-72-74-78	295	$2,266.00
Ken Mcdonald	T65	74-69-77-75	295	$2,266.00
Dick Mast	T70	72-73-73-78	296	$2,189.00
John Wilson	T70	74-69-80-73	296	$2,189.00
Billy Ray Brown	T72	71-72-77-77	297	$2,134.00
Robin Freeman	T72	71-73-76-77	297	$2,134.00
D.A. Weibring	T72	75-70-74-78	297	$2,134.00
John Cook	T75	71-74-82-72	299	$2,079.00
Jay Delsing	T75	71-74-75-79	299	$2,079.00
Steve Brodie	T77	72-71-77-81	301	$2,035.00
Ryan Howison	T77	73-70-80-78	301	$2,035.00
Carl Paulson	79	71-74-81-79	305	$2,002.00
Bruce Lietzke	80	72-73-82-79	306	$1,980.00

The following players did not finish (C=cut, W=withdrew, D=disqualified)

C—146- Michael Allen, Chip Beck, Mark Brooks, Tom Byrum, Marco Dawson, Mike Donald, Brad Faxon, Marco Gortana, Brian Henninger, Jonathan Kaye, J.L. Lewis, Dennis Paulson, Joey Sindelar, Craig Stadler, Ted Tryba, Bobby Wadkins. **147-** John Adams, Guy Boros, Patrick Burke, Bruce Fleisher, Fred Funk, Kirk Johnson, Larry Nelson, Ted Schulz, Jeff Sluman, Dicky Thompson, Tommy Tolles. **148-** Pat Bates, Rick Fehr, Steve Hart, Don Reese, Mike Smith, Scott Verplank. **149-** Ronnie Black, Clark Dennis, Mike Sullivan, Harry Taylor, Jeff Woodland. **150-** Scott Ford, Pete Jordan, Skip Kendall. **151-** Brian Kamm, Steve Lowery. **152-** Nolan Henke. **153-** Ricky Arnett, Emlyn Aubrey. **154-** Scott Hoch. **155-** Jeff Gibralter, Gary Hallberg, Mark Wurtz. **156-** Tray Tyner, Willie Wood. **157-** J.P. Hayes, Martin Lusk, Ron Streck. **160-** Elroy Marti, Jr. **163-** Vic Yannuzzi. **W—217-** Bob Gilder, **73-** Dave Stockton, Jr., **74-** Brad Bryant, Neal Lancaster, Tim Loustalot, Doug Martin, **75-** Howard Twitty, **76-** Hubert Green, Jay Williamson, **78-** John Daly, Tony Sills, **79-**Clark Burroughs, **80-** Joe Acosta, Jr., **81-** Kenny Knox, **83-** Chris DiMarco. **D—145-** Mike Reid, **72-** Paul Stankowski, **77-** Bob Burns.

LACANTERA TEXAS OPEN

TOURNAMENT HISTORY

Year	Winner	Score	Runner-up	Score	Location	Par/Yards
1922	Bob MacDonald	281	Cyril Walker	282	Brackenridge Park GC, San Antonio, TX	71/6185
1923	*Walter Hagen	279	Bill Mehlhorn	279	Brackenridge Park GC, San Antonio, TX	71/6185
1924	Joe Kirkwood	279	George Kerrigan	286	Brackenridge Park GC, San Antonio, TX	71/6185
			James Ockenden			
1925	Joe Turnesa	284	Macdonald Smith	285	Brackenridge Park GC, San Antonio, TX	71/6185
1926	Mac Smith	288	Bobby Cruickshank	289	Brackenridge Park GC, San Antonio, TX	71/6185
1927	Bobby Cruickshank	272	Larry Nabholtz	295	Willow Springs GC, San Antonio, TX	72/6930
1928	Bill Mehlhorn	297	Harry Cooper	298	Willow Springs GC, San Antonio, TX	72/6930
1929	Bill Mehlhorn	277	Horton Smith	281	Brackenridge Park GC, San Antonio, TX	71/6185
1930	Denny Shute	277	Ed Dudley	280	Brackenridge Park GC, San Antonio, TX	71/6185
			Al Espinosa			
			Neil McIntyre			
1931	Abe Espinosa	281	Harry Cooper	283	Brackenridge Park GC, San Antonio, TX	71/6185
			Joe Turnesa			
			Frank Walsh			
1932	Clarence Clark	287	Gus Moreland	288	Brackenridge Park GC, San Antonio, TX	71/6185
			Gene Sarazen			
1933	No Tournament					
1934	Wiffy Cox	283	Byron Nelson	284	Brackenridge Park GC, San Antonio, TX	71/6185
			Craig Wood			
1935-1938	No Tournaments					
1939	Dutch Harrison	271	Sam Byrd	273	Brackenridge Park GC, San Antonio, TX	71/6185
1940	*Byron Nelson	271	Ben Hogan	271	Brackenridge Park GC, San Antonio, TX	71/6185
1941	Lawson Little	273	Ben Hogan	276	Willow Springs GC, San Antonio, TX	72/6930
1942	*Chick Harbert	272	Ben Hogan	272	Willow Springs GC, San Antonio, TX	72/6930
1943	No Tournament					
1944	Johnny Revolta	273	Harold McSpaden	274	Willow Springs GC, San Antonio, TX	72/6930
			Byron Nelson			
1945	Sam Byrd	268	Byron Nelson	269	Willow Springs GC, San Antonio, TX	72/6930
1946	Ben Hogan	264	Sam Byrd	270	Willow Springs GC, San Antonio, TX	72/6930
1947	Ed Oliver	265	Jimmy Demaret	266	Willow Springs GC, San Antonio, TX	72/6930
1948	Sam Snead	264	Jimmy Demaret	266	Willow Springs GC, San Antonio, TX	72/6930
1949	Dave Douglas	268	Sam Snead	269	Willow Springs GC, San Antonio, TX	72/6930
1950	Sam Snead	265	Jimmy Demaret	266	Brackenridge Park GC, San Antonio, TX	71/6185
					Ft. Sam Houston GC, San Antonio, TX	72/6566
1951	*Dutch Harrison	265	Doug Ford	265	Brackenridge Park GC, San Antonio, TX	71/6185
					Ft. Sam Houston GC, San Antonio, TX	72/6566
1952	Jack Burke, Jr.	260	Doug Ford	266	Brackenridge Park GC, San Antonio, TX	71/6185
1953	Tony Holguin	264	Doug Ford	265	Brackenridge Park GC, San Antonio, TX	71/6185
1954	Chandler Harper	259	Johnny Palmer	261	Brackenridge Park GC, San Antonio, TX	71/6185
1955	Mike Souchak	257	Fred Haas	264	Brackenridge Park GC, San Antonio, TX	71/6185
1956	Gene Littler	276	Mike Fetchick	278	Ft. Sam Houston GC, San Antonio, TX	72/6566
			Frank Stranahan			
			Ernie Vossler			
1957	Jay Hebert	271	Ed Furgol	272	Brackenridge Park GC, San Antonio, TX	71/6185
1958	Bill Johnston	274	Bob Rosburg	277	Brackenridge Park GC, San Antonio, TX	71/6185
1959	Wes Ellis	276	Bill Johnston	278	Brackenridge Park GC, San Antonio, TX	71/6185
			Tom Nieporte			
1960	Arnold Palmer	276	Doug Ford	278	Ft. Sam Houston GC, San Antonio, TX	72/6566
			Frank Stranahan			
1961	Arnold Palmer	270	Al Balding	271	Oak Hills CC, San Antonio, TX	70/6576
1962	Arnold Palmer	273	Joe Campbell	274	Oak Hills CC, San Antonio, TX	70/6576
			Gene Littler			
			Mason Rudolph			
			Doug Sanders			
1963	Phil Rodgers	268	Johnny Pott	270	Oak Hills CC, San Antonio, TX	70/6576
1964	Bruce Crampton	273	Bob Charles	274	Oak Hills CC, San Antonio, TX	70/6576
			Chi Chi Rodriguez			

LACANTERA TEXAS OPEN

TOURNAMENT HISTORY

Year	Winner	Score	Runner-up	Score	Location	Par/Yards
1965	Frank Beard	270	Gardner Dickinson	273	Oak Hills CC, San Antonio, TX	70/6576
1966	Harold Henning	272	Wes Ellis Gene Littler Ken Still	275	Oak Hills CC, San Antonio, TX	70/6576
1967	Chi Chi Rodriguez	277	Bob Charles Bob Goalby	278	Pecan Valley CC, San Antonio, TX	71/7183
1968	No Tournament					
1969	*Deane Beman	274	Jack McGowan	274	Pecan Valley CC, San Antonio, TX	71/7183
SAN ANTONIO TEXAS OPEN						
1970	Ron Cerrudo	273	Dick Lotz	278	Pecan Valley CC, San Antonio, TX	71/7183
1971	No Tournament					
1972	Mike Hill	273	Lee Trevino	275	Woodlake GC, San Antonio, TX	72/7143
1973	Ben Crenshaw	270	Orville Moody	272	Woodlake GC, San Antonio, TX	71/6990
1974	Terry Diehl	269	Mike Hill	270	Woodlake GC, San Antonio, TX	72/7143
1975	*Don January	275	Larry Hinson	275	Woodlake GC, San Antonio, TX	72/7143
1976	*Butch Baird	273	Miller Barber	273	Woodlake GC, San Antonio, TX	72/7143
1977	Hale Irwin	266	Miller Barber	268	Oak Hills CC, San Antonio, TX	70/6576
1978	Ron Streck	265	Hubert Green Lon Hinkle	266	Oak Hills CC, San Antonio, TX	70/6576
1979	Lou Graham	268	Eddie Pearce Bill Rogers Doug Tewell	269	Oak Hills CC, San Antonio, TX	70/6576
1980	Lee Trevino	265	Terry Diehl	266	Oak Hills CC, San Antonio, TX	70/6576
TEXAS OPEN						
1981	*Bill Rogers	266	Ben Crenshaw	266	Oak Hills CC, San Antonio, TX	70/6576
1982	Jay Haas	262	Curtis Strange	265	Oak Hills CC, San Antonio, TX	70/6576
1983	Jim Colbert	261	Mark Pfeil	266	Oak Hills CC, San Antonio, TX	70/6576
1984	Calvin Peete	266	Bruce Lietzke	269	Oak Hills CC, San Antonio, TX	70/6576
1985	*John Mahaffey	268	Jodie Mudd	268	Oak Hills CC, San Antonio, TX	70/6576
VANTAGE CHAMPIONSHIP						
1986	~Ben Crenshaw	196	Payne Stewart	197	Oak Hills CC, San Antonio, TX	70/6576
TEXAS OPEN PRESENTED BY NABISCO						
1988	Corey Pavin	259	Robert Wrenn	267	Oak Hills CC, San Antonio, TX	70/6576
1989	Donnie Hammond	258	Paul Azinger	265	Oak Hills CC, San Antonio, TX	70/6576
H-E-B TEXAS OPEN						
1990	Mark O'Meara	261	Gary Hallberg	262	Oak Hills CC, San Antonio, TX	70/6576
1991	*Blaine McCallister	269	Gary Hallberg	269	Oak Hills CC, San Antonio, TX	70/6576
1992	*Nick Price	263	Steve Elkington	263	Oak Hills CC, San Antonio, TX	71/6650
1993	*Jay Haas	263	Bob Lohr	263	Oak Hills CC, San Antonio, TX	71/6650
TEXAS OPEN						
1994	Bob Estes	265	Gil Morgan	266	Oak Hills CC, San Antonio, TX	71/6650
LACANTERA TEXAS OPEN						
1995	Duffy Waldorf	268	Justin Leonard	274	LaCantera GC, San Antonio, TX	72/6899

Tournament Record: 257 -- Mike Souchak, 1995 (Brackenridge Park GC)
Current Course Record: 64 -- Loren Roberts, 1995

KEY: * = Playoff ~ = Weather-shortened

1995 TOUR CHAMPIONSHIP

Southern Hills CC, Tulsa, OK
Par: 35-35—70 Yards: 6,834

Purse: $3,000,000
October 26-29, 1995

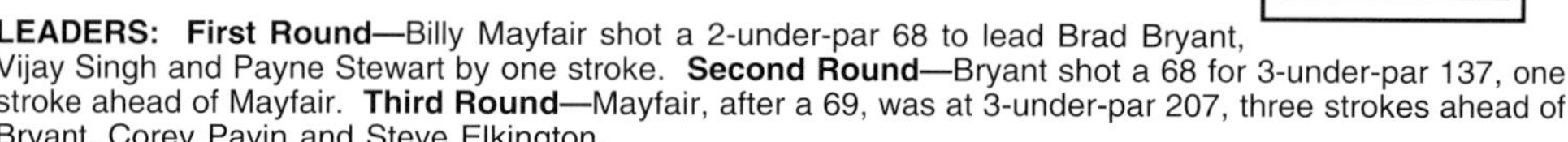

LEADERS: First Round—Billy Mayfair shot a 2-under-par 68 to lead Brad Bryant, Vijay Singh and Payne Stewart by one stroke. **Second Round**—Bryant shot a 68 for 3-under-par 137, one stroke ahead of Mayfair. **Third Round**—Mayfair, after a 69, was at 3-under-par 207, three strokes ahead of Bryant, Corey Pavin and Steve Elkington.

PRO-AM: $10,000. Individual—Justin Leonard, Nick Price, Tom Lehman, Corey Pavin and Woody Austin, 69, $720 each. Team—Fred Funk, Kirk Triplett and Phil Mickelson, 58, $833.33.

WEATHER: Sunny and windy each day with highs near 70.

Winner: Billy Mayfair 68-70-69-73 280 $540,000.00

Player	Pos.	Scores	Total	Money
Steve Elkington	T 2	71-72-67-73	283	$265,500.00
Corey Pavin	T 2	72-70-68-73	283	$265,500.00
Woody Austin	T 4	71-68-73-72	284	$132,000.00
Scott Simpson	T 4	71-70-74-69	284	$132,000.00
Vijay Singh	6	69-71-72-73	285	$108,000.00
Brad Bryant	T 7	69-68-73-76	286	$99,000.00
Justin Leonard	T 7	70-70-72-74	286	$99,000.00
David Duval	T 9	74-69-71-73	287	$87,600.00
Greg Norman	T 9	72-70-74-71	287	$87,600.00
Loren Roberts	11	73-68-74-73	288	$81,000.00
Tom Lehman	12	71-70-73-76	290	$76,800.00
Nick Faldo	T13	76-72-73-70	291	$71,400.00
Mark O'Meara	T13	71-74-71-75	291	$71,400.00
Bob Tway	15	70-75-72-75	292	$66,000.00
Ernie Els	T16	71-74-75-73	293	$60,900.00
Peter Jacobsen	T16	73-70-73-77	293	$60,900.00
Davis Love III	T16	74-73-74-72	293	$60,900.00
Payne Stewart	T16	69-75-74-75	293	$60,900.00
Jay Haas	T20	75-74-73-72	294	$55,800.00
Lee Janzen	T20	75-70-71-78	294	$55,800.00
Kenny Perry	T20	76-72-70-76	294	$55,800.00
Kirk Triplett	T20	77-71-69-77	294	$55,800.00
Phil Mickelson	24	79-73-68-75	295	$52,800.00
Ben Crenshaw	T25	74-73-73-76	296	$51,000.00
Jim Gallagher, Jr.	T25	74-73-75-74	296	$51,000.00
Mark Calcavecchia	T27	72-75-73-77	297	$49,200.00
Fred Funk	T27	74-75-72-76	297	$49,200.00
Scott Hoch	T27	75-72-71-79	297	$49,200.00
Nick Price	30	77-73-74-75	299	$48,000.00

THE TOUR CHAMPIONSHIP

TOURNAMENT HISTORY

Year	Winner	Score	Runner-up	Score	Location	Par/Yards
NABISCO CHAMPIONSHIPS OF GOLF						
1987	Tom Watson	268	Chip Beck	270	Oak Hills CC, San Antonio, TX	70/6576
NABISCO GOLF CHAMPIONSHIPS						
1988	*Curtis Strange	279	Tom Kite	279	Pebble Beach GL, Monterey Peninsula, CA	72/6815
	(won playoff with birdie on second extra hole)					
NABISCO CHAMPIONSHIPS						
1989	*Tom Kite	276	Payne Stewart	276	Harbour Town GL, Hilton Head, SC	71/6657
	(won playoff with par on second extra hole)					
1990	*Jodie Mudd	273	Billy Mayfair	273	Champions GC, Houston, TX	71/7187
	(won playoff with birdie on first extra hole)					
THE TOUR CHAMPIONSHIP						
1991	*Craig Stadler	279	Russ Cochran	279	Pinehurst No. 2, Pinehurst, NC	71/7005
	(won playoff with birdie on second extra hole)					
1992	Paul Azinger	276	Lee Janzen Corey Pavin	279	Pinehurst No. 2, Pinehurst, NC	71/7005
1993	Jim Gallagher, Jr.	277	David Frost John Huston Greg Norman Scott Simpson	278	The Olympic Club, San Francisco, CA	71/6812
1994	*Mark McCumber	274	Fuzzy Zoeller	274	The Olympic Club, San Francisco, CA	71/6812
	(won playoff with birdie on first extra hole)					
1995	Billy Mayfair	280	Steve Elkington Corey Pavin	283	Southern Hills CC, Tulsa, OK	70/6834

NOTE: Each year, the top 30 PGA TOUR members on the money list compete at the season-ending TOUR Championship. The 1996 TOUR Championship will be played at Southern Hills CC in Tulsa, OK.

Tournament Record: 268 -- Tom Watson, 1987 (Oak Hills CC)
Tournament 18-Hole Record: 63 -- Wayne Levi, 1989 (Harbour Town GL); Wayne Levi, 1990 (Champions GC); Jim Gallagher, Jr., 1993 (Olympic Club)

KEY: *= Playoff

1995 LINCOLN-MERCURY KAPALUA INTERNATIONAL

Kapalua Resort, Kapalua, Maui, HI
Plantation Course Par: 36-37—73 Yards: 7,263
Bay Course Par: 35-36—71 Yards: 6,600

Purse: $1,000,000
November 2-5, 1995

LEADERS: First Round—Gary McCord (PC) fired a 7-under-par 66 for a one-stroke lead over Darren Clarke (BC), Jim Furyk (BC) and Mike Standly (BC). **Second Round**—Furyk (PC), at 14-under-par 130, led by three strokes over Russ Cochran (BC) and Davis Love III (PC). **Third Round**—Furyk, at 16-under-par 201, led by two strokes over Steve Pate, Jim McGovern and Hale Irwin.

WEATHER: Partly cloudy with little wind both Thursday and Friday. Windy and cloudy during the morning and then sunny with a light breeze Saturday afternoon. Sunday was beautiful with a light breeze.

Winner: Jim Furyk 65-65-71-70—271 $180,000.00

Player	Pos.	Scores	Money
Russ Cochran	T2	67-66-73-67—273	$70,950.00
Barry Lane	T2	66-69-69-69—273	$70,950.00
Jim McGovern	T2	66-69-68-70—273	$70,950.00
Ben Crenshaw	T5	67-67-71-69—274	$34,000.00
Tom Lehman	T5	67-69-69-69—274	$34,000.00
Steve Jones	T7	73-65-72-65—275	$26,500.00
Marco Dawson	T7	67-67-73-68—275	$26,500.00
Fred Couples	T9	68-72-69-67—276	$21,333.34
Kirk Triplett	T9	68-66-74-68—276	$21,333.33
Hale Irwin	T9	68-67-68-73—276	$21,333.33
Dave Stockton, Jr.	T12	69-68-74-66—277	$18,500.00
Neal Lancaster	T12	72-68-68-69—277	$18,500.00
Jay Delsing	T14	72-67-72-67—278	$14,485.72
John Schroeder	T14	67-72-72-67—278	$14,485.71
Guy Boros	T14	68-70-74-66—278	$14,485.71
Bob Lohr	T14	66-73-71-68—278	$14,485.71
Sandy Lyle	T14	68-68-73-69—278	$14,485.71
Peter Jacobsen	T14	68-66-71-73—278	$14,485.71
Steve Pate	T14	71-67-65-75—278	$14,485.71
Billy Andrade	T21	69-70-69-71—279	$11,850.00
Davis Love III	T21	69-64-73-73—279	$11,850.00
Lennie Clements	T23	69-72-69-70—280	$10,612.50
Nolan Henke	T23	69-68-73-70—280	$10,612.50
Mike Heinen	T23	67-67-74-72—280	$10,612.50
Gary McCord	T23	66-72-70-72—280	$10,612.50
Jay Don Blake	T27	69-67-75-70—281	$9,550.00
Duffy Waldorf	T27	70-69-73-69—281	$9,550.00
Brian Claar	T27	69-71-66-75—281	$9,550.00
Scott Simpson	T30	72-68-70-72—282	$9,050.00
Blaine McCallister	T30	69-73-70-70—282	$9,050.00
Jerry Pate	T32	67-72-74-70—283	$8,700.00
John Adams	T32	66-71-72-74—283	$8,700.00
Howard Twitty	T32	67-72-69-75—283	$8,700.00
Mike Standly	T32	65-70-72-76—283	$8,700.00
Robin Freeman	36	71-71-70-72—284	$8,450.00
Mike Hulbert	T37	72-65-75-73—285	$8,300.00
Tom Purtzer	T37	73-65-72-75—285	$8,300.00
Mike Sullivan	T37	73-62-78-72—285	$8,300.00
Doug Martin	T40	73-69-71-73—286	$8,175.00
Chip Beck	T40	72-70-72-72—286	$8,175.00
Woody Austin	T42	75-65-73-74—287	$8,025.00
Roger Maltbie	T42	67-68-79-73—287	$8,025.00
Andy Bean	T42	75-66-74-72—287	$8,025.00
Steve Lowery	T42	70-70-78-69—287	$8,025.00
Darren Clarke	T46	65-70-78-75—288	$7,850.00
Ted Tryba	T46	70-70-75-73—288	$7,850.00
John Cook	T46	74-67-76-71—288	$7,850.00
Brandel Chamblee	49	67-75-74-73—289	$7,750.00
John Mahaffey	50	70-71-75-74—290	$7,700.00
John Morse	51	74-70-77-70—291	$7,650.00
Michael Bradley	T52	74-68-75-75—292	$7,635.00
Ed Dougherty	T52	74-71-75-72—292	$7,635.00
David Feherty	54	71-75-72-75—293	$7,620.00
Grant Waite	55	68-78-75-77—298	$7,610.00

The following players did not finish **(C=cut, W=withdrew, D=disqualified)**

D—Robert Gamez, $7,600.00.

LINCOLN-MERCURY KAPALUA INTERNATIONAL

TOURNAMENT HISTORY

Year	Winner	Score	Runner-up	Score	Location	Par/Yards
KAPALUA INTERNATIONAL						
1983	Greg Norman	268			Bay Course, Kapalua GC, Kapalua, Maui, HI	71/6731
1984	Sandy Lyle	266			Bay Course, Kapalua GC, Kapalua, Maui, HI	71/6731
ISUZU KAPALUA INTERNATIONAL						
1985	Mark O'Meara	275	Corey Pavin		Bay Course, Kapalua GC, Kapalua, Maui, HI	72/6731
1986	Andy Bean	278	Davis Love III	280	Bay Course, Kapalua GC, Kapalua, Maui, HI	72/6731
1987	Andy Bean	267	Lanny Wadkins	270	Bay Course, Kapalua GC, Kapalua, Maui, HI	72/6731
1988	Bob Gilder	266	John Mahaffey	268	Bay Course, Kapalua GC, Kapalua, Maui, HI	72/6731
1989	*Peter Jacobsen	270	Steve Pate	270	Bay Course, Kapalua GC, Kapalua, Maui, HI	72/6731
1990	David Peoples	264	Davis Love III	269	Bay Course, Kapalua GC, Kapalua, Maui, HI	71/6731
PING KAPALUA INTERNATIONAL						
1991	*Mike Hulbert	276	Davis Love III	276	Plantation Course, Kapalua GC, Kapalua, Maui, HI	73/7263
LINCOLN-MERCURY KAPALUA INTERNATIONAL						
1992	Davis Love III	275	Mike Hulbert	276	Plantation Course, Kapalua GC, Kapalua, Maui, HI	73/7263
					Bay Course, Kapalua GC, Kapalua, Maui, HI	71/6731
1993	Fred Couples	274	Blaine McCallister	278	Plantation Course, Kapalua GC, Kapalua, Maui, HI	73/7263
					Bay Course, Kapalua GC, Kapalua, Maui, HI	71/6731
1994	Fred Couples	279	Bob Gilder	281	Plantation Course, Kapalua GC, Kapalua, Maui, HI	73/7263
					Bay Course, Kapalua GC, Kapalua, Maui, HI	71/6731
1995	Jim Furyk	271	Russ Cochran	273	Plantation Course, Kapalua GC, Kapalua, Maui, HI	73/7263
			Barry Lane		Bay Course, Kapalua GC, Kapalua, Maui, HI	71/6731
			Jim McGovern			

Tournament Record:	264 -- David Peoples, 1990	
Current Course Record:	Plantation Course	64 -- Davis Love III, 1995
	Bay Course	62 -- Mike Sullivan, 1995

KEY: *= Playoff

WORLD CUP OF GOLF BY HEINEKEN

TPC at Mission Hills, Shenzhen, China **Purse: $1,500,000**
Par: 36-36—72 Yards: 7,102 **November 9-12, 1995**

LEADERS: First Round—Fred Couples (68) and Davis Love III (65) of the United States had an 11-under-par total of 133 and led by three strokes over Sweden (Jesper Parnevik-67 and Jarmo Sandelin-69) at 8-under-par 136. **Second Round**—Couples (69) and Love (67) added an 8-under-par total of 136 for a 19-under-par 269, and they led by four strokes over Sweden (Parnevik-66 and Sandelin-71) at 15-under-par 273. **Third Round**—Couples (70) and Love (68) increased their lead to 10 strokes with a 6-under-par 138 for the day and total of 25-under-par 407. Japan at 15-under-par 417 moved into second place with Hisayuki Sasaki (62-69-67—198) and Hiroshi Goda (77-72-70—219).

INTERNATIONAL TROPHY (INDIVIDUAL) LEADERS: First Round—Hisayuki Sasaki of Japan set a World Cup record with 10-under-par 29-33—62 (11 birdies, 1 bogey). Davis Love III of the United States was second at 7-under-par 30-35—65. **Second Round**—Sasaki added a 3-under-par 69 for 13-under-par 131. Love was only one stroke back at 12-under-par 132 after a 67. **Third Round**—Sasaki, with a 5-under-par 67, moved to 18-under-par 198 and had a two-stroke lead over Love, 68 for 16-under-par 200.

WINNER: UNITED STATES - 543 (-33)

Davis Love III	**65-67-68-67**	**267**	**$200,000.00**
Fred Couples	**68-69-70-69**	**276**	**$200,000.00**

2 AUSTRALIA - 557 (-19)			
Brett Ogle	70-71-69-68	278	$100,000.00
Robert Allenby	68-73-68-70	279	$100,000.00
T3 SCOTLAND - 558 (-18)			
Sam Torrance	68-70-64-69	271	$56,250.00
Andrew Coltart	70-74-72-71	287	$56,250.00
T3 JAPAN - 558 (-18)			
Hisayuki Sasaki	62-69-67-69	267	$56,250.00
Hiroshi Goda	77-72-70-72	291	$56,250.00
5 NEW ZEALAND - 559 (-17)			
Frank Nobilo	73-70-70-71	284	$40,000.00
Michael Campbell	69-71-67-68	275	$40,000.00
T6 FRANCE - 561 (-15)			
Jean Van De Velde	69-72-68-69	278	$26,250.00
Jean Louis Guepy	72-69-72-70	285	$26,250.00
T6 IRELAND - 561 (-15)			
Philip Walton	73-71-71-71	286	$26,250.00
Darren Clarke	68-69-69-69	275	$26,250.00
8 SOUTH AFRICA - 563 (-13)			
Hendrick Buhrmann	74-73-70-71	288	$16,000.00
Retief Goosen	71-66-66-72	275	$16,000.00
9 SWEDEN - 564 (-12)			
Jarmo Sandelin	69-71-73-74	287	$14,000.00
Jesper Parnevik	67-66-73-71	277	$14,000.00
T10 ZIMBABWE - 565 (-11)			
Tony Johnstone	67-78-68-71	284	$11,000.00
Mark McNulty	71-72-69-69	281	$11,000.00
T10 MEXICO - 565 (-11)			
Esteban Toledo	70-67-68-73	278	$11,000.00
Rafael Alarcon	72-70-73-72	287	$11,000.00
T12 SWITZERLAND - 566 (-10)			
Andre Bossert	71-73-72-67	283	$8,000.00
Paolo Quirici	73-72-72-66	283	$8,000.00
T12 ITALY - 566 (-10)			
Silvio Grappasonni	72-75-72-73	292	$8,000.00
Costantino Rocca	70-68-64-72	274	$8,000.00
14 GERMANY - 567 (-9)			
Sven Struver	73-73-69-70	285	$6,500.00
Alexander Cejka	71-70-72-69	282	$6,500.00

WORLD CUP OF GOLF BY HEINEKEN

15 SPAIN - 569 (-7)			
Santiago Luna	66-71-69-70	276	$5,500.00
Ignacio Garrido	74-75-75-69	293	$5,500.00
16 WALES - 570 (-6)			
Phillip Price	73-70-72-72	287	$5,000.00
Mark Mouland	68-74-71-70	283	$5,000.00
17 CANADA - 571 (-5)			
Jim Rutledge	72-76-71-73	292	$4,500.00
Rick Gibson	67-73-71-68	279	$4,500.00
18 HOLLAND - 572 (-4)			
Rolf Muntz	73-75-68-70	286	$4,400.00
Joost Steenkamer	70-70-73-73	286	$4,400.00
19 FINLAND - 579 (2)			
Anssi Kankkonen	72-71-73-68	284	$4,300.00
Kalle Vainola	76-70-75-73	294	$4,300.00
T20 PHILIPPINES - 580 (4)			
Frankie Minoza	71-74-71-71	287	$4,100.00
Robert Pactolerin	72-74-74-73	293	$4,100.00
T20 PARAGUAY - 580 (4)			
Gregorio Nelson Cabrera	70-74-75-75	294	$4,100.00
Marco Ruiz	74-71-71-70	286	$4,100.00
T20 ENGLAND - 580 (4)			
Paul Broadhurst	73-74-76-75	298	$4,100.00
Mark Roe	68-69-72-73	282	$4,100.00
23 ARGENTINA - 582 (6)			
Cesar Monasterio	75-77-74-76	302	$3,900.00
Eduardo Romero	67-76-70-67	280	$3,900.00
T24 REPUBLIC OF KOREA - 583 (7)			
Sang Ho Choi	71-72-72-72	287	$3,750.00
Kwang-Soo Choi	78-73-73-72	296	$3,750.00
T24 DENMARK - 583 (7)			
Steen Tinning	75-71-72-74	292	$3,750.00
Anders Sorensen	73-74-79-75	291	$3,750.00
26 THAILAND - 585 (9)			
Thamnoon Sriroj	70-67-74-73	284	$3,600.00
Udorn Duangdecha	80-76-73-72	301	$3,600.00
27 CHINA - 588 (12)			
Cheng Jun	76-74-74-72	296	$3,500.00
Zhang Lianwei	75-74-68-75	292	$3,500.00
28 VENEZUELA - 589 (13)			
Henrique Lavie	78-72-73-70	293	$3,400.00
Emilio Miartuz	76-74-72-74	296	$3,400.00
29 MALAYSIA - 590 (14)			
Mohammed Ali Kadir	70-76-78-73	297	$3,300.00
Marimuthu Ramayah	70-76-74-73	293	$3,300.00
30 COLOMBIA - 596 (20)			
Jesus Amaya	76-73-74-80	303	$3,200.00
Angel Romero	73-72-75-73	293	$3,200.00
31 SRI LANKA - 603 (27)			
Nandesena Perera	77-71-75-74	297	$3,100.00
Koswinna Chandradasa	78-74-77-77	306	$3,100.00
32 PERU - 634 (58)			
Luis Felipe Graf	74-77-84-81	316	$3,000.00
Niceforo Quispe	84-81-77-76	318	$3,000.00

INTERNATIONAL TROPHY

1 Davis Love III, USA*	65-67-68-67	267	$100,000.00
2 Hisayuki Sasaki, Japan	62-69-67-69	267	$50,000.00
3 Sam Torrance, Scotland	68-70-64-69	271	$25,000.00
4 Costantino Rocca, Italy	70-68-64-72	274	$15,000.00
T5 Darren Clarke, Ireland	68-69-69-69	275	$3,333.33
T5 Retief Goosen, South Africa	71-66-66-72	275	$3,333.33
T5 Michael Campbell, New Zealand	69-71-67-68	275	$3,333.00

* Won playoff.

1995 FRANKLIN TEMPLETON SHARK SHOOTOUT

Franklin Templeton
SHARK
SHOOTOUT
HOSTED BY GREG NORMAN
SHERWOOD COUNTRY CLUB

Sherwood CC, Thousand Oaks, CA | **Purse: $1,100,000**
Par: 36-36--72 Yards: 7,025 | **November 17-19, 1995**

Round #1 format: *Modified Alternate Shot*
Round #2 format: *Best Ball*
Round #3 format: *Scramble*

LEADERS: First Round--Mark Calcavecchia/Steve Elkington and Jay Haas/Tom Kite posted 8-under-par 64s in the alternate shot format and held a one-stroke lead over Chip Beck/Lee Janzen and Ray Floyd/Greg Norman. **Second Round--**Calcavecchia/Elkington, after an 11-under-par 61 in the best ball format, stood at 19-under-par 125. That was good for a two-stroke lead over David Duval/Tom Lehman.

WEATHER: Sunny and clear all week, with temperatures in the upper 70s.

Winners: Mark Calcavecchia/Steve Elkington 64-61-59--184 $150,000.00

2.	Lee Janzen/Chip Beck	65-63-57	185	$85,000.00 each
T3.	Fred Couples/Brad Faxon	68-62-57	187	$51,000.00 each
	Tom Lehman/David Duval	66-61-60	187	$51,000.00 each
5.	Greg Norman/Ray Floyd	65-65-58	188	$41,500.00 each
T6.	Hale Irwin/Bruce Lietzke	67-63-59	189	$37,750.00 each
	Tom Kite/Jay Haas	64-66-59	189	$37,750.00 each
8.	Arnold Palmer/Peter Jacobsen	66-67-59	192	$34,000.00 each
9.	Curtis Strange/Mark O'Meara	69-67-58	194	$32,000.00 each
10.	Fuzzy Zoeller/John Daly	69-68-60	197	$30,000.00 each

TOURNAMENT HISTORY

Year	Winner	Score	Location	Par/Yards
RMCC INVITATIONAL				
1989	Curtis Strange/ Mark O'Meara	190	Sherwood CC Thousand Oaks, CA	72/7025
1990	Ray Floyd/ Fred Couples	182	Sherwood CC Thousand Oaks, CA	72/7025
SHARK SHOOTOUT BENEFITING RMCC				
1991	Tom Purtzer/ Lanny Wadkins	189	Sherwood CC Thousand Oaks, CA	72/7025
FRANKLIN FUNDS SHARK SHOOT OUT				
1992	Davis Love III/ Tom Kite	191	Sherwood CC Thousand Oaks, CA	72/7025
1993	Steve Elkington/ Ray Floyd	188	Sherwood CC Thousand Oaks, CA	72/7025
1994	Fred Couples/ Brad Faxon	190	Sherwood CC Thousand Oaks, CA	72/7025
1995	Mark Calcavecchia/ Steve Elkington	184	Sherwood CC Thousand Oaks, CA	72/7025

Tournament Record: 182 -- Ray Floyd/Fred Couples (1990)

1995 SKINS GAME

Bighorn GC, Palm Desert, CA **Purse: $540,000**
Par: 36-36--72 **Yards: 6,850** **Nov. 25-26, 1995**

WEATHER: Clear and sunny both days with highs in the upper 80s.

Holes 1-6:	$20,000
Holes 7-12:	$30,000
Holes 13-18:	$40,000

Hole	(par)	
1	(5)	Couples, Pavin, Jacobsen halve with birdie
2	(4)	Four players halve with par
3	(5)	Couples and Jacobsen halve with birdie
4	(3)	Four players halve with par
5	(4)	Pavin chips in for eagle-2 from 25-ft behind pin/collects $100,000 (five skins)
6	(4)	Pavin and Watson halve with par
7	(4)	Pavin wins with birdie/collects $50,000 (two skins)
8	(3)	Jacobsen wins with birdie/collects $30,000
9	(4)	Watson and Jacobsen halve with birdie
10	(4)	Couples, Pavin and Jacobsen halve with par
11	(3)	Pavin wins with birdie/collects $90,000
12	(5)	Couples and Pavin halve with par
13	(4)	Couples and Watson halve with birdie
14	(4)	Four players halve with par
15	(5)	Jacobsen and Watson halve with birdie
16	(4)	Four players halve with par
17	(3)	Jacobsen and Watson halve with par
18	(4)	Couples and Jacobsen halve with birdie
		NOTE: The 18th hole was for seven skins and a Skins Game record $270,000.

Playoffs:

18	(4)	Couples/Pavin advance with birdie, Jacobsen/Watson eliminated
17	(3)	Couples and Pavin halve with par
18	(4)	Couples and Pavin halve with par
17	(3)	Couples and Pavin halve with par
18	(4)	Couples wins with birdie/collects $270,000

Final Standings:

Fred Couples	$270,000 (8 skins)
Corey Pavin	$240,000 (10 skins)
Peter Jacobsen	$30,000 (1 skin)
Tom Watson	no skins

TOURNAMENT HISTORY

Year	Winner	Winnings	Location	Par/Yards
1983	Gary Player	$170,000	Desert Highlands CC, Scottsdale, AZ	72/7100
1984	Jack Nicklaus	$240,000	Desert Highlands CC, Scottsdale, AZ	72/7100
1985	Fuzzy Zoeller	$255,000	Bear Creek CC, Murietta, CA	72/7024
1986	Fuzzy Zoeller	$370,000	TPC at PGA West, La Quinta, CA	72/7271
1987	Lee Trevino	$310,000	TPC at PGA West, La Quinta, CA	72/7271
1988	Ray Floyd	$290,000	TPC at PGA West, La Quinta, CA	72/7271
1989	Curtis Strange	$265,000	TPC at PGA West, La Quinta, CA	72/7271
1990	Curtis Strange	$225,000	TPC at PGA West, La Quinta, CA	72/7271
1991	Payne Stewart	$260,000	TPC at PGA West, La Quinta, CA	72/7271
1992	Payne Stewart	$220,000	Bighorn GC, Palm Desert, CA	72/6848
1993	Payne Stewart	$280,000	Bighorn GC, Palm Desert, CA	72/6848
1994	Tom Watson	$210,000	Bighorn GC, Palm Desert, CA	72/6848
1995	Fred Couples	$270,000	Bighorn GC, Palm Desert, CA	72/6848

Tournament Record: $370,000 — Fuzzy Zoeller (1986)

1995 JCPENNEY CLASSIC

Innisbrook Hilton Resort, Tarpon Springs, FL Purse: $1,300,000
Par: 36-35--71 Yards: 7,054/6,394 November 30-December 3, 1995

LEADERS: First Round--The team of Jay Delsing/Val Skinner posted a 62 to lead Robert Gamez/Helen Alfredsson, Mark McCumber/Laura Davies and Michael Bradley/Katie Peterson-Parker by one shot. **Second Round--**McCumber/Davies led Delsing/Skinner by a stroke. **Third Round--** Davis Love III/Beth Daniel and Delsing/Skinner shared a one shot lead over four teams.

PRO-AM: $10,000. Tuesday: Individual--Steve Jones, 65, $250. Team--Skip Kendall, 60, $225. Wednesday: Individual--Mark McCumber, 65, $250. Team--Mark McCumber, 59, $250.

WEATHER: Beautiful all week.

WINNERS: Davis Love III/Beth Daniel 66-65-63-63 257 $162,500.00

2.	Robert Gamez/Helen Alfredsson	63-67-65-64	259	$79,000.00
3.	Jesper Parnevik/Annika Sorenstam	67-66-64-63	260	$52,000.00
4.	Mark McCumber/Laura Davies	63-65-67-67	262	$39,500.00
5.	Jay Delsing/Val Skinner	62-67-65-69	63	$29,750.00
T6.	Kenny Perry/Michelle McGann	69-63-68-64	264	$22,755.00
	Michael Bradley/Katie Peterson-Parker	63-68-64-69	264	$22,755.00
T8.	Billy Mayfair/Brandie Burton	69-68-64-64	265	$14,406.67
	John Huston/Liselotte Neumann	66-68-64-67	265	$14,406.67
	Billy Andrade/Kris Tschetter	66-65-65-69	265	$14,406.67
T11.	Bill Glasson/Kelly Robbins	70-65-66-65	266	$10,275.00
	Dan Forsman/Pam Wright	64-67-67-68	266	$10,275.00
T13.	Doug Martin/Carin Hjalmarsson	66-64-69-68	267	$8,390.00
	Steve Jones/Barb Thomas	65-65-68-69	267	$8,390.00
	Glen Day/Melissa McNamara	68-63-67-69	267	$8,390.00
	Bob Lohr/Marianne Morris	68-64-66-69	267	$8,390.00
T17.	Jim Gallagher, Jr./Jackie Gallagher-Smith	65-70-66-67	268	$6,230.00
	Brad Bryant/Marta Figueras-Dotti	70-64-65-69	268	$6,230.00
	Jay Haas/Cathy Gerring	66-68-63-71	268	$6,230.00
	Gene Sauers/Hollis Stacy	64-66-65-73	268	$6,230.00
21.	Steve Stricker/Vicki Goetze	65-65-67-72	269	$5,300.00
T22.	Kirk Triplett/Julie Larsen	66-67-68-69	270	$5,000.00
	Gary Koch/Tammie Green	67-66-68-69	270	$5,000.00
	Mike Brisky/Barb Mucha	68-67-66-69	270	$5,000.00
	John Adams/Alice Miller	65-66-67-72	270	$5,000.00
T26.	Mark Brooks/Cindy Figg-Currier	67-68-67-69	271	$4,395.00
	Jeff Sluman/Dottie Mochrie	67-69-66-69	271	$4,395.00
	Curt Byrum/Jan Stephenson	68-69-66-68	271	$4,395.00
	Jim Furyk/Lisa Kiggens	68-70-65-68	271	$4,395.00
	Dillard Pruitt/Amy Fruhwirth	66-69-69-67	271	$4,395.00
	Marco Dawson/Elaine Crosby	66-70-70-65	271	$4,395.00
	Tom Purtzer/Juli Inkster	67-73-66-65	271	$4,395.00
T33.	Jim McGovern/Dale Eggeling	68-68-67-69	272	$3,850.00
	Fred Funk/Tina Barrett	70-67-68-67	272	$3,850.00
T35.	Larry Rinker/Laurie Rinker-Graham	66-70-68-69	273	$3,627.50
	Jim Albus/Margaret Platt	67-70-67-69	273	$3,627.50
T37.	Nolan Henke/Terry-Jo Myers	69-67-67-71	274	$3,233.75
	Brian Claar/Jane Geddes	67-68-69-70	274	$3,233.75
	Woody Austin/Page Dunlap	67-70-68-69	274	$3,233.75
	Jonathan Kaye/Tracy Hanson	67-66-65-76	274	$3,233.75
	Robin Freeman/Amy Alcott	67-70-69-68	274	$3,233.75
	John Mahaffey/Cindy Rarick	68-70-68-68	274	$3,233.75
	Jay Overton/Tracy Kerdyk	69-69-68-68	274	$3,233.75
	D.A. Weibring/Chris Johnson	69-67-71-67	274	$3,233.75
45.	Lee Rinker/Colleen Walker	68-69-69-69	275	$3,000.00
T46.	Guy Boros/Michele Redman	69-70-68-69	276	$2,925.00
	Mike Hulbert/Donna Andrews	67-72-69-68	276	$2,925.00
48.	Scott Gump/Karen Weiss	69-70-67-71	277	$2,850.00
49.	Jim Dent/Kim Williams	67-68-70-73	278	$2,800.00
50.	Tom Wargo/Nancy Scranton	68-70-70-72	280	$2,750.00
51.	Jay Don Blake/Emilee Klein	70-71-68-76	285	$2,700.00
52.	Larry Laoretti/Karen Noble	72-73-70-72	287	$2,650.00

JCPENNEY CLASSIC

TOURNAMENT HISTORY

Year	Winner	Score	Location	Par/Yards
HAIG & HAIG SCOTCH FOURSOME				
1960	*Jim Turnesa		Pinecrest Lake Club, Avon Park, FL	72/6449
	Gloria Armstrong	+139	Harder Hall, Sebring, FL	72/6300
1961	Dave Ragan		Pinecrest Lake Club, Avon Park, FL	72/6449
	Mickey Wright	272	Harder Hall, Sebring, FL	72/6300
1962	Mason Rudolph		Pinecrest Lake Club, Avon Park, FL	72/6449
	Kathy Whitworth	272	Harder Hall, Sebring, FL	72/6300
1963	Dave Ragan		Pinecrest Lake Club, Avon Park, FL	72/6449
	Mickey Wright	273	Harder Hall, Sebring, FL	72/6300
1964	Sam Snead		Pinecrest Lake Club, Avon Park, FL	72/6449
	Shirley Englehorn	272	Harder Hall, Sebring, FL	72/6300
1965	Gardner Dickinson			
	Ruth Jessen	281	La Costa CC, Encinitas, CA	72/6607
1966	Jack Rule			
	Sandra Spuzich	276	La Costa CC, Encinitas, CA	72/6607
PEPSI-COLA MIXED TEAM				
1976	Chi Chi Rodriguez			
	JoAnn Washam	275	Doral CC, Miami, FL	72/6939
1977	Jerry Pate			
	Hollis Stacy	270	Bardmoor CC, Largo, FL	M-72/6957, W-72/6464
1978	*Lon Hinkle			
	Pat Bradley	267	Bardmoor CC, Largo, FL	M-72/6957, W-72/6464
JCPENNEY CLASSIC				
1979	Dave Eichelberger			
	Murle Breer	268	Bardmoor CC, Largo, FL	M-72/6957, W-72/6464
1980	Curtis Strange			
	Nancy Lopez	268	Bardmoor CC, Largo, FL	M-72/6957, W-72/6464
1981	Tom Kite			
	Beth Daniel	270	Bardmoor CC, Largo, FL	M-72/6957, W-72/6464
1982	John Mahaffey			
	JoAnne Carner	268	Bardmoor CC, Largo, FL	M-72/6957, W-72/6464
1983	Fred Couples			
	Jan Stephenson	264	Bardmoor CC, Largo, FL	M-72/6957, W-72/6464
1984	Mike Donald			
	Vicki Alvarez	270	Bardmoor CC, Largo, FL	M-72/6957, W-72/6464
1985	Larry Rinker			
	Laurie Rinker	267	Bardmoor CC, Largo, FL	M-72/6957, W-72/6464
1986	Tom Purtzer			
	Juli Inkster	267	Bardmoor CC, Largo, FL	M-72/6957, W-72/6464
1987	Steve Jones			
	Jane Crafter	268	Bardmoor CC, Largo, FL	M-72/6957, W-72/6464
1988	John Huston			
	Amy Benz	269	Bardmoor CC, Largo, FL	M-72/6957, W-72/6464
1989	*Bill Glasson			
	Pat Bradley	267	Bardmoor CC, Largo, FL	M-72/6957, W-72/6464
1990	Davis Love III			
	Beth Daniel	266	Innisbrook Resort, Tarpon Springs, FL	M-71/7031, W-71/6400
1991	*Billy Andrade			
	Kris Tschetter	266	Innisbrook Resort, Tarpon Springs, FL	M-71/7031, W-71/6400
1992	Dan Forsman			
	Dottie Mochrie	264	Innisbrook Resort, Tarpon Springs, FL	M-71/7031, W-71/6400
1993	Mike Springer			
	Melissa McNamara	265	Innisbrook Resort, Tarpon Springs, FL	M-71/7031, W-71/6400
1994	*Brad Bryant			
	Marta Figueras-Dotti	262	Innisbrook Resort, Tarpon Springs, FL	M-71/7031, W-71/6400
1995	Davis Love III			
	Beth Daniel	257	Innisbrook Resort, Tarpon Springs, FL	M-71/7054, W-71/6394

Tournament Record: 257 -- Davis Love/Beth Daniel (1995)
KEY: *= Playoff

1995 PGA TOUR QUALIFYING TOURNAMENT

Bear Lakes CC, West Palm Beach, FL
The Lakes (host): Par: 36-36--72 Yards: 7,062
The Links: Par: 36-36--72 Yards: 6,948
November 29-December 4, 1995

A total of 1,000 applications were accepted, with 15 regionals held to reduce the field to 190 players for the final tournament. The top 40 and ties received their PGA TOUR cards for 1996, and the remainder became members of the 1996 NIKE TOUR.

1.	Carl Paulson	70-65-69-65-59-71--409
2.	Omar Uresti	70-67-71-67-68-67--410
	Steve Hart	67-70-68-69-58-58--410
4.	Shane Bertsch	71-68-68-69-69-66--411
	Joey Gullion	71-68-72-64-69-67--411
	Olin Browne	70-68-65-68-70-70--411
	Tom Byrum	71-68-68-71-64-69--411
	Kevin Sutherland	70-67-66-68-68-72--411
9.	Tim Herron	71-69-65-68-69-70--412
	Russ Cochran	69-70-69-67-66-71--412
11.	Steve Jurgensen	68-70-68-70-67-70--413
12.	Clarence Rose	67-67-68-72-69-71--414
	David Peoples	69-68-68-67-70-72--414
	Scott Medlin	69-69-69-71-64-72--414
15.	Robert Wrenn	67-68-70-71-74-65--415
	Lucas Parsons	67-68-69-68-73-70--415
	Paul Stankowski	66-67-69-77-66-70--415
	Hisayuki Sasaki	74-64-70-69-68-70--415
	Brian Tennyson	69-71-68-65-70-72--415
20.	Billy Ray Brown	75-68-68-67-71-67--416
	Frank Lickliter, Jr.	73-75-65-67-67-69--416
	Len Mattiace	71-68-72-69-67-69--416
	Jeff Gallagher	66-74-66-72-69-69--416
	Ronnie Black	71-68-70-64-72-71--416
	Steve Rintoul	72-65-69-70-69-71--416
26.	Scott Dunlap	70-73-68-71-68-67--417
	Joe Daley	67-71-73-69-68-69--417
	Bart Bryant	70-68-69-70-69-71--417
29.	Jarmo Sandelin	74-72-67-68-70-67--418
	John Maginnes	71-71-69-68-72-67--418
	Taylor Smith	69-69-71-73-69-67--418
	Greg Kraft	71-73-67-67-71-69--418
	Jeff Julian	73-67-74-67-68-69--418
	Jay Williamson	70-68-68-72-70-70--418
	Joel Edwards	67-70-66-70-72-73--418
	Mike Swartz	70-65-70-69-71-73--418
37.	Jeff Hart	67-73-69-74-67-69--419
	Andy Bean	74-67-70-68-71-69--419
	Gary Rusnak	73-72-66-72-68-68--419
	John Elliott	70-69-72-69-70-69--419
	Ron Whittaker	74-68-69-70-71-67--419
	Bryan Gorman	72-68-67-70-71-71--419

SUMMARY OF PAST QUALIFYING TOURNAMENTS

DATE	SITE	MEDALIST	CARDS GRANTED	APPLICANTS	FINAL FIELD	FORMAT
1965	PGA National GC Palm Beach Gardens, FL	John Schlee	17	49	49	144 holes
1966	PGA National GC Palm Beach Gardens, FL	Harry Toscano	32	99	99	144 holes
1967	PGA National GC Palm Beach Gardens, FL	Bobby Cole	30	111	111	144 holes
Spring 1968	PGA National GC Palm Beach Gardens, FL	Bob Dickson	15	81	81	144 holes
Fall 1968	PGA National GC Palm Beach Gardens, FL	Grier Jones	30	79	79	144 holes
Spring 1969	PGA National GC. Palm Beach Gardens, FL	Bob Eastwood	15	91	91	144 holes
Fall 1969	PGA National GC Palm Beach Gardens, FL	Doug Olson	12	182	48	144 holes
1970	Tucson CC Tucson, AZ	Robert Barbarossa	18	250	60	72 holes, after nine 54-hole District Qualifiers
1971	PGA National GC Palm Beach Gardens, FL	Bob Zender	23	357	75	108 holes, after three 72-hole Regional Qualifiers
1972	Silverado CC Napa, CA	Larry Stubblefield John Adams	25	468	81	108 holes, after three 72-hole Regional Qualifiers
1973	Perdido Bay CC Pensacola, FL Dunes G.C. N. Myrtle Beach, SC	Ben Crenshaw	23	373	78	144 holes, after three 72-hole RegionalQualifiers
1974	Silverado CC Napa CA Canyon C.C. Palm Springs, CA	Fuzzy Zoeller	19	447	78	144 holes, after three 72-hole Regional Qualifiers
Spring 1975	Bay Tree Plantation N. Myrtle Beach, SC	Joey Dills	13	233	233	108 holes
Fall 1975	Walt Disney World Lake Buena Vista, FL	Jerry Pate	25	380	380	108 holes
Spring 1976	Bay Tree Plantation N. Myrtle Beach, SC	Bob Shearer Woody Blackburn	15	276	276	108 holes
Fall 1976	Rancho Viejo CC Valley International CC Brownsville, TX	Keith Fergus	29	349	349	108 holes
Spring 1977	Pinehurst CC Pinehurst, NC	Phil Hancock	26	408	408	108 holes

SUMMARY OF PAST QUALIFYING TOURNAMENTS

DATE	SITE	MEDALIST	CARDS GRANTED	APPLICANTS	FINAL FIELD	FORMAT
Fall 1977	Pinehurst CC Pinehurst, NC	Ed Fiori	34	660	144	72 holes, after Sectional Qualifiers
Spring 1978	U. of New Mexico GC Albuquerque, NM	Wren Lum	28	502	150	72 holes, after five 72-hole Regional Qualifiers
Fall 1978	Waterwood Nat'l.CC Huntsville, TX	Jim Thorpe John Fought	27	606	120	72 holes, after five 72-hole Regional Qualifiers
Spring 1979	Pinehurst CC Pinehurst, NC	Terry Mauney	25	521	150	72 holes, after five 72-hole Regional Qualifiers
Fall 1979	Waterwood Nat'l. CC Huntsville, TX	Tom Jones	27	652	120	72 holes, after five 72-hole Regional Qualifiers
Spring 1980	Pinehurst C.C. Pinehurst, NC	Jack Spradlin	27	553	150	72 holes, after five 72-hole Regional Qualifiers
Fall 1980	Ft. Washington G&CC Fresno, Calif.	Bruce Douglass	27	621	120	72 holes, after five 72-hole Regional Qualifiers
Spring 1981	Walt Disney World Golf Resort Lake Buena Vista, FL	Billy Glisson	25	556	150	72 holes, after five 72-hole Regional Qualifiers
Fall 1981	Waterwood Nat'l. CC Huntsville, TX	Robert Thompson Tim Graham	34	513	120	72 holes, after six 72-hole Regional Qualifiers
1982	Tournament Players Club & Sawgrass Country Club Ponte Vedra, FL	Donnie Hammond	50	696	200	108 holes after eight Regional Qualifiers
1983	Tournament Players Club Ponte Vedra, FL	Willie Wood	57	624	144	108 holes after nine Regional Qualifiers
1984	La Quinta Hotel and GC Mission Hills CC La Quinta, CA	Paul Azinger	50	800	160	108 holes after 10 Regional Qualifiers
1985	Grenelefe Golf and Tennis Club Haines City, FL	Tom Sieckmann	50	825	162	108 holes after 11 Regional Qualifiers
1986	PGA West (Stadium Golf Course) La Quinta Hotel Golf & Tennis Resort (Dunes Course) La Quinta, CA	Steve Jones	53	750	186	108 holes after 14 Regionals
1987	Matanzas Woods GC Pine Lakes CC Palm Coast, FL	John Huston	54	800	183	108 holes after 11 Regionals

SUMMARY OF PAST QUALIFYING TOURNAMENTS

DATE	SITE	MEDALIST	CARDS GRANTED	APPLICANTS	FINAL FIELD	FORMAT
1988	La Quinta Hotel (Dunes Course) PGA West Jack Nicklaus Resort Course La Quinta, CA	Robin Freeman	52	750	183	108 holes after 11 Regionals
1989	TPC at The Woodlands The Woodlands Inn & CC The Woodlands, TX	David Peoples	59	825	180	108 holes after 11 Regionals
1990	La Quinta Hotel (Dunes Course) PGA West Jack Nicklaus Resort Course La Quinta, CA	Duffy Waldorf	49	835	182	108 holes after 11 Regionals
1991	Grenelefe Resort & Conference Center Haines City, FL	Mike Standly	48	850	181	108 holes after 12 Regionals
1992	TPC at The Woodlands The Woodlands Inn & CC The Woodlands, TX	Massy Kuramato Skip Kendall Brett Ogle Perry Moss Neale Smith	43	800	188	108 holes after 13 Regionals
1993	La Quinta Hotel (Dunes Course) PGA West Jack Nicklaus Resort Course La Quinta, CA	Ty Armstrong Dave Stockton, Jr. Robin Freeman	46	800	191	108 holes after 13 Regionals
1994	Grenelefe Resort & Conference Center Haines City, FL	Woody Austin	46	1000	185	108 holes after 13 Regionals
1995	Bear Lakes CC (Lakes and Links Courses) W. Palm Beach, FL	Carl Paulson	42	1000	190	108 holes after 15 Regionals

NOTE: The American Professional Golfers also held a School in the fall of 1968, graduating 21. The 144-hole competition was played at Doral CC. The medalist was Martin Roesink.

DINERS CLUB MATCHES

PGA West (Nicklaus Resort Course), La Quinta, CA **Purse: $2,110,000**
Par: 36-36--72 Yards: 6,214 (LPGA) **December 7-10, 1995**
6,870 (Senior PGA TOUR)
7,112 (PGA TOUR)

PGA TOUR

First Round (Losing teams received $15,000 per player)

Kirk Triplett/Steve Stricker d. Jeff Maggert/Jim McGovern, 2 up.
Tom Lehman/Duffy Waldorf d. Jay Haas/Curtis Strange, 1 up.
Bob Tway/Scott Verplank d. Billy Mayfair/Mark Calcavecchia, 1 up.
David Duval/Woody Austin d. Justin Leonard/Jeff Sluman, 2 and 1.
Tom Kite/Billy Andrade d. Fred Funk/Blaine McCallister, 19 holes.
Kenny Perry/John Huston d. Peter Jacobsen/Brian Henninger, 3 and 2.
Phil Mickelson/Paul Azinger d. Lee Janzen/Payne Stewart, 2 up.
Jim Gallagher, Jr./Steve Lowery d. Scott Simpson/Larry Mize, 2 and 1.

Quarterfinals (Losing teams received $20,000 per player)

Lehman/Waldorf d. Triplett/Stricker, 1 up
Tway/Verplank d. Duval/Austin, 2 up
Perry/Huston d. Kite/Andrade, 2 and 1
Gallagher/Lowery d. Mickelson/Azinger, 2 and 1

Semifinals (Losing teams received $35,000 per player)

Lehman/Waldorf d. Tway/Verplank, 23 holes.
Perry/Huston d. Gallagher/Lowery, 5 and 4.

Final

Lehman/Waldorf ($125,000 each) d. Perry/Huston ($50,000 each), 1 up.

Senior PGA TOUR

Quarterfinals (Losing teams received $15,000 per player)

Ray Floyd/Dave Eichelberger d. Jack Nicklaus/Arnold Palmer, 3 and 2.
Dave Stockton/Hale Irwin d. Tom Weiskopf/Isao Aoki, 2 and 1.
George Archer/Dale Douglass d. Chi Chi Rodriguez/Jim Albus, 1 up.
Jim Colbert/Bob Murphy d. J.C. Snead/Gibby Gilbert, 2 and 1.

Semifinals (Losing teams received $35,000 per player)

Stockton/Irwin d. Floyd/Eichelberger, 5 and 3.
Colbert/Murphy d. Archer/Douglass, 24 holes.

Final

Colbert/Murphy ($125,000 each) d. Stockton/Irwin ($50,000 each), 1 up.

LPGA

Quarterfinals (Losing teams received $15,000 per player)

Kelly Robbins/Tammy Green d. Jenny Lidback/Alicia Dibos, 3 and 2.
Nanci Bowen/Annika Sorenstam d. Beth Daniel/Meg Mallon, 19 holes.
Laura Davies/Mardi Lunn d. Donna Andrews/Michelle McGann, 4 and 3.
Dottie Pepper/Juli Inkster d. Betsy King/Val Skinner, 1 up.

Semifinals (Losing teams received $35,000 per player)

Robbins/Green d. Bowen/Sorenstam, 3 and 2.
Davies/Lunn d. Pepper/Inkster, 2 and 1.

Final

Robbins/Green ($125,000 each) d. Davies/Lunn ($50,000 each), 1 up.

TOURNAMENT HISTORY

1994	PGA TOUR	Jeff Maggert/Jim McGovern d. Lee Janzen/Rocco Mediate, 19 holes.
	Senior PGA TOUR	Dave Eichelberger/Ray Floyd d. Jack Nicklaus/Arnold Palmer, 19 holes.
	LPGA	Tammie Green/Kelly Robbins d. Juli Inkster/Dottie Mochrie, 2 and 1.

PGA TOUR

Robert Trent Jones Golf Club, site of a United States victory in the inaugural Presidents Cup Match, will be the venue for the 1996 Presidents Cup Sept. 13-15 on Lake Manassas in Prince William County, VA.

THE PRESIDENTS CUP

The Presidents Cup Match was conceived as a means of giving many of the world's best (non-European) players an opportunity to compete in international team match play competition. A biennial event played in non-Ryder Cup years, the second Presidents Cup will be held this year, September 13-15, at Robert Trent Jones Golf Club on Lake Manassas in Prince William County, VA.

The first Presidents Cup Match was contested September 16-18, 1994 at Robert Trent Jones GC. The United States Team, captained by Hale Irwin, defeated the International side of David Graham, 20-12. Graham returns as captain of the Internationals in September. Arnold Palmer, no stranger to high-level international competition, succeeds Irwin as captain of the U.S. Team.

Members of the U.S. squad will be selected based on official earnings from the start of the 1995 season through the 1996 NEC World Series of Golf. All 1996 money is doubled. International Team players are chosen on the basis of Sony World Rankings at the conclusion of the 1996 NEC World Series of Golf. International Teams do not include any players eligible for the European Ryder Cup team.

The rankings are used for selection of 10 members of each squad. Two captain's choices apiece round out the 12-man teams.

The Presidents Cup competition consists of 10 matches (five foursomes and five four-ball matches) each of the first two days. Each member of the two 12-man squads must play each day.

There are 12 singles matches involving all players on the final Sunday, which this year is September 15. All singles matches will be played to conclusion. No singles matches will be halved, or tied. All matches are worth one point each, for a total of 32 points.

If, at any time, a Presidents Cup Match is deadlocked at the end of singles play, there will be a sudden-death playoff between two players designated in advance by the respective captains.

As is the case with virtually all activity involving the PGA TOUR, charity is the ultimate winner at the Presidents Cup.

There is no purse for the players. Net revenues are divided into 26 equal shares, which the players and captains designate for charities or golf-related projects of their choice. Contributions in their names are made through PGA TOUR Charities, Inc.

Former President Gerald R. Ford presided over the first Presidents Cup Match as Honorary Chairman. Former President George H.W. Bush, like Ford an avid golfer, will serve as Honorary Chairman of this year's Presidents Cup Match.

Members of the Presidents Cup Committee include, among others, representatives of the PGA Tour of Australasia, PGA of South Africa, Asia-Pacific Golf Confederation and the Royal and Ancient Golf Club of St. Andrews.

THE PRESIDENTS CUP

Robert Trent Jones GC, Lake Manassas, VA
Par: 36-36--72 Yards: 7,238 September 16-18, 1994

1994 MATCHES

FIRST DAY

Four-Ball--United States 5, International 0

Corey Pavin/Jeff Maggert (U.S.) def. Steve Elkington/Vijay Singh, 2&1
Jay Haas/Scott Hoch (U.S.) def. Fulton Allem/David Frost, 6&5
Davis Love III/Fred Couples (U.S.) def. Nick Price/Bradley Hughes, 1 up
John Huston/Jim Gallagher, Jr. (U.S.) def. Craig Parry/Robert Allenby, 4&2
Tom Lehman/Phil Mickelson (U.S.) def. Frank Nobilo/Peter Senior, 3&2

Foursomes--United States 2 1/2, International 2 1/2

Hale Irwin/Loren Roberts (U.S.) def. Frost/Allem, 3&1
Haas/Hoch (U.S.) def. Parry/Tsukasa Watanabe, 4&3
Nobilo/Allenby (Int.) def. Pavin/Maggert, 2&1
Elkington/Singh (Int.) def. Mickelson/Lehman, 2&1
Price/Mark McNulty (Int.) halved with Love/Gallagher

Totals: United States 7 1/2, International 2 1/2

SECOND DAY

Four-Ball--International 3 1/2, United States 1 1/2

Allem/McNulty (Int.) def. Gallagher/Huston, 4&3
Watanabe/Singh (Int.) def. Haas/Hoch, 3&1
Parry/Hughes (Int.) def. Roberts/Lehman, 4&3
Couples/Love (U.S.) def. Nobilo/Allenby, 2 up
Price/Elkington (Int.) halved with Mickelson/Pavin

Totals: United States 9, International 6

Foursomes--United States 3, International 2

Frost/Senior (Int.) def. Irwin/Haas, 6&5
Pavin/Roberts (U.S.) def. Parry/Allem, 1 up
Singh/Elkington (Int.) def. Maggert/Huston, 3&2
Love/Gallagher (U.S.) def. Nobilo/Allenby, 7&5
Mickelson/Lehman (U.S.) def. Hughes/McNulty, 3&2

Totals: United States 12, International 8

THIRD DAY

Singles--United States 8, International 4

Irwin (U.S.) def. Allenby, 1 up
Haas (U.S.) def. McNulty, 4&3
Gallagher (U.S.) def. Watanabe, 4&3
Mickelson (U.S.) halved with Allem
Singh (Int.) halved with Lehman
Senior (Int.) def. Huston, 3&2
Hoch (U.S.) halved with Frost
Maggert (U.S.) def. Hughes, 2&1
Nobilo (Int.) halved with Roberts
Couples (U.S.) def. Price, 1 up
Love (U.S.) def. Elkington, 1 up
Parry (Int.) def. Pavin, 1 up

Totals: United States 20, International 12

RYDER CUP MATCHES

The Ryder Cup Matches developed from a match played between representatives of the American and British Professional Golfers' Association in England in 1926. That unofficial match, incidentally, was won by the British 13 1/2 to 1 1/2.

Following this highly successful exhibition, Samuel A. Ryder, a wealthy British seed merchant, offered to donate a solid gold trophy bearing his name to be competed for in a series of matches between professionals of the two nations.

From the start of the series through the 1959 Ryder Cup matches, the competition was comprised of four foursome matches one day and eight singles matches the other day, each at 36 holes.

In 1961, the format was changed to provide for four 18-hole foursomes the morning of the first day and four more that afternoon, then for eight 18-hole singles the morning of the second day and eight more that afternoon. As in the past, one point was at stake in each match, so the total number of points was doubled.

In 1963, for the first time, a day of four-ball matches augmented the program to add new interest to the overall competition. This brought the total number of points to 32.

In 1977, the format was altered once again. This time there were five foursomes on the opening day, five four-ball matches on the second day, and 10 singles matches on the final day. This reduced the total number of points to 20.

For 1979, eligibility for the Great Britain-Ireland side was expanded to include all British PGA/European TPD members who are residents of European nations.

The 1997 Ryder Cup Matches will be played September 26-28, 1997, at Valderrama, Costa del Sol, Spain.

Year	Played At	Date	Result			
1927	Worcester Country Club, Worcester, MA	June 3-4	U.S.	9 1/2	Britain	2 1/2
1929	Moortown, England	April 26-27	Britain	7	U.S.	5
1931	Scioto Country Club, Columbus, OH	June 26-27	U.S.	9	Britain	3
1933	Southport & Ainsdale Courses, England	June 26-27	Britain	6 1/2	U.S.	5 1/2
1935	Ridgewood Country Club, Ridgewood, NJ	Sept. 28-29	U S.	9	Britain	3
1937	Southport & Ainsdale Courses, England	June 29-30	U.S.	8	Britain	4
	Ryder Cup Matches not held during World War II years.					
1947	Portland Golf Club, Portland, OR	Nov. 1-2	U.S.	11	Britain	1
1949	Ganton Golf Course, Scarborough, England	Sept 16-17	U.S.	7	Britain	5
1951	Pinehurst Country Club, Pinehurst, NC	Nov. 2-4	U.S.	9 1/2	Britain	2 1/2
1953	Wentworth, England	Oct. 2-3	U.S.	6 1/2	Britain	5 1/2
1955	Thunderbird Ranch and CC, Palm Springs, CA	Nov. 5-6	U.S.	8	Britain	4
1957	Lindrick Golf Club, Yorkshire, England	Oct. 4-5	Britain	7 1/2	U.S	4 1/2
1959	Eldorado Country Club, Palm Desert, CA	Nov. 6-7	U.S.	8 1/2	Britain	3 1/2
1961	Royal Lytham and St. Anne's Golf Club, St. Anne's-On-The-Sea, England	Oct. 13-14	U.S.	14 1/2	Britain	9 1/2
1963	East Lake Country Club, Atlanta, GA	Oct. 11-13	U.S.	23	Britain	9
1965	Royal Birkdale Golf Club, Southport, England	Oct. 7-9	U.S.	19 1/2	Britain	12 1/2
1967	Champions Golf Club, Houston, TX	Oct. 20-22	U.S.	23 1/2	Britain	8 1/2
1969	Royal Birkdale Golf Club, Southport, England	Sept.18-20	U.S.	16-Tie	Britain	16
1971	Old Warson Country Club, St. Louis, MO	Sept. 16-18	U S.	18 1/2	Britain	13 1/2
1973	Muirfield, Scotland	Sept. 20-22	U.S.	19	Britain	13
1975	Laurel Valley Golf Club, Ligonier, PA	Sept. 19-21	U.S.	21	Britain	11
1977	Royal Lytham and St. Anne's Golf Club, St. Anne's-On-The-Sea, England	Sept. 15-17	U.S	12 1/2	Britain	7 1/2
1979	Greenbrier, White Sulphur Springs, WV	Sept. 13-15	U.S.	17	Europe	11
1981	Walton Heath Golf Club, Surrey, England	Sept. 18-20	U.S.	18 1/2	Europe	9 1/2
1983	PGA National GC, Palm Beach Gardens, FL	Oct. 14-16	U.S.	14 1/2	Europe	13 1/2
1985	The Belfry Golf Club, Sutton Coldfield, England	Sept. 13-15	Europe	16 1/2	U.S.	11 1/2
1987	Muirfield Village Golf Club, Dublin, OH	Sept. 24-27	Europe	15	U.S.	13
1989	The Belfry Golf Club, Sutton Coldfield, England	Sept. 22-24	U.S.	14-Tie	Europe	14
1991	The Ocean Course, Kiawah Island, SC	Sept. 26-29	U.S.	14 1/2	Europe	13 1/2
1993	The Belfry Golf Club, Sutton Coldfield, England	Sept. 24-26	U.S.	15	Europe	13
1995	Oak Hill CC, Rochester, NY	Sept. 22-24	Europe	14 1/2	U.S.	13 1/2

(The United States leads the series, 23-6-2.)

THE RYDER CUP

The 1995 U.S. Ryder Cup Team was selected by way of Ryder Cup points earned from the beginning of 1994 through the 1995 PGA Championship. The top 10 point-getters qualified for the 12-man team. U.S. Captain Lanny Wadkins selected Fred Couples and Curtis Strange to complete the team.

Points were awarded to the first 10 positions in each PGA TOUR event on the following basis, with points weighted toward the 1995 season:

PGA Championship, U.S. Open, Masters Tournament and the British Open (1994/1995): 1st—225/300; 2nd—135/180; 3rd—120/160; 4th—105/140; 5th—90/120; 6th—75/100; 7th—60/80; 8th—45/60; 9th—30/40; 10th—15/20.

All other PGA TOUR events (1994/1995): 1st—75/150; 2nd—45/90; 3rd—40/80; 4th—35/70; 5th—30/60; 6th—25/50; 7th—2040; 8th—15/30; 9th—10/20; 10th—5/10.

If a player who was ineligible finished in one of those positions, no points were awarded for that position. In order to be eligible, a player must be a U.S. citizen and a member of the PGA of America.

1995 MATCH RESULTS

FIRST DAY

Foursomes—Europe 2, United States 2

Corey Pavin/Tom Lehman (USA) def. Nick Faldo/Colin Montgomerie, 1 up
Costantino Rocca/Sam Torrance (Europe) def. Fred Couples/Jay Haas, 3 & 2
Davis Love III/Jeff Maggert (USA) def. Howard Clark/Mark James, 4 & 3
Per-Ulrik Johansson/Bernhard Langer (Europe) def. Ben Crenshaw/Curtis Strange, 1 up

Four-Ball—United States 3, Europe 1

Severiano Ballesteros/David Gilford (Europe) def. Brad Faxon/Peter Jacobsen, 4 & 3
Jeff Maggert/Loren Roberts (USA) def. Costantino Rocca/Sam Torrance, 6 & 5
Fred Couples/Davis Love III (USA) def. Nick Faldo/Colin Montgomerie, 3 & 2
Phil Mickelson/Corey Pavin (USA) def. Per-Ulrik Johansson/Bernhard Langer, 6 & 4

Day One Totals: United States 5, Europe 3

SECOND DAY

Foursomes—Europe 3, United States 1

Nick Faldo/Colin Montgomerie (Europe) def. Jay Haas/Curtis Strange, 4 & 2
Costantino Rocca/Sam Torrance (Europe) def. Davis Love III/Jeff Maggert, 6 & 5
Peter Jacobsen/Loren Roberts (USA) def. Philip Walton/Ian Woosnam, 1 up
David Gilford/Bernhard Langer (Europe) def. Tom Lehman/Corey Pavin, 4 & 3

Four-Ball—United States 3, Europe 1

Fred Couples/Brad Faxon (USA) def. Colin Montgomerie/Sam Torrance, 4 & 2
Costantino Rocca/Ian Woosnam (Europe) def. Ben Crenshaw/Davis Love III, 3 & 2
Jay Haas/Phil Mickelson (USA) def. Severiano Ballesteros/David Gilford, 3 & 2
Corey Pavin/Loren Roberts (USA) def. Nick Faldo/Bernhard Langer, 1 up

Day Two Totals: United States 9, Europe 7

FINAL DAY

Singles—Europe 7 1/2, United States 4 1/2

Tom Lehman (USA) def. Severiano Ballesteros, 4 & 3
Howard Clark (Europe) def. Peter Jacobsen, 1 up
Mark James (Europe) def. Jeff Maggert, 4 & 3
Fred Couples (USA) halved with Ian Woosnam (Europe)
Davis Love III (USA) def. Costantino Rocca, 3 & 2
David Gilford (Europe) def. Brad Faxon, 1 up
Colin Montgomerie (Europe) def. Ben Crenshaw, 3 & 1
Nick Faldo (Europe) def. Curtis Strange, 1 up
Sam Torrance (Europe) def. Loren Roberts, 2 & 1
Corey Pavin (USA) def. Bernhard Langer, 3 & 2
Phillip Walton (Europe) def. Jay Haas, 1 up
Phil Mickelson (USA) def. Per-Ulrik Johansson, 2 & 1

Final Total: Europe 14 1/2, United States 13 1/2

WORLD CUP OF GOLF

Fred Couples and Davis Love III were part of history and made history at the 41st World Cup of Golf, played at the TPC at Mission Hills in Shenzhen, China in November 1995.

The competition among 32 teams from around the world was the first major international golf competition in the People's Republic of China. And with their 14-stroke victory over Robert Allenby and Brett Ogle of Australia, Couples and Love became the first team to win four consecutive World Cups, extending their own record. They also equaled Jack Nicklaus and Arnold Palmer's record of four team victories; Palmer and Nicklaus won the World Cup in 1963-64 and 1966-67.

The 42nd World Cup of Golf will be staged this year at the Erinvale Golf Club near Cape Town, South Africa. Dates of the competition are November 21-24.

YEAR	COUNTRY	WINNING TEAM MEMBERS	INDIVIDUAL MEDALIST
1953	Argentina	Antonio Cerda, Roberto De Vicenzo	Antonio Cerda, Argentina
1954	Australia	Peter Thomson, Kel Nagle	Stan Leonard, Canada
1955	United States	Chick Harbert, Ed Furgol	Ed Furgol, United States
1956	United States	Ben Hogan, Sam Snead	Sam Snead, United States
1957	Japan	Torakichi Nakamura, Koichi Ono	Torakichi Nakamura, Japan
1958	Ireland	Harry Bradshaw, Christy O'Connor	Angel Miguel, Spain
1959	Australia	Peter Thomson, Kel Nagle	Stan Leonard, Canada
1960	United States	Sam Snead, Arnold Palmer	Flory Von Donck, Belgium
1961	United States	Sam Snead, Jimmy Demaret	Sam Snead, United States
1962	United States	Sam Snead, Arnold Palmer	Roberto De Vicenzo, Argentina
1963	United States	Arnold Palmer, Jack Nicklaus	Jack Nicklaus, United States
1964	United States	Arnold Palmer, Jack Nicklaus	Jack Nicklaus, United States
1965	South Africa	Gary Player, Harold Henning	Gary Player, South Africa
1966	United States	Jack Nicklaus, Arnold Palmer	George Knudson, Canada
1967	United States	Jack Nicklaus, Arnold Palmer	Arnold Palmer, United States
1968	Canada	Al Balding, George Knudson	Al Balding, Canada
1969	United States	Orville Moody, Lee Trevino	Lee Trevino, United States
1970	Australia	Bruce Devlin, David Graham	Roberto De Vicenzo, Argentina
1971	United States	Jack Nicklaus, Lee Trevino	Jack Nicklaus, United States
1972	Taiwan	Hsieh Min Nan, Lu Liang Huan	Hsieh Min Nan, Taiwan
1973	United States	Jack Nicklaus, Johnny Miller	Johnny Miller, United States
1974	South Africa	Bobby Cole, Dale Hayes	Bobby Cole, South Africa
1975	United States	Johnny Miller, Lou Graham	Johnny Miller, United States
1976	Spain	Seve Ballesteros, Manuel Pinero	Ernesto Acosta, Mexico
1977	Spain	Seve Ballesteros, Antonio Garrido	Gary Player, South Africa
1978	United States	John Mahaffey, Andy North	John Mahaffey, United States
1979	United States	John Mahaffey, Hale Irwin	Hale Irwin, United States
1980	Canada	Dan Halldorson, Jim Nelford	Sandy Lyle, Scotland
1981	Not played		
1982	Spain	Manuel Pinero, Jose Maria Canizares	Manuel Pinero, Spain
1983	United States	Rex Caldwell, John Cook	Dave Barr, Canada
1984	Spain	Jose Maria Canizares, Jose Rivero	Jose Maria Canizares
1985	Canada	Dan Halldorson, Dave Barr	Howard Clark, England
1986	Not played		
1987	Wales	Ian Woosnam, David Llewellyn	Ian Woosnam, Wales
1988	United States	Ben Crenshaw, Mark McCumber	Ben Crenshaw, United States
1989	Australia	Wayne Grady, Peter Fowler	Peter Fowler, Australia
1990	Germany	Bernhard Langer, Torsten Gideon	Payne Stewart, United States
1991	Sweden	Anders Forsbrand, Per Ulrik Johansson	Ian Woosnam, Wales
1992	United States	Fred Couples, Davis Love III	Brett Ogle, Australia
1993	United States	Fred Couples, Davis Love III	Bernhard Langer, Germany
1994	United States	Fred Couples, Davis Love III	Fred Couples, United States
1995	United States	Fred Couples, Davis Love III	Davis Love III, United States

(See 1995 World Cup of Golf summary on pages 398-399.)

Andersen Consulting World Championship of Golf

On October 19, 1994, plans were announced for the Andersen Consulting World Championship of Golf, an international match-play competition designed to determine "the best professional golfer in the world." First-round and regional finals competition produced four regional champions.

The four — Mark McCumber (United States), David Frost (Rest of the World), Barry Lane (Europe) and Massy Kuramoto (Japan) — met at Grayhawk Golf Club in Scottsdale, AZ December 30-31, 1995 to determine the first "World Champion." That first winner earned $1 million from the total purse of $3.65 million, as will the 1996 champion.

But whereas finalists for that first championship were determined through play at two sites each (except for Japan) over a period of months, all regional competition (first-round, semifinals and championship) in the Andersen Consulting World Championship of Golf will take place at one site over two days.

Eight players from each of the four regions ("Rest of the World" is now known as International) comprise the 32-man field. Seven players from each region are invited based on the Sony World Rankings. The eighth competitor is a sponsor's invitation and seeded eighth.

The Andersen Consulting World Championship of Golf is sanctioned by all five of the world's major tours — the PGA TOUR, the PGA European Tour, the Japan PGA Tour, the PGA Tour of Australasia and the FNB Tour in South Africa.

The schedule of matches for 1996 is as follows:

Date	Championship	Site
March 2-3	Japan Championship	Kagoshima, Japan
April 22-23	U.S. Championship (Great Waters Course) Lake Oconee, GA	Reynolds Plantation
May 20-21	European Championship	London, England
July 29-30	International Championship (River Course) Kohler, WI	Blackwolf Run
Jan. 4-5, 1997	World Championship Scottsdale, AZ	Grayhawk Golf Club

ESPN will provide 38 hours of coverage of the 1996 tournament, with same-day, prime-time coverage of the April 22 U.S. matches and both days of the International competition. The World Championship semifinals will be aired live on January 4, 1997. The World Championship match will be broadcast live by ABC Sports.

There also will be same-day coverage of Day 2 of the U.S. competition and the European matches; the Japan Championship will air in June. ESPN also will air two preview shows, one on April 19 and a World Championship Preview on January 5, 1997.

WINNERS OF MAJOR U.S. AMATEUR EVENTS

NCAA CHAMPIONS (SINCE 1949)

Year	Winner
1949	Harvie Ward, North Carolina
1950	Fred Wampler, Purdue
1951	Tom Nieporte, Ohio State
1952	Jim Vickers, Oklahoma
1953	Earl Moeller, Oklahoma State
1954	Hillman Robbins, Memphis State
1955	Joe Campbell, Purdue
1956	Rick Jones, Ohio State
1957	Rex Baxter Jr. Houston
1958	Phil Rodgers, Houston
1959	Dick Crawford, Houston
1960	Dick Crawford, Houston
1961	Jack Nicklaus, Ohio State
1962	Kermit Zarley, Houston
1963	R.H. Sikes, Arkansas
1964	Terry Small, San Jose State
1965	Marty Fleckman, Houston
1966	Bob Murphy, Florida
1967	Hale Irwin, Colorado
1968	Grier Jones, Oklahoma State
1969	Bob Clark, Los Angeles State
1970	John Mahaffey, Houston
1971	Ben Crenshaw, Texas
1972	Ben Crenshaw, Texas
	Tom Kite, Texas
1973	Ben Crenshaw, Texas
1974	Curtis Strange, Wake Forest
1975	Jay Haas, Wake Forest
1976	Scott Simpson, USC
1977	Scott Simpson, USC
1978	David Edwards, Oklahoma State
1979	Gary Hallberg, Wake Forest
1980	Jay Don Blake, Utah State
1981	Ron Commans, USC
1982	Billy Ray Brown, Houston
1983	Jim Carter, Anzona State
1984	John Inman, North Carolina
1985	Clark Burroughs, Ohio State
1986	Scott Verplank, Oklahoma State
1987	Brian Watts, Oklahoma State
1988	E.J. Pfister, Oklahoma State
1989	Phil Mickelson, Arizona State
1990	Phil Mickelson, Arizona State
1991	Warren Schutte, Nevada-Las Vegas
1992	Phil Mickelson, Arizona State
1993	Todd Demsey, Arizona State
1994	Justin Leonard, Texas
1995	Chip Spratlin, Auburn

U.S. AMATEUR CHAMPIONS (SINCE 1949)

Year	Match Play
1949	Charles R. Coe
1950	Sam Urzetta
1951	Billy Maxwell
1952	Jack Westland
1953	Gene A. Littler
1954	Arnold Palmer
1955	E. Harvie Ward, Jr.
1956	E. Harvie Ward, Jr.
1957	Hillman Robbins, Jr.
1958	Charles R. Coe
1959	Jack W. Nicklaus
1960	Deane R. Beman
1961	Jack W. Nicklaus
1962	Labron E. Harris Jr.
1963	Deane R. Beman
1964	William C. Campbell

Stroke Play

Year	Winner	Score
1965	Robert J. Murphy	291
1966	Gary Cowan	285
1967	Robert B. Dickson	285
1968	Bruce Fleisher	284
1969	Steven N. Melnyk	286
1970	Lanny Wadkins	*279
1971	Gary Cowan	280
1972	Vinny Giles	285

Match Play

Year	Winner
1973	Craig Stadler
1974	Jerry Pate
1975	Fred Ridley
1976	Bill Sander
1977	John Fought
1978	John Cook
1979	Mark O'Meara
1980	Hal Sutton
1981	Nathaniel Crosby
1982	Jay Sigel
1983	Jay Sigel
1984	Scott Verplank
1985	Sam Randolph
1986	Buddy Alexander
1987	Bill Mayfair
1988	Eric Meeks
1989	Chris Patton
1990	Phil Mickelson
1991	Mitch Voges
1992	Justin Leonard
1993	John Harris
1994	Tiger Woods
1995	Tiger Woods

U.S. PUBLIC LINKS CHAMPIONS (SINCE 1949)

Year	Match Play
1949	Kenneth J. Towns
1950	Stanley Bielat
1951	Dave Stanley
1952	Omer L. Bogan
1953	Ted Richards, Jr.
1954	Gene Andrews
1955	Sam D. Kocsis
1956	James H. Buxbaum
1957	Don Essig, III
1958	Daniel D. Sikes, Jr.
1959	William A Wright
1960	Verne Callison
1961	Richard H. Sikes
1962	Richard H. Sikes
1963	Robert Lunn
1964	William McDonald
1965	Arne Dokka
1966	Lamont Kaser

Stroke Play

Year	Winner	Score
1967	Verne Callison	287
1968	Gene Towry	292
1969	J. M. Jackson	292
1970	Robert Risch	293
1971	Fred Haney	290
1972	Bob Allard	285
1973	Stan Stopa	294
1974	Chas. Barenaba	290

Match Play

Year	Winner
1975	Randy Barenaba
1976	Eddie Mudd
1977	Jerry Vidovic
1978	Dean Prince
1979	Dennis Walsh
1980	Jodie Mudd
1981	Jodie Mudd
1982	Billy Tuten
1983	Billy Tuten
1984	Bill Malley
1985	Jim Sorenson
1986	Bill Mayfair
1987	Kevin Johnson
1988	Ralph Howe
1989	Tim Hobby
1990	Mike Combs
1991	David Berganio, Jr.
1992	Warren Schutte
1993	David Berganio, Jr.
1994	Guy Yamamoto
1995	Chris Wollman

Corey Pavin successfully defended his Nissan Open crown in February, then in June made the U.S. Open his first major win and 13th PGA TOUR title.

PGA TOUR

1995 PGA TOUR FACTS AND FIGURES

1995 OFFICIAL PGA TOUR MONEY LIST

	Name	Events	Wins	Money
1.	GREG NORMAN	16	3	$1,654,959
2.	BILLY MAYFAIR	28	2	1,543,192
3.	LEE JANZEN	28	3	1,378,966
4.	COREY PAVIN	22	2	1,340,079
5.	STEVE ELKINGTON	21	2	1,254,352
6.	DAVIS LOVE III	24	1	1,111,999
7.	PETER JACOBSEN	25	2	1,075,057
8.	JIM GALLAGHER, JR.	27	2	1,057,241
9.	VIJAY SINGH	22	2	1,018,713
10.	MARK O'MEARA	27	2	914,129
11.	DAVID DUVAL @	26		881,436
12.	PAYNE STEWART	27	1	866,219
13.	MARK CALCAVECCHIA	29	1	843,552
14.	ERNIE ELS	18	1	842,590
15.	TOM LEHMAN	18	1	830,231
16.	JAY HAAS	27		822,259
17.	SCOTT SIMPSON	25		795,798
18.	SCOTT HOCH	28	1	792,643
19.	NICK FALDO	19	1	790,961
20.	BOB TWAY	27	1	787,348
21.	KENNY PERRY	25	1	773,388
22.	JUSTIN LEONARD	31		748,793
23.	BEN CRENSHAW	23	1	737,475
24.	WOODY AUSTIN +	34	1	736,497
25.	BRAD BRYANT	31	1	723,834
26.	FRED FUNK	32	2	717,232
27.	LOREN ROBERTS	23	1	678,335
28.	PHIL MICKELSON	24	1	655,777
29.	KIRK TRIPLETT	27		644,607
30.	NICK PRICE	18		611,700
31.	JEFF SLUMAN	29		563,681
32.	HAL SUTTON	31	1	554,733
33.	JIM FURYK	31	1	535,380
34.	JEFF MAGGERT	23		527,952
35.	DUFFY WALDORF	26	1	525,622
36.	D.A. WEIBRING	24	1	517,065
37.	BRAD FAXON	25		471,887
38.	STEVE LOWERY	30		463,858
39.	TED TRYBA	35	1	451,983
40.	STEVE STRICKER	23		438,931
41.	BOB ESTES	24		433,992
42.	JOHN MORSE	24	1	416,803
43.	BILL GLASSON	22		412,094
44.	JIM MCGOVERN	31		402,587
45.	CRAIG STADLER	21		402,316
46.	BERNHARD LANGER *	7		394,877
47.	MARK MCCUMBER	19		375,923
48.	MARK BROOKS	29		366,860
49.	CURTIS STRANGE	24		358,175
50.	DAVID FROST	21		357,658
51.	LENNIE CLEMENTS	24		355,130
52.	MIKE HEINEN	29		350,920
53.	COLIN MONTGOMERIE *	8		335,617
54.	JAY DON BLAKE	26		333,551
55.	SCOTT VERPLANK	25		332,886
56.	BRETT OGLE	20		326,932
57.	JOHN DALY	23	1	321,748
58.	TOM WATSON	16		320,785
59.	BOB LOHR	28		314,947
60.	GENE SAUERS	23		311,578
61.	MIKE HULBERT	31		311,055
62.	GUY BOROS	34		303,654
63.	FRED COUPLES	15		299,259
64.	JOHN HUSTON	27		294,574
65.	CRAIG PARRY	24		293,413
66.	JOE OZAKI	20		290,001
67.	LARRY MIZE	22		$289,576
68.	ROBIN FREEMAN	30		283,756
69.	BILLY ANDRADE	29		276,494
70.	BRUCE LIETZKE	16		269,394
71.	MARCO DAWSON #	25		261,214
72.	ANDREW MAGEE	27		256,918
73.	GIL MORGAN	21		255,565
74.	JOHN ADAMS #	25		243,366
75.	BRIAN CLAAR	30		241,107
76.	GRANT WAITE	26		240,722
77.	BLAINE MCCALLISTER	26		238,847
78.	NOLAN HENKE	25		237,141
79.	STEVE JONES	24		234,749
80.	JAY DELSING	27		230,769
81.	DOUG MARTIN #	29		227,463
82.	DON POOLEY	22		226,804
83.	DAVID EDWARDS	22		225,857
84.	JESPER PARNEVIK	19		222,458
85.	MICHAEL BRADLEY	27		214,469
86.	BRANDEL CHAMBLEE	25		213,796
87.	JOSE MARIA OLAZABAL	10		213,415
88.	DILLARD PRUITT	25		210,453
89.	ROBERT GAMEZ	27		206,588
90.	JOEY SINDELAR	24		202,896
91.	GLEN DAY	32		201,809
92.	MIKE BRISKY #	30		194,874
93.	DAN FORSMAN	23		194,539
94.	JONATHAN KAYE #	25		191,883
95.	HALE IRWIN	14		190,961
96.	LEE RINKER +	29		187,065
97.	JOHN COOK	27		186,977
98.	COSTANTINO ROCCA *	2		185,500
99.	SCOTT GUMP @	29		184,828
100.	PAUL AZINGER	23		182,595
101.	NEAL LANCASTER	29		182,219
102.	JIM CARTER @	30		180,664
103.	CHARLIE RYMER +	28		180,401
104.	TOM KITE	25		178,580
105.	MIKE STANDLY	30		177,920
106.	IAN WOOSNAM *	8		174,464
107.	CURT BYRUM	33		173,838
108.	KEN GREEN	23		173,577
109.	KELLY GIBSON #	33		173,425
110.	FUZZY ZOELLER	15		170,706
111.	CHIP BECK	29		170,081
112.	MARK WIEBE	23		168,832
113.	MIKE SULLIVAN	26		167,486
114.	BRIAN HENNINGER	28		166,730
115.	BOBBY WADKINS	30		166,527
116.	TOMMY TOLLES +	27		166,431
117.	DAN POHL	15		166,219
118.	BRIAN KAMM	30		165,235
119.	PATRICK BURKE #	24		162,892
120.	JOHN MAHAFFEY	25		156,608
121.	PHIL BLACKMAR #	24		154,801
122.	ED DOUGHERTY	15	1	154,007
123.	DAVID OGRIN	30		151,419
124.	DAVE STOCKTON,JR	32		149,579
125.	JOHN WILSON	30		149,280
126.	RICK FEHR	24		147,766
127.	JOE ACOSTA, JR. #	26		147,745
128.	SCOTT MCCARRON #	25		147,371
129.	PAUL GOYDOS	35		146,423
130.	KEITH FERGUS +	26		146,359
131.	RUSS COCHRAN	26		145,663
132.	TOM BYRUM	14		145,427

* Non-PGA TOUR Member   @ 1994 NIKE TOUR Grad   # 1994 Qualifying Tournament Grad
+ Q-school Grad/NIKE TOUR member

1995 OFFICIAL PGA TOUR MONEY LIST (cont.)

	Name	Events	Money
133.	PAUL STANKOWSKI	31	$144,558
134.	PETE JORDAN	18	143,936
135.	MICHAEL CAMPBELL *	3	141,388
136.	DONNIE HAMMOND	24	141,150
137.	HOWARD TWITTY	29	140,695
138.	BOB GILDER	30	139,361
139.	GREG KRAFT	35	137,655
140.	EMLYN AUBREY @	30	137,020
141.	TOMMY ARMOUR III @	30	134,407
142.	TRAY TYNER +	31	126,339
143.	RONNIE BLACK #	29	122,188
144.	TOM PURTZER	19	120,717
145.	JAY WILLIAMSON #	22	120,180
146.	BART BRYANT #	27	119,201
147.	DAVE BARR	27	118,218
148.	DUDLEY HART #	30	116,334
149.	JOEL EDWARDS	31	114,285
150.	CHRIS PERRY @	30	113,632
151.	TONY SILLS #	24	113,186
152.	STEVE RINTOUL	34	112,877
153.	J.P. HAYES +	27	111,696
154.	BRUCE FLEISHER #	22	108,830
155.	ROCCO MEDIATE	18	105,618
156.	OMAR URESTI +	31	104,876
157.	STEVEN BOTTOMLEY	1	104,738
158.	DENNIS PAULSON	30	103,411
159.	MIKE REID	23	102,809
160.	GARY HALLBERG	28	99,332
161.	DICKY PRIDE	31	97,712
162.	LANNY WADKINS	21	97,485
163.	HARRY TAYLOR #	29	94,265
164.	SKIP KENDALL @	31	93,606
165.	CLARK DENNIS	33	92,077
166.	DAVID FEHERTY	26	90,274
167.	STEPHEN KEPPLER *	6	90,040
168.	STEVE PATE	32	89,758
169.	DAVID PEOPLES	15	86,679
170.	ED FIORI	15	83,852
171.	JERRY HAAS @	29	78,769
172.	ED HUMENIK	32	78,150
173.	BRUCE VAUGHAN @	30	77,561
174.	CHRIS DIMARCO	33	74,698
175.	BILL BRITTON #	24	73,574
176.	ROBERT ALLENBY *	9	73,288
177.	STEVE GOTSCHE #	28	70,425
178.	BILL PORTER +	25	68,390
179.	JACK NICKLAUS	11	68,180
180.	RAY FLOYD	4	65,031
181.	MARK MCNULTY	10	64,795
182.	WILLIE WOOD	11	64,697
183.	CARL PAULSON #	21	64,501
184.	SEVE BALLESTEROS *	9	64,345
185.	MARK CARNEVALE	29	62,206
186.	JERRY PATE	22	62,001
187.	ROGER MALTBIE	11	61,664
188.	JUMBO OZAKI *	6	60,292
189.	MARK WURTZ #	28	59,949
190.	J.L. LEWIS #	28	59,750
191.	BOB BURNS	31	59,243
192.	STEWART CINK *	6	58,426
193.	MIGUEL JIMENEZ *	5	57,196
194.	SAM TORRANCE *	2	56,970
195.	KAWIKA COTNER #	26	56,625
196.	BILLY RAY BROWN	24	56,111
197.	MICHAEL ALLEN #	21	55,825
198.	MIKE SPRINGER	28	55,146

	Name	Events	Money
199.	FULTON ALLEM	21	$54,239
200.	JEFF LEONARD #	26	53,444
201.	DICKY THOMPSON #	25	53,380
202.	MARK JAMES *	1	53,167
203.	FRANK NOBILO *	5	52,119
204.	RAY STEWART #	21	48,965
205.	MIKE SMITH +	25	48,088
206.	PAT BATES @	31	48,049
207.	DANNY BRIGGS *	4	46,415
208.	WAYNE LEVI	20	46,095
209.	DOUG TEWELL	21	45,878
210.	WAYNE GRADY	16	45,218
211.	SCOTT DUNLAP *	2	44,000
212.	JODIE MUDD	9	43,200
213.	GREG TWIGGS	9	42,474
214.	LARRY NELSON	21	40,689
215.	SEAN MURPHY *	3	40,115
216.	TOM HEARN #	21	39,163
217.	DON REESE #	26	38,905
218.	ANDREW COLTART *	3	36,683
219.	KEITH CLEARWATER	28	34,354
220.	JOEY RASSETT #	22	34,132
221.	BRIAN WATTS *	3	33,725
222.	PETER SENIOR *	4	33,391
223.	BARRY LANE *	3	33,080
224.	PER-ULRIK JOHANSSON	3	32,659
225.	DAVID ISHII *	3	31,200
226.	MARK ROE *	2	30,934
227.	TED SCHULZ	16	29,290
228.	YOSHINORI MIZUMAKI	15	28,292
229.	HISAYUKI SASAKI *	2	27,855
230.	DAVID GILFORD *	3	26,993
231.	DICK MAST	13	26,623
232.	DAVE RUMMELLS	10	26,095
233.	EDUARDO ROMERO #	15	24,942
234.	RICHARD ZOKOL	10	23,371
235.	SANDY LYLE *	7	22,908
236.	PETER MITCHELL *	1	21,533
237.	RETIEF GOOSEN *	3	20,652
238.	ROCKY WALCHER *	4	20,300
239.	TREVOR DODDS *	3	20,122
240.	WAYNE WESTNER *	1	18,750
241.	BRAD SHERFY *	3	18,112
242.	MIKE SMALL *	2	17,875
243.	TIM LOUSTALOT +	22	17,077
244.	KATSUYOSHI TOMORI *	1	16,455
245.	GARY MCCORD	5	15,813
246.	ANTHONY GILLIGAN *	2	15,350
247.	EIJI MIZOGUCHI *	2	14,650
247.	RON WHITTAKER *	4	14,650
249.	DARREN CLARKE *	1	12,955
249.	ROSS DRUMMOND *	1	12,955
251.	JIM THORPE	15	12,945
252.	ANTHONY RODRIGUEZ *	4	12,847
253.	STEVE BRODIE	8	11,461
254.	WARREN BENNETT *	1	11,245
255.	RYAN HOWISON #	19	11,078
256.	ANDERS FORSBRAND *	1	10,128
256.	TOMMY NAKAJIMA *	2	10,128
258.	LARRY RINKER	8	9,975
259.	MORRIS HATALSKY	5	9,833
260.	RUSSELL CLAYDON *	1	9,411
260.	PETER O'MALLEY *	1	9,411
262.	KENNY KNOX	11	9,010
263.	PAUL BROADHURST *	1	8,733
263.	DERRICK COOPER *	1	8,733

* Non-PGA TOUR Member @ 1994 NIKE TOUR Grad # 1994 Qualifying Tournament Grad + Q-school Grad/NIKE TOUR member

1995 OFFICIAL PGA TOUR MONEY LIST (cont.)

	Name	Events	Money
263.	MARTIN GATES *	1	$8,733
263.	EDUARDO HERRERA *	1	8,733
263.	PAUL LAWRIE *	1	8,733
268.	REX CALDWELL	6	8,694
269.	PETER BAKER *	1	7,935
269.	MATS HALLBERG *	1	7,935
269.	OLLE KARLSSON *	1	7,935
269.	JONATHAN LOMAS *	1	7,935
269.	GARY PLAYER	2	7,935
269.	JOSE RIVERO	1	7,935
275.	SCOTT FORD #	19	7,608
276.	FRANK CONNER	2	7,480
277.	ANDY BEAN	14	7,405
278.	RYOKEN KAWAGISHI *	1	7,178
278.	DEAN ROBERTSON *	1	7,178
278.	JARMO SANDELIN *	1	7,178
281.	BRADLEY HUGHES *	6	7,146
281.	CHRISTIAN PENA *	2	7,146
283.	MARK HAYES	6	7,061
283.	CLARENCE ROSE	2	7,061
285.	PHILIP WALTON *	2	6,750
286.	MARK DAVIS *	1	6,579
286.	WAYNE RILEY *	2	6,579
288.	SIMON BURNELL *	1	6,380
288.	JOSE COCERES *	1	6,380
288.	JOHN HAWKSWORTH *	1	6,380
288.	PEDRO LINHART *	1	6,380
288.	BILL LONGMUIR *	1	6,380
288.	MARK NICHOLS *	1	6,380
288.	LEE WESTWOOD *	1	6,380
295.	HUBERT GREEN	17	6,200
296.	MATT GOGEL *	1	5,843
297.	MIKE DONALD	15	5,760
298.	BUDDY GARDNER	6	5,622
299.	BOBBY CLAMPETT	9	5,472
300.	BOB BOYD *	2	5,400
301.	CLARK BURROUGHS +	15	5,218
302.	JOHN SCHROEDER	6	5,122
303.	JIM HALLET *	3	4,956
303.	SAM RANDOLPH	1	4,956
305.	GREG BRUCKNER *	1	4,834
306.	JERRY KELLY *	2	4,733
307.	ROBERT HOYT *	1	4,550
308.	BILL KRATZERT	10	4,548
309.	ERNIE GONZALEZ	3	4,227
310.	YOSHINORI KANEKO *	2	4,205
311.	ALAN T. PATE *	3	4,160
312.	MIKE TAYLOR *	1	4,035

	Name	Events	Money
313.	BRANDT JOBE *	4	$3,969
314.	ALLEN M. DOYLE *	2	3,264
315.	DAVID GRAHAM	5	3,196
316.	WAYNE DEFRANCESCO *	2	3,163
317.	JIMMY GREEN *	1	3,162
318.	DAVE STOCKTON	1	3,122
319.	KATSUMASA MIYAMOTO *	1	3,075
320.	JOHN CONNELLY *	3	3,039
321.	MARCO GORTANA *	2	2,940
322.	J.B. SNEVE *	1	2,925
323.	MARK PFEIL	4	2,890
324.	JOHN MAGINNES *	1	2,807
325.	RICHARD SADLER *	1	2,790
326.	STEVE HART #	17	2,748
327.	ROGER SALAZAR *	1	2,730
328.	GREG POWERS	4	2,712
329.	TIM SIMPSON	1	2,688
330.	JOEY GULLION *	1	2,574
331.	BOBBY DOOLITTLE *	1	2,508
332.	GEORGE BURNS	7	2,463
332.	P.H. HORGAN III *	2	2,463
334.	MASSY KURAMOTO *	2	2,460
335.	MIKE MCCULLOUGH	2	2,376
336.	KAZUHIRO TAKAMI *	2	2,328
337.	RAY FREEMAN *	1	2,314
338.	DOUG DUNAKEY *	1	2,309
339.	IKUO SHIRAHAMA *	1	2,304
340.	EDDIE PEARCE *	1	2,280
341.	PETE MATHEWS *	2	2,268
342.	KEN MCDONALD *	1	2,266
343.	RICHARD BACKWELL *	1	2,250
344.	CHRIS VAN DER VELDE	2	2,244
345.	JOHN SIKES *	1	2,236
346.	KEVIN BURTON *	1	2,232
347.	CRAIG KANADA *	1	2,220
348.	TOM SULLIVAN *	1	2,208
349.	STEVE LAMONTAGNE *	2	2,176
350.	BOBBY TRACY *	1	2,088
351.	JOHN GODWIN *	2	2,040
352.	BARRY CHEESMAN *	1	1,960
352.	KEN SCHALL *	1	1,960
354.	RODNEY BUTCHER *	1	1,860
355.	DAVE RUETER *	1	1,780
356.	VANCE HEAFNER	2	1,690
357.	BARRY JAECKEL	8	1,540
357.	MAC O'GRADY	5	1,540
357.	MIKE TSCHETTER *	1	1,540

* Non-PGA TOUR Member @ 1994 NIKE TOUR Grad # 1994 Qualifying Tournament Grad
+ Q-school Grad/NIKE TOUR member

1995 PGA TOUR FACTS AND FIGURES

LOW 9:	28 (7-under)	*Brad Faxon*, PGA Championship
	29 (7-under)	*Jim Gallagher, Jr., Mark Brooks, Kenny Perry,* Bob Hope Chrysler Classic, *Jay Delsing,* FedEx St. Jude Classic, *Dave Stockton, Jr., Brad Bryant*, Walt Disney World/Oldsmobile Golf Classic
	30 (7-under)	*Hal Sutton*, B.C. Open
LOW 18:	61 (10-under)	*Hal Sutton*, B.C. Open
	61 (9-under)	*Ernie Els,* GTE Byron Nelson Classic
	62 (10-under)	*Jim Furyk*, Buick Open, *Carl Paulson*, Walt Disney World/Oldsmobile Golf Classic
	62 (9-under)	*Kenny Perry*, Nissan Open
LOW FIRST 18:	62 (10-under)	*Carl Paulson*, Walt Disney World/Oldsmobile Golf Classic
	62 (9-under)	*Glen Day*, *Mike Standly*, FedEx St. Jude Classic
LOW FIRST 36:	127 (15-under)	*Jim Gallagher, Jr.* (65-62), FedEx St. Jude Classic
LOW 36: (any rounds)	126 (14-under)	*Ernie Els* (61-65), GTE Byron Nelson Classic (Rounds 2-3)
	127 (15-under)	*Jim Gallagher, Jr.* (65-62), FedEx St. Jude Classic (Rounds 1-2)
	127 (15-under)	*Billy Andrade* (65-62), Canon Greater Hartford Open (Rounds 2-3)
LOW FIRST 54:	195 (18-under)	*Jim Gallagher, Jr.* (65-62-68), FedEx St. Jude Classic
	195 (18-under)	*Fred Funk* (66-63-66), Ideon Classic at Pleasant Valley
	195 (15-under)	*Ernie Els* (69-61-65), GTE Byron Nelson Classic
	196 (20-under)	*Harry Taylor* (66-64-66), Bob Hope Chrysler Classic
LOW 54: (any rounds)	194 (16-under)	*Ernie Els* (61-65-68), GTE Byron Nelson Classic (Rounds 2-3-4)
	196 (20-under)	*Harry Taylor* (66-64-66), Bob Hope Chrysler Classic (Rounds 1-2-3)
LOW FIRST 72:	263 (17-under)	*Ernie Els,* GTE Byron Nelson Classic
	268 (20-under)	*Duffy Waldorf*, LaCantera Texas Open
	264 (23-under)	*Billy Mayfair, Jim Furyk*, Las Vegas Invitational
	265 (23-under)	*Kenny Perry,* Bob Hope Chrysler Classic
LOW 90:	331 (28-under)	*Jim Furyk*, Las Vegas Invitational
HIGH 90:	335 (25-under)	*Kenny Perry*, Bob Hope Chrysler Classic
HIGH WINNING SCORE:	280 (even par)	*Corey Pavin,* U.S. Open, *Billy Mayfair*, THE TOUR Championship
	283 (5-under)	*Lee Janzen,* THE PLAYERS Championship
LARGEST WINNING MARGIN:	6 strokes	*Duffy Waldorf,* LaCantera Texas Open
LOW START BY WINNER:	63 (9-under)	*Kenny Perry,* Bob Hope Chrysler Classic; *Woody Austin*, Buick Open
HIGH START BY WINNER:	73 (3-over)	*Greg Norman*, NEC World Series of Golf
	73 (1-over)	*Payne Stewart*, Shell Houston Open; *Billy Mayfair,* Motorola Western Open
LOW FINISH BY WINNER:	61 (10-under)	*Hal Sutton*, B.C. Open
HIGH FINISH BY WINNER:	73 (3-over)	*Billy Mayfair*, THE TOUR Championship
	73 (2-over)	*Fred Funk,* Ideon Classic at Pleasant Valley
LARGEST 18-HOLE LEAD:	2 strokes	*John Huston,* Mercedes Championships; *Duffy Waldorf,* Phoenix Open; *Mark Brooks*, Nestle Invitational; *Woody Austin*, Buick Open
LARGEST 36-HOLE LEAD:	4 strokes	*Tom Lehman,* MCI Classic; *D.A. Weibring*, Quad City Classic
LARGEST 54-HOLE LEAD:	5 strokes	*Scott Hoch,* Shell Houston Open
LOW 36-HOLE CUT:	139 (3-under)	FedEx St. Jude Classic
	139 (1-under)	GTE Byron Nelson Classic
	140 (4-under)	Buick Open
HIGH 36-HOLE CUT:	149 (5-over)	THE PLAYERS Championship
	148 (4-over)	British Open Championship
	146 (6-over)	U.S. Open Championship

1995 PGA TOUR FACTS AND FIGURES *(cont'd.)*

LOW 54-HOLE CUT:	208 (8-under) 208 (7-under)	Walt Disney World/Oldsmobile Golf Classic Las Vegas Invitational
HIGH 54-HOLE CUT:	215 (1-under)	AT&T Pebble Beach National Pro-Am
FEWEST TO MAKE 36-HOLE CUT:	70	Phoenix Open
MOST TO MAKE 36-HOLE CUT:	103 88	British Open (10-stroke rule) Quad City Classic
FEWEST TO MAKE 54-HOLE CUT:	70	Walt Disney World/Oldsmobile Golf Classic
MOST TO MAKE 54-HOLE CUT:	80	Las Vegas Invitational
MOST CONSECUTIVE EVENTS IN THE MONEY:	14	*Jay Haas*
CONSECUTIVE YEARS WITH WIN:	4	*Ben Crenshaw, Lee Janzen & Greg Norman* (1992 through 1995)

DOUBLE EAGLE: *Per-Ulrik Johansson*, PGA Championship (Riviera CC #11); *J.L. Lewis*, Greater Milwaukee Open (Brown Deer Park GC #4)

HOLES IN ONE: (35) *Richard Zokol,* United Airlines Hawaiian Open; *David Graham,* AT&T Pebble Beach National Pro-Am; *Ray Stewart, Chris DiMarco, John Huston, Jim Gallagher, Jr.,* Bob Hope Chrysler Classic; *Craig Stadler,* Nissan Open; *Phil Mickelson,* THE PLAYERS Championship; *Brian Claar,* Freeport-McMoRan Classic; *Gil Morgan,* MCI Classic; *Michael Bradley, Andy North,* Kmart Greater Greensboro Open; *Phil Mickelson, Bob Lohr,* Shell Houston Open; *Wayne Grady, Dave Barr,* BellSouth Classic; *Tommy Tolles, Donnie Hammond,* GTE Byron Nelson Classic; *Jim McGovern,* Buick Classic; *Jeff Maggert,* Colonial National Invitation; *Gary Hallberg,* U.S. Open; *Dan Pohl,* Canon Greater Hartford Open; *Kawika Cotner,* FedEx St. Jude Classic; *Scott Gump, Joel Edwards,* Motorola Western Open; *Larry Rinker,* Anheuser-Busch Golf Classic; *Fuzzy Zoeller, Lee Janzen,* PGA Championship; *Lennie Clements,* Greater Milwaukee Open; *Willie Wood, Gary Hallberg,* B.C. Open; *Jeff Sluman,* Buick Challenge; *Bill Glasson, D.A. Weibring, Robin Freeman,* Las Vegas Invitational

THREE EAGLES ONE ROUND: *Tommy Tolles*, Bell Canadian Open; *John Adams*, Buick Challenge

TWO EAGLES ONE ROUND: *Steve Jones, Brian Claar,* United Airlines Hawaiian Open; *Phil Mickelson,* Northern Telecom Open; *Dan Forsman,* Phoenix Open; *Davis Love III,* AT&T Pebble Beach National Pro-Am; *Jim Gallagher, Jr.,* Bob Hope Chrysler Classic; *Steve Rintoul,* Honda Classic; *Mark McNulty,* Nestle Invitational; *Davis Love III,* Freeport-McMoRan Classic; *John Wilson, Brian Kamm, Grant Waite,* FedEx St. Jude Classic; *Pete Jordan,* Deposit Guaranty Golf Classic; *Mark Wiebe,* Sprint International; *Andrew Magee,* Bell Canadian Open; *Ernie Gonzalez,* Quad City Classic; *Dan Forsman,* Walt Disney World/Oldsmobile Golf Classic; *Kelly Gibson, Dennis Paulson, D.A. Weibring,* Las Vegas Invitational

BEST BIRDIE STREAK: 7 *Jay Delsing,* FedEx St. Jude Classic

BEST EAGLE/BIRDIE STREAK: *Keith Fergus* (4 birdies, 1 eagle), United Airlines Hawaiian Open; *Ben Crenshaw* (4 birdies, 1 eagle), Phoenix Open

BEST COME FROM BEHIND LAST DAY TO WIN: 7 strokes *Jim Gallagher, Jr.,* Kmart Greater Greensboro Open; *Payne Stewart,* Shell Houston Open

FIRST-TIME WINNERS: *John Morse,* United Airlines Hawaiian Open; *Ted Tryba,* Anheuser-Busch Golf Classic; *Ed Dougherty,* Deposit Guaranty Golf Classic; *Woody Austin,* Buick Open; *Brad Bryant,* Walt Disney World/Oldsmobile Golf Classic; *Jim Furyk,* Las Vegas Invitational; *Duffy Waldorf,* LaCantera Texas Open

1995 PGA TOUR FACTS AND FIGURES *(cont'd.)*

COURSE RECORDS: (No Ties)		
	63 (9-under)	*Lee Janzen,* La Costa CC, Mercedes Championships
	64 (8-under)	*Brad Faxon,* Poppy Hills CC, AT&T Pebble Beach Nat'l Pro-Am
	63 (9-under)	*Kenny Perry,* Indian Ridge CC, Bob Hope Chrysler Classic
	61 (9-under)	*Ernie Els,* Cottonwood Valley, GTE Byron Nelson Classic
	63 (7-under)	*Fuzzy Zoeller,* TPC at River Highlands, Canon Greater Hartford Open
	62 (8-under)	*Billy Andrade,* TPC at River Highlands, Canon Greater Hartford Open
	63 (9-under)	*Jonathan Kaye,* Annandale GC, Deposit Guaranty Golf Classic
	62 (10-under)	*Jim Furyk,* Warwick Hills CC, Buick Open
	61 (10-under)	*Hal Sutton,* En-Joie GC, B.C. Open
	63 (9-under)	*Mike Heinen,* Callaway Gardens Mtn View Course, Buick Challenge

TOURNAMENT RECORDS:

Peter Jacobsen, 271 (17-under), AT&T Pebble Beach National Pro-Am
Ernie Els, 263 (17-under), GTE Byron Nelson Classic
Steve Elkington, Colin Montgomerie, 267 (17-under), PGA Championship

MOST CONSECUTIVE ROUNDS PAR OR BETTER:

27 *Kirk Triplett* (Motorola Western Open 1, Anheuser-Busch Golf Classic 4, Deposit Guaranty Golf Classic 4, PGA Championship 4, B.C. Open 4, Buick Challenge 4, Las Vegas Invitational 5, LaCantera Texas Open (1)

MULTIPLE WINNERS:

Lee Janzen (3), THE PLAYERS Championship, Kemper Open, Sprint International
Greg Norman (3), Memorial Tournament, Canon Greater Hartford Open, NEC World Series of Golf
Vijay Singh (2), Phoenix Open, Buick Classic
Peter Jacobsen (2), AT&T Pebble Beach Pro-Am, Buick Invitational of California
Corey Pavin (2), Nissan Open, U.S. Open
Jim Gallagher, Jr. (2), Kmart Greater Greensboro Open, FedEx St. Jude Classic
Steve Elkington (2), Mercedes Championships, PGA Championship
Mark O'Meara (2), Honda Classic, Bell Canadian Open
Fred Funk (2), Ideon Classic at Pleasant Valley, Buick Challenge
Billy Mayfair (2), Motorola Western Open, THE TOUR Championship

PLAYOFFS:

Mercedes Championships	*Steve Elkington* def. *Bruce Lietzke,* birdie on 2nd extra hole
Phoenix Open	*Vijay Singh* def. *Billy Mayfair,* par on 1st extra hole
Freeport-McMoRan Classic	*Davis Love III* def. *Mike Heinen,* birdie on 2nd extra hole
MCI Classic	*Bob Tway* def. *Nolan Henke* and *David Frost,* par on 2nd extra hole
Shell Houston Open	*Payne Stewart* def. *Scott Hoch,* par on 1st extra hole
Buick Classic	*Vijay Singh* def. *Doug Martin,* birdie on 5th extra hole
Kemper Open	*Lee Janzen* def. *Corey Pavin,* birdie on 1st extra hole
British Open	*John Daly* def. *Costantino Rocca,* 15-19 in 4-hole playoff
Buick Open	*Woody Austin* def. *Mike Brisky,* par on 2nd extra hole
PGA Championship	*Steve Elkington* def. *Colin Montgomerie,* birdie on 1st extra hole
NEC World Series of Golf	*Greg Norman* def. *Nick Price & Billy Mayfair,* birdie on 1st extra hole
Bell Canadian Open	*Mark O'Meara* def. *Bob Lohr,* par on 1st extra hole

THE LAST TIME

WINNERS

Last to win back-to-back events	Peter Jacobsen, 1995 AT&T Pebble Beach National Pro-Am, Buick Invitational of California
Last to win three consecutive events	Gary Player, 1978 Masters, T of C, Houston Open
Last to win three consecutive starts	Nick Price, 1993 Hartford, Western, FedEx St. Jude
Last to successfully defend title	Loren Roberts, 1994-95 Nestle Invitational
Last lefthander to win	Phil Mickelson, 1995 Northern Telecom Open
Last Monday Open Qualifier to win	Fred Wadsworth, 1986 Southern Open
Last rookie to win	Woody Austin, 1995 Buick Open
Last rookie to win twice	Robert Gamez, 1990 Northern Telecom Tucson Open and Nestle Invitational
Last amateur to win	Phil Mickelson, 1991 Northern Telecom Open
Last to win in first-ever TOUR start	Jim Benepe, 1988 Beatrice Western Open
Last to win in first start as official member of PGA TOUR	Robert Gamez, 1990 Northern Telecom Tucson Open
Last wire-to-wire winner (no ties)	Bob Estes, 1994 Texas Open
Last to win with even-par score	Billy Mayfair, 1995 TOUR Championship
Last to win with over-par score	Bruce Lietzke, 1981 Byron Nelson Classic, plus-1
Last to win with no bogeys over 72 holes	Lee Trevino, 1974 Greater New Orleans Open
Last time player shot 80 and won	Kenny Knox, 1986 Honda Classic (third round)
Last to repeat as money leader	Nick Price, 1993, 1994
Last to win by holing final shot from off thegreen	Greg Norman, 1995 NEC World Series of Golf (66-foot chip shot)
Last grandfather to win	Johnny Miller, 1994 AT&T Pebble Beach National Pro-Am

TOURNAMENT FINISHES

Last 36-hole event	1994 Deposit Guaranty Golf Classic
Last 54-hole event	1995 Walt Disney World/Oldsmobile Golf Classic
Last Monday finish	1994 Southwestern Bell Colonial
Last Monday U.S. Open playoff finish	1994 Ernie Els defeated Loren Roberts, Colin Montgomerie
Last Tuesday finish	1980 Joe Garagiola-Tucson Open
Last 36-hole final day	1994 Buick Open
Last 54-hole final day	1925 Shawnee Open (Willie Macfarlane/Willie Klein 18-hole playoff after field completed 36 holes)
Last time cut made after 18 holes	1987 Beatrice Western Open

WEATHER

Last time tournament rained out	1991 Independent Insurance Agent Open
Last time it snowed during tournament	1987 Greater Greensboro Open

DOUBLE EAGLES, ACES & EAGLES

Last time back-to-back eagles	Dave Stockton, Jr., 1994 Walt Disney/Oldsmobile Classic
Last time double eagle	J.L. Lewis, 1995 Greater Milwaukee Open
Last time three eagles in same round	John Adams, 1995 Buick Challenge
Last time four aces same day, same hole	1989 U.S. Open, Doug Weaver, Mark Wiebe, Jerry Pate, Nick Price on hole No. 6, 160 yards, all used a 7-iron.

PLAYOFFS

Last one-hole playoff	1995 Bell Canadian Open (Mark O'Meara def. Bob Lohr)
Last two-hole playoff	1995 Buick Open (Woody Austin def. Mike Brisky)
Last three-hole playoff	1993 Buick Classic (Vijay Singh def. Mark Wiebe)
Last four-hole playoff	1995 British Open (John Daly def. Costantino Rocca)
Last five-hole playoff	1995 Buick Classic (Vijay Singh def. Doug Martin)
Last six-hole playoff	1986 Kemper Open (Greg Norman def. Larry Mize)
Last seven-hole playoff	1991 New England Classic (Bruce Fleisher def. Ian Baker-Finch)
Last eight-hole playoff	1983 Phoenix Open (Bob Gilder def. Johnny Miller, Mark O'Meara and Rex Caldwell)
Last 11-hole playoff (PGA TOUR record for sudden death)	1949 Motor City Open (Middlecoff and Mangrum co-winners)
Last 18-hole playoff (plus)	1994 U.S. Open (Ernie Els def. Loren Roberts and Colin Montgomerie; Montgomerie eliminated via 18-hole playoff; Els won on 20th extra hole)
Last 18-hole-plus playoff in PGA TOUR event	1972 Tucson Open [21 holes] (Miller Barber def. George Archer)
Last 36-hole playoff in PGA TOUR event	1947 All-American Open (Bobby Locke def. Ed Oliver)
Last 54-hole playoff in PGA TOUR event	1926 Metropolitan Open (Macdonald Smith def. Gene Sarazen)
Last 72-hole playoff (two 36-hole rounds)	1931 U.S. Open Championship (Billy Burke def. George Von Elm)

THE LAST TIME *(continued)*

PLAYOFFS (cont'd.)

Last playoff won with eagle	1992 Bob Hope Chrysler Classic (John Cook defeated Gene Sauers, Tom Kite, Mark O'Meara and Rick Fehr)
Last playoff won with birdie	1995 NEC World Series of Golf (Greg Norman def. Nick Price and Billy Mayfair)
Last playoff won with bogey	1988 Phoenix Open (Sandy Lyle def. Fred Couples, third extra hole)
Last two-man playoff	1995 Bell Canadian Open (Mark O'Meara def. Bob Lohr)
Last three-man playoff	1995 NEC World Series of Golf (Greg Norman def. Nick Price and Billy Mayfair)
Last four-man playoff	1990 Doral Ryder Open (Greg Norman def. Paul Azinger, Mark Calcavecchia and Tim Simpson)
Last five-man playoff	1993 Buick Southern Open (John Inman def. Bob Estes, Billy Andrade, Brad Bryant and Mark Brooks)
Last six-man playoff	1994 GTE Byron Nelson Classic (Neal Lancaster def. Tom Byrum, Mark Carnevale, David Edwards, Yoshinori Mizumaki and David Ogrin)
Last five-team playoff	1985 Chrysler Team Championship
Last tie/no playoff in PGA TOUR event	1952 Jacksonville Open (Sam Snead forfeited to Doug Ford after 72 holes)

1995 PGA TOUR TOURNAMENT SUMMARY

* Denotes first-time winner

TOURNAMENT	COURSE	WINNER	SCORE	UNDER PAR	MARGIN	MONEY	RUNNERS-UP
1. Mercedes Championships	La Costa Resort Carlsbad, CA	Steve Elkington	278	10	playoff	$180,000	Bruce Lietzke
2. United Airlines Hawaiian Open	Waialae CC Honolulu, HI	*John Morse	269	19	3	$216,000	Tom Lehman Duffy Waldorf
3. Northern Telecom Open	Tucson National Starr Pass GC Tucson, AZ	Phil Mickelson	269	18	1	$225,000	Jim Gallagher, Jr. Scott Simpson
4. Phoenix Open	TPC of Scottsdale Scottsdale, AZ	Vijay Singh	269	15	playoff	$234,000	Billy Mayfair
5. AT&T Pebble Beach National Pro-Am	Pebble Beach GL Spyglass Hill CC Poppy Hills CC Pebble Beach, CA	Peter Jacobsen	271	17	2	$252,000	David Duval
6. Buick Invitational of California	Torrey Pines GC North and South Courses La Jolla, CA	Peter Jacobsen (2)	269	19	4	$216,000	Hal Sutton Mark Calcavecchia Mike Hulbert Kirk Triplett
7. Bob Hope Chrysler Classic	Indian Ridge CC Bermuda Dunes CC Indian Wells, CC La Quinta CC Palm Desert, CA	Kenny Perry	335	25	1	$216,000	David Duval
8. Nissan Open	Riviera CC Pacific Palisades, CA	Corey Pavin	268	16	3	$216,000	Jay Don Blake Kenny Perry
9. Doral-Ryder Open	Doral Resort & CC Miami, FL	Nick Faldo	273	15	1	$270,000	Greg Norman Peter Jacobsen
10. Honda Classic	Weston Hills CC Ft. Lauderdale, FL	Mark O'Meara	275	9	1	$216,000	Nick Faldo
11. Nestle Invitational	Bay Hill Club Orlando, FL	Loren Roberts	272	16	2	$216,000	Brad Faxon
12 THE PLAYERS Championship	TPC at Sawgrass Ponte Vedra, FL	Lee Janzen	283	5	1	$540,000	Bernhard Langer
13. Freeport-McMoRan Classic	English Turn G&CC New Orleans, LA	Davis Love III	274	14	playoff	$216,000	Mike Heinen
14. Masters Tournament	Augusta National GC Augusta, GA	Ben Crenshaw	274	14	1	$396,000	Davis Love III
15. MCI Classic	Harbour Town GL Hilton Head Island, SC	Bob Tway	275	9	playoff	$234,000	Nolan Henke David Frost
16. Kmart Greater Greensboro Open	Forest Oaks CC Greensboro, NC	Jim Gallagher, Jr.	274	14	1	$270,000	Jeff Sluman Peter Jacobsen
17. Shell Houston Open	TPC at The Woodlands The Woodlands, TX	Payne Stewart	276	12	playoff	$252,000	Scott Hoch
18. BellSouth Classic	Atlanta CC Marietta, GA	Mark Calcavecchia	271	17	2	$234,000	Jim Gallagher,Jr.
19. GTE Byron Nelson Classic	TPC at Four Seasons Resort—Las Colinas Cottonwood Valley GC Irving, TX	Ernie Els	263	17	3	$234,000	Robin Freeman Mike Heinen D.A. Weibring
20. Buick Classic	Westchester CC Rye, NY	Vijay Singh (2)	278	6	playoff	$216,000	Doug Martin
21. Colonial National Invitation	Colonial CC Fort Worth, TX	Tom Lehman	271	9	1	$252,000	Craig Parry
22. Memorial Tournament	Muirfield Village GC Dublin, OH	Greg Norman	269	19	4	$306,000	Steve Elkington Mark Calcavecchia David Duval
23. Kemper Open	TPC at Avenel Potomac, MD	Lee Janzen (2)	272	1	playoff	$252,000	Corey Pavin
24. U.S. Open	Shinnecock Hills GC Southampton, NY	Corey Pavin (2)	280	level	2	$350,000	Greg Norman
25. Canon Greater Hartford Open	TPC at River Highlands Cromwell, CT	Greg Norman (2)	267	13	2	$216,000	Dave Stockton, Jr. Kirk Triplett Grant Waite

1995 PGA TOUR TOURNAMENT SUMMARY

* Denotes first-time winner

TOURNAMENT	COURSE	WINNER	SCORE	UNDER PAR	MARGIN	MONEY	RUNNERS-UP
26. FedEx St. Jude Classic	TPC at Southwind Memphis, TN	Jim Gallagher, Jr. (2)	267	17	1	$225,000	Ken Green Jay Delsing
27. Motorola Western Open	Cog Hill G&CC Lemont, IL	Billy Mayfair	279	9	1	$360,000	Jay Haas Justin Leonard Jeff Maggert
28 Anheuser-Busch Golf Classic	Kingsmill GC Williamsburg, VA	*Ted Tryba	272	12	1	$198,000	Scott Simpson
29. Deposit Guaranty Golf Classic	Annandale GC Madison, MS	*Ed Dougherty	272	16	2	$126,000	Gil Morgan
30. British Open	St. Andrews GC Old Course Fife, Scotland	John Daly	282	6	playoff	$199,375	Costantino Rocca
31. Ideon Classic at Pleasant Valley	Pleasant Valley CC Sutton, MA	Fred Funk	268	16	1	$180,000	Jim McGovern
32. Buick Open	Warwick Hills G&CC Grand Blanc, MI	*Woody Austin	270	18	playoff	$216,000	Mike Brisky
33. PGA Championship	Riviera CC Pacific Palisades, CA	Steve Elkington (2)	267	17	playoff	$360,000	Colin Montgomerie
34. Sprint International	Castle Pines GC Castle Rock, CO	Lee Janzen (3)	34 points	-	1 point	$270,000	Ernie Els
35. NEC World Series of Golf	Firestone CC Akron, OH	Greg Norman (3)	278	2	playoff	$360,000	Nick Price Billy Mayfair
36. Greater Milwaukee Open	Brown Deer Park GC Milwaukee, WI	Scott Hoch	269	15	3	$180,000	Marco Dawson
37. Bell Canadian Open	Glen Abbey GC Oakville, Ontario, Canada	Mark O'Meara (2)	274	14	playoff	$234,000	Bob Lohr
38. B.C. Open	En-Joie GC Endicott, NY	Hal Sutton	269	15	1	$180,000	Jim McGovern
39. Quad City Classic	Oakwood CC Coal Valley, IL (tournament reduced to 54 holes due to rain)	D.A. Weibring	197	13	1	$180,000	Jonathan Kaye
40. Buick Challenge	Callaway Gardens Mountain View Course Pine Mountain, GA	Fred Funk (2)	272	16	1	$180,000	Loren Roberts John Morse
41. Walt Disney World/ Oldsmobile Golf Classic	Three Disney Courses Magnolia, Palm and Lake Buena Vista Lake Buena Vista, FL (tournament reduced to 54 holes due to rain)	*Brad Bryant	198	18	1	$216,000	Hal Sutton Ted Tryba
42. Las Vegas Invitational	TPC at Summerlin Las Vegas CC Las Vegas Hilton CC Las Vegas, NV	*Jim Furyk	329	28	1	$270,000	Billy Mayfair
43. LaCantera Texas Open	LaCantera GC San Antonio, TX	*Duffy Waldorf	268	20	6	$198,000	Justin Leonard
44. THE TOUR Championship	Southern Hills CC Tulsa, OK	Billy Mayfair (2)	280	even	3	$540,000	Corey Pavin Steve Elkington
45. Lincoln-Mercury Kapalua Int'l	Kapalua Resort Kapalua Maui, HI	Jim Furyk	271	19	2	$180,000	Russ Cochran Barry Lane Jim McGovern
46. World Cup of Golf	TPC at Mission Hills Shenzhen, China	United States (Fred Couples/ Davis Love III)	545	33	14	$200,000 each	Australia
47. Franklin Templeton Shark Shoot-Out	Sherwood CC Thousand Oaks, CA	Mark Calcavecchia/ Steve Elkington	184	32	1	$150,000 each	Lee Janzen/ Chip Beck
48. Skins Game	Bighorn GC Palm Desert, CA	Fred Couples	-	-	-	$270,000	Corey Pavin
49. JCPenney Classic	Innisbrook Hilton Tarpon Springs, FL	Davis Love III/ Beth Daniel	257	27	2	$162,500	Robert Gamez/ Helen Alfredsson

1995 PGA TOUR STATISTICAL LEADERS

(minimum of 50 rounds)

DRIVING DISTANCE

	NAME	RDS.	YARDS
1.	JOHN DALY	75	289.0
2.	DAVIS LOVE III	89	284.6
3.	DENNIS PAULSON	82	284.1
4.	VIJAY SINGH	79	283.5
5.	KELLY GIBSON	101	280.2
6.	JOHN ADAMS	81	278.9
6.	BRETT OGLE	64	278.9
8.	CARL PAULSON	62	278.2
9.	WOODY AUSTIN	114	277.5
10.	FRED COUPLES	54	276.3
11.	ROBERT GAMEZ	82	275.8
12.	JIM GALLAGHER, JR.	99	275.4
13.	TOM PURTZER	58	275.3
14.	STEVE STRICKER	83	275.2
15.	CHARLIE RYMER	75	274.4
16.	DAVID DUVAL	89	274.3
16.	ERNIE ELS	60	274.3
18.	DUFFY WALDORF	90	274.2
19.	MICHAEL BRADLEY	88	274.0
20.	JOHN HUSTON	81	273.9
21.	GREG NORMAN	58	273.4
22.	TOM WATSON	56	273.2
23.	NICK PRICE	66	273.0
24.	PETER JACOBSEN	93	272.9
25.	MARK CALCAVECCHIA	105	272.5

DRIVING ACCURACY

	NAME	RDS.	PCT.
1.	FRED FUNK	112	81.3
2.	DOUG TEWELL	55	80.3
3.	LARRY MIZE	70	79.6
4.	DAVID EDWARDS	74	79.1
5.	BRUCE LIETZKE	53	78.8
6.	BRUCE FLEISHER	69	78.7
7.	LENNIE CLEMENTS	93	78.3
8.	CURTIS STRANGE	84	77.9
9.	NICK FALDO	72	77.8
9.	BILL PORTER	76	77.8
11.	FULTON ALLEM	55	77.7
12.	TIM LOUSTALOT	55	77.2
13.	JUSTIN LEONARD	110	77.1
14.	HAL SUTTON	94	77.0
15.	SCOTT GUMP	93	76.9
16.	LOREN ROBERTS	83	76.8
17.	NICK PRICE	66	76.3
18.	TOM HEARN	57	76.2
18.	TRAY TYNER	82	76.2
20.	BLAINE MCCALLISTER	90	76.1
21.	JOHN MORSE	71	75.8
21.	DICKY THOMPSON	70	75.8
23.	GRANT WAITE	84	75.6
23.	D.A. WEIBRING	83	75.6
25.	LEE RINKER	91	75.4

GREENS IN REGULATION

	NAME	RDS.	PCT.
1.	LENNIE CLEMENTS	93	72.3
2.	BART BRYANT	82	71.4
3.	CRAIG STADLER	69	71.3
3.	GRANT WAITE	84	71.3
5.	DAVE BARR	79	70.9
6.	SCOTT GUMP	93	70.7
7.	SCOTT SIMPSON	88	70.6
8.	MARK O'MEARA	96	70.5
9.	TOM LEHMAN	65	70.4
9.	TOM PURTZER	58	70.4
11.	JOEY SINDELAR	71	70.3
12.	PETER JACOBSEN	93	70.2
13.	HAL SUTTON	94	70.0
14.	EMLYN AUBREY	86	69.8
15.	JOHN MAHAFFEY	81	69.7
15.	KIRK TRIPLETT	100	69.7
17.	STEVE JONES	80	69.6
17.	TOM KITE	87	69.6
19.	GIL MORGAN	71	69.5
20.	TOM WATSON	56	69.4
21.	PATRICK BURKE	75	69.3
22.	JOHN ADAMS	81	69.2
22.	LARRY MIZE	70	69.2
22.	FUZZY ZOELLER	55	69.2
25.	MARK BROOKS	93	69.1

PUTTING LEADERS

	NAME	RDS.	AVG.
1.	JIM FURYK	102	1.708
2.	SCOTT HOCH	100	1.737
3.	GENE SAUERS	75	1.740
4.	PETE JORDAN	59	1.744
5.	BRAD FAXON	87	1.749
6.	PAYNE STEWART	97	1.750
7.	PAUL AZINGER	76	1.751
7.	BOB ESTES	91	1.751
7.	JAY HAAS	88	1.751
7.	STEVE LOWERY	107	1.751
7.	FUZZY ZOELLER	55	1.751
12.	KIRK TRIPLETT	100	1.752
13.	JIM GALLAGHER, JR.	99	1.753
13.	DAVIS LOVE III	89	1.753
15.	BOB TWAY	94	1.754
16.	JUSTIN LEONARD	110	1.757
16.	SCOTT SIMPSON	88	1.757
16.	JOHN WILSON	95	1.757
19.	DAVID FROST	72	1.758
19.	JOHN HUSTON	81	1.758
21.	COREY PAVIN	79	1.759
21.	DON POOLEY	77	1.759
23.	BILL GLASSON	73	1.760
23.	NICK PRICE	66	1.760
25.	BOB LOHR	95	1.761

1995 PGA TOUR Statistical Leaders *(cont'd.)*

(minimum of 50 rounds)

TOTAL DRIVING

	NAME	RDS.	TOTAL
1.	NICK PRICE	18	40
2.	HAL SUTTON	31	58
3.	PETER JACOBSEN	25	60
4.	GREG NORMAN	16	63
5.	GRANT WAITE	26	73
6.	BILL GLASSON	22	82
7.	BRUCE LIETZKE	16	83
8.	TOM WATSON	16	87
9.	DAVID DUVAL	26	102
10.	CRAIG STADLER	21	103
11.	DAVIS LOVE III	24	104
12.	TOMMY ARMOUR III	30	108
13.	PHIL MICKELSON	24	112
14.	BILLY MAYFAIR	28	116
14.	FUZZY ZOELLER	15	116
16.	STEVE ELKINGTON	21	117
17.	LEE RINKER	29	119
18.	KIRK TRIPLETT	27	120
19.	STEVE STRICKER	23	122
20.	JEFF MAGGERT	23	123
21.	BLAINE MCCALLISTER	26	125
21.	DUFFY WALDORF	26	125
23.	ERNIE ELS	18	126
24.	CARL PAULSON	21	132
25.	ROBERT GAMEZ	27	133

EAGLE LEADERS

	NAME	RDS.	TOTAL
1.	KELLY GIBSON	101	16
2.	PAUL AZINGER	76	15
3.	DAVIS LOVE III	89	14
4.	JOHN ADAMS	81	13
5.	WOODY AUSTIN	114	12
5.	MICHAEL BRADLEY	88	12
5.	MARK CALCAVECCHIA	105	12
5.	JIM GALLAGHER, JR.	99	12
5.	JAY HAAS	88	12
5.	MIKE STANDLY	93	12
5.	TOMMY TOLLES	79	12
12.	MARK BROOKS	93	11
12.	SCOTT MCCARRON	77	11
12.	VIJAY SINGH	79	11
15.	JOE ACOSTA, JR.	74	10
15.	BRAD BRYANT	95	10
15.	DAN FORSMAN	77	10
15.	BRIAN KAMM	90	10
15.	STEVE LOWERY	107	10
20.	16 TIED WITH		9

BIRDIE LEADERS

	NAME	RDS.	TOTAL
1.	STEVE LOWERY	107	410
2.	WOODY AUSTIN	114	404
2.	JIM FURYK	102	404
4.	KIRK TRIPLETT	100	399
5.	JUSTIN LEONARD	110	386
6.	CURT BYRUM	106	380
6.	FRED FUNK	112	380
8.	MARK CALCAVECCHIA	105	372
9.	SCOTT HOCH	100	371
10.	PAUL GOYDOS	109	366
11.	KELLY GIBSON	101	361
11.	MARK O'MEARA	96	361
13.	JIM GALLAGHER, JR.	99	360
13.	HAL SUTTON	94	360
15.	PAYNE STEWART	97	358
16.	MIKE HULBERT	102	355
17.	BOB TWAY	94	354
18.	BRAD BRYANT	95	353
18.	JEFF SLUMAN	101	353
20.	ROBIN FREEMAN	97	348
21.	LENNIE CLEMENTS	93	346
21.	JIM MCGOVERN	97	346
23.	GUY BOROS	97	343
24.	JOHN WILSON	95	342
25.	2 TIED WITH		341

SAND SAVES

	NAME	RDS.	PCT.
1.	BILLY MAYFAIR	99	68.6
2.	STEVE ELKINGTON	72	68.2
3.	DAVID FROST	72	66.9
4.	DAVID FEHERTY	71	64.1
5.	DAVID OGRIN	91	62.5
6.	BEN CRENSHAW	80	61.4
7.	BILL BRITTON	67	61.3
7.	ERNIE ELS	60	61.3
9.	GREG NORMAN	58	61.0
10.	JEFF SLUMAN	101	60.8
11.	BOB ESTES	91	60.7
12.	FRED FUNK	112	60.6
12.	LANNY WADKINS	59	60.6
14.	JERRY HAAS	82	60.3
15.	BRAD FAXON	87	59.7
15.	DENNIS PAULSON	82	59.7
17.	NOLAN HENKE	81	59.6
18.	JOHN ADAMS	81	59.0
19.	JIM CARTER	96	58.9
19.	CURTIS STRANGE	84	58.9
21.	EMLYN AUBREY	86	58.8
21.	FUZZY ZOELLER	55	58.8
23.	BRUCE FLEISHER	69	58.7
24.	TOMMY TOLLES	79	58.6
24.	TRAY TYNER	82	58.6

1995 PGA TOUR Statistical Leaders *(cont'inued)*

(minimum of 50 rounds)

SCORING AVERAGE

	NAME	RDS.	AVG.
1.	GREG NORMAN	58	69.06
2.	STEVE ELKINGTON	72	69.59
3.	ERNIE ELS	60	69.81
3.	NICK PRICE	66	69.81
5.	NICK FALDO	72	69.85
5.	TOM LEHMAN	65	69.85
7.	VIJAY SINGH	79	69.92
8.	BOB TWAY	94	69.93
9.	SCOTT SIMPSON	88	69.99
10.	PETER JACOBSEN	93	70.03
11.	COREY PAVIN	79	70.04
12.	DAVIS LOVE III	89	70.09
13.	JAY HAAS	88	70.18
14.	LOREN ROBERTS	83	70.21
15.	FRED COUPLES	54	70.22
15.	KIRK TRIPLETT	100	70.22
17.	JUSTIN LEONARD	110	70.23
17.	PAYNE STEWART	97	70.23
17.	SCOTT VERPLANK	85	70.23
20.	MARK O'MEARA	96	70.25
21.	MARK MCCUMBER	66	70.27
22.	MARK CALCAVECCHIA	105	70.28
22.	PETE JORDAN	59	70.28
24.	BILLY MAYFAIR	99	70.29
24.	STEVE STRICKER	83	70.29

ALL AROUND

	NAME		TOTAL
1.	JUSTIN LEONARD	31	323
2.	JEFF SLUMAN	29	326
3.	KIRK TRIPLETT	27	339
4.	DAVID DUVAL	26	348
5.	MARK CALCAVECCHIA	29	350
6.	JIM GALLAGHER, JR.	27	353
7.	SCOTT VERPLANK	25	378
8.	JOHN ADAMS	25	381
9.	STEVE LOWERY	30	395
10.	BRAD BRYANT	31	397
10.	DUFFY WALDORF	26	397
12.	JAY HAAS	27	398
13.	DAVIS LOVE III	24	399
14.	HAL SUTTON	31	407
15.	BILLY MAYFAIR	28	420
16.	MARK BROOKS	29	423
16.	BILL GLASSON	22	423
18.	PETER JACOBSEN	25	425
19.	GREG NORMAN	16	426
20.	BOB TWAY	27	439
21.	STEVE STRICKER	23	441
22.	ANDREW MAGEE	27	442
23.	STEVE ELKINGTON	21	450
24.	SCOTT HOCH	28	452
25.	KENNY PERRY	25	455

1995 PGA TOUR STATISTICAL HIGH/LOWS

Those with 50 rounds or more based on 188 ranked players.

STATISTICAL CATEGORY	HIGHEST	AVERAGE	LOWEST
Driving Distance	289.0	263.5	246.6
Driving Accuracy	81.3%	67.3%	54.6%
Greens in Regulation	72.3%	64.3%	57.4%
Putting	1.708	1.787	1.856
Par Breakers	22.7%	19.1%	14.0%
Eagles	16	5	0
Birdies	410	273	135
Scoring Average	69.06	71.17	73.14
Sand Saves	68.6%	52.3%	32.3%

YEAR-BY-YEAR STATISTICAL LEADERS

SCORING AVERAGE

1980	Lee Trevino	69.73
1981	Tom Kite	69.80
1982	Tom Kite	70.21
1983	Raymond Floyd	70.61
1984	Calvin Peete	70.56
1985	Don Pooley	70.36
1986	Scott Hoch	70.08
1987	David Frost	70.09
1988	Greg Norman	69.38
1989	Payne Stewart	*69.485
1990	Greg Norman	69.10
1991	Fred Couples	69.59
1992	Fred Couples	69.38
1993	Greg Norman	68.90
1994	Greg Norman	68.81
1995	Greg Norman	69.06

DRIVING DISTANCE

1980	Dan Pohl	274.3
1981	Dan Pohl	280.1
1982	Bill Calfee	275.3
1983	John McComish	277.4
1984	Bill Glasson	276.5
1985	Andy Bean	278.2
1986	Davis Love III	285.7
1987	John McComish	283.9
1988	Steve Thomas	284.6
1989	Ed Humenik	280.9
1990	Tom Purtzer	279.6
1991	John Daly	288.9
1992	John Daly	283.4
1993	John Daly	288.9
1994	Davis Love III	283.8
1995	John Daly	289.0

DRIVING ACCURACY

1980	Mike Reid	79.5%
1981	Calvin Peete	81.9
1982	Calvin Peete	84.6
1983	Calvin Peete	81.3
1984	Calvin Peete	77.5
1985	Calvin Peete	80.6
1986	Calvin Peete	81.7
1987	Calvin Peete	83.0
1988	Calvin Peete	82.5
1989	Calvin Peete	82.6
1990	Calvin Peete	83.7
1991	Hale Irwin	78.3
1992	Doug Tewell	82.3
1993	Doug Tewell	82.5
1994	David Edwards	81.6
1995	Fred Funk	81.3

GREENS IN REGULATION

1980	Jack Nicklaus	72.1%
1981	Calvin Peete	73.1
1982	Calvin Peete	72.4
1983	Calvin Peete	71.4
1984	Andy Bean	72.1
1985	John Mahaffey	71.9
1986	John Mahaffey	72.0
1987	Gil Morgan	73.3
1988	John Adams	73.9
1989	Bruce Lietzke	72.6
1990	Doug Tewell	70.9
1991	Bruce Lietzke	73.3
1992	Tim Simpson	74.0
1993	Fuzzy Zoeller	73.6
1994	Bill Glasson	73.0
1995	Lennie Clements	72.3

PUTTING

1980	Jerry Pate	28.81
1981	Alan Tapie	28.70
1982	Ben Crenshaw	28.65
1983	Morris Hatalsky	27.96
1984	Gary McCord	28.57
1985	Craig Stadler	*28.627
1986	Greg Norman	1.736
1987	Ben Crenshaw	1.743
1988	Don Pooley	1.729
1989	Steve Jones	1.734
1990	Larry Rinker	*1.7467
1991	Jay Don Blake	*1.7326
1992	Mark O'Meara	1.731
1993	David Frost	1.739
1994	Loren Roberts	1.737
1995	Jim Furyk	1.708

ALL-AROUND

1987	Dan Pohl	170
1988	Payne Stewart	170
1989	Paul Azinger	250
1990	Paul Azinger	162
1991	Scott Hoch	283
1992	Fred Couples	256
1993	Gil Morgan	252
1994	Bob Estes	227
1995	Justin Leonard	323

SAND SAVES

1980	Bob Eastwood	65.4%
1981	Tom Watson	60.1
1982	Isao Aoki	60.2
1983	Isao Aoki	62.3
1984	Peter Oosterhuis	64.7
1985	Tom Purtzer	60.8
1986	Paul Azinger	63.8
1987	Paul Azinger	63.2
1988	Greg Powers	63.5
1989	Mike Sullivan	66.0
1990	Paul Azinger	67.2
1991	Ben Crenshaw	64.9
1992	Mitch Adcock	66.9
1993	Ken Green	64.4
1994	Corey Pavin	65.4
1995	Billy Mayfair	68.6

PAR BREAKERS (category discontinued)

1980	Tom Watson	.213
1981	Bruce Lietzke	.225
1982	Tom Kite	*.2154
1983	Tom Watson	.211
1984	Craig Stadler	.220
1985	Craig Stadler	.218
1986	Greg Norman	.248
1987	Mark Calcavecchia	.221
1988	Ken Green	.236
1989	Greg Norman	.224
1990	Greg Norman	.219

TOTAL DRIVING

1991	Bruce Lietzke	42
1992	Bruce Lietzke	50
1993	Greg Norman	41
1994	Nick Price	43
1995	Nick Price	40

EAGLES

1980	Dave Eichelberger	16
1981	Bruce Lietzke	12
1982	Tom Weiskopf	10
	J.C. Snead	10
	Andy Bean	10
1983	Chip Beck	15
1984	Gary Hallberg	15
1985	Larry Rinker	14
1986	Joey Sindelar	16
1987	Phil Blackmar	20
1988	Ken Green	21
1989	Lon Hinkle	14
	Duffy Waldorf	14
1990	Paul Azinger	14
1991	Andy Bean	15
	John Huston	15
1992	Dan Forsman	18
1993	Davis Love III	15
1994	Davis Love III	18
1995	Kelly Gibson	16

BIRDIES

1980	Andy Bean	388
1981	Vance Heafner	388
1982	Andy Bean	392
1983	Hal Sutton	399
1984	Mark O'Meara	419
1985	Joey Sindelar	411
1986	Joey Sindelar	415
1987	Dan Forsman	409
1988	Dan Forsman	465
1989	Ted Schulz	415
1990	Mike Donald	401
1991	Scott Hoch	446
1992	Jeff Sluman	417
1993	John Huston	426
1994	Brad Bryant	397
1995	Steve Lowery	410

** had to be carried a decimal further to determine winner*

TOUGHEST HOLES ON THE 1995 PGA TOUR

RANK	GOLF COURSE	HOLE #	PAR	AVG. SCORE	AVG. OVER PAR	EAGLES	BIRDIES	PARS	BOGEYS	DOUBLE BOGEYS	TRIPLE BOGEY+	TOURNAMENT NAME
1	ST. ANDREWS GOLF CLUB	17	4	4.617	.617		13	232	229	39	9	British Open
2	GLEN ABBEY GC	9	4	4.539	.539		42	210	158	48	12	Bell Canadian Open
3	TPC AT SAWGRASS	18	4	4.515	.515		25	229	135	41	8	THE PLAYERS Championship
4	WESTCHESTER CC	12	4	4.472	.472		24	239	174	23	3	Buick Classic
5	WESTCHESTER CC	15	4	4.446	.446		24	248	167	22	2	Buick Classic
6	WESTCHESTER CC	11	4	4.439	.439		16	271	149	24	3	Buick Classic
7	OAKWOOD CC	4	4	4.415	.415		20	199	147	13		Quad Cities Open
8	SHINNECOCK HILLS CLUB	6	4	4.410	.410		16	261	156	22	1	U.S. Open Championship
9	WESTCHESTER CC	8	4	4.404	.404		25	268	145	21	4	Buick Classic
10	FIRESTONE CC (South)	4	4	4.399	.399		14	98	65	5	2	NEC World Series of Golf
11	SHINNECOCK HILLS CLUB	18	4	4.395	.395	1	26	256	147	19	7	U.S. Open Championship
12	EN-JOIE GC	15	4	4.392	.392		26	241	167	16	1	B.C. Open
13	WESTON HILLS CC	15	4	4.388	.388		24	273	122	22	8	Honda Classic
14	ST. ANDREWS GOLF CLUB	11	3	3.383	.383		31	292	175	18	6	British Open Championship
15	PEBBLE BCH GOLF LINKS	8	4	4.380	.380		13	147	69	12	4	AT&T Pebble Beach National Pro-Am
15	LACANTERA CC	12	4	4.380	.380		44	258	108	36	9	LaCantera Texas Open
17	FIRESTONE CC (South)	6	4	4.372	.372		11	110	53	8	2	NEC World Series of Golf
18	PEBBLE BCH GOLF LINKS	9	4	4.367	.367		16	137	78	14		AT&T Pebble Beach National Pro-Am
18	SOUTHERN HILLS CC	18	4	4.367	.367		9	65	40	5	1	THE TOUR Championship
20	COLONIAL CC	5	4	4.350	.350		25	228	91	24	4	Colonial
20	FIRESTONE CC (South)	9	4	4.350	.350		11	104	62	5	1	NEC World Series of Golf
20	SOUTHERN HILLS CC	9	4	4.350	.350		9	71	32	6	2	THE TOUR Championship
23	FIRESTONE CC (South)	18	4	4.339	.339		13	103	59	8		NEC World Series of Golf
24	TUCSON NAT'L GOLF	10	4	4.337	.337		19	185	93	14	1	Northern Telecom Open
25	SHINNECOCK HILLS CLUB	9	4	4.333	.333		27	271	141	14	3	U.S. Open Championship
25	SOUTHERN HILLS CC	2	4	4.333	.333		8	67	42	3		THE TOUR Championship
25	SOUTHERN HILLS CC	12	4	4.333	.333		7	70	39	4		THE TOUR Championship
28	PEBBLE BCH GOLF LINKS	10	4	4.322	.322		21	144	62	16	2	AT&T Pebble Beach National Pro-Am
29	WESTON HILLS CC	9	4	4.321	.321	1	32	272	122	21	2	Honda Classic
30	SHINNECOCK HILLS CLUB	10	4	4.318	.318		32	277	123	18	6	U.S. Open Championship
30	GLEN ABBEY GC	11	4	4.318	.318		46	284	98	31	10	Bell Canadian Open
32	LA COSTA CC	5	4	4.317	.317		11	66	42	4		Mercedes Championships
33	TORREY PINES (South)	7	4	4.316	.316		30	179	104	10	3	Buick Invitational of California
33	WAIALAE CC	4	3	3.316	.316	1	34	257	130	17	2	United Airlines Hawaiian Open
35	LACANTERA CC	17	3	3.312	.312		34	281	110	24	6	LaCantera Texas Open
36	ST. ANDREWS GOLF CLUB	13	4	4.308	.308		41	304	157	15	5	British Open Championship
37	TPC AT SAWGRASS	7	4	4.304	.304		33	273	112	18	3	THE PLAYERS Championship
38	RIVIERA CC	2	4	4.302	.302		25	276	128	14	1	Nissan Open
38	TPC AT AVENEL	12	4	4.302	.302		40	275	101	28	4	Kemper Open
40	WESTON HILLS CC	5	3	3.301	.301		28	296	105	18	4	Honda Classic
41	SOUTHERN HILLS CC	16	4	4.300	.300		7	78	27	8		THE TOUR Championship
42	RIVIERA CC	2	4	4.299	.299		25	274	132	10	1	PGA Championship
43	TORREY PINES (South)	4	4	4.298	.298		23	190	106	7		Buick Invitational
44	TPC AT SAWGRASS	5	4	4.297	.297		25	279	124	10	1	THE PLAYERS Championship
45	COG HILL G&CC	13	4	4.295	.295		41	271	109	26	4	Motorola Western Open
46	TPC AT SAWGRASS	13	3	3.293	.293	1	47	254	104	27	5	THE PLAYERS Championship
47	WESTON HILLS CC	16	4	4.290	.290		31	285	114	14	5	Honda Classic
48	BROWN DEER PARK GC	10	4	4.287	.287		34	272	131	14		Greater Milwaukee Open
49	SPYGLASS HILL GC	8	4	4.283	.283		14	107	53	6		AT&T Pebble Beach National Pro-Am
49	INDIAN RIDGE CC	5	3	3.283	.283	1	12	82	18	11	3	Bob Hope Chrysler Classic
49	SHINNECOCK HILLS CLUB	12	4	4.283	.283		42	264	133	15	2	U.S. Open Championship
52	WAIALAE CC	5	4	4.282	.282	1	27	280	119	12	2	United Airlines Hawaiian Open

PLAYER PERFORMANCE CHART

TOP 50 MONEY WINNERS ON THE 1995 PGA TOUR

LEGEND:

- ☐ Did not play
- T7 Final position
- (1) (2) Involved in play-off
- MC Missed cut
- WD Withdrew

	1. Greg Norman	2. Billy Mayfair	3. Lee Janzen	4. Corey Pavin	5. Steve Elkington	6. Davis Love III	7. Peter Jacobsen	8. Jim Gallagher, Jr.	9. Vijay Singh	10. Mark O'Meara	11. David Duval	12. Payne Stewart	13. Mark Calcavecchia	14. Ernie Els	15. Tom Lehman	16. Jay Haas	17. Scott Simpson	18. Scott Hoch	19. Nick Faldo	20. Bob Tway	21. Kenny Perry	22. Justin Leonard	23. Ben Crenshaw	24. Woody Austin	25. Brad Bryant
Mercedes Championships	18		T9	T12	(1)	T59									T5			11			T16		T5		
United Airlines Hawaiian Open		MC		T36			T47	T27	T47	T47	T14		T14		T2		T65	76				MC		T58	MC
Northern Telecom Open		MC	T25					T2	MC	T45	T6	MC	T32			MC	T2	T32	T25	T6	72	MC		T6	MC
Phoenix Open		(2)	63		T26		MC	MC	(1)			T4	T7		T22	MC			T54	T41	T41	MC	3	T35	MC
AT&T Pebble Bch Ntl. Pro-Am			MC	T65	T19	T3	1	MC	MC	T9	2	5	T13		MC		MC		T9		T3	T43	T13	MC	T63
Buick Invitational of California		T48			MC	T12	1			T58	T63	T16	T2			MC	MC		MC	MC			T41	MC	T12
Bob Hope Chrysler Classic				T70				T14		T16	2					MC	T16	T54		T16	1	T14		T67	
Nissan Open		T35	T46	1	T14	T35	T35						T41			T7	T4	T23		T19	T2	T52	T61	MC	
Doral-Ryder Open	T2	T43	MC		T4	T4	T2	T33	T12	T10	T17	76	T33	T17		T17		MC	1	T67	MC	T4	MC	T7	WD
Honda Classic			T27					T59	T31	1		MC	T47		T31				2	T13		T31		T13	
Nestle Invitational	T11	MC	T65	T37		T16	3	T37	T20	T42	T53	T31	T53	T42	T37	T5	T11	MC	T5		T53	MC	T42	WD	MC
THE PLAYERS Championship	T37	T18	1	T3	WD	T6	T29	T23	T43	MC	MC	T3	T18	T68	T14	MC	T11	WD	MC	T68	T55	T34	MC		T6
Freeport-McMoRan Classic		T15				(1)		MC			3						T8					T39	MC	T15	T8
Masters Tournament	T3		T12	T17	T5	2	T31		TMC	T31		T41	T41	MC	40	T3		T17	T24		T12		1		MC
MCI Classic	WD	T56	MC	T53		T68	T20		MC	T61	MC	T24		T7	T24	MC		T20	T4	(1)	T24	T44		T4	
Kmart Gr. Greensboro Open		MC	T41		MC	T19	T2	1	T7	MC	T14	MC	5			MC	T29			MC	T36	T14		MC	T25
Shell Houston Open			T59		MC		T59		T8		T27	(1)	T59				T19	(2)				T32	T59	MC	T19
BellSouth Classic		T29		MC		T22		2			T15		1					T7		MC				MC	
GTE Byron Nelson Classic		T48		T16	T32					T16		T32	T16	1		MC	T56	T21	T21	T9	T5	T26	T48	T74	T32
Buick Classic			T18		T18			T40	(1)		T8			T4	T14				T4	T14			T26	MC	T29
Colonial National Invitation		T8	MC	MC	T15	T58	T23	MC		MC	T12	T52	T8	MC	1	MC	T33	T52		T29	T33	T5	MC	4	T23
Memorial Tournament	1	MC	T19	MC	T2	T53	T13	T38	T11	T38	T2	T59	T2	T13	T29	T5	T21	T38	T13	T29	T11	MC	T5	T38	T21
Kemper Open	T4	T42	(1)	(2)		T4			T4	T4		T9				T31	T14	T21			T9	T4		MC	MC
U.S. Open	2		T13	1	T36	T4	T51	T62	T10		T28	T21	MC	MC	3	T4	T28	T56	T46	T10	MC		T71		T13
Canon Greater Hartford Open	1	T51		T11					T15	T28	MC		MC								MC	MC			
Federal-Express St. Jude Cl.		MC	T45				T26	1				MC		T26		T11	T39			T5		T53		MC	
Motorola Western Open		1	MC	T60	T29	T60	T60	MC	66	WD	T68		T25	MC		T2	T2	T10		T6		T2	MC	T10	T57
Anheuser-Busch Golf Classic								T18				T11				T34	2	T3						T27	
Deposit Guaranty Golf Classic																									
British Open	T15		T24	T8	T6	T98	T31	T55	T6	T49	T20	T11	T24	T11		T79	MC	T68	T40	MC		T58	T15		MC
Ideon Classic		T33					T22						T27								T11			T11	
Buick Open		MC									MC	8		T3	T9	T33		T33	T57		T11	T17	MC	(1)	T11
PGA Championship	T20	T23	T23	MC	(1)	MC	T23	T44	MC	T6	MC	T13	MC	T3	MC	T8	T54		T31	MC	T49	18	T44	T23	MC
Sprint International	T8		1			T8	MC			MC	5		T26	2	T14	T3	MC	MC		T42		T62		MC	T26
NEC World Series of Golf	1	(T2)	T18	T20	DQ	T12	17	T6	T4	T20		T25	T25	T28	T12				T12	11	31		T42	T37	
Greater Milwaukee Open		T34	T34					T3		T10			MC			T10		1				T17		T54	MC
Bell Canadian Open		T34	MC					T24		1		MC	T45							T9		T29		T67	T14
B.C. Open						MC	T20									T5									MC
Quad City Classic																		T5		T27					
Buick Challenge	T20	T58			MC			T20			MC						MC	T8				T18	T30	T24	T12
Walt Disney World/Olds Cl.			T21	T49				T49		MC		T28					WD	T21		T4				MC	1
Las Vegas Invitational		2				T7	MC			T4			T39							T25	MC	T23		T71	T4
LaCantera Texas Open											T50	T15				8		MC			T15	2			WD
THE TOUR Championship	T9	1	T20	T2	T2	T16	T16	T25	6	T13	T9	T16	T27	T16	12	T20	T4	T27	T13	15	T20	T7	T25	T4	T7

continued on page 434

PLAYER PERFORMANCE CHART

TOP 50 MONEY WINNERS ON THE 1995 PGA TOUR

LEGEND:

- ☐ Did not play
- T7 Final position
- ① ② Involved in play-off
- MC Missed cut
- WD Withdrew

	26. Fred Funk	27. Loren Roberts	28. Phil Mickelson	29. Kirk Tripplet	30. Nick Price	31. Jeff Sluman	32. Hal Sutton	33. Jim Furyk	34. Jeff Maggert	35. Duffy Waldorf	36. D.A. Weibring	37. Brad Faxon	38. Steve Lowery	39. Ted Tryba	40. Steve Stricker	41. Bob Estes	42. John Morse	43. Bill Glasson	44. Jim McGovern	45. Craig Stadler	46. Bernhard Langer	47. Mark McCumber	48. Mark Brooks	49. Curtis Strange	50. David Frost
Mercedes Championships		T24	19										22			T12		3		4		T16	15		
United Airlines Hawaiian Open	T74							T18	MC	T2			T42	T74	T36		1	T4	T27	T27			T7	T42	
Northern Telecom Open	T73	T58	1	76		MC	T15	5	T25	MC	MC			T32	T25	T32	MC		MC				T58	MC	
Phoenix Open	MC	T29	T35	T35		MC	MC	T12	MC	T54		MC	T7	MC	T12	T29	T18	T41	T51					MC	
AT&T Pebble Bch Ntl. Pro-Am	T21	T31	MC	T21		T57	T21	T21	T21	T31	MC	T6	T21	MC	T13		MC		WD	T31			T21		T50
Buick Invitational of California	T26	T26	T16	T2			T2			MC		T32	T26	MC	T41	T16	T81	MC		T12				T63	
Bob Hope Chrysler Classic	T28			T16		MC	MC	T16			MC			T54		T49							T7	T3	
Nissan Open			MC	T25		T14		T9		T46	T66	T52	T14	MC		T14			MC	T4			MC		
Doral-Ryder Open	T33	T43				T12	T33	T58			T33	MC	T10	MC	9		T67	T17	T43	MC	T40	T12	MC	T43	
Honda Classic	MC		MC		T13									MC	T13				T13		T13	T13		T31	
Nestle Invitational	T16	1	MC	MC	T14	T26	MC	MC	T16	T5	64	2	MC		4	T53	T67	T20			T31	T5	T20	T16	MC
THE PLAYERS Championship	T61	T34	T14	67	T37	T49	MC	MC	T18	MC	T43	T49	DQ	MC	T11	T34	MC	MC	MC	T14	2	T23	MC	T23	T37
Freeport-McMoRan Classic	T39			T10			MC	T63	T5	71			T24	WD									MC		T60
Masters Tournament		T24	T7		MC	T41	MC		MC	T24		T17	MC			T29	MC	MC	MC	MC	T31	T35	MC	9	T5
MCI Classic	T44	T13	T13	T44	T7	MC		T56		T37	T24	T56	T7	MC	T24	MC	T56		T33			T4	MC		(T2)
Kmart Gr. Greensboro Open		T14		T14		T2	T12	T51	T47			T7	T51	T7	T7		MC		MC	MC					
Shell Houston Open	T12		MC	T12	MC		T41	T46	T19		MC			MC			DQ		MC	T41			T32	T32	
BellSouth Classic	T66		MC	T68		MC	T33	MC						T68	T12	T22		MC	T45			MC	T66	T4	T42
GTE Byron Nelson Classic		T9				T26	WD		T32		T2		T11	MC		T55				T11			T11		MC
Buick Classic	T4							T40		T55		T29	T14	MC	T60				T14	T12					T50
Colonial National Invitation	T33	T46	T33	T33	T12	T23		MC	T8	MC	3	T5	T33	MC		MC		MC	T46			T5	MC	T58	T15
Memorial Tournament	T13		T59	MC	10	T19	T66	T53	MC	T47	T47	T47			T66	T3		T13	T38	T47		T21	T38	T62	T5
Kemper Open	MC		MC		T9	T38	T21	MC	T31	MC	MC	T31	T42	MC			MC	T16					MC		
U.S. Open	MC	WD	T4		T13	T13	T36		T4	T13		T56	T56	T51	T13	MC		T4	T45		T36	T13		T36	MC
Canon Greater Hartford Open				T2		MC						T66		T74	T57	T8	MC						MC		MC
Federal-Express St. Jude Cl.				T14	MC		MC		WD	T21	T14			T14		T14		T45	MC	T26			T11	20	
Motorola Western Open	MC		T43	MC	T13	MC	MC	WD	T2	T40	T52		T6	T60	T43	T6	MC	T13	MC			MC	T20	MC	T29
Anheuser-Busch Golf Classic	T8			T11		T8	MC	MC		T45				1					T18			T11		T6	
Deposit Guaranty Golf Classic	T11			T4				MC																	
British Open		MC	T40		T40				T68			T15	T79			T8	MC	T24		MC	T24	MC	T3	MC	T31
Ideon Classic	1					T56		T27	T74		T15	MC	T11	T27		T18		WD	2						
Buick Open	T11	MC			T17	T3	MC	T11	T70		T57	T46		T57			MC		T33					MC	
PGA Championship	T39	T58	MC	T13	T39	T8	MC	T13	T3	T20	T31	5	T8	MC	T23	T6	MC	MC	MC	T8		MC	T31	T17	T67
Sprint International	T55		MC	T11			MC	T42		T26	T14	MC	MC	MC	T26				MC	T14					
NEC World Series of Golf	T18	T9	T4		(T2)									T12		T28	44					T12			
Greater Milwaukee Open		T27				T3	T27	T58		T6	T10	WD	T6		MC	T10	T54		MC				MC	T17	
Bell Canadian Open					3	MC	4	MC			T55		T45	WD	MC		T29	T5	T45	MC		T22	T14	MC	T14
B.C. Open	T28	MC		T3		T7	1	T17				T20	T28	T59				WD	2	T3					MC
Quad City Classic							T52				1								4			T38			T67
Buick Challenge	1	T2		T4		T4	T40	T56		T24			T24	T40	T8		T2	T74	MC				MC		T34
Walt Disney World/Olds Cl.	T37						T2	T49		T37			T21	T2	MC		T63					MC	T37		
Las Vegas Invitational			T30	T10		T54	MC	1	MC	146	MC	T64	T59	T71				T10	T25	77			T30	MC	MC
LaCantera Texas Open	MC	T3		T50		MC	T59		T38	1	T72	MC	MC	MC		T22	T3		T13	MC			MC		
THE TOUR Championship	T27	11	24	T20	30																				

A playoff winner at the Mercedes Championships to open the 1995 season, Steve Elkington captured the PGA Championship in August.

PGA TOUR

ALL-TIME PGA TOUR RECORDS

ALL-TIME PGA TOUR RECORDS

All information based on official PGA TOUR cosponsored or approved events.

SCORING RECORDS

72 holes:

257—(60-68-64-65) by **Mike Souchak**, at Brackenridge Park Golf Course, San Antonio, TX, in 1955 Texas Open (27-under-par).

258—(65-64-65-64) by **Donnie Hammond**, at Oak Hills CC, San Antonio, TX, in 1989 Texas Open Presented by Nabisco (22-under-par).

259—(62-68-63-66) by **Byron Nelson**, at Broadmoor Golf Club. Seattle, WA, in 1945 Seattle Open (21-under-par).

259—(70-63-63-63) by **Chandler Harper,** at Brackenridge Park Golf Course, San Antonio, TX, in 1954 Texas Open (25-under-par).

259—(63-64-66-66) by **Tim Norris**, at Wethersfield CC, Hartford, CT, in 1982 Sammy Davis Greater Hartford Open (25-under-par).

259—(64-63-66-66) by **Corey Pavin,** at Oak Hills CC, San Antonio, TX, in 1988 Texas Open Presented by Nabisco (21-under-par).

259—(68-63-64-64) by **David Frost,** at Oakwood CC, Coal Valley, IL, in 1993 Hardee's Golf Classic (21-under-par).

90 holes:

325—(67-67-64-65-62) by **Tom Kite,** at four courses, Palm Springs, CA, in the 1993 Bob Hope Chrysler Classic (35-under-par).

329—(69-65-67-62-66) by **Andrew Magee**, at three courses, Las Vegas, NV, in the 1991 Las Vegas Invitational (31-under-par).

329—(70-64-65-64-66) by **D.A. Weibring**, at three courses, Las Vegas, NV, in the 1991 Las Vegas Invitational (31-under-par).

Most shots under par:
72 holes:

27— **Mike Souchak** in winning the 1955 Texas Open with 257.
27— **Ben Hogan** in winning the 1945 Portland Invitational with 261.
26— **Gay Brewer** in winning the 1967 Pensacola Open with 262.
26— **Robert Wrenn** in winning the 1987 Buick Open with 262.
26— **Chip Beck** in winning the 1988 USF&G Classic with 262.
26— **John Huston** in winning the 1992 Walt Disney World/Oldsmobile Classic with 262.

90 holes:

35— **Tom Kite** in winning the 1993 Bob Hope Chrysler Classic with 325.
31— **Andrew Magee** in winning the 1991 Las Vegas Invitational with 329.
31— **D.A. Weibring** in finishing second in the 1991 Las Vegas Invitational with 329 (lost playoff).

54 holes:
Opening rounds:

191—(66-64-61) by **Gay Brewer,** at Pensacola CC, Pensacola, FL, in winning 1967 Pensacola Open (25-under-par).

191—(65-62-64) by **Johnny Palmer**, at Brackenridge Park Golf Course, San Antonio, Texas, in 1954 Texas Open (22-under-par)

192—(60-68-64) by **Mike Souchak**, at Brackenridge Park Golf Course. San Antonio, TX, in 1955 Texas Open (21-under-par).

192—(64-63-65) by **Bob Gilder**, at Westchester CC, Harrison, NY, in 1982 Manufacturers Hanover Westchester Classic (18-under-par).

Consecutive rounds

189—(63-63-63) by **Chandler Harper** in the last three rounds of the 1954 Texas Open at Brackenridge (24-under-par).

ALL-TIME PGA TOUR RECORDS

All information based on official PGA TOUR cosponsored or approved events.

36 holes:
Opening rounds

126—(64-62) by **Tommy Bolt,** at Cavalier Yacht & Country Club, Virginia Beach, VA, in 1954 Virginia Beach Open (12-under-par).

126—(64-62) by **Paul Azinger**, at Oak Hills CC, San Antonio, TX, in 1989 Texas Open Presented by Nabisco (14-under-par).

Consecutive rounds

125—(64-61) by **Gay Brewer** in the middle rounds of the 1967 Pensacola Open at Pensacola CC, Pensacola, FL (19-under-par).

125—(63-62) by **Ron Streck** in the last two rounds of the 1978 Texas Open at Oak Hills Country Club, San Antonio, TX (15-under-par).

125—(62-63) by **Blaine McCallister** in the middle two rounds of the 1988 Hardee's Golf Classic at Oakwood CC, Coal Valley, IL (15-under-par).

18 holes:

59— by **Al Geiberger**, at Colonial Country Club, Memphis, TN, in second round of 1977 Memphis Classic (13-under-par).

59— by **Chip Beck**, at Sunrise Golf Club, Las Vegas, NV, in third round of 1991 Las Vegas Invitational (13-under-par).

60— by **Al Brosch**, at Brackenridge Park Golf Course, San Antonio, TX, in third round of 1951 Texas Open (11-under-par).

60— by **Bill Nary**, at El Paso Country Club, El Paso, TX, in third round of 1952 El Paso Open (11-under-par).

60— by **Ted Kroll**, at Brackenridge Park Golf Course, San Antonio, TX, in third round of 1954 Texas Open (11-under-par).

60— by **Wally Ulrich**, at Cavalier Yacht and Country Club, Virginia Beach, VA, in second round of 1954 Virginia Beach Open (9-under-par).

60— by **Tommy Bolt**, at Wethersfield Country Club, Hartford, CT, in second round of 1954 Insurance City Open (11-under-par).

60— by **Mike Souchak** at Brackenridge Park Golf Course, San Antonio, TX, in first round of 1955 Texas Open (11-under-par).

60— by **Sam Snead**, at Glen Lakes Country Club, Dallas, TX, in second round of 1957 Dallas Open (11-under-par).

60— by **David Frost**, at Randolph Park Golf Course, Tucson, AZ, in second round of 1990 Northern Telecom Tucson Open (12-under-par).

60— by **Davis Love III**, at Waialae Country Club, Honolulu, HI, in second round of 1994 United Airlines Hawaiian Open (12-under-par).

9 holes:

27— by **Mike Souchak**, at Brackenridge Park Golf Course, San Antonio, TX, on par-35 second nine of first round in 1955 Texas Open.

27— by **Andy North** at En-Joie Golf Club, Endicott, NY, on par-34 second nine of first round in 1975 B.C. Open.

Best Vardon Trophy scoring average:
Non-adjusted:

69.23—Sam Snead in 1950 (6646 strokes, 96 rounds).
69.30—Ben Hogan in 1948 (5267 strokes, 76 rounds).
69.37—Sam Snead in 1949 (5064 strokes, 73 rounds).

Adjusted (since 1988):

68.81—Greg Norman in 1994.
68.90—Greg Norman in 1993.
69.06—Greg Norman in 1995.

ALL-TIME PGA TOUR RECORDS

All information based on official PGA TOUR cosponsored or approved events.

Most birdies in a row:

8— **Bob Goalby** at Pasadena Golf Club, St. Petersburg, FL, during fourth round of 1961 St. Petersburg Open.
Fuzzy Zoeller, at Oakwood Country Club, Coal Valley, IL, during first round of 1976 Quad Cities Open.
Dewey Arnette, Warwick Hills GC, Grand Blanc, MI, during first round of the 1987 Buick Open.

Best birdie-eagle streak:

7— **Al Geiberger,** 6 birdies and 1 eagle, at Colonial Country Club, Memphis, TN, during second round of 1977 Danny Thomas Memphis Classic.
Webb Heintzelman, 5 birdies, 1 eagle and 1 birdie, in 1989 Las Vegas Invitational.

Most birdies in a row to win:

6— by **Mike Souchak** to win 1956 St. Paul Open (last 6 holes)
5— by **Jack Nicklaus** to win 1978 Jackie Gleason Inverrary Classic (last 5 holes).
5— by **Tom Weiskopf** to win 1971 Kemper Open (last 4 regulation holes + 1 extra hole)
NOTE: John Cook birdied final hole of regulation at 1992 Bob Hope Chrysler Classic, then birdied first 3 holes of playoff and eagled final hole to win

VICTORY RECORDS

Most victories during career (PGA TOUR cosponsored and/or approved tournaments only):

81— Sam Snead
70— Jack Nicklaus
63— Ben Hogan
60— Arnold Palmer
52— Byron Nelson
51— Billy Casper

Most consecutive years winning at least one tournament:

17— Jack Nicklaus (1962-78)
17— Arnold Palmer (1955-71)
16— Billy Casper (1956-71)

Most consecutive victories:

11— **Byron Nelson**, from Miami Four Ball March 8-11, 1945, through Canadian Open, August 2-4, 1945. Tournament, site, dates, score, purse-Miami Four Ball (with Jug McSpaden), Miami Springs Course, Miami, FL, March 8-11, won 8-6, $1,500; Charlotte Open, Myers Park Golf Club, Charlotte, NC, March 16-21, 272, $2000; Greensboro Open, Starmount Country Club, Greensboro, NC, March 23-25, 271, $1000; Durham Open, Hope Valley Country Club, Durham, NC, March 30-April 1, 276, $1000; Atlanta Open, Capital City Course, Atlanta, GA, April 5-8, 263, $2000; Montreal Open, Islemere Golf and Country Club, Montreal, Que., June 7-10, 268, $2000; Philadelphia Inquirer Invitational, Llanerch Country Club, Phila., PA, June 14-17, 269, $3000; Chicago Victory National Open, Calumet Country Club, Chicago, IL, June 29-July 1, 275, $2000; PGA Championship, Moraine Country Club, Dayton, OH, July 9-15,4-3, $3750; Tam O'Shanter Open, Tam O'Shanter Country Club, Chicago, IL, July 26-30, 269, $10,000; Canadian Open, Thornhill Country Club, Toronto, Ont., August 2-4, 280, $2000; Winnings for streak $30,250. NOTE: Nelson won a 12th event in Spring Lake, NJ which is not counted as official, as its $2,500 purse was below the PGA $3000 minimum.
6— **Ben Hogan**, in 1948: From June 12 to August 22 — U.S. Open, Inverness Round Robin, Motor City Open, Reading Open, Western Open, Denver Open Invitational.
4— **Jackie Burke, Jr.**, in 1952: From February 14 to March 9 — Texas Open, Houston Open, Baton Rouge Open, St. Petersburg Open.
Walter Hagen in 1923.
Joe Kirkwood, Sr. in 1924.
Bill Mehlhorn in 1929.
Horton Smith in 1929.

All information based on official PGA TOUR cosponsored or approved events.

Most consecutive victories (cont'd.):

3— **Paul Runyan** in 1933.
Henry Picard in 1939.
Jimmy Demaret in 1940.
Ben Hogan in 1940
Byron Nelson in 1945-1946.
Ben Hogan in 1953.
Walter Hagen in 1923.
Joe Kirkwood, Sr., in 1924.
Bill Mehlhorn in 1929.
Horton Smith in 1929.
Paul Runyan in 1933.
Henry Picard in 1939.
Jimmy Demaret in 1940.
Ben Hogan in 1940.
Byron Nelson in 1944, 1945-46.
Sam Snead in 1945.
Ben Hogan in 1946 (twice).
Bobby Locke in 1947.
Cary Middlecoff in 1951.
Jim Ferrier in 1951.
Billy Casper in 1960.
Arnold Palmer in 1960, 1962.
Johnny Miller in 1974.
Hubert Green in 1976.
Gary Player in 1978.
Tom Watson in 1980.
Nick Price in 1993.

Most victories in a single event:

8— **Sam Snead**, Greater Greensboro Open: 1938, 1946, 1949, 1950, 1955, 1956, 1960, 1965 (27-year span also record for time between first and last victories in the same event).
6— **Sam Snead**, Miami Open: 1937, 1939, 1946, 1950, 1951, 1955.
6— **Jack Nicklaus**, Masters: 1963, 1965, 1966, 1972, 1975, 1986.
5— **Walter Hagen**, PGA Championship:1921, 1924, 1925, 1926, 1927.
Ben Hogan, Colonial NIT: 1946, 1947, 1952, 1953, 1959.
Arnold Palmer, Bob Hope Desert Classic: 1960, 1962, 1968, 1971, 1973.
Jack Nicklaus, Tournament of Champions: 1963, 1964, 1971, 1973, 1977.
Jack Nicklaus, PGA Championship: 1963, 1971, 1973, 1975, 1980.
Walter Hagen, Western Open: 1916, 1921, 1926, 1927, 1932.

Most consecutive victories in a single event:

5— **Sam Snead**, Goodall Palm Beach Round Robin, 1938, 1952, 1954, 1955, 1957.
4— **Walter Hagen**, PGA Championship, 1924-1927.
4— **Gene Sarazen**, Miami Open, 1926 (schedule change), 1928, 1929, 1930.
3— **Willie Anderson**, U.S. Open, 1903-1905.
3— **Walter Hagen**, Metropolitan Open (1916, 1919-1920; no event held 1917-1918 due to World War I.
3— **Gene Sarazen**, Miami Beach Open, 1927, 1928, 1929.
3— **Ralph Guldahl**, Western Open, 1936-1938.
3— **Ben Hogan**, Asheville Land of the Sky Open, 1940-1942.
3— **Gene Littler**, Tournament of Champions, 1955-1957.
3— **Billy Casper**, Portland Open, 1959-1961.
3— **Arnold Palmer**, Texas Open, 1960-1962, Phoenix Open, 1961-1963.
3— **Jack Nicklaus**, Disney World Golf Classic, 1971-1973.
3— **Johnny Miller**, Tucson Open, 1974-1976.
3— **Tom Watson**, Byron Nelson Classic, 1978-1980.

ALL-TIME PGA TOUR RECORDS

All information based on official PGA TOUR cosponsored or approved events.

Most victories in a calendar year:

18— **Byron Nelson** (1945)
13— **Ben Hogan** (1946)
11— **Sam Snead** (1950)
10— **Ben Hogan** (1948)
9— **Paul Runyan** (1933)
8— **Horton Smith** (1929)
8— **Gene Sarazen** (1930)
8— **Byron Nelson** (1944)
8— **Arnold Palmer** (1960)
8— **Johnny Miller** (1974)
8— **Sam Snead** (1938)
7— 11 times

Most first-time winners during one calendar year:

14— 1991
12— 1979, 1980, 1986
11— 1977, 1985, 1988
10— 1968, 1969, 1971, 1974, 1983, 1987, 1990, 1994

Most years between victories:

15 years, 5 months, 10 days—Butch Baird (1961-1976)
12 years, 5 months, 21 days— Howard Twitty (1980-1993)
11 years, 9 months—Leonard Thompson (1977-1989)
11 years, 3 months, 27 days— Bob Murphy (1975-1986)
11 years, 22 days—Bob Rosburg (1961-1972)

Most years from first victory to last:

28 years, 11 months, 20 days—Ray Floyd (1963-1992)
28 years, 8 months, 25 days—Sam Snead (1936-1965)
23 years, 11 months, 5 days—Macdonald Smith (1912-1936)
23 years, 9 months, 27 days—Jack Nicklaus (1962-1986)
23 years, 3 months, 7 days—Gene Littler (1954-1977)
22 years, 10 months, 19 days—Jim Barnes (1914-1937)
22 years, 4 months, 25 days—Johnny Miller (1971-1994)
22 years, 4 months, 20 days—Hale Irwin (1971-1994)

Youngest winners:

Johnny McDermott, 19 years, 10 months, 1911 U.S. Open.
Gene Sarazen, 20 years, 5 days, 1922 Southern Open.
Charles Evans, Jr. (amateur), 20 years, 1 month, 15 days, 1910 Western Open.
Francis Ouimet (amateur), 20 years, 4 months, 12 days, 1913 U.S. Open.
Gene Sarazen, 20 years, 4 months, 18 days, 1922 U.S. Open.
Horton Smith, 20 years, 5 months, 13 days, 1928 Oklahoma City Open.
Gene Sarazen, 20 years, 5 months, 22 days, 1922 PGA.
Ray Floyd, 20 years, 6 months, 13 days, 1963 St. Petersburg Open.
Phil Mickelson (amateur), 20 years, 6 months, 28 days, 1991 Northern Telecom Open.
Horton Smith, 20 years, 7 months, 1 day, 1928 Catalina Island Open.
Tom Creavy, 20 years, 7 months, 16 days, 1931 PGA.

Oldest winners:

Sam Snead, 52 years,10 months, 8 days, 1965 Greater Greensboro Open.
Art Wall, 51 years, 7 months, 10 days, 1975 Greater Milwaukee Open.
Jim Barnes, 51 years, 3 months, 7 days, 1937 Long Island Open.
John Barnum, 51 years, 1 month, 5 days, 1962 Cajun Classic.
Ray Floyd, 49 years, 6 months, 4 days, 1992 Doral-Ryder Open.

Oldest first-time winner:

John Barnum, 51 years, 1 month, 5 days, 1962 Cajun Classic.

ALL-TIME PGA TOUR RECORDS

All information based on official PGA TOUR cosponsored or approved events.

Widest winning margin: strokes

16— **Joe Kirkwood, Sr.**, 1924 Corpus Christi Open.
Bobby Locke, 1948 Chicago Victory National Championship.
14— **Ben Hogan**, 1945 Portland Invitational.
Johnny Miller, 1975 Phoenix Open.
13— **Byron Nelson,** 1945 Seattle Open.
Gene Littler, 1955 Tournament of Champions.
12— **Byron Nelson**, 1939 Phoenix Open.
Arnold Palmer, 1962 Phoenix Open.
Jose Maria Olazabal, 1990 NEC World Series of Golf.

PLAYOFF RECORDS

Longest sudden-death playoffs (holes):

11— **Cary Middlecoff** and **Lloyd Mangrum** were declared co-winners by mutual agreement in the 1949 Motor City Open.
8— **Dick Hart** defeated **Phil Rodgers** in the 1965 Azalea Open.
8— **Lee Elder** defeated **Lee Trevino** in the 1978 Greater Milwaukee Open.
8— **Dave Barr** defeated **Woody Blackburn**, **Dan Halldorson**, **Frank Conner**, **Victor Regalado** in the 1981 Quad Cities Open.
8— **Bob Gilder** defeated **Rex Caldwell, Johnny Miller**, **Mark O'Meara** in the 1983 Phoenix Open.

Most players in a sudden-death playoff:

6— 1994 GTE Byron Nelson Classic—**Neal Lancaster** defeated **Tom Byrum**, **Mark Carnevale**, **David Edwards**, **Yoshinori Mizumaki** and **David Ogrin**.
5— Five times, most recently 1993 Buick Southern Open—**John Inman** defeated **Billy Andrade**, **Brad Bryant**, **Mark Brooks** and **Bob Estes**.
5— Teams at the 1985 Chrysler Team Championship.

Most playoffs, season:

16— 1988, 1991
15— 1972

PUTTING RECORDS

Fewest putts, one round:

18— **Sam Trahan**, at Whitemarsh Valley Country Club, in final round of 1979 IVB Philadephia Golf Classic.
18— **Mike McGee**, at Colonial CC, in first round of 1987 Federal Express St. Jude Classic.
18— **Kenny Knox**, at Harbour Town GL, in first round of 1989 MCI Heritage Classic.
18— **Andy North**, at Kingsmill GC, in second round of 1990 Anheuse-Busch Golf Classic.
18— **Jim McGovern,** at TPC at Southwind, in second round of 1992 Federal Express St. Jude Classic.

Fewest putts, four rounds:

93— **Kenny Knox** in 1989 MCI Heritage Classic at Harbour Town Golf Links.
94— **Bob Tway** in 1986 MCI Heritage Classic at Harbour Town Golf Links.
95— **George Archer** in 1980 Sea Pines Heritage Classic at Harbour Town Golf Links.
95— **Lennie Clements** in 1986 PGA Championship at the Inverness Club.
95— **Andy Bean** in 1990 MCI Heritage Classic at Harbour Town Golf Links.
95— **Mark O'Meara** in 1989 GTE Byron Nelson Classic at the TPC at Las Colinas.

Fewest putts, nine holes:

7— **Bill Nary**, at the El Paso Country Club, on the back nine of the third round in the 1952 El Paso Open.
8— **Jim Colbert**, at the Deerwood Club, on the front nine of the last round in 1967 Greater Jacksonville Open.
8— **Sam Trahan**, at Whitemarsh Valley Country Club, on the back nine of the last round in the1979 IVB Philadelphia Golf Classic.

All information based on official PGA TOUR cosponsored or approved events.

Fewest putts, nine holes (cont'd.):

- **8—** **Bill Calfee**, at Forest Oaks CC, on the back nine of the third round of the 1980 Greater Greensboro Open.
- **8—** **Kenny Knox**, at Harbour Town GL, on the back nine of the first round of the 1989 MCI Heritage Classic.
- **8—** **John Inman**, at Harbour Town GL, on the front nine of the fourth round of the 1994 MCI Heritage Classic.

MISCELLANEOUS RECORDS

Most consecutive events without missing cut:

- **113—Byron Nelson**, during the 1940s (Nelson's finishes technically were "in the money").
- **105—Jack Nicklaus**, from Sahara Open, November 1970, through World Series of Golf, September 1976 (missed cut in 1976 World Open).
- **86—** **Hale Irwin**, from Tucson Open, February 1975, through conclusion of 1978 season (missed cut in first start of 1979 season at Bing Crosby)
- **72—** **Dow Finsterwald**, from Carling Golf Classic, September 1955, through Houston Invitational, February, 1958.

Youngest pro shooting age:

- **66—** (4 under, 4th round), **Sam Snead** (age 67), 1979 Quad Cities Open.
- **67—** (3 under, 2nd round), **Sam Snead** (age 67), 1979 Quad Cities Open.

MONEY-WINNING RECORDS

Most money won in a single season:

$1,654,959 by **Greg Norman** in 1995
$1,543,192 by **Billy Mayfair** in 1995
$1,499,927 by **Nick Price** in 1994
$1,478,557 by **Nick Price** in 1993
$1,458,456 by **Paul Azinger** in 1993

Most money won by a rookie:

$881,436 by **David Duval** in 1995
$748,793 by **Justin Leonard** in 1995
$736,497 by **Woody Austin** in 1995
$684,440 by **Ernie Els** in 1994
$657,831 by **Vijay Singh** in 1993

Most money won by a second-year player:

$842,590 by **Ernie Els** in 1995
$693,658 by **Billy Mayfair** in 1990
$652,780 by **Bob Tway** in 1986
$628,735 by **Phil Mickelson** in 1993

Most money won in first two seasons:

$1,527,030 by **Ernie Els** (1994-1995)
$983,790 by **Vijay Singh** (1993-1994)
$962,238 by **John Daly** (1991-1992)
$816,803 by **Bob Tway** (1985-1986)
$805,650 by **Billy Mayfair** (1989-1990)

Most consecutive years $100,000 or more:

- **22—** **Tom Watson** (1974-present)
- **20—** **Tom Kite** (1976-present)
- **19—** **Bruce Lietzke** (1977-present)

ALL-TIME PGA TOUR RECORDS

All information based on official PGA TOUR cosponsored or approved events.

Most consecutive years $200,000 or more:

14— **Tom Kite** (1981-1994)
12— **Curtis Strange** (1980-1991)
12— **Tom Watson** (1977-1988)
12— **Mark O'Meara** (1984-present)
10— **Payne Stewart** (1984-1993)
10— **Ben Crenshaw** (1986-present)

Most consecutive years $500,000 or more:

7— **Paul Azinger** (1987-1993)
7— **Chip Beck** (1987-1993)
6— **Fred Couples** (1989-1994)
6— **Nick Price** (1990-present)
5— **Payne Stewart** (1986-1990)
5— **Greg Norman** (1986-1990)
5— **Corey Pavin** (1991-present)

Most consecutive years $1 million or more:

3— **Nick Price** (1992-1994)
3— **Greg Norman** (1993-present)

Most consecutive years Top 10 Money List:

17— **Jack Nicklaus** (1962-1978)
15— **Arnold Palmer** (1957-1971)

Most years Top 10 Money List:

18— **Jack Nicklaus**
15— **Arnold Palmer**, **Sam Snead**

Most years leading Money List:

8— **Jack Nicklaus**

Most consecutive years leading Money List:

4— **Tom Watson** (1977-1980)

Most money won in a single season without a victory:

$1,016,804 by **Fuzzy Zoeller** in 1994

ALL-TIME PGA TOUR RECORDS

All information based on official PGA TOUR cosponsored or approved events.

$1 MILLION IN A SINGLE SEASON

1.	Greg Norman	$1,654,959	1995
2.	Billy Mayfair	1,543,192	1995
3.	Nick Price	1,499,927	1994
4.	Nick Price	1,478,557	1993
5.	Paul Azinger	1,458,456	1993
6.	Tom Kite	1,395,278	1989
7.	Lee Janzen	1,378,966	1995
8.	Greg Norman	1,359,653	1993
9.	Fred Couples	1,344,188	1992
10.	Corey Pavin	1,340,079	1995
11.	Greg Norman	1,330,307	1994
12.	Steve Elkington	1,254,352	1995
13.	Mark McCumber	1,208,209	1994
14.	Payne Stewart	1,201,301	1989
15.	Davis Love III	1,191,630	1992
16.	John Cook	1,165,606	1992
17.	Greg Norman	1,165,477	1990
18.	Curtis Strange	1,147,644	1988
19.	Nick Price	1,135,773	1992
20.	Davis Love, III	1,111,999	1995
21.	Jim Gallagher, Jr.	1,078,870	1993
22.	Peter Jacobsen	1,075,057	1995
23.	Jim Gallagher, Jr.	1,057,241	1995
24.	Tom Lehman	1,031,144	1994
25.	David Frost	1,030,717	1993
26.	Wayne Levi	1,024,647	1990
27.	Vijay Singh	1,018,713	1995
28.	Fuzzy Zoeller	1,016,804	1994
29.	Loren Roberts	1,015,671	1994

FIRST-YEAR PLAYERS TO EARN $300,000 OR MORE

1.	David Duval	$881,436	1995
2.	Justin Leonard	748,793	1995
3.	Woody Austin	736,497	1995
4.	Ernie Els	684,440	1994
5.	Vijay Singh	657,831	1993
6.	John Daly	574,783	1991
7.	Robert Gamez	461,407	1990
8.	Mike Heinen	390,963	1994
9.	Glen Day	357,236	1994
10.	Brett Ogle	337,374	1993
11.	Steve Stricker	334,409	1994
12.	Keith Clearwater	320,007	1987
13.	Dicky Pride	305,769	1994

BIGGEST ONE-SEASON GAINS

	Season	Money	Season	Money	Gain
1. Billy Mayfair	1994	$158,159	1995	$1,543,192	$1,385,033
2. Steve Elkington	1994	294,943	1995	1,254,352	954,409
3. Lee Janzen	1994	442,588	1995	1,378,966	936,378
4. Peter Jacobsen	1994	211,762	1995	1,075,057	863,295
5. Mark McCumber	1993	363,269	1994	1,208,209	844,940
6. Jim Gallagher, Jr.	1994	325,976	1995	1,057,241	844,940
7. Payne Stewart	1994	145,687	1995	866,219	720,532
8. Mark O'Meara	1994	214,070	1995	914,129	700,059
9. Loren Roberts	1993	316,506	1994	1,015,671	699,165
10. Vijay Singh	1994	325,959	1995	1,018,913	692,754

Single Tournament Stat Records--PGA TOUR *(1980 thru 1995)*

72-HOLE EVENTS

Driving Distance	John Daly	331.4	1991	Kemper
Driving Accuracy	Calvin Peete	56 of 56	1986	Memorial
	Calvin Peete	56 of 56	1987	Memorial
	David Frost	56 of 56	1988	Tucson
	Brian Claar	56 of 56	1992	Memorial
Greens In Reg.	Peter Jacobsen	69 of 72	1995	AT&T
Putts	Kenny Knox	93	1989	MCI
Birdies	Chip Beck	29	1988	Walt Disney World
	Davis Love III	29	1990	Walt Disney World
Eagles	Dave Eichelberger	5	1980	Hawaii
	Davis Love III	5	1994	Hawaii

54-HOLE EVENTS

Driving Distance	John Daly	306.3	1993	Houston
Driving Accuracy	Keith Fergus	41 of 42	1981	AT&T
	Fulton Allem	41 of 42	1993	Houston
	John Dowdall	41 of 42	1993	Houston
Greens In Reg.	Mike Heinen	53 of 54	1995	Walt Disney World
Putts	Jonathan Kaye	70	1995	Quad City
Birdies	Hale Irwin	20	1981	Houston
	Robert Wrenn	20	1992	San Diego
	John Huston	20	1993	Houston
	B. McCallister	20	1993	Houston
Eagles	Bob Eastwood	3	1986	San Diego
	Bill Glasson	3	1986	San Diego
	Dan Forsman	3	1992	San Diego

90-HOLE EVENTS

Driving Distance	Davis Love III	304.3	1993	Las Vegas
Driving Accuracy	Doug Tewell	64 of 70	1992	Las Vegas
Greens In Reg.	John Mahaffey	82 of 90	1989	Las Vegas
Putts	Jeff Sluman	129	1991	Las Vegas
Birdies	Tom Kite	37	1993	Bob Hope
Eagles	Andy Bean	4	1986	Las Vegas
	Roger Maltbie	4	1986	Las Vegas
	Andy Bean	4	1990	Bob Hope
	David Frost	4	1990	Las Vegas
	Robert Wrenn	4	1990	Las Vegas
	Craig Stadler	4	1991	Las Vegas
	Ted Schulz	4	1992	Las Vegas
	Fuzzy Zoeller	4	1992	Las Vegas
	Davis Love III	4	1993	Las Vegas

GROWTH OF PGA TOUR PURSES

YEAR	NO.OF EVENTS	TOTAL PURSE	YEAR	NO.OF EVENTS	TOTAL PURSE
1938	38	$158,000	1967	37	$3,979,162
1939	28	121,000	1968	45	5,077,600
1940	27	117,000	1969	47	5,465,875
1941	30	169,200	1970	55	6,751,523
1942	21	116,650	1971	63	7,116,000
1943	3	17,000	1972	71	7,596,749
1944	22	150,500	1973	75	8,657,225
1945	36	435,380	1974	57	8,165,941
1946	37	411,533	1975	51	7,895,450
1947	31	352,500	1976	49	9,157,522
1948	34	427,000	1977	48	9,688,977
1949	25	338,200	1978	48	10,337,332
1950	33	459,950	1979	46	12,801,200
1951	30	460,200	1980	45	13,371,786
1952	32	498,016	1981	45	14,175,393
1953	32	562,704	1982	46	15,089,576
1954	26	600,819	1983	45	17,588,242
1955	36	782,010	1984	46	21,251,382
1956	36	847,070	1985	47	25,290,526
1957	32	820,360	1986	46	25,442,242
1958	39	1,005,800	1987	46	32,106,093
1959	43	1,225,205	1988	47	36,959,307
1960	41	1,335,242	1989	44	41,288,787
1961	45	1,461,830	1990	44	46,251,831
1962	49	1,790,320	1991	44	49,628,203
1963	43	2,044,900	1992	44	49,386,906
1964	41	2,301,063	1993	43	53,203,611
1965	36	2,848,515	1994	43	56,416,080
1966	36	3,704,445	1995	44	62,250,000

LEADERS IN CAREER MONEY EARNINGS

1.	GREG NORMAN	$9,592,829
2.	TOM KITE	9,337,998
3.	PAYNE STEWART	7,389,479
4.	NICK PRICE	7,338,119
5.	FRED COUPLES	7,188,408
6.	COREY PAVIN	7,175,523
7.	TOM WATSON	7,072,113
8.	PAUL AZINGER	6,957,324
9.	BEN CRENSHAW	6,845,235
10.	CURTIS STRANGE	6,791,618
11.	MARK O'MEARA	6,126,466
12.	LANNY WADKINS	6,028,855
13.	CRAIG STADLER	6,008,753
14.	MARK CALCAVECCHIA	5,866,716
15.	HALE IRWIN	5,845,024
16.	CHIP BECK	5,755,844
17.	BRUCE LIETZKE	5,710,262
18.	DAVIS LOVE III	5,623,890
19.	SCOTT HOCH	5,465,898
20.	DAVID FROST	5,458,172
21.	JACK NICKLAUS	5,440,357
22.	JAY HAAS	5,426,821
23.	RAY FLOYD	5,194,044
24.	GIL MORGAN	4,991,433
25.	FUZZY ZOELLER	4,918,771
26.	MARK MCCUMBER	4,799,702
27.	SCOTT SIMPSON	4,768,955
28.	LARRY MIZE	4,584,287
29.	JIM GALLAGHER, JR.	4,583,940
30.	PETER JACOBSEN	4,547,564
31.	STEVE ELKINGTON	4,525,487
32.	HAL SUTTON	4,486,587
33.	JOHN COOK	4,461,954
34.	WAYNE LEVI	4,237,387
35.	LEE JANZEN	3,910,397
36.	JEFF SLUMAN	3,860,431
37.	JOHN MAHAFFEY	3,828,008
38.	BOB TWAY	3,815,540
39.	LOREN ROBERTS	3,809,733
40.	STEVE PATE	3,661,591
41.	DAVID EDWARDS	3,646,275
42.	D.A. WEIBRING	3,612,373
43.	JOEY SINDELAR	3,565,399
44.	BRAD FAXON	3,537,539
45.	LEE TREVINO	3,478,450
46.	JOHN HUSTON	3,408,018
47.	BILLY MAYFAIR	3,397,626
48.	TIM SIMPSON	3,351,476
49.	KEN GREEN	3,347,802
50.	LARRY NELSON	3,313,938
51.	MARK BROOKS	$3,300,176
52.	TOM PURTZER	3,250,834
53.	ANDY BEAN	3,250,480
54.	BILL GLASSON	3,230,227
55.	MIKE REID	3,131,821
56.	DAN FORSMAN	3,040,150
57.	GENE SAUERS	3,002,576
58.	DAN POHL	2,909,071
59.	TOM LEHMAN	2,902,257
60.	MIKE HULBERT	2,878,027
61.	BRAD BRYANT	2,866,233
62.	KENNY PERRY	2,844,072
63.	ANDREW MAGEE	2,832,873
64.	DON POOLEY	2,811,123
65.	JODIE MUDD	2,806,955
66.	JEFF MAGGERT	2,753,797
67.	JOHNNY MILLER	2,746,425
68.	BLAINE MCCALLISTER	2,678,444
69.	RUSS COCHRAN	2,668,983
70.	HOWARD TWITTY	2,665,173
71.	BOB GILDER	2,636,473
72.	RICK FEHR	2,620,197
73.	HUBERT GREEN	2,586,664
74.	DONNIE HAMMOND	2,567,729
75.	BOBBY WADKINS*	2,448,213
76.	DOUG TEWELL	2,424,476
77.	ROCCO MEDIATE	2,367,238
78.	BOB ESTES	2,332,399
79.	BILLY ANDRADE	2,311,290
80.	MARK WIEBE	2,305,739
81.	CALVIN PEETE	2,302,363
82.	BOB LOHR	2,287,789
83.	JAY DON BLAKE	2,276,989
84.	DAVE BARR	2,270,323
85.	TOM WEISKOPF	2,241,688
86.	J.C. SNEAD	2,219,171
87.	NOLAN HENKE	2,215,189
88.	PHIL MICKELSON	2,204,542
89.	FRED FUNK	2,191,458
90.	ROGER MALTBIE	2,164,079
91.	STEVE JONES	2,129,428
92.	GARY HALLBERG	2,128,311
93.	DUFFY WALDORF	2,113,447
94.	MIKE SULLIVAN	2,077,400
95.	KEITH CLEARWATER	2,056,142
96.	FULTON ALLEM	2,031,256
97.	VIJAY SINGH	2,002,503
98.	IAN BAKER-FINCH	1,998,078
99.	NICK FALDO	1,977,198
100.	MIKE DONALD	1,938,765

* = Non-winner

PAST LEADING MONEY-WINNERS

1934	Paul Runyan	$6,767.00
1935	Johnny Revolta	9,543.00
1936	Horton Smith	7,682.00
1937	Harry Cooper	14,138.69
1938	Sam Snead	19,534.49
1939	Henry Picard	10,303.00
1940	Ben Hogan	10,655.00
1941	Ben Hogan	18,358.00
1942	Ben Hogan	13,143.00
1943	No Statistics Compiled	
1944	Byron Nelson (War Bonds)	37,967.69
1945	Byron Nelson (War Bonds)	63,335.66
1946	Ben Hogan	42,556.16
1947	Jimmy Demaret	27,936.83
1948	Ben Hogan	32,112.00
1949	Sam Snead	31,593.83
1950	Sam Snead	35,758.83
1951	Lloyd Mangrum	26,088.83
1952	Julius Boros	37,032,97
1953	Lew Worsham	34,002.00
1954	Bob Toski	65,819.81
1955	Julius Boros	63,121.55
1956	Ted Kroll	72,835.83
1957	Dick Mayer	65,835.00
1958	Arnold Palmer	42,607.50
1959	Art Wall	53,167.60
1960	Arnold Palmer	75,262.85
1961	Gary Player	64,540.45
1962	Arnold Palmer	81,448.33
1963	Arnold Palmer	128,230.00
1964	Jack Nicklaus	113,284.50
1965	Jack Nicklaus	$140,752.14
1966	Billy Casper	121,944.92
1967	Jack Nicklaus	188,998.08
1968	Billy Casper	205,168.67
1969	Frank Beard	164,707.11
1970	Lee Trevino	157,037.63
1971	Jack Nicklaus	244,490.50
1972	Jack Nicklaus	320,542.26
1973	Jack Nicklaus	308,362.10
1974	Johnny Miller	353,021.59
1975	Jack Nicklaus	298,149.17
1976	Jack Nicklaus	266,438.57
1977	Tom Watson	310,653.16
1978	Tom Watson	362,428.93
1979	Tom Watson	462,636.00
1980	Tom Watson	530,808.33
1981	Tom Kite	375,698.84
1982	Craig Stadler	446,462.00
1983	Hal Sutton	426,668.00
1984	Tom Watson	476,260.00
1985	Curtis Strange	542,321.00
1986	Greg Norman	653,296.00
1987	Curtis Strange	925,941.00
1988	Curtis Strange	1,147,644.00
1989	Tom Kite	1,395,278.00
1990	Greg Norman	1,165,477.00
1991	Corey Pavin	979,430.00
1992	Fred Couples	1,344,188.00
1993	Nick Price	1,478,557.00
1994	Nick Price	1,499,927.00
1995	Greg Norman	1,654,959.00

*TOTAL MONEY LISTED BEGINNING IN 1968 THROUGH 1974. ** OFFICIAL MONEY LISTED BEGINNING IN 1975.

ALL-TIME TOUR WINNERS

1.	Sam Snead	81
2.	Jack Nicklaus	70
3.	Ben Hogan	63
4.	Arnold Palmer	60
5.	Byron Nelson	52
6.	Billy Casper	51
T7.	Walter Hagen	40
	Cary Middlecoff	40
9.	Gene Sarazen	38
10.	Lloyd Mangrum	36
T11.	Horton Smith	32
	Tom Watson	32
T13.	Harry Cooper	31
	Jimmy Demaret	31
15.	Leo Diegel	30
T16.	Gene Littler	29
	Paul Runyan	29
18.	Lee Trevino	27
19.	Henry Picard	26
T20.	Tommy Armour	24
	Macdonald Smith	24
	Johnny Miller	24
T23.	Johnny Farrell	22
	Ray Floyd	22
T25.	Willie Macfarlane	21
	Gary Player	21
	Craig Wood	21
	Lanny Wadkins	21
T29.	James Barnes	20
	Hale Irwin	20
	Bill Mehlhorn	20
	Doug Sanders	20
T33.	Ben Crenshaw	19
	Doug Ford	19
	Hubert Green	19
	Tom Kite	19
T37.	Julius Boros	18
	Jim Ferrier	18
	E.J. Harrison	18
	Johnny Revolta	18
T41.	Jack Burke	17
	Bobby Cruickshank	17
	Harold McSpaden	17
	Curtis Strange	17
45.	Ralph Guldahl	16
T46.	Tommy Bolt	15
	Ed Dudley	15
	Greg Norman	15
	Denny Shute	15
	Mike Souchak	15
	Tom Weiskopf	15

MOST TOUR WINS YEAR BY YEAR

Year	Player	Wins
1916	James Barnes	3
	Walter Hagen	3
1917	James Barnes	2
	Mike Brady	2
1918	Jock Hutchison	1
	Walter Hagen	1
	Patrick Doyle	1
1919	James Barnes	5
1920	Jock Hutchison	4
1921	James Barnes	4
1922	Gene Sarazen	3
	Walter Hagen	3
1923	Walter Hagen	5
	Joe Kirkwood, Sr	5
1924	Joe Kirkwood, Sr	4
	Walter Hagen	4
1925	Leo Diegel	5
1926	Bill Mehlhorn	5
	Macdonald Smith	5
1927	Johnny Farrell	7
1928	Bil Mehlhorn	7
1929	Horton Smith	8
1930	Gene Sarazen	8
1931	Wiffy Cox	4
1932	Craig Wood	3
	Gene Sarazen	3
	Olin Dutra	3
	Mike Turnesa	3
	Tommy Armour	3
1933	Paul Runyan	9
1934	Paul Runyan	7
1935	Johnny Revolta	5
	Henry Picard	5
1936	Ralph Guldahl	3
	Henry Picard.	3
	Jimmy Hines	3
1937	Harry Cooper	8
1938	Sam Snead	8
1939	Henry Picard	8
1940	Jimmy Demaret	6
1941	Sam Snead	7
1942	Ben Hogan	6
1943	Sam Byrd	1
	Harold McSpaden	1
	Steve Warga	1
1944	Byron Nelson	8
1945	Byron Nelson	18
1946	Ben Hogan	13
1947	Ben Hogan	7
1948	Ben Hogan	10
1949	Cary Middlecoff	7
1950	Sam Snead	11
1951	Cary Middlecoff	6
1952	Jack Burke, Jr	5
	Sam Snead	5
1953	Ben Hogan	4
	Lloyd Mangrum	4
1954	Bob Toski	4
1955	Cary Middlecoff	6
1956	Mike Souchak	4
1957	Arnold Palmer	4
1958	Ken Venturi	4
1959	Gene Littler	5
1960	Arnold Palmer	8
1961	Arnold Palmer	5
	Doug Sanders	5
1962	Arnold Palmer	7
1963	Arnold Palmer	7
1964	Jack Nicklaus	4
	Billy Casper	4
	Tony Lema	4
1965	Jack Nicklaus	5
1966	Billy Casper	4
1967	Jack Nicklaus	5
1968	Billy Casper	6
1969	Dave Hill	3
	Billy Casper	3
	Jack Nicklaus	3
	Ray Floyd	3
1970	Billy Casper	4
1971	Jack Nicklaus	5
	Lee Trevino	5
1972	Jack Nicklaus	7
1973	Jack Nicklaus	7
1974	Johnny Miller	8
1975	Jack Nicklaus	5
1976	Ben Crenshaw	3
	Hubert Green	3
1977	Tom Watson	4
1978	Tom Watson	5
1979	Tom Watson	5
1980	Tom Watson	6
1981	Tom Watson	3
	Bruce Lietzke	3
	Ray Floyd	3
	Bill Rogers,	3
1982	Craig Stadler	4
	Calvin Peete	4
1983	Fuzzy Zoeller	2
	Lanny Wadkins	2
	Calvin Peete	2
	Hal Sutton	2
	Gil Morgan	2
	Mark McCumber	2
	Jim Colbert	2
	Seve Ballesteros	2
1984	Tom Watson	3
	Denis Watson	3
1985	Lanny Wadkins	3
	Curtis Strange	3
1986	Bob Tway	4
1987	Curtis Strange	3
	Paul Azinger	3
1988	Curtis Strange	4
1989	Tom Kite	3
	Steve Jones	3
1990	Wayne Levi	4
1991	Ian Woosnam	2
	Corey Pavin	2
	Billy Andrade	2
	Tom Purtzer	2
	Mark Brooks	2
	Nick Price	2
	Fred Couples	2
	Andrew Magee	2
1992	Fred Couples	3
	Davis Love III	3
	John Cook	3
1993	Nick Price	4
1994	Nick Price	5
1995	Greg Norman	3
	Lee Janzen	3

INDIVIDUAL PLAYOFF RECORDS

AARON, Tommy -- (0-4) 1963: lost to Tony Lema, Memphis Open; lost to Arnold Palmer, Cleveland Open. 1972: lost to George Archer, Glen Campbell Los Angeles Open; lost to George Archer, Greater Greensboro Open.

ADAMS, John -- (0-1) 1982: lost to Jay Haas, Hall of Fame Classic.

ALEXANDER, Skip -- (1-0) 1950: defeated Ky Laffoon, Empire State Open.

ALLIN, Buddy -- (1-0) 1971: defeated Dave Eichelberger, Rod Funseth, Greater Greensboro Open.

ALLISS, Percy -- (0-1) 1931: lost to Walter Hagen, Canadian Open.

ANDERSON, Willie -- (2-0) 1901: defeated Alex Smith, U.S. Open. 1903: defeated David Brown, U.S. Open.

ANDRADE, Billy -- (1-1) 1991: defeated Jeff Sluman, Kemper Open. 1993: lost to John Inman, Buick Southern Open.

ARCHER, George -- (4-3) 1965: defeated Bob Charles, Lucky International Open. 1969: lost to Jack Nicklaus, Kaiser International. 1970: lost to George Knudson, Robinson Open. 1971: defeated Lou Graham, J.C. Snead, Greater Hartford Open. 1972: defeated Tommy Aaron, Dave Hill, Glen Campbell Los Angeles Open; lost to Miller Barber, Bing Crosby National Pro-Am; defeated Tommy Aaron, Greater Greensboro Open.

ARMOUR, Tommy -- (2-2) 1920: lost to J. Douglas Edgar, Canadian Open. 1927: defeated Harry Cooper, U.S. Open. 1930: defeated Leo Diegel, Canadian Open. 1936: lost to Willie Macfarlane, Walter Olson Open.

AUSTIN, Woody -- (1-0) 1995: defeated Mike Brisky, Buick Open.

AZINGER, Paul -- (1-2) 1989: lost to Steve Jones, Bob Hope Chrysler Classic. 1990: lost to Greg Norman, Doral-Ryder Open. 1993: defeated Greg Norman, PGA Championship.

BAIRD, Butch-- (1-0) 1976: defeated Miller Barber, San Antonio Texas Open.

BAKER-FINCH, Ian-- (0-1) 1991: lost to Bruce Fleisher, New England Classic.

BALDING, Al-- (1-3) 1957: defeated Al Besselink, Havana Invitational. 1959: lost to Don Whitt, Memphis Open. 1961: lost to Arnold Palmer, San Diego Open. 1964: lost to George Knudson, Fresno Open.

BALLESTEROS, Seve-- (1-2) 1987: lost to Larry Mize, Masters Tournament; lost to J.C. Snead, Manufacturers Hanover Westchester Classic. 1988: defeated David Frost, Greg Norman, Ken Green, Manufacturers Hanover Westchester Classic.

BARBER, Jerry-- (1-0) 1961: defeated Don January, PGA Championship.

BARBER, Miller-- (3-4) 1964: lost to Gary Player, Pensacola Open. 1967: defeated Gary Player, Oklahoma City Open. 1970: defeated Bob Charles, Howie Johnson, Greater New Orleans Open. 1972: defeated George Archer, Dean Martin Tucson Open. 1973: lost to Jack Nicklaus, Greater New Orleans Open; lost to Bert Greene, Ligget and Myers Open. 1976: lost to Butch Baird, San Antonio Texas Open.

BARNES, James-- (0-3) 1916: lost to Walter Hagen, Metropolitan Open. 1920: lost to Walter Hagen, Metropolitan Open. 1923: lost to Robert MacDonald, Metropolitan Open.

BARR, Dave-- (1-2) 1981: defeated Woody Blackburn, Frank Conner, Dan Halldorson, Victor Regalado, Quad Cities Open. 1986: lost to Corey Pavin, Greater Milwaukee Open. 1988: lost to Mark Brooks, Canon Sammy Davis, Jr.-Greater Hartford Open.

BARRON, Herman-- (1-0) 1946: defeated Lew Worsham, Philadelphia Inquirer Open.

BAYER, George-- (2-2) 1957: lost to Doug Ford, Western Open. 1958: defeated Sam Snead, Havana International. 1960: defeated Jack Fleck, St. Petersburg Open. 1961: lost to Eric Monti, Ontario Open.

BEAN, Andy-- (3-3) 1978: defeated Lee Trevino, Danny Thomas Memphis Classic; defeated Bill Rogers, Western Open. 1979: lost to Lon Hinkle, Bing Crosby National Pro-Am. 1984: lost to Bruce Lietzke, Honda Classic; lost to Jack Nicklaus, Memorial Tournament. 1986: defeated Hubert Green, Doral-Eastern Open.

BEARD, Frank-- (0-3) 1968: lost to Jack Nicklaus, American Golf Classic. 1969: lost to Larry Hinson, Greater New Orleans Open. 1974: lost to Johnny Miller, World Open.

BECK, Chip-- (0-2) 1988: lost to Bob Lohr, Walt Disney World/Oldsmobile Classic. 1991: lost to Brad Faxon, Buick Open.

BEMAN, Deane-- (1-1) 1968: lost to Arnold Palmer, Bob Hope Desert Classic. 1969: defeated Jack McGowan, Texas Open.

BESSELINK, Al-- (2-2) 1955: defeated Don Fairfield, West Palm Beach Open. 1957: lost to Ed Furgol, Caliente Open; defeated Bob Rosburg, Caracas Open; lost to Al Balding, Havana Invitational.

BIES, Don-- (1-0) 1975: defeated Hubert Green, Sammy Davis, Jr.-Greater Hartford Open.

BLACK, Ronnie-- (1-1) 1983: defeated Sam Torrance, Southern Open. 1989: lost to Wayne Grady, Manufacturers Hanover Westchester Classic.

BLACKBURN, Woody-- (1-1) 1981: lost to Dave Barr, Quad Cities Open. 1985: defeated Ron Streck, Isuzu-Andy Williams-San Diego Open.

BLACKMAR, Phil-- (1-1) 1985: defeated Jodie Mudd, Dan Pohl, Canon Sammy Davis, Jr.-Greater Hartford Open. 1988: defeated Payne Stewart, Provident Classic.

BLANCAS, Homero-- (1-1) 1969: lost to Larry Ziegler, Michigan Golf Classic. 1972: defeated Lanny Wadkins, Phoenix Open.

BLOCKER, Chris-- (0-1) 1970: lost to Doug Sanders, Bahama Islands Open.

INDIVIDUAL PLAYOFF RECORDS (continued)

BOLT, Tommy-- (3-3) 1952: defeated Jack Burke, Jr., Dutch Harrison, Los Angeles Open; lost to Jack Burke, Jr., Baton Rouge Open. 1954: defeated Earl Stewart, Insurance City Open. 1955: lost to Sam Snead, Miami Beach Open. 1960: defeated Ben Hogan, Gene Littler, Memphis Open. 1961: lost to Dave Hill, Home of the Sun Open.

BOROS, Julius-- (4-5) 1952: defeated Cary Middlecoff, World Championship of Golf. 1954: defeated George Fazio, Carling's World Open. 1958: lost to Sam Snead, Dallas Open. 1959: lost to Jack Burke, Jr., Houston Classic. 1963: defeated Arnold Palmer, Jacky Cupit, U.S. Open; lost to Arnold Palmer, Western Open. 1964: defeated Doug Sanders, Greater Greensboro Open. 1969: lost to Gene Littler, Greater Greensboro Open. 1975: lost to Gene Littler, Westchester Classic.

BRADLEY, Jackson-- (0-1) 1955: lost to Henry Ransom, Rubber City Open.

BRADY, Mike-- (1-2) 1911: lost to John McDermott, U.S. Open. 1916: defeated Patrick Doyle, Massachusetts Open. 1919: lost to Walter Hagen, U.S. Open.

BRANCA, Tee-- (0-1) 1938: lost to Al Zimmerman, Utah Open.

BREWER, Gay-- (2-5) 1959: lost to Arnold Palmer, West Palm Beach Open. 1965: defeated Doug Sanders, Greater Seattle Open; defeated Bob Goalby, Hawaiian Open. 1966: lost to Jack Nicklaus, Masters Tournament; lost to Arnold Palmer, Tournament of Champions. 1969: lost to Dave Hill, IVB-Philadelphia Classic. 1974: lost to Jim Colbert, American Golf Classic.

BRISKY, Mike-- (0-1) 1995: lost to Woody Austin, Buick Open.

BRITTON, Bill-- (0-1) 1982: lost to Hal Sutton, Walt Disney World Golf Classic.

BROOKS, Mark-- (2-2) 1988: defeated Dave Barr, Joey Sindelar, Canon Sammy Davis, Jr.-Greater Hartford Open; lost to Tom Purtzer, Gatlin Brothers Southwest Classic. 1991: defeated Gene Sauers, Kmart Greater Greensboro Open. 1993: lost to John Inman, Buick Southern Open.

BROWN, Billy Ray-- (2-0) 1991: defeated Corey Pavin, Rick Fehr, Canon Greater Hartford Open. 1992: defeated Ray Floyd, Ben Crenshaw, Bruce Lietzke, GTE Byron Nelson Classic.

BROWN, David-- (0-1) 1903: lost to Willie Anderson, U.S. Open.

BROWN, Pete-- (1-1) 1964: lost to Billy Casper, Alamden Open. 1970: defeated Tony Jacklin, Andy Williams San Diego Open.

BRYANT, Brad-- (0-1) 1993: lost to John Inman, Buick Southern Open.

BURKE, Billy-- (2-0) 1929: defeated Bill Mehlhorn, Glens Falls Open. 1931: defeated George Von Elm, U.S.Open.

BURKE, Jr., Jack-- (4-4) 1952: lost to Tommy Bolt, Los Angeles Open; defeated Bill Nary, Tommy Bolt, Baton Rouge Open: defeated Dick Mayer, Miami Open; lost to Cary Middlecoff, Kansas City Open. 1955: lost to Henry Ransom, Rubber City Open. 1958: lost to Art Wall, Rubber City Open. 1959: defeated Julius Boros, Houston Classic. 1961: defeated Billy Casper, Johnny Pott, Buick Open.

BURNS, George-- (0-2) 1984: lost to Gary Koch, Bay Hill Classic. 1985: lost to Roger Maltbie, Manufacturers Hanover Westchester Classic.

BYMAN, Bob-- (1-0) 1979: defeated John Schroeder, Bay Hill Citrus Classic.

BYRD, Sam-- (1-0) 1945: defeated Dutch Harrison, Mobile Open.

BYRUM, Tom-- (0-1) 1994: lost to Neal Lancaster, GTE Byron Nelson Classic.

CADLE, George-- (0-1) 1983: lost to Morris Hatalsky, Greater Milwaukee Open.

CALCAVECCHIA, Mark-- (0-3) 1987: lost to Fred Couples, Byron Nelson Classic. 1990: lost to Greg Norman, Doral-Ryder Open. 1993: lost to Billy Mayfair, Greater Milwaukee Open.

CALDWELL, Rex-- (0-2) 1983: lost to Keith Fergus, Bob Hope Desert Classic; lost to Bob Gilder, Phoenix Open.

CAMPBELL, Joe-- (1-2) 1962: lost to Doug Ford, Bing Crosby National Pro-Am. 1966: defeated Gene Littler, Tucson Open. 1967: lost to Randy Glover, Azalea Open.

CARNEVALE, Mark-- (0-1) 1994: lost to Neal Lancaster, GTE Byron Nelson Classic.

CASPER, Billy-- (8-8) 1958: defeated Ken Venturi, Greater New Orleans Open. 1961: lost to Jack Burke, Jr., Buick Open. 1964: defeated Pete Brown, Jerry Steelsmith, Almaden Open. 1965: lost to Wes Ellis, San Diego Open; defeated Johnny Pott, Insurance City Open. 1966: defeated Arnold Palmer, U.S. Open. 1967: defeated Art Wall, Canadian Open; defeated Al Geiberger, Carling World Open; lost to Dudley Wysong, Hawaiian Open. 1968: lost to Johnny Pott, Bing Crosby National Pro-Am. 1969: lost to Jack Nicklaus, Kaiser International. 1970: defeated Hale Irwin, Los Angeles Open; defeated Gene Littler, Masters Tournament. 1971: lost to Bob Lunn, Glen Campbell Los Angeles Open. 1972: lost to Chi Chi Rodriguez, Byron Nelson Classic. 1975: lost to Jack Nicklaus, World Open

CHARLES, Bob-- (0-2) 1965: lost to George Archer, Lucky International Open. 1970: lost to Miller Barber, Greater New Orleans Open.

CHEN, Tze-Chung-- (1-1) 1983: lost to Fred Couples, Kemper Open. 1987: defeated Ben Crenshaw, Los Angeles Open.

CHRISTIAN, Neil--(0-1) 1937: lost to Lawson Little, San Francisco Match Play.

CLAMPETT, Bobby-- (0-2) 1981: lost to John Cook, Bing Crosby National Pro-Am; lost to Hale Irwin, Buick Open.

CLARK, Jimmy-- (1-1) 1952: defeated Jim Turnesa, Ft. Wayne Open. 1955: lost to Bo Wininger, Baton Rouge Open.

COCHRAN, Russ-- (0-1) 1991: lost to Craig Stadler, THE TOUR Championship.

COLBERT, Jim-- (2-0) 1974: defeated Ray Floyd, Gay Brewer, Forrest Fezler, American Golf Classic. 1983: defeated Fuzzy Zoeller, Colonial National Invitation.

COLLINS, Bill-- (1-3) 1960: lost to Jack Fleck, Phoenix Open; defeated Arnold Palmer, Houston Classic; lost to Arnold Palmer, Insurance City Open. 1962: lost to Al Johnston, Hot Springs Open.

CONGDON, Charles-- (0-1) 1948: lost to Ed Oliver, Tacoma Open.

CONNER, Frank-- (0-2) 1981: lost to Dave Barr, Quad Cities Open. 1982: lost to Tom Watson, Sea Pines Heritage Classic.

COOK, John-- (3-3) 1981: defeated Hale Irwin, Ben Crenshaw, Bobby Clampett, Barney Thompson, Bing Crosby National Pro-Am. 1983: defeated Johnny Miller, Canadian Open. 1986: lost to Donnie Hammond, Bob Hope Chrysler Classic. 1990: lost to Tom Kite, Federal Express St. Jude Classic; lost to Bob Tway, Las Vegas Invitational. 1992: defeated Gene Sauers, RIck Fehr, Mark O'Meara, Tom Kite, Bob Hope Chrysler Classic.

COOPER, Harry-- (3-4) 1927: lost to Tommy Armour, U.S. Open. 1934: defeated Ky Laffoon, Western Open; lost to Johnny Revolta, St. Paul Open. 1936: defeated Dick Metz, St. Paul Open; lost to Leonard Dodson, St. Petersburg Open. 1937: defeated Horton Smith, Ralph Guldahl, St. Petersburg Open. 1938: lost to Sam Snead, Canadian Open.

COOPER, Pete-- (1-1) 1958: defeated Wes Ellis, Jr., West Palm Beach Open. 1959: lost to Arnold Palmer, West Palm Beach Open.

COUPLES, Fred-- (4-4) 1983: defeated Tze-Chung Chen, Barry Jaeckel, Gil Morgan, Scott Simpson, Kemper Open. 1986: lost to Tom Kite, Western Open. 1987: defeated Mark Calcavecchia, Byron Nelson Classic. 1988: lost to Sandy Lyle, Phoenix Open. 1992: defeated Davis Love III, Nissan Los Angeles Open; lost to Corey Pavin, Honda Classic. 1993: defeated Robert Gamez, Honda Classic. 1994: lost to Phil Mickelson, Mercedes Championships.

COURTNEY, Chuck-- (0-1) 1972: lost to DeWitt Weaver, Southern Open.

COX, Wiffy-- (1-1) 1931: defeated Joe Turnesa, North & South Open. 1936: defeated Bill Mehlhorn, Sacramento Open.

CRAMPTON, Bruce-- (0-2) 1970: lost to Gibby Gilbert, Houston Champions International. 1974: lost to Richie Karl, B.C. Open.

CRENSHAW, Ben-- (0-8) 1978: lost to Tom Watson, Bing Crosby National Pro-Am. 1979: lost to Larry Nelson, Western Open; lost to David Graham, PGA Championship. 1981: lost to John Cook, Bing Crosby National Pro-Am; lost to Bill Rogers, Texas Open. 1987: lost to Tze-Chung Chen, Los Angeles Open. 1989: lost to David Frost, NEC World Series of Golf. 1992: lost to Billy Ray Brown, GTE Byron Nelson Classic.

CRUICKSHANK, Bobby-- (1-3) 1923: lost to Robert T. Jones, Jr., U.S. Open. 1926: lost to Johnny Farrell, Florida Open; lost to Bill Mehlhorn, South Central Open. 1935: defeated Johnny Revolta, Orlando Open.

CUPIT, Jacky-- (1-2) 1961: lost Dave Marr, Greater Seattle Open. 1963: lost to Julius Boros, U.S. Open. 1966: defeated Chi Chi Rodriguez, Cajun Classic Open.

DALY, John-- (1-0) 1995: defeated Costantino Rocca, British Open.

DEMARET, Jimmy-- (4-5) 1940: defeated Toney Penna, Western Open. 1947: lost to Dave Douglas, Orlando Open. 1948: lost to Lloyd Mangrum, Lower Rio Grande Open; defeated Otto Greiner, St. Paul Open. 1949: lost to Ben Hogan, Long Beach Open; defeated Ben Hogan, Phoenix Open; lost to Johnny Palmer, World Championship of Golf. 1957: defeated Ken Venturi, Mike Souchak, Thunderbird Invitational. 1964: lost to Tommy Jacobs, Palm Springs Golf Classic.

DEVLIN, Bruce-- (0-3) 1968: lost to Johnny Pott, Bing Crosby National Pro-Am. 1969: lost to Bert Yancey, Atlanta Classic. 1972: lost to David Graham, Cleveland Open.

DICKINSON, Gardner-- (1-2) 1956: lost to Art Wall, Ft. Wayne Open. 1969: lost to Raymond Floyd, Greater Jacksonville Open. 1971: defeated Jack Nicklaus, Atlanta Golf Classic.

DIEGEL, LEO-- (3-2) 1922: lost to Abe Mitchell, Southern Open. 1924: defeated Will MacFarlane, Shawnee Open. 1927: defeated Fred McLeod, Middle Adlantic Open. 1930: lost to Tommy Armour, Canadian Open; defeated Gene Sarazen, Oregon Open.

DIEHL, Terry-- (0-1) 1976: lost to Tom Kite, IVB-Bicentennial Golf Classic.

DODSON, Leonard-- (3-1) 1936: lost to Ray Mangrum, Wildwood New Jersey Open; defeated Harry Cooper, St. Petersburg Open. 1937: defeated Horton Smith, Hollywood Open. 1941: defeated Dutch Harrison, Ben Hogan, Oakland Open.

DONALD, Mike-- (1-1) 1989: defeated Tim Simpson, Hal Sutton, Anheuser-Busch Golf Classic. 1990: lost to Hale Irwin, U.S. Open.

DOUGHERTY, Ed-- (0-1) 1990: lost to Jim Gallagher, Jr., Greater Milwaukee Open.

DOUGLAS, Dave-- (1-1) 1947: defeated Jimmy Demaret, Herman Keiser, Orlando Open. 1951: lost to Cary Middlecoff, Kansas City Open.

DOUGLASS, Dale-- (0-3) 1968: lost to Chi Chi Rodriguez, Sahara Invitational. 1970: lost to Don January, Greater Jacksonville Open. 1971: lost to Tom Weiskopf, Kemper Open.

DOW, Willie-- (0-1) 1934: lost to Ralph Stonehouse, Miami Open.

DOYLE, Patrick-- (0-1) 1916: lost to Mike Brady, Massachusetts Open.

DUDLEY, Ed-- (1-1) 1936: defeated Charles Lacey, Philadelphia Open. 1937: lost to Dick Metz, Thomasville Open.

DUTRA, Olin-- (1-0) 1930: defeated Joe Kirkwood, Sr., Long Beach Open.

EASTWOOD, Bob-- (1-0) 1985: defeated Payne Stewart, Byron Nelson Classic.

EDGAR, J. Douglas-- (1-0) 1920: defeated Tommy Armour, Charles Murray, Canadian Open.

EDWARDS, Danny-- (1-0) 1983: defeated Morris Hatalsky, Miller High Life-Quad Cities Open.

EDWARDS, David-- (1-1) 1992: defeated Rick Fehr, Memorial Tournament. 1994: lost to Neal Lancaster, GTE Byron Nelson Classic.

EICHELBERGER, Dave-- (1-1) 1971: lost to Buddy Allin, Greater Greensboro Open. 1981: defeated Bob Murphy, Mark O'Meara, Tallahassee Open.

ELDER, Lee-- (2-2) 1968: lost to Jack Nicklaus, American Golf Classic. 1972: lost to Lee Trevino, Greater Hartford Open. 1974: defeated Peter Oosterhuis, Monsanto Open. 1978: defeated Lee Trevino, Greater Milwaukee Open.

ELKINGTON, Steve-- (3-3) 1992: defeated Brad Faxon, Infiniti Tournament of Champions; lost to Dan Forsman, Buick Open; lost to Nick Price, H-E-B Texas Open. 1993: lost to Rocco Mediate, Kmart Greater Greensboro Open. 1995: defeated Bruce Lietzke, Mercedes Championships; defeated Colin Montgomerie, PGA Championship.

ELLIS, Wes-- (1-1) 1958: lost to Pete Cooper, West Palm Beach Open. 1965: defeated Billy Casper, San Diego Open.

ELS, Ernie-- (1-0) 1994: defeated Loren Roberts, Colin Montgomerie, U.S. Open.

ESPINOSA, Al-- (0-1) 1929: lost to Robert T. Jones, Jr., U.S. Open.

ESPINOSA, Abe-- (0-1) 1924: lost to Macdonald Smith, Northern California Open.

ESTES, Bob-- (0-2) 1989: lost to Mike Hulbert, B.C. Open. 1993: lost to John Inman, Buick Southern Open.

FAIRFIELD, Don-- (0-2) 1955: lost to Al Besselink, West Palm Beach Open. 1959: lost to Dow Finsterwald, Kansas City Open.

FALDO, Nick-- (2-1) 1988: lost to Curtis Strange, U.S. Open. 1989: defeated Scott Hoch, Masters Tournament. 1990: defeated Ray Floyd, Masters Tournament.

FARRELL, Johnny-- (3-2) 1926: defeated Bobby Cruickshank, Florida Open. 1928: lost to Gene Sarazen, Nassau Bahamas Open; defeated Robert T. Jones, Jr., U.S. Open. 1930: lost to Willie Macfarlane, Metropolitan Open. 1936: defeated Vic Ghezzi, New Jersey Open.

FAXON, Brad-- (1-2) 1991: defeated Chip Beck, Buick Open. 1992: lost to Steve Elkington, Infiniti Tournament of Champions; lost to Dan Forsman, Buick Open.

FAZIO, George-- (1-3) 1946: defeated Dick Metz, Canadian Open. 1948: lost to Lloyd Mangrum, Utah Open. 1950: lost to Ben Hogan, U.S. Open. 1954: lost to Julius Boros, Carling's World Open.

FEHR, Rick-- (0-4) 1991: lost to Billy Ray Brown, Canon Greater Hartford Open. 1992: lost to John Cook, Bob Hope Chrysler Classic; lost to David Edwards, Memorial Tournament. 1994: lost to Steve Lowery, Sprint International.

FERGUS, Keith-- (2-0) 1982: defeated Ray Floyd, Georgia-Pacific Atlanta Classic. 1983: defeated Rex Caldwell, Bob Hope Desert Classic.

FERRIER, Jim-- (2-1) 1947: defeated Fred Haas, Jr., St. Paul Open. 1950: defeated Sam Snead, St. Paul Open. 1953: lost to Cary Middlecoff, Houston Open.

FETCHICK, Mike-- (2-0) 1956: defeated Lionel Hebert, St. Petersburg Open; defeated Jay Hebert, Don January, Doug Ford, Western Open.

FEZLER, Forrest-- (0-1) 1974: lost to Jim Colbert, American Golf Classic.

FINSTERWALD, Dow-- (2-4) 1956: lost to Doug Sanders, Canadian Open. 1957: defeated Don Whitt, Tucson Open. 1958: lost to Art Wall, Rubber City Open. 1959: lost to Art Wall, Buick Open; defeated Don Fairfield, Kansas City Open. 1962: lost to Arnold Palmer, Masters Tournament.

FIORI, Ed-- (2-0) 1979: defeated Tom Weiskopf, Southern Open. 1982: defeated Tom Kite, Bob Hope Desert Classic.

FLECK, Jack-- (3-2) 1955: defeated Ben Hogan, U.S. Open. 1960: defeated Bill Collins, Phoenix Open; lost to George Bayer, St. Petersburg Open; lost to Arnold Palmer, Insurance City Open. 1961: defeated Bob Rosburg, Bakersfield Open.

FLECKMAN, Marty-- (1-0) 1967: defeated Jack Montgomery, Cajun Classic Open.

FLEISHER, Bruce-- (1-0) 1991: defeated Ian Baker-Finch, New England Classic.

FLOYD, Raymond-- (4-11) 1969: defeated Gardner Dickinson, Greater Jacksonville Open. 1971: lost to Arnold Palmer, Bob Hope Desert Classic. 1973: lost to Jack Nicklaus, Bing Crosby National Pro-Am. 1974: lost to Jim Colbert, American Golf Classic. 1975: lost to J.C.Snead, Andy Williams San Diego Open. 1976: defeated Jerry McGee, World Open. 1980: defeated Jack Nicklaus, Doral-Eastern Open. 1981: lost to Bruce Lietzke, Wickes Andy Williams-San Diego Open; defeated Barry Jaeckel, Curtis Strange, Tournament Players Championship. 1982: lost to Keith Fergus, Georgia-Pacific Atlanta Classic; lost to Craig Stadler, World Series of Golf. 1985: lost to Roger Maltbie, Manufacturers Hanover Westchester Classic. 1986: defeated Mike Sullivan, Lon Hinkle, Walt Disney World/Oldsmobile Classic. 1990: lost to Nick Faldo, Masters Tournament. 1992: lost to Billy Ray Brown, GTE Byron Nelson Classic.

FORD, Doug-- (5-7) 1951: lost to Dutch Harrison, Texas Open; lost to Cary Middlecoff, Kansas City Open. 1952: defeated Sam Snead, Jacksonville Open. 1953: lost to Earl Stewart, Greensboro Open. 1954: defeated Marty Furgol, Greater Greensboro Open. 1955: lost to Henry Ransom, Rubber City Open; lost to Ted Kroll, Philadelphia Daily News Open. 1956: lost to Mike Fetchick, Western Open. 1957: lost to Arnold Palmer, Rubber City Open; defeated George Bayer, Gene Littler, Billy Maxwell, Western Open. 1961: defeated Arnold Palmer, "500" Festival Open. 1962: defeated Joe Campbell, Bing Crosby National Pro-Am.

FORSMAN, Dan-- (1-0) 1992: defeated Steve Elkington, Brad Faxon, Buick Open.

FOUGHT, John-- (1-0) 1979: defeated Jim Simons, Buick Goodwrench Open.

FROST, David-- (2-3) 1986: lost to Tom Kite, Western Open. 1988: lost to Seve Ballesteros, Manufacturers Hanover Westchester Classic; defeated Bob Tway, Southern Open. 1989: defeated Ben Crenshaw, NEC World Series of Golf. 1995: lost to Bob Tway, MCI Classic.

FUNSETH, Rod-- (0-1) 1971: lost to Buddy Allin, Greater Greensboro Open.

FURGOL, Ed-- (2-1) 1954: defeated Cary Middlecoff, Phoenix Open. 1956: lost to Bob Rosburg, Motor City Open. 1957: defeated Al Besselink, Caliente Open.

FURGOL, Marty-- (0-1) 1954: lost to Doug Ford, Greater Greensboro Open.

GALLAGHER, Jr., Jim-- (1-1) 1990: defeated Ed Dougherty, Billy Mayfair, Greater Milwaukee Open. 1991: lost to Tom Purtzer, NEC World Series of Golf.

GAMEZ, Robert-- (0-1) 1993: lost to Fred Couples, Honda Classic.

GARDNER, Buddy-- (0-1) 1987: lost to Jay Haas, Big "I" Houston Open.

GEIBERGER, Al-- (1-1) 1967: lost to Billy Casper, Carling World Open. 1975: defeated Gary Player, MONY Tournament of Champions.

GHEZZI, Vic-- (2-4) 1935: defeated Johnny Revolta, Los Angeles Open. 1936: lost to Johnny Farrell, New Jersey Open. 1939: lost to Henry Picard, Metropolitan Open. 1941: defeated Byron Nelson, PGA Championship. 1946: lost to Lloyd Mangrum, U.S. Open. 1948: lost to Ed Oliver, Tacoma Open.

GILBERT, Gibby-- (1-0) 1970: defeated Bruce Crampton, Houston Champions International.

GILDER, Bob-- (1-0) 1983: defeated, Rex Caldwell, Johnny Miller, Mark O'Meara, Phoenix Open.

GLOVER, Randy-- (1-0) 1967: defeated Joe Campbell, Azalea Open.

GOALBY, Bob-- (2-1) 1962: defeated Art Wall, Insurance City Open. 1965: lost to Gay Brewer, Hawaiian Open. 1969: defeated Jim Wiechers, Robinson Open.

GOLDEN, John-- (2-0) 1931: defeated George Von Elm, Agua Caliente Open. 1932: defeated Craig Wood, North & South Open.

GRADY, Wayne-- (1-0) 1989: defeated Ronnie Black, Manufacturers Hanover Westchester Classic.

GRAHAM, David-- (2-1) 1972: defeated Bruce Devlin, Cleveland Open; lost to Lou Graham, Liggett and Myers Open. 1979: defeated Ben Crenshaw, PGA Championship.

GRAHAM, Lou-- (3-1) 1971: lost to George Archer, Greater Hartford Open. 1972: defeated Hale Irwin, David Graham, Larry Ziegler, Liggett and Myers Open. 1975: defeated John Mahaffey, U.S. Open. 1979: defeated Bobby Wadkins, IVB-Philadelphia Classic.

GREEN, Hubert-- (2-3) 1971: defeated Don January, Houston Champions International. 1975: lost to Don Bies, Sammy Davis, Jr.-Greater Hartford Open. 1978: defeated Bill Kratzert, Hawaiian Open; lost to Gil Morgan, World Series of Golf. 1986: lost to Andy Bean, Doral-Eastern Open.

GREEN, Ken-- (0-2) 1988: lost to Sandy Lyle, Kmart Greater Greensboro Open; lost to Seve Ballesteros, Manufacturers Hanover Westchester Classic.

GREENE, Bert-- (1-0) 1973: defeated Miller Barber, Ligget and Myers Open.

GREINER, Otto-- (0-1) 1948: lost to Jimmy Demaret, St. Paul Open.

GULDAHL, Ralph-- (2-2) 1936: lost to Macdonald Smith, Seattle Open. 1937: lost to Harry Cooper, St. Petersburg Open; defeated Horton Smith, Western Open. 1939: defeated Denny Shute, Gene Sarazen, Dapper Dan Open.

INDIVIDUAL PLAYOFF RECORDS (continued)

HAAS, Jr., Fred-- (2-3) 1947: lost to Jim Ferrier, St. Paul Open. 1948: lost to Ed Oliver, Tacoma Open; defeated Ben Hogan, Johnny Palmer, Portland Open. 1949: defeated Bob Hamilton, Miami Open. 1955: lost to Shelly Mayfield, Thunderbird Invitational.

HAAS, Jay-- (3-0) 1982: defeated John Adams, Hall of Fame Classic. 1987: defeated Buddy Gardner, Big "I" Houston Open. 1993: defeated Bob Lohr, H-E-B Texas Open.

HAGEN, Walter-- (5-1) 1916: defeated James Barnes, Charles Hoffner, Metropolitan Open. 1919: defeated Mike Brady, U.S. Open. 1920: defeated James Barnes, Metropolitan Open. 1923: lost to Gene Sarazen, PGA Championship; defeated Bill Mehlhorn, Texas Open. 1931: defeated Percy Alliss, Canadian Open.

HALLBERG, Gary-- (0-2) 1984: lost to Gary Koch, Isuzu-Andy Williams-San Diego Open. 1991: lost to Blaine McCallister, H-E-B Texas Open.

HALLDORSON, Dan-- (0-1) 1981: lost to Dave Barr, Quad Cities Open.

HALLET, Jim-- (0-2) 1990: lost to Kenny Knox, Buick Southern Open. 1991: lost to Ian Woosnam, USF&G Classic.

HAMILTON, Bob-- (0-1) 1949: lost to Fred Haas, Jr., Miami Open.

HAMMOND, Donnie-- (1-0) 1986: defeated John Cook, Bob Hope Chrysler Classic.

HAMPTON, Harry-- (0-1) 1923: lost to George McLean, Shawnee Open.

HARBERT, Chick-- (2-1) 1942: defeated Ben Hogan, Texas Open; defeated Dutch Harrison, St. Paul Open. 1950: lost to Henry Ransom, World Championship of Golf.

HARNEY, Paul-- (0-1) 1963: lost to Arnold Palmer, Thunderbird Classic.

HARPER, Chandler-- (1-1) 1938: lost to Johnny Revolta, St. Petersburg Open. 1953: defeated Ted Kroll, El Paso Open.

HARRIS, Jr., Labron-- (1-1) 1968: lost to Bob Murphy, Philadelphia Golf Classic. 1971: defeated Bert Yancey, Robinson Open.

HARRISON, Dutch-- (1-8) 1939: lost to Dick Metz, Oakland Open. 1941: lost to Leonard Dodson, Oakland Open. 1942: lost to Chick Harbert, St. Paul Open. 1945: lost to Sam Byrd, Mobile Open. 1946: lost to Johnny Palmer, Nashville Invitational. 1948: lost to Ben Hogan, Motor City Open; lost to Lloyd Mangrum, World's Championship of Golf. 1951: defeated Doug Ford, Texas Open. 1952: lost to Tommy Bolt, Los Angeles Open.

HART, Dick-- (1-0) 1965: defeated Phil Rogers, Azalea Open.

HATALSKY, Morris-- (2-1) 1983: defeated George Cadle, Greater Milwaukee Open; lost to Danny Edwards, Miller High Life-Quad Cities Open. 1988: defeated Tom Kite, Kemper Open.

HAWKINS, Fred-- (0-1) 1959: lost to Ben Hogan, Colonial National Invitation.

HAYES, Mark-- (0-2) 1979: lost to Lon Hinkle, Bing Crosby National Pro-Am. 1981: lost to Larry Nelson, Greater Greensboro Open.

HEAFNER, Clayton-- (1-1) 1942: lost to Byron Nelson, Tam O' Shanter Open. 1947: defeated Lew Worsham, Jacksonville Open.

HEARD, Jerry-- (0-1) 1974: lost to Bob Menne, Kemper Open.

HEBERT, Jay-- (2-1) 1956: lost to Mike Fetchick, Western Open. 1961: defeated Ken Venturi, Houston Classic; defeated Gary Player, American Golf Classic.

HEBERT, Lionel-- (1-1) 1956: lost to Mike Fetchick, St. Petersburg Open. 1962: defeated Gary Player, Gene Littler, Memphis Open.

HEINEN, Mike-- (0-1) 1995: lost to Davis Love III, Freeport-McMoRan Classic.

HENKE, Nolan-- (0-1) 1995: lost to Bob Tway, MCI Classic.

HENNING, Harold--(0-1) 1969: lost to Charles Sifford, Los Angeles Open.

HENNINGER, Brian--(1-0) 1994: defeated Mike Sullivan, Deposit Guaranty Classic.

HILL, Dave-- (4-2) 1961: defeated Tommy Bolt, Bud Sullivan, Home of the Sun Open. 1963: defeated Mike Souchak, Hot Springs Open. 1969: defeated Gay Brewer, Tommy Jacobs, R.H. Sikes, IVB-Philadelphia Classic; lost to Bob Lunn, Greater Hartford Open. 1972: lost to George Archer, Glen Campbell Los Angeles Open. 1975: defeated Rik Massengale, Sahara Invitational.

HINKLE, Lon-- (1-2) 1977: lost to Ed Sneed, Tallahassee Open. 1979: defeated Andy Bean, Mark Hayes, Bing Crosby National Pro-Am. 1986: lost to Ray Floyd, Walt Disney World/Oldsmobile Classic.

HINSON, Larry-- (1-1) 1969: defeated Frank Beard, Greater New Orleans Open. 1975: lost to Don January, San Antonio Texas Open.

HISKEY, Babe-- (1-0) 1965: defeated Dudley Wysong, Cajun Classic.

HOCH, Scott-- (1-2) 1989: lost to Nick Faldo, Masters Tournament; defeated Robert Wrenn, Las Vegas Invitational. 1995: lost to Payne Stewart, Shell Houston Open.

HOFFNER, Charles-- (0-1) 1916: lost to Walter Hagen, Metropolitan Open.

HOGAN, Ben-- (8-12) 1940: lost to Byron Nelson, Texas Open. 1941: lost to Leonard Dodson, Oakland Open. 1942: defeated Jimmy Thomson, Los Angeles Open; lost to Chick Harbert, Texas Open; lost to Byron Nelson, Masters Tournament. 1944: lost to Harold McSpaden, Chicago Victory Open. 1945: defeated Harold McSpaden, Montgomery Invitational. 1946: defeated Herman Keiser, Phoenix Open; lost to Ray Mangrum, Pensacola Open. 1948: defeated Dutch Harrison, Motor City Open; defeated Ed Oliver, Western Open; lost to Fred Haas, Jr., Portland Open. 1949: defeated Jimmy Demaret, Long Beach Open; lost to Jimmy Demaret, Phoenix Open. 1950: lost to Sam Snead, Los Angeles Open; defeated Lloyd Mangrum, George Fazio, U.S. Open. 1954: lost to Sam Snead, Masters Tournament. 1955: lost to Jack Fleck, U.S. Open. 1959: defeated Fred Hawkins, Colonial National Invitation. 1960: lost to Tommy Bolt, Memphis Open.

HOLSCHER, Bud-- (0-1) 1956: lost to Dick Mayer, Philadelphia Daily News Open.

HULBERT, Mike-- (2-0) 1989: defeated Bob Estes, B.C. Open. 1991: defeated Kenny Knox, Anheuser-Busch Golf Classic.

HUNTER, Willie-- (1-0) 1927: defeated Harold Sampson, California Open.

HUSTON, John-- (0-1) 1993: lost to Jim McGovern, Shell Houston Open.

INMAN, John-- (1-0) 1993: defeated Bob Estes, Mark Brooks, Brad Bryant, Billy Andrade, Buick Southern Open.

IRWIN, Hale-- (4-5) 1970: lost to Billy Casper, Los Angeles Open. 1972: lost to Lou Graham, Liggett and Myers Open. 1976: defeated Kermit Zarley, Florida Citrus Open; lost to Roger Maltbie, Memorial Tournament. 1981: lost to John Cook, Bing Crosby National Pro-Am; defeated Bobby Clampett, Peter Jacobsen, Gil Morgan, Buick Open. 1984: defeated Jim Nelford, Bing Crosby National Pro-Am. 1990: defeated Mike Donald, U.S. Open. 1991: lost to Kenny Perry, Memorial Tournament.

JACKLIN, Tony-- (1-1) 1970: lost to Pete Brown, Andy Williams San Diego Open. 1972: defeated John Jacobs, Greater Jacksonville Open.

JACOBS, John-- (0-1) 1972: lost to Tony Jacklin, Greater Jacksonville Open.

JACOBS, Tommy-- (2-2) 1962: defeated Johnny Pott, San Diego Open. 1964: defeated Jimmy Demaret, Palm Springs Golf Classic. 1966: lost to Jack Nicklaus, Masters Tournament. 1969: lost to Dave Hill, IVB-Philadelphia Classic.

JACOBSEN, Peter-- (1-3) 1981: lost to Hale Irwin, Buick Open. 1984: defeated Payne Stewart, Colonial National Invitation. 1985: lost to Curtis Strange, Honda Classic. 1989: lost to Mark McCumber, Beatrice Western Open.

JAECKEL, Barry-- (1-2) 1978: defeated Bruce Lietzke, Tallahassee Open. 1981: lost to Ray Floyd, Tournament Players Championship. 1983: lost to Fred Couples, Kemper Open.

JANUARY, Don-- (3-5) 1956: lost to Mike Fetchick, Western Open. 1961: lost to Jerry Barber, PGA Championship. 1964: lost to Chi Chi Rodriguez, Lucky International Open. 1967: defeated Don Massengale, PGA Championship. 1969: lost to Jack Nicklaus, Kaiser International. 1970: defeated Dale Douglass, Greater Jacksonville Open. 1971: lost to Hubert Green, Houston Champions International. 1975: defeated Larry Hinson, San Antonio Texas Open.

JANZEN, Lee-- (1-0) 1995: defeated Corey Pavin, Kemper Open.

JENKINS, Tom-- (0-1) 1981: lost to Bruce Lietzke, Wickes Andy Williams-San Diego Open.

JOHNSON, Howie-- (1-1) 1958: defeated Arnold Palmer, Azalea Open. 1970: lost to Miller Barber, Greater New Orleans Open.

JOHNSTON, Al-- (1-0) 1962: defeated Bill Collins, Hot Springs Open.

JONES, Grier-- (2-0) 1972: defeated Bob Murphy, Hawaiian Open; defeated Dave Marad, Robinson's Fall Classic.

JONES, Jr., Robert T.-- (2-2) 1923: defeated Bobby Cruickshank, U.S. Open. 1925: lost to Willie Macfarlane, U.S. Open. 1928: lost to Johnny Farrell, U.S. Open. 1929: defeated Al Espinosa, U.S. Open.

JONES, Steve-- (2-1) 1988: defeated Bob Tway, AT&T Pebble Beach National Pro-Am. 1989: defeated Sandy Lyle, Paul Azinger, Bob Hope Chrysler Classic. 1990: lost to Payne Stewart, MCI Heritage Classic.

KARL, Richie-- (1-0) 1974: defeated Bruce Crampton, B.C. Open.

KEISER, Herman-- (0-2) 1946: lost Ben Hogan, Phoenix Open. 1947: lost to Dave Douglas, Orlando Open.

KIRKWOOD, Sr., Joe-- (1-1) 1923: defeated Macdonald Smith, California Open. 1930: lost to Olin Dutra, Long Beach Open.

KITE, Tom-- (6-4) 1976: defeated Terry Diehl, IVB-Bicentennial Golf Classic. 1982: lost to Ed Fiori, Bob Hope Desert Classic; defeated Jack Nicklaus, Denis Watson, Bay Hill Classic. 1986: defeated Fred Couples, David Frost, Nick Price, Western Open. 1988: lost to Morris Hatalsky, Kemper Open; lost to Curtis Strange, Nabisco Championships. 1989: defeated Davis Love III, Nestle Invitational; defeated Payne Stewart, Nabisco Championships. 1990: defeated John Cook, Federal Express St. Jude Classic. 1992: lost to John Cook, Bob Hope Chrysler Classic.

KLEIN, Willie-- (0-1) 1925: lost to Willie Macfarlane, Shawnee Open.

KNOX, Kenny-- (1-1) 1990: defeated Jim Hallet, Buick Southern Open. 1991: lost to Mike Hulbert, Anheuser-Busch Golf Classic.

KNUDSON, George-- (3-0) 1963: defeated Mason Rudolph, Portland Open. 1964: defeated Al Balding, Fresno Open. 1970: defeated George Archer, Robinson Open.

KOCH, Gary-- (2-0) 1984: defeated Gary Hallberg, Isuzu-Andy Williams-San Diego Open; defeated George Burns, Bay Hill Classic.

KRATZERT, Bill-- (0-1) 1978: lost to Hubert Green, Hawaiian Open.

KROLL, Ted-- (1-7) 1952: lost to Cary Middlecoff, Motor City Open. 1953: lost to Chandler Harper, El Paso Open; lost to Cary Middlecoff, Carling's Open. 1954: lost to Lloyd Mangrum, Western Open. 1955: defeated Doug Ford, Philadelphia Daily News Open. 1956: lost to Arnold Palmer, Insurance City Open. 1960: lost to Johnny Pott, Dallas Open. 1961: lost to Billy Maxwell, Insurance City Open.

LACEY, Charles-- (0-1) 1936: lost to Ed Dudley, Philadelphia Open.

LAFFOON, Ky-- (1-3) 1934: defeated Paul Runyan, Glens Falls Open; lost to Harry Cooper, Western Open; lost to Johnny Revolta, St. Paul Open. 1950: lost to Skip Alexander, Empire State Open.

LANCASTER, Neal-- (1-0) 1994: defeated Tom Byrum, Mark Carnevale, David Edwards, Yoshinori Mizumaki, David Ogrin, GTE Byron Nelson Classic.

LANGER, Bernhard-- (1-1) 1985: defeated Bobby Wadkins, Sea Pines Heritage Classic. 1986: lost to Bob Tway, Shearson Lehman Brothers-Andy Williams Open.

LEMA, Tony-- (3-1) 1962: defeated Bob Rosburg, Orange County Open. 1963: defeated Tommy Aaron, Memphis Open; lost to Arnold Palmer, Cleveland Open. 1964: defeated Arnold Palmer, Cleveland Open.

LEONARD, Stan-- (1-1) 1955: lost to Gene Littler, Labatt Open. 1960: defeated Art Wall, Western Open.

LEVI, Wayne-- (2-1) 1980: defeated Gil Morgan, Pleasant Valley Jimmy Fund Classic. 1984: lost to Jack Renner, Hawaiian Open. 1985: defeated Steve Pate, Georgia Pacific Atlanta Classic.

LIETZKE, Bruce-- (6-5) 1977: defeated Gene Littler, Joe Garagiola-Tucson Open; lost to Jack Nicklaus, MONY Tournament of Champions. 1978: lost to Barry Jaeckel, Tallahassee Open. 1981: defeated Ray Floyd, Tom Jenkins, Wickes Andy Williams-San Diego Open; defeated Tom Watson, Byron Nelson Classic. 1984: defeated Andy Bean, Honda Classic. 1988: defeated Clarence Rose, GTE Byron Nelson Classic. 1992: lost to Billy Ray Brown, GTE Byron Nelson Classic; defeated Corey Pavin, Southwestern Bell Colonial; lost to Greg Norman, Canadian Open. 1995: lost to Steve Elkington, Mercedes Championships.

LITTLE, Lawson-- (2-0) 1937: defeated Neil Christian, San Francisco Match Play. 1940: defeated Gene Sarazen, U.S. Open.

LITTLER, Gene-- (3-8) 1955: defeated Stan Leonard, Labatt Open. 1956: lost to Peter Thomson, Texas International Open. 1957: lost to Doug Ford, Western Open. 1960: lost to Tommy Bolt, Memphis Open. 1962: lost to Lionel Hebert, Memphis Open. 1966: lost to Joe Campbell, Tucson Open. 1969: defeated Orville Moody, Julius Boros, Tom Weiskopf, Greater Greensboro Open. 1970: lost to Billy Casper, Masters Tournament. 1975: defeated Julius Boros, Westchester Classic. 1977: lost to Bruce Lietzke, Joe Garagiola-Tucson Open; lost to Lanny Wadkins, PGA Championship.

LOCKE, Bobby-- (3-0) 1947: defeated Ed Oliver, All American Open. 1949: defeated Frank Stranahan, Cavalier Specialist Tournament. 1950: defeated Lloyd Mangrum, All American Tournament.

LOHR, Bob-- (1-2) 1988: defeated Chip Beck, Walt Disney World/Oldsmobile Classic. 1993: lost to Jay Haas, H-E-B Texas Open. 1995: lost to Mark O'Meara, Bell Canadian Open.

LOVE III, Davis-- (1-3) 1989: lost to Tom Kite, Nestle Invitational. 1991: lost to Tom Purtzer, NEC World Series of Golf. 1992: lost to Fred Couples, Nissan Los Angeles Open. 1995: defeated Mike Heinen, Freeport McMoRan Classic.

LOWERY, Steve-- (1-0) 1994: defeated Rick Fehr, Sprint International.

LUNN, Bob-- (2-0) 1969: defeated Dave Hill, Greater Hartford Open. 1971: defeated Billy Casper, Glen Campbell Los Angeles Open.

LUTHER, Ted-- (1-0) 1935: defeated Felix Serafin, Hershey Open.

LYLE, Sandy-- (3-1) 1987: defeated Jeff Sluman, Tournament Players Championship. 1988: defeated Fred Couples, Phoenix Open; defeated Ken Green, Kmart Greater Greensboro Open. 1989: lost to Steve Jones, Bob Hope Chrysler, Classic.

MacDONALD, Robert-- (1-0) 1923: defeated James Barnes, Metropolitan Open.

MACFARLANE, Willie-- (4-2) 1924: lost Leo Diegel, Shawnee Open. 1925: defeated Robert T. Jones, Jr., U.S. Open; defeated Willie Klein, Shawnee Open. 1930: defeated Johnny Farrell, Metropolitan Open. 1933: lost to Denny Shute, Gasparilla Open. 1936: defeated Tommy Armour, Walter Olson Open.

MAGEE, Andrew-- (1-0) 1991: defeated D.A. Weibring, Las Vegas Invitational.

MAHAFFEY, John-- (3-2) 1975: lost to Lou Graham, U.S. Open. 1978: defeated Jerry Pate, Tom Watson, PGA Championship. 1984: defeated Jim Simons, Bob Hope Desert Classic. 1985: lost to Mark Wiebe, Anheuser-Busch Golf Classic; defeated Jodie Mudd, Texas Open.

MALTBIE, Roger-- (2-1) 1976: defeated Hale Irwin, Memorial Tournament. 1985: defeated George Burns, Ray Floyd, Manufacturers Hanover Westchester Classic. 1986: lost to Mac O'Grady, Canon Sammy Davis, Jr.-Greater Hartford Open.

MANERO, Tony-- (0-1) 1937: lost to Ray Mangrum, Miami Open.

MANGRUM, Lloyd-- (5-3-1) 1946: defeated Vic Ghezzi, Byron Nelson, U.S. Open. 1948: defeated Jimmy Demaret, Lower Rio Grande Open; defeated Sam Snead, Dutch Harrison, World's Championship of Golf; defeated George Fazio, Utah Open. 1949: lost to Sam Snead, Greater Greensboro Open; tied Cary Middlecoff, Motor City Open. 1950: lost to Ben Hogan, U.S. Open; lost to Bobby Locke, All American Tournament.1954: defeated Ted Kroll, Western Open.

MANGRUM, Ray-- (3-1) 1936: lost to Henry Picard, North & South Open; defeated Leonard Dodson, Wildwood New Jersey Open. 1937: defeated Tony Manero, Miami Open. 1946: defeated Ben Hogan, Pensacola Open.

MARAD, Dave-- (0-1) 1972: lost to Grier Jones, Robinson's Fall Classic.

MARR, Dave-- (2-0) 1961: defeated Bob Rosburg, Jacky Cupit, Greater Seattle Open. 1962: defeated Jerry Steelsmith, Azalea Open.

MARTIN, Doug-- (0-1) 1995: lost to Vijay Singh, Buick Classic.

MASSENGALE, Don-- (0-1) 1967: lost to Don January, PGA Championship.

MASSENGALE, Rik-- (0-1) 1975: lost to Dave Hill, Sahara Invitational.

MAXWELL, Billy-- (1-2) 1955: lost to Bo Wininger, Baton Rouge Open. 1957: lost to Doug Ford, Western Open. 1961: defeated Ted Kroll, Insurance City Open.

MAYFAIR, Billy-- (1-4) 1990: lost to Jim Gallagher, Jr., Greater Milwaukee Open; lost to Jodie Mudd, Nabisco Championships. 1993:defeated Mark Calcavecchia, Ted Schulz, Greater Milwaukee Open. 1995: lost to Vijay Singh, Phoenix Open; lost to Greg Norman, NEC World Series of Golf.

MAYER, Dick-- (2-1) 1952: lost to Jack Burke, Jr., Miami Open. 1956: defeated Bud Holscher, Philadelphia Daily News Open. 1957: defeated Cary Middlecoff, U.S. Open.

MAYFIELD, Shelley-- (1-1) 1953: lost to Cary Middlecoff, Houston Open. 1955: defeated Mike Souchak and Fred Haas, Jr., Thunderbird Invitational.

McCALLISTER, Blaine-- (1-1) 1986: lost to Gene Sauers, Bank of Boston Classic. 1991: defeated Gary Hallberg, H-E-B Texas Open.

McCUMBER, Mark-- (2-0) 1989: defeated Peter Jacobsen, Beatrice Western Open. 1994: defeated Fuzzy Zoeller, THE TOUR Championship.

McDERMOTT, John-- (1-1) 1910: lost to Alex Smith, U.S. Open. 1911: defeated Mike Brady, George Simpson, U.S. Open.

McGEE, Jerry-- (0-1) 1976: lost to Ray Floyd, World Open.

McGOVERN, Jim-- (1-0) 1993: defeated John Huston, Shell Houston Open.

McGOWAN, Jack-- (0-1) 1969: lost to Deane Beman, Texas Open.

McLEAN, George-- (1-0) 1923: defeated Harry Hampton, Shawnee Open.

McLENDON, Mac-- (1-0) 1978: defeated Mike Reid, Pensacola Open.

McLEOD, Fred-- (1-1) 1908: defeated Willie Smith, U.S. Open. 1927: lost to Leo Diegel, Middle Atlantic Open.

McMULLIN, John-- (0-1) 1958: lost to Sam Snead, Dallas Open.

McSPADEN, Harold-- (3-4) 1937: lost to Denny Shute, PGA Championship. 1940: lost to Sam Snead, Canadian Open. 1943: defeated Buck White, All American Open. 1944: defeated Byron Nelson, Phoenix Open; defeated Ben Hogan, Chicago Victory Open. 1945: lost to Byron Nelson, New Orleans Open; lost to Ben Hogan, Montgomery Invitational.

MEDIATE, Rocco-- (2-0) 1991: defeated Curtis Strange, Doral-Ryder Open. 1993: defeated Steve Elkington, Kmart Greater Greensboro Open.

MEHLHORN, Bill-- (4-3) 1923: lost to Walter Hagen, Texas Open. 1926: defeated Bobby Cruickshank, South Central Open; defeated Gene Sarazen, South Florida Open. 1928: defeated Fred Morrison, Hawaiian Open. 1929: defeated Bobby Cruickshank, Horton Smith, South Central Open; lost to Billy Burke, Glens Falls Open. 1936: lost to Wiffy Cox, Sacramento Open.

MENNE, Bob-- (1-1) 1970: lost to Lee Trevino, National Airlines Open. 1974: defeated Jerry Heard, Kemper Open.

METZ, Dick-- (2-2) 1936: lost to Harry Cooper, St. Paul Open. 1937: defeated Ed Dudley, Thomasville Open. 1939: defeated Dutch Harrison, Oakland Open. 1946: lost to George Fazio, Canadian Open.

MICKELSON, Phil-- (1-0) 1994: defeated Fred Couples, Mercedes Championships.

MIDDLECOFF, Cary-- (7-6-1) 1947: defeated George Schoux, Charlotte Open. 1948: lost to Ed Oliver, Tacoma Open. 1949: tied Lloyd Mangrum, Motor City Open. 1950: defeated Ed Oliver, St. Louis Open. 1951: defeated Doug Ford, Dave Douglas, Kansas City Open. 1952: defeated Ted Kroll, Motor City Open; lost

MIDDLECOFF, Cary (cont'd.)-- to Julius Boros, World Championship of Golf: defeated Jack Burke, Jr., Kansas City Open. 1953: defeated Shelley Mayfield, Jim Ferrier, Earl Stewart, Billy Nary, Houston Open; defeated Ted Kroll, Carling's Open; lost to Art Wall, Ft. Wayne Open. 1954: lost to Ed Furgol, Phoenix Open. 1956: lost to Peter Thomson, Texas International Open. 1957: lost to Dick Mayer, U.S. Open.

MILLER, Johnny-- (1-5) 1972: lost to Jack Nicklaus, Bing Crosby National Pro-Am. 1974: defeated Frank Beard, Bob Murphy, Jack Nicklaus, World Open. 1979: lost to Tom Watson, Colgate Hall of Fame Classic. 1982: lost to Tom Watson, Glen Campbell Los Angeles Open. 1983: lost to Bob Gilder, Phoenix Open; lost to John Cook, Canadian Open.

MILLER, Massie-- (0-1) 1929: lost to Joe Turnesa, Lannin Memorial Tournament.

MITCHELL, Abe-- (1-0) 1922: defeated Leo Diegel, Southern Open.

MITCHELL, Bobby-- (1-0) 1972: defeated Jack Nicklaus, Tournament of Champions.

MIZE, Larry-- (1-2) 1986: lost to Greg Norman, Kemper Open. 1987: defeated Greg Norman, Seve Ballesteros, Masters Tournament. 1990: lost to Payne Stewart, MCI Heritage Classic.

MIZUMAKI, Yoshinori-- (0-1) 1994: lost to Neal Lancaster, GTE Byron Nelson Classic.

MONTGOMERIE, Colin-- (0-2) 1994: lost to Ernie Els, U.S. Open. 1995: lost to Steve Elkington, PGA Championship.

MONTGOMERY, Jack-- (0-1) 1967: lost to Marty Fleckman, Cajun Classic Open.

MONTI, Eric-- (1-0) 1961: defeated George Bayer, Bobby Nichols, Ontario Open.

MOODY, Orville-- (0-2) 1969: lost to Gene Littler, Greater Greensboro Open. 1973: lost to Jack Nicklaus, Bing Crosby National Pro-Am.

MORGAN, Gil-- (3-4) 1978: defeated Hubert Green, World Series of Golf. 1979: defeated Larry Nelson, Danny Thomas-Memphis Classic. 1980: lost to Wayne Levi, Pleasant Valley Jimmy Fund Classic. 1981: lost to Hale Irwin, Buick Open. 1983: defeated Lanny Wadkins, Curtis Strange, Joe Garagiola-Tucson Open; lost to Fred Couples, Kemper Open. 1990: lost to Tony Sills, Independent Insurance Agent Open.

MORRISON, Fred-- (0-1) 1928: lost to Bill Mehlhorn, Hawaiian Open.

MUDD, Jodie-- (2-2) 1985: lost to Phil Blackmar, Canon Sammy Davis, Jr.-Greater Hartford Open; lost to John Mahaffey, Texas Open. 1989: defeated Larry Nelson, GTE Byron Nelson Classic. 1990: defeated Billy Mayfair, Nabisco Championships.

MURPHY, Bob-- (1-5) 1968: defeated Labron Harris, Jr., Philadelphia Golf Classic. 1970: lost to Lee Trevino, Tucson Open. 1972: lost to Grier Jones, Hawaiian Open. 1973: lost to Bobby Nichols, Westchester Classic. 1974: lost to Johnny Miller, World Open. 1981: lost to Dave Eichelberger, Tallahassee Open.

MURRAY, Charles-- (0-1) 1920: lost to J. Douglas Edgar, Canadian Open.

NAGLE, Kel-- (0-1) 1965: lost to Gary Player, U.S. Open.

NARY, Bill-- (0-2) 1952: lost to Jack Burke, Jr., Baton Rouge Open. 1953: lost to Cary Middlecoff, Houston Open.

NELFORD, Jim-- (0-1) 1984: lost to Hale Irwin, Bing Crosby National Pro-Am.

NELSON, Byron-- (6-6) 1939: defeated Craig Wood, Denny Shute, U.S. Open; lost to Henry Picard, PGA Championship. 1940: defeated Ben Hogan, Texas Open. 1941: lost to Horton Smith, Florida West Coast Open; lost to Vic Ghezzi, PGA Championship. 1942: defeated Ben Hogan, Masters Tournament; defeated Clayton Heafner, Tam O' Shanter Open. 1944: lost to Harold McSpaden, Phoenix Open. 1945: defeated Sam Snead, Charlotte Open; defeated Harold McSpaden, New Orleans Open; lost to Sam Snead, Gulfport Open. 1946: lost to Lloyd Mangrum, U.S. Open.

NELSON, Larry-- (3-2) 1979: lost to Gil Morgan, Danny Thomas-Memphis Classic; defeated Ben Crenshaw, Western Open. 1981: defeated Mark Hayes, Greater Greensboro Open. 1987: defeated Lanny Wadkins, PGA Championship. 1989: lost to Jodie Mudd, GTE Byron Nelson Classic.

NEWTON, Jack-- (1-0) 1978: defeated Mike Sullivan, Buick-Goodwrench Open.

NICHOLS, Bobby-- (2-2) 1961: lost to Eric Monti, Ontario Open. 1962: defeated Dan Sikes, Jack Nicklaus, Houston Classic. 1973: defeated Bob Murphy, Westchester Classic. 1975: lost to J.C. Snead, Andy Williams San Diego Open.

NICKLAUS, Jack-- (13-10) 1962: lost to Bobby Nichols, Houston Classic; defeated Arnold Palmer, U.S. Open. 1963: defeated Gary Player, Palm Springs Golf Classic; lost to Arnold Palmer, Western Open. 1965: lost to Doug Sanders, Pensacola Open; defeated Johnny Pott, Memphis Open. 1966: defeated Tommy Jacobs, Gay Brewer, Masters Tournament. 1968: defeated Frank Beard, Lee Elder, American Golf Classic. 1969: defeated George Archer, Billy Casper, Don January, Kaiser International. 1970: defeated Arnold Palmer, Byron Nelson Classic. 1971: lost to Gardner Dickinson, Atlanta Golf Classic; lost to Lee Trevino, U.S. Open. 1972: defeated Johnny Miller, Bing Crosby National Pro-Am; lost to Bobby Mitchell, Tournament of Champions. 1973: defeated Ray Floyd, Orville Moody, Bing Crosby National Pro-Am; defeated Miller Barber, Greater New Orleans Open. 1974: lost to Johnny Miller, World Open. 1975: lost to Tom Weiskopf,

NICKLAUS, Jack (cont'd.)-- Canadian Open; defeated Billy Casper, World Open. 1977: defeated Bruce Lietzke, MONY Tournament of Champions. 1980: lost to Ray Floyd, Doral-Eastern Open. 1982: lost to Tom Kite, Bay Hill Classic. 1984: defeated Andy Bean, Memorial Tournament.

NICOLETTE, Mike-- (1-0) 1983: defeated Greg Norman, Bay Hill Classic.

NORMAN, Greg-- (4-7) 1983: lost to Mike Nicolette, Bay Hill Classic. 1984: lost to Fuzzy Zoeller, U.S. Open; lost to Tom Watson, Western Open. 1986: defeated Larry Mize, Kemper Open. 1987: lost to Larry Mize, Masters Tournament. 1988: lost to Curtis Strange, Independent Insurance Agent Open; lost to Seve Ballesteros, Manufacturers Hanover Westchester Classic. 1990: defeated Paul Azinger, Mark Calcavecchia, Tim Simpson, Doral-Ryder Open. 1992: defeated Bruce Lietzke, Canadian Open. 1993: lost to Paul Azinger, PGA Championship. 1995: defeated Billy Mayfair, Nick Price, NEC World Series of Golf.

O'GRADY, Mac-- (1-0) 1986: defeated Roger Maltbie, Canon Sammy Davis, Jr.-Greater Hartford Open.

OGRIN, David-- (0-2) 1985: lost to Hal Sutton, St. Jude Memphis Classic. 1994: lost to Neal Lancaster, GTE Byron Nelson Classic.

OLIVER, Ed-- (1-3) 1947: lost to Bobby Locke, All American Open. 1948: lost to Ben Hogan, Western Open; defeated Cary Middlecoff, Fred Haas, Jr., Charles Congdon, Vic Ghezzi, Tacoma Open. 1950: lost to Cary Middlecoff, St. Louis Open.

O'MEARA, Mark-- (2-4) 1981: lost to Dave Eichelberger, Tallahassee Open. 1983: lost to Bob Gilder, Phoenix Open. 1991: lost to Corey Pavin, Bob Hope Chrysler Classic. 1992: lost to John Cook, Bob Hope Chrysler Classic; defeated Jeff Sluman, AT&T Pebble Beach National Pro-Am. 1995: defeated Bob Lohr, Bell Canadian Open.

OOSTERHUIS, Peter-- (0-1) 1974: lost to Lee Elder, Monsanto Open.

OUIMET, Francis-- (1-0) 1913: defeated Harry Vardon, Edward Ray, U.S. Open.

PALMER, Arnold-- (14-10) 1956: defeated Ted Kroll, Insurance City Open. 1957: defeated Doug Ford, Rubber City Open. 1958: lost to Howie Johnson, Azalea Open. 1959: defeated Gay Brewer, Pete Cooper, West Palm Beach Open. 1960: lost to Bill Collins, Houston Classic; defeated Bill Collins, Jack Fleck, Insurance City Open. 1961: defeated Al Balding, San Diego Open; defeated Doug Sanders, Phoenix Open; lost to Doug Ford, "500" Festival Open. 1962: defeated Gary Player, Dow Finsterwald, Masters Tournament; defeated Johnny Pott, Colonial National Invitation; lost to Jack Nicklaus, U.S. Open. 1963: defeated Paul Harney, Thunderbird Classic; lost to Julius Boros, U.S. Open; defeated Tommy Aaron, Tony Lema, Cleveland Open; defeated Julius Boros, Jack Nicklaus, Western Open. 1964: lost to Gary Player, Pensacola Open; lost to Tony Lema, Cleveland Open. 1966: lost to Doug Sanders, Bob Hope Desert Classic; defeated Gay Brewer, Tournament of Champions; lost to Billy Casper, U.S. Open. 1968: defeated Deane Beman, Bob Hope Desert Classic. 1970: lost to Jack Nicklaus, Byron Nelson Classic. 1971: defeated Ray Floyd, Bob Hope Desert Classic.

PALMER, Johnny-- (2-1) 1946: defeated Dutch Harrison, Nashville Invitational. 1948: lost to Fred Haas, Jr., Portland Open. 1949: defeated Jimmy Demaret, World Championship of Golf.

PATE, Jerry-- (1-2) 1977: defeated Dave Stockton, Phoenix Open. 1978: lost to John Mahaffey, PGA Championship. 1980: lost to Doug Tewell, Sea Pines Heritage Classic.

PATE, Steve-- (0-2) 1985: lost to Wayne Levi, Georgia Pacific Atlanta Classic. 1991: lost to Corey Pavin, BellSouth Atlanta Classic.

PAVIN, Corey-- (5-3) 1986: defeated Dave Barr, Greater Milwaukee Open. 1987: defeated Craig Stadler, Hawaiian Open. 1991: defeated Mark O'Meara, Bob Hope Chrysler Classic; defeated Steve Pate, BellSouth Atlanta Classic; lost to Billy Ray Brown, Canon Greater Hartford Open. 1992: defeated Fred Couples, Honda Classic; lost to Bruce Lietzke, Southwestern Bell Colonial. 1995: lost to Lee Janzen, Kemper Open.

PEETE, Calvin-- (0-1) 1986: lost to Curtis Strange, Houston Open.

PENNA, Toney: (0-1) 1940: lost to Jimmy Demaret, Western Open.

PERRY, Kenny-- (1-0) 1991: defeated Hale Irwin, Memorial Tournament.

PICARD, Henry-- (3-1) 1936: defeated Ray Mangrum, North & South Open. 1939: lost to Sam Snead, St. Petersburg Open; defeated Paul Runyan, Vic Ghezzi, Metropolitan Open; defeated Byron Nelson, PGA Championship.

PLAYER, Gary-- (3-10) 1958: lost to Sam Snead, Dallas Open. 1959: lost to Don Whitt, Memphis Open. 1961: lost to Jay Hebert, American Golf Classic. 1962: lost to Arnold Palmer, Masters Tournament; lost to Lionel Hebert, Memphis Open. 1963: lost to Jack Nicklaus, Palm Springs Golf Classic. 1964: defeated Arnold Palmer, Miller Barber, Pensacola Open. 1965: defeated Kel Nagle, U.S. Open. 1967: lost to Miller Barber, Oklahoma City Open. 1968: lost to Steve Reid, Azalea Open. 1971: defeated Hal Underwood, Greater Jacksonville Open; lost to Tom Weiskopf, Kemper Open. 1975: lost to Al Geiberger, MONY Tournament of Champions.

INDIVIDUAL PLAYOFF RECORDS (continued)

POHL, Dan-- (1-2) 1982: lost to Craig Stadler, Masters Tournament. 1985: lost to Phil Blackmar, Canon Sammy Davis, Jr.-Greater Hartford Open. 1986: defeated Payne Stewart, Colonial National Invitation.

POTT, Johnny-- (2-5) 1960: defeated Bo Wininger, Ted Kroll, Dallas Open. 1961: lost to Jack Burke, Jr., Buick Open. 1962: lost to Tommy Jacobs, San Diego Open; lost to Arnold Palmer, Colonial National Invitation. 1965: lost to Jack Nicklaus, Memphis Open; lost to Billy Casper, Insurance City Open. 1968: defeated Billy Casper, Bruce Devlin, Bing Crosby National Pro-Am.

PRICE, Nick-- (2-2) 1986: lost to Tom Kite, Western Open. 1992: defeated Steve Elkington, H-E-B Texas Open. 1994: defeated Scott Simpson, Southwestern Bell Colonial. 1995: lost to Greg Norman, NEC World Series of Golf.

PRIDE, Dicky-- (1-0) 1994: defeated Gene Sauers, Hal Sutton, Federal Express St. Jude Classic.

PURTZER, Tom-- (2-0) 1988: defeated Mark Brooks, Gatlin Brothers Southwest Classic. 1991: defeated Davis Love III, Jim Gallagher, NEC World Series of Golf.

RAGAN, Jr., Dave-- (1-0) 1962: defeated Doug Sanders, West Palm Beach Open.

RANSOM, Henry-- (2-0) 1950: defeated Chick Harbert, World Championship of Golf. 1955: defeated Jack Burke, Jr., Doug Ford, Jackson Bradley, Rubber City Open.

RAY, Edward-- (0-1) 1913: lost to Francis Ouimet, U.S. Open.

REGALADO, Victor-- (0-1) 1981: lost to Dave Barr, Quad Cities Open.

REID, Mike-- (1-2) 1978: lost to Mac McLendon, Pensacola Open. 1985: lost to Hal Sutton, Southwest Golf Classic. 1988: defeated Tom Watson, NEC World Series of Golf.

REID, Steve-- (1-0) 1968: defeated Gary Player, Azalea Open.

RENNER, Jack-- (1-0) 1984: defeated Wayne Levi, Hawaiian Open.

REVOLTA, Johnny-- (2-2) 1934: defeated Ky Laffoon and Harry Cooper, St. Paul Open. 1935: lost to Vic Ghezzi, Los Angeles Open; lost to Bobby Cruickshank, Orlando Open. 1938: defeated Chandler Harper, St. Petersburg Open.

ROBERTS, Loren-- (0-1) 1994: lost to Ernie Els, U.S. Open.

ROCCA, Costantino-- (0-1) 1995: lost to John Daly, British Open

RODRIGUEZ, Chi Chi-- (3-1) 1964: defeated Don January, Lucky International Open. 1966: lost to Jacky Cupit, Cajun Classic Open. 1968: defeated Dale Douglass, Sahara Invitational. 1972: defeated Billy Casper, Byron Nelson Classic.

RODGERS, Phil-- (0-1) 1965: lost to Dick Hart, Azalea Open.

ROGERS, Bill-- (1-2) 1978: lost to Andy Bean, Western Open. 1979: lost to Tom Watson, Byron Nelson Classic. 1981: defeated Ben Crenshaw, Texas Open.

ROSBURG, Bob-- (1-5) 1956: defeated Ed Furgol, Motor City Open. 1957: lost to Al Besselink, Caracas Open. 1958: lost to Art Wall, Eastern Open. 1961: lost to Dave Marr, Greater Seattle Open; lost to Jack Fleck, Bakersfield Open. 1962: lost to Tony Lema, Orange County Open.

ROSE, Clarence-- (0-1) 1988: lost to Bruce Lietzke, GTE Byron Nelson Classic.

RUDOLPH, Mason-- (0-1) 1963: lost to George Knudson, Portland Open.

RUNYAN, Paul-- (1-2) 1934: lost to Ky Laffoon, Glens Falls Open; defeated Craig Wood, PGA Championship. 1939: lost to Henry Picard, Metropolitan Open.

SAMPSON, Harold-- (0-1) 1927: lost to Willie Hunter, California Open.

SANDERS, Doug-- (5-4) 1956: defeated Dow Finsterwald, Canadian Open. 1961: lost to Arnold Palmer, Phoenix Open. 1962: lost to Dave Ragan, Jr., West Palm Beach Open. 1964: lost to Julius Boros, Greater Greensboro Open. 1965: defeated Jack Nicklaus, Pensacola Open; lost to Gay Brewer, Greater Seattle Open. 1966: defeated Arnold Palmer, Bob Hope Desert Classic; defeated Tom Weiskopf, Greater Greensboro Open. 1970: defeated Chris Blocker, Bahama Islands Open.

SARAZEN, Gene-- (3-7) 1923: defeated Walter Hagen, PGA Championship. 1926: lost to Macdonald Smith, Metropolitan Open; lost to Bill Mehlhorn, South Florida Open. 1927: lost to Joe Turnesa, Ridgewood CC Open. 1928: defeated Johnny Farrell, Nassau Bahamas Open. 1930: lost to Leo Diegel, Oregon Open. 1935: defeated Craig Wood, Augusta National Invitational. 1938: lost to Sam Snead, Goodall Round Robin. 1939: lost to Ralph Guldahl, Dapper Dan Open. 1940: lost to Lawson Little, U.S. Open.

SAUERS, Gene-- (1-3) 1986: defeated Blaine McCallister, Bank of Boston Classic. 1991: lost to Mark Brooks, Kmart Greater Greensboro Open. 1992: lost to John Cook, Bob Hope Chrysler Classic. 1994: lost to Dicky Pride, Federal Express St. Jude Classic.

SCHLEE, John-- (0-1) 1973: lost to Ed Sneed, Kaiser International

SCHOUX, George-- (0-1) 1947: lost to Cary Middlecoff, Charlotte Open.

SCHROEDER, John-- (0-1) 1979: lost to Bob Byman, Bay Hill Citrus Classic.

SCHULZ, Ted-- (0-1) 1993: lost to Billy Mayfair, Greater Milwaukee Open.

INDIVIDUAL PLAYOFF RECORDS (continued)

SERAFIN, Felix-- (0-1) 1935: lost to Ted Luther, Hershey Open.

SHEARER, Bob-- (0-1) 1982: lost to Ed Sneed, Michelob-Houston Open.

SHEPPARD, Charles-- (0-1) 1938: lost to Al Zimmerman, Utah Open.

SHUTE, Denny-- (4-3) 1929: lost to Horton Smith, Fort Myers Open. 1933: defeated Willie Macfarlane, Gasparilla Open. 1934: defeated Horton Smith, Gasparilla Open. 1937: defeated Jug McSpaden, PGA Championship. 1939: lost to Byron Nelson, U.S. Open; lost to Ralph Guldahl, Dapper Dan Open; defeated Horton Smith, Glens Falls Open.

SIECKMANN, Tom-- (1-0) 1988: defeated Mark Wiebe, Anheuser-Busch Golf Classic.

SIFFORD, Charles-- (1-0) 1969: defeated Harold Henning, Los Angeles Open.

SIKES, Dan-- (0-2) 1962: lost to Bobby Nichols, Houston Classic. 1973: lost to Lanny Wadkins, Byron Nelson Golf Classic.

SIKES, R.H.-- (0-1) 1969: lost to Dave Hill, IVB-Philadelpha Classic.

SILLS, Tony-- (1-0) 1990: defeated Gil Morgan, Independent Insurance Agent Open.

SIMONS, Jim-- (0-3) 1979: lost to John Fought, Buick Goodwrench Open. 1980: lost to Howard Twitty, Sammy Davis, Jr.-Greater Hartford Open. 1984: lost to John Mahaffey, Bob Hope Desert Classic.

SIMPSON, George-- (0-1) 1911: lost to John McDermott, U.S. Open.

SIMPSON, Scott-- (1-3) 1983: lost to Fred Couples, Kemper Open. 1989: defeated Bob Tway, BellSouth Atlanta Golf Classic. 1991: lost to Payne Stewart, U.S. Open. 1994: lost to Nick Price, Southwestern Bell Colonial.

SIMPSON, Tim-- (0-2) 1989: lost to Mike Donald, Anheuser-Busch Golf Classic. 1990: lost to Greg Norman, Doral-Ryder Open.

SINDELAR, Joey-- (1-1) 1988: lost to Mark Brooks, Canon Sammy Davis, Jr.-Greater Hartford Open. 1990: defeated Willie Wood, Hardee's Golf Classic.

SINGH, Vijay-- (3-0) 1993: defeated Mark Wiebe, Buick Classic. 1995: defeated Billy Mayfair, Phoenix Open; defeated Doug Martin, Buick Classic.

SLUMAN, Jeff-- (0-3) 1987: lost to Sandy Lyle, Tournament Players Championship. 1991: lost to Billy Andrade, Kemper Open. 1992: lost to Mark O'Meara, AT&T Pebble Beach National Pro-Am.

SMITH, Alex-- (1-1) 1901: lost to Willie Anderson, U.S. Open. 1910: defeated John McDermott, Macdonald Smtih, U.S. Open.

SMITH, Horton-- (3-6) 1929: lost to Bill Mehlhorn, South Central Open; defeated Denny Shute, Fort Myers Open. 1934: Lost to Denny Shute, Gasparilla Open. 1937: lost to Harry Cooper, St. Petersburg Open; lost to Ralph Guldahl, Western Open; lost to Leonard Dodson, Hollywood Open. 1939: lost to Denny Shute, Glens Falls Open. 1941: defeated Byron Nelson, Florida West Coast Open.

SMITH, Macdonald-- (3-2) 1910: lost to Alex Smith, U.S. Open. 1923: lost to Joe Kirkwood, Sr., California Open. 1924: defeated Abe Espinosa, Northern California Open. 1926: defeated Gene Sarazen, Metropolitan Open. 1936: defeated Ralph Guldahl, Seattle Open.

SMITH, Willie-- (0-1) 1908: lost to Fred McLeod, U.S. Open.

SNEAD, J.C.-- (3-1) 1971: lost to George Archer, Greater Hartford Open. 1975: defeated Ray Floyd, Bobby Nichols, Andy Williams San Diego Open. 1981: defeated Mike Sullivan, Southern Open. 1987: defeated Seve Ballesteros, Manufacturers Hanover Westchester Classic.

SNEAD, Sam-- (10-8) 1938: defeated Harry Cooper, Canadian Open; defeated Gene Sarazen, Goodall Round Robin. 1939: defeated Henry Picard, St. Petersburg Open. 1940: defeated Harold McSpaden, Canadian Open. 1945: lost to Byron Nelson, Charlotte Open; defeated Byron Nelson, Gulfport Open. 1947; lost to Lew Worsham, U.S. Open. 1948: lost to Lloyd Mangrum, World's Championship of Golf. 1949: defeated Lloyd Mangrum, Greater Greensboro Open. 1950: defeated Ben Hogan, Los Angeles Open; lost to Jim Ferrier, St. Paul Open. 1952: lost to Doug Ford, Jacksonville Open. 1953: lost to Earl Stewart, Greensboro Open. 1954: defeated Ben Hogan, Masters Tournament. 1955: defeated Tommy Bolt, Miami Open. 1956: defeated Fred Wampler, Greater Greensboro Open. 1958: defeated Gary Player, Julius Boros, John McMullin, Dallas Open; lost to George Bayer, Havana International.

SNEED, Ed-- (3-1) 1973: defeated John Schlee, Kaiser International. 1977: defeated Lon Hinkle, Tallahassee Open. 1979: lost to Fuzzy Zoeller, Masters Tournament. 1982: defeated Bob Shearer, Michelob-Houston Open.

SOUCHAK, Mike-- (0-3) 1955: lost to Shelley Mayfield, Thunderbird Invitational. 1957: lost to Jimmy Demaret, Thunderbird Invitational. 1963: lost to Dave Hill, Hot Springs Open.

STADLER, Craig-- (3-2) 1982: defeated Dan Pohl, Masters Tournament; defeated Ray Floyd, World Series of Golf. 1985: lost to Lanny Wadkins, Bob Hope Desert Classic. 1987: lost to Corey Pavin, Hawaiian Open. 1991: defeated Russ Cochran, THE TOUR Championship.

STEELSMITH, Jerry-- (0-2) 1962: lost to Dave Marr, Azalea Open. 1964: lost to Billy Casper, Almaden Open.

STEWART, Jr., Earl-- (1-2) 1953: lost to Cary Middlecoff, Houston Open; defeated Sam Snead, Doug Ford, Art Wall, Greensboro Open. 1954: lost to Tommy Bolt, Insurance City Open.

STEWART, Payne-- (3-5) 1984: lost to Peter Jacobsen, Colonial National Invitation. 1985: lost to Bob Eastwood, Byron Nelson Classic. 1986: lost to Dan Pohl, Colonial National Invitation. 1988: lost to Phil Blackmar, Provident Classic. 1989: lost to Tom Kite, Nabisco Championships. 1990: defeated Steve Jones, Larry Mize, MCI Heritage Classic. 1991: defeated Scott Simpson, U.S. Open. 1995: defeated Scott Hoch, Shell Houston Open.

STILL, Ken-- (1-0) 1970: defeated Lee Trevino, Bert Yancey, Kaiser International.

STOCKTON, Dave-- (0-1) 1977: lost to Jerry Pate, Phoenix Open.

STONEHOUSE, Ralph-- (1-0) 1934: defeated Willie Dow, Miami Open.

STRANAHAN, Frank-- (0-1) 1949: lost to Bobby Locke, Cavalier Specialist Tournament.

STRANGE, Curtis-- (6-3) 1980: defeated Lee Trevino, Michelob Houston Open. 1981: lost to Ray Floyd, Tournament Players Championship. 1983: lost to Gil Morgan, Joe Garagiola-Tucson Open. 1985: defeated Peter Jacobsen, Honda Classic. 1986: defeated Calvin Peete, Houston Open. 1988: defeated Greg Norman, Independent Insurance Agent Open; defeated Nick Faldo, U.S. Open; defeated Tom Kite, Nabisco Championships. 1991: lost to Rocco Mediate, Doral-Ryder Open.

STRECK, Ron-- (0-1) 1985: lost to Woody Blackburn, Isuzu-Andy Williams-San Diego Open.

SULLIVAN, Bud-- (0-1) 1961: lost to Dave Hill, Home of the Sun Open.

SULLIVAN, Mike-- (0-4) 1978: lost to Jack Newton, Buick-Goodwrench Open. 1981: lost to J.C. Snead, Southern Open. 1986: lost to Ray Floyd, Walt Disney World/Oldsmobile Classic. 1994: lost to Brian Henninger, Deposit Guaranty Golf Classic.

SUTTON, Hal-- (2-2) 1982: defeated Bill Britton, Walt Disney World Golf Classic. 1985: defeated David Ogrin, St. Jude Memphis Classic; defeated Mike Reid, Southwest Golf Classic. 1989: lost to Mike Donald, Anheuser-Busch Golf Classic. 1994: lost to Dicky Pride, Federal Express St. Jude Classic.

TEWELL, Doug-- (1-0) 1980: defeated Jerry Pate, Sea Pines Heritage Classic.

THOMPSON, Barney-- (0-1) 1981: lost to John Cook, Bing Crosby National Pro-Am.

THOMSON, Jimmy-- (0-1) 1942: lost to Ben Hogan, Los Angeles Open.

THOMSON, Peter-- (0-1) 1956: defeated Gene Littler, Cary Middlecoff, Texas International Open.

THORPE, Jim-- (0-1) 1985: lost to Scott Verplank, Western Open.

TORRANCE, Sam-- (0-1) 1983: lost to Ronnie Black, Southern Open.

TREVINO, Lee-- (5-5) 1970: defeated Bob Murphy, Tucson Open; defeated Bob Menne, National Airlines Open; lost to Ken Still, Kaiser International. 1971: defeated Jack Nicklaus, U.S. Open; lost to Tom Weiskopf, Kemper Open; defeated Art Wall, Canadian Open. 1972: defeated Lee Elder, Greater Hartford Open. 1978: lost to Andy Bean, Danny Thomas-Memphis Classic; lost to Lee Elder, Greater Milwaukee Open. 1980: lost to Curtis Strange, Michelob Houston Open.

TROMBLEY, Bill-- (0-1) 1956: lost to Art Wall, Ft. Wayne Open.

TWAY, Bob-- (3-3) 1986: defeated Bernhard Langer, Shearson Lehman Brothers-Andy Williams Open. 1988: lost to Steve Jones, AT&T Pebble Beach National Pro-Am; lost to David Frost, Southern Open. 1989: lost to Scott Simpson, BellSouth Atlanta Golf Classic. 1990: defeated John Cook, Las Vegas Inviational. 1995: defeated Nolan Henke, David Frost, MCI Classic.

TWITTY, Howard-- (1-0) 1980: defeated Jim Simons, Sammy Davis, Jr.-Greater Hartford Open.

TURNESA, Jim-- (0-1) 1952: lost to Jimmy Clark, Ft. Wayne Open.

TURNESA, Joe-- (2-1) 1927: defeated Gene Sarazen, Ridgewood CC Open. 1929: defeated Massie Miller, Lannin Memorial Tournament. 1931: lost to Wiffy Cox, North & South Open.

ULOZAS, Tom-- (0-1) 1972: lost to Bert Yancey, American Golf Classic.

UNDERWOOD, Hal-- (0-1) 1971: lost to Gary Player, Greater Jacksonville Open.

VALENTINE, Tommy-- (0-1) 1981: lost to Tom Watson, Atlanta Classic.

VARDON, Harry-- (0-1) 1913: lost to Francis Ouimet, U.S. Open.

VENTURI, Ken-- (0-3) 1957: lost to Jimmy Demaret, Thunderbird Invitational. 1958: lost to Billy Casper, Greater New Orleans Open. 1961: lost to Jay Hebert, Houston Classic.

VERPLANK, Scott-- (1-0) 1985: defeated Jim Thorpe, Western Open.

VON ELM, George-- (0-2) 1931: lost to John Golden, Agua Caliente Open. 1931: lost to Billy Burke, U.S. Open.

WADKINS, Bobby-- (0-2) 1979: lost to Lou Graham, IVB-Philadelphia Classic. 1985: lost to Bernhard Langer, Sea Pines Heritage Classic.

WADKINS, Lanny-- (3-3) 1972: lost to Homero Blancas, Phoenix Open. 1973: defeated Dan Sikes, Byron Nelson Golf Classic. 1977: defeated Gene Littler, PGA Championship. 1983: lost to Gil Morgan, Joe Garagiola-Tucson Open. 1985: defeated Craig Stadler, Bob Hope Desert Classic. 1987: lost to Larry Nelson, PGA Championship.

WALL, Art-- (5-5) 1953: lost to Earl Stewart, Greensboro Open; defeated Cary Middlecoff, Ft. Wayne Open. 1956: defeated Bill Trombley, Gardner Dickinson, Jr., Ft. Wayne Open. 1958: defeated Dow Finsterwald, Rubber City Open; defeated Jack Burke, Jr., Bob Rosburg, Eastern Open. 1959: defeated Dow Finsterwald, Buick Open. 1960: lost to Stan Leonard, Western Open. 1962: lost to BobGoalby, Insurance City Open. 1967: lost to Billy Casper, Canadian Open. 1971: lost to Lee Trevino, Canadian Open.

WAMPLER, Fred-- (0-1) 1956: lost to Sam Snead, Greater Greensboro Open.

WATSON, Denis-- (0-1) 1982: lost to Tom Kite, Bay Hill Classic.

WATSON, Tom-- (8-4) 1978: defeated Ben Crenshaw, Bing Crosby National Pro-Am; lost to John Mahaffey, PGA Championship. 1979: lost to Fuzzy Zoeller, Masters Tournament; defeated Bill Rogers, Byron Nelson Classic; defeated Johnny Miller, Colgate Hall of Fame Classic. 1980: defeated D.A. Weibring, Andy Williams-San Diego Open. 1981: lost to Bruce Lietzke, Byron Nelson Classic; defeated Tommy Valentine, Atlanta Classic. 1982: defeated Johnny Miller, Glen Campbell Los Angeles Open; defeated Frank Conner, Sea Pines Heritage Classic. 1984: defeated Greg Norman, Western Open. 1988: lost to Mike Reid, NEC World Series of Golf.

WEAVER, DeWitt-- (1-0) 1972: defeated Chuck Courtney, Southern Open.

WEIBRING, D.A.-- (0-2) 1980: lost to Tom Watson, Andy Williams-San Diego Open. 1991: lost to Andrew Magee, Las Vegas Invitational.

WEISKOPF, Tom-- (2-3) 1966: lost to Doug Sanders, Greater Greensboro Open. 1969: lost to Gene Littler, Greater Greensboro Open. 1971: defeated Dale Douglass, Gary Player, Lee Trevino, Kemper Open. 1975: defeated Jack Nicklaus, Canadian Open. 1979: lost to Ed Fiori, Southern Open.

WHITE, Buck-- (0-1) 1943: lost to Harold McSpaden, All American Open.

WHITT, Don-- (1-1) 1957: lost to Dow Finsterwald, Tucson Open. 1959: defeated Gary Player, Al Balding, Memphis Open.

WIEBE, Mark-- (1-2) 1985: defeated John Mahaffey, Anheuser-Busch Golf Classic. 1988: lost to Tom Sieckmann, Anheuser-Busch Golf Classic. 1993: lost to Vijay Singh, Buick Classic.

WIECHERS, Jim-- (0-1) 1969: lost to Bob Goalby, Robinson Open.

WININGER, BO-- (1-1) 1955: defeated Jimmy Clark, Billy Maxwell, Baton Rouge Open. 1960: lost to Johnny Pott, Dallas Open.

WOOD, Craig-- (0-4) 1932: lost to John Golden, North & South Open. 1934: lost to Paul Runyan, PGA Championship. 1935: lost to Gene Sarazen, Augusta National Invitational. 1939: lost to Byron Nelson, U.S. Open.

WOOD, Willie-- (0-1) 1990: lost to Joey Sindelar, Hardee's Golf Classic.

WOOSNAM, Ian-- (1-0) 1991: defeated Jim Hallet, USF&G Classic.

WORSHAM, Lew-- (1-2) 1946: lost to Herman Barron, Philadelphia Inquirer Open. 1947: lost to Clayton Heafner, Jacksonville Open. 1947: defeated Sam Snead, U.S. Open.

WRENN, Robert-- (0-1) 1989: lost to Scott Hoch, Las Vegas Invitational.

WYSONG, Dudley-- (1-1) 1965: lost to Babe Hiskey, Cajun Classic. 1967: defeated Billy Casper, Hawaiian Open.

YANCEY, Bert-- (2-2) 1969: defeated Bruce Devlin, Atlanta Classic. 1970: lost to Ken Still, Kaiser International. 1971: lost to Labron Harris, Jr., Robinson Open. 1972: defeated Tom Ulozas, American Golf Classic.

ZARLEY, Kermit-- (0-1) 1976: lost to Hale Irwin, Florida Citrus Open.

ZIEGLER, Larry-- (1-1) 1969: defeated Homero Blancas, Michigan Golf Classic. 1972: lost to Lou Graham, Liggett and Myers Open.

ZIMMERMAN, Al-- (1-0) 1938: defeated Tee Branca, Charles Sheppard, Utah Open.

ZOELLER, Fuzzy-- (2-2) 1979: defeated Ed Sneed, Tom Watson, Masters Tournament. 1983: lost to Jim Colbert, Colonial National Invitation. 1984: defeated Greg Norman, U.S. Open. 1994: lost to Mark McCumber, THE TOUR Championship.

PGA TOUR FACTS AND FIGURES (1970-95)

LOW 9:

1995 --	28 (7-under)	Brad Faxon, PGA Championship
	29 (7-under)	Jim Gallagher, Jr., Mark Brooks, Kenny Perry, Bob Hope Chrysler Classic; Jay Delsing, FedEx St. Jude Classic; Dave Stockton, Jr., Brad Bryant, Walt Disney World/Oldsmobile Golf Classic.
	30 (7-under)	Hal Sutton, B.C. Open.
1994 --	29 (7 under)	Davis Love III, Hawaiian; Lennie Clements, Bob Hope; Ronnie Black, Buick Invitational; Larry Nelson, Doral-Ryder; Dennis Paulson, Freeport-McMoRan; Brian Henninger, New England.
	29 (6 under)	Steve Lamontagne, Honda; Guy Boros, Southwestern Bell Colonial.
	29 (5 under)	Glen Day, B.C. Open.
1993 --	28 (7 under)	Keith Clearwater, Wayne Levi, Southwestern Bell Colonial.
	29 (7 under)	Fuzzy Zoeller, Tom Kite, Bob Hope; Greg Norman, Buick Open; Dan Halldorson, Milwaukee.
1992 --	29 (7 under)	Gil Morgan, Neal Lancaster, Bob Hope; Greg Norman, Buick Open; Mark Calcavecchia, Masters, Jim McGovern, Federal Express; John Cook, Las Vegas.
	29 (6 under)	Dillard Pruitt, Phoenix; Robin Freeman, Byron Nelson; David Frost, Hardee's; Donnie Hammond, David Edwards, Texas.
1991 --	28 (7 under)	Andrew Magee, Los Angeles.
	28 (6 under)	Emlyn Aubrey, Chattanooga.
1990 --	28 (7 under)	Kenny Knox, Chattanooga.
	29 (7 under)	Tom Kite, Bob Hope.
	29 (6 under)	David Frost, Tucson; Mike Hulbert, Colonial; Kirk Triplett, Buick Classic; Howard Twitty, David Peoples, Southern; Steve Jones, Billy Ray Brown, John Dowdall, Texas.
	29 (5 under)	Chris Perry, Brad Fabel, Canon GHO.
1989 --	28 (8 under)	Steve Pate, Bob Hope; Webb Heintzelman, Las Vegas.
1988 --	28 (7 under)	Mike Sullivan, Texas.
	29 (7 under)	Sandy Lyle, Pebble Beach; Dave Eichelberger, Hawaiian; Gil Morgan, Andy Williams; Ken Green, Milwaukee; Mike Donald, Walt Disney; Mark Wiebe, Ken Green,Tucson.
1987 --	29 (7 under)	Dewey Arnette, Trevor Dodds, Buick.
	30 (7 under)	Joey Sindelar, B.C. Open.
	29 (6 under)	Payne Stewart, Phoenix; David Frost, Andy Williams; Wayne Levi, Hartford; Curtis Strange, Anheuser-Busch; Dave Rummells, Dave Stockton, Hardee's; Robert Thompson, Provident.
1986 --	29 (7 under)	Hubert Green, Doral; Mike Sullivan, Houston; Charles Bolling, Las Vegas.
	29 (6 under)	Willie Wood, Westchester; Mike Smith, Hardee's; Mike Donald, Southern.
1985 --	29 (7 under)	Jim Thorpe, Milwaukee.
	29 (6 under)	John Mahaffey, Bob Hope; Larry Mize, Los Angeles; Tom Watson, Colonial; Roger Maltbie, Westchester; Brad Fabel, Quad Cities; Mike Gove, Texas; Ken Brown, Pensacola.
1984 --	29 (6 under)	George Burns, Colonial; Mike McCullough, Canadian; Mark O'Meara, Hartford.
	30 (6 under)	Gibby Gilbert, Bob Hope; Willie Wood, Phoenix; Greg Norman, Bay Hill; David Graham, T of C; Payne Stewart, Memorial; Tom Kite, Westchester; Tommy Valentine, Mike Donald, Atlanta; Gary Player, PGA; Rod Nuckolls, Steve Brady, Denis Watson, Buick; Lon Hinkle, Scott Simpson, Las Vegas; George Archer, Bank of Boston; Mark Lye, Larry Rinker, Walt Disney.
1983 --	28 (7 under)	Jeff Sluman, Quad Cities.
	28 (6 under)	Mark O'Meara, B.C. Open.
	29 (7 under)	Hubert Green, Bob Hope; Craig Stadler, Buick.
	29 (6 under)	Jon Chaffee, Rick Pearson, Quad Cities; Gibby Gilbert, PGA; Lanny Wadkins, Anheuser-Busch; George Cadle, Jim Colbert, Texas; Gary Hallberg, Pensacola.
1982 --	29 (7 under)	George Burns, Hartford.
	29 (6 under)	Scott Hoch, Houston; Gary Koch, Bob Eastwood, Allen Miller, Quad Cities; Fred Couples, PGA; Isao Aoki, Hartford.
1981 --	29 (6 under)	Mike Holland, Anheuser-Busch; Fuzzy Zoeller, Hartford; Bob Gilder, Southern.
1980 --	29 (7 under)	Bob Murphy, Tallahassee; Curtis Strange, Houston; John Fought, Buick.
	29 (6 under)	Gary Koch, Byron Nelson.
1979 --	29 (7 under)	Kermit Zarley, Doral-Eastern; Andy Bean, Atlanta.
	29 (6 under)	Pat McGowan, Phoenix; Brad Bryant, Quad Cities; Allen Miller, Hartford.
1978 --	29 (7 under)	Gary Koch, Houston.
	29 (6 under)	Rod Funseth, Hartford; Ron Streck, Texas.
	29 (5 under)	Rod Curl, B.C. Open.
1977 --	29 (7 under)	Graham Marsh, T of C; Bobby Wadkins, Memorial; Al Geiberger, Memphis; Lanny Wadkins, Milwaukee; Rik Massengale, Pleasant Valley; Florentino Molina, Hartford; Leonard Thompson, Hall of Fame.
	29 (6 under)	Fred Marti, Pleasant Valley; Rod Curl, IVB; Bruce Lietzke, Hartford; Tom Weiskopf, World Series.
1976 --	28 (8 under)	Jim Colbert, Bob Hope; Fuzzy Zoeller, Quad Cities.
1975 --	27 (7 under)	Andy North, B.C. Open.
	28 (7 under)	Bruce Crampton, Sahara.
	29 (7 under)	Hale Irwin, Phoenix; Tom Weiskopf, Westchester.
	29 (6 under)	Jim Simons, Hartford.

LOW 9 (cont'd.):

1974 --	29 (7 under)	Tom Kite, Doral-Eastern; Dan Sikes, New Orleans; Tom Watson, Hartford.
	29 (6 under)	Raymond Floyd, American Classic.
1973 --	28 (7 under)	Bert Yancey, American Classic.
1972 --	29 (7 under)	Babe Hiskey, Inverrary; Bert Yancey, Walt Disney.
	29 (7 under)	Dwight Nevil, Southern; Cesar Sanudo, Sahara.
1971 --	28 (7 under)	Jim Jamieson, Robinson.
1970 --	29 (6 under)	Dave Hill, Cleveland; George Knudson, Robinson; Wilf Homenuik, Azalea.
	29 (5 under)	Lou Graham, Memphis.

LOW 18:

1995 --	61 (10-under)	Hal Sutton, B.C. Open
	61 (9-under)	Ernie Els, GTE Byron Nelson Classic
	62 (10-under)	Jim Furyk, Buick Open; Carl Paulson, Walt Disney World/Oldsmobile Golf Classic.
	62 (9-under)	Kenny Perry, Nissan Open.
1994 --	60 (12 under)	Davis Love III, Hawaiian.
1993 --	61 (10 under)	Jay Delsing, Federal Express.
	61 (9 under)	Billy Mayfair, Byron Nelson; Keith Clearwater, Lee Janzen, Colonial.
1992 --	62 (10 under)	David Love III, Kmart GGO; Fred Funk, Houston; John Cook, Las Vegas; Lee Janzen, John Huston, Walt Disney.
	62 (8 under)	David Frost, Hardee's; Nick Price, Texas.
1991 --	59 (13 under)	Chip Beck, Las Vegas.
1990 --	60 (12 under)	David Frost, Tucson.
1989 --	61 (11 under)	Jim Carter, Centel; Bob Tway, Walt Disney.
1988 --	61 (11 under)	Ken Green, Milwaukee; Mark Wiebe, Tucson.
	61 (9 under)	Dave Barr, Southern.
1987 --	61 (11 under)	David Edwards, Bob Hope.
	61 (9 under)	Mike Smith, Hardee's.
1986 --	61 (10 under)	Don Pooley, Phoenix.
	61 (9 under)	Rod Curl, Southern.
	62 (10 under)	George Burns, Las Vegas; Greg Norman, Canadian.
1985 --	62 (10 under)	Jim Thorpe, Milwaukee.
	62 (9 under)	Larry Mize, Los Angeles; Jay Delsing, B.C. Open.
	62 (8 under)	Bill Glasson, Las Vegas; Ron Streck, Quad Cities.
1984 --	61 (11 under)	Mark Lye, Walt Disney.
1983 --	61 (10 under)	George Archer, Los Angeles.
	62 (10 under)	John Fought, Bob Hope; Tom Kite, Bing Crosby
	62 (9 under)	Andy Bean, Canadian; Curtis Strange, Hartford.
	62 (8 under)	Jon Chaffee, Quad Cities; Craig Stadler, Jim Colbert, Texas.
1982 --	61 (10 under)	Dana Quigley, Hartford.
	61 (9 under)	Hale Irwin, Southern.
	62 (10 under)	Larry Rinker, Tallahassee.
1981 --	62 (10 under)	Nick Faldo, Hale Irwin, Hawaiian.
	62 (9 under)	Andy Bean, Bay Hill; Ron Streck, Houston; Leonard Thompson, Canadian; Mark O'Meara, Hartford.
1980 --	62 (9 under)	Jim Simons, Hartford.
	62 (8 under)	George Burns, Texas.
	63 (9 under)	Andy Bean, Hawaiian; Bob Shearer, Atlanta; Bob Mann, Pensacola.
1979 --	61 (11 under)	Jerry McGee, Kemper; Andy Bean, Atlanta.
	61 (10 under)	Ben Crenshaw, Phoenix.
1978 --	62 (10 under)	Dave Eichelberger, Atlanta.
	62 (9 under)	Joe Inman, Hartford.
	62 (8 under)	Hubert Green, Ron Streck, San Antonio.
1977 --	59 (13 under)	Al Geiberger, Memphis.
1976 --	62 (10 under)	Gary Player, Florida Citrus.
1975 --	61 (11 under)	Johnny Miller, Tucson.
	61 (10 under)	Johnny Miller, Phoenix.
1974 --	61 (11 under)	Bert Yancey, Bob Hope.
1973 --	62 (9 under)	Jack Nicklaus, Ohio Kings Island; Gibby Gilbert, Tom Watson, World Open.
	62 (8 under)	J.C. Snead, Phoenix.
	63 (9 under)	Dave Stockton, Milwaukee; Hubert Green, Disney.
	63 (8 under)	Johnny Miller, U.S. Open; Hubert Green (twice), Hartford; John Schroeder, Quad Cities.
	63 (7 under)	Dick Rhyan, Southern.
1972 --	61 (10 under)	Homero Blancas, Phoenix.
1971 --	62 (9 under)	Billy Casper, Phoenix; Charles Coody, Cleveland.
	62 (8 under)	Larry Ziegler, Dave Eichelberger, Memphis; Bobby Mitchell, Southern.
1970 --	61 (10 under)	Johnny Miller, Phoenix.

PGA TOUR FACTS AND FIGURES (1970-95) *...continued*

LOW FIRST 18:

1995 --	62 (10-under)	Carl Paulson, Walt Disney World/Oldsmobile Golf Classic.
	62 (9-under)	Glen Day, Mike Standly, FedEx St. Jude Classic.
1994 --	61 (10 under)	Bob Lohr, Anheuser-Busch.
1993 --	62 (9 under)	Mike Sith, Texas.
	63 (9 under)	Howard Twitty, Hawaiian; Billy Andrade, Northern Telecom.
	63 (8 under)	Jim Gallagher, Jr., TOUR Championship.
	63 (7 under)	Jeff Woodland, Hardee's.
1992 --	62 (10 under)	Lee Janzen, Walt Disney.
	62 (8 under)	David Frost, Hardee's.
1991 --	61 (11 under)	Robert Gamez, Milwaukee.
	61 (9 under)	Marco Dawson, Chattanooga.
1990 --	61 (9 under)	Jose Maria Olazabal, World Series.
	62 (10 under)	Pat McGowan, Tucson.
	62 (9 under)	Larry Silveira, Federal Express.
	62 (8 under)	Howard Twitty, Southern.
1989 --	61 (11 under)	Bob Tway, Walt Disney.
1988 --	62 (10 under)	Bob Lohr, Walt Disney.
1987 --	61 (11 under)	David Edwards, Bob Hope.
1986 --	62 (8 under)	Ernie Gonzalez, Deposit Guaranty.
	63 (9 under)	George Burns, Hawaiian.
	63 (8 under)	Hubert Green, Phoenix.
	63 (7 under)	Bob Lohr, Hardee's.
1985 --	62 (8 under)	Bill Glasson, Las Vegas.
	63 (9 under)	Fred Couples, Honda; John Mahaffey, USF&G.
	63 (8 under)	Lanny Wadkins, Los Angeles; Mac O'Grady, Byron Nelson; John Cook, Pensacola.
1984 --	62 (9 under)	Lon Hinkle, Las Vegas.
1983 --	62 (8 under)	Craig Stadler, Texas.
	63 (9 under)	Craig Stadler, Bob Hope, Fuzzy Zoeller, Las Vegas.
	63 (8 under)	Mark O'Meara, B.C. Open, Mark Lye, Pensacola.
	63 (7 under)	Tom Byrum, Quad Cities.
1982 --	62 (10 under)	Larry Rinker, Tallahassee.
1981 --	63 (8 under)	Lon Nielsen, Hartford.
	63 (7 under)	Dan Halldorson, Tucson; Craig Stadler, Texas.
	64 (8 under)	Skip Dunaway, USF&G.
	64 (7 under)	Tom Watson, Bay Hill; Calvin Peete, B.C. Open.
1980 --	62 (9 under)	Jim Simons, Hartford.
	63 (9 under)	Bob Shearer, Atlanta.
	63 (7 under)	Bruce Lietzke, Colonial; Jack Nicklaus, Tom Weiskopf, U.S. Open; Scott Hoch, Quad Cities.
1979 --	61 (11 under)	Jerry McGee, Greensboro.
1978 --	62 (10 under)	Dave Eichelberger, Atlanta.
	62 (8 under)	Hubert Green, Texas.
1977 --	63 (8 under)	J.C. Snead, Hall of Fame.
	63 (7 under)	Charles Coody, Texas.
	64 (8 under)	Rik Massengale, Bob Hope; George Burns, Buick.
	64 (7 under)	Fred Marti, Pleasant Valley; Lee Elder, Hartford.
	64 (6 under)	Jerry Pate, Southern.
1976 --	63 (9 under)	Johnny Miller, Kaiser International.
	63 (8 under)	Fuzzy Zoeller, Quad Cities; David Graham, Carlton White, Westchester; Buddy Allin, B.C. Open.
	64 (8 under)	Rod Curl, Hawaiian; Ken Still, Milwaukee.
1975 --	63 (8 under)	Andy North, B.C. Open; Miller Barber, Sahara.
	64 (8 under)	Johnny Miller, Bob Hope; Bob Stanton, Inverrary.
	64 (7 under)	Tom Weiskopf, Greensboro; Andy North, Pensacola; Dennis Meyer, Hartford.
1974 --	62 (10 under)	Johnny Miller, Tucson.
1973 --	62 (9 under)	Gibby Gilbert, World Open.
	62 (8 under)	J.C. Snead, Phoenix.
	63 (8 under)	Hubert Green, Hartford.
	64 (8 under)	Jack Nicklaus, Bob Hope; Gibby Gilbert, Chi Chi Rodriguez, Florida Citrus; Lee Trevino, Doral-Eastern; Tom Weiskopf, Westchester.
1972 --	63 (8 under)	Bert Yancey, Hartford.
	64 (8 under)	DeWitt Weaver, Westchester.
	64 (7 under)	Dave Hill, Monsanto.
	64 (6 under)	Deane Beman, St. Louis.
1971 --	63 (9 under)	Joel Goldstrand, Hartford.
1970 --	63 (7 under)	Dave Hill, Memphis.
	64 (8 under)	Arnold Palmer, Florida Citrus; Bob Menne, National Airlines.
	64 (7 under)	Bert Greene, Phoenix; Arnold Palmer, Tommy Aaron, Greensboro; Tommy Aaron, Sahara.

LOW FIRST 36:

1995 --	127 (15-under)	Jim Gallagher, Jr., FedEx St. Jude Classic.
1994 --	127 (15 under)	Bob Estes, Texas.
	128 (16 under)	Davis Love III, Hawaiian; Scott Hoch, Bob Hope.
1993 --	129 (15 under)	Blaine McCallister, Houston.
	129 (11 under)	Dan Forsman, Byron Nelson; Fulton Allem, Colonial.
1992 --	128 (14 under)	Roger Maltbie, Texas.
	130 (10 under)	David Frost, Hardee's.
	130 (12 under)	Davis Love III, Los Angeles; Dan Forsman, Federal Express.
	131 (13 under)	Tom Watson, Brad Faxon, Mike Springer, Buick Invitational.
1991 --	127 (17 under)	Robert Gamez, Milwaukee.
	127 (13 under)	Lennie Clements, Chattanooga.
1990 --	128 (16 under)	Tim Simpson, Walt Disney.
	128 (12 under)	Jose Maria Olazabal, World Series; Peter Persons, Chattanooga; Steve Jones, Texas.
1989 --	126 (14 under)	Paul Azinger, Texas.
	128 (16 under)	Dan Pohl, Honda.
1988 --	127 (13 under)	Corey Pavin, Texas.
	129 (15 under)	Jeff Sluman, Greensboro; Larry Nelson, Atlanta; Bob Lohr, Disney.
1987 --	128 (16 under)	Robert Wrenn, Buick.
	128 (14 under)	Joey Sindelar, B.C. Open.
1986 --	128 (12 under)	Hal Sutton, Phoenix; Ernie Gonzalez, Pensacola.
1985 --	128 (12 under)	Tim Simpson, Southern.
1984 --	130 (14 under)	Chip Beck, Walt Disney.
	130 (11 under)	Lon Hinkle, Las Vegas.
	130 (10 under)	Jim Colbert, Texas.
1983 --	128 (12 under)	Jim Colbert, Texas.
	129 (15 under)	Craig Stadler, Bob Hope.
1982 --	127 (15 under)	Tim Norris, Hartford.
	127 (13 under)	Bob Gilder, Westchester.
1981 --	129 (13 under)	Lon Nielsen, Hartford.
1980 --	129 (13 under)	Curtis Strange, Houston.
	129 (11 under)	Scott Hoch, Quad Cities.
	131 (13 under)	Tom Watson, T of C.
	131 (9 under)	Mike Sullivan, Southern.
1979 --	128 (14 under)	Ben Crenshaw, Phoenix.
1978 --	128 (14 under)	Phil Hancock, Hartford.
	128 (12 under)	Ben Crenshaw, Texas.
1977 --	127 (15 under)	Hale Irwin, Hall of Fame.
1976 --	130 (12 under)	Roger Maltbie, Phoenix; Buddy Allin, B.C. Open; Rik Massengale, Hartford.
	131 (13 under)	Raymond Floyd, Masters.
	132 (12 under)	Fuzzy Zoeller, Milwaukee.
1975 --	128 (14 under)	Johnny Miller, Phoenix.
	129 (15 under)	Tom Weiskopf, Westchester.
	129 (13 under)	Jack Nicklaus, Heritage.
1974 --	130 (12 under)	Dave Stockton, Hartford.
	132 (12 under)	Jack Nicklaus, Hawaiian; Hubert Green, Memphis.
1973 --	129 (11 under)	J.C. Snead, Phoenix.
	131 (13 under)	Buddy Allin, Florida Citrus.
	131 (11 under)	Jim Wiechers, Hartford.
	133 (11 under)	John Schlee, Kaiser International.
1972 --	131 (13 under)	Dwight Nevil, Westchester.
	131 (9 under)	Deane Beman, St. Louis.
1971 --	129 (13 under)	Miller Barber, Paul Harney, Gene Littler, Phoenix.
1970 --	130 (12 under)	Bobby Mitchell, Azalea.

LOW FIRST 54 HOLES:

1995 --	195 (18-under)	Jim Gallagher, Jr., FedEx St. Jude Classic.
	195 (18-under)	Fred Funk, Ideon Classic
	195 (15-under)	Ernie Els, GTE Byron Nelson Classic.
	196 (20-under)	Harry Taylor, Bob Hope Chrysler Classic.
1994 --	195 (18 under)	Bob Estes, Texas.
	197 (19 under)	Lennie Clements, Bob Hope; Greg Norman, PLAYERS.
1993 --	195 (21 under)	Greg Norman, Doral-Ryder.
	195 (15 under)	David Frost, Hardee's.
1992 --	194 (16 under)	David Frost, Hardee's.
	196 (20 under)	Ted Schulz, Mark O'Meara, Walt Disney.
	197 (16 under)	Nick Price, Texas.
1991 --	195 (18 under)	Hal Sutton, Kemper.
	195 (15 under)	Lance Ten Broeck, Chattanooga.
	196 (20 under)	Chip Beck, Bruce Lietzke, Las Vegas.
1990 --	193 (23 under)	Tim Simpson, Walt Disney.
	193 (17 under)	Peter Persons, Chattanooga.

LOW FIRST 54 (cont'd.):

1989 --	194 (16 under)	John Daly, Chattanooga; Donnie Hammond, Texas.
	197 (19 under)	Gene Sauers, Hawaiian.
1988 --	193 (17 under)	Blaine McCallister, Hardee's; Corey Pavin, Texas.
1987 --	195 (21 under)	Robert Wrenn, Buick.
1986 --	196 (17 under)	Hal Sutton, Phoenix.
	196 (14 under)	Ben Crenshaw, Vantage.
	199 (17 under)	Calvin Peete, T of C.
1985 --	197 (13 under)	Jodie Mudd, Texas; Tim Simpson, Southern.
	198 (18 under)	Craig Stadler, Bob Hope; Mark O'Meara, Hawaiian; Woody Blackburn, San Diego.
1984 --	196 (20 under)	Larry Nelson, Walt Disney.
1983 --	194 (16 under)	Jim Colbert, Texas.
	198 (15 under)	Jack Renner, Hartford.
	199 (17 under)	Craig Stadler, Bob Hope.
1982 --	192 (18 under)	Bob Gilder, Westchester.
	193 (20 under)	Tim Norris, Hartford.
1981 --	196 (20 under)	Bruce Lietzke, Bob Hope; Hale Irwin, Hawaiian.
1980 --	195 (18 under)	Curtis Strange, Houston.
	200 (19 under)	Jim Colbert, Tucson.
1979 --	197 (16 under)	Wayne Levi, Houston.
	197 (13 under)	Doug Tewell, Texas.
	198 (18 under)	Hubert Green, Hawaiian; Andy Bean, Atlanta.
1978 --	198 (18 under)	Andy Bean, Houston.
	198 (12 under)	Ben Crenshaw, Texas.
1977 --	196 (17 under)	Bill Kratzert, Hartford; Hale Irwin, Hall of Fame.
1976 --	200 (16 under)	J.C. Snead, San Diego.
	200 (13 under)	Roger Maltbie, Phoenix; Al Geiberger, Greensboro; Rik Massengale, J.C. Snead, Hartford.
	200 (10 under)	Lee Trevino, Colonial.
1975 --	196 (17 under)	Johnny Miller, Phoenix.
1974 --	198 (18 under)	Terry Diehl, Texas.
1973 --	198 (18 under)	Buddy Allin, Florida Citrus.
1972 --	198 (12 under)	Deane Beman, St. Louis.
	201 (15 under)	George Knudson, Kaiser International.
1971 --	194 (19 under)	Paul Harney, Phoenix.
1970 --	198 (15 under)	Bob Murphy, Hartford; Bobby Mitchell, Azalea.
	198 (12 under)	Homero Blancas, Memphis.

LOW FIRST 72:

1995 --	263 (17-under)	Ernie Els, GTE Byron Nelson Classic.
	268 (20-under)	Duffy Waldorf, LaCantera Texas Open.
	264 (23-under)	Billy Mayfair, Jim Furyk, Las Vegas Invitational.
	265 (23-under)	Kenny Perry, Bob Hope.
1994 --	264 (24 under)	Scott Hoch, Bob Hope; Greg Norman, PLAYERS.
1993 --	259 (21 under)	David Frost, Hardee's.
	263 (25 under)	Tom Kite, Bob Hope.
1992 --	262 (26 under)	John Huston, Walt Disney.
1991 --	260 (20 under)	Dillard Pruitt, Chattanooga.
	263 (21 under)	Billy Andrade, Jeff Sluman, Kemper.
	263 (25 under)	Bruce Lietzke, Craig Stadler, D.A. Weibring, Andrew Magee, Las Vegas.
1990 --	260 (20 under)	Peter Persons, Chattanooga.
	264 (24 under)	Bob Tway, Las Vegas; Tim Simpson, Walt Disney.
1989 --	258 (22 under)	Donnie Hammond, Texas.
	266 (22 under)	Blaine McCallister, Honda; Scott Hoch, Las Vegas.
1988 --	259 (21 under)	Corey Pavin, Texas.
	262 (26 under)	Chip Beck, USF&G.
1987 --	262 (26 under)	Robert Wrenn, Buick.
1986 --	267 (21 under)	Calvin Peete, T of C.
	267 (17 under)	Hal Sutton, Phoenix; Rick Fehr, B.C. Open.
1985 --	264 (20 under)	Lanny Wadkins, Los Angeles.
	264 (16 under)	Tim Simpson, Southern.
	267 (21 under)	Mark O'Meara, Hawaiian; Lanny Wadkins, Disney World.
1984 --	265 (15 under)	Hubert Green, Southern.
	266 (22 under)	Larry Nelson, Disney World.
1983 --	261 (19 under)	Jim Colbert, Texas.
	266 (18 under)	Mark McCumber, Pensacola.
	267 (20 under)	Fuzzy Zoeller, Las Vegas.
	268 (20 under)	Isao Aoki, Hawaiian.
1982 --	259 (25 under)	Tim Norris, Hartford.
1981 --	264 (20 under)	Hubert Green, Hartford.
	265 (23 under)	Hale Irwin, Hawaiian.
	265 (15 under)	Johnny Miller, Tucson.

PGA TOUR FACTS AND FIGURES (1970-95) *...continued*

LOW FIRST 72 (cont'd.):

1980 -- 265 (15 under) Lee Trevino, Texas.
266 (22 under) Andy Bean, Hawaiian; Bill Kratzert, Milwaukee.
270 (22 under) Jim Colbert, Tucson.
266 (18 under) Curtis Strange, Lee Trevino, Houston; Howard Twitty, Jim Simons, Hartford.
1979 -- 265 (23 under) Andy Bean, Atlanta.
1978 -- 264 (24 under) Rod Funseth, Hartford.
1977 -- 264 (20 under) Hale Irwin, Hall of Fame.
1976 -- 266 (18 under) Rik Massengale, Hartford.
268 (16 under) Bob Gilder, Phoenix; Al Geiberger, Greensboro; John Lister, Quad Cities.
269 (19 under) Jack Nicklaus, TPC.
1975 -- 260 (24 under) Johnny Miller, Phoenix.
263 (25 under) Johnny Miller, Tucson.
1974 -- 267 (21 under) Lee Trevino, New Orleans.
1973 -- 264 (20 under) Billy Casper, Hartford.
265 (23 under) Buddy Allin, Florida Citrus.
1972 -- 267 (21 under) Jack Nicklaus, Walt Disney.
1971 -- 261 (23 under) Miller Barber, Phoenix.
1970 -- 267 (17 under) Bob Murphy, Hartford.
267 (13 under) Dave Hill, Memphis.

LOW 90:

1995 -- 331 (28-under) Jim Furyk, Las Vegas.
1994 -- 332 (27 under) Bruce Lietzke, Las Vegas.
1993 -- 325 (35 under) Tom Kite, Bob Hope.
1992 -- 336 (24 under) John Cook, Gene Sauers, Rick Fehr, Mark O'Meara, Tom Kite, Bob Hope.
1991 -- 329 (31 under) Andrew Magee, D.A. Weibring, Las Vegas.
1990 -- 334 (26 under) Bob Tway, Las Vegas.
1989 -- 336 (24 under) Scott Hoch, Robert Wrenn, Las Vegas.
1988 -- 338 (22 under) Jay Haas, Bob Hope.
1987 -- 341 (19 under) Corey Pavin, Bob Hope.
1986 -- 333 (27 under) Greg Norman, Las Vegas.
1985 -- 333 (27 under) Lanny Wadkins, Bob Hope.
1984 -- 340 (20 under) John Mahaffey, Jim Simons, Bob Hope.
1983 -- 335 (25 under) Keith Fergus, Rex Caldwell, Bob Hope.
1982 -- 335 (25 under) Ed Fiori, Bob Hope.
1981 -- 335 (25 under) Bruce Lietzke, Bob Hope.
1980 -- 343 (17 under) Craig Stadler, Bob Hope.
1979 -- 343 (17 under) John Mahaffey, Bob Hope.
1978 -- 339 (21 under) Bill Rogers, Bob Hope.
1977 -- 337 (23 under) Rik Massengale, Bob Hope.
1976 -- 344 (16 under) Johnny Miller, Bob Hope.
1975 -- 339 (21 under) Johnny Miller, Bob Hope.
1974 -- 341 (19 under) Hubert Green, Bob Hope.
1973 -- 343 (17 under) Arnold Palmer, Bob Hope.
1972 -- 344 (16 under) Bob Rosburg, Bob Hope.
1971 -- 342 (18 under) Arnold Palmer, Bob Hope.
1970 -- 339 (21 under) Bruce Devlin, Bob Hope.

HIGHEST WINNING SCORE:

1995 -- 280 (even par) Corey Pavin, U.S. Open, Billy Mayfair, TOUR Championship.
. 283 (5-under) Lee Janzen, THE PLAYERS.
1994 -- 281 (7 under) Johnny Miller, AT&T.
279 (5 under) Ernie Els, U.S. Open.
1993 -- 281 (7 under) Mike Standly, Freeport-McMoRan; Rocco Mediate, Kmart GGO.
280 (4 under) Vijay Singh, Buick Classic.
1992 -- 285 (3 under) Tom Kite, U.S. Open.
1991 -- 282 (6 under) Payne Stewart, U.S. Open.
279 (1 under) Tom Purtzer, World Series.
279 (5 under) Craig Stadler, TOUR Championship.
279 (9 under) Steve Pate, Honda.
1990 -- 282 (6 under) John Huston, Honda; Steve Elkington, Kmart GGO; Wayne Grady, PGA.
216 (even) Greg Norman, Memorial (54 holes).
1989 -- 283 (5 under) Nick Faldo, Masters.
278 (2 under) Curtis Strange, U.S. Open.
1988 -- 281 (7 under) Sandy Lyle, Masters.
1987 -- 287 (1 under) Larry Nelson, PGA.
1986 -- 287 (1 under) Kenny Knox, Honda.
279 (1 under) Raymond Floyd, U.S. Open.
1985 -- 285 (3 under) Joey Sindelar, Greensboro.
279 (1 under) Andy North, U.S. Open.

HIGHEST WINNING SCORE (cont'd.):

1984 --	276 (4 under)	Fuzzy Zoeller, U.S. Open.
	280 (8 under)	Bruce Lietzke, Honda; Jack Nicklaus, Memorial; Greg Norman, Kemper; Tom Watson, Western.
1983 --	287 (1 under)	Fred Couples, Kemper.
1982 --	278 (2 under)	Craig Stadler, World Series.
	285 (3 under)	Danny Edwards, Greensboro.
1981 --	281 (1 over)	Bruce Lietzke, Byron Nelson.
1980 --	280 (4 under)	Doug Tewell, Heritage.
1979 --	284 (even)	Hale Irwin, U.S. Open.
1978 --	289 (1 over)	Jack Nicklaus, TPC.
1977 --	289 (1 over)	Mark Hayes, TPC.
1976 --	288 (4 over)	Al Geiberger, Western.
	288 (even)	Roger Maltbie, Memorial.
	281 (1 over)	Dave Stockton, PGA.
1975 --	287 (3 over)	Lou Graham, U.S. Open.
1974 --	287 (7 over)	Hale Irwin, U.S. Open.
	287 (3 over)	Tom Watson, Western.
1973 --	283 (5 under)	Tommy Aaron, Masters; Dave Hill, Memphis.
	277 (3 under)	Lanny Wadkins, Byron Nelson.
1972 --	290 (2 over)	Jack Nicklaus, U.S. Open.
1971 --	283 (3 over)	Gene Littler, Colonial.
1970 --	282 (2 over)	Gibby Gilbert, Houston.

LARGEST WINNING MARGIN:

1995 --	6 strokes	Duffy Waldorf, LaCantera Texas Open.
1994 --	6 strokes	Nick Price, PGA.
1993 --	8 strokes	Davis Love III, Las Vegas.
1992 --	9 strokes	Fred Couples, Nestle.
1991 --	4 strokes	Lanny Wadkins, Hawaiian; Paul Azinger, Pebble Beach.
1990 --	12 strokes	Jose Maria Olazabal, World Series.
1989 --	7 strokes	Mark Calcavecchia, Phoenix; Donnie Hammond, Texas.
1988 --	8 strokes	Corey Pavin, Texas.
1987 --	7 strokes	Tom Kite, Kemper; Robert Wrenn, Buick; Ken Brown, Southern.
1986 --	7 strokes	Doug Tewell, Los Angeles; Greg Norman, Las Vegas.
1985 --	7 strokes	Lanny Wadkins, Los Angeles.
1984 --	6 strokes	George Archer, Bank of Boston; Hubert Green, Southern.
1983 --	5 strokes	Gary Koch, Doral; Lanny Wadkins, Greensboro; David Graham, Houston; Jim Colbert, Texas.
1982 --	7 strokes	Craig Stadler, Kemper; Calvin Peete, B.C. Open; Calvin Peete, Pensacola.
1981 --	7 strokes	Andy Bean, Bay Hill.
1980 --	7 strokes	Larry Nelson, Atlanta; Jack Nicklaus, PGA.
1979 --	8 strokes	Andy Bean, Atlanta.
1978 --	5 strokes	Andy Bean, Kemper; Tom Kite, B.C. Open.
1977 --	7 strokes	Jerry Pate, Southern; Rik Massengale, Bob Hope.
1976 --	8 strokes	Raymond Floyd, Masters.
1975 --	14 strokes	Johnny Miller, Phoenix.
1974 --	8 strokes	Lee Trevino, New Orleans; Johnny Miller, Kaiser International.
1973 --	8 strokes	Buddy Allin, Florida Citrus.
1972 --	9 strokes	Jack Nicklaus, Walt Disney.
1971 --	8 strokes	Jack Nicklaus, T of C.
1970 --	7 strokes	Frank Beard, T of C; Tony Jacklin, U.S. Open.

LOW START BY A WINNER:

1995 --	63 (9-under)	Kenny Perry, Bob Hope; Woody Austin, Buick Open.
1994 --	62 (9 under)	Bob Estes, Texas.
1993 --	63 (9 under)	Howard Twitty, Hawaiian.
	63 (8 under)	Jim Gallagher, Jr., TOUR Championship.
1992 --	62 (8 under)	David Frost, Hardee's.
1991 --	63 (9 under)	Mark Brooks, Milwaukee.
1990 --	61 (9 under)	Jose Maria Olazabal, World Series.
1989 --	64 (8 under)	Greg Norman, Milwaukee.
1988 --	62 (10 under)	Bob Lohr, Walt Disney.
1987 --	64 (8 under)	Mike Reid, Tucson.
1986 --	64 (7 under)	Hal Sutton, Phoenix.
1985 --	63 (8 under)	Lanny Wadkins, Los Angeles.
	64 (8 under)	Tom Kite, T of C.
1984 --	64 (6 under)	Peter Jacobsen, Colonial.
1983 --	63 (9 under)	Fuzzy Zoeller, Las Vegas.
1982 --	63 (8 under)	Tim Norris, Hartford.
	63 (7 under)	Jay Haas, Texas.

PGA TOUR FACTS AND FIGURES (1970-95) *...continued*

LOW START BY A WINNER (cont'd.):

1981 -- 65 (7 under) Bruce Lietzke, Bob Hope; Hale Irwin, Buick.
65 (6 under) David Graham, Phoenix; Morris Hatalsky, Hall of Fame.
1980 -- 63 (7 under) Bruce Lietzke, Colonial; Jack Nicklaus, U.S. Open; Scott Hoch, Quad Cities.
65 (7 under) Tom Watson, T of C.
66 (7 under) Jim Colbert, Tucson.
1979 -- 61 (11 under) Jerry McGee, Kemper.
1978 -- 63 (9 under) Tom Watson, Tucson.
1977 -- 64 (8 under) Rik Massengale, Bob Hope.
64 (6 under) Jerry Pate, Southern.
65 (6 under) Graham Marsh, Heritage; Hale Irwin, Hall of Fame.
66 (6 under) Tom Watson, Bing Crosby, San Diego.
1976 -- 63 (8 under) David Graham, Westchester.
1975 -- 64 (8 under) Johnny Miller, Bob Hope.
1974 -- 62 (10 under) Johnny Miller, Tucson.
1973 -- 64 (8 under) Lee Trevino, Doral-Eastern.
1972 -- 64 (7 under) Dave Hill, Monsanto.
65 (7 under) Grier Jones, Hawaiian.
1971 -- 64 (8 under) Arnold Palmer, Westchester.
64 (7 under) Dave Eichelberger, Milwaukee.
1970 -- 63 (7 under) Dave Hill, Memphis.

HIGH START BY A WINNER:

1995 -- 73 (3 over) Greg Norman, NEC World Series of Golf.
73 (1-over) Payne Stewart, Shell Houston Open; Billy Mayfair, Motorola Western.
1994 -- 74 (2 over) Jose Maria Olazabal, Masters.
1993 -- 75 (3 over) Phil Mickelson, Buick Invitational.
1992 -- 73 (1 over) Greg Norman, Canadian.
1991 -- 73 (1 over) Ian Woosnam, USF&G.
72 (2 over) Tom Purtzer, World Series.
1990 -- 72 (even) David Ishii, Hawaiian.
1989 -- 76 (4 over) Steve Jones, Bob Hope; Mike Sullivan, IIAO.
1988 -- 73 (1 over) Curtis Strange, Memorial.
1987 -- 75 (3 over) Lanny Wadkins, Doral.
1986 -- 75 (5 over) Raymond Floyd, U.S. Open.
1985 -- 72 (even) Bernhard Langer, Masters; Bill Glasson, Kemper.
1984 -- 73 (1 over) Greg Norman, Canadian.
71 (1 over) Fuzzy Zoeller, U.S. Open.
1983 -- 75 (4 over) Larry Nelson, U.S. Open.
1982 -- 75 (3 over) Craig Stadler, Masters.
1981 -- 74 (2 over) Ed Fiori, Western.
1980 -- 74 (2 over) Raymond Floyd, Doral-Eastern.
1979 -- 76 (4 over) Fuzzy Zoeller, San Diego.
1978 -- 76 (4 over) Bruce Lietzke, Canadian.
75 (4 over) John Mahaffey, PGA.
1977 -- 72 (even) Mark Hayes, TPC; Jack Nicklaus, Memorial; Al Geiberger, Memphis.
1976 -- 75 (3 over) Ben Crenshaw, Pebble Beach.
73 (3 over) Lee Trevino, Colonial.
1975 -- 74 (3 over) Lou Graham, U.S. Open.
1974 -- 73 (3 over) Hale Irwin, U.S. Open; Lee Trevino, PGA.
1973 -- 73 (2 over) Rod Funseth, Los Angeles.
1972 -- 73 (1 over) Gary Player, New Orleans.
72 (1 over) Deane Beman, Quad Cities.
71 (1 over) Gary Player, PGA.
1971 -- 75 (7 over) Buddy Allin, Greensboro.
1970 -- 76 (4 over) Pete Brown, San Diego.

LOW FINISH BY A WINNER:

1995 -- 61 (10-under) Hal Sutton, B.C. Open.
1994 -- 64 (7 under) Bill Glasson, Phoenix.
65 (7 under) Bruce Lietzke, Las Vegas
64 (6 under) Nick Price, Colonial.
1993 -- 62 (10 under) Tom Kite, Bob Hope.
62 (8 under) Fulton Allem, World Series.
1992 -- 62 (10 over) Davis Love III, Greensboro; John Huston, Disney.
1991 -- 64 (8 under) Mark Brooks, Greensboro; Mark O'Meara, Disney.
64 (7 under) Bruce Fleisher, New England.
64 (6 under) Tom Purtzer, Colonial; D.A. Weibring, Hardee's.
64 (6 under) Dillard Pruitt, Chattanooga.
1990 -- 62 (10 under) Greg Norman, Doral.
1989 -- 63 (9 under) Bill Britton, Centel.
1988 -- 64 (8 under) Tom Purtzer, Southwest; Chip Beck, USF&G.

LOW FINISH BY A WINNER (cont'd.):

1987 -- 63 (9 under) Larry Nelson, Walt Disney.
1986 -- 62 (9 under) Mac O'Grady, Hartford.
1985 -- 63 (9 under) Lanny Wadkins, Walt Disney.
1984 -- 63 (8 under) Gary Koch, Bay Hill, Ronnie Black, Anheuser-Busch.
1983 -- 63 (9 under) Calvin Peete, Atlanta.
1982 -- 63 (7 under) Payne Stewart, Quad Cities.
65 (7 under) Lanny Wadkins, Buick Open.
1981 -- 62 (9 under) Ron Streck, Houston.
1980 -- 65 (5 under) Lee Trevino, Texas; Tom Watson, WSOG.
66 (6 under) Andy Bean, Hawaiian; Raymond Floyd, Doral-Eastern; Bill Kratzert, Milwaukee.
1979 -- 64 (7 under) Lou Graham, IVB.
65 (7 under) Calvin Peete, Milwaukee.
1978 -- 62 (8 under) Ron Streck, Texas.
1977 -- 64 (6 under) Mike Hill, Ohio Kings Island.
65 (7 under) Miller Barber, Anheuser-Busch.
1976 -- 63 (9 under) Johnny Miller, Bob Hope.
63 (7 under) Jerry Pate, Canadian.
65 (7 under) Jack Nicklaus, TPC.
1975 -- 61 (11 under) Johnny Miller, Tucson.
1974 -- 64 (7 under) Dave Stockton, Quad Cities.
65 (7 under) Hubert Green, Bob Hope; Lee Trevino, New Orleans; Dave Hill, Houston.
1973 -- 63 (8 under) Johnny Miller, U.S. Open.
1972 -- 64 (8 under) Grier Jones, Hawaiian; Jack Nicklaus, Walt Disney.
1971 -- 65 (7 under) George Archer, San Diego.
65 (6 under) Miller Barber, Phoenix; Bobby Mitchell, Cleveland.
1970 -- 63 (8 under) George Knudson, Robinson.

HIGH FINISH BY A WINNER:

1995 -- 73 (3-over) Billy Mayfair, TOUR Championship.
73 (2-over) Fred Funk, Ideon Classic.
1994 -- 74 (2 over) Johnny Miller, AT&T.
1993 -- 71 (1 over) Scott Simpson, Byron Nelson.
71 (1 under) Brett Ogle, Pebble Beach.
1992 -- 72 (even) Steve Elkington, T of C; Tom Kite, U.S. Open; David Frost, Hardee's.
1991 -- 75 (3 over) Steve Pate, Honda.
1990 -- 72 (even) Mark O'Meara, Pebble Beach; David Ishii, Hawaiian; Dan Forsman, Shearson Lehman.
71 (even) Payne Stewart, MCI.
1989 -- 72 (1 over) Wayne Grady, Westchester.
72 (even) Bill Glasson, Doral-Ryder.
70 (even) Curtis Strange, U.S. Open.
1988 -- 74 (2 over) Steve Jones, Pebble Beach; Curtis Strange, Nabisco.
1987 -- 72 (1 over) Paul Azinger, Hartford.
71 (1 over) Curtis Strange, World Series.
72 (even) Larry Nelson, PGA.
1986 -- 71 (1 over) Dan Pohl, World Series.
71 (even) Hal Sutton, Phoenix.
71 (1 under) John Mahaffey, TPC; Bob Murphy, Canadian.
1985 -- 74 (2 over) Curtis Strange, Honda; Scott Verplank, Western.
74 (4 over) Andy North, U.S. Open.
1984 -- 73 (1 over) Greg Norman, Kemper.
1983 -- 77 (5 over) Fred Couples, Kemper.
1982 -- 75 (3 over) Danny Edwards, Greensboro.
1981 -- 75 (3 over) Larry Nelson, Greensboro.
1980 -- 74 (3 over) Dave Eichelberger, Bay Hill.
1979 -- 77 (5 over) Lon Hinkle, Bing Crosby.
1978 -- 75 (3 over) Jack Nicklaus, TPC.
1977 -- 74 (2 over) Gene Littler, Houston; Lee Trevino, Canadian.
73 (2 over) Jerry Pate, Phoenix.
1976 -- 76 (4 over) Roger Maltbie, Memorial.
1975 -- 73 (2 over) Lou Graham, U.S. Open.
73 (1 over) Gene Littler, Bing Crosby.
72 (1 over) Tom Jenkins, IVB.
71 (1 over) Jack Nicklaus, PGA.
1974 -- 73 (3 over) Hale Irwin, U.S. Open.
73 (1 over) Allen Miller, Tallahassee.
1973 -- 75 (4 over) Homero Blancas, Monsanto.
1972 -- 74 (2 over) Jack Nicklaus, Masters, U.S. Open; Gary Player, PGA.
73 (3 over) Jerry Heard, Colonial.
1971 -- 74 (4 over) Jerry Heard, American Classic.
1970 -- 72 (1 over) Billy Casper, Los Angeles.
72 (even) Bob Stone, Citrus Open; Ken Still, Kaiser International.

LARGEST 18-HOLE LEAD:

1995 --	2 strokes	John Huston, Mercedes Championships; Duffy Waldorf, Phoenix Open; Mark Brooks, Nestle Invitational; Woody Austin, Buick Open.
1994 --	4 strokes	Jose Maria Olazabal, Freeport-McMoRan.
1993 --	5 strokes	Jim Gallagher, Jr., TOUR Championship.
1992 --	3 strokes	Billy Ray Brown, PLAYERS.
1991 --	3 strokes	Lanny Wadkins, T of C, Scott Hoch, Buick Open.
1990 --	4 strokes	Fred Couples, Memorial; Jose Maria Olazabal, World Series.
1989 --	4 strokes	Bob Tway, Disney World.
1988 --	3 strokes	Davis Love III, Phoenix; Jeff Sluman, Southern.
1987 --	4 strokes	Mike Sullivan, Honda.
1986 --	3 strokes	Fred Couples, Kemper.
1985 --	4 strokes	Tom Kite, T of C.
1984 --	3 strokes	David Graham, T of C; Ralph Landrum, Pensacola.
1983 --	4 strokes	George Burns, Kemper.
1982 --	4 strokes	Terry Mauney, Los Angeles; Larry Rinker, Tallahassee.
1981 --	3 strokes	Calvin Peete, B.C. Open.
1980 --	2 strokes	Dan Pohl, Bay Hill; Jerry Pate, Heritage; Tom Purtzer, Greensboro; Bob Murphy, Tallahassee; Tom Watson, Byron Nelson, World Series; Bruce Lietzke, Colonial; Bob Shearer, Atlanta; Scott Hoch, Quad Cities; Jim Simons, Hartford; Barry Jaeckel, Hall of Fame.
1979 --	4 strokes	Mark Lye, Atlanta; Dana Quigley, Hall of Fame.
1978 --	3 strokes	Tom Watson, Tucson, Bing Crosby; Jeff Hewes, Canadian.
1977 --	3 strokes	Rik Massengale, Bob Hope; Fred Marti, Pleasant Valley.
1976 --	3 strokes	Mike Reid (amateur), U.S. Open.
1975 --	3 strokes	Bob Stanton, Inverrary; Jack Nicklaus, Heritage; Tom Weiskopf, Greensboro; David Graham, Western.
1974 --	4 strokes	Johnny Miller, Tucson.
1973 --	5 strokes	Gibby Gilbert, World.
1972 --	3 strokes	Jack Nicklaus, Bing Crosby.
1971 --	3 strokes	Charles Coody, Masters.
1970 --	3 strokes	Rod Funseth, San Antonio.

LARGEST 36-HOLE LEAD:

1995 --	4 strokes	Tom Lehman, MCI Classic; D.A. Weibring, Quad City Classic.
1994 --	5 strokes	Nick Price, PGA.
1993 --	3 strokes	Payne Stewart, Buick Invitational; Steve Stricker, Canadian; Tom Lehman, Buick Southern.
1992 --	4 strokes	Davis Love III, Los Angeles; Chip Beck, Freeport-McMoRan; Bruce Lietzke, Canadian.
1991 --	4 strokes	Blaine McCallister, Texas; Jeff Maggert, IIAO.
1990 --	9 strokes	Jose Maria Olazabal, World Series.
1989 --	5 strokes	Fuzzy Zoeller, Memorial.
1988 --	4 strokes	Paul Azinger, Bay Hill; Larry Nelson, Atlanta.
1987 --	7 strokes	Joey Sindelar, B.C. Open.
1986 --	5 strokes	Sandy Lyle, Greensboro.
1985 --	5 strokes	Calvin Peete, Phoenix.
1984 --	6 strokes	Nick Price, Canadian.
1983 --	6 strokes	Hal Sutton, Anheuser-Busch.
1982 --	6 strokes	Roger Maltbie, Colonial.
1981 --	4 strokes	Jack Nicklaus, Masters; Leonard Thompson, Canadian.
1980 --	5 strokes	Rex Caldwell, Buick.
1979 --	4 strokes	Ben Crenshaw, Phoenix; Tom Watson, Memorial.
1978 --	5 strokes	Mac McLendon, Pensacola.
1977 --	6 strokes	Al Geiberger, Memphis.
1976 --	6 strokes	Bob Dickson, Western.
1975 --	7 strokes	Tom Weiskoipf, Westchester.
1974 --	6 strokes	Johnny Miller, Heritage.
1973 --	4 strokes	Billy Casper, Bing Crosby; Tom Watson, Hawaiian; Lee Trevino, Doral-Eastern; Jack Nicklaus, Atlanta; Forrest Fezler, American Classic.
1972 --	4 strokes	Homero Blancas, Phoenix; Chris Blocker, Florida Citrus; Dave Hill, Monsanto.
1971 --	3 strokes	Jerry Heard, American Classic; Billy Casper, Kaiser International.
1970 --	4 strokes	Grier Jones, Monsanto.

LARGEST 54-HOLE LEAD:

1995 --	5 strokes	Scott Hoch, Shell Houston Open.
1994 --	5 strokes	Steve Elkington, Buick Southern.
1993 --	6 strokes	Greg Norman, Doral-Ryder.
1992 --	6 strokes	Fred Couples, Nestle.
1991 --	5 strokes	Steve Pate, Honda.
1990 --	8 strokes	Jose Maria Olazabal, World Series.
1989 --	4 strokes	Ian Baker-Finch, Colonial; Greg Norman, Milwaukee; John Daly, Chattanooga.
1988 --	5 strokes	Corey Pavin, Texas.

PGA TOUR FACTS AND FIGURES (1970-95) ...*continued*

LARGEST 54-HOLE LEAD (cont'd.):

1987 --	8 strokes	Joey Sindelar, Buick.
1986 --	5 strokes	Fuzzy Zoeller, Pebble Beach; Calvin Peete, USF&G; Mark Calcavecchia, Southwest.
1985 --	5 strokes	Corey Pavin, Colonial.
1984 --	7 strokes	Greg Norman, Kemper.
1983 --	6 strokes	Mike Nicolette, Bay Hill; Hal Sutton, Anheuser-Busch.
1982 --	7 strokes	Craig Stadler, Tucson.
1981 --	5 strokes	Bruce Lietzke, Bob Hope; Hale Irwin, Hawaiian; Jay Haas, Milwaukee.
1980 --	7 strokes	Jim Colbert, Tucson; Seve Ballesteros, Masters.
1979 --	8 strokes	Tom Watson, Heritage.
1978 --	5 strokes	Tom Watson, PGA; Tom Kite, B.C. Open.
1977 --	6 strokes	Lee Trevino, Canadian.
1976 --	8 strokes	Raymond Floyd, Masters.
1975 --	7 strokes	Johnny Miller, Phoenix.
1974 --	6 strokes	Jack Nicklaus, Hawaiian.
1973 --	9 strokes	Jack Nicklaus, Ohio Kings Island.
1972 --	8 strokes	Jim Jamieson, Western.
1971 --	5 strokes	Jack Nicklaus, T of C; Jerry Heard, American Classic.
1970 --	4 strokes	Ron Cerrudo, San Antonio; Bob Stone, Citrus Open; Tony Jacklin, U.S. Open; Bob Murphy, Hartford; Bobby Mitchell, Azalea.

LOW 36-HOLE CUT:

1995 --	139 (3-under)	FedEx St. Jude Classic.
	139 (1-under)	GTE Byron Nelson Classic.
	140 (4-under)	Buick Open.
1994 --	139 (3 under)	Texas.
	140 (even)	Hardee's.
	141 (3 under)	Hawaiian, Buick Invitational.
1993 --	140 (4 under)	Shell Houston.
	140 (2 under)	H-E-B Texas.
1992 --	139 (1 under)	Byron Nelson.
	139 (3 under)	Federal Express, Texas.
	140 (4 under)	Buick Invitational.
1991 --	137 (3 under)	Chattanooga.
	140 (4 under)	Milwaukee, Shearson Lehman.
	140 (2 under)	Phoenix, Anheuser-Busch, New England.
1990 --	138 (2 under)	Chattanooga, Texas.
	141 (3 under)	Milwaukee.
1989 --	137 (3 under)	Byron Nelson, Texas.
1988 --	141 (3 under)	Andy Williams, USF&G.
	139 (1 under)	Hardee's, Provident, Texas.
1987 --	140 (4 under)	Andy Williams.
	139 (1 under)	Byron Nelson, Hardee's.
1986 --	141 (3 under)	Buick.
	139 (1 under)	Vantage.
1985 --	139 (5 under)	San Diego.
1984 --	141 (3 under)	San Diego.
	141 (1 under)	Phoenix.
1983 --	139 (3 under)	Hartford.
	139 (1 under)	Texas.
1982 --	139 (3 under)	Hartford.
1981 --	139 (3 under)	Hartford.
1980 --	140 (2 under)	Hartford.
	141 (3 under)	Milwaukee.
1979 --	140 (even)	Tucson.
	141 (1 under)	Phoenix, Houston.
	142 (2 under)	Hawaiian, Pensacola.
1978 --	140 (2 under)	Hartford.
	142 (2 under)	Anheuser-Busch.
	140 (even)	Texas.
1977 --	142 (2 under)	Buick.
1976 --	142 (even)	Phoenix, Hartford.
	143 (1 under)	Hawaiian, San Diego.
	144 (even)	Florida Citrus.
1975 --	142 (even)	Hartford, Sahara.
	144 (even)	Inverrary, Houston, Westchester, Texas, Kaiser International.
1974 --	141 (1 under)	Greensboro, Hartford.
	142 (2 under)	Kemper, Texas.
	143 (1 under)	San Diego.
1973 --	140 (2 under)	Hartford.
1972 --	141 (1 under)	Hartford.

LOW 36-HOLE CUT (cont'd.):

1971 --	137 (5 under)	Phoenix.
1970 --	140 (even)	Memphis.
	141 (1 under)	Azalea.
	141 (1 over)	Magnolia.
	143 (1 under)	Citrus Invitational.

HIGH 36-HOLE CUT:

1995 --	149 (5-over)	THE PLAYERS
	148 (4-over)	British Open
	146 (6-over)	U.S. Open
1994 --	148 (4 over)	Doral-Ryder.
	147 (5 over)	Honda, U.S. Open.
1993 --	152 (8 over)	Freeport-McMoRan.
1992 --	148 (4 over)	Nestle.
	148 (6 over)	PGA.
1991 --	149 (5 over)	USF&G.
1990 --	157 (13 over)	Memorial.
1989 --	150 (6 over)	Memorial.
1988 --	149 (5 over)	Memorial.
1987 --	151 (7 over)	Honda, PGA.
1986 --	150 (10 over)	U.S. Open.
	150 (6 over)	St. Jude Classic.
1985 --	150 (6 over)	Memorial.
1984 --	151 (9 over)	Los Angeles.
	151 (7 over)	Memorial.
1983 --	152 (10 over)	Bay Hill.
1982 --	149 (5 over)	Memorial, Kemper, Western.
	147 (7 over)	Colonial.
1981 --	152 (8 over)	Memorial.
1980 --	150 (6 over)	Memorial, Western.
	149 (9 over)	PGA.
1979 --	157 (13 over)	Memorial.
1978 --	153 (9 over)	TPC.
1977 --	155 (11 over)	TPC.
1976 --	157 (13 over)	Memorial.
1975 --	151 (9 over)	Western.
1974 --	151 (9 over)	Heritage.
	149 (9 over)	PGA.
1973 --	151 (7 over)	Masters.
	149 (9 over)	American Classic.
1972 --	154 (10 over)	U.S. Open.
	150 (10 over)	PGA.
1971 --	152 (10 over)	Heritage.
1970 --	153 (9 over)	U.S. Open.
	151 (9 over)	Heritage.
	151 (7 over)	Masters.
	150 (10 over)	PGA.

FEWEST TO MAKE 36-HOLE CUT:

1995 -- 70 at Phoenix Open
1994 -- 70 at Buick Classic, Federal Express.
1993 -- 70 at New England.
1992 -- 70 at Texas.
1991 -- 70 at Buick Classic, Chattanooga.
1990 -- 70 at Canadian, Texas.
1989 -- 70 at Doral-Ryder, Memorial, Atlanta, Hardee's, PGA.
1988 -- 70 at Phoenix.
1987 -- 70 at Buick, Centel.
1986 -- 70 at Hawaiian, Heritage, Buick, Anhueser-Busch.
1985 -- 70 at Atlanta, Quad Cities.
1984 -- 70 at Atlanta, PGA, Milwaukee.
1983 -- 70 at Hawaii, Atlanta, Memorial.
1982 -- 70 at Houston, Disney World.
1981 -- 70 at Inverrary.
1980 -- 70 at Doral-Eastern.
1979 -- 70 at Byron Nelson, Pensacola.
1978 -- 70 at Tucson, San Diego, Byron Nelson, American Optical, Westchester.
1977 -- 70 at Hawaiian.
1976 -- 70 at Heritage.
1975 -- 70 at B.C. Open.
1974 -- 70 at Greensboro, American Classic, Sahara.

PGA TOUR FACTS AND FIGURES (1970-95) *...continued*

FEWEST TO MAKE 36-HOLE CUT (cont'd.):
1973 -- 70 at Jacksonville, IVB, Southern, Kaiser International.
1972 -- 70 at Monsanto, Colonial, Cleveland.
1971 -- 70 at Los Angeles, Tucson, Kaiser International.
1970 -- 70 at San Diego, Canadian, PGA.

FEWEST TO MAKE 54-HOLE CUT:
1995 -- 70 at Walt Disney World.
1994 -- 72 at AT&T Pebble Beach.
1993 -- 73 at Walt Disney World.
1992 -- 72 at Las Vegas Invitational.
1991 -- 73 at AT&T Pebble Beach.
1990 -- 78 at AT&T Pebble Beach.
1989 -- 73 at Las Vegas Invitational.
1988 -- 72 at Las Vegas Invitational.
1987 -- 70 at Las Vegas Invitational.
1986 -- 71 at AT&T Pebble Beach.
1985 -- 70 at Las Vegas Invitational.
1984 -- 73 at Bing Crosby.
1983 -- 75 at Bing Crosby.
1982 -- 70 at Walt Disney World.
1981 -- 77 at Bing Crosby.
1980 -- 75 at Bing Crosby.
1979 -- 78 at Bing Crosby.
1978 -- 70 at Bing Crosby.
1977 -- 73 at Bing Crosby.
1976 -- 76 at Bing Crosby.
1975 -- 75 at Bing Crosby.
1974 -- 71 at Bing Crosby.
1973 -- 71 at Bing Crosby.
1972 -- 70 at Bing Crosby.
1971 -- 80 at Bing Crosby.
1970 -- 71 at Bing Crosby.

MOST TO MAKE 36-HOLE CUT:
1995 -- 103 at British Open (10-stroke rule).
88 at Quad City Classic.
1994 -- 88 at Buick Southern Open.
1993 -- 90 at Buick Invitational.
1992 -- 85 at PGA.
1991 -- 84 at Hardee's.
1990 -- 88 at Buick Classic.
1989 -- 85 at Phoenix.
1988 -- 89 at Milwaukee.
1987 -- 87 at USF&G.
1986 -- 86 at Phoenix, Southern.
1985 -- 83 at Buick.
1984 -- 89 at LaJet.
1983 -- 87 at PGA.
1982 -- 90 at Texas.
1981 -- 91 at Hartford.
1980 -- 83 at Phoenix.
1979 -- 88 at Quad Cities.
1978 -- 85 at New Orleans.
1977 -- 86 at Doral-Eastern.
1976 -- 85 at Westchester.
1975 -- 86 at San Diego.
1974 -- 84 at B.C. Open.
1973 -- 90 at Phoenix.
1972 -- 86 at St. Louis.
1971 -- 88 at Hartford.
1970 -- 85 at Kaiser International, Sahara.

MOST TO MAKE 54-HOLE CUT:
1995 -- 80 at Las Vegas Invitational.
1994 -- 77 at Walt Disney World.
1993 -- 82 at AT&T Pebble Beach.
1992 -- 82 at AT&T Pebble Beach.
1991 -- 80 at Walt Disney World.
1990 -- 86 at Las Vegas Invitational.
1989 -- 82 at Walt Disney World.

MOST TO MAKE 54-HOLE CUT (cont'd.):
1988 -- 76 at AT&T Pebble Beach.
1987 -- 82 at AT&T Pebble Beach.
1986 -- 81 at Las Vegas Invitational.
1985 -- 74 at Walt Disney World.
1984 -- 83 at Walt Disney World.
1983 -- 80 at Walt Disney World.
1982 -- 77 at Bing Crosby.
1981 -- 77 at Bing Crosby.
1980 -- 75 at Bing Crosby.
1979 -- 78 at Bing Crosby.
1978 -- 70 at Bing Crosby.
1977 -- 73 at Bing Crosby.
1976 -- 76 at Bing Crosby.
1975 -- 72 at Bing Crosby.
1974 -- 71 at Bing Crosby.
1973 -- 71 at Bing Crosby.
1972 -- 70 at Bing Crosby.
1971 -- 80 at Bing Crosby.
1970 -- 71 at Bing Crosby.

MOST TIED FOR LEAD, 18 HOLES:
1995 -- 5 at Buick Invitational of California
1994 -- 5 at Western, Deposit Guaranty, Federal Express St. Jude
1993 -- 7 at Phoenix
1992 -- 6 at Kmart Greater Greeensboro
1991 -- 5 at USF&G
1990 -- 4 at Bob Hope Chrysler, Phoenix, USF&G
1989 -- 5 at Kmart Greater Greensboro
1988 -- 6 at Buick Open
1987 -- 7 at Western
1986 -- 6 at Shearson Lehman-Andy Williams
1985 -- 4 at Bob Hope, Isuzu Andy Williams, Hawaiian, Colonial
1984 -- 7 at Los Angeles
1983 -- 4 at Phoenix
1982 -- 5 at Greater Milwaukee
1981 -- 5 at Hawaiian
1980 -- 4 at Kemper
1979 -- 5 at Greater Greensboro, U.S. Open
1978 -- 7 at TPC
1977 -- 7 at U.S. Open
1976 -- 4 at Houston, Pensacola
1975 -- 6 at Tallahassee
1974 -- 5 at B.C.
1973 -- 6 at Southern
1972 -- 6 at U.S. Open
1971 -- 4 at Canadian, Greater Hartford
1970 -- 7 at Coral Springs

MOST TIED FOR LEAD, 36 HOLES:
1995 -- 5 at B.C.
1994 -- 4 at Northern Telecom
1993 -- 4 at Nissan Los Angeles, Deposit Guaranty, H-E-B Texas, Las Vegas
1992 -- 4 at Kemper
1991 -- 3 at Honda, Buick Classic
1990 -- 3 at Bob Hope Chrysler, AT&T Pebble Beach
1989 -- 4 at Kmart Greater Greensboro
1988 -- 6 at Honda
1987 -- 5 at Doral-Ryder
1986 -- 4 at Memorial
1985 -- 3 at Los Angeles, Doral-Eastern, Masters, St. Jude Memphis
1984 -- 3 at Los Angeles, Doral-Eastern, PGA
1983 -- 3 at MONY T of C, Miller High Life Quad Cities, Panasonic Las Vegas, Walt Disney World
1982 -- 6 at TPC
1981 -- 3 at Danny Thomas Memphis, Pleasant Valley
1980 -- 4 at Memorial, B.C.
1979 -- 3 at Hawaiian, Tallahassee
1978 -- 5 at Sea Pines Heritage
1977 -- 7 at Westchester
1976 -- 4 at Greater Greensboro, Pleasant Valley
1975 -- 6 at Sahara
1974 -- 4 at U.S. Open

MOST TIED FOR LEAD, 36 HOLES (cont'd.):
1973 -- 6 at Liggett & Myers, Shrine Robinson
1972 -- 6 at U.S. Open
1971 -- 6 at National Airlines
1970 -- 3 at Colonial, Dow Jones

MOST TIED FOR LEAD, 54 HOLES:
1995 -- 4 at MCI
1994 -- 3 at Northern Telecom, Phoenix, Shell Houston, Federal Express St. Jude, Las Vegas
1993 -- 4 at NEC World Series, H-E-B Texas
1992 -- 4 at GTE Byron Nelson
1991 -- 4 at Las Vegas
1990 -- 3 at Nestle, Buick Southern
1989 -- 3 at Manufacturers Hanover Westchester, Canon Greater Hartford, NEC World Series
1988 -- 4 at Provident, Centel
1987 -- 4 at Las Vegas
1986 -- 4 at Buick Open, Federal Express St. Jude
1985 -- 3 at Doral-Eastern, TPC, Houston, Pensacola
1984 -- 5 at Las Vegas
1983 -- 5 at Colonial
1982 -- 3 at Miller High-Life Quad Cities
1981 -- 3 at Memorial, Anheuser-Busch
1980 -- 3 at Doral-Eastern, World Series
1979 -- 3 at Glen Campbell Los Angeles
1978 -- 5 at First NBC New Orleans
1977 -- 3 at Kemper, Western
1976 -- 5 at IVB-Philadelphia
1975 -- 4 at San Antonio-Texas
1974 -- 4 at Glen Campbell Los Angeles, Houston, Southern
1973 -- 4 at U.S. Open
1972 -- 3 at Jackie Gleason's Inverrary, Greater Jacksonville, Liggett & Myers, Southern
1971 -- 5 at Andy Williams San Diego
1970 -- 4 at Greater Greensboro

MOST CONSECUTIVE EVENTS IN THE MONEY (ongoing at conclusion of season):
1995 -- 14, Jay Haas.
1994 -- 25, Fred Couples.
1993 -- 25, Steve Elkington.
1992 -- 19, Tom Kite.
1991 -- 18, Fred Couples.
1990 -- 17, Larry Mize.
1989 -- 33, Tom Kite.
1988 -- 15, Ben Crenshaw.
1987 -- 19, Greg Norman.
1986 -- 16, Gene Sauers.
1985 -- 14, Tom Kite, Scott Hoch.
1984 -- 21, Jack Nicklaus.
1983 -- 26, Hale Irwin.
1982 -- 53, Tom Kite.
1981 -- 35, Tom Kite.
1980 -- 28, Tom Watson.
1979 -- 17, Hubert Green, Bill Rogers.
1978 -- 86, Hale Irwin.
1977 -- 54, Hale Irwin.
1976 -- 105, Jack Nicklaus.
1975 -- 91, Jack Nicklaus.
1974 -- 74, Jack Nicklaus.
1973 -- 56, Jack Nicklaus.
1972 -- 37, Jack Nicklaus.

CONSECUTIVE YEARS WITH WIN:
1995 -- 4, Ben Crenshaw, Lee Janzen and Greg Norman (1992 through 1995).
1994 -- 5, Fred Couples (1990-94).
1993 -- 7, Paul Azinger (1987-93).
1992 -- 6, Paul Azinger (1987-92).
1991 -- 5, Paul Azinger (1987-91).
1990 -- 4, Paul Azinger (1987-90).
1989 -- 7, Curtis Strange (1983-89).
1988 -- 6, Curtis Strange (1983-88).
1987 -- 7, Tom Kite (1981-87).
1986 -- 6, Tom Kite (1981-86).
1985 -- 5, Hale Irwin, Tom Kite (1981-85).

CONSECUTIVE YEARS WITH WIN (cont'd.):
1984 -- 4, Hale Irwin, Tom Kite (1981-84).
1983 -- 4, Johnny Miller (1980-83).
1982 -- 6, Bruce Lietzke, Tom Watson (1977-82).
1981 -- 14, Lee Trevino (1968-81).
1980 -- 13, Lee Trevino (1968-80).
1979 -- 12, Lee Trevino (1968-79).
1978 -- 17, Jack Nicklaus (1962-78).
1977 -- 16, Jack Nicklaus (1962-77).
1976 -- 15, Jack Nicklaus (1962-76).
1975 -- 14, Jack Nicklaus (1962-75).
1974 -- 13, Jack Nicklaus (1962-74).
1973 -- 12, Jack Nicklaus (1962-73).
1972 -- 11, Jack Nicklaus (1962-72).
1971 -- 16, Billy Casper (1956-71).
1970 -- 15, Billy Casper (1956-70).

THREE EAGLES IN ONE ROUND:
1995 -- Tommy Tolles, Canadian; John Adams, Buick Challenge.
1994 -- Davis Love, Hawaiian; Dave Stockton, Jr., Disney.
1992 -- Dan Forsman, Honda; Don Pooley, Texas.
1990 -- David Frost, Las Vegas.
1981 -- Bruce Lietzke, Hawaiian; Howard Twitty, Pensacola.

DOUBLE-EAGLES:
1995 -- Per-Ulrik Johansson, PGA Championship (Riviera CC #11); J.L. Lewis, Milwaukee (Brown Deer Park GC #4)
1994 -- Olin Browne, Northern Telecom (Tucson National #2); Jeff Maggert, Masters (Augusta National #13); Mike Donald, Texas (Oak Hills #15).
1993 -- Massy Kuramoto, Deposit Guaranty (Hattiesburg #3); Tom Sieckmann, Kmart GGO (Forest Oaks #9); Bobby Wadkins, Memorial (Muirfield Village #15); Darrell Kestner, PGA (Inverness #13).
1992 -- Mark O'Meara, Bob Hope (Indian Wells #18); Billy Andrade, Las Vegas (LVCC #2).
1991 -- Payne Stewart, Pebble Beach (Spyglass #7); Mark Brooks, Kemper (TPC Avenel #6); Lon Hinkle, Anheuser-Busch (Kingsmill #13); John Daly, Western (Cog Hill #5); Davis Love III, World Series (Firestone #2).
1990 -- Tom Pernice, Phoenix (TPC Scottsdale #15); Gary Koch, Anheuser-Busch (Kingsmill #3); Steve Pate, Jim Gallagher, Jr., International (Castle Pines #17); Greg Bruckner, Southern (Green Island #18).
1989 -- Bill Britton, Anheuser-Busch (Kingsmill #3).
1988 -- Mike Reid, Los Angeles (Riviera #1); Jim Booros, Provident (Valleybrook #17).
1987 -- David Edwards, Andy Williams (Torrey Pines South #17); Dan Halldorson, Provident (Valleybrook #8).
1986 -- Mike Hulbert, Pebble Beach (Cypress Point #10).
1985 -- None.
1984 -- Hal Sutton, Byron Nelson (Las Colinas #7); John Adams, Canadian (Glen Abbey #16).
1983 -- None.
1982 -- Bob Gilder, Westchester (Westchester #18); Pat McGowan, Walt Disney (Palm Course #1).
1981 -- Jim Thorpe, LaJet (Fairway Oaks).
1980 -- Bruce Lietzke, Inverrary (Inverrary); Fred Marti, Milwaukee (Tuckaway); Stanton Altgelt, IVB (Whitemarsh Valley).
1979 -- Rik Massengale, Tucson (Randolph North); Bob Murphy, Tallahassee (Killearn).
1978 -- Terry Mauney, Hawaiian (Waialae); George Burns, Colonial (Colonial); Jim Nelford, Tommy Valentine, Atlanta (Atlanta CC).
1977 -- Joe Inman, Bob Hope (La Quinta).
1976 -- Lyn Lott, World (Pinehurst No. 2 #16).
1975 -- Lee Elder, Greensboro (Sedgefield); Miller Barber, Canadian (Royal Montreal).
1974 -- George Knudson, Bob Hope (Indian Wells); Larry Wise, Greensboro (Sedgefield).
1973 -- Jerry Heard, Milwaukee (Tuckaway).
1972 -- Bob Murphy, Bing Crosby (Pebble Beach #2); Roy Pace, Houston (Westwood #13).
1971 -- Rod Curl, Greensboro (Sedgefield); Larry Ziegler, Westchester (Westchester).
1970 -- Rod Curl, Memphis (Colonial); Mike Hill, AVCO (Pleasant Valley).

LONGEST BIRDIE STREAK:
1995 -- 7 Jay Delsing, FedEx St. Jude Classic.
1994 -- 7 Keith Clearwater, Colonial.
1992 -- 6 Gil Morgan, Bob Hope; Ed Fiori, Phoenix; Mark Calcavecchia, Masters; Fred Funk, Houston; Tom Kite, BellSouth; Andy Dillard, U.S. Open; Andy Bean, Chattanooga.
1991 -- 6 Mark Lye, Phoenix; Bill Sander, Shearson Lehman; Mark Brooks, Kmart GGO; Karl Kimball, Milwaukee; Chip Beck, Las Vegas.
1990 -- 7 Steve Elkington, Bob Hope; Scott Verplank, Milwaukee.
1989 -- 7 Wayne Grady, Shearson Lehman.
1988 -- 7 Nick Faldo, T of C.
1987 -- 8 Dewey Arnette, Buick.

PGA TOUR FACTS AND FIGURES (1970-95) *...continued*

LONGEST BIRDIE STREAK (cont'd.):

1986 -- 6 Doug Tewell, Los Angeles; Don Pooley, USF&G; Dave Rummells, TPC; Jack Nicklaus, Memorial; Kenny Knox, Buick; Mark Calcavecchia, Milwaukee.
1985 -- 7 Hubert Green, Western.
1984 -- 7 Tommy Valentine, Atlanta; Mike McCullough, Canadian; Rod Nuckolls, Buick.
1983 -- 6 Bill Kratzert, Los Angeles; Mike Sullivan, David Graham, Buick.
1982 -- 7 Scott Hoch, Bob Hope.
1981 -- 6 Tom Kite, Pensacola.
1980 -- 7 George Burns, Westchester; John Fought, Buick.
1979 -- 7 John Mahaffey, Bob Hope.
1978 -- 6 Bob Gilder, Doral-Eastern.
1977 -- 7 Bobby Walzel, Pensacola.
1976 -- 8 Fuzzy Zoeller, Quad Cities.
1975 -- 6 Johnny Miller, Masters.
1974 -- 6 Gary McCord, Bing Crosby; Mike McCullough, Bob Hope; Ben Crenshaw, San Diego.
1973 -- 6 Dan Sikes, Westchester; Hale Irwin, World Open.
1972 -- 7 Bert Yancey, Walt Disney.
1971 -- 6 Gibby Gilbert, Westchester.
1970 -- 6 Frank Beard, T of C; Wilf Homenuik, Azalea.

LONGEST BIRDIE/EAGLE STREAK (5 or more):

1995 -- 5 Keith Fergus (4 birdies, 1 eagle), Hawaiian; Ben Crenshaw (4 birdies, 1 eagle), Phoenix.
1994 -- 5 Ken Green, Phoenix (B,E,B,E,B).
1993 -- 5 Rick Fehr, Bob Hope (B,E,B,B,B).
1992 -- 5 Chris Tucker, Federal Express (B,E,B,B,B); Lee Janzen, Disney, (E,B,B,B,B).
1991 -- 6 Robert Gamez, Milwaukee (B,B,B,E,B,B).
1990 -- 6 David Frost, Tucson (B,B,B,B,B,E).
1989 -- 7 Webb Heintzelman, Las Vegas (B,B,B,B,B,E,B).
1986 -- 5 Raymond Floyd, Bob Hope (E,B,B,B,B); Denis Watson, Hartford (B,E,B,B,B).
1983 -- 6 Craig Stadler, Buick (B,B,E,B,B,B).
1977 -- 7 Al Geiberger, Memphis (B,B,B,B,E,B,B).
1975 -- 5 Bob Mitchell, Memphis (B,B,B,B,E).

BEST COME-FROM-BEHIND, FINAL-ROUND WIN:

1995 -- 7 strokes, Jim Gallagher, Jr., Kmart GGO; Payne Stewart, Shell Houston Open.
1994 -- 7 strokes, Nick Price, Colonial.
1993 -- 5 strokes, Vijay Singh, Buick Classic.
1992 -- 5 strokes, Lanny Wadkins, Canon GHO; David Edwards, Memorial; Mark Carnevale, Chattanooga.
1991 -- 7 strokes, Mark Brooks, Kmart GGO; Fulton Allem, IIAO.
1990 -- 8 strokes, Chip Beck, Buick Open.
1989 -- 7 strokes, Mike Sullivan, IIAO.
1988 -- 7 strokes, Sandy Lyle, Phoenix.
1987 -- 6 strokes, Corey Pavin, Hawaiian; Larry Nelson, Walt Disney.
1986 -- 7 strokes, Tom Kite, Western.
1985 -- 8 strokes, Hal Sutton, Memphis.
1984 -- 7 strokes, Ronnie Black, Anheuser-Busch.
1983 -- 8 strokes, Mark Lye, Bank of Boston.
1982 -- 6 strokes, Tom Kite, Bay Hill.
1981 -- 6 strokes, Raymond Floyd, TPC.
1980 -- 6 strokes, Peter Jacobsen, Buick.
1979 -- 6 strokes, Raymond Floyd, Greensboro; Lou Graham, IVB; Fuzzy Zoeller, Masters.
1978 -- 7 strokes, Gary Player, Masters, T of C; John Mahaffey, PGA.
1977 -- 6 strokes, Lanny Wadkins, PGA; Miller Barber, Anheuser-Busch.
1976 -- 5 strokes, Al Geiberger, Western.
1975 -- 7 strokes, Roger Maltbie, Quad Cities.
1974 -- 6 strokes, Tom Watson, Western.
1973 -- 6 strokes, Johnny Miller, U.S. Open.
1972 -- 5 strokes, Grier Jones, Hawaiian.
1971 -- 5 strokes, Gene Littler, Colonial.
1970 -- 7 strokes, Pete Brown, San Diego.

THREE OR MORE VICTORIES:

1995 -- 3 Lee Janzen, PLAYERS, Kemper, Sprint; Greg Norman, Memorial, Hartford, NEC WSOG.
1994 -- 5 Nick Price, Honda, Colonial, Western, PGA, Canadian.
3 Mark McCumber, Anheuser-Busch, Hardee's, TOUR Championship.
1993 -- 4 Nick Price, PLAYERS, Canon GHO, Western, Federal Express.
3 Paul Azinger, Memorial, New England, PGA.
1992 -- 3 Fred Couples, Los Angeles, Nestle, Masters; Davis Love III, PLAYERS, MCI, Kmart GGO; John Cook, Bob Hope, Hawaiian, Las Vegas.
1991 -- NONE
1990 -- 4 Wayne Levi, Atlanta, Western, Canon GHO, Canadian.
1989 -- 3 Tom Kite, Nestle, PLAYERS, Nabisco.

THREE OR MORE VICTORIES (cont'd.):

Year	Wins	Players
1988 --	4	Curtis Strange, Houston, Memorial, U.S. Open, Nabisco.
	3	Sandy Lyle, Phoenix, Greensboro, Masters.
1987 --	3	Curtis Strange, Canadian, St. Jude, World Series; Paul Azinger, Phoenix, Las Vegas, Hartford.
1986 --	4	Bob Tway, Andy Williams, Westchester, Atlanta, PGA.
	3	Fuzzy Zoeller, Pebble Beach, Heritage, Anheuser-Busch.
1985 --	3	Curtis Strange, Honda, Las Vegas, Canadian; Lanny Wadkins, Bob Hope, Los Angeles, Disney.
1984 --	3	Tom Watson, Tucson Match Play, T of C, Western; Denis Watson, Buick, World Series, Las Vegas.
1983 --	NONE	
1982 --	4	Calvin Peete, Milwaukee, Anheuser-Busch, B.C. Open, Pensacola; Craig Stadler, Tucson, Masters, Kemper, World Series.
	3	Tom Watson, Los Angeles, Heritage, U.S. Open; Raymond Floyd, Memorial, Memphis, PGA; Lanny Wadkins, Phoenix, T of C, Buick; Bob Gilder, Byron Nelson, Westchester, Bank of Boston.
1981 --	3	Bruce Lietzke, Bob Hope, San Diego, Byron Nelson; Tom Watson, Masters, New Orleans, Atlanta; Raymond Floyd, Doral-Eastern, TPC, Westchester; Bill Rogers, Heritage, World Series,Texas.
1980 --	6	Tom Watson, San Diego, Los Angeles, T of C, New Orleans, Byron Nelson, World Series.
	3	Lee Trevino, TPC, Memphis, Texas.
1979 --	5	Tom Watson, Heritage, T of C, Byron Nelson, Memorial, Hall of Fame.
	3	Lou Graham, IVB, American Optical, Texas.
1978 --	5	Tom Watson, Tucson, Bing Crosby, Byron Nelson, Hall of Fame, Anheuser-Busch.
	3	Gary Player, Masters, T of C, Houston; Andy Bean, Kemper, Memphis, Western; Jack Nicklaus, Inverrary, TPC, IVB.
1977 --	4	Tom Watson, Pebble Beach, San Diego, Masters, Western.
	3	Jack Nicklaus, Inverrary, T of C, Memorial; Hale Irwin, Atlanta, Hall of Fame, Texas.
1976 --	3	Hubert Green, Doral-Eastern, Jacksonville, Heritage; Ben Crenshaw, Pebble Beach, Hawaiian, Ohio Kings Island.
1975 --	5	Jack Nicklaus, Doral-Eastern, Heritage, Masters, PGA, World.
	4	Johnny Miller, Tucson, Phoenix, Bob Hope, Kaiser International.
	3	Gene Littler, Bing Crosby, Memphis, Westchester.
1974 --	8	Johnny Miller, Bing Crosby, Phoenix, Tucson, Heritage, T of C, Westchester, World, Kaiser International.
	3	Hubert Green, Bob Hope, Jacksonville, IVB; Dave Stockton, Los Angeles, Quad Cities, Hartford.
1973 --	7	Jack Nicklaus, Bing Crosby, New Orleans, T of C, Atlanta, PGA, Ohio Kings Island, Walt Disney.
	4	Tom Weiskopf, Colonial, Kemper, IVB, Canadian; Bruce Crampton, Phoenix, Tucson, Houston, American Classic.
1972 --	7	Jack Nicklaus, Bing Crosby, Doral-Eastern, Masters, U.S. Open, Westchester, Match Play, Walt Disney.
	3	Lee Trevino, Memphis, Hartford, St. Louis.
1971 --	5	Lee Trevino, Tallahassee, Memphis, U.S. Open, Canadian, Sahara.
	4	Jack Nicklaus, PGA, T of C, Byron Nelson, Walt Disney.
	3	Arnold Palmer, Bob Hope, Florida Citrus, Westchester.
1970 --	4	Billy Casper, Los Angeles, Masters, IVB, AVCO.

WIRE-TO-WIRE WINNERS (no ties):

1995 --	NONE
1994 --	Greg Norman, PLAYERS; Mike Springer, Kmart GGO; Bob Estes, Texas.
1993 --	Howard Twitty, Hawaiian; Nick Price, Western.
1992 --	Fred Couples, Nestle; David Frost, Hardee's.
1991 --	NONE
1990 --	Jose Maria Olazabal, World Series; Tim Simpson, Disney.
1989 --	Ian Baker-Finch, Colonial.
1988 --	Steve Pate, T of C; Larry Nelson, Atlanta; Bob Lohr, Disney; Curtis Strange, Nabisco.
1987 --	Joey Sindelar, B.C. Open; Tom Watson, Nabisco.
1986 --	NONE
1985 --	Tom Kite, T of C.
1984 --	Greg Norman, Kemper.
1983 --	Hal Sutton, PGA; Nick Price, World Series.
1982 --	Bob Gilder, Westchester; Ray Floyd, PGA; Tim Norris, Hartford.
1981 --	NONE
1980 --	Tom Watson, T of C, Byron Nelson; Bruce Lietzke, Colonial; Scott Hoch, Quad Cities.
1979 --	Bruce Lietzke, Tucson; Tom Watson, Heritage, T of C.
1978 --	Tom Watson, Tucson.
1977 --	Rik Massengale, Bob Hope; Andy Bean, Doral-Eastern; Lee Trevino, Canadian; Jerry Pate, Southern.
1976 --	Raymond Floyd, Masters; Mark Hayes, Byron Nelson.
1975 --	Johnny Miller, Tucson; Tom Weiskopf, Greensboro; Al Geiberger, TPC.
1974 --	Johnny Miller, Tucson, Heritage; Allen Miller, Tallahassee; Ed Sneed, Milwaukee.
1973 --	Lee Trevino, Doral-Eastern; Homero Blancas, Monsanto.
1972 --	Jack Nicklaus, Masters; Dave Hill, Monsanto.
1971 --	Jack Nicklaus, PGA; Arnold Palmer, Westchester.
1970 --	Tony Jacklin, U.S. Open.

Needing a victory to qualify for the 1995 Masters Tournament, Davis Love III won the 1995 Freeport-McMoRan Classic and then finished one stroke behind Ben Crenshaw at Augusta National.

PGA TOUR AWARDS

Three of the PGA TOUR's major awards — **PGA TOUR Player of the Year**, **PGA TOUR Rookie of the Year** and the **PGA TOUR Comeback Award** — were presented January 4, 1996 at the annual PGA TOUR Awards Dinner at La Costa.

Recipients of the Player of the Year, Rookie of the Year and Comeback Awards:

PGA TOUR Player of the Year

1990	Wayne Levi
1991	Fred Couples
1992	Fred Couples
1993	Nick Price
1994	Nick Price
1995	Greg Norman

PGA TOUR Rookie of the Year

1990	Robert Gamez
1991	John Daly
1992	Mark Carnevale
1993	Vijay Singh
1994	Ernie Els
1995	Woody Austin

PGA TOUR Comeback Player Award

1991	Bruce Fleisher, D.A. Weibring
1992	John Cook
1993	Howard Twitty
1994	Hal Sutton
1995	Bob Tway

PGA TOUR LIFETIME ACHIEVEMENT AWARD

The first **PGA TOUR Lifetime Achievement Award** also was presented January 4, 1996 at the annual PGA TOUR Awards Dinner. The PGA TOUR Lifetime Achievement Award honors those individuals "who have made outstanding contributions to the PGA TOUR over an extended period of time through their performances on the golf course as well as (through) their actions off the course in serving as ambassadors of the game."

The recipient of the first Lifetime Achievement Award was announced at La Costa.

ARNOLD PALMER AWARD

Awarded each year to the PGA TOUR's leading money winner.

1981	Tom Kite	$ 375,699
1982	Craig Stadler	$ 446,462
1983	Hal Sutton	$ 426,668
1984	Tom Watson	$ 476,260
1985	Curtis Strange	$ 542,321
1986	Greg Norman	$ 653,296
1987	Curtis Strange	$ 925,941
1988	Curtis Strange	$1,147,644
1989	Tom Kite	$1,395,278
1990	Greg Norman	$1,165,477
1991	Corey Pavin	$ 979,430
1992	Fred Couples	$1,344,188
1993	Nick Price	$1,478,557
1994	Nick Price	$1,499,927
1995	Greg Norman	$1,654,959

BYRON NELSON AWARD

The Byron Nelson Award was presented on the PGA TOUR for the first time in 1995 to honor the TOUR's scoring leader.

1995	Greg Norman	69.06

PGA TOUR CHARITY OF THE YEAR AWARD

The PGA TOUR Charity of the Year Award was started in 1987. Charities are nominated by the American Golf Sponsors and voted on by the Tournament Policy Board.

Year	Charity	Tournament
1987	Egleston Hospital for Children	BellSouth Classic
1988	Siskin Memorial Foundation	Chattanooga Classic
1989	Bobby Benson Foundation	United Airlines Hawaiian Open
1990	Salesmanship Club	GTE Byron Nelson Classic
1991	Arrowhead Ranch for Boys	Hardee's Golf Classic
1992	United Health Services System	B.C. Open
1993	Chinquapin School	Shell Houston Open
1994	Louisiana Children's Research Center for Development and Learning	Freeport-McMoRan Classic
1995	The Pro Kids Golf Academy	Buick Invitational

CARD WALKER AWARD

The Card Walker Award is given annually by the PGA TOUR to the person or group who has made significant contributions to the support of Junior Golf.

Year	Recipient	Year	Recipient
1981	Mrs. Lou Smith	1989	Selina Johnson
1982	Frank Emmet	1990	Tucson Conquistadores
1983	Jack Nicklaus	1991	American Junior Golf Association
1984	Sally Carroll	1992	Bill Dickey
1985	Don Padgett, Sr.	1993	Western Golf Association
1986	Chi Chi Rodriguez	1994	Fred Engh
1987	James S. Kemper	1995	Ryder System, Inc.
1988	William V. Powers	1996	Sandy LaBauve

PGA TOUR PLAYERS OF THE MONTH

Beginning with the 1994 season, a PGA TOUR Player of the Month is selected from January through October by a five-member media panel. The monthly winners receive special medals commemorating their selection.

1994 PLAYERS OF THE MONTH

January .... Phil Mickelson
February .... Corey Pavin
March .... Greg Norman
April .... Hale Irwin
May .... Tom Lehman
June .... Ernie Els
July .... Nick Price
August .... Nick Price
September ..... Mark McCumber
October .... Mark McCumber

1995 PLAYERS OF THE MONTH

January .... Phil Mickelson
February .... Peter Jacobsen
March .... Nick Faldo
April .... Davis Love III
May .... Ernie Els
June .... Greg Norman
July .... John Daly
August .... Steve Elkington
September ..... Hal Sutton
October .... Billy Mayfair

OTHER AWARDS WON BY PGA TOUR GOLFERS

SPORTING NEWS MAN OF THE YEAR

1971 .... Lee Trevino

SPORTS ILLUSTRATED SPORTSMAN OF THE YEAR

1960 .... Arnold Palmer
1964 .... Ken Venturi
1971 .... Lee Trevino
1978 .... Jack Nicklaus

ASSOCIATED PRESS MALE ATHLETE OF THE YEAR

1932 .... Gene Sarazen
1944 .... Byron Nelson
1945 .... Byron Nelson
1953 .... Ben Hogan
1971 .... Lee Trevino

VARDON TROPHY

The Vardon Trophy, named in honor of famed British golfer Harry Vardon, was placed in competition among American professionals in 1937. It was the successor to the Harry E. Radix Trophy, which had been awarded annually to the professional having the finest tournament record in the U.S. The Vardon Trophy is a bronze-colored plaque measuring 39" by 27" and features sculpted hands replicating Vardon's famed overlapping grip. From 1947 to 1987, the Vardon Trophy was awarded to the professional golfer with the lowest scoring average. In 1988, the criteria was adjusted to award the Vardon Trophy to the touring professional with the lowest adjusted scoring average. It is based on a minimum of 60 official rounds in events cosponsored or approved by the PGA TOUR, with no incomplete rounds (i.e. stipulated rounds as defined by the Rules of Golf, as approved by the USGA and the Royal & Ancient Golf Club of St. Andrews, Scotland). The adjusted score is computed from the average score of the field at each tournament. As a result, a player's adjusted score may be higher or lower than his actual score. For example, a player shoots 70 each day at a tournament while the field average was 73. His 280 total would then be adjusted to 268, since he actually played 12 shots better than the field during the tournament. Any player with an incomplete round will be ineligible to win the Vardon Trophy.

Year	Winner	Average
1937	Harry Cooper	*500
1938	Sam Snead	*520
1939	Byron Nelson	*473
1940	Ben Hogan	*423
1941	Ben Hogan	*494
1942-1946	No Award-World War II	
1947	Jimmy Demaret	69.90
1948	Ben Hogan	69.30
1949	Sam Snead	69.37
1950	Sam Snead	69.23
1951	Lloyd Mangrum	70.05
1952	Jack Burke	70.54
1953	Lloyd Mangrum	70.22
1954	E. J. Harrison	70.41
1955	Sam Snead	69.86
1956	Cary Middlecoff	70.35
1957	Dow Finsterwald	70.30
1958	Bob Rosburg	70.11
1959	Art Wall	70.35
1960	Billy Casper	69.95
1961	Arnold Palmer	69.85
1962	Arnold Palmer	70.27
1963	Billy Casper	70.58
1964	Arnold Palmer	70.01
1965	Billy Casper	70.85
1966	Billy Casper	70.27
1967	Arnold Palmer	70.18
1968	Billy Casper	69.82
1969	Dave Hill	70.34
1970	Lee Trevino	70.64
1971	Lee Trevino	70.27
1972	Lee Trevino	70.89
1973	Bruce Crampton	70.57
1974	Lee Trevino	70.53
1975	Bruce Crampton	70.51
1976	Don January	70.56
1977	Tom Watson	70.32
1978	Tom Watson	70.16
1979	Tom Watson	70.27
1980	Lee Trevino	69.73
1981	Tom Kite	69.80
1982	Tom Kite	70.21
1983	Raymond Floyd	70.61
1984	Calvin Peete	70.56
1985	Don Pooley	70.36
1986	Scott Hoch	70.08
1987	Dan Pohl	70.25
1988	Chip Beck	69.46
1989	Greg Norman	69.49
1990	Greg Norman	69.10
1991	Fred Couples	69.59
1992	Fred Couples	69.38
1993	Nick Price	69.11
1994	Greg Norman	68.81
1995	Steve Elkington	69.62

*Point system used, 1937—'41.

PGA PLAYER OF THE YEAR AWARD

The PGA Player of the Year Award is given to the top PGA TOUR player based on tournament wins, official money standing and scoring average. The point system for selecting the Player of the Year was amended in 1982, as follows: 30 points for winning PGA Championship, U.S. Open, British Open or Masters; 20 points for winning the NEC World Series of Golf or THE PLAYERS Championship; 10 points for winning all other designated PGA TOUR events. In addition, there is a 50-point bonus for winning two majors, 75-point bonus for winning three, 100-point bonus for winning four. For top 10 finishes on the PGA TOUR's official money list and scoring average list, the point value is: first, 20 points, then 18, 16, 14, 12, 10, 8, 6, 4, 2. Any incomplete rounds in the scoring average list will result in a .10 penalty per incomplete round.

1948—Ben Hogan
1949—Sam Snead
1950—Ben Hogan
1951—Ben Hogan
1952—Julius Boros
1953—Ben Hogan
1954—Ed Furgol
1955—Doug Ford
1956—Jack Burke
1957—Dick Mayer
1958—Dow Finsterwald
1959—Art Wall
1960—Arnold Palmer
1961—Jerry Barber
1962—Arnold Palmer
1963—Julius Boros
1964—Ken Venturi
1965—Dave Marr
1966—Billy Casper
1967—Jack Nicklaus
1968—Not Awarded
1969—Orville Moody
1970—Billy Casper
1971—Lee Trevino
1972—Jack Nicklaus
1973—Jack Nicklaus
1974—Johnny Miller
1975—Jack Nicklaus
1976—Jack Nicklaus
1977—Tom Watson
1978—Tom Watson
1979—Tom Watson
1980—Tom Watson
1981—Bill Rogers
1982—Tom Watson
1983—Hal Sutton
1984—Tom Watson
1985—Lanny Wadkins
1986—Bob Tway
1987—Paul Azinger
1988—Curtis Strange
1989—Tom Kite
1990—Nick Faldo
1991—Corey Pavin
1992—Fred Couples
1993—Nick Price
1994—Nick Price
1995—Greg Norman

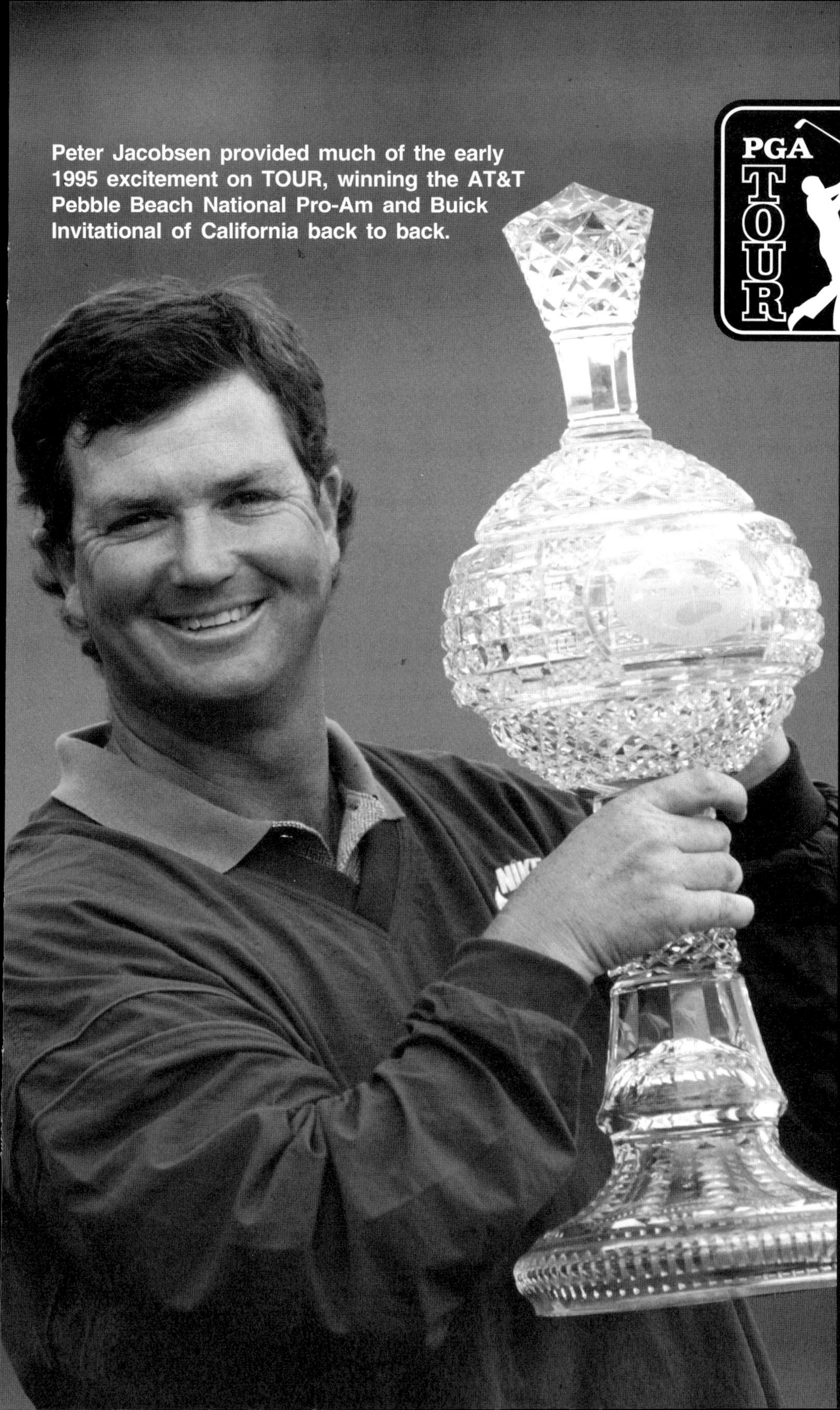

PGA TOUR

Peter Jacobsen provided much of the early 1995 excitement on TOUR, winning the AT&T Pebble Beach National Pro-Am and Buick Invitational of California back to back.

PGA TOUR MARKETING

PGA TOUR LICENSING

Formed in February 1995, PGA TOUR Licensing was established to manage the domestic licensing interests of the PGA TOUR, Senior PGA TOUR and certain tournaments of both TOURs.

The goal of PGA TOUR Licensing is to further expand the public's awareness of the PGA TOUR marks and to help develop the PGA TOUR as the world's premier golf property.

PGA TOUR Licensing is building a family of manufacturers dedicated to producing upscale merchandise which reflects the tradition and quality of the PGA TOUR.

Products featuring the PGA TOUR marks will include a comprehensive apparel offering, headwear, golf accessories (i.e. golf gloves, golf bags, divot repair tools, ball markers and bag tags), pewter giftwear, luggage, financial instruments, publications, home furnishings, collectibles and other related products. Merchandise will begin appearing in retail outlets, including PGA TOUR Shops, pro shops, department stores and specialty stores, as early as the first quarter of 1996 and will be widely available for the year-end holiday season.

PGA TOUR Licensing is a joint venture between The Paradies Shops and Battle Enterprises, Inc., both Atlanta-based companies.

The Paradies Shops currently manages 13 PGA TOUR Shops in airports, as well as three in other retail locations throughout the country. In addition to the 16 PGA TOUR Shops, The Paradies Shops also operate more than 200 news, gift and specialty shops throughout the United States.

Battle Enterprises, Inc. (BEI), a full-service licensing representative, also is the sister company of The Collegiate Licensing Company, a licensing representative for more than 150 colleges, universities, bowl games and athletic conferences.

PGA TOUR MARKETING PARTNERS

ANHEUSER-BUSCH

One of golf's most enduring corporate supporters, Anheuser-Busch is one of the PGA TOUR's leading sponsors.

Through the years Michelob, which is brewed by Anheuser-Busch, has sponsored thousands of local golf tournaments, a host of touring pros and a long list of professional tournaments, including the newly renamed Michelob Championship at Kingsmill.

Primary features of the Michelob/PGA TOUR relationship include Michelob as the "Official Sponsor of the PGA TOUR's 19th Hole," a unique interactive display, and presenting sponsor for THE TOUR Championship, as well as media-driven national promotions and extensive participation in television's TOUR coverage.

In addition, O'Doul's TOUR program includes network television advertising, national point-of-sale promotions and tournament sampling opportunities.

O'Doul's is the "Official Non-Alcoholic Beer of the PGA TOUR and Senior PGA TOUR."

AT&T

AT&T enters its third year as the "Official Telecommunications Company of the PGA TOUR and the Senior PGA TOUR." As part of this agreement, AT&T provides phones for player use in locker rooms at TOUR and Senior TOUR events, as well as special rates on AT&T telecommunications equipment.

AT&T entertains its clients through pro-am spots and corporate hospitality at TOUR and Senior TOUR events throughout the year, and is a major advertiser on TOUR telecasts. Future involvement will include TOUR-themed offers to AT&T's residential customers. AT&T continues its title sponsorship of the AT&T Pebble Beach National Pro-Am.

BAYER ASPIRIN

Bayer Aspirin is the "Official Pain Reliever of the PGA TOUR and Senior PGA TOUR" and is provided to players via the Centinela Fitness Training Facilities.

Bayer, a long-time industry leader for pain relief and prevention, conducts consumer sampling at a number of tournaments and advertises in such TOUR products as *ON TOUR* Magazine and "Inside the Senior PGA TOUR."

Bayer, along with the American Heart Association and PGA TOUR, sponsors "Strokes Against Stroke," a national awareness and fund-raising program to help fight stroke. Team Bayer, comprised of several PGA TOUR and Senior TOUR players, raises funds on behalf of Bayer Aspirin during tournaments in May — Stroke Awareness Month.

BUICK

Buick Motor Division is a long-time marketing partner and "Official Car of the PGA TOUR." The relationship between the TOUR and Buick over the last 30 years has led to sponsorship of PGA TOUR tournaments across the country.

It all began with the Buick Open, now the TOUR event with the longest continuing sponsorship. The tournament is played in Flint, MI, Buick's "hometown." Each year, countless Buick employees use their vacation time to volunteer at the event, which they consider their own.

Buick's partnership with the TOUR includes the sponsorship of four tournaments: the Buick Open (Flint, MI); the Buick Challenge (Callaway Gardens, GA); the Buick Invitational (San Diego, CA); and the Buick Classic (Rye, NY).

To enhance fans' awareness of Buick tournaments, the company has set up a nationwide sweepstakes that encourages fans to test drive and register to win a Buick. The company has said its golf-related promotions are the most successful it has ever run.

COCA-COLA

The Coca-Cola Company is entering its fifth year of sponsorship as the "Official Soft Drink of the PGA TOUR." Coca-Cola Scoreboards will travel to 38 PGA TOUR tournaments in 1996, providing up-to-the-minute scores, weather warnings and other important information for golf fans.

The Coca-Cola classic Clinics, scheduled at 38 tournaments in 1996, provide an opportunity for children in the community to receive tips from TOUR professionals. They also have a chance to win a "Coca-Cola classic Behind The Scenes VIP Tour" of the tournament. The winner has an opportunity to meet some TOUR players and visit the media room, the scoreboard trailer and the TV compound.

Coca-Cola utilizes its relationship with the TOUR as an entertainment opportunity for its clients, as well as in promotional programs at retail. In 1996, 41 PGA TOUR tournaments will serve Coca-Cola products.

DELTA AIR LINES

Delta Air Lines is the "Official Airline of the PGA TOUR, Senior PGA TOUR and NIKE TOUR." Delta offers TOUR players preferred rates on air travel and awards tournament winners with Frequent Flyer mileage. Delta is involved with over 65 tournaments on the three tours through advertising or hospitality.

Delta prints PGA TOUR, Senior PGA TOUR and NIKE TOUR schedules in its timetables, includes PGA TOUR stories in *Sky* Magazine and airs TOUR features on inflight video programs. Delta rewards its most frequent flyers with sweepstakes programs featuring a chance to win trips to TOUR events and pro-am spots.

PGA TOUR MARKETING PARTNERS *continued*

EASTMAN KODAK

In its capacity as the "Official Film, Photographic Paper and Processing Company of the PGA TOUR," the company furnishes the PGA TOUR with film supplies for its photographers and tournament operations staff.

IBM

In one of the most appropriate sports collaborations ever, IBM entered into an agreement with the PGA TOUR to develop the IBM Scoring System. This is an agreement that benefits everyone, from the players to the media to the television viewers to the spectators at each TOUR event.

The IBM Scoring System is so fast that scoring updates are seen just seconds after a player completes a hole. Players and galleries on the course know where the field stands at all times. Remote computers keep fans informed at other locations, such as hospitality areas, host hotels, etc.

The TOUR's agreement with IBM as the "Official Computer of the PGA TOUR" runs through 1998.

PGA TOUR MARKETING PARTNERS *continued*

MASTERCARD

MasterCard, one of the TOUR's newer corporate marketing partners, will become a major sponsor of the PGA TOUR and Senior PGA TOUR. MasterCard is the "Official Credit Card" of the PGA TOUR and Senior PGA TOUR. It also will sponsor scoreboard signage on both TOURs that will travel to approximately 80 tournaments in 1996, providing information to fans, players and media alike.

MasterCard is title sponsor of the MasterCard Colonial on the PGA TOUR. It will become title sponsor of the Senior Tournament of Champions, to be renamed the MasterCard Championship, in 1997 when that event moves to Hualalai, Hawaii, a PGA TOUR Resort.

MasterCard also will sponsor the MasterCard Grand Masters, a separate Senior TOUR competition for players 60 and older.

MasterCard's sponsorship is integrated across all aspects of the TOUR, and will help MasterCard build its brand and service relationships with member banks.

MERRILL LYNCH

Merrill Lynch sponsors the popular Merrill Lynch Shoot-Outs at PGA TOUR and Senior PGA TOUR events. The 10-man, nine-hole elimination competitions culminate at year-end finals. The Shoot-Outs are crowd pleasers wherever they are played. ABC will televise the Shoot-Out Final for the PGA TOUR; ESPN will air the Senior PGA TOUR Shoot-Out Final. Results from the 1995 Merrill Lynch Shoot-Out Series on the PGA TOUR and a schedule for 1996 can be found on page 497.

PGA TOUR MARKETING PARTNERS *continued*

NATIONAL CAR RENTAL

National Car Rental is the "Official Car Rental Company of the PGA TOUR and the Senior PGA TOUR." National offers TOUR players preferred rental car rates and other benefits, such as Emerald Club Memberships. National awards tournament winners on both TOURs with a free week of a full-size rental car in recognition of their achievements. National rental cars and vans are used at several TOUR tournaments to fulfill their transportation needs. Emerald Club members benefit from the sponsorship through special PGA TOUR-themed offers outlined in Emerald Club newsletters.

RESOURCE

In response to the growing awareness of the relationship between proper diet and sports performance, ReSource has joined the PGA TOUR and Senior PGA TOUR as the "Official Nutritional Drink."

ReSource is developed by Sandoz Nutrition, a world leader in nutritional products for more than 75 years. ReSource will be provided to players on both the PGA TOUR and Senior TOUR.

ReSource will promote its relationship with the TOUR through a variety of media products, including ON TOUR Magazine, "Inside the Senior PGA TOUR" and advertising within televised TOUR events.

ROYAL CARIBBEAN CRUISE LINE

Royal Caribbean Cruise Line

Royal Caribbean is the "Official Cruise Line of the PGA TOUR." The company offers special Golf Ahoy! cruises along with special cruise rates for TOUR members. In 1996, for the seventh consecutive year, the Royal Caribbean Classic will be played at Key Biscayne, FL as part of the Senior PGA TOUR.

PGA TOUR MARKETING PARTNERS *continued*

SKYTEL

SkyTel, as the "Official Wireless Messaging Company of the PGA TOUR," supports the TOUR by providing SkyPagers for use in several areas of the TOUR. SkyTel also seeks to have pro-am guests and tournament volunteers use SkyPagers to help them communicate better throughout tournament week. SkyTel, whose products are targeted to the business traveler, is a natural partner when considering the nature of the TOUR's business.

Publications

BUSINESSWEEK

Once again in 1996, *BusinessWeek* will publish two special supplements dealing exclusively with the PGA TOUR. In January, "The 1996 Senior TOUR Journal" will be published. "The Business of the PGA TOUR" will be published in April. *BusinessWeek* also publishes *ON TOUR* Magazine for PGA TOUR Partners.

GOLF MAGAZINE

Golf Magazine covers the PGA TOUR in *TOUR Magazine*. This insert appears in the magazine's February issue and as a handout at most PGA TOUR events. *Golf Magazine* also produces a supplement that is distributed at NIKE TOUR events.

PGA TOUR PARTNERS

Created in 1991, PGA TOUR Partners offers golfers and golf fans the opportunity to become a valuable part of the PGA TOUR.

For a nominal annual membership fee, Partners offers the most dedicated golf fan a chance to go "inside the ropes" by providing unique benefits that bring them closer to players, tournaments and courses of the PGA TOUR. 1996 benefits include:

- ***ON TOUR* Magazine** — *ON TOUR* is published by the TOUR exclusively for TOUR players, officials, Partners and the golf media. Ten times each year, Partners receive issues featuring instruction, player profiles and other unique insights. Since its premier issue in 1993, ON TOUR has proven to be a member favorite.

- **Complimentary VIP Pass to a TOUR Tournament** — Partners are the TOUR's guest for a day at one of more than 40 tournaments around the country. Partners even can give their pass to a friend or family member.

- **Partners Fantasy Challenge** — This interactive game allows Partners to choose their dream team, follow tournament results and have the chance to win great prizes, including pro-am spots. Partners are passionate about this fantasy game. TOUR players often get mail from Partners expressing their interest in the player's performance.

- **Credentials, Travel and Merchandise** — Partners receive a personalized, engraved bag tag and ID card to identify themselves as a member. Partners Classics are handicapped tournaments held at TOUR host sites exclusively for members and their guests. Partners also are offered special TOUR merchandise.

More importantly, the program funds the PGA TOUR Charity Team Competition (see pages 501-504). Since 1991, Partners has distributed more than $8 million to worthy nonprofit organizations throughout the country.

Partners memberships make great personal or business gifts. Call 1-800-545-9920 for more information.

MERRILL LYNCH SHOOT-OUT SERIES

A 10-man competition covering nine holes of play, the Merrill Lynch Shoot-Out Series, now in its ninth season, will be held at 18 different PGA TOUR events in 1996, with the weekly winners collecting $5,000 from the $15,100 purse.

What is a Shoot-Out? The format is easy to understand and a pleasure to watch. Ten players begin. On each hole, the player with the highest score is dropped from the field. If there is a tie, those players participate in a sudden-death playoff where a pitch shot, a chip or a long putt is executed to eliminate the player farthest from the hole.

Weekly Shoot-Outs: The 1996 Merrill Lynch Shoot-Out Series competitions will be held on Tuesday of tournament week. The field for each Shoot-Out consists of that tournament's defending champion, the six leading money winners entered in that tournament and three sponsor selections.

Shoot-Out Championship: The field for the final competition consists of the top three money winners on the 1996 PGA TOUR Official Money List and seven sponsor selections. Ten players will vie for $600,000 in prize money, with $150,000 going to the winner. Curtis Strange won the title in 1995 at the Mid Ocean Club in Tucker's Town, Bermuda. The Merrill Lynch Shoot-Out Championship returns to Bermuda for the third year on October 15, 1996.

1995 MERRILL LYNCH SHOOT-OUT WINNERS

AT&T Pebble Beach National Pro-Am	Ben Crenshaw
Bob Hope Chrysler Classic	Scott Hoch
Nissan Open	Brad Faxon
THE PLAYERS Championship	Fred Funk
Freeport-McMoRan Classic	Jim Furyk
MCI Classic	Steve Stricker
Kmart Greater Greensboro Open	Brad Faxon (2)
Shell Houston Open	Scott Simpson
BellSouth Classic	David Duval
GTE Byron Nelson Classic	Jeff Sluman
Kemper Open	Jay Haas
FedEx St. Jude Classic	Woody Austin
NEC World Series of Golf	Woody Austin (2)
Greater Milwaukee Open	John Daly
B.C. Open	Kirk Triplett
Quad City Classic	Rained out
Walt Disney World/Oldsmobile Golf Classic	Rained out
Las Vegas Invitational	Woody Austin (3)

1996 MERRILL LYNCH SHOOT-OUT SCHEDULE

Bob Hope Chrysler Classic	Jan. 16
AT&T Pebble Beach National Pro-Am	Jan. 30
Nissan Open	Feb.20
Freeport•McDermott Classic	Mar. 19
THE PLAYERS Championship	Mar. 26
BellSouth Classic	Apr. 2
MCI Classic	Apr. 16
Kmart Greater Greensboro Open	Apr. 23
Shell Houston Open	Apr. 30
GTE Byron Nelson Classic	May 7
Kemper Open	May 21
FedEx St. Jude Classic	June 18
NEC World Series of Golf	Aug. 20
Greater Milwaukee Open	Aug. 27
Quad City Classic	Sept. 10
B.C. Open	Sept. 17
Las Vegas Invitational	Oct. 1
Walt Disney World/Oldsmobile Golf Classic	Oct. 15
Merrrill Lynch Shoot-Out Championship	Oct. 15

CHAMPIONSHIP WINNERS

1987	Fuzzy Zoeller
1988	David Frost
1989	Chip Beck
1990	John Mahaffey
1991	Davis Love III
1992	Chip Beck
1993	Davis Love III
1994	Corey Pavin
1995	Curtis Strange

1996 CHAMPIONSHIP PRIZE MONEY BREAKDOWN

1st	$150,000
2nd	90,000
3rd	55,000
4th	50,000
5th	45,000
6th	44,000
7th	43,000
8th	42,000
9th	41,000
10th	40,000

WEEKLY PRIZE MONEY BREAKDOWN

1st	$5,000
2nd	3,000
3rd	1,500
4th	1,100
5th	1,000
6th	900
7th	800
8th	700
9th	600
10th	500

CENTINELA FITNESS CENTER

The "Official Hospital of the PGA TOUR" since 1984, Centinela Hospital Medical Center in Inglewood, CA again will sponsor the Centinela Hospital Player Fitness Center (CHPFC) on TOUR in 1996.

One of the TOUR's most popular innovations, the CHPFC is a mobile gymnasium that includes state-of-the-art exercise equipment, television, stereo, three treatment tables, various physical therapy modalities and a full line of vitamins.

Staffed by qualified physical therapists, the CHPFC travels to the vast majority of TOUR events across the country, providing both rehabilitative and preventive care for TOUR members.

During its 13 years on TOUR, the Centinela Hospital Player Fitness Center has attracted the interest of virtually every player, with at least 80 percent using the mobile unit on a regular basis. Housed in a 45-foot-long trailer (expandable to 24 feet wide when parked), the Centinela Hospital Player Fitness Center enables TOUR pros to maintain peak levels of performance at absolutely no cost to the individual players.

According to Dr. Frank Jobe, Medical Director of the PGA TOUR and team physician of the Los Angeles Dodgers, "Centinela Hospital Medical Center provides each player with a personal physical conditioning program based on that individual's current level of conditioning." Dr. Jobe works with Dr. Lewis Yocum, Assistant Medical Director of the PGA TOUR and orthopedic consultant for the California Angels.

The CHPFC has made its impact, with many players finding the center and available technicians an invaluable aid to their success on TOUR. In fact, many players have commented that they would have been unable to compete in some tournaments without the facility.

"If they'd had this setup several years ago," Fuzzy Zoeller said, "it might have saved me from having back surgery."

"If it wasn't for the Centinela Hospital Player Fitness Center," said Curtis Strange, "I wouldn't be here."

Centinela Hospital Medical Center's Biomechanics Laboratory has done research and testing on professional golfers' swings and, based on the results, developed scientific exercise programs that are available through books and videotapes. These programs, designed by Dr. Jobe and Dr. Yocum, have helped countless golfers stretch their potentials while minimizing the risk of injury. For more information, contact Centinela Hospital Medical Center.

Bayer Aspirin supports the Centinela Hospital Player Fitness Centers by providing players with one of the leading pain-relievers on the market. Bayer also conducts consumer sampling at tournaments and explores new ways to provide better healthcare products for golfers.

The products contributed by sponsors of the Centinela Hospital Player Fitness Centers have helped make the facility such a success that a similar fitness van has been operating on the Senior PGA TOUR since 1986.

The Centinela Hospital Player Fitness Centers are out on TOUR in 1996.

Jim Gallagher, Jr., with victories at the Greater Greensboro Open and FedEx St. Jude Classic, went over $1 million for the second time in his career in 1995.

PGA TOUR EVENTS RAISED $25.2 MILLION FOR CHARITY IN '95

Charity, as the old line goes, begins at home.

That was certainly true on the PGA TOUR in 1995, when TOUR events raised $25.2 million for charities in tournament hometowns.

"We are very proud that our events have such a positive impact on the communities in which they are played every year," said TOUR Commissioner Timothy W. Finchem. "Providing the very best playing opportunities for our members while contributing to charities are at the heart of everything we do.

"The American Golf Sponsors and the thousands of volunteers who work at our events deserve a great deal of credit for what they accomplish in their communities week in and week out," Finchem noted.

The $25.2 million total surpassed the previous one-year record of $24.7 million, set in 1994. Charity dollars from the Senior PGA TOUR and NIKE TOUR will push the total 1995 PGA TOUR contributions to charity well over the $30 million mark for the second year in a row.

Since the first charity donation tournament in 1938, more than $275 million has been raised by the events on the three tours operated by the PGA TOUR. The $300 million barrier will fall sometime during the 1996 season.

A Brief History of TOUR Charitable Contributions

1938	First contribution	$ 10,000	(Palm Beach Invitational)
1950	Contributions reach	$ 1,000,000	
1960	Contributions reach	$ 5,000,000	
1976	TOUR reaches	$10,000,000	
1977	AGS formed	$ 3,300,000	for year
1978		$ 4,300,000	"
1979	$20 million overall	$ 4,400,000	"
1980		$ 4,500,000	"
1981	$30 million overall	$ 6,800,000	"
1982		$ 7,200,000	"
1983		$ 7,800,000	"
1984	$50 million overall	$ 9,400,000	"
1985		$11,300,000	"
1986		$16,100,000	"
1987	$100 million overall	$17,600,000	"
1988	$125 million overall	$18,390,000	"
1989	$145 million overall	$19,779,000	"
1990	$165 million overall	$20,191,000	"
1991	$185 million overall	$19,534,000	"
1992	$200 million overall	$22,223,055	"
1993	$230 million overall	$22,752,137	"
1994	$250 million overall	$24,701,631	"
1995	$275 million overall	$25,200,000	"

CHARITY is the leading winner on the **PGA TOUR**

CHARITY TEAM COMPETITION CUMULATIVE TOTALS

	1986	1987	1988	1989	1990	1991	1992	1993	1994	1995	TOTAL
Mercedes Championships	$1,562	$300,000	$7,500	$500,000	$12,000	$8,500	$120,000	$17,600	$17,600	$100,000	$1,084,762
Walt Disney World/Oldsmobile Golf Classic	500,000	130,000	11,500	90,000	9,250	70,000	10,000	17,600	100,000	60,000	998,350
MCI Classic	1,562	5,555	250,000	10,500	90,000	500,000	10,000	28,000	17,600	20,000	933,217
Shell Houston Open	11,500	5,555	500,000	27,000	24,000	28,000	10,000	100,000	17,600	20,000	743,655
Phoenix Open	14,000	5,555	27,000	8,500	500,000	24,000	10,000	17,600	17,600	20,000	644,255
Las Vegas Invitational	26,000	500,000	21,000	17,000	21,000	50,000	10,000	17,600	17,600	20,000	700,200
JCPenney Classic	120,000	13,000	150,000	10,000	25,000	9,750	180,000	17,600	17,600	20,000	562,950
Honda Classic	16,000	38,000	5,500	12,500	250,000	150,000	10,000	40,000	17,600	20,000	559,600
Sprint International	18,000	60,000	9,000	250,000	40,000	80,000	10,000	17,600	17,600	20,000	522,200
Buick Open	1,562	100,000	125,000	7,500	125,000	11,000	10,000	17,600	75,000	40,000	512,662
Quad City Classic	1,562	50,000	80,000	19,000	11,500	250,000	10,000	50,000	17,600	20,000	509,662
B.C. Open	20,000	70,000	60,000	125,000	14,000	27,000	75,000	26,000	17,600	50,000	484,600
THE PLAYERS Championship	300,000	5,555	24,000	7,000	28,000	15,000	10,000	25,000	35,000	20,000	469,555
United Airlines Hawaiian Open	1,562	200,000	9,500	50,000	10,500	9,000	100,000	35,000	30,800	20,000	466,362
Freeport•McDermott Classic	32,000	5,555	23,000	40,000	150,000	19,000	30,000	17,600	17,600	20,000	354,755
Greater Milwaukee Open	1,562	20,500	20,000	80,000	30,000	125,000	10,000	17,600	17,600	20,000	342,262
Deposit Guaranty Golf Classic	60,000	5,555	10,000	150,000	8,500	13,000	40,000	17,600	17,600	20,000	342,255
Buick Invitational	40,000	90,000	10,500	9,000	10,000	30,000	60,000	17,600	17,600	55,000	339,700
MasterCard Colonial	1,562	80,000	50,000	13,500	13,500	100,000	10,000	17,600	27,000	20,000	333,162
Buick Challenge	200,000	5,555	7,000	20,000	11,000	12,000	10,000	17,600	25,000	20,000	328,155
Canon Greater Hartford Open	22,000	5,555	6,000	70,000	60,000	25,000	10,000	17,600	26,000	75,000	317,155
CVS Charity Classic	80,000	33,000	15,500	60,000	20,000	26,000	10,000	17,600	17,600	20,000	299,700
Greater Greensboro Open	140,000	5,555	5,000	28,000	9,500	21,000	35,000	17,600	17,600	20,000	299,255
Nissan Open	35,000	5,555	90,000	30,000	16,000	40,000	10,000	17,600	17,600	20,000	281,755
BellSouth Classic	1,562	10,000	12,500	22,000	19,000	90,000	10,000	75,000	17,600	20,000	277,662
Bob Hope Chrysler Classic	1,562	5,555	11,000	100,000	17,000	60,000	10,000	17,600	17,600	35,000	275,317

CHARITY TEAM COMPETITION CUMULATIVE TOTALS

	1986	1987	1988	1989	1990	1991	1992	1993	1994	1995	TOTAL
Buick Classic	$50,000	$18,000	$18,000	$13,000	$70,000	$11,500	$10,000	$17,600	$17,600	$20,000	$245,700
Sazale Classic	100,000	12,000	8,500	8,000	100,000	16,000					244,500
Kemper Open	24,000	5,555	100,000	12,000	15,000	17,000	10,000	17,600	17,600	20,000	238,755
AT&T Pebble Beach National Pro-Am	1,562	5,555	70,000	15,000	22,000	22,000	10,000	17,600	17,600	20,000	201,317
Lincoln-Mercury Kapalua International		5,555	25,000	11,000	80,000	12,500	10,000	17,600	17,600	20,000	199,255
NEC World Series of Golf	1,562	5,555	17,000	6,000	50,000	20,000	10,000	17,600	17,600	45,000	190,317
Motorola Western Open	1,562	16,000	29,000	9,500	23,000	18,000	10,000	17,600	40,000	20,000	184,662
GTE Byron Nelson Classic	1,562	5,555	30,000	21,000	9,000	9,250	10,000	30,800	28,000	37,500	182,667
LaCantera Texas Open			13,000	25,000	27,000	14,000	45,000	17,600	17,600	20,000	179,200
Nortel Open	29,000	15,000	12,000	26,000	13,000	10,500	10,000	17,600	17,600	20,000	170,700
THE TOUR Championship	1,562	5,555	6,500	18,000	26,000	13,500	10,000	17,600	50,000	20,000	168,717
FedEx St. Jude Classic	10,000	25,500	13,500	23,000	9,750	10,000	10,000	27,000	17,600	20,000	166,350
Chattanooga Classic	12,500	43,000	28,000	24,000	12,500	9,500	25,000				154,500
Bell Canadian Open		11,000	22,000	11,500	18,000	23,000	10,000	17,600	17,600	20,000	150,700
Pensacola Open	70,000	23,000	14,000	6,500							113,500
Gatlin Brothers Southwest Classic	45,000	28,000	26,000								99,000
Bay Hill Invitational								17,600	17,600	42,500	77,700
Memorial Tournament		5,555	8,000					17,600	17,600	20,000	68,755
Doral-Ryder Open								17,600	17,600	20,000	55,200
Michelob Championship at Kingsmill								17,600	17,600	20,000	55,200
Centel Classic	1,562	14,000	19,000	14,000							48,562
Franklin Templeton Shark Shootout										20,000	20,000
PGA Championship	1,562										1,562
TOTALS	$2,000,000	2,000,000	2,000,000	2,000,000	2,000,000	2,000,000	1,000,000	1,000,000	1,000,000	1,180,000	$16,200,000

FINAL 1995 PGA TOUR CHARITY TEAM COMPETITION STANDINGS

	TOURNAMENT NAME	TOURNAMENT TOTAL	TOURNAMENT BONUS
1.	MERCEDES CHAMPIONSHIPS	2,816,847	$100,000
2.	CANON GREATER HARTFORD OPEN	2,250,480	75,000
3.	WALT DISNEY WORLD/OLDSMOBILE CLASSIC	2,129,561	60,000
4.	BUICK INVITATIONAL OF CALIFORNIA	2,010,906	55,000
5.	B.C. OPEN	1,904,867	50,000
6.	NEC WORLD SERIES OF GOLF	1,873,872	45,000
7.	NESTLE INVITATIONAL	1,833,793	42,500
8.	BUICK OPEN	1,792,493	40,000
9.	GTE BYRON NELSON CLASSIC	1,758,225	37,500
10.	BOB HOPE CHRYSLER CLASSIC	1,686,414	35,000
11.	MCI CLASSIC	1,593,290	20,000
12.	UNITED AIRLINES HAWAIIAN OPEN	1,585,951	20,000
13.	BELLSOUTH CLASSIC	1,511,567	20,000
14.	LAS VEGAS INVITATIONAL	1,495,033	20,000
15.	BELL CANADIAN OPEN	1,476,106	20,000
16.	GREATER MILWAUKEE OPEN	1,465,576	20,000
17.	FREEPORT-MCMORAN CLASSIC	1,460,164	20,000
18.	HONDA CLASSIC	1,428,151	20,000
19.	NORTHERN TELECOM OPEN	1,393,736	20,000
20.	LINCOLN-MERCURY KAPALUA INTERNATIONAL	1,247,293	20,000
21.	THE TOUR CHAMPIONSHIP	1,210,041	20,000
22.	SHELL HOUSTON OPEN	1,173,988	20,000
23.	FRANKLIN TEMPLETON SHARK SHOOTOUT	1,171,625	20,000
24.	DEPOSIT GUARANTY GOLF CLASSIC	1,162,233	20,000
25.	NISSAN OPEN	1,132,244	20,000
26.	KEMPER OPEN	1,078,461	20,000
27.	ANHEUSER-BUSCH GOLF CLASSIC	1,062,989	20,000
28.	FEDEX ST. JUDE CLASSIC	980,831	20,000
29.	JCPENNEY CLASSIC	947,386	20,000
30.	IDEON CLASSIC AT PLEASANT VALLEY	936,187	20,000
31.	AT&T PEBBLE BEACH NATIONAL PRO-AM	914,116	20,000
32.	MEMORIAL TOURNAMENT	894,502	20,000
33.	DORAL-RYDER OPEN	830,548	20,000
34.	BUICK CLASSIC	813,724	20,000
35.	MOTOROLA WESTERN OPEN	803,630	20,000
36.	PHOENIX OPEN	786,401	20,000
37.	SPRINT INTERNATIONAL	784,766	20,000
38.	COLONIAL NATIONAL INVITATION	784,281	20,000
39.	BUICK CHALLENGE	756,207	20,000
40.	KMART GREATER GREENSBORO OPEN	708,569	20,000
41.	LACANTERA TEXAS OPEN	672,244	20,000
42.	QUAD CITY CLASSIC	556,701	20,000
43.	THE PLAYERS CHAMPIONSHIP	482,907	20,000
		Total	$1,200,000

1996 PGA TOUR CHARITY TEAM COMPETITION DRAFT

1. **NORTEL OPEN**
   1. Phil Mickelson
   2. Don Pooley
   3. Brandel Chamblee
   4. Bob Gilder

2. **FREEPORT•MCDERMOTT CLASSIC**
   1. Greg Norman
   2. Grant Waite
   3. Mike Standly
   4. Brian Tennyson

3. **FEDEX ST. JUDE CLASSIC**
   1. Lee Janzen
   2. Russ Cochran
   3. Lanny Wadkins
   4. David Peoples

4. **KEMPER OPEN**
   1. Corey Pavin
   2. Rocco Mediate
   3. Dave Stockton, Jr.
   4. Robert Wrenn

5. **NISSAN OPEN**
   1. Nick Price
   2. David Edwards
   3. Marco Dawson
   4. Joey Gullion

6. **MEMORIAL TOURNAMENT**
   1. Jim Gallagher, Jr.
   2. Gene Sauers
   3. Doug Martin
   4. Jack Nicklaus

7. **DEPOSIT GUARANTY GOLF CLASSIC**
   1. Davis Love III
   2. Glen Day
   3. Scott Gump
   4. Joel Edwards

8. **HONDA CLASSIC**
   1. Ernie Els
   2. John Morse
   3. John Adams
   4. Brad Fabel

9. **THE TOUR CHAMPIONSHIP**
   1. Steve Elkington
   2. Gil Morgan
   3. Franklin Langham
   4. Emlyn Aubrey

10. **LAS VEGAS INVITATIONAL**
    1. Tom Lehman
    2. Curt Byrum
    3. Tom Byrum
    4. Wayne Grady

11. **GREATER MILWAUKEE OPEN PRESENTED BY LITE BEER**
    1. Fred Couples
    2. Mike Hulbert
    3. Jerry Kelly
    4. Ian Baker-Finch

12. **BELL CANADIAN OPEN**
    1. Justin Leonard
    2. Joey Sindelar
    3. Phil Blackmar
    4. Jay Williamson

13. **DORAL-RYDER OPEN**
    1. Nick Faldo
    2. Bob Lohr
    3. Tom Purtzer
    4. Mark Carnevale

14. **AT&T PEBBLE BEACH NATIONAL PRO-AM**
    1. Mark O'Meara
    2. Dan Forsman
    3. Brian Henninger
    4. Steve Hart

15. **BUICK CLASSIC**
    1. Vijay Singh
    2. Guy Boros
    3. Charlie Rymer
    4. Shane Bertsch

16. **SPRINT INTERNATIONAL**
    1. David Duval
    2. Joe Ozaki
    3. Mark Wiebe
    4. Doug Tewell

17. **MCI CLASSIC**
    1. Payne Stewart
    2. Jay Don Blake
    3. Dillard Pruitt
    4. Hale Irwin

18. **SHELL HOUSTON OPEN**
    1. Jeff Maggert
    2. Robert Gamez
    3. Rick Fehr
    4. Gary Hallberg

19. **MASTERCARD COLONIAL**
    1. Billy Mayfair
    2. Craig Parry
    3. Michael Bradley
    4. Roger Maltbie

20. **KMART GREATER GREENSBORO OPEN**
    1. Ben Crenshaw
    2. Mike Heinen
    3. Pete Jordan
    4. Chris Perry

21. **UNITED AIRLINES HAWAIIAN OPEN**
    1. Peter Jacobsen
    2. Lennie Clements
    3. Brian Claar
    4. Bart Bryant

22. **PHOENIX OPEN**
    1. Mark Calcavecchia
    2. Nolan Henke
    3. Jim Carter
    4. Howard Twitty

23. **BUICK CHALLENGE**
    1. John Daly
    2. Steve Jones
    3. Neal Lancaster
    4. Hugh Royer III

24. **CVS CHARITY CLASSIC**
    1. Jay Haas
    2. Andrew Magee
    3. Jay Delsing
    4. Olin Browne

25. **LINCOLN-MERCURY KAPALUA INTERNATIONAL***
    1. Scott Hoch
    2. Larry Mize
    3. David Ogrin
    4. John Wilson

26. **FRANKLIN TEMPLETON SHARK SHOOTOUT***
    1. Brad Faxon
    2. Jesper Parnevik
    3. Kelly Gibson
    4. Keith Clearwater

27. **QUAD CITY CLASSIC**
    1. Loren Roberts
    2. John Cook
    3. Dicky Price
    4. Steve Pate

28. **LACANTERA TEXAS OPEN**
    1. Duffy Waldorf
    2. Blaine McCallister
    3. Mike Brisky
    4. Paul Goydos

29. **JCPENNEY CLASSIC***
    1. Brad Bryant
    2. Fuzzy Zoeller
    3. Jonathan Kaye
    4. Ed Dougherty

30. **BELLSOUTH CLASSIC**
    1. Scott Simpson
    2. Sandy Lyle
    3. Lee Rinker
    4. Ken Green

31. **MICHELOB CHAMPIONSHIP AT KINGSMILL**
    1. Curtis Strange
    2. Ted Tryba
    3. Bobby Wadkins
    4. Donnie Hammond

32. **THE PLAYERS CHAMPIONSHIP**
    1. Kenny Perry
    2. Mark McCumber
    3. Stuart Appleby
    4. Brian Kamm

33. **MOTOROLA WESTERN OPEN**
    1. Chip Beck
    2. Brett Ogle
    3. Allen Doyle
    4. Hisayuki Sasaki

34. **BOB HOPE CHRYSLER CLASSIC**
    1. Kirk Triplett
    2. Robin Freeman
    3. Mike Sullivan
    4. Scott McCarron

35. **GTE BYRON NELSON CLASSIC**
    1. D.A. Weibring
    2. Bruce Lietzke
    3. Carl Paulson
    4. Sean Murphy

36. **BUICK OPEN**
    1. Woody Austin
    2. Bob Estes
    3. Fulton Allem
    4. Mike Springer

37. **BAY HILL INVITATIONAL PRESENTED BY OFFICE DEPOT**
    1. Steve Lowery
    2. Billy Andrade
    3. Billy Ray Brown
    4. Tom Scherrer

38. **NEC WORLD SERIES OF GOLF**
    1. Bob Tway
    2. Scott Verplank
    3. Tommy Armour III
    4. John Mahaffey

39. **B.C. OPEN**
    1. Hal Sutton
    2. Bill Glasson
    3. Paul Stankowski
    4. Lucas Parsons

40. **BUICK INVITATIONAL**
    1. Craig Stadler
    2. David Frost
    3. Chris Smith
    4. Keith Fergus

41. **WALT DISNEY WORLD/ OLDSMOBILE GOLF CLASSIC**
    1. Jeff Sluman
    2. John Huston
    3. Mike Reid
    4. Patrick Burke

42. **CANON GREATER HARTFORD OPEN**
    1. Paul Azinger
    2. Tom Kite
    3. Dudley Hart
    4. Omar Uresti

43. **MERCEDES CHAMPIONSHIPS**
    1. Steve Stricker
    2. Fred Funk
    3. Joe Acosta, Jr.
    4. David Toms

44. **DINERS CLUB MATCHES***
    1. Jim McGovern
    2. Mark Brooks
    3. Greg Kraft
    4. Dan Pohl

45. **GREATER VANCOUVER OPEN**
    1. Jim Furyk
    2. Tom Watson
    3. Dave Barr
    4. Tommy Tolles

** Unofficial Event*

After winning the Phoenix Open and the Buick Classic in 1995, Vijay Singh owns three victories in three years on TOUR–and all have come via playoffs.

TOURNAMENT PLAYERS CLUBS

An original concept of the PGA TOUR, Tournament Players Clubs have gone from a dream to a Network that now encompasses 15 courses in 10 states and, with the addition of Non-Domestic TPCs, three foreign countries. Last November, the TPC at Mission Hills near Shenzhen became the first facility to serve as host for a major golf competition in the People's Republic of China when it was the venue for the 41st World Cup of Golf.

It was the TOUR's view that the spectator had been left out in golf course design throughout the years. When it came time for the PGA TOUR to build its own course, the opportunity presented itself to design a course that not only challenged the players but also allowed spectators to see the action as never before.

It's called "Stadium Golf"—and once you've viewed a tournament on a Stadium Golf Course, you'll understand why the network has grown in such a short period of time.

Spectator mounds afford fans unrestricted views, whether on tee shots, fairway shots or on the greens. In fact, the 18th hole at the original TPC at Sawgrass can accommodate crowds of some 30,000 people--all with a clear view of the action. You won't see any periscopes at an event on a Tournament Players Club golf course.

The Network began in 1980 with the TPC at Sawgrass, which annually is host to THE PLAYERS Championship, and quickly grew into the present number of 15. All TPCs are designed to serve as host sites for PGA TOUR or Senior PGA TOUR events, and the clubs have been designed by some of the top architects in the business — Pete Dye, Arnold Palmer, Arthur Hills, Jay Morrish, Mark McCumber, Tom Weiskopf, Bob Von Hagge and Jack Nicklaus, to name just a few.

In addition, one of the things that adds a bit of spice to all TPCs is that a PGA TOUR player (or, in some cases, two) is assigned to serve as consultant to the designer. Ed Sneed, Fuzzy Zoeller, Hubert Green, Craig Stadler, Ben Crenshaw, Al Geiberger and Chi Chi Rodriguez have been among those lending their expertise to the TPC Network.

The Network, in reality, is a nationwide country club. A premium membership at one TPC affords the member a chance to play at any of the other clubs across the country and an opportunity to view the greatest players in the world in action on his own course once a year.

Since the Tournament Players Club at Sawgrass opened, the TPC Network truly has become "the best set of clubs in America."

TPC Network — Domestic

	Club	Architect	Consultant	Host
1.	**TPC at Sawgrass** Ponte Vedra, FL	Pete Dye	--	THE PLAYERS Championship
2.	**TPC at Eagle Trace** Coral Springs, FL	Arthur Hills	--	--
3.	**TPC at River Highlands** Cromwell, CT	Pete Dye/ Robert Weed	Howard Twitty/ Roger Maltbie	Canon Greater Hartford Open
4.	**TPC at Prestancia** Sarasota, FL	Ron Garl	Mike Souchak	--
5.	**TPC at Avenel** Potomac, MD	Ault, Clark & Associates	Ed Sneed	Kemper Open
6.	**TPC of Scottsdale** Scottsdale, AZ	Jay Morrish/ Tom Weiskopf	Jim Colbert/ Howard Twitty	Phoenix Open
7.	**TPC at Piper Glen** Charlotte, NC	Arnold Palmer	--	PaineWebber Invitational
8.	**TPC at Southwind** Memphis, TN	Ron Prichard	Hubert Green/ Fuzzy Zoeller	FedEx St. Jude Classic
9.	**TPC of Michigan** Dearborn, MI	Jack Nicklaus	--	FORD SENIOR PLAYERS Championship
10.	**TPC of Tampa Bay** Tampa, FL	Robert Weed	Chi Chi Rodriguez	GTE Suncoast Classic
11.	**TPC at Summerlin** Las Vegas, NV	Robert Weed	Fuzzy Zoeller	Las Vegas Invitational Invitational & Las Vegas Senior Classic by TrueGreen-ChemLawn
12.	**TPC at Heron Bay** Coral Springs, FL (first quarter 1996 opening)	Mark McCumber	--	Honda Classic

Tournament Players Courses (Licensed Facilities)

	Club	Architect	Consultant	Host
1.	**TPC at The Woodlands** The Woodlands, TX	Bob Von Hagge	--	Shell Houston Open
2.	**TPC at Four Seasons Resort-Las Colinas** Irving, TX	Jay Morrish	Ben Crenshaw/ Byron Nelson	GTE Byron Nelson Classic
3.	**TPC at PGA West** La Quinta, CA	Pete Dye	--	--

Future TPCs (Announced, Planned or Under Construction)

Club	Architect	Consultant	Host
TPC at Jasna Polana Princeton, NJ	Gary Player	--	--
TPC at Sugarloaf Atlanta, GA	Greg Norman	--	--
TPC at The Canyons Las Vegas, NV	Robert Weed	Raymond Floyd	--

TPCs — Non-Domestic

TPC of Batoh
Tochigi Prefecture, Japan

TPC of Mito
Ibaraki Prefecture, Japan

TPC Mission Hills
Kanchanaburi, Thailand

TPC Mission Hills
Khao Yai, Thailand

TPC Mission Hills
Shenzhen, China

PGA TOUR PRODUCTIONS

PGA TOUR Productions is the television, film and video production company of the PGA TOUR.

Most people know PGA TOUR Productions by its award-winning "Inside the PGA TOUR" and "Inside the Senior PGA TOUR" programs, which are broadcast each week on ESPN and are celebrating their 12th and sixth seasons, respectively.

Productions is a diverse company delivering a wide range of creative services to an international clientele. Its film capacity has expanded to include production of the TOUR's "Anything's Possible" public service announcement (PSA) campaign, as well as numerous other commercials, tournament and pro-am highlight programs, corporate and promotional sales videos and home videos.

In addition to the "Inside" shows, Productions has developed an expertise in delivering live and live-to-tape golf events, including the Merrill Lynch Senior TOUR Shoot-Out Championship, the 1995 Remax North American Long Drive Championship and the Andersen Consulting World Championship of Golf.

PGA TOUR Productions also serves its worldwide clientele by producing, in conjunction with the networks, international live telecasts of select PGA TOUR events. More than 100 million viewers in more than 100 countries enjoy PGA TOUR events and programming enhanced by PGA TOUR Productions.

Along with the latest in television and communications technology, PGA TOUR Productions houses the world's most extensive library of golf footage. In the near future, PGA TOUR Productions will move its headquarters to the World Golf Hall of Fame complex located in Florida's St. Johns County.

WORLD GOLF VILLAGE

Ruffin Beckwith
Executive Director

Jerri Moon
Administrative Assistant

Florida's First Coast, home of THE PLAYERS Championship since 1977 and the PGA TOUR since 1979, will soon welcome one of the most exciting projects in the history of the game of golf: the World Golf Village.

Situated on Interstate 95 in St. Johns County, just 22 miles south of Jacksonville and eight miles northwest of St. Augustine, the World Golf Village will offer year-round golf and resort facilities, anchored by the new 75,000-square-foot World Golf Hall of Fame. Additional amenities will include a major hotel and conference center, 54 holes of golf, a PGA TOUR Golf Academy, both corporate and vacation villas, an upscale festival shopping area, the International Golf Library and Resource Center, new video and television studios for PGA TOUR Productions, a Mayo Clinic Sports Medicine facility and more. The first phase of the World Golf Village is scheduled to open in late 1997.

The new Hall of Fame will contain a 325-seat, big-screen theater, along with 36,000 square feet of exhibits that balance the history and traditions of the game with more contemporary interactive exhibits. They are being designed by Ralph Applebaum Associates of New York, designers of the acclaimed Holocaust Museum, and the work is being overseen by an Advisory Board that includes representatives of all major golf organizations, among them the PGA TOUR, LPGA, PGA of America, USGA, Royal & Ancient, Augusta National, National Golf Foundation and the PGA Tours of Europe, South Africa, Australasia and Japan.

"This endeavor represents the first time that all the major entities in the game have united behind a project of this magnitude," says World Golf Village Executive Director Ruffin Beckwith. "We believe this is destined to become something very special for the game of golf, for its great players and for all its fans and supporters."

Also within the building will be exhibits honoring the members of the restructured World Golf Hall of Fame, which includes all inductees into the old World Golf Hall of Fame in Pinehurst, NC, as well as all members of the LPGA Hall of Fame. Details of the restructuring will be announced later this year, with the first elections under the new structure to occur shortly thereafter.

"Nothing is as important to the game as the great players and other individuals who have contributed to golf's traditions of honor, integrity and competitive excellence," Beckwith said. "More than anything, we hope this new facility is an appropriate tribute to their accomplishments."

The World Golf Village is part of a 6,300-acre development called St. Johns, which will also include 7,200 residences and more than six million square feet of office, commercial and industrial space.

WORLD GOLF HALL OF FAME

Artist's Rendering of World Golf Hall of Fame

MEMBERS OF THE WORLD GOLF HALL OF FAME

INDUCTED VIA THE FORMER WORLD GOLF HALL OF FAME IN PINEHURST, NC (selected by the Golf Writers Association of America):

1974 Patty Berg, Walter Hagen, Ben Hogan, Robert T. Jones, Byron Nelson, Jack Nicklaus, Francis Ouimet, Arnold Palmer, Gary Player, Gene Sarazen, Sam Snead, Harry Vardon, Babe Zaharias
1975 Willie Anderson, Fred Corcoran, Joseph C. Dey, Chick Evans, Tom Morris, Jr., John H. Taylor, Glenna C. Vare, Joyce Wethered
1976 Tommy Armour, James Braid, Tom Morris, Sr., Jerome Travers, Mickey Wright
1977 Bobby Locke, John Ball, Herb Graffis, Donald Ross
1978 Billy Casper, Harold Hilton, Dorothy Campbell Hurd Howe, Bing Crosby, Clifford Roberts
1979 Louise Suggs, Walter Travis
1980 Lawson Little, Henry Cotton
1981 Lee Trevino, Ralph Guldahl
1982 Julius Boros, Kathy Whitworth
1983 Bob Hope, Jimmy Demaret
1985 JoAnne Carner
1986 Cary Middlecoff
1987 Robert Trent Jones, Betsy Rawls
1988 Tom Watson, Peter Thomson, Bob Harlow
1989 Raymond Floyd, Nancy Lopez, Roberto De Vicenzo, Jim Barnes
1990 William C. Campbell, Paul Runyan, Gene Littler, Horton Smith
1992 Hale Irwin, Chi Chi Rodriguez, Richard Tufts, Harry Cooper

INDUCTED VIA THE LPGA HALL OF FAME:

1951 Betty Jameson
1977 Sandra Haynie, Carol Mann
1991 Pat Bradley
1993 Patty Sheehan
1994 Dinah Shore
1995 Betsy King

Mark O'Meara returned to form in 1995 with victories at the Honda Classic and the Bell Canadian Open. His earnings total of $914,129 was the best of his 15 years on TOUR.

PGA TOUR MEDIA REGULATIONS

General Regulations:
The following regulations are to be followed by *all* members of the media:

1 An armband is necessary to walk inside the gallery ropes. Remain not more than an arm's length from the ropes, so as to blend into the gallery and appear to be a part of the gallery at all times.

2. Players are not to be distracted during play. Do not interview players or ask them to pose for photographs during their rounds.

3. Do not interview players or ask them to pose for photographs during their practice sessions before a round, except by prior arrangement with the player.

4. If an interview is to be conducted in the practice areas, either the range or the putting green, it must be done by prior arrangement with the player, up against the ropes and not in the middle of the areas where it could be distracting to other players.

5. Do not disturb players at their 18th green and/or scoring tent until after they have checked, signed and returned their scorecards. Media are not allowed in the scoring tent.

Working Press Regulations:
To avoid embarrassment to you and distraction to the contestants:

1. Do not walk or stand in playing areas.

2. Follow directions of marshals and other officials.

3. Do not interview during play. The leading players each day -- and others requested -- will be interviewed following their rounds in the Press Room interview area.

Tape Recorder Regulations:
1. All tape recorder work should be done in the proximity of the Press Room and/or clubhouse.

2. Tape recorders are not permitted in the locker room.

3. Tape recorders are not permitted within the playing area of the golf course unless written permission has been granted from PGA TOUR.

Weather Delay Guidelines:
1. During weather delay situations, no one other than players and essential staff will be permitted in the locker room. This means the media is not permitted in the locker room in such situations. However, whenever possible, arrangements will be made to provide players for interviews during such situations.

2. Fully accredited members of the news media will be welcome in the locker room at all other times to carry out their assigned duties. (Note: Cameras and tape recorders are not permitted in the locker room.)

PGA TOUR PHOTOGRAPHY REGULATIONS

Photo credentials will be issued only to personnel on assignment from recognized and accredited publications or news services. Requests for credentials must be made by the appropriate news agency, not by the photographer.

Photographic likenesses of PGA TOUR, Senior PGA TOUR and NIKE TOUR players may be used only for legitimate newspaper and magazine coverage of the events in which they are competing.

Commercial exploitation of these likenesses without written consent of the players and PGA TOUR is prohibited.

A limited number of photo armbands (or photo bibs), which permit the wearer access inside the gallery ropes, may be issued. Photographers who do not have armbands or bibs must stay outside the gallery ropes. Photographic assistants will not be issued armbands or bibs.

Cameras may be used only by accredited media representatives who have been assigned photo credentials, and such use is subject to the following conditions:

1. Photographers with photo armbands must stay within one arm's length of the ropes at all times. Photographers without armbands are not permitted inside the ropes at any time.

2. The use of golf carts is prohibited at all times.

3. Photographers must not position themselves in the line of play. If requested to move by a player, his caddie or an official, the photographer will do so without delay or discussion.

4. No photograph shall be taken until a player has completed his stroke.

5. Players should not be asked to pose during a round.

6. Noise-free equipment must be used at all times.

7. Cameras are not permitted in the scoring tent or in the locker rooms.

The Photographer shall indemnify, defend and hold the Tournament and the PGA TOUR and their respective officers, agents, representatives, successors and assigns harmless from and against any and all expenses, lawsuits, damages, costs and liabilities (including reasonable attorney's fees and expenses) incurred by, arising from or in connection with (1) the unauthorized use of photographs taken by the Photographer, whether such unauthorized use is by the Photographer, the company designating the Photographer to use the credential on its behalf, or some third party to whom the photographs are distributed; (2) any injuries resulting from acts or omissions by the Photographer or some third party to whom the Photographer directly or indirectly distributed the material; (3) any cameras, wires, cables or other equipment brought to the premises by the Photographer, or (4) the use of any photographs of any matter other than coverage of the Tournament.

PGA TOUR TELEVISION COVERAGE REGULATIONS

The PGA TOUR retains exclusive television rights (including but not limited to broadcast, cable, home video) to all events on the PGA TOUR, Senior PGA TOUR and NIKE TOUR. No live or tape-delayed broadcast of any portion of any PGA TOUR, Senior PGA TOUR or NIKE TOUR event is permitted without the prior written consent of the PGA TOUR.

In most cases, play-by-play television rights have been sold for network broadcast.

Stations or networks which have not purchased the rights to originate play-by-play coverage of events from the PGA TOUR are permitted to broadcast highlights coverage of such events only under the following conditions:

1. Televised coverage shall not be in excess of three minutes of highlights daily from each TOUR (and six minutes total for all three TOURS) and may not purport to be live, play-by-play coverage from the course. Requests for expanded coverage must be submitted in writing to the PGA TOUR.

2. All highlights coverage must be part of regularly scheduled news and/or sports programs.

3. Highlights from any day's play may not be broadcast or used for any other purpose after seven days from the conclusion of play each day.

4. No action footage of any day's play may be broadcast until that day's live or tape-delayed coverage by the television network is concluded.

5. No footage may be inserted into any commercial announcement or sold to any other broadcast entity or agency.

6. As the exclusive rights holder, PGA TOUR is the absolute owner of all footage shot at the tournament site (golf action or other footage) and may request copies of any footage shot at PGA TOUR, Senior PGA TOUR and NIKE TOUR events. Such footage will be provided to the TOUR at cost upon request.

7. The use of golf carts is prohibited at all times.

8. Only personnel with appropriate credentials will be allowed inside the gallery ropes, and they must stay within one arm's length of the ropes at all times. All support personnel must remain outside the ropes.

PGA TOUR RADIO COVERAGE REGULATIONS

The PGA TOUR retains exclusive national radio rights to all events on the PGA TOUR, Senior PGA TOUR and NIKE TOUR.

No live or tape-delayed broadcast of any portion of any PGA TOUR, Senior PGA TOUR or NIKE TOUR event is permitted without the prior written consent of the PGA TOUR.

In some cases, play-by-play radio rights have been sold for network broadcast.

Stations or networks which have not purchased the rights to originate play-by-play coverage of events from the PGA TOUR are permitted to broadcast highlights coverage of such events only under the following conditions:

1. Coverage shall not be in excess of three minutes of highlights and may not purport to be live, play-by-play coverage from the course.

2. All highlights coverage must be part of regularly scheduled news and/or sports programs and may not be broadcast after seven days from the conclusion of play on that day.

3. As the exclusive rightsholder, PGA TOUR may request copies of any coverage of PGA TOUR, Senior PGA TOUR and NIKE TOUR events. Such coverage will be provided to the TOUR at cost upon request.

4. The use of golf carts is prohibited at all times.

5. Only personnel with appropriate credentials will be permitted into the media center and locker room areas.

6. Radio broadcasters are not permitted inside the gallery ropes at any time.

7. Broadcasters are not permitted to talk to players during play or after the round until the player has signed his scorecard.

8. Tape recorders are not permitted in the locker room.

PRIZE MONEY DISTRIBUTION CHARTS

PRO-AM CHARTS

$7,500
Individual & team

POSITION	PRIZE
1	$750
2	600
3	525
4	450
5	375
6	300
7	225
8	200
9	175
10	150

$10,000
Individual & team

POSITION	PRIZE
1	$1,000
2	800
3	700
4	600
5	500
6	400
7	310
8	260
9	230
10	200

POSITION	$1,000,000 PRIZE	$1,200,000 PRIZE	$1,250,000 PRIZE	$1,300,000 PRIZE	$1,350,000 PRIZE
1	$180,000	$216,000	$225,000	$234,000	$243,000
2	108,000	129,600	35,000	140,400	$145,800
3	68,000	81,600	85,000	88,400	$91,800
4	48,000	57,600	60,000	62,400	$64,800
5	40,000	48,000	50,000	52,000	$54,000
6	36,000	43,200	45,000	46,800	$48,600
7	33,500	40,200	41,875	43,550	$45,225
8	31,000	37,200	38,750	40,300	$41,850
9	29,000	34,800	36,250	37,700	$39,150
10	27,000	32,400	33,750	35,100	$36,450
11	25,000	30,000	31,250	32,500	$33,750
12	23,000	27,600	28,750	29,900	$31,050
13	21,000	25,200	26,250	27,300	$28,350
14	19,000	22,800	23,750	24,700	$25,650
15	18,000	21,600	22,500	23,400	$24,300
16	17,000	20,400	21,250	22,100	$22,950
17	16,000	19,200	20,000	20,800	$21,600
18	15,000	18,000	18,750	19,500	$20,250
19	14,000	16,800	17,500	18,200	$18,900
20	13,000	15,600	16,250	16,900	$17,550
21	12,000	14,400	15,000	15,600	$16,200
22	11,200	13,440	14,000	14,560	$15,120
23	10,400	12,480	13,000	13,520	$14,040
24	9,600	11,520	12,000	12,480	$12,960
25	8,800	10,560	11,000	11,440	$11,880
26	8,000	9,600	10,000	10,400	$10,800
27	7,700	9,240	9,625	10,010	$10,395
28	7,400	8,880	9,250	9,620	$9,990
29	7,100	8,520	8,875	9,230	$9,585
30	6,800	8,160	8,500	8,840	$9,180
31	6,500	7,800	8,125	8,450	$8,775
32	6,200	7,440	7,750	8,060	$8,370
33	5,900	7,080	7,375	7,670	$7,965
34	5,650	6,780	7,065	7,345	$7,628
35	5,400	6,480	6,750	7,020	$7,290
36	5,150	6,180	6,435	6,695	$6,953
37	4,900	5,880	6,125	6,370	$6,615
38	4,700	5,640	5,875	6,110	$6,345
39	4,500	5,400	5,625	5,850	$6,075
40	4,300	5,160	5,375	5,590	$5,805
41	4,100	4,920	5,125	5,330	$5,535
42	3,900	4,680	4,875	5,070	$5,265
43	3,700	4,440	4,625	4,810	$4,995
44	3,500	4,200	4,375	4,550	$4,725
45	3,300	3,960	4,125	4,290	$4,455
46	3,100	3,720	3,875	4,030	$4,185
47	2,900	3,480	3,625	3,770	$3,915
48	2,740	3,288	3,425	3,562	$3,699
49	2,600	3,120	3,250	3,380	$3,510
50	2,520	3,024	3,150	3,276	$3,402
51	2,460	2,952	3,075	3,198	$3,321
52	2,400	2,880	3,000	3,120	$3,240
53	2,360	2,832	2,950	3,068	$3,186
54	2,320	2,784	2,900	3,016	$3,132
55	2,300	2,760	2,875	2,990	$3,105
56	2,280	2,736	2,850	2,964	$3,078
57	2,260	2,712	2,825	2,938	$3,051
58	2,240	2,688	2,800	2,912	$3,024
59	2,220	2,664	2,775	2,886	$2,997
60	2,200	2,640	2,750	2,860	$2,970
61	2,180	2,616	2,725	2,834	$2,943
62	2,160	2,592	2,700	2,808	$2,916
63	2,140	2,568	2,675	2,782	$2,889
64	2,120	2,544	2,650	2,756	$2,862
65	2,100	2,520	2,625	2,730	$2,835
66	2,080	2,495	2,600	2,704	$2,808
67	2,060	2,472	2,575	2,678	$2,781
68	2,040	2,448	2,550	2,652	$2,754
69	2,020	2,424	2,525	2,626	$2,727
70	2,000	2,400	2,500	2,600	$2,700

PRIZE MONEY DISTRIBUTION CHARTS

POSITION	$1,400,000 PRIZE	$1,500,000 PRIZE	$1,600,000 PRIZE	$1,800,000 PRIZE	$2,000,000 PRIZE	$3,000,000 PRIZE
1	$252,000	$270,000	$288,000	$324,000	$360,000	$540,000
2	151,200	162,000	$172,800	$194,400	$216,000	$324,000
3	95,200	102,000	$108,800	$122,400	$136,000	$204,000
4	67,200	72,000	$76,800	$86,400	$96,000	$144,000
5	56,000	60,000	$64,000	$72,000	$80,000	$120,000
6	50,400	54,000	$57,600	$64,800	$72,000	$108,000
7	46,900	50,250	$53,600	$60,300	$67,000	$100,500
8	43,400	46,500	$49,600	$55,800	$62,000	$93,000
9	40,600	43,500	$46,400	$52,200	$58,000	$87,000
10	37,800	40,500	$43,200	$48,600	$54,000	$81,000
11	35,000	37,500	$40,500	$45,000	$50,000	$75,000
12	32,200	34,500	$36,800	$41,400	$46,000	$69,000
13	29,400	31,500	$33,600	$37,800	$42,000	$63,000
14	26,600	28,500	$30,400	$34,200	$38,000	$57,000
15	25,200	27,000	$28,800	$32,400	$36,000	$54,000
16	23,800	25,500	$27,200	$30,600	$34,000	$51,000
17	22,400	24,000	$25,600	$28,800	$32,000	$48,000
18	21,000	22,500	$24,000	$27,000	$30,000	$45,000
19	19,600	21,000	$22,400	$25,200	$28,000	$42,000
20	18,200	19,500	$20,800	$23,400	$26,000	$39,000
21	16,800	18,000	$19,200	$21,600	$24,000	$36,000
22	15,680	16,800	$17,920	$20,160	$22,400	$33,600
23	14,560	15,600	$16,640	$18,720	$20,800	$31,200
24	13,440	14,400	$15,360	$17,280	$19,200	$28,800
25	12,320	13,200	$14,080	$15,840	$17,600	$26,400
26	11,200	12,000	$12,800	$14,400	$16,000	$24,000
27	10,785	11,550	$12,320	$13,860	$15,400	$23,100
28	10,360	11,100	$11,840	$13,320	$14,800	$22,200
29	9,940	10,650	$11,360	$12,780	$14,200	$21,300
30	9,520	10,200	$10,880	$12,240	$13,600	$20,400
31	9,100	9,750	$10,400	$11,700	$13,000	$19,500
32	8,680	9,300	8,060	$11,160	$12,400	$18,600
33	8,260	8,850	7,670	$10,620	$11,800	$17,700
34	7,910	8,475	7,345	$10,170	$11,300	$16,950
35	7,560	8,100	7,020	$9,720	$10,800	$16,200
36	7,210	7,725	6,695	$9,270	$10,300	$15,450
37	6,860	7,350	6,370	$8,820	$9,800	$14,700
38	6,580	7,050	6,110	$8,460	$9,400	$14,100
39	6,300	6,750	5,850	$8,100	$9,000	$13,500
40	6,020	6,450	5,590	$7,740	$8,600	$12,900
41	5,740	6,150	5,330	$7,380	$8,200	$12,300
42	5,460	5,850	5,070	$7,020	$7,800	$11,700
43	5,180	5,550	4,810	$6,660	$7,400	$11,100
44	4,900	5,250	4,550	$6,300	$7,000	$10,500
45	4,620	4,950	4,290	$5,940	$6,600	$9,900
46	4,340	4,650	4,030	$5,580	$6,200	$9,300
47	4,060	4,350	3,770	$5,220	$5,800	$8,700
48	3,836	4,110	3,562	$4,932	$5,480	$8,220
49	3,640	3,900	3,380	$4,680	$5,200	$7,800
50	3,528	3,780	3,276	$4,536	$5,040	$7,560
51	3,444	3,690	3,198	$4,428	$4,920	$7,380
52	3,360	3,600	3,120	$4,320	$4,800	$7,200
53	3,304	3,540	3,068	$4,248	$4,720	$7,080
54	3,248	3,480	3,016	$4,176	$4,640	$6,960
55	3,220	3,450	2,990	$4,140	$4,600	$6,900
56	3,192	3,420	2,964	$4,104	$4,560	$6,840
57	3,164	3,390	2,938	$4,068	$4,520	$6,780
58	3,136	3,360	2,912	$4,032	$4,480	$6,720
59	3,108	3,330	2,886	$3,996	$4,440	$6,660
60	3,080	3,300	2,860	$3,960	$4,400	$6,600
61	3,052	3,270	2,834	$3,924	$4,360	$6,540
62	3,024	3,240	2,808	$3,888	$4,320	$6,480
63	2,996	3,210	2,782	$3,852	$4,280	$6,420
64	2,968	3,180	2,756	$3,816	$4,240	$6,360
65	2,940	3,150	2,730	$3,780	$4,200	$6,300
66	2,912	3,120	2,704	$3,744	$4,160	$6,240
67	2,884	3,090	2,678	$3,708	$4,120	$6,180
68	2,856	3,060	2,652	$3,672	$4,080	$6,120
69	2,828	3,030	2,626	$3,636	$4,040	$6,060
70	2,800	3,000	2,600	$3,600	$4,000	$6,000

SONY RANKING

Originally formulated in 1986, the Sony Ranking is a computerized system that provides a reference source to the relative performance of the world's leading professional golfers.

The Sony Ranking is issued every Monday, following completion of the previous week's tournaments from around the world. The official events from the world's leading tours are taken into account. Points are generally awarded according to the players' finishing positions and are related to the number and ranking of the players in the respective tournament fields. However, the Masters Tournament, U.S. Open, British Open, PGA Championship and THE PLAYERS Championship are rated separately to reflect the higher quality of the events and the stronger fields participating.

The Sony Ranking had previously been based on a three-year "rolling" period weighted in favor of the more recent results. But from December 31, 1995, the system was changed to a two-year "rolling" period, with the points accumulated in the most recent 52-week period doubled.

Each player is then ranked according to his average points per tournament, which is determined by dividing his total number of points by the number of tournaments he has played over that two-year period. There is a minimum requirement of 20 tournaments for each 52-week period.

For example, if a player were in 32 tournaments in the most recent 52 weeks and 15 events in the previous 52 weeks, his divisor would be 52 (32 plus 20). A player who was in 32 tournaments in each year would have a divisor of 64 (32 plus 32).

The winners of the Masters, U.S. Open, British Open and PGA Championship are awarded 50 points (doubled to 100 in current year). THE PLAYERS Championship is among several tournaments at the next level whose winner is awarded 40 points (80 in the current year). The winner of a tournament with a relatively strong field would receive approximately 25-30 points (50-60 in current year).

The Sony Ranking International Advisory Committee, a worldwide panel which includes a representative from the PGA TOUR, meets periodically to review and monitor the Sony Ranking system in order to recommend refinements or modifications for the consideration of the Championship Committee of the Royal and Ancient Golf Club of St. Andrews, the sanctioning body of the Sony Ranking.

The Sony Ranking is available each week at PGA TOUR sites. The top 20 as of December 3, 1995 (based on the new two-year system) was as follows:

POS.	PLAYER	AVERAGE	POS.	PLAYER	AVERAGE
1.	Greg Norman	13.76	11.	Jumbo Ozaki	7.10
2.	Nick Price	11.19	12.	Jose Maria Olazabal	6.34
3.	Ernie Els	10.38	13.	Loren Roberts	6.20
4.	Bernhard Langer	9.62	14.	Sam Torrance	5.46
5.	Corey Pavin	9.35	15.	Peter Jacobsen	5.35
6.	Colin Montgomerie	9.33	16.	Lee Janzen	5.11
7.	Nick Faldo	8.63	17.	Vijay Singh	5.11
8.	Steve Elkington	7.59	18.	Mark McCumber	5.10
9.	Tom Lehman	7.31	19.	Davis Love III	4.89
10.	Fred Couples	7.22	20.	Ben Crenshaw	4.83

Nick Price finished in the Top 30 for the sixth consecutive year and seventh time in nine seasons in 1995. He also led the TOUR in total driving for the second year in a row.

PGA TOUR

PGA TOUR STAFF

OFFICE OF THE COMMISSIONER

Michael L. Starks
Vice President
Corporate Affairs

Sid T. Wilson
Vice President
Player Relations

John White
Director
Senior PGA TOUR
Player Relations

Marty Caffey
Manager
PGA TOUR Player Relations

Sara Moores
Manager
TOUR Wives Associations

Patty Cianfrocca
Executive Assistant

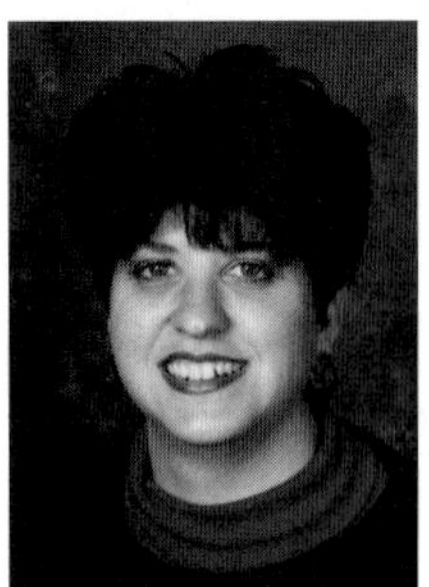

Jodi Herb
Administrative Assistant
Player Relations

Marie Holeva
Administrative
Assistant

Cathie Hurlburt
Assistant to the
Commissioner

Charles L. Zink
Executive Vice President
Chief Financial Officer

Charles L. Zink is Executive Vice President and Chief Financial Officer. His areas of responsibility are **Communications**, **Finance and Administration**, the **Tournament Players Clubs**, the **World Golf Village**, **Corporate Marketing**, **Retail Licensing** and **Business Development**.

John Morris is Vice President of Communications; Helen Atter is Vice President of Corporate Compliance; and Ron Price is Vice President of Finance and Administration. Vernon Kelly is President and Joe Walser is Chief Operating Officer of PGA TOUR Golf Course Properties. Ruffin Beckwith is Executive Director of the World Golf Village.

Leo McCullagh is Vice President of Marketing and Retail Licensing and Tom Wade is Vice President of Business Development.

COMMUNICATIONS

John Morris
Vice President of
Communications

Dave Lancer
Director
of Information

Chuck Adams
Director
Editorial Projects

Chris Smith
Director
Special Projects

John Snow
Director
Creative Services

Denise Taylor
Manager
Media Relations

James Cramer
Media Official
PGA TOUR/NIKE TOUR

Bob Hyde
Media Official
NIKE TOUR

Mark Mitchell
Media Official
PGA TOUR

Lee Patterson
Media Official
PGA TOUR

Wes Seeley
Media Official
PGA TOUR

Dave Senko
Media Official
Senior PGA TOUR

COMMUNICATIONS

Phil Stambaugh
Media Official
Senior PGA TOUR

Stan Badz
Staff Photographer

Sam Greenwood
Staff Photographer

Mike Smith
Senior Graphic Designer
Creative Services

Sally Peterson
Production Coordinator
Creative Services

Eric Francis
Graphic Designer
Creative Services

Holly Carothers
Administrative Assistant
to Vice President

Gray Autrey
Communications
Assistant
PGA TOUR

Kim Delaney
Communications
Assistant
NIKE TOUR

Michelle Falcone
Administrative
Assistant
Photography

Dianne Reed
Communications
Assistant
Senior PGA TOUR

CORPORATE MARKETING / RETAIL LICENSING

Leo McCullagh
Vice President
Marketing and Retail Licensing

Jeff Monday
Vice President
Retail Licensing

Tim Benton
Corporate Marketing
Manager

Donna Fiedorowicz
Corporate Marketing
Manager

Sheila McLenaghan
Corporate Marketing
Manager

Carol Curry
Director of Marketing
Services/Corp. Hospitality

Linda Dutcher
Corporate Marketing
Coordinator

Mike Mueller
Assistant Corporate
Marketing Manager

Tom Jaronski
Assistant Corporate
Marketing Manager

Kathy Sutton
Administrative
Assistant

BUSINESS DEVELOPMENT

Tom Wade
Vice President
Business Development

Jon Podany
Director
Business Development

Steve Horner
Manager
Business Development

Barry Hyde
Manager
Bus. Development Accounts

TOURNAMENT PLAYERS CLUBS

Vernon Kelly
President
PGA TOUR Golf
Course Properties

Joe Walser
Chief Operating
Officer
PGA TOUR Golf
Course Properties

Pete Davison
Vice President,
Operations
PGA TOUR Golf
Course Properties

Keith Tomlinson
Vice President,
TPC Development
PGA TOUR Golf
Course Properties

Chris Wilkerson
Director of Construction
PGA TOUR Golf
Course Properties

Mike Diffenderfer
National Director
Membership/Marketing

Mike Hawkins
National Food &
Beverage Manager

Cal Roth
National Director
Golf Course
Maintenance Operations

Chris Gray
Director of Design

Ricardo Guzman
Design Associate

Jayne Davison
Director of Merchandising

FINANCE AND ADMINISTRATION

Helen Atter
Vice President
Corporate Compliance

Ron Price
Vice President
Finance and Administration

Steve Winsor
Vice President of Finance
PGA TOUR Golf
Course Properties

Linda Altman
Director
Human Resources

Jerry Hawks
Director
Information Services

Andrea King
Treasury and
Administration

Jeanne Lightcap
Controller
PGA TOUR

Jack Daughtry
Manager
Information Support

Steve Evans
Manager
Information Systems

Roberta Blackwell
Controller
Club Operations

Karen Boliek
Financial Controller

Margaret Lewis
Director of Travel

Denise Brown
Tax Manager

Cindy Ross
Administrative Assistant

W. William Calfee
Executive Vice President
Competition

W. William Calfee, a one-time member of the PGA TOUR and formerly its Vice President of Player Relations, is Executive Vice President of Competition.

Calfee has responsibility for the **Competition and Rules** function on all three TOURs—the PGA TOUR, Senior PGA TOUR and NIKE TOUR. He also has overall charge of **agronomy**, **scoring** and other aspects of **on-site tournament operations**.

David Eger serves under Calfee as Vice President of Competition.

COMPETITION AND RULES

David Eger
Vice President
Competition

Arvin Ginn
Tournament
Director

Ben Nelson
Tournament
Director

Mike Shea
Senior Director
of Rules

George Boutell
Tournament Official
Scottsdale, AZ

Jon Brendle
Tournament Official
Orlando, FL

Wade Cagle
Tournament Supervisor
Alpharetta, GA

Frank Kavanaugh
Tournament Official
Pattenburg, NJ

Vaughn Moise
Tournament Official
Kingwood, TX

Mark Russell
Tournament Official
Orlando, FL

Glen Tait
Tournament Official
LaMesa, CA

Slugger White
Tournament Official
Ormond Beach, FL

COMPETITION AND RULES

Cliff Holtzclaw
Membership Services Coordinator

Robin Leaptrott
Administrative Assistant

Barbara Potts
Assistant Membership Services Coordinator

Karen Rose
Tournament Competitions Coordinator

SCOREBOARD / TOURNAMENT OPERATIONS

Jack White
Director of Tournament Operations

Irv Batten
Scorekeeper

Randall Kato
Tournament Operations

Steve Mahady
Tournament Operations

Todd Morton
Tournament Operations

Rich Pierson
Assistant Manager

Don Wallace
General Manager

AGRONOMY

Allan MacCurrach
Senior Agronomist

Tom Brown
Agronomist

Jeff Haley
Agronomist

Dennis Leger
Agronomist

Edward L. Moorhouse
Executive Vice President
and General Counsel

Edward L. Moorhouse is Executive Vice President and Chief Legal Officer, responsible for **Government**, **International** and **Legal Affairs**, **Television**, **Broadcasting** and **PGA TOUR Productions**.

Mike Bodney is Vice President of International Affairs; Richard Bowers is Vice President of Government Affairs; and Jim Triola is Associate General Counsel.

Donna Orender is Vice President of Television and Productions, overseeing Television and Broadcasting and PGA TOUR Productions. Under Orender are John Evenson, Vice President of Broadcasting; and Jack Peter, Vice President of Production for PGA TOUR Productions.

TELEVISION AND BROADCASTING

Donna Orender
Vice President
Television & Productions

John Evenson
Vice President
Broadcasting

Terri Montville
Broadcasting
Manager

Abbe Moody
Administrative
Assistant

GOVERNMENT / INTERNATIONAL / LEGAL

Mike Bodney
Vice President
International Affairs

Richard Bowers
Vice President
Government Relations

Jim Triola
Associate General
Counsel

Rick Anderson
Senior Counsel

Lisa Selph
Administrative Assistant

PGA TOUR PRODUCTIONS

Jack Peter
Vice President
Production

Roger Stevenson
Vice President
Operations

Jim Pierson
Director of Sales

Tom Alter
Senior Producer

Al Brito
Senior Producer

Michael O'Connell
Senior Coordinating
Producer

Scott Rinehart
Manager, Library

Scott Goodall
Manager, Field Operations

Seth Giambalvo
Producer

Rick Persons
Producer

Glenn Rocha
Producer

Lowell Thaler
Producer

Marion Stratford
Producer

Ed Waud
Producer

Kristin H. Kristen
Coordinator,
Special Projects

Charlene Landen
Assistant Controller

Stephen C. Rankin is Executive Vice President for **Tournament Sponsor Affairs**. As such, he supervises sponsor relations on the three TOURs.

The TOUR's **Championship Management** Department, which conducts six events for the three TOURs, also falls under Rankin's supervision.

Henry Hughes works under Rankin in **Sponsor Affairs** as well as **Championship Management**.

Stephen C. Rankin
Executive Vice President
Tournament Sponsor Affairs

TOURNAMENT SPONSOR AFFAIRS

Henry Hughes
Vice President
Tournament Sponsor Affairs

Duke Butler
Vice President

Ric Clarson
Vice President

Erica de la Uz
Administrative
Assistant

Evanne DiGenti
Administrative
Assistant

Cheryl Webb
Sponsor Services
Coordinator

CHAMPIONSHIP MANAGEMENT

Brian Goin
General Manager

Paul Hardwick
Director of
Operations

Ana Leaird
Director
Public Relations & Media

Jan Leone
Director of Marketing

Ron Cross
Tournament Director
NIKE TOUR
Championship

Marlene Livaudais
Tournament Director
THE TOUR
Championship

Anne Mullen
Tournament Director
Energizer SENIOR
TOUR Championship

Greg Wheeler
Tournament Director
FORD SENIOR PLAYERS
Championship

Brian Kemp
Tournament Operations
Manager and National
Purchasing Manager

Debbie Jones
Accounting Manager

Norma Long
Client Services
Manager

1996 COMPLETE SCHEDULES

Week of	PGA TOUR	SENIOR PGA TOUR	NIKE TOUR
Jan. 1-7	Mercedes Championships		
8-14	Nortel Open		
15-21	Bob Hope Chrysler Classic	Puerto Rico Sr. Tourn.of Champions	
22-28	Phoenix Open	+Senior Skins Game	
29-4	AT&T Pebble Beach National Pro-Am	Royal Caribbean Classic	
Feb. 5-11	Buick Invitational	Greater Naples IntelliNet Challenge	
12-18	United Airlines Hawaiian Open	GTE Suncoast Classic	
19-25	Nissan Open	Senior Golf Classic	NIKE San Jose Open
26-3	Doral-Ryder Open	FHP Health Care Classic	NIKE Inland Empire Open
March 4-10	Honda Classic	+Senior Slam	
11-17	Bay Hill Invitational	Toshiba Senior Classic	NIKE Monterrey Open
18-24	Freeport•McDermott Classic	+Liberty Mutual Legends of Golf	
25-31	THE PLAYERS Championship	SBC Dominion Seniors	NIKE Louisiana Open
April 1-7	BellSouth Classic	The Tradition	NIKE Tallahassee Opem
8-14	*Masters Tournament		NIKE South Carolina Classic
15-21	MCI Classic	*PGA Seniors' Championship	NIKE Alabama Classic
22-28	Greater Greensboro/Andersen Consulting	Las Vegas Senior Classic	NIKE Shreveport Open
29-5	Shell Houston Open	World Seniors Invitational	TBA
May 6-12	GTE Byron Nelson Classic	Nationwide Championship	TBA
13-19	MasterCard Colonial	Cadillac NFL Golf Classic	NIKE Carolina Classic
20-26	Kemper Open	BellSouth Senior Classic at Opryland	NIKE Greater Greenville Classic
27-2	Memorial Tournament	Bruno's Memorial Classic	NIKE Dominion Open
June 3-9	Buick Classic	Pittsburgh Senior Classic	NIKE Cleveland Open
10-16	*U.S. Open Championship	Canadian Senior Open	NIKE Knoxville Open
17-23	FedEx St. Jude Classic	Bell Atlantic Classic	NIKE Ozarks Open
24-30	Canon Greater Hartford Open	Kroger Senior Classic	NIKE Dakota Dunes Open
July 1-7	Motorola Western Open	*U.S. Senior Open	
8-14	Michelob Championship At Kingsmill	FORD SENIOR PLAYERS Championship	NIKE Buffalo Open
15-21	*British Open/Deposit Guaranty Golf Classic	Burnet Senior Classic	NIKE Philadelphia Open
22-28	CVS Charity Classic	Ameritech Senior Open	NIKE Miami Open
29-4	Buick Open	VFW Senior Championship	NIKE Gateway Classic
Aug. 5-11	*PGA Championship	First of America Classic	NIKE Wichita Open
12-18	Sprint International	Northville Long Island Classic	NIKE Texarkana Open
19-25	NEC WSOG/Greater Vancouver Open	Bank of Boston Senior Golf Classic	NIKE Permian Basin Open
26-1	Greater Milwaukee Open	Franklin Quest Championship	
Sept. 2-8	Bell Canadian Open	Boone Valley Classic	
9-15	Quad City Classic/+Presidents Cup	Bank One Classic	NIKE Utah Classic
16-22	B.C. Open	Brickyard Crossing Championship	NIKE Boise Open
23-29	Buick Challenge	Vantage Championship	NIKE Tri-Cities Open
30-6	Las Vegas Invitational	Ralphs Senior Classic	NIKE Olympia Open
Oct. 7-13	LaCantera Texas Open	The Transamerica	
14-20	Walt Disney World/Oldsmobile Classic	Raley's Gold Rush Classic	NIKE TOUR Championship
21-27	THE TOUR Championship	Hyatt Regency Maui Kaanapali Classic	
28-3		Emerald Coast Classic	
Nov. 4-10	+Lincoln-Mercury Kapalua International	Energizer SENIOR TOUR Championship	
11-17	+Franklin Templeton Shark Shootout		
18-24	+World Cup of Golf		
25-1	+Skins Game		
Dec. 2-8	+JCPenney Classic		
9-15	+Diners Club Matches	+Diners Club Matches	
16-22		+Lexus Challenge	

** = non-PGA TOUR cosponsored event*
+ = unofficial event

INDEX

INDEX

INDEX

INDEX